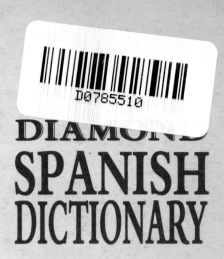

DIAMOND
SPANISH
DICTIONARY

D0785510

DIAMOND
SPANISH
DICTIONARY

SPANISH · ENGLISH   ENGLISH · SPANISH

Mike Gonzalez

This edition published 1994 by
Diamond Books
77–85 Fulham Palace Road
Hammersmith, London W6 8JB

© William Collins Sons & Co. Ltd. 1982

Reprinted 1992

Latest reprint 1994

contributors
Margaret Tejerizo, John Forry,
Carmen Billinghurst, Liam Kane, Pat Feehan

editorial staff
Irene Lakhani

All rights reserved

Printed in Great Britain

INTRODUCCIÓN

INTRODUCTION

Quien desee leer y entender el inglés encontrará en este diccionario un extenso léxico moderno que abarca una amplia gama de locuciones de uso corriente. Igualmente encontrará, en su debido orden alfabético, las abreviaturas, las siglas, los nombres geográficos más conocidos y, además, las principales formas de verbo irregulares, donde se le referirá a las respectivas formas de base, hallándose allí la traducción.

Quien aspire comunicarse y expresarse en lengua extranjera, hallará aquí una clara y detallada explicación de las palabras básicas, empleándose un sistema de indicadores que le remitirán a la traducción más apta y le señalarán su correcto uso.

The user whose aim is to read and understand Spanish will find a comprehensive and up-to-date wordlist including numerous phrases in current use. He will also find listed alphabetically the main irregular forms with a cross-reference to the basic form where a translation is given, as well as some of the most common abbreviations, acronyms and geographical names.

The user who wishes to communicate and to express himself in the foreign language will find clear and detailed treatment of all the basic words, with numerous indicators pointing to the appropriate translation, and helping him to use it correctly.

Spanish	Abbr.	English
adjetivo, locución adjetivo	a	adjective, adjectival phrase
abreviatura	ab(b)r	abbreviation
adverbio, locución adverbial	ad	adverb, adverbial phrase
administración, lengua administrativa	ADMIN	administration
agricultura	AGR	agriculture
América Latina	AM	Latin America
anatomía	ANAT	anatomy
arquitectura	ARQ, ARCH	architecture
astrología, astronomía	ASTRO	astrology, astronomy
el automóvil	AUT(O)	the motor car and motoring
aviación, viajes aéreos	AVIAT	flying, air travel
biología	BIO(L)	biology
botánica, flores	BOT	botany
inglés británico	Brit	British English
química	CHEM	chemistry
conjunción	conj	conjunction
lengua familiar	col	colloquial usage
comercio, finanzas, banca	COM(M)	commerce, finance, banking
construcción	CONSTR	building
compuesto	cpd	compound element
cocina	CULIN	cookery
determinante, artículo	det	determiner, article
economía	ECON	economics
electricidad, electrónica	ELEC	electricity, electronics
enseñanza, sistema escolar y universitario	ESCOL	schooling, schools and universities
especialmente	esp	especially
exclamación, interjección	excl	exclamation, interjection
femenino	f	feminine
lengua familiar	fam	colloquial usage
ferrocarril	FERRO	railways
uso figurado	fig	figurative use
fotografía	FOTO	photography
(verbo inglés) del cual la partícula es inseparable	fus	(phrasal verb) where the particle is inseparable
generalmente	gen	generally
geografía, geología	GEO	geography, geology
geometría	GEOM	geometry
invariable	inv	invariable
irregular	irg	irregular
lo jurídico	JUR	law
gramática, lingüística	LING	grammar, linguistics
masculino	m	masculine

matemáticas	**MAT(H)**	mathematics
medicina	**MED**	medical term, medicine
masculino/femenino	**m/f**	masculine/feminine
lo militar, ejército	**MIL**	military matters
música	**MUS**	music
sustantivo, nombre	**n**	noun
navegación, náutica	**NAUT**	sailing, navigation
sustantivo numérico	**num**	numeral noun
complemento	**obj**	(grammatical) object
	o.s.	oneself
peyorativo	**pey, pej**	derogatory, pejorative
fotografía	**PHOT**	photography
fisiología	**PHYSIOL**	physiology
plural	**pl**	plural
política	**POL**	politics
participio de pasado	**pp**	past participle
prefijo	**pref**	prefix
preposición	**prep**	preposition
pronombre	**pron**	pronoun
psicología, psiquiatría	**PSICO, PSYCH**	psychology, psychiatry
tiempo pasado	**pt**	past tense
sustantivo no empleado en el plural	**q**	collective (uncountable) noun, not used in plural
ferrocarril	**RAIL**	railways
religión, lo eclesiástico	**REL**	religion, church service
	sb	somebody
escolar, universitario	**SCOL**	schools, universities
singular	**sg**	singular
	sth	something
sujeto	**su(b)j**	(grammatical) subject
sufijo	**suff**	suffix
tauromaquia	**TAUR**	bullfighting
técnica, tecnología	**TEC(H)**	technical term, technology
telecomunicaciones	**TELEC, TEL**	telecommunications
televisión	**TV**	television
imprenta, tipografía	**TYP**	typography, printing
inglés norteamericano	**US**	American English
verbo	**vb**	verb
verbo intransitivo	**vi**	intransitive verb
verbo pronominal	**vr**	reflexive verb
verbo transitivo	**vt**	transitive verb
zoología, animales	**ZOOL**	zoology
marca registrada	**®**	registered trademark
indica un equivalente cultural	**≈**	introduces a cultural equivalent

SPANISH PRONUNCIATION

Consonants

c	[k]	caja	c before a, o or u is pronounced as in cat
ce, ci	[θe, θi]	cero cielo	c before e or i is pronounced as in thin
ch	[tʃ]	chiste	ch is pronounced as ch in chair
d	[d, ð]	danés ciudad	at the beginning of a phrase or after l or n, d is pronounced as in English. In any other position it is pronounced like th in the
g	[g, ɣ]	gafas paga	g before a, o or u is pronounced as in gap, if at the beginning of a phrase or after n. In other positions the sound is softened
ge, gi	[xe, xi]	gente girar	g before e or i is pronounced similar to ch in Scottish loch
h		haber	h is always silent in Spanish
j	[x]	jugar	j is pronounced similar to ch in Scottish loch
ll	[ʎ]	talle	ll is pronounced like the lli in million
ñ	[ɲ]	niño	ñ is pronounced like the ni in onion
q	[k]	que	q is pronounced as k in king
r, rr	[r, rr]	quitar garra	r is always pronounced in Spanish, unlike the silent r in dancer. rr is trilled, like a Scottish r
s	[s]	quizás isla	s is usually pronounced as in pass, but before b, d, g, l, m or n it is pronounced as in rose
v	[b, ß]	vía dividir	v is pronounced something like b. At the beginning of a phrase or after m or n it is pronounced as b in boy. In any other position the sound is softened
z	[θ]	tenaz	z is pronounced as th in thin

b, f, k, l, m, n, p, t and x are pronounced as in English.

Vowels

[a]	p*a*ta	not as long as *a* in f*a*r. When followed by a consonant in the same syllable (i.e. in a closed syllable), as in am*a*nte, the *a* is short, as in b*a*t
[e]	m*e*	like *e* in th*ey*. In a closed syllable, as in g*e*nte, the *e* is short as in p*e*t
[i:]	p*i*no	as in m*ea*n or mach*i*ne
[o]	l*o*	as in l*o*cal. In a closed syllable, as in c*o*ntrol, the *o* is short as in c*o*t
[u:]	l*u*nes	as in r*u*le. It is silent after *q*, and in *gue, gui*, unless marked *güe, güi* e.g. antig*ü*edad

Diphthongs

ai, ay	b*ai*le	as *i* in r*i*de
au	*au*to	as *ou* in sh*ou*t
ei, ey	bu*ey*	as *ey* in gr*ey*
eu	d*eu*da	both elements pronounced independently [e] + [u:]
oi, oy	h*oy*	as *oy* in t*oy*

Stress

The rules of stress in Spanish are as follows:
(a) when a word ends in a vowel or in *n* or *s*, the second last syllable is stressed: pat*a*ta, pat*a*tas, c*o*me, c*o*men
(b) when a word ends in a consonant other than *n* or *s*, the stress falls on the last syllable: par*e*d, habl*a*r
(c) when the rules set out in a and b are not applied, an acute accent appears over the stressed vowel: com*ú*n, geograf*í*a, ingl*é*s

In the phonetic transcription, the symbol ['] precedes the syllable on which the stress falls.

PRONUNCIACIÓN INGLESA

Vocales y diptongos

	Ejemplo inglés	Ejemplo español/explicación
ɑː	father	Entre a de padre y o de noche
ʌ	but, come	a muy breve
æ	man, cat	Se mantienen los labios en la posición de e en pena y luego se pronuncia el sonido a
ə	father, ago	Sonido indistinto parecido a una e u o casi mudas
əː	bird, heard	Entre e abierta, y o cerrada, sonido alargado
ɛ	get, bed	como en perro
ɪ	it, big	Más breve que en si
iː	tea, see	Como en fino
ɔ	hot, wash	Como en torre
ɔː	saw, all	Como en por
u	put, book	Sonido breve, más cerrado que burro
uː	too, you	Sonido largo, como en uno
aɪ	fly, high	Como en fraile
au	how, house	Como en pausa
ɛə	there, bear	Casi como en vea, pero el sonido a se mezcla con el indistinto [ə]
eɪ	day, obey	e cerrada seguida por una i débil
ɪə	here, hear	Como en manía, mezclándose el sonido a con el indistinto [ə]
əu	go, note	[ə] seguido por una breve u
ɔɪ	boy, oil	Como en voy
uə	poor, sure	u bastante larga más el sonido indistinto [ə]

Consonantes

	Ejemplo inglés	Ejemplo español/explicación
d	men*d*ed	Como en con*d*e, an*d*ar
g	*g*o, *g*et, bi*g*	Como en *g*rande, *g*ol
dʒ	*g*in, ju*dg*e	Como en la *ll* andaluza y en *G*eneralitat (catalán)
ŋ	si*ng*	Como en ví*n*culo
h	*h*ouse, *h*e	Como la jota hispanoamericana
j	*y*oung, *y*es	Como en *y*a
k	*c*ome, mo*ck*	Como en *c*aña, Es*c*ocia
r	*r*ed, t*r*ead	Se pronuncia con la punta de la lengua hacia atrás y sin hacerla vibrar
s	*s*and, ye*s*	Como en ca*s*a, *s*esión
z	ro*s*e, *z*ebra	Como en de*s*de, mi*s*mo
ʃ	*sh*e, ma*ch*ine	Como en *ch*ambre (francés), ro*x*o (portugués)
tʃ	*ch*in, ri*ch*	Como en *ch*ocolate
v	*v*alley	Como en f, pero se retiran los dientes superiores vibrándolos contra el labio inferior
w	*w*ater, *wh*ich	Como en la *u* de h*u*evo, p*u*ede
ʒ	vi*s*ion	Como en *j*ournal (francés)
θ	*th*ink, my*th*	Como en re*c*eta, *z*apato
ð	*th*is, *th*e	Como en la *d* de habla*d*o, verda*d*

b, p, f, m, n, l, t iguales que en español
El signo * indica que la r final escrita apenas se pronuncia en inglés británico cuando la palabra siguiente empieza con vocal. El signo ['] indica la sílaba acentuada.

ESPAÑOL - INGLÉS
SPANISH - ENGLISH

A

a [a] *prep* (*a + el = al*) (*lugar*) at, in, on; (*dirección*) to; (*destino*) to, towards; (*tiempo*) at; ~ **la derecha/ izquierda** on the right/left; **al lado de** beside, at the side of; **subir ~ un avión/tren** to get on or board a plane/train; **hablar ~ larga distancia** to speak long distance; ~ **las cuatro** at four o'clock; ¿~ **qué hora?** at what time?; ~ **los 30 años** at 30 years of age; **al día siguiente** the next day; ~ **eso de las cuatro** at about four o'clock; **al poco tiempo** a short time later; **al verlo yo** when I saw it; (*manera*): **hacerlo ~ la fuerza** to do it by force; **ir ~ caballo/pie** to go on horseback/foot; (*evaluación*): **poco ~ poco** little by little; **de dos ~ tres** from two to three; **ocho horas al día** eight hours a *or* per day; ~ **50 ptas el kilo** 50 pesetas a kilo; (*con verbo*): **empezó ~ llover** it started raining; **enseñar ~ leer** to teach to read; **voy ~ llevarlo** I am going to carry it; (*complemento de objeto*): **quiero ~ mis padres** (*not translated*) I love my parents; (*complemento circunstancial*): **cercano ~** near (to); **por miedo ~** out of fear of; (*frases elípticas*): ¡~ **comer!** let's eat!; ¿~ **qué viene eso?** what's the meaning of this?; ~ **ver** let's see.

abacero, a [aßa'θero, a] *nm/f* grocer.

abad, esa [a'ßað, 'ßesa] *nm/f* abbot/abbess; ~**ía** *nf* abbey.

abajo [a'ßaxo] *ad* (*situación*) down, below, underneath; (*en casa*) downstairs; (*dirección*) down, downwards; ~ **de** *prep* below, under; **el piso de ~** the downstairs flat; **la parte de ~** the lower part; ¡~ **el gobierno!** down with the government!; **cuesta/río ~** downhill/downstream; **de arriba ~** from top to bottom; **el ~ firmante** the undersigned; **más ~** lower *or* further down; **echar ~** to bring down.

abalanzar [aßalan'θar] *vt* to weigh; (*equilibrar*) to balance; (*arrojar*) to hurl; ~**se** *vr*: ~**se sobre** *o* **contra** to throw o.s. at.

abandonado, a [aßando'naðo, a] *a* derelict; (*desatendido*) abandoned; (*desierto*) deserted; (*descuidado*) neglected.

abandonar [aßando'nar] *vt* (*dejar*) to leave, abandon, desert; (*descuidar*) to neglect; (*ceder, dejar de*) to give up; ~**se** *vr*: ~**se a** to abandon o.s. to.

abandono [aßan'dono] *nm* (*acto*) desertion, abandonment; (*estado*) abandon, neglect; (*renuncia*) withdrawal, retirement; **perdió por ~** he lost by default.

abanicar [aßani'kar] *vt* to fan; **abanico** *nm* fan; (*NAUT*) derrick.

abaratar [aßara'tar] *vt* to lower (the price of) // *vi*, ~**se** *vr* to go *or* come down in price.

abarcar [aßar'kar] *vt* to include, embrace; (*AM*) to monopolize.

abarrotar [aßarro'tar] *vt* to bar; (*NAUT*) to stow; (*fig*) to overstock.

abarrote [aßa'rrote] *nm* packing; ~**s** *nmpl* (*AM*) groceries, provisions; ~**ro, a** *nm/f* (*AM*) grocer.

abastecer [aßaste'θer] *vt* to supply; **abastecimiento** *nm* supply; (*suministrar*) supplying.

abasto [a'ßasto] *nm* supply; (*abundancia*) abundance; **dar ~ con** to manage to finish.

abatido, a [aßa'tiðo, a] *a* dejected, downcast.

abatimiento [aßati'mjento] *nm* (*acto*) demolition; (*moral*) dejection, depression.

abatir [aßa'tir] *vt* (*muro*) to demolish; (*pájaro*) to shoot, bring down; (*fig*) to depress; (*humillar*) to humiliate // *vi* to go off course; ~**se** *vr* to be depressed; ~**se sobre** to swoop *or* pounce on.

abdicación [aßðika'θjon] *nf* abdication; **abdicar** *vi* to abdicate.

abdomen [aß'ðomen] *nm* abdomen.

abecedario [aßeθe'ðarjo] *nm* alphabet; (*libro*) spelling book.

abedul [aße'ðul] *nm* birch.

abeja [a'ßexa] *nf* bee.

aberración [aßerra'θjon] *nf* aberration.

abertura [aßer'tura] *nf* opening, gap; (*fig*) openness.

abeto [a'ßeto] *nm* fir.

abierto, a [a'ßjerto, a] *pp de* **abrir** // *a* open; (*AM*) generous.

abigarrado, a [aßiʝa'rraðo, a] *a* multi-coloured.

abismar [aßis'mar] *vt* to humble, cast down; ~**se** *vr* to sink; ~**se en** (*fig*) to be plunged into.

abismo [a'ßismo] *nm* abyss.

abjurar [aßxu'rar] *vt*, *vi* to abjure, forswear.

ablandar [aßlan'dar] *vt* to soften up; (*AUTO*) to run in // *vi*, ~**se** *vr* to grow softer.

ablución [aßlu'θjon] *nf* ablution.

abnegación [aßneʝa'θjon] *nf* self-denial; **abnegarse** *vr* to act unselfishly.

abobado, a [aβo'βaðo, a] *a* silly.

abobar [aβo'βar] *vt* to daze.

abocar [aβo'kar] *vt* to seize in one's mouth; ~ **se** *vr* to approach.

abochornar [aβotʃor'nar] *vt* to embarrass; ~**se** *vr* to get flustered; (*BOT*) to wilt.

abofetear [aβofete'ar] *vt* to slap (in the face).

abogacía [aβoɣa'θia] *nf* legal profession; (*ejercicio*) practice of the law; **abogado** *nm* lawyer.

abogar [aβo'ɣar] *vi*: ~ **por** to plead for; (*fig*) to advocate.

abolengo [aβo'lengo] *nm* ancestry, lineage.

abolición [aβoli'θjon] *nf* abolition.

abolir [aβo'lir] *vt* to abolish; (*cancelar*) to cancel.

abolladura [aβoʎa'ðura] *nf* dent; (*chichón, choque*) bump; **abollar** *vt* to dent; to raise a bump on.

abominación [aβomina'θjon] *nf* abomination.

abonado, a [aβo'naðo, a] *a* (*deuda*) paid // *nm/f* subscriber.

abonar [aβo'nar] *vt* (*deuda*) to settle; (*terreno*) to fertilize; (*idea*) to endorse; ~**se** *vr* to subscribe; **abono** *nm* payment; fertilizer; subscription.

abordar [aβor'ðar] *vt* to board; (*fig*) to broach.

aborigen [aβo'rixen] *nm* aborigine.

aborrecer [aβorre'θer] *vt* to hate, loathe; **aborrecible** *a* hateful, loathsome.

abortar [aβor'tar] *vi* (*malparir*) to have a miscarriage; (*deliberadamente*) to have an abortion; **hacerse** ~ to have an abortion; **aborto** *nm* miscarriage; abortion.

abotonar [aβoto'nar] *vt* to button (up), do up // *vi* to bud.

abovedado, a [aβoβe'ðaðo, a] *a* vaulted, domed.

abrasar [aβra'sar] *vt* to burn (up); (*AGR*) to dry up, parch.

abrazar [aβra'θar] *vt* to embrace.

abrazo [a'βraθo] *nm* embrace, hug; **un** ~ (*en carta*) with best wishes.

abrelatas [aβre'latas] *nm inv* tin opener.

abreviar [aβre'βjar] *vt* to abbreviate; (*texto*) to abridge; (*plazo*) to reduce; **abreviatura** *nf* abbreviation.

abrigar [aβri'ɣar] *vt* (*proteger*) to shelter; (*suj: ropa*) to keep warm; (*fig*) to cherish; **abrigo** *nm* shelter; (*apoyo*) support; (*prenda*) coat, overcoat.

abril [a'βril] *nm* April.

abrir [a'βrir] *vt* to open (up) // *vi* to open; ~**se** *vr* to open (up); (*extenderse*) to open out; (*cielo*) to clear; ~**se paso** to find *or* force a way through.

abrochar [aβro'tʃar] *vt* (*vestido*) to button (up); (*AM*) to staple; (*zapato*) to buckle; (*atar*) to lace up.

abrumar [aβru'mar] *vt* to overwhelm; (*sobrecargar*) to weigh down; (*agotar*) to wear out; ~ **se** *vr* to become foggy.

abrupto, a [a'βrupto, a] *a* abrupt; (*empinado*) steep.

absceso [aβs'θeso] *nm* abscess.

absolución [aβsolu'θjon] *nf* (*REL*) absolution; (*JUR*) pardon; (: *de acusado*) acquittal.

absoluto, a [aβso'luto, a] *a* absolute; **en** ~ *ad* in no way, not at all.

absolver [aβsol'βer] *vt* to absolve; (*JUR*) to pardon; (: *acusado*) to acquit.

absorber [aβsor'βer] *vt* to absorb; (*embeber*) to soak up.

absorción [aβsor'θjon] *nf* absorption.

absorto, a [aβ'sorto, a] *pp de* **absorber** // *a* absorbed, engrossed.

abstemio, a [aβs'temjo, a] *a* teetotal.

abstención [aβsten'θjon] *nf* abstention; **abstenerse** *vr*: **abstenerse de** to abstain *or* refrain from.

abstinencia [aβsti'nenθja] *nf* abstinence; (*ayuno*) fasting.

abstracción [aβstrak'θjon] *nf* abstraction; (*despiste*) absent-mindedness; ~ **hecha de** leaving aside.

abstraer [aβstra'er] *vt* to abstract // *vi*: ~ **de** to leave aside; ~**se** *vr* to be/become absorbed.

abstraído, a [aβstra'iðo, a] *a* preoccupied; (*despistado*) absent-minded.

absuelto [aβ'swelto] *pp de* **absolver.**

absurdo, a [aβ'surðo, a] *a* absurd.

abuelo, a [a'βwelo, a] *nm/f* grandfather/mother.

abulia [a'βulja] *nf* spinelessness, weakness.

abultado, a [aβul'taðo, a] *a* bulky.

abultar [aβul'tar] *vt* to enlarge; (*aumentar*) to increase; (*fig*) to exaggerate // *vi* to be bulky.

abundancia [aβun'danθja] *nf* abundance, plenty; **abundante** *a* abundant, plentiful; **abundar** *vi* to abound, be plentiful.

aburrido, a [aβu'rriðo, a] *a* (*hastiado*) bored; (*que aburre*) boring; **aburrimiento** *nm* boredom, tedium; **aburrir** *vt* to bore; **aburrirse** *vr* to be bored, get bored.

abusar [aβu'sar] *vi* to go too far; ~ **de** to abuse; **abuso** *nm* imposition; abuse.

abyecto, a [aβ'jekto, a] *a* wretched, abject.

A.C. *abr de* **Año de Cristo** A.D. (Anno Domini).

a/c *abr de* **al cuidado de** c/o (care of).

acá [a'ka] *ad* (*lugar*) here; (*tiempo*) now.

acabado, a [aka'βaðo, a] *a* finished, complete; (*perfecto*) perfect; (*agotado*) worn out; (*fig*) masterly // *nm* finish.

acabar [aka'βar] *vt* (*llevar a su fin*) to finish, complete; (*llegar al final de*) to finish, conclude; (*perfeccionar*) to complete; (*consumir*) to use up; (*rematar*) to finish off // *vi* to finish, end, come to an end; ~ **con** to put an end to; ~ **de llegar** to have just arrived; ~ **por** to end (up) by; ~**se** *vr* to finish, stop; (*terminarse*) to be over; (*agotarse*) to run out; **¡se acabó** that's enough!; it's all over!

academia [aka'ðemja] *nf* academy; **académico**, a *a* academic.

acaecer [akae'θer] *vi* to happen, occur; **acaecimiento** *nm* occurrence, happening.

acalorar [akalo'rar] *vt* to heat; (*fig*) to inflame; ~**se** *vr* (*fig*) to get heated.

acampar [akam'par] *vi* to camp.

acanalar [akana'lar] *vt* to groove; (*ondular*) to corrugate.

acantilado, a [akanti'laðo, a] *a* steep, sheer // *nm* cliff.

acaparar [akapa'rar] *vt* to monopolize; (*acumular*) to hoard.

acariciar [akari'θjar] *vt* to caress; (*fig*) to cherish.

acarrear [akarre'ar] *vt* to transport; (*fig*) to cause, result in; **acarreo** *nm* transport, haulage; (*precio*) carriage.

acaso [a'kaso] *ad* perhaps, maybe // *nm* chance; **por si** ~ just in case; **si** ~ in case; **al** ~ at random.

acatamiento [akata'mjento] *nm* respect; (*reverencia*) reverence; (*deferencia*) deference; **acatar** *vt* to respect; to revere; (*obedecer*) to obey.

acatarrarse [akata'rrarse] *vr* to catch a cold.

acaudalado, a [akauða'laðo, a] *a* well-off; **acaudalar** *vt* to accumulate.

acaudillar [akauði'ʎar] *vt* to lead, command.

acceder [akθe'ðer] *vi* to accede, agree.

accesible [akθe'siβle] *a* accessible.

acceso [ak'θeso] *nm* access, entry; (*camino*) access road; (*MED*) attack, fit.

accesorio, a [akθe'sorjo, a] *a, nm* accessory.

accidentado, a [akθiðen'taðo, a] *a* uneven; (*áspero*) rough; (*montañoso*) hilly; (*azaroso*) eventful // *nm/f* injured person.

accidental [akθiðen'tal] *a* accidental; **accidentarse** *vr* to have an accident.

accidente [akθi'ðente] *nm* accident; (*MED*) faint; ~**s** *nmpl* unevenness *sg*, roughness *sg*.

acción [ak'θjon] *nf* action; (*acto*) action, act, deed; (*COM*) share; (*JUR*) action, lawsuit; ~ **ordinaria/preferente** ordinary/preference share; **accionar** *vt* to work, operate // *vi* to gesticulate.

accionista [akθjo'nista] *nm/f* shareholder.

acebo [a'θeβo] *nm* holly; (*árbol*) holly tree.

acechanza [aθe'tʃanθa] *nf* = **acecho**.

acechar [aθe'tʃar] *vt* to spy on; (*aguardar*) to lie in wait for; **acecho** *nm* spying, watching; ambush.

acedía [aθe'ðia] *nf* acidity; (*MED*) heartburn; (*fig*) sourness.

aceitar [aθei'tar] *vt* to oil, lubricate; **aceite** *nm* oil; (*de oliva*) olive oil; **aceitera** *nf* oilcan; **aceitoso**, a *a* oily.

aceituna [aθei'tuna] *nf* olive.

acelerar [aθele'rar] *vt* to accelerate.

acento [a'θento] *nm* accent; (*acentuación*) stress; **acentuar** *vt* to accent; to stress; (*fig*) to accentuate.

acepción [aθep'θjon] *nf* meaning; (*preferencia*) preference.

acepillar [aθepi'ʎar] *vt* to brush; (*alisar*) to plane.

aceptación [aθepta'θjon] *nf* acceptance; (*aprobación*) approval; **aceptar** *vt* to accept; to approve.

acequia [a'θekja] *nf* irrigation ditch.

acera [a'θera] *nf* pavement.

acerado, a [aθe'raðo, a] *a* steel; (*afilado*) sharp; (*fig: duro*) steely; (*: mordaz*) biting.

acerbo, a [a'θerβo, a] *a* bitter; (*fig*) harsh.

acerca [a'θerka]: ~ **de** *ad* about, concerning.

acercar [aθer'kar] *vt* to bring or move nearer; ~**se** *vr* to approach, come near.

acero [a'θero] *nm* steel.

acérrimo, a [a'θerrimo, a] *a* out-and-out, staunch.

acertado, a [aθer'taðo, a] *a* correct; (*apropiado*) apt; (*sensato*) sensible.

acertar [aθer'tar] *vt* (*dar en: el blanco*) to hit; (*llegar a encontrar*) to get right; (*adivinar*) to guess; (*alcanzar*) to achieve // *vi* to get it right, be right; ~ **a** to manage to; ~ **con** to happen on.

acertijo [aθer'tixo] *nm* riddle, puzzle.

acervo [a'θerβo] *nm* heap; ~ **común** undivided estate.

acicalar [aθika'lar] *vt* to polish; (*adornar*) to bedeck; ~**se** *vr* to smarten o.s. up.

acicate [aθi'kate] *nm* spur.

acidez [aθi'ðeθ] *nf* acidity.

ácido, a ['aθiðo, a] *a* sour, acid // *nm* acid.

acierto [a'θjerto] *nm* success; (*buen paso*) wise move; (*solución*) solution; (*habilidad*) skill, ability.

aclamación [aklama'θjon] *nf* acclamation; (*aplausos*) applause; **aclamar** *vt* to acclaim; to applaud.

aclaración [aklara'θjon] *nf* rinsing, rinse; (*clasificación*) classification.

aclarar [akla'rar] *vt* to clarify, explain; (*ropa*) to rinse // *vi* to clear up; ~**se** *vr*: ~ **se la garganta** to clear one's throat.

aclimatación [aklimata'θjon] *nf* acclimatization; **aclimatar** *vt* to acclimatize; **aclimatarse** *vr* to become acclimatized.

acobardar [akoβar'ðar] *vt* to daunt, intimidate.

acodarse [ako'ðarse] *vr*: ~ **en** to lean on.

acogedor, a [akoxe'ðor, a] *a* welcoming; (*hospitalario*) hospitable; **acoger** *vt* to welcome; (*abrigar*) to shelter; **acogerse** *vr* to take refuge; **acogida** *nf* reception; refuge.

acolchar [akol'tʃar] *vt* to pad; (*tapizar*) to upholster; (*fig*) to cushion.

acometer [akome'ter] *vt* to attack; (*emprender*) to undertake; **acometida** *nf* attack, assault.

acomodadizo, a [akomoða'ðiθo, a] *a* obliging, acquiescent.

acomodado, a [akomo'ðaðo, a] *a* suitable; (*precio*) moderate; (*persona*) well-to-do.

acomodador, a [akomoða'ðor, a] *nm/f* usher/ette.

acomodar [akomo'ðar] *vt* to adjust; (*alojar*) to accommodate; (*convenir*) to suit; (*reparar*) to repair; (*reconciliar*) to reconcile // *vi* to suit, be suitable; ~**se** *vr* to conform; (*instalarse*) to install o.s.; (*adaptarse*) to adapt o.s.

acomodo [ako'moðo] *nm* arrangement; (*puesto*) post.

acompañar [akompa'ɲar] *vt* to accompany; (*documentos*) to enclose.

acondicionar [akondiθjo'nar] *vt* to arrange, prepare; (*determinar*) to condition.

acongojar [akongo'xar] *vt* to distress, grieve.

aconsejar [akonse'xar] *vt* to advise, counsel; ~**se** *vr*: ~**se con** to consult.

acontecer [akonte'θer] *vi* to happen, occur; **acontecimiento** *nm* event.

acopio [a'kopjo] *nm* store, stock; (*asamblea*) gathering.

acoplamiento [akopla'mjento] *nm* coupling, joint; **acoplar** *vt* to fit, couple; (*unir*) to connect.

acorazado, a [akora'θaðo, a] *a* armour-plated, armoured // *nm* battleship.

acordar [akor'ðar] *vt* (*resolver*) to agree, resolve; (*recordar*) to remind; (*MUS*) to tune; ~**se** *vr* to agree; ~**se (de)** to remember; **acorde** *a* in agreement; (*MUS*) harmonious // *nm* chord.

acordeón [akorðe'on] *nm* accordion.

acordonado, a [akorðo'naðo, a] *a* cordoned-off.

acorralar [akorra'lar] *vt* to round up, corral.

acortar [akor'tar] *vt* to shorten; (*duración*) to cut short; (*cantidad*) to reduce; ~**se** *vr* to become shorter.

acosar [ako'sar] *vt* to pursue relentlessly; (*fig*) to hound, pester.

acostar [akos'tar] *vt* (*en cama*) to put to bed; (*en suelo*) to lay down; (*barco*) to bring alongside; ~**se** *vr* to go to bed; to lie down.

acostumbrar [akostum'brar] *vt*: ~ **a uno a** to accustom sb to // *vi*: ~ **a** to be used to; ~**se** *vr*: ~**se a** to get used to.

acotación [akota'θjon] *nf* marginal note; (*GEO*) elevation mark; (*de límite*) boundary mark; (*TEATRO*) stage direction.

acre ['akre] *a* sharp, bitter; (*fig*) biting // *nm* acre.

acrecentar [akreθen'tar] *vt* to increase, augment.

acreditar [akreði'tar] *vt* (*garantizar*) to vouch for, guarantee; (*autorizar*) to authorize; (*dar prueba de*) to prove; (*COM: abonar*) to credit; (*embajador*) to accredit; ~ **se** *vr* to become famous.

acreedor, a [akree'ðor, a] *a*: ~ **a** worthy of // *nm/f* creditor.

acribillar [akriβi'ʎar] *vt*: ~ **a balazos** to riddle with bullets.

acrimonia [akri'monja], **acritud** [akri-'tuð] *nf* acrimony.

acta ['akta] *nf* certificate; (*de comisión*) minutes *pl*, record; ~ **de nacimiento/matrimonial** birth/marriage certificate; ~ **notarial** affidavit.

actitud [akti'tuð] *nf* attitude; (*postura*) posture.

activar [akti'βar] *vt* to activate; (*acelerar*) to expedite.

actividad [aktiβi'ðað] *nf* activity.

activo, a [ak'tiβo, a] *a* active; (*vivo*) lively // *nm* assets *pl*.

acto ['akto] *nm* act, action; (*ceremonia*) ceremony; (*TEATRO*) act; **en el** ~ immediately.

actor [ak'tor] *nm* actor; (*JUR*) plaintiff.

actora [ak'tora] *a*: **parte** ~ prosecution; (*demandante*) plaintiff.

actriz [ak'triθ] *nf* actress.

actuación [aktwa'θjon] *nf* action; (*comportamiento*) conduct, behaviour; (*JUR*) proceedings *pl*; (*desempeño*) performance.

actual [ak'twal] *a* present(-day), current; ~**idad** *nf* present, present time; ~**idades** *nfpl* news *sg*; (*película, nodo*) newsreel *sg*; **en la** ~**idad** nowadays, at the present time.

actualizar [aktwali'θar] *vt* to update, modernize.

actualmente [aktwal'mente] *ad* now, nowadays, at present.

actuar [ak'twar] *vi* (*obrar*) to work, operate; (*actor*) to act, perform // *vt* to work, operate; ~ **de** to act as.

actuario [ak'twarjo] *nm* clerk; (*COM*) actuary.

acuarela [akwa'rela] *nf* watercolour.

acuario [a'kwarjo] *nm* aquarium; **A**~ (*ASTRO*) Aquarius.

acuático, a [a'kwatiko, a] *a* aquatic.

acuciar [aku'θjar] *vt* to urge on.

acuclillarse [akukli'ʎarse] *vr* to crouch down.

acudir [aku'ðir] *vi* to come along, turn up; ~ **a** to turn to; ~ **en ayuda de** to go to the aid of.

acuerdo *etc vb ver* **acordar** // [a'kwerðo] *nm* agreement; **¡de** ~**!** agreed!; **de** ~ **con** (*persona*) in agreement with; (*acción, documento*) in accordance with.

acumulador [akumula'ðor] *nm* storage battery; **acumular** *vt* to accumulate, collect.

acuñar [aku'ɲar] *vt* (*moneda*) to coin, mint; (*poner cuñas*) to wedge.

acuoso, a [a'kwoso, a] *a* watery.

acurrucarse [akurru'karse] *vr* to crouch; (*ovillarse*) to curl up.

acusación [akusa'θjon] *nf* accusation; **acusar** *vt* to accuse; (*revelar*) to reveal; (*denunciar*) to denounce.

acuse [a'kuse] *nm*: ~ **de recibo**

acknowledgement of receipt.

acústico, a [a'kustiko, a] *a* acoustic // *nm* hearing aid.

achacar [atʃa'kar] *vt* to attribute.

achacoso, a [atʃa'koso, a] *a* sickly.

achaque [a'tʃake] *nm* ailment.

achicar [atʃi'kar] *vt* to reduce; (*humillar*) to humiliate; (*NAUT*) to bale out.

achicoria [atʃi'korja] *nf* chicory.

achicharrar [atʃitʃa'rrar] *vt* to scorch, burn.

adagio [a'ðaxjo] *nm* adage; (*MUS*) adagio.

adaptación [aðapta'θjon] *nf* adaptation; **adaptar** *vt* to adapt; (*acomodar*) to fit.

a. de C. *abr* = **a. de J.C.**

A. de C. *abr* = **A.C.**

adecuado, a [aðe'kwaðo, a] *a* adequate; (*apto*) suitable; (*oportuno*) appropriate; **adecuar** *vt* to adapt; to make suitable.

a. de J.C. *abr de* **antes de Jesucristo** B.C. (before Christ).

adelantado, a [aðelan'taðo, a] *a* advanced; (*reloj*) fast; **pagar por** ~ to pay in advance; **adelantamiento** *nm* advance, advancement; (*AUTO*) overtaking; (*progreso*) progress.

adelantar [aðelan'tar] *vt* to move forward; (*avanzar*) to advance; (*acelerar*) to speed up // *vi*, ~**se** *vr* to go forward, advance; (*AUTO*) to overtake.

adelante [aðe'lante] *ad* forward(s), onward(s), ahead // *excl* come in!; **de hoy en** ~ from now on; **más** ~ later on; (*más allá*) further on.

adelanto [aðe'lanto] *nm* advance; (*mejora*) improvement; (*progreso*) progress.

adelgazar [aðelɣa'θar] *vt* to thin (down); (*afilar*) to taper // *vi*, ~**se** *vr* to grow thin.

ademán [aðe'man] *nm* gesture; **ademanes** *nmpl* manners; **en** ~ **de** as if to.

además [aðe'mas] *ad* besides; (*por otra parte*) moreover; (*también*) also; ~ **de** besides, in addition to.

adentro [a'ðentro] *ad* inside, in; **mar** ~ out at sea; **tierra** ~ inland.

adepto, a [a'ðepto, a] *nm/f* supporter.

aderezar [aðere'θar] *vt* to prepare; (*persona, ensalada*) to dress; (*comida*) to season; ~**se** *vr* to dress up; **aderezo** *nm* preparation; dressing; seasoning.

adeudar [aðeu'ðar] *vt* to owe // *vi* to become related by marriage; ~**se** *vr* to run into debt.

adherirse [aðe'rirse] *vr*: ~ **a** to adhere to.

adhesión [aðe'sjon] *nf* adhesion; (*fig*) adherence.

adición [aði'θjon] *nf* addition.

adicionar [aðiθjo'nar] *vt* to add.

adicto, a [a'ðikto, a] *a*: ~ **a** given to; (*dedicado*) devoted to // *nm/f* supporter, follower.

adiestrar [aðjes'trar] *vt* to train, teach; (*conducir*) to guide, lead; ~**se** *vr* to practise; (*enseñarse*) to train o.s.

adinerado, a [aðine'raðo, a] *a* wealthy.

adiós [a'ðjos] *excl* (*para despedirse*) goodbye!, cheerio!; (*para saludar*) hello!

aditivo [aði'tiβo] *nm* additive.

adivinanza [aðiβi'nanθa] *nf* riddle; **adivinar** *vt* to prophesy; (*conjeturar*) to guess; **adivino, a** *nm/f* fortune-teller.

adj *a abr de* **adjunto** encl. (enclosed).

adjetivo [aðxe'tiβo] *nm* adjective.

adjudicación [aðxuðika'θjon] *nf* award; **adjudicar** *vt* to award; **adjudicarse** *vr*: **adjudicarse algo** to appropriate sth.

adjuntar [aðxun'tar] *vt* to attach, enclose; **adjunto, a** *a* attached, enclosed // *nm/f* assistant.

administración [aðministra'θjon] *nf* administration; (*dirección*) management; **administrador, a** *nm/f* administrator; manager/ess.

administrar [aðminis'trar] *vt* to administer; **administrativo, a** *a* administrative.

admirable [aðmi'raβle] *a* admirable; **admiración** *nf* admiration; (*asombro*) wonder; (*LING*) exclamation mark; **admirar** *vt* to admire; (*extrañar*) to surprise; **admirarse** *vr* to be surprised.

admisible [aðmi'siβle] *a* admissible.

admitir [aðmi'tir] *vt* to admit; (*aceptar*) to accept.

admonición [aðmoni'θjon] *nf* warning.

adobe [a'ðoβe] *nm* adobe, sun-dried brick.

adolecer [aðole'θer] *vi* to be ill, fall ill; ~ **de** to suffer from.

adolescente [aðoles'θente] *nm/f* adolescent.

adonde [a'ðonðe] *conj* (to) where.

adónde [a'ðonðe] *ad* = **dónde**.

adopción [aðop'θjon] *nf* adoption.

adoptar [aðop'tar] *vt* to adopt.

adoquín [aðo'kin] *nm* paving stone.

adorar [aðo'rar] *vt* to adore.

adormecer [aðorme'θer] *vt* to put to sleep; ~**se** *vr* to become sleepy, fall asleep.

adornar [aðor'nar] *vt* to adorn.

adorno [a'ðorno] *nm* adornment; (*decoración*) decoration.

adquiero *etc vb ver* **adquirir**.

adquirir [aðki'rir] *vt* to acquire, obtain.

adquisición [aðkisi'θjon] *nf* acquisition.

adrede [a'ðreðe] *ad* on purpose.

adscribir [aðskri'βir] *vt* to appoint.

aduana [a'ðwana] *nf* customs *pl*.

aduanero, a [aðwa'nero, a] *a* customs *cpd* // *nm/f* customs officer.

aducir [aðu'θir] *vt* to adduce; (*dar como prueba*) to offer as proof.

adueñarse [aðwe'ɲarse] *vr*: ~ **de** to take possession of.

adulación [aðula'θjon] *nf* flattery.

adular [aðu'lar] *vt* to flatter.

adulterar [aðulte'rar] *vt* to adulterate // *vi* to commit adultery.

adulterio [aðul'terjo] *nm* adultery.

adulto, a [a'ðulto, a] *a, nm/f* adult.

adusto, a [a'ðusto, a] *a* stern; (*austero*) austere.

advenedizo, a [aðßene'ðiðo, a] *nm/f* upstart.

advenimiento [aðßeni'mjento] *nm* arrival; (*al trono*) accession.

adverbio [að'ßerßjo] *nm* adverb.

adversario, a [aðßer'sarjo, a] *nm/f* adversary.

adversidad [aðßersi'ðað] *nf* adversity; (*contratiempo*) setback.

adverso, a [að'ßerso, a] *a* adverse; (*opuesto*) opposite.

advertencia [aðßer'tenðja] *nf* warning; (*prefacio*) preface, foreword.

advertir [aðßer'tir] *vt* to notice; (*avisar*) to warn // *vi*: ~ **en** to notice.

Adviento [að'ßjento] *nm* Advent.

adyacente [aðja'ßente] *a* adjacent.

aéreo, a [a'ereo, a] *a* aerial.

aerodeslizador [aeroðesliða'ðor], **aerodeslizante** [aeroðesli'ßante] *nm* hovercraft.

aeronáutica [aero'nautika] *nf* aeronautics *sg*.

aeropuerto [aero'pwerto] *nm* airport.

afabilidad [afaßili'ðað] *nf* friendliness; **afable** *a* affable.

afán [a'fan] *nm* hard work; (*deseo*) desire.

afanar [afa'nar] *vt* to harass; ~**se** *vr*: ~**se por** to strive to; **afanoso, a** *a* hard; (*trabajador*) industrious.

afear [afe'ar] *vt* to make ugly; (*mutilar*) to deface.

afección [afek'ßjon] *nf* affection; (*MED*) disease.

afectación [afekta'ßjon] *nf* affectation; **afectado, a** *a* affected; **afectar** *vt* to affect.

afectísimo, a [afek'tisimo, a] *a* affectionate; ~ **suyo** yours truly.

afecto, a [a'fekto, a] *a* affectionate // *nm* affection; ~ a fond of.

afectuoso, a [afek'twoso, a] *a* affectionate.

afeitar [afei'tar] *vt* to shave; ~**se** *vr* to shave.

afeminado, a [afemi'naðo, a] *a* effeminate.

aferrado, a [afe'rraðo, a] *a* stubborn.

aferrar [afe'rrar] *vt* to moor; (*fig*) to grasp // *vi* to moor.

afianzamiento [afjanßa'mjento] *nm* strengthening; (*garantía*) guarantee; (*COM*) security; **afianzar** *vt* to strengthen; to guarantee; to secure; **afianzarse** *vr* to become established.

afición [afi'ßjon] *nf* fondness, liking; **la** ~ the fans *pl*; **pinto por** ~ I paint as a hobby; **aficionado, a** *a* keen, enthusiastic; amateur // *nm/f* enthusiast, fan; amateur.

aficionar [afiðjo'nar] *vt*: ~ **a uno a algo** to make sb like sth; ~**se** *vr*: ~**se a algo** to grow fond of sth.

afilado, a [afi'laðo, a] *a* sharp.

afilar [afi'lar] *vt* to sharpen.

afiliarse [afi'ljarse] *vr* to become affiliated to.

afín [a'fin] *a* bordering, adjacent; (*parecido*) similar; (*conexo*) related.

afinar [afi'nar] *vt* (*TEC*) to refine; (*MUS*) to tune // *vi* to play/sing in tune.

afinidad [afini'ðað] *nf* affinity; (*parentesco*) relationship; **por** ~ by marriage.

afirmación [afirma'ßjon] *nf* affirmation; **afirmar** *vt* to affirm, state; (*sostener*) to strengthen; **afirmativo, a** *a* affirmative.

aflicción [aflik'ßjon] *nf* affliction; (*dolor*) grief.

afligir [afli'xir] *vt* to afflict; (*apenar*) to distress; ~**se** *vr* to grieve.

aflojar [aflo'xar] *vt* to slacken; (*desatar*) to loosen, undo; (*relajar*) to relax // *vi* to drop; (*bajar*) to go down; ~**se** *vr* to relax.

afluente [aflu'ente] *a* flowing; (*elocuente*) eloquent // *nm* tributary.

afluir [aflu'ir] *vi* to flow.

afmo, a *abr de* **afectísimo(a) suyo(a)**.

afónico, a [a'foniko, a] *a* (*ronco*) hoarse; (*sin voz*) voiceless.

afortunado, a [afortu'naðo, a] *a* fortunate, lucky.

afrancesado, a [afranße'saðo, a] *a* francophile; (*pey*) frenchified.

afrenta [a'frenta] *nf* affront, insult; (*deshonra*) dishonour, shame; **afrentar** *vt* to affront; to dishonour; **afrentarse** *vr* to be ashamed; **afrentoso, a** *a* insulting.

África ['afrika] *nf* Africa; ~ **del Sur** South Africa; **africano, a** *a*, *nm/f* African.

afrontar [afron'tar] *vt* to confront; (*poner cara a cara*) to bring face to face.

afuera [a'fwera] *ad* out, outside; ~**s** *nfpl* outskirts, suburbs.

agachar [aɣa'tʃar] *vt* to bend, bow; ~**se** *vr* to stoop, bend.

agalla [a'ɣaʎa] *nf* (*ZOOL*) gill; ~**s** *nfpl* (*MED*) tonsillitis *sg*; (*ANAT*) tonsils.

agarradera [aɣarra'ðera] *nf* (*AM*), **agarradero** [aɣarra'ðero] *nm* handle; ~**s** *npl* pull *sg*, influence *sg*.

agarrado, a [aɣa'rraðo, a] *a* mean, stingy.

agarrar [aɣa'rrar] *vt* to grasp, grab; (*AM*) to take, catch // *vi* (*planta*) to take root; ~**se** *vr* to hold on (tightly).

agarrotar [aɣarro'tar] *vt* (*llo*) to tie tightly; (*persona*) to squeeze tightly; (*reo*) to garrotte; ~**se** *vr* (*motor*) to seize up; (*MED*) to stiffen.

agasajar [aɣasa'xar] *vt* to treat well, fête; **agasajo** *nm* lavish hospitality.

agencia [a'xenðja] *nf* agency; ~ **de viajes/inmobiliaria** travel/estate agency.

agenda [a'xenda] *nf* diary.

agente [a'xente] *nm* agent; (*de policía*) policeman; ~ **femenino** policewoman.

ágil ['axil] *a* agile, nimble; **agilidad** *nf* agility, nimbleness.

agio ['axjo] *nm* speculation.

agiotista [axjo'tista] *nm* (stock)jobber; (*especulador*) speculator.

agitación [axita'θjon] nf shaking, waving, stirring; (del mar) roughness; (fig) agitation.

agitar [axi'tar] vt to wave, shake, stir; (fig) to stir up, excite; ~se vr to get excited.

aglomerar [axlome'rar] vt, ~se vr to agglomerate, crowd together.

agnóstico, a [ax'nostiko, a] a, nm/f agnostic.

agobiar [axo'βjar] vt to weigh down; (oprimir) to oppress; (cargar) to burden.

agolparse [axol'parse] vr to crowd together.

agonía [axo'nia] nf agony, anguish.

agonizante [axoni'θante] a dying.

agonizar [axoni'θar] vi (también estar agonizando) to be dying.

agosto [a'xosto] nm August.

agotado, a [axo'taðo, a] a exhausted; (libros) out of print; (acabado) finished; (mercancías) sold out; **agotamiento** nm exhaustion.

agotar [axo'tar] vt to exhaust; (consumir) to drain; (recursos) to use up, deplete; ~se vr to be exhausted; (acabarse) to run out; (libro) to go out of print.

agraciar [axra'θjar] vt (JUR) to pardon; (con premio) to reward.

agradable [axra'ðaβle] a pleasing, pleasant, nice.

agradar [axra'ðar] vt, vi to please.

agradecer [axraðe'θer] vt to thank; (favor etc) to be grateful for; **agradecimiento** nm thanks pl; gratitude.

agrado [a'xraðo] nm affability; (gusto) liking.

agrandar [axran'dar] vt to enlarge; (fig) to exaggerate; ~se vr to get bigger.

agrario, a [a'xrarjo, a] a agrarian.

agravar [axra'βar] vt to make heavier; (irritar) to aggravate; (oprimir) to oppress; ~se vr to worsen, get worse.

agraviar [axra'βjar] vt to offend; (ser injusto con) to wrong; ~se vr to take offence; **agravio** nm offence; wrong; (ofensa) grievance.

agregado [axre'xaðo] nm aggregate; (persona) attaché.

agregar [axre'xar] vt to gather; (añadir) to add; (persona) to appoint.

agresión [axre'sjon] nf aggression; **agresivo, a** a aggressive.

agriar [a'xrjar] vt to (turn) sour; ~se vr to turn sour.

agricultor, a [axrikul'tor, a] nm/f farmer; **agricultura** nf agriculture, farming.

agridulce [axri'ðulθe] a bittersweet.

agrietarse [axrje'tarse] vr to crack; (la piel) to chap.

agrio, a [a'xrjo, a] a bitter.

agronomía [axrono'mia] nf agronomy, agriculture.

agrupación [axrupa'θjon] nf group; (acto) grouping.

agrupar [axru'par] vt to group.

agua ['axwa] nf water; (lluvia) rain; (NAUT) wake; (ARQ) slope of a roof; ~s nfpl (de piedra) water sg, sparkle sg; (MED) water sg, urine sg; (NAUT) waters; ~s abajo/arriba downstream/upstream; ~ bendita/destilada/potable holy/distilled/drinking water; ~ corriente running water; ~ de colonia eau de cologne; ~s jurisdiccionales territorial waters; ~s mayores excrement sg.

aguacate [axwa'kate] nm avocado pear.

aguacero [axwa'θero] nm (heavy) shower.

aguado, a [a'xwaðo, a] a watery, watered down // nf (AGR) watering place; (NAUT) water supply; (ARTE) water-colour.

aguafiestas [axwa'fjestas] nm/f inv spoilsport.

aguafuerte [axwa'fwerte] nf etching.

aguamar [axwa'mar] nm jellyfish.

aguantable [axwan'taβle] a bearable; **aguantar** vt to bear, put up with; (contener) to hold; (sostener) to hold up // vi to last; **aguantarse** vr to restrain o.s.

aguar [a'xwar] vt to water down.

aguardar [axwar'ðar] vt to wait for.

aguardiente [axwar'ðjente] nm brandy.

aguarrás [axwa'rras] nm turpentine.

agudeza [axu'ðeθa] nf sharpness; (ingenio) wit; **agudo, a** a sharp; (voz) high-pitched, piercing; (dolor, enfermedad) acute.

agüero [a'xwero] nm omen; (pronóstico) prediction.

aguijar [axi'xar] vt to goad; (incitar) to urge on // vi to hurry along.

aguijón [axi'xon] nm sting; (BOT) spine; (estímulo, fig) spur; **aguijonear** vt = aguijar.

águila ['axila] nf eagle; (fig) genius.

aguileño, a [axi'leno, a] a aquiline; (facciones) sharp-featured.

aguinaldo [axi'naldo] nm Christmas box.

aguja [a'xuxa] nf needle; (de reloj) hand; (ARQ) spire; (TEC) firing-pin; ~s nfpl (ZOOL) ribs; (FERRO) points.

agujerear [axuxere'ar] vt to make holes in; **agujero** nm hole.

agujetas [axu'xetas] nfpl stitch sg; (rigidez) stiffness sg.

aguzar [axu'θar] vt to sharpen; (fig) to incite.

ahí [a'i] ad there; de ~ que so that, with the result that; ~ llega here he comes; por ~ that way; (allá) over there.

ahijado, a [ai'xaðo, a] nm/f godson/daughter.

ahínco [a'inko] nm earnestness.

ahitar [ai'tar] vt to surfeit; ~se vr to stuff o.s.

ahíto, a [a'ito, a] a: estoy ~ I have indigestion // nm indigestion.

ahogar [ao'xar] vt to drown; (asfixiar) to suffocate, smother; (fuego) to put out; ~se vr (en el agua) to drown; (suicidio) to drown o.s.; (por asfixia) to suffocate.

ahogo [a'oxo] nm shortness of breath; (fig) financial difficulty.

ahondar [aon'dar] vt to deepen, make

deeper; (*fig*) to go deeply into // *vi:* ~ **en** to go deeply into.

ahora [a'ora] *ad* now; (*poco tiempo ha*) a moment ago, just now; (*dentro de poco*) in a moment // *conj* now; ~ **voy** I'm coming; ~ **mismo** right now; ~ **bien** now then; **por** ~ for the present.

ahorcar [aor'kar] *vt* to hang; ~**se** *vr* to hang o.s.

ahorita [ao'rita] *ad* (*fam*) right now.

ahorrar [ao'rrar] *vt* (*dinero*) to save; (*esfuerzos*) to save, avoid; **ahorro** *nm* economy, saving; (*frugalidad*) thrift; **ahorros** *nmpl* savings.

ahuecar [awe'kar] *vt* to hollow (out); (*voz*) to deepen; ~**se** *vr* to give o.s. airs.

ahumar [au'mar] *vt* to smoke, cure; (*llenar de humo*) to fill with smoke // *vi* to smoke; ~**se** *vr* to fill with smoke.

ahuyentar [aujen'tar] *vt* to drive off, frighten off; (*fig*) to dispel; ~**se** *vr* to run away.

airado, a [ai'raðo, a] *a* angry; **airar** *vt* to anger; **airarse** *vr* to get angry.

aire ['aire] *nm* air; (*viento*) wind; (*corriente*) draught; (*MUS*) tune; ~**s** *nmpl*: **darse** ~**s** to give o.s. airs; **al** ~ **libre** in the open air; ~ **acondicionado** air conditioning; **aireso, a** *a* windy; draughty; (*fig*) graceful.

aislador [aisla'ðor] *nm* insulator; **aislar** *vt* to isolate; (*ELEC*) to insulate.

ajar [a'xar] *vt* to spoil; (*fig*) to abuse.

ajedrez [axe'ðreθ] *nm* chess.

ajeno, a [a'xeno, a] *a* (*que pertenece a otro*) somebody else's; (*impropio*) inappropriate; (*extraño*) alien, foreign; ~ **a** foreign to; ~ **de** free from, devoid of.

ajetreo [axe'treo] *nm* bustle.

ají [a'xi] *nm* chili, red pepper; (*salsa*) chili sauce.

ajo ['axo] *nm* garlic; ~ **porro** *o* **puerro** leek.

ajorca [a'xorka] *nf* bracelet.

ajuar [a'xwar] *nm* household furnishings *pl*; (*de novia*) trousseau; (*de niño*) layette.

ajustado, a [axus'taðo, a] *a* (*tornillo*) tight; (*cálculo*) right; (*ropa*) tight-fitting; (*DEPORTE: resultado*) close.

ajustar [axus'tar] *vt* (*adaptar*) to adjust; (*encajar*) to fit; (*TEC*) to engage; (*contratar*) to hire; (*IMPRENTA*) to make up; (*apretar*) to tighten; (*concertar*) to agree (on); (*reconciliar*) to reconcile; (*cuenta*) to settle // *vi* to fit; ~**se** *vr* to come to an agreement.

ajuste [a'xuste] *nm* adjustment; (*TEC: costura*) fitting; (*acuerdo*) compromise; (*de cuenta*) settlement.

al [al] = **a + el**, ver **a**.

ala ['ala] *nf* wing; (*de sombrero*) brim; (*futbolista*) winger.

alabanza [ala'ßanθa] *nf* praise.

alabar [ala'ßar] *vt* to praise; ~**se** *vr*: ~**se de** to boast of (being).

alabear [alaße'ar] *vt*, ~**se** *vr* to warp.

alacena [ala'θena] *nf* cupboard.

alacrán [ala'kran] *nm* scorpion.

alambicado, a [alambi'kaðo, a] *a* distilled; (*fig*) affected.

alambicar [alambi'kar] *vt* to distil.

alambique [alam'bike] *nm* still.

alambrado [alam'braðo] *nm* wire fence; (*red*) wire netting; **alambre** *nm* wire; **alambre de púas** barbed wire; **alambrista** *nm/f* tightrope walker.

alameda [ala'meða] *nf* (*plantío*) poplar grove; (*lugar de paseo*) avenue, tree-lined walk.

álamo ['alamo] *nm* poplar; ~ **temblón** aspen.

alano [a'lano] *nm* mastiff.

alar [a'lar] *nm* eaves *pl*.

alarde [a'larðe] *nm* (*MIL*) review; (*ostentación*) show, display; **hacer** ~ **de** to boast of.

alargar [alar'var] *vt* to lengthen, extend; (*paso*) to hasten; (*brazo*) to stretch out; (*cuerda*) to pay out; (*conversación*) to spin out; ~**se** *vr* to get longer; ~**se en** to enlarge upon; (*pey*) to drag out.

alarido [ala'riðo] *nm* shriek.

alarma [a'larma] *nf* alarm.

alazán [ala'θan] *nm* sorrel.

alba ['alßa] *nf* dawn.

albacea [alßa'θea] *nm/f* executor/trix.

Albania [al'ßanja] *nf* Albania.

albañal [alßa'ɲal] *nm* drain, sewer.

albañil [alßa'ɲil] *nm* bricklayer; (*cantero*) mason.

albaricoque [alßari'koke] *nm* apricot.

albedrío [alße'ðrio] *nm*: **libre** ~ free will.

alberca [al'ßerka] *nf* reservoir.

albergar [alßer'var] *vt*, ~**se** *vr* to shelter.

albergue [al'ßerve] *nm* shelter, refuge; ~ **de juventud** youth hostel.

albóndiga [al'ßondiva] *nf* meatball.

albor [al'ßor] *nm* whiteness; (*amanecer*) dawn; ~**ada** *nf* dawn; (*diana*) reveille; ~**ear** *vi* to dawn.

albornoz [alßor'noθ] *nm* (*de los árabes*) burnous; (*para el baño*) bathrobe.

alborotar [alßoro'tar] *vi* to make a row // *vt* to agitate, stir up; ~**se** *vr* to get excited; (*mar*) to get rough; **alboroto** *nm* row, uproar.

alborozar [alßoro'θar] *vt* to gladden; ~**se** *vr* to rejoice.

alborozo [alßo'roθo] *nm* joy.

albricias [al'ßriθjas] *nfpl* reward *sg* // *excl* good news!

álbum ['alßum] *nm* album.

albumen [al'ßumen] *nm* egg white.

alcachofa [alka'tʃofa] *nf* artichoke.

alcalde [al'kalde] *nm* mayor.

alcaldía [alkal'dia] *nf* mayoralty; (*lugar*) mayor's office.

alcance [al'kanθe] *nm* reach; (*COM*) adverse balance; (*de periódico*) stop-press (news); **de pocos** ~**s** not very clever; ~ **de última hora** late postal collection.

alcancía [alkan'θia] *nf* money box.

alcantarilla [alkanta'ri/a] *nf* (*de aguas*

cloacales) sewer; (*en la calle*) gutter.

alcanzar [alkan'θar] *vt* (*algo: con la mano, el pie*) to reach; (*alguien en el camino*) to catch up with; (*autobús*) to catch; (*suj: bala*) to hit, strike // *vi*: ~ **a hacer** to manage to do.

alcatraz [alka'traθ] *nm* gannet.

alcázar [al'kaθar] *nm* fortress; (*palacio*) royal palace; (*NAUT*) quarter-deck.

alcoba [al'koβa] *nf* bedroom.

alcohol [al'kol] *nm* alcohol; **alcohólico, a** a alcoholic; ~ **ismo** *nm* alcoholism.

alcornoque [alkor'noke] *nm* cork tree.

aldaba [al'daβa] *nf* (door) knocker.

aldea [al'dea] *nf* village; ~ **no, a** a village *cpd* // *nm/f* villager.

aleación [alea'θjon] *nf* alloy.

aleccionar [alekθjo'nar] *vt* to instruct; (*adiestrar*) to train.

alegación [aleɣa'θjon] *nf* allegation; **alegar** *vt* to allege; (*JUR*) to plead; (*AM*) to dispute, argue.

alegato [ale'ɣato] *nm* (*JUR*) allegation; (*AM*) argument.

alegoría [aleɣo'ria] *nf* allegory.

alegrar [ale'ɣrar] *vt* (*causar alegría*) to cheer (up); (*fuego*) to poke; (*fiesta*) to liven up; ~ **se** *vr* to get merry *or* tight; ~ **se de** to be glad about.

alegre [a'leɣre] a happy, cheerful; (*fam*) merry, tight; (*licencioso*) risqué, blue; **alegría** *nf* happiness; merriment.

alejamiento [alexa'mjento] *nm* removal; (*distancia*) remoteness.

alejar [ale'xar] *vt* to remove; (*fig*) to estrange; ~ **se** *vr* to move away.

aleluya [ale'luja] *nm* (*canto*) hallelujah; (*Pascuas*) Easter time // *nf* Easter print.

alemán, ana [ale'man, ana] a, *nm/f* German // *nm* (*lengua*) German.

Alemania [ale'manja] *nf*: ~ **Federal/Oriental** West/East Germany.

alentado, a [alen'taðo, a] *pp de* alentar // a brave; (*orgulloso*) proud; (*fuerte*) strong.

alentador, a [alenta'ðor, a] a encouraging.

alentar [alen'tar] *vt* to encourage; ~ **se** *vr* to cheer up.

alerce [a'lerθe] *nm* larch.

alergia [a'lerxja] *nf* allergy.

alero [a'lero] *nm* (*de tejado*) eaves *pl*; (*de carruaje*) mudguard.

alerta [a'lerta] a, *nm* alert.

aleta [a'leta] *nf* (*de pez*) fin; (*de ave*) wing; (*de coche*) mudguard.

aletargar [aletar'xar] *vt* to make drowsy; (*entumecer*) to make numb; ~ **se** *vr* to grow drowsy; to become numb.

aletazo [ale'taθo] *nm* wingbeat, flap of the wing.

aletear [alete'ar] *vi* to flutter.

aleve [a'leβe] a treacherous.

alevosía [aleβo'sia] *nf* treachery.

alfabeto [alfa'βeto] *nm* alphabet.

alfarería [alfare'ria] *nf* pottery; (*tienda*) pottery shop; **alfarero** *nm* potter.

alférez [al'fereθ] *nm* (*MIL*) second lieutenant; (*NAUT*) ensign.

alfiler [alfi'ler] *nm* pin; (*broche*) clip; ~ **de seguridad** safety pin.

alfombra [al'fombra] *nf* carpet; (*más pequeña*) rug; **alfombrar** *vt* to carpet; **alfombrilla** *nf* rug, mat; (*MED*) German measles.

alforja [al'forxa] *nf* saddlebag.

alforza [al'forθa] *nf* pleat.

alga ['alɣa] *nf* seaweed, alga.

algarabía [alɣara'βia] *nf* (*fam*) gibberish; (*BOT*) cornflower.

algarrobo [alɣa'rroβo] *nm* carob tree.

algazara [alɣa'θara] *nf* din, uproar.

álgebra ['alxeβra] *nf* algebra.

algo ['alɣo] *pron* something; anything // *ad* somewhat, rather; **por** ~ **será** there must be some reason for it.

algodón [alɣo'ðon] *nm* cotton; (*planta*) cotton plant; (*dulce*) candy floss; ~ **hidrófilo** cotton wool.

algodonero, a [alɣoðo'nero, a] a cotton *cpd* // *nm/f* cotton grower // *nm* cotton plant.

alguacil [alɣwa'θil] *nm* bailiff; (*TAUR*) mounted official.

alguien ['alɣjen] *pron* someone, somebody, anybody.

alguno, a [al'ɣuno, a], **algún** [al'ɣun] a some, any // *pron* some; one; someone, somebody; ~ **que otro libro** some book or other; **algún día iré** I'll go one *or* some day; **sin interés** ~ without the slightest interest; ~ **que otro** an occasional one; ~ **s piensan** some (people) think.

alhaja [a'laxa] *nf* jewel; (*tesoro*) precious object, treasure; (*pey*) rogue.

aliado, a [a'ljaðo, a] a allied.

alianza [a'ljanθa] *nf* alliance.

aliar [a'ljar] *vt* to ally; ~ **se** *vr* to form an alliance.

alias ['aljas] *ad* alias.

alicantino, a [alikan'tino, a] a of *or* from Alicante.

alicates [ali'kates] *nmpl*: ~ **de uñas** nail clippers.

aliciente [ali'θjente] *nm* incentive; (*atracción*) attraction.

alienación [aljena'θjon] *nf* alienation.

aliento [a'ljento] *nm* breath; (*respiración*) breathing; **sin** ~ breathless.

aligerar [alixe'rar] *vt* to lighten; (*reducir*) to shorten; (*aliviar*) to alleviate; (*mitigar*) to ease.

alimaña [ali'maɲa] *nf* pest.

alimentación [alimenta'θjon] *nf* (*comida*) food; (*acción*) feeding; (*tienda*) grocer's (shop); **alimentar** *vt* to feed; (*nutrir*) to nourish; **alimentarse** *vr* to feed.

alimenticio, a [alimen'tiθjo, a] a nourishing.

alimento [ali'mento] *nm* food; (*nutrición*) nourishment; ~ **s** *nmpl* (*JUR*) alimony *sg*.

alinear [aline'ar] *vt* to align; ~ **se** *vr*: ~ **se en** to fall in with.

aliñar [ali'nar] vt to adorn; (*preparar*) to prepare; (*CULIN*) to season; **aliño** nm decoration; (*esmero*) neatness; (*CULIN*) dressing.

alisar [ali'sar] vt to smooth; (*pulir*) to polish.

aliso [a'liso] nm alder.

alistamiento [alista'mjento] nm recruitment; **alistar** vt to recruit; (*inscribir*) to enrol; **alistarse** vr to enlist; to enrol.

aliviar [ali'βjar] vt (*carga*) to lighten; (*persona*) to relieve; (*dolor*) to alleviate; ~ se vr: ~se de to unburden o.s. of.

alivio [a'liβjo] nm alleviation, relief.

aljibe [al'xiβe] nm cistern; (*AUTO*) oil tanker.

aljofaina [alxo'faina] nf = jofaina.

alma ['alma] nf soul; (*persona*) person; (*que anima*) life and soul; (*TEC*) core.

almacén [alma'θen] nm (*depósito*) warehouse, store; (*MIL*) magazine; (*AM*) shop; **almacenes** nmpl department store sg; **almacenaje** nm storage.

almacenar [almaθe'nar] vt to store, put in storage; (*proveerse*) to stock up (with); **almacenero** nm warehouseman.

almanaque [alma'nake] nm almanac.

almeja [al'mexa] nf shellfish, clam.

almendra [al'mendra] nf almond; **almendro** nm almond tree.

almiar [al'mjar] nm hayrick.

almíbar [al'miβar] nm syrup; **almibarado, a** a syrupy.

almidón [almi'ðon] nm starch; **almidonar** vt to starch.

almirantazgo [almiran'taθvo] nm admiralty; **almirante** nm admiral.

almohada [almo'aða] nf pillow; (*funda*) pillowcase; **almohadilla** nf cushion; (*TEC*) pad; (*AM*) pincushion.

almoneda [almo'neða] nf auction; (*liquidación*) clearance sale.

almorranas [almo'rranas] nfpl piles, haemorrhoids.

almorzar [almor'θar] vt: ~ una tortilla to have an omelette for lunch // vi to (have) lunch.

almuerzo [al'mwerθo] nm lunch.

alnado, a [al'naðo, a] nm/f stepson/daughter.

alocado, a [alo'kaðo, a] a crazy.

alojamiento [aloxa'mjento] nm lodging(s) (pl); (*viviendas*) housing.

alojar [alo'xar] vt to lodge; ~se vr to lodge, stay.

alondra [a'londra] nf lark, skylark.

alpargata [alpar'ɣata] nf rope-soled sandal; (*de lona*) canvass shoe.

Alpes ['alpes] nmpl: los ~ the Alps.

alpinismo [alpi'nismo] nm mountaineering, climbing; **alpinista** nm/f mountaineer, climber.

alquería [alke'ria] nf farmhouse.

alquilar [alki'lar] vt to rent (out), let, hire (out); (*de inquilino*) to rent, hire; se

alquilan casas houses to let.

alquiler [alki'ler] nm renting, letting, hiring; (*arriendo*) rent, hire charge; de ~ for hire.

alquimia [al'kimja] nf alchemy.

alquitrán [alki'tran] nm tar.

alrededor [alreðe'ðor] ad around, about; ~es nmpl surroundings; ~ de prep around, about; mirar a su ~ to look (round) about one.

alta ['alta] nf ver **alto**.

altanería [altane'ria] nf haughtiness, arrogance; **altanero, a** a arrogant, haughty.

altar [al'tar] nm altar.

altavoz [alta'βoθ] nm loudspeaker; (*amplificador*) amplifier.

alteración [altera'θjon] nf alteration; (*alboroto*) disturbance; (*discusión*) quarrel; **alterar** vt to alter; to disturb; **alterarse** vr (*alimento etc*) to go bad or off; (*voz*) to falter; (*persona*) to get upset.

altercado [alter'kaðo] nm argument.

alternar [alter'nar] vt to alternate // vi, ~se vr to alternate; (*turnar*) to take turns; ~ con to mix with; **alternativo, a** a alternative; (*alterno*) alternating // nf alternative; (*elección*) choice; **alternativas** nfpl ups and downs.

alteza [al'teθa] nf (*tratamiento*) highness; (*altura*) height.

altibajos [alti'βaxos] nmpl ups and downs.

altiplanicie [altipla'niθje] nf, **altiplano** [alti'plano] nm high plateau.

altisonante [altiso'nante] a high-flown.

altitud [alti'tuð] nf altitude.

altivez [alti'βeθ] nf haughtiness, arrogance; **altivo, a** a haughty, arrogant.

alto, a ['alto, a] a high; (*de tamaño*) tall; (*precio, importante*) high; (*sonido*) high, sharp; (*noble*) high, lofty // nm halt; (*MUS*) alto; (*GEO*) hill; (*AM*) pile // ad (*de sitio*) high; (*de sonido*) loud, loudly // nf (*certificate of*) discharge // excl halt!; tiene 2 metros de ~ he is 2 metres tall; en ~ a mar on the high seas; en voz ~a in a loud voice; las ~as horas de la noche the small hours; en lo ~ de at the top of; pasar por ~ to overlook; dar de ~a to discharge.

altoparlante [altopar'lante] nm (*AM*) loudspeaker.

altura [al'tura] nf height; (*NAUT*) depth; (*GEO*) latitude; tiene 1.80 de ~ he is 1 metre 80cm tall; a esta ~ del año at this time of the year.

alubia [a'luβja] nf French bean, kidney bean.

alucinación [aluθina'θjon] nf hallucination; **alucinar** vi to hallucinate // vt to deceive; (*fascinar*) to fascinate.

alud [a'luð] nm avalanche.

aludir [alu'ðir] vi: ~ a to allude to; darse por ~ to take the hint.

alumbrado [alum'braðo] nm lighting; **alumbramiento** nm lighting; (*MED*) childbirth, delivery.

alumbrar [alum'brar] vt to light (up); (ciego) to restore the sight of // vi to give birth.

aluminio [alu'minjo] nm aluminium.

alumno, a [a'lumno, a] nm/f pupil, student.

alunizar [aluni'θar] vi to land on the móon.

alusión [alu'sjon] nf allusion.

alusivo, a [alu'siβo, a] a allusive.

aluvión [alu'βjon] nm alluvium; (fig) flood.

alza ['alθa] nf rise; ~s nfpl sights.

alzada [al'θaða] nf (de caballos) height; (JUR) appeal.

alzamiento [alθa'mjento] nm (aumento) rise, increase; (acción) lifting, raising; (mejor postura) higher bid; (rebelión) rising; (COM) fraudulent bankruptcy.

alzar [al'θar] vt to lift (up); (precio, muro) to raise; (cuello de abrigo) to turn up; (AGR) to gather in; (IMPRENTA) to gather; ~se vr to get up, rise; (rebelarse) to revolt; (COM) to go fraudulently bankrupt; (JUR) to appeal.

allá [a'ʎa] ad (lugar) there; (por ahí) over there; (tiempo) then; ~ abajo down there; más ~ further on; más ~ de beyond; ¡ ~ tu! that's your problem!

allanar [aʎa'nar] vt to flatten, level (out); (igualar) to smooth (out); (fig) to subdue; (JUR) to burgle, break into; ~se vr to fall down; ~ se a to submit to, accept.

allegado, a [aʎe'vaðo, a] a near, close // nm/f relation.

allegar [aʎe'var] vt to gather (together); (añadir) to add; ~ se vr to approach.

allí [a'ʎi] ad there; ~ mismo right there; por ~ over there; (por ese camino) that way.

ama ['ama] nf lady of the house; (dueña) owner; (institutriz) governess; (madre adoptiva) foster mother; ~ de cría o de leche wet-nurse; ~ de llaves housekeeper.

amabilidad [amaβili'ðað] nf kindness; (simpatía) niceness; **amable** a kind; nice.

amado, a [a'maðo, a] nm/f beloved, sweetheart.

amaestrar [amaes'trar] vt to train; (preparar) to coach.

amagar [ama'var] vt, vi to threaten; **amago** nm threat; (gesto) threatening gesture; (MED) symptom.

amalgama [amal'vama] nf amalgam; **amalgamar** vt to amalgamate; (combinar) to combine, mix.

amamantar [amaman'tar] vt to suckle, nurse.

amanecer [amane'θer] vi to dawn // nm dawn; el niño amaneció afiebrado the child woke up with a fever.

amanerado, a [amane'raðo, a] a affected.

amansar [aman'sar] vt to tame; (templar) to subdue.

amante [a'mante] a: ~ de fond of // nm/f lover.

amapola [ama'pola] nf poppy.

amar [a'mar] vt to love.

amargado, a [amar'vaðo, a] a bitter; **amargar** vt to make bitter; (fig) to embitter; **amargarse** vr to get bitter.

amargo, a [a'marvo, a] a bitter; **amargura** nf bitterness.

amarillento, a [amari'ʎento, a] a yellowish; (tez) sallow; **amarillo, a** a, nm yellow.

amarrar [ama'rrar] vt to moor; (sujetar) to tie up.

amartelar [amarte'lar] vt to make jealous; (enamorar) to win the heart of; ~se vr: ~se de to fall in love with.

amartillar [amarti'ʎar] vt = **martillar.**

amasar [ama'sar] vt to knead; (mezclar) to mix, prepare; (MED) to massage; (confeccionar) to concoct; **amasijo** nm kneading; mixing; (masa) dough; (pasta) paste; (fig) hotchpotch.

amateur ['amatur] nm/f amateur.

amatista [ama'tista] nf amethyst.

amazona [ama'θona] nf horsewoman; A~s nm: el A~s the Amazon.

ambages [am'baxes] nmpl: sin ~ in plain language.

ámbar ['ambar] nm amber.

ambición [ambi'θjon] nf ambition; **ambicionar** vt to aspire to; **ambicioso, a** a ambitious.

ambidextro, a [ambi'ðekstro, a] a ambidextrous.

ambiente [am'bjente] nm atmosphere; (medio) environment.

ambigüedad [ambixwe'ðað] nf ambiguity; **ambiguo, a** a ambiguous.

ámbito ['ambito] nm compass; (campo) field; (límite) boundary; (fig) scope.

ambos, as ['ambos, as] apl, pron pl both.

ambulancia [ambu'lanθja] nf ambulance.

ambulante [ambu'lante] a walking cpd, itinerant.

ambulatorio [ambula'torio] nm national health clinic.

amedrentar [ameðren'tar] vt to scare.

amén [a'men] excl amen; ~ de except for.

amenaza [ame'naθa] nf threat; **amenazar** vt, vi to threaten.

amenguar [amen'vwar] vt to diminish; (fig) to dishonour.

amenidad [ameni'ðað] nf pleasantness.

ameno, a [a'meno, a] a pleasant.

América [a'merika] nf America; ~ del Norte/del Sur North/South America; ~ Central/Latina Central/Latin America; **americano, a** a a, nm/f American // nf coat, jacket.

ametralladora [ametraʎa'ðora] nf machine gun.

amigable [ami'vaβle] a friendly.

amígdala [a'mivðala] nf tonsil; **amigdalitis** nf tonsillitis.

amigo, a [a'mivo, a] a friendly // nm/f friend.

amilanar [amila'nar] vt to scare.

aminorar [amino'rar] *vt* to diminish; (*reducir*) to reduce.

amistad [amis'taδ] *nf* friendship; ~es *nfpl* friends; **amistoso, a** *a* friendly.

amnesia [am'nesja] *nf* amnesia.

amnistía [amnis'tia] *nf* amnesty.

amo ['amo] *nm* owner; (*dueño*) boss; ~ de **casa** householder.

amodorrarse [amoδo'rrarse] *vr* to get sleepy.

amolar [amo'lar] *vt* to sharpen; (*fig*) to bore.

amoldar [amol'dar] *vt* to mould; (*adaptar*) to adapt.

amonestación [amonesta'θjon] *nf* warning; **amonestaciones** *nfpl* marriage banns; **amonestar** *vt* to warn; to publish the banns of.

amontonar [amonto'nar] *vt* to collect, pile up; ~se *vr* to crowd together; (*acumularse*) to pile up.

amor [a'mor] *nm* love; (*amante*) lover; **hacer el** ~ to make love; (*cortejar*) to court.

amoratado, a [amora'taδo, a] *a* purple, blue with cold.

amordazar [amorδa'θar] *vt* to muzzle; (*fig*) to gag.

amorío [amo'rio] *nm* (*fam*) love affair.

amoroso, a [amo'roso, a] *a* affectionate, loving.

amortajar [amorta'xar] *vt* to shroud.

amortiguador [amortigwa'δor] *nm* shock absorber; (*parachoques*) bumper; (*silenciador*) silencer; **amortiguar** *vt* to deaden; (*ruido*) to muffle; (*color*) to soften.

amortización [amortiθa'θjon] *nf* redemption, repayment.

amotinar [amoti'nar] *vt* to stir up, incite (to riot); ~se *vr* to mutiny.

amparar [ampa'rar] *vt* to protect; ~se *vr* to seek protection; (*abrigar*) to shelter; **amparo** *nm* help, protection.

ampliación [amplja'θjon] *nf* enlargement; (*extensión*) extension; **ampliar** *vt* to enlarge; to extend.

amplificación [amplifika'θjon] *nf* enlargement; **amplificador** *nm* amplifier; **amplificar** *vt* to amplify.

amplio, a ['ampljo, a] *a* spacious; (*de falda etc*) full; (*extenso*) extensive; (*ancho*) wide; **amplitud** *nf* spaciousness; extent; (*fig*) amplitude.

ampolla [am'poλa] *nf* blister; (*MED*) ampoule.

amputar [ampu'tar] *vt* to cut off, amputate.

amueblar [amwe'βlar] *vt* to furnish.

amurallar [amura'λar] *vt* to wall up/in.

anacronismo [anakro'nismo] *nm* anachronism.

ánade ['anaδe] *nm* duck.

anadear [anaδe'ar] *vi* to waddle.

anales [a'nales] *nmpl* annals.

analfabetismo [analfaβe'tismo] *nm* illiteracy; **analfabeto, a** *a* illiterate.

análisis [a'nalisis] *nm* analysis.

analizar [anali'θar] *vt* to analyse.

analogía [analo'xia] *nf* analogy.

anana(s) [ana'na(s)] *nm* pineapple.

anaquel [ana'kel] *nm* shelf.

anarquía [anar'kia] *nf* anarchy; **anarquismo** *nm* anarchism; **anarquista** *nm/f* anarchist.

anatomía [anato'mia] *nf* anatomy.

anciano, a [an'θjano, a] *a* old, aged // *nm/f* old man/woman // *nm* elder.

ancla ['ankla] *nf* anchor; ~dero *nm* anchorage; **anclar** *vi* to (drop) anchor.

ancho, a ['antʃo, a] *a* wide; (*falda*) full; (*fig*) liberal // *nm* width; (*FERRO*) gauge; **ponerse** ~ to get conceited; **estar a sus** ~**as** to be at one's ease.

anchoa [an'tʃoa] *nf* anchovy.

anchura [an'tʃura] *nf* width; (*extensión*) wideness; (*fig*) freedom.

andaderas [anda'δeras] *nfpl* baby walker sg.

andadura [anda'δura] *nf* gait, pace.

Andalucía [andalu'θia] *nf* Andalusia; **andaluz, a** *a, nm/f* Andalusian.

andamio [an'damjo], **andamiaje** [anda'mjaxe] *nm* scaffold.

andar [an'dar] *vt* to go, cover, travel // *vi* to go, walk, travel; (*funcionar*) to go, work; (*estar*) to be // *nm* walk, gait, pace; ~se *vr* to go away; ~ **a pie/a caballo/en bicicleta** to go on foot/on horseback/by bicycle; **¡anda!, ¡andando!** go on!; (*vamos*) come on!; (*bien*) well!; **anda en los 40** he's about 40.

andariego, a [anda'rjeɣo, a] *a* fond of travelling.

andén [an'den] *nm* (*FERRO*) platform; (*NAUT*) quayside; (*AUTO*) hard shoulder.

Andes ['andes] *nmpl*: **los** ~ the Andes.

Andorra [an'dorra] *nf* Andorra.

andrajo [an'draxo] *nm* rag; ~**so, a** *a* ragged.

andurriales [andu'rrjales] *nmpl* out-of-the-way place sg.

anduve *etc vb ver* **andar**.

anécdota [a'nekδota] *nf* anecdote, story.

anegar [ane'ɣar] *vt* to flood; (*ahogar*) to drown; ~se *vr* to drown; (*hundirse*) to sink.

anemia [a'nemja] *nf* anaemia.

anestésico [anes'tesiko] *nm* anaesthetic.

anexar [anek'sar] *vt* to annex; (*documento*) to attach; **anexo, a** *a* attached // *nm* annexe.

anfibio, a [an'fiβjo, a] *a* amphibious // *nm* amphibian.

anfiteatro [anfite'atro] *nm* amphitheatre; (*TEATRO*) dress circle.

anfitrión, ona [anfi'trjon, ona] *nm/f* host.

ángel ['anxel] *nm* angel; **angélico, a**, **angélical** *a* angelic(al).

angina [an'xina] *nf* (*MED*) inflammation of the throat; ~ **de pecho** angina (pectoris).

anglicano, a [angli'kano, a] *a, nm/f* Anglican.

angosto, a [an'gosto, a] *a* narrow.

angostura [angos'tura] *nf* narrowness; (*paso*) narrow passage.

anguila [an'gila] *nf* eel; **~s** *nfpl* slipway *sg.*

ángulo ['angulo] *nm* angle; (*esquina*) corner; (*curva*) bend.

angustia [an'gustja] *nf* anguish; **angustiar** *vt* to distress, grieve.

anhelante [ane'lante] *a* eager; (*deseoso*) longing; **anhelar** *vt* to be eager for; to long for, desire // *vi* to pant, gasp; **anhelo** *nm* eagerness; desire.

anidar [ani'ðar] *vi* to nest.

anillo [a'niʎo] *nm* ring; **~ de boda** wedding ring.

ánima ['anima] *nf* soul; **las ~s** the Angelus (bell) *sg.*

animación [anima'θjon] *nf* liveliness; (*vitalidad*) life; (*actividad*) bustle; **animado, a** *a* lively; (*vivaz*) animated.

animadversión [animaðßer'sjon] *nf* ill-will, antagonism.

animal [ani'mal] *a* animal; (*fig*) stupid // *nm* animal; (*fig*) fool; (*bestia*) brute.

animar [ani'mar] *vt* (BIO) to animate, give life to; (*fig*) to liven up, brighten up, cheer up; (*estimular*) to stimulate; **~se** *vr* to cheer up, feel encouraged; (*decidirse*) to make up one's mind.

ánimo ['animo] *nm* soul, mind; (*valentía*) courage // *excl* cheer up!

animosidad [animosi'ðað] *nf* animosity.

animoso, a [ani'moso, a] *a* brave; (*vivo*) lively.

aniquilar [aniki'lar] *vt* to annihilate, destroy; **~se** *vr* to be wiped out, disappear; (*empeorarse*) to deteriorate.

anís [a'nis] *nm* aniseed.

aniversario [anißer'sarjo] *nm* anniversary.

anoche [a'notʃe] *ad* last night; **antes de ~** the night before last.

anochecer [anotʃe'θer] *vi* to get dark // *nm* nightfall, dark.

anomalía [anoma'lia] *nf* anomaly.

anonadamiento [anonaða'mjento] *nm* annihilation; (*desaliento*) discouragement; **anonadar** *vt* to annihilate; to discourage; **anonadarse** *vr* to get discouraged.

anónimo, a [a'nonimo, a] *a* anonymous; (*COM*) limited // *nm* anonymity.

anormal [anor'mal] *a* abnormal.

anotación [anota'θjon] *nf* note.

anotar [ano'tar] *vt* to note down; (*comentar*) to annotate.

ansia ['ansja] *nf* anxiety; (*añoranza*) yearning; **ansiar** *vt* to long for.

ansiedad [ansje'ðað] *nf* anxiety.

ansioso, a [an'sjoso, a] *a* anxious; (*anhelante*) eager.

antagónico, a [anta'voniko, a] *a* antagonistic; (*opuesto*) contrasting; **antagonista** *nm/f* antagonist.

antaño [an'taɲo] *ad* long ago.

Antártico [an'tartiko] *nm*: **el ~** the Antarctic.

ante ['ante] *prep* before, in the presence of; (*encarado con*) faced with // *nm* suede, buckskin; **~ todo** above all.

anteanoche [antea'notʃe] *ad* the night before last.

anteayer [antea'jer] *ad* the day before yesterday.

antebrazo [ante'ßraðo] *nm* forearm.

antecedente [anteθe'ðente] *a* previous // *nm* antecedent; **~s** *nmpl* record *sg*, background *sg.*

anteceder [anteθe'ðer] *vt* to precede, go before.

antecesor, a [anteθe'sor, a] *nm/f* predecessor; (*antepasado*) ancestor.

antedicho, a [ante'ðitʃo, a] *a* aforementioned.

antelación [antela'θjon] *nf*: **con ~** in advance.

antemano [ante'mano]: **de ~** *ad* beforehand, in advance.

antena [an'tena] *nf* antenna; (*de televisión etc*) aerial.

anteojo [ante'oxo] *nm* eyeglass; **~s** *nmpl* spectacles, glasses.

antepasados [antepa'saðos] *nmpl* ancestors.

antepecho [ante'petʃo] *nm* guardrail, parapet; (*repisa*) ledge, sill.

anteponer [antepo'ner] *vt* to place in front; (*fig*) to prefer; **~se** *vr*: **~se a** to overcome.

anteproyecto [antepro'jekto] *nm* preliminary sketch; (*fig*) blueprint.

anterior [ante'rjor] *a* preceding, previous; **~idad** *nf*: **con ~idad a** prior to, before.

antes ['antes] *ad* sooner; (*primero*) first; (*con prioridad*) before; (*hace tiempo*) previously, once; (*más bien*) rather // *prep*: **~ de** before // *conj*: **~ (de) que** before; **~ bien** (but) rather; **dos días ~** two days before *or* previously; **~ muerto que esclavo** better dead than enslaved; **tomo el avión ~ que el barco** I take the plane rather than the boat; **cuanto ~, lo ~ posible** as soon as possible.

antesala [ante'sala] *nf* anteroom.

antibiótico [anti'ßjotiko] *nm* antibiotic.

anticipación [antiθipa'θjon] *nf* anticipation; (*COM*) advance; **con 10 minutos de ~** 10 minutes early; **anticipado, a** *a* (in) advance.

anticipar [antiθi'par] *vt* to anticipate; (*adelantar*) to bring forward; (*COM*) to advance; **~se** *vr*: **~se a su época** to be ahead of one's time.

anticipo [anti'θipo] *nm* = **anticipación.**

anticonceptivo, a [antikonθep'tißo, a] *a, nm* contraceptive.

anticongelante [antikonxe'lante] *nm* antifreeze.

anticuado, a [anti'kwaðo, a] *a* out-of-date, old-fashioned; (*desusado*) obsolete.

anticuario [anti'kwarjo] *nm* antique dealer.

antídoto [an'tiðoto] *nm* antidote.
antifaz [anti'faθ] *nm* mask; (*velo*) veil.
antigualla [anti'ɣwaʎa] *nf* antique; (*reliquia*) relic.
antiguamente [antiɣwa'mente] *ad* formerly; (*hace mucho tiempo*) long ago.
antigüedad [antiɣwe'ðað] *nf* antiquity; (*artículo*) antique; (*rango*) seniority; **antiguo, a** *a* old, ancient; (*que fue*) former.
antílope [an'tilope] *nm* antelope.
antillano, a [anti'ʎano, a] *a, nm/f* West Indian.
Antillas [an'tiʎas] *nfpl:* **las ~** the West Indies.
antipara [anti'para] *nf* screen.
antipatía [antipa'tia] *nf* antipathy, dislike; **antipático, a** *a* disagreeable, unpleasant.
antisemita [antise'mita] *nm/f* antisemite.
antítesis [an'titesis] *nf* antithesis.
antojadizo, a [antoxa'ðiθo, a] *a* capricious.
antojarse [anto'xarse] *vr* (*desear*): **se me antoja comprarlo** I have a mind to buy it; (*pensar*): **se me antoja que** I have a feeling that.
antojo [an'toxo] *nm* caprice, whim; (*rosa*) birthmark; (*lunar*) mole.
antología [antolo'xia] *nf* anthology.
antorcha [an'tortʃa] *nf* torch.
antro ['antro] *nm* cavern.
antropófago, a [antro'pofaɣo, a] *a, nm/f* cannibal.
antropología [antropolo'xia] *nf* anthropology.
anual [a'nwal] *a* annual.
anualidad [anwali'ðað] *nf* annuity.
anuario [a'nwarjo] *nm* yearbook.
anublar [anu'βlar] *vt* to cloud; (*oscurecer*) to darken; **~se** *vr* to become cloudy, cloud over; (*BOT*) to wither.
anudar [anu'ðar] *vt* to knot, tie; (*unir*) to join; **~se** *vr* to get tied up.
anulación [anula'θjon] *nf* annulment; (*cancelación*) cancellation; **anular** *vt* to annul; to cancel; (*revocar*) to revoke, repeal // *nm* ring finger.
anunciación [anunθja'θjon] *nf* announcement; **anunciar** *vt* to announce; (*proclamar*) to proclaim; (*COM*) to advertise.
anuncio [a'nunθjo] *nm* announcement; (*señal*) sign; (*COM*) advertisement; (*cartel*) poster.
anzuelo [an'θwelo] *nm* hook; (*para pescar*) fish hook.
añadidura [aɲaði'ðura] *nf* addition, extra; **por ~** besides, in addition.
añadir [aɲa'ðir] *vt* to add.
añejo [a'ɲexo, a] *a* old.
añicos [a'ɲikos] *nmpl:* **hacer ~** to smash, shatter.
año ['aɲo] *nm* year; **¡Feliz A~ Nuevo!** Happy New Year!; **tener 15 ~s** to be 15 (years old); **los ~s 60** the sixties; **~ bisiesto/escolar** leap/school year.

añoranza [aɲo'ranθa] *nf* nostalgia; (*anhelo*) longing.
apacentar [apaθen'tar] *vt* to pasture, graze.
apacible [apa'θiβle] *a* gentle, mild.
apaciguar [apaθi'ɣwar] *vt* to pacify, calm (down).
apadrinar [apaðri'nar] *vt* to sponsor, support; (*REL*) to act as godfather to.
apagado, a [apa'ɣaðo, a] *a* out; (*volcán*) extinct; (*cal*) slaked; (*color*) dull; (*voz*) quiet, timid; (*sonido*) muted, muffled; (*apático*) listless.
apagar [apa'ɣar] *vt* to put out; (*sonido*) to silence, muffle; (*sed*) to quench; (*fig*) to kill.
apagón [apa'ɣon] *nm* blackout, power cut.
apalabrar [apala'βrar] *vt* to agree to; (*obrero*) to engage.
apalear [apale'ar] *vt* to beat, thrash; (*AGR*) to winnow.
apañar [apa'ɲar] *vt* to pick up; (*asir*) to take hold of, grasp; (*vestir*) to dress up; (*reparar*) to mend, patch up; **~se** *vr* to manage, get along.
aparador [apara'ðor] *nm* sideboard; (*escaparate*) shop window.
aparato [apa'rato] *nm* apparatus; (*máquina*) machine; (*doméstico*) appliance; (*boato*) ostentation; **~so, a** *a* showy, ostentatious.
aparcamiento [aparka'mjento] *nm* car park.
aparcar [apar'kar] *vt, vi* to park.
aparecer [apare'θer] *vi*, **~se** *vr* to appear.
aparejado, a [apare'xaðo, a] *a* fit, suitable.
aparejar [apare'xar] *vt* to prepare; (*caballo*) to saddle, harness; (*NAUT*) to fit out, rig out; **aparejo** *nm* preparation; harness; rigging; (*de poleas*) block and tackle.
aparentar [aparen'tar] *vt* to feign; (*parecer*) to look, seem (to be).
aparente [apa'rente] *a* apparent; (*adecuado*) suitable.
aparición [apari'θjon] *nf* appearance; (*de libro*) publication.
apariencia [apa'rjenθja] *nf* (outward) appearance; **en ~** outwardly, seemingly.
apartado, a [apar'taðo, a] *a* separate; (*lejano*) remote // *nm* post office box; (*tipográfico*) paragraph.
apartamento [aparta'mento] *nm* apartment, flat.
apartamiento [aparta'mjento] *nm* separation; (*aislamiento*) remoteness; (*AM*) apartment, flat.
apartar [apar'tar] *vt* to separate; (*quitar*) to remove; (*MINEROLOGÍA*) to extract; **~se** *vr* to separate, part; (*irse*) to move away, keep away; **aparte** *ad* (*separadamente*) separately; (*además*) besides // *nm* aside; (*tipográfico*) new paragraph.
apasionado, a [apasjo'naðo, a] *a* passionate; biassed, prejudiced.

apasionar [apasjo'nar] *vt* to arouse passion in; ~**se** *vr* to get excited.

apatía [apa'tia] *nf* apathy.

apático, a [a'patiko, a] *a* apathetic.

apdo *nm abr de* **apartado** (de correos).

apeadero [apea'ðero] *nm* halt, wayside station.

apearse [ape'arse] *vr* to dismount; (*bajarse*) to get down/out.

apedrear [apeðre'ar] *vt* to stone.

apegarse [ape'varse] *vr*: ~**se a** to become attached to; **apego** *nm* attachment, fondness.

apelación [apela'θjon] *nf* appeal.

apelante [ape'lante] *nm/f* appellant.

apelar [ape'lar] *vi* to appeal; ~ **a** to resort to.

apellidar [apeʎi'ðar] *vt* to call, name; ~**se** *vr* to be called; **apellido** *nm* surname, name.

apenar [ape'nar] *vt* to grieve, trouble; ~**se** *vr* to grieve.

apenas [a'penas] *ad* scarcely, hardly // *conj* as soon as, no sooner.

apéndice [a'pendiθe] *nm* appendix; **apendicitis** *nf* appendicitis.

apercibir [aperθi'ßir] *vt* to prepare; (*avisar*) to warn; (*JUR*) to summon; (*AM*) to notice, see; ~**se** *vr* to get ready.

aperitivo [aperi'tißo] *nm* aperitif.

apertura [aper'tura] *nf* opening.

apesadumbrar [apesaðum'brar] *vt* to grieve, sadden; ~**se** *vr* to distress o.s.

apestar [apes'tar] *vt* to infect // *vi* to stink.

apetecer [apete'θer] *vt*: ¿**te apetece una tortilla?** do you fancy an omelette?; **apetecible** *a* desirable; (*llamativo*) attractive.

apetito [ape'tito] *nm* appetite; ~**so, a** *a* appetizing; (*fig*) tempting.

apiadarse [apja'ðarse] *vr*: ~ **de** to take pity on.

ápice ['apiθe] *nm* apex; (*fig*) whit, iota.

apio ['apjo] *nm* celery.

aplacar [apla'kar] *vt* to placate; ~**se** *vr* to calm down.

aplanamiento [aplana'mjento] *nm* smoothing, levelling.

aplanar [apla'nar] *vt* to smooth, level; (*allanar*) to roll flat, flatten.

aplastar [aplas'tar] *vt* to squash (flat); (*fig*) to crush.

aplaudir [aplau'ðir] *vt* to applaud.

aplauso [a'plauso] *nm* applause; (*fig*) approval, acclaim.

aplazamiento [aplaθa'mjento] *nm* postponement, adjournment; **aplazar** *vt* to postpone, defer.

aplicación [aplika'θjon] *nf* application; (*esfuerzo*) effort.

aplicado, a [apli'kaðo, a] *a* diligent, hard-working.

aplicar [apli'kar] *vt* (*ejecutar*) to apply; ~**se** *vr* to apply o.s.

aplomo [a'plomo] *nm* aplomb, self-assurance.

apocado, a [apo'kaðo, a] *a* timid.

apocamiento [apoka'mjento] *nm* timidity; (*depresión*) depression.

apocar [apo'kar] *vt* to reduce; ~**se** *vr* to feel small, feel humiliated.

apodar [apo'ðar] *vt* to nickname.

apoderado [apoðe'raðo] *nm* agent, representative; **apoderar** *vt* to authorize, empower; (*JUR*) to grant (a) power of attorney to; **apoderarse** *vr*: **apoderarse de** to take possession of.

apodo [a'poðo] *nm* nickname.

apogeo [apo'xeo] *nm* peak, summit.

apología [apolo'xia] *nf* eulogy; (*defensa*) defence.

apoplejía [apople'xia] *nf* apoplexy, stroke.

aporrear [aporre'ar] *vt* to beat (up); **aporreo** *nm* beating.

aportar [apor'tar] *vt* to contribute // *vi* to reach port; ~**se** *vr* (*AM*) to arrive, come.

aposentar [aposen'tar] *vt* to lodge, put up; **aposento** *nm* lodging; (*habitación*) room.

apostar [apos'tar] *vt* to bet, stake; (*destinar*) to station, post // *vi* to bet.

apostilla [apos'tiʎa] *nf* note, comment.

apóstol [a'postol] *nm* apostle.

apóstrofe [a'postrofe] *nm* insult; (*reprimenda*) reprimand.

apóstrofo [a'postrofo] *nm* apostrophe.

apostura [apos'tura] *nf* neatness, elegance.

apoyar [apo'jar] *vt* to lean, rest; (*fig*) to support, back; ~**se** *vr*: ~**se en** to lean on; **apoyo** *nm* support, backing; (*sostén*) prop.

apreciable [apre'θjaßle] *a* considerable; (*fig*) esteemed.

apreciación [apreθja'θjon] *nf* appreciation; (*COM*) valuation; **apreciar** *vt* to evaluate, assess; (*COM*) to appreciate, value.

aprecio [a'preθjo] *nm* valuation, estimate; (*fig*) appreciation.

aprehender [apreen'der] *vt* to apprehend, seize; **aprehensión** *nf* detention, capture.

apremiante [apre'mjante] *a* urgent, pressing; **apremiar** *vt* to compel, force // *vi* to be urgent, press; **apremio** *nm* compulsion; urgency.

aprender [apren'der] *vt*, *vi* to learn.

aprendiz, a [apren'diθ, a] *nm/f* apprentice; (*principiante*) learner; ~**aje** *nm* apprenticeship.

aprensión [apren'sjon] *nm* apprehension, fear; (*delicadeza*) squeamishness; **aprensivo, a** *a* apprehensive; (*nervioso*) nervous, timid.

apresar [apre'sar] *vt* to seize; (*capturar*) to capture.

aprestar [apres'tar] *vt* to prepare, get ready; (*TEC*) to prime, size; ~**se** *vr* to get ready.

apresurado, a [apresu'raðo, a] *a* hurried,

hasty; **apresuramiento** *nm* hurry, haste.
apresurar [apresu'rar] *vt* to hurry, accelerate; ~se *vr* to hurry, make haste.
apretado, a [apre'taðo, a] *a* tight; (*escritura*) cramped; (*difícil*) difficult; (*fam*) stingy.
apretar [apre'tar] *vt* to squeeze, press; (*TEC*) to tighten; (*presionar*) to press together, pack // *vi* to be too tight; (*insistir*) to insist.
apretón [apre'ton] *nm* squeeze; (*abrazo*) hug; (*aglomeración*) crush; (*dificultad*) difficulty, jam; (*carrera*) dash, sprint; ~ **de manos** handshake; **apretura** *nf* squeeze; hug; crush; difficulty, jam; (*escasez*) scarcity.
aprieto [a'prjeto] *nm* squeeze, press; (*dificultad*) difficulty, jam.
aprisionar [aprisjo'nar] *vt* to imprison.
aprobación [aproßa'θjon] *nf* approval; (*de examen*) pass; (*nota*) pass mark; **aprobar** *vt* to approve (of); to pass (*//*) to pass.
apropiación [apropja'θjon] *nf* appropriation.
apropiado, a [apro'pjaðo, a] *a* appropriate.
apropiar [apro'pjar] *vt* to adapt, make fit; ~se *vr*: ~se de to appropriate.
aprovechado, a [aproße'tʃaðo, a] *a* diligent, hardworking; (*económico*) thrifty; (*pey*) unscrupulous, grasping; **aprovechamiento** *nm* use, exploitation.
aprovechar [aproße'tʃar] *vt* to use, exploit, profit from; (*sacar partido de*) to take advantage of // *vi* to progress, improve; ~se *vr*: ~se de to make use of, take advantage of; ¡**que aproveche!** enjoy your meal!
aproximación [aproksima'θjon] *nf* approximation; (*cercanía*) nearness; (*de lotería*) consolation prize; **aproximado, a** *a* approximate; **aproximar** *vt* to bring nearer; **aproximarse** *vr* to come near, approach.
aptitud [apti'tuð] *nf* aptitude; (*idoneidad*) suitability.
apto, a ['apto, a] *a* suitable.
apuesto, a [a'pwesto, a] *a* neat, elegant // *nf* bet, wager.
apuntador [apunta'ðor] *nm* prompter.
apuntalar [apunta'lar] *vt* to prop up.
apuntar [apun'tar] *vt* (*con arma*) to aim at; (*con dedo*) to point at or to; (*anotar*) to note (down); (*TEATRO*) to prompt; (*dinero*) to stake; ~se *vr* to score a point.
apunte [a'punte] *nm* note.
apuñalar [apuɲa'lar] *vt* to stab.
apurado, a [apu'raðo, a] *a* needy; (*difícil*) difficult, dangerous; (*agotado*) exhausted; (*AM*) hurried, rushed.
apurar [apu'rar] *vt* (*purificar*) to purify; (*agotar*) to drain; (*recursos*) to use up; (*molestar*) to annoy; ~se *vr* to worry; (*AM*) to hurry.
apuro [a'puro] *nm* (*aprieto*) fix, jam; (*escasez*) want, hardship; (*aflicción*) distress; (*AM*) haste, urgency.

aquejar [ake'xar] *vt* to distress, grieve; (*MED*) to afflict.
aquel, aquella, aquellos, as [a'kel, a'keʎa, a'keʎos, as] *det* that; (*pl*) those.
aquél, aquélla, aquéllos, as [a'kel, a'keʎa, a'keʎos, as] *pron* that (one); (*pl*) those (ones).
aquello [a'keʎo] *pron* that, that business.
aquí [a'ki] *ad* (*lugar*) here; (*tiempo*) now; ~ **arriba** up here; ~ **mismo** right here; ~ **yace** here lies; **de** ~ **a siete días** a week from now.
aquietar [akje'tar] *vt* to quieten (down), calm (down).
árabe ['araße] *a* Arab, Arabian, Arabic // *nm/f* Arab // *nm* (*lengua*) Arabic.
Arabia Saudita [araßjasau'ðita] *nf* Saudi Arabia.
arado [a'raðo] *nm* plough.
aragonés, esa [arayo'nes, esa] *a, nm/f* Aragonese.
arancel [aran'θel] *nm* tariff, duty; ~ **de aduanas** customs duty.
araña [a'raɲa] *nf* (*ZOOL*) spider; (*de luces*) chandelier.
arañar [ara'ɲar] *vt* to scratch.
arañazo [ara'ɲaθo] *nm* scratch.
arar [a'rar] *vt* to plough, till.
arbitrador, a [arßitra'ðor, a] *nm/f* arbiter.
arbitraje [arßi'traxe] *nm* arbitration.
arbitrar [arßi'trar] *vt* to arbitrate in; (*DEPORTE*) to referee // *vi* to arbitrate.
arbitrariedad [arßitrarje'ðað] *nf* arbitrariness; (*acto*) arbitrary act; **arbitrario, a** *a* arbitrary.
arbitrio [ar'ßitrjo] *nm* free will; (*JUR*) adjudication, decision.
árbitro ['arßitro] *nm* arbitrator; (*DEPORTE*) referee; (*TENIS*) umpire.
árbol ['arßol] *nm* (*BOT*) tree; (*NAUT*) mast; (*TEC*) axle, shaft; **arbolado, a** *a* wooded, tree-lined // *nm* woodland.
arboladura [arßola'ðura] *nf* rigging; **arbolar** *vt* to hoist, raise; **arbolarse** *vr* to rear up.
arboleda [arßo'leða] *nf* grove, plantation.
arbusto [ar'ßusto] *nm* bush, shrub.
arca ['arka] *nf* chest, box; (*caja fuerte*) strongbox.
arcada [ar'kaða] *nf* arcade; (*de puente*) arch, span; ~s *nfpl* retching *sg*.
arcaduz [arka'ðuθ] *nm* pipe, conduit.
arcaico, a [ar'kaiko, a] *a* archaic.
arce ['arθe] *nm* maple tree.
arcediano [arθe'ðjano] *nm* archdeacon.
arcilla [ar'θiʎa] *nf* clay.
arco ['arko] *nm* arch; (*MAT*) arc; (*MIL, MUS*) bow; ~ **iris** rainbow.
archipiélago [artʃi'pjelavo] *nm* archipelago.
archivar [artʃi'ßar] *vt* to file (away); **archivo** *nm* archive(s) (*pl*).
arder [ar'ðer] *vi, vt* to burn.
ardid [ar'ðið] *nm* ruse.

ardiente [ar'öjente] a burning; (*apasionado*) ardent.

ardilla [ar'ðiʎa] nf squirrel.

ardor [ar'ðor] nm (*calor*) heat, warmth; (*fig*) ardour; ~ **de estómago** heartburn; ~**oso**, a a = **ardiente**.

arduo, a ['arðwo, a] a arduous.

área ['area] nf area; (*DEPORTE*) penalty area.

arena [a'rena] nf sand; (*de una lucha*) arena; (*MED*) stone.

arenal [are'nal] nm sandy ground; (*arena movediza*) quicksand.

arengar [aren'gar] vt to harangue.

arenisco, a [are'nisko, a] a sandy // nf sandstone; (*cascajo*) grit.

arenoso, a [are'noso, a] a sandy.

arenque [a'renke] nm herring.

arete [a'rete] nm earring.

argamasa [arva'masa] nf mortar, plaster; **argamasar** vt to mortar, plaster.

Argel [ar'xel] n Algiers; ~**ia** nf Algeria; **argelino, a** a, nm/f Algerian.

argentino, a [arxen'tino, a] a Argentinian; (*de plata*) silvery // nm/f Argentinian // nf: **A**~**a** Argentina.

argolla [ar'voʎa] nf (*large*) ring; (*juego*) croquet.

argot [ar'vo] nm slang.

argucia [ar'vuθja] nf subtlety, sophistry.

argüir [ar'xwir] vt to deduce; (*discutir*) to argue; (*indicar*) to indicate, imply; (*censurar*) to reproach // vi to argue.

argumentación [arvumenta'θjon] nf (line of) argument; **argumentar** vt, vi to argue.

argumento [arvu'mento] nm argument; (*de obra*) plot.

aria ['arja] nf aria.

aridez [ari'ðeθ] nf aridity, dryness.

árido, a ['ariðo, a] a arid, dry; ~**s** nmpl dry goods.

Aries ['arjes] nm Aries.

ariete [a'rjete] nm battering ram.

ario, a ['arjo, a] a Aryan.

arisco, a [a'risko, a] a surly; (*insociable*) unsociable.

aristócrata [aris'tokrata] nm/f aristocrat.

aritmética [arit'metika] nf arithmetic.

arma ['arma] nf arm; ~**s** nfpl arms; ~ **blanca** blade, knife; (*espada*) sword; ~ **de fuego** firearm; ~**s cortas** small arms.

armadillo [arma'ðiʎo] nm armadillo.

armado, a [ar'maðo, a] a armed; (*TEC*) reinforced // nf armada; (*flota*) fleet.

armadura [arma'ðura] nf (*MIL*) armour; (*TEC*) framework; (*ZOOL*) skeleton; (*FÍSICA*) armature.

armamento [arma'mento] nm armament; (*NAUT*) fitting-out.

armar [ar'mar] vt (*soldado*) to arm; (*máquina*) to assemble; (*navío*) to fit out; ~**la**, ~ **un lío** to start a row.

armario [ar'marjo] nm wardrobe.

armatoste [arma'toste] nm large useless object, contraption.

armazón [arma'θon] nf body, chassis; (*de mueble etc*) frame; (*ARQ*) skeleton.

armería [arme'ria] nf (*museo*) military museum; (*tienda*) gunsmith's.

armiño [ar'mino] nm stoat; (*piel*) ermine.

armisticio [armis'tiθjo] nm armistice.

armonía [armo'nia] nf harmony.

armónica [ar'monika] nf harmonica.

armonioso, a [armo'njoso, a] a harmonious.

arnés [ar'nes] nm armour; **arneses** nmpl harness sg.

aro ['aro] nm ring; (*tejo*) quoit; (*pendiente*) earring.

aroma [a'roma] nm aroma.

aromático, a [aro'matiko, a] a aromatic.

arpa ['arpa] nf harp.

arpía [ar'pia] nf shrew.

arpista [ar'pista] nm/f harpist.

arpón [ar'pon] nm harpoon.

arquear [arke'ar] vt to arch, bend; ~**se** vr to arch, bend; **arqueo** nm (*gen*) arching, curve; (*de navío*) tonnage.

arqueología [arkeolo'xia] nf archaeology; **arqueólogo, a** nm/f archaeologist.

arquero [ar'kero] nm archer, bowman.

arquetipo [arke'tipo] nm archetype.

arquitecto [arki'tekto] nm architect; **arquitectura** nf architecture.

arrabal [arra'βal] nm suburb; (*AM*) slum.

arraigado, a [arrai'vaðo, a] a deep-rooted; (*fig*) established.

arraigar [arrai'var] vt to establish // vi, ~**se** vr to take root.

arrancar [arran'kar] vt (*sacar*) to pull up, extract, pull out; (*separar*) to snatch (away), wrest; (*fig*) to extract // vi to start, pull out.

arranque [a'rranke] nm sudden start; (*AUTO*) start; (*fig*) fit, outburst.

arras ['arras] nfpl pledge sg, security sg.

arrasar [arra'sar] vt (*aplanar*) to level, flatten; (*destruir*) to demolish; (*llenar*) to fill up // vi to clear.

arrastrado, a [arras'traðo, a] a poor, wretched; (*AM*) servile.

arrastrar [arras'trar] vt to drag (along); (*fig*) to drag down, degrade; (*suj: agua, viento*) to carry away // vi to drag, trail on the ground; ~**se** vr to crawl; (*fig*) to grovel; **llevar algo arrastrado** to drag sth along.

arrastre [a'rrastre] nm drag, dragging; (*DEPORTE*) crawl.

arrayán [arra'jan] nm myrtle.

arrear [arre'ar] vt to drive, urge on; (*enganchar*) to harness // vi to hurry along; ¡**arre**(**a**)! get up!, gee up!

arrebatado, a [arreβa'taðo, a] a rash, impetuous; (*repentino*) sudden, hasty.

arrebatar [arreβa'tar] vt to snatch (away), seize; (*fig*) to captivate; ~**se** vr to get carried away, get excited.

arrebato [arre'βato] nm fit of rage, fury; (*éxtasis*) rapture.

arreglado, a [arre'vlaðo, a] a (*ordenado*)

neat, orderly; (*moderado*) moderate, reasonable.

arreglar [arre'xlar] *vt* (*poner orden*) to tidy up; (*algo roto*) to fix, repair; (*problema*) to solve; (*MUS*) to arrange; ~**se** *vr* to reach an understanding; **arreglárselas** (*fam*) to get by, manage.

arreglo [a'rrexlo] *nm* settlement; (*orden*) order; (*acuerdo*) agreement; (*MUS*) arrangement, setting.

arremangar [arreman'gar] *vt* to roll up, turn up; ~**se** *vr* to roll up one's sleeves.

arremeter [arreme'ter] *vt* to attack, assault.

arrendador, a [arrenda'ðor, a] *nm/f* landlord/lady; (*inquilino*) tenant.

arrendamiento [arrenda'mjento] *nm* letting; (*alquilar*) hiring; (*contrato*) lease; (*alquiler*) rent; **arrendar** *vt* to let, lease; to rent; **arrendatario, a** *nm/f* tenant.

arreo [a'rreo] *nm* adornment; ~**s** *nmpl* harness *sg*, trappings.

arrepentimiento [arrepenti'mjento] *nm* regret, repentance.

arrepentirse [arrepen'tirse] *vr*: ~ **de** to regret, repent of.

arrestar [arres'tar] *vt* to arrest; (*encarcelar*) to imprison; **arresto** *nm* arrest; (*MIL*) detention; (*audacia*) boldness, daring; **arresto domiciliario** house arrest.

arriar [a'rrjar] *vt* (*velas, bandera*) to lower, strike; (*un cable*) to pay out; ~**se** *vr* to flood.

arriba [a'rriβa] *ad* (*posición*) above, overhead, on top; (*en casa*) upstairs; (*dirección*) up, upwards; ~ **de** above, higher (up) than; ~ **del todo** at the very top; **el piso de** ~ the flat upstairs; **de** ~ **abajo** from top to bottom; **calle** ~ up the street; **lo** ~ **mencionado** the aforementioned; ~ **de 20 pesetas** more than 20 pesetas; ¡~ **las manos!** hands up!

arribar [arri'βar] *vi* to put into port; (*llegar*) to arrive.

arribista [arri'βista] *nm/f* parvenu/e, upstart.

arriendo [a'rrjendo] *nm* = **arrendamiento**.

arriero [a'rrjero] *nm* muleteer.

arriesgado, a [arrjes'yaðo, a] *a* (*peligroso*) risky; (*audaz*) bold, daring; **arriesgar** *vt* to risk; (*poner en peligro*) to endanger; **arriesgarse** *vr* to take a risk.

arrimar [arri'mar] *vt* (*acercar*) to bring close; (*poner de lado*) to set aside; ~**se** *vr* to come close or closer; ~**se a** to lean on; **arrimo** *nm* approach; (*fig*) support.

arrinconado, a [arrinko'naðo, a] *a* forgotten, neglected; **arrinconar** *vt* to put in a corner; (*fig*) to put on one side; (*abandonar*) to push aside; **arrinconarse** *vr* to withdraw from the world.

arrodillarse [arroði'Aarse] *vr* to kneel, kneel down.

arrogancia [arro'xanθja] *nf* arrogance; **arrogante** *a* arrogant.

arrojar [arro'xar] *vt* to throw, hurl; (*humo*) to emit, give out; (*COM*) to yield, produce; ~**se** *vr* to throw or hurl o.s.

arrojo [a'rroxo] *nm* daring.

arrollador, a [arroʎa'ðor, a] *a* crushing, overwhelming.

arropar [arro'par] *vt* to cover, wrap up; ~**se** *vr* to wrap o.s. up.

arrope [a'rrope] *nm* syrup.

arrostrar [arros'trar] *vt* to face (up to); ~**se** *vr* to rush into the fight.

arroyo [a'rrojo] *nm* stream; (*de la calle*) gutter.

arroz [a'rroθ] *nm* rice; ~ **con leche** rice pudding.

arruga [a'rruxa] *nf* fold; (*de cara*) wrinkle; (*de vestido*) crease; **arrugar** *vt* to fold; to wrinkle; to crease; **arrugarse** *vr* to get creased.

arruinar [arrwi'nar] *vt* to ruin, wreck; ~**se** *vr* to be ruined.

arrullar [arru'Aar] *vi* to coo // *vt* to lull to sleep.

arsenal [arse'nal] *nm* naval dockyard; (*MIL*) arsenal.

arsénico [ar'seniko] *nm* arsenic.

arte ['arte] *nm* (*gen m en sg y siempre f en pl*) art; (*maña*) skill, guile; ~**s** *nfpl* arts.

artefacto [arte'fakto] *nm* appliance; (*ARQUEOLOGÍA*) artefact.

artejo [ar'texo] *nm* knuckle.

arteria [ar'terja] *nf* artery.

artesanía [artesa'nia] *nf* craftsmanship; (*artículos*) handicrafts *pl*; **artesano** *nm* artisan, craftsman.

ártico, a ['artiko, a] *a* Arctic // *nm*: el Á~ the Arctic.

articulación [artikula'θjon] *nf* articulation; (*MED, TEC*) joint; **articulado, a** *a* articulated; jointed; **articular** *vt* to articulate; to join together.

artículo [ar'tikulo] *nm* article; (*cosa*) thing, article; ~**s** *nmpl* goods.

artífice [ar'tifiθe] *nm* artist, craftsman; (*fig*) architect.

artificial [artifi'θjal] *a* artificial.

artificio [arti'fiθjo] *nm* art, skill; (*artesanía*) craftsmanship; (*astucia*) cunning; ~**so, a** *a* skilful, clever; cunning.

artillería [artiʎe'ria] *nf* artillery.

artillero [arti'Aero] *nm* artilleryman, gunner.

artimaña [arti'mana] *nf* trap, snare; (*astucia*) cunning.

artista [ar'tista] *nm/f* (*pintor*) artist, painter; (*TEATRO*) artist, artiste; **artístico, a** *a* artistic.

artritis [ar'tritis] *nf* arthritis.

arzobispo [arθo'βispo] *nm* archbishop.

as [as] *nm* ace.

asa ['asa] *nf* handle; (*fig*) lever.

asado [a'saðo] *nm* roast (meat).

asador [asa'ðor] *nm* spit.

asalariado, a [asala'rjaðo, a] *a* paid, wage-earning // *nm/f* wage earner.

asaltabancos [asalta'baŋkos] nm inv bank robber.

asaltador, a [asalta'ðor, a], **asaltante** [asal'tante] nm/f assailant; **asaltar** vt to attack, assault; (fig) to assail; **asalto** nm attack, assault; (DEPORTE) round.

asamblea [asam'blea] nf assembly; (reunión) meeting.

asar [a'sar] vt to roast.

asbesto [as'βesto] nm asbestos.

ascendencia [asθen'denθja] nf ancestry; (AM) ascendancy.

ascender [asθen'der] vi (subir) to ascend, rise; (ser promovido) to gain promotion // vt to promote; ~ a to amount to; **ascendiente** nm ascendency, influence // nm/f ancestor.

ascensión [asθen'sjon] nf ascent; la A~ the Ascension.

ascensionista [asθensjo'nista] nm/f balloonist.

ascenso [as'θenso] nm ascent; (promoción) promotion.

ascensor [asθen'sor] nm lift, elevator.

ascético, a [as'θetiko, a] a ascetic.

asco ['asko] nm loathing, disgust; (cosa) loathsome thing; **el ajo me da** ~ I hate or loathe garlic.

ascua ['askwa] nf ember.

aseado, a [ase'aðo, a] a clean; (arreglado) tidy; (pulcro) smart; **asear** vt to clean, wash; to tidy (up); (adornar) to adorn.

asediar [ase'ðjar] vt to besiege, lay siege to; (fig) to chase, pester; **asedio** nm siege; (COM) run.

asegurado, a [aseɣu'raðo, a] a insured; **asegurador, a** nm/f insurer; underwriter.

asegurar [aseɣu'rar] vt (consolidar) to secure, fasten; (dar garantía de) to guarantee; (preservar) to safeguard; (afirmar, dar por cierto) to assure, affirm; (tranquilizar) to reassure; (tomar un seguro) to insure; ~se vr to assure o.s., make sure.

asemejarse [aseme'xarse] vr to be alike; ~ a to be like, resemble.

asentado, a [asen'taðo, a] a established, settled.

asentar [asen'tar] vt (sentar) to seat, sit down; (poner) to place, establish; (alisar) to level, smooth down or out; (anotar) to note down; (afirmar) to affirm, assert; (afinar) to sharpen, hone // vi to be suitable, suit.

asentir [asen'tir] vi to assent, agree.

aseo [a'seo] nm cleanliness; ~s nmpl toilet sg, cloakroom sg.

asequible [ase'kiβle] a attainable, available.

aserradero [aserra'ðero] nm sawmill; **aserrar** vt to saw.

aserrín [ase'rrin] nm sawdust.

asesinar [asesi'nar] vt to murder; (POL) to assassinate; (fig) to pester; **asesinato** nm murder; assassination.

asesino, a [ase'sino, a] nm/f murderer, killer; (POL) assassin.

asesor, a [ase'sor, a] nm/f adviser, consultant.

asfalto [as'falto] nm asphalt.

asfixia [as'fiksja] nf suffocation.

asfixiar [asfik'sjar] vt, ~se vr to asphyxiate, suffocate.

asgo etc vb ver **asir**.

así [a'si] ad (de esta manera) so, in this way, like this, thus; (aunque) although; (tan luego como) as soon as; ~ que so, therefore; ~ como as well as; ~ y todo even so; ¿no es ~? isn't it?, didn't you? etc.

Asia ['asja] nf Asia; **asiático, a** a Asiatic, Asian.

asidero [asi'ðero] nm handle.

asiduidad [asiðwi'ðað] nf assiduousness; **asiduo, a** a assiduous; (frecuente) frequent // nm/f regular (customer).

asiento [a'sjento] nm (mueble) seat, chair; (de coche, en tribunal etc) seat; (localidad) seat, place; (fundamento) site; (colocación) establishment; (depósito) sediment; (cordura) good sense; ~ delantero/trasero front/back seat.

asignación [asiɣna'θjon] nf (atribución) assignment; (reparto) allocation; (cita) appointment; (sueldo) salary; **asignar** vt to assign, allocate.

asignatura [asiɣna'tura] nf subject.

asilo [a'silo] nm (refugio) asylum, refuge; (establecimiento) home, institution.

asimilación [asimila'θjon] nf assimilation.

asimilar [asimi'lar] vt to assimilate; ~se vr: ~se a to resemble; (incorporarse) to become assimilated to.

asimismo [asi'mismo] ad in the same way, likewise.

asir [a'sir] vt to seize, grasp.

asistencia [asis'tenθja] nf audience; (MED) attendance; (ayuda) assistance; **asistir** vt to assist // vi to attend, be present.

asma ['asma] nf asthma.

asno ['asno] nm donkey; (fig) ass.

asociación [asoθja'θjon] nf association; (COM) partnership; ~ **aduanera** customs union; **asociado, a** a associate // nm/f associate; partner.

asociar [aso'θjar] vt to combine.

asolear [asole'ar] vt to put in the sun; ~se vr to sunbathe.

asomar [aso'mar] vt to show, stick out // vi to appear; ~se vr to appear, show up; ~ **la cabeza por la ventana** to put one's head out of the window.

asombrar [asom'brar] vt (causar admiración, sorpresa) to amaze, astonish; (asustar) to frighten; (dar sombra a) to shade; ~se vr to be amazed; to be frightened; **asombro** nm amazement, astonishment; fright; **asombroso, a** a astonishing, amazing.

asomo [a'somo] nm hint, sign; (apariencia) appearance.

aspa ['aspa] nf (cruz) cross; (de molino) sail.

aspar [as'par] *vt* to reel, wind; (*fig*) to vex, annoy.

aspaviento [aspa'βjento] *nm* exaggerated display of feeling; (*fam*) fuss.

aspecto [as'pekto] *nm* (*apariencia*) look, appearance; (*fig*) aspect.

aspereza [aspe'reθa] *nf* roughness; (*agrura*) sourness; (*severidad*) harshness, surliness; **áspero, a** *a* rough; bitter, sour; harsh.

aspersión [asper'sjon] *nf* sprinkling.

áspid ['aspið] *nm* asp.

aspiración [aspira'θjon] *nf* breath, inhalation; (*MUS*) short pause; **aspiraciones** *nfpl* (*AM*) aspirations.

aspiradora [aspira'ðora] *nf* vacuum cleaner.

aspirar [aspi'rar] *vt* to breathe in // *vi*: ~ a to aspire to.

aspirina [aspi'rina] *nf* aspirin.

asquear [aske'ar] *vt* to sicken // *vi* to be sickening; ~**se** *vr* to feel disgusted; **asqueroso, a** *a* disgusting, sickening.

asta ['asta] *nf* lance; (*arpón*) spear; (*mango*) shaft, handle; (*ZOOL*) horn; **a media** ~ at half mast.

astilla [as'tiʎa] *nf* splinter; (*pedacito*) chip; ~**s** *nfpl* firewood *sg*.

astillero [asti'ʎero] *nm* shipyard.

astringente [astrin'xente] *a, nm* astringent.

astringir [astrin'xir] *vt* to bind.

astro ['astro] *nm* star.

astrología [astrolo'xia] *nf* astrology; **astrólogo, a** *nm/f* astrologer.

astronauta [astro'nauta] *nm/f* astronaut.

astronomía [astrono'mia] *nf* astronomy; **astrónomo** *nm* astronomer.

astucia [as'tuθja] *nf* astuteness; (*destreza*) clever trick; **astuto, a** *a* astute; (*taimado*) cunning.

asueto [a'sweto] *nm* holiday; (*tiempo libre*) time off *q*.

asumir [asu'mir] *vt* to assume.

asunción [asun'θjon] *nf* assumption.

asunto [a'sunto] *nm* (*tema*) matter, subject; (*negocio*) business.

asustar [asus'tar] *vt* to frighten; ~**se** *vr* to be/become frightened.

atacar [ata'kar] *vt* to attack.

atadura [ata'ðura] *nf* bond, tie.

atajo [a'taxo] *nm* short cut; (*DEPORTE*) tackle.

ataque [a'take] *nm* attack; ~ **cardíaco** heart attack.

atar [a'tar] *vt* to tie, tie up; ~**se** *vr* (*fig*) to be or get embarrassed.

atardecer [ataröe'θer] *vi* to get dark // *nm* evening; (*crepúsculo*) dusk.

atareado, a [atare'aðo, a] *a* busy.

atarear [atare'ar] *vt* to give a job to; ~**se** *vr* to be busy, keep busy.

atascamiento [ataska'mjento] *nm* = atasco.

atascar [atas'kar] *vt* to clog up; (*obstruir*) to jam; (*fig*) to hinder; ~**se** *vr* to stall;

(*cañería*) to get clogged up; **atasco** *nm* obstruction; (*AUTO*) traffic jam.

ataúd [ata'uð] *nm* coffin.

ataviar [ata'βjar] *vt* to deck, array; ~**se** *vr* to dress up.

atavío [ata'βio] *nm* attire, dress; ~**s** *nmpl* finery *sg*.

atemorizar [atemori'θar] *vt* to frighten, scare; ~**se** *vr* to get scared.

Atenas [a'tenas] *n* Athens.

atención [aten'θjon] *nf* attention; (*bondad*) kindness; (*cortesía*) civility // *excl* (be) careful!, look out!

atender [aten'der] *vt* to attend to, look after // *vi* to pay attention.

atenerse [ate'nerse] *vr*: ~ a to abide by, adhere to.

atentado [aten'taðo] *nm* crime, illegal act; (*asalto*) assault; (*contra la vida de uno*) attempt on sb's life.

atentar [aten'tar] *vi*: ~ a o contra to commit an outrage against.

atento, a [a'tento, a] *a* attentive, observant; (*cortés*) polite, thoughtful.

atenuación [atenwa'θjon] *nf* attenuation, lessening; **atenuante** *a* attenuating, extenuating; **atenuar** *vt* to attenuate; (*disminuir*) to lessen, minimize.

ateo, a [a'teo, a] *a* atheistic // *nm/f* atheist.

aterrador, a [aterra'ðor, a] *a* frightening.

aterrar [ate'rrar] *vt* to pull down, demolish; (*AGR*) to cover with earth; (*espantar*) to frighten; ~**se** *vr* to be frightened.

aterrizar [aterri'θar] *vi* to land.

aterrorizar [aterrori'θar] *vt* to terrify; (*MIL, POL*) to terrorize.

atesorar [ateso'rar] *vt* to hoard, store up.

atestar [ates'tar] *vt* to pack, stuff; (*JUR*) to attest, testify to.

atestiguar [atesti'ɣwar] *vt* to testify to, bear witness to.

atiborrar [atiβo'rrar] *vt* to fill, stuff; ~**se** *vr* to stuff o.s.

ático ['atiko] *nm* attic.

atildar [atil'dar] *vt* to criticize; ~**se** *vr* to spruce o.s. up.

atisbar [atis'βar] *vt* to spy on; (*echar ojeada*) to peep at.

atizar [ati'θar] *vt* to poke; (*horno etc*) to stoke; (*fig*) to stir up, rouse.

atlántico, a [at'lantiko, a] *a* Atlantic // *nm*: **el (océano) A**~ the Atlantic (Ocean).

atlas ['atlas] *nm* atlas.

atleta [at'leta] *nm* athlete; **atlético, a** *a* athletic; **atletismo** *nm* athletics *sg*.

atmósfera [at'mosfera] *nf* atmosphere.

atolondramiento [atolondra'mjento] *nm* bewilderment; (*insensatez*) silliness.

atollar [ato'ʎar] *vi*, ~**se** *vr* to get stuck; (*fig*) to get into a jam.

atómico, a [a'tomiko, a] *a* atomic.

atomizador [atomiθa'ðor] *nm* atomizer.

átomo ['atomo] *nm* atom.

atónito, a [a'tonito, a] *a* astonished, amazed.

atontado, a [aton'taðo, a] *a* stunned; (*bobo*) silly, daft.

atontar [aton'tar] *vt* to stun; **~se** *vr* to become bewildered.

atormentar [atormen'tar] *vt* to torture; (*molestar*) to torment; (*acosar*) to plague, harass.

atornillar [atorni'ʎar] *vt* to screw on *or* down.

atracar [atra'kar] *vt* (*NAUT*) to moor; (*robar*) to hold up, rob; (*fam*) to stuff (with food) // *vi* to moor.

atracción [atrak'θjon] *nf* attraction.

atraco [a'trako] *nm* holdup, robbery.

atractivo, a [atrak'tiβo, a] *a* attractive // *nm* attraction; (*belleza*) attractiveness.

atraer [atra'er] *vt* to attract.

atrancar [atran'kar] *vt* (*con tranca, barra*) to bar, bolt.

atrapar [atra'par] *vt* to trap; (*fig*) to take in, deceive.

atrás [a'tras] *ad* (*movimiento*) back, backwards; (*lugar*) behind; (*tiempo*) previously; **ir hacia ~** to go back *or* backwards; to go to the rear; **estar ~** to be behind *or* at the back.

atrasado, a [atra'saðo, a] *a* slow; (*pago*) overdue, late; (*país*) backward.

atrasar [atra'sar] *vi* to be slow; **~se** *vr* to remain behind; (*llegar tarde*) to arrive late; **atraso** *nm* slowness; lateness, delay; (*de país*) backwardness; **atrasos** *nmpl* arrears.

atravesar [atraβe'sar] *vt* (*cruzar*) to cross (over); (*traspasar*) to pierce, go through; (*poner al través*) to lay *or* put across; **~se** *vr* to come in between; (*intervenir*) to interfere.

atrayente [atra'jente] *a* attractive.

atreverse [atre'βerse] *vr* to dare; (*insolentarse*) to be insolent; **atrevido, a** *a* daring; insolent; **atrevimiento** *nm* daring; insolence.

atribuir [atriβu'ir] *vt* to attribute; (*funciones*) to confer.

atribular [atriβu'lar] *vt* to afflict, distress; **~se** *vr* to grieve, be distressed.

atributo [atri'βuto] *nm* attribute.

atrocidad [atroθi'ðað] *nf* atrocity, outrage.

atropellar [atrope'ʎar] *vt* (*derribar*) to knock over, knock down; (*empujar*) to push (aside); (*pasar por encima de*) to run over, run down; (*agraviar*) to insult; **~se** *vr* to act hastily; **atropello** *nm* accident; push; insult; (*agravio*) wrong; (*atrocidad*) outrage.

atroz [a'troθ] *a* atrocious, awful.

atto, a *abr de* **atento**.

atuendo [a'twendo] *nm* dress.

atún [a'tun] *nm* tuna, tunny.

aturdir [atur'ðir] *vt* to stun; (*de ruido*) to deafen; (*fig*) to dumbfound, bewilder.

audacia [au'ðaθja] *nf* boldness, audacity; **audaz** *a* bold, audacious; (*descarado*) cheeky, impudent.

audible [au'ðiβle] *a* audible.

audición [auði'θjon] *nf* hearing; (*TEATRO*) audition.

audiencia [au'ðjenθja] *nf* audience; (*JUR*) high court.

auditor [auði'tor] *nm* (*JUR*) judge-advocate; (*COM*) auditor.

auditorio [auði'torjo] *nm* audience; (*sala*) auditorium.

auge ['auxe] *nm* boom; (*clímax*) climax.

augurar [auɣu'rar] *vt* to predict; (*presagiar*) to portend; **augurio** *nm* omen; **augurios** *nmpl* good wishes.

aula ['aula] *nf* classroom.

aullar [au'ʎar] *vi* to howl, yell.

aullido [au'ʎiðo] *nm* howl, yell.

aumentar [aumen'tar] *vt* (*precios, sueldo*) to raise; (*producción*) to increase; (*con microscopio, anteojos*) to magnify // *vi*, **~se** *vr* to increase; (*subirse*) to rise; (*multiplicarse*) to multiply; **aumento** *nm* increase; rise.

aun [a'un] *ad* even.

aún [a'un] *ad* still, yet.

aunque [a'unke] *conj* though, although, even though, even if.

aura ['aura] *nf* gentle breeze; (*fig*) popularity.

aureola [aure'ola] *nf* halo.

auricular [auriku'lar] *nm* (*dedo*) little finger; (*del teléfono*) earpiece, receiver; **~es** *nmpl* headphones.

ausencia [au'senθja] *nf* absence.

ausentarse [ausen'tarse] *vr* to go/stay away, absent o.s.

ausente [au'sente] *a* absent.

auspicios [aus'piθjos] *nmpl* auspices; (*protección*) protection *sg*.

austeridad [austeri'ðað] *nf* austerity; **austero, a** *a* austere.

austral [aus'tral] *a* southern.

Australia [aus'tralja] *nf* Australia; **australiano, a** *a, nm/f* Australian.

Austria ['austrja] *nf* Austria; **austríaco, a** *a, nm/f* Austrian.

autenticar [autenti'kar] *vt* to authenticate; **auténtico, a** *a* authentic.

auto ['auto] *nm* (*JUR*) edict, decree; (: *orden*) writ; (*fam*) car; **~s** *nmpl* (*JUR*) proceedings; (: *acta*) court record *sg*.

autobiografía [autoβjoɣra'fia] *nf* autobiography.

autobús [auto'βus] *nm* bus.

autocar [auto'kar] *nm* coach.

autócrata [au'tokrata] *nm/f* autocrat.

autóctono, a [au'toktono, a] *a* native, indigenous.

autodefensa [autoðe'fensa] *nf* self-defence.

autodeterminación [autoðetermina'θjon] *nf* self-determination.

autoescuela [autoes'kwela] *nf* driving school.

autógrafo [au'toɣrafo] *nm* autograph.

autómata [au'tomata] *nm* automaton.

automático, a [auto'matiko, a] *a* automatic.

automotor, triz [automo'tor, 'triz] *a* self-propelled // *nm* Diesel train.

automóvil [auto'moβil] *nm* (motor) car, automobile; **automovilístico, a** *a* driving *cpd*, motoring *cpd*.

autonomía [autono'mia] *nf* autonomy; **autónomo, a** *a* autonomous.

autopista [auto'pista] *nf* motorway.

autopsia [au'topsja] *nf* autopsy.

autor, a [au'tor, a] *nm/f* author.

autoridad [autori'ðað] *nf* authority; **autoritario, a** *a* authoritarian.

autorización [autoriθa'θjon] *nf* authorization; **autorizado, a** *a* authorized; (*aprobado*) approved; **autorizar** *vt* to authorize; to approve.

autorretrato [autorre'trato] *nm* self-portrait.

autoservicio [autoser'βiθjo] *nm* self-service restaurant.

autostop [auto'stop] *nm* hitch-hiking; **hacer el ~** to hitch-hike; **~ista** *nm/f* hitch-hiker.

autosuficiencia [autosufi'θjenθja] *nf* self-sufficiency.

auxiliar [auksi'ljar] *vt* to help // *nm/f* assistant; **auxilio** *nm* assistance, help; **primeros auxilios** first aid *sg*.

Av *abr de* **Avenida**.

aval [a'βal] *nm* guarantee; (*persona*) guarantor.

avalancha [aβa'lantʃa] *nf* avalanche.

avaluar [aβa'lwar] *vt* to value, appraise.

avance [a'βanθe] *nm* advance; (*pago*) advance payment.

avanzar [aβan'θar] *vt, vi,* **~se** *vr* to advance.

avaricia [aβa'riθja] *nf* avarice, greed; **avariento, a** *a* avaricious, greedy.

avaro, a [a'βaro, a] *a* miserly, mean // *nm/f* miser.

avasallar [aβasa'ʎar] *vt* to subdue, subjugate; **~se** *vr* to submit.

Avda *abr de* **Avenida**.

ave ['aβe] *nf* bird; **~ de rapiña** bird of prey.

avellana [aβe'ʎana] *nf* hazelnut; **avellano** *nm* hazel tree.

avemaría [aβema'ria] *nf* Hail Mary, Ave Maria.

avena [a'βena] *nf* oats *pl*.

avenencia [aβe'nenθja] *nf* agreement; (*COM*) bargain.

avenida [aβe'niða] *nf* (*calle*) avenue; (*de río*) flood, spate.

avenir [aβe'nir] *vt* to reconcile; **~se** *vr* to come to an agreement, reach a compromise.

aventajado, a [aβenta'xaðo, a] *a* outstanding; **aventajar** *vt* (*sobrepasar*) to surpass, outstrip; (*preferir*) to prefer; **aventajarse** *vr* to surpass or excel o.s.

aventar [aβen'tar] *vt* to fan, blow;

(*esparcir*) to scatter; (*grano*) to winnow; **~se** *vr* to fill with air.

aventura [aβen'tura] *nf* adventure; (*casualidad*) chance; **aventurado, a** *a* risky; **aventurero, a** *a* adventurous.

avergonzar [aβerɣon'θar] *vt* to shame; (*desconcertar*) to embarrass; **~se** *vr* to be ashamed; to be embarrassed.

avería [aβe'ria] *nf* damage; (*TEC*) breakdown, fault.

averiguación [aβeriɣwa'θjon] *nf* investigation; (*determinación*) ascertainment; **averiguar** *vt* to investigate; to find out, ascertain.

aversión [aβer'sjon] *nf* aversion, dislike.

avestruz [aβes'truθ] *nm* ostrich.

avezarse [aβe'θarse] *vr:* **~se a algo** to grow used to sth.

aviación [aβja'θjon] *nf* aviation *q*; (*fuerzas aéreas*) air force.

aviador, a [aβja'ðor, a] *nm/f* aviator, airman/woman.

avicultura [aβikul'tura] *nf* poultry farming.

avidez [aβi'ðeθ] *nf* avidity, eagerness; **ávido, a** *a* avid, eager.

avinagrado, a [aβina'xraðo, a] *a* sour, acid; **avinagrarse** *vr* to turn sour.

avío [a'βio] *nm* preparation; **~s** *nmpl* gear *sg*, kit *sg*.

avión [a'βjon] *nm* aeroplane; (*ave*) martin; **~ de reacción** jet plane.

avisar [aβi'sar] *vt* (*advertir*) to warn, notify; (*informar*) to tell; (*aconsejar*) to advise, counsel; **aviso** *nm* warning; (*noticia*) notice; (*prudencia*) caution, discretion.

avispa [a'βispa] *nf* wasp.

avispado, a [aβis'paðo, a] *a* sharp, clever.

avispar [aβis'par] *vt* to spur (on); **~se** *vr* to fret, worry.

avispero [aβis'pero] *nm* wasp's nest.

avispón [aβis'pon] *nm* hornet.

avistar [aβis'tar] *vt* to sight, spot; **~se** *vr* to have an interview.

avituallar [aβitwa'ʎar] *vt* to supply with food.

avivar [aβi'βar] *vt* to strengthen, intensify; **~se** *vr* to revive, acquire new life.

avizorar [aβiθo'rar] *vt* to spy on.

axila [ak'sila] *nf* armpit.

axioma [ak'sjoma] *nm* axiom.

ay [ai] *excl* (*dolor*) ow!, ouch!; (*aflicción*) oh!, oh dear!; **¡~ de mí!** poor me!; **¡~ del quel** pity help or woe betide whoever!

aya ['aja] *nf* governess; (*niñera*) children's nurse.

ayer [a'jer] *ad, nm* yesterday; **antes de ~** the day before yesterday.

ayo ['ajo] *nm* tutor.

ayuda [a'juða] *nf* help, assistance; (*MED*) enema; (*AM*) laxative // *nm* page; **ayudante, a** *nm/f* assistant, helper; (*ESCOL*) assistant; (*MIL*) adjutant; **ayudar** *vt* to help, assist.

ayunar [aju'nar] *vi* to fast; **ayunas** *nfpl*: **estar en ayunas** (*no haber comido*) to be fasting; (*ignorante*) to be in the dark; **ayuno** *nm* fasting; ignorance.

ayuntamiento [ajunta'mjento] *nm* (*consejo*) council; (*edificio*) town hall; (*cópula*) sexual intercourse.

azabache [aθa'βatʃe] *nm* jet.

azada [a'θaða] *nf* hoe.

azafata [aθa'fata] *nf* air hostess.

azafrán [aθa'fran] *nm* saffron.

azahar [aθa'ar] *nm* orange/lemon blossom.

azar [a'θar] *nm* (*casualidad*) chance, fate; (*desgracia*) misfortune, accident; **por** ~ by chance; **al** ~ at random.

azarearse [aθare'arse] *vr* = **azorarse**.

azogue [a'θoxe] *nm* mercury.

azoramiento [aθora'mjento] *nm* alarm; (*confusión*) confusion.

azorar [aθo'rar] *vt* to alarm; ~**se** *vr* to get alarmed.

Azores [a'θores] *nmpl*: **los** ~ the Azores.

azotar [aθo'tar] *vt* to whip, beat; (*pegar*) to spank; **azote** *nm* (*látigo*) whip; (*latigazo*) lash, stroke; (*en las nalgas*) spank; (*calamidad*) calamity.

azotea [aθo'tea] *nf* terrace roof.

azteca [aθ'teka] *a*, *nm/f* Aztec.

azúcar [a'θukar] *nm* sugar; **azucarado, a** a sugary, sweet.

azucarero, a [aθuka'rero, a] *a* sugar *cpd* // *nm* sugar bowl.

azucena [aθu'θena] *nf* white lily.

azufre [a'θufre] *nm* sulphur.

azul [a'θul] *a*, *nm* blue.

azulejo [aθu'lexo] *nm* glazed tile.

azuzar [aθu'θar] *vt* to incite, egg on.

B

B.A. *abr de* **Buenos Aires.**

baba ['baβa] *nf* spittle, saliva; **babear** *vi* to drool, slaver.

babel [ba'βel] *nm o f* bedlam.

babero [ba'βero] *nm* bib.

babor [ba'βor] *nm* port (side).

babucha [ba'βutʃa] *nf* slipper.

bacalao [baka'lao] *nm* cod(fish).

bacía [ba'θia] *nf* basin, bowl.

bacín [ba'θin] *nm* chamber pot.

bacteria [bak'terja] *nf* bacterium, germ.

báculo ['bakulo] *nm* stick, staff.

bache ['batʃe] *nm* pothole, rut; (*fig*) bad patch.

bachillerato [batʃiʎe'rato] *nm* (*ESCOL*) school-leaving examination.

bagaje [ba'xaxe] *nm* baggage.

bagatela [baɣa'tela] *nf* trinket, trifle.

bahía [ba'ia] *nf* bay.

bailar [bai'lar] *vt*, *vi* to dance; ~**ín, ina** *nm/f* (*ballet*) dancer; **baile** *nm* dance; (*formal*) ball.

baja ['baxa] *nf ver* **bajo.**

bajada [ba'xaða] *nf* descent; (*camino*) slope; (*de aguas*) ebb.

bajamar [baxa'mar] *nf* low tide.

bajar [ba'xar] *vi* to go/come down; (*temperatura, precios*) to drop, fall; (*de coche*) to get out; (*de autobús*) to get off // *vt* (*cabeza*) to bow, bend; (*escalera*) to go/come down; (*precio, voz*) to lower; (*llevar abajo*) to take down; ~**se** *vr* to bend down; to get out of; to get off; (*fig*) to humble o.s.

bajeza [ba'xeθa] *nf* baseness *q*; (*una* ~) vile deed.

bajío [ba'xio] *nm* shoal, sandbank; (*AM*) lowlands *pl*.

bajo, a ['baxo, a] *a* (*terreno*) low(-lying); (*mueble, número, precio*) low; (*piso*) ground; (*de estatura*) small, short; (*color*) pale; (*sonido*) faint, soft, low; (*voz: en tono*) deep; (*metal*) base; (*humilde*) low, humble // *ad* (*hablar*) low, quietly; (*volar*) low // *prep* under, below, underneath // *nm* (*MUS*) bass // *nf* drop, fall; (*MIL*) casualty; ~ **la lluvia** in the rain; **dar de** ~**a** (*soldado*) to discharge; (*empleado*) to dismiss, sack.

bajón [ba'xon] *nm* (*MUS*) bassoon; (*baja*) decline, fall, drop.

bajorrelieve [baxorre'ljeβe] *nm* bas-relief.

bala ['bala] *nf* bullet.

baladí [bala'ði] *a* a trivial.

baladrón, ona [bala'ðron, ona] *a* boastful.

bálago ['balaɣo] *nm* thatch.

balance [ba'lanθe] *nm* (*balanceo*) oscillation, rocking; (*NAUT*) roll; (*COM*) balance; (: *libro*) balance sheet; (: *cuenta general*) stocktaking; ~**ar** *vt* to balance // *vi*, ~**arse** *vr* to swing (to and fro); (*vacilar*) to hesitate; **balanceo** *nm* swinging.

balanza [ba'lanθa] *nf* balance, scales *pl*; ~ **comercial** balance of trade; ~ **de pagos** balance of payments; (*ASTRO*): **B**~ = **Libra.**

balar [ba'lar] *vi* to bleat.

balazo [ba'laθo] *nm* (*golpe*) shot; (*herida*) bullet wound.

balbucear [balβuθe'ar] *vi*, *vt* to stammer, stutter; **balbuceo** *nm* stammering, stuttering.

balbucir [balβu'θir] *vi*, *vt* to stammer, stutter.

balcón [bal'kon] *nm* balcony.

baldaquín [balda'kin], **baldaquino** [balda'kino] *nm* canopy.

baldar [bal'dar] *vt* to cripple.

balde ['balde] *nm* bucket, pail; **de** ~ *ad* (for) free, for nothing; **en** ~ *ad* in vain.

baldío, a [bal'dio, a] *a* uncultivated // *nm* waste land.

baldón [bal'don] *nm* (*injuria*) insult.

baldosa [bal'dosa] *nf* paving stone.

Baleares [bale'ares] *nfpl*: **las (Islas)** ~ the Balearic Islands.

balido [ba'liðo] *nm* bleat, bleating.

balística [ba'listika] *nf* ballistics *pl*.

baliza [ba'liθa] *nf* (*AVIAT*) beacon; (*NAUT*) buoy.

balneario, a [balne'arjo, a] *a*: **estación** ~ a bathing resort // *nm* spa, health resort.

balón [ba'lon] *nm* ball.

baloncesto [balon'θesto] *nm* basketball.

balsa ['balsa] *nf* raft; (*BOT*) balsa wood.

bálsamo ['balsamo] *nm* balsam, balm.

baluarte [ba'lwarte] *nm* bastion, bulwark.

ballena [ba'ʎena] *nf* whale.

ballesta [ba'ʎesta] *nf* crossbow; (*AUTO*) spring.

ballet [ba'le] *nm* ballet.

bambolear [bambole'ar] *vi*, ~**se** *vr* to swing, sway; (*silla*) to wobble; **bamboleo** *nm* swinging, swaying; wobbling.

bambú [bam'bu] *nm* bamboo.

banca ['banka] *nf* (*asiento*) bench; (*COM*) banking; ~**da** *nf* (*banco*) stone bench; (*TEC*) bench.

bancario, a [ban'karjo, a] *a* banking *cpd*, bank *cpd*.

bancarrota [banka'rrota] *nf* (*esp fraudulent*) bankruptcy.

banco ['banko] *nm* bench; (*ESCOL*) desk; (*COM*) bank; (*GEO*) stratum; ~ **de crédito/de ahorros** credit/ savings bank; ~ **de arena** sandbank; ~ **de hielo** iceberg.

banda ['banda] *nf* band; (*pandilla*) gang; (*NAUT*) side, edge; **la B**~ **Oriental** Uruguay; ~ **sonora** soundtrack.

bandada [ban'daða] *nf* (*de pájaros*) flock; (*de peces*) shoal.

bandeja [ban'dexa] *nf* tray.

bandera [ban'dera] *nf* (*de tela*) flag; (*estandarte*) banner.

banderilla [bande'riʎa] *nf* banderilla.

banderola [bande'rola] *nf* banderole, pennant.

bandidaje [bandi'ðaxe] *nm* banditry; **bandido** *nm* bandit.

bando ['bando] *nm* (*edicto*) edict, proclamation; (*facción*) faction; **los** ~**s** the banns.

bandolero [bando'lero] *nm* bandit, brigand.

banquero [ban'kero] *nm* banker.

banqueta [ban'keta] *nf* (*asiento*) bench; (*escabel*) stool.

banquete [ban'kete] *nm* banquet; (*para convidados*) formal dinner.

banquillo [ban'kiʎo] *nm* (*JUR*) dock, prisoner's bench; (*banco*) bench; (*para los pies*) footstool.

bañador [baɲa'ðor] *nm* swimming costume.

bañar [ba'ɲar] *vt* (*niño*) to bath, bathe; (*objeto*) to dip; (*de barniz*) to coat; ~**se** *vr* (*en el mar*) to bathe, swim; (*en la bañera*) to bath, have a bath.

bañera [ba'ɲera] *nf* bath(tub).

bañero [ba'ɲero] *nm* lifeguard.

bañista [ba'ɲista] *nm/f* bather.

baño ['baɲo] *nm* (*en bañera*) bath; (*en río*) dip, swim; (*cuarto*) bathroom; (*bañera*) bath(tub); (*capa*) coating.

baptista [bap'tista] *nm/f* baptist.

baqueta [ba'keta] *nf* (*MUS*) drumstick.

bar [bar] *nm* bar.

barahúnda [bara'unda] *nf* uproar, hubbub.

baraja [ba'raxa] *nf* pack (of cards); **barajar** *vt* (*naipes*) to shuffle; (*fig*) to jumble up.

baranda [ba'randa] *nf* rail, railing.

barandilla [baran'diʎa] *nf* rail, railing.

baratija [bara'tixa] *nf* trinket.

baratillo [bara'tiʎo] *nm* (*tienda*) junkshop; (*subasta*) bargain sale; (*conjunto de cosas*) secondhand goods *pl*.

barato, a [ba'rato, a] *a* cheap // *nm* bargain sale // *ad* cheap, cheaply; **baratura** *nf* cheapness.

baraúnda [bara'unda] *nf* = **barahúnda**.

barba ['barβa] *nf* (*ANAT*) chin; (*pelo*) beard, whiskers *pl*.

barbacoa [barβa'koa] *nf* (*parrilla*) barbecue; (*carne*) barbecued meat.

barbado, a [bar'βaðo, a] *a* bearded // *nm* seedling.

barbaridad [barβari'ðað] *nf* barbarity; (*acto*) barbarism; (*atrocidad*) outrage; **una** ~ (*fam*) a huge amount; **¡qué** ~**!** (*fam*) how awful!

barbarie [bar'βarje] *nf*, **barbarismo** [barβa'rismo] *nm* barbarism; (*crueldad*) barbarity.

bárbaro, a ['barβaro, a] *a* barbarous, cruel; (*grosero*) rough, uncouth // *nm/f* barbarian // *ad*: **lo pasamos** ~ (*fam*) we had a tremendous time; **¡qué** ~**!** (*fam*) how marvellous!; **un éxito** ~ (*fam*) a terrific success; **es un tipo** ~ (*fam*) he's a splendid chap.

barbear [barβe'ar] *vt* (*AM*) to shave.

barbecho [bar'βetʃo] *nm* fallow land.

barbero [bar'βero] *nm* barber, hairdresser.

barbilampiño [barβilam'piɲo] *a* smooth-faced; (*fig*) inexperienced.

barbilla [bar'βiʎa] *nf* chin, tip of the chin.

barbotar [barβo'tar], **barbotear** [barβote'ar] *vt*, *vi* to mutter, mumble.

barbudo, a [bar'βuðo, a] *a* bearded.

barca ['barka] *nf* (*small*) boat; ~ **de pesca** fishing boat; ~ **de pasaje** ferry; ~**za** *nf* barge; ~**za de desembarco** landing craft.

barcelonés, esa [barθelo'nes, esa] *a* of or from Barcelona.

barco ['barko] *nm* boat; (*buque*) ship; ~ **de carga** cargo boat.

bardar [bar'ðar] *vt* to thatch.

barítono [ba'ritono] *nm* baritone.

barman ['barman] *nm* barman.

Barna *abr de* **Barcelona**.

barniz [bar'niθ] *nm* varnish; (*en la loza*) glaze; (*fig*) veneer; ~ **para las uñas** nail varnish; ~**ar** *vt* to varnish; (*loza*) to glaze.

barómetro [ba'rometro] *nm* barometer.

barquero [bar'kero] *nm* boatman.

barquillo [bar'kiʎo] *nm* cone, cornet.

barra ['barra] *nf* bar, rod; (*de un bar, café*) bar; (*de pan*) small loaf; (*palanca*) lever; ~ **de carmín** *o* **de labios** lipstick.

barraca [ba'rraka] *nf* hut, cabin.

barranca [ba'rranka] *nf* ravine, gully; **barranco** *nm* ravine; (*fig*) difficulty.

barrena [ba'rrena] *nf* drill; **barrenar** *vt* to drill (through), bore; **barreno** *nm* large drill, borer.

barrer [ba'rrer] *vt* to sweep; (*quitar*) to sweep away.

barrera [ba'rrera] *nf* barrier.

barriada [ba'rrjaða] *nf* quarter, district.

barricada [barri'kaða] *nf* barricade.

barrido [ba'rriðo] *nm*, **barrida** [ba'rriða] *nf* sweep, sweeping.

barriga [ba'rriʁa] *nf* belly; (*panza*) paunch; **barrigón, ona, barrigudo, a** *a* fat, potbellied.

barril [ba'rril] *nm* barrel, cask.

barrio ['barrjo] *nm* (*en el pueblo*) district, quarter; (*fuera del pueblo*) suburb.

barro ['barro] *nm* (*lodo*) mud; (*objetos*) earthenware; (*MED*) pimple.

barroco, a [ba'rroko, a] *a, nm* baroque.

barroso, a [ba'rroso, a] *a* (*lodoso*) muddy; (*MED*) pimply.

barruntar [barrun'tar] *vt* (*conjeturar*) to guess; (*presentir*) to suspect; **barrunto** *nm* guess; suspicion.

bartola [bar'tola]: **a la** ~ *ad*: **tirarse a la** ~ to take it easy, do nothing.

bártulos ['bartulos] *nmpl* things, belongings.

barullo [ba'ruʎo] *nm* row, uproar.

basa ['basa] *nf* base; (*fig*) basis; ~**mento** *nm* base, plinth.

basar [ba'sar] *vt* to base; ~**se** *vr*: ~**se en** to be based on.

basca ['baska] *nf* nausea.

báscula ['baskula] *nf* (platform) scales *pl*.

base ['base] *nf* base; **a** ~ **de** on the basis of.

básico, a ['basiko, a] *a* basic.

basílica [ba'silika] *nf* basilica.

bastante [bas'tante] *a* (*suficiente*) enough, sufficient; (*no poco(s)*) quite a lot of // *a* (*suficientemente*) enough, sufficiently; (*muy*) quite, rather.

bastar [bas'tar] *vi* to be enough *or* sufficient; ~**se** *vr* to be self-sufficient; ~ **para** to be enough to; **¡basta!** (that's) enough!

bastardilla [bastar'ðiʎa] *nf* italics *pl*.

bastardo, a [bas'tarðo, a] *a, nm/f* bastard.

bastidor [basti'ðor] *nm* frame; (*de coche*) chassis.

basto, a ['basto, a] *a* coarse, rough; ~**s** *nmpl* (*NAIPES*) clubs.

bastón [bas'ton] *nm* (*gen*) stick, staff; (*para el paseo*) walking stick.

basura [ba'sura] *nf* rubbish, refuse.

basurero [basu'rero] *nm* (*hombre*) dustman; (*lugar*) rubbish dump; (*cubo*) (rubbish) bin.

bata ['bata] *nf* (*salto de cama*) dressing gown, housecoat; (*de alumno etc*) smock, overall.

batalla [ba'taʎa] *nf* battle; **de** ~ everyday, for everyday use.

batallar [bata'ʎar] *vi* to fight.

batallón [bata'ʎon] *nm* battalion.

bate ['bate] *nm* bat; ~**ador** *nm* batter, batsman.

batería [bate'ria] *nf* battery; (*MUS*) drums *pl*; ~ **de cocina** kitchen utensils *pl*.

batido, a [ba'tiðo, a] *a* (*camino*) beaten, well-trodden // *nm* (*CULIN*) batter; ~ **de leche** milk shake.

batidora [bati'ðora] *nf* beater, mixer.

batir [ba'tir] *vt* to beat, strike; (*vencer*) to beat, defeat; (*revolver*) to beat, mix; (*acuñar*) to strike, mint; (*pelo*) to comb; ~**se** *vr* to fight; ~ **palmas** to clap, applaud.

batuta [ba'tuta] *nf* baton.

baúl [ba'ul] *nm* trunk; (*AUTO*) boot.

bautismo [bau'tismo] *nm* baptism, christening.

bautizar [bauti'θar] *vt* to baptize, christen; (*fam*) to water down; **bautizo** *nm* baptism, christening.

bayo, a ['bajo, a] *a* bay // *nf* berry.

bayoneta [bajo'neta] *nf* bayonet.

baza ['baθa] *nf* trick.

bazar [ba'θar] *nm* bazaar.

bazofia [ba'θofja] *nf* left-overs *pl*.

beato, a [be'ato, a] *a* blessed; (*piadoso*) pious // *nm/f* lay brother/sister.

bebé [be'βe] *nm* baby.

bebedero, a [beβe'ðero, a] *a* drinkable // *nm* (*para animales*) drinking trough; (*de vasija*) spout.

bebedizo, a [beβe'ðiθo, a] *a* drinkable // *nm* potion.

bebedor, a [beβe'ðor, a] *a* hard-drinking.

beber [be'βer] *vt, vi* to drink.

bebida [be'βiða] *nf* drink.

beca ['beka] *nf* grant, scholarship.

befa ['befa] *nf* ver **befo**.

befar [be'far] *vt* to scoff at.

befo, a ['befo, a] *a* thick-lipped // *nm* lip // *nf*: **hacer** ~**a de** to jeer, mock.

beldad [bel'dað] *nf* beauty.

belfo, a ['belfo, a] = **befo**.

belga ['belʁa] *a, nm/f* Belgian.

Bélgica ['belxika] *nf* Belgium.

bélico, a ['beliko, a] *a* warlike, martial; **belicoso, a** *a* (*guerrero*) warlike; (*agresivo*) aggressive, bellicose.

beligerante [belive'rante] *a* belligerent.

bellaco, a [be'ʎako, a] *a* sly, cunning // *nm* villain, rogue; **bellaquería** *nf* (*acción*) dirty trick; (*calidad*) wickedness.

belleza [be'ʎeθa] *nf* beauty.

bello, a ['beʎo, a] *a* beautiful, lovely; ~**as artes** fine arts.

bellota [be'ʎota] *nf* acorn.

bemol [be'mol] *nm* (*MUS*) flat; **esto tiene** ~**es** (*fam*) this is a real problem.

bendecir [bende'θir] *vt* to bless.

bendición [bendi'θjon] *nf* blessing.

bendito, a [ben'dito, a] *pp de* **bendecir** // *a* holy; (*afortunado*) lucky; (*feliz*) happy; (*sencillo*) simple // *nm/f* simple soul.

benedictino, a [benedik'tino, a] *a, nm* Benedictine.

beneficencia [benefi'θenθja] *nf* charity.

beneficiar [benefi'θjar] *vt* (*hacer bien a*) to benefit, be of benefit to; (*tierra*) to cultivate; (*mina*) to exploit; (*mineral*) to process, treat; ~**se** *vr* to benefit, profit; ~**io, a** *nm/f* beneficiary.

beneficio [bene'fiθjo] *nm* (*bien*) benefit, advantage; (*ganancia*) profit, gain; (*AGR*) cultivation; ~**so, a** *a* beneficial.

benéfico, a [be'nefiko, a] *a* beneficent, charitable.

beneplácito [bene'plaθito] *nm* approval, consent.

benevolencia [beneβo'lenθja] *nf* benevolence, kindness; **benévolo, a** *a* benevolent, kind.

benignidad [beniγni'ðað] *nf* (*afabilidad*) kindness; (*suavidad*) mildness; **benigno, a** *a* kind; mild.

beodo, a [be'oðo, a] *a* drunk.

berenjena [beren'xena] *nf* aubergine, eggplant.

Berlín [ber'lin] *n* Berlin; **berlinés, esa** *a* of or from Berlin // *nm/f* Berliner.

bermejo, a [ber'mexo, a] *a* red.

Berna ['berna] *n* Berne.

berrear [berre'ar] *vi* to bellow, low.

berrido [be'rriðo] *nm* bellow, bellowing.

berrinche [be'rrintʃe] *nm* (*fam*) temper, tantrum.

berro ['berro] *nm* watercress.

berza ['berθa] *nf* cabbage.

besar [be'sar] *vt* to kiss; (*fig*) to graze; ~**se** *vr* to kiss (one another); **beso** *nm* kiss.

bestia ['bestja] *nf* beast, animal; (*fig*) idiot; ~ **de carga** beast of burden.

bestial [bes'tjal] *a* bestial; (*fam*) terrific; ~**idad** *nf* bestiality; (*fam*) stupidity.

besuquear [besuke'ar] *vt* to cover with kisses; ~**se** *vr* to kiss and cuddle.

betún [be'tun] *nm* bitumen, asphalt; (*para calzado*) shoe polish.

biberón [biβe'ron] *nm* feeding bottle.

Biblia ['biβlja] *nf* Bible.

bíblico, a ['biβliko, a] *a* biblical.

bibliografía [biβljoγra'fia] *nf* bibliography.

biblioteca [biβljo'teka] *nf* library; (*mueble*) bookshelves *pl*; ~ **de consulta** reference library; ~**rio, a** *nm/f* librarian.

B.I.C. *nf abr de* **Brigada de Investigación Criminal** CID (Criminal Investigation Department); FBI (Federal Bureau of Investigation) (*US*).

bicarbonato [bikarβo'nato] *nm* bicarbonate.

bicicleta [biθi'kleta] *nf* bicycle, bike.

bicho ['bitʃo] *nm* (*animal*) small animal; (*sabandija*) bug, insect; (*TAUR*) bull.

bidé [bi'ðe] *nm* bidet.

bien [bjen] *nm* good; (*interés*) advantage, benefit // *ad* well; (*correctamente*) properly, right; (*oler*) nice; (*muy*) very; **más ~** rather // *excl*: ¡(muy) ~! well done! // *conj*: **no ~ llovió, bajó la temperatura** no sooner had it rained than the temperature dropped; ~ **que** although; ~**es inmuebles/muebles** real estate *sg*/personal property *sg*; ~**es de consumo** consumer goods; ~**es raíces** real estate *sg*.

bienal [bje'nal] *a* biennial.

bienandanza [bjenan'danθa] *nf* happiness.

bienaventurado, a [bjenaβentu'raðo, a] *a* (*feliz*) happy, fortunate; (*sencillo*) simple, naïve.

bienestar [bjenes'tar] *nm* well-being.

bienhechor, a [bjene'tʃor, a] *a* beneficent.

bienvenida [bjenβe'niða] *nf* welcome; **bienvenido** *excl* welcome!

biftec [bif'tek] *nm* (beef)steak.

bifurcación [bifurka'θjon] *nf* fork.

bigamia [bi'γamja] *nf* bigamy; **bígamo, a** *a* bigamous // *nm/f* bigamist.

bigote [bi'γote] *nm* moustache; **bigotudo, a** *a* moustached.

bilbaíno, a [bilβa'ino, a] *a* of or from Bilbao.

bilingüe [bi'lingwe] *a* bilingual.

billar [bi'ʎar] *nm* billiards *sg*; (*lugar*) billiard hall.

billete [bi'ʎete] *nm* ticket; (*de banco*) banknote; (*carta*) note; ~ **simple** single (ticket); ~ **de ida y vuelta** return (ticket); ~ **kilométrico** runabout ticket.

billetera [biʎe'tera] *nf*, **billetero** [biʎe'tero] *nm* wallet.

billón [bi'ʎon] *nm* billion.

bimensual [bimen'swal] *a* twice monthly.

bimotor [bimo'tor] *a* twin-engined // *nm* twin-engined plane.

binóculo [bi'nokulo] *nm* pince-nez.

biografía [bjoγra'fia] *nf* biography; **biógrafo, a** *nm/f* biographer.

biología [bjolo'xia] *nf* biology; **biológico, a** *a* biological; **biólogo, a** *nm/f* biologist.

biombo ['bjombo] *nm* (folding) screen.

biopsia [bi'opsja] *nf* biopsy.

biplano [bi'plano] *nm* biplane.

birlar [bir'lar] *vt* (*derribar*) to knock down; (*matar*) to kill; (*fam*) to pinch.

bis [bis] *excl* encore! // *ad*: **viven en el 27 ~** they live at 27a.

bisabuelo, a [bisa'βwelo, a] *nm/f* great-grandfather/mother.

bisagra [bi'saγra] *nf* hinge.

bisbisar [bisβi'sar], **bisbisear** [bisβise'ar] *vt* to mutter, mumble.

bisexual [bisek'swal] *a* bisexual.

bisiesto [bi'sjesto] *a*: **año ~** leap year.

bisnieto, a [bis'njeto, a] *nm/f* great-grandson/daughter.

bisonte [bi'sonte] *nm* bison.

bisoño, a [bi'soɲo, a] *a* green, inexperienced.

bistec [bis'tek], **bisté** [bis'te] *nm* steak.
bisturí [bistu'ri] *nm* scalpel.
bisuteria [bisute'ria] *nf* imitation *or* costume jewellery.
bizarría [biθa'rria] *nf* (*valor*) bravery; (*generosidad*) generosity; **bizarro, a** *a* brave; generous.
bizcar [biθ'kar] *vi* to squint; **bizco, a** *a* cross-eyed.
bizcocho [biθ'kotʃo] *nm* (*CULIN*) sponge cake.
bizquear [biθke'ar] *vi* to squint.
blanco, a ['blanko, a] *a* white // *nm/f* white man/woman, white // *nm* (*color*) white; (*intervalo*) space, interval; (*en texto*) blank; (*MIL, fig*) target // *nf* (*MUS*) minim; **en ~** blank; **noche en ~** sleepless night; **estar sin ~** to be broke.
blancura [blan'kura] *nf* whiteness.
blandir [blan'dir] *vt* to brandish.
blando, a ['blando, a] *a* soft; (*tierno*) tender, gentle; (*carácter*) mild; (*fam*) cowardly; **blandura** *nf* softness; tenderness; mildness.
blanquear [blanke'ar] *vt* to whiten; (*fachada*) to whitewash; (*paño*) to bleach // *vi* to turn white; **blanquecino, a** *a* whitish; **blanqueo** *nm* whitewashing; bleaching.
blanquillo, a [blan'kiʎo, a] *a* white.
blasfemar [blasfe'mar] *vi* to blaspheme, curse; **blasfemia** *nf* blasphemy.
blasón [bla'son] *nm* coat of arms; (*fig*) honour; **blasonar** *vt* to emblazon // *vi* to boast, brag.
bledo ['bleðo] *nm*: **(no) me importa un ~** I don't care two hoots.
blindaje [blin'daxe] *nm* armour, armour-plating; **blindar** *vt* to armour, armour-plate.
bloc [blok] *nm* writing pad.
bloque ['bloke] *nm* block; (*POL*) bloc; **~ de cilindros** cylinder block.
bloquear [bloke'ar] *vt* to blockade; **bloqueo** *nm* blockade; (*COM*) freezing, blocking.
bluejean ['bludʒin] *nm inv* jeans *pl*.
blusa ['blusa] *nf* (*de alumno*) smock; (*de mujer*) blouse.
boardilla [boar'ðiʎa] *nf* = **buhardilla**.
boato [bo'ato] *nm* show, ostentation.
bobada [bo'βaða], **bobería** [boβe'ria] *nf* foolish action/ statement.
bobina [bo'βina] *nf* (*TEC*) bobbin; (*FOTO*) spool; (*ELEC*) coil; **bobinar** *vt* to wind.
bobo, a ['boβo, a] *a* (*tonto*) daft, silly; (*cándido*) naïve // *nm* (*TEATRO*) clown, funny man, fool.
boca ['boka] *nf* mouth; (*de crustáceo*) pincer; (*de cañón*) muzzle; (*de vino*) flavour, taste; (*entrada*) mouth, entrance; **~s** *nfpl* (*de río*) mouth *sg*; **~ abajo/arriba** face down/up; **a ~ de jarro** point-blank; **se me hace la ~ agua** my mouth is watering.
bocacalle [boka'kaʎe] *nf* entrance to a street.

bocadillo [boka'ðiʎo] *nm* (*emparedado*) sandwich; (*comida ligera*) snack.
bocado [bo'kaðo] *nm* mouthful, bite; (*de caballo*) bridle; **~ de Adán** Adam's apple.
bocanada [boka'naða] *nf* (*de vino*) mouthful, swallow; (*de aire*) gust, puff.
boceto [bo'θeto] *nm* sketch, outline.
bocina [bo'θina] *nf* (*MUS*) trumpet; (*AUTO*) horn; (*para hablar*) megaphone; (*para sordos*) ear trumpet.
bocha ['botʃa] *nf* bowl; **~s** *nfpl* bowls.
bochinche [bo'tʃintʃe] *nm* (*fam*) uproar.
bochorno [bo'tʃorno] *nm* (*calor*) sultry weather; (*vergüenza*) embarrassment; **~so, a** *a* sultry; embarrassing; (*sofocante*) stuffy.
boda ['boða] *nf* (*también* **~s** *nfpl*) wedding, marriage; (*fiesta*) wedding reception; **~s de plata/de oro** silver/golden wedding.
bodega [bo'ðeva] *nf* (*de vino*) (wine) cellar; (*depósito*) storeroom; (*de barco*) hold.
bodegón [boðe'von] *nm* cheap restaurant; (*ARTE*) still life.
bofe ['bofe] *nm* (*también* **~s** *nmpl*) lung.
bofetada [bofe'taða] *nf* slap (in the face).
bofetón [bofe'ton] *nm* punch (in the face).
boga ['boɣa] *nf* (*NAUT*) rowing; (*fig*) vogue, fashion // *nm/f* rower; **en ~** in vogue; **bogar** *vi* (*remar*) to row; (*navegar*) to sail.
Bogotá [boɣo'ta] *n* Bogota; **bogotano, a** *a* of or from Bogota.
bohardilla [boar'ðiʎa] *nf* = **buhardilla**.
bohemio, a [bo'emjo, a] *a, nm/f* Bohemian.
boicot [boi'kot] *nm* boycott; **~ear** *vt* to boycott; **~eo** *nm* boycott.
boina ['boina] *nf* beret.
bola ['bola] *nf* (*gen*) ball; (*canica*) marble; (*NAIPES*) (grand) slam; (*betún*) shoe polish; **~ de billar** billiard ball; **~ de nieve** snowball.
bolchevique [boltʃe'βike] *nm/f* Bolshevik.
boleadoras [bolea'ðoras] *nfpl* (*AM*) bolas.
bolera [bo'lera] *nf* skittle alley.
boleta [bo'leta] *nf* (*billete*) ticket; (*permiso*) pass, permit.
boletín [bole'tin] *nm* bulletin; (*periódico*) journal, review; (*billete*) ticket; **~ escolar** school report; **~ de noticias** news bulletin; **~ de pedido** application form; **~ de precios** price list; **~ de prensa** press release.
boleto [bo'leto] *nm* ticket.
boliche [bo'litʃe] *nm* (*bola*) jack; (*juego*) bowls *sg*; (*lugar*) bowling alley.
bolígrafo [bo'livrafo] *nm* ball-point pen.
bolívar [bo'liβar] *nm* monetary unit of Venezuela.
Bolivia [bo'liβja] *nf* Bolivia; **boliviano, a** *a, nm/f* Bolivian.
bolo ['bolo] *nm* skittle; (*píldora*) (large) pill; (*juego de*) **~s** skittles *sg*.
bolsa ['bolsa] *nf* (*cartera*) purse; (*saco*) bag; (*ANAT*) cavity, sac; (*COM*) stock exchange; (*MINERÍA*) pocket; **~ de agua**

caliente hot water bottle; ~ **de aire** air pocket; ~ **de papel** paper bag.

bolsillo [bol'siʎo] *nm* pocket; (*cartera*) purse; **de** ~ pocket(-size).

bolsista [bol'sista] *nm/f* stockbroker.

bolso ['bolso] *nm* (*bolsa*) bag; (*de mujer*) handbag.

bollo ['boʎo] *nm* (*pan*) roll; (*bulto*) bump, lump; (*abolladura*) dent.

bomba ['bomba] *nf* (*MIL*) bomb; (*TEC*) pump // *a* (*fam*): **noticia** ~ shattering piece of news // *ad* (*fam*): **pasarlo** ~ to have a great time; ~ **atómica/de humo/de retardo** atomic/smoke/ time bomb; ~ **de gasolina** petrol pump; ~ **de mano** grenade; ~ **lacrimógena** tear gas bomb.

bombardear [bombarðe'ar] *vt* to bombard; (*MIL*) to bomb; **bombardeo** *nm* bombardment; bombing.

bombardero [bombar'ðero] *nm* bomber.

bombear [bombe'ar] *vt* (*agua*) to pump (out or up); (*MIL*) to bomb; ~**se** *vr* to warp.

bombero [bom'bero] *nm* fireman.

bombilla [bom'biʎa] *nf* bulb.

bombín [bom'bin] *nm* bowler hat.

bombo ['bombo] *nm* (*MUS*) bass drum; (*TEC*) drum.

bombón [bom'bon] *nm* chocolate.

bonachón, ona [bona'tʃon, ona] *a* good-natured, easy-going.

bonaerense [bonae'rense] *a* of or from Buenos Aires.

bonancible [bonan'θiβle] *a* (*tiempo*) fair, calm.

bonanza [bo'nanθa] *nf* (*NAUT*) fair weather; (*fig*) bonanza; (*MINERÍA*) rich pocket or vein.

bondad [bon'dað] *nf* goodness, kindness; **tenga la** ~ **de** (*please*) be good enough to; ~**oso, a** a good, kind.

bonito, a [bo'nito, a] *a* (*lindo*) pretty; (*agradable*) nice.

bono ['bono] *nm* voucher; (*FIN*) bond.

boquear [boke'ar] *vi* to gasp.

boquerón [boke'ron] *nm* (*anchoa*) anchovy; (*agujero*) large hole.

boquete [bo'kete] *nm* gap, hole.

boquiabierto, a [bokia'βjerto, a] *a* open-mouthed (in astonishment).

boquilla [bo'kiʎa] *nf* (*para riego*) nozzle; (*para cigarro*) cigarette holder; (*MUS*) mouthpiece.

borbollar [borβo'ʎar], **borbollear** [borβoʎe'ar], **borbotar** [borβo'tar] *vi* to bubble.

borbotón [borβo'ton] *nm* bubbling.

bordado [bor'ðaðo] *nm* embroidery.

bordar [bor'ðar] *vt* to embroider.

borde ['borðe] *nm* edge, border; (*de camino etc*) side; (*en la costura*) hem; **al** ~ **de** (*fig*) on the verge or brink of; ~**ar** *vt* to border.

bordo ['borðo] *nm* (*NAUT*) side; **a** ~ **on** board.

Borinquén [borin'ken] *nm* Puerto Rico;

borinqueño, a a, *nm/f* Puerto Rican.

borra ['borra] *nf* (*pelusa*) fluff; (*sedimento*) sediment.

borrachera [borra'tʃera] *nf* (*ebriedad*) drunkenness; (*orgía*) spree, binge.

borracho, a [bo'rratʃo, a] *a* drunk // *nm/f* (*que bebe mucho*) drunkard, drunk; (*temporalmente*) drunk, drunk man/woman.

borrador [borra'ðor] *nm* (*escritura*) first draft, rough sketch; (*cuaderno*) scribbling pad; (*goma*) rubber, eraser.

borrajear [borraxe'ar] *vt, vi* to scribble.

borrar [bo'rrar] *vt* to erase, rub out.

borrascoso, a [borras'koso, a] *a* stormy.

borrica [bo'rrika] *nf* she-donkey; (*fig*) stupid woman; ~**da** *nf* foolish action/statement.

borrico [bo'rriko] *nm* donkey; (*fig*) stupid man.

borrón [bo'rron] *nm* (*mancha*) stain; (*proyecto*) rough draft; (*de cuadro*) sketch.

borroso, a [bo'rroso, a] *a* vague, unclear; (*escritura*) illegible.

bosque ['boske] *nm* wood, forest.

bosquejar [boske'xar] *vt* to sketch; **bosquejo** *nm* sketch.

bosta ['bosta] *nf* dung, manure.

bostezar [boste'θar] *vi* to yawn; **bostezo** *nm* yawn.

bota ['bota] *nf* (*saco*) leather wine bottle; (*calzado*) boot.

botadura [bota'ðura] *nf* launching.

botánico, a [bo'taniko, a] *nm/f* botanist // *nf* botany.

botar [bo'tar] *vt* to throw, hurl; (*NAUT*) to launch; (*fam*) to throw out // *vi* to bounce.

bote ['bote] *nm* (*salto*) bounce; (*golpe*) thrust; (*vasija*) tin, can; (*embarcación*) boat; **de** ~ **en** ~ packed, jammed full; ~ **salvavidas** lifeboat.

botella [bo'teʎa] *nf* bottle.

botica [bo'tika] *nf* chemist's (shop), pharmacy; ~**rio,** a *nm/f* chemist, pharmacist.

botija [bo'tixa] *nf* (*earthenware*) jug; **botijo** *nm* (*earthenware*) jug; (*tren*) excursion train.

botín [bo'tin] *nm* (*calzado*) half boot; (*polaina*) spat; (*MIL*) booty.

botiquín [boti'kin] *nm* (*armario*) medicine cabinet; (*portátil*) first-aid kit.

botón [bo'ton] *nm* button; (*BOT*) bud; (*de florete*) tip; ~ **de oro** buttercup.

botones [bo'tones] *nm* buttons *sg*, bellboy.

bóveda [bo'βeða] *nf* (*ARQ*) vault.

boxeador [boksea'ðor] *nm* boxer.

boxeo [bok'seo] *nm* boxing.

boya ['boja] *nf* (*NAUT*) buoy; (*flotador*) float.

bozal [bo'θal] *a* (*novato*) raw, green; (*tonto*) stupid; (*salvaje*) wild // *nm* (*de caballo*) halter; (*de perro*) muzzle.

bracear [braθe'ar] *vi* (*agitar los brazos*) to wave one's arms; (*nadar*) to swim (the crawl).

bracero [bra'θero] *nm* labourer; (*en el campo*) farmhand.

bracete [bra'θete]: **de ~ ad** arm in arm.

braga [ˈbraɣa] *nf* (*cuerda*) sling, rope; (*de bebé*) nappy; **~s** *nfpl* (*de mujer*) panties.

bragueta [braˈɣeta] *nf* fly, flies *pl*.

braille [breil] *nm* braille.

bramar [braˈmar] *vi* to bellow, roar; **bramido** *nm* bellow, roar.

brasa [ˈbrasa] *nf* live coal.

brasero [braˈsero] *nm* brazier.

Brasil [braˈsil] *nm*: **el ~ Brazil**; **brasileño, a** *a, nm/f* Brazilian.

bravata [braˈβata] *nf* boast.

braveza [braˈβeθa] *nf* (*valor*) bravery; (*ferocidad*) ferocity.

bravío, a [braˈβio, a] *a* wild; (*feroz*) fierce.

bravo, a [ˈbraβo, a] *a* (*valiente*) brave; (*bueno*) fine, splendid; (*feroz*) ferocious; (*salvaje*) wild // *excl* bravo!; **bravura** *nf* bravery; ferocity; (*pey*) boast.

braza [ˈbraθa] *nf* fathom; **nadar a la ~** to swim the breast-stroke.

brazada [braˈθaða] *nf* stroke.

brazado [braˈθaðo] *nm* armful.

brazalete [braθaˈlete] *nm* (*pulsera*) bracelet; (*banda*) armband.

brazo [ˈbraθo] *nm* arm; (*zool*) foreleg; (*bot*) limb, branch; **a ~ partido** hand-to-hand; **del ~** arm in arm.

brea [ˈbrea] *nf* pitch, tar.

brebaje [breˈβaxe] *nm* potion.

brecha [ˈbretʃa] *nf* breach, gap, opening.

brega [ˈbreɣa] *nf* (*lucha*) struggle; (*trabajo*) hard work.

breve [ˈbreβe] *a* short, brief // *nf* breve; **~dad** *nf* brevity, shortness.

brezal [breˈθal] *nm* moor(land), heath; **brezo** *nm* heather.

bribón, ona [briˈβon, ona] *a* idle, lazy // *nm/f* (*vagabundo*) vagabond; (*pícaro*) rascal, rogue.

bricolaje [brikoˈlaxe] *nm* do-it-yourself, DIY.

brida [ˈbriða] *nf* bridle, rein; (*tec*) clamp; **a toda ~** at top speed.

bridge [britʃ] *nm* bridge.

brigada [briˈɣaða] *nf* (*unidad*) brigade; (*trabajadores*) squad, gang // *nm* ≈ staff-sergeant, sergeant-major.

brillante [briˈʎante] *a* brilliant // *nm* diamond; **brillar** *vi* to shine.

brillo [ˈbriʎo] *nm* shine; (*brillantez*) brilliance; (*fig*) splendour; **sacar ~ a** to polish.

brincar [brinˈkar] *vi* to skip about, hop about, jump about; **está que brinca** he's hopping mad.

brinco [ˈbrinko] *nm* hop, skip, jump.

brindar [brinˈdar] *vi*: **~ a o por** to drink (a toast) to // *vt* to offer, present.

brindis [ˈbrindis] *nm* toast; (*taur*) (ceremony of) dedicating the bull.

brío [ˈbrio] *nm* spirit, dash; **brioso, a** *a* spirited, dashing.

brisa [ˈbrisa] *nf* breeze.

británico, a [briˈtaniko, a] *a* British // *nm/f* Briton, British person.

brocal [broˈkal] *nm* rim.

brocha [ˈbrotʃa] *nf* brush.

broche [ˈbrotʃe] *nm* brooch; **~ para papeles** (*am*) paper clip.

broma [ˈbroma] *nf* (*bulla*) fun; (*chanza*) joke; **en ~** in fun, as a joke; **bromear** *vi* to joke.

bromista [broˈmista] *a* fond of joking // *nm/f* joker, wag.

bronca [ˈbronka] *nf* row.

bronce [ˈbronθe] *nm* bronze; **~ado, a** *a* bronze; (*por el sol*) tanned // *nm* (sun)tan; (*tec*) bronzing.

broncearse [bronθeˈarse] *vr* to get a suntan.

bronco, a [ˈbronko, a] *a* (*superficie*) rough; (*manera*) rude, surly; (*voz*) harsh.

bronquitis [bronˈkitis] *nf* bronchitis.

brotar [broˈtar] *vi* (*bot*) to sprout; (*aguas*) to gush (forth), flow; (*med*) to break out; **brote** *nm* (*bot*) shoot; (*med, fig*) outbreak.

bruces [ˈbruθes]: **de ~ ad**: **caer o dar de ~** to fall headlong, fall flat; **estar de ~** to lie face downwards.

bruja [ˈbruxa] *nf* witch; (*lechuza*) owl; **brujería** *nf* witchcraft.

brujo [ˈbruxo] *nm* wizard, magician.

brújula [ˈbruxula] *nf* compass.

bruma [ˈbruma] *nf* mist; **brumoso, a** *a* misty.

bruñido [bruˈɲiðo] *nm* polish; **bruñir** *vt* to polish.

brusco, a [ˈbrusko, a] *a* (*súbito*) sudden; (*áspero*) brusque.

Bruselas [bruˈselas] *n* Brussels.

brutal [bruˈtal] *a* brutal; (*fig*) sudden; **~idad** *nf* brutality.

bruto, a [ˈbruto, a] *a* (*idiota*) stupid; (*bestial*) brutish; (*peso*) gross; (*diamante etc*) raw, uncut; **en ~** raw, unworked.

Bs.As. *abr de* **Buenos Aires**.

buba [ˈbuβa] *nf* tumour.

bucal [buˈkal] *a*: **por vía ~** by *or* through the mouth, orally.

bucear [buθeˈar] *vi* to dive // *vt* to explore; **buceo** *nm* diving; (*fig*) investigation.

bucle [ˈbukle] *nm* curl.

budismo [buˈðismo] *nm* Buddhism.

buenamente [bwenaˈmente] *ad* (*fácilmente*) easily; (*voluntariamente*) willingly.

buenaventura [bwenaβenˈtura] *nf* (*suerte*) good luck; (*adivinación*) fortune.

bueno, a [ˈbweno, a], **buen** [bwen] *a* (*amable*) kind; (*med*) well; (*guapo*) attractive; **¡~as!** hello!; **buen día, ~os días** good morning!; good afternoon!; hello!; **~as tardes** good afternoon!; good evening!; **~as noches** good night!; **¡buen sinvergüenza resultó!** a fine rascal he turned out to be // *excl* right!, all right!; **~, ¿y qué?** well, so what?

buey [bwei] *nm* ox.

búfalo [ˈbufalo] *nm* buffalo.

bufanda [buˈfanda] *nf* scarf, muffler.

bufar [buˈfar] *vi* to snort.

bufete [bu'fete] *nm* (*mesa*) desk; (*de abogado*) lawyer's office.
bufo, a ['bufo, a] *a* comic.
bufón, ona [bu'fon, ona] *a* funny // *nm* clown.
buhardilla [buar'ðiʎa] *nf* (*ventana*) skylight; (*desván*) attic.
búho ['buo] *nm* owl; (*fig*) hermit, recluse.
buhonero [buo'nero] *nm* pedlar.
buitre ['bwitre] *nm* vulture.
bujía [bu'xia] *nf* (*vela*) candle; (*ELEC*) candle (power); (*AUTO*) spark plug.
bula ['bula] *nf* (*papal*) bull.
bulbo ['bulβo] *nm* bulb.
búlgaro, a ['bulxaro, a] *a, nm/f* Bulgarian.
bulto ['bulto] *nm* (*paquete*) package; (*fardo*) bundle; (*tamaño*) size, bulkiness; (*MED*) swelling, lump; (*silueta*) vague shape; (*estatua*) bust, statue; **de mucho/poco ~** important/unimportant.
bulla ['buʎa] *nf* (*ruido*) uproar; (*de gente*) crowd.
bullicio [bu'ʎiθjo] *nm* (*ruido*) uproar; (*movimiento*) bustle.
bullir [bu'ʎir] *vi* (*hervir*) to boil; (*burbujear*) to bubble; (*mover*) to move, stir.
buñuelo [bu'ŋwelo] *nm* fritter.
buque ['buke] *nm* ship, vessel.
burbuja [bur'βuxa] *nf* bubble; **burbujear** *vi* to bubble.
burdel [bur'ðel] *nm* brothel.
burdo, a ['burðo, a] *a* coarse, rough.
burgués, esa [bur'xes, esa] *a* middle-class, bourgeois; **burguesía** *nf* middle class, bourgeoisie.
burla ['burla] *nf* (*mofa*) gibe; (*broma*) joke; (*engaño*) trick.
burladero [burla'ðero] *nm* (*bullfighter's*) refuge.
burlador, a [burla'ðor, a] *a* mocking // *nm* (*bromista*) joker; (*libertino*) seducer.
burlar [bur'lar] *vt* (*engañar*) to deceive; (*seducir*) to seduce // *vi*, **~se** *vr* to joke; **~se de** to make fun of.
burlesco, a [bur'lesko, a] *a* burlesque.
burlón, ona [bur'lon, ona] *a* mocking.
burocracia [buro'kraθja] *nf* civil service; (*pey*) bureaucracy.
burócrata [bu'rokrata] *nm/f* civil servant; (*pey*) bureaucrat.
burra ['burra] *nf* (she-)donkey; (*fig*) stupid woman.
burro ['burro] *nm* donkey; (*fig*) ass, idiot.
bursátil [bur'satil] *a* stock-exchange *cpd*.
busca ['buska] *nf* search, hunt; **en ~ de** in search of.
buscapleitos [buska'pleitos] *nm/f inv* troublemaker.
buscar [bus'kar] *vt* to look for, search for, seek // *vi* to look, search, seek; **se busca empleado** employee wanted.
buscón, ona [bus'kon, ona] *a* thieving // *nm* petty thief // *nf* whore.
busilis [bu'silis] *nm* (*fam*) snag.
busque *etc vb ver* **buscar.**

búsqueda ['buskeða] *nf* = **busca.**
busto ['busto] *nm* bust.
butaca [bu'taka] *nf* armchair; (*de cine, teatro*) stall, seat.
butano [bu'tano] *nm* butane.
buzo ['buθo] *nm* diver.
buzón [bu'θon] *nm* letter box; (*en la calle*) pillar box.

C

c. *abr de* **capítulo.**
C. *abr de* **centígrado; compañía.**
C/ *abr de* **calle.**
c.a. *abr de* **corriente alterna.**
cabal [ka'βal] *a* (*exacto*) exact; (*correcto*) right, proper; (*acabado*) finished, complete; **~es** *nmpl*: **estar en sus ~es** to be in one's right mind.
cabalgadura [kaβalɣa'ðura] *nf* mount, horse.
cabalgar [kaβal'xar] *vt, vi* to ride.
caballa [ka'βaʎa] *nf* mackerel.
caballeresco, a [kaβaʎe'resko, a] *a* noble, chivalrous.
caballería [kaβaʎe'ria] *nf* mount; (*MIL*) cavalry.
caballeriza [kaβaʎe'riθa] *nf* stable; **caballerizo** *nm* groom, stableman.
caballero [kaβa'ʎero] *nm* rider, horseman; (*hombre galante*) gentleman; (*de la orden de caballería*) knight; (*hidalgo*) noble(man); (*señor, término de cortesía*) sir.
caballerosidad [kaβaʎerosi'ðað] *nf* chivalry.
caballo [ka'βaʎo] *nm* horse; (*AJEDREZ*) knight; (*NAIPES*) queen; **~ de vapor** *o* **de fuerza** horsepower.
cabaña [ka'βaɲa] *nf* (*casita*) hut, cabin; (*rebaño*) flock.
cabaré, cabaret (*pl* **cabarets**) [kaβa're] *nm* cabaret.
cabás [ka'βas] *nm* satchel.
cabecear [kaβeθe'ar] *vt* to head // *vi* to nod; (*negar*) to shake one's head.
cabecera [kaβe'θera] *nf* (*gen*) head; (*de distrito*) chief town; (*IMPRENTA*) headline.
cabecilla [kaβe'θiʎa] *nm/f* ringleader; (*fig: fam*) hothead.
cabellera [kaβe'ʎera] *nf* hair; (*de cometa*) tail.
cabello [ka'βeʎo] *nm* (*también* **~s** *nmpl*) hair *sg*; **cabelludo, a** *a* hairy.
caber [ka'βer] *vi* (*entrar*) to fit, go; (*tener lugar*) to have enough room; **caben 3 más** there's room for 3 more.
cabestrillo [kaβes'triʎo] *nm* sling.
cabestro [ka'βestro] *nm* halter.
cabeza [ka'βeθa] *nf* head; (*POL*) chief, leader; **~da** *nf* (*golpe*) butt; (*al dormirse*) nod.
cabezudo, a [kaβe'θuðo, a] *a* bigheaded; (*fig*) pigheaded.
cabida [ka'βiða] *nf* space.
cabildo [ka'βildo] *nm* (*de iglesia*) chapter; (*POL*) town council.

cabina [ka'βina] *nf* booth; (*de camión*) cabin.

cabizbajo, a [kaβiθ'βaxo, a] *a* crestfallen, dejected.

cable ['kaβle] *nm* cable; **~grama** *nm* cablegram.

cabo ['kaβo] *nm* (*de objeto*) end, extremity; (*de tiempo, proceso*) end; (*persona*) head, chief; (*MIL*) corporal; (*NAUT*) rope, cable; (*GEO*) cape; **al ~ de 3 días** after 3 days; **al fin y al ~** in the end.

cabra ['kaβra] *nf* (she-)goat, nanny goat.

cabré *etc vb ver* **caber.**

cabria ['kaβrja] *nf* hoist, derrick.

cabrío, a [ka'βrio, a] *a* goatish; **macho ~** (he-)goat, billy goat.

cabriola [ka'βrjola] *nf* caper.

cabritilla [kaβri'tiʎa] *nf* kid, kidskin.

cabrito [ka'βrito] *nm* kid.

cabrón [ka'βron] *nm* cuckold; (*fig: fam*) bastard (*fam!*).

cacahuete [kaka'wete] *nm* peanut, monkey nut.

cacao [ka'kao] *nm* cocoa; (*BOT*) cacao.

cacarear [kakare'ar] *vi* (*persona*) to boast; (*gallo*) to cackle.

cacería [kaθe'ria] *nf* hunting, shooting.

cacerola [kaθe'rola] *nf* pan, saucepan.

cacique [ka'θike] *nm* chief, local ruler; (*POL*) local boss; **caciquismo** *nm* (system of) dominance by the local boss.

caco ['kako] *nm* pickpocket.

cacto ['kakto], **cactus** ['kaktus] *nm* cactus.

cacumen [ka'kumen] *nm* (*fig: fam*) acumen.

cachar [ka'tʃar] *vt* to smash, break.

cacharro [ka'tʃarro] *nm* earthenware pot.

cachear [katʃe'ar] *vt* to search, frisk.

cachemira [katʃe'mira] *nf* cashmere.

cacheo [ka'tʃeo] *nm* searching, frisking.

cachimba [ka'tʃimba] *nf*, **cachimbo** [ka'tʃimbo] *nm* pipe.

cachiporra [katʃi'porra] *nf* truncheon.

cachivache [katʃi'βatʃe] *nm* pot; (*utensilio*) utensil; (*persona*) good-for-nothing.

cacho, a ['katʃo, a] *a* bent, crooked // *nm* (small) bit.

cachondeo [katʃon'deo] *nm* (*fam*) farce, joke.

cachondo, a [ka'tʃondo, a] *a* (*ZOOL*) on heat; (*vulg*) randy, sexy; (*gracioso*) funny.

cachorro, a [ka'tʃorro, a] *nm/f* (*perro*) pup, puppy; (*león*) cub.

cada ['kaða] *a inv* each; (*antes de número*) every; **~ día** each day, every day; **~ uno/a** each one, every one; **~ vez más** more and more; **uno de ~ diez** one out of every ten.

cadalso [ka'ðalso] *nm* scaffold.

cadáver [ka'ðaβer] *nm* (dead) body, corpse.

cadena [ka'ðena] *nf* chain; (*TV*) channel; **trabajo en ~** assembly line work.

cadencia [ka'ðenθja] *nf* cadence, rhythm.

cadera [ka'ðera] *nf* hip.

cadete [ka'ðete] *nm* cadet.

caducar [kaðu'kar] *vi* (*permiso, ley*) to lapse, expire; (*persona*) to become senile; **caduco, a** *a* expired; (*persona*) very old.

C.A.E. *abr de* **cóbrese al entregar** COD (cash on delivery).

caer [ka'er] *vi*, **~se** *vr* to fall (down); **~ bien/mal** to make a good/bad impression; **el pago cae mañana** the payment is due tomorrow; **~ en la cuenta** to catch on.

café [ka'fe] (*pl* **~s**) *nm* (*bebida, planta*) coffee; (*lugar*) café // *a* (*color*) brown; **cafetal** *nm* coffee plantation.

cafetero, a [kafe'tero, a] *a* coffee *cpd* // *nf* coffee pot.

cáfila ['kafila] *nf* (*de personas*) group; (*de ovejas*) flock.

caída [ka'iða] *nf* (*gen*) fall; (*declive*) slope; (*disminución*) fall, drop.

caigo *etc vb ver* **caer.**

caimán [kai'man] *nm* alligator.

caimiento [kai'mjento] *nm* fall, falling.

caja ['kaxa] *nf* box; (*para reloj*) case; (*de ascensor*) shaft; (*COM*) cashbox; (*donde se hacen los pagos*) cashdesk; **~ de ahorros** savings bank; **~ de cambios** gearbox; **~ fuerte, ~ de caudales** safe, strongbox.

cajero, a [ka'xero, a] *nm/f* cashier.

cajetilla [kaxe'tiʎa] *nf* small box; (*de cigarrillos*) packet.

cajón [ka'xon] *nm* big box; (*de mueble*) drawer.

cal [kal] *nf* lime.

cala ['kala] *nf* (*GEO*) cove, inlet; (*de barco*) hold; (*MED*) suppository.

calabaza [kala'βaθa] *nf* (*BOT*) pumpkin.

calabozo [kala'βoθo] *nm* prison (cell).

calamar [kala'mar] *nm* squid.

calambre [ka'lambre] *nm* cramp.

calamidad [kalami'ðað] *nf* calamity, disaster.

calamina [kala'mina] *nf* calamine.

calaña [ka'laɲa] *nf* model, pattern.

calar [ka'lar] *vt* to soak, drench; (*penetrar*) to pierce, penetrate; (*comprender*) to see through; (*vela, red*) to lower; **~se las gafas** to stick one's glasses on.

calavera [kala'βera] *nf* skull.

calcañar [kalka'ɲar], **calcañal** [kalka-'ɲal], **calcaño** [kal'kaɲo] *nm* heel.

calcar [kal'kar] *vt* (*reproducir*) to trace; (*imitar*) to copy.

calceta [kal'θeta] *nf* (knee-length) stocking; **hacer ~** to knit; **calcetín** *nm* sock.

calcina [kal'θina] *nf* concrete.

calcinar [kalθi'nar] *vt* to burn, blacken.

calcio ['kalθjo] *nm* calcium.

calco ['kalko] *nm* tracing.

calcomanía [kalkoma'nia] *nm* transfer.

calculadora [kalkula'ðora] *nf* calculator; **~ de bolsillo** pocket calculator.

calcular [kalku'lar] *vt* (*MAT*) to calculate, compute; (*suponer, creer*) to reckon, expect; **cálculo** nm calculation; reckoning.

caldear [kalde'ar] vt to warm (up), heat (up); (los metales) to weld.

caldera [kal'dera] nf boiler.

calderilla [kalde'riʎa] nf (REL) vessel for holy water; (moneda) small change.

caldero [kal'dero] nm small boiler.

calderón [kalde'ron] nm cauldron.

caldo ['kaldo] nm stock; (consomé) consommé; (para la ensalada) dressing.

calefacción [kalefak'θjon] nf heating.

calendario [kalen'darjo] nm calendar.

calentador [kalenta'ðor] nm heater.

calentar [kalen'tar] vt to heat (up); ~se vr to heat up, warm up; (fig) to get heated.

calentura [kalen'tura] nf (MED) fever, (high) temperature; **calenturiento, a** a feverish.

calero, a [ka'lero, a] a lime cpd.

calibrar [kali'βrar] vt to gauge, measure; **calibre** nm (de cañón) calibre, bore; (diámetro) diameter; (fig) calibre.

calidad [kali'ðað] nf quality; **en ~ de** in the capacity of.

cálido, a ['kaliðo, a] a hot; (fig) warm.

caliente [ka'ljente] a hot; (sin exceso) warm; (fig) fiery; (disputa) heated.

calificación [kalifika'θjon] nf qualification; (de alumno) grade, mark.

calificado, a [kalifi'kaðo, a] a qualified, competent; (trabajador) skilled.

calificar [kalifi'kar] vt to qualify; (enaltecer) to distinguish; (alumno) to grade, mark; (determinar) to describe.

calma ['kalma] nf calm; (pachorra) slowness.

calmante [kal'mante] nm sedative, tranquillizer.

calmar [kal'mar] vt to calm, calm down // vi (tempestad) to abate; (mente etc) to become calm.

calmoso, a [kal'moso, a], **calmudo, a** [kal'muðo, a] a calm, quiet.

calofrío [kalo'frio] nm = **escalofrío**.

calor [ka'lor] nm heat; (~ agradable) warmth.

caloría [kalo'ria] nf calorie.

calorífero, a [kalo'rifero, a] a heat-producing, heat-giving // nm heating system.

calumnia [ka'lumnja] nf calumny, slander; **calumnioso, a** a slanderous.

caluroso, a [kalu'roso, a] a hot; (sin exceso) warm; (fig) enthusiastic.

calva ['kalβa] nf bald patch; (en bosque) clearing.

calvario [kal'βarjo] nm stations pl of the cross.

calvicie [kal'βiθje] nf baldness.

calvo, a ['kalβo, a] a bald; (terreno) bare, barren; (tejido) threadbare.

calza ['kalθa] nf wedge, chock.

calzado, a [kal'θaðo, a] a shod // nm footwear // nf roadway, highway.

calzador [kalθa'ðor] nm shoehorn.

calzar [kal'θar] vt to put on; (un mueble) to put a wedge under; ~se vr: ~se los zapatos to put on one's shoes; ¿qué (número) calza? what size do you wear or take?

calzón [kal'θon] nm (también **calzones** nmpl) shorts pl.

calzoncillos [kalθon'θiʎos] nmpl underpants.

callado, a [ka'ʎaðo, a] a quiet.

callar [ka'ʎar] vt to keep quiet about, say nothing about // vi, ~se vr to keep quiet, be silent.

calle ['kaʎe] nf street; (DEPORTE) lane; ~ arriba/abajo up/down the street; ~ de un solo sentido one-way street.

calleja [ka'ʎexa] nf alley, narrow street; **callejear** vi to wander about the streets; **callejero, a** a street cpd.

callejón [kaʎe'xon] nm alley, passage; ~ sin salida one-way street.

callejuela [kaʎe'xwela] nf side-street, alley.

callista [ka'ʎista] nm/f chiropodist.

callo ['kaʎo] nm callus; (en el pie) corn; ~s nmpl tripe sg; ~so, a a horny, rough.

cama ['kama] nf bed; (GEO) stratum; ~ de matrimonio double bed.

camada [ka'maða] nf litter; (de personas) gang, band.

camafeo [kama'feo] nm cameo.

camandulear [kamandule'ar] vi to be a hypocrite.

cámara ['kamara] nf (gen) chamber; (habitación) room; (sala) hall; (CINE) cine camera; (fotográfica) camera; ~ de aire inner tube.

camarada [kama'raða] nm comrade, companion.

camarera [kama'rera] nf (en restaurante) waitress; (en casa, hotel) maid.

camarero [kama'rero] nm waiter.

camarilla [kama'riʎa] nf (clan) clique; (POL) lobby.

camarín [kama'rin] nm dressing room.

camarón [kama'ron] nm shrimp.

camarote [kama'rote] nm cabin.

cambiable [kam'bjaβle] a (variable) changeable, variable; (intercambiable) interchangeable.

cambiante [kam'bjante] a variable // nm moneychanger.

cambiar [kam'bjar] vt (gen) to change; (de moneda) to change; (dinero) to exchange // vi (gen) to change; ~se vr (mudarse) to move; (de ropa) to change; ~(se) de... to change one's ... .

cambio ['kambjo] nm change; (trueque) exchange; (COM) rate of exchange; (oficina) (foreign) exchange office; (dinero menudo) small change; **en ~** on the other hand; (en lugar de eso) instead; ~ **de velocidades** gear lever; ~ **de vía** points pl.

cambista [kam'bista] nm (COM) exchange broker; (FERRO) switchman.

camelar [kame'lar] *vt* (*galantear*) to flirt with; (*engañar*) to cajole.

camello [ka'meʎo] *nm* camel.

camilla [ka'miʎa] *nf* (*cama*) cot; (*MED*) stretcher.

caminante [kami'nante] *nm/f* traveller.

caminar [kami'nar] *vi* (*marchar*) to walk, go; (*viajar*) to travel, journey // *vt* (*recorrer*) to cover, travel.

caminata [kami'nata] *nf* long walk.

camino [ka'mino] *nm* (*gen*) way, road; (*senda*) track; **a medio ~** halfway (there); **en el ~** on the way, en route.

camión [ka'mjon] *nm* lorry, truck.

camisa [ka'misa] *nf* shirt; (*BOT*) skin; **~ de dormir** nightdress; **~ de fuerza** straitjacket; **camisería** *nf* outfitter's (shop).

camiseta [kami'seta] *nf* (*prenda*) vest; (*de deportista*) singlet.

camisón [kami'son] *nm* nightdress, nightgown.

campamento [kampa'mento] *nm* camp.

campana [kam'pana] *nf* bell; **~da** *nf* peal; **~rio** *nm* belfry.

campanilla [kampa'niʎa] *nf* (*campana*) small bell; (*burbuja*) bubble.

campaña [kam'paɲa] *nf* (*MIL*, *POL*) campaign; (*campo*) countryside.

campar [kam'par] *vi* to camp; (*sobresalir*) to excel, stand out.

campeón, ona [kampe'on, ona] *nm/f* champion; **campeonato** *nm* championship.

campesino, a [kampe'sino, a] *a* country *cpd*, rural // *nm/f* countryman/woman; (*agricultor*) farmer.

campestre [kam'pestre] *a* country *cpd*, rural.

camping ['kampin] *nm* camping; (*lugar*) campsite; **hacer ~** to go camping.

campiña [kam'piɲa] *nf* countryside.

campo ['kampo] *nm* (*fuera de la ciudad*) country, countryside; (*AGR*, *ELEC*) field; (*de fútbol*) ground, pitch; (*de golf*) course; (*de tenis*) court; (*MIL*) camp.

camposanto [kampo'santo] *nm* cemetery.

camuflaje [kamu'flaxe] *nm* camouflage.

Canadá [kana'ða] *nm* Canada; **canadiense** *a*, *nm/f* Canadian // *nf* fur-lined jacket.

canal [ka'nal] *nm* canal; (*GEO*) channel, strait; (*de televisión*) channel; (*de tejado*) gutter; **~izar** *vt* to channel.

canalón [kana'lon] *nm* (*conducto vertical*) drainpipe; (*del tejado*) gutter.

canalla [ka'naʎa] *nf* rabble, mob // *nm* swine, rotter.

canapé [kana'pe] (*pl* **~s**) *nm* sofa, settee; (*CULIN*) canapé.

canario, a [ka'narjo, a] *a*, *nm/f* (native) of the Canary Isles // *nm* canary.

canasta [ka'nasta] *nf* (round) basket; **canasto** *nm* large basket.

cancelación [kanθela'θjon] *nf* cancellation.

cancelar [kanθe'lar] *vt* to cancel; (*una deuda*) to write off.

cáncer ['kanθer] *nm* (*MED*) cancer; **C~** (*ASTRO*) Cancer.

canciller [kanθi'ʎer] *nm* chancellor.

canción [kan'θjon] *nf* song; **~ de cuna** lullaby; **cancionero** *nm* song book.

candado [kan'daðo] *nm* padlock.

candela [kan'dela] *nf* candle.

candelero [kande'lero] *nm* (*para vela*) candlestick; (*de aceite*) oil lamp.

candente [kan'dente] *a* red-hot; (*fig*) burning.

candidato [kandi'ðato] *nm/f* candidate.

candidez [kandi'ðeθ] *nf* (*sencillez*) simplicity; (*simpleza*) naiveté; **cándido, a** *a* simple; naive.

candil [kan'dil] *nm* oil lamp; **~eja** *nf* small oil lamp.

candor [kan'dor] *nm* (*sinceridad*) frankness; (*inocencia*) innocence.

canela [ka'nela] *nf* cinnamon.

canelón [kane'lon] *nm* (*canal*) drainpipe; (*carámbano*) icicle.

cangrejo [kan'grexo] *nm* crab.

canguro [kan'guro] *nm* kangaroo.

caníbal [ka'niβal] *a*, *nm/f* cannibal.

canica [ka'nika] *nf* marble.

canijo, a [ka'nixo, a] *a* frail, sickly.

canino, a [ka'nino, a] *a* canine // *nm* canine (tooth).

canjear [kanxe'ar] *vt* to exchange.

cano, a ['kano, a] *a* grey-haired, white-haired.

canoa [ka'noa] *nf* canoe.

canon ['kanon] *nm* canon; (*pensión*) rent; (*COM*) tax.

canónigo [ka'noniβo] *nm* canon.

canonizar [kanoni'θar] *vt* to canonize.

canoro, a [ka'noro, a] *a* melodious.

cansado, a [kan'saðo, a] *a* tired, weary; (*tedioso*) tedious, boring.

cansancio [kan'sanθjo] *nm* tiredness, fatigue.

cansar [kan'sar] *vt* (*fatigar*) to tire, tire out, weary; (*aburrir*) to bore; (*fastidiar*) to bother; **~se** *vr* to tire, get tired; (*aburrirse*) to get bored.

cantante [kan'tante] *a* singing // *nm/f* singer.

cantar [kan'tar] *vt* to sing // *vi* (*gen*) to sing; (*insecto*) to chirp; (*rechinar*) to squeak // *nm* (*acción*) singing; (*canción*) song; (*poema*) poem.

cántara ['kantara] *nf* large pitcher.

cántaro ['kantaro] *nm* pitcher, jug.

cantatriz [kanta'triθ] *nf* singer.

cante ['kante] *nm*: **~ jondo** flamenco singing.

cantera [kan'tera] *nf* quarry.

cantidad [kanti'ðað] *nf* quantity, amount.

cantilena [kanti'lena] *nf* = **cantinela**.

cantimplora [kantim'plora] *nf* (*frasco*) water bottle, canteen; (*sifón*) syphon.

cantina [kan'tina] *nf* canteen; (*de estación*) buffet; (*sótano*) wine cellar.

cantinela [kanti'nela] *nf* ballad, song.

canto ['kanto] *nm* (*gen*) singing; (*canción*) song; (*borde*) edge, rim; (*de un cuchillo*) back; ~ **rodado** boulder.

cantor, a [kan'tor, a] *nm/f* singer.

canturrear [kanturre'ar], **canturriar** [kantu'rrjar] *vi* to sing softly.

caña ['kaɲa] *nf* (*bot: tallo*) stem, stalk; (*carrizo*) reed; (*de cerveza*) glass; (*ANAT: del brazo*) long bone; (: *de la pierna*) shinbone; (*MINERÍA*) gallery; ~ **de azúcar** sugar cane.

cañada [ka'ɲaða] *nf* (*entre dos montañas*) gully, ravine; (*camino*) cattle track.

caño ['kaɲo] *nm* (*tubo*) tube, pipe; (*MIL*) cannon; (*de fusil*) barrel; (*GEO*) canyon, gorge.

cañón [ka'ɲon] *nm* (*tubo*) tube, pipe; (*de aguas servidas*) sewer; (*MUS*) pipe; (*NAUT*) navigation channel; (*de fuente*) jet.

cañonero [kaɲo'nero] *nm* gunboat.

caoba [ka'oβa] *nf* mahogany.

caos ['kaos] *nm* chaos.

cap. *abr de* **capítulo**.

capa ['kapa] *nf* cloak, cape; (*GEO*) layer, stratum; (*pretexto*) pretence.

capacidad [kapaθi'ðað] *nf* (*medida*) capacity; (*aptitud*) capacity, ability.

capacitación [kapaθita'θjon] *nf* training.

capar [ka'par] *vt* to castrate, geld.

caparazón [kapara'θon] *nm* shell.

capataz [kapa'taθ] *nm* foreman.

capaz [ka'paθ] *a* able, capable; (*amplio*) capacious, roomy.

capcioso, a [kap'θjoso, a] *a* wily, deceitful.

capellán [kape'ʎan] *nm* chaplain; (*sacerdote*) priest.

caperuza [kape'ruθa] *nf* hood; **caperucita** *nf*: **Caperucita Roja** Little Red Riding Hood.

capilla [ka'piʎa] *nf* chapel; (*capucha*) hood, cowl.

capital [kapi'tal] *a* capital // *nm* (*COM*) capital // *nf* capital; ~ **social** share capital.

capitalismo [kapita'lismo] *nm* capitalism; **capitalista** *a, nm/f* capitalist.

capitalizar [kapitali'θar] *vt* to capitalize.

capitán [kapi'tan] *nm* captain.

capitana [kapi'tana] *nf* flagship.

capitanear [kapitane'ar] *vt* to captain.

capitolio [kapi'toljo] *nm* capitol.

capitoné [kapito'ne] *nm* removal van.

capitulación [kapitula'θjon] *nf* (*rendición*) capitulation, surrender; (*acuerdo*) agreement, pact.

capitular [kapitu'lar] *vi* to come to terms, make an agreement // *a* chapter *cpd*.

capítulo [ka'pitulo] *nm* chapter; ~**s** *nmpl*: ~**s matrimoniales** marriage contract *sg*.

capó [ka'po] *nm* bonnet.

caporal [kapo'ral] *nm* chief, leader.

capota [ka'pota] *nf* (*de mujer*) bonnet; (*de coche*) hood, roof.

capote [ka'pote] *nm* (*abrigo, de militar*)

greatcoat; (*de torero*) cloak; (*NAIPES*) slam.

Capricornio [kapri'kornjo] *nm* Capricorn.

capricho [ka'pritʃo] *nm* whim, caprice; ~**so, a** *a* capricious.

cápsula ['kapsula] *nf* capsule; (*de botella*) cap.

captar [kap'tar] *vt* to win (over).

captura [kap'tura] *nf* capture; (*JUR*) arrest; **capturar** *vt* to capture; to arrest.

capucha [ka'putʃa] *nf* hood, cowl.

cara ['kara] *nf* (*ANAT*) face; (*aspecto*) appearance; (*de moneda*) face; (*de disco*) side; (*fig*) boldness; ~ **a** *ad* facing; **de** ~ opposite, facing; **dar la** ~ to face the consequences; ¿~ **o cruz?** heads or tails?

carabina [kara'βina] *nf* carbine, rifle.

caracol [kara'kol] *nm* (*ZOOL*) snail; (*concha*) shell.

caracolear [karakole'ar] *vi* to prance about.

carácter [ka'rakter] (*pl* **caracteres**) *nm* character.

característico, a [karakte'ristiko, a] *a* characteristic // *nf* characteristic.

caracterizar [karakteri'θar] *vt* (*distinguir*) to characterize, typify; (*honrar*) to confer (a) distinction on.

caramba [ka'ramba] *excl* well!, good gracious!

carámbano [ka'rambano] *nm* icicle.

caramelo [kara'melo] *nm* (*dulce*) sweet; (*dulce de* ~) toffee; (*azúcar fundida*) caramel.

caramillo [kara'miʎo] *nm* (*flauta*) recorder; (*montón*) untidy heap; (*chisme, enredo*) bit of gossip.

carapacho [kara'patʃo] *nm* shell, carapace.

caraqueño, a [kara'keɲo, a] *a, nm/f* (*native*) of Caracas.

carátula [ka'ratula] *nf* (*careta, máscara*) mask; (*TEATRO*): **la** ~ the stage.

caravana [kara'βana] *nf* caravan; (*fig*) group; (*sucesión de autos*) stream; (*embotellamiento*) traffic jam.

carbón [kar'βon] *nm* coal; **papel** ~ carbon paper; **carbonero** *nm/f* coal merchant; **carbonilla** *nf* coal dust.

carbonizar [karβoni'θar] *vt* to carbonize; (*quemar*) to char.

carbono [kar'βono] *nm* carbon.

carburador [karβura'ðor] *nm* carburettor.

carcajada [karka'xaða] *nf* (loud) laugh, guffaw.

cárcel ['karθel] *nf* prison, jail; (*TEC*) clamp; **carcelero, a** *a* prison *cpd* // *nm/f* warder.

carcomer [karko'mer] *vt* to bore into, eat into; (*fig*) to undermine; ~**se** *vr* to become worm-eaten; (*fig*) to decay.

carcomido, a [karko'miðo, a] *a* worm-eaten; (*fig*) rotten.

cardenal [karðe'nal] *nm* (*REL*) cardinal; (*equimosis*) bruise.

cárdeno, a ['karðeno, a] *a* purple; (*lívido*) livid.

cardíaco, a [kar'ðiako, a] *a* cardiac, heart *cpd*.

cardinal [karði'nal] *a* cardinal.

cardo ['karðo] *nm* thistle.

cardumen [kar'ðumen] *nm* shoal.

carear [kare'ar] *vt* to bring face to face; (*comparar*) to compare; ~**se** *vr* to come face to face, meet.

carecer [kare'θer] *vi*: ~ **de** to lack, be in need of.

carencia [ka'renθja] *nf* lack; (*escasez*) shortage; (*MED*) deficiency.

carente [ka'rente] *a*: ~ **de** lacking, devoid of.

carestía [kares'tia] *nf* (*escasez*) scarcity, shortage; (*COM*) high cost.

careta [ka'reta] *nf* mask.

carga ['karɣa] *nf* (*peso, ELEC*) load; (*de barco*) cargo, freight; (*MIL*) charge; (*obligación, responsabilidad*) duty, obligation.

cargadero [karɣa'ðero] *nm* goods platform, loading bay.

cargado, a [kar'ɣaðo, a] *a* loaded; (*ELEC*) live; (*café, te*) strong; (*el cielo*) overcast.

cargamento [karɣa'mento] *nm* (*acción*) loading; (*mercancías*) load, cargo.

cargar [kar'ɣar] *vt* (*barco, arma*) to load; (*ELEC*) to charge; (*COM: algo en cuenta*) to charge, debit; (*MIL: enemigo*) to charge // *vi* to load (up); (*inclinarse*) to lean; ~ **con** to pick up, carry away.

cargo ['karɣo] *nm* (*puesto*) post, office; (*responsabilidad*) duty, obligation; (*fig*) weight, burden; (*JUR*) charge; **hacerse** ~ **del gobierno** to take charge of the government.

carguero [kar'ɣero] *nm* freighter, cargo boat; (*avión*) freight plane.

caribe [ka'riße] *a, nm/f* (native) of the Caribbean.

Caribe [ka'riße] *nm*: **el** ~ the Caribbean.

caricatura [karika'tura] *nf* caricature.

caricia [ka'riθja] *nf* caress.

caridad [kari'ðað] *nf* charity.

cariño [ka'riɲo] *nm* affection, love; (*caricia*) caress; (*en carta*) love...; ~**so, a** *a* affectionate.

caritativo, a [karita'tißo, a] *a* charitable.

carmesí [karme'si] *a, nm* crimson.

carnal [kar'nal] *a* carnal; **primo** ~ first cousin.

carnaval [karna'ßal] *nm* carnival.

carne ['karne] *nf* flesh; (*CULIN*) meat; **echar** ~**s** to put on weight.

carnero [kar'nero] *nm* sheep, ram; (*carne*) mutton.

carnet [kar'ne] *nm*: ~ **de conducir** driving licence.

carnicería [karniθe'ria] *nf* butcher's (shop); (*mercado*) meat market.

carnicero, a [karni'θero, a] *a* carnivorous // *nm/f* butcher // *nm* carnivore.

carnívoro, a [kar'nißoro, a] *a* carnivorous.

carnoso, a [kar'noso, a] *a* beefy, fat.

caro, a ['karo, a] *a* dear; (*COM*) dear, expensive // *ad* dear, dearly.

carpeta [kar'peta] *nf* table cover; (*para documentos*) folder, file.

carpintería [karpinte'ria] *nf* carpentry, joinery; **carpintero** *nm* carpenter.

carraspera [karras'pera] *nf* hoarseness.

carrera [ka'rrera] *nf* (*DEPORTE*) running; (*espacio recorrido*) run; (*certamen*) race; (*trayecto*) course; (*profesión*) career; (*ESCOL*) course.

carreta [ka'rreta] *nf* wagon, cart.

carrete [ka'rrete] *nm* reel, spool; (*TEC*) coil.

carretel [karre'tel] *nm* reel, spool.

carretera [karre'tera] *nf* (main) road, highway.

carretilla [karre'tiʎa] *nf* trolley; (*AGR*) (wheel)barrow.

carril [ka'rril] *nm* furrow; (*de autopista*) lane; (*FERRO*) rail.

carrillo [ka'rriʎo] *nm* (*ANAT*) cheek; (*TEC*) pulley.

carrizo [ka'rriθo] *nm* reed.

carro ['karro] *nm* cart, wagon; (*MIL*) tank; (*AM. coche*) car.

carrocería [karroθe'ria] *nf* bodywork, coachwork.

carta ['karta] *nf* letter; (*CULIN*) menu; (*naipe*) card; (*mapa*) map; (*JUR*) document; ~ **de crédito** credit card; ~ **certificada** registered letter.

cartel [kar'tel] *nm* (*anuncio*) poster, placard; (*alfabeto*) wall chart; (*COM*) cartel.

cartera [kar'tera] *nf* (*de bolsillo*) wallet; (*de colegial, cobrador*) satchel; (*de señora*) handbag; (*para documentos*) briefcase; (*COM, POL*) portfolio.

cartero [kar'tero] *nm* postman.

cartón [kar'ton] *nm* cardboard; (*ARTE*) cartoon.

cartucho [kar'tutʃo] *nm* (*MIL*) cartridge.

casa ['kasa] *nf* house; (*hogar*) home; (*edificio*) building; (*COM*) firm, company; (*de tablero de ajedrez*) square; ~ **consistorial** town hall; ~ **de huéspedes** boarding house; ~ **de socorro** first aid post; ~ **editorial** publishing house.

casamiento [kasa'mjento] *nm* marriage, wedding.

casar [ka'sar] *vt* to marry; (*JUR*) to quash, annul // *nm* hamlet; ~**se** *vr* to marry, get married.

cascada [kas'kaða] *nf* waterfall.

cascar [kas'kar] *vt*, ~**se** *vr* to crack, split, break (open).

cáscara ['kaskara] *nf* (*de huevo, fruta seca*) shell; (*de fruta*) skin; (*de limón*) peel.

casco ['kasko] *nm* (*de bombero, soldado*) helmet; (*cráneo*) skull; (*de botella, obús*) fragment; (*BOT: de cebolla*) skin; (*tonel*) cask, barrel; (*NAUT: de barco*) hull; (*ZOOL: de caballo*) hoof; (*botella*) empty bottle.

caserío [kase'rio] *nm* hamlet; (*casa*) country house.

casero, a [ka'sero, a] *a* domestic, household *cpd* // *nm/f* (*propietario*) landlord/lady; (*portero*) caretaker; (*COM*) house agent.

caseta [ka'seta] *nf* hut; (*para bañista*) cubicle; (*de feriantes*) stall.

casi ['kasi] *ad* almost; ~ **te caes** you almost fell.

casilla [ka'siʎa] *nf* (*casita*) hut, cabin; (*TEATRO*) box office; (*de ajedrez*) square.

casino [ka'sino] *nm* club.

caso ['kaso] *nm* case; **en** ~ **de...** in case of...; **el** ~ **es que** the fact is that; **hacer** ~ **a** to pay attention to; **hacer** *o* **venir al** ~ to be relevant.

caspa ['kaspa] *nf* dandruff.

cassette [ka'set] *nf* cassette.

casta ['kasta] *nf* caste; (*raza*) breed; (*linaje*) lineage.

castaña [kas'taɲa] *nf* chestnut.

castaño, a [kas'taɲo, a] *a* chestnut-brown // *nm* chestnut tree.

castañuela [kasta'ɲwela] *nf* castanet.

castellano, a [kaste'ʎano, a] *a* Castilian // *nm* (*lengua*) Castilian, Spanish.

castidad [kasti'ðað] *nf* chastity, purity.

castigar [kasti'ɣar] *vt* to punish; (*DEPORTE*) to penalize; (*afligir*) to afflict; **castigo** *nm* punishment; (*DEPORTE*) penalty.

castillo [kas'tiʎo] *nm* castle.

castizo, a [kas'tiθo, a] *a* (*LING*) pure; (*de buena casta*) purebred, pedigree.

casto, a ['kasto, a] *a* chaste, pure.

castor [kas'tor] *nm* beaver.

castrar [kas'trar] *vt* to castrate.

casual [ka'swal] *a* fortuitous, accidental; ~**idad** *nf* chance, accident; (*combinación de circunstancias*) coincidence.

cataclismo [kata'klismo] *nm* cataclysm.

catalán, ana [kata'lan, ana] *a, nm/f* Catalan, Catalonian.

catalizador [kataliθa'ðor] *nm* catalyst.

catálogo [ka'taloɣo] *nm* catalogue.

Cataluña [kata'luɲa] *nf* Catalonia.

cataplasma [kata'plasma] *nf* poultice.

catar [ka'tar] *vt* to taste, sample.

catarata [kata'rata] *nf* (*GEO*) waterfall, falls *pl*; (*MED*) cataract.

catarro [ka'tarro] *nm* catarrh; (*constipado*) cold.

catástrofe [ka'tastrofe] *nf* catastrophe.

catedral [kate'ðral] *nf* cathedral.

catedrático, a [kate'ðratiko, a] *nm/f* professor.

categoría [kateɣo'ria] *nf* category; (*rango*) rank, standing; (*calidad*) quality.

categórico, a [kate'ɣoriko, a] *a* categorical.

catolicismo [katoli'θismo] *nm* Catholicism.

católico, a [ka'toliko, a] *a, nm/f* Catholic.

catorce [ka'torθe] *num* fourteen.

caución [kau'θjon] *nf* bail; **caucionar** *vt* to prevent, guard against; (*JUR*) to bail, go bail for.

caucho ['kautʃo] *nm* rubber.

caudal [kau'ðal] *nm* (*de río*) volume, flow;

(*fortuna*) wealth; (*abundancia*) abundance; ~**oso, a** *a* (*río*) large; (*aguas*) copious; (*persona*) wealthy, rich.

caudillo [kau'ðiʎo] *nm* leader, chief.

causa ['kausa] *nf* cause; (*razón*) reason; (*JUR*) lawsuit, case; **causar** *vt* to cause.

cáustico, a ['kaustiko, a] *a* caustic.

cautela [kau'tela] *nf* caution, cautiousness; **cauteloso, a** *a* cautious, wary, careful.

cautivar [kauti'ßar] *vt* to capture; (*fig*) to captivate.

cautiverio [kauti'ßerjo] *nm*, **cautividad** [kautißi'ðað] *nf* captivity.

cautivo, a [kau'tißo, a] *a, nm/f* captive.

cauto, a ['kauto, a] *a* cautious, careful.

cavar [ka'ßar] *vt* to dig.

caverna [ka'ßerna] *nf* cave, cavern.

cavidad [kaßi'ðað] *nf* cavity.

cavilar [kaßi'lar] *vt* to ponder.

cayado [ka'jaðo] *nm* (*de pastor*) staff, crook; (*de obispo*) crozier.

cayó *etc vb ver* **caer.**

caza ['kaθa] *nf* (*gen*) hunting, shooting; (*una* ~) hunt, chase; (*animales*) game // *nm* (*AVIAT*) fighter.

cazador [kaθa'ðor] *nm* hunter.

cazar [ka'θar] *vt* to hunt; (*perseguir*) to chase; (*coger*) to catch.

cazo ['kaθo] *nm* saucepan.

cazuela [ka'θwela] *nf* pan; (*guisado*) casserole.

cebada [θe'ßaða] *nf* barley.

cebar [θe'ßar] *vt* (*animal*) to fatten (up); (*anzuelo*) to bait; (*MIL, TEC*) to prime; (*pasión*) to nourish; (*ira*) to inflame.

cebo ['θeßo] *nm* (*para animales*) feed, food; (*para peces, fig*) bait; (*de arma*) charge.

cebolla [θe'ßoʎa] *nf* onion.

cebra [θe'ßra] *nf* zebra.

cecear [θeθe'ar] *vi* to lisp; **ceceo** *nm* lisp.

cedazo [θe'ðaθo] *nm* sieve.

ceder [θe'ðer] *vt* to hand over, give up, part with // *vi* (*renunciar*) to give in, yield; (*disminuir*) to diminish, decline; (*romperse*) to give way.

cedro ['θeðro] *nm* cedar.

cédula ['θeðula] *nf* certificate, document; ~ **de aduana** customs permit.

C.E.E. *nf abr de* **Comunidad Económica Europea** E.E.C. (European Economic Community).

cegar [θe'xar] *vt* to blind; (*fig: pozo*) to block up, fill up // *vi* to go blind, ~**se** *vr* to be blinded (*de by*).

ceguedad [θeɣe'ðað], **ceguera** [θe'ɣera] *nf* blindness.

ceja ['θexa] *nf* eyebrow.

cejar [θe'xar] *vi* to move back, go back; (*fig*) to back down.

cejijunto, a [θexi'xunto, a] *a* with bushy eyebrows; (*fig*) scowling.

celada [θe'laða] *nf* ambush, trap.

celador, a [θela'ðor, a] *nm/f* (*de edificio*) watchman; (*de museo etc*) attendant.

celar [θe'lar] *vt* (*vigilar*) to watch over; (*encubrir*) to conceal, hide.

celda ['θelda] nf cell.

celebración [θeleßra'θjon] nf celebration.

celebrar [θele'ßrar] vt to celebrate; (alabar) to praise // vi to be glad; ~se vr to occur, take place.

célebre ['θelebre] a famous; (chistoso) witty, funny.

celebridad [θeleßri'ðað] nf (gen) fame; (persona) celebrity; (festividad) celebration(s) (pl).

celeste [θe'leste] a celestial, heavenly.

celestial [θeles'tjal] a celestial, heavenly.

celibato [θeli'ßato] nm celibacy.

célibe ['θelißе] a celibate // nm/f unmarried person.

celo ['θelo] nm zeal; (REL) fervour; (pey) envy; (de animales) rut, heat; ~s nmpl jealousy sg.

celofán [θelo'fan] nm cellophane.

celoso, a [θe'loso, a] a (envidioso) jealous; (trabajo) zealous; (desconfiado) suspicious.

celta ['θelta] nm/f Celt.

célula ['θelula] nf cell.

cementar [θemen'tar] vt to cement.

cementerio [θemen'terjo] nm cemetery, graveyard.

cemento [θe'mento] nm cement; (hormigón) concrete.

cena ['θena] nf evening meal.

cenagal [θena'val] nm bog, quagmire.

cenar [θe'nar] vt to have for supper // vi to dine.

cenicero [θeni'θero] nm ashtray.

cenit [θe'nit] nm zenith.

ceniza [θe'niθa] nf ash, ashes pl.

censo ['θenso] nm (empadronamiento) census; (JUR) tax; (renta) rent; (carga sobre una casa) mortgage.

censor [θen'sor] nm censor.

censura [θen'sura] nf (POL) censorship; (moral) censure, criticism.

censurar [θensu'rar] vt (idea) to censure; (cortar: película) to censor.

centella [θen'teʎa] nf spark.

centellar [θente'ʎar], **centellear** [θenteʎe'ar] vi (metal) to gleam; (estrella) to twinkle; (fig) to sparkle; **centelleo** nm gleam(ing); twinkling; sparkling.

centenar [θente'nar] nm hundred.

centenario, a [θente'narjo, a] a centenary.

centésimo, a [θen'tesimo, a] a hundredth.

centígrado, a [θen'tixraðo, a] a centigrade.

centímetro [θen'timetro] nm centimetre.

céntimo, a ['θentimo, a] a hundredth // nm cent.

centinela [θenti'nela] nm sentry, guard.

central [θen'tral] a central // nf head office; (TEC) plant; (TELEC) exchange.

centralización [θentraliθa'θjon] nf centralization.

centralizar [θentrali'θar] vt to centralize.

centrar [θen'trar] vt to centre.

céntrico, a ['θentriko, a] a centre.

centro ['θentro] nm centre.

centroamericano, a [θentroameri'kano, a] a, nm/f Central American.

ceñidor [θeni'ðor] nm sash.

ceñir [θe'nir] vt (rodear) to encircle, surround; (ajustar) to fit (tightly); (apretar) to tighten.

ceño ['θeno] nm frown, scowl; **fruncir el ~** to frown, knit one's brow.

cepillar [θepi'ʎar] vt to brush; (madera) to plane (down); **cepillo** nm (gen) brush; (TEC) plane.

cera ['θera] nf wax.

cerámico, a [θe'ramiko, a] a ceramic // nf ceramics sg.

cerca ['θerka] nf fence // ad near, nearby, close; ~s nmpl foreground sg; ~ de prep near, close to.

cercanía [θerka'nia] nf nearness, closeness; ~s nfpl outskirts.

cercano, a [θer'kano, a] a close, near.

cercar [θer'kar] vt to fence in; (rodear) to surround.

cerciorar [θerθjo'rar] vt (informar) to inform; (asegurar) to assure; ~se vr (descubrir) to find out; (asegurarse) to make sure.

cerco ['θerko] nm (AGR) enclosure; (AM) fence; (MIL) siege.

cerdo ['θerðo] nm pig.

cereal [θere'al] nm cereal.

cerebro [θe'reßro] nm brain; (fig) brains pl.

ceremonia [θere'monja] nf ceremony; **ceremonial** a, nm ceremonial; **ceremonioso, a** a ceremonious; (cumplido) formal.

cereza [θe'reθa] nf cherry.

cerilla [θe'riʎa] nf (fósforo) match.

cerner [θer'ner] vt to sift, sieve; (fig) to scan, watch // vi to blossom; (lloviznar) to drizzle; ~se vr to hover.

cernidor [θerni'ðor] nm sieve.

cero ['θero] nm nothing, zero.

cerrado, a [θe'rraðo, a] a closed, shut; (con llave) locked; (tiempo) cloudy, overcast; (curva) sharp; (acento) thick, broad.

cerradura [θerra'ðura] nf (acción) closing; (mecanismo) lock.

cerraja [θe'rraxa] nf lock.

cerrar [θe'rrar] vt to close, shut; (paso, carretera) to close; (grifo) to turn off; (trato, cuenta, negocio) to close; ~ con llave to lock // vi to close, shut; (la noche) to come down; ~se vr to close, shut.

cerro ['θerro] nm hill.

cerrojo [θe'rroxo] nm (herramienta) bolt; (de puerta) latch.

certamen [θer'tamen] nm competition, contest.

certero, a [θer'tero, a] a accurate; (cierto) sure, certain.

certeza [θer'teθa], **certidumbre** [θerti-'ðumbre] nf certainty.

certificado [θertifi'kaðo] nm certificate.

certificar [θertifi'kar] vt (asegurar,

atestar) to certify; (*carta*) to register.
cervato [θer'βato] *nm* fawn.
cervecería [θerβeθe'ria] *nf* (*fábrica*) brewery; (*tienda*) public house.
cerveza [θer'βeθa] *nf* beer.
cesación [θesa'θjon] *nf* cessation; (*suspensión*) suspension.
cesante [θe'sante] *a* out of a job.
cesar [θe'sar] *vi* to cease, stop.
cese ['θese] *nm* (*de trabajo*) dismissal; (*de pago*) suspension.
césped ['θespeδ] *nm* grass, lawn.
cesta ['θesta] *nf* basket; **cesto** *nm* (large) basket, hamper.
ch... *ver bajo la letra* CH, *después de* C.
Cía *abr de* **compañía.**
cianuro [θja'nuro] *nm* cyanide.
ciar [θjar] *vi* to go backwards.
cicatriz [θika'triθ] *nf* scar.
ciclismo [θi'klismo] *nm* cycling.
ciclo ['θiklo] *nm* cycle.
ciclón [θi'klon] *nm* cyclone.
ciego, a ['θjeɣo, a] *a* blind // *nm/f* blind man/woman.
cielo ['θjelo] *nm* sky; (*REL*) heaven; ¡~ sí good heavens!
ciempiés [θjem'pjes] *nm* centipede.
cien [θjen] *num ver* **ciento.**
ciénaga ['θjenaxa] *nf* marsh, swamp.
ciencia ['θjenθja] *nf* science; ~-**ficción** *nf* science fiction.
cieno ['θjeno] *nm* mud, mire.
científico, a [θjen'tifiko, a] *a* scientific // *nm/f* scientist.
ciento ['θjento], **cien** *num* hundred; **pagar al 10 por** ~ to pay at 10 per cent.
cierne ['θjerne] *nm*: **en** ~ in blossom.
cierre ['θjerre] *nm* closing, shutting; (*con llave*) locking; ~ **a cremallera** zip fastener.
cierro *etc vb ver* **cerrar.**
cierto, a ['θjerto, a] *a* sure, certain; (*un tal*) a certain; (*correcto*) right, correct; ~ **hombre** a certain man; **sí, es** ~ yes, that's correct.
ciervo ['θjerβo] *nm* (*especie*) deer; (*macho*) stag.
cierzo ['θjerθo] *nm* north wind.
cifra ['θifra] *nf* number, numeral; (*cantidad*) number, quantity; (*secreta*) code; (*siglas*) abbreviation.
cifrar [θi'frar] *vt* to code, write in code; (*resumir*) to abridge.
cigarra [θi'ɣarra] *nf* cicada.
cigarrera [θiɣa'rrera] *nf* cigar case.
cigarrillo [θiɣa'rriʎo] *nm* cigarette.
cigarro [θi'ɣarro] *nm* cigarette; (*puro*) cigar.
cigüeña [θi'ɣweɲa] *nf* stork.
cilíndrico, a [θi'lindriko, a] *a* cylindrical.
cilindro [θi'lindro] *nm* cylinder; (*rodillo*) roller.
cima ['θima] *nf* (*de montaña*) top, peak; (*de árbol*) top; (*fig*) summit, height.
címbalo ['θimbalo] *nm* cymbal.
cimbrar [θim'brar], **cimbrear** [θimbre-

'ar] *vt* to brandish; ~**se** *vr* (*al viento*) to sway.
cimentar [θimen'tar] *vt* to lay the foundations of.
cimiento [θi'mjento] *nm* foundation.
cinc [θink] *nm* zinc.
cincel [θin'θel] *nm* chisel; ~**ar** *vt* to chisel.
cinco ['θinko] *num* five.
cincuenta [θin'kwenta] *num* fifty.
cincho ['θintʃo] *nm* sash, belt.
cine ['θine] *nm* cinema.
cinematográfico, a [θinemato'ɣrafiko, a] *a* cine-, film *cpd*.
cínico, a ['θiniko, a] *a* cynical // *nm/f* cynic.
cinismo [θi'nismo] *nm* cynicism.
cinta ['θinta] *nf* band, strip; (*de seda, lana, algodón*) ribbon, tape; (*película*) reel; (*de máquina de escribir*) ribbon; (*métrica*) tape measure; (*magnetofónica*) tape; (*adhesiva*) adhesive tape.
cinto ['θinto] *nm* belt, girdle.
cintura [θin'tura] *nf* waist.
cinturón [θintu'ron] *nm* belt; ~ **de seguridad** safety belt.
ciprés [θi'pres] *nm* cypress (tree).
circo ['θirko] *nm* circus.
circuito [θir'kwito] *nm* circuit.
circulación [θirkula'θjon] *nf* circulation; (*AUTO*) traffic.
circular [θirku'lar] *a, nf* circular // *vi, vt* to circulate.
círculo ['θirkulo] *nm* circle.
circuncidar [θirkunθi'dar] *vt* to circumcise; **circuncisión** *nf* circumcision; **circunciso, a** *pp de* **circuncidar** // *a* circumcised.
circundar [θirkun'dar] *vt* to surround.
circunferencia [θirkunfe'renθja] *nf* circumference.
circunlocución [θirkunloku'θjon] *nf*, **circunloquio** [θirkun'lokjo] *nm* circumlocution.
circunscribir [θirkunskri'βir] *vt* to circumscribe; ~**se** *vr* to be limited.
circunscripción [θirkunskrip'θjon] *nf* division; (*POL*) constituency.
circunspección [θirkunspek'θjon] *nf* circumspection.
circunspecto, a [θirkuns'pekto, a] *a* circumspect, cautious.
circunstancia [θirkuns'tanθja] *nf* circumstance.
circunstante [θirkuns'tante] *nm/f* onlooker, bystander.
cirio ['θirjo] *nm* (wax) candle.
ciruela [θi'rwela] *nf* plum; ~ **pasa** prune.
cirugía [θiru'xia] *nf* surgery; ~ **estética** plastic surgery.
cirujano [θiru'xano] *nm* surgeon.
cisne ['θisne] *nm* swan.
cisterna [θis'terna] *nf* cistern.
cita ['θita] *nf* appointment, engagement; (*de novios*) date; (*referencia*) quotation.
citación [θita'θjon] *nf* (*JUR*) summons *sg*; (*referencia*) quotation.

citar [θi'tar] *vt* (*gen*) to make an appointment with; (*JUR*) to summons; (*un autor, texto*) to quote.

citrón [θi'tron] *nm* lemon.

ciudad [θju'ðað] *nf* town; (*capital de país etc*) city; ~**ano, a** *nm/f* citizen; ~**ela** *nf* citadel, fortress.

cívico, a ['θiβiko, a] *a* civic.

civil [θi'βil] *a* civil // *nm* (*guardia*) policeman; ~**idad** *nf* civility, courtesy.

civilización [θiβiliθa'θjon] *nf* civilization.

civilizar [θiβili'θar] *vt* to civilize.

civismo [θi'βismo] *nm* public spirit.

cizaña [θi'θaɲa] *nf* discord.

clamar [kla'mar] *vt* to clamour for // *vi* to cry out, clamour.

clamor [kla'mor] *nm* (*grito*) cry, shout; (*gemido*) whine; (*de campana*) knell; (*fig*) clamour, protest.

clamorear [klamore'ar] *vt* to clamour for // *vi* (*campana*) to toll; **clamoreo** *nm* clamour(ing).

clandestino, a [klandes'tino, a] *a* clandestine; (*POL*) underground.

clara ['klara] *nf* (*de huevo*) white of an egg; (*del día*) bright interval.

claraboya [klara'βoja] *nf* skylight.

clarear [klare'ar] *vi* (*el día*) to dawn; (*el cielo*) to clear up, brighten up; ~**se** *vr* to be transparent.

claridad [klari'ðað] *nf* (*del día*) brightness; (*de estilo*) clarity.

clarificar [klarifi'kar] *vt* to clarify.

clarín [kla'rin] *nm* bugle.

clarinete [klari'nete] *nm* clarinet.

clarividencia [klariβi'ðenθja] *nf* clairvoyance; (*fig*) far-sightedness.

claro, a ['klaro, a] *a* (*gen*) clear; (*luminoso*) bright; (*poco subido*) light; (*evidente*) clear, evident; (*ralo*) sparse; (*poco espeso*) thin // *nm* (*en escritura*) space; (*en bosque*) clearing // *ad* clearly // *excl* of course!

clase ['klase] *nf* class; ~ **alta/media/obrera** upper/middle/working class.

clásico, a ['klasiko, a] *a* classical; (*fig*) classic.

clasificación [klasifika'θjon] *nf* classification; (*DEPORTE*) league.

clasificar [klasifi'kar] *vt* to classify.

claudicar [klauði'kar] *vi* to limp; (*fig*) to back down.

claustro ['klaustro] *nm* cloister.

cláusula ['klausula] *nf* clause.

clausura [klau'sura] *nf* closing, closure.

clavar [kla'βar] *vt* (*clavo*) to knock in, drive in; (*cuchillo, tenedor*) to stick, thrust; (*mirada*) to fix.

clave ['klaβe] *nf* key; (*MUS*) clef.

clavel [kla'βel] *nm* carnation.

clavícula [kla'βikula] *nf* collar bone.

clavija [kla'βixa] *nf* peg, dowel, pin; (*ELEC*) plug.

clavo ['klaβo] *nm* (*de metal*) nail; (*BOT*) clove; (*callo*) corn.

claxon ['klakson] *nm* horn.

clemencia [kle'menθja] *nf* mercy, clemency; **clemente** *a* merciful, clement.

cleptómano, a [klep'tomano, a] *nm/f* kleptomaniac.

clerical [kleri'kal] *a* clerical // *nm* clergyman.

clérigo ['klerixo] *nm* clergyman.

clero ['klero] *nm* clergy.

cliente ['kljente] *nm/f* client, customer.

clientela [kljen'tela] *nf* clientele, customers *pl*.

clima ['klima] *nm* climate.

clínica ['klinika] *nf* clinic; (*particular*) private hospital.

clip [klip] *nm* paper clip.

clorhídrico, a [klo'ridriko, a] *a* hydrochloric.

cloroformo [kloro'formo] *nm* chloroform.

club [klub] (*pl* ~**s** *o* ~**es**) *nm* club.

C.N.T. *abr de* **Confederación Nacional de Trabajo.**

coacción [koak'θjon] *nf* coercion, compulsion.

coalición [koali'θjon] *nf* coalition.

coartar [koar'tar] *vt* to limit, restrict.

cobarde [ko'βarðe] *a* cowardly // *nm* coward; **cobardía** *nf* cowardice.

cobertizo [koβer'tiθo] *nm* shelter.

cobertor [koβer'tor] *nm* bedspread.

cobertura [koβer'tura] *nf* cover.

cobija [ko'βixa] *nf* roof; **cobijar** *vt* (*cubrir*) to cover; (*abrigar*) to shelter.

cobra ['koβra] *nf* cobra.

cobrador [koβra'ðor] *nm* (*de autobús*) conductor; (*de impuestos, gas*) collector.

cobrar [ko'βrar] *vt* (*cheque*) to cash; (*sueldo*) to collect, draw; (*objeto*) to recover; (*precio*) to charge; (*deuda*) to collect // *vi* to draw one's pay; ~**se** *vr* to recover, get well; **cóbrese al entregar** cash on delivery (COD).

cobre ['koβre] *nm* copper; ~**s** *nmpl* brass instruments.

cobro ['koβro] *nm* recovery; (*paga*) payment.

cocaína [koka'ina] *nf* cocaine.

cocción [kok'θjon] *nf* cooking.

cocear [koθe'ar] *vi* to kick.

cocer [ko'θer] *vt, vi* to cook; (*en agua*) to boil; (*en horno*) to bake; ~**se** *vr* to suffer intensely.

cocido [ko'θiðo] *nm* stew.

cocina [ko'θina] *nf* kitchen; (*aparato*) cooker, stove; (*acto*) cookery; **cocinar** *vt, vi* to cook.

cocinero, a [koθi'nero, a] *nm/f* cook.

coco ['koko] *nm* (*árbol*) coconut palm; (*fruto*) coconut.

cocodrilo [koko'ðrilo] *nm* crocodile.

coche ['kotʃe] *nm* car, motorcar; (*de tren, de caballos*) coach, carriage; (*fúnebre*) hearse; (*para niños*) pram; ~ **celular** Black Maria, prison van.

coche-cama [kotʃekama] (*pl* **coches-camas**) *nm* sleeping car, sleeper.

cochera [ko'tʃera] nf garage.
cochero [ko'tʃero] nm coachman.
cochino, a [ko'tʃino, a] a filthy, dirty // nm pig.
codazo [ko'ðaθo] nm jab, poke (with the elbow).
codear [koðe'ar] vi to elbow, jostle; ~se vr: ~se con to rub shoulders with.
códice ['koðiðe] nm manuscript, codex.
codicia [ko'ðiθja] nf greed; (fig) lust; **codiciar** vt to covet; **codicioso, a** a covetous.
código ['koðiɣo] nm code; ~ civil common law.
codillo [ko'ðiʎo] nm (ZOOL) knee; (TEC) elbow (joint).
codo ['koðo] nm (ANAT. de tubo) elbow; (ZOOL) knee.
codorniz [koðor'niθ] nf quail.
coerción [koer'θjon] nf coercion.
coetáneo, a [koe'taneo, a] a contemporary.
coexistencia [koeksis'tenðja] nf coexistence; **coexistir** vi to coexist.
cofradía [kofra'ðia] nf brotherhood, fraternity.
cofre ['kofre] nm chest.
coger [ko'xer] vt (gen) to take (hold of); (objeto caído) to pick up; (frutas) to pick, harvest; (resfriado, ladrón, pelota) to catch // vi: ~ por el buen camino to take the right road; ~se vr to catch; (robar) to steal.
cogida [ko'xiða] nf gathering, harvesting; (de peces) catch.
cogote [ko'ɣote] nm back or nape of the neck.
cohabitar [koaβi'tar] vi to live together, cohabit.
cohechar [koe'tʃar] vt to bribe; **cohecho** nm (acción) bribery; (soborno) bribe.
coherente [koe'rente] a coherent.
cohesión [koe'sjon] nm cohesion.
cohete [ko'ete] nm rocket.
cohibición [koiβi'θjon] nf restraint, restriction.
cohibir [koi'βir] vt to restrain, restrict.
coincidencia [koinθi'ðenðja] nf coincidence; (acuerdo) agreement.
coincidir [koinθi'ðir] vi (en idea) to coincide, agree; (en lugar) to coincide.
coito ['koito] nm intercourse, coitus.
cojear [koxe'ar] vi (persona) to limp, hobble; (mueble) to wobble, rock.
cojera [ko'xera] nf lameness; (andar cojo) limp.
cojín [ko'xin] nm cushion; **cojinete** nm small cushion, pad; (TEC) ball bearing.
cojo, a ['koxo, a] a (que no puede andar) lame; (manco) crippled; (mueble) shaky // nm/f lame person; cripple.
col [kol] nf cabbage; ~ de Bruselas Brussels sprouts.
cola ['kola] nf (gen) tail; (de gente) queue; (lugar) end, last place; (para pegar) glue, gum; **hacer la** ~ to queue (up).

colaborador, a [kolaβora'ðor, a] nm/f collaborator.
colaborar [kolaβo'rar] vi to collaborate.
coladera [kola'ðera] nf strainer.
coladura [kola'ðura] nf (filtración) straining; (residuo) grounds pl, dregs pl.
colapso [ko'lapso] nm collapse; ~ nervioso nervous breakdown.
colar [ko'lar] vt (líquido) to strain off; (ropa) to bleach; (metal) to cast // vi to ooze, seep (through); ~se vr to slip in or past.
colateral [kolate'ral] nm collateral.
colcha ['koltʃa] nf bedspread.
colchón [kol'tʃon] nm mattress.
colear [kole'ar] vi to wag its tail.
colección [kolek'θjon] nf collection; **coleccionista** nm/f collector.
colecta [ko'lekta] nf collection.
colectar [kolek'tar] vt to collect.
colectivo, a [kolek'tiβo, a] a collective, joint.
colector [kolek'tor] nm collector; (sumidero) sewer.
colega [ko'leɣa] nm/f colleague.
colegio [ko'lexjo] nm (gen) college; (escuela) (private) school; (de abogados etc) association.
colegir [kole'xir] vt (juntar, reunir) to collect, gather; (deducir) to infer, conclude.
cólera ['kolera] nf (ira) anger; (MED) cholera.
colérico, a [ko'leriko, a] a angry, furious.
coleta [ko'leta] nf pigtail.
colgadero [kolɣa'ðero] nm (gancho) hook; (percha) hanger.
colgadura [kolɣa'ðura] nf hangings pl, drapery.
colgante [kol'xante] a hanging // nm drop earring.
colgar [kol'ɣar] vt to hang (up); (ropa) to hang (out); (teléfono) to hang up // vi to hang.
coliflor [koli'flor] nf cauliflower.
colilla [ko'liʎa] nf fag end, butt.
colina [ko'lina] nf hill.
colindante [kolin'dante] a adjacent, neighbouring.
colindar [kolin'dar] vi to adjoin, be adjacent.
colisión [koli'sjon] nf collision; (choque) crash.
colmado, a [kol'maðo, a] a abundant, copious; (cuchara etc) heaped.
colmar [kol'mar] vt to fill to the brim; (fig) to fulfil, realize.
colmena [kol'mena] nf beehive.
colmillo [kol'miʎo] nm (diente) eye tooth; (de elefante) tusk; (de perro) fang.
colmo ['kolmo] nm height, summit.
colocación [koloka'θjon] nf placing; (empleo) job, position; (de mueble) place, position.
colocar [kolo'kar] vt to place, put,

position; (*poner en empleo*) to find a job for.

Colombia [ko'lombja] *nf* Colombia; **colombiano, a** *a, nm/f* Colombian.

colon ['kolon] *nm* colon.

colonia [ko'lonja] *nf* colony; (*de casas*) housing estate; (*agua de* ~) cologne.

colonización [koloniθa'θjon] *nf* colonization.

colonizador, a [koloniθa'δor, a] *a* colonizing // *nm/f* colonist, settler.

colonizar [koloni'θar] *vt* to colonize.

coloquio [ko'lokjo] *nm* conversation; (*congreso*) conference.

color [ko'lor] *nm* colour.

colorado, a [kolo'raδo, a] *a* (*que tiene color*) coloured; (*rojo*) red.

colorar [kolo'rar] *vt* to colour; (*teñir*) to dye.

colorear [kolore'ar] *vt* to colour // *vi* to redden.

colorido [kolo'riδo] *nm* colouring.

colosal [kolo'sal] *a* colossal.

columbrar [kolum'brar] *vt* to glimpse, spy.

columna [ko'lumna] *nf* column; (*pilar*) pillar; (*apoyo*) support.

columpiar [kolum'pjar] *vt*, ~**se** *vr* to swing; **columpio** *nm* swing.

collar [ko'ʌar] *nm* necklace; (*de perro*) collar.

coma ['koma] *nf* comma // *nm* coma.

comadre [ko'maδre] *nf* (*partera*) midwife; (*madrina*) godmother; (*vecina*) neighbour; ~**ar** *vi* to gossip.

comandancia [koman'danθja] *nf* command.

comandante [koman'dante] *nm* commandant.

comandar [koman'dar] *vt* to command.

comarca [ko'marka] *nf* region.

comarcar [komar'kar] *vi*: ~ **con** to border on, be adjacent to.

combar [kom'bar] *vt* to bend, curve.

combate [kom'bate] *nm* fight; (*fig*) battle; **combatiente** *nm* combatant.

combatir [komba'tir] *vt* to fight, combat.

combinación [kombina'θjon] *nf* combination; (*QUÍMICA*) compound; (*bebida*) cocktail; (*plan*) scheme, setup.

combinar [kombi'nar] *vt* to combine.

combustible [kombus'tiβle] *nm* fuel.

combustión [kombus'tjon] *nf* combustion.

comedia [ko'meδja] *nf* comedy; (*TEATRO*) play, drama.

comediante [kome'δjante] *nm/f* (comic) actor/actress.

comedido, a [kome'δiδo, a] *a* moderate; (*cortés*) courteous.

comedirse [kome'δirse] *vr* to behave moderately; (*ser cortés*) to be courteous.

comedor, a [kome'δor, a] *nm/f* (*persona*) glutton // *nm* (*habitación*) dining room; (*restaurante*) restaurant; (*cantina*) canteen.

comentador, a [komenta'δor, a] *nm/f* = **comentarista.**

comentar [komen'tar] *vt* to comment on; (*fam*) to discuss.

comentario [komen'tarjo] *nm* comment, remark; (*literario*) commentary; ~**s** *nmpl* gossip *sg*.

comentarista [komenta'rista] *nm/f* commentator.

comento [ko'mento] *nm* = **comentario.**

comenzar [komen'θar] *vt, vi* to begin, start, commence.

comer [ko'mer] *vt* (*gen*) to eat; (*DAMAS, AJEDREZ*) to take, capture // *vi* to eat; (*almorzar*) to have lunch; ~**se** *vr* to eat up.

comercial [komer'θjal] *a* commercial; (*relativo al negocio*) business *cpd.*

comerciante [komer'θjante] *nm/f* trader, merchant.

comerciar [komer'θjar] *vi* to trade, do business.

comercio [ko'merθjo] *nm* commerce; (*tráfico*) trade; (*negocio*) business; (*fig*) dealings *pl.*

comestible [komes'tiβle] *a* eatable, edible // *nm* foodstuff.

cometa [ko'meta] *nm* comet // *nf* kite.

cometer [kome'ter] *vt* to commit.

cometido [kome'tiδo] *nm* (*misión*) task, assignment; (*deber*) commitment.

comezón [kome'θon] *nf* itch, itching.

cómico, a ['komiko, a] *a* comic(al) // *nm/f* comedian; (*de teatro*) (comic) actor/actress.

comida [ko'miδa] *nf* (*alimento*) food; (*almuerzo, cena*) meal; (*de mediodía*) lunch.

comienzo [ko'mjenθo] *nm* beginning, start.

comillas [ko'miʌas] *nfpl* inverted commas.

comisario [komi'sarjo] *nm* commissary; (*POL*) commissar.

comisión [komi'sjon] *nf* commission.

comité [komi'te] *nm* committee.

como ['komo] *ad* as; (*tal* ~) like; (*aproximadamente*) about, approximately // *conj* (*ya que, puesto que*) as, since; (*en seguida que*) as soon as; ¡~ **no!** of course!; ~ **no lo haga hoy** unless he does it today; ~ **si** as if; **es tan alto** ~ **ancho** it is as high as it is wide.

cómo ['komo] *ad* how?, why? // *excl* what?, I beg your pardon? // *nm*: **el** ~ **y el porqué** the whys and wherefores.

comodidad [komoδi'δaδ] *nf* comfort; **venga a su** ~ come at your convenience.

comodín [komo'δin] *nm* joker.

cómodo, a ['komoδo, a] *a* comfortable; (*práctico, de fácil uso*) convenient.

compacto, a [kom'pakto, a] *a* compact.

compadecer [kompaδe'θer] *vt* to pity, be sorry for; ~**se** *vr*: ~**se de** to pity, be sorry for.

compadre [kom'paδre] *nm* (*padrino*) godfather; (*amigo*) friend, pal.

compañero, a [kompa'ɲero, a] *nm/f* companion; ~ **de clase** classmate.

compañía [kompa'ɲia] *nf* company.

comparación [kompara'θjon] *nf* comparison; **en** ~ **con** in comparison with.

comparar [kompa'rar] *vt* to compare.

comparativo, a [kompara'tiβo, a] *a* comparative.

comparecer [kompare'θer] *vi* to appear (in court).

compartimiento [komparti'mjento] *nm* division; (*distribución*) distribution; (*FERRO*) compartment.

compartir [kompar'tir] *vt* to divide (up), share (out).

compás [kom'pas] *nm* (*MUS*) beat, rhythm; (*MAT*) compasses *pl*; (*NAUT*) compass.

compasión [kompa'sjon] *nf* compassion, pity.

compasivo, a [kompa'siβo, a] *a* compassionate.

compatibilidad [kompatiβili'ðað] *nf* compatibility.

compatible [kompa'tiβle] *a* compatible.

compatriota [kompa'trjota] *nm/f* compatriot.

compeler [kompe'ler] *vt* to compel.

compendiar [kompen'djar] *vt* to summarize; (*libro*) to abridge; **compendio** *nm* summary; abridgement.

compensación [kompensa'θjon] *nf* compensation.

compensar [kompen'sar] *vt* to compensate.

competencia [kompe'tenθja] *nf* (*incumbencia*) domain, field; (*aptitud, idoneidad*) competence; (*rivalidad*) competition.

competente [kompe'tente] *a* (*persona, jurado, tribunal*) competent; (*conveniente*) fit, suitable.

competición [kompeti'θjon] *nf* competition.

competir [kompe'tir] *vi* to compete.

compilar [kompi'lar] *vt* to compile.

complacencia [kompla'θenθja] *nf* (*placer*) pleasure; (*satisfacción*) satisfaction; (*buena voluntad*) willingness.

complacer [kompla'θer] *vt* to please; ~**se** *vr* to be pleased.

complaciente [kompla'θjente] *a* kind, obliging, helpful.

complejo, a [kom'plexo, a] *a, nm* complex.

complementario, a [komplemen'tarjo, a] *a* complementary.

completar [komple'tar] *vt* to complete.

completo, a [kom'pleto, a] *a* complete; (*perfecto*) perfect; (*lleno*) full // *nm* full complement.

complicar [kompli'kar] *vt* to complicate.

cómplice ['kompliθe] *nm/f* accomplice.

complot [kom'plot] *nm* plot; (*conspiración*) conspiracy.

componenda [kompo'nenda] *nf* compromise; (*pey*) shady deal.

componer [kompo'ner] *vt* to make up, put together; (*MUS, LITERATURA, IMPRENTA*) to compose; (*algo roto*) to mend, repair; (*adornar*) to adorn; (*arreglar*) to arrange; (*reconciliar*) to reconcile; ~**se** *vr*: ~**se de** to consist of.

comportamiento [komporta'mjento] *nm* behaviour, conduct.

comportarse [kompor'tarse] *vr* to behave.

composición [komposi'θjon] *nf* composition.

compositor, a [komposi'tor, a] *nm/f* composer.

compostura [kompos'tura] *nf* (*reparación*) mending, repair; (*arreglo*) arrangement; (*acuerdo*) agreement; (*actitud*) composure.

compra ['kompra] *nf* purchase; ~**s** *nfpl* purchases, shopping *sg*.

comprador, a [kompra'ðor, a] *nm/f* buyer, purchaser.

comprar [kom'prar] *vt* to buy, purchase.

comprender [kompren'der] *vt* to understand; (*incluir*) to comprise, include.

comprensión [kompren'sjon] *nf* understanding; (*totalidad*) comprehensiveness.

comprensivo, a [kompren'siβo, a] *a* comprehensive; (*actitud*) understanding.

compresión [kompre'sjon] *nf* compression.

comprimir [kompri'mir] *vt* to compress; (*fig*) to control.

comprobante [kompro'βante] *a* verifying, supporting // *nm* proof.

comprobar [kompro'βar] *vt* to check; (*probar*) to prove; (*TEC*) to check, test.

comprometer [komprome'ter] *vt* to compromise; (*exponer*) to endanger; ~**se** *vr* to compromise o.s.; (*involucrarse*) to get involved.

compromiso [kompro'miso] *nm* (*obligación*) obligation; (*cometido*) commitment; (*convenio*) agreement; (*dificultad*) awkward situation.

compuesto, a [kom'pwesto, a] *a*: ~ **de** composed of, made up of // *nm* compound.

compulsión [kompul'sjon] *nf* compulsion.

compunción [kompun'θjon] *nf* compunction, regret.

computador [komputa'ðor] *nm*, **computadora** [komputa'ðora] *nf* computer.

comulgar [komul'xar] *vi* to receive communion.

común [ko'mun] *a* common // *nm*: **el** ~ the community.

comunicación [komunika'θjon] *nf* communication; (*ponencia*) report.

comunicar [komuni'kar] *vt, vi*, ~**se** *vr* to communicate; **comunicativo, a** *a* communicative.

comunidad [komuni'ðað] *nf* community.

comunión [komu'njon] *nf* communion.

comunismo [komu'nismo] *nm*

communism; **comunista** *a*, *nm/f* communist.

con [kon] *prep* with; (*a pesar de*) in spite of; ~ **que** so, and so; ~ **apretar el botón** by pressing the button.

concebir [konθe'βir] *vt*, *vi* to conceive.

conceder [konθe'δer] *vt* to concede.

concejo [kon'θexo] *nm* council.

concentración [konθentra'θjon] *nf* concentration.

concentrar [konθen'trar] *vt*, ~**se** *vr* to concentrate.

concepción [konθep'θjon] *nf* conception.

concepto [kon'θepto] *nm* concept.

concertar [konθer'tar] *vt* (*MUS*) to harmonize; (*acordar: precio*) to agree; (: *tratado*) to conclude; (*trato*) to arrange, fix up; (*combinar: esfuerzos*) to coordinate; (*reconciliar: personas*) to reconcile // *vi* to harmonize, be in tune.

concesión [konθe'sjon] *nf* concession.

conciencia [kon'θjenθja] *nf* conscience.

concienzudo, a [konθjen'θuδo, a] *a* conscientious.

concierto [kon'θjerto] *nm* concert; (*obra*) concerto.

conciliar [konθi'ljar] *vt* to reconcile.

concilio [kon'θiljo] *nm* council.

conciso, a [kon'θiso, a] *a* concise.

concluir [konklu'ir] *vt*, *vi*, ~**se** *vr* to conclude.

conclusión [konklu'sjon] *nf* conclusion.

concordar [konkor'δar] *vt* to reconcile // *vi* to agree, tally; **concordia** *nf* concord, harmony.

concretar [konkre'tar] *vt* to make concrete, make more specific; ~**se** *vr* to become more definite.

concreto, a [kon'kreto, a] *a*, *nm* (*AM*) concrete; **en** ~ (*en resumen*) to sum up; (*específicamente*) specifically; **no hay nada en** ~ there's nothing definite.

concurrir [konku'rrir] *vi* (*juntarse: ríos*) to meet, come together; (: *personas*) to gather, meet; (*ponerse de acuerdo, coincidir*) to concur; (*competir*) to compete; (*contribuir*) to contribute.

concurso [kon'kurso] *nm* (*de público*) crowd; (*ESCOL, DEPORTE, competencia*) competition; (*coincidencia*) coincidence; (*ayuda*) help, cooperation.

concusión [konku'sjon] *nf* concussion.

concha ['kontʃa] *nf* shell.

conde ['konde] *nm* count.

condecorar [kondeko'rar] *vt* to decorate.

condena [kon'dena] *nf* sentence.

condenación [kondena'θjon] *nf* (*gen*) condemnation; (*condena*) sentence; (*REL*) damnation.

condenar [konde'nar] *vt* to condemn; (*JUR*) to convict; ~**se** *vr* (*JUR*) to confess (one's guilt); (*REL*) to be damned.

condensar [konden'sar] *vt* to condense.

condescender [kondesθen'der] *vi* to acquiesce, comply.

condición [kondi'θjon] *nf* condition;

condicionado, a *a* conditioned.

condicional [kondiθjo'nal] *a* conditional.

condimento [kondi'mento] *nm* seasoning.

condolerse [kondo'lerse] *vr* to sympathize.

conducir [kondu'θir] *vt* to take, convey; (*AUTO*) to drive // *vi* to drive; (*fig*) to lead; ~**se** *vr* to behave.

conducta [kon'dukta] *nf* conduct, behaviour.

conducto [kon'dukto] *nm* pipe, tube; (*fig*) channel.

conductor, a [konduk'tor, a] *a* leading, guiding // *nm* (*FÍSICA*) conductor; (*de vehículo*) driver.

conduje *etc vb ver* **conducir.**

conduzco *etc vb ver* **conducir.**

conectar [konek'tar] *vt* to connect (up), plug in.

conejo [ko'nexo] *nm* rabbit.

conexión [konek'sjon] *nf* connection.

confeccionar [konfekθjo'nar] *vt* to make (up).

confederación [konfeδera'θjon] *nf* confederation.

conferencia [konfe'renθja] *nf* conference; (*lección*) lecture; (*TELEC*) call.

conferir [konfe'rir] *vt* to award.

confesar [konfe'sar] *vt* to confess, admit.

confesión [konfe'sjon] *nf* confession.

confesionario [konfesjo'narjo] *nm* confessional.

confiado, a [kon'fjaδo, a] *a* (*crédulo*) trusting; (*presumido*) confident; (*pey*) conceited, vain.

confianza [kon'fjanθa] *nf* trust; (*aliento, confidencia*) confidence; (*familiaridad*) intimacy, familiarity; (*pey*) vanity, conceit.

confiar [kon'fjar] *vt* to entrust // *vi* to trust.

confidencia [konfi'δenθja] *nf* confidence.

confidencial [konfiδen'θjal] *a* confidential.

confidente [konfi'δente] *nm/f* confidant/e; (*policial*) informer.

configurar [konfiɣu'rar] *vt* to shape, form.

confín [kon'fin] *nm* limit; ~**es** *nmpl* edges.

confinar [konfi'nar] *vi* to confine; (*desterrar*) to banish.

confirmar [konfir'mar] *vt* to confirm.

confiscar [konfis'kar] *vt* to confiscate.

confitería [konfite'ria] *nf* confectionery; (*tienda*) confectioner's (shop).

confitura [konfi'tura] *nf* jam.

conflicto [kon'flikto] *nm* conflict; (*fig*) clash.

conformar [konfor'mar] *vt* to shape, fashion // *vi* to agree; ~**se** *vr* to conform; (*resignarse*) to resign o.s.

conforme [kon'forme] *a* (*gen*) alike, similar; (*de acuerdo*) agreed, in agreement; (*resignado*) resigned // *ad* as // *excl* agreed! // *nm* agreement // *prep*: ~ **a** in accordance with.

conformidad [konformi'ðað] nf (semejanza) similarity; (acuerdo) agreement; (resignación) resignation.

confortable [konfor'taβle] a comfortable.

confortar [konfor'tar] vt to comfort.

confrontar [konfron'tar] vt to confront; (dos personas) to bring face to face; (cotejar) to compare // vi to border.

confundir [konfun'dir] vt to blur; (equivocar) to mistake, confuse; (mezclar) to mix; (turbar) to confuse; ~se vr to become blurred; (turbarse) to get confused; (equivocarse) to make a mistake; (mezclarse) to mix.

confusión [konfu'sjon] nf confusion.

confuso, a [kon'fuso, a] a confused.

congelar [konxe'lar] vt to freeze; ~se vr (sangre, grasa) to congeal.

congeniar [konxe'njar] vi to get on (well).

conglomeración [konglomera'θjon] nf conglomeration.

congoja [kon'goxa] nf distress, grief.

congratular [kongratu'lar] vt to congratulate.

congregación [kongreβa'θjon] nf congregation.

congresista [kongre'sista] nm/f delegate, congressman/woman.

congreso [kon'greso] nm congress.

conjetura [konxe'tura] nf guess; conjeturar vt to guess.

conjugar [konxu'xar] vt to combine, fit together; (un verbo) to conjugate.

conjunción [konxun'θjon] nf conjunction.

conjunto, a [kon'xunto, a] a joint, united // nm whole; (MUS) group; en ~ as a whole.

conmemoración [konmemora'θjon] nf commemoration.

conmemorar [konmemo'rar] vt to commemorate.

conmigo [kon'miɣo] pron with me; with myself.

conminar [konmi'nar] vt to threaten.

conmiseración [konmisera'θjon] nf pity, commiseration.

conmoción [konmo'θjon] nf shock; (MED) concussion; (fig) upheaval.

conmovedor, a [konmoβe'ðor, a] a touching, moving; (impresionante) exciting.

conmover [konmo'βer] vt to shake, disturb; (fig) to move.

conmutador [konmuta'ðor] nm switch.

conocedor, a [konoθe'ðor, a] a expert, knowledgeable // nm/f expert.

conocer [kono'θer] vt (gen) to know; (por primera vez) to meet, get to know; (entender) to know about; (reconocer) to know, recognize; ~se vr (una persona) to know o.s.; (dos personas) to (get to) know each other.

conocido, a [kono'θiðo, a] a (well-)known // nm/f acquaintance.

conocimiento [konoθi'mjento] nm knowledge; (MED) consciousness; ~s nmpl (personas) acquaintances; (ciencia) knowledge sg.

conozco etc vb ver conocer.

conque ['konke] conj and so, so then.

conquista [kon'kista] nf conquest.

conquistador, a [konkista'ðor, a] a conquering // nm conqueror.

conquistar [konkis'tar] vt to conquer.

consagrar [konsa'xrar] vt (REL) to consecrate; (fig) to devote.

consciente [kons'θjente] a conscious.

consecución [konseku'θjon] nf acquisition; (de fin) attainment.

consecuencia [konse'kwenθja] nf consequence, outcome; (firmeza) consistency.

consecuente [konse'kwente] a consistent.

consecutivo, a [konseku'tiβo, a] a consecutive.

conseguir [konse'xir] vt to get, obtain; (sus fines) to attain.

consejero, a [konse'xero, a] nm/f adviser, consultant; (POL) councillor.

consejo [kon'sexo] nm advice; (POL) council.

consenso [kon'senso] nm consensus.

consentimiento [konsenti'mjento] nm consent.

consentir [konsen'tir] vt (permitir, tolerar) to consent to; (mimar) to pamper, spoil; (admitir) to admit // vi to agree, consent.

conserje [kon'serxe] nm caretaker; (portero) porter.

conserva [kon'serβa] nf (acción) preserving; (alimento) preserved food.

conservación [konserβa'θjon] nf conservation; (de alimentos, vida) preservation.

conservador, a [konserβa'ðor, a] a preservative; (POL) conservative // nm/f conservative; (de museo) keeper.

conservar [konser'βar] vt to conserve, keep; (alimentos, vida) to preserve; ~se vr to survive.

considerable [konsiðe'raβle] a considerable.

consideración [konsiðera'θjon] nf consideration; (estimación) respect.

considerado, a [konsiðe'raðo, a] a (prudente, reflexivo) considerate; (respetado) respected.

considerar [konsiðe'rar] vt to consider.

consigna [kon'sivna] nf (orden) order, instruction; (para equipajes) left-luggage office.

consigo [kon'sivo] pron (m) with him; (f) with her; (Vd.) with you; (reflexivo) with o.s.

consiguiente [konsi'vjente] a consequent; por ~ and so, therefore, consequently.

consistente [konsis'tente] a consistent; (sólido) solid, firm; (válido) sound.

consistir [konsis'tir] vi: ~ en (componerse de) to consist of; (ser resultado de) to be due to.

consolación [konsola'θjon] nf consolation.

consolar [konso'lar] *vt* to console.
consolidar [konsoli'ðar] *vt* to consolidate.
consomé [konso'me] *nm* consommé, clear soup.
consonante [konso'nante] *a* consonant, harmonious // *nf* consonant.
conspicuo, a [kons'pikwo, a] *a* conspicuous.
conspiración [konspira'θjon] *nf* conspiracy.
conspirador, a [konspira'ðor, a] *nm/f* conspirator.
conspirar [konspi'rar] *vi* to conspire.
constante [kons'tante] *a* constant.
constar [kons'tar] *vi* (*evidenciarse*) to be clear *or* evident; ~ **de** to consist of.
consternación [konsterna'θjon] *nf* consternation.
constipación [konstipa'θjon] *nf* = **constipado**.
constipado, a [konsti'paðo, a] *a*: **estar** ~ to have a cold // *nm* cold.
constitución [konstitu'θjon] *nf* constitution; **constitucional** *a* constitutional.
constituir [konstitu'ir] *vt* (*formar, componer*) to constitute, make up; (*fundar, erigir, ordenar*) to constitute, establish.
constitutivo, a [konstitu'tiβo, a] *a* constitutive, constituent.
constituyente [konstitu'jente] *a* constituent.
constreñir [konstre'ɲir] *vt* (*obligar*) to compel, oblige; (*restringir*) to restrict.
construcción [konstruk'θjon] *nf* construction, building.
constructor, a [konstruk'tor, a] *nm/f* builder.
construir [konstru'ir] *vt* to build, construct.
consuelo [kon'swelo] *nm* consolation, solace.
cónsul ['konsul] *nm* consul; **consulado** *nm* consulate.
consulta [kon'sulta] *nf* consultation.
consultar [konsul'tar] *vt* to consult.
consultorio [konsul'torjo] *nm* information bureau; (MED) surgery.
consumar [konsu'mar] *vt* to complete, carry out; (*crimen*) to commit; (*matrimonio*) to consummate.
consumición [konsumi'θjon] *nf* consumption; (*bebida*) drink; (*en restaurante*) meal.
consumidor, a [konsumi'ðor, a] *nm/f* consumer.
consumir [konsu'mir] *vt* to consume; ~**se** *vr* to be consumed; (*persona*) to waste away.
consumo [kon'sumo] *nm*, **consunción** [konsun'θjon] *nf* consumption.
contabilidad [kontaβili'ðað] *nf* accounting, book-keeping; (*profesión*) accountancy.
contacto [kon'takto] *nm* contact.
contado, a [kon'taðo, a] *a*: ~**s** (*escasos*)

numbered, scarce, few // *nm*: **al** ~ for cash.
contador [konta'ðor] *nm* (*aparato*) meter; (COM) accountant; (*de café*) counter.
contagiar [konta'xjar] *vt* (*enfermedad*) to pass on, transmit; (*persona*) to infect; ~**se** *vr* to become infected.
contagio [kon'taxjo] *nm* infection.
contagioso, a [konta'xjoso, a] *a* infectious; (*fig*) catching.
contaminación [kontamina'θjon] *nf* contamination.
contaminar [kontami'nar] *vt* to contaminate.
contar [kon'tar] *vt* (*páginas, dinero*) to count; (*anécdota*) to tell // *vi* to count; ~ **con** to rely on, count on.
contemplación [kontempla'θjon] *nf* contemplation.
contemplar [kontem'plar] *vt* to contemplate; (*mirar*) to look at.
contemporáneo, a [kontempo'raneo, a] *a, nm/f* contemporary.
contender [konten'der] *vi* (*gen*) to contend; (*en un concurso*) to compete.
contener [konte'ner] *vt* to contain, hold; (*retener*) to hold back, contain.
contenido, a [konte'niðo, a] *a* (*moderado*) restrained; (*reprimido*) suppressed // *nm* contents *pl*, content.
contentar [konten'tar] *vt* (*satisfacer*) to satisfy; (*complacer*) to please; ~**se** *vr* to be satisfied.
contento, a [kon'tento, a] *a* contented, content; (*alegre*) pleased; (*feliz*) happy // *nm* contentment; (*felicidad*) happiness.
contestación [kontesta'θjon] *nf* answer, reply.
contestar [kontes'tar] *vt* to answer, reply; (JUR) to corroborate, confirm.
contigo [kon'tiɣo] *pron* with you.
contiguo, a [kon'tiɣwo, a] *a* (*de al lado*) next; (*vecino*) adjacent, adjoining.
continental [kontinen'tal] *a* continental.
continente [konti'nente] *a, nm* continent.
contingencia [kontin'xenθja] *nf* contingency; (*riesgo*) risk; **contingente** *a, nm* contingent.
continuación [kontinwa'θjon] *nf* continuation; **a** ~ then, next.
continuar [konti'nwar] *vt* to continue, go on with // *vi* to continue, go on.
continuidad [kontinwi'ðað] *nf* continuity.
continuo, a [kon'tinwo, a] *a* (*sin interrupción*) continuous; (*acción perseverante*) continual.
contorno [kon'torno] *nm* outline; (GEO) contour; ~**s** *nmpl* neighbourhood *sg*, environs.
contorsión [kontor'sjon] *nf* contortion.
contra ['kontra] *prep, ad* against // *nm* con.
contraataque [kontraa'take] *nm* counter-attack.
contrabajo [kontra'βaxo] *nm* double bass.

contrabandista [kontraßan'dista] *nm/f* smuggler.

contrabando [kontra'ßando] *nm* (*acción*) smuggling; (*mercancías*) contraband.

contracción [kontrak'θjon] *nf* contraction; (*encogimiento*) shrinkage.

contracepción [kontraθep'θjon] *nf* contraception.

contraceptivo [kontraθep'tißo] *nm* contraceptive.

contradecir [kontraðe'θir] *vt* to contradict.

contradicción [kontraðik'θjon] *nf* contradiction.

contradictorio, a [kontraðik'torjo, a] *a* contradictory.

contraer [kontra'er] *vt* to contract; (*encoger*) to shrink; (*limitar*) to restrict; ~**se** *vr* to contract; to shrink; (*limitarse*) to limit o.s.

contragolpe [kontra'ɣolpe] *nm* backlash.

contrahacer [kontraa'θer] *vt* to copy, imitate; (*falsificar*) to forge.

contramaestre [kontrama'estre] *nm* foreman.

contrapelo [kontra'pelo]: **a** ~ *ad* the wrong way.

contrapesar [kontrape'sar] *vt* to counterbalance; (*fig*) to offset.

contrariar [kontra'rjar] *vt* (*oponerse*) to oppose; (*poner obstáculo*) to impede; (*enfadar*) to vex.

contrariedad [kontrarje'ðað] *nf* (*oposición*) opposition; (*obstáculo*) obstacle, setback; (*disgusto*) vexation, annoyance.

contrario, a [kon'trarjo, a] *a* contrary; (*de persona*) opposed; (*sentido, lado*) opposite // *nm/f* enemy, adversary; (*DEPORTE*) opponent; **de lo** ~ otherwise.

contrarrestar [kontrarres'tar] *vt* to counteract; (*pelota*) to return.

contrastar [kontras'tar] *vt* to resist // *vi* to contrast.

contraste [kon'traste] *nm* contrast.

contratante [kontra'tante] *nm/f* contractor.

contratar [kontra'tar] *vt* (*firmar un acuerdo para*) to contract for; (*empleados, obreros*) to hire, engage; ~**se** *vr* to sign on.

contratiempo [kontra'tjempo] *nm* setback.

contratista [kontra'tista] *nm/f* contractor.

contrato [kon'trato] *nm* contract.

contravención [kontraßen'θjon] *nf* contravention, violation.

contravenir [kontraße'nir] *vi*: ~ **a** to contravene, violate.

contraventana [kontraßen'tana] *nf* shutter.

contribución [kontrißu'θjon] *nf* (*municipal etc*) tax; (*ayuda*) contribution.

contribuir [kontrißu'ir] *vt, vi* to contribute; (*COM*) to pay (in taxes).

contribuyente [kontrißu'jente] *nm/f* (*COM*) taxpayer; (*que ayuda*) contributor.

control [kon'trol] *nm* control; (*inspección*) inspection, check; ~**ar** *vt* to control; to inspect, check.

controversia [kontro'ßersja] *nf* controversy.

convalecencia [konßale'θenθja] *nf* convalescence.

convalecer [konßale'θer] *vi* to convalesce, get better.

convaleciente [konßale'θjente] *a, nm/f* convalescent.

convencer [konßen'θer] *vt* to convince; (*persuadir*) to persuade.

convencimiento [konßenθi'mjento] *nm* convincing; (*persuasión*) persuasion; (*certidumbre*) conviction.

convención [konßen'θjon] *nf* convention.

convencional [konßenθjo'nal] *a* conventional.

convenido, a [konße'niðo, a] *a* agreed.

conveniencia [konße'njenθja] *nf* suitability; (*conformidad*) agreement; (*utilidad, provecho*) usefulness; ~**s** *nfpl* conventions; (*COM*) property *sg*.

conveniente [konße'njente] *a* suitable; (*útil*) useful.

convenio [kon'ßenjo] *nm* agreement, treaty.

convenir [konße'nir] *vi* (*estar de acuerdo*) to agree; (*ser conveniente*) to suit, be suitable; ~**se** *vr* to agree.

convento [kon'ßento] *nm* monastery; (*de monjas*) convent.

converger [konßer'xer], **convergir** [konßer'xir] *vi* to converge.

conversación [konßersa'θjon] *nf* conversation.

conversar [konßer'sar] *vi* to talk, converse.

conversión [konßer'sjon] *nf* conversion.

convertir [konßer'tir] *vt* to convert.

convicción [konßik'θjon] *nf* conviction.

convicto, a [kon'ßikto, a] *a* convicted, found guilty; (*condenado*) condemned.

convidado, a [konßi'ðaðo, a] *nm/f* guest.

convidar [konßi'ðar] *vt* to invite.

convincente [konßin'θente] *a* convincing.

convite [kon'ßite] *nm* invitation; (*banquete*) banquet.

convivencia [konßi'ßenθja] *nf* coexistence, living together.

convocar [konßo'kar] *vt* to summon, call (together).

convulsión [konßul'sjon] *nf* convulsion.

conyugal [konju'val] *a* conjugal.

coñac [ko'nak] *nm* cognac, brandy.

cooperación [koopera'θjon] *nf* cooperation.

cooperar [koope'rar] *vi* to cooperate.

cooperativo, a [koopera'tißo, a] *a* cooperative // *nf* cooperative.

coordinación [koorðina'θjon] *nf* coordination.

coordinar [koorði'nar] *vt* to coordinate.

copa ['kopa] *nf* cup; (*vaso*) glass; (*de árbol*) top; (*de sombrero*) crown; **~s** *nfpl* (*NAIPES*) ≈ hearts.

copia ['kopja] *nf* copy; **copiar** *vt* to copy.

copioso, a [ko'pjoso, a] *a* copious, plentiful.

copita [ko'pita] *nf* (small) glass; (*GOLF*) tee.

copla ['kopla] *nf* verse; (*canción*) (popular) song.

coqueta [ko'keta] *a* flirtatious, coquettish; **coquetear** *vi* to flirt.

coraje [ko'raxe] *nm* courage; (*ánimo*) spirit; (*ira*) anger.

coral [ko'ral] *a* choral // *nf* choir.

corazón [kora'θon] *nm* heart.

corazonada [koraθo'naða] *nf* impulse; (*presentimiento*) presentiment, hunch.

corbata [kor'βata] *nf* tie.

corcovado, a [korko'βaðo, a] *a* hunchbacked.

corchete [kor'tʃete] *nm* catch, clasp.

corcho ['kortʃo] *nm* cork; (*PESCA*) float.

cordel [kor'ðel] *nm* cord, line.

cordero [kor'ðero] *nm* lamb.

cordial [kor'ðjal] *a* cordial; **~idad** *nf* warmth, cordiality.

cordillera [korði'ʎera] *nf* range, chain (of mountains).

Córdoba ['korðoβa] *n* Cordoba; **cordobés, esa** *a* of or from Cordoba.

cordón [kor'ðon] *nm* (*cuerda*) cord, string; (*de zapatos*) lace; (*policía*) cordon.

corneta [kor'neta] *nf* bugle.

coro ['koro] *nm* chorus; (*conjunto de cantores*) choir.

corolario [koro'larjo] *nm* corollary.

corona [ko'rona] *nf* crown; (*de flores*) garland; **~ción** *nf* coronation; **coronar** *vt* to crown.

coronel [koro'nel] *nm* colonel.

coronilla [koro'niʎa] *nf* crown (of the head).

corporación [korpora'θjon] *nf* corporation.

corporal [korpo'ral] *a* corporal.

corpulento, a [korpu'lento a] *a* (*árbol*) stout; (*persona*) well-built.

corral [ko'rral] *nm* farmyard; **~illo** *nm* playpen.

correa [ko'rrea] *nf* strap; (*cinturón*) belt.

corrección [korrek'θjon] *nf* correction; (*reprensión*) rebuke; **correccional** *nm* reformatory.

correcto, a [ko'rrekto, a] *a* correct; (*persona*) well-mannered.

corredor, a [korre'ðor, a] *a* running; (*rápido*) fast // *nm* (*COM*) agent, broker; (*pasillo*) corridor, passage; (*DEPORTE*) runner.

corregir [korre'xir] *vt* (*error*) to correct; (*amonestar, reprender*) to rebuke, reprimand; **~se** *vr* to reform.

correo [ko'rreo] *nm* post, mail; (*persona*) courier; (*cartero*) postman; **C~** Post Office; **~ aéreo** airmail.

correr [ko'rrer] *vt* to run; (*viajar*) to cover, travel; (*cortinas*) to draw; (*cerrojo*) to shoot // *vi* to run; (*líquido*) to run, flow; (*moneda*) to pass, be valid; **~se** *vr* to slide, move; (*colores*) to run.

correspondencia [korrespon'denθja] *nf* correspondence; (*FERRO*) connection.

corresponder [korrespon'der] *vi* to correspond; (*convenir*) to be suitable; (*pertenecer*) to belong; (*tocar*) to concern; **~se** *vr* (*por escrito*) to correspond; (*amarse*) to have mutual affection.

correspondiente [korrespon'djente] *a* corresponding // *nm* correspondent.

corrido, a [ko'rriðo, a] *a* (*avergonzado*) abashed; (*fluido*) fluent // *nf* run, dash; (*de toros*) bullfight; **3 noches ~as** 3 nights running; **un kilo ~** a good kilo.

corriente [ko'rrjente] *a* (*agua*) running; (*fig*) flowing; (*dinero etc*) current; (*común*) ordinary, normal // *nf* current // *nm* current month.

corrillo [ko'rriʎo] *nm* huddle; (*fig*) clique.

corro ['korro] *nm* ring, circle (of people).

corroborar [korroβo'rar] *vt* to corroborate.

corroer [korro'er] *vt* to corrode; (*GEO*) to erode.

corromper [korrom'per] *vt* (*madera*) to rot; (*alimento*) to turn bad; (*fig*) to corrupt.

corrosivo, a [korro'siβo, a] *a* corrosive.

corrupción [korrup'θjon] *nf* rot, decay; (*fig*) corruption.

corsé [kor'se] *nm* corset.

cortado, a [kor'taðo, a] *a* (*con cuchillo*) cut; (*leche*) sour; (*confuso*) confused; (*disconcertado*) embarrassed; (*estilo*) abrupt // *nm* white coffee (with just a little milk).

cortador, a [korta'ðor, a] *a* cutting // *nf* cutter, slicer.

cortadura [korta'ðura] *nf* cut.

cortar [kor'tar] *vt* to cut; (*el agua*) to cut off; (*un pasaje*) to cut out // *vi* to cut; **~se** *vr* (*turbarse*) to become embarrassed; (*leche*) to turn, curdle; **~se el pelo** to have one's hair cut.

corte ['korte] *nm* cut, cutting; (*filo*) edge; (*de tela*) piece, length; **las C~s** the Spanish Parliament.

cortedad [korte'ðað] *nf* shortness; (*fig*) bashfulness, timidity.

cortejar [korte'xar] *vt* to court.

cortejo [kor'texo] *nm* entourage; **~ túnebre** funeral procession.

cortés [kor'tes] *a* courteous, polite.

cortesía [korte'sia] *nf* courtesy.

corteza [kor'teθa] *nf* (*de árbol*) bark; (*de pan*) crust.

cortina [kor'tina] *nf* curtain.

corto, a ['korto, a] *a* (*breve*) short; (*tímido*) bashful; (*poco inteligente*) not very clever; **~ de vista** short-sighted; **estar ~ de fondos** to be short of funds.

corvo, a ['korβo, a] *a* curved.

cosa ['kosa] *nf* thing; (*asunto*) affair; **~ de** about; **eso es ~ mía** that's my affair.

cosecha [ko'setʃa] *nf* (*AGR*) harvest; (*de vino*) vintage.

cosechar [kose'tʃar] *vt* to harvest, gather (in).

coser [ko'ser] *vt* to sew.

cosmético, a [kos'metiko, a] *a, nm* cosmetic.

cosquillas [kos'kiʎas] *nfpl*: **hacer ~** to tickle; **tener ~** to be ticklish.

cosquilloso, a [koski'ʎoso, a] *a* ticklish; (*fig*) touchy.

costa ['kosta] *nf* (*gasto*) cost; (*GEO*) coast.

costado [kos'taðo] *nm* side.

costal [kos'tal] *nm* sack.

costar [kos'tar] *vt* (*valer*) to cost; (*necesitar*) to require, need; **me cuesta hacer** I find it hard to do.

Costa Rica [kosta'rika] *nf* Costa Rica; **costarricense, costarriqueño, a** *a, nm/f* Costa Rican.

coste ['koste] *nm* = **costo**.

costilla [kos'tiʎa] *nf* rib; (*CULIN*) chop.

costo ['kosto] *nm* cost, price; **~ de la vida** cost of living; **~so, a** *a* costly, expensive.

costra ['kostra] *nf* crust; (*MED*) scab.

costumbre [kos'tumbre] *nf* custom, habit.

costura [kos'tura] *nf* sewing, needlework; (*de medias*) seam.

costurera [kostu'rera] *nf* dressmaker.

costurero [kostu'rero] *nm* sewing box *or* case.

cotejar [kote'xar] *vt* to compare.

cotejo [ko'texo] *nm* comparison.

cotidiano, a [koti'ðjano, a] *a* daily, day to day.

cotización [kotiθa'θjon] *nf* (*COM*) quotation, price; (*cuota*) dues *pl*.

cotizar [koti'θar] *vt* (*COM*) to quote, price; **~se** *vr*: **~se a** to sell at, fetch.

coto ['koto] *nm* (*terreno cercado*) enclosure; (*de caza*) reserve.

coyote [ko'jote] *nm* coyote, prairie wolf.

coyuntura [kojun'tura] *nf* (*ANAT*) joint; (*oportunidad*) opportunity.

cráneo ['kraneo] *nm* skull, cranium.

cráter ['krater] *nm* crater.

creación [krea'θjon] *nf* creation.

creador, a [krea'ðor, a] *a* creative // *nm/f* creator.

crear [kre'ar] *vt* to create, make.

crecer [kre'θer] *vi* (*niño*) to grow; (*precio*) to rise; (*días*) to get longer; (*mar*) to swell.

crecido, a [kre'θiðo, a] *a* (*persona, planta*) full-grown; (*cantidad*) large; (*fig*) conceited.

creciente [kre'θjente] *a* (*persona*) growing; (*cantidad*) increasing; (*luna*) crescent // *nm* crescent // *nf* flood.

crecimiento [kreθi'mjento] *nm* growth; (*aumento*) increase.

credenciales [kreðen'θjales] *nfpl* credentials.

crédito ['kreðito] *nm* credit.

credo ['kreðo] *nm* creed.

crédulo, a ['kreðulo, a] *a* credulous.

creencia [kre'enθja] *nf* belief.

creer [kre'er] *vt, vi* to think, believe; **~se** *vr* to believe o.s. (to be); **¡ya lo creo!** I should think so!

creíble [kre'iβle] *a* credible, believable.

crema ['krema] *nf* cream; (*de huevo*) custard.

cremallera [krema'ʎera] *nf* zip (fastener).

crepúsculo [kre'puskulo] *nm* twilight, dusk.

crespón [kres'pon] *nm* crêpe.

creta ['kreta] *nf* chalk.

creyente [kre'jente] *nm/f* believer.

creyó *etc vb ver* **creer.**

cría ['kria] *nf* (*de animales*) rearing, breeding; (*animal*) baby animal; (*niño*) child.

criadero [kria'ðero] *nm* nursery; (*ZOOL*) breeding place.

criado, a [kri'aðo, a] *a* bred, reared // *nm* servant // *nf* servant, maid; **mal/bien ~** badly/well brought up.

criador [kria'ðor] *nm* breeder.

crianza [kri'anθa] *nf* rearing, breeding; (*fig*) breeding.

criar [kri'ar] *vt* to suckle, feed; (*educar*) to bring up; (*producir*) to grow, produce; (*animales*) to breed.

criatura [kria'tura] *nf* creature; (*niño*) baby, (small) child.

criba ['kriβa] *nf* sieve; **cribar** *vt* to sieve.

crimen ['krimen] *nm* crime.

criminal [krimi'nal] *a, nm/f* criminal.

crin [krin] *nf* (*también* **~es** *nfpl*) mane.

crisis ['krisis] *nf inv* crisis.

crispar [kris'par] *vt* (*músculo*) to make contract; (*nervios*) to set on edge.

cristal [kris'tal] *nm* crystal; (*de ventana*) glass, pane; (*lente*) lens; **~ino, a** *a* crystalline; (*fig*) clear // *nm* lens of the eye; **~izar** *vt, vi* to crystallize.

cristiandad [kristjan'dað] *nf* Christianity.

cristianismo [kristja'nismo] *nm* Christianity.

cristiano, a [kris'tjano, a] *a, nm/f* Christian.

Cristo ['kristo] *nm* (*dios*) Christ; (*crucifijo*) crucifix.

criterio [kri'terjo] *nm* criterion; (*juicio*) judgement.

criticar [kriti'kar] *vt* to criticize.

crítico, a ['kritiko, a] *a* critical // *nm* critic // *nf* criticism.

cromo ['kromo] *nm* chrome.

crónico, a ['kroniko, a] *a* chronic // *nf* chronicle, account.

cronista [kro'nista] *nm/f* chronicler.

cruce ['kruθe] *nm* crossing; (*de carreteras*) crossroads.

crucificar [kruθifi'kar] *vt* to crucify.

crucifijo [kruθi'fixo] *nm* crucifix.

crucigrama [kruθi'ɤrama] *nm* crossword (puzzle).

crudo, a ['kruðo, a] *a* raw; (*no maduro*) unripe; (*petróleo*) crude; (*rudo, cruel*) cruel.

cruel [krwel] *a* cruel.
crueldad [krwel'ðað] *nf* cruelty.
crujido [kru'xiðo] *nm* creak.
crujir [kru'xir] *vi* (*madera*) to creak; (*dedos*) to crack; (*dientes*) to grind; (*nieve, arena*) to crunch.
cruz [kruθ] *nf* cross; (*de moneda*) tails *sg*.
cruzado, a [kru'θaðo, a] *a* crossed // *nm* crusader // *nf* crusade.
cruzar [kru'θar] *vt* to cross; ~**se** *vr* to cross; (*personas*) to pass each other.
cuaderno [kwa'ðerno] *nm* notebook; (*de escuela*) exercise book; (*NAUT*) logbook.
cuadra ['kwaðra] *nf* (*caballeriza*) stable; (*gran sala*) hall.
cuadrado, a [kwa'ðraðo, a] *a* square // *nm* (*MAT*) square; (*regla*) ruler.
cuadrar [kwa'ðrar] *vt* to square // *vi*: ~ **con** to square with, tally with; ~**se** *vr* (*soldado*) to stand to attention.
cuadrilla [kwa'ðriʎa] *nf* party, group.
cuadro ['kwaðro] *nm* square; (*de vidrio*) frame; (*PINTURA*) painting; (*TEATRO*) scene.
cuádruplo, a ['kwaðruplo, a], **cuádruple** ['kwaðruple] *a* quadruple.
cuajar [kwa'xar] *vt* to thicken; (*leche*) to curdle; (*sangre*) to congeal; (*adornar*) to adorn; ~**se** *vr* to curdle; to congeal; (*llenarse*) to fill up.
cual [kwal] *ad* like, as // *pron*: **el** ~ *etc* which; (*persona: sujeto*) who; (: *objeto*) whom // *a* such as; **cada** ~ each one; ~ **más,** ~ **menos** some more, some less; **tal** ~ just as it is.
cuál [kwal] *pron interr* which (one).
cualesquier(a) [kwales'kjer(a)] *pl* de **cualquier(a).**
cualidad [kwali'ðað] *nf* quality.
cualquiera [kwal'kjera], **cualquier** [kwal'kjer] *a* any // *pron* anybody, anyone; (*quienquiera*) whoever; **en cualquier parte** anywhere; ~ **que sea** whichever it is; (*persona*) whoever it is.
cuando ['kwando] *ad* when; (*aún si*) if, even if // *conj* (*puesto que*) since // *prep*: **yo,** ~ **niño...** when I was a child...; ~ **no sea así** even if it is not so; ~ **más** the more; ~ **menos** the less; ~ **no** if not, otherwise; **de** ~ **en** ~ from time to time.
cuándo ['kwando] *ad* when; ¿**desde** ~?, ¿**de** ~ **acá?** since when?
cuanto, a ['kwanto, a] *a* all that, as much as // *pron* all that (which), as much as; **llévate todo** ~ **quieras** take as much as you like; **en** ~ (*en seguida que*) as soon as; (*ya que*) since, inasmuch as; **en** ~ **profesor** as a teacher; **en** ~ **a** as for; ~ **más difícil sea** the more difficult it is; ~ **más hace (tanto) menos avanza** the more he does, the less he progresses; ~ **antes** as soon as possible; **unos** ~**s libros** a few books.
cuánto, a ['kwanto, a] *a* what a lot of; (*interr: sg*) how much?; (: *pl*) how many? // *pron, ad* how; (*interr: sg*) how much?; (: *pl*) how many?; ¡~ **a gente!** what a lot of people!; ¿~ **cuesta?** how much does it cost?; ¿**a** ~**s estamos?** what's the date?; **Señor no sé** ~**s** Mr. So-and-So.
cuarenta [kwa'renta] *num* forty.
cuarentena [kwaren'tena] *nf* quarantine.
cuartear [kwarte'ar] *vt* to quarter; (*dividir*) to divide up; ~**se** *vr* to crack, split.
cuartel [kwar'tel] *nm* (*de ciudad*) quarter, district; (*MIL*) barracks *pl*; ~ **general** headquarters *pl*.
cuarteto [kwar'teto] *nm* quartet.
cuarto, a ['kwarto, a] *a* fourth // *nm* (*MAT*) quarter, fourth; (*habitación*) room // *nf* (*MAT*) quarter, fourth; (*palmo*) span; ~ **de baño** bathroom; ~ **de hora** quarter (of an) hour.
cuatro ['kwatro] *num* four.
cuba ['kuβa] *nf* cask, barrel; (*fig*) drunkard.
Cuba ['kuβa] *nf* Cuba; **cubano, a** *a*, *nm/f* Cuban.
cúbico, a ['kuβiko, a] *a* cubic.
cubierto, a [ku'βjerto, a] *pp de* **cubrir** // *a* covered // *nm* cover; (*en la mesa*) place; ~**s** *nmpl* cutlery *sg* // *nf* cover, covering; (*neumático*) tyre; (*NAUT*) deck; **a** ~ **de** covered with or in.
cubo ['kuβo] *nm* cube; (*de madera*) bucket, tub; (*TEC*) drum.
cubrir [ku'βrir] *vt* to cover; ~**se** *vr* (*cielo*) to become overcast.
cucaracha [kuka'ratʃa] *nf* cockroach.
cuchara [ku'tʃara] *nf* spoon; (*TEC*) scoop; ~**da** *nf* spoonful; ~**dita** *nf* teaspoonful.
cucharita [kutʃa'rita] *nf* teaspoon.
cucharón [kutʃa'ron] *nm* ladle.
cuchichear [kutʃitʃe'ar] *vi* to whisper.
cuchilla [ku'tʃiʎa] *nf* (large) knife; (*de arma blanca*) blade.
cuchillo [ku'tʃiʎo] *nm* knife.
cuello ['kweʎo] *nm* (*ANAT*) neck; (*de vestido, camisa*) collar.
cuenca ['kwenka] *nf* (*escudilla*) hollow; (*ANAT*) eye socket; (*GEO*) bowl, deep valley.
cuenta ['kwenta] *nf* (*cálculo*) count, counting; (*en café, restaurante*) bill; (*COM*) account; (*de collar*) bead; (*fig*) account; **a fin de** ~**s** in the end; **caer en la** ~ to catch on; **darse** ~ **de** to realize; **tener en** ~ to bear in mind; **echar** ~**s** to take stock; ~ **corriente/de ahorros** current/savings account.
cuento *etc vb ver* **contar** // ['kwento] *nm* story.
cuerdo, a ['kwerðo, a] *a* sane; (*prudente*) wise, sensible // *nf* rope; (*hilo*) string; (*de reloj*) spring; **dar** ~**a a un reloj** to wind up a clock.
cuerno ['kwerno] *nm* horn.
cuero ['kwero] *nm* (*ZOOL*) skin, hide; (*TEC*) leather; **en** ~**s** stark naked; ~ **cabelludo** scalp.
cuerpo ['kwerpo] *nm* body.
cuesta ['kwesta] *nf* slope; (*en camino etc*) hill; ~ **arriba/abajo** uphill/downhill; **a** ~**s** on one's back.
cuestión [kwes'tjon] *nf* matter, question,

issue; (*riña*) quarrel, dispute.

cuesto *etc vb ver* **costar.**

cueva ['kweβa] *nf* cave; (*bodega*) cellar.

cuidado [kwi'ðaðo] *nm* care, carefulness; (*preocupación*) care, worry; *excl* careful!, look out!

cuidadoso, a [kwiða'ðoso, a] *a* careful; (*preocupado*) anxious.

cuidar [kwi'ðar] *vt* (MED) to care for; (*ocuparse de*) to take care of, look after // *vi:* ~ **de** to take care of, look after; ~**se** *vr* to look after o.s.; ~**se de hacer algo** to take care not to do something.

culebra [ku'leβra] *nf* snake.

culebrear [kuleβre'ar] *vi* to wriggle along; (*río*) to meander.

culinario, a [kuli'narjo, a] *a* culinary, cooking *cpd.*

culminación [kulmina'θjon] *nf* culmination.

culo ['kulo] *nm* bottom, backside.

culpa ['kulpa] *nf* fault; (JUR) guilt; **tener la** ~ (**de**) to be to blame (for).

culpabilidad [kulpaβili'ðað] *nf* guilt.

culpable [kul'paβle] *a* guilty // *nm/f* culprit.

culpar [kul'par] *vt* to blame; (*acusar*) to accuse.

cultivador, a [kultiβa'ðor, a] *nm/f* farmer // *nf* cultivator.

cultivar [kulti'βar] *vt* to cultivate.

cultivo [kul'tiβo] *nm* cultivation; (*plantas*) crop.

culto, a ['kulto, a] *a* (*cultivado*) cultivated; (*que tiene cultura*) cultured // *nm* (*homenaje*) worship; (*religión*) cult.

cultura [kul'tura] *nf* culture.

cumbre ['kumbre] *nf* summit, top.

cumpleaños [kumple'aɲos] *nm* birthday.

cumplido, a [kum'pliðo, a] *a* complete, perfect; (*abundante*) plentiful; (*cortés*) courteous // *nm* compliment; (*cortesía*) courtesy.

cumplimentar [kumplimen'tar] *vt* to congratulate.

cumplimiento [kumpli'mjento] *nm* (*de un deber*) fulfilment; (*acabamiento*) completion; (*cumplido*) compliment.

cumplir [kum'plir] *vt* (*orden*) to carry out, obey; (*promesa*) to carry out, fulfil; (*condena*) to serve; (*años*) to reach, attain // *vi:* ~ **con** (*deberes*) to carry out, fulfil; ~**se** *vr* (*plazo*) to expire.

cuna ['kuna] *nf* cradle, cot.

cuñado, a [ku'ɲaðo, a] *nm/f* brother/sister-in-law.

cuota ['kwota] *nf* (*parte proporcional*) share; (*cotización*) fee, dues *pl.*

cupe *etc vb ver* **caber.**

cura ['kura] *nf* (*curación*) cure; (*método curativo*) treatment // *nm* priest.

curación [kura'θjon] *nf* cure; (*acción*) curing.

curar [ku'rar] *vt* (*herida*) to treat, dress; (*enfermo*) to cure; (*carne, pescado*) to cure,

salt; (*cuero*) to tan // *vi,* ~**se** *vr* to get well, recover.

curiosear [kurjose'ar] *vt* to glance at, look over // *vi* to look round, wander round.

curiosidad [kurjosi'ðað] *nf* curiosity.

curioso, a [ku'rjoso, a] *a* curious // *nm/f* bystander, onlooker.

cursi ['kursi] *a* (*fam*) in bad taste, vulgar.

cursivo, a [kur'siβo, a] *a* italic // *nf* italics *pl.*

curso ['kurso] *nm* course; **en** ~ (*año*) current; (*proceso*) going on, under way.

curvo, a ['kurβo, a] *a* (*gen*) curved; (*torcido*) bent // *nf* (*gen*) curve, bend.

custodia [kus'toðja] *nf* care, safekeeping, custody.

custodiar [kusto'ðjar] *vt* (*guardar*) to keep, take care of; (*vigilar*) to guard, watch over.

custodio [kus'toðjo] *nm* guardian, keeper.

cutis ['kutis] *nm* skin, complexion.

cuyo, a ['kujo, a] *pron* (*de quien*) whose, of whom; (*de que*) of which.

CH

chabacano, a [tʃaβa'kano, a] *a* vulgar, coarse.

chacal [tʃa'kal] *nm* jackal.

chacota [tʃa'kota] *nf* fun (and games).

chal [tʃal] *nm* shawl.

chalán [tʃa'lan] *nm* (*pey*) shady dealer.

chaleco [tʃa'leko] *nm* waistcoat, vest (US); ~ **salvavidas** life jacket.

chalupa [tʃa'lupa] *nf* launch, boat.

champán [tʃam'pan] *nm,* **champaña** [tʃam'paɲa] *nm* champagne.

champiñón [tʃampi'ɲon] *nm* mushroom.

champú [tʃam'pu] *nm* shampoo.

chamuscar [tʃamus'kar] *vt* to scorch, sear, singe.

chantaje [tʃan'taxe] *nm* blackmail.

chapa ['tʃapa] *nf* (*de metal*) plate, sheet; (*de madera*) board, panel.

chaparrón [tʃapa'rron] *nm* downpour, cloudburst.

chapotear [tʃapote'ar] *vt* to sponge down // *vi* (*fam*) to splash about.

chapucero, a [tʃapu'θero, a] *a* rough, crude // *nm/f* bungler.

chapurrar [tʃapu'rrar], **chapurrear** [tʃapurre'ar] *vt* (*idioma*) to speak badly; (*bebidas*) to mix.

chapuzar [tʃapu'θar] *vi* to duck.

chaqueta [tʃa'keta] *nf* jacket.

charca ['tʃarka] *nf* pond, pool.

charco ['tʃarko] *nm* pool, puddle.

charla ['tʃarla] *nf* talk, chat; (*conferencia*) lecture.

charlar [tʃar'lar] *vi* to talk, chat.

charlatán, ana [tʃarla'tan, ana] *nm/f* chatterbox; (*embaidor*) trickster; (*curandero*) charlatan.

charol [tʃa'rol] *nm* varnish; (*cuero*) patent leather.

chascarrillo [tʃaska'rriʎo] *nm* (*fam*) funny story.

chasco ['tʃasko] *nm* (*broma*) trick, joke; (*desengaño*) disappointment.

chasquear [tʃaske'ar] *vt* (*engañar*) to disappoint; (*bromear*) to play a trick on; (*látigo*) to crack; (*lengua*) to click.

chasquido [tʃas'kiðo] *nm* (*de lengua*) click; (*de látigo*) crack.

chato, a ['tʃato, a] *a* flat // *excl* hey handsome/beautiful!

chaval, a [tʃa'ßal, a] *nm/f* lad/girl.

checo(e)slovaco, a [tʃeko(e)slo'ßako, a] *a, nm/f* Czech, Czechoslovak.

Checo(e)slovaquia [tʃeko(e)slo'ßakja] *nf* Czechoslovakia.

cheque ['tʃeke] *nm* cheque.

chequeo [tʃe'keo] *nm* (*MED*) check-up; (*AUTO*) service.

chequera [tʃe'kera] *nf* cheque-book.

chico, a ['tʃiko, a] *a* small, little // *nm/f* (*niño, niña*) child; (*muchacho, muchacha*) boy/girl.

chicharrón [tʃitʃa'rron] *nm* crackling.

chichón [tʃi'tʃon] *nm* bump, hump.

chiflado, a [tʃi'flaðo, a] *a* daft, barmy.

chiflar [tʃi'flar] *vt* to hiss, boo; ~**se** *vr*: ~**se por** to be/go crazy about.

chile ['tʃile] *nm* chilli, red pepper.

Chile ['tʃile] *nm* Chile; **chileno** *a, nm/f* Chilean.

chillar [tʃi'ʎar] *vi* (*persona*) to yell, scream; (*animal salvaje*) to howl; (*cerdo*) to squeal; (*puerta*) to creak.

chillido [tʃi'ʎiðo] *nm* (*de persona*) yell, scream; (*de animal*) howl; (*de frenos*) screech(ing).

chillón, ona [tʃi'ʎon, ona] *a* (*niño*) noisy; (*color*) loud, gaudy.

chimenea [tʃime'nea] *nf* chimney; (*hogar*) fireplace.

China ['tʃina] *nf*: **la ~** China.

chinche ['tʃintʃe] *nf* bug; (*TEC*) drawing pin // *nm/f* nuisance, pest.

chino, a ['tʃino, a] *a, nm/f* Chinese // *nm* (*lengua*) Chinese.

Chipre ['tʃipre] *nf* Cyprus; **chipriota, chiprlote** *a, nm/f* Cypriot.

chiquito, a [tʃi'kito, a] *a* very small, tiny // *nm/f* kid.

chirle ['tʃirle] *a* watery, wishy-washy.

chirriar [tʃi'rrjar] *vi* (*goznes*) to creak, squeak; (*pájaros*) to chirp, sing.

chirrido [tʃi'rriðo] *nm* creak(ing). squeak(ing); (*de pájaros*) chirp(ing).

chis [tʃis] *excl* sh!

chisme ['tʃisme] *nm* (*habladurías*) piece of gossip; (*fam: objeto*) thing, thingummyjig.

chismoso, a [tʃis'moso, a] *a* gossiping // *nm/f* gossip.

chispa ['tʃispa] *nf* spark; (*fig*) sparkle; (*ingenio*) wit; (*fam*) drunkenness.

chispeante [tʃispe'ante] *a* sparkling, scintillating.

chispear [tʃispe'ar] *vi* to spark; (*lloviznar*) to drizzle.

chisporrotear [tʃisporrote'ar] *vi* (*fuego*) to throw out sparks; (*leña*) to crackle; (*aceite*) to hiss, splutter.

chiste ['tʃiste] *nm* joke, funny story.

chistoso, a [tʃis'toso, a] *a* (*gracioso*) funny, amusing; (*bromista*) witty.

chivo, a ['tʃißo, a] *nm/f* (billy/nanny-)goat.

chocante [tʃo'kante] *a* startling; (*extraño*) odd; (*ofensivo*) shocking; (*antipático*) annoying.

chocar [tʃo'kar] *vi* (*coches, trenes*) to collide, crash // *vt* to shock; (*sorprender*) to startle; ~ **con** to collide with; (*fig*) to run into *or* up against; ¡**chócala!** put it there!

chocolate [tʃoko'late] *a, nm* chocolate.

chochear [tʃotʃe'ar] *vi* to dodder, be senile.

chocho, a ['tʃotʃo, a] *a* doddering, senile; (*fig*) soft, doting.

chollo ['tʃoʎo] *nm* (*fam*) bargain, snip.

choque ['tʃoke] *nm* (*impacto*) impact; (*golpe*) jolt; (*AUTO*) crash; (*ELEC, MED*) shock; (*MIL*) clash; (*fig*) conflict.

chorizo [tʃo'riðo] *nm* hard pork sausage, salami.

chorrear [tʃorre'ar] *vi* to gush, spout (out); (*gotear*) to drip, trickle.

chorro ['tʃorro] *nm* jet; (*fig*) stream.

choza ['tʃoða] *nf* hut, shack.

chuleta [tʃu'leta] *nf* chop, cutlet.

chulo ['tʃulo] *nm* (*pícaro*) rascal; (*fam: joven lindo*) dandy.

chupado, a [tʃu'paðo, a] *a* (*delgado*) skinny, gaunt; (*ajustado*) tight.

chupar [tʃu'par] *vt* to suck; (*absorber*) to absorb; ~**se** *vr* to grow thin.

churro, a ['tʃurro, a] *a* coarse // *nm* fritter.

chuscada [tʃus'kaða] *nf* funny remark, joke.

chusco, a ['tʃusko, a] *a* funny; (*persona*) coarse but amusing.

chusma ['tʃusma] *nf* rabble, mob.

D

D. *abr de* **Don**.

Da. *abr de* **Doña**.

dactilógrafo, a [dakti'loɤrafo, a] *nm/f* typist.

dádiva ['daðißa] *nf* (*donación*) donation; (*regalo*) gift.

dado, a ['daðo, a] *pp de* **dar** // *nm* die; ~**s** *nmpl* dice; ~ **que** *conj* given that.

dador, a [da'ðor, a] *nm/f* (*gen*) giver.

dama ['dama] *nf* (*gen*) lady; (*AJEDREZ*) queen; ~**s** *nfpl* draughts.

damasco [da'masko] *nm* (*tela*) damask.

damnificar [damnifi'kar] *vt* (*gen*) to harm; (*persona*) to injure.

danés, esa [da'nes, esa] *a* Danish // *nm/f* Dane.

danzar [dan'θar] *vt, vi* to dance.

dañar [da'ɲar] *vt* (*objeto*) to damage;

(*persona*) to hurt; ~**se** *vr* to get hurt.

dañino, a [da'ɲino, a] *a* harmful.

daño ['daɲo] *nm* (*a un objeto*) damage; (*a una persona*) harm, injury; ~**s y perjuicios** (*JUR*) damages; **hacer** ~ **a** to damage; to harm, injure.

dar [dar] *vt* (*gen*) to give; (*TEATRO*) to perform, put on; (*película*) to show; (*intereses*) to yield; (*naipes*) to deal; (*la hora*): ~ **las 3** to strike 3 // *vi*: ~ **a** to look out on(to), overlook; ~ **con** (*persona etc*) to meet, run into; (*idea*) to hit on; ~ **contra** to knock against, bang into; ~ **de cabeza** to fall on one's head; ~ **en** (*objeto*) to strike, hit; (*broma*) to catch on to; ~ **de sí** to give, stretch; ~**se** *vr* (*pasar*) to happen; (*presentarse*) to occur; ~**se a** to be given to; ~**se por** to consider o.s.; **dárselas de** to pose as; ~ **de comer/beber a uno** to give sb sth to eat/drink; **da lo mismo** *o* **qué más da** it's all the same; ~ **en el blanco** to hit the mark; **me da pena** it saddens me; ~**se prisa** to hurry (up).

dardo ['darðo] *nm* dart.

dársena ['darsena] *nf* dock.

datar [da'tar] *vi*: ~ **de** to date from.

dátil ['datil] *nm* date.

dato ['dato] *nm* fact, piece of information.

d. de J. C. *abr de* **después de Jesucristo** A.D. (Anno Domini).

de [de] *prep* of; from; **libro** ~ **cocina** cookery book; **el hombre** ~ **largos cabellos** the man with long hair; **guantes** ~ **cuero** leather gloves; **fue a Londres** ~ **profesor** he went to London as a teacher; **una** ~ **dos** one or the other; ~ **mañana** in the morning; **vestido** ~ **negro** dressed in black; **más/menos** ~ more/less than; ~ **cabeza** on one's head; ~ **cara a** facing.

deambular [deambu'lar] *vi* to stroll, wander.

debajo [de'βaxo] *ad* underneath; ~ **de** below, under; **por** ~ **de** beneath.

debate [de'βate] *nm* debate; **debatir** *vt* to debate.

deber [de'βer] *nm* duty // *vt* to owe // *vi*: **debe (de)** it must, it should; **debo hacerlo** I must do it; **debe de ir** he should go; ~**se** *vr*: ~**se a** to be owing *or* due to.

debido, a [de'βiðo, a] *a* proper, just; ~ **a** due to, because of.

débil ['deβil] *a* (*persona, carácter*) weak; (*luz*) dim; **debilidad** *nf* weakness; dimness; **debilidad senil** senility.

debilitar [deβili'tar] *vt* to weaken; ~**se** *vr* to grow weak.

débito ['deβito] *nm* debit.

década ['dekaða] *nf* decade.

decadencia [deka'ðenθja] *nf* decadence.

decaer [deka'er] *vi* (*declinar*) to decline; (*debilitarse*) to weaken.

decaimiento [dekai'mjento] *nm* (*declinación*) decline; (*desaliento*) discouragement; (*MED: empeoramiento*) weakening; (: *estado débil*) weakness.

decano, a [de'kano, a] *nm/f* dean.

decapitar [dekapi'tar] *vt* to behead.

decena [de'θena] *nf*: **una** ~ ten (or so).

decencia [de'θenθja] *nf* (*modestia*) modesty; (*honestidad*) respectability.

decente [de'θente] *a* (*correcto*) seemly, proper; (*honesto*) respectable.

decepción [deθep'θjon] *nf* disappointment; **decepcionar** *vt* to disappoint.

decidir [deθi'ðir] *vt* (*persuadir*) to convince, persuade; (*resolver*) to decide // *vi* to decide; ~**se** *vr*: ~**se a** to make up one's mind to.

décimo, a ['deθimo, a] *a* tenth // *nm* tenth.

decir [de'θir] *vt* (*expresar*) to say; (*contar*) to tell; (*hablar*) to speak // *nm* saying; ~**se** *vr*: **se dice que** it is said that; ~ **para/entre sí** to say to o.s.; **querer** ~ to mean.

decisión [deθi'sjon] *nf* (*resolución*) decision; (*firmeza*) decisiveness.

decisivo, a [deθi'siβo, a] *a* decisive.

declamar [dekla'mar] *vt, vi* to declaim.

declaración [deklara'θjon] *nf* (*manifestación*) statement; (*explicación*) explanation; **declarar** *vt* to declare, state; to explain // *vi* to declare; (*JUR*) to testify; **declararse** *vr* to propose.

declinar [dekli'nar] *vt* (*gen*) to decline; (*JUR*) to reject // *vi* (*el día*) to draw to a close; (*salud*) to deteriorate.

declive [de'kliβe] *nm* (*cuesta*) slope; (*inclinación*) incline.

decolorarse [dekolo'rarse] *vr* to become discoloured.

decoración [dekora'θjon] *nf* decoration.

decorado [deko'raðo] *nm* scenery, set.

decorar [deko'rar] *vt* to decorate; **decorativo, a** *a* ornamental, decorative.

decoro [de'koro] *nm* (*respeto*) respect; (*dignidad*) decency; (*recato*) decorum, propriety; ~**so, a** (*decente*) decent; (*modesto*) modest; (*digno*) proper.

decrecer [dekre'θer] *vi* to decrease, diminish.

decrépito, a [de'krepito, a] *a* decrepit.

decretar [dekre'tar] *vt* to decree; **decreto** *nm* decree.

dedal [de'ðal] *nm* thimble.

dedicación [deðika'θjon] *nf* dedication; **dedicar** *vt* (*libro*) to dedicate; (*tiempo, dinero*) to devote; (*palabras: decir, consagrar*) to dedicate, devote; **dedicatoria** *nf* (*de libro*) dedication.

dedo ['deðo] *nm* finger; ~ (**del pie**) toe; ~ **pulgar** thumb; ~ **índice** index finger; ~ **mayor** *o* **cordial** middle finger; ~ **anular** ring finger; ~ **meñique** little finger.

deducción [deðuk'θjon] *nf* deduction.

deducir [deðu'θir] *vt* (*concluir*) to deduce, infer; (*COM*) to deduct.

defecto [de'fekto] *nm* defect, flaw; (*ELEC*) fault; **defectuoso, a** *a* defective, faulty.

defender [defen'der] *vt* to defend.

defensa [de'fensa] *nf* defence; (*DEPORTE*)

back; **defensivo, a** a defensive // nf: **a la defensiva** on the defensive.
defensor, a [defen'sor, a] a defending // nm/f (abogado) defending counsel; (protector) protector.
deficiencia [defi'θjenθja] nf deficiency; **deficiente** a (defectuoso) defective; (imperfecto) deficient, wanting.
déficit ['defiθit] nm deficit.
definición [defini'θjon] nf definition.
definir [defi'nir] vt (determinar) to determine, establish; (decidir) to define; (aclarar) to clarify; **definitivo, a** a definitive; **en definitiva** definitively.
deformación [deforma'θjon] nf (alteración) deformation; (distorsión) distortion.
deformar [defor'mar] vt (gen) to deform; ~se vr to become deformed; **deforme** a (informe) deformed; (feo) ugly; (mal hecho) misshapen.
defraudar [defrau'ðar] vt (decepcionar) to disappoint; (estafar) to cheat, defraud; (engañar) to deceive.
defunción [defun'θjon] nf decease, demise.
degeneración [dexenera'θjon] nf (de las células) degeneration; (moral) degeneracy; **degenerar** vi to degenerate.
degollar [dexo'ʎar] vt (animal) to slaughter; (decapitar) to behead, decapitate.
degradar [dexra'ðar] vt to debase, degrade; ~se vr to demean o.s.
degüello [de'xweʎc] nm: **entrar a** ~ **to** slaughter, put to the sword.
degustación [dexusta'θjon] nf sampling, tasting.
deidad [dei'ðað] nf deity, divinity.
deificar [deifi'kar] vt (persona) to deify.
dejación [dexa'θjon] nf (abandono) abandonment.
dejadez [dexa'ðeθ] nf (negligencia) neglect; (descuido) untidiness, carelessness; **dejado, a** a (negligente) careless; (indolente) lazy.
dejar [de'xar] vt (gen) to leave; (permitir) to allow, let; (abandonar) to abandon, forsake; (beneficios) to produce, yield // vi: ~ **de** (parar) to stop; (no hacer) to fail to; ~ **a un lado** to leave or set aside.
dejo ['dexo] nm (LING) accent; (sabor fuerte) tang; (sabor que queda) aftertaste.
del [del] = **de** + **el**, ver **de**.
delantal [delan'tal] nm apron.
delante [de'lante] ad in front; (enfrente) opposite; (adelante) ahead; ~ **de** in front of, before.
delantero, a [delan'tero, a] a front // nm (DEPORTE) forward // nf (de vestido, casa) front part; (DEPORTE) forward line; **llevar la** ~ **a** a uno to be ahead of sb.
delatar [dela'tar] vt to inform on or against, betray; **delator, a** nm/f informer.
delegación [delexa'θjon] nf delegation; (COM) office, branch; ~ **de policía** police station; ~ **municipal** local government

office; **delegado, a** nm/f delegate; (COM) agent; **delegar** vt to delegate.
deleitar [delei'tar] vt to delight; ~se vr: ~se **con** o **en** to delight in, take pleasure in; **deleite** nm delight, pleasure.
deletrear [deletre'ar] vi to spell (out); (fig) to interpret, decipher; **deletreo** nm spelling; interpretation, decipherment.
deleznable [deleθ'naβle] a inv (frágil) fragile; (resbaloso) slippery; (fugaz) fleeting.
delfín [del'fin] nm dolphin.
delgadez [delxa'ðeθ] nf thinness, slimness; **delgado, a** a (gen) thin; (persona) slim, thin; (tierra) poor; (tela etc) light, delicate.
deliberación [deliβera'θjon] nf deliberation; **deliberar** vt to debate, discuss.
delicadeza [delika'ðeθa] nf (gen) delicacy; (refinamiento, sutileza) refinement.
delicado, a [deli'kaðo, a] a (gen) delicate; (sensible) sensitive; (quisquilloso) touchy.
delicia [de'liθja] nf delight.
delicioso, a [deli'θjoso, a] a (gracioso) delightful, agreeable; (placentero) pleasant; (exquisito) delicious.
delincuencia [delin'kwenθja] nf delinquency; **delincuente** nm/f delinquent, criminal.
delinquir [delin'kir] vi to commit an offence.
delirante [deli'rante] a delirious; **delirar** vi to be delirious, rave.
delirio [de'lirjo] nm (MED) delirium; (palabras insensatas) wanderings pl, ravings pl.
delito [de'lito] nm (infracción) offence; (crimen) crime; ~ **político/común** political/common crime.
demagogo [dema'xoxo] nm demagogue.
demanda [de'manda] nf (pedido, COM) demand; (petición) request; (JUR) action, lawsuit; **demandante** nm/f claimant.
demandar [deman'dar] vt (gen) to demand; (JUR) to sue.
demarcación [demarka'θjon] nf (de terreno) demarcation; **demarcar** vt to demarcate.
demás [de'mas] a: **los** ~ **niños** the other children, the remaining children // pron: **los/las** ~ the others, the rest (of them); **lo** ~ the rest (of it) // ad besides.
demasía [dema'sia] nf (exceso) excess, surplus; (atrevimiento) boldness; (insolencia) outrage; **comer en** ~ to eat to excess.
demasiado, a [dema'sjaðo, a] a too, too much; ~s too many // ad too, too much; **¡es** ~! it's too much!
demencia [de'menθja] nf (locura) madness; **demente** nm/f lunatic // a mad, insane.
democracia [demo'kraθja] nf democracy.
demócrata [de'mokrata] nm/f democrat; **democrático, a** a democratic.

demoler [demo'ler] vt to demolish; **demolición** nf demolition.

demonio [de'monjo] nm devil, demon; ¡~s! hell!, confound it!; ¿cómo ~s? how the hell?

demora [de'mora] nf delay; **demorar** vt (retardar) to delay, hold back; (dilatar) to hold up // vi to linger, stay on.

demostración [demostra'θjon] nf (de teorema) demonstration; (de afecto) show, display.

demostrar [demos'trar] vt (probar) to prove; (mostrar) to show; (manifestar) to demonstrate; **demostrativo**, a a demonstrative.

denegar [dene'xar] vt (rechazar) to refuse; (JUR) to reject.

denigrar [deni'xrar] vt (desacreditar, infamar) to denigrate; (injuriar) to insult.

denominación [denomina'θjon] nf (nombramiento) designation; (clase) denomination.

denotar [deno'tar] vt (indicar) to indicate; (significar) to denote.

densidad [densi'ðað] nf (FÍSICA) density; (fig) thickness.

denso, a ['denso, a] a (apretado) solid; (espeso, pastoso) thick; (fig) heavy.

dentadura [denta'ðura] nf (set of) teeth pl; ~ postiza false teeth pl.

dentera [den'tera] nf (sensación desagradable) the shivers pl, the shudders pl; (envidia) envy, jealousy; (deseo) desire.

dentista [den'tista] nm/f dentist.

dentro ['dentro] ad inside // prep: ~ de in, inside, within; vayamos a ~ let's go inside; mirar por ~ to look inside; ~ de tres meses within three months.

denuedo [de'nweðo] nm boldness, daring.

denuncia [de'nunθja] nf (delación) denunciation; (acusación) accusation; (de accidente) report; **denunciar** vt to report; (delatar) to inform on or against.

departamento [departa'mento] nm (sección administrativa) department, section; (de caja, tren) compartment; (AM: piso) apartment, flat.

dependencia [depen'denθja] nf dependence; (POL) dependency; (COM) office, section.

depender [depen'der] vi: ~ de to depend on.

dependienta [depen'djenta] nf saleswoman, shop assistant; **dependiente** a dependent // nm salesman.

deplorable [deplo'raβle] a deplorable; **deplorar** vt to deplore.

deponer [depo'ner] vt to lay down // vi (JUR) to give evidence; (declarar) to testify.

deportar [depor'tar] vt to deport.

deporte [de'porte] nm sport; **deportista** a sports cpd // nm/f sportsman/woman.

depositante [deposi'tante], **depositador, a** [deposita'ðor, a] nm/f depositor.

depositar [deposi'tar] vt (dinero) to deposit; (mercaderías) to put away, store;

(AM: persona) to confide; ~se vr to settle; ~lo, a nm/f trustee.

depósito [de'posito] nm (gen) deposit; (de mercaderías) warehouse, store; (de agua, gasolina etc) tank; ~ de equipajes cloakroom.

depravar [depra'βar] vt to deprave; ~se vr to become depraved.

depreciar [depre'θjar] vt to depreciate, reduce the value of; ~se vr to depreciate, lose value.

depredación [depreða'θjon] nf (saqueo, pillaje) pillage; (malversación) depredation.

depresión [depre'sjon] nf depression.

deprimido, a [depri'miðo, a] a depressed.

deprimir [depri'mir] vt to depress; ~se vr (persona) to become depressed.

depuración [depura'θjon] nf purification; (POL) purge; **depurar** vt to purify; (purgar) to purge.

derecha [de'retʃa] nf right(-hand) side; (POL) right.

derechamente [deretʃa'mente] ad (dirección) straight.

derecho, a [de'retʃo, a] a right, right-hand // nm (privilegio) right; (lado) right(-hand) side; (leyes) law // ad straight, directly; ~s nmpl (de aduana) duty sg; (de autor) royalties; tener ~ a to have a right to.

deriva [de'riβa] nf: ir o estar a la ~ to drift, be adrift.

derivación [deriβa'θjon] nf derivation.

derivar [deri'βar] vt (gen) to derive; (desviar) to drift; ~se vr to derive, be derived; to drift.

derramamiento [derrama'mjento] nm (de sangre) shedding; (dispersión) spilling.

derramar [derra'mar] vt to spill; (echar) to pour out; (dispersar) to scatter; ~se vr to pour out; ~ lágrimas to weep.

derrame [de'rrame] nm (de líquido) spilling; (de sangre) shedding; (de tubo etc) overflow; (perdida) loss, leakage; (MED) discharge; (declive) slope.

derredor [derre'ðor] ad: al o en ~ de around, about.

derretido, a [derre'tiðo, a] a melted, molten.

derretir [derre'tir] vt (gen) to melt; (nieve) to thaw; (fig) to squander; ~se vr to melt.

derribar [derri'βar] vt to knock down; (construcción) to demolish; (persona, gobierno, político) to bring down; ~se vr to fall down.

derrocar [derro'kar] vt (despeñar) to demolish, knock down; (gobierno) to bring down, overthrow.

derrochar [derro'tʃar] vt to squander **derroche** nm (despilfarro) waste squandering.

derrota [de'rrota] nf (camino, vereda) road, route; (NAUT) course; (MIL) defeat rout; (fig) disaster; **derrotar** vt (gen) to defeat; (destruir) to ruin; **derrotero** n (rumbo) course.

derrumbar [derrum'bar] *vt* to throw down; ~**se** *vr* (*despeñarse*) to collapse; (*precipitarse*) to throw o.s. down.

desabotonar [desaβoto'nar] *vt* to unbutton, undo // *vi* to open out; ~**se** *vr* to come undone.

desabrido, a [desa'βriðo, a] *a* (*insípido, soso*) insipid, tasteless; (*persona*) rude, surly; (*respuesta*) sharp.

desabrochar [desaβro'tʃar] *vt* (*botones, broches*) to undo, unfasten; (*fig*) to expose; ~**se** *vr* to confide, unburden o.s.

desacato [desa'kato] *nm* (*falta de respeto*) disrespect; (*irreverencia*) insulting behaviour; (*JUR*) contempt.

desacertado, a [desaθer'taðo, a] *a* (*equivocado*) mistaken; (*inoportuno*) unwise.

desacertar [desaθer'tar] *vi* (*errar*) to be mistaken; (*desatinar*) to act unwisely.

desacierto [desa'θjerto] *nm* mistake, error.

desacomodar [desakomo'ðar] *vt* (*molestar*) to put out, inconvenience; **desacomodo** *nm* (*incomodidad*) inconvenience; (*molestia*) trouble.

desaconsejado, a [desakonse'xaðo, a] *a* ill-advised; **desaconsejar** *vt* to dissuade, advise against.

desacordarse [desakor'ðarse] *vr* (*MUS*) to get out of tune; **desacorde** *a inv* discordant.

desacreditar [desakreði'tar] *vt* (*desprestigiar*) to discredit, bring into disrepute; (*denigrar*) to run down.

desacuerdo [desa'kwerðo] *nm* (*conflicto*) discord, disagreement; (*error*) error, blunder.

desafecto, a [de.sa'fekto, a] *a* (*opuesto*) disaffected // *nm* (*hostilidad*) disaffection.

desafiar [desa'fjar] *vt* (*retar*) to challenge; (*enfrentarse a*) to defy.

desafilar [desafi'lar] *vt* to blunt; ~**se** *vr* to become blunt.

desafinado, a [desafi'naðo] *a*: estar ~ to be out of tune; **desafinarse** *vr* (*MUS*) to go out of tune.

desafío [desa'fio] *nm* (*reto*) challenge; (*combate*) duel; (*resistencia*) defiance; (*competencia*) competition.

desafortunado, a [desafortu'naðo, a] *a* (*desgraciado*) unfortunate, unlucky.

desagradable [desaɣra'ðaßle] *a* (*fastidioso, enojoso*) unpleasant; (*irritante*) disagreeable.

desagradar [desaɣra'ðar] *vi* (*disgustar*) to displease; (*molestar*) to bother; **desagradecido, a** *a* ungrateful.

desagrado [desa'ɣraðo] *nm* (*disgusto*) displeasure; (*contrariedad*) dissatisfaction.

desagraviar [desaɣra'βjar] *vt* to make amends to; **desagravio** *nm* (*recompensa*) amends; (: *en efectivo*) compensation.

desaguadero [desaɣwa'ðero] *nm* drain.

desagüe [des'aɣwe] *nm* (*de un líquido*) drainage; (*cañería*) drainpipe.

desaguisado, a [desaɣi'saðo, a] *a* illegal // *nm* outrage.

desahogado, a [desao'xaðo, a] *a* (*descarado*) brazen, impudent; (*holgado*) comfortable; (*espacioso*) roomy.

desahogar [desao'xar] *vt* (*consolar*) to console; (*aliviar*) to ease, relieve; (*ira*) to vent; ~**se** *vr* (*distenderse*) to take it easy; (*desfogarse*) to let off steam.

desahogo [desa'oxo] *nm* (*alivio*) relief; (*comodidad*) comfort, ease; (*descaro*) impudence.

desahuciar [desau'θjar] *vt* (*enfermo*) to give up hope for; (*inquilino*) to evict; **desahucio** *nm* eviction.

desairado, a [desai'raðo, a] *a* (*menospreciado*) disregarded; (*desgarbado*) shabby.

desairar [desai'rar] *vt* (*menospreciar*) to slight, snub; (*ultrajar*) to dishonour.

desaire [des'aire] *nm* (*afrenta*) rebuff; (*menosprecio*) slight; (*falta de garbo*) unattractiveness, lack of charm.

desajustar [desaxus'tar] *vt* (*desarreglar*) to disarrange; (*desconcertar*) to throw off balance; ~**se** *vr* to get out of order; (*cintura*) to loosen.

desajuste [desa'xuste] *nm* (*de máquina*) disorder; (*situación*) imbalance.

desalentador, a [desalenta'ðor, a] *a* disheartening; **desalentar** *vt* (*desanimar*) to discourage; **desalentar a uno** to make sb breathless.

desaliento [desa'ljento] *nm* discouragement.

desalinear [desaline'ar] *vt* to throw out of the straight; ~**se** *vr* to go off the straight.

desaliño [desa'liɲo] *nm* (*negligencia*) slovenliness.

desalmado, a [desal'maðo, a] *a* (*cruel*) cruel, heartless.

desalojamiento [desaloxa'mjento] *nm* ousting; (*cambio de residencia*) removal; (: *forzado*) eviction.

desalojar [desalo'xar] *vt* (*expulsar, echar*) to eject; (*abandonar*) to abandon, evacuate // *vi* to move out.

desamarrar [desama'rrar] *vt* to untie; (*NAUT*) to cast off.

desamor [desa'mor] *nm* (*frialdad*) indifference; (*odio*) dislike; (*enemistad*) enmity.

desamparado, a [desampa'raðo, a] *a* (*persona*) helpless; (*lugar: expuesto*) exposed; (*desierto*) deserted.

desamparar [desampa'rar] *vt* (*abandonar*) to desert, abandon; (*JUR*) to leave defenceless; (*barco*) to abandon.

desandar [desan'dar] *vt*: ~ **lo andado** o **el camino** to retrace one's steps.

desanimado, a [desani'maðo, a] *a* (*persona*) downhearted; (*espectáculo, fiesta*) dull; **desanimar** *vt* (*desalentar*) to discourage; (*deprimir*) to depress.

desapacible [desapa'θißle] *a* (*gen*) unpleasant; (*carácter*) disagreeable; (*voz*) harsh.

desaparecer [desapare'θer] vt (gen) to hide // vi (gen) to disappear; (el sol, la luz) to vanish; **desaparición** nf disappearance.

desapego [desa'peɣo] nm (frialdad) coolness; (distancia) detachment.

desapercibido, a [desaperθi'βiðo, a] a (desprevenido) unprepared; **pasar** ~ to go unnoticed.

desaplicación [desaplika'θjon] nf (negligencia) slackness; (ocio) laziness; **desaplicado, a** a slack; lazy.

desaprensivo, a [desapren'siβo, a] a unscrupulous.

desaprobar [desapro'βar] vt (reprobar) to disapprove of; (condenar) to condemn; (no consentir) to reject.

desaprovechado, a [desaproβe'tʃaðo, a] a (improductivo) unproductive; (atrasado) backward; **desaprovechar** vt to waste.

desarmar [desar'mar] vt (MIL, fig) to disarm; (TEC) to take apart, dismantle; **desarme** nm disarmament.

desarraigar [desarrai'ɣar] vt to uproot; **desarraigo** nm uprooting.

desarreglado, a [desarre'ɣlaðo, a] a (TEC) out of order; (desordenado) disorderly, untidy.

desarreglar [desarre'ɣlar] vt (desordenar) to disarrange; (mecánica) to put out of order; (trastocar) to upset, disturb.

desarreglo [desa'rreɣlo] nm (de casa, persona) untidiness; (desorden) disorder.

desarrollar [desarro'ʎar] vt (gen) to develop; (extender) to unfold; ~se vr to develop; (extenderse) to open (out); (film) to develop; **desarrollo** nm development.

desarticular [desartiku'lar] vt (hueso) to put out; (objeto) to take apart; (fig) to break up.

desaseo [desa'seo] nm (suciedad) slovenliness; (desarreglo) untidiness.

desasir [desa'sir] vt to loosen; ~se vr to extricate o.s.; ~se de to let go, give up.

desasosegar [desasose'ɣar] vt (inquietar) to disturb; (afligir) to make uneasy; ~se vr to become uneasy.

desasosiego [desaso'sjeɣo] nm (intranquilidad) uneasiness; (aflicción) restlessness; (ansiedad) anxiety.

desastrado, a [desas'traðo, a] a (desaliñado) shabby; (sucio) dirty; (desgraciado, adverso) wretched.

desastre [de'sastre] nm disaster; **desastroso, a** a disastrous.

desatado, a [desa'taðo, a] a (desligado) untied; (violento) violent, wild.

desatar [desa'tar] vt (nudo) to untie; (paquete) to undo; (separar) to detach; ~se vr (zapatos) to come untied; (tormenta) to break.

desatender [desaten'der] vt (no prestar atención a) to disregard; (abandonar) to neglect; (invitado) to slight.

desatento, a [desa'tento, a] a (distraído) inattentive; (descortés) discourteous.

desatinado, a [desati'naðo, a] a (disparatado) wild, reckless; (absurdo) foolish, silly; **desatinar** vi (desvariar) to behave foolishly; **desatino** nm (idiotez) foolishness, folly; (error) blunder.

desautorizado, a [desautori'θaðo, a] a unauthorized; **desautorizar** vt (oficial) to deprive of authority; (informe) to deny.

desavenencia [desaβe'nenθja] nf (desacuerdo) disagreement; (discrepancia) rift, quarrel.

desaventajado, a [desaβenta'xaðo, a] a (inferior) inferior; (poco ventajoso) disadvantageous.

desayunar [desaju'nar] vi to have breakfast // vt to have for breakfast; **desayuno** nm breakfast.

desazón [desa'θon] nf (insipidez) tastelessness; (angustia) anxiety; (fig) annoyance.

desazonar [desaθo'nar] vt to make tasteless; (fig) to annoy, upset; ~se vr (enojarse) to be annoyed; (preocuparse) to worry, be anxious; (MED) to be off colour.

desbandarse [desβan'darse] vr (MIL) to disband; (fig) to flee in disorder.

desbarajuste [desβara'xuste] nm confusion, disorder.

desbaratar [desβara'tar] vt (deshacer, destruir) to ruin; (malgastar) to squander; (mecánica) to take apart.

desbordar [desβor'ðar] vt (sobrepasar) to go beyond; (exceder) to exceed // vi, ~se vr (río) to overflow; (entusiasmo) to erupt; (persona) to express one's feelings freely.

descabalgar [deskaβal'ɣar] vi to dismount.

descabellado, a [deskaβe'ʎaðo, a] a (disparatado) wild, crazy; (insensato) ridiculous.

descabellar [deskaβe'ʎar] vt to ruffle; (TAUR: toro) to give the coup de grace to.

descabezar [deskaβe'θar] vt (persona) to behead; (árbol) to lop; ~se vr (AGR) to shed the grain; (fig) to rack one's brains.

descafeinado [deskafei'naðo] nm decaffeinated coffee.

descalabro [deska'laβro] nm blow; (desgracia) misfortune.

descalzar [deskal'θar] vt (zapato) to take off; **descalzo, a** a barefoot(ed); (fig) destitute.

descaminado, a [deskami'naðo, a] a (equivocado) on the wrong road; (fig) misguided.

descaminar [deskami'nar] vt (alguien) to misdirect; (: fig) to lead astray; ~se vr (en la ruta) to go the wrong way; (fig) to go astray.

descansado, a [deskan'saðo, a] a (gen) rested; (que tranquiliza) restful; **descansar** vt (gen) to rest // vi to rest, have a rest; (echarse) to lie down.

descanso [des'kanso] nm (reposo) rest; (alivio) relief; (pausa) break; (DEPORTE) interval, half time.

descarado, a [deska'raðo, a] a (sin

vergüenza) shameless; (*insolente*) cheeky; **descararse** *vr* to be insolent *or* cheeky.
descarga [des'karɣa] *nf* (*ARQ. ELEC. MIL*) discharge; (*NAUT*) unloading.
descargadero [deskarɣa'ðero] *nm* wharf.
descargar [deskar'ɣar] *vt* to unload; (*golpe*) to let fly; ~**se** *vr* to unburden o.s.; **descargo** *nm* unloading; (*COM*) receipt; (*JUR*) evidence.
descarnado, a [deskar'naðo, a] *a* scrawny; (*fig*) bare.
descaro [des'karo] *nm* (*atrevimiento*) shamelessness, nerve; (*insolencia*) cheek.
descarriar [deska'rrjar] *vt* (*descaminar*) to misdirect; (*fig*) to lead astray; ~**se** *vr* (*perderse*) to lose one's way; (*separarse*) to stray; (*pervertirse*) to err, go astray.
descarrilamiento [deskarrila'mjento] *nm* (*de tren*) derailment.
descartar [deskar'tar] *vt* (*rechazar*) to reject; (*poner a un lado*) to set aside; (*eliminar*) to rule out; ~**se** *vr* (*NAIPES*) to discard; ~**se de** to shirk; **descartado, a** *a* rejected; set aside, eliminated.
descendencia [desθen'denθja] *nf* (*origen*) origin, descent; (*hijos*) offspring.
descender [desθen'der] *vt* (*bajar: escaleras*) to go down; (: *equipajes*) to take down // *vi* to descend; (*temperatura, nivel*) to fall, drop; ~ **de** to be descended from.
descendiente [desθen'djente] *nm/f* descendant.
descenso [des'θenso] *nm* descent; (*de temperatura*) drop.
descifrar [desθi'frar] *vt* to decipher.
descolgar [deskol'ɣar] *vt* (*bajar*) to take down; (*teléfono*) to pick up; ~**se** *vr* to let o.s. down.
descolorir [deskolo'rir], **descolorar** [deskolo'rar] *vt* = **decolorar**.
descomedido, a [deskome'ðiðo, a] *a* (*descortés*) rude; (*excesivo*) excessive.
descompaginar [deskompaxi'nar] *vt* (*desordenar*) to disarrange, mess up.
descompasado, a [deskompa'saðo, a] *a* (*sin proporción*) out of all proportion; (*excesivo*) excessive.
descomponer [deskompo'ner] *vt* (*desordenar*) to disarrange, disturb; (*TEC*) to put out of order; (*dividir*) to break down (into parts); (*fig*) to provoke; ~**se** *vr* (*corromperse*) to rot, decompose; (*el tiempo*) to change (for the worse); (*TEC*) to break down; (*irritarse*) to lose one's temper.
descomposición [deskomposi'θjon] *nf* (*gen*) breakdown; (*de fruta etc*) decomposition.
descompostura [deskompos'tura] *nf* (*TEC*) breakdown; (*desorganización*) disorganization; (*desorden*) untidiness.
descompuesto, a [deskom'pwesto, a] *a* (*corrompido*) decomposed; (*roto*) broken; (*descarado*) brazen; (*furioso*) angry.
desconcertado, a [deskonθer'taðo, a] *a* disconcerted, bewildered.
desconcertar [deskonθer'tar] *vt*

(*confundir*) to baffle; (*incomodar*) to upset, put out; (*TEC*) to put out of order; (*ANAT*) to dislocate; ~**se** *vr* (*turbarse*) to be upset.
desconcierto [deskon'θjerto] *nm* (*gen*) disorder; (*daño*) damage; (*desorientación*) uncertainty; (*inquietud*) uneasiness.
desconectar [deskonek'tar] *vt* to disconnect.
desconfianza [deskon'fjanθa] *nf* distrust; **desconfiar** *vi* to be distrustful; **desconfiar de** to distrust, suspect.
desconocer [deskono'θer] *vt* (*alguien*) to ignore; (*ignorar*) not to know, be ignorant of; (*no recordar*) to fail to remember; (*no aceptar*) to deny; (*repudiar*) to disown.
desconocimiento [deskonoθi'mjento] *nm* (*falta de conocimientos*) ignorance; (*repudio*) disregard; (*ingratitud*) ingratitude.
desconsiderado, a [deskonsiðe'raðo, a] *a* (*descuidado*) inconsiderate; (*insensible*) thoughtless.
desconsolar [deskonso'lar] *vt* to distress; ~**se** *vr* to despair.
desconsuelo [deskon'swelo] *nm* (*tristeza*) distress; (*desesperación*) despair.
descontar [deskon'tar] *vt* (*deducir*) to take away, deduct; (*rebajar*) to discount; (*predecir, dar por cierto*) to take for granted.
descontento, a [deskon'tento, a] *a* dissatisfied // *nm* dissatisfaction, discontent.
descorazonar [deskoraθo'nar] *vt* to discourage, dishearten.
descorchar [deskor'tʃar] *vt* to uncork.
descortés [deskor'tes] *a* (*mal educado*) discourteous; (*grosero*) rude.
descoser [desko'ser] *vt* to unstitch; ~**se** *vr* to come apart (at the seams).
descosido, a [desko'siðo, a] *a* (*costura*) unstitched; (*indiscreto*) indiscreet; (*desordenado*) disjointed.
descoyuntar [deskojun'tar] *vt* (*ANAT*) to dislocate.
descrédito [des'kreðito] *nm* discredit.
descreído, a [deskre'iðo, a] *a* (*incrédulo*) incredulous; (*falto de fe*) unbelieving.
describir [deskri'ßir] *vt* to describe.
descripción [deskrip'θjon] *nf* description.
descrito [des'krito] *pp de* **describir**.
descuajar [deskwa'xar] *vt* (*disolver*) to melt; (*planta*) to pull out by the roots.
descubierto, a [desku'ßjerto, a] *pp de* **descubrir** // *a* uncovered, bare; (*persona*) bareheaded; **al** ~ in the open.
descubrimiento [deskußri'mjento] *nm* (*hallazgo*) discovery; (*revelación*) revelation.
descubrir [desku'ßrir] *vt* to discover, find; (*inaugurar*) to unveil; (*vislumbrar*) to detect; (*revelar*) to reveal, show; (*quitar la tapa*) to uncover; ~**se** *vr* to reveal o.s.; (*quitarse sombrero*) to take off one's hat; (*confesar*) to confess.
descuento [des'kwento] *nm* discount; ~ **jubilatorio** retirement pension.

descuidado, a [deskwi'ðaðo, a] *a* (*sin cuidado*) careless; (*desordenado*) untidy; (*olvidadizo*) forgetful; (*dejado*) neglected; (*desprevenido*) unprepared.

descuidar [deskwi'ðar] *vt* (*dejar*) to neglect; (*olvidar*) to overlook // *vi*, **~se** *vr* (*distraerse*) to be careless; (*estar desaliñado*) to let o.s. go; (*desprevenirse*) to drop one's guard; ¡**descuida!** don't worry!; **descuido** *nm* (*dejadez*) carelessness; (*olvido*) negligence.

desde ['desðe] *ad* from; ~ **que** *conj* since; ~ **lejos** from afar; ~ **ahora en adelante** from now onwards; ~ **hace 3 días** for 3 days now; ~ **luego** of course.

desdecirse [desðe'θirse] *vr* (*de promesa*) to go back on one's word.

desdén [des'ðen] *nm* scorn.

desdeñar [desðe'nar] *vt* (*despreciar*) to scorn.

desdicha [des'ðitʃa] *nf* (*desgracia*) misfortune; (*infelicidad*) unhappiness; **desdichado, a** *a* (*sin suerte*) unlucky; (*infeliz*) unhappy.

desdoblar [desðo'ßlar] *vt* (*extender*) to spread out; (*desplegar*) to unfold; (*separar en dos*) to split.

desear [dese'ar] *vt* to want, desire, wish for.

desecar [dese'kar] *vt*, **~se** *vr* to dry up.

desechar [dese'tʃar] *vt* (*basura*) to throw out *or* away; (*ideas*) to reject, discard; **desechos** *nmpl* rubbish *sg*, waste *sg*.

desembalar [desemba'lar] *vt* to unpack.

desembarazado, a [desembara'θaðo, a] *a* (*libre*) clear, free; (*desenvuelto*) free and easy.

desembarazar [desembara'θar] *vt* (*desocupar*) to clear; (*desenredar*) to free; **~se** *vr*: **~se de** to free o.s. of, get rid of.

desembarcar [desembar'kar] *vt*, *vi*, **~se** *vr* to land.

desembocadura [desemboka'ðura] *nf* (*de río*) mouth; (*de calle*) opening.

desembocar [desembo'kar] *vi* to flow into; (*fig*) to result in.

desembolso [desem'bolso] *nm* payment; **~s** *nmpl* expenses; ~ **inicial** deposit, down payment.

desemejante [deseme'xante] *a* dissimilar, unlike; **desemejanza** *nf* dissimilarity.

desempeñar [desempe'nar] *vt* (*cargo*) to hold; (*papel*) to perform; (*lo empeñado*) to redeem; **~se** *vr* to get out of debt; ~ **un papel** to play (a role).

desempeño [desem'peno] *nm* redeeming; (*de cargo*) occupation; (*TEATRO*, *fig*) performance.

desempleado, a [desemple'aðo, a] *nm/f* unemployed person; **desempleo** *nm* unemployment.

desencadenar [desenkaðe'nar] *vt* to unchain; (*ira*) to unleash; **~se** *vr* to break loose; (*tormenta*) to burst.

desencajar [desenka'xar] *vt* (*hueso*) to put out of joint; (*mandíbula*) to dislocate;

(*mecanismo*, *pieza*) to disconnect, disengage.

desencanto [desen'kanto] *nm* disillusionment.

desenfadado, a [desenfa'ðaðo, a] *a* (*desenvuelto*) uninhibited; (*descarado*) forward; **desenfado** *nm* (*libertad*) freedom; (*comportamiento*) free and easy manner; (*descaro*) forwardness.

desenfrenado, a [desenfre'naðo, a] *a* (*descontrolado*) uncontrolled; (*inmoderado*) unbridled; **desenfreno** *nm* (*vicio*) wildness; (*de las pasiones*) lack of self-control.

desengañar [desenga'nar] *vt* to disillusion; **~se** *vr* to become disillusioned; **desengaño** *nm* disillusionment; (*decepción*) disappointment.

desenlace [desen'laθe] *nm* outcome.

desenmarañar [desenmara'nar] *vt* (*desenredar*) to disentangle; (*fig*) to unravel.

desenredar [desenre'ðar] *vt* to resolve; (*intriga*) to unravel; **~se** *vr* to extricate o.s.

desentenderse [desenten'derse] *vr*: ~ **de** to pretend to be ignorant about; (*apartarse*) to have nothing to do with.

desenterrar [desente'rrar] *vt* to exhume; (*tesoro*, *fig*) to unearth, dig up.

desentrañar [desentra'nar] *vt* to disembowel; (*misterio*) to unravel.

desentumecer [desentume'θer] *vt* (*pierna etc*) to stretch; (*DEPORTE*) to loosen up.

desenvoltura [desenßol'tura] *nf* (*libertad*, *gracia*) ease; (*descaro*) free and easy manner; (*desvergüenza*) forwardness.

desenvolver [desenßol'ßer] *vt* (*paquete*) to unwrap; (*madeja*) to disentangle; (*fig*) to develop; **~se** *vr* (*desarrollarse*) to unfold, develop; (*arreglárselas*) to extricate o.s.

deseo [de'seo] *nm* desire, wish; **~so, a**: **estar ~so de** to be anxious to.

desequilibrado, a [desekili'ßraðo, a] *a* unbalanced.

desertar [deser'tar] *vi* to desert.

desesperación [desespera'θjon] *nf* (*impaciencia*) desperation, despair; (*irritación*) fury.

desesperar [desespe'rar] *vt* to drive to despair; (*exasperar*) to drive to distraction // *vi*: ~ **de** to despair of; **~se** *vr* to despair; lose hope.

desestimar [desesti'mar] *vt* (*menospreciar*) to have a low opinion of; (*rechazar*) to reject.

desfachatez [desfatʃa'teθ] *nf* (*insolencia*) impudence; (*descaro*) cheek.

desfalco [des'falko] *nm* embezzlement.

desfallecer [desfaʎe'θer] *vi* (*perder las fuerzas*) to become weak; (*desvanecerse*) to faint.

desfavorable [desfaßo'raßle] *a* unfavourable.

desfigurar [desfiɣu'rar] *vt* (*cara*) to disfigure; (*cuerpo*) to deform.

desfilar [desfi'lar] *vi* to parade; **desfile** *nm* procession.

desgaire [des'ɣaire] *nm* (*desaliño, desgano*) slovenliness; (*menosprecio*) disdain.

desgajar [desɣa'xar] *vt* (*arrancar*) to tear off; (*romper*) to break off; **~se** *vr* to come off.

desgana [des'ɣana] *nf* (*falta de apetito*) loss of appetite; (*renuencia*) unwillingness; **desganarse** *vr* to lose one's appetite; (*cansarse*) to become bored.

desgarrar [desɣa'rrar] *vt* to tear (up); (*fig*) to shatter; **desgarro** *nm* (*muscular*) tear; (*aflicción*) grief; (*descaro*) impudence.

desgastar [desɣas'tar] *vt* (*deteriorar*) to wear away or down; (*estropear*) to spoil; **~se** *vr* to get worn out; **desgaste** *nm* wear (and tear); (*MED*) weakening, decline.

desgracia [des'ɣraθja] *nf* misfortune; (*accidente*) accident; (*vergüenza*) disgrace; (*contratiempo*) setback; **por ~** unfortunately.

desgraciado, a [desɣra'θjaðo, a] *a* (*infortunado*) unlucky, unfortunate; (*miserable*) wretched; (*infeliz*) miserable; (*feo*) ugly; (*desagradable*) unpleasant.

desgreñado, a [desɣre'paðo, a] *a* dishevelled.

deshacer [desa'θer] *vt* (*casa*) to break up; (*dañar*) to damage; (*TEC*) to take apart; (*enemigo*) to defeat; (*diluir*) to melt; (*contrato*) to break; (*intriga*) to solve; **~se** *vr* (*disolverse*) to melt; (*despedazarse*) to come apart *or* undone; **~se de** to get rid of; **~se en lágrimas** to burst into tears.

deshecho, a [des'etʃo, a] *a* undone.

deshelar [dese'lar] *vt* (*cañería*) to thaw; (*heladera*) to defrost.

desheredar [desere'ðar] *vt* to disinherit.

deshielo [des'jelo] *nm* (*de cañería*) thaw; (*de heladera*) defrosting.

deshilar [desi'lar] *vt* (*tela*) to unravel.

deshonesto, a [deso'nesto, a] *a* indecent.

deshonra [des'onra] *nf* (*deshonor*) dishonour; (*vergüenza*) shame; **deshonrar** *vt* to dishonour; (*insultar*) to insult.

deshora [des'ora]: **a ~** *ad* at the wrong time.

desierto, a [de'sjerto, a] *a* (*casa, calle, negocio*) deserted // *nm* desert.

designar [desiɣ'nar] *vt* (*nombrar*) to designate; (*indicar*) to fix.

designio [de'siɣnjo] *nm* (*proyecto*) plan; (*destino*) fate.

desigual [desi'ɣwal] *a* (*terreno*) uneven; (*lucha etc*) unequal.

desilusión [desilu'sjon] *nf* disappointment, disillusionment; **desilusionar** *vt* to disappoint; **desilusionarse** *vr* to become disillusioned.

desinfectar [desinfek'tar] *vt* to disinfect.

desinflar [desin'flar] *vt* to deflate.

desintegración [desinteɣra'θjon] *nf* disintegration.

desinterés [desinte'res] *nm* (*objetividad*) disinterestedness; (*altruismo*) unselfishness.

desistir [desis'tir] *vi* (*renunciar*) to stop, desist.

desleal [desle'al] *a* (*infiel*) disloyal; **~tad** *nf* disloyalty.

deslenguado, a [deslen'ɡwaðo, a] *a* (*grosero*) foul-mouthed.

desligar [desli'ɣar] *vt* (*desatar*) to untie, undo; (*separar*) to separate; **~se** *vr* (*dos personas*) to break up, separate; (*de un compromiso*) to extricate o.s.

desliz [des'liθ] *nm* (*de coche*) skid; (*de persona*) slip, slide; (*fig*) lapse; **~ar** *vt* to slip, slide; **~arse** *vr* (*escurrirse: persona*) to slip, slide; (*coche*) to skid; (*aguas mansas*) to flow gently; (*error*) to slip in.

deslucido, a [deslu'θiðo, a] *a* (*gen*) dull; (*torpe*) awkward, graceless; (*marchitado*) tarnished.

deslumbrar [deslum'brar] *vt* to dazzle.

desmán [des'man] *nm* (*exceso*) outrage; (*abuso de poder*) abuse.

desmandarse [desman'darse] *vr* (*abusarse*) to behave badly; (*excederse*) to get out of hand; (*caballo*) to bolt.

desmantelar [desmante'lar] *vt* (*deshacer*) to dismantle; (*casa*) to strip.

desmayado, a [desma'jaðo, a] *a* (*sin sentido*) unconscious; (*carácter*) dull; (*débil*) faint, weak.

desmayar [desma'jar] *vi* to lose heart; **~se** *vr* (*MED*) to faint; **desmayo** *nm* (*desvanecimiento*) faint; (*sin conciencia*) unconsciousness; (*depresión*) dejection.

desmedido, a [desme'ðiðo, a] *a* excessive; **desmedirse** *vr* to go too far, forget o.s.

desmejorar [desmexo'rar] *vt* (*dañar*) to impair, spoil; (*MED*) to weaken.

desmembrar [desmem'brar] *vt* (*MED*) to dismember; (*fig*) to separate.

desmentir [desmen'tir] *vt* (*contradecir*) to contradict; (*refutar*) to deny // *vi*: **~ de** to refute, **~se** *vr* to contradict o.s.

desmenuzar [desmenu'θar] *vt* (*deshacer*) to crumble; (*examinar*) to examine closely.

desmerecer [desmere'θer] *vt* to be unworthy of // *vi* (*deteriorarse*) to deteriorate.

desmesurado, a [desmesu'raðo, a] *a* disproportionate.

desmontar [desmon'tar] *vt* (*deshacer*) to dismantle; (*tierra*) to level // *vi* to dismount.

desmoralizar [desmorali'θar] *vt* to demoralize.

desmoronar [desmoro'nar] *vt* to wear away, erode; **~se** *vr* (*edificio, dique*) to fall into disrepair; (*sociedad*) to decay; (*economía*) to decline.

desnivel [desni'βel] *nm* (*de terreno*) unevenness; **paso a ~** (*AUTO*) flyover.

desnudar [desnu'ðar] *vt* (*desvestir*) to

undress; (*despojar*) to strip; **~se** *vr* (*desvestirse*) to get undressed; **desnudo, a** *a* naked // *nm/f* nude; **desnudo de** devoid *or* bereft of.

desobedecer [desoβeðe'θer] *vt, vi* to disobey; **desobediencia** *nf* disobedience.

desocupación [desokupa'θjon] *nf* (*ocio*) leisure; (*desempleo*) unemployment; **desocupado, a** *a* at leisure; unemployed; (*deshabitado*) empty, vacant; **desocupar** *vt* to vacate.

desodorante [desoðo'rante] *nm* deodorant.

desolación [desola'θjon] *nf* (*lugar*) desolation; (*fig*) grief; **desolar** *vt* to ruin, lay waste; **desolarse** *vr* to grieve.

desorden [des'orðen] *nm* confusion; (*político*) disorder.

desorganizar [desorγani'θar] *vt* (*desordenar*) to disorganize; (*deshacer*) to disrupt.

desorientar [desorjen'tar] *vt* (*extraviar*) to mislead; (*confundir, desconcertar*) to confuse; **~se** *vr* (*perderse*) to lose one's way.

despabilado, a [despaβi'laðo, a] *a* (*despierto*) wide-awake; (*fig*) alert, sharp.

despabilar [despaβi'lar] *vt* (*vela*) to snuff; (*el ingenio*) to sharpen; (*fortuna, negocio*) to squander // *vi*, **~se** *vr* to wake up.

despacio [des'paθjo] *ad* slowly.

despachar [despa'tʃar] *vt* (*negocio*) to do, complete; (*enviar*) to send, dispatch; (*vender*) to sell, deal in; (*billete*) to issue; (*mandar ir*) to send away.

despacho [des'patʃo] *nm* (*oficina*) office; (*de paquetes*) dispatch; (*venta*) sale; (*comunicación*) message; (*eficacia*) efficiency; (*rapidez*) promptness.

desparramar [desparra'mar] *vt* (*esparcir*) to scatter; (*noticia*) to spread; (*dinero, fortuna*) to squander; (*líquido*) to spill.

despavorido, a [despaβo'riðo, a] *a* terrified.

despectivo, a [despek'tiβo, a] *a* (*despreciativo*) derogatory; (*LING*) pejorative.

despecho [des'petʃo] *nm* spite; **a ~ de** in spite of.

despedazar [despeða'θar] *vt* to tear to pieces.

despedida [despe'ðiða] *nf* (*adiós*) farewell; (*de obrero*) sacking.

despedir [despe'ðir] *vt* (*visita*) to see off, show out; (*licenciar: empleado*) to discharge; (*inquilino*) to evict; (*objeto*) to hurl; (*flecha*) to fire; (*olor etc*) to give out *or* off; **~se** *vr*: **~se de** to say goodbye to.

despegar [despe'γar] *vt* to unstick // *vi* to take off, **~se** *vr* to come loose, come unstuck; **despegue** *nm* detachment.

despegue [des'peγe] *nm* takeoff.

despeinado, a [despei'naðo, a] *a* dishevelled, unkempt.

despejado, a [despe'xaðo, a] *a* (*lugar*) clear, free; (*cielo*) cloudless, clear; (*persona*) wide-awake.

despejar [despe'xar] *vt* (*gen*) to clear; (*misterio*) to clarify, clear up // *vi* (*el tiempo*) to clear; **~se** *vr* (*tiempo, cielo*) to clear (up); (*misterio*) to become clearer; (*persona*) to relax.

despejo [des'pexo] *nm* (*de casa, calle etc*) brightness; (*desenvoltura*) self-confidence; (*talento, ingenio*) alertness.

despensa [des'pensa] *nf* larder.

despeñadero [despeɲa'ðero] *nm* (*GEO*) cliff, precipice.

desperdicio [desper'ðiθjo] *nm* (*despilfarro*) squandering; (*residuo*) waste.

desperezarse [despere'θarse] *vr* to stretch (o.s.).

desperfecto [desper'fekto] *nm* (*deterioro*) slight damage; (*defecto*) flaw, imperfection.

despertador [desperta'ðor] *nm* alarm clock.

despertar [desper'tar] *vt* (*persona*) to wake up; (*vocación*) to awaken; (*recuerdos*) to revive; (*apetito*) to arouse // *vi*, **~se** *vr* to awaken, wake up // *nm* awakening.

despido [des'piðo] *nm* dismissal, sacking.

despierto *etc vb ver* **despertar**.

despierto, a [des'pjerto, a] *a* awake; (*fig*) sharp, alert.

despilfarro [despil'farro] *nm* (*derroche*) squandering; (*lujo desmedido*) extravagance.

despistar [despis'tar] *vt* to throw off the track *or* scent; (*fig*) to mislead, confuse; **~se** *vr* to take the wrong road; (*fig*) to become confused.

desplazamiento [desplaθa'mjento] *nm* displacement; **~ de tierras** landslip.

desplegar [desple'γar] *vt* (*tela, papel*) to unfold, open out; (*bandera*) to unfurl.

despoblar [despo'βlar] *vt* (*de gente*) to depopulate.

despojar [despo'xar] *vt* (*alguien: de sus bienes*) to divest of, deprive of; (*casa*) to strip, leave bare; (*alguien: de su cargo*) to strip of; **despojo** *nm* (*acto*) plundering; (*objetos*) plunder, loot; **despojos** *nmpl* waste *sg*; (*rocas, ladrillos*) debris *sg*.

desposado, a [despo'saðo, a] *a, nm/f* newly-wed.

desposeer [despose'er] *vt* (*despojar*) to dispossess.

déspota ['despota] *nm* despot.

despreciar [despre'θjar] *vt* (*desdeñar*) to despise, scorn; (*afrentar*) to slight; **desprecio** *nm* scorn, contempt; slight.

desprender [despren'der] *vt* (*separar*) to separate; (*desatar*) to unfasten; (*olor*) to give off; **~se** *vr* (*botón: caerse*) to fall off; (*: abrirse*) to unfasten; (*olor, perfume*) to be given off; **~se de** to follow from; **se desprende que** it transpires that.

desprendimiento [desprendi'mjento] *nm* (*gen*) loosening; (*de botón que se cae*) detachment; (*de botón que se abre*)

unfastening; (*generosidad*) disinterestedness; (*indiferencia*) detachment; (*de
gas*) release; (*de tierra, rocas*) landslide.

despreocupado, a [despreoku'paðo, a] *a*
(*sin preocupación*) unworried, nonchalant;
(*desprejuiciado*) impartial; (*negligente*)
careless; **despreocuparse** *vr* to be
carefree; **despreocuparse de** to have no
interest in.

desprevenido, a [despreße'niðo, a] *a* (*no
preparado*) unprepared, unready.

desproporción [despropor'θjon] *nf*
disproportion, lack of proportion.

después [des'pwes] *ad* afterwards, later;
(*próximo paso*) next; ~ **de comer** after
lunch; **un año** ~ a year later; ~ **se
debatió el tema** next the matter was
discussed; ~ **de corregido el texto** after
the text had been corrected; ~ **de todo**
after all.

desquite [des'kite] *nm* (*satisfacción*)
satisfaction; (*venganza*) revenge.

destacar [desta'kar] *vt* to emphasize,
point up; (*MIL*) to detach, detail // *vi*, ~**se**
vr (*resaltarse*) to stand out; (*persona*) to be
outstanding or exceptional.

destajo [des'taxo] *nm*: **trabajar a** ~ to do
piecework.

destapar [desta'par] *vt* (*gen*) to open;
(*cacerola*) to take the lid off, uncover;
~**se** *vr* (*revelarse*) to reveal one's true
character.

destartalado, a [destarta'laðo, a] *a*
(*desordenado*) untidy; (*ruinoso*)
tumbledown.

destello [des'teʎo] *nm* (*de estrella*)
twinkle; (*de faro*) signal light.

destemplado, a [destem'plaðo, a] *a* (*MUS*)
out of tune; (*voz*) harsh; (*MED*) out of sorts,
indisposed.

desteñir [deste'nir] *vt* to fade // *vi*, ~**se**
vr (*color*) to fade; **esta tela no destiñe**
this fabric will not run.

desterrar [deste'rrar] *vt* (*exilar*) to exile;
(*fig*) to banish, dismiss.

destierro [des'tjerro] *nm* exile.

destilación [destila'θjon] *nf* distillation;
destilar *vt* to distil; **destilería** *nf*
distillery.

destinar [desti'nar] *vt* to destine;
(*funcionario*) to appoint, assign; (*fondos*) to
set aside (*a* for); ~**se** *vr* to be destined.

destinatario, a [destina'tarjo, a] *nm/f*
addressee.

destino [des'tino] *nm* (*suerte*) destiny; (*de
viajero*) destination; (*función*) use.

destituir [destitu'ir] *vt* to dismiss.

destornillador [destorniʎa'ðor] *nm*
screwdriver; **destornillar** *vt*,
destornillarse *vr* (*tornillo*) to unscrew.

destreza [des'treθa] *nf* (*habilidad*) skill;
(*maña*) dexterity; (*facilidad*) handiness.

destrozar [destro'θar] *vt* (*romper*) to
smash, break (up); (*estropear*) to ruin;
(*deshacer*) to shatter; (*el corazón*) to
break.

destrozo [des'troθo] *nm* (*acción*)

destruction; (*desastre*) smashing; ~**s** *nmpl*
(*pedazos*) pieces; (*daños*) havoc *sg*.

destrucción [destruk'θjon] *nf* destruction.

destruir [destru'ir] *vt* to destroy.

desunir [desu'nir] *vt* to separate; (*TEC*) to
disconnect; (*fig*) to cause a quarrel or rift
between.

desusado, a [desu'saðo, a] *a* (*anticuado*)
obsolete.

desvalido, a [desßa'liðo, a] *a*
(*desprotegido*) destitute; (*POL*)
underprivileged; (*sin fuerzas*) helpless.

desván [des'ßan] *nm* attic.

desvanecer [desßane'θer] *vt* (*disipar*) to
dispel; (*borrar*) to blur; ~**se** *vr* (*humo*) to
vanish, disappear; (*color*) to fade;
(*recuerdo*) to fade away.

desvanecimiento [desßaneθi'mjento] *nm*
(*desaparición*) disappearance; (*de colores*)
fading; (*evaporación*) evaporation; (*MED*)
fainting fit.

desvariar [desßa'rjar] *vi* (*enfermo*) to be
delirious; **desvarío** *nm* delirium.

desvelar [desße'lar] *vt* to keep awake;
~**se** *vr* to stay awake; (*fig*) to be vigilant
or watchful; **desvelo** *nm* lack of sleep;
(*insomnio*) sleeplessness; (*fig*) vigilance.

desventaja [desßen'taxa] *nf* disadvantage.

desventura [desßen'tura] *nf* misfortune.

desvergonzado, a [desßerxon'θaðo, a] *a*
shameless.

desvergüenza [desßer'ɣwenθa] *nf*
(*descaro*) shamelessness; (*insolencia*)
impudence; (*mala conducta*) effrontery.

desviación [desßja'θjon] *nf* deviation.

desviar [des'ßjar] *vt* to turn aside; (*río*) to
alter the course of; (*navío*) to divert, reroute; (*conversación*) to sidetrack; ~**se** *vr*
(*apartarse del camino*) to turn aside,
deviate; (: *barco*) to go off course.

desvío [des'ßio] *nm* (*desviación*) detour,
diversion; (*fig*) indifference.

desvirtuar [desßir'twar] *vt*, ~**se** *vr* to
spoil.

desvivirse [desßi'ßirse] *vr*: ~ **por** to long
for, crave for.

detallar [deta'ʎar] *vt* to detail; (*COM*) to
sell retail.

detalle [de'taʎe] *nm* detail; (*fig*) gesture,
token; **al** ~ in detail.

detallista [deta'ʎista] *nm/f* retailer.

detener [dete'ner] *vt* (*tren, persona*) to
stop; (*JUR*) to arrest; (*objeto*) to keep; ~**se**
vr to stop; (*demorarse*): ~**se en** to delay
over, linger over.

detenido, a [dete'niðo, a] *a* (*preso*)
arrested, under arrest; (*minucioso*)
detailed; (*tímido*) timid // *nm/f* person
under arrest, prisoner.

detergente [deter'xente] *nm* detergent.

deteriorar [deterjo'rar] *vt* to spoil,
damage; ~**se** *vr* to deteriorate;
(*relaciones*) to become damaged;
deterioro *nm* deterioration.

determinación [determina'θjon] *nf*
(*empeño*) determination; (*decisión*)

decision; **determinar** vt (*plazo*) to fix; (*precio*) to settle; **determinarse** vr to decide.

detestar [detes'tar] vt to detest.

detonar [deto'nar] vi to detonate.

detrás [de'tras] ad behind; (*atrás*) at the back; ~ **de** behind.

detrimento [detri'mento] nm harm, damage; **en** ~ **de** to the detriment of.

deuda ['deuða] nf (*condición*) indebtedness, debt; (*cantidad*) debt.

deudor, a [deu'ðor, a] a: **saldo** ~ **debit** balance // nm/f debtor.

devaluación [deβalwa'θjon] nf devaluation.

devastar [deβas'tar] vt (*destruir*) to devastate.

devoción [deβo'θjon] nf devotion.

devolución [deβolu'θjon] nf devolution; (*reenvío*) return, sending back; (*reembolso*) repayment.

devolver [deβol'βer] vt (*gen*) to return; (*carta al correo*) to send back; (*COM*) to repay, refund; (*visita, la palabra*) to return.

devorar [deβo'rar] vt to devour.

devoto, a [de'βoto, a] a devout // nm/f admirer.

di vb ver **dar; decir.**

día ['dia] nm day; ¿**qué** ~ **es?** what's the date?; **estar/poner al** ~ to be/keep up to date; **el** ~ **de hoy/de mañana** today/tomorrow; **al** ~ **siguiente** on the following day; **vivir al** ~ to live from hand to mouth; **de** ~ by day, in daylight; **en pleno** ~ in full daylight.

diablo ['djaβlo] nm devil; **diablura** nf prank; **diabluras** nfpl mischief sg.

diabólico, a [dja'βoliko, a] a diabolical.

diafragma [dja'fraɣma] nm diaphragm.

diagnosis [djaɣ'nosis] nf, **diagnóstico** [djaɣ'nostiko] nm diagnosis.

dialecto [dja'lekto] nm dialect.

diálogo ['djaloɣo] nm dialogue.

diamante [dja'mante] nm diamond.

diapositiva [djaposi'tiβa] nf (*FOTO*) slide, transparency.

diario, a [a, 'djarjo, a] a daily // nm newspaper.

diarrea [dja'rrea] nf diarrhoea.

dibujar [diβu'xar] vt to draw, sketch; **dibujo** nm drawing; **dibujos animados** cartoons.

diccionario [dikθjo'narjo] nm dictionary.

dice etc vb ver **decir.**

diciembre [di'θjembre] nm December.

dictado [dik'taðo] nm dictation.

dictador [dikta'ðor] nm dictator; **dictadura** nf dictatorship.

dictamen [dik'tamen] nm (*opinión*) opinion; (*juicio*) judgment.

dicho, a ['ditʃo, a] pp de **decir** // a: **en** ~**s países** in the aforementioned countries // nm saying // nf happiness.

diente ['djente] nm (*ANAT, TEC*) tooth; (*ZOOL*) fang; (: *de elefante*) tusk; (*de ajo*) clove; **da** ~ **con** ~ his teeth are

chattering; **hablar entre** ~**s** to mutter, mumble.

dieron vb ver **dar.**

diesel ['disel] a: **motor** ~ diesel engine.

dieta ['djeta] nf diet.

diez [djeθ] num ten.

diferencia [dife'renθja] nf difference; **diferenciar** vt to differentiate between // vi to differ; **diferenciarse** vr to differ, be different; (*distinguirse*) to distinguish o.s.

diferente [dife'rente] a different.

difícil [di'fiθil] a difficult.

dificultad [difikul'taθ] nf difficulty; (*problema*) trouble.

dificultar [difikul'tar] vt (*complicar*) to complicate, make difficult; (*estorbar*) to obstruct.

difundir [difun'dir] vt (*esparcir*) to spread, diffuse; (*divulgar*) to divulge; ~**se** vr to spread (out).

difunto, a [di'funto, a] a dead, deceased // nm/f deceased (person).

digerir [dixe'rir] vt to digest; (*fig*) to absorb.

digital [dixi'tal] a digital.

dignarse [diɣ'narse] vr to deign to.

dignidad [diɣni'ðað] nf dignity; (*honra*) honour.

digno, a ['diɣno, a] a worthy.

digo etc vb ver **decir.**

dije etc vb ver **decir.**

dilatación [dilata'θjon] nf (*expansión*) dilation.

dilatado, a [dila'taðo, a] a dilated; (*ancho*) widened; (*largo*) long drawn-out; (*extenso*) extensive.

dilatar [dila'tar] vt (*cuerpo*) to dilate; (*prolongar*) to stretch; (*en el tiempo*) to prolong.

dilema [di'lema] nm dilemma.

diligencia [dili'xenθja] nf diligence; (*ocupación*) errand, job; ~**s** nfpl (*JUR*) formalities; **diligente** a diligent.

diluir [dilu'ir] vt to dilute.

diluvio [di'luβjo] nm deluge, flood.

dimensión [dimen'sjon] nf dimension.

diminuto, a [dimi'nuto, a] a tiny.

dimitir [dimi'tir] vi to resign.

dimos vb ver **dar.**

Dinamarca [dina'marka] nf Denmark; **dinamarqués, esa** a Danish // nm/f Dane.

dinámico, a [di'namiko, a] a dynamic.

dinamita [dina'mita] nf dynamite.

dínamo ['dinamo] nf dynamo.

dineral [dine'ral] nm large sum of money, fortune.

dinero [di'nero] nm money; ~ **efectivo** cash, ready cash.

dio vb ver **dar.**

dios [djos] nm god.

diosa ['djosa] nf goddess.

diplomacia [diplo'maθja] nf diplomacy; (*fig*) tact; **diplomático, a** a diplomatic // nm/f diplomat.

diputado, a [dipu'taðo, a] nm/f delegate; (*Cortes*) deputy.

diré etc vb ver **decir.**

dirección [direk'θjon] nf direction; (*señas*) address; (AUTO) steering; (*gerencia*) management; (POL) leadership; ~ **única** o **obligatoria** o **prohibida** one-way.

directo, a [di'rekto, a] a direct; **transmitir en** ~ to broadcast live.

director, a [direk'tor, a] a leading // nm/f director; ~ **de cine/de escena** producer/stage manager.

dirigir [diri'xir] vt to direct; (*carta*) to address; (*obra de teatro, film*) to produce, direct; (*coche, barco*) to steer; (*avión*) to fly; (MUS) to conduct; (*comercio*) to manage; ~**se vr:** ~**se a** to go towards, make one's way towards; (*fig*) to speak to.

discernir [disθer'nir] vt (*distinguir, discriminar*) to discern.

disciplina [disθi'plina] nf discipline; **disciplinar** vt to discipline.

discípulo, a [dis'θipulo, a] nm/f disciple.

disco ['disko] nm disc; (DEPORTE) discus; (TELEC) dial; (AUTO) signal; (*fam*) boring affair; ~ **de larga duración/de duración extendida** long-playing record (L.P.)/extended play record (E.P.); ~ **de freno** brake disc.

discordia [dis'korðja] nf discord.

discoteca [disko'teka] nf discotheque.

discreción [diskre'θjon] nf discretion; (*reserva*) prudence; (*secreto*) secrecy; **comer a** ~ to eat as much as one wishes; **discrecional** a (*facultativo*) discretionary.

discrepancia [diskre'panθja] nf (*diferencia*) discrepancy; (*desacuerdo*) disagreement.

discreto, a [dis'kreto, a] a (*diplomático*) discreet; (*sensato*) sensible; (*listo*) shrewd; (*reservado*) quiet; (*sobrio*) sober; (*retraído*) unobtrusive; (*razonable*) reasonable.

discriminación [diskrimina'θjon] nf discrimination.

disculpa [dis'kulpa] nf excuse; (*pedir perdón*) apology; **disculpar** vt to excuse, pardon; **disculparse** vr to excuse o.s.; to apologize.

discurrir [disku'rrir] vt to invent // vi (*pensar, reflexionar*) to think, meditate; (*recorrer*) to roam, wander; (*el tiempo*) to pass, flow by.

discurso [dis'kurso] nm speech; (*razonamiento*) reasoning power.

discutir [disku'tir] vt (*debatir*) to discuss; (*pelear*) to argue about; (*contradecir*) to contradict.

diseminar [disemi'nar] vt to disseminate, spread.

diseño [di'seɲo] nm (*dibujo*) design.

disfraz [dis'fraθ] nm (*máscara*) disguise; (*excusa*) pretext; ~**ar** vt to disguise; ~**arse vr:** ~**arse de** to disguise o.s. as.

disfrutar [disfru'tar] vt to enjoy // vi to enjoy o.s.; ~ **de** to enjoy, possess.

disgustar [disɣus'tar] vt (*no gustar*) to displease; (*contrariar, enojar*) to annoy,

upset; ~**se vr** to be annoyed; (*dos personas*) to fall out.

disgusto [dis'ɣusto] nm (*repugnancia*) disgust; (*contrariedad*) annoyance; (*tristeza*) grief; (*riña*) quarrel; (*avería*) misfortune.

disidente [disi'ðente] nm dissident.

disimular [disimu'lar] vt (*ocultar*) to hide, conceal; (*perdonar*) to excuse // vi to dissemble.

disipar [disi'par] vt to dispel; (*fortuna*) to squander; ~**se vr** (*nubes*) to vanish; (*indisciplinarse*) to dissipate.

disminución [disminu'θjon] nf diminution.

disminuir [disminu'ir] vt (*acortar*) to decrease; (*achicar*) to diminish; (*estrechar*) to lessen.

disoluto, a [diso'luto, a] a dissolute.

disolver [disol'βer] vt (*gen*) to dissolve; ~**se vr** to be dissolved.

disparar [dispa'rar] vt, vi to shoot, fire.

disparate [dispa'rate] nm (*tontería*) foolish remark; (*error*) blunder.

disparo [dis'paro] nm shot.

dispensar [dispen'sar] vt to dispense; (*disculpar*) to excuse.

dispersar [disper'sar] vt to disperse; ~**se vr** to scatter.

disponer [dispo'ner] vt (*arreglar*) to arrange; (*ordenar*) to put in order; (*preparar*) to prepare, get ready // vi: ~ **de** to have, own; ~**se vr:** ~**se para** to prepare to, prepare for.

disponible [dispo'niβle] a available.

disposición [disposi'θjon] nf arrangement, disposition; (*aptitud*) aptitude; **a la** ~ **de** at the disposal of.

dispuesto, a [dis'pwesto, a] pp de **disponer** // a (*arreglado*) arranged; (*preparado*) disposed.

disputar [dispu'tar] vt (*discutir*) to dispute, question; (*contender*) to contend for // vi to argue.

distanciar [distan'θjar] vt to space out; ~**se vr** to become estranged.

distante [dis'tante] a distant.

diste, distéis vb ver **dar.**

distinción [distin'θjon] nf (*gen*) distinction; (*claridad*) clarity; (*elegancia*) elegance; (*honor*) honour.

distinguir [distin'ɡir] vt to distinguish; (*escoger*) to single out; ~**se vr** to be distinguished.

distinto, a [dis'tinto, a] a different; (*claro*) clear.

distracción [distrak'θjon] nf (*pasatiempo*) hobby, pastime; (*olvido*) absent-mindedness, distraction.

distraer [distra'er] vt (*entretener*) to entertain; (*divertir*) to amuse; (*fondos*) to embezzle; ~**se vr** (*entretenerse*) to amuse o.s.; (*perder la concentración*) to allow one's attention to wander.

distraído, a [distra'iðo, a] a (*gen*) absent-minded; (*entretenido*) amusing.

distribuir [distriβu'ir] vt to distribute.

distrito [dis'trito] *nm* (*sector, territorio*) region; (*barrio*) district.
disturbio [dis'turβjo] *nm* disturbance.
disuadir [diswa'ðir] *vt* to dissuade.
disuelto [di'swelto] *pp de* **disolver**.
divagar [diβa'xar] *vi* (*desviarse*) to digress; (*errar*) to wander.
diván [di'βan] *nm* divan.
divergencia [diβer'xenθja] *nf* divergence.
diversidad [diβersi'ðað] *nf* diversity, variety.
diversificar [diβersifi'kar] *vt* to diversify.
diversión [diβer'sjon] *nf* (*gen*) entertainment; (*actividad*) hobby, pastime.
diverso, a [di'βerso, a] *a* diverse; **~s** sundry.
divertir [diβer'tir] *vt* (*entretener, recrear*) to amuse, entertain; (*apartar, distraer*) to divert; **~se** *vr* (*pasarlo bien*) to have a good time; (*distraerse*) to amuse o.s.
dividir [diβi'ðir] *vt* (*gen*) to divide; (*separar*) to separate; (*distribuir*) to distribute, share out.
divino, a [di'βino, a] *a* divine.
divisa [di'βisa] *nf* (*emblema, moneda*) emblem, badge; **~s** *nfpl* currency *sg*.
división [diβi'sjon] *nf* (*gen*) division; (*de partido*) split; (*de país*) partition; (*LING*) hyphen; (*divergencia*) divergence.
divorciar [diβor'θjar] *vt* to divorce; **~se** *vr* to get divorced; **divorcio** *nm* divorce.
divulgar [diβul'xar] *vt* (*desparramar*) to spread; (*hacer circular*) to divulge, circulate; **~se** *vr* to leak out.
doblar [do'βlar] *vt* (*gen*) to double; (*papel*) to fold; (*caño*) to bend; (*la esquina*) to turn, go round; (*film*) to dub // *vi* to turn; (*campana*) to toll; **~se** *vr* (*plegarse*) to fold up; (*encorvarse*) to bend; **~se de risa/dolor** to be doubled up with laughter/pain.
doble ['doβle] *a* (*gen*) double; (*de dos aspectos*) dual; (*fig*) two-faced // *nm* double; (*campana*) toll(ing); **~s** *nmpl* (*DEPORTE*) doubles *sg* // *nm/f* (*TEATRO*) double, stand-in; **con ~ sentido** with a double meaning.
doblegar [doβle'xar] *vt* to fold, crease; **~se** *vr* to yield.
doce ['doθe] *num* twelve.
docena [do'θena] *nf* dozen.
dócil ['doθil] *a* (*pasivo*) docile; (*obediente*) obedient.
doctor, a [dok'tor, a] *nm/f* doctor.
doctrina [dok'trina] *nf* doctrine, teaching.
documentación [dokumenta'θjon] *nf* documentation, papers *pl*.
documento [doku'mento] *nm* (*certificado*) document.
dólar ['dolar] *nm* dollar.
doler [do'ler] *vt, vi* to hurt; (*fig*) to grieve; **~se** *vr* (*de su situación*) to grieve, feel sorry; (*de las desgracias ajenas*) to sympathize; **me duele el brazo** my arm hurts.
dolor [do'lor] *nm* pain; (*fig*) grief, sorrow.

domar [do'mar], **domesticar** [domesti'kar] *vt* to tame.
domicilio [domi'θiljo] *nm* home; **~ particular** private residence; **~ social** head office.
dominante [domi'nante] *a* dominant; (*person*) domineering.
dominar [domi'nar] *vt* (*gen*) to dominate; (*idiomas etc*) to have a command of // *vi* to dominate, prevail; **~se** *vr* to control o.s.
domingo [do'mingo] *nm* Sunday.
dominio [do'minjo] *nm* (*tierras*) domain; (*autoridad*) power, authority; (*de las pasiones*) grip, hold; (*de varios idiomas*) command.
don [don] *nm* (*talento*) gift; **~ Juan Gómez** Mr Juan Gomez *or* Juan Gomez Esq.
donaire [do'naire] *nm* charm.
doncella [don'θeʎa] *nf* (*criada*) maid; (*muchacha*) girl.
donde ['donde] *ad* where // *prep*: **el coche está allí ~ el farol** the car is over there by the lamppost *or* where the lamppost is; **por ~** through which; **en ~** where, in which.
dónde ['donde] *ad interr* where?; **¿a ~ vas?** where are you going (to)?; **¿de ~ vienes?** where have you come from?; **¿por ~?** where?, whereabouts?
dondequiera [donde'kjera] *ad* anywhere; **por ~** everywhere, all over the place // *conj*: **~ que** wherever.
doña ['dona] *nf título de mujer que no se traduce.*
dorado, a [do'raðo, a] *a* (*color*) golden; (*TEC*) gilt.
dormir [dor'mir] *vt*: **~ la siesta por la tarde** to have an afternoon nap // *vi* to sleep; **~se** *vr* to go to sleep.
dormitar [dormi'tar] *vi* to doze.
dormitorio [dormi'torjo] *nm* bedroom; **~ común** dormitory.
dos [dos] *num* two.
dosis ['dosis] *nf inv* dose, dosage.
dotado, a [do'taðo, a] *a* gifted; **~ de** endowed with.
dotar [do'tar] *vt* to endow; **dote** *nf* dowry; **dotes** *nfpl* gifts.
doy *vb ver* **dar**.
drama ['drama] *nm* drama.
dramaturgo [drama'turxo] *nm* dramatist, playwright.
droga ['droxa] *nf* drug.
drogadicto, a [droxa'ðikto, a] *nm/f* drug addict.
ducha ['dutʃa] *nf* (*baño*) shower; (*MED*) douche; **ducharse** *vr* to take a shower.
duda ['duða] *nf* doubt.
dudoso, a [du'ðoso, a] *a* (*incierto*) hesitant; (*sospechoso*) doubtful.
duelo ['dwelo] *nm* (*combate*) duel; (*luto*) mourning.
duende ['dwende] *nm* imp, goblin.
dueño, a ['dweɲo, a] *nm/f* (*propietario*)

owner; (de casa) landlord/lady; (empresario) employer.

duermo etc vb ver **dormir.**

dulce ['dulθe] a sweet // ad gently, softly // nm sweet.

dulzura [dul'θura] nf sweetness; (ternura) gentleness.

duplicar [dupli'kar] vt (hacer el doble de) to duplicate; ~se vr to double.

duque ['duke] nm duke.

duquesa [du'kesa] nf duchess.

duración [dura'θjon] nf duration.

duradero, a [dura'θero, a] a lasting.

durante [du'rante] ad during.

durar [du'rar] vi (permanecer) to last; (recuerdo) to remain.

dureza [du'reθa] nf (calidad) hardness.

durmí etc vb ver **dormir.**

durmiente [dur'mjente] nm/f sleeper.

duro, a ['duro, a] a (gen) hard; (carácter) tough // ad hard // nm (moneda) five peseta coin/note.

E

e [e] conj and.

E abr de **este.**

ebanista [eßa'nista] nm cabinetmaker.

ébano ['eßano] nm ebony.

ebrio, a ['eßrjo, a] a drunk.

ebullición [eßuʎi'θjon] nf boiling; (fig) ferment.

eclesiástico, a [ekle'sjastiko, a] a ecclesiastical.

eclipse [e'klipse] nm eclipse.

eco ['eko] nm echo; **tener ~** to catch on.

ecología [ekolo'xia] nf ecology.

economato [ekono'mato] nm cooperative store.

economía [ekono'mia] nf (sistema) economy; (cualidad) thrift.

económico, a [eko'nomiko, a] a (barato) cheap, economical; (persona) thrifty; (COM: plan) financial; (: situación) economic.

economista [ekono'mista] nm/f economist.

ecuador [ekwa'ðor] nm equator; **el E~** Ecuador.

ecuánime [e'kwanime] a (carácter) level-headed; (estado) calm.

ecuestre [e'kwestre] a equestrian.

echar [e'tʃar] vt to throw; (agua, vino) to pour (out); (empleado: despedir) to fire, sack; (bigotes) to grow; (hojas) to sprout; (cartas) to post; (humo) to emit, give out // vi: **~ a correr/llorar** to break into a run/burst into tears; **~se** vr to lie down; **~ llave a** to lock (up); **~ abajo** (gobierno) to overthrow; (edificio) to demolish; **~ mano a** to lay hands on.

edad [e'ðað] nf age; **¿qué ~ tienes?** how old are you?; **tiene ocho años de ~** he is eight (years old); **de ~ mediana/avanzada** middle-aged/ advanced in years; **la E~ Media** the Middle Ages.

edición [eði'θjon] nf (acto) publication; (ejemplar) edition.

edicto [e'ðikto] nm edict, proclamation.

edificio [eði'fiθjo] nm building; (fig) edifice, structure.

editar [eði'tar] vt (publicar) to publish; (preparar textos) to edit.

editor, a [eði'tor, a] nm/f (que publica) publisher; (de periódico etc) editor // a: **casa ~a** publishing house; **~ial** a editorial // nm leading article, editorial; **casa ~ial** publishing house.

educación [eðuka'θjon] nf education; (crianza) upbringing; (modales) (good) manners pl.

educar [eðu'kar] vt to educate; (criar) to bring up; (voz) to train.

EE. UU. nmpl abr de **Estados Unidos** USA (United States of America).

efectivo, a [efek'tißo, a] a effective; (real) actual, real // nm: **pagar en ~** to pay (in) cash; **hacer ~ un cheque** to cash a cheque.

efecto [e'fekto] nm effect, result; **~s** nmpl goods; (COM) assets; **en ~** in fact; (respuesta) exactly, indeed.

efectuar [efek'twar] vt to carry out; (viaje) to make.

eficacia [efi'kaθja] nf (de persona) efficiency; (de medicamento) effectiveness.

eficaz [efi'kaθ] a (persona) efficient; (acción) effective.

egipcio, a [e'xipθjo, a] a, nm/f Egyptian.

Egipto [e'xipto] nm Egypt.

egoísmo [eʁo'ismo] nm egoism.

egoísta [eʁo'ista] a egoistical, selfish // nm/f egoist.

egregio, a [e'ʁrexjo, a] a eminent, distinguished.

Eire ['eire] nm Eire.

ej. abr de **ejemplo.**

eje ['exe] nm (GEO, MAT) axis; (de rueda) axle; (de máquina) shaft, spindle; **la idea ~** the central idea.

ejecución [exeku'θjon] nf (gen) execution; (cumplimiento) fulfilment; (actuación) performance; (JUR: embargo de deudor) attachment, distraint.

ejecutar [exeku'tar] vt (gen) to execute, carry out; (matar) to execute; (cumplir) to fulfil; (MUS) to perform; (JUR: embargar) to attach, distrain (on).

ejecutivo, a [exeku'tißo, a] a executive; **el poder ~** the Executive (Power).

ejemplar [exem'plar] a exemplary // nm example; (ZOOL) specimen; (de libro) copy; (de periódico) number, issue.

ejemplo [e'xemplo] nm example; **por ~** for example.

ejercer [exer'θer] vt to exercise; (influencia) to exert; (un oficio) to practise // vi (practicar) to practise (de as); (tener oficio) to hold office.

ejercicio [exer'θiθjo] nm exercise; (período) tenure; **~ comercial** financial year.

ejército [e'xerθito] nm army; **entrar en**

el ~ to join the army, join up.

el [el] *det* the.

él [el] *pron* (*persona*) he; (*cosa*) it; (*después de prep: persona*) him; (: *cosa*) it.

elaborar [elaβo'rar] *vt* to elaborate; (*hacer*) to make; (*preparar*) to prepare; (*trabajar*) to work; (*calcular*) to work out.

elasticidad [elasti\u03b8i'\u00f0a\u00f0] *nf* elasticity; **elástico, a** *a* elastic; (*flexible*) flexible // *nm* elastic.

elección [elek'\u03b8jon] *nf* election; (*selección*) choice, selection.

electorado [elekto'ra\u00f0o] *nm* electorate, voters *pl.*

electricidad [elektri\u03b8i'\u00f0a\u00f0] *nf* electricity.

electricista [elektri'\u03b8ista] *nm/f* electrician.

eléctrico, a [e'lektriko, a] *a* electric // *nm* electric train.

electrizar [elektri'\u03b8ar] *vt* to electrify.

electro... [elektro] *pref* electro...; ~**cardiógrafo** *nm* electrocardiograph; ~**cución** *nf* electrocution; ~**cutar** *vt* to electrocute, ~**chapado, a** *a* electroplated; **electrodo** *nm* electrode; ~**domésticos** *nmpl* (*electrical*) household appliances; ~**imán** *nm* electromagnet; ~**magnético, a** *a* electromagnetic; ~**motor** *nm* electric motor.

electrónico, a [elek'troniko, a] *a* electronic // *nf* electronics *sg.*

electrotecnia [elektro'teknja] *nf* electrical engineering; **electrotécnico, a** *nm/f* electrical engineer.

electrotermo [elektro'termo] *nm* immersion heater.

elefante [ele'fante] *nm* elephant; ~ **marino** elephant seal.

elegancia [ele'xan\u03b8ja] *nf* (*gracia*) elegance, grace; (*estilo*) stylishness; **elegante** *a* elegant, graceful; stylish, fashionable.

elegía [ele'xia] *nf* elegy.

elegir [ele'xir] *vt* (*escoger*) to choose, select; (*optar*) to opt for; (*presidente*) to elect.

elemental [elemen'tal] *a* (*claro, obvio*) elementary; (*fundamental*) elemental, fundamental.

elemento [ele'mento] *nm* element; (*fig*) ingredient; ~**s** *nmpl* elements, rudiments.

elevación [eleβa'\u03b8jon] *nf* elevation; (*acto*) raising, lifting; (*de precios*) rise; (*GEO etc*) height, altitude; (*de persona*) loftiness; (*pey*) conceit, pride.

elevar [ele'βar] *vt* to raise, lift (up); (*precio*) to put up; ~**se** *vr* (*edificio*) to rise; (*precios*) to go up; (*transportarse, enajenarse*) to get carried away; (*engreírse*) to become conceited.

eliminar [elimi'nar] *vt* to eliminate, remove.

eliminatoria [elimina'torja] *nf* heat, preliminary (round).

elite [e'lite] *nf* elite.

elocuencia [elo'kwen\u03b8ja] *nf* eloquence.

elogiar [elo'xjar] *vt* to praise, eulogize;

elogio *nm* praise; (*tributo*) tribute.

eludir [elu'\u00f0ir] *vt* (*evitar*) to avoid, evade; (*escapar*) to escape, elude.

ella ['e\u028ea] *pron* (*persona*) she; (*cosa*) it; (*después de prep: persona*) her; (: *cosa*) it.

ellas ['e\u028eas] *pron* (*personas y cosas*) they; (*después de prep*) them.

ello ['e\u028eo] *pron* it.

ellos ['e\u028eos] *pron* they; (*después de prep*) them.

emanar [ema'nar] *vi*: ~ **de** to emanate from, come from; (*derivar de*) to originate in.

emancipar [eman\u03b8i'par] *vt* to emancipate; ~**se** *vr* to become emancipated, free o.s.

embadurnar [emba\u00f0ur'nar] *vt* to smear.

embajada [emba'xa\u00f0a] *nf* embassy; (*mensaje*) message, errand.

embajador, a [embaxa'\u00f0or, a] *nm/f* ambassador/ambassadress.

embalar [emba'lar] *vt* (*envolver*) to parcel, wrap (up); (*envasar*) to package // *vi* to sprint.

embarazada [embara'\u03b8a\u00f0a] *a* pregnant // *nf* pregnant woman.

embarazar [embara'\u03b8ar] *vt* to obstruct, hamper; (*a una mujer*) to make pregnant; ~**se** *vr* (*aturdirse*) to become embarrassed; (*confundirse*) to get into a muddle; (*mujer*) to become pregnant.

embarazo [emba'ra\u00f0o] *nm* (*de mujer*) pregnancy; (*impedimento*) obstacle, obstruction; (*timidez*) embarrassment.

embarcación [embarka'\u03b8jon] *nf* (*barco*) boat, craft; (*acto*) embarkation.

embarcadero [embarka'\u00f0ero] *nm* pier, landing stage.

embarcar [embar'kar] *vt* (*cargamento*) to ship, stow; (*persona*) to embark, put on board; ~**se** *vr* to embark, go on board.

embargar [embar'\u00f0ar] *vt* (*impedir*) to impede, hinder; (*JUR*) to seize, impound.

embarque [em'barke] *nm* shipment, loading.

embaular [embau'lar] *vt* to pack (into a trunk); (*fig*) to stuff o.s. with.

embebecerse [embeβe'\u00f0erse] *vr* (*extasiarse*) to be lost in wonder, be amazed.

embeber [embe'βer] *vt* (*absorber*) to absorb, soak up; (*empapar*) to saturate // *vi* to shrink; ~**se** *vr*: ~**se en la lectura** to be engrossed *or* absorbed in a book.

embellecer [embe\u028ee'\u00f0er] *vt* to embellish, beautify.

embestida [embes'ti\u00f0a] *nf* attack, onslaught; (*carga*) charge; **embestir** *vt* to attack, assault; to charge, attack // *vi* to attack.

emblema [em'blema] *nm* emblem.

embobado, a [embo'βa\u00f0o, a] *a* (*atontado*) stunned, bewildered.

embocadura [emboka'\u00f0ura] *nf* narrow entrance; (*de río*) mouth; (*MUS*) mouthpiece.

émbolo ['embolo] *nm* (*AUTO*) piston.

embolsar [embol'sar] vt to pocket, put in one's pocket.

emborrachar [emborra'tʃar] vt to intoxicate, make drunk; ~se vr to get drunk.

emboscada [embos'kaða] nf (celada) ambush.

embotar [embo'tar] vt to blunt, dull; ~se vr (adormecerse) to go numb.

embotellar [embote'ʎar] vt to bottle; ~se vr (circulación) to get into a jam.

embozar [embo'θar] vt to muffle (up).

embragar [embra'xar] vi to let in the clutch.

embrague [em'braxe] nm (también pedal de ~) clutch.

embravecer [embraße'θer] vt to enrage, infuriate; ~se vr to become furious; (el mar) to get rough; (tormenta) to rage.

embriagado, a [embrja'xaðo, a] a (emborrachado) intoxicated, drunk.

embriagar [embrja'xar] vt (emborrachar) to intoxicate, make drunk; (alegrar) to delight; ~se vr (emborracharse) to get drunk.

embriaguez [embrja'xeθ] nf (borrachera) drunkenness; (fig) rapture, delight.

embrollar [embro'ʎar] vt (el asunto) to confuse, complicate; (persona) to involve, embroil; ~se vr (confundirse) to get into a muddle or mess; ~se con uno to get into an argument with sb.

embrollo [em'broʎo] nm (enredo) muddle, confusion; (aprieto) fix, jam; (pey: engaño) fraud; (: trampa) trick.

embromar [embro'mar] vt (burlarse de) to tease, make fun of.

embrutecer [embrute'θer] vt (brutalizar) to brutalize; (depravar) to deprave; (atontar) to stupefy; ~se vr to become brutal; to become depraved.

embudo [em'buðo] nm funnel; (fig: engaño) fraud; (: trampa) trick.

embuste [em'buste] nm trick; (impostura) imposture; (mentira) lie; (hum) fib; ~ro, a a lying, deceitful // nm/f (tramposo) cheat; (impostor) impostor; (mentiroso) liar; (hum) fibber.

embutido [embu'tiðo] nm (CULIN) sausage; (TEC) inlay.

embutir [embu'tir] vt (TEC) to inlay; (llenar) to pack tight, cram, stuff.

emergencia [emer'xenθja] nf emergency; (surgimiento) emergence.

emerger [emer'xer] vi to emerge, appear.

emigración [emixra'θjon] nf (éxodo) migration; (destierro) emigration.

emigrar [emi'xrar] vi (pájaros) to migrate; (personas) to emigrate.

eminencia [emi'nenθja] nf eminence; eminente a eminent, distinguished; (GEO) high.

emisario [emi'sarjo] nm emissary.

emisión [emi'sjon] nf (acto) emission; (COM etc) issue; (RADIO, TV: acto) broadcasting; (: programa) broadcast, programme.

emisora [emi'sora] nf (de onda corta) shortwave radio station; (aparato) broadcasting station.

emitir [emi'tir] vt (olor etc) to emit, give off; (moneda etc) to issue; (opinión) to express; (RADIO) to broadcast.

emoción [emo'θjon] nf emotion; (excitación) excitement; (turbación) worry, anxiety.

emocionante [emoθjo'nante] a (excitante) exciting, thrilling; (conmovedor) moving, touching; (impresionante) striking, impressive.

emocionar [emoθjo'nar] vt (excitar) to excite, thrill; (conmover) to move, touch; (impresionar) to impress.

empacho [em'patʃo] nm (MED) indigestion; (fig) embarrassment.

empalagoso, a [empala'xoso, a] a cloying; (fig) tiresome.

empalmar [empal'mar] vt to join, connect // vi (dos caminos) to meet, join; **empalme** nm joint, connection; junction; (de trenes) connection.

empanada [empa'naða] nf pie, patty.

empantanarse [empanta'narse] vr to get swamped; (fig) to get bogged down.

empañar [empa'ɲar] vt (niño) to swaddle, wrap up; ~se vr (nublarse) to get misty, steam up.

empapar [empa'par] vt (mojar) to soak, saturate; (absorber) to soak up, absorb; ~se vr: ~se de to soak up.

empapelar [empape'lar] vt (paredes) to paper; (envolver con papel) to wrap (up) in paper.

empaquetar [empake'tar] vt to pack, parcel up.

empastar [empas'tar] vt (embadurnar) to paste; (diente) to fill.

empatar [empa'tar] vi to draw, tie; **empate** nm draw, tie.

empedernido, a [empeðer'niðo, a] a hard, heartless; (fijado) hardened, inveterate.

empedernir [empeðer'nir] vt to harden.

empedrado, a [empe'ðraðo, a] a paved // nm paving; **empedrar** vt to pave.

empeñado, a [empe'ɲaðo, a] a (objeto) pawned; (persona) determined.

empeñar [empe'ɲar] vt (objeto) to pawn, pledge; (persona) to compel; ~se vr (obligarse) to bind o.s., pledge o.s.; (endeudarse) to get into debt; ~se en to be set on, be determined to.

empeño [em'peɲo] nm (cosa prendada) pledge; (determinación, insistencia) determination, insistence; **banco de ~s** pawnshop.

empeorar [empeo'rar] vt to make worse, worsen // vi to get worse, deteriorate.

empequeñecer [empekeɲe'θer] vt to dwarf; (fig) to belittle.

emperador [empera'ðor] nm emperor.

emperatriz [empera'triθ] nf empress.

empezar [empe'θar] vt, vi to begin, start.

empiezo etc vb ver **empezar**.

empinar [empi'nar] *vt* to raise (up) // *vi* (*fam*) to drink, booze (*fam*); ~**se** *vr* (*persona*) to stand on tiptoe; (*animal*) to rear up; (*camino*) to climb steeply; (*edificio*) to tower.

empírico, a [em'piriko, a] *a* empirical.

emplasto [em'plasto], **emplaste** [em-'plaste] *nm* (*MED*) plaster; (: *cataplasma*) poultice; (*componenda*) compromise.

emplazamiento [emplaθa'mjento] *nm* site, location; (*JUR*) summons *sg*.

emplazar [empla'θar] *vt* (*ubicar*) to site, place, locate; (*JUR*) to summons; (*convocar*) to summon.

empleado, a [emple'aðo, a] *nm/f* (*gen*) employee; (*de banco etc*) clerk.

emplear [emple'ar] *vt* (*usar*) to use, employ; (*dar trabajo a*) to employ; ~**se** *vr* (*conseguir trabajo*) to be employed; (*ocuparse*) to occupy o.s.

empleo [em'pleo] *nm* (*puesto*) job; (*puestos: colectivamente*) employment; (*uso*) use, employment.

empobrecer [empoβre'θer] *vt* to impoverish; ~**se** *vr* to become poor or impoverished; **empobrecimiento** *nm* impoverishment.

emporio [em'porjo] *nm* emporium, trading centre; (*gran almacén*) department store.

emprender [empren'der] *vt* (*empezar*) to begin, embark on; (*acometer*) to tackle, take on.

empreñar [empre'ɲar] *vt* to make pregnant; ~**se** *vr* to become pregnant.

empresa [em'presa] *nf* enterprise.

empréstito [em'prestito] *nm* (public) loan.

empujar [empu'xar] *vt* to push, shove; **empuje** *nm* thrust; (*presión*) pressure; (*fig*) vigour, drive.

empujón [empu'xon] *nm* push, shove.

empuñar [empu'ɲar] *vt* (*asir*) to grasp, take (firm) hold of.

emular [emu'lar] *vt* to emulate; (*rivalizar*) to rival.

émulo, a ['emulo, a] *nm/f* rival, competitor.

en [en] *prep* (*gen*) in; (*sobre*) on, upon; **meter** ~ **el bolsillo** to put in or into one's pocket; (*lugar*): **vivir** ~ **Toledo** to live in Toledo; ~ **casa** at home; (*tiempo*): **lo terminó** ~ **6 días** he finished it in 6 days; ~ **el mes de enero** in the month of January; ~ **aquel momento/aquella época** at that moment/that time; ~ **aquel día/aquella ocasión** on that day/that occasion; ~ **serio** seriously; ~ **fin** well, well then; **ir de puerta** ~ **puerta** to go from door to door; ~ **tren** by train.

enajenación [enaxena'θjon] *nf*, **enajenamiento** [enaxena'mjento] *nm* alienation; (*fig: distracción*) absent-mindedness; (: *embelesamiento*) rapture, trance; (*extrañamiento*) estrangement.

enajenar [enaxe'nar] *vt* to alienate; (*fig*)

to carry away; ~**se** *vr* (*de un bien*) to deprive o.s.; (*amigos*) to become estranged, fall out.

enamorado, a [enamo'raðo, a] *a* in love; **enamorar** *vt* to inspire love; **enamorarse** *vr* to fall in love.

enano, a [e'nano, a] *a* tiny // *nm/f* dwarf.

enardecer [enarðe'θer] *vt* (*pasiones*) to fire, inflame; (*persona*) to fill with enthusiasm; (: *llenar de ira*) to fill with anger; ~**se** *vr* to get excited; (*entusiasmarse*) to get enthusiastic (*por* about); (*de cólera*) to blaze.

encabezamiento [enkaβeθa'mjento] *nm* (*de carta*) heading; (*de periódico*) headline; (*preámbulo*) foreword, preface; (*registro*) roll, register.

encabezar [enkaβe'θar] *vt* (*manifestación*) to lead, head; (*lista*) to be at the top of; (*carta*) to put a heading to; (*libro*) to entitle; (*empadronar*) to register.

encadenar [enkaðe'nar] *vt* to chain (together); (*poner grilletes a*) to shackle.

encajar [enka'xar] *vt* (*ajustar*) to fit (into); (*golpe*) to give, deal; (*entrometer*) to insert // *vi* to fit (well); (*fig: corresponder a*) to match; ~**se** *vr* to intrude; ~**se en un sillón** to squeeze into a chair.

encaje [en'kaxe] *nm* (*labor*) lace; (*inserción*) insertion; (*ajuste*) fitting.

encajonar [enkaxo'nar] *vt* to box (up), put in a box.

encaminar [enkami'nar] *vt* to direct, send; ~**se** *vr*: ~**se a** to set out for.

encandilar [enkandi'lar] *vt* to dazzle; (*fuego*) to poke.

encantador, a [enkanta'ðor, a] *a* charming, lovely // *nm/f* magician, enchanter/tress.

encantar [enkan'tar] *vt* to charm, delight; (*hechizar*) to bewitch, cast a spell on; **encanto** *nm* (*magia*) spell, charm; (*fig*) charm, delight.

encarcelar [enkarθe'lar] *vt* to imprison, jail.

encarecer [enkare'θer] *vt* to put up the price of; (*pedir*) tc recommend, urge // *vi*, ~**se** *vr* to get dearer.

encarecimiento [enkareθi'mjento] *nm* price increase; (*pedido insistente*) urging.

encargado, a [enkar'ɣaðo, a] *a* in charge // *nm/f* agent, representative; (*responsable*) person in charge; ~ **de negocios** chargé d'affaires.

encargar [enkar'ɣar] *vt* to entrust; (*recomendar*) to urge, recommend; ~**se** *vr*: ~**se de** to look after, take charge of.

encargo [en'karɣo] *nm* (*pedido*) assignment, job; (*responsabilidad*) responsibility; (*recomendación*) recommendation; (*COM*) order.

encarnación [enkarna'θjon] *nf* incarnation, embodiment.

encarrilar [enkarri'lar] *vt* to correct, put on the right track; (*tren*) to put back on the rails.

encausar [enkau'sar] *vt* to prosecute, sue.

encauzar [enkau'θar] *vt* to channel.

enceguecer [enθeɣe'θer] *vt* to blind // *vi*, ~**se** *vr* to go blind.

encendedor [enθende'dor] *nm* lighter.

encender [enθen'der] *vt* (*con fuego*) to light; (*incendiar*) to set fire to; (*luz, radio*) to put on, switch on; (*inflarse*) to inflame; ~**se** *vr* to catch fire; (*excitarse*) to get excited; (*de cólera*) to flare up; (*el rostro*) to blush.

encendido [enθen'diðo] *nm* ignition.

encerrar [enθe'rrar] *vt* (*confinar*) to shut in, shut up; (*comprender, incluir*) to include, contain.

encía [en'θia] *nf* gum.

encierro [en'θjerro] *nm* shutting in, shutting up; (*calabozo*) prison.

encima [en'θima] *ad* (*sobre*) above, over; (*además*) besides; ~ **de** (*en*) on, on top of; (*sobre*) above, over; (*además de*) besides, on top of; **por** ~ **de** over; ¡**llevas dinero** ~? have you any money on you?; **se me vino** ~ it got on top of me.

encinta [en'θinta] *a* pregnant.

enclavar [enkla'βar] *vt* (*clavar*) to nail; (*atravesar*) to pierce; (*sitio*) to set; (*fig: fam*) to swindle.

encoger [enko'xer] *vt* (*gen*) to shrink, contract; (*fig: asustar*) to scare; (: *desanimar*) to discourage; ~**se** *vr* to shrink, contract; (*fig*) to cringe; ~**se de hombros** to shrug one's shoulders.

encojar [enko'xar] *vt* to lame; (*tullir*) to cripple; ~**se** *vr* to go lame; to become crippled.

encolar [enko'lar] *vt* (*engomar*) to glue, paste; (*pegar*) to stick down.

encolerizar [enkoleri'θar] *vt* to anger, provoke; ~**se** *vr* to get angry.

encomendar [enkomen'dar] *vt* to entrust, commend; ~**se** *vr*: ~**se a** to put one's trust in.

encomiar [enko'mjar] *vt* to praise, pay tribute to.

encomienda [enko'mjenda] *nf* (*encargo*) charge, commission; (*precio*) price; (*elogio*) tribute; ~ **postal** (*AM*) parcel post.

encomio [en'komjo] *nm* praise, tribute.

enconado, a [enko'naðo, a] *a* (*MED*) inflamed; (: *dolorido*) sore; (*fig*) angry.

enconar [enko'nar] *vt* (*MED*) to inflame; (*fig*) to anger, irritate; ~**se** *vr* (*MED*) to become inflamed; (*fig*) to get angry or irritated.

encono [en'kono] *nm* (*rencor*) rancour, spite; (*odio*) ill-feeling.

encontrado, a [enkon'traðo, a] *a* (*contrario*) contrary, conflicting; (*hostil*) hostile.

encontrar [enkon'trar] *vt* (*hallar*) to find; (*inesperadamente*) to meet, run into; ~**se** *vr* to meet (each other); (*situarse*) to be (situated); (*entrar en conflicto*) to crash, collide; ~**se con** to meet (with); ~**se bien de salud** to feel well.

encorvar [enkor'βar] *vt* to curve;

(*inclinar*) to bend (down); ~**se** *vr* to bend down, bend over, stoop.

encrespar [enkres'par] *vt* (*cabellos*) to curl; (*agua*) to ripple; (*fig*) to anger, irritate; ~**se** *vr* (*el mar*) to get rough; (*fig*) to get annoyed, irritated.

encrucijada [enkruθi'xaða] *nf* crossroads *sg*; (*empalme*) junction.

encuadernación [enkwaðerna'θjon] *nf* binding.

encuadernador, a [enkwaðerna'ðor, a] *nm/f* bookbinder.

encuadrar [enkwa'ðrar] *vt* (*retrato*) to frame; (*ajustar*) to fit, insert; (*encerrar*) to contain.

encubrir [enku'βrir] *vt* (*ocultar*) to hide, conceal; (*criminal*) to harbour, shelter.

encuentro *etc vb ver* **encontrar** // [en-'kwentro] *nm* (*de personas*) meeting; (*de trenes*) collision, crash; (*DEPORTE*) match, game; (*MIL*) encounter.

encuesta [en'kwesta] *nf* inquiry, investigation; ~ **judicial** post mortem.

encumbrado, a [enkum'braðo, a] *a* (*edificio*) lofty, towering; (*persona*) eminent, distinguished.

encumbrar [enkum'brar] *vt* (*edificio*) to raise; (*elevar*) to elevate; (*persona*) to exalt; ~**se** *vr* to rise, tower; (*fig*) to become conceited.

encharcado, a [entʃar'kaðo, a] *a* still; (*estancado*) stagnant.

enchufar [entʃu'far] *vt* (*ELEC*) to plug in; (*TEC*) to connect, fit together; **enchufe** *nm* (*ELEC. clavija*) plug; (: *toma*) plug, socket; (*de dos tubos*) joint, connection; (*fam: influencia*) contact, connection; (: *puesto*) cushy job.

endemoniado, a [endemo'njaðo, a] *a* possessed (of the devil); (*endiabolado*) devilish; (*furioso*) furious, wild.

endentar [enden'tar] *vt*, *vi* to engage, mesh.

enderezar [endere'θar] *vt* (*poner derecho*) to straighten (out); (: *verticalmente*) to set upright; (*carta*) to address; (*fig*) to straighten or sort out; (*dirigir*) to direct; ~**se** *vr* (*persona sentado*) to stand up; (*fig*) to correct one's ways.

endeudarse [endeu'ðarse] *vr* to get into debt.

endiablado, a [endja'βlaðo, a] *a* devilish, diabolical; (*hum*) mischievous; (*fig*) furious, angry.

endomingarse [endomin'garse] *vr* to dress up, put on one's best clothes.

endosar [endo'sar] *vt* (*cheque etc*) to endorse.

endulzar [endul'θar] *vt* to sweeten; (*fig*) to soften.

endurecer [endure'θer] *vt* to harden; (*fig*) to harden, toughen; ~**se** *vr* to harden, grow hard.

endurecido, a [endure'θiðo, a] *a* (*duro*) hard; (*fig*) hardy, tough; **estar** ~ **a algo** to be hardened or used to sth.

endurecimiento [endureθi'mjento] *nm*

(acto) hardening; *(tenacidad)* toughness; *(crueldad)* cruelty; *(insensibilidad)* callousness.

enemigo, a [ene'miɤo, a] *a* enemy, hostile // *nm/f* enemy // *nf* enmity, hostility.

enemistad [enemis'tað] *nf* enmity.

enemistar [enemis'tar] *vt* to make enemies of, cause a rift between; ~**se** *vr* to become enemies; *(amigos)* to fall out.

energía [ener'xia] *nf (vigor)* energy, drive; *(TEC, ELEC)* energy, power.

enérgico, a [e'nerxiko, a] *a (gen)* energetic; *(voz, modales)* forceful.

enero [e'nero] *nm* January.

enfadar [enfa'ðar] *vt* to anger, annoy; ~**se** *vr* to get angry or annoyed.

enfado [en'faðo] *nm (enojo)* anger, annoyance; *(disgusto)* trouble, bother; ~**so, a** *a* annoying; *(aburrido)* tedious.

énfasis ['enfasis] *nm* emphasis, stress.

enfático, a [en'fatiko, a] *a* emphatic; *(afectado)* pompous.

enfermar [enfer'mar] *vt* to make ill // *vi* to fall ill, be taken ill.

enfermedad [enferme'ðað] *nf* illness; ~ **venérea** venereal disease.

enfermería [enferme'ria] *nf* infirmary; *(de colegio etc)* sick bay.

enfermero, a [enfer'mero, a] *nm/f* male nurse/nurse.

enfermizo, a [enfer'miθo, a] *a (persona)* sickly, unhealthy; *(lugar)* unhealthy.

enfermo, a [en'fermo, a] *a* ill, sick // *nm/f* invalid, sick person; *(en hospital)* patient.

enflaquecer [enflake'θer] *vt (adelgazar)* to make thin; *(debilitar)* to weaken; ~**se** *vr (adelgazarse)* to become thin, lose weight; *(debilitarse)* to grow weak; *(fig)* to lose heart.

enfocar [enfo'kar] *vt (foto etc)* to focus; *(problema etc)* to approach, look at.

enfoque [en'foke] *nm* focus.

enfrentar [enfren'tar] *vt (peligro)* to face (up to), confront; *(oponer, carear)* to put face to face; ~**se** *vr (dos personas)* to face or confront each other; *(dos equipos)* to meet; ~**se a o con** to face up to, confront.

enfrente [en'frente] *ad* opposite; ~ **de** *prep* opposite, facing; **la casa de** ~ the house opposite, the house across the street.

enfriamiento [enfria'mjento] *nm* chilling, refrigeration; *(MED)* cold, chill.

enfriar [enfri'ar] *vt (alimentos)* to cool, chill; *(algo caliente)* to cool down; *(habitación)* to air, freshen; ~**se** *vr* to cool down; *(MED)* to catch a chill; *(amistad)* to cool.

enfurecer [enfure'θer] *vt* to enrage, madden; ~**se** *vr* to become furious, fly into a rage; *(mar)* to get rough.

engalanar [engala'nar] *vt (adornar)* to adorn; *(ciudad)* to decorate; ~**se** *vr* to get dressed up.

enganchar [engan'tʃar] *vt (gen)* to hook; *(ropa)* to hang up; *(dos vagones)* to hitch up; *(TEC)* to couple, connect; *(MIL)* to

recruit; *(fig: fam: persona)* to rope into; ~**se** *vr (MIL)* to enlist, join up.

enganche [en'gantʃe] *nm* hook; *(TEC)* coupling, connection; *(acto)* hooking (up); *(: ropa)* hanging up; *(MIL)* recruitment, enlistment.

engañar [enga'ɲar] *vt* to deceive; *(trampear)* to cheat, swindle; ~**se** *vr (equivocarse)* to be wrong; *(disimular la verdad)* to deceive or kid o.s.

engaño [en'gaɲo] *nm* deceit; *(trampa)* trick, swindle; *(error)* mistake, misunderstanding; *(ilusión)* delusion; ~**so, a** *a (tramposo)* crooked; *(mentiroso)* dishonest, deceitful; *(aspecto)* deceptive; *(consejo)* misleading, wrong.

engarzar [engar'θar] *vt (joya)* to set, mount; *(fig)* to link, connect.

engatusar [engatu'sar] *vt (fam)* to coax.

engendrar [enxen'drar] *vt* to breed; *(procrear)* to beget; *(fig)* to cause, produce; **engendro** *nm (BIO)* foetus; *(fig)* monstrosity; *(idea)* brainchild.

engolfarse [engol'farse] *vr:* ~ **en** to bury o.s in, become deeply involved in.

engomar [engo'mar] *vt* to gum, glue, stick.

engordar [engor'ðar] *vt* to fatten // *vi* to get fat, put on weight.

engranaje [engra'naxe] *nm* gear.

engranar [engra'nar] *vt* to put into gear // *vi* to interlock.

engrandecer [engrande'θer] *vt* to enlarge, magnify; *(alabar)* to praise, speak highly of; *(exagerar)* to exaggerate.

engrasar [engra'sar] *vt (TEC: poner grasa)* to grease; *(: lubricar)* to lubricate, oil; *(manchar)* to make greasy; *(animal)* to fatten.

engreído, a [engre'iðo, a] *a* vain, conceited; **engreírse** *vr* to become conceited.

engrosar [engro'sar] *vt (ensanchar)* to enlarge; *(aumentar)* to increase; *(hinchar)* to swell // *vi* to get fat; ~**se** *vr* to increase; to swell.

enhebrar [ene'βrar] *vt* to thread.

enhorabuena [enora'βwena] *nf* congratulations *pl* // *ad* well and good.

enigma [e'niɣma] *nm* enigma; *(problema)* puzzle; *(misterio)* mystery.

enjabonar [enxaβo'nar] *vt* to soap; *(fam: adular)* to soft-soap; *(: regañar)* to scold.

enjambre [en'xamβre] *nm* swarm.

enjaular [enxau'lar] *vt* to put in a cage; *(fam)* to jail, lock up.

enjuagar [enxwa'ɤar] *vt (ropa)* to rinse (out).

enjugar [enxu'ɤar] *vt* to wipe (off); *(lágrimas)* to dry; *(déficit)* to wipe out.

enjuiciar [enxwi'θjar] *vt (JUR: procesar)* to prosecute, try; *(fig)* to judge.

enjuto, a [en'xuto, a] *a* dry, dried up; *(fig)* lean, skinny.

enlace [en'laθe] *nm* link, connection; *(relación)* relationship; *(casamiento)* marriage; *(de carretera, trenes)* connection; **agente**

de ~ broker; ~ **sindical** shop steward.

enlazar [enla'θar] vt (atar) to tie; (conectar) to link, connect; (AM) to lasso; ~**se** vr (novios) to get married; (dos familias) to become related by marriage; (conectarse) to link (up), be linked.

enlodar [enlo'ðar], **enlodazar** [enloða-'θar] vt to muddy, cover in mud; (fig: manchar) to stain; (: rebajar) to debase.

enloquecer [enloke'θer] vt to drive mad // vi, ~**se** vr to go mad.

enlutar [enlu'tar] vt to dress in mourning; ~**se** vr to go into mourning.

enmarañar [enmara'ɲar] vt (enredar) to tangle (up), entangle; (complicar) to complicate; (confundir) to confuse; ~**se** vr (enredarse) to become entangled; (confundirse) to get confused; (nublarse) to cloud over.

enmascarar [enmaska'rar] vt to mask; ~**se** vr to put on a mask; ~**se de** to masquerade as.

enmendar [enmen'dar] vt to emend, correct; (constitución etc) to amend; (compensar) to make good; (comportamiento) to reform; ~**se** vr to reform, mend one's ways; **enmienda** nf correction; amendment; reform; (compensación) compensation, indemnity.

enmohecerse [enmoe'θerse] vr (metal) to rust, go rusty; (muro, plantas) to get mouldy.

enmudecer [enmuðe'θer] vt to silence // vi, ~**se** vr (perder el habla) to go silent; (guardar silencio) to keep quiet.

ennegrecer [ennevre'θer] vt (poner negro) to blacken; (oscurecer) to darken; ~**se** vr to turn black; (oscurecerse) to get dark.

ennoblecer [ennoβle'θer] vt to ennoble; (fig) to embellish, adorn.

enojadizo, a [enoxa'ðiθo, a] a irritable, short-tempered.

enojar [eno'xar] vt (encolerizar) to anger; (disgustar) to annoy, upset; ~**se** vr to get angry; to get annoyed.

enojo [e'noxo] nm (cólera) anger; (disgusto) annoyance; ~**s** nmpl trials, problems; ~**so, a** a annoying.

enorgullecerse [enorɣuʎe'θerse] vr to be proud; ~ **de** to pride o.s. on, be proud of.

enorme [e'norme] a enormous, huge; (fig) monstrous; **enormidad** nf hugeness, immensity; (despropósito) absurdity, piece of nonsense; (perversidad) monstrosity.

enraizar [enrai'θar] vi to take root.

enredadera [enreða'ðera] nf (BOT) creeper, climbing plant.

enredar [enre'ðar] vt (ovillo) to tangle (up), entangle; (peces) to net; (situación) to complicate, confuse; (meter cizaña) to sow discord among or between; (implicar) to embroil, implicate; ~**se** vr to get entangled, get tangled (up); (situación) to get complicated; (persona) to get embroiled; (AM. fam) to meddle.

enredo [en'reðo] nm (maraña) tangle;

(confusión) mix-up, confusion; (intriga) intrigue.

enrevesado, a [enreβe'saðo, a] a unruly, uncontrollable; (enredado) complicated, involved.

enriquecer [enrike'θer] vt to make rich, enrich; ~**se** vr to get rich.

enrojecer [enroxe'θer] vt to redden // vi, ~**se** vr (metal) to become red hot; (persona) to blush.

enrollar [enro'ʎar] vt to roll (up), wind (up).

enroscar [enros'kar] vt (torcer, doblar) to coil (round), wind; (tornillo, rosca) to screw in; ~**se** vr to coil, wind.

ensalada [ensa'laða] nf salad; **ensaladilla** nf Russian salad.

ensalzar [ensal'θar] vt (alabar) to praise, extol; (exaltar) to exalt.

ensambladura [ensambla'ðura] nf, **ensamblaje** [ensam'blaxe] nm assembly; (TEC) joint; **ensamblar** vt to assemble.

ensanchar [ensan'tʃar] vt (hacer más ancho) to widen; (agrandar) to enlarge, expand; ~**se** vr to get wider, expand; (pey) to give o.s. airs; **ensanche** nm (de vestido, calle) widening; (de negocio) expansion.

ensangrentar [ensangren'tar] vt to stain with blood; ~**se** vr (fig) to get angry.

ensañar [ensa'ɲar] vt to enrage; ~**se** vr: ~**se con** to delight in tormenting.

ensartar [ensar'tar] vt (gen) to string (together); (aguja) to thread.

ensayar [ensa'jar] vt to test, try (out); (TEATRO) to rehearse.

ensayista [ensa'jista] nm/f essayist.

ensayo [en'sajo] nm test, trial; (QUÍMICA) experiment; (TEATRO) rehearsal; (DEPORTE) try; (obra literaria) essay.

ensenada [ense'naða] nf inlet, cove.

enseñanza [ense'ɲanθa] nf (educación) education; (acción) teaching; (doctrina) teaching, doctrine.

enseñar [ense'ɲar] vt (educar) to teach; (instruir) to teach, instruct; (mostrar, señalar) to show.

enseres [en'seres] nmpl goods and chattels, things.

ensimismarse [ensimis'marse] vr (abstraerse) to become lost in thought; (estar absorto) to be lost in thought; (AM) to become conceited.

ensoberbecerse [ensoβerβe'θerse] vr to become proud; (hacerse arrogante) to become arrogant; (mar) to get rough.

ensordecer [ensorðe'θer] vt to deafen // vi to go deaf.

ensortijar [ensorti'xar] vt, ~**se** vr (cabellos) to curl.

ensuciar [ensu'θjar] vt (manchar) to dirty, soil; (fig) to defile; ~**se** vr (mancharse) to get dirty; (fig) to dirty/wet o.s.

ensueño [en'sweɲo] nm (sueño) dream, fantasy; (ilusión) illusion; (soñando despierto) reverie.

entablado [enta'βlaðo] nm (piso)

floorboards pl; (armazón) boarding.

entablar [enta'βlar] vt (recubrir) to board (up); (AJEDREZ, DAMAS) to set up; (conversación) to strike up; (JUR) to file // vi to draw.

entallar [enta'ʎar] vt (piedra) to sculpt; (madera) to carve; (grabar) to engrave; (traje) to tailor // vi: **el traje entalla bien** the suit fits well.

entender [enten'der] vt (comprender) to understand; (darse cuenta) to realize; (creer, pensar) to think, believe; (querer decir) to mean // vi: ~ **de** to know all about; ~ **en** to deal with, have to do with; ~**se** vr (comprenderse) to be understood; (ponerse de acuerdo) to understand one another, have an understanding; (aliarse) to agree, reach an agreement; (fam) to have an affair; **me entiendo con la mecánica** I'm (quite) good at mechanics.

entendido, a [enten'diðo, a] a (comprendido) understood; (hábil) skilled; (inteligente) knowledgeable // nm/f (experto) expert; (docto) knowledgeable person // excl agreed!; **entendimiento** nm (comprensión) understanding; (facultad intelectual) the mind, intellect; (juicio) judgement.

enterado, a [ente'raðo, a] a well-informed; **estar** ~ **de** to know about, be aware of.

enteramente [entera'mente] ad entirely, completely.

enterar [ente'rar] vt (informar) to inform, tell; ~**se** vr to find out, get to know.

entereza [ente'reθa] nf (totalidad) entirety; (fig: energía) strength of mind; (honradez) integrity; (severidad) strictness, severity.

enternecer [enterne'θer] vt (ablandar) to soften; (apiadar) to touch, move; ~**se** vr to be touched, be moved.

entero, a [en'tero, a] a (total) whole, entire; (fig: recto) honest; (: firme) firm, resolute // nm (COM: punto) point; (AM: pago) payment.

enterrador [enterra'ðor] nm gravedigger.

enterrar [ente'rrar] vt to bury.

entibiar [enti'βjar] vt to cool; (fig) to cool (down).

entidad [enti'ðað] nf (empresa) firm, company; (organismo) body; (sociedad) society; (FILOSOFIA) entity.

entiendo etc vb ver **entender.**

entierro [en'tjerro] nm (acción) burial; (funeral) funeral.

entomología   [entomolo'xia]   nf entomology.

entonación [entona'θjon] nf (LING) intonation; (fig) conceit.

entonado, a [ento'naðo, a] a (MUS) in tune; (fig) conceited.

entonar [ento'nar] vt (canción) to intone; (colores) to tone; (MED) to tone up // vi to be in tune; ~**se** vr (engreírse) to give o.s. airs.

entonces [en'tonθes] ad then, at that time;

desde ~ since then; **en aquel** ~ at that time; (pues) ~ and so.

entornar [entor'nar] vt (puerta, ventana) to half close, leave ajar; (los ojos) to screw up.

entorpecer [entorpe'θer] vt (adormecer los sentidos) to dull, benumb; (impedir) to obstruct, hinder; (: tránsito) to slow down, delay; **entorpecimiento** nm numbness; slowing-down, delay; (letargia) lethargy.

entrado, a [en'traðo, a] a: ~ **en años** elderly; **una vez** ~ **el verano** in the summer(time), when summer comes // nf (acción) entry, access; (sitio) entrance, way in; (COM) receipts pl, takings pl; (CULIN) entree; (DEPORTE) innings sg; (TEATRO) house, audience; (para el cine etc) ticket; (COM): ~**as y salidas** income and expenditure; (TEC): ~**a de aire** air intake or inlet.

entrante [en'trante] a next, coming // nm inlet; **ser** ~ **en una casa** to have the run of a house.

entraña [en'traɲa] nf (fig: centro) heart, core; (raíz) root; ~**s** nfpl (ANAT) entrails; **entrañable** a close, intimate.

entrar [en'trar] vt (introducir) to bring in // vi (meterse) to go/come in, enter; (comenzar): ~ **diciendo** to begin by saying; **no me entra** I can't get the hang of it; **el año que entra** next year.

entre ['entre] prep (dos) between; (más de dos) among(st); **pensaba** ~ **mí** I thought to myself.

entreabrir [entrea'βrir] vt to half-open, open halfway.

entrecejo [entre'θexo] nm: **fruncir el** ~ to frown.

entredicho [entre'ðitʃo] nm prohibition, ban; (JUR) injunction.

entrega [en'treɣa] nf (de mercancías) delivery; (rendición) surrender; **novela por** ~**s** serial, novel in instalments.

entregar [entre'ɣar] vt (dar) to hand (over), deliver; (ceder) to give up; ~**se** vr (rendirse) to surrender, give in, submit; (dedicarse) to devote o.s.

entrelazar [entrela'θar] vt to entwine.

entremés [entre'mes] nm (CULIN) side-dish; **entremeses** nmpl hors d'œuvres.

entremeter [entreme'ter] vt to insert, put in; ~**se** vr to meddle, interfere; **entremetido, a** a meddling, interfering.

entremezclar [entremeθ'klar] vt, ~**se** vr to intermingle.

entrenador [entrena'ðor] nm trainer, coach; **entrenarse** vr to train.

entreoír [entreo'ir] vt to half hear.

entresacar [entresa'kar] vt to pick out, select.

entresuelo [entre'swelo] nm (sótano) basement.

entretanto [entre'tanto] ad meanwhile, meantime; **en el** ~ in the meantime.

entretejer [entrete'xer] vt to interweave.

entretener [entrete'ner] vt (divertir) to entertain, amuse; (detener) to hold up, delay; (*cuidar*) to maintain; ~**se** *vr* (*divertirse*) to amuse o.s.; (*retrasarse*) to delay, linger; **entretenido, a** *a* entertaining, amusing; **entretenimiento** *nm* entertainment, amusement; (*cuidado*) upkeep, maintenance.

entrever [entre'ßer] *vt* to glimpse, catch a glimpse of.

entreverar [entreße'rar] *vt* to mix (up).

entrevista [entre'ßista] *nf* interview; **entrevistar** *vt* to interview; **entrevistarse** *vr* to have an interview.

entristecer [entriste'θer] *vt* to sadden, grieve; ~**se** *vr* to grow sad.

entrometer [entrome'ter] *etc* = **entremeter** *etc*.

entroncar [entron'kar] *vi* to be connected *or* related.

entronque [en'tronke] *nm* connection, link.

entuerto [en'twerto] *nm* wrong, injustice.

entumecer [entume'θer] *vt* to numb, benumb; ~**se** *vr* (*por el frío*) to go *or* become numb; **entumecido, a** *a* numb, stiff.

enturbiar [entur'ßjar] *vt* (*el agua*) to disturb, make cloudy; (*fig*) to fog, confuse; ~**se** *vr* (*oscurecerse*) to become cloudy; (*fig*) to get confused, become obscure.

entusiasmar [entusjas'mar] *vt* to excite, fill with enthusiasm; (*gustar mucho*) to delight; ~**se** *vr*: ~**se con** *o* **por** to get enthusiastic *or* excited about.

entusiasmo [entu'sjasmo] *nm* enthusiasm; (*deleite*) delight; (*excitación*) excitement.

entusiasta [entu'sjasta] *a* enthusiastic // *nm/f* enthusiast.

enumerar [enume'rar] *vt* to enumerate.

enunciación [enunθja'θjon] *nf*, **enunciado** [enun'θjaðo] *nm* enunciation; (*declaración*) declaration, statement; **enunciar** *vt* to enunciate; to declare, state.

envainar [enßai'nar] *vt* to sheathe.

envalentonar [enßalento'nar] *vt* to give courage to; ~**se** *vr* to take courage, become bolder; (*pey: jactarse*) to boast, brag.

envanecer [enßane'θer] *vt* to make conceited; ~**se** *vr* to grow vain *or* conceited.

envasar [enßa'sar] *vt* (*empaquetar*) to pack, wrap; (*enfrascar*) to bottle; (*enlatar*) to tin; (*embolsar*) to pocket // *vi* (*fig: fam: vino*) to knock back; **envase** *nm* packing, wrapping; bottling; tinning, canning; pocketing; (*recipiente*) container; (*paquete*) package; (*botella*) bottle; (*lata*) tin, can.

envejecer [enßexe'θer] *vt* to make old, age // *vi*, ~**se** *vr* (*volverse viejo*) to grow old; (*fig*) to become old-fashioned.

envenenar [enßene'nar] *vt* to poison; (*fig*) to embitter.

envergadura [enßerxa'ðura] *nf* (*fig*) scope, compass.

envés [en'ßes] *nm* (*de tela*) back, wrong side.

enviar [en'ßjar] *vt* to send.

envidia [en'ßiðja] *nf* (*deseo ferviente*) envy; (*celos*) jealousy; **envidiar** *vt* (*desear*) to envy; (*tener celos de*) to be jealous of.

envilecer [enßile'θer] *vt* to debase, degrade; ~**se** *vr* to lower o.s.

envío [en'ßio] *nm* (*acción*) sending; (*de mercancías*) consignment; (*COM*) remittance.

enviudar [enßju'ðar] *vi* to be widowed.

envoltura [enßol'tura] *nf* (*cobertura*) cover; (*embalaje*) wrapper, wrapping; (*funda*) case.

envolver [enßol'ßer] *vt* to wrap (up); (*cubrir*) to cover; (*enemigo*) to surround; (*implicar*) to involve, implicate; ~**se** *vr* (*cubrirse*) to wrap o.s. up; (*implicarse*) to become involved.

envuelto [en'ßwelto] *pp de* **envolver**.

enzarzar [enθar'θar] *vt* (*fig*) to involve (in a dispute).

épico, a ['epiko, a] *a* epic // *nf* epic.

epidemia [epi'ðemja] *nf* epidemic; **epidémico, a** *a* epidemic.

epifanía [epifa'nia] *nf* Epiphany.

epilepsia [epi'lepsja] *nf* epilepsy.

epílogo [e'piloxo] *nm* epilogue.

episodio [epi'soðjo] *nm* episode.

epístola [e'pistola] *nf* epistle; (*fam*) letter.

epitafio [epi'tafjo] *nm* epitaph.

época ['epoka] *nf* period, time; (*HISTORIA*) age, epoch; **hacer** ~ to be epoch-making.

equidad [eki'ðað] *nf* equity.

equilibrar [ekili'ßrar] *vt* to balance; **equilibrio** *nm* balance, equilibrium; **equilibrista** *nm/f* (*funámbulo*) tightrope walker; (*acróbata*) acrobat.

equipaje [eki'paxe] *nm* luggage; (*equipo*) equipment, kit; (*NAUT: tripulación*) crew; ~ **de mano** hand luggage.

equipar [eki'par] *vt* (*proveer*) to equip.

equipararse [ekipa'rarse] *vr*: ~ **con** to be on a level with.

equipo [e'kipo] *nm* (*materiales*) equipment; (*grupo*) team; (: *de obreros*) shift.

equis ['ekis] *nf* (the letter) X.

equitación [ekita'θjon] *nf* (*acto*) riding; (*arte*) horsemanship.

equitativo, a [ekita'tißo, a] *a* equitable, fair.

equivalente [ekißa'lente] *a*, *nm* equivalent; **equivaler** *vi* to be equivalent *or* equal.

equivocación [ekißoka'θjon] *nf* mistake, error; **equivocarse** *vr* to be wrong, make a mistake; **equivocarse de camino** to take the wrong road; **equívoco, a** *a* (*dudoso*) suspect; (*ambiguo*) ambiguous // *nm* ambiguity; (*juego de palabras*) play on words.

era *vb ver* **ser** // ['era] *nf* era, age.

erais *vb ver* **ser**.

éramos vb ver **ser**.

eran vb ver **ser**.

erario [e'rarjo] nm exchequer, treasury.

eras vb ver **ser**.

eres vb ver **ser**.

erguir [er'xir] vt to raise, lift; (poner derecho) to straighten; ~se vr to straighten up; (fig) to swell with pride.

erigir [eri'xir] vt to erect, build; ~se vr: ~se en to set o.s. up as.

erizado, a [eri'θaðo, a] a bristly.

erizarse [eri'θarse] vr to stand on end.

erizo [e'riθo] nm hedgehog; (~ de mar) sea-urchin.

ermitaño, a [ermi'taɲo, a] nm/f hermit.

erótico, a [e'rotiko, a] a erotic; **erotismo** nm eroticism.

erradicar [erraði'kar] vt to eradicate.

errado, a [e'rraðo, a] a mistaken, wrong.

errante [e'rrante] a wandering, errant.

errar [e'rrar] vi (vagar) to wander, roam; (equivocarse) to err, make a mistake // vt: ~ el camino to take the wrong road; ~ el tiro to miss.

erróneo, a [e'rroneo, a] a (equivocado) wrong, mistaken; (falso) false, untrue.

error [e'rror] nm error, mistake; ~ de imprenta misprint.

eructar [eruk'tar] vt to belch.

erudición [eruði'θjon] nf erudition, learning.

erudito, a [eru'ðito, a] a erudite, learned.

erupción [erup'θjon] nf eruption; (MED) rash.

es vb ver **ser**.

esa, esas det ver **ese**.

ésa, ésas pron ver **ese**.

esbelto, a [es'βelto, a] a slim, slender.

esbozo [es'βoθo] nm sketch, outline.

escabeche [eska'βetʃe] nm brine; (de aceitunas etc) pickle; **pescado en** ~ pickled fish.

escabel [eska'βel] nm (low) stool.

escabroso, a [eska'βroso, a] a (accidentado) rough, uneven; (fig) tough, difficult; (: atrevido) risqué.

escabullirse [eskaβuʎirse] vr to slip away; (irse) to clear out.

escala [es'kala] nf (proporción, MUS) scale; (de mano) ladder; (AVIAT) stopover; **hacer** ~ en to stop or call in at; ~ de colores range of colours.

escalafón [eskala'fon] nm (escala de salarios) salary scale, wage scale; (lista etc) list; (registro) register.

escalar [eska'lar] vt (montaña etc) to climb, scale; (casa) to burgle, break into.

escalera [eska'lera] nf stairs pl, staircase; (escala) ladder; (NAIPES) run; ~ **mecánica** escalator; ~ **de caracol** spiral staircase.

escalinata [eskali'nata] nf outside staircase.

escalofrío [eskalo'frio] nm chill; ~s nmpl (fig) shivers; **escalofriante** a chilling.

escalón [eska'lon] nm step, stair; (de escalera) rung.

escama [es'kama] nf (de pez, serpiente) scale; (de jabón) flake; (fig) resentment.

escamado, a [eska'maðo, a] a wary, cautious.

escamotar [eskamo'tar], **escamotear** [eskamote'ar] vt (quitar) to lift, swipe (fam); (hacer desaparecer) to make disappear.

escampar [eskam'par] vb impersonal to stop raining; (del cielo) to clear (up).

escandalizar [eskandali'θar] vt to scandalize, shock; ~se vr to be shocked; (ofenderse) to be offended.

escándalo [es'kandalo] nm scandal; (alboroto, tumulto) row, uproar; **escandaloso, a** a scandalous, shocking.

escandinavo, a [eskandi'naβo, a] a, nm/f Scandinavian.

escaño [es'kaɲo] nm bench; (POL) seat.

escapar [eska'par] vi (gen) to escape, run away; (DEPORTE) to break away; ~se vr to escape, get away; (gas) to leak (out).

escaparate [eskapa'rate] nm shop window; (AM) wardrobe.

escape [es'kape] nm (de gas) leak; (de motor) exhaust; (de persona) escape.

escarabajo [eskara'βaxo] nm beetle; ~s nmpl (fam) scribble sg.

escaramuza [eskara'muθa] nf skirmish; (fig) brush.

escarbar [eskar'βar] vt (gallina) to scratch; (dientes) to pick; (orejas) to clean; (fig) to inquire into, investigate.

escarcha [es'kartʃa] nf frost.

escarlata [eskar'lata] a inv scarlet; **escarlatina** nf scarlet fever.

escarmentar [eskarmen'tar] vt to punish severely // vi to learn one's lesson; **escarmiento** nm (ejemplo) lesson, example; (castigo) punishment.

escarnecer [eskarne'θer] vt to mock, ridicule; **escarnio, escarnecimiento** nm mockery; (injuria) insult.

escarpado, a [eskar'paðo, a] a (abrupto) sheer; (inclinado) steep; (accidentado) craggy.

escasear [eskase'ar] vt to skimp (on) // vi to be scarce.

escasez [eska'seθ] nf (falta) shortage, scarcity; (pobreza) poverty; (mezquindad) meanness.

escaso, a [es'kaso, a] a (poco) scarce; (raro) rare; (ralo) thin, sparse; (limitado) limited.

escatimar [eskati'mar] vt (limitar) to skimp (on); (reducir) to curtail, cut down.

escena [es'θena] nf scene.

escenario [esθe'narjo] nm (TEATRO) stage; (CINE) set; (fig) scene.

escepticismo [esθepti'θismo] nm scepticism; **escéptico, a** a sceptical // nm/f sceptic.

esclarecer [esklare'θer] vt (iluminar) to light up, illuminate; (misterio, problema) to shed light on; (ennoblecer) to ennoble.

esclavitud [esklaβi'tuð] *nf* slavery.

esclavizar [esklaβi'θar] *vt* to enslave.

esclavo, a [es'klaβo, a] *nm/f* slave.

escoba [es'koβa] *nf* broom.

escocer [esko'θer] *vt* to annoy // *vi* to burn, sting; ~**se** *vr* to chafe, get chafed.

escocés, esa [esko'θes, esa] *a* Scottish // *nm/f* Scotsman/woman, Scot.

Escocia [es'koθja] *nf* Scotland.

escoger [esko'xer] *vt* to choose, pick, select; **escogido, a** *a* chosen, selected; (*calidad*) choice, select; **escogimiento** *nm* choice.

escolar [esko'lar] *a* school *cpd* // *nm/f* schoolboy/girl, pupil.

escolta [es'kolta] *nf* escort; **escoltar** *vt* to escort.

escombro [es'kombro] *nm* mackerel; ~**s** *nmpl* (*basura*) rubbish *sg*; (*restos*) debris *sg*.

esconder [eskon'der] *vt* to hide, conceal; ~**se** *vr* to hide; **escondite** *nm* hiding place; (*juego*) hide-and-seek.

escondrijo [eskon'drixo] *nm* hiding-place, hideout.

escopeta [esko'peta] *nf* shotgun.

escoplo [es'koplo] *nm* chisel.

Escorpio [es'korpjo] *nm* Scorpio.

escorpión [eskor'pjon] *nm* scorpion.

escote [es'kote] *nm* (*de vestido*) low neck; (*parte*) share; **pagar a** ~ to share the expenses.

escotillón [eskoti'ʎon] *nm* trapdoor.

escozor [esko'θor] *nm* (*dolor*) sting(ing); (*fig*) grief, heartache.

escribano, a [eskri'βano, a], **escribiente** [eskri'βjente] *nm/f* clerk.

escribir [eskri'βir] *vt, vi* to write; ~ **a máquina** to type; **¿cómo se escribe?** how do you spell it?

escrito, a [es'krito, a] *pp de* **escribir** // *nm* (*documento*) document; (*manuscrito*) text, manuscript; **por** ~ in writing.

escritor, a [eskri'tor, a] *nm/f* writer.

escritorio [eskri'torjo] *nm* desk; (*oficina*) office.

escritura [eskri'tura] *nf* (*acción*) writing; (*caligrafía*) (hand)writing; (*JUR*: *documento*) deed.

escrúpulo [es'krupulo] *nm* scruple; (*minuciosidad*) scrupulousness; **escrupuloso, a** *a* scrupulous.

escrutar [eskru'tar] *vt* to scrutinize, examine; (*votos*) to count.

escrutinio [eskru'tinjo] *nm* (*examen atento*) scrutiny; (*recuento de votos*) poll; (*resultado de elección*) voting, ballot.

escuadra [es'kwaðra] *nf* (*MIL etc*) squad; (*NAUT*) squadron; (*de coches etc*) fleet; **escuadrilla** *nf* (*de aviones*) squadron; (*AM*: *de obreros*) gang.

escuadrón [eskwa'ðron] *nm* squadron.

escuálido, a [es'kwaliðo, a] *a* (*flaco, macilento*) pale, wan; (*sucio*) squalid.

escuchar [esku'tʃar] *vt* to listen to // *vi* to listen.

escudilla [esku'ðiʎa] *nf* bowl, basin.

escudo [es'kuðo] *nm* shield.

escudriñar [eskuðri'nar] *vt* (*examinar*) to investigate, examine closely; (*mirar de lejos*) to scan.

escuela [es'kwela] *nf* school.

escueto, a [es'kweto, a] *a* plain, unadorned.

esculpir [eskul'pir] *vt* to sculpt; (*grabar*) to engrave; (*tallar*) to carve; **escultor, a** *nm/f* sculptor/tress; **escultura** *nf* sculpture.

escupidora [eskupi'ðora], **escupidera** [eskupi'ðera] *nf* spittoon; (*orinal*) bedpan.

escupir [esku'pir] *vt, vi* to spit (out).

escurridero [eskurri'ðero] *nm* draining-board.

escurridizo, a [eskurri'ðiθo, a] *a* slippery.

escurrir [esku'rrir] *vt* (*ropa*) to wring out; (*verduras*) to strain; (*platos*) to drain // *vi* (*los líquidos*) to drip; (*resbalarse*) to slip, slide; ~**se** *vr* (*gotear*) to drip; (*secarse*) to drain; (*resbalarse*) to slip, slide; (*escaparse*) to slip away.

ese, esa, esos, esas ['ese, 'esa, 'esos, 'esas] *det* (*sg*) that; (*pl*) those.

ése, esa, esos, esas ['ese, 'esa, 'esos, 'esas] *pron* (*sg*) that (one); (*pl*) those (ones); ~... **éste**... the former... the latter...; **¡no me vengas con** ~**as** don't give me any more of that nonsense.

esencia [e'senθja] *nf* essence; **esencial** *a* essential.

esfera [es'fera] *nf* sphere; (*de reloj*) face; **esférico, a** *a* spherical.

esforzado, a [esfor'θaðo, a] *a* (*enérgico*) energetic, vigorous; (*valiente*) brave.

esforzar [esfor'θar] *vt* (*fortalecer*) to strengthen; (*alentar*) to encourage; ~**se** *vr* to exert o.s., make an effort.

esfuerzo [es'fwerθo] *nm* effort; (*TEC*) stress; (*valor*) courage, spirit.

esfumarse [esfu'marse] *vr* to fade away.

esgrima [es'ɣrima] *nf* fencing.

esguince [es'ɣinθe] *nm* (*MED*) sprain; (*ademán*) swerve, dodge; (*ceño*) scowl, frown.

eslabón [esla'βon] *nm* link; **eslabonar** *vt* to link, connect.

esmaltar [esmal'tar] *vt* to enamel; (*las uñas*) to paint, varnish; **esmalte** *nm* enamel; **esmalte de uñas** nail varnish, nail polish.

esmerado, a [esme'raðo, a] *a* careful, neat.

esmeralda [esme'ralda] *nf* emerald.

esmerarse [esme'rarse] *vr* (*aplicarse*) to take great pains, exercise great care; (*brillar*) to shine, do well.

esmero [es'mero] *nm* (great) care.

esnob [es'nob] *a inv* (*persona*) snobbish; (*coche etc*) posh // *nm/f* snob; ~**ismo** *nm* snobbery.

eso ['eso] *pron* that, that thing *or* matter; ~ **de su coche** all that about his car; ~ **de ir al cine** all that about going to the cinema, the idea of going to the cinema; **a** ~ **de las cinco** at about five o'clock; **en**

~ thereupon, at that point; ~ **es** that's it; ;~ **sí que es vidal** now this is really living!; **por ~ te lo dije** that's why I told you.

esos ['esos] *det ver* **ése**.

ésos ['esos] *pron ver* **ése**.

espabilar [espaßi'lar] *vt* (*vela*) to snuff; ~**se** *vr* (*despertarse*) to wake up; (*animarse*) to liven up, look lively.

espacial [espa'θjal] *a inv* (*del espacio*) space *cpd*.

espaciar [espa'θjar] *vt* to space (out); (*divulgar*) to spread; ~ **se** *vr*: ~**se en un tema** to enlarge on a subject.

espacio [es'paθjo] *nm* space; (*MUS*) interval; (*emisión*) (short) programme, spot; **el ~** space; ~**so, a** *a* spacious, roomy; (*lento*) slow.

espada [es'paða] *nf* sword; ~**s** *nfpl* (*NAIPES*) spades.

espaguetis [espa'xetis] *nmpl* spaghetti *sg*.

espalda [es'palda] *nf* (*gen*) back; ~**s** *nfpl* (*hombros*) shoulders; **a ~s de uno** behind sb's back; **cargado de ~s** round-shouldered; **tenderse de ~s** to lie (down) on one's back; **volver la ~ a alguien** to give sb the cold shoulder.

espaldar [espal'dar] *nm* (*de asiento*) back.

espaldilla [espal'ðiʎa] *nf* shoulder-blade.

espantadizo, a [espanta'ðiθo, a] *a* timid, easily frightened.

espantajo [espan'taxo] *nm*, **espantapájaros** [espanta'paxaros] *nmpl* scarecrow *sg*.

espantar [espan'tar] *vt* (*asustar*) to frighten, scare; (*ahuyentar*) to frighten off; (*asombrar*) to horrify, appal; ~**se** *vr* to get frightened or scared; to be appalled.

espanto [es'panto] *nm* (*susto*) fright; (*terror*) terror; (*fantasma*) ghost; (*asombro*) astonishment; ~**so, a** *a* frightening; terrifying; astonishing.

España [es'paɲa] *nf* Spain; **español, a** *a* Spanish // *nm/f* Spaniard // *nm* (*lengua*) Spanish.

esparadrapo [espara'ðrapo] *nm* sticking plaster.

esparcido, a [espar'θiðo, a] *a* scattered; (*fig*) jolly, cheerful.

esparcimiento [esparθi'mjento] *nm* (*de líquido*) spilling; (*dispersión*) spreading; (*derramamiento*) scattering; (*fig*) cheerfulness.

esparcir [espar'θir] *vt* to spread; (*derramar*) to scatter; (*líquido*) to spill; ~**se** *vr* to spread (out); to scatter; to spill; (*divertirse*) to enjoy o.s.

espárrago [es'parraɣo] *nm* asparagus.

espasmo [es'pasmo] *nm* spasm.

especia [es'peθja] *nf* spice.

especial [espe'θjal] *a* special; ~**idad** *nf* speciality.

especie [es'peθje] *nf* (*BIO*) species; (*clase*) kind, sort; (*asunto*) matter; (*comentario*) remark, comment; **en ~** in kind.

especificar [espeθifi'kar] *vt* to specify; **específico, a** *a* specific.

espécimen [es'peθimen] (*pl* **especímenes**) *nm* specimen.

especioso, a [espe'θjoso, a] *a* (*perfecto*) perfect; (*fig*) deceitful.

espectáculo [espek'takulo] *nm* (*gen*) spectacle; (*TEATRO etc*) show.

espectador, a [espekta'ðor, a] *nm/f* spectator.

espectro [es'pektro] *nm* ghost; (*fig*) spectre.

especular [espeku'lar] *vt, vi* to speculate; **especulativo, a** *a* speculative.

espejismo [espe'xismo] *nm* mirage.

espejo [es'pexo] *nm* mirror; (*fig*) model; ~ **de retrovisión** rear-view mirror.

espeluznante [espeluθ'nante] *a inv* horrifying, hair-raising.

espera [es'pera] *nf* (*pausa, intervalo*) wait, period of waiting; (*JUR*: *plazo*) respite; **en ~ de** waiting for; (*con expectativa*) expecting.

esperanza [espe'ranθa] *nf* (*confianza*) hope; (*expectativa*) expectation; (*perspectiva*) prospect; **esperanzar** *vt* to give hope to.

esperar [espe'rar] *vt* (*aguardar*) to wait for; (*tener expectativa de*) to expect; (*desear*) to hope for // *vi* to wait; to expect; to hope.

esperma [es'perma] *nf* sperm.

espesar [espe'sar] *vt* to thicken; ~**se** *vr* to thicken, get thicker.

espeso, a [es'peso, a] *a* thick; **espesor** *nm* thickness.

espetar [espe'tar] *vt* (*pollo*) to put on a spit *or* skewer; (*pregunta*) to pop; (*dar*: *reto, sermón*) to give.

espetón [espe'ton] *nm* (*asador*) spit, skewer; (*aguja*) large pin; (*empujón*) jab, poke.

espía [es'pia] *nm/f* spy; **espiar** *vt* (*observar*) to spy on; (*acechar*) to watch out for.

espina [es'pina] *nf* thorn; (*de madera, astilla*) splinter; (*de pez*) bone; ~ **dorsal** spine.

espinaca [espi'naka] *nf* spinach.

espinar [espi'nar] *vt* (*herir*) to prick; (*fig*) to sting, hurt.

espinazo [espi'naθo] *nm* spine, backbone.

espino [es'pino] *nm* hawthorn.

espinoso, a [espi'noso, a] *a* (*planta*) thorny, prickly; (*fig*) bony.

espionaje [espjo'naxe] *nm* spying, espionage.

espiral [espi'ral] *a, nf* spiral.

espirar [espi'rar] *vt* to breathe out, exhale.

espiritista [espiri'tista] *a, nm/f* spiritualist.

espíritu [es'piritu] *nm* spirit; **espiritual** *a* spiritual.

espita [es'pita] *nf* tap; (*fig*: *fam*) drunkard.

esplendidez [esplendi'ðeθ] *nf* (*abundancia*) lavishness; (*magnificencia*) splendour.

esplendor [esplen'dor] *nm* splendour.

espolear [espole'ar] *vt* to spur on.

espolvorear [espolßore'ar] *vt* (*echar polvos*) to dust; (*esparcir*) to dust, sprinkle.

esponja [es'ponxa] *nf* sponge; (*fig*) sponger.

esponjarse [espon'xarse] *vr* (*fam*: *hincharse*) to swell with pride; (: *de salud*) to glow with health.

esponjoso, a [espon'xoso, a] *a* spongy, porous.

espontaneidad [espontanei'ðað] *nf* spontaneity; **espontáneo, a** *a* spontaneous.

esposa [es'posa] *nf* wife; **~s** *nfpl* handcuffs; **esposar** *vt* to handcuff.

esposo [es'poso] *nm* husband.

espuela [es'pwela] *nf* spur.

espuma [es'puma] *nf* foam; (*de cerveza*) froth, head; (*de jabón*) lather; **espumoso, a** *a* frothy, foamy; (*vino*) sparkling.

esqueleto [eske'leto] *nm* skeleton.

esquema [es'kema] *nm* (*diagrama*) diagram; (*dibujo*) plan; (*plan*) scheme; (*FILOSOFÍA*) schema.

esquí [es'ki] (*pl* **esquís**) *nm* (*objeto*) ski; (*deporte*) skiing.

esquilar [eski'lar] *vt* to shear.

esquilmar [eskil'mar] *vt* (*cosechar*) to harvest; (*empobrecer*: *suelo*) to exhaust; (*fig*) to skin.

esquimal [eski'mal] *a*, *nm/f* Eskimo.

esquina [es'kina] *nf* corner.

esquirol [eski'rol] *nm* (*fam*) blackleg.

esquivar [eski'ßar] *vt* to avoid; (*evadir*) to dodge, elude; **~se** *vr* to withdraw.

esquivez [eski'ßeθ] *nf* (*altanería*) aloofness; (*desdeño*) scorn, disdain; **esquivo, a** *a* (*altanero*) aloof; (*desdeñoso*) scornful, disdainful.

esta ['esta] *det ver* **este**.

ésta ['esta] *pron ver* **éste**.

está *vb ver* **estar**.

estabilidad [estaßili'ðað] *nf* stability; **estable** *a* stable.

establecer [estaße'θer] *vt* to establish; **~se** *vr* to establish o.s.; (*echar raíces*) to settle; **establecimiento** *nm* establishment.

estaca [es'taka] *nf* stake, post; (*para tiendas*) peg.

estacada [esta'kaða] *nf* (*cerca*) fence, fencing; (*palenque*) stockade.

estación [esta'θjon] *nf* station; (*del año*) season; **~ de autobuses** bus station.

estacionamiento [estaθjona'mjento] *nm* (*AUTO*) parking; (*MIL*) stationing; (*colocación*) placing.

estacionar [estaθjo'nar] *vt* (*AUTO*) to park; (*MIL*) to station; (*colocar*) to place; **~lo, a** a stationary; (*COM*: *mercado*) slack.

estadio [es'taðjo] *nm* (*fase*) stage, phase; (*DEPORTE*) stadium.

estadista [esta'ðista] *nm* (*POL*) statesman; (*ESTADÍSTICA*) statistician.

estadística [esta'ðistika] *nf* (*una* **~**) figure, statistic; (*ciencia*) statistics *sg*.

estado [es'taðo] *nm* (*POL*: *condición*) state; (*social*) status; **~ de las cuentas** statement of accounts; **~ mayor** staff; **E~s Unidos (EE. UU.)** United States (USA).

estafa [es'tafa] *nf* swindle, trick; **estafar** *vt* to swindle, defraud.

estafeta [esta'feta] *nf* (*correo*) post; (*oficina de correos*) post office; **~ diplomática** diplomatic bag.

estallar [esta'ʎar] *vi* to burst; (*explotar*) to explode; (*epidemia, rebelión*) to break out; **~ en llanto** to burst into tears; **estallido** *nm* explosion; (*fig*) outbreak.

estampa [es'tampa] *nf* (*imagen*) image; (*impresión, imprenta*) print, engraving; (*imagen, figura*: *de persona*) appearance; (*fig*: *huella*) footprint.

estampado, a [es'tam'paðo, a] *a* printed // *nm* (*impresión*: *acción*) printing; (: *efecto*) print; (*marca*) stamping.

estampar [estam'par] *vt* (*imprimir*) to print; (*marcar*) to stamp; (*metal*) to engrave; (*poner sello en*) to stamp; (*fig*) to stamp, imprint.

estampida [estam'piða] *nf* stampede; (*estampido*) bang, report.

estampido [estam'piðo] *nm* bang, report.

estampilla [estam'piʎa] *nf* stamp.

están *vb ver* **estar**.

estancar [estan'kar] *vt* (*aguas*) to hold up, hold back; (*COM*) to monopolize; (*fig*) to block, hold up; **~se** *vr* to stagnate.

estancia [es'tanθja] *nf* (*permanencia*) stay; (*sala*) living-room; (*AM*) farm, ranch; **estanciero** *nm* farmer, rancher.

estanco, a [es'tanko, a] *a* watertight // *nm* (*monopolio*) state monopoly; (*tienda*) tobacconist's (shop).

estandarizar [estandari'θar] *vt* to standardize.

estandarte [estan'darte] *nm* banner, standard.

estanque [es'tanke] *nm* (*lago*) pool, pond; (*AGR*) reservoir.

estanquero, a [estan'kero, a], **estanquillero, a** [estanki'ʎero, a] *nm/f* tobacconist.

estante [es'tante] *nm* (*armario*) rack, stand; (*biblioteca*) bookcase; (*anaquel*) shelf; (*AM*) prop; **estantería** *nf* shelving, shelves *pl*.

estantigua [estan'tixwa] *nf* (*fantasma*) apparition.

estaño [es'tano] *nm* tin.

estar [es'tar] *vi* (*gen*) to be; (*en casa*) to be in; (*ubicarse*) to be found; (*presente*) to be present; **estamos a 2 de mayo** it is the 2nd May; **¿cómo está Ud?** how are you?; **~ enfermo** to be ill; **~ viejo/joven** (*parecerse*) to seem old/young; (*seguido de una preposición*): **¿a cuánto estamos de Madrid?** how far are we from Madrid?; **~ de fiesta** *o* **vacaciones** to be on holiday; **las uvas están a 5 pesetas** grapes are at 5 pesetas; **María no está** María isn't in; **~ por** (: *moción*) to be in favour of; (: *persona*) to support, back; **está por hacer** it remains to be done; **¿estamos?** are we agreed?

estas ['estas] *det ver* **este**.

éstas ['estas] *pron ver* **éste**.

estás *vb ver* **estar**.

estatal [esta'tal] *a inv* state *cpd*.

estático, a [es'tatiko, a] *a* static.

estatificar [estatifi'kar] *vt* to nationalize.

estatua [es'tatwa] *nf* statue.

estatuir [estatu'ir] *vt* (*establecer*) to establish; (*determinar*) to prove.

estatura [esta'tura] *nf* stature, height.

estatuto [esta'tuto] *nm* (*JUR*) statute; (*de ciudad*) bye-law; (*de comité*) rule.

este ['este] *nm* east.

este, esta, estos, estas ['este, 'esta, 'estos, 'estas] *det* (*sg*) this; (*pl*) these.

éste, ésta, éstos, éstas ['este, 'esta, 'estos, 'estas] *pron* (*sg*) this (one); (*pl*) these (ones); **~... ése...** the latter... the former...

esté *etc vb ver* **estar**.

estela [es'tela] *nf* wake, wash; (*fig*) trail.

estenografía [estenoɤra'fia] *nf* shorthand, stenography.

estepa [es'tepa] *nf* (*GEO*) steppe.

estera [es'tera] *nf* mat(ting).

estereo... [estereo] *pref* stereo...; **~fónico, a** a stereophonic; **~tipar** *vt* to stereotype; **~tipo** *nm* stereotype.

estéril [es'teril] *a* sterile, barren; (*fig*) vain, futile.

esterlina [ester'lina] *a.* **libra ~** pound sterling.

estético, a [es'tetiko, a] *a* aesthetic // *nf* aesthetics *sg*.

estiércol [es'tjerkol] *nm* dung, manure.

estigma [es'tiɤma] *nm* stigma.

estilar [esti'lar] *vi,* **~se** *vr* to be in fashion, be used, be worn.

estilo [es'tilo] *nm* style; (*TEC*) stylus; (*DEPORTE*) stroke; **algo por el ~** something of the sort.

estima [es'tima] *nf* esteem, respect.

estimación [estima'θjon] *nf* (*evaluación*) estimation; (*aprecio, afecto*) esteem, regard.

estimar [esti'mar] *vt* (*evaluar*) to estimate; (*valorar*) to value; (*apreciar*) to esteem, respect; (*pensar, considerar*) to think, reckon; **¡se estima!** thanks very much!

estimulante [estimu'lante] *a* stimulating // *nm* stimulant; **estimular** *vt* to stimulate; (*excitar*) to excite; (*animar*) to encourage; **estímulo** *nm* stimulus; (*ánimo*) encouragement.

estío [es'tio] *nm* summer.

estipulación [estipula'θjon] *nf* stipulation, condition; **estipular** *vt* to stipulate.

estirado, a [esti'raðo, a] *a* (*tenso*) (stretched *or* drawn) tight; (*fig*) stiff, pompous.

estirar [esti'rar] *vt* to stretch; (*conversa-*

ción, presupuesto) to stretch out; **~se** *vr* to stretch.

estirón [esti'ron] *nm* pull, tug; (*crecimiento*) spurt, sudden growth; **dar un ~** to shoot up.

estirpe [es'tirpe] *nf* stock, lineage.

estival [esti'βal] *a* summer *cpd*.

esto ['esto] *pron* this, this thing *or* matter; **~ de la boda** this business about the wedding.

estofa [es'tofa] *nf* (*tela*) quilting; (*calidad, clase*) quality, class.

estofado, a [esto'faðo, a] *a* (*CULIN*) stewed; (*bordado*) quilted // *nm* stew.

estofar [esto'far] *vt* (*bordar*) to quilt; (*CULIN*) to stew.

estoico, a [es'toiko, a] *a* (*FILOSOFÍA*) stoic(al); (*fig*) cold, indifferent.

estólido, a [es'toliðo, a] *a* stupid.

estómago [es'tomaɤo] *nm* stomach; **tener ~** to be thick-skinned.

estorbar [estor'βar] *vt* to hinder, obstruct; (*fig*) to bother, disturb // *vi* to be in the way; **estorbo** *nm* (*molestia*) bother, nuisance; (*obstáculo*) hindrance, obstacle.

estornudar [estornu'ðar] *vi* to sneeze.

estos ['estos] *det ver* **este**.

éstos ['estos] *pron ver* **éste**.

estoy *vb ver* **estar**.

estrafalario, a [estrafa'larjo, a] *a* odd, eccentric; (*desarreglado*) slovenly, sloppy.

estragar [estra'var] *vt* to deprave, corrupt; (*deteriorar*) to ruin; **estrago** *nm* ruin, destruction; **hacer estragos en** to wreak havoc among.

estragón [estra'von] *nm* (*CULIN*) tarragon.

estrangul [estran'gul] *nm* mouthpiece.

estrangulación [estrangula'θjon] *nf* strangulation.

estrangulador, a [estrangula'ðor, a] *nm/f* strangler // *nm* (*TEC*) throttle; (*AUTO*) choke.

estrangulamiento [estrangula'mjento] *nm* (*AUTO*) bottleneck.

estrangular [estrangu'lar] *vt* (*persona*) to strangle; (*MED*) to strangulate.

estraperlo [estra'perlo] *nm* black market.

estratagema [estrata'xema] *nf* (*MIL*) stratagem; (*astucia*) cunning.

estrategia [estra'texja] *nf* strategy; **estratégico, a** a strategic.

estratificar [estratifi'kar] *vt* to stratify.

estrato [es'trato] *nm* stratum, layer.

estrechar [estre'tʃar] *vt* (*reducir*) to narrow; (*vestido*) to take in; (*persona*) to hug, embrace; **~se** *vr* (*reducirse*) to narrow, grow narrow; (*apretarse*) to embrace; (*reducir los gastos*) to economize; **~ la mano** to shake hands; **~ amistad con alguien** to become very friendly with sb.

estrechez [estre'tʃeθ] *nf* narrowness; (*de ropa*) tightness; (*intimidad*) intimacy; (*COM*) want *or* shortage of money; **estrecheces** *nfpl* financial difficulties; **~ de conciencia** small-mindedness; **~ de miras** narrow-mindedness.

estrecho, a [es'tret∫o, a] *a* narrow; (*apretado*) tight; (*íntimo*) close, intimate; (*miserable*) mean // *nm* strait.

estregar [estre'var] *vt* (*sobar*) to rub (hard); (*rascar*) to scrape.

estrella [es'treʎa] *nf* star; ~ **de mar** starfish.

estrellar [estre'ʎar] *vt* (*hacer añicos*) to smash (to pieces); (*huevos*) to fry; ~**se** *vr* to smash; (*chocarse*) to crash; (*fracasar*) to be smashed to pieces.

estremecer [estreme'θer] *vt* to shake; ~**se** *vr* to shake, tremble; **estremecimiento** *nm* (*conmoción*) tremor; (*sobresalto*) shock; (*temblor*) trembling, shaking.

estrenar [estre'nar] *vt* (*vestido*) to wear for the first time; (*casa*) to move into; (*película, obra de teatro*) to present for the first time; ~**se** *vr* (*persona*) to make one's début; **estreno** *nm* (*primer uso*) first use; (*en un empleo*) début, first appearance; (*CINE etc*) première.

estreñir [estre'nir] *vt* to constipate; ~**se** *vr* to become constipated.

estrépito [es'trepito] *nm* noise, racket; (*fig*) fuss; **estrepitoso, a** *a* noisy; (*fiesta*) rowdy, boisterous.

estría [es'tria] *nf* groove.

estribar [estri'βar] *vi*: ~ **en** to rest on, be supported by.

estribo [es'triβo] *nm* (*de jinete*) stirrup; (*de coche, tren*) step; (*de puente*) support; (*fig*) basis, foundation; (*GEO*) spur.

estribor [estri'βor] *nm* starboard.

estricnina [estrik'nina] *nf* strychnine.

estricto, a [es'trikto, a] *a* (*riguroso*) strict; (*severo*) severe.

estro ['estro] *nm* inspiration.

estropajo [estro'paxo] *nm* scourer.

estropear [estrope'ar] *vt* (*arruinar*) to spoil; (*dañar*) to damage; (*lisiar*) to maim; (*tullir*) to cripple; ~**se** *vr* (*objeto*) to get damaged; (*persona*) to be crippled.

estructura [estruk'tura] *nf* structure.

estruendo [es'trwendo] *nm* (*ruido*) racket, din; (*fig: alboroto*) uproar, turmoil; (*pompa*) pomp.

estrujar [estru'xar] *vt* (*apretar*) to squeeze; (*aplastar*) to crush; (*magullar*) to bruise; (*fig*) to drain, bleed.

estuario [es'twarjo] *nm* estuary.

estuche [es'tut∫e] *nm* box, case.

estudiante [estu'ðjante] *nm/f* student; **estudiantil** *a inv* student *cpd*.

estudiantina [estuðjan'tina] *nf* student music group.

estudiar [estu'ðjar] *vt* to study.

estudio [es'tuðjo] *nm* study; (*CINE, ARTE, RADIO*) studio; ~**s** *nmpl* studies; (*erudición*) learning *sg*; ~**so, a** *a* studious.

estufa [es'tufa] *nf* heater, fire.

estulticia [estul'tiθja] *nf* foolishness.

estupefacto, a [estupe'fakto, a] *a* speechless, thunderstruck.

estupendo, a [estu'pendo, a] *a* wonderful,

terrific; (*fam*) great; ¡~! that's great!, fantastic!

estupidez [estupi'ðeθ] *nf* (*torpeza*) stupidity; (*tontería*) piece of nonsense.

estúpido, a [es'tupiðo, a] *a* stupid, silly.

estupor [estu'por] *nm* stupor; (*fig*) astonishment, amazement.

estupro [es'tupro] *nm* rape.

estuve *etc vb ver* **estar**.

etapa [e'tapa] *nf* stage; (*DEPORTE*) leg; (*parada*) stopping place; (*fig*) stage, phase.

eternidad [eterni'ðað] *nf* eternity; **eterno, a** *a* eternal, everlasting.

ético, a ['etiko, a] *a* ethical // *nf* ethics *pl*.

etíope [e'tiope] *a, nm/f* Ethiopian.

Etiopía [etjo'pia] *nf* Ethiopia.

etiqueta [eti'keta] *nf* (*modales*) etiquette; (*papel*) label, tag.

eucalipto [euka'lipto] *nm* eucalyptus.

Eucaristía [eukaris'tia] *nf* Eucharist.

eufemismo [eufe'mismo] *nm* euphemism.

euforia [eu'forja] *nf* euphoria.

eugenesia [euxe'nesja] *nf*, **eugenismo** [euxe'nismo] *nm* eugenics *sg*.

eunuco [eu'nuko] *nm* eunuch.

Europa [eu'ropa] *nf* Europe; **europeo, a** *a, nm/f* European.

éuscaro, a ['euskaro, a] *a* Basque // (*lengua*) Basque.

Euskadi [eus'kaði] *nm* the Basque Provinces *pl*.

eutanasia [euta'nasja] *nf* euthanasia.

evacuación [eβakwa'θjon] *nf* evacuation; **evacuar** *vt* to evacuate.

evadir [eβa'ðir] *vt* to evade, avoid; ~**se** *vr* to escape.

evaluar [eβa'lwar] *vt* to evaluate.

evangélico, a [eβan'xeliko, a] *a* evangelic(al).

evangelio [eβan'xeljo] *nm* gospel.

evaporación [eβapora'θjon] *nf* evaporation.

evaporar [eβapo'rar] *vt* to evaporate; ~**se** *vr* to vanish.

evasión [eβa'sjon] *nf* escape, flight; (*fig*) evasion.

evasivo, a [eβa'siβo, a] *a* evasive, non-committal.

evento [e'βento] *nm* unforeseen event; (*eventualidad*) eventuality; **a cualquier** ~ in any event.

eventual [eβen'twal] *a* possible, conditional (upon circumstances); (*trabajador*) casual, temporary.

evidencia [eβi'ðenθja] *nf* (*certidumbre*) evidence, proof; **evidenciar** *vt* (*hacer patente*) to make evident; (*probar*) to prove, show; **evidenciarse** *vr* to be evident.

evidente [eβi'ðente] *a* obvious, clear, evident.

evitar [eβi'tar] *vt* (*evadir*) to avoid; (*impedir*) to prevent.

evocar [eβo'kar] *vt* to evoke, call forth.

evolución [eβolu'θjon] *nf* (*desarrollo*) evolution, development; (*cambio*) change;

(MIL) manoeuvre; **evolucionar** vi to evolve; (MIL, AVIAT) to manoeuvre.

ex [eks] a ex-; **el ~ ministro** the former minister, the ex-minister.

exacerbar [eksaβer'βar] vt to irritate, annoy; (agravar) to aggravate.

exactitud [eksakti'tuð] nf exactness; (precisión) accuracy; (puntualidad) punctuality; **exacto, a** a exact; accurate; punctual; **¡exacto!** exactly!

exageración [eksaxera'θjon] nf exaggeration; **exagerar** vt, vi to exaggerate.

exaltado, a [eksal'taðo, a] a (apasionado) over-excited, worked-up; (exagerado) extreme; (excitado) elated.

exaltar [eksal'tar] vt to exalt, glorify; **~ se** vr (excitarse) to get excited or worked-up; (arrebatarse) to get carried away.

examen [ek'samen] nm examination.

examinar [eksami'nar] vt to examine; **~se** vr to be examined, sit an examination.

exangüe [ek'sangwe] a (desangrado) bloodless; (sin fuerzas) weak.

exasperar [eksaspe'rar] vt to exasperate; **~ se** vr to get exasperated, lose patience.

Exca. abr de **Excelencia.**

excedente [eksθe'ðente] a, nm excess, surplus.

exceder [eksθe'ðer] vt to exceed, surpass; **~ se** vr (extralimitarse) to go too far; (sobrepasarse) to excel o.s.

excelencia [eksθe'lenθja] nf excellence; **E~** Excellency; **excelente** a excellent.

excelso, a [eks'θelso, a] a lofty, sublime.

excentricidad [eksθentriθi'ðað] nf eccentricity; **excéntrico, a** a, nm/f eccentric.

excepción [eksθep'θjon] nf exception; **excepcional** a exceptional.

excepto [eks'θepto] ad excepting, except (for).

exceptuar [eksθep'twar] vt to except, exclude.

excesivo, a [eksθe'siβo, a] a excessive.

exceso [eks'θeso] nm (gen) excess; (COM) surplus.

excitación [eksθita'θjon] nf (sensación) excitement; (acción) excitation.

excitado, a [eksθi'taðo, a] a excited; (emociones) aroused; **excitar** vt to excite; (incitar) to urge; **excitarse** vr to get excited.

exclamación [eksklama'θjon] nf exclamation; **exclamar** vi to exclaim.

excluir [eksklu'ir] vt to exclude; (dejar fuera) to shut out; (descartar) to reject; **exclusión** nf exclusion; (descarte) rejection; **con exclusión de** excluding.

exclusiva [eksklu'siβa], **exclusividad** [eksklusiβi'ðað] nf exclusiveness; (PRENSA) exclusive; (COM) sole right or agency.

exclusivo, a [eksklu'siβo, a] a exclusive; (único) sole.

Excmo. abr de **excelentísimo.**

excomulgar [ekskomul'var] vt (REL) to excommunicate; (excluir) to ban, banish.

excomunión [ekskomu'njon] nf excommunication.

excoriar [eksko'rjar] vt to flay, skin.

excursión [ekskur'sjon] nf excursion, outing; **excursionismo** nm sightseeing.

excusa [eks'kusa] nf excuse; (disculpa) apology.

excusado, a [eksku'saðo, a] a unnecessary; (disculpado) excused, forgiven // nm lavatory, toilet.

excusar [eksku'sar] vt to excuse; (evitar) to avoid; (impedir) to prevent; **~ se** vr (rehusarse) to decline a request; (disculparse) to apologize.

execrar [ekse'krar] vt to loathe.

exención [eksen'θjon] nf exemption.

exento, a [ek'sento, a] pp de **eximir** // a exempt; **~ de derechos** tax-free.

exequias [ek'sekjas] nfpl funeral rites, obsequies.

exhalación [eksala'θjon] nf (del aire) exhalation; (vapor) fumes pl; (rayo) shooting star.

exhalar [eksa'lar] vt to exhale, breathe out; (olor etc) to give off; (suspiro) to breathe, heave.

exhausto, a [ek'sausto, a] a exhausted.

exhibición [eksiβi'θjon] nf exhibition, display, show.

exhibir [eksi'βir] vt to exhibit, display, show.

exhortación [eksorta'θjon] nf exhortation; **exhortar** vt: **exhortar a** to exhort to.

exigencia [eksi'xenθja] nf demand, requirement; **exigente** a demanding.

exigir [eksi'xir] vt (gen) to demand, require; (pago) to exact.

exilio [ek'siljo] nm exile.

eximio, a [ek'simjo, a] a (excelente) choice, select; (eminente) distinguished, eminent.

eximir [eksi'mir] vt to exempt.

existencia [eksis'tenθja] nf existence; **~ s** nfpl stock(s) (pl).

existir [eksis'tir] vi to exist, be.

éxito ['eksito] nm (resultado) result, outcome; (triunfo) success; **tener ~** to be successful.

exonerar [eksone'rar] vt to exonerate; **~ de una obligación** to free from an obligation.

exorcizar [eksorθi'θar] vt to exorcize.

exótico, a [ek'sotiko, a] a exotic.

expandir [ekspan'dir] vt to expand.

expansión [ekspan'sjon] nf expansion.

expatriarse [ekspa'trjarse] vr to emigrate; (POL) to go into exile.

expectativa [ekspekta'tiβa] nf (espera) expectation; (perspectiva) prospect.

expedición [ekspeði'θjon] nf (excursión) expedition; (envío) shipment; (rapidez) speed.

expediente [ekspe'ðjente] nm expedient; (JUR: procedimento) action, proceedings pl; (: papeles) dossier, file, record.

expedir [ekspe'ðir] *vt* (*despachar*) to send, forward; (*libreta cívica, pasaporte*) to issue; (*fig*) to deal with.

expedito, a [ekspe'ðito, a] *a* (*libre*) clear, free; (*pronto*) prompt, speedy.

expendedor, a [ekspende'ðor, a] *nm/f* (*vendedor*) dealer; (*aparato*) (vending) machine; **~ de cigarrillos** cigarette machine.

expendeduría [ekspendedu'ria] *nf* shop; (*estanco*) tobacconist's (shop).

expensas [eks'pensas] *nfpl* expenses; **a ~ de** at the expense of.

experiencia [ekspe'rjenθja] *nf* experience; (*científica*) experiment.

experimentado, a [eksperimen'taðo, a] *a* experienced.

experimentar [eksperimen'tar] *vt* (*en laboratorio*) to experiment with; (*probar*) to test, try out; (*notar, observar*) to experience; (*sufrir*) to suffer; **experimento** *nm* experiment.

experto, a [eks'perto, a] *a* (*práctico*) expert; (*diestro*) skilled, experienced // *nm/f* expert.

expiar [ekspi'ar] *vt* to atone for.

expirar [ekspi'rar] *vi* to expire.

explayar [ekspla'jar] *vt* to extend, expand; **~se** *vr* to extend, spread; **~se con uno** to confide in sb.

explicación [eksplika'θjon] *nf* explanation; **explicar** *vt* to explain; **explicarse** *vr* to explain (o.s.).

explícito, a [eks'pliθito, a] *a* explicit.

explorador, a [eksplora'ðor, a] *nm/f* (*pionero*) explorer; (*MIL*) scout // *nm* (*MED*) probe; (*TEC*) (radar) scanner; **los E~es** the Scouts.

explorar [eksplo'rar] *vt* to explore; (*MED*) to probe; (*radar*) to scan.

explosión [eksplo'sjon] *nf* explosion; **explosivo, a** *a* explosive.

explotación [eksplota'θjon] *nf* exploitation; (*de planta etc*) running, operation; **explotar** *vt* to exploit; to run, operate // *vi* to explode.

exponer [ekspo'ner] *vt* to expose; (*cuadro*) to display; (*vida*) to risk; (*idea*) to explain; **~se** *vr* to expose o.s., leave o.s. open.

exportación [eksporta'θjon] *nf* (*acción*) export; (*mercancías*) exports *pl*; **exportar** *vt* to export.

exposición [eksposi'θjon] *nf* (*gen*) exposure; (*de arte*) show, exhibition; (*petición*) petition; (*explicación*) explanation; (*narración*) account, statement.

exposímetro [ekspo'simetro] *nm* (*FOTO*) exposure meter.

exprés [eks'pres] *nm* (*AM*) express (train).

expresar [ekspre'sar] *vt* to express; **expresión** *nf* expression; **expresiones** *nfpl* regards.

expreso, a [eks'preso, a] *pp de* **expresar** // *a* (*claro*) specific, clear; (*rápido*) fast // *nm*: **mandar por ~** to send by express (delivery).

exprimir [ekspri'mir] *vt* (*fruta*) to squeeze (out); (*ropa*) to wring out; (*fig*) to express emphatically.

expropiar [ekspro'pjar] *vt* to expropriate.

expuesto, a [eks'pwesto, a] *a* exposed; (*cuadro etc*) on show, on display.

expugnar [ekspuɣ'nar] *vt* to take by storm.

expulsar [ekspul'sar] *vt* (*echar*) to eject; (*arrojar*) to throw out; (*expeler*) to expel; (*desalojar*) to drive out; (*despedir*) to sack, fire; (*a un futbolista*) to send off; **expulsión** *nf* expulsion; sending-off.

expurgar [ekspur'ɣar] *vt* to expurgate.

exquisito, a [ekski'sito, a] *a* exquisite; (*agradable*) delightful.

éxtasis ['ekstasis] *nm* ecstasy.

extender [eksten'der] *vt* (*gen*) to extend; (*los brazos*) to stretch out, hold out; (*mapa*) to spread (out), open (out); (*mantequilla*) to spread; (*certificado*) to issue; (*cheque, recibo*) to make out; (*documento*) to draw up; **~se** *vr* (*gen*) to extend; (*en el suelo*) to stretch out; (*epidemia*) to spread; **extendido, a** *a* (*abierto*) spread out, open; (*brazos*) outstretched; (*prevaleciente*) widespread; **extensión** *nf* (*de país*) expanse, stretch; (*de libro*) extent; (*de tiempo*) length, duration; (*AM*) extension; **en toda la extensión de la palabra** in every sense of the word; **extenso, a** *a* extensive; (*prevaleciente*) widespread.

extenuar [ekste'nwar] *vi* (*agotar*) to exhaust; (*debilitar*) to weaken.

exterior [ekste'rjor] *a inv* (*de fuera*) external; (*afuera*) outside, exterior; (*apariencia*) outward; (*comercio*) foreign // *nm* (*gen*) exterior, outside; (*aspecto*) outward appearance; (*DEPORTE*) wing(er); **el ~** foreign parts *pl*; **al ~** outwardly, on the surface.

exterminar [ekstermi'nar] *vt* to exterminate; **exterminio** *nm* extermination.

externo, a [eks'terno, a] *a* (*exterior*) external, outside; (*superficial*) outward // *nm/f* day pupil.

extinguir [ekstin'gir] *vt* (*fuego*) to extinguish, put out; (*raza, población*) to wipe out; **~se** *vr* (*fuego*) to go out; (*BIO*) to die out, become extinct.

extinto, a [eks'tinto, a] *a* extinct.

extintor [ekstin'tor] *nm* (fire) extinguisher.

extra ['ekstra] *a, nm/f* extra // *nm* extra; (*bono*) bonus.

extracción [ekstrak'θjon] *nf* extraction; (*en lotería*) draw.

extracto [eks'trakto] *nm* extract.

extraer [ekstra'er] *vt* to extract, take out.

extralimitarse [ekstralimi'tarse] *vr* to go too far.

extranjero, a [ekstran'xero, a] *a* foreign // *nm/f* foreigner // *nm* foreign lands *pl*; **en el ~** abroad.

extrañar [ekstra'nar] *vt* (*desterrar*) to exile; (*sorprender*) to find strange *or* odd;

(AM) to miss; ~se vr (sorprenderse) to be amazed, be surprised; (distanciarse) to become estranged, grow apart.

extrañeza [ekstra'neθa] nf (rareza) strangeness, oddness; (asombro) amazement, surprise.

extraño, a [eks'trano, a] a (extranjero) foreign; (raro, sorprendente) strange, odd.

extraordinario, a [ekstraorði'narjo, a] a extraordinary; (edición, número) special // nm (plato) special dish; (de periódico) special edition; **horas ~as** overtime sg.

extravagancia [ekstraβa'vanθja] nf extravagance; **extravagante** a extravagant; (extraño) strange, odd; (excéntrico) eccentric; (estrafalario) outlandish.

extraviado, a [ekstra'βjaðo, a] a lost, missing.

extraviar [ekstra'βjar] vt (desviar) to mislead; (perder) to lose, misplace; ~se vr to lose one's way, get lost.

extravío [ekstra'βio] nm loss; (fig) deviation.

extremar [ekstre'mar] vt to carry to extremes; ~se vr to do one's utmost, make every effort.

extremaunción [ekstremaun'θjon] nf extreme unction.

extremeño, a [ekstre'meno, a] a, nm/f Extremaduran.

extremidad [ekstremi'ðað] nf (punta) extremity; (fila) edge; ~es nfpl (ANAT) extremities.

extremo, a [eks'tremo, a] a extreme; (último) last // nm end; (límite, grado sumo) extreme; **en último** ~ as a last resort; ~ **derecho/izquierdo** outside-right/ outside-left.

extrínseco, a [eks'trinseko, a] a extrinsic.

extrovertido, a [ekstroβer'tiðo, a] a, nm/f extrovert.

exuberancia [eksuβe'ranθja] nf exuberance; **exuberante** a exuberant; (fig) luxuriant, lush.

exvoto [eks'βoto] nm votive offering.

eyacular [ejaku'lar] vt, vi to ejaculate.

F

f.a.b. abr de **franco a bordo** f.o.b. (free on board).

fábrica ['faβrika] nf factory; **marca de ~** trademark; **precio de ~** factory price.

fabricación [faβrika'θjon] nf (manufactura) manufacture; (producción) production; **de ~ casera** home-made; ~ **en serie** mass production.

fabricante [faβri'kante] nm/f manufacturer.

fabricar [faβri'kar] vt (hacer) to manufacture, make; (construir) to build; (elaborar) to fabricate, devise.

fabril [fa'βril] a: **industria ~** manufacturing industry.

fábula ['faβula] nf (cuento) fable; (chisme) rumour.

facción [fak'θjon] nf (POL) faction; (del rostro) feature.

fácil ['faθil] a (simple) easy; (probable) likely.

facilidad [faθili'ðað] nf (capacidad) ease; (sencillez) simplicity; (de palabra) fluency; ~**es** nfpl facilities.

facilitar [faθili'tar] vt (hacer fácil) to make easy; (proporcionar) to provide; (hacer posible) to arrange; (hacer más fácil) to facilitate.

fácilmente ['faθilmente] ad easily.

factible [fak'tiβle] a feasible.

factor [fak'tor] nm factor.

factura [fak'tura] nf (cuenta) bill; (hechura) manufacture; **facturar** vt (COM) to invoice, charge for.

facultad [fakul'tað] nf (aptitud, ESCOL etc) faculty; (poder) power.

facha ['fatʃa] nf (fam: aspecto) look; (: desagradable) unpleasant sight.

fachada [fa'tʃaða] nf (ARQ) façade, front.

faena [fa'ena] nf (trabajo) work; (quehacer) task, job; ~ **s de la casa** housework sg.

fagot [fa'got] nm (MUS) bassoon.

faisán [fai'san] nm pheasant.

faja ['faxa] nf (para la cintura) sash; (de mujer) corset; (de tierra) strip; (venda) bandage.

falange [fa'lanxe] nf (POL) Falange.

falda ['falda] nf (prenda de vestir) skirt.

falibilidad [faliβili'ðað] nf fallibility.

fálico, a ['faliko, a] a phallic.

falo ['falo] nm phallus.

falsedad [false'ðað] nf (hipocresía) falseness; (mentira) falsehood.

falsificar [falsifi'kar] vt (firma etc) to forge; (voto etc) to rig; (moneda) to counterfeit.

falso, a ['falso, a] a (gen) false; (erróneo) mistaken; (moneda etc) fake; **en ~** falsely.

falta ['falta] nf (defecto) fault, flaw; (privación) lack, want; (ausencia) absence; (carencia) shortage; (equivocación) mistake; (DEPORTE) foul; **hacer ~** to be missing or lacking.

faltar [fal'tar] vi (escasear) to be lacking, be wanting; (ausentarse) to be absent, be missing; (fallar: mecanismo) to go wrong, break down; **faltan 2 horas para llegar** there are 2 hours to go till arrival; ~ **el respeto a alguien** to be disrespectful to sb; **echar a ~ a alguien** to miss sb; **¡no faltaba más!** that's the last straw!

falto, a ['falto, a] a (desposeído) deficient, lacking; (necesitado) poor, wretched.

falla ['faʎa] nf (defecto) fault, flaw; (fracaso) failure.

fallar [fa'ʎar] vt (JUR) to pronounce sentence on // vi (memoria) to fail; (motor) to miss.

fallecer [faʎe'θer] vi to pass away, die; **fallecimiento** nm decease, demise.

fallo ['faʎo] nm (JUR) verdict, ruling; (fracaso) failure.

fama ['fama] nf (renombre) fame; (reputación) reputation.

familia [fa'milja] nf family.

familiar [fami'ljar] a (relativo a la familia) family cpd; (conocido, informal) familiar // nm relative; ~**idad** nf (gen) familiarity; (informalidad) homeliness; ~**izarse** vr to familiarize o.s. with.

famoso, a [fa'moso, a] a (renombrado) famous; (fam: fabuloso) great.

fanático, a [fa'natiko, a] a fanatical // nm/f (gen) fanatic; (CINE etc) fan; (de deportes) supporter; **fanatismo** nm fanaticism.

fanfarrón, ona [fanfa'rron, ona] a boastful; (pey) showy.

fango ['fango] nm mud; ~**so, a** a muddy.

fantasía [fanta'sia] nf fantasy, imagination; (fam) conceit, vanity; **joyas de ~** imitation jewellery sg.

fantasma [fan'tasma] nm (espectro) ghost, apparition.

fantástico, a [fan'tastiko, a] a fantastic.

farmacéutico, a [farma'θeutiko, a] a pharmaceutical // nm/f chemist, pharmacist.

farmacia [far'maθja] nf chemist's (shop), pharmacy; ~ **de turno** all-night chemist.

faro ['faro] nm (NAUT. torre) lighthouse; (AUTO) headlamp; ~**s laterales** sidelights; ~**s traseros** rear lights.

farol [fa'rol] nm (luz) lantern, lamp; (de calle) streetlamp.

farsa ['farsa] nf (gen) farce.

farsante [far'sante] nm/f fraud, fake.

fascinar [fasθi'nar] vt (deslumbrar) to fascinate.

fascismo [fas'θismo] nm fascism; **fascista** a, nm/f fascist.

fase ['fase] nf phase.

fastidiar [fasti'ðjar] vt (disgustar) to annoy, bother; (estropear) to spoil; (aburrir) to bore; ~**se** vr (dañarse) to harm o.s.; (disgustarse) to get annoyed or cross.

fastidio [fas'tiðjo] nm (disgusto) annoyance; (tedio) boredom; ~**so, a** a (molesto) annoying; (aburrido) tedious.

fatal [fa'tal] a (gen) fatal; (inevitable) unavoidable; (desgraciado) ill-fated; (fam: malo, pésimo) awful; ~**idad** nf (destino) fate; (mala suerte) misfortune.

fatiga [fa'tiɣa] nf (cansancio) fatigue, weariness; **fatigar** vt to tire, weary; **fatigarse** vr to get tired; **fatigoso, a** a (cansador) tiring; (aburrido) tiresome.

fatuo, a ['fatwo, a] a (vano) fatuous; (presuntuoso) conceited.

fauces ['fauθes] nfpl jaws, mouth sg.

favor [fa'ßor] nm favour; **entrada de ~** complimentary ticket; **haga el ~ de...** would you be so good as to..., kindly...; **por ~ please**; ~**able** a favourable.

favorecer [faßore'θer] vt (gen) to favour; (vestido etc) to become, flatter; **este peinado le favorece** this hairstyle suits her.

favorito, a [faßo'rito, a] a, nm/f favourite.

faz [faθ] nf: **la ~ de la tierra** the face of the earth.

fe [fe] nf (REL) faith; (confianza) belief; (documento) certificate; (lealtad) fidelity, loyalty; **prestar ~ a** to believe, credit; **actuar con buena/mala ~** to act in good/bad faith; **dar ~ de** to bear witness to.

fealdad [feal'daθ] nf ugliness.

febrero [fe'ßrero] nm February.

febril [fe'ßril] a feverish.

fecundar [fekun'dar] vt (generar) to fertilize, make fertile; **fecundo, a** a (fértil) fertile; (prolífico) prolific; (fructífero) fruitful; (abundante) abundant; (productivo) productive.

fecha ['fetʃa] nf date; **en ~ próxima** soon; **hasta la ~** to date, so far; **poner ~** to date; **con ~ adelantada** post-dated.

federación [federa'θjon] nf federation.

federal [feðe'ral] a federal; ~**ismo** nm federalism.

felicidad [feliθi'ðað] nf (satisfacción, contento) happiness; (suerte feliz) (good) luck; ~**es** nfpl best wishes, congratulations.

felicitación [feliθita'θjon] nf congratulation; **felicitar** vt to congratulate.

feligrés, esa [feli'ɣres, esa] nm/f parishioner.

feliz [fe'liθ] a (contento) happy; (afortunado) lucky.

felonía [felo'nia] nf felony, crime.

felpudo [fel'puðo] nm doormat.

femenino, a [feme'nino, a] a, nm feminine.

feminista [femi'nista] nf feminist.

fénix ['feniks] nm (ave) phoenix.

fenómeno [fe'nomeno] nm phenomenon; (fig) freak, accident // a inv great // excl smashing!, marvellous!

feo, a ['feo, a] a (gen) ugly; (desagradable) bad, nasty.

féretro ['feretro] nm (ataúd) coffin; (sarcófago) bier.

feria ['ferja] nf (gen) fair; (AM) village market; (día de asueto) holiday, rest day.

fermentar [fermen'tar] vi to ferment.

ferocidad [feroθi'ðað] nf fierceness, ferocity.

feroz [fe'roθ] a (cruel) cruel; (salvaje) fierce.

férreo, a ['ferreo, a] a iron.

ferretería [ferrete'ria], **ferrería** [ferre'ria] nf (trastes) ironmongery; (tienda) ironmonger's shop), hardware store.

ferrocarril [ferroka'rril] nm railway; ~ **de cremallera** rack railway.

fértil ['fertil] a (productivo) fertile; (rico) rich; **fertilidad** nf (gen) fertility; (productividad) fruitfulness; **fertilizar** vt to fertilize.

fervor [fer'ßor] nm fervour; ~**oso, a** a fervent.

festejar [feste'xar] vt (agasajar) to

entertain lavishly; (*galantear*) to court; (*su cumpleaños*) to celebrate; **festejo** *nm* (*diversión*) entertainment; (*galanteo*) courtship; (*fiesta*) celebration.

festividad [festiβi'ðað] *nf* festivity.

festivo, a [fes'tiβo, a] *a* (*de fiesta*) festive; (*fig*) witty; (*CINE, LITERATURA*) humorous.

fétido, a ['fetiðo, a] *a* (*hediondo*) foul-smelling; (*podrido*) rotten.

fiado [fi'aðo] *nm*: **comprar al ~** to buy on credit.

fiador, a [fia'ðor, a] *nm/f* (*JUR*) surety, guarantor; (*COM*) backer // *nm* (*de arma*) safety catch; (*cerrojo*) tumbler; **salir ~ por alguien** to go bail for sb.

fiambre ['fjambre] *nm* cold meat.

fianza ['fjanθa] *nf* surety; (*JUR*): **libertad bajo ~** release on bail.

fiar [fi'ar] *vt* (*salir garante de*) to guarantee; (*vender a crédito*) to sell on credit // *vi* to trust; **~se** *vr* to trust (in), rely on; **~se de uno** to rely on sb.

fiasco ['fjasko] *nm* fiasco.

fibra ['fiβra] *nf* fibre.

ficción [fik'θjon] *nf* fiction.

ficticio, a [fik'tiθjo, a] *a* (*imaginario*) fictitious; (*falso*) fabricated.

ficha ['fitʃa] *nf* (*en juegos*) token, counter; (*tarjeta*) (index) card; (*ELEC*) plug; **fichar** *vt* (*archivar*) to file, index; **estar fichado** to have a record; **fichero** *nm* card index.

fidelidad [fiðeli'ðað] *nf* (*lealtad*) fidelity, loyalty; **alta ~** high fidelity, hi-fi.

fideos [fi'ðeos] *nmpl* noodles.

fiebre ['fjeβre] *nf* (*MED*) fever; (*fig*) feverish excitement; **~ amarilla/del heno** yellow/hay fever; **~ palúdica** malaria; **tener ~** to have a temperature.

fiel [fjel] *a* (*leal*) faithful, loyal; (*fiable*) reliable; (*exacto*) accurate, exact // *nm* inspector; (*aguja*) needle, pointer; **los ~es** the faithful.

fieltro ['fjeltro] *nm* felt.

fiereza [fje'reθa] *nf* (*bravura*) fierceness; (*fealdad*) ugliness.

fiero, a ['fjero, a] *a* (*cruel*) cruel; (*feroz*) fierce; (*duro*) harsh // *nf* (*animal feroz*) wild animal or beast.

fiesta ['fjesta] *nf* party; (*de pueblo*) festival; **~s** *nfpl* (*caricias*) endearments; (*vacaciones*) holiday *sg*; (*broma*) jokes; (*juerga*) fun and games; (*REL*): **~ de guardar** day of obligation.

figura [fi'xura] *nf* (*gen*) figure; (*forma, imagen*) shape, form; (*cara*) face; (*TEATRO*) marionette; (*NAIPES*) face card.

figurar [fixu'rar] *vt* (*representar*) to represent; (*fingir*) to figure // *vi* to figure; **~se** *vr* (*imaginarse*) to imagine; (*suponer*) to suppose.

fijar [fi'xar] *vt* (*gen*) to fix; (*estampilla*) to affix, stick (on); (*fig*) to settle (on), decide; **~ con hilos** to sew on; **~se** *vr*: **~se en** to notice.

fijo, a ['fixo, a] *a* (*gen*) fixed; (*firme*) firm; (*permanente*) permanent // *ad*: **mirar ~** to stare.

fila ['fila] *nf* row; (*cola, columna*) queue; (*cadena*) line; **ponerse en ~** to line up, get into line.

filántropo [fi'lantropo] *nm* philanthropist.

filatelia [fila'telja] *nf* philately.

filete [fi'lete] *nm* (*carne*) steak; (*pescado*) fillet.

filial [fi'ljal] *a* filial // *nf* subsidiary.

Filipinas [fili'pinas] *nfpl*: **las ~** the Philippines.

filmar [fil'mar] *vt* to film, shoot.

filo ['filo] *nm* (*gen*) edge; **sacar ~ a** to sharpen; **al ~ del mediodía** at about midday; **de doble ~** double-edged.

filosofía [filoso'fia] *nf* philosophy; **filósofo** *nm* philosopher.

filtrar [fil'trar] *vt, vi* to filter, strain; **~se** *vr* to filter; (*fig*) to dwindle; **filtro** *nm* (*TEC, utensilio*) filter; (*CULIN*) strainer.

fin [fin] *nm* (*gen*) end; (*objetivo*) aim, purpose; **al ~ y al cabo** when all's said and done; **a ~ de** in order to; **por ~** finally; **en ~** in short; **~ de semana** weekend; **~al a final** // *nm* end, conclusion // *nf* final; **~alista** *nm/f* finalist; **~alizar** *vt* to end, finish // *vi*, **~alizarse** *vr* to end, come to an end.

financiar [finan'θjar] *vt* to finance; **financiero, a** *a* financial.

finca ['finka] *nf* country estate; (*casa*) country house.

fingir [fin'xir] *vt* (*simular*) to simulate; (*pretextar*) to sham, fake // *vi* (*aparentar*) to pretend, feign; **~se** *vr* to pretend to be.

finlandés, esa [finlan'des, esa] *a* Finnish // *nm/f* Finn // *nm* (*lengua*) Finnish.

Finlandia [fin'landja] *nf* Finland.

fino, a ['fino, a] *a* (*gen*) fine; (*delgado*) slender; (*puro*) pure; (*de buenas maneras*) polite, refined; (*inteligente*) shrewd.

firma ['firma] *nf* signature; (*COM*) firm, company; **firmar** *vt* to sign.

firme ['firme] *a* (*gen*) firm; (*estable*) stable; (*sólido*) solid; (*compacto*) compact; (*constante*) steady; (*decidido*) resolute // *nm* road (surface); **~mente** *ad* firmly; **~za** *nf* firmness; (*constancia*) steadiness; (*solidez*) solidity.

fiscal [fis'kal] *a* fiscal // *nm* Public Prosecutor.

fisgar [fis'xar] *vt* to pry into; (*pescar*) to spear, harpoon.

físico, a ['fisiko, a] *a* physical // *nm* physique // *nm/f* physicist // *nf* physics *sg*.

flaco, a ['flako, a] *a* (*muy delgado*) skinny, lean; (*débil*) weak, feeble.

flagrante [fla'xrante] *a* flagrant.

flamante [fla'mante] *a* brilliant; (*nuevo*) brand-new.

flamenco, a [fla'menko, a] *a* (*de Flandes*) Flemish; (*agitanado*) gipsy // *nm* (*canto y baile*) flamenco.

flan [flan] *nm* creme caramel.

flaqueza [fla'keθa] *nf* (*delgadez*) leanness; (*fig*) weakness.

flash [flaʃ] *nm* (*FOTO*) flash.

flauta ['flauta] *nf* flute.

fleco ['fleko] nm fringe.

flecha ['fletʃa] nf arrow.

flema ['flema] nm phlegm.

flequillo [fle'kiʎo] nm (pelo) fringe.

flete ['flete] nm (carga) freight; (alquiler) charter; (precio) freightage.

flexible [flek'siβle] a flexible.

flojo, a ['floxo, a] a (gen) loose; (sin fuerzas) limp; (débil) weak.

flor [flor] nf flower; (piropo) compliment; a ~ de on the surface of; ~ecer vi (BOT) to flower; (fig) to flourish; ~eciente a (BOT) in flower, flowering; (fig) thriving.

flota ['flota] nf fleet.

flotar [flo'tar] vi (gen) to float; (colgar) to hang; **flote** nm: **a flote** afloat; **sacar a flote** (fig) to get back on one's feet.

fluctuar [fluk'twar] vi (oscilar) to fluctuate; (vacilar) to waver.

fluidez [flui'ðeθ] nf fluidity; (fig) fluency.

fluído, a ['fluiðo, a] a, nm fluid.

fluir [flu'ir] vi to flow.

flujo ['fluxo] nm flow; ~ y reflujo ebb and flow; ~ de sangre (MED) loss of blood.

foca ['foka] nf seal.

foco ['foko] nm focus; (ELEC) floodlight.

fogón [fo'ɣon] nm (de cocina) stove.

fogoso, a [fo'ɣoso, a] a spirited.

follaje [fo'ʎaxe] nm foliage.

folleto [fo'ʎeto] nm pamphlet.

fomentar [fomen'tar] vt (MED) to foment; **fomento** nm (MED) fomentation; (promoción) promotion; **Ministerio de Fomento** Ministry of Public Works.

fonda ['fonda] nf inn; (restaurante) buffet.

fondo ['fondo] nm (de mar) bottom; (cuarto) back; (ARTE etc) background; (reserva) fund; ~s nmpl (COM) funds, resources; **una investigación a** thorough investigation; **en el ~ at** bottom, deep down.

fontanería [fontane'ria] nf plumbing; **fontanero** nm plumber.

forastero, a [foras'tero, a] a (extraño) alien, strange // nm/f stranger.

forcejear [forθexe'ar] vi (luchar) to struggle; (esforzarse) to make violent efforts.

forjar [for'xar] vt to forge.

forma ['forma] nf (figura) form, shape; (molde) mould, pattern; (MED) fitness; (método) way, means; **las ~s** the conventions.

formación [forma'θjon] nf (gen) formation; (educación) education.

formal [for'mal] a (gen) formal; (fig: persona) serious; ~idad nf. formality; seriousness.

formar [for'mar] vt (componer) to form, shape; (constituir) to make up, constitute; (ESCOL) to train, educate; ~se vr (cobrar forma) to form, take form; (hacer línea) to form up; (desarrollarse) to develop.

formidable [formi'ðaβle] a (temible) formidable; (asombroso) tremendous.

formulario [formu'larjo] nm form.

fornido, a [for'niðo, a] a strapping, well-built.

foro ['foro] nm (gen) forum; (JUR) court.

forrar [fo'rrar] vt (abrigo) to line; (libro) to cover; **forro** nm (de cuaderno) cover; (costura) lining; (de sillón) upholstery; **forro de freno** brake lining.

fortalecer [fortale'θer] vt to strengthen.

fortaleza [forta'leθa] nf (gen) strength; (determinación) resolution.

fortuito, a [for'twito, a] a accidental.

fortuna [for'tuna] nf (suerte) fortune, (good) luck; (riqueza, caudal) fortune, wealth.

forzar [for'θar] vt (puerta) to force (open); (casa) to break into; (compeler) to compel.

forzoso, a [for'θoso, a] a necessary.

fosa ['fosa] nf (sepultura) grave; (en tierra) pit; (MED) cavity.

fósforo ['fosforo] nm (metaloide) phosphorus; (AM) match.

foso ['foso] nm ditch; (TEATRO) pit; (AUTO): ~ de reconocimiento inspection pit.

foto ['foto] nf photo, snap(shot); ~**copia** nf photocopy; ~**copiador** nm photocopier; ~**copiar** vt to photocopy.

fotografía [fotoɣra'fia] nf (gen) photography; (una ~) photograph; **fotografiar** vt to photograph.

fotógrafo, a [fo'toɣrafo, a] nm/f photographer.

fracaso [fra'kaso] nm (desgracia, revés) failure; **fracasar** vi (gen) to fail.

fracción [frak'θjon] nf fraction; (POL) faction; **fraccionar** vt to divide, break up.

fractura [frak'tura] nf fracture, break.

fragancia [fra'vanðja] nf (olor) fragrance; (perfume) perfume.

frágil ['fraxil] a (débil) fragile; (quebradizo) breakable; **fragilidad** nf fragility; (de persona) frailty.

fragmento [fraɣ'mento] nm (pedazo) fragment.

fragor [fra'ɣor] nm (ruido intenso) din; (de gente) uproar.

fragua ['fraɣwa] nf forge; **fraguar** vt to forge; (fig) to concoct // vi to harden.

fraile ['fraile] nm (REL) friar; (: monje) monk.

frambuesa [fram'bwesa] nf raspberry.

francés, esa [fran'θes, esa] a French // nm/f Frenchman/woman // nm (lengua) French.

Francia ['franθja] nf France.

franco, a ['franko, a] a (leal, abierto) frank, open; (generoso, liberal) generous, liberal; (COM: exento) free // nm franc.

francotirador, a [frankotira'ðor, a] nm/f sniper.

franela [fra'nela] nf flannel.

franja ['franxa] nf fringe.

franquear [franke'ar] vt (camino) to clear; (carta, paquete postal) to frank, stamp; (obstáculo) to overcome; ~se vr (ceder) to give way; (confiarse a alguien) to unburden o.s.

franqueo [fraŋ'keo] *nm* postage.
franqueza [fraŋ'keθa] *nf* (*candor*) frankness; (*generosidad*) generosity.
frasco ['frasko] *nm* bottle; (*al vacío*) (vacuum) flask.
frase ['frase] *nf* sentence; ~ **hecha** set phrase.
fraude ['frauðe] *nm* (*cualidad*) dishonesty; (*acto*) fraud; **fraudulento, a** *a* fraudulent.
frecuencia [fre'kwenθja] *nf* frequency; **con** ~ frequently, often.
fregadero [freɣa'ðor] *nm* sink.
fregar [fre'ɣar] *vt* (*frotar*) to scrub; (*platos*) to wash (up); (*AM*) to annoy.
freír [fre'ir] *vt* to fry.
frenar [fre'nar] *vt* to brake; (*fig*) to check.
frenesí [frene'si] *nm* frenzy; **frenético, a** *a* frantic.
freno ['freno] *nm* (*TEC, AUTO*) brake; (*de cabalgadura*) bit; (*fig*) check.
frente ['frente] *nm* (*ARQ, POL*) front; (*de objeto*) front part // *nf* forehead, brow; **en** ~ **de** in front of; (*en situación opuesta de*) opposite; **chocar de** ~ to crash head-on; **hacer** ~ **a** to face up to.
fresa ['fresa] *nf* strawberry.
fresco, a ['fresko, a] *a* (*nuevo*) fresh; (*frío*) cool // *nm* (*aire*) fresh air; (*ARTE*) fresco; (*fam*) shameless person; (*persona insolente*) impudent person // *nf* cool part of the day; **tomar el** ~ to get some fresh air; **frescura** *nf* freshness; (*descaro*) cheek, nerve; (*calma*) calmness.
frialdad [frial'dað] *nf* (*gen*) coldness; (*indiferencia*) indifference.
fricción [frik'θjon] *nf* (*gen*) friction; (*acto*) rub(bing); (*MED*) massage.
frigidez [frixi'ðeθ] *nf* frigidity.
frigorífico [friɣo'rifiko] *nm* refrigerator.
frijol [fri'xol] *nm* kidney bean.
frío, a ['frio, a] *a* cold // *nm* cold(ness).
frito, a ['frito, a] *a* fried; **me trae** ~ **ese hombre** I'm sick and tired of that man.
frívolo, a ['friβolo, a] *a* frivolous.
frontera [fron'tera] *nf* frontier; **fronterizo, a** *a* frontier *cpd*; (*contiguo*) bordering.
frontón [fron'ton] *nm* (*DEPORTE*) pelota court.
frotar [fro'tar] *vt* to rub; ~**se** *vr*: ~**se las manos** to rub one's hands.
fructífero, a [fruk'tifero, a] *a* fruitful.
frugal [fru'ɣal] *a* frugal.
fruncir [frun'θir] *vt* to pucker; (*costura*) to pleat; ~ **el ceño** to knit one's brow.
frustrar [frus'trar] *vt* to frustrate.
fruta ['fruta] *nf* fruit; **frutería** *nf* fruit shop.
fue *vb ver* **ser, ir**.
fuego ['fweɣo] *nm* (*gen*) fire; (*MED*) rash; **a** ~ **lento** on a low flame or gas; **¿tienes** ~? have you a light?
fuente ['fwente] *nf* (*de una plaza*) fountain; (*manantial, fig*) spring; (*origen*) source; (*plato*) large dish.
fuera *etc vb ver* **ser, ir** // ['fwera] *ad*

out(side); (*en otra parte*) away; (*excepto, salvo*) except, save // *prep*: ~ **de** outside; (*fig*) besides; ~ **de sí** beside o.s.
fuerte ['fwerte] *a* (*gen*) strong; (*golpe*) hard; (*ruido*) loud; (*comida*) rich; (*lluvia*) heavy; (*dolor*) intense // *ad* strongly; hard; loud(ly).
fuerza ['fwerθa] *nf* (*fortaleza*) strength; (*TEC, ELEC*) power; (*coacción*) force; (*MIL*) forces *pl*; **a** ~ **de** by dint of; **cobrar** ~**s** to recover one's strength; **tener** ~**s para** to have the strength to; **a la** ~, **por** ~ forcibly, by force.
fuga ['fuɣa] *nf* (*huida*) flight, escape; (*de gas*) leak; **fugarse** *vr* to flee, escape; **fugaz** *a* fleeting; **fugitivo, a** *a*, *nm/f* fugitive.
fui *vb ver* **ser, ir**.
fulano, a [fu'lano, a] *nm/f* so-and-so, what's-his-name.
fulgor [ful'xor] *nm* brilliance.
fumar [fu'mar] *vi* to smoke; ~**se** *vr* (*disipar*) to squander; ~ **en pipa** to smoke a pipe.
funámbulo, a [fu'nambulo, a] *nm/f* tightrope-walker.
función [fun'θjon] *nf* function; (*de puesto*) duties *pl*; (*espectáculo*) show; **entrar en funciones** to take up one's duties; **funcionar** *vi* (*gen*) to function; (*máquina*) to work.
funcionario, a [funθjo'narjo, a] *nm/f* official; (*público*) civil servant.
funda ['funda] *nf* (*gen*) cover; (*de almohada*) pillowcase.
fundación [funda'θjon] *nf* foundation.
fundamental [fundamen'tal] *a* fundamental, basic.
fundamentar [fundamen'tar] *vt* (*poner base*) to lay the foundations of; (*establecer*) to found; (*fig*) to base; **fundamento** *nm* (*base*) foundation.
fundar [fun'dar] *vt* to found; (*dotar de fondos*) to endow; ~**se** *vr*: ~**se en** to be founded on.
fundición [fundi'θjon] *nf* fusing; (*fábrica*) foundry.
fundir [fun'dir] *vt* (*gen*) to fuse; (*metal*) to smelt, melt down; (*COM*) to merge; (*estatua*) to cast; ~**se** *vr* (*sólido*) to merge, blend; (*unirse*) to fuse together.
fúnebre ['funeβre] *a* funeral *cpd*, funereal.
funeral [fune'ral] *nm* funeral.
furgón [fur'xon] *nm* wagon.
furia ['furja] *nf* (*ira*) fury; (*violencia*) violence; **furibundo, a** *a* furious; **furioso, a** *a* (*iracundo*) furious; (*violento*) violent; **furor** *nm* (*cólera*) rage.
furtivo, a [fur'tiβo, a] *a* furtive.
furúnculo [fu'runkulo] *nm* (*MED*) boil.
fusible [fu'siβle] *nm* fuse.
fusil [fu'sil] *nm* rifle; ~**ar** *vt* to shoot.
fusión [fu'sjon] *nf* (*gen*) melting; (*unión*) fusion; (*COM*) merger.
fútbol ['futβol] *nm* football; **futbolín** *nm* table football; **futbolista** *nm* footballer.

fútil ['futil] a trifling; **futilidad, futileza** nf trviality.

futuro, a [fu'turo, a] a, nm future.

G

gabacho, a [ga'ßatʃo, a] a Pyrenean; (fam) frenchified // nm/f Pyrenean villager.

gabán [ga'ßan] nm overcoat.

gabardina [gaßar'ðina] nf raincoat, gabardine.

gabinete [gaßi'nete] nm (POL) cabinet; (estudio) study; (de abogados etc) office.

gaceta [ga'θeta] nf gazette; **gacetilla** nf (en periódico) news in brief; (de personalidades) gossip column.

gacha ['gatʃa] nf mush; ~**s** nfpl porridge sg.

gafas ['gafas] nfpl glasses; ~ **oscuras** dark glasses.

gaita ['gaita] nf flute; (~ gallega) bagpipes pl.

gajes ['gaxes] nmpl (salario) pay; **los ~ del oficio** occupational hazards.

gajo ['gaxo] nm (gen) bunch; (de árbol) bough; (de naranja) segment.

gala ['gala] nf full dress; (fig: lo mejor) cream, flower; ~**s** nfpl finery sg; **estar de ~** to be in one's best clothes; **hacer ~ de** to display, show off.

galán [ga'lan] nm lover, gallant; (hombre atractivo) ladies' man; (TEATRO): **primer ~** leading man.

galano, a [ga'lano, a] a (elegante) elegant; (bien vestido) smart.

galante [ga'lante] a gallant; **galantear** vt (hacer la corte a) to court, woo; **galanteo** nm (coqueteo) flirting; (de pretendiente) wooing; **galantería** nf (caballerosidad) gallantry; (cumplido) politeness; (comentario) compliment.

galaxia [ga'laksja] nf galaxy.

galera [ga'lera] nf (nave) galley; (carro) wagon; (MED) hospital ward; (IMPRENTA) galley.

galería [gale'ria] nf (gen) gallery; (balcón) veranda(h); (de casa) corridor.

Gales ['gales] nm Wales; **galés, esa** a Welsh // nm/f Welshman/woman // nm (lengua) Welsh.

galgo, a ['galxo, a] nm/f greyhound.

galimatías [galima'tias] nmpl (lenguaje) gibberish, nonsense sg.

galón [ga'lon] nm (MIL) stripe; (medida) gallon.

galopar [galo'par] vi to gallop; **galope** nm gallop.

galvanizar [galßani'θar] vt to galvanize.

gallardía [gaʎar'ðia] nf (galantería) dash; (valor) bravery; (elegancia) elegance.

gallego, a [ga'ʎexo, a] a, nm/f Galician.

galleta [ga'ʎeta] nf biscuit.

gallina [ga'ʎina] nf hen // nm (fam) coward; ~ **ciega** blind man's buff.

gallo ['gaʎo] nm cock, rooster.

gama ['gama] nf (MUS) scale; (fig) range.

gamba ['gamba] nf prawn.

gamberro, a [gam'berro, a] nm/f hooligan, lout.

gamuza [ga'muθa] nf chamois.

gana ['gana] nf (deseo) desire, wish; (apetito) appetite; (voluntad) will; (añoranza) longing; **de buena ~** willingly; **de mala ~** reluctantly; **me da la ~ de** I feel like, I want to; **tener ~s de** to feel like.

ganadería [ganaðe'ria] nf (ganado) livestock; (ganado vacuno) cattle pl; (cría, comercio) cattle raising.

ganado [ga'naðo] nm livestock; ~ **lanar** sheep pl; ~ **vacuno** cattle pl; ~ **porcino** pigs pl.

ganador, a [gana'ðor, a] a winning // nm/f winner.

ganancia [ga'nanθja] nf (lo ganado) gain; (aumento) increase; (beneficio) profit; ~**s** nfpl (ingresos) earnings; (beneficios) profit sg, winnings.

ganapán [gana'pan] nm (obrero casual) odd-job man; (individuo tosco) lout.

ganar [ga'nar] vt (obtener) to get, obtain; (sacar ventaja a) (COM) to earn; (DEPORTE, premio) to win; (derrotar a) to beat; (alcanzar) to reach // vi (DEPORTE) to win; ~**se** vr: ~**se la vida** to earn one's living.

gancho ['gantʃo] nm (gen) hook; (colgador) hanger.

gandul, a [gan'dul, a] a, nm/f good-for-nothing.

ganga ['ganga] nf (cosa buena y barata) bargain; (buena situación) cushy job.

gangrena [gan'grena] nf gangrene.

gansada [gan'saða] nf (fam) stupid thing to do.

ganso, a ['ganso, a] nm/f (ZOOL) gander/goose; (fam) idiot.

ganzúa [gan'θua] nf skeleton key // nm/f burglar.

gañán [ga'ɲan] nm farmhand, farm labourer.

garabato [gara'ßato] nm (gancho) hook; (garfio) grappling iron; (escritura) scrawl, scribble; (fam) sex appeal.

garaje [ga'raxe] nm garage.

garante [ga'rante] a responsible // nm/f guarantor.

garantía [garan'tia] nf guarantee.

garantizar [garanti'θar], **garantir** [garan'tir] vt (hacerse responsable de) to vouch for; (asegurar) to guarantee.

garbanzo [gar'ßanθo] nm chickpea.

garbo ['garßo] nm grace, elegance; ~**so, a** a graceful, elegant.

garfa ['garfa] nf claw.

garfio ['garfjo] nm grappling iron.

garganta [gar'xanta] nf (interna) throat; (externa, de botella) neck; **gargantilla** nf necklace.

gárgara ['garxara] nf gargle, gargling.

gárgola ['garxola] nf gargoyle.

garita [ga'rita] nf cabin, hut; (MIL) sentry box; (de camión) cab.

garra ['garra] nf (de gato, TEC) claw; (de ave) talon; (fam) hand, paw (fam).

garrafa [ga'rrafa] nf carafe, decanter.

garrido, a [ga'rriðo, a] a handsome.

garrote [ga'rrote] nm (palo) stick; (porra) cudgel; (suplicio) garrotte; (MED) tourniquet.

garrulería [garrule'ria] nf chatter.

gárrulo, a ['garrulo, a] a (charlatán) talkative; (ave) twittering; (arroyo) murmuring.

garzo, a ['garθo, a] a blue // nf heron.

gas [gas] nm gas.

gasa ['gasa] nf gauze.

gaseoso, a [gase'oso, a] a gassy, fizzy // nf lemonade, fizzy drink; (fam) pop.

gasolina [gaso'lina] nf petrol, gas(oline) (US); **gasolinera** nf petrol station.

gasómetro [ga'sometro] nm gasometer.

gastado, a [gas'taðo, a] a (rendido) spent; (raído) worn, threadbare; (usado: frase etc) trite.

gastar [gas'tar] vt (dinero, tiempo) to spend; (fuerzas) to use up; (desperdiciar) to waste; (llevar) to wear; ~se vr to wear out; (estropearse) to waste; ~ bromas to crack jokes.

gasto ['gasto] nm (desembolso) expenditure, spending; (consumo, uso) use; ~s nmpl (desembolsos) expenses; (cargos) charges, costs.

gatear [gate'ar] vi (andar a gatas) to go on all fours; (trepar) to climb // vt to scratch.

gatillo [ga'tiʎo] nm (de arma de fuego) trigger; (de dentista) forceps.

gato, a [ga'to, a] nm/f cat // nm (TEC) jack; **andar a ~** as to go on all fours.

gatuno, a [ga'tuno, a] a feline.

gaucho, a ['gautʃo] nm gaucho.

gaveta [ga'βeta] nf drawer.

gavilla [ga'βiʎa] nf sheaf.

gaviota [ga'βjota] nf seagull.

gay [ge] a gay, homosexual.

gayo, a ['gajo, a] a gay, merry.

gazapera [gaθa'pera] nf (conejera) rabbit warren; (de gente) den of thieves; **gazapo** nm young rabbit; (fam) sly fellow.

gazmoño, a [gaθ'moɲo, a], **gazmoñero, a** [gaθmo'ɲero, a] nm/f prude; (pretencioso) prig; (hipócrita) hypocrite.

gazpacho [gaθ'patʃo] nm gazpacho, cold vegetable soup.

gelatina [xela'tina] nf (plato) jelly; (polvos etc) gelatine.

gema ['xema] nf gem.

gemelo, a [xe'melo, a] a, nm/f twin; ~s nmpl (de camisa) cufflinks; **G~s** (ASTRO) Gemini sg; ~s de campo field glasses.

gemido [xe'miðo] nm (quejido) moan, groan; (aullido) howl.

gemir [xe'mir] vi (quejarse) to moan, groan; (aullar) to howl.

genealogía [xenealo'xia] nf genealogy.

generación [xenera'θjon] nf generation.

generador [xenera'ðor] nm generator.

general [xene'ral] a general // nm general; **por lo o en ~** in general; ~**idad** nf generality; **G~itat** nf Catalan parliament; ~**ización** nf generalization; ~**izar** vt to generalize; ~**izarse** vr to become generalised, spread; ~**mente** ad generally.

generar [xene'rar] vt to generate.

genérico, a [xe'neriko, a] a generic.

género ['xenero] nm (clase) kind, sort; (tipo) type; (BIO) genus; (LING) gender; (COM) material; ~ **humano** human race.

generosidad [xenerosi'ðað] nf generosity; **generoso, a** a generous.

genial [xe'njal] a inspired; (idea) brilliant; (afable) genial.

genio ['xenjo] nm (carácter) nature, disposition; (humor) temper; (facultad creadora) genius; **de mal ~** bad-tempered.

gente ['xente] nf (personas) people pl; (raza) race; (nación) nation; (parientes) relatives pl.

gentil [xen'til] a (elegante) graceful; (encantador) charming; ~**eza** nf grace; charm; (cortesía) courtesy.

gentío [xen'tio] nm crowd, throng.

genuflexión [xenuflek'sjon] nf genuflexion.

genuino, a [xe'nwino, a] a genuine.

geografía [xeoɣra'fia] nf geography.

geología [xeolo'xia] nf geology.

geometría [xeome'tria] nf geometry.

gerencia [xe'renθja] nf management; **gerente** nm (supervisor) manager; (jefe) director.

germen ['xermen] nm germ.

germinar [xermi'nar] vi to germinate.

gesticulación [xestikula'θjon] nf (ademán) gesticulation; (mueca) grimace.

gestión [xes'tjon] nf management; (diligencia, acción) negotiation; (esfuerzo) effort; **gestionar** vt (lograr) to try to arrange; (llevar) to manage; (discutir) to negotiate.

gesto ['xesto] nm (mueca) grimace; (ademán) gesture.

gestoría [xesto'ria] nf estate agent's.

Gibraltar [xiβral'tar] nm Gibraltar.

gigante [xi'vante] a, nm/f giant.

gilipollas [xili'poʎas] excl (fam) bastard! (fam).

gimnasia [xim'nasja] nf gymnastics pl; **gimnasio** nm gymnasium; **gimnasta** nm/f gymnast.

gimotear [ximote'ar] vi to whine, whimper.

ginebra [xi'neβra] nf gin.

ginecólogo, a [xine'koloɣo, a] nm/f gynecologist.

gira ['xira] nf tour, trip.

girar [xi'rar] vt (dar la vuelta) to turn (around); (: rápidamente) to spin; (COM: cheque) to draw; (comerciar: letra de cambio) to issue // vi to turn (round); (rápido) to spin; (COM) to draw.

girasol [xira'sol] *nm* sunflower.

giratorio, a [xira'torjo, a] *a* (*gen*) revolving; (*puente*) swing.

giro ['xiro] *nm* (*movimiento*) turn, revolution; (*LING*) expression; (*COM*) draft; ~ **bancario/postal** money/ postal order.

gitano, a [xi'tano, a] *a, nm/f* gypsy.

glacial [gla'θjal] *a* icy, freezing.

glándula ['glandula] *nf* gland.

globo ['gloβo] *nm* (*esfera*) globe, sphere; (*aerostato, juguete*) balloon.

gloria ['glorja] *nf* glory; **gloriarse** *vr* to boast.

glorieta [glo'rjeta] *nf* (*de jardín*) bower, arbour; (*plazoleta*) roundabout.

glorificar [glorifi'kar] *vt* (*enaltecer*) to glorify, praise; ~**se** *vr*: ~**se de** to boast of.

glorioso, a [glo'rjoso, a] *a* glorious.

glosa ['glosa] *nf* comment; **glosar** *vt* (*comentar*) to comment on; (*fig*) to criticize.

glosario [glo'sarjo] *nm* glossary.

glotón, ona [glo'ton, ona] *a* gluttonous, greedy; **glotonería** *nf* gluttony, greed.

gobernación [goβerna'θjon] *nf* government, governing; **gobernador, a** *a* governing // *nm* governor; **gobernante** *a* governing.

gobernar [goβer'nar] *vt* (*dirigir*) to guide, direct; (*regir*) to rule, govern // *vi* to govern; (*NAUT*) to steer.

gobierno [go'βjerno] *nm* (*POL*) government; (*dirección*) guidance, direction; (*NAUT*) steering.

goce ['goθe] *nm* enjoyment.

gol [gol] *nm* goal.

gola ['gola] *nf* gullet; (*garganta*) throat.

golf [golf] *nm* golf.

golfa ['golfa] *nf* (*fam*) tart, whore.

golfo ['golfo] *nm* (*GEO*) gulf; (*fam: niño*) urchin; (*gamberro*) lout.

golondrina [golon'drina] *nf* swallow.

golosina [golo'sina] *nf* (*gen*) titbit; (*dulce*) sweet; **goloso, a** *a* sweet-toothed.

golpe ['golpe] *nm* (*gen*) blow; (*de puño*) punch; (*de mano*) smack; (*de corazón*) beat; (*de remo*) stroke; (*fig: choque*) clash; **no dar** ~ to be bone idle; **de un** ~ **with one blow; de** ~ **suddenly;** ~ **de estado** coup d'état; **golpear** *vt, vi* to strike, knock; (*asestar*) to beat; (*de puño*) to punch; (*golpetear*) to tap.

goma ['goma] *nf* (*caucho*) rubber; (*elástico*) elastic; ~ **espuma** foam rubber; ~ **de pegar** gum, glue.

gomita [go'mita] *nf* elastic band.

góndola ['gondola] *nf* (*barco*) gondola; (*de tren*) goods wagon.

gordo, a ['gorðo, a] *a* (*gen*) fat; (*persona*) plump; (*tela*) coarse; (*fam*) enormous; **el premio** ~ (*en lotería*) first prize; **gordura** *nf* fat; (*corpulencia*) fatness, stoutness.

gorgojo [gor'xoxo] *nm* (*insecto*) grub; (*fam*) runt.

gorila [go'rila] *nm* gorilla.

gorjear [gorxe'ar] *vi* to twitter, chirp; **gorjeo** *nm* twittering, chirping.

gorra ['gorra] *nf* (*gen*) cap; (*de niño*) bonnet; (*militar*) bearskin // *nm* scrounger.

gorrión [go'rrjon] *nm* sparrow.

gorro ['gorro] *nm* (*gen*) cap; (*de niño, mujer*) bonnet.

gorrón [go'rron] *nm* pebble.

gota ['gota] *nf* (*gen*) drop; (*de sudor*) bead; (*MED*) gout; **gotear** *vi* to drip; (*lloviznar*) to drizzle; **gotera** *nf* leak.

gótico, a ['gotiko, a] *a* Gothic.

gozar [go'θar] *vi* to enjoy o.s.; ~ **de** (*disfrutar*) to enjoy; (*poseer*) to possess.

gozne ['goθne] *nm* hinge.

gozo ['goθo] *nm* (*alegría*) joy; (*placer*) pleasure; ~**so, a** *a* joyous, joyful.

grabación [graβa'θjon] *nf* recording.

grabado [gra'βaðo] *nm* print, engraving; **grabador** *nm* engraver.

grabadora [graβa'ðora] *nf* tape-recorder.

grabar [gra'βar] *vt* to engrave; (*discos, cintas*) to record.

gracejo [gra'θexo] *nm* (*humor*) wit, humour; (*elegancia*) grace.

gracia ['graθja] *nf* (*encanto*) grace, gracefulness; (*chiste*) joke; (*humor*) humour, wit; ¡~**s!** thanks!; **¡muchas** ~**s!** thanks very much!; ~**s** a thanks to; **tener** ~ to be funny; (*ser divertido*) to be enjoyable; **no me hace** ~ I am not keen; **gracioso, a** *a* (*divertido*) funny, amusing; (*cómico*) comical // *nm* (*TEATRO*) comic character.

grada ['graða] *nf* (*de escalera*) step; (*de anfiteatro*) tier, row.

gradación [graða'θjon] *nf* gradation.

gradería [graðe'ria] *nf* (*gradas*) (flight of) steps *pl*; (*de anfiteatro*) tiers *pl*, rows *pl*; ~ **cubierta** covered stand.

grado ['graðo] *nm* degree; (*de aceite, vino*) grade; (*grada*) step; (*MIL*) rank; **de buen** ~ willingly.

graduación [graðwa'θjon] *nf* (*del alcohol*) proof, strength; (*ESCOL*) graduation.

gradual [gra'ðwal] *a* gradual.

graduar [gra'ðwar] *vt* (*gen*) to graduate; (*clasificar*) to grade; (*MIL*) to commission; ~**se** *vr* to graduate.

gráfico, a ['grafiko, a] *a* graphic // *nm* diagram // *nf* graph.

grajo ['graxo] *nm* rook.

Gral *abr de* **General.**

gramática [gra'matika] *nf* grammar.

gramo ['gramo] *nm* gramme.

gran [gran] *a ver* **grande.**

grana ['grana] *nf* (*BOT*) seedling; (*ZOOL*) cochineal; (*color, tela*) scarlet.

Granada [gra'naða] *n* Granada.

granada [gra'naða] *nf* pomegranate; (*MIL*) grenade; **granadina** *nf* grenadine.

granadino, a [grana'ðino, a] *a* of Granada // *nm/f* native *or* inhabitant of Granada.

granado, a [gra'naðo, a] *a* choice, select // *nm* pomegranate tree.

granar [gra'nar] *vi* to seed.

granate [gra'nate] *nm* garnet.

Gran Bretaña [granbre'taɲa] *nf* Great Britain.

grande ['grande], **gran** [gran] *a* (*de tamaño*) big, large; (*alto*) tall; (*distinguido*) great; (*impresionante*) grand // *nm* grandee; **grandeza** *nf* greatness.

grandioso, a [gran'djoso, a] *a* magnificent, grand.

grandor [gran'dor] *nm* size.

granel [gra'nel]: **a ~** *ad* in abundance; (*COM*) in bulk.

granero [gra'nero] *nm* granary, barn.

granito [gra'nito] *nm* (*AGR*) small grain; (*roca*) granite; (*MED*) pimple.

granizado [grani'θaðo] *nm* iced drink; **granizar** *vi* to hail; **granizo** *nm* hail.

granja ['granxa] *nf* (*gen*) farm; (*lechería*) dairy; (*café*) milk bar.

granjear [granxe'ar] *vt* (*cobrar*) to earn; (*ganar*) to win; (*avanzar*) to gain; **granjería** *nf* (*COM*) profit; (*AGR*) farming.

grano ['grano] *nm* grain; (*semilla*) seed; (*baya*) berry; (*MED*) pimple; **~s** *nmpl* cereals.

granoso, a [gra'noso, a] *a* granulated.

granuja [gra'nuxa] *nf* grape seed // *nm* rogue; (*golfillo*) urchin.

grapa ['grapa] *nf* staple; (*TEC*) clamp.

grasa ['grasa] *nf* (*gen*) grease; (*de cocina*) fat, lard; (*sebo*) suet; (*mugre*) filth; (*escoria*) dross; **grasiento, a** *a* greasy; (*de aceite*) oily.

gratificación [gratifika'θjon] *nf* (*propina*) tip; (*bono*) bonus; (*recompensa*) reward; **gratificar** *vt* to tip; to reward.

gratis ['gratis] *ad* free.

gratitud [grati'tuð] *nf* gratitude.

grato, a ['grato, a] *a* (*agradable*) pleasant, agreeable; (*bienvenido*) welcome.

gratuito, a [gra'twito, a] *a* (*gratis*) free; (*sin razón*) gratuitous.

gravamen [gra'ßamen] *nm* (*carga*) burden; (*impuesto*) tax.

gravar [gra'ßar] *vt* to burden.

grave ['graße] *a* heavy; (*serio*) grave, serious; **~dad** *nf* gravity.

grávido, a [gra'ßiðo, a] *a* (*preñada*) pregnant; (*lleno, cargado*) full.

gravitación [graßita'θjon] *nf* gravitation; **gravitar** *vi* to gravitate; **gravitar sobre** to rest on.

gravoso, a [gra'ßoso, a] *a* (*pesado*) burdensome; (*costoso*) costly.

graznar [graθ'nar] *vi* (*cuervo*) to squawk; (*pato*) to quack; (*hablar ronco*) to croak; **graznido** *nm* squawk; croak.

Grecia ['greθja] *nf* Greece

greguería [greɣe'ria] *nf* hubbub.

gremio ['gremjo] *nm* (*sindicato*) trade union; (*asociación*) professional association.

greña ['greɲa] *nf* (*cabellos*) shock of hair;

(*maraña*) tangle; **greñudo, a** *a* (*persona*) dishevelled; (*hair*) tangled.

gresca ['greska] *nf* uproar.

grey [grei] *nf* flock.

griego, a ['grjeɣo, a] *a, nm/f* Greek.

grieta ['grjeta] *nf* crack; **grietarse** *vr* = **agrietarse**.

grifo, a ['grifo, a] *a* curly, kinky // *nm* tap.

grillo ['griʎo] *nm* (*ZOOL*) cricket; (*BOT*) shoot; **~s** *nmpl* shackles, irons.

gripe ['gripe] *nf* flu, influenza.

gris [gris] *a* (*color*) grey.

grita ['grita] *nf* uproar; **gritar** *vt, vi* to shout, yell; **grito** *nm* shout, yell; (*de horror*) scream; **a grito pelado** at the top of one's voice.

grosella [gro'seʎa] *nf* (red)currant; **~ negra** blackcurrant.

grosería [grose'ria] *nf* (*actitud*) rudeness; (*comentario*) vulgar comment; **grosero, a** *a* (*poco cortés*) rude; (*ordinario*) vulgar, crude.

grosor [gro'sor] *nm* thickness.

grotesco, a [gro'tesko, a] *a* grotesque.

grúa ['grua] *nf* (*TEC*) crane; (*de petróleo*) derrick.

grueso, a ['grweso, a] *a* thick; (*voluminoso*) stout // *nm* bulk // *nf* gross; **el ~ de** the bulk of.

grulla ['gruʎa] *nf* crane.

gruñido [gru'niðo] *nm* grunt; (*fig*) grumble; **gruñir** *vi* (*animal*) to growl; (*fam*) to grumble.

grupa ['grupa] *nf* (*ZOOL*) rump.

grupo ['grupo] *nm* group; (*TEC*) unit, set.

gruta ['gruta] *nf* grotto.

guadamecí [gwaðame'θi], **guadamecil** [gwaðame'θil] *nm* embossed leather.

guadaña [gwa'ðaɲa] *nf* scythe; **guadañar** *vt* to scythe, mow.

guano ['gwano] *nm* (*AM*) guano.

guante ['gwante] *nm* glove.

guapo, a ['gwapo, a] *a* good-looking, attractive; (*hombre*) handsome; (*elegante*) smart // *nm* lover, gallant.

guarda ['gwarða] *nm* guard, keeper // *nf* guarding; (*custodia*) custody; **~bosque** *nm* gamekeeper; **~costas** *nm inv* coastguard vessel; **~dor, a** a protective // *nm/f* guardian, protector; **~espaldas** *nm/f inv* bodyguard; **~polvo** *nm* dust cover; (*de niño*) smock; (*para el trabajo*) overalls *pl*; **guardar** *vt* (*gen*) to keep; (*vigilar*) to guard, watch over; (*dinero: ahorrar*) to save, put by; **guardarse** *vr* (*preservarse*) to protect o.s.; (*evitar*) to avoid; **guardarropa** *nm* (*armario*) wardrobe; (*en establecimiento público*) cloakroom.

guardería [gwarðe'ria] *nf* (children's) nursery.

guardia ['gwarðja] *nf* (*MIL*) guard; (*cuidado*) care, custody // *nm* (*policía*) policeman; **estar de ~** to be on guard; **montar ~** to mount guard; **G~ Civil** Civil Guard; **G~ Nacional** police; **~ urbano** traffic policeman.

guardián, ana [gwar'ðjan, ana] nm/f (gen) guardian, keeper; (sereno) watchman.

guardilla [gwar'ðiʎa] nf attic.

guarecer [gware'θer] vt (proteger) to ·protect; (abrigar) to shelter; ~se vr to take refuge.

guarida [gwa'riða] nf (de animal) den, lair; (refugio) refuge.

guarismo [gwa'rismo] nm figure, number.

guarnecer [gwarne'θer] vt (equipar) to provide; (adornar) to adorn; (TEC) to reinforce; **guarnición** nf (de vestimenta) trimming; (de piedra) mount; (CULIN) garnish; (arneses) harness; (MIL) garrison.

guarro, a ['gwarro, a] nm/f pig.

guasa ['gwasa] nf joke; **guasón, ona** a witty; (bromista) joking // nm/f wit; joker.

Guatemala [gwate'mala] nf Guatemala.

gubernativo, a [guβerna'tiβo, a] a governmental.

guedeja [ge'ðexa] nf long hair; (de león) mane.

guerra ['gerra] nf war; (pelea) struggle; ~ fría cold war; **dar** ~ to annoy; **guerrear** vi to wage war; **guerrero, a** a fighting; (carácter) warlike // nm/f warrior.

guerrilla [ge'rriʎa] nf guerrilla warfare; (tropas) guerrilla band or group.

guía ['gia] nm/f guide // nf (libro) guidebook; ~ **de ferrocarriles** railway timetable; ~ **de teléfonos** telephone directory; **guiar** vt to guide, direct; (AUT) to steer; **guiarse** vr: **guiarse por** to be guided by.

guija ['gixa] nf, **guijarro** [gi'xarro] nm pebble; (camino) cobblestone.

guijo ['gixo] nm gravel; (de playa) shingle.

guillotina [giʎo'tina] nf guillotine.

guinda ['ginda] nf morello cherry.

guindar [gin'dar] vt to hoist.

guindilla [gin'diʎa] nf Guinea pepper.

guiñapo [gi'ɲapo] nm (harapo) rag; (persona) reprobate, rogue.

guiñar [gi'ɲar] vi to wink; (parpadear) to blink.

guión [gi'on] nm (conductor) leader; (LING) hyphen, dash; (CINE) script; **guionista** nm/f scriptwriter.

guirnalda [gir'nalda] nf garland.

guisa ['gisa] nf: **a** ~ **de** as, like, in the way of.

guisado [gi'saðo] nm stew.

guisante [gi'sante] nm pea; ~ **de olor** sweet pea.

guisar [gi'sar] vt, vi to cook; **guiso** nm cooked dish.

guita ['gita] nf twine.

guitarra [gi'tarra] nf guitar.

gula ['gula] nf gluttony, greed.

gusano [gu'sano] nm maggot; (lombriz) earthworm; ~ **de luz** glow-worm; ~ **de seda** silk-worm.

gustar [gus'tar] vt to taste, sample // vi to please, be pleasing; ~ **de algo** to like or

enjoy sth; **me gustan las uvas** I like grapes.

gusto ['gusto] nm (sentido, sabor) taste; (placer) pleasure; **tiene** ~ **a menta** it tastes of mint; **tener buen** ~ to have good taste; **sentirse a** ~ to feel at ease; **mucho** ~ **en conocerle** pleased to meet you; **el** ~ **es mío** the pleasure is mine; **con** ~ willingly, gladly; ~**so, a** a (sabroso) tasty; (agradable) pleasant.

gutural [gutu'ral] a guttural.

H

ha vb ver **haber**.

haba ['aβa] nf bean.

Habana [a'βana] nf: **la** ~ Havana.

habano [a'βano] nm Havana cigar.

haber [a'βer] vb auxiliar to have; **de** ~**lo sabido** if I had known (it); ~ **de** to have to // vb impersonal: **hay** there is/are; **hay que** it is necessary to, one must; **¿qué hay?** how's it going?; **no hay de qué** don't mention it // nm (ingreso) income; (COM: crédito) credit; ~**es** nmpl assets.

habichuela [aβi't∫wela] nf kidney bean.

hábil ['aβil] a (listo) clever, smart; (capaz) fit, capable; (experto) expert; **día** ~ working day; **habilidad** nf (gen) skill, ability; (inteligencia) cleverness.

habilitación [aβilita'θjon] nf qualification; (colocación de muebles) fitting out; (financiamiento) financing.

habilitar [aβili'tar] vt (capacitar) to enable; (dar instrumentos) to equip; (financiar) to finance.

hábilmente [aβil'mente] ad skilfully, expertly.

habitación [aβita'θjon] nf (cuarto) room; (casa) dwelling, abode; (BIO: morada) habitat; ~ **sencilla** o **particular** single room; ~ **doble** o **matrimonial** double room.

habitante [aβi'tante] nm/f inhabitant.

habitar [aβi'tar] vt (residir en) to inhabit; (ocupar) to occupy // vi to live.

hábito ['aβito] nm habit; **habitual** a habitual.

habituar [aβi'twar] vt to accustom; ~**se** vr: ~**se a** to get used to.

habla ['aβla] nf (capacidad de hablar) speech; (idioma) language; (dialecto) dialect; **perder el** ~ to become speechless; **de** ~ **francesa** French-speaking; **estar al** ~ to be in contact; **¡González al** ~! Gonzalez speaking!

hablador, a [aβla'ðor, a] a talkative // nm/f chatterbox.

habladuría [aβlaðu'ria] nf rumour; (sarcasmo) sarcastic comment; ~**s** nfpl gossip sg.

hablar [a'βlar] vt to speak, talk // vi to speak; ~**se** vr to speak to each other; ~ **con** to speak to; ~ **de** to speak of or about; **'se habla inglés'** 'English spoken here'.

hablilla [a'βliʎa] nf story, rumour.

habré *etc vb ver* **haber.**

hacedero, a [aθe'θero, a] *a* feasible.

hacedor, a [aθe'ðor, a] *nm/f* maker.

hacendoso, a [aθen'doso, a] *a* industrious.

hacer [a'θer] *vt* (*gen*) to make; (*crear*) to create; (*TEC*) to manufacture; (*preparar*) to prepare; (*ejecutar*) to do, execute; (*obligar*) to force, compel // *vi* (*comportarse*) to act, behave; (*disimular*) to pretend; (*importar*) to be important, matter; (*convenir, ser apto*) to be suitable; **~se** *vr* (*fabricarse*) to be made, be done; (*volverse*) to become; (*acostumbrarse a*) to get used to; **~ la maleta** to pack; **~ una pregunta** to ask a question; **~ una visita** to visit; **~ bien/mal** to act rightly/wrongly; **hace frío/calor** it's cold/hot; **hace dos años** two years ago; **hace poco** a little while ago; **~ el malo** (*TEATRO*) to play (the part of) the villain; **¿qué ~?** what is to be done?; **~ como que o como si** to act as though *or* as if; **~ de** to act as; **me hice un traje** I had a suit made; **~se el sordo** to turn a deaf ear; **~se viejo** to grow old; **~se con algo** to get hold of sth; **~se a un lado** to stand aside.

hacia [a'θja] *prep* (*en dirección de*) towards; (*cerca de*) near; **~ arriba/abajo** up(wards)/down(wards); **~ mediodía** about noon.

hacienda [a'θjenda] *nf* (*propiedad*) property; (*estancia*) farm, ranch; (*AM*) plantation; **~ pública** public finance; (*Ministerio de*) **H~** Treasury, Exchequer.

hacina [a'θina] *nf* pile, stack.

hacha [a'tʃa] *nf* axe; (*antorcha*) torch.

hache [a'tʃe] *nf* (the letter) H.

hada ['aða] *nf* fairy.

hago *etc vb ver* **hacer.**

Haití [ai'ti] *nm* Haiti.

halagar [ala'ɣar] *vt* (*mostrar afecto*) to show affection to; (*lisonjear*) to flatter.

halago [a'laɣo] *nm* pleasure, delight; (*atractivo*) attraction; (*adulación*) flattery; **halagüeño, a** *a* pleasing; attractive; flattering.

halcón [al'kon] *nm* falcon, hawk.

hálito ['alito] *nm* breath.

hallar [a'ʎar] *vt* (*gen*) to find; (*descubrir*) to discover; (*toparse con*) to run up against; **~se** *vr* to be (situated); **hallazgo** *nm* discovery; (*cosa*) find.

hamaca [a'maka] *nf* hammock; **~ plegable** deckchair.

hambre ['ambre] *nf* hunger; (*carencia*) famine; (*fig*) longing; **tener ~** to be hungry; **~ar** *vi, vt* to starve; **hambriento, a** *a* hungry, starving.

hamburguesa [ambur'ɣesa] *nf* hamburger.

hampa ['ampa] *nf* underworld; **hampón** *nm* tough.

han *vb ver* **haber.**

haragán, ana [ara'ɣan, ana] *a, nm/f* good-for-nothing; **haraganear** *vi* to idle, loaf about.

harapiento, a [ara'pjento, a] *a* tattered, in rags; **harapo** *nm* rag.

haré *etc vb ver* **hacer.**

harina [a'rina] *nf* flour; (*polvo*) powder; **harinero, a** *nm/f* flour merchant; **harinoso, a** *a* floury.

hartar [ar'tar] *vt* to satiate, glut; (*fig*) to tire, sicken; **~se** *vr* (*de comida*) to fill o.s., gorge o.s.; (*cansarse*) to get fed up (*de with*); **hartazgo** *nm* surfeit, glut; **harto, a** *a* (*lleno*) full; (*cansado*) fed up // *ad* (*bastante*) enough; (*muy*) very; **estar harto de** to be fed up with; **hartura** *nf* (*exceso*) surfeit; (*abundancia*) abundance; (*satisfacción*) satisfaction.

has *vb ver* **haber.**

hasta ['asta] *ad* even // *prep* (*alcanzando a*) as far as, up/down to; (*de tiempo: a tal hora*) till, until; (*antes de*) before // *conj*: **~ que** until; **~ luego/la vista** see you soon.

hastiar [as'tjar] *vt* (*gen*) to weary; (*aburrir*) to bore; (*asquear*) to disgust; **~se** *vr*: **~se de** to get fed up with; **hastío** *nm* weariness; boredom; disgust.

hato ['ato], **hatillo** [a'tiʎo] *nm* belongings *pl*, kit; (*víveres*) provisions *pl*; (*banda*) gang, group; (*montón*) bundle, heap.

hay *vb ver* **haber.**

Haya ['aja] *nf*: **la ~** The Hague.

haya *etc vb ver* **haber** // ['aja] *nf* beech tree; **hayal, hayedo** *nm* beech grove.

haz [aθ] *vb ver* **hacer** // *nm* bundle, bunch; (*rayo: de luz*) beam.

hazaña [a'θaɲa] *nf* feat, exploit.

hazmerreír [aθmerre'ir] *nm* laughing stock.

he *vb ver* **haber.**

hebilla [e'βiʎa] *nf* buckle, clasp.

hebra ['eβra] *nf* thread; (*BOT: fibra*) fibre, grain; **tabaco de ~** loose tobacco.

hebreo, a [e'βreo, a] *a, nm/f* Hebrew // *nm* (*lengua*) Hebrew.

hectárea [ek'tarea] *nf* hectare.

hechizar [etʃi'θar] *vt* to cast a spell on, bewitch.

hechizo, a [e'tʃiθo, a] *a* (*gen*) false, artificial; (*removible*) detachable // *nm* witchcraft, magic; (*acto de magia*) spell, charm.

hecho, a ['etʃo, a] *pp de* **hacer** // *a* complete; (*maduro*) mature; (*costura*) ready-to-wear // *nm* deed, act; (*dato*) fact; (*cuestión*) matter; (*suceso*) event // *excl* agreed!, done!; **¡bien ~!** well done!; **de ~** in fact, as a matter of fact.

hechura [e'tʃura] *nf* making, creation; (*producto*) product; (*forma*) form, shape; (*de persona*) build; (*TEC*) craftsmanship; **~s** *nfpl* (*COSTURA*) cost of making up *sg*.

heder [e'ðer] *vi* to stink, smell; (*fig*) to be unbearable.

hediondez [eðjon'deθ] *nf* stench, stink; (*cosa*) stinking thing; **hediondo, a** *a* stinking; (*insoportable*) repulsive, unbearable.

hedor [e'ðor] *nm* stench.

helado, a [e'laðo, a] *a* frozen; (*glacial*) icy; (*fig*) chilly, cold // *nm* ice-cream // *nf* frost.

helar [e'lar] *vt* to freeze, ice (up); (*dejar atónito*) to amaze; (*desalentar*) to discourage // *vi*, ~**se** *vr* to freeze.

hélice ['eliθe] *nf* spiral; (*TEC*) propeller.

helicóptero [eli'koptero] *nm* helicopter.

hembra ['embra] *nf* (*BOT, ZOOL*) female; (*mujer*) woman; (*TEC*) nut.

hemorragia [emo'rraxja] *nf* haemorrhage.

hemorroides [emo'rroiðes] *nfpl* haemorrhoids.

hemos *vb ver* **haber.**

henchir [en'tʃir] *vt* to fill, stuff; ~**se** *vr* (*llenarse de comida*) to stuff o.s. (with food); (*inflarse*) to swell (up).

hender [en'der] *vt* to cleave, split; **hendidura** *nf* crack, split; (*GEO*) fissure.

heno ['eno] *nm* hay.

herbicida [erβi'θiða] *nm* weed-killer.

heredad [ere'ðað] *nf* landed property; (*granja*) farm.

heredar [ere'ðar] *vt* to inherit; **heredero, a** *nm/f* heir/heiress.

hereje [e'rexe] *nm/f* heretic; **herejía** *nf* heresy.

herencia [e'renθja] *nf* inheritance.

herido, a [e'riðo, a] *a* injured, wounded // *nm/f* casualty // *nf* wound, injury; (*insulto*) insult.

herir [e'rir] *vt* to wound, injure; (*fig*) to offend.

hermanar [erma'nar] *vt* to match; (*unir*) to join.

hermandad [erman'dað] *nf* brotherhood.

hermano, a [er'mano, a] *nm/f* brother/sister; ~ **gemelo** twin brother; ~ **político** brother-in-law; ~**a política** sister-in-law.

hermético, a [er'metiko, a] *a* hermetic; (*fig*) watertight.

hermoso, a [er'moso, a] *a* beautiful, lovely; (*estupendo*) splendid; (*guapo*) handsome; **hermosura** *nf* beauty.

héroe ['eroe] *nm* hero; **heroico, a** *a* heroic.

heroína [ero'ina] *nf* (*mujer*) heroine; (*droga*) heroin.

heroísmo [ero'ismo] *nm* heroism.

herrador [erra'ðor] *nm* blacksmith; **herradura** *nf*: **curva en herradura** hairpin bend.

herramienta [erra'mjenta] *nf* tool; (*conjunto*) set of tools.

herrería [erre'ria] *nf* smithy; (*TEC*) forge; **herrero** *nm* blacksmith.

herrumbre [e'rrumbre] *nf* rust.

hervidero [erβi'ðero] *nm* (*burbujeo*) boiling, seething; (*fuente*) hot spring.

hervir [er'βir] *vi* (*gen*) to boil; (*burbujear*) to bubble; (*fig*): ~ **de** to teem with; ~ **a**

fuego lento to simmer; **hervor** *nm* boiling; (*fig*) ardour, fervour.

heterogéneo, a [etero'xeneo, a] *a* heterogeneous.

heterosexual [eterosek'swal] *a* heterosexual.

hice *etc vb ver* **hacer.**

hidráulico, a [i'ðrauliko, a] *a* hydraulic // *nf* hydraulics *sg*.

hidro... [iðro] *pref* hydro..., water-...; ~**ala** *nf* hovercraft; ~**avión** *nm* seaplane; ~**eléctrico, a** *a* hydroelectric; ~**fobia** *nf* hydrophobia, rabies; **hidrófugo, a** *a* damp-proof; **hidrógeno** *nm* hydrogen.

hiedra ['jeðra] *nf* ivy.

hiel [jel] *nf* gall, bile; (*fig*) bitterness.

hiela *etc vb ver* **helar.**

hielo ['jelo] *nm* (*gen*) ice; (*escarza*) frost; (*fig*) coldness, reserve.

hiena ['jena] *nf* hyena.

hierba ['jerβa] *nf* (*BOT*) grass; (*MED*) herb; **mala** ~ weed; (*fig*) evil influence; ~**buena** *nf* mint.

hierro ['jerro] *nm* (*metal*) iron; (*objeto*) iron object; (*herramienta*) tool; ~ **acanalado** corrugated iron; ~ **colado** *o* **fundido** cast iron.

hígado ['iβaðo] *nm* liver.

higiene [i'xjene] *nf* hygiene; **higiénico, a** *a* hygienic.

higo ['iβo] *nm* fig; ~ **paso** *o* **seco** dried fig; **higuera** *nf* fig tree.

hijastro, a [i'xastro, a] *nm/f* stepson/daughter.

hijo, a ['ixo, a] *nm/f* son/daughter, child; ~**s** *nmpl* children, sons and daughters; ~ **de papá/mamá** daddy's/mummy's boy; ~ **de puta** bastard, son of a bitch.

hilado, a [i'laðo, a] *a* spun // *nm* yarn.

hilandero, a [ilan'dero, a] *nm/f* spinner.

hilar [i'lar] *vt* to spin; ~ **delgado** to split hairs.

hilera [i'lera] *nf* row, file.

hilo ['ilo] *nm* (*gen*) thread; (*BOT*) fibre; (*metal*) wire; (*de agua*) trickle, thin stream; (*de luz*) beam, ray.

hilvanar [ilβa'nar] *vt* to tack; (*fig*) to do hurriedly.

Himalayas [ima'lajas] *nfpl*: **las** ~ the Himalayas.

himno ['imno] *nm* hymn; ~ **nacional** national anthem.

hincapié [inka'pje] *nm*: **hacer** ~ **en** to emphasize.

hincar [in'kar] *vt* to drive (in), thrust (in); ~**se** *vr*: ~**se de rodillas** to kneel down.

hinchado, a [in'tʃaðo, a] *a* (*gen*) swollen; (*persona*) pompous.

hinchar [in'tʃar] *vt* (*gen*) to swell; (*inflar*) to blow up, inflate; (*fig*) to exaggerate; ~**se** *vr* (*inflarse*) to swell up; (*fam*: *llenarse*) to stuff o.s.; **hinchazón** *nf* (*MED*) swelling; (*altivez*) arrogance.

hinojo [i'noxo] *nm* fennel.

hipar [i'par] *vi* to hiccup; (*perro*) to pant.

hipnotismo [ipno'tismo] *nm* hypnotism; **hipnotizar** *vt* to hypnotize.
hipo ['ipo] *nm* hiccups *pl.*
hipocresía [ipokre'sia] *nf* hypocrisy; **hipócrita** *a* hypocritical // *nm/f* hypocrite.
hipódromo [i'poðromo] *nm* racetrack.
hipopótamo [ipo'potamo] *nm* hippopotamus.
hipoteca [ipo'teka] *nf* mortgage.
hipótesis [i'potesis] *nf* hypothesis.
hiriente [i'rjente] *a* offensive, cutting.
hirsuto, a [ir'suto, a] *a* hairy; (*fig*) rough.
hispánico, a [is'paniko, a] *a* Hispanic.
hispano, a [is'pano, a] *a* Hispanic, Spanish, Hispano-; **H~américa** *nf* Spanish *or* Latin America; **~americano** *a a, nm/f* Spanish *or* Latin American.
histeria [is'terja] *nf* hysteria.
historia [is'torja] *nf* (*gen*) history; (*cuento*) story, tale; **~s** *nfpl* (*chismes*) gossip *sg*; **dejarse de ~s** to come to the point; **pasar a la ~** to go down in history; **~dor, a** *nm/f* historian; **historiar** *vt* to chronicle, write the history of; **histórico, a** *a* historical; (*fig*) historic.
historieta [isto'rjeta] *nf* tale, anecdote; (*dibujos*) strip cartoon.
hito ['ito] *nm* (*gen*) landmark; (*objetivo*) goal, target.
hizo *vb ver* **hacer.**
hocico [o'θiko] *nm* snout; (*fig*) grimace; **caer o dar de ~s** to fall on one's face.
hockey ['xoki] *nm* hockey; **~ sobre patines o hielo** ice hockey.
hogar [o'xar] *nm* fireplace, hearth; (*casa*) home; (*vida familiar*) home life; **~eño, a** *a* home; (*persona*) home-loving.
hoguera [o'xera] *nf* (*gen*) bonfire; (*llamas*) blaze.
hoja ['oxa] *nf* (*gen*) leaf; (*de flor*) petal; (*de papel*) sheet; (*página*) page; **~ de afeitar** razor blade; **~ de estaño** tinfoil.
hojalata [oxa'lata] *nf* tin(plate).
hojear [oxe'ar] *vt* to leaf through, turn the pages of.
hola ['ola] *excl* hello!
Holanda [o'landa] *nf* Holland; **holandés, esa** *a* Dutch // *nm/f* Dutchman/woman // *nm* (*lengua*) Dutch.
holgado, a [ol'xaðo, a] *a* loose, baggy; (*libre*) free; (*desempleado*) idle; (*rico*) well-to-do.
holganza [ol'xanθa] *nf* (*ocio*) leisure; (*pereza*) idleness; (*diversión*) amusement.
holgar [ol'xar] *vi* (*descansar*) to rest; (*sobrar*) to be superfluous; **~se** *vr* to enjoy o.s.; **huelga decir que** it goes without saying that.
holgazán, ana [olxa'θan, ana] *a* idle, lazy // *nm/f* loafer.
holgura [ol'xura] *nf* looseness, bagginess; (*TEC*) play, free movement; (*vida*) comfortable living, luxury.
hollar [o'ʎar] *vt* to tread (on), trample.
hollín [o'ʎin] *nm* soot.
hombradía [ombra'ðia] *nf* manliness.

hombre ['ombre] *nm* (*gen*) man(kind); (*uno*) man // *excl* (*claro*) of course!; (*para énfasis*) man, old boy; (*sorpresa*) you don't say!; **~ de negocios** businessman; **~-rana** frogman; **~ de pro o de provecho** honest man.
hombrera [om'brera] *nf* shoulder strap.
hombro ['ombro] *nm* shoulder.
hombruno, a [om'bruno, a] *a* mannish.
homenaje [ome'naxe] *nm* (*gen*) homage; (*lealtad*) allegiance; (*tributo*) tribute.
homicida [omi'θiða] *a* homicidal // *nm/f* murderer; **homicidio** *nm* murder, homicide.
homosexual [omosek'swal] *a, nm/f* homosexual.
hondo, a ['ondo, a] *a* deep; (*profundo*) low // *nm* depth(s) (*pl*), bottom; **~nada** *nf* hollow, depression; (*cañón*) ravine; (*GEO*) lowland; **hondura** *nf* depth, profundity.
Honduras [on'duras] *nf* Honduras.
hondureño, a [ondu'reɲo, a] *a, nm/f* Honduran.
honestidad [onesti'ðað] *nf* purity, chastity; (*decencia*) decency; **honesto, a** *a* chaste, decent, honest; (*justo*) just.
hongo ['ongo] *nm* (*BOT. gen*) fungus; (: *comestible*) mushroom; (: *venenoso*) toadstool.
honor [o'nor] *nm* (*gen*) honour; (*gloria*) glory; **en ~ a la verdad** to be fair; **~able** *a* honourable.
honorario, a [ono'rarjo, a] *a* honorary; **~s** *nmpl* fees.
honra ['onra] *nf* (*gen*) honour; (*nombre*) reputation; **~dez** *nf* honesty; (*de persona*) integrity; **~do, a** *a* honest, upright.
honrar [on'rar] *vt* to honour; **~se** *vr*: **~se con algo/de hacer algo** to be honoured by/to do sth.
honroso, a [on'roso, a] *a* (*honrado*) honourable; (*respetado*) respectable.
hora ['ora] *nf* (*gen*) time; (*específica*) hour; **¿qué ~ es?** what time is it?; **¿a qué ~?** at what time?; **media ~** half an hour; **a la ~ de recreo** at playtime; **a primera ~** first thing (in the morning); **a última ~** at the last moment; **en las altas ~s** in the small hours; **¡a buena ~!** it's high time!; **dar la ~** to strike the hour; **~s de oficina/de trabajo** office/working hours; **~s de visita** visiting times; **~s extras o extraordinarias** overtime *sg*; **~s punta** rush hours.
horadar [ora'ðar] *vt* to drill, bore.
horario, a [o'rarjo, a] *a* hourly, hour *cpd* // *nm* timetable.
horca ['orka] *nf* gallows *sg.*
horcajadas [orka'xaðas]: **a ~** *ad* astride.
horda ['orða] *nf* horde.
horizontal [oriθon'tal] *a* horizontal; **horizonte** *nm* horizon.
horma ['orma] *nf* mould.
hormiga [or'miva] *nf* ant; **~s** *nfpl* (*MED*) pins and needles.
hormigón [ormi'von] *nm* concrete; **~**

armado/pretensado reinforced/pre-stressed concrete.

hormigueo [ormi'ɤeo] nm (comezón) itch; (fig) uneasiness; (amontonamiento) swarming.

hormona [or'mona] nf hormone.

hornillo [or'niʎo] nm small furnace; (cocina) portable stove.

horno ['orno] nm (CULIN) oven; (TEC) furnace; alto ~ blast furnace.

horóscopo [o'roskopo] nm horoscope.

horquilla [or'kiʎa] nf hairpin; (AGR) pitchfork.

horrendo, a [o'rrendo, a] a horrendous, frightful.

horrible [o'rriβle] a horrible, dreadful.

horripilante [orripi'lante] a hair-raising; (espeluznante) creepy.

horripilar [orripi'lar] vt: ~ a uno to horrify sb; ~se vr to be horrified.

horror [o'rror] nm horror, dread; (atrocidad) atrocity; ¡qué ~! (fam) oh, my God!; ~izar vt to horrify, frighten; ~izarse vr to be horrified; ~oso, a a horrifying, ghastly.

hortaliza [orta'liθa] nf vegetable.

hortelano, a [orte'lano, a] nm/f (market) gardener.

hosco, a ['osko, a] a dark; (triste, ceñudo) sullen, gloomy.

hospedar [ospe'ðar] vt to put up, lodge; ~se vr to stay, lodge.

hospital [ospi'tal] nm hospital.

hospitalario, a [ospita'larjo, a] a hospitable; **hospitalidad** nf hospitality.

hosquedad [oske'ðað] nf sullenness.

hostal [os'tal] nm small hotel.

hostelero, a [oste'lero, a] nm/f innkeeper, landlord/lady.

hostería [oste'ria] nf hostelry.

hostia ['ostja] nf host, consecrated wafer; (fam: golpe) whack, punch // excl: ¡~s! damn it!

hostigar [osti'ɤar] vt to whip; (fig) to harass, pester.

hostil [os'til] a hostile; ~idad nf hostility.

hotel [o'tel] nm hotel; ~ero, a a hotel cpd // nm/f hotelier.

hoy [oi] ad (este día) today; (el ahora) now(adays) // nm present time; ~ (en) día now(adays).

hoya ['oja] nf pit; (sepulcro) grave; (GEO) valley.

hoyo ['ojo] nm hole, pit; **hoyuelo** nm dimple.

hoz [oθ] nf sickle.

hube etc vb ver **haber**.

hucha ['utʃa] nf money box; (fig) nest egg.

hueco, a ['weko, a] a (vacío) hollow, empty; (blanco: papel) blank; (resonante) booming // nm hollow, cavity.

huelga etc vb ver **holgar** // ['welɤa] nf strike; **declararse en** ~ to go on strike, come out on strike; ~ **de brazos caídos/de hambre** sit-down/hunger strike; ~ **patronal** lockout.

huelgo etc vb ver **holgar** // ['welɤo] nm breath; (espacio) room, space.

huelguista [wel'ɤista] nm/f striker.

huelo etc vb ver **oler.**

huella ['weʎa] nf (acto de pisar, pisada) tread(ing); (marca del paso) footprint, footstep; (: de animal, máquina) track; ~ **digital** fingerprint; ~ **del sonido** sound track.

huérfano, a ['werfano, a] a orphan(ed) // nm/f orphan.

huerta ['werta] nf market garden; (área de regadío) irrigated region.

huerto ['werto] nm orchard.

hueso ['weso] nm (ANAT) bone; (de fruta) stone.

huésped, a ['wespeð, a] nm/f (invitado) guest; (habitante) resident; (anfitrión) host.

huesudo, a [we'suðo, a] a bony, big-boned.

huevo ['weβo] nm egg; ~ **en cáscara/escalfado/estrellado** o **frito/pasado por agua** boiled/poached/fried/soft-boiled egg; ~s **revueltos** scrambled eggs.

huida [u'iða] nf escape, flight.

huidizo, a [ui'ðiθo, a] a (tímido) shy; (pasajero) fleeting.

huir [u'ir] vt (escapar) to flee, escape (from); (evadir) to avoid; ~se vr (escaparse) to escape; (el tiempo) to fly.

hule ['ule] nm (goma) rubber; (encerado) oilskin.

humanidad [umani'ðað] nf (los hombres) man(kind); (cualidad) humanity.

humanizar [umani'θar] vt to humanize.

humano, a [u'mano, a] a (gen) human; (humanitario) humane // nm human; ser ~ human being.

humareda [uma'reða] nf cloud of smoke.

humear [ume'ar] vi to smoke.

humedad [ume'ðað] nf (del clima) humidity; (de pared etc) dampness; a prueba de ~ damp-proof; **humedecer** vt to moisten, wet; **humedecerse** vr to get wet.

húmedo, a ['umeðo, a] a (mojado) damp, wet; (tiempo etc) humid.

humildad [umil'dað] nf humility, humbleness; **humilde** a humble, modest; (pequeño: voz) small.

humillación [umiʎa'θjon] nf humiliation; **humillante** a humiliating; **humillar** vt to humiliate; **humillarse** vr to humble o.s., grovel.

humo ['umo] nm (de fuego) smoke; (gas nocivo) fumes pl; ~s nmpl (fig) conceit sg.

humor [u'mor] nm (disposición) mood, temper; (lo que divierte) humour; de buen/mal ~ in a good/bad mood; ~ada nf witticism; ~ismo nm humour; ~ista nm/f humorist; ~ístico, a a funny, humorous.

hundido, a [un'diðo, a] a (de mejillas) sunken; (de ojos) deep-set.

hundimiento [undi'mjento] nm (gen) sinking; (colapso) collapse.

hundir [un'dir] vt to sink; (edificio, plan) to

ruin, destroy; ~**se** *vr* to sink, collapse.
húngaro, a ['ungaro, a] *a, nm/f*
Hungarian.
Hungría [un'gria] *nf* Hungary.
huracán [ura'kan] *nm* hurricane.
huraño, a [u'raño, a] *a* shy; (*antisocial*)
unsociable.
hurgar [ur'xar] *vt* to poke, jab; (*remover*)
to stir (up).
hurgonear [urxone'ar] *vt* to poke.
hurón, ona [u'ron, ona] *a* unsociable //
nm (ZOOL) ferret; (*persona tímida*) shy
person; (*persona arisca*) unsociable person.
hurtadillas [urta'ðiʎas]: **a ~** *ad*
stealthily, on the sly.
hurtar [ur'tar] *vt* to steal; ~**se** *vr* to hide,
withdraw; **hurto** *nm* theft, stealing.
husmear [usme'ar] *vt* (*oler*) to sniff out,
scent; (*fam*) to pry into // *vi* to smell bad;
husmo *nm* strong smell.
huyo *etc vb ver* **huir.**

I

iba *etc vb ver* **ir.**
ibérico, a [i'ßeriko, a] *a* Iberian.
iberoamericano, a [ißeroameri'kano, a]
a, nm/f Spanish American.
íbice ['ißiθe] *nm* ibex.
ibicenco, a [ißi'θenko, a] *a* Ibizan.
Ibiza [i'ßiθa] *nf* Ibiza.
ibón [i'ßon] *nm* lake, tarn.
iceberg ['aisßerx] *nm* iceberg.
ícono ['ikono] *nm* ikon, icon.
iconoclasta [ikono'klasta] *a* iconoclastic
// *nm/f* iconoclast.
ictericia [ikte'riθja] *nf* jaundice.
ida ['iða] *nf* going, departure; **~ y vuelta**
round trip, return.
idea [i'ðea] *nf* idea; **darse/hacerse una
~ de...** to get an idea of... .
ideal [iðe'al] *a, nm* ideal; ~**ista** *nm/f*
idealist; ~**izar** *vt* to idealize.
idear [iðe'ar] *vt* to think up; (*aparato*) to
invent; (*viaje*) to plan.
ídem ['iðem] *pron* ditto.
idéntico, a [i'ðentiko, a] *a* identical.
identidad [iðenti'ðað] *nf* identity; **carné
de ~** identity card.
identificación [iðentifika'θjon] *nf*
identification; **identificar** *vt* to identify;
identificarse *vr:* **identificarse con** to
identify o.s. with.
ideología [iðeolo'xia] *nf* ideology;
ideológico, a *a* ideological.
idioma [i'ðjoma] *nm* (*gen*) language; (*giro*)
idiom.
idiota [i'ðjota] *a* idiotic // *nm/f* idiot;
idiotez *nf* idiocy.
idólatra [i'ðolatra] *nm/f* idolater/tress;
idolatría *nf* idolatry.
ídolo ['iðolo] *nm* idol.
idóneo, a [i'ðoneo, a] *a* (*apto*) fit; (*conveniente*) suitable.
iglesia [i'xlesja] *nf* church.
ignición [ixni'θjon] *nf* ignition.

ignominia [ixno'minja] *nf* ignominy;
ignominioso, a *a* ignominious.
ignorado, a [ixno'raðo, a] *a* unknown;
(*dato*) obscure.
ignorancia [ixno'ranθja] *nf* ignorance;
ignorante *a* ignorant, uniformed // *nm/f*
ignoramus.
ignorar [ixno'rar] *vt* not to know, be
ignorant of.
ignoto, a [ix'noto, a] *a* unknown.
igual [i'xwal] *a* (*gen*) equal; (*similar*) like,
similar; (*mismo*) (the) same; (*constante*)
constant; (*temperatura*) even // *nm/f*
equal; **al ~ que** *prep, conj* like, just like.
igualada [ixwa'laða] *nf* equaliser.
igualar [ixwa'lar] *vt* (*gen*) to equalize,
make equal; (*allanar, nivelar*) to level (off),
even (out); ~**se** *vr* (*platos de balanza*) to
balance out; (*equivaler*) to be equal.
igualdad [ixwal'dað] *nf* equality;
(*similaridad*) sameness; (*uniformidad*)
evenness, uniformity.
igualmente [ixwal'mente] *ad* equally;
(*también*) also, likewise // *excl* the same
to you.
ikurriña [iku'rriɲa] *nf* Basque flag.
ilegal [ile'xal] *a* illegal.
ilegítimo, a [ile'xitimo, a] *a* illegitimate.
ileso, a [i'leso, a] *a* unhurt.
ilícito, a [i'liθito] *a* illicit.
ilimitado, a [ilimi'taðo, a] *a* unlimited.
ilógico, a [i'loxiko, a] *a* illogical.
iluminación [ilumina'θjon] *nf* (*gen*)
illumination; (*alumbrado*) lighting.
iluminar [ilumi'nar] *vt* to illuminate, light
(up); (*fig*) to enlighten.
ilusión [ilu'sjon] *nf* illusion; (*quimera*)
delusion; (*esperanza*) hope; **ilusionado, a**
a excited.
ilusionista [ilusjo'nista] *nm/f* conjurer.
iluso, a [i'luso, a] *a* easily deceived.
ilusorio, a [ilu'sorjo, a] *a* (*de ilusión*)
illusory, deceptive; (*esperanza*) vain.
ilustración [ilustra'θjon] *nf* illustration;
(*saber*) learning, erudition; **la I~** the En-
lightenment; **ilustrado, a** *a* illustrated;
learned.
ilustrar [ilus'trar] *vt* (*gen*) to illustrate;
(*instruir*) to instruct; (*explicar*) to explain,
make clear; ~**se** *vr* to acquire
knowledge.
ilustre [i'lustre] *a* famous, illustrious.
imagen [i'maxen] *nf* (*gen*) image; (*dibujo*)
picture; (*semejanza*) likeness.
imaginación [imaxina'θjon] *nf*
imagination.
imaginar [imaxi'nar] *vt* (*gen*) to imagine;
(*idear*) to think up; (*suponer*) to suppose;
~**se** *vr* to imagine; ~**lo, a** *a* imaginary;
imaginativo, a *a* imaginative.
imán [i'man] *nm* magnet.
imbécil [im'beθil] *nm/f* imbecile, idiot;
imbecilidad *nf* imbecility.
imbuir [imbu'ir] *vt* to imbue.
imitación [imita'θjon] *nf* imitation; **imitar**

vt to imitate; (*parodiar, remedar*) to mimic, ape.

impaciencia [impa'θjenθja] *nf* impatience; **impaciente** *a* impatient; (*nervioso*) anxious.

impacto [im'pakto] *nm* impact.

impar [im'par] *a* odd.

imparcial [impar'θjal] *a* impartial, fair; ~ **idad** *nf* impartiality, fairness.

impartir [impar'tir] *vt* to impart, give.

impasible [impa'siβle] *a* impassive.

impavidez [impaβi'ðeθ] *nf* fearlessness, intrepidness; **impávido, a** *a* fearless, intrepid.

impecable [impe'kaβle] *a* impeccable.

impedimento [impeði'mento] *nm* impediment, obstacle.

impedir [impe'ðir] *vt* (*obstruir*) to impede, obstruct; (*estorbar*) to prevent.

impeler [impe'ler] *vt* to drive, propel; (*fig*) to impel.

impenetrabilidad [impenetraβili'ðað] *nf* impenetrability; **impenetrable** *a* impenetrable; (*fig*) incomprehensible.

impenitente [impeni'tente] *a* unrepentant.

impensado, a [impen'saðo, a] *a* unexpected.

imperar [impe'rar] *vi* (*reinar*) to rule, reign; (*fig*) to prevail, reign; (*precio*) to be current.

imperativo, a [impera'tiβo, a] *a* (*persona*) imperious; (*urgente, LING*) imperative.

imperceptible [imperθep'tiβle] *a* imperceptible.

imperdible [imper'ðiβle] *nm* safety pin.

imperdonable [imperðo'naβle] *a* unforgivable, inexcusable.

imperfección [imperfek'θjon] *nf* imperfection.

imperfecto, a [imper'fekto, a] *a* imperfect.

imperial [impe'rjal] *a* imperial; ~ **ismo** *nm* imperialism.

impericia [impe'riθja] *nf* (*torpeza*) unskilfulness; (*inexperiencia*) inexperience.

imperio [im'perjo] *nm* empire; (*reino, dominación*) rule, authority; (*fig*) pride, haughtiness; ~ **so, a** *a* imperious; (*urgente*) urgent; (*imperativo*) imperative.

impermeable [imperme'aβle] *a* impermeable; (*a prueba de agua*) waterproof // *nm* raincoat.

impersonal [imperso'nal] *a* impersonal.

impertérrito, a [imper'territo, a] *a* undaunted.

impertinencia [imperti'nenθja] *nf* (*inoportunidad*) irrelevancy; (*insolencia*) impertinence; **impertinente** *a* irrelevant; impertinent.

imperturbable [impertur'βaβle] *a* imperturbable.

ímpetu ['impetu] *nm* (*impulso*) impetus, impulse; (*impetuosidad*) impetuosity; (*violencia*) violence.

impetuosidad [impetwosi'ðað] *nf* impetuousness; (*violencia*) violence; **impetuoso, a** *a* impetuous; (*persona*) headstrong; (*río*) rushing, violent; (*acto*) hasty.

impío, a [im'pio, a] *a* impious, ungodly.

implacable [impla'kaβle] *a* implacable.

implicar [impli'kar] *vt* (*gen*) to implicate, involve; (*entrañar*) to imply.

implícito, a [im'pliθito, a] *a* (*tácito*) implicit; (*sobreentendido*) implied.

implorar [implo'rar] *vt* to beg, implore.

imponente [impo'nente] *a* (*impresionante*) impressive, imposing; (*solemne*) grand // *nm/f* investor.

imponer [impo'ner] *vt* (*gen*) to impose; (*informar*) to inform, instruct; (*exigir*) to exact, command; (*com*) to invest; ~ **se** *vr* to assert o.s.; (*prevalecer*) to prevail.

impopular [impopu'lar] *a* unpopular.

importación [importa'θjon] *nf* (*acto*) importing; (*objetos*) imports *pl*.

importancia [impor'tanθja] *nf* importance; (*valor*) value, significance; (*extensión*) size, magnitude; **importante** *a* important; valuable, significant.

importar [impor'tar] *vt* (*del extranjero*) to import; (*valer*) to amount to, be worth // *vi* to be important, matter; **me importa el rábano** I don't give a damn; **no importa** it doesn't matter.

importe [im'porte] *nm* (*total*) amount; (*valor*) value.

importunar [importu'nar] *vt* to bother, pester.

importuno, a [impor'tuno, a] *a* (*inoportuno, molesto*) inopportune; (*indiscreto*) troublesome.

imposibilidad [imposiβili'ðað] *nf* impossibility; **imposibilitar** *vt* to make impossible, prevent; (*incapacitar*) to disable, cripple.

imposible [impo'siβle] *a* (*gen*) impossible; (*insoportable*) unbearable, intolerable.

imposición [imposi'θjon] *nf* imposition; (*com*) tax; (*enganche*) deposit.

impostor, a [impos'tor, a] *nm/f* impostor; **impostura** *nf* fraud, imposture.

impotencia [impo'tenθja] *nf* impotence; **impotente** *a* impotent, powerless.

impracticable [imprakti'kaβle] *a* (*irrealizable*) impracticable; (*intransitable*) impassable.

imprecar [impre'kar] *vi* to curse.

impregnar [impreɣ'nar] *vt* to impregnate; ~ **se** *vr* to become impregnated.

imprenta [im'prenta] *nf* (*gen*) printing; (*aparato*) press; (*casa*) printer's; (*letra*) print.

imprescindible [impresθin'diβle] *a* essential, indispensable.

impresión [impre'sjon] *nf* (*gen*) impression; (*IMPRENTA*) printing; (*edición*) edition; (*FOTO*) print; (*marca*) imprint; ~ **digital** fingerprint.

impresionable [impresjo'naβle] *a*

(*sensible*) impressionable; (*excitable*) emotional.

impresionante [impresjo'nante] *a* impressive; (*tremendo*) tremendous; (*maravilloso*) great, marvellous.

impresionar [impresjo'nar] *vt* (*conmover*) to move; (*afectar*) to impress, strike; (*película fotográfica*) to expose; ~**se** *vr* to be impressed; (*conmoverse*) to be moved.

impreso, a [im'preso, a] *pp de* **imprimir** // a printed // *nm* printed paper/book *etc.*

impresor [impre'sor] *nm* printer.

imprevisto, a [impre'ßisto, a] *a* (*gen*) unforeseen; (*inesperado*) unexpected.

imprimir [impri'mir] *vt* to imprint, impress, stamp; (*textos*) to print.

improbabilidad [improßaßili'ðað] *nf* (*sin seguridad*) improbability; (*inverosimilitud*) unlikelihood; **improbable** *a* improbable; unlikely.

improcedente [improθe'ðente] *a* (*inconveniente*) unsuitable; (*inadecuado*) inappropriate.

improductivo, a [improðuk'tißo, a] *a* unproductive.

improperio [impro'perjo] *nm* insult, taunt.

impropiedad [impropje'ðað] *nf* impropriety (of language).

impropio, a [im'propjo, a] *a* improper.

imprévido, a [im'proßiðo, a] *a* improvident.

improvisación [improßisa'θjon] *nf* improvisation; **improvisado, a** *a* improvised; **improvisar** *vt* to improvise.

improviso, a [impro'ßiso, a], **improvisto, a** [impro'ßisto, a] *a* unexpected, unforeseen; **de** ~ unexpectedly, suddenly.

imprudencia [impru'ðenθja] *nf* imprudence; (*indiscreción*) indiscretion; (*descuido*) carelessness; **imprudente** *a* imprudent; indiscreet; (*irreflexivo*) unwise.

impúdico, a [im'puðiko, a] *a* shameless, immodest; (*lujurioso*) lecherous, lewd.

impudor [impu'ðor] *nm* shamelessness, immodesty; (*lujuria*) lechery, lewdness.

impuesto, a [im'pwesto, a] *a* imposed; (*informado*) informed // *nm* tax.

impugnar [impuƔ'nar] *vt* = **impeler**.

impulsar [impul'sar] *vt* = **impeler**.

impulsión [impul'sjon] *nf* (*TEC*) propulsion; (*fig*) impulse.

impulso [im'pulso] *nm* impulse; (*fuerza, empuje*) thrust, drive; (*rapto*) urge, impulse.

impune [im'pune] *a* unpunished; **impunidad** *nf* impunity.

impureza [impu'reθa] *nf* impurity; (*fig*) lewdness; **impuro, a** *a* impure; lewd.

imputación [imputa'θjon] *nf* imputation.

imputar [impu'tar] *vt* (*atribuir*) to attribute to; (*cargar*) to impute to.

inacabable [inaka'ßaßle] *a* (*infinito*) endless; (*interminable*) interminable.

inaccesible [inakθe'sißle] *a* inaccessible.

inacción [inak'θjon] *nf* (*gen*) inaction; (*desocupación*) inactivity; (*ocio*) idleness.

inaceptable [inaθep'taßle] *a* inacceptable.

inactividad [inaktißi'ðað] *nf* inactivity; (*pereza*) laziness, idleness; (*COM*) dullness; **inactivo, a** *a* inactive.

inadaptación [inaðapta'θjon] *nf* maladjustment.

inadecuado, a [inaðe'kwaðo, a] *a* (*insuficiente*) inadequate; (*inapto*) unsuitable.

inadmisible [inaðmi'sißle] *a* inadmissible.

inadvertencia [inaðßer'tenθja] *nf* oversight.

inadvertido, a [inaðßer'tiðo, a] *a* (*distraído*) inattentive; (*no visto*) unnoticed; (*descuidado*) careless.

inagotable [inaƔo'taßle] *a* inexhaustible.

inaguantable [inaƔwan'taßle] *a* unbearable.

inalterable [inalte'raßle] *a* immutable, unchangeable; (*permanente*) permanent.

inanición [inani'θjon] *nf* starvation.

inanimado, a [inani'maðo, a] *a* inanimate.

inapto, a [in'apto] *a* unsuited.

inaudito, a [inau'ðito, a] *a* unheard-of.

inauguración [inauƔura'θjon] *nf* inauguration; (*de exposición*) opening; **inaugurar** *vt* to inaugurate; to open.

I.N.B. *abr de* **Instituto Nacional de Bachillerato** ≈ secondary school.

inca ['inka] *nm/f* Inca; ~**ico, a** *a* a Inca.

incalculable [inkalku'laßle] *a* incalculable.

incandescente [inkandes'θente] *a* incandescent.

incansable [inkan'saßle] *a* tireless, untiring.

incapacidad [inkapaθi'ðað] *nf* incapacity; (*incompetencia*) incompetence; ~ **física/mental** physical/mental incapacity *or* disability.

incapacitar [inkapaθi'tar] *vt* (*inhabilitar*) to incapacitate, render unfit; (*descalificar*) to disqualify.

incapaz [inka'paθ] *a* incapable.

incautación [inkauta'θjon] *nf* confiscation; **incautarse** *vr*: **incautarse de** to seize, confiscate.

incauto, a [in'kauto, a] *a* (*imprudente*) incautious, unwary.

incendiar [inθen'djar] *vt* to set on fire; (*fig*) to inflame; ~**se** *vr* to catch fire; ~**io, a** *a* incendiary; (*fig*) inflammatory.

incendio [in'θendjo] *nm* fire.

incentivo [inθen'tißo] *nm* incentive.

incertidumbre [inθerti'ðumßre] *nf* (*inseguridad*) uncertainty; (*duda*) doubt.

incesante [inθe'sante], **incesable** [inθe'saßle] *a* incessant.

incesto [in'θesto] *nm* incest.

incidencia [inθi'ðenθja] *nf* (*accidente*) incident; (*MAT*) incidence.

incidente [inθi'ðente] *a* incidental // *nm* incident.

incidir [inθi'ðir] *vi* (*influir*) to influence; (*afectar*) to affect; ~ **en un error** to fall into error.

incienso [in'θjenso] *nm* incense.

incierto, a [in'θjerto, a] *a* uncertain.

incineración [inθinera'θjon] *nf* incineration; (*de cadáveres*) cremation; **incinerar** *vt* to burn; to cremate.

incipiente [inθi'pjente] *a* incipient.

incisión [inθi'sjon] *nf* incision.

incisivo, a [inθi'siβo, a] *a* sharp, cutting; (*fig*) incisive.

incitación [inθita'θjon] *nf* incitement.

incitante [inθi'tante] *a* (*estimulante*) exciting; (*provocativo*) provocative; **incitar** *vt* to incite, rouse.

incivil [inθi'βil] *a* rude, uncivil.

inclemencia [inkle'menθja] *nf* (*severidad*) harshness, severity; (*del tiempo*) inclemency; **inclemente** *a* harsh, severe; inclement.

inclinación [inklina'θjon] *nf* (*gen*) inclination; (*de tierras*) slope, incline; (*de cabeza*) nod, bow; (*fig*) leaning, bent.

inclinar [inkli'nar] *vt* to incline; (*cabeza*) to nod, bow; (*tierras*) to slope; (*persuadir*) to persuade; ~**se** *vr* to bow; (*encorvarse*) to stoop; ~**se a** to take after, resemble; ~**se ante** to bow down to; **me inclino a pensar que** I'm inclined to think that.

inclito, a ['inklito, a] *a* illustrious, renowned.

incluir [inklu'ir] *vt* to include; (*incorporar*) to incorporate; (*meter*) to enclose.

inclusive [inklu'siβe] *ad* inclusive // *prep* including.

incluso, a [in'kluso, a] *a* included // *ad* inclusively; (*hasta*) even.

incógnito, a [in'koɣnito, a] *a* unknown // *nm*: **de** ~ incognito // *nf* unknown factor.

incoherente [inkoe'rente] *a* incoherent.

incoloro, a [inko'loro, a] *a* colourless.

incólume [in'kolume] *a* (*gen*) safe; (*indemne*) unhurt, unharmed.

incomodar [inkomo'ðar] *vt* to inconvenience; (*molestar*) to bother, trouble; (*fastidiar*) to annoy; ~**se** *vr* to put o.s. out; (*fastidiarse*) to get annoyed.

incomodidad [inkomoði'ðað] *nf* inconvenience; (*fastidio, enojo*) annoyance; (*de vivienda*) discomfort.

incómodo, a [in'komoðo, a] *a* (*inconfortable*) uncomfortable; (*molesto*) annoying; (*inconveniente*) inconvenient.

incomparable [inkompa'raβle] *a* incomparable.

incompatible [inkompa'tiβle] *a* incompatible.

incompetencia [inkompe'tenθja] *nf* incompetence; **incompetente** *a* incompetent.

incompleto, a [inkom'pleto, a] *a* incomplete, unfinished.

incomprensible [inkompren'siβle] *a* incomprehensible.

incomunicado, a [inkomuni'kaðo, a] *a* (*aislado*) cut off, isolated; (*confinado*) in solitary confinement.

inconcebible [inkonθe'βiβle] *a* inconceivable.

inconcluso, a [inkon'kluso, a] *a* (*inacabado*) unfinished; (*incompleto*) incomplete.

incondicional [inkondiθjo'nal] *a* unconditional; (*apoyo*) wholehearted; (*partidario*) staunch.

inconexo, a [inko'nekso, a] *a* (*gen*) unconnected; (*desunido*) disconnected.

inconfundible [inkonfun'diβle] *a* unmistakable.

incongruente [inkon'grwente] *a* incongruous.

inconmensurable [inkonmensu'raβle] *a* immeasurable, vast.

inconsciencia [inkons'θjenθja] *nf* unconsciousness; (*fig*) thoughtlessness; **inconsciente** *a* unconscious; thoughtless.

inconsecuencia [inkonse'kwenθja] *nf* inconsistency; **inconsecuente** *a* inconsistent.

inconsiderado, a [inkonsiðe'raðo, a] *a* inconsiderate.

inconsistente [inkonsis'tente] *a* weak; (*tela*) flimsy.

inconstancia [inkons'tanθja] *nf* (*inconsecuencia, veleidad*) inconstancy; (*inestabilidad*) unsteadiness; **inconstante** *a* inconstant.

incontestable [inkontes'taβle] *a* unanswerable; (*innegable*) undeniable.

incontinencia [inkonti'nenθja] *nf* incontinence; **incontinente** *a* incontinent.

inconveniencia [inkonβe'njenθja] *nf* unsuitability, inappropriateness; (*incorrección*) impoliteness; **inconveniente** *a* unsuitable; impolite // *nm* obstacle; (*desventaja*) disadvantage.

incorporación [inkorpora'θjon] *nf* incorporation; (*del cuerpo*) sitting/standing up; **incorporar** *vt* to incorporate; **incorporarse** *vr* to sit/stand up.

incorrección [inkorrek'θjon] *nf* (*gen*) incorrectness, inaccuracy; (*descortesía*) bad-mannered behaviour; **incorrecto, a** *a* (*gen*) incorrect, wrong; (*facciones*) irregular, odd; (*comportamiento*) bad-mannered.

incorregible [inkorre'xiβle] *a* incorrigible.

incorruptible [inkorrup'tiβle] *a* incorruptible; ~ **a la intemperie** rustproof.

incredulidad [inkreðuli'ðað] *nf* incredulity; (*escepticismo*) scepticism; **incrédulo, a** *a* incredulous, unbelieving; sceptical.

increíble [inkre'iβle] *a* incredible.

incremento [inkre'mento] *nm* increment; (*aumento*) rise, increase.

increpar [inkre'par] *vt* to reprimand.

incruento, a [in'krwento, a] a bloodless.
incrustar [inkrus'tar] vt to incrust; (*piedras: en joya*) to inlay.
incubar [inku'ßar] vt to incubate; (*fig*) to hatch.
inculcar [inkul'kar] vt to inculcate.
inculpar [inkul'par] vt (*acusar*) to accuse; (*achacar, atribuir*) to charge, blame.
inculto, a [in'kulto, a] a (*persona*) uneducated, uncultured; (*terreno*) uncultivated // nm/f ignoramus.
incumplimiento [inkumpli'mjento] nm non-fulfilment; ~ **de contrato** breach of contract.
incurrir [inku'rrir] vi: ~ **en** to incur; (*crimen*) to commit; ~ **en un error** to fall into error.
indagación [indaɣa'θjon] nf investigation; (*búsqueda*) search; (*JUR*) inquest; **indagar** vt to investigate; to search; (*averiguar*) to ascertain.
indecente [inde'θente] a indecent, improper; (*lascivo*) obscene.
indecible [inde'θiβle] a unspeakable; (*indescriptible*) indescribable.
indeciso, a [inde'θiso, a] a (*por decidir*) undecided; (*vacilante*) hesitant; (*resultado*) indecisive.
indefectible [indefek'tiβle] a unfailing.
indefenso, a [inde'fenso, a] a defenceless.
indefinido, a [indefi'niðo, a] a indefinite; (*vago*) vague, undefined.
indeleble [inde'leβle] a indelible.
indemnizar [indemni'θar] vt to indemnify; (*compensar*) to compensate.
independencia [independen'denθja] nf independence.
independiente [independ'djente] a (*libre*) independent; (*autónomo*) self-sufficient.
indeterminado, a [indetermi'naðo, a] a indefinite; (*desconocido*) indeterminate.
India ['indja] nf: la ~ India.
indicación [indika'θjon] nf indication; (*señal*) sign; (*sugerencia*) suggestion, hint; (*de termómetro*) reading.
indicador [indika'ðor] nm indicator; (*TEC*) gauge, meter.
indicar [indi'kar] vt (*mostrar*) to indicate, show; (*termómetro etc*) to read, register; (*señalar*) to point to.
índice ['indiθe] nm index; (*catálogo*) catalogue; (*ANAT*) index finger, forefinger; (*de cuadrante*) pointer, needle; (*de reloj*) hand.
indicio [in'diθjo] nm indication, sign; (*huella*) trace; (*pesquisa*) clue.
indiferencia [indife'renθja] nf indifference; (*apatía*) apathy; **indiferente** a indifferent.
indígena [in'dixena] a indigenous, native; (*aborigen*) aboriginal // nm/f native; aborigine.
indigencia [indi'xenθja] nf poverty, need.
indigestión [indixes'tjon] nf indigestion.
indigesto, a [indi'xesto, a] a undigested; (*indigestible*) indigestible; (*fig*) turgid.

indignación [indiɣna'θjon] nf indignation; **indignado, a** a indignant.
indignar [indiɣ'nar] vt to anger, make indignant; ~**se** vr: ~**se de** o **por** to get indignant about.
indignidad [indiɣni'ðað] nf (*insulto*) indignity, insult; (*ruindad*) vile act; **indigno, a** a (*despreciable*) low, contemptible; (*inmerecido*) unworthy.
indio, a ['indjo, a] a, nm/f Indian.
indirecta [indi'rekta] nf insinuation, innuendo; (*sugerencia*) hint.
indirecto, a [indi'rekto, a] a indirect.
indiscreción [indiskre'θjon] nf (*imprudencia*) indiscretion; (*irreflexión*) tactlessness; (*acto*) gaffe, tactless act.
indiscreto, a [indis'kreto, a] a indiscreet.
indiscutible [indisku'tiβle] a indisputable, unquestionable.
indispensable [indispen'saβle] a indispensable.
indisponer [indispo'ner] vt to spoil, upset; (*salud*) to make ill; ~**se** vr to fall ill; ~**se con uno** to fall out with sb.
indisposición [indisposi'θjon] nf indisposition.
indistinto, a [indis'tinto, a] a indistinct; (*vago*) vague.
individual [indiβi'ðwal] a individual; (*habitación*) single // nm (*DEPORTE*) singles sg.
individuo, a [indi'βiðwo, a] a individual // nm individual; (*miembro, socio*) member, fellow.
indiviso, a [indi'βiso, a] a undivided.
índole ['indole] nf (*naturaleza*) nature; (*clase*) sort, kind.
indolencia [indo'lenθja] nf indolence, laziness.
indomable [indo'maβle] a indomitable; (*animal*) untameable; (*fig*) unmanageable.
indómito, a [in'domito, a] a indomitable.
inducir [indu'θir] vt to induce; (*inferir*) to infer; (*persuadir*) to persuade.
indudable [indu'ðaβle] a undoubted; (*incuestionable*) unquestionable.
indulgencia [indul'xenθja] nf indulgence.
indultar [indul'tar] vt (*perdonar*) to pardon, reprieve; (*librar de pago*) to exempt; **indulto** nm pardon; exemption.
industria [in'dustrja] nf industry; (*habilidad*) skill; **industrial** a industrial // nm industrialist.
industrioso, a [indus'trjoso, a] a industrious.
inédito, a [in'eðito, a] a (*libro*) unpublished; (*nuevo*) unheard-of.
inefable [ine'faβle] a ineffable, indescribable.
ineficaz [inefi'kaθ] a (*inútil*) ineffective; (*ineficiente*) inefficient.
ineludible [inelu'ðiβle] a inescapable, unavoidable.
ineptitud [inepti'tuð] nf ineptitude, incompetence; **inepto, a** a inept, incompetent.

inequívoco, a [ine'kiβoko, a] *a* unequivocal; (*inconfundible*) unmistakable.
inercia [in'erθja] *nf* inertia; (*fig*) passivity.
inerme [in'erme] *a* (*sin armas*) unarmed; (*indefenso*) defenceless.
inerte [in'erte] *a* inert; (*fig*) passive.
inesperado, a [inespe'raðo, a] *a* unexpected, unforeseen.
inestable [ines'taβle] *a* unstable.
inevitable [ineβi'taβle] *a* inevitable.
inexactitud [ineksakti'tuð] *nf* inaccuracy; **inexacto, a** *a* inaccurate; (*falso*) untrue.
infamar [infa'mar] *vt* to dishonour; (*calumniar*) to defame, slander.
infame [in'fame] *a* infamous // *nm/f* vile person; **infamia** *nf* infamy; (*deshonra*) disgrace.
infancia [in'fanθja] *nf* infancy, childhood.
infante [in'fante] *nm* (*niño*) infant, child; (*hijo del rey*) prince.
infantería [infante'ria] *nf* infantry.
infantil [infan'til] *a* (*pueril, aniñado*) infantile; (*cándido*) childlike; (*literatura*) children's.
infarto [in'farto] *nm* heart attack.
infatigable [infati'vaβle] *a* tireless, untiring.
infausto, a [in'fausto, a] *a* unlucky.
infección [infek'θjon] *nf* infection; **infeccioso, a** *a* infectious.
infectar [infek'tar] *vt* to infect; ~**se** *vr* to become infected.
infelicidad [infeliθi'ðað] *nf* unhappiness.
infeliz [infe'liθ] *a* unhappy, wretched // *nm/f* wretch.
inferior [infe'rjor] *a* inferior; (*situación*) lower // *nm/f* inferior, subordinate.
inferir [infe'rir] *vt* (*deducir*) to infer, deduce; (*causar*) to cause.
infestar [infes'tar] *vt* (*infectar*) to infect; (*apestar*) to infest; (*fig*) to harass.
inficionar [infiθjo'nar] *vt* to infect; (*fig*) to corrupt.
infidelidad [infiðeli'ðað] *nf* (*gen*) infidelity, unfaithfulness; (*REL*) lack of faith.
infiel [in'fjel] *a* unfaithful, disloyal; (*falso*) inaccurate // *nm/f* infidel, unbeliever.
infierno [in'fjerno] *nm* hell.
ínfimo, a ['infimo, a] *a* vile, mean.
infinidad [infini'ðað] *nf* infinity; (*abundancia*) great quantity.
infinito, a [infi'nito, a] *a, nm* infinite.
inflación [infla'θjon] *nf* (*hinchazón*) swelling; (*monetaria*) inflation; (*fig*) conceit; **inflacionario, a** *a* inflationary.
inflamar [infla'mar] *vt* to set on fire; (*MED*) to inflame; ~**se** *vr* to catch fire; (*fig*) to become inflamed.
inflar [in'flar] *vt* (*hinchar*) to inflate, blow up; (*fig*) to exaggerate; ~**se** *vr* to swell (up); (*fig*) to get conceited.
inflexible [inflek'siβle] *a* inflexible; (*irrompible*) unbending; (*fig*) strict.
infligir [infli'xir] *vt* to inflict.

influencia [influ'enθja] *nf* influence; **influenciar** *vt* to influence.
influir [influ'ir] *vt* to influence.
influjo [in'fluxo] *nm* influence.
influyente [influ'jente] *a* influential.
información [informa'θjon] *nf* information; (*noticias*) news *sg*; (*JUR*) inquiry.
informal [infor'mal] *a* (*gen*) irregular, incorrect; (*persona*) unreliable; (*poco serio*) frivolous; (*trabajo*) disorganized; (*comportamiento*) unconventional.
informalidad [informali'ðað] *nf* (*impuntualidad*) unpunctuality; (*incorrección*) bad manners *pl*; (*ligereza*) frivolity.
informante [infor'mante] *nm/f* informant.
informar [infor'mar] *vt* (*gen*) to inform; (*revelar*) to reveal, make known // *vi* (*JUR*) to plead; (*denunciar*) to inform; (*dar cuenta de*) to report on; ~**se** *vr* to find out; ~**se de** to inquire into.
informe [in'forme] *a* shapeless // *nm* report.
infortunio [infor'tunjo] *nm* misfortune.
infracción [infrak'θjon] *nf* infraction, infringement; (*transgresión*) transgression.
infranqueable [infranke'aβle] *a* impassable; (*impracticable*) insurmountable.
infringir [infrin'xir] *vt* to infringe, contravene.
infructuoso, a [infruk'twoso, a] *a* fruitless, unsuccessful.
infundado, a [infun'daðo, a] *a* groundless, unfounded.
infundir [infun'dir] *vt* to infuse, instil.
ingeniar [inxe'njar] *vt* to think up, devise; ~**se** *vr*: ~**se para** to manage to.
ingeniería [inxenje'ria] *nf* engineering; **ingeniero, a** *nm/f* engineer; **ingeniero agrónomo/de sonido** agronomist/sound engineer.
ingenio [in'xenjo] *nm* (*talento*) talent; (*agudeza*) wit; (*habilidad*) ingenuity, inventiveness; (*TEC*): ~ **azucarero** sugar refinery.
ingenioso, a [inxe'njoso, a] *a* ingenious, clever; (*divertido*) witty.
ingénito, a [in'xenito, a] *a* innate.
ingenuidad [inxenwi'ðað] *nf* ingenuousness; (*candor*) candour; **ingenuo, a** *a* ingenuous.
ingerencia [inxe'renθja] *nf* = **injerencia**.
ingerir [inxe'rir] *vt* to ingest; (*tragar*) to swallow; (*consumir*) to consume.
Inglaterra [ingla'terra] *nf* England.
ingle ['ingle] *nf* groin.
inglés, esa [in'gles, esa] *a* English // *nm/f* Englishman/woman // *nm* (*lengua*) English.
ingratitud [ingrati'tuð] *nf* ingratitude; **ingrato, a** *a* (*gen*) ungrateful; (*desagradable*) unpleasant.
ingrediente [ingre'ðjente] *nm* ingredient.

ingresar [ingre'sar] vt (dinero) to deposit // vi to come in; ~ **en un club** to join a club; ~ **en el hospital** to go into hospital.

ingreso [in'greso] nm (entrada) entry; (: en hospital etc) admission; (de dinero) income, takings pl.

inhábil [in'aβil] a unskilful, clumsy; **día** ~ non-working day.

inhabitable [inaβi'taβle] a uninhabitable.

inherente [ine'rente] a inherent.

inhibir [ini'βir] vt to inhibit; (REL) to restrain.

inhospitalario, a [inospita'larjo, a] a inhospitable.

inhumano, a [inu'mano, a] a inhuman.

I. N. I. ['ini] nm abr de **Instituto Nacional de Industria** = National Enterprise Board.

inicial [ini'θjal] a, nf initial.

iniciar [ini'θjar] vt (persona) to initiate; (estudios) to begin, commence; (conversación) to start up.

iniciativa [iniθja'tiβa] nf initiative; **la** ~ **privada** private enterprise.

inicuo, a [in'ikwo, a] a iniquitous.

ininterrumpido, a [ininterrum'pido, a] a uninterrupted.

injerencia [inxe'renθja] nf interference.

injertar [inxer'tar] vt to graft; (inyectar) to inject; **injerto** nm graft.

injuria [in'xurja] nf (agravio, ofensa) offence; (insulto) insult; (daño) harm; **injuriar** vt to insult; to harm; **injurioso, a** a offensive; insulting; harmful.

injusticia [inxus'tiθja] nf injustice.

injusto, a [in'xusto, a] a unjust, unfair.

inmadurez [inmaðu'reθ] nf immaturity.

inmarcesible [inmarθe'siβle], **inmarchitable** [inmartʃi'taβle] a imperishable.

inmediaciones [inmeðja'θjones] nfpl neighbourhood sg, environs.

inmediato, a [inme'ðjato, a] a immediate; (contiguo) adjoining; (rápido) prompt; (próximo) close, next; **de** ~ immediately.

inmejorable [inmexo'raβle] a unsurpassable; (precio) unbeatable.

inmenso, a [in'menso, a] a immense, huge.

inmerecido, a [inmere'θiðo, a] a undeserved.

inmigración [inmixra'θjon] nf immigration.

inmiscuirse [inmisku'irse] vr to interfere, meddle.

inmobiliario, a [inmoβi'ljarjo, a] a real-estate cpd // nf estate agency.

inmoderado, a [inmoðe'raðo, a] a immoderate, excessive.

inmolar [inmo'lar] vt to immolate, sacrifice.

inmoral [inmo'ral] a immoral.

inmortal [inmor'tal] a immortal; ~**izar** vt to immortalize.

inmotivado, a [inmoti'βaðo, a] a motiveless.

inmóvil [in'moβil] a immobile;

(inamovible) immovable; (invariable) unchanging; (parado) still, stationary.

inmueble [in'mweβle] nm property.

inmundicia [inmun'diθja] nf filth; **inmundo, a** [in'mundo, a] a filthy.

inmunidad [inmuni'ðað] nf immunity.

inmutar [inmu'tar] vt to alter; ~**se** vr to turn pale.

innato, a [in'nato, a] a innate.

innecesario, a [inneθe'sarjo, a] a unnecessary.

innoble [in'noβle] a ignoble.

innocuo, a [in'nokwo, a] a innocuous.

innovación [innoβa'θjon] nf innovation; **innovar** vt to introduce.

inocencia [ino'θenθja] nf innocence.

inocentada [inoθen'taða] nf practical joke.

inocente [ino'θente] a (ingenuo) naive, simple; (inculpable) innocent // nm/f simpleton.

inodoro [ino'ðoro] nm toilet, lavatory.

inofensivo, a [inofen'siβo, a] a inoffensive.

inolvidable [inolβi'ðaβle] a unforgettable.

inoperante [inope'rante] a unworkable.

inopinado, a [inopi'naðo, a] a unexpected.

inoportuno, a [inopor'tuno, a] a untimely; (molesto) inconvenient.

inoxidable [inoksi'ðaβle] a: **acero** ~ stainless steel.

inquebrantable [inkeβran'taβle] a unbreakable.

inquietar [inkje'tar] vt to worry, trouble, disturb; ~**se** vr to worry, get upset; **inquieto, a** a anxious, worried; **inquietud** nf anxiety, worry.

inquilino, a [inki'lino, a] nm/f tenant.

inquirir [inki'rir] vt to enquire into, investigate.

insaciable [insa'θjaβle] a insatiable.

insalubre [insa'luβre] a unhealthy.

inscribir [inskri'βir] vt to inscribe; (lista) to list; (censo) to register; ~**se** vr to register; (ESCOL etc) to enrol.

inscripción [inskrip'θjon] nf inscription; (ESCOL etc) enrolment; (censo) registration.

insecto [in'sekto] nm insect.

inseguridad [insexuri'ðað] nf insecurity.

inseguro, a [inse'xuro, a] a insecure; (inconstante) unsteady; (incierto) uncertain.

insensato, a [insen'sato, a] a foolish, stupid.

insensibilidad [insensiβili'ðað] nf (gen) insensitivity; (dureza de corazón) callousness.

insensible [insen'siβle] a (gen) insensitive; (duro) callous; (movimiento) imperceptible; (sin sentido) numb.

insertar [inser'tar] vt to insert.

inservible [inser'βiβle] a useless.

insidioso, a [insi'ðjoso, a] a insidious.

insignia [in'siɣnja] nf (señal distintivo)

badge; (*estandarte*) flag; (*condecoración*) decoration.

insignificante [insiɣnifiˈkante] *a* insignificant.

insinuar [insiˈnwar] *vt* to insinuate, imply; ~**se** *vr*: ~**se con uno** to ingratiate o.s. with sb.

insípido, a [inˈsipiðo, a] *a* insipid.

insistencia [insisˈtenθja] *nf* (*obstinación*) insistence; (*porfía*) persistence.

insistir [insisˈtir] *vi* to insist; ~ **en algo** to stress sth.

insolación [insolaˈθjon] *nf* (MED) sunstroke.

insolencia [insoˈlenθja] *nf* insolence; **insolente** *a* insolent.

insólito, a [inˈsolito, a] *a* unusual.

insoluble [insoˈluβle] *a* insoluble.

insolvencia [insolˈβenθja] *nf* insolvency.

insomnio [inˈsomnjo] *nm* insomnia.

insondable [insonˈdaβle] *a* bottomless.

insoportable [insoporˈtaβle] *a* unbearable.

inspección [inspekˈθjon] *nf* inspection, check; **inspeccionar** *vt* (*examinar*) to inspect, examine; (*controlar*) to check.

inspector, a [inspekˈtor, a] *nm/f* inspector.

inspiración [inspiraˈθjon] *nf* inspiration; **inspirar** *vt* to inspire; (MED) to inhale; **inspirarse** *vr*: **inspirarse en** to be inspired by.

instalar [instaˈlar] *vt* (*establecer*) to instal; (*erguir*) to set up, erect; ~**se** *vr* to establish o.s.

instancia [insˈtanθja] *nf* (JUR) petition; (*ruego*) request; **en última** ~ in the last resort.

instantáneo, a [instanˈtaneo, a] *a* instant, instantaneous // *nf* snap(shot).

instante [insˈtante] *nm* instant, moment.

instar [insˈtar] *vt* to press, urge // *vi* to be pressing *or* urgent.

instigar [instiˈɣar] *vt* to instigate.

instinto [insˈtinto] *nm* instinct; **por** ~ instinctively.

institución [instituˈθjon] *nf* institution, establishment.

instituir [instituˈir] *vt* to establish; (*fundar*) to found; **instituto** *nm* (*gen*) institute; (*escuela*) high school.

instrucción [instrukˈθjon] *nf* instruction.

instructivo, a [instrukˈtiβo, a] *a* instructive.

instruir [instruˈir] *vt* (*gen*) to instruct; (*enseñar*) to teach, educate; (MIL, DEPORTE) to train.

instrumento [instruˈmento] *nm* (*gen*) instrument; (*herramienta*) tool, implement.

insubordinarse [insuβorðiˈnarse] *vr* to rebel.

insuficiencia [insufiˈθjenθja] *nf* (*carencia*) lack; (*inadecuación*) inadequacy; **insuficiente** *a* (*gen*) insufficient; (*incompetente*) incompetent; (*nota*) inadequate.

insufrible [insuˈfriβle] *a* insufferable.

insular [insuˈlar] *a* insular.

insulsez [insulˈseθ] *nf* (*insipidez*) insipidity; (*fig*) dullness.

insultar [insulˈtar] *vt* to insult; **insulto** *nm* insult.

insuperable [insupeˈraβle] *a* (*excelente*) unsurpassable; (*arduo*) insurmountable.

insurgente [insurˈxente] *a, nm/f* insurgent.

insurrección [insurrekˈθjon] *nf* insurrection, rebellion.

intacto, a [inˈtakto, a] *a* intact.

intachable [intaˈtʃaβle] *a* irreproachable.

integral [inteˈɣral] *a*: **pan** ~ wholemeal bread.

integrar [inteˈɣrar] *vt* to make up, compose; (COM) to repay; (MAT) to integrate.

integridad [inteɣriˈðað] *nf* wholeness; (*carácter*) integrity; **íntegro, a** *a* whole, entire; (*honrado*) honest.

intelectual [intelekˈtwal] *a, nm/f* intellectual.

inteligencia [inteliˈxenθja] *nf* intelligence; (*ingenio*) ability; **inteligente** *a* intelligent.

intemperancia [intempeˈranθja] *nf* excess, intemperance.

intemperie [intemˈperje] *nf* bad weather; **a la** ~ outdoors, in the open air.

intempestivo, a [intempesˈtiβo, a] *a* untimely.

intención [intenˈθjon] *nf* (*gen*) intention; (*propósito*) purpose; **con segundas intenciones** maliciously; **de primera** ~ provisionally; **con** ~ deliberately.

intencionado, a [intenθjoˈnaðo, a] *a* deliberate; **bien/mal** ~ well-meaning/ill-disposed.

intendencia [intenˈdenθja] *nf* management, administration.

intenso, a [inˈtenso, a] *a* intense; (*impresión*) vivid; (*sentimiento*) profound, deep.

intentar [intenˈtar] *vt* (*tratar*) to try, attempt; **intento** *nm* (*intención*) intention, purpose; (*tentativa*) attempt.

intercalar [interkaˈlar] *vt* to insert.

intercambio [interˈkambjo] *nm* exchange, swap.

interceder [interθeˈðer] *vi* to intercede.

intercesión [interθeˈsjon] *nf* intercession.

interés [inteˈres] *nm* (*gen*) interest; (*parte*) share, part; (*pey*) self-interest; **intereses creados** vested interests.

interesado, a [intereˈsaðo, a] *a* interested; (*prejuiciado*) prejudiced; (*pey*) mercenary, self-seeking.

interesar [intereˈsar] *vt, vi* to interest, be of interest to; ~**se** *vr*: ~**se en** *o* **por** to take an interest in.

interferir [interfeˈrir] *vt* to interfere with; (TELEC) to jam // *vi* to interfere.

interior [inteˈrjor] *a* inner, inside; (COM) domestic, internal // *nm* interior, inside; (*fig*) soul, mind; **Ministerio del I**~ Home Office.

interjección [interxek'θjon] *nf* interjection.

interlocutor, a [interloku'tor] *nm/f* speaker.

intermediario, a [interme'δjarjo, a] *nm/f* intermediary // *nm* middleman.

intermedio, a [inter'meδjo, a] *a* intermediate // *nm* interval.

interminable [intermi'naβle] *a* endless.

intermitente [intermi'tente] *a* intermittent // *nm* indicator.

internacional [internaθjo'nal] *a* international.

internar [inter'nar] *vt* to intern; (*loco*) to commit; ~**se** *vr* (*en un hospital*) to go into hospital; (*penetrar*) to penetrate.

interno, a [in'terno, a] *a* internal, interior; (*POL etc*) domestic // *nm/f* (*alumno*) boarder.

interpelar [interpe'lar] *vt* (*rogar*) to implore; (*hablar*) to speak to.

interponer [interpo'ner] *vt* to interpose, put in; ~**se** *vr* to intervene.

interposición [interposi'θjon] *nf* insertion.

interpretación [interpreta'θjon] *nf* interpretation; **interpretar** *vt* to interpret; **intérprete** *nm/f* interpreter; (*traductor*) translator; (*músico, TEATRO*) performer, artist(e).

interrogación [interroxa'θjon] *nf* interrogation; (*LING*) question mark; **interrogar** *vt* to interrogate, question.

interrumpir [interrum'pir] *vt* to interrupt; (*ELEC*) to switch off, cut off.

interrupción [interrup'θjon] *nf* interruption.

interruptor [interrup'tor] *nm* (*ELEC*) switch.

intersección [intersek'θjon] *nf* intersection.

interurbano, a [interur'βano, a] *a*: **llamada** ~ a trunk call.

intervalo [inter'βalo] *nm* interval; (*descanso*) break; a ~**s** at intervals, every now and then.

intervenir [interβe'nir] *vt* (*controlar*) to control, supervise; (*MED*) to operate on // *vi* (*participar*) to take part, participate; (*mediar*) to intervene.

interventor, a [interβen'tor, a] *nm/f* inspector; (*COM*) auditor.

interviú [inter'βju] *nf* interview.

intestino, a [intes'tino, a] *a* internal; (*doméstico*) domestic // *nm* intestine.

intimar [inti'mar] *vt* to intimate, announce // *vi* to become friendly.

intimidad [intimi'δaδ] *nf* intimacy; (*confianza*) confidence; (*familiaridad*) familiarity; (*vida privada*) private life; (*soledad*) privacy.

íntimo, a ['intimo, a] *a* intimate.

intolerable [intole'raβle] *a* intolerable, unbearable.

intransitable [intransi'taβle] *a* impassable.

intrepidez [intrepi'δeθ] *nf* courage,

bravery; **intrépido, a** *a* intrepid.

intriga [in'trixa] *nf* intrigue; (*plan*) plot; **intrigar** *vt, vi* to intrigue.

intrincado, a [intrin'kaδo, a] *a* intricate.

intrínseco, a [in'trinseko, a] *a* intrinsic.

introducción [introδuk'θjon] *nf* introduction.

introducir [introδu'θir] *vt* (*gen*) to introduce; (*hacer penetrar*) to insert.

intruso, a [in'truso, a] *a* intrusive // *nm/f* intruder.

intuición [intwi'θjon] *nf* intuition.

inundación [inunda'θjon] *nf* flood(ing); **inundar** *vt* to flood; (*fig*) to swamp, inundate.

inusitado, a [inusi'taδo, a] *a* unusual.

inútil [in'util] *a* useless; (*esfuerzo*) vain, fruitless; **inutilidad** *nf* uselessness.

inutilizar [inutili'θar] *vt* to make useless, render useless; ~**se** *vr* to become useless.

invadir [inβa'δir] *vt* to invade.

inválido, a [in'βaliδo, a] *a* invalid // *nm/f* invalid.

invariable [inβa'rjaβle] *a* invariable.

invasión [inβa'sjon] *nf* invasion.

invasor, a [inβa'sor, a] *a* invading // *nm/f* invader.

invención [inβen'θjon] *nf* invention.

inventar [inβen'tar] *vt* to invent.

inventario [inβen'tarjo] *nm* inventory.

inventiva [inβen'tiβa] *nf* inventiveness.

inventor, a [inβen'tor, a] *nm/f* inventor.

inverosímil [inβero'simil] *a* implausible; (*improbable*) unlikely, improbable.

inversión [inβer'sjon] *nf* (*COM*) investment; (*AUTO*) reversing; **inversionista** *nm/f* investor.

inverso, a [in'βerso, a] *a* inverse, opposite; **en el orden** ~ in reverse order; **a la** ~ **a** inversely, the other way round.

invertir [inβer'tir] *vt* (*COM*) to invest; (*volcar*) to turn upside down; (*tiempo etc*) to spend; (*AUTO*) to reverse.

investigación [inβestiνa'θjon] *nf* investigation; (*estudio*) research; **investigar** *vt* to investigate; (*estudiar*) to do research into.

inveterado, a [inβete'raδo, a] *a* inveterate, confirmed.

invicto, a [in'βikto, a] *a* unconquered.

invierno [in'βjerno] *nm* winter.

invitar [inβi'tar] *vt* to invite; (*incitar*) to entice; (*pagar*) to buy, pay for.

invocar [inβo'kar] *vt* to invoke, call on.

inyección [injek'θjon] *nf* injection.

inyectar [injek'tar] *vt* to inject.

ir [ir] *vi* (*gen*) to go; (*viajar*) to travel; (*ropa*) to suit; ~ **caminando** to walk; ~ **en coche/bicicleta/caballo/a pie** to drive/cycle/ride/walk; **¡voy!** I'm coming!; ~ **de viaje** to travel, go away; **voy para viejo** I'm getting on (in years); ~ **por algo** to go for/go and get sth; **¡qué va!** (*no diga*) you don't say!; (: *¡no!*) no way!, rubbish!; **¡vamos!** come on!; **vaya susto que me has dado** what a fright you gave me; **~se** vr to go away, leave; (mano etc) to slip; ¡vete! go away!

ira ['ira] nf anger, rage.

iracundo, a [ira'kundo, a] a irascible; (colérico) irate.

Irán [i'ran] nm Iran; **iraní, esa, iraní** a, nm/f Iranian.

iris ['iris] nm (arco ~) rainbow; (ANAT) iris.

Irlanda [ir'landa] nf Ireland; **irlandés, esa** a Irish // nm/f Irishman/woman.

ironía [iro'nia] nf irony; **irónico, a** a ironic(al).

irreal [irre'al] a unreal.

irreflexión [irreflek'sjon] nf thoughtlessness.

irremediable [irreme'ðjaβle] a incurable, hopeless.

irresoluto, a [irreso'luto, a] a irresolute, hesitant.

irrespetuoso, a [irrespe'twoso, a] a disrespectful.

irresponsable [irrespon'saβle] a irresponsible.

irrigar [irri'xar] vt to irrigate.

irrisorio, a [irri'sorjo, a] a derisory, ridiculous.

irritar [irri'tar] vt to irritate, annoy.

irrupción [irrup'θjon] nf irruption; (invasión) invasion.

isla ['isla] nf island.

islandés, esa [islan'des, esa] a Icelandic // nm/f Icelander.

Islandia [is'landja] nf Iceland.

isleño, a [is'leɲo, a] a island cpd // nm/f islander.

Israel [isra'el] nm Israel; **israelí** a, nm/f Israeli.

istmo ['istmo] nm isthmus.

Italia [i'talja] nf Italy; **italiano, a** a a, nm/f Italian.

itinerario [itine'rarjo] nm itinerary, route.

izar [i'θar] vt to hoist.

izquierdista [iθkjer'ðista] nm/f left-winger, leftist.

izquierdo, a [iθ'kjerðo, a] a left // nf left; a **la ~a** on the left.

J

jabalí [xaβa'li] nm wild boar.

jabalina [xaβa'lina] nf javelin.

jabón [xa'βon] nm soap; **jabonar** vt to soap.

jaca ['xaka] nf pony.

jacinto [xa'θinto] nm hyacinth.

jactancia [xak'tanθja] nf boasting, boastfulness.

jactarse [xak'tarse] vr to boast, brag.

jadeante [xaðe'ante] a panting, gasping; **jadear** vi to pant, gasp for breath; **jadeo** nm panting, gasping.

jaez [xa'eθ] nm (de caballerías) harness; (clase) kind, sort.

jaguar [xa'ɣwar] nm jaguar.

jalar [xa'lar] vt to pull, haul.

jalbegue [xal'βeɣe] nm (pintura) whitewash; (fig) make-up.

jalea [xa'lea] nf jelly.

jaleo [xa'leo] nm racket, uproar; (baile) Andalusian popular dance; **estar de ~** to be having a good time; **armar un ~** to kick up a din.

Jamaica [xa'maika] nf Jamaica.

jamás [xa'mas] ad never; (sin negación) ever.

jamón [xa'mon] nm ham.

Japón [xa'pon] nm: **el ~** Japan; **japonés, esa** a, nm/f Japanese.

jaque ['xake] nm cheque; (fam) bully; **~ mate** checkmate.

jaqueca [xa'keka] nf (severe) headache, migraine.

jarabe [xa'raβe] nm syrup.

jarcia ['xarθja] nf (NAUT) ropes pl, rigging; (para pescar) (fishing) tackle; (confusión, revoltijo) jumble, mess.

jardín [xar'ðin] nm garden; **jardinería** nf gardening; **jardinero, a** nm/f gardener.

jarra ['xarra] nf jar.

jarro ['xarro] nm jug.

jaula ['xaula] nf cage.

jauría [xau'ria] nf pack of hounds.

J. C. abr de **Jesucristo**.

jefatura [xefa'tura] nf: **~ de policía** police headquarters sg.

jefe ['xefe] nm (gen) chief, head; (patrón) boss; **~ de camareros** head waiter; **~ de cocina** chef; **~ de estación** station-master; **~ de estado** head of state; **~ supremo** commander-in-chief; **ser el ~** (fig) to be the boss.

jengibre [xen'xiβre] nm ginger.

jeque ['xeke] nm sheik.

jerarquía [xerar'kia] nf (orden) hierarchy; (rango) rank; **jerárquico, a** a hierarchic(al).

jerez [xe'reθ] nm sherry.

jerga ['xerɣa] nf (tela) coarse cloth; (lenguaje) jargon, slang.

jerigonza [xeri'ɣonθa] nf (jerga) jargon, slang; (galimatías) nonsense, gibberish.

jeringa [xe'ringa] nf syringe; (AM) annoyance, bother; **~ de engrase** grease gun; **jeringar** vt to syringe; (inyectar) to inject; (AM) to annoy, bother.

jeroglífico [xero'ɣlifiko] nm hieroglyphic.

jersé, jersey (pl **jerseys**) [xer'sei] nm jersey, pullover, jumper.

Jerusalén [xerusa'len] n Jerusalem.

Jesucristo [xesu'kristo] n Jesus Christ.

jesuita [xe'swita] a, nm Jesuit.

Jesús [xe'sus] nm Jesus; ¡~! good heavens!; (al estornudar) bless you!

jícara ['xikara] nf small cup.

jifero, a [xi'fero, a] a (fam) filthy // nm butcher's knife; (matarife) butcher, slaughterer.

jinete [xi'nete] nm (horse)rider.

jipijapa [xipi'xapa] nm (AM) straw hat.

jira ['xira] *nf* (*de tela*) strip; (*excursión*) picnic.

jirafa [xi'rafa] *nf* giraffe.

jirón [xi'ron] *nm* rag, shred.

jocosidad [xokosi'ðað] *nf* humour; (*chiste*) joke.

jocoso, a [xo'koso, a] *a* humorous, jocular.

jofaina [xo'faina] *nf* washbasin.

jornada [xor'naða] *nf* day's journey; (*camino o viaje entero*) journey; (*día de trabajo*) working day; (*fig*) lifetime.

jornal [xor'nal] *nm* (day's) wage; ~**ero** *nm* (day) labourer.

joroba [xo'roßa] *nf* hump, hunched back; (*fam*) nuisance; ~**do, a** a hunchbacked // *nm/f* hunchback.

jota ['xota] *nf* letter J; (*danza*) Aragonese dance; (*fam*) iota; **no saber** ~ to have no idea.

joven ['xoßen] *a* young // *nm* young man, youth // *nf* young woman, girl.

jovial [xo'ßjal] *a* cheerful, jovial; ~**idad** *nf* cheerfulness, joviality.

joya ['xoja] *nf* jewel, gem; (*fig: persona*) gem; **joyería** *nf* (*joyas*) jewellery; (*tienda*) jeweller's (shop); **joyero** *nm* (*persona*) jeweller; (*caja*) jewel case.

juanete [xwa'nete] *nf* bunion.

jubilación [xußila'θjon] *nf* (*retiro*) retirement; (*alegría*) jubilation.

jubilar [xußi'lar] *vt* to pension off, retire; (*fam*) to discard // *vi* to rejoice; ~**se** *vr* to retire.

jubileo [xußi'leo] *nm* (*indulgencia*) jubilee; (*fam*) comings and goings *pl*.

júbilo ['xußilo] *nm* joy, jubilation, rejoicing; ~**so, a** a jubilant.

judaísmo [xuða'ismo] *nm* Judaism.

judía [xu'ðia] *nf* Jewess; (*CULIN*) bean.

judicatura [xuðika'tura] *nf* (*cargo de juez*) office of judge; (*magistratura*) judicature.

judicial [xuði'θjal] *a* judicial.

judío, a [xu'ðio, a] *a* Jewish // *nm/f* Jew/ess.

juego etc *vb ver* **jugar** // ['xweɣo] *nm* (*gen*) play; (*pasatiempo, partido*) game; (*en casino*) gambling; (*conjunto*) set; **fuera de** ~ (*persona*) offside; (*pelota*) out of play.

juerga ['xwerɣa] *nf* good time; (*fiesta*) party; **ir de** ~ to go out on a spree.

jueves ['xweßes] *nm inv* Thursday.

juez [xweθ] *nm* judge; ~ **de línea** linesman; ~ **de salida** starter.

jugada [xu'ɣaða] *nf* play; **buena** ~ good move/shot/stroke *etc*.

jugador, a [xuɣa'ðor, a] *nm/f* player; (*en casino*) gambler.

jugar [xu'ɣar] *vt, vi* to play; (*en casino*) to gamble; ~**se** *vr* to gamble (away).

juglar [xu'ɣlar] *nm* minstrel.

jugo ['xuɣo] *nm* (*BOT*) juice; (*fig*) essence, substance; ~**so, a** a juicy; (*fig*) substantial, important.

juguete [xu'ɣete] *nm* toy; (*TEATRO*) sketch; ~**ar** *vi* to play; ~**ría** *nf* toyshop.

juguetón, ona [xuɣe'ton, ona] *a* playful.

juicio ['xwiθjo] *nm* judgement; (*sana razón*) sanity, reason; (*opinión*) opinion; **estar fuera de** ~ to be out of one's mind; ~**so, a** a wise, sensible.

julio ['xuljo] *nm* July.

jumento, a [xu'mento, a] *nm/f* donkey.

junco ['xunko] *nm* rush, reed.

jungla ['xungla] *nf* jungle.

junio ['xunjo] *nm* June.

junta ['xunta] *nf ver* **junto**.

juntamente [xunta'mente] *ad* (*conjuntamente*) together; (*al mismo tiempo*) together, at the same time.

juntar [xun'tar] *vt* to join, unite; (*maquinaria*) to assemble, put together; (*dinero*) to collect; (*puerta*) to half-close, leave ajar; ~**se** *vr* to join, meet; (*reunirse: personas*) to meet, assemble; (*arrimarse*) to approach, draw closer; (*vivir juntos*) to live together; ~**se con uno** to join sb.

junto, a ['xunto, a] *a* (*unido*) joined, united; (*anexo*) near, close; (*continuo, próximo*) next, adjacent // *ad*: **todo** ~ all at once // *nf* (*asamblea*) meeting, assembly; (*comité, consejo*) board, council, committee; (*articulación*) joint; ~ **a** near (to), next to; ~**s** together.

juntura [xun'tura] *nf* (*punto de unión*) join, junction; (*articulación*) joint.

jurado [xu'raðo] *nm* (*JUR*) juror; (: *conjunto de* ~**s**) jury; (*de concurso*) panel (of judges); (: *individuo*) member of a panel.

juramentar [xuramen'tar] *vt* to swear in, administer the oath to; ~**se** *vr* to be sworn in, take the oath.

juramento [xura'mento] *nm* oath; (*maldición*) oath, curse; **prestar** ~ to take the oath; **tomar** ~ **a** to swear in, administer the oath to.

jurar [xu'rar] *vt, vi* to swear; ~ **en falso** to commit perjury; **jurárselas a uno** to have it in for sb.

jurídico, a [xu'riðiko, a] *a* legal.

jurisdicción [xurisðik'θjon] *nf* (*poder, autoridad*) jurisdiction; (*territorio*) district.

jurisprudencia [xurispru'ðenθja] *nf* jurisprudence.

jurista [xu'rista] *nm/f* jurist.

justamente [xusta'mente] *ad* justly, fairly; (*precisamente*) just, precisely, exactly.

justicia [xus'tiθja] *nf* justice; (*equidad*) fairness, justice; **justiciero, a** a just, righteous.

justificación [xustifika'θjon] *nf* justification; **justificar** *vt* to justify.

justo, a ['xusto, a] *a* (*equitativo*) just, fair, right; (*preciso*) exact, correct; (*ajustado*) tight // *ad* (*precisamente*) exactly, precisely.

juvenil [xuße'nil] *a* youthful.

juventud [xußen'tuð] *nf* (*adolescencia*) youth; (*jóvenes*) young people *pl*.

juzgado [xuθ'ɣaðo] *nm* tribunal; (*JUR*) court.

juzgar [xuθ'ɣar] *vt* to judge; **a** ~ **por...** to judge by..., judging by... .

K

kg abr de **kilogramo.**
kilo ['kilo] nm kilo // pref: ~**gramo** nm
kilogramme; ~**litro** nm kilolitre;
~**metraje** nm distance in kilometres;
kilómetro nm kilometre; ~**vatio** nm
kilowatt.
kiosco ['kjosko] nm = **quiosco.**
km abr de **kilómetro.**
kv abr de **kilovatio.**

L

l abr de **litro.**
la [la] det the // pron her; (Ud.) you; (cosa)
it // nm (MUS) la; ~ **del sombrero rojo**
the girl in the red hat.
laberinto [laße'rinto] nm labyrinth.
labia ['laßja] nf fluency; (pey) glibness.
labial [la'ßjal] a labial; **lectura** ~ lip-
reading.
labio ['laßjo] nm lip.
labor [la'ßor] nf labour; (AGR) farm work;
(tarea) job, task; (costura) needlework;
~**able** a workable; **día** ~**able** working
day; ~**ar** vi to work; ~**eo** nm (AGR)
cultivation; (de minas) working; ~**ioso, a**
a (persona) hard-working; (trabajo) tough;
~**ista** a: **Partido L**~**ista** Labour Party.
labrado, a [la'ßraðo, a] a worked;
(cincelado) carved; (metal) wrought // nm
(AGR) cultivated field.
labrador, a [laßra'ðor, a] a farming //
nm/f farmer.
labrantío, a [laßran'tio, a] a arable.
labranza [la'ßranθa] nf (AGR) cultivation.
labrar [la'ßrar] vt (gen) to work; (madera
etc) to carve; (fig) to cause.
labriego, a [la'ßrjexo, a] nm/f peasant.
laca ['laka] nf lacquer.
lacayo [la'kajo] nm lackey.
lacerar [laθe'rar] vt to lacerate.
lacio, a ['laθjo, a] a (pelo) lank;
(movimiento) limp; (BOT) withered.
lacónico, a [la'koniko, a] a laconic.
lacrar [la'krar] vt (MED) to injure the
health of; (dañar) to harm; (cerrar) to seal
(with sealing wax); ~**se** vr to harm o.s.;
lacre nm sealing wax.
lacrimoso, a [lakri'moso, a] a tearful.
lactar [lak'tar] vt, vi to suckle.
ladear [laðe'ar] vt to tip, tilt; (ciudad,
colina) to skirt // vi to tilt; ~**se** vr to lean.
ladera [la'ðera] nf slope.
ladino, a [la'ðino, a] a cunning.
lado ['laðo] nm (gen) side; (fig) protection;
(MIL) flank; **al** ~ **de** beside; **poner de** ~
to put on its side; **poner a un** ~ to put
aside; **por todos** ~**s** on all sides, all
round.
ladrar [la'ðrar] vi to bark; **ladrido** nm
bark, barking.
ladrillo [la'ðriʎo] nm (gen) brick; (azulejo)
tile; (color) brick red.

ladrón, ona [la'ðron, ona] nm/f thief.
lagar [la'xar] nm (wine/oil) press.
lagarto [la'xarto] nm (ZOOL) lizard; (fig:
fam) sharp customer; ~ **de Indias**
alligator.
lago ['laxo] nm lake.
lágrima ['laxrima] nf tear; **lagrimar** vi to
weep.
laguna [la'xuna] nf (lago) lagoon; (hueco)
gap.
laico, a ['laiko, a] a lay.
lamentable [lamen'taßle] a lamentable,
regrettable; (miserable) pitiful.
lamentar [lamen'tar] vt (sentir) to regret;
(deplorar) to lament; ~**se** vr to lament;
lamento nm lament.
lamer [la'mer] vt to lick.
lámina ['lamina] nf (plancha delgada)
sheet; (para estampar, estampa) plate;
laminar vt (en libro) to laminate.
lámpara ['lampara] nf lamp; ~ **de
alcohol/gas** spirit/gas lamp; ~ **de
bolsillo** torch; ~ **de pie** standard lamp.
lampiño [lam'piɲo] a clean-shaven.
lana ['lana] nf wool.
lance ['lanθe] nm (golpe) stroke; (suceso)
event, incident; (riña) quarrel; (tirada)
throw; **libros de** ~ second-hand books.
lancha ['lantʃa] nf launch; ~ **automóvil**
motorboat; ~ **de pesca** fishing boat; ~
salvavidas/torpedera lifeboat/torpedo
boat; **lanchero** nm boatman.
lanero, a [la'nero, a] a woollen.
langosta [lan'gosta] nf (insecto) locust;
(crustáceo) lobster; (fig) plague;
langostín, langostino nm prawn.
languidecer [langiðe'θer] vi to languish;
languidez nf languour; **lánguido, a** a (gen)
languid; (sin energía) listless.
lanilla [la'niʎa] nf nap.
lanudo, a [la'nuðo, a] a woolly.
lanza ['lanθa] nf (arma) lance, spear; (de
vagón) pole.
lanzadera [lanθa'ðera] nf shuttle.
lanzamiento [lanθa'mjento] nm (gen)
throwing; (NAUT, COM) launch, launching;
~ **de pesos** putting the shot.
lanzar [lan'θar] vt (gen) to throw;
(DEPORTE) to bowl; (NAUT, COM) to launch;
(JUR) to evict; (MED) to vomit; ~**se** vr to
throw o.s.
laña ['laɲa] nf clamp.
lapa ['lapa] nf limpet.
lapicero [lapi'θero] nm propelling pencil.
lápida ['lapiða] nf stone; ~ **mortuoria**
headstone; ~ **conmemorativa** memorial
stone; **lapidar** vt to stone; **lapidario, a** a,
nm lapidary.
lápiz ['lapiθ] nm pencil; ~ **de color**
coloured pencil; ~ **de labios** lipstick.
lapón, ona [la'pon, ona] nm/f Laplander,
Lapp.
lapso ['lapso] nm (de tiempo) interval;
(error) error.
largar [lar'xar] vt (soltar) to release;
(aflojar) to loosen; (lanzar) to launch;

(*fam*) to let fly; (*pelota*) to throw; (*velas*) to unfurl; (*AM*) to throw; ~**se** *vr* (*fam*) to beat it; (*NAUT*) to set sail; ~**se a** (*AM*) to start to.

largo, a ['larɣo, a] *a* (*longitud*) long; (*tiempo*) lengthy; (*persona: alta*) tall; (*fig*) generous // *nm* length; (*MUS*) largo // *ad* widely; **dos años** ~**s** two long years; **tiene 9 metros de** ~ it is 9 metres long; **a lo** ~ **de** along.

largueza [lar'ɣeθa] *nf* generosity.

lárice ['lariθe] *nm* larch.

laringe [la'rinxe] *nf* larynx; **laringitis** *nf* laryngitis.

larva ['larβa] *nf* larva.

las [las] *det* the // *pron* them; ~ **que cantan** the ones/women/girls who sing.

lascivo, a [las'θiβo, a] *a* lewd.

láser ['laser] *nm* laser.

lasitud [lasi'tuð] *nf* lassitude, weariness.

lástima ['lastima] *nf* (*pena*) pity; (*queja*) complaint; **dar** ~ to be pitiful; **es** ~ **que** it's a pity that; **¡qué** ~**!** what a pity!; **ella está hecha una** ~ she looks pitiful.

lastimar [lasti'mar] *vt* (*herir*) to wound; (*ofender*) to offend; (*compadecer*) to pity; ~**se** *vr* to hurt o.s.; ~**se de** to feel sorry for; **lastimero, a, lastimoso, a** a pitiful, pathetic.

lastre ['lastre] *nm* (*TEC, NAUT*) ballast; (*fig*) dead weight.

lata ['lata] *nf* (*metal*) tin; (*caja*) tin, can; (*fam*) nuisance; **hoja de** ~ tin(plate); **en** ~ tinned; **dar (la)** ~ to be a nuisance.

latente [la'tente] *a* latent.

lateral [late'ral] *a* side, lateral // *nm* (*TEATRO*) wings.

latido [la'tiðo] *nm* (*del corazón*) beat; (*de perro*) yelp.

latifundio [lati'fundjo] *nm* large estate; **latifundista** *nm/f* owner of a large estate.

latigazo [lati'ɣaθo] *nm* (*golpe*) lash; (*sonido*) crack; (*fig: regaño*) sharp reproof; (*fam: bebida*) swig.

látigo ['latiɣo] *nm* whip.

latín [la'tin] *nm* Latin.

latino, a [la'tino, a] *a* Latin; ~**americano, a** a, *nm/f* Latin-American.

latir [la'tir] *vi* (*corazón, pulso*) to beat; (*perro*) to yelp.

latitud [lati'tuð] *nf* (*GEO*) latitude; (*fig*) breadth.

lato, a ['lato, a] *a* broad.

latón [la'ton] *nm* brass.

latoso, a [la'toso, a] *a* (*cansado*) annoying; (*aburrido*) boring.

latrocinio [latro'θinjo] *nm* robbery.

laúd [la'uð] *nm* lute.

laudo ['lauðo] *nm* (*JUR*) decision.

laureado, a [laure'aðo, a] *a* honoured // *nm* laureate.

laurel [lau'rel] *nm* (*BOT*) laurel; (*CULIN*) bay.

lava ['laβa] *nf* lava.

lavabo [la'βaβo] *nm* washbasin.

lavadero [laβa'ðero] *nm* laundry.

lavado [la'βaðo] *nm* washing; (*de ropa*) laundry; (*ARTE*) wash; ~ **de cerebro** brainwashing; ~ **en seco** dry cleaning.

lavadora [laβa'ðora] *nf* washing machine.

lavamanos [laβa'manos] *nm inv* washbasin.

lavandería [laβande'ria] *nf* laundry; ~ **automática** launderette.

lavaplatos [laβa'platos] *nm o f inv* dishwasher.

lavar [la'βar] *vt* to wash; (*borrar*) to wipe away; ~**se** *vr* to wash o.s.; ~**se las manos** to wash one's hands; ~ **y marcar** (*pelo*) to shampoo and set; ~ **en seco** to dry clean.

lavavajillas [laβaβa'xiʎas] *nm inv* dishwasher.

laxante [lak'sante] *nm* laxative.

laya ['laja] *nf* spade; **de la misma** ~ (*fig*) of the same sort.

lazada [la'θaða] *nf* bow.

lazo ['laθo] *nm* knot; (*lazada*) bow; (*para animales*) lasso; (*trampa*) snare; (*de camino*) hairpin bend; (*vínculo*) tie.

lb(s) *abr de* **libra(s)**.

le [le] *pron* (*directo*) him; (: *usted*) you; (*indirecto*) to him; (: *usted*) to you.

leal [le'al] *a* loyal; ~**tad** *nf* loyalty.

lebrel [le'βrel] *nm* greyhound.

lección [lek'θjon] *nf* lesson.

lector, a [lek'tor, a] *nm/f* reader.

lectura [lek'tura] *nf* reading.

leche ['letʃe] *nf* milk; **tener mala** ~ to be nasty; ~ **condensada/en polvo** condensed/powdered milk; ~ **desnatada** skimmed milk; ~ **de magnesia** milk of magnesia; ~**ra** *nf* (*vendedora*) milkmaid; (*para hervir*) milk pan; (*para servir*) milkjug; (*AM*) cow; ~**ría** *nf* dairy.

lecho ['letʃo] *nm* (*cama*) bed; (*de río*) bottom; (*GEO*) layer.

lechón [le'tʃon] *nm* sucking pig.

lechoso, a [le'tʃoso, a] *a* milky.

lechuga [le'tʃuɣa] *nf* lettuce.

lechuza [le'tʃuθa] *nf* owl.

leer [le'er] *vt* to read.

legación [leɣa'θjon] *nf* legation.

legado [le'ɣaðo] *nm* (*don*) bequest; (*herencia*) legacy; (*enviado*) legate.

legajo [le'ɣaxo] *nm* file.

legal [le'ɣal] *a* (*gen*) legal; (*persona*) trustworthy; ~**idad** *nf* legality; ~**izar** *vt* to legalize; (*documento*) to authenticate.

légamo ['leɣamo] *nm* (*cieno*) mud, ooze.

legar [le'ɣar] *vt* to bequeath, leave; **legatario, a** *nm/f* legatee.

legión [le'xjon] *nf* legion; **legionario, a** *a* legionary // *nm* legionnaire.

legislación [lexisla'θjon] *nf* legislation; **legislar** *vt* to legislate.

legitimar [lexiti'mar] *vt* to legitimize; **legítimo, a** *a* (*genuino*) authentic; (*legal*) legitimate.

lego, a ['leɣo, a] *a* (*REL*) secular; (*ignorante*) ignorant // *nm* layman.

legua ['leɣwa] *nf* league.

leguleyo [leɣu'lexo] *nm* (*pey*) petty lawyer.

legumbre [le'ɣumbre] *nf* vegetable.

leído, a [le'iðo, a] *a* well-read.

lejanía [lexa'nia] *nf* distance; **lejano, a** *a* far-off; (*en el tiempo*) distant; (*fig*) remote.

lejía [le'xia] *nf* bleach.

lejos ['lexos] *ad* far, far away; **a lo ~** in the distance; **de o desde ~** from afar; **~ de** *prep* far from.

lelo, a ['lelo, a] *a* silly; (*fig*) open-mouthed // *nm/f* idiot.

lema ['lema] *nm* motto; (*POL*) slogan.

lencería [lenθe'ria] *nf* drapery.

lengua ['lengwa] *nf* tongue; **~ moderna** modern language; **morderse la ~** to hold one's tongue.

lenguado [len'gwaðo] *nm* sole.

lenguaje [len'gwaxe] *nm* language.

lenguaraz [lengwa'raθ] *a* talkative; (*pey*) foul-mouthed.

lengüeta [len'gweta] *nf* (*ANAT*) epiglottis; (*de balanza, zapatos, MUS*) tongue; (*herramienta*) needle.

lenidad [leni'ðað] *nf* lenience.

lente ['lente] *nm o f* lens; (*lupa*) magnifying glass; **~s** *npl* glasses; **~s de contacto** contact lenses.

lenteja [len'texa] *nf* lentil; **lentejuela** *nf* sequin.

lentitud [lenti'tuð] *nf* slowness; **con ~** slowly.

lento, a ['lento, a] *a* slow.

leña ['leɲa] *nf* firewood; **~dor, a, ~tero, a** *nm/f* woodcutter.

leño ['leɲo] *nm* (*trozo de árbol*) log; (*madera*) timber; (*fig*) blockhead.

Leo ['leo] *nm* Leo.

león [le'on] *nm* lion; (*AM*) puma; **~ marino** sea lion; **leonino, a** *a* leonine.

leontina [leon'tina] *nf* watch chain.

leopardo [leo'parðo] *nm* leopard.

lepra ['lepra] *nf* leprosy; **leproso, a** *nm/f* leper.

lerdo, a ['lerðo, a] *a* (*lento*) slow; (*patoso*) clumsy.

les [les] *pron* (*directo*) them; (: *ustedes*) you; (*indirecto*) to them; (: *ustedes*) to you.

lesbiana [les'βjana] *a, nf* lesbian.

lesión [le'sjon] *nf* (*daño*) lesion; (*fig*) injury; **lesionado, a** *a* injured // *nm/f* injured person.

letal [le'tal] *a* lethal.

letanía [leta'nia] *nf* litany.

letargo [le'tarɣo] *nm* (*MED*) lethargy.

letra ['letra] *nf* letter; (*escritura*) handwriting; (*MUS*) lyrics *pl*; **~ de cambio** bill of exchange; **~ de imprenta** print; **~do, a** *a* learned; (*fam*) pedantic // *nm* lawyer; **letrero** *nm* (*cartel*) sign; (*etiqueta*) label.

leva ['leβa] *nf* (*NAUT*) weighing anchor; (*MIL*) levy; (*TEC*) lever.

levadizo [leβa'ðiθo] *a*: **puente ~** drawbridge.

levadura [leβa'ðura] *nf* (*para el pan*) yeast; (*de la cerveza*) brewer's yeast.

levantamiento [leβanta'mjento] *nm* raising, lifting; (*rebelión*) revolt, rising; **~ de pesos** weight-lifting.

levantar [leβan'tar] *vt* (*gen*) to raise; (*del suelo*) to pick up; (*hacia arriba*) to lift (up); (*plan*) to make, draw up; (*mesa*) to clear away; (*campamento*) to strike; (*fig*) to cheer up, hearten; **~se** *vr* to get up; (*enderezarse*) to straighten up; (*rebelarse*) to rebel; **~ el ánimo** to cheer up.

levante [le'βante] *nm* east coast; **el L~** the Near East, the Levant.

levar [le'βar] *vi* to weigh anchor; **~se** *vr* to set sail.

leve ['leβe] *a* light; (*fig*) trivial; **~dad** *nf* lightness.

levita [le'βita] *nf* frock coat.

léxico ['leksiko] *nm* lexicon, dictionary.

ley [lei] *nf* (*gen*) law; (*fig*) loyalty; (*metal*) standard.

leyenda [le'jenda] *nf* legend.

leyó *etc vb ver* **leer**.

liar [li'ar] *vt* to tie (up); (*unir*) to bind; (*envolver*) to wrap (up); (*enredar*) to confuse; (*cigarrillo*) to roll; **~se** *vr* (*fam*) to get involved; **~se a palos** to get involved in a fight.

Líbano ['liβano] *nm*: **el ~** the Lebanon.

libar [li'βar] *vt* to suck.

libelo [li'βelo] *nm* satire, lampoon; (*JUR*) petition.

libélula [li'βelula] *nf* dragonfly.

liberación [liβera'θjon] *nf* liberation; (*de la cárcel*) release.

liberal [liβe'ral] *a, nm/f* liberal; **~idad** *nf* liberality; (*lujo*) lavishness.

liberar [liβe'rar] *vt* to liberate.

libertad [liβer'tað] *nf* liberty; (*soltura*) freedom; **~ de culto/de prensa/de comercio** freedom of worship/the press/of trade; **~ condicional** probation; **~ bajo palabra** parole; **~ bajo fianza** bail.

libertar [liβer'tar] *vt* (*preso*) to set free; (*de una obligación*) to release; (*eximir*) to exempt.

libertino, a [liβer'tino, a] *a* loose-living // *nm/f* libertine.

libra ['liβra] *nf* pound; **L~** (*ASTRO*) Libra; **~ esterlina** pound sterling.

librador, a [liβra'ðor, a] *nm/f* drawer.

libramiento [liβra'mjento] *nm* rescue; (*COM*) delivery.

libranza [li'βranθa] *nf* (*COM*) draft; (*de letra de cambio*) bill of exchange.

librar [li'βrar] *vt* (*de peligro*) to save; (*batalla*) to wage, fight; (*de impuestos*) to exempt; (*secreto*) to reveal; (*mercancías*) to draw; (*cheque*) to make out; (*JUR*) to exempt // *vi* to give birth; **~se** *vr*: **~se de** to escape from, free o.s. from.

libre ['liβre] *a* (*gen*) free; (*lugar*) unoccupied; (*asiento*) vacant; (*de impuestos*) tax-free; (*de deudas*) free of debts; (*pey*) outspoken; **tiro ~** free kick; **los 100 metros ~** the 100 metres freestyle (race); **al aire ~** in the open air.

librería [liβre'ria] nf (biblioteca) library; (comercio) bookshop; **librero, a** nm/f bookseller.

libreta [li'βreta] nf notebook; ~ **de ahorros** savings book; ~ **de banco** bank book.

libro ['liβro] nm book; ~ **en rústica/en pasta** o **encuadernado** paperback/hardback; ~ **de bolsillo** paperback; ~ **de caja** cashbook; ~ **de cheques** cheque book; ~ **de inventario** stock-list; ~ **de pedidos** order book; ~ **de texto** textbook.

Lic. abr de **licenciado, a.**

licencia [li'θenθja] nf (gen) licence; (permiso) permission; ~ **por enfermedad/con goce de sueldo** sick leave/paid leave; ~ **de caza/de conductor** game/driving licence; ~ **de derecho/de letras** law/arts degree; ~**do, a** a licensed // nm/f graduate; **licenciar** vt (empleado) to dismiss; (permitir) to permit, allow; (soldado) to discharge; (estudiante) to confer a degree upon; **licenciarse** vr: **licenciarse en letras** to graduate in arts.

licencioso, a [liθen'θjoso, a] a licentious.

liceo [li'θeo] nm (high) school.

licitador [liθita'ðor] nm bidder; (AM) auctioneer; **licitar** vt to bid for; (AM) to sell by auction.

lícito, a ['liθito, a] a (legal) lawful; (justo) fair, just; (permisible) permissible.

licor [li'kor] nm spirits pl; (preparado) liqueur.

licuadora [likwa'ðora] nf food-mixer, liquidizer; **licuar** vt to liquidize.

lid [lið] nf combat; (fig) controversy.

líder ['liðer] nm/f leader; **liderato** nm leadership.

lidia ['liðja] nf bullfight; **toros de** ~ fighting bulls; **lidiar** vt, vi to fight.

liebre ['ljeβre] nf hare.

lienzo ['ljenθo] nm linen; (ARTE) canvas; (pañuelo) handkerchief; (ARQ) wall.

liga ['liɣa] nf (de medias) garter, suspender; (confederación) league; (venda) band; (aleación) alloy; (BOT) mistletoe.

ligadura [liɣa'ðura] nf bond, tie; (MED, MUS) ligature.

ligamento [liɣa'mento] nm (ANAT) ligament; (atadura) tie; (unión) bond.

ligar [li'ɣar] vt (atar) to tie; (unir) to join; (MED) to bind up; (MUS) to slur; (metales) to alloy // vi to mix, blend; (fam) to pick up; (entenderse) to get on (well); ~**se** vr to commit o.s.

ligereza [lixe'reθa] nf lightness; (rapidez) swiftness; (agilidad) agility; (superficialidad) flippancy.

ligero, a [li'xero, a] a (de peso) light; (tela) thin; (rápido) swift, quick; (ágil) agile, nimble; (de importancia) slight; (de carácter) flippant, superficial // ad: **a la** ~**a** superficially.

lija [li'xa] nf (ZOOL) dogfish; **(papel de)** ~ sandpaper.

lila ['lila] nf lilac // nm (fam) twit.

lima ['lima] nf file; (BOT) lime; ~ **de carpintero** file; ~ **de uñas** nail-file; **limar** vt to file.

limitación [limita'θjon] nf limitation, limit.

limitar [limi'tar] vt to limit; (reducir) to reduce, cut down // vi: ~ **con** to border on; ~**se** vr: ~**se a** to limit o.s. to.

límite ['limite] nm (gen) limit; (fin) end; (frontera) border; ~ **de velocidad** speed limit.

limítrofe [li'mitrofe] a bordering, neighbouring.

limón [li'mon] nm lemon // a: **amarillo** ~ lemon-yellow; **limonada** nf lemonade; **limonero** nm lemon tree.

limosna [li'mosna] nf alms pl; **vivir de** ~ to live on charity.

limpiabotas [limpja'βotas] nm inv bootblack, shoeshine boy/girl.

limpiaparabrisas [limpjapara'βrisas] nm inv windscreen wiper.

limpiar [lim'pjar] vt (gen) to clean; (con trapo) to wipe; (quitar) to wipe away; (zapatos) to shine, polish; (fig) to clean up.

limpieza [lim'pjeθa] nf (estado) cleanliness; (acto) cleaning; (: de las calles) cleansing; (: de zapatos) polishing; (habilidad) skill; (fig) clean-up; (pureza) purity; (MIL): **operación de** ~ mopping-up operation; ~ **en seco** dry cleaning.

limpio, a ['limpjo, a] a clean; (moralmente) pure; (COM) clear, net; (fam) honest // ad: **jugar** ~ to play fair // nm: **pasar en** ~ to make a fair copy.

linaje [li'naxe] nm lineage, family; **linajudo, a** a highborn.

linaza [li'naθa] nf linseed; **aceite de** ~ linseed oil.

lince ['linθe] nm lynx.

linchar [lin'tʃar] vt to lynch.

lindante [lin'dante] a adjoining; ~ **con** bordering on.

lindar [lin'dar] vi to adjoin; ~ **con** to border on; **linde** nm o f boundary; **lindero, a** a adjoining // nm boundary.

lindo, a ['lindo, a] a pretty, lovely // ad (AM): **nos divertimos de lo** ~ we had a marvellous time; **canta muy** ~ he/she sings beautifully.

línea ['linea] nf (gen) line; ~ **aérea** airline; ~ **delantera** (DEPORTE) forward line; ~ **de meta** goal line; (de carrera) finishing line; ~ **de saque** service line, base line; ~ **recta** straight line.

lingüista [lin'gwista] nm/f linguist.

linimento [lini'mento] nm liniment.

lino ['lino] nm linen; (BOT) flax.

linóleo [li'noleo] nm lino, linoleum.

linterna [lin'terna] nf lantern, lamp; ~ **eléctrica** o **a pilas** torch.

lío ['lio] nm bundle; (fam) fuss; (desorden) muddle, mess; **armar un** ~ to make a fuss.

liquidación [likiða'θjon] nf liquidation; **venta de** ~ clearance sale.

liquidar [liki'ðar] vt (*licuar*) to liquidize; (*eliminar*) to liquidate; (*mercaderías*) to sell off; (*pagar*) to pay off; (*terminar*) to wind up; (AM) to ruin; **~se** vr to liquefy.

líquido, a ['likiðo, a] a liquid; (*ganancia*) net; (AM) accurate // nm liquid; **~ imponible** net taxable income.

lira ['lira] nf (MUS) lyre; (*moneda*) lira.

lirio ['lirjo] nm (BOT) iris.

Lisboa [lis'βoa] n Lisbon.

lisiado, a [li'sjaðo, a] a injured // nm/f cripple.

lisiar [li'sjar] vt to maim; **~se** vr to injure o.s.

liso, a ['liso, a] a (*terreno*) flat; (*cabello*) straight; (*superficie*) even; (*tela*) smooth.

lisonja [li'sonxa] nf flattery; **lisonjear** vt to flatter; (*fig*) to please; **lisonjero, a** a (*gen*) flattering; (*agradable*) gratifying, pleasing // nm/f flatterer.

lista ['lista] nf (*gen*) list; (*de alumnos*) school register; (*de libros*) catalogue; (*de correos*) poste restante; (*de platos*) menu; (*de precios*) price list; **pasar ~** to call the roll; **~ de espera** waiting list; **tela a ~s** striped material.

listado, a [lis'taðo, a] a striped.

listo, a ['listo, a] a (*perspicaz*) smart, clever; (*preparado*) ready.

listón [lis'ton] nm (*tela*) ribbon; (*de madera, metal*) strip.

litera [li'tera] nf (*en barco, tren*) berth; (*en dormitorio*) bunk, bunk bed.

literato, a [lite'rato, a] a literary // nm/f writer.

literatura [litera'tura] nf literature.

litigar [liti'xar] vt to fight // vi (JUR) to go to law; (*fig*) to dispute, argue.

litigio [li'tixjo] nm (JUR) lawsuit; (*fig*): **en ~ con** in dispute with.

litografía [litoxra'fia] nf lithography; (*una ~*) lithograph.

litoral [lito'ral] a coastal // nm coast, seaboard.

litro ['litro] nm litre.

liviano, a [li'βjano, a] a (*persona*) fickle; (*cosa, objeto*) trivial.

lívido, a ['liβiðo, a] a livid; (AM) pale.

ll... ver bajo la letra LL, después de L.

lo [lo] det neuter def art; **~ bueno** the good // pron (*persona*) him; (*cosa*) it.

loa ['loa] nf praise; **loable** a praiseworthy; **loar** vt to praise.

lobato [lo'βato] nm wolf cub.

lobo ['loβo] nm wolf; **~ de mar** sea dog; **~ marino** seal.

lóbrego, a ['loβreɣo, a] a dark; (*fig*) gloomy.

lóbulo ['loβulo] nm lobe.

locación [loka'θjon] nf lease.

local [lo'kal] a local // nm place, site; (*oficinas*) premises pl; **~idad** nf (*barrio*) locality; (*lugar*) location; (TEATRO) seat, ticket; **~izar** vt (*ubicar*) to locate, find; (*restringir*) to localize; (*situar*) to place.

loco, a ['loko, a] a mad // nm/f lunatic, mad person.

locomoción [lokomo'θjon] nf locomotion.

locomotora [lokomo'tora] nf engine.

locuaz [lo'kwaθ] a loquacious.

locución [loku'θjon] nf expression.

locura [lo'kura] nf madness; (*acto*) crazy act.

lodo ['loðo] nm mud; **~s** nmpl (MED) mudbath sg.

lógico, a ['loxiko, a] a logical // nf logic.

logística [lo'xistika] nf logistics pl.

lograr [lo'xrar] vt to achieve; (*obtener*) to get, obtain; **~ hacer** to manage to do; **~ que uno venga** to manage to get sb to come.

logro ['loxro] nm achievement, success; **prestar a ~** to lend at a high rate of interest.

loma ['loma] nf hillock.

lombriz [lom'briθ] nf worm; **~ solitaria** tapeworm.

lomo ['lomo] nm (*de animal*) back; (*de cerdo*) pork loin; (*de vaca*) rib steak; (*de libro*) spine.

lona ['lona] nf canvas.

Londres ['londres] n London.

longaniza [longa'niθa] nf pork sausage.

longitud [lonxi'tuð] nf length; (GEO) longitude; **tener 3 metros de ~** to be 3 metres long; **~ de onda** wavelength.

lonja ['lonxa] nf slice; (*de jamón*) rasher; **~ de pescado** fish market.

lontananza [lonta'nanθa] nf background.

loor [lo'or] nm praise.

loro ['loro] nm parrot.

los [los] det the // pron them; (*ustedes*) you; **mis libros y ~ de Ud** my books and yours.

losa ['losa] nf stone; **~ sepulcral** gravestone.

lote ['lote] nm portion; (COM) lot.

lotería [lote'ria] nf lottery; (*juego*) lotto.

loza ['loθa] nf crockery.

lozanía [loθa'nia] nf (*lujo*) luxuriance; (*orgullo*) pride; **lozano, a** a luxuriant; (*animado*) lively; (*altanero*) haughty.

lubricante [luβri'kante] nm lubricant; **lubricar** vt to lubricate.

lucero [lu'θero] nm (ASTRO) bright star; (*fig*) brilliance.

lucidez [luθi'ðeθ] nf lucidity; **lúcido, a** a lucid.

luciente [lu'θjente] a shining.

luciérnaga [lu'θjernaɣa] nf glow-worm.

lucimiento [luθi'mjento] nm (*brillo*) brilliance; (*éxito*) success.

lucir [lu'θir] vt to illuminate, light (up); (*fig*) to show off // vi (*brillar*) to shine; (*tener éxito*) to be successful; **~se** vr to dress up.

lucrarse [lu'krarse] vr to enrich o.s.

lucro ['lukro] nm profit, gain.

luctuoso, a [luk'twoso, a] a mournful.

lucha ['lutʃa] nf fight, struggle; **~ de**

clases class struggle; ~ **libre** wrestling; **luchar** vi to fight.

ludibrio [lu'ðiβrjo] nm mockery.

luego ['lweɣo] ad (después) next; (más tarde) later, afterwards; (pronto) soon; **desde** ~ of course; **tan** ~ **como** as soon as.

lugar [lu'ɣar] nm place; (sitio) spot; **en** ~ **de** instead of; **hacer** ~ to make room; **fuera de** ~ out of place; **tener** ~ to take place; ~ **común** commonplace.

lugareño, a [luɣa'reɲo, a] a village cpd // nm/f villager.

lúgubre ['luɣuβre] a mournful.

lujo ['luxo] nm luxury; (fig) profusion, abundance; ~**so, a** a luxurious.

lujuria [lu'xurja] nf lust; (fig) lewdness.

lumbre ['lumbre] nf (gen) light.

lumbrera [lum'brera] nf luminary; (en techo) skylight; (de barco) vent, port.

luminoso, a [lumi'noso, a] a luminous, shining.

luna ['luna] nf moon; (de un espejo) glass; (de gafas) lens; (fig) crescent; ~ **llena/nueva** full/new moon; **estar con** ~ to have one's head in the clouds.

lunar [lu'nar] a lunar // nm (ANAT) mole; **tela a** ~**es** spotted material.

lunes ['lunes] nm inv Monday.

luneta ₁lu'neta] nf lens.

lupa ['lupa] nf magnifying glass.

lustrar [lus'trar] vt (mueble) to polish; (zapatos) to shine; **lustre** nm polish; (fig) lustre; **dar lustre a** to polish; **lustroso, a** a shining.

luterano, a [lute'rano, a] a Lutheran.

luto ['luto] nm mourning; (congoja) grief, sorrow; ~**s** nmpl mourning clothes; **llevar el** o **vestirse de** ~ to be in mourning.

Luxemburgo [luksem'burɣo] nm Luxembourg.

luz [luθ] (pl **luces**) nf light; **dar a** ~ **un niño** to give birth to a child; **sacar a** ~ to bring to light; (ELEC): **dar** ~ to switch on the light; **prender/apagar la** ~ to put the light on/off; **a todas luces** by any reckoning; **hacer la** ~ **sobre** to shed light on; **tener pocas luces** to be dim or stupid; ~ **roja/verde** red/green light; (AUTO): ~ **de costado** sidelight; ~ **de freno** brake light; ~ **del relámpago** flashlight; **luces de tráfico** traffic lights; **traje de luces** bullfighter's costume.

LL

llaga ['ʎaɣa] nf wound.

llama ['ʎama] nf flame; (ZOOL) llama.

llamada [ʎa'maða] nf call; ~ **al orden** call to order; **toque de** ~ (MIL) call-up; ~ **a pie de página** reference note.

llamamiento [ʎama'mjento] nm call.

llamar [ʎa'mar] vt to call; (atención) to attract // vi (por teléfono) to telephone; (a la puerta) to knock/ring; (por señas) to beckon; (MIL) to call up; ~**se** vr to be called, be named; **¿cómo se llama Usted?** what's your name?

llamarada [ʎama'raða] nf (llamas) blaze; (rubor) flush; (fig) flare-up.

llamativo, a [ʎama'tiβo, a] a showy; (color) loud.

llamear [ʎame'ar] vi to blaze.

llaneza [ʎa'neθa] nf (gen) simplicity; (honestidad) straightforwardness, frankness.

llano, a ['ʎano, a] a (superficie) flat; (persona) straightforward; (estilo) clear // nm plain, flat ground.

llanta ['ʎanta] nf (wheel) rim; (AM): ~ **de goma** tyre.

llanto ['ʎanto] nm weeping.

llanura [ʎa'nura] nf plain.

llave ['ʎaβe] nf key; (del agua) tap; (MECÁNICA) spanner; (de la luz) switch; (MUS) key; ~ **inglesa** monkey wrench; ~ **de contacto** (AUTO) ignition key; **echar** ~ **a** to lock up; ~**ro** nm keyring; **llavín** nm latchkey.

llegada [ʎe'ɣaða] nf arrival.

llegar [ʎe'ɣar] vi to arrive; (alcanzar) to reach; (bastar) to be enough; ~**se** vr: ~**se a** to approach; ~ **a** to manage to, succeed in; ~ **a ser** to become; ~ **a las manos de** to come into the hands of.

llenar [ʎe'nar] vt (gen) to fill; (espacio) to cover; (formulario) to fill in or up; (deber) to fulfil; (fig) to heap.

lleno, a ['ʎeno, a] a full, filled; (repleto) full up // nm (abundancia) abundance; (ASTRO) full moon; (TEATRO) full house; **dar de** ~ **contra un muro** to hit a wall head-on.

llevadero, a [ʎeβa'ðero, a] a bearable, tolerable.

llevar [ʎe'βar] vt (gen) to take; (ropa) to wear; (cargar) to carry; (quitar) to take away; (conducir a alguien) to drive; (cargar hacia) to transport; (traer: dinero) to carry; (conducir) to lead; (MAT) to carry; ~**se** vr to carry off, take away; **llevamos dos días aquí** we have been here for two days; **él me lleva 2 años** he's 2 years older than me; (COM): ~ **los libros** to keep the books; ~**se bien** to get on well (together).

llorar [ʎo'rar] vt, vi to weep; ~ **de risa** to cry with laughter.

lloriquear [ʎorike'ar] vi to snivel, whimper.

lloro ['ʎoro] nm weeping; **llorón, ona** a tearful // nm/f cry-baby; ~**so, a** a (gen) weeping, tearful; (triste) sad, sorrowful.

llover [ʎo'βer] vi to rain; ~**se** vr (techo) to leak.

llovizna [ʎo'βiθna] nf drizzle; **lloviznar** vi to drizzle.

llueve etc vb ver **llover**.

lluvia ['ʎuβja] nf rain; ~ **radioactiva** radioactive fallout; **lluvioso, a** a rainy.

M

m *abr de* **metro; minuto.**

macarrones [maka'rrones] *nmpl* macaroni *sg.*

macerar [maθe'rar] *vt* to macerate; *(fig)* to mortify; **~se** *vr* to mortify o.s.

maceta [ma'θeta] *nf (de flores)* pot of flowers; *(para plantas)* flowerpot; *(mazo pequeño)* mallet.

macilento, a [maθi'lento, a] *a* wan; *(ojeroso)* haggard.

macis ['maθis] *nf* mace.

macizo, a [ma'θiθo, a] *a* massive; *(puerta)* solid // *nm* mass, chunk; *(de edificios)* block; *(AUTO)* solid tyre.

mácula ['makula] *nf* stain, blemish; *(ANAT)* blind spot.

machacar [matʃa'kar] *vt* to crush, pound // *vi* to go on, keep on.

machamartillo [matʃamar'tiʎo]: **a ~** *ad*: **cumplir a ~** to carry out a task to the letter; **eran cristianos a ~** they were totally convinced Christians.

machete [ma'tʃete] *nm (AM)* machete, (large) knife.

macho ['matʃo] *a* male; *(fig)* virile // *nm* male; *(fig)* he-man.

machucar [matʃu'kar] *vt* to pound.

madeja [ma'ðexa] *nf (de lana)* skein, hank; *(de pelo)* mop.

madera [ma'ðera] *nf* wood; *(fig)* nature, character; **una ~** a piece of wood.

madero [ma'ðero] *nm* beam; *(fig)* ship.

madrastra [ma'ðrastra] *nf* stepmother.

madre ['maðre] *a* mother *cpd*; *(AM)* tremendous // *nf* mother; *(ANAT)* womb; *(AGR)* main channel; *(de vino etc)* dregs *pl*; *(de río)* bed; **~ política/soltera** mother-in-law/unmarried mother.

madreperla [maðre'perla] *nf* mother-of-pearl.

madreselva [maðre'selβa] *nf* honeysuckle.

madriguera [maðri'ɣera] *nf* burrow.

madrileño, a [maðri'leɲo, a] *a of or from* Madrid // *nm/f* native of Madrid.

madrina [ma'ðrina] *nf (protectora)* godmother; *(ARQ)* prop, shore; *(TEC)* brace; **~ de boda** bridesmaid.

madrugada [maðru'ɣaða] *nf* early morning; *(alba)* dawn, daybreak; **madrugador, a** *a* early-rising; **madrugar** *vi* to get up early; *(fig)* to get ahead.

madurar [maðu'rar] *vt*, *vi (fruta)* to ripen; *(fig)* to mature; **madurez** *nf* ripeness; maturity; **maduro, a** *a* ripe; mature.

maestra [ma'estra] *nf ver* **maestro.**

maestría [maes'tria] *nf* mastery; *(habilidad)* skill, expertise.

maestro, a [ma'estro, a] *a* masterly; *(perito)* skilled, expert; *(principal)* main; *(educado)* trained // *nm/f* master/mistress; *(que enseña)* teacher // *nm (autoridad)* authority; *(MUS)* maestro;

(AM) skilled workman; **obra ~a** masterpiece; **~ albañil** master mason.

magia ['maxja] *nf* magic; **mágico, a** *a* magic(al) // *nm/f* magician.

magisterio [maxis'terjo] *nm (enseñanza)* teaching; *(profesión)* teaching profession; *(maestros)* teachers *pl.*

magistrado [maxis'traðo] *nm* magistrate.

magistral [maxis'tral] *a* magisterial; *(fig)* masterly.

magnánimo, a [maɣ'nanimo, a] *a* magnanimous.

magnate [maɣ'nate] *nm* magnate, tycoon.

magnético, a [maɣ'netiko, a] *a* magnetic; **magnetizar** *vt* to magnetize.

magnetofón [maɣneto'fon], **magnetófono** [maɣne'tofono] *nm* tape recorder; **magnetofónico, a**: **cinta magnetofónica** recording tape.

magnífico, a [maɣ'nifiko, a] *a* splendid, magnificent, wonderful.

magnitud [maɣni'tuð] *nf* magnitude.

mago, a ['maɣo, a] *nm/f* magician; **los Reyes M~s** the Magi, the Three Wise Men.

magro, a ['maɣro, a] *a (persona)* thin, lean; *(carne)* lean.

magullar [maɣu'ʎar] *vt (amoratar)* to bruise; *(dañar)* to damage; *(fam: golpear)* to bash, beat.

mahometano, a [maome'tano, a] *a* Mohammedan.

maíz [ma'iθ] *nm* maize, sweet corn.

majada [ma'xaða] *nf (abrigo)* sheepfold; *(abono)* dung.

majadero, a [maxa'ðero, a] *a* silly, stupid // *nm (TEC)* pestle; *(canilla)* bobbin.

majar [ma'xar] *vt* to crush, grind; *(fig)* to bother, pester.

majestad [maxes'taθ] *nf* majesty; **majestuoso, a** *a* majestic.

majo, a ['maxo, a] *a* nice; *(guapo)* attractive, good-looking; *(lujoso)* smart.

mal [mal] *ad* badly; *(equivocadamente)* wrongly; *(con dificultad)* with difficulty // *a* = **malo** // *nm* evil; *(desgracia)* misfortune; *(daño)* harm, hurt; *(MED)* illness; **¡menos ~!** just as well!; **~ que bien** rightly or wrongly.

malabarismo [malaβa'rismo] *nm* juggling; **malabarista** *nm/f* juggler.

malaconsejado, a [malakonse'xaðo, a] *a* ill-advised.

malagueño, a [mala'ɣeɲo, a] *a of or from* Málaga.

malaria [ma'larja] *nf* malaria.

malbaratar [malβara'tar] *vt (malgastar)* to squander; *(malvender)* to sell off cheap.

malcontento, a [malkon'tento, a] *a* discontented.

malcriado, a [mal'krjaðo, a] *a (grosero)* rude, bad-mannered; *(consentido)* spoiled.

maldad [mal'daθ] *nf* evil, wickedness.

maldecir [malde'θir] *vt* to curse // *vi*: **~ de** to speak ill of.

maldición [maldi'θjon] *nf* curse.

maldito, a [mal'dito, a] *pp de* **maldecir** // *a* (*condenado*) damned; (*perverso*) wicked // *nf*: **soltar la** ~ **a** to talk too much.

maleante [male'ante] *a* wicked // *nm/f* malefactor; **malear** *vt* to spoil; (*fig*) to corrupt.

malecón [male'kon] *nm* pier, jetty.

maledicencia [maleði'θenθja] *nf* slander, scandal.

maleficiar [malefi'θjar] *vt* to harm, damage; (*hechizar*) to bewitch; **maleficio** *nm* curse, spell.

malestar [males'tar] *nm* (*gen*) discomfort; (*fig*) uneasiness; (*POL*) unrest.

maleta [ma'leta] *nf* case, suitcase; (*AUTO*) boot; **maletín** *nm* small case, bag.

malevolencia [maleßo'lenθja] *nf* malice, spite; **malévolo, a** *a* malicious, spiteful.

maleza [ma'leθa] *nf* (*hierbas malas*) weeds *pl*; (*arbustos*) thicket.

malgastar [malɣas'tar] *vt* (*tiempo, dinero*) to waste; (*salud*) to ruin.

malhechor, a [male'tʃor, a] *nm/f* malefactor; (*criminal*) criminal.

malicia [ma'liθja] *nf* (*maldad*) wickedness; (*astucia*) slyness, guile; (*mala intención*) malice, spite; (*carácter travieso*) mischievousness; ~**s** *nfpl* suspicions; **malicioso, a** *a* wicked, evil; sly, crafty; malicious, spiteful; mischievous.

malignidad [maliɣni'ðað] *nf* (*MED*) malignancy; (*malicia*) malice.

maligno, a [ma'liɣno, a] *a* evil; (*malévolo*) malicious; (*MED*) malignant.

malo, a ['malo, a] *a* bad; (*falso*) false // *nm/f* villain // *nf* spell of bad luck; **estar** ~ to be ill; **estar de** ~**as** to be in a bad mood.

malograr [malo'ɣrar] *vt* to spoil; (*plan*) to upset; (*tiempo, ocasión*) to waste; ~**se** *vr* (*plan etc*) to fail, come to grief; (*persona*) to die before one's time; **malogro** *nm* (*fracaso*) failure; (*pérdida*) waste; (*muerte*) early death.

malparado, a [malpa'raðo, a] *a*: **salir** ~ to come off badly.

malparir [malpa'rir] *vi* to have a miscarriage.

malquistar [malkis'tar] *vt* to estrange, cause a rift with/between.

malsano, a [mal'sano, a] *a* unhealthy.

Malta ['malta] *nf* Malta.

maltratar [maltra'tar] *vt* to ill-treat; **maltrato** *nm* ill-treatment; (*ofensa*) abuse, insults *pl*.

maltrecho, a [mal'tretʃo, a] *a* battered, damaged.

malvado, a [mal'ßaðo, a] *a* evil, villainous.

malvavisco [malßa'ßisko] *nm* marshmallow.

malversar [malßer'sar] *vt* to embezzle, misappropriate.

Malvinas [mal'ßinas]: **Islas** ~ *nfpl* Falkland Islands.

malla ['maʎa] *nf* mesh; (*de baño*) bathing costume; ~**s** *nfpl* tights; ~ **de alambre** wire mesh; **hacer** ~ to knit.

Mallorca [ma'ʎorka] *nf* Majorca.

mama ['mama] *nf* (*de animal*) teat; (*de persona*) breast.

mamá [ma'ma] (*pl* ~**s**) *nf* (*fam*) mum, mummy.

mamar [ma'mar] *vt* (*pecho*) to suck; (*fig*) to absorb, assimilate // *vi* to suck.

mamarracho [mama'rratʃo] *nm* sight, mess.

mampara [mam'para] *nf* (*entre habitaciones*) partition; (*biombo*) screen.

mampostería [mamposte'ria] *nf* masonry.

mampuesto [mam'pwesto] *nm* (*piedra*) rough stone; (*muro*) wall, parapet; **de** ~ spare, emergency.

mamut [ma'mut] *nm* mammoth.

manada [ma'naða] *nf* (*rebaño*) herd; (*de ovejas*) flock; (*de lobos*) pack.

manantial [manan'tjal] *nm* spring; (*fuente*) fountain; (*fig*) source.

manar [ma'nar] *vt* to run with, flow with // *vi* to run, flow; (*abundar*) to abound.

mancebo [man'θeßo] *nm* (*joven*) young man; (*soltero*) bachelor; (*dependiente*) assistant.

mancilla [man'θiʎa] *nf* stain, blemish.

manco, a ['manko, a] *a* one-armed, one-handed; (*fig*) defective, faulty.

mancomún [manko'mun]: **de** ~ *ad* jointly, together; **mancomunar** *vt* to unite, bring together; (*recursos*) to pool; (*JUR*) to make jointly responsible; **mancomunarse** *vr* to unite, merge; **mancomunidad** *nf* union, association; (*POL*) commonwealth; (*JUR*) joint responsibility.

mancha ['mantʃa] *nf* stain, mark; (*boceto*) sketch, outline; **manchar** *vt* (*gen*) to stain, mark; (*ensuciar*) to soil, dirty.

manchego, a [man'tʃeɣo, a] *a* of or from La Mancha.

mandadero [manda'ðero] *nm* messenger; (*niño*) errand boy.

mandado [man'daðo] *nm* (*orden*) order; (*comisión*) commission, errand.

mandamiento [manda'mjento] *nm* (*orden*) order, command; (*REL*) commandment; ~ **judicial** warrant.

mandar [man'dar] *vt* (*ordenar*) to order; (*dirigir*) to lead, command; (*enviar*) to send; (*pedir*) to order, ask for // *vi* to be in charge; (*pey*) to be bossy; ~**se** *vr* (*MED*) to get about by o.s.; ¿**mande?** pardon?; ~ **hacer un traje** to have a suit made; ~**se cambiar** to go away, leave.

mandarín [manda'rin] *nm* mandarin // *nf* tangerine, mandarin.

mandatario, a [manda'tarjo, a] *nm/f* (*representante*) agent; (*AM*) leader.

mandato [man'dato] *nm* (*orden*) order; (*POL*) term of office; (: *territorio*) mandate; ~ **judicial** (*search*) warrant.

mandíbula [man'dißula] *nf* jaw.

mandil [man'dil] *nm* (*delantal*) apron; (*vestido*) pinafore dress.

mando ['mando] nm (MIL) command; (de país) rule; (el primer lugar) lead; (POL) term of office; (TEC) control; ~ **a la izquierda** left-hand drive; ~ **remoto** remote control.

mandolina [mando'lina] nf mandolin(e).

mandón, ona [man'don, ona] a bossy, domineering.

manea [ma'nea] nf hobble.

manejable [mane'xaβle] a manageable.

manejar [mane'xar] vt (gen) to manage; (máquina) to work, operate; (idioma, caballo etc) to handle; (casa) to run, manage; (AM) to drive; ~**se** vr (comportarse) to act, behave; (arreglárselas) to manage; (MED) to get about unaided; **manejo** nm management; handling; running; driving; (facilidad de trato) ease, confidence; **manejos** nmpl intrigues.

manera [ma'nera] nf way, manner, fashion; ~**s** nfpl manners; ~ **de ser** way of life; (aire) manner; **de ninguna** ~ no way, by no means; **de otra** ~ otherwise; **de todas** ~**s** at any rate; **no hay** ~ **de persuadirle** there's no way of convincing him.

manga ['manga] nf (de camisa) sleeve; (de riego) hose; (tromba) downpour; (filtro) filter; (NAUT) beam.

mangana [man'gana] nf lasso.

mango ['mango] nm handle; (BOT) mango.

mangonear [mangone'ar] vt to manage, boss about // vi (meterse) to meddle, interfere; (ser mandón) to boss people about.

manguera [man'gera] nf (de riego) hose; (tubo) pipe.

maní [ma'ni] nm (AM) peanut.

manía [ma'nia] nf (MED) mania; (capricho) rage, craze; (disgusto) dislike; (malicia) spite; **maníaco, a** a maniac(al) // nm/f maniac.

maniatar [manja'tar] vt to tie the hands of.

maniático, a [ma'njatiko, a] a maniac(al) // nm/f maniac.

manicomio [mani'komjo] nm asylum, mental hospital.

manifestación [manifesta'θjon] nf (declaración) statement, declaration; (demostración) show, manifestation; (POL) demonstration.

manifestar [manifes'tar] vt to show, manifest; (declarar) to state, declare; **manifiesto, a** a clear, manifest // nm manifesto.

manija [ma'nixa] nf handle.

manilla [ma'niʎa] nf: ~**s de hierro** handcuffs.

maniobra [ma'njoβra] nf manœuvring; (maneja) handling; (fig) manœuvre; (estratagema) stratagem; ~**s** nfpl manœuvres; **maniobrar** vt to manœuvre; (manejar) to handle.

manipulación [manipula'θjon] nf manipulation; **manipular** vt to manipulate; (manejar) to handle.

maniquí [mani'ki] nm dummy // nf model.

manirroto, a [mani'rroto, a] a lavish, extravagant // nm/f spendthrift.

manivela [mani'βela] nf crank.

manjar [man'xar] nm (tasty) dish; ~ **blanco** blancmange.

mano ['mano] nf hand; (ZOOL) foot, paw; (de pintura) coat; (serie) lot, series; a ~ by hand; **a la** ~ on hand, within reach; **a** ~ **derecha/izquierda** on the right(-hand side)/left(-hand side); **de primera** ~ (at) first hand; **de segunda** ~ (at) second hand; **robo a** ~ **armada** armed robbery; ~ **de obra** labour, manpower; **estrechar la** ~ **a uno** to shake sb's hand.

manojo [ma'noxo] nm handful, bunch; ~ **de llaves** bunch of keys.

manoseado, a [manose'aðo, a] a well-worn; **manosear** vt (tocar) to handle, touch; (desordenar) to mess up, rumple; (insistir en) to overwork; (AM) to caress, fondle.

manotazo [mano'taθo] nm slap, smack.

mansalva [man'salβa]: a ~ ad without risk, without any danger.

mansedumbre [manse'ðumbre] nf gentleness, meekness.

mansión [man'sjon] nf mansion.

manso, a ['manso, a] a gentle, mild, meek; (animal) tame.

manta ['manta] nf blanket; (abrigo) shawl.

manteca [man'teka] nf fat; ~ **de cacahuete/cacao** peanut/cocoa butter; ~ **de cerdo** lard.

mantecado [mante'kaðo] nm ice-cream.

mantel [man'tel] nm tablecloth.

mantener [mante'ner] vt (gen) to support, maintain; (alimentar) to sustain; (conservar) to keep; (TEC) to maintain, service; ~**se** vr (seguir de pie) to be still standing; (no ceder) to hold one's ground; (subsistir) to sustain o.s., keep going; **mantenimiento** nm maintenance; sustenance; (sustento) support.

mantequera [mante'kera] nf (para hacer) churn; (para servir) butter dish.

mantequilla [mante'kiʎa] nf butter.

mantilla [man'tiʎa] nf mantilla; ~**s** nfpl baby clothes.

manto ['manto] nm (capa) cloak; (chal) shawl; (de ceremonia) robe, gown.

mantón [man'ton] nm shawl.

manual [ma'nwal] a manual // nm manual, handbook.

manufactura [manufak'tura] nf manufacture; (fábrica) factory.

manuscrito, a [manus'krito, a] a hand-written // nm manuscript.

manutención [manuten'θjon] nf maintenance; (sustento) support.

manzana [man'θana] nf apple; (ARQ) block.

manzanilla [manθa'niʎa] nf (planta) camomile; (infusión) camomile tea; (vino) manzanilla.

manzano [man'θano] nm apple tree.

maña ['maɲa] *nf* (*gen*) skill, dexterity; (*pey*) guile; (*costumbre*) habit; (*una* ~) trick, knack.

mañana [ma'ɲana] *ad* tomorrow // *nm* future // *nf* morning; **de o por la** ~ in the morning; **¡hasta** ~**!** see you tomorrow!; ~ **por la** ~ tomorrow morning; **mañanero, a** *a* early-rising.

mañoso, a [ma'ɲoso, a] *a* (*hábil*) skilful; (*astuto*) smart, clever.

mapa ['mapa] *nm* map.

maque ['make] *nm* lacquer.

maqueta [ma'keta] *nf* (*scale*) model.

maquillaje [maki'ʎaxe] *nm* make-up; (*acto*) making up; **maquillar** *vt* to make up; **maquillarse** *vr* to put on (some) make-up.

máquina ['makina] *nf* machine; (*de tren*) locomotive, engine; (*cámara*) camera; (*fig*) machinery; (: *proyecto*) plan, project; **escrito a** ~ typewritten; ~ **de afeitar** (safety) razor; ~ **de escribir** typewriter; ~ **de coser/lavar** sewing/washing machine.

maquinación [makina'θjon] *nf* machination, scheme, plot.

maquinal [maki'nal] *a* (*fig*) mechanical, automatic.

maquinaria [maki'narja] *nf* (*máquinas*) machinery; (*mecanismo*) mechanism, works *pl*.

maquinista [maki'nista] *nm* (*de tren*) engine driver; (*TEC*) operator; (*NAUT*) engineer.

mar [mar] *nm o f* sea; (*marea*) tide; ~ **adentro** *o* **afuera** out at sea; **en alta** ~ on the high seas; **la** ~ **de** (*fam*) lots of; **el M~ Negro/Báltico** the Black/Baltic Sea.

maraña [ma'raɲa] *nf* (*maleza*) thicket; (*confusión*) tangle.

maravilla [mara'βiʎa] *nf* marvel, wonder; (*BOT*) marigold; **maravillar** *vt* to astonish, amaze; **maravillarse** *vr* to be astonished, be amazed; **maravilloso, a** *a* wonderful, marvellous.

marca ['marka] *nf* (*gen*) mark; (*sello*) stamp; (*COM*) make, brand; **de** ~ excellent, outstanding; ~ **de fábrica** trademark.

marcado, a [mar'kaðo, a] *a* marked, strong.

marcar [mar'kar] *vt* (*gen*) to mark; (*número de teléfono*) to dial; (*gol*) to score; (*números*) to record, keep a tally of; (*el pelo*) to set; (*fig*) to indicate, point to // *vi* (*DEPORTE*) to score; (*TELEC*) to dial; ~**se** *vr* (*NAUT*) to take one's bearings; (*fig*) to make one's mark, stand out.

marcial [mar'θjal] *a* martial, military.

marciano, a [mar'θjano, a] *a* Martian.

marco ['marko] *nm* frame; (*DEPORTE*) goal-posts *pl*; (*moneda*) mark; (*fig*) framework; ~ **de chimenea** mantelpiece.

marcha ['martʃa] *nf* march; (*TEC*) running, working; (*AUTO*) gear; (*velocidad*) speed;

(*fig*) progress; (*dirección*) course; **poner en** ~ to put into gear; **dar** ~ **atrás** to reverse, put into reverse; **estar en** ~ to be under way, be in motion.

marchante, a [mar'tʃante, a] *nm/f* dealer, merchant; (*AM. cliente*) client, customer; (: *buhonero*) pedlar.

marchar [mar'tʃar] *vi* to go; (*funcionar*) to work, go; ~**se** *vr* to go (away), leave.

marchitar [martʃi'tar] *vt* to wither, dry up; ~**se** *vr* (*BOT*) to wither; (*fig*) to go into a decline; **marchito, a** *a* withered, faded; (*fig*) in decline.

marea [ma'rea] *nf* tide; (*llovizna*) drizzle.

marear [mare'ar] *vt* (*NAUT*) to sail, navigate; (*fig*) to annoy, upset; (*MED*): ~ **a uno** to make sb feel sick; ~**se** *vr* (*tener náuseas*) to feel/be sick; (*desvanecerse*) to feel faint; (*aturdirse*) to feel dizzy; (*fam*: *emborracharse*) to get a bit drunk.

maremoto [mare'moto] *nm* tidal wave.

mareo [ma'reo] *nm* (*náusea*) sick feeling; (*aturdimiento*) dizziness; (*fam*: *lata*) nuisance.

marfil [mar'fil] *nm* ivory.

margarina [marɣa'rina] *nf* margarine.

margarita [marɣa'rita] *nf* (*BOT*) daisy; (*perla*) pearl.

margen ['marxen] *nm* (*borde*) edge, border; (*fig*) margin, space // *nf* bank; **dar** ~ **para** to give an opportunity for; **mantenerse al** ~ to keep out (of things).

marica [ma'rika] *nm* magpie; (*fam*) sissy.

maricón [mari'kon] *nm* (*fam*) queer (*fam*).

marido [ma'riðo] *nm* husband.

marijuana [mari'xwana] *nf* marijuana, cannabis.

marina [ma'rina] *nf* navy; ~ **mercante** merchant navy.

marinero, a [mari'nero, a] *a* sea *cpd*; (*barco*) seaworthy // *nm* sailor, seaman.

marino, a [ma'rino, a] *a* sea *cpd*, marine // *nm* sailor.

marioneta [marjo'neta] *nf* puppet.

mariposa [mari'posa] *nf* butterfly.

mariscos [ma'riskos] *nmpl* shellfish, seafood *sg*.

marisma [ma'risma] *nf* marsh, swamp.

marítimo, a [ma'ritimo, a] *a* sea *cpd*, maritime.

marmita [mar'mita] *nf* pot.

mármol ['marmol] *nm* marble; **marmóreo, a** *a* marble.

marqués, esa [mar'kes, esa] *nm/f* marquis/marchioness.

marrar [ma'rrar] *vi* to miss.

marrón [ma'rron] *a* brown.

marroquí [marro'ki] *a* Moroccan // *nm* Morocco (leather).

Marruecos [ma'rrwekos] *nm* Morocco.

Marsellas [mar'seʎas] *n* Marseille.

martes ['martes] *nm inv* Tuesday.

martillar [marti'ʎar] *vt* to hammer.

martillo [mar'tiʎo] *nm* hammer; ~

neumático pneumatic drill; ~ **de orejas** claw-hammer.

mártir ['martir] *nm/f* martyr; **martirio** *nm* martyrdom; (*fig*) torture, torment.

marxismo [mark'sismo] *nm* Marxism; **marxista** *nm/f* Marxist.

marzo ['marθo] *nm* March.

mas [mas] *conj* but.

más [mas] *a, ad* more; (*superlativo*) most // *conj* and, plus; **es** ~ **de medianoche** it's after midnight; **el libro** ~ **leído del año** the most-read book of the year; **¡qué perro** ~ **feo!** what an ugly dog!; ~ **de**, ~ **de lo que**, ~ **que** more than; ~ **bien** rather; ~ **o menos** more or less.

masa ['masa] *nf* (*mezcla*) dough; (*volumen*) volume, mass; (*FÍSICA*) mass; (*ELEC*) earth; **en** ~ **en masse**; **las** ~**s** the masses.

masacre [ma'sakre] *nm* massacre.

masaje [ma'saxe] *nm* massage.

mascar [mas'kar] *vt* to chew; (*fig*) to mumble, mutter.

máscara ['maskara] *nf* (*gen*) mask // *nm/f* masked person; **mascarada** *nf* masquerade.

masculino, a [masku'lino, a] *a* masculine; (*BIO*) male.

mascullar [masku'ʎar] *vt* to mumble, mutter.

masilla [ma'siʎa] *nf* putty.

masivo, a [ma'siβo, a] *a* (*enorme*) massive; (*en masa*) mass, en masse.

masón [ma'son] *nm* (free)mason.

masoquista [maso'kista] *nm/f* masochist.

masticar [masti'kar] *vt* to chew; (*fig*) to ponder.

mástil ['mastil] *nm* (*de navío*) mast; (*de guitarra*) neck; (*sostén*) post, support.

mastín [mas'tin] *nm* mastiff; ~ **danés** Great Dane.

masturbación [masturβa'θjon] *nf* masturbation; **masturbarse** *vr* to masturbate.

mata ['mata] *nf* bush, shrub; (*de hierbas*) tuft; (*campo*) field; (*AM*) clump (of trees).

matadero [mata'ðero] *nm* slaughterhouse, abattoir.

matador, a [mata'ðor, a] *a* killing // *nm/f* killer // *nm* (*TAUR*) matador, bullfighter.

matanza [ma'tanθa] *nf* (*de personas*) killing; (*de animales*) slaughter(ing).

matar [ma'tar] *vt, vi* to kill; ~**se** *vr* (*suicidarse*) to kill o.s., commit suicide; (*por otro*) to be killed; ~ **el hambre** to stave off hunger.

mate ['mate] *a* (*sin brillo: color*) dull // *nm* (*en ajedrez*) (check)mate; (*AM: hierba*) maté; (: *vasija*) gourd.

matemáticas [mate'matikas] *nfpl* mathematics; **matemático, a** *a* mathematical // *nm/f* mathematician.

materia [ma'terja] *nf* (*gen*) matter; (*TEC*) material; **en** ~ **de** on the subject of; ~ **prima** raw material; **material** *a* material; (*dolor*) physical // *nm* material; (*TEC*) equipment; **materialismo** *nm*

materialism; **materialista** *a* materialist(ic); **materialmente** *ad* materially; (*fig*) absolutely.

maternal [mater'nal] *a* motherly, maternal.

maternidad [materni'ðað] *nf* motherhood, maternity; **materno, a** *a* motherly, maternal; (*lengua*) mother *cpd*.

matinal [mati'nal] *a* morning *cpd*.

matiz [ma'tiθ] *nm* shade; ~**ar** *vt* (*dar tonos de*) to tinge, tint; (*variar*) to vary; (*ARTE*) to blend.

matón [ma'ton] *nm* bully.

matorral [mato'rral] *nm* thicket.

matraca [ma'traka] *nf* rattle.

matrícula [ma'trikula] *nf* (*registro*) register; (*AUTO*) registration number; (: *placa*) licence plate; **matricular** *vt* to register, enrol.

matrimonial [matrimo'njal] *a* matrimonial.

matrimonio [matri'monjo] *nm* (*boda*) wedding; (*pareja*) (married) couple; (*unión*) marriage.

matriz [ma'triθ] *nf* womb; (*TEC*) mould; **casa** ~ (*COM*) head office.

matrona [ma'trona] *nf* (*persona de edad*) matron; (*partera*) midwife.

matute [ma'tute] *nm* contraband.

maullar [mau'ʎar] *vi* to mew, miaow.

mausoleo [mauso'leo] *nm* mausoleum.

maxilar [maksi'lar] *nm* jaw(bone).

máxima ['maksima] *ver* **máximo**.

máxime ['maksime] *ad* especially.

máximo, a ['maksimo, a] *a* maximum; (*más alto*) highest; (*más grande*) greatest // *nm* maximum // *nf* maxim.

mayo ['majo] *nm* May.

mayonesa [majo'nesa] *nf* mayonnaise.

mayor [ma'jor] *a* (*gen*) main, chief; (*adulto*) adult; (*de edad avanzada*) elderly; (*MUS*) major; (*comparativo*: de tamaño) bigger; (: *de edad*) older; (*superlativo*: de tamaño) biggest; (: *de edad*) oldest // *nm* chief, boss; **al por** ~ wholesale; ~ **de edad** adult; ~**es** *nmpl* ancestors.

mayoral [majo'ral] *nm* foreman.

mayordomo [major'ðomo] *nm* (*criado*) butler; (*de hotel*) steward.

mayoría [majo'ria] *nf* majority, greater part.

mayorista [majo'rista] *nm/f* wholesaler.

mayúsculo, a [ma'juskulo, a] *a* (*fig*) big, tremendous // *nf* capital (letter).

mazapán [maθa'pan] *nm* marzipan.

mazo ['maθo] *nm* (*martillo*) mallet; (*de flores*) bunch; (*fig*) bore; (*DEPORTE*) bat; (*palo*) club.

me [me] *pron* (*directo*) me; (*indirecto*) (to) me; (*reflexivo*) (to) myself; **¡démelo!** give it to me!

mecánico, a [me'kaniko, a] *a* mechanical // *nm/f* mechanic // *nf* (*estudio*) mechanics *sg*; (*mecanismo*) mechanism.

mecanismo [meka'nismo] *nm* mechanism; (*marcha*) gear.

mecanografía [mekanoɤra'fia] nf typewriting; **mecanógrafo, a** nm/f typist.

mecedor, a [meθe'ðor, a] a rocking // nm (columpio) swing // nf rocking chair.

mecer [me'θer] vt (cuna) to rock; (líquido) to stir; **~se** vr to rock; (ramo) to sway.

mechero [me'tʃero] nm (cigarette) lighter.

mechón [me'tʃon] nm (gen) tuft; (manojo) bundle; (de pelo) lock.

medalla [me'ðaʎa] nf medal.

media ['meðja] nf ver **medio**.

mediado, a [me'ðjaðo, a] a half-full; (trabajo) half-complete; a ~s de in the middle of, halfway through.

mediano, a [me'ðjano, a] a (regular) medium, average; (mediocre) mediocre; (indiferente) indifferent.

medianoche [meðja'notʃe] nf midnight.

mediante [me'ðjante] ad by (means of), through.

mediar [me'ðjar] vi (llegar a la mitad) to get to the middle, get halfway; (estar en medio) to be in the middle; (interceder) to mediate, intervene.

medicación [meðika'θjon] nf medication, treatment.

medicamento [meðika'mento] nm medicine, drug.

medicina [meði'θina] nf medicine.

medición [meði'θjon] nf measurement.

médico, a ['meðiko, a] a medical // nm/f doctor.

medida [me'ðiða] nf (gen) measure; (medición) measurement; (prudencia) moderation, prudence; **en cierta/gran ~** up to a point/to a great extent; **un traje a la ~** made-to-measure suit; **~ de cuello** collar size; **a ~ de** in proportion to; (de acuerdo con) in keeping with.

medio, a ['meðjo, a] a half (a); (punto) mid, middle; (promedio) average // ad half // nm (centro) middle, centre; (promedio) average; (DEPORTE) half-back; (método) means, way; (ambiente) environment // nf (prenda de vestir) stocking; (promedio) average; **~s** nmpl means, resources; **~ litro** half a litre; **las tres y ~a** half past three; **M~ Oriente** Middle East; **a ~ terminar** half finished; **pagar a ~as** to share the cost; **hacer ~a** to knit.

mediocre [me'ðjokre] a middling, average; (pey) mediocre.

mediodía [meðjo'ðia] nm midday, noon.

medir [me'ðir] vt (gen) to measure; (pesar) to weigh up // vi to measure.

meditar [meði'tar] vt to ponder, think over, meditate (on); (planear) to think out.

mediterráneo, a [meðite'rraneo, a] a Mediterranean // nm: **el M~** the Mediterranean.

medroso, a [me'ðroso, a] a fearful, timid.

medusa [me'ðusa] nf jellyfish.

megáfono [me'ɤafono] nm megaphone.

megalómano, a [meɤa'lomano, a] nm/f megalomaniac.

mejicano, a [mexi'kano, a] a, nm/f Mexican.

Méjico ['mexiko] nm Mexico.

mejilla [me'xiʎa] nf cheek.

mejor [me'xor] a, ad (comparativo) better; (superlativo) best; **a lo ~** probably; (quizá) maybe; **~ dicho** rather; **tanto ~** so much the better.

mejora [me'xora] nf improvement; **mejorar** vt to improve, make better // vi, **mejorarse** vr to improve, get better.

melancólico, a [melan'koliko, a] a (triste) sad, melancholy; (soñador) dreamy.

melena [me'lena] nf (de persona) long hair; (del león) mane.

melocotón [meloko'ton] nm peach.

melodía [melo'ðia] nf melody; (aire) tune.

melodrama [melo'ðrama] nm melodrama; **melodramático, a** a melodramatic.

melón [me'lon] nm melon.

meloso, a [me'loso, a] a honeyed, sweet.

mellizo, a [me'ʎiθo, a] a, nm/f twin.

membrete [mem'brete] nm letterhead.

memorable [memo'raβle] a memorable.

memorándum [memo'randum] nm (libro) notebook; (comunicación) memorandum.

memoria [me'morja] nf (gen) memory; (informe) report; **~s** nfpl (de autor) memoirs.

mencionar [menθjo'nar] vt to mention.

mendigar [mendi'ɤar] vt to beg (for).

mendigo, a [men'diɤo, a] nm/f beggar.

mendrugo [men'druɤo] nm crust.

menear [mene'ar] vt to move; (fig) to handle; **~se** vr to shake; (balancearse) to sway; (moverse) to move; (fig) to get a move on.

menester [menes'ter] nm (necesidad) necessity; (ocupación) job; **~es** nmpl (deberes) duties; (instrumentos) tackle sg, tools; **es ~** it is necessary.

mengua ['mengwa] nf (disminución) decrease; (falta) lack; (pobreza) poverty; (fig) discredit; **~do, a** a cowardly, timid; (cicatero) mean.

menguante [men'gwante] a decreasing, diminishing; **menguar** vt to lessen, diminish; (fig) to discredit // vi to diminish, decrease; (fig) to decline.

menopausia [meno'pausja] nf menopause.

menor [me'nor] a (más pequeño: comparativo) smaller; (: superlativo) smallest; (más joven: comparativo) younger; (: superlativo) youngest; (MUS) minor // nm/f (joven) young person, juvenile; **no tengo la ~ idea** I haven't the slightest idea; **al por ~** retail; **~ de edad** person under age.

menos ['menos] a (comparativo: sg) less; (: pl) fewer; (superlativo: sg) least; (: pl) fewest // ad (comparativo) less; (superlativo) least // conj except // nm (MAT) minus; **es lo ~ que puedo hacer**

it's the least I can do; **lo ~ posible** as little as possible; **a ~ que** unless; **te echo de ~** I miss you; **al o por lo ~** at least.

menoscabar [menoska'ßar] *vt* (*estropear*) to damage, harm; (*acortar*) to lessen, reduce; (*fig*) to discredit.

menospreciar [menospre'θjar] *vt* to underrate, undervalue; (*despreciar*) to scorn, despise; **menosprecio** *nm* underrating, undervaluation; scorn, contempt.

mensaje [men'saxe] *nm* message; **~ro, a** *nm/f* messenger.

menstruar [mens'trwar] *vi* to menstruate; **menstruo** *nm* menstruation, period.

mensual [men'swal] *a* monthly; **100 ptas ~es** 100 ptas. a month.

menta ['menta] *nf* mint.

mental [men'tal] *a* mental.

mentar [men'tar] *vt* to mention, name.

mente ['mente] *nf* mind.

mentecato, a [mente'kato, a] *a* silly, stupid // *nm/f* fool, idiot.

mentir [men'tir] *vi* to lie; **~a** *nf* (*una ~a*) lie; (*acto*) lying; (*invención*) fiction; **parece ~a que...** it seems incredible that..., I can't believe that...; **~oso, a** *a* lying; (*texto*) full of errors // *nm/f* liar.

mentís [men'tis] *nm*: **dar el ~ a** to deny.

menú [me'nu] *nm* menu.

menudeo [menu'ðeo] *nm*: **vender al ~** to sell retail.

menudo, a [me'nuðo, a] *a* (*pequeño*) small, tiny; (*sin importancia*) petty, insignificant; (*exacto*) exact, meticulous; **¡~ negocio!** (*fam*) some deal!; **a ~** often, frequently; **por ~** in detail.

meñique [me'ɲike] *nm* little finger.

meollo [me'oʎo] *nm* (*gen*) marrow; (*fig*) core.

mercadería [merkaðe'ria] *nf* commodity; **~s** *nfpl* goods, merchandise *sg*.

mercado [mer'kaðo] *nm* market; **M~ Común** Common Market.

mercadotecnia [merkaðo'teknja] *nf* marketing.

mercancía [merkan'θia] *nf* commodity; **~s** *nfpl* goods, merchandise *sg*.

mercantil [merkan'til] *a* mercantile, commercial.

mercenario, a [merθe'narjo, a] *a, nm* mercenary.

mercurio [mer'kurjo] *nm* mercury.

merecer [mere'θer] *vt* to deserve, merit // *vi* to be deserving, be worthy; **merece la pena** it's worthwhile; **merecido, a** *a* (well) deserved; **llevar su merecido** to get one's deserts.

merendar [meren'dar] *vt* to have for tea // *vi* to have tea; (*en el campo*) to have a picnic.

merengue [me'renge] *nm* meringue.

merienda [me'rjenda] *nf* (light) tea, afternoon snack; (*de campo*) picnic.

mérito ['merito] *nm* merit; (*valor*) worth, value.

merluza [mer'luθa] *nf* hake.

merma ['merma] *nf* decrease; (*pérdida*) wastage; **mermar** *vt* to reduce, lessen // *vi*, **mermarse** *vr* to decrease, dwindle; (*fig*) to waste away.

mermelada [merme'laða] *nf* jam.

mero, a ['mero, a] *a* mere.

mes [mes] *nm* month; (*salario*) month's pay.

mesa ['mesa] *nf* table; (*de trabajo*) desk; (*GEO*) plateau; (*ARQ*) landing; **~ directiva** board; **poner/quitar la ~** to lay/clear the table.

meseta [me'seta] *nf* (*GEO*) meseta, tableland; (*ARQ*) landing.

mesón [me'son] *nm* olde-worlde bar.

mestizo, a [mes'tiθo, a] *a* half-caste, of mixed race; (*ZOOL*) crossbred // *nm/f* half-caste, half-breed.

mesura [me'sura] *nf* (*moderación*) moderation, restraint; (*dignidad*) dignity, calm; (*cortesía*) courtesy.

meta ['meta] *nf* goal; (*de carrera*) finish.

metáfora [me'tafora] *nf* metaphor.

metal [me'tal] *nm* (*materia*) metal; (*MUS*) brass; (*fig*) quality; **metálico, a** *a* metallic; (*de metal*) metal // *nm* cash.

metalurgia [meta'lurxja] *nf* metallurgy.

meteoro [mete'oro] *nm* meteor.

meter [me'ter] *vt* (*colocar*) to put, place; (*introducir*) to put in, insert; (*añadir*) to add; (*involucrar*) to involve; (*causar*) to make, cause; **~se** *vr*: **~se en** to go into, enter; (*fig*) to interfere in, meddle in; **~se a** to start; **~se a escritor** to become a writer; **~se con alguien** to provoke sb, pick a quarrel with sb.

meticuloso, a [metiku'loso, a] *a* meticulous, thorough.

metódico, a [me'toðiko, a] *a* methodical.

metodismo [meto'ðismo] *nm* Methodism.

método ['metoðo] *nm* method.

metralleta [metra'ʎeta] *nf* submachine gun.

métrico, a ['metriko, a] *a* metric.

metro ['metro] *nm* metre; (*tren*) underground, subway.

México ['meksiko] *nm* Mexico.

mezcla ['meθkla] *nf* mixture; (*ARQ*) mortar; **mezclar** *vt* to mix (up); (*naipes*) to shuffle; **mezclarse** *vr* to mix, mingle; **mezclarse en** to get mixed up in, get involved in.

mezquino, a [meθ'kino, a] *a* (*cicatero*) mean; (*pobre*) miserable.

mezquita [meθ'kita] *nf* mosque.

mi [mi] *det* my.

mí [mi] *pron* me; myself.

miaja ['mjaxa] *nf* crumb.

microbús [mikro'ßus] *nm* minibus.

micrófono [mi'krofono] *nm* microphone.

microlentillas [mikrolen'tiʎas] *nfpl* contact lenses.

microscopio [mikro'skopjo] *nm* microscope.

miedo ['mjeðo] *nm* fear; (*nerviosismo*) apprehension, nervousness; **tener ~ to**

be afraid; **de ~** wonderful, marvellous; **hace un frio de ~** (fam) it's terribly cold; **~so, a** a fearful, timid.

miel [mjel] nf honey.

miembro ['mjembro] nm limb; (socio) member; **~ viril** penis.

mientes ['mjentes] nfpl: **no parar ~ en** to pay no attention to; **traer a las ~** to recall.

mientras ['mjentras] conj while; (duración) as long as // ad meanwhile; **~ tanto** meanwhile; **~ más tiene, más quiere** the more he has, the more he wants.

miércoles ['mjerkoles] nm inv Wednesday.

mierda ['mjerða] nf (fam) shit.

miga ['miɣa] nf crumb; (fig) essence; **hacer buenas ~s** (fam) to get on well.

migración [miɣra'θjon] nf migration.

mil [mil] num thousand; **dos ~ libras** two thousand pounds.

milagro [mi'laɣro] nm miracle; **~so, a** a miraculous.

mili ['mili] nf: **hacer la ~** (fam) to do one's military service.

milicia [mi'liθja] nf (MIL) militia; (: arte) art of war; (servicio militar) military service.

milímetro [mi'limetro] nm millimetre.

militante [mili'tante] a militant.

militar [mili'tar] a (del ejército) military; (guerrero) warlike // nm/f soldier // vi to serve in the army; (fig) to be a member of a party.

milla ['miʎa] nf mile.

millar [mi'ʎar] nm thousand.

millón [mi'ʎon] num million; **millonario, a** nm/f millionaire.

mimar [mi'mar] vt (gen) to spoil, pamper; (al poderoso) to flatter.

mimbre ['mimbre] nm wicker.

mímica ['mimika] nf (para comunicarse) sign language; (imitación) mimicry.

mimo ['mimo] nm (caricia) affectionate caress; (de niño) spoiling; (TEATRO) mime.

mina ['mina] nf mine; **minar** vt to mine; (fig) to undermine.

mineral [mine'ral] a mineral // nm (GEO) mineral; (mena) ore.

minero, a [mi'nero, a] a mining // nm/f miner.

miniatura [minja'tura] a inv, nf miniature.

minifalda [mini'falda] nf miniskirt.

mínimo, a ['minimo, a] a, nm minimum.

ministerio [minis'terjo] nm Ministry; **M~ de Hacienda/del Exterior** Treasury/Foreign Office.

ministro [mi'nistro] nm minister.

minorar [mino'rar] vt to reduce.

minoría [mino'ria] nf minority.

minucioso, a [minu'θjoso, a] a thorough, meticulous; (prolijo) very detailed.

minúsculo, a [mi'nuskulo, a] a tiny, minute // nf small letter.

minuta [mi'nuta] nf (de comida) menu;

(borrador) rough draft; (apunte) note.

minutero [minu'tero] nm minute hand.

minuto [mi'nuto] nm minute.

mío, a ['mio, a] pron: **el ~** mine; **un amigo ~** a friend of mine; **lo ~** what is mine.

miope [mi'ope] a short-sighted.

mira ['mira] nf (de arma) sight(s) (pl); (fig) aim, intention; **estar a la ~** to be on the look-out, keep watch; **~da** nf look, glance; (expresión) look, expression; **echar una ~da a** to glance at; **~do, a** a (sensato) sensible; (considerado) considerate; **bien/mal ~do** well/not well thought of.

mirador [mira'ðor] nm viewpoint, vantage point.

mirar [mi'rar] vt to look at; (observar) to watch; (considerar) to consider, think over; (vigilar, cuidar) to watch, look after // vi to look; (ARQ) to face; **~se** vr (dos personas) to look at each other; **~ bien/mal** to think highly of/have a poor opinion of; **~se al espejo** to look at o.s. in the mirror.

mirlo ['mirlo] nm blackbird.

misa ['misa] nf mass.

miserable [mise'raßle] a (avaro) mean, stingy; (nimio) miserable, paltry; (lugar) squalid; (fam) vile, despicable // nm/f (indigente) wretch, poor person; (perverso) rotter.

miseria [mi'serja] nf misery; (pobreza) poverty; (tacañería) meanness, stinginess; (condiciones) squalor; **una ~** a pittance.

misericordia [miseri'korðja] nf (compasión) compassion, pity; (piedad) mercy.

misil [mi'sil] nm missile.

misión [mi'sjon] nf mission; **misionero, a** nm/f missionary.

mismo, a ['mismo, a] a (semejante) same; (después de pronombre) -self; (para énfasis) very; **el ~ traje** the same suit; **en ese ~ momento** at that very moment; **vino el ~ Ministro** the minister himself came; **yo ~ lo vi** I saw it myself; **lo ~ the same** (thing); **da lo ~** it's all the same; **quedamos en las ~as** we're no further forward // ad: **aquí/hoy ~** right here/this very day; **ahora ~** right now // conj: **lo ~ que** just like, just as; **por lo ~** for the same reason.

misterio [mis'terjo] nm (gen) mystery; (lo secreto) secrecy.

mitad [mi'tað] nf (medio) half; (centro) middle; **a ~ de precio** (at) half-price; **en o a ~ del camino** halfway along the road; **cortar por la ~** to cut through the middle.

mitin ['mitin] nm meeting.

mito ['mito] nm myth.

mixto, a ['miksto, a] a mixed.

mobiliario [moßi'ljarjo] nm furniture.

mocedad [moθe'ðað] nf youth.

moción [mo'θjon] nf motion.

mochila [mo'tʃila] nf rucksack.

moda ['moða] *nf* (*gen*) fashion; (*estilo*) style: **de** *o* **a la** ~ in fashion, fashionable; **pasado** *o* **fuera de** ~ out of fashion.
modales [mo'ðales] *nmpl* manners.
modalidad [moðali'ðað] *nf* kind, variety.
modelar [moðe'lar] *vt* to model.
modelo [mo'ðelo] *a inv, nm/f* model.
moderado, a [moðe'raðo, a] *a* moderate.
moderar [moðe'rar] *vt* to moderate; (*violencia*) to restrain, control; (*velocidad*) to reduce; ~**se** *vr* to restrain o.s., control o.s.
modernizar [moðerni'θar] *vt* to modernize.
moderno, a [mo'ðerno, a] *a* modern; (*actual*) present-day.
modestia [mo'ðestja] *nf* modesty; **modesto, a** *a* modest.
módico, a ['moðiko, a] *a* moderate, reasonable.
modificar [moðifi'kar] *vt* to modify.
modista [mo'ðista] *nm/f* dressmaker.
modo ['moðo] *nm* (*manera, forma*) way, manner; (*MUS*) mode; ~**s** *nmpl* manners; **de ningún** ~ in no way; **de todos** ~**s** at any rate; ~ **de empleo** directions *pl* (for use).
modorra [mo'ðorra] *nf* drowsiness.
modular [moðu'lar] *vt* to modulate.
mofa ['mofa] *nf* mockery, ridicule; **hacer** ~ **de** to mock; **mofar** *vi* to mock, scoff; **mofarse** *vr*: **mofarse de** to mock, scoff at.
mohino, a [mo'ino, a] *a* (*triste*) gloomy, depressed; (*enojado*) sulky.
moho ['moo] *nm* (*BOT*) mould; (*oxidación*) rust; ~**so, a** *a* mouldy; rusty.
mojar [mo'xar] *vt* to wet; (*humedecer*) to damp(en), moisten; (*calar*) to soak // *vi*: ~ **en** to get involved in; ~**se** *vr* to get wet.
mojón [mo'xon] *nm* (*en un camino*) signpost; (*montón*) heap, pile.
molde ['molde] *nm* mould; (*de costura*) pattern; (*fig*) model; **el vestido le está de** ~ the dress is just right for her; ~**ar** *vt* to mould.
mole ['mole] *nf* mass, bulk.
moledora [mole'ðora] *nf* grinder, mill.
moler [mo'ler] *vt* to grind, crush; (*cansar*) to tire out, exhaust; (*irritar*) to annoy.
molestar [moles'tar] *vt* (*gen*) to bother; (*fastidiar*) to annoy; (*incomodar*) to inconvenience, put out // *vi* to be a nuisance; ~**se** *vr* to bother; (*incomodarse*) to go to trouble; (*ofenderse*) to take offence.
molestia [mo'lestja] *nf* (*gen*) bother, trouble; (*incomodidad*) inconvenience; (*MED*) discomfort; **es una** ~ it's a nuisance; **molesto, a** *a* (*que causa molestia*) annoying; (*incómodo*) inconvenient; (*inquieto*) uncomfortable, ill at ease; (*enfadado*) annoyed.
molinillo [moli'niʎo] *nm*: ~ **de café/carne** coffee grinder/mincer.

molino [mo'lino] *nm* (*edificio*) mill; (*máquina*) grinder.
momentáneo, a [momen'taneo, a] *a* momentary.
momento [mo'mento] *nm* (*gen*) moment; (*TEC*) momentum; **de** ~ at the moment, for the moment.
momia ['momja] *nf* mummy.
monarca [mo'narka] *nm/f* monarch, ruler; **monarquía** *nf* monarchy; **monarquista** *nm/f* royalist, monarchist.
monasterio [monas'terjo] *nm* monastery.
mondar [mon'dar] *vt* (*limpiar*) to clean; (*podar*) to prune, trim; (*pelar*) to peel; ~**se** *vr*: ~**se los dientes** to pick one's teeth.
moneda [mo'neða] *nf* (*tipo de dinero*) currency, money; (*pieza*) coin; **una** ~ **de 5p a 5p piece**; **monedero** *nm* purse; **monetario, a** *a* monetary, financial.
monja ['monxa] *nf* nun.
monje ['monxe] *nm* monk.
mono, a ['mono, a] *a* (*bonito*) lovely, pretty; (*gracioso*) nice, charming // *nm/f* monkey, ape // *nm* (*overoles*) overalls *pl*.
monopolio [mono'poljo] *nm* monopoly; **monopolizar** *vt* to monopolize.
monoriel [mono'riel] *nm* monorail.
monotonía [monoto'nia] *nf* (*sonido*) monotone; (*fig*) monotony.
monótono, a [mo'notono, a] *a* monotonous.
monstruo ['monstrwo] *nm* monster // *a* fantastic; ~**so, a** *a* monstrous.
monta ['monta] *nf* total, sum; **de poca** ~ unimportant, of little account.
montaje [mon'taxe] *nm* assembly; (*ARQ*) erection; (*TEATRO*) décor; (*CINE*) montage.
montaña [mon'tana] *nf* (*monte*) mountain; (*sierra*) mountains *pl*, mountainous area; (*AM*) forest; ~ **rusa** roller coaster; **montañés, esa** *a* mountain *cpd* // *nm/f* highlander; (*de Santander*) native of the Santander region.
montar [mon'tar] *vt* (*subir a*) to mount, get on; (*caballo etc*) to ride; (*TEC*) to assemble, put together; (*ARQ*) to erect; (*negocio*) to set up; (*arma*) to cock; (*colocar*) to lift on to // *vi* to mount, get on; (*sobresalir*) to overlap; ~ **a** to amount to, come to; ~ **en cólera** to get angry.
montaraz [monta'raθ] *a* mountain *cpd*, highland *cpd*; (*salvaje*) wild, untamed; (*pey*) uncivilized.
monte ['monte] *nm* (*montaña*) mountain; (*bosque*) woodland; (*área sin cultivar*) wild area, wild country; ~ **de Piedad** pawnshop; ~ **alto** forest; ~ **bajo** scrub(land).
monto ['monto] *nm* total, amount.
montón [mon'ton] *nm* heap, pile; (*fig*): **un** ~ **de** heaps of, lots of.
monumento [monu'mento] *nm* monument.
monzón [mon'θon] *nm* monsoon.
moña ['mona] *nf* hair ribbon.
moño ['mono] *nm* bun.

morado, a [mo'raðo, a] a purple; (*violado*) violet // *nm* bruise // *nf* (*casa*) dwelling, abode; (*período*) stay.

moral [mo'ral] a moral // *nf* (*ética*) ethics; (*moralidad*) morals *pl*, morality; (*ánimo*) morale.

moraleja [mora'lexa] *nf* moral.

moralizar [morali'θar] *vt* to moralize.

morboso, a [mor'βoso, a] a morbid.

morcilla [mor'θiʎa] *nf* blood sausage, black pudding.

mordaz [mor'ðaθ] a biting, scathing.

mordaza [mor'ðaθa] *nf* (*para la boca*) gag; (*TEC*) clamp.

morder [mor'ðer] *vt* to bite; (*mordisquear*) to nibble; (*consumir*) to eat away, eat into; **mordisco** *nm* bite.

moreno, a [mo'reno, a] a (*color*) (dark) brown; (*de tez*) dark; (*de pelo* ~) darkhaired; (*negro*) Negro.

moretón [more'ton] *nm* (*fam*) bruise.

morfina [mor'fina] *nf* morphine.

moribundo, a [mori'βundo, a] a dying.

morir [mo'rir] *vi* (*gen*) to die; (*fuego*) to die down; (*luz*) to go out; ~ **se** *vr* (*gen*) to die; (*pierna etc*) to go to sleep, go numb; (*fig*) to be dying; **fue muerto en un accidente** he was killed in an accident; ~ **se por algo** to be dying for sth.

morisco, a [mo'risko, a], **moro, a** ['moro, a] a Moorish // *nm/f* Moor.

morral [mo'rral] *nm* haversack.

morsa ['morsa] *nf* walrus.

mortaja [mor'taxa] *nf* shroud; (*TEC*) mortise; (*AM*) cigarette paper.

mortal [mor'tal] a mortal; (*golpe*) deadly; ~ **idad, mortandad** *nf* mortality.

mortero [mor'tero] *nm* mortar.

mortífero, a [mor'tifero, a] a deadly, lethal.

mortificar [mortifi'kar] *vt* (*MED*) to damage, affect seriously; (*fig*) to mortify; ~ **se** *vr* to be (very) embarrassed.

mosca ['moska] *nf* fly.

Moscú [mos'ku] *n* Moscow.

mosquitero [moski'tero] *nm* mosquito net.

mosquito [mos'kito] *nm* mosquito.

mostaza [mos'taθa] *nf* mustard.

mostrador [mostra'ðor] *nm* (*de tienda*) counter; (*de café*) bar; (*de reloj*) face, dial.

mostrar [mos'trar] *vt* (*gen*) to show; (*exhibir*) to display, exhibit; (*explicar*) to explain; ~ **se** *vr*: ~ **se amable** to be kind, to prove to be kind; **no se muestra muy inteligente** he doesn't seem (to be) very intelligent.

mostrenco, a [mos'trenko, a] a ownerless, unclaimed; (*perro*) stray; (*persona*) homeless; (*fam*) dense, slow.

mota ['mota] *nf* speck, tiny piece; (*en diseño*) dot.

mote ['mote] *nm* (*apodo*) nickname; (*sentencia*) motto.

motín [mo'tin] *nm* (*del pueblo*) revolt, rising; (*del ejército*) mutiny.

motivar [moti'βar] *vt* (*causar*) to cause, motivate; (*explicar*) to explain, justify; **motivo, a** a motive // *nm* motive, reason.

moto ['moto] *nf*, **motocicleta** [motoθi'kleta] *nf* motorbike.

motoniveladora [motoniβela'ðora] *nf* bulldozer.

motor [mo'tor] *nm* motor, engine; ~ **a chorro** *o* **de reacción/de explosión** jet engine/internal combustion engine.

motora [mo'tora] *nf*, **motorbote** [motor'βote] *nm* motorboat.

motosierra [moto'sjerra] *nf* mechanical saw.

movedizo, a [moβe'ðiθo, a] a easily moved, movable; (*inseguro*) unsteady; (*fig*) unsettled, changeable; (*persona*) fickle.

mover [mo'βer] *vt* (*gen*) to move; (*cabeza*) to shake; (*accionar*) to drive; (*fig*) to cause, provoke; ~ **se** *vr* to move; (*fig*) to get a move on.

móvil ['moβil] a mobile; (*pieza de máquina*) moving; (*mueble*) movable // *nm* motive; **movilidad** *nf* mobility; **movilizar** *vt* to mobilize.

movimiento [moβi'mjento] *nm* (*gen*) movement; (*TEC*) motion; (*actividad*) activity; **el M**~ the Falangist Movement.

mozo, a ['moθo, a] a (*joven*) young; (*soltero*) single, unmarried // *nm/f* (*joven*) youth, lad/girl; (*criado*) servant // *nm* (*camarero*) waiter.

muchacho, a [mu'tʃatʃo, a] *nm/f* (*niño*) boy/girl; (*criado*) servant/servant or maid.

muchedumbre [mutʃe'ðumbre] *nf* crowd.

mucho, a ['mutʃo, a] a (*sg*) a lot of; (*gen en frase negativa o interrogativa*) much; (*pl*) many, a lot of, lots of // ad (*en cantidad*) a lot, a great deal, much; (*del tiempo*) long; (*muy*) very // *pron*: **tengo** ~ **que hacer** I have a lot to do; ~ **s dicen que** a lot of people say that; **ni** ~ **menos** far from it.

mudanza [mu'ðanθa] *nf* (*cambio*) change; (*de casa*) move; ~ **s** *nfpl* (*fig*) moodiness *sg*.

mudar [mu'ðar] *vt* to change; (*ZOOL*) to shed // *vi* to change; ~ **se** *vr* (*la ropa*) to change; (*de casa*) to move (house).

mudo, a ['muðo, a] a dumb; (*callado, CINE*) silent.

mueble ['mweβle] *nm* piece of furniture; ~ **s** *nmpl* furniture *sg*; ~ **ría** *nf* furniture shop.

mueca ['mweka] *nf* face, grimace; **hacer** ~ **s** a to make faces at.

muela ['mwela] *nf* (*diente*) tooth; (: *de atrás*) molar.

muelle ['mweʎe] a (*blando*) soft; (*elástico*) springy; (*fig*) soft, easy // *nm* spring; (*NAUT*) wharf; (*malecón*) jetty.

muero *etc vb ver* **morir.**

muerte ['mwerte] *nf* death; (*homicidio*) murder; **dar** ~ **a** to kill.

muerto, a ['mwerto, a] *pp de* **morir** // a dead; (*color*) dull // *nm/f* dead man/woman; (*difunto*) deceased;

(*cadáver*) corpse; **estar ~ de cansancio** to be dead tired.

muestra ['mwestra] *nf* (*señal*) indication, sign; (*demostración*) demonstration; (*prueba*) proof; (*estadística*) sample; (*modelo*) model, pattern; (*testimonio*) token; **muestreo** *nm* sample, sampling.

muestro *etc vb ver* **mostrar**.

muevo *etc vb ver* **mover**.

mugir [mu'xir] *vi* (*vaca*) to moo; (*persona*) to roar, howl.

mugre ['muxre] *nf* dirt, filth; **mugriento, a** *a* dirty, filthy.

mujer [mu'xer] *nf* (*de sexo femenino*) woman; (*esposa*) wife; **~iego** *nm* womaniser.

mula ['mula] *nf* mule.

muladar [mula'ðar] *nm* dungheap, dung-hill.

muleta [mu'leta] *nf* (*para andar*) crutch; (*TAUR*) stick with red cape attached; (*fig*) prop, support.

multa ['multa] *nf* fine; **multar** *vt* to fine.

multicopista [multiko'pista] *nm* duplicator.

múltiple ['multiple] *a* multiple; (*pl*) many, numerous.

multiplicar [multipli'kar] *vt* (*MAT*) to multiply; (*fig*) to increase; **~se** *vr* (*BIO*) to multiply; (*fig*) to attend to a lot of things at one time.

multitud [multi'tuð] *nf* (*gentío, muchedumbre*) crowd; **~ de** lots of.

mullido, a [mu'ʎiðo, a] *a* (*cama*) soft; (*hierba*) soft, springy // *nm* stuffing, filling.

mundano, a [mun'dano, a] *a* worldly; (*de moda*) fashionable.

mundial [mun'djal] *a* world-wide, universal; (*guerra, récord*) world *cpd*.

mundo ['mundo] *nm* world; **todo el ~** everybody; **tener ~** to be experienced, know one's way around.

munición [muni'θjon] *nf* (*MIL*) stores *pl*, supplies *pl*; (*de arma*) ammunition.

municipio [muni'θipjo] *nm* (*municipalidad*) town council, corporation; (*comuna*) town, municipality.

muñeca [mu'neka] *nf* (*ANAT*) wrist; (*juguete*) doll; (*maniquí*) dummy.

muñeco [mu'neko] *nm* (*figura*) figure; (*marioneta*) puppet; (*maniquí*) dummy; (*fig*) puppet, pawn.

muralla [mu'raʎa] *nf* (city) wall(s) (*pl*).

murciélago [mur'θjelaxo] *nm* bat.

murmullo [mur'muʎo] *nm* murmur(ing); (*cuchicheo*) whispering; (*de arroyo*) murmur, rippling.

murmuración [murmura'θjon] *nf* gossip; **murmurar** *vi* to murmur, whisper; (*criticar*) to criticize; (*cotillear*) to gossip.

muro ['muro] *nm* wall.

muscular [musku'lar] *a* muscular.

músculo ['muskulo] *nm* muscle.

museo [mu'seo] *nm* museum.

musgo ['musxo] *nm* moss.

músico, a ['musiko, a] *a* musical // *nm/f* musician // *nf* music.

musitar [musi'tar] *vt, vi* to mutter, mumble.

muslo ['muslo] *nm* thigh.

mustio, a ['mustjo, a] *a* (*persona*) depressed, gloomy; (*planta*) faded, withered.

musulmán, ana [musul'man, ana] *nm/f* Moslem.

mutación [muta'θjon] *nf* (*BIO*) mutation; (*cambio*) (sudden) change.

mutilar [muti'lar] *vt* to mutilate; (*a una persona*) to maim.

mutuamente [mutwa'mente] *ad* mutually; **mutuo, a** *a* mutual.

muy [mwi] *ad* very; (*demasiado*) too; **M~ Señor mío** Dear Sir; **~ de noche** very late at night; **eso es ~ de él** that's just like him.

N

N *abr de* **norte**.

n/ *abr de* **nuestro, a.**

nabo ['naβo] *nm* turnip; (*raíz*) root.

nácar ['nakar] *nm* mother-of-pearl.

nacer [na'θer] *vi* to be born; (*de huevo*) to hatch; (*vegetal*) to sprout; (*río*) to rise; **~ al amor** to awaken to love; **nació una sospecha en su mente** a suspicion formed in her mind; **nacido, a** *a* born; **recién nacido** newborn; **naciente** *a* new, emerging; (*sol*) rising; **nacimiento** *nm* birth; (*fig*) birth, origin; (*de Navidad*) Nativity; (*linaje*) descent, family; (*de río*) source.

nación [na'θjon] *nf* nation; **nacional** *a* national; **nacionalismo** *nm* nationalism; **nacionalista** *nm/f* nationalist; **nacionalizar** *vt* to nationalize; **nacionalizarse** *vr* to become naturalized.

nada ['naða] *pron* nothing // *ad* not at all. in no way; **no decir ~** to say nothing, not to say anything; **de ~** don't mention it.

nadaderas [naða'ðeras] *nfpl* waterwings.

nadador, a [naða'ðor, a] *nm/f* swimmer.

nadar [na'ðar] *vi* to swim.

nadie ['naðje] *pron* nobody, no-one; **~ habló** nobody spoke; **no había ~** there was nobody there, there wasn't anybody there.

nado ['naðo]: **a ~** *ad*: **pasar a ~** to swim across.

naipe ['naipe] *nm* playing card; **~s** *nmpl* cards.

nalgas ['nalxas] *nfpl* buttocks.

nana ['nana] *nf* (*fam: abuela*) grandma (*fam*), granny (*fam*); (: *canción*) lullaby.

naranja [na'ranxa] *a, nf* orange; **media ~** (*fam*) better half (*fam*); **~da, a** *a* orange // *nf* orangeade; **naranjo** *nm* orange tree.

narciso [nar'θiso] *nm* narcissus.

narcótico, a [nar'kotiko, a] *a, nm* narcotic; **narcotizar** *vt* to drug.

nardo ['narðo] nm lily.

narigón, ona [nari'ɣon, ona], **narigudo, a** [nari'ɣuðo, a] a big-nosed.

nariz [na'riθ] nf nose; **narices** nfpl nostrils; **en las narices de uno** under one's (very) nose.

narración [narra'θjon] nf narration; **narrador, a** nm/f narrator.

narrar [na'rrar] vt to narrate, recount; **narrativa** nf narrative, story.

nata ['nata] nf cream.

natación [nata'θjon] nf swimming.

natal [na'tal] a: **ciudad ~** home town; **~icio** nm birthday; **~idad** nf birth rate.

natillas [na'tiʎas] nfpl custard sg.

natividad [natiβi'ðað] nf nativity.

nativo, a [na'tiβo, a] a native; (innato) innate, natural // nm/f native.

nato, a ['nato, a] a born; **un músico ~** a born musician.

natural [natu'ral] a natural; (fruta etc) fresh // nm/f native // nm nature; **~eza** nf nature; (género) nature, kind; **~eza muerta** still life; **~idad** nf naturalness; **~ización** nf naturalization; **~izarse** vr to become naturalized; (aclimatarse) to become acclimatized; **~mente** ad naturally.

naufragar [naufra'ɣar] vi to sink; **naufragio** nm shipwreck; **náufrago, a** nm/f castaway, shipwrecked person.

náusea ['nausea] nf nausea; **me da ~** it makes me feel sick; **nauseabundo, a** a nauseating, sickening.

náutico, a ['nautiko, a] a nautical.

nava ['naβa] nf (GEO) level plain.

navaja [na'βaxa] nf (cortaplumas) clasp knife, penknife; (de barbero, peluquero) razor.

navarro, a [na'βarro, a] a Navarrese.

nave ['naβe] nf (barco) ship, vessel; (ARQ) nave; **~ espacial** spaceship.

navegación [naβeɣa'θjon] nf navigation; (viaje) sea journey; **~ aérea** air traffic; **~ costera** coastal shipping; **navegante** nm/f navigator; **navegar** vi (barco) to sail; (avión) to fly // vt to sail; to fly; (dirigir el rumbo) to navigate.

navidad [naβi'ðað] nf Christmas; **navideño, a** a Christmas cpd.

navío [na'βio] nm ship.

nazi ['naθi] a, nm/f Nazi.

neblina [ne'βlina] nf mist.

nebuloso, a [neβu'loso, a] a foggy; (calinoso) misty; (cielo) cloudy; (indefinido) nebulous, vague // nf nebula.

necedad [neθe'ðað] nf foolishness; (una ~) foolish act.

necesario, a [neθe'sarjo, a] a necessary.

neceser [neθe'ser] nm vanity case; (bolsa) holdall; **~ de viaje** travelling case.

necesidad [neθesi'ðað] nf need; (lo inevitable) necessity; (miseria) poverty, need; **en caso de ~** in case of need or emergency; **hacer sus ~es** to relieve o.s.

necesitado, a [neθesi'taðo, a] a needy, poor; **~ de** in need of.

necesitar [neθesi'tar] vt to need, require // vi: **~ de** to have need of.

necio, a ['neθjo, a] a foolish.

necrología [nekrolo'xia] nf obituary.

necrópolis [ne'kropolis] nf cemetery.

nectarina [nekta'rina] nf nectarine.

nefando, a [ne'fando, a] a unspeakable.

nefasto, a [ne'fasto, a] a ill-fated, unlucky.

negación [neɣa'θjon] nf negation; (rechazo) refusal, denial.

negar [ne'ɣar] vt (renegar, rechazar) to refuse; (prohibir) to refuse, deny; (desmentir) to deny; **~se** vr: **~se a** to refuse to.

negativo, a [neɣa'tiβo, a] a, nm negative // nf (gen) negative; (rechazo) refusal, denial.

negligencia [neɣli'xenθja] nf negligence; **negligente** a negligent.

negociable [neɣo'θjaβle] a (COM) negotiable.

negociado [neɣo'θjaðo] nm department, section.

negociante [neɣo'θjante] nm/f businessman/woman; (comerciante) merchant.

negociar [neɣo'θjar] vt, vi to negotiate; **~ en** to deal in, trade in.

negocio [ne'ɣoθjo] nm (COM) business; (asunto) affair, business; (operación comercial) deal, transaction; (AM) firm; (lugar) place of business; **los ~s** business sg; **hacer ~** to do business.

negro, a ['neɣro, a] a black; (suerte) awful // nm black // nm/f Negro/Negress, black // nf (MUS) crotchet; **negrura** nf blackness.

nene, a ['nene, a] nm/f baby, small child; (fam) dear.

nenúfar [ne'nufar] nm water lily.

neologismo [neolo'xismo] nm neologism.

neoyorquino, a [neojor'kino, a] a (of) New York.

nepotismo [nepo'tismo] nm nepotism.

nervio ['nerβjo] nm (ANAT) nerve; (: tendón) tendon; (fig) vigour; **~sidad** nf nervousness, nerves pl; **~so, a, nervudo, a** a nervous.

neto, a ['neto, a] a clear; (verdad etc) pure; (limpio) clean; (COM) net.

neumático, a [neu'matiko, a] a pneumatic // nm tyre; **~ de recambio** spare tyre.

neuralgia [neu'ralxja] nf neuralgia.

neurastenia [neuras'tenja] nf nervous exhaustion.

neuritis [neu'ritis] nf neuritis.

neurólogo, a [neu'roloɣo, a] nm/f neurologist.

neurosis [neu'rosis] nf inv neurosis.

neutral [neu'tral] a neutral; **~izar** vt to neutralize; (contrarrestar) to counteract.

neutro, a ['neutro, a] a (BIO) neuter, sexless; (LING) neuter.

neutrón [neu'tron] *nm* neutron; **bomba de neutrones** neutron bomb.

nevada [ne'βaða] *nf* snowstorm; (*caída de nieve*) snowfall.

nevar [ne'βar] *vi* to snow; **nevasca** *nf* snowstorm.

nevera [ne'βera] *nf* refrigerator, icebox.

nevisca [ne'βiska] *nf* flurry of snow; (*aguanieve*) sleet; **neviscar** *vi* to snow lightly; to sleet.

ni [ni] *conj* nor, neither; (~ *siquiera*) not ... even; ~ **que** not even if; ~ **blanco** ~ **negro** neither white nor black.

Nicaragua [nika'raɣwa] *nf* Nicaragua; **nicaragüense** *a, nm/f* Nicaraguan.

nicotina [niko'tina] *nf* nicotine.

nicho ['nitʃo] *nm* niche.

nido [niðo] *nm* nest; (*fig*) hiding place; (*lugar predilecto*) haunt.

niebla ['njeβla] *nf* fog; (*neblina*) mist.

niego *etc vb ver* **negar**.

nieto, a ['njeto, a] *nm/f* grandson/daughter; ~**s** *nmpl* grandchildren.

nieva *etc vb ver* **nevar**.

nieve ['njeβe] *nf* snow.

nigromancia [niɣro'manθja] *nf* necromancy, black magic.

nihilismo [nii'lismo] *nm* nihilism.

Nilo ['nilo] *nm*: **el** ~ the Nile.

nimbo ['nimbo] *nm* (*aureola*) halo; (*nube*) nimbus.

nimiedad [nimje'ðað] *nf* small-mindedness; (*prolijidad*) long-windedness; (*trivialidad*) triviality.

nimio, a ['nimjo, a] *a* (*insignificante*) trivial, insignificant; (*escrupuloso*) fussy, overparticular.

ninfa ['ninfa] *nf* nymph.

ninfómana, a [nin'fomana] *nf* nymphomaniac.

ninguno, a [nin'guno, a], **ningún** [nin'gun] *a* no // *pron* (*nadie*) nobody; (*ni uno*) none, not one; (*ni uno ni otro*) neither; **de** ~**a manera** by no means, not at all.

niña ['niɲa] *nf ver* **niño**.

niñera [ni'ɲera] *nf* nursemaid, nanny; **niñería** *nf* childish act.

niñez [ni'ɲeθ] *nf* childhood; (*infancia*) infancy.

niño, a ['niɲo, a] *a* (*joven*) young; (*inmaduro*) immature // *nm* (*chico*) boy, child // *nf* (*chica*) girl, child; (*ANAT*) pupil.

nipón, ona [ni'pon, ona] *a, nm/f* Japanese.

níquel ['nikel] *nm* nickel; **niquelar** *vt* (*TEC*) to nickel-plate.

nitidez [niti'ðeθ] *nf* (*claridad*) clarity; (: *de atmósfera*) brightness; (: *de imagen*) sharpness; **nítido, a** *a* clear; sharp.

nitrato [ni'trato] *nm* nitrate.

nitrógeno [ni'troxeno] *nm* nitrogen.

nitroglicerina [nitroɣliθe'rina] *nf* nitroglycerine.

nivel [ni'βel] *nm* (*GEO*) level; (*norma*) level, standard; (*altura*) height; ~ **de aceite** oil level; ~ **de aire** spirit level; ~ **de vida** standard of living; ~**ar** *vt*

(*terreno*) to level out; (*equilibrar: mueble*) to even up; (*COM*) to balance.

NN. UU. *nfpl abr de* **Naciones Unidas** U.N. *sg* (United Nations).

no [no] *ad* no; not; (*con verbo*) not // *excl* no!; ~ **tengo nada** I don't have anything, I have nothing; ~ **es el mío** it's not mine; **ahora** ~ not now; ¿~ **lo sabes?** don't you know?; ~ **mucho** not much; ~ **bien termine, lo entregaré** as soon as I finish I'll hand it over; ¡**a que** ~ **lo sabes!** I bet you don't know!; ¡**cuándo** *o* **cómo** ~! of course!; **los países** ~ **alineados** the non-aligned countries; **el** ~ **conformismo** non-conformism; **la** ~ **intervención** non-intervention.

NO *abr de* **noroeste**.

no. *abr de* **número**.

noble ['noβle] *a, nm/f* noble; ~**za** *nf* nobility.

noción [no'θjon] *nf* notion.

nocivo, a [no'θiβo, a] *a* harmful.

noctambulismo [noktambu'lismo] *nm* sleepwalking; **noctámbulo, a** *nm/f* sleepwalker.

nocturno, a [nok'turno, a] *a* (*de la noche*) nocturnal, night *cpd*; (*de la tarde*) evening *cpd* // *nm* nocturne.

noche ['notʃe] *nf* night, night-time; (*la tarde*) evening; (*fig*) darkness; **de** ~, **por la** ~ at night.

nochebuena [notʃe'βwena] *nf* Christmas Eve.

nochevieja [notʃe'βjexa] *nf* New Year's Eve.

nodriza [no'ðriθa] *nf* wet nurse.

nogal [no'ɣal] *nm* walnut tree.

nómada ['nomaða] *a* nomadic // *nm/f* nomad.

nombradía [nombra'ðia] *nf* fame.

nombramiento [nombra'mjento] *nm* naming; (*a un empleo*) appointment.

nombrar [nom'brar] *vt* (*designar*) to name; (*mencionar*) to mention; (*dar puesto a*) to appoint.

nombre ['nombre] *nm* name; (*sustantivo*) noun; (*fama*) renown; ~ **y apellidos** name in full; ~ **común/propio** common/proper noun; ~ **de pila/de soltera** Christian/maiden name.

nomenclatura [nomenkla'tura] *nf* nomenclature.

nomeolvides [nomeol'βiðes] *nm inv* forget-me-not.

nómina ['nomina] *nf* (*lista*) list; (*COM*) payroll.

nominal [nomi'nal] *a* nominal.

nominativo, a [nomina'tiβo, a] *a* (*COM*): **cheque** ~ **a X** cheque made out to X.

non [non] *a* odd, uneven // *nm* odd number.

nonada [no'naða] *nf* trifle.

nono, a ['nono, a] *a* ninth.

nordeste [nor'ðeste] *a* north-east, north-eastern, north-easterly // *nm* north-east.

nórdico, a ['norðiko, a] *a* (*del norte*) northern, northerly; (*escandinavo*) Nordic.

noria ['norja] *nf* (AGR) waterwheel; (*de carnaval*) big wheel.

normal [nor'mal] *a* (*corriente*) normal; (*habitual*) usual, natural; (**gasolina**) ~ two-star petrol; **~idad** *nf* normality; **restablecer la ~idad** to restore order; **~izar** *vt* (*reglamentar*) to normalize; (TEC) to standardize; **~izarse** *vr* to return to normal.

normando, a [nor'mando, a] *a, nm/f* Norman.

noroeste [noro'este] *a* north-west, north-western, north-westerly // *nm* north-west.

norte ['norte] *a* north, northern, northerly // *nm* north; (fig) guide.

norteamericano, a [norteameri'kano, a] *a, nm/f* (North) American.

noruego, a [no'rweɣo, a] *a, nm/f* Norwegian; N~a *nf* Norway.

nos [nos] *pron* (*directo*) us; (*indirecto*) us; to us; for us; from us; (*reflexivo*) (to) ourselves; (*recíproco*) (to) each other; ~ **levantamos a las 7** we get up at 7.

nosotros [no'sotros] *pron* (*sujeto*) we; (*después de prep*) us.

nostalgia [nos'talxja] *nf* nostalgia.

nota ['nota] *nf* note; (ESCOL) mark.

notabilidad [notaβili'ðað] *nf* (*persona*) notable.

notable [no'taβle] *a, nm/f* notable.

notación [nota'θjon] *nf* (*nota*) note; (MAT, MUS) notation.

notar [no'tar] *vt* (*advertir*) to notice, note; (*anotar, asentar*) to note (down); (*censurar*) to criticize; **~se** *vr* to be obvious.

notarial [nota'rjal] *a*: **acta** ~ affidavit.

notario [no'tarjo] *nm* notary.

noticia [no'tiθja] *nf* (*información*) piece of news; **las ~s** the news *sg*; **tener ~s de alguien** to hear from sb.

noticiar [noti'θjar] *vt* to notify; **~lo** *nm* (CINE) newsreel; (TV) news bulletin; **noticioso, a** *a* well-informed.

notificación [notifika'θjon] *nf* notification; **notificar** *vt* to notify, inform.

notoriedad [notorje'ðað] *nf* fame, renown; **notorio, a** *a* (*público*) well-known; (*evidente*) obvious.

novato, a [no'βato, a] *a* inexperienced // *nm/f* beginner.

novecientos [noβe'θjentos] *num* nine hundred.

novedad [noβe'ðað] *nf* (*calidad de nuevo*) newness; (*noticia*) piece of news; (*cambio*) change, (new) development.

novedoso, a [noβe'ðoso, a] *a* novel.

novel [no'βel] *a* new; (*inexperto*) inexperienced // *nm/f* beginner.

novela [no'βela] *nf* novel.

novelero, a [noβe'lero, a] *a* highly imaginative; (*voluble*) fickle; (*chismoso*) gossipy.

novelesco, a [noβe'lesko, a] *a* fictional; (*romántico*) romantic; (*fantástico*) fantastic.

noveno, a [no'βeno, a] *a* ninth.

noventa [no'βenta] *num* ninety.

novia ['noβja] *nf ver* **novio**.

noviazgo [no'βjaɣo] *nm* engagement.

novicio [no'βiθjo, a] *nm/f* novice.

noviembre [no'βjembre] *nm* November.

novilla [no'βiʎa] *nf* heifer; **~da** *nf* (TAUR) bullfight with young bulls; **novillero** *nm* novice bullfighter; **novillo** *nm* young bull; **hacer novillos** (*fam*) to play truant.

novio, a ['noβjo, a] *nm/f* boyfriend/girlfriend; (*prometido*) fiancé/fiancée; (*recién casado*) bridegroom/bride; **los ~s** the newly-weds.

N. S. *abr de* **Nuestro Señor.**

nubarrón [nuβa'rron] *nm* storm cloud.

nube ['nuβe] *nf* cloud.

nublado, a [nu'βlaðo, a] *a* cloudy // *nm* storm cloud; **nublar** *vt* (*oscurecer*) to darken; (*confundir*) to cloud; **nublarse** *vr* to grow dark.

nuca ['nuka] *nf* nape of the neck.

nuclear [nukle'ar] *a* nuclear.

núcleo [nu'kleo] *nm* (*centro*) core; (FÍSICA) nucleus.

nudillo [nu'ðiʎo] *nm* knuckle.

nudo ['nuðo] *nm* (*gen*) knot; (*unión*) bond; (*de problema*) crux; (*de comunicaciones*) centre; **~so, a** *a* knotty.

nuera ['nwera] *nf* daughter-in-law.

nuestro, a ['nwestro, a] *det* our // *pron* ours; ~ **padre** our father; **un amigo** ~ a friend of ours; **es el** ~ it's ours.

nueva ['nweβa] *nf ver* **nuevo**.

nuevamente [nweβa'mente] *ad* (*otra vez*) again; (*de nuevo*) anew.

nueve ['nweβe] *num* nine.

nuevo, a ['nweβo, a] *a* (*gen*) new // *nf* piece of news; **de** ~ again; N~a **York** *nf* New York; N~a **Zelandia** *nf* New Zealand.

nuez [nweθ] (*pl* **nueces**) *nf* (*fruto*) nut; (*del nogal*) walnut; ~ **de Adán** Adam's apple; ~ **moscada** nutmeg.

nulidad [nuli'ðað] *nf* (*incapacidad*) incompetence; (*abolición*) nullity.

nulo, a ['nulo, a] *a* (*inepto, torpe*) useless; (*inválido*) (null and) void; (DEPORTE) drawn, tied.

núm. *abr de* **número.**

numen ['numen] *nm* inspiration.

numeración [numera'θjon] *nf* (*cifras*) numbers *pl*; (*arábiga, romana etc*) numerals *pl*.

numeral [nume'ral] *nm* numeral.

numerar [nume'rar] *vt* to number.

numerario [nume'rarjo] *nm* hard cash.

numérico, a [nu'meriko, a] *a* numerical.

número ['numero] *nm* (*gen*) number; (*tamaño: de zapato*) size; (*ejemplar: de diario*) number, issue; **sin** ~ numberless, unnumbered; ~ **de matrícula/telefónico** registration/telephone number; ~ **atrasado** back number.

numeroso, a [nume'roso, a] *a* numerous.

nunca ['nunka] *ad* (*jamás*) never; ~ **lo pensé** I never thought it; **no vino** ~ he

never came; ~ **más** never again.
nuncio ['nunθjo] *nm* (*REL*) nuncio.
nupcias ['nupθjas] *nfpl* wedding *sg*, nuptials.
nutria ['nutrja] *nf* otter.
nutrición [nutri'θjon] *nf* nutrition.
nutrido, a [nu'triðo, a] *a* (*alimentado*) nourished; (*fig: grande*) large; (*abundante*) abundant.
nutrir [nu'trir] *vt* (*alimentar*) to nourish; (*dar de comer*) to feed; (*alentar*) to encourage; (*esperanzas*) to cherish; **nutritivo, a** *a* nourishing, nutritious.
nylon [ni'lon] *nm* nylon.

Ñ

ñame ['ɲame] *nm* yam.
ñaque ['ɲake] *nm* junk.
ñato, a ['ɲato, a] *a* (*AM*) snub-nosed.
ñoñería [ɲoɲe'ria], **ñoñez** [ɲo'ɲeθ] *nf* insipidness.
ñoño, a ['ɲoɲo, a] *a* (*AM: tonto*) silly, stupid; (*soso*) insipid; (*persona*) spineless.

O

o [o] *conj* or.
O *abr de* **oeste**.
o/ *abr de* **orden**.
oasis [o'asis] *nm* oasis.
obcecar [oβθe'kar] *vt* to blind.
obedecer [oβeðe'θer] *vt* to obey; **obediencia** *nf* obedience; **obediente** *a* obedient.
obertura [oβer'tura] *nf* overture.
obesidad [oβesi'ðað] *nf* obesity; **obeso, a** *a* obese.
obispo [o'βispo] *nm* bishop.
objeción [oβxe'θjon] *nf* objection; **objetar** *vt, vi* to object.
objetivo, a [oβxe'tiβo, a] *a, nm* objective.
objeto [oβ'xeto] *nm* (*cosa*) object; (*fin*) aim.
oblicuo, a [o'βlikwo, a] *a* oblique; (*mirada*) sidelong.
obligación [oβliɣa'θjon] *nf* obligation; (*COM*) bond.
obligar [oβli'ɣar] *vt* to force; ~**se** *vr* to bind o.s.; **obligatorio, a** *a* compulsory, obligatory.
oboe [o'βoe] *nm* oboe.
obra ['oβra] *nf* (*gen*) work; (*hechura*) piece of work; (*ARQ*) construction, building; (*TEATRO*) play; ~ **maestra** masterpiece; (**Ministerio de**) **O**~**s Públicas** Ministry of Public Works; **en** ~ **de** in about; **por** ~ **de** thanks to (the efforts of); **obrar** *vt* to work; (*tener efecto*) to have an effect on // *vi* to act, behave; (*tener efecto*) to have an effect; **la carta obra en su poder** the letter is in his/her possession; **obrero, a** *a* working, labour *cpd*; **clase obrera** working class // *nm/f* (*gen*) worker; (*sin oficio*) labourer.

obscenidad [oβsθeni'ðað] *nf* obscenity; **obsceno, a** *a* obscene.
obscu... = oscu... .
obsequiar [oβse'kjar] *vt* (*ofrecer*) to present with; (*agasajar*) to make a fuss of, lavish attention on; **obsequio** *nm* (*regalo*) gift; (*cortesía*) courtesy, attention; **obsequioso, a** *a* attentive.
observación [oβserβa'θjon] *nf* observation; (*reflexión*) remark.
observancia [oβser'βanθja] *nf* observance.
observar [oβser'βar] *vt* to observe; (*anotar*) to notice; ~**se** *vr* to keep to, observe.
obsesión [oβse'sjon] *nf* obsession; **obsesionar** *vt* to obsess.
obstaculizar [oβstakuli'θar] *vt* (*dificultar*) to hinder; (*impedir*) to stand in the way of.
obstáculo [oβ'stakulo] *nm* (*gen*) obstacle; (*impedimento*) hindrance, drawback.
obstante [oβ'stante]: **no** ~ *ad* nevertheless // *prep* in spite of.
obstar [oβ'star] *vi*: ~ **a** to hinder.
obstetricia [oβste'triθja] *nf* obstetrics *sg*; **obstétrico, a** *a* obstetric // *nm/f* obstetrician.
obstinado, a [oβsti'naðo, a] *a* (*gen*) obstinate; (*terco*) stubborn.
obstinarse [oβsti'narse] *vr* to be obstinate; ~ **en** to persist in.
obstrucción [oβstruk'θjon] *nf* obstruction; **obstruir** *vt* to obstruct.
obtener [oβte'ner] *vt* (*conseguir*) to obtain; (*ganar*) to gain.
obtuso, a [oβ'tuso, a] *a* (*filo*) blunt; (*MAT, fig*) obtuse.
obviar [oβ'βjar] *vt* to clear away // *vi* to stand in the way.
obvio, a ['oββjo, a] *a* obvious.
ocasión [oka'sjon] *nf* (*oportunidad*) opportunity, chance; (*momento*) occasion, time; (*causa*) cause; **de** ~ secondhand; **ocasionar** *vt* to cause.
ocaso [o'kaso] *nm* (*oeste*) west; (*fig*) decline.
occidente [okθi'ðente] *nm* west.
océano [o'θeano] *nm* ocean; **el** ~ **Índico** the Indian Ocean.
O.C.E.D. *nf abr de* **Organización de Cooperación Económica y Desarrollo** OECD (Organization for Economic Cooperation and Development).
ocio ['oθjo] *nm* (*tiempo*) leisure; (*pey*) idleness; ~**s** *nmpl* pastime *sg*; ~**sidad** *nf* idleness; ~**so, a** *a* (*inactivo*) idle; (*inútil*) useless.
octanaje [okta'naxe] *nm*: **de alto** ~ high octane; **octano** *nm* octane.
octavín [okta'βin] *nm* piccolo.
octavo, a [ok'taβo, a] *a* eighth.
octogenario, a [oktoxe'narjo, a] *a* octogenarian.
octubre [ok'tuβre] *nm* October.
ocular [oku'lar] *a* ocular, eye *cpd*; **testigo** ~ eyewitness.

oculista [oku'lista] *nm/f* oculist.

ocultar [okul'tar] *vt* (*esconder*) to hide; (*callar*) to withhold; **oculto, a** *a* hidden; (*fig*) secret.

ocupación [okupa'θjon] *nf* occupation.

ocupado, a [oku'paðo, a] *a* (*persona*) busy; (*sitio*) occupied; (*teléfono*) engaged; **ocupar** *vt* (*gen*) to occupy; **ocuparse** *vr*: **ocuparse con** *o* **de** *o* **en** (*gen*) to concern o.s. with; (*cuidar*) to look after.

ocurrencia [oku'rrenθja] *nf* (*ocasión*) occurrence; (*agudeza*) witticism.

ocurrir [oku'rrir] *vi* to happen; **~se** *vr*: **se me ocurre que...** it occurs to me that... .

ochenta [o'tʃenta] *num* eighty.

ocho ['otʃo] *num* eight.

odiar [o'ðjar] *vt* to hate; **odio** *nm* (*gen*) hate, hatred; (*disgusto*) dislike; **odioso, a** *a* (*gen*) hateful; (*malo*) nasty.

O.E.A. *nf abr de* **Organización de Estados Americanos** O.A.S. (Organization of American States).

oeste [o'este] *nm* west; **una película del ~** a western.

ofender [ofen'der] *vt* (*agraviar*) to offend; (*ser ofensivo a*) to be offensive to; **~se** *vr* to take offence; **ofensa** *nf* offence; **ofensivo, a** *a* (*insultante*) insulting; (*MIL*) offensive // *nf* offensive.

oferta [o'ferta] *nf* offer; (*propuesta*) proposal; **la ~ y la demanda** supply and demand; **artículos en ~** goods on offer.

oficial [ofi'θjal] *a* official // *nm* official; (*MIL*) officer.

oficina [ofi'θina] *nf* office; **oficinista** *nm/f* clerk.

oficio [o'fiθjo] *nm* (*profesión*) profession; (*puesto*) post; (*REL*) service; **ser del ~** to be an old hand; **tener mucho ~** to have a lot of experience; **~ de difuntos** funeral service; **de ~** officially.

oficiosidad [ofiθjosi'ðað] *nf* helpfulness; (*pey*) officiousness.

oficioso, a [ofi'θjoso, a] *a* (*diligente*) attentive; (*pey*) officious; (*no oficial*) unofficial, informal.

ofrecer [ofre'θer] *vt* (*dar*) to offer; (*proponer*) to propose; **~se** *vr* (*persona*) to offer o.s., volunteer; (*situación*) to present itself; **¿qué se le ofrece?, ¿se le ofrece algo?** what can I do for you?, can I get you anything?

ofrecimiento [ofreθi'mjento] *nm* offer, offering.

ofrendar [ofren'dar] *vt* to offer, contribute.

oftálmico, a [of'talmiko, a] *a* ophthalmic.

ofuscación [ofuska'θjon] *nf*, **ofuscamiento** [ofuska'mjento] *nm* (*fig*) bewilderment; **ofuscar** *vt* (*confundir*) to bewilder; (*enceguecer*) to dazzle, blind.

oída [o'iða] *nf* hearing; **de ~s** by hearsay.

oído [o'iðo] *nm* ear; (*sentido*) hearing.

oigo *etc vb ver* **oír.**

oír [o'ir] *vt* (*gen*) to hear; (*atender a*) to listen to; **¡oiga!** listen!; **~ misa** to attend mass.

O.I.T. *nf abr de* **Organización Internacional del Trabajo** I.L.O. (International Labour Organization).

ojal [o'xal] *nm* buttonhole.

ojalá [oxa'la] *excl* if only it were so!, some hope(s)! // *conj* if only...!, would that...!; **~ que venga hoy** I hope he comes today.

ojeada [oxe'aða] *nf* glance; **ojear** *vt* (*mirar fijo*) to stare at; (*examinar*) to eye; (*mirar de reojo*) to glance at.

ojera [o'xera] *nf*: **tener ~s** to have rings or circles under the eyes.

ojeriza [oxe'riθa] *nf* ill-will.

ojeroso, a [oxe'roso, a] *a* haggard.

ojete [o'xete] *nm* eye(let).

ojo ['oxo] *nm* eye; (*de puente*) span; (*de cerradura*) keyhole // *excl* careful!; **tener ~ para** to have an eye for; **~ de buey** porthole.

ola ['ola] *nf* wave.

olé [o'le] *excl* bravo!, olé!

oleada [ole'aða] *nf* big wave, swell; (*fig*) surge.

oleaje [ole'axe] *nm* swell.

óleo ['oleo] *nm* oil; **oleoducto** *nm* (oil) pipeline.

oler [o'ler] *vt* (*gen*) to smell; (*husmear*) to pry into; (*fig*) to sniff out // *vi*: **~ a** to smell of.

olfatear [olfate'ar] *vt* to smell; (*fig*) to sniff out; (*husmear*) to pry into; **olfato** *nm* sense of smell.

oliente [o'ljente] *a* smelling; **bien/mal ~** sweet-/foul-smelling.

oligarquía [oliɣar'kia] *nf* oligarchy.

olimpíada [olim'piaða] *nf*: **las O~s** the Olympics.

oliva [o'liβa] *nf* (*aceituna*) olive; (*árbol*) olive tree; **aceite de ~** olive oil; **olivo** *nm* olive tree.

olmo ['olmo] *nm* elm (tree).

olor [o'lor] *nm* smell; **~oso, a** *a* scented.

olvidadizo, a [olβiða'ðiθo, a] *a* (*desmemoriado*) forgetful; (*distraído*) absent-minded.

olvidar [olβi'ðar] *vt* to forget; (*omitir*) to omit; **~se** *vr* to forget o.s.; **se me olvidó** I forgot.

olvido [ol'βiðo] *nm* oblivion.

olla ['oʎa] *nf* pan; (*comida*) stew; **~ a presión** *o* **autopresión** pressure cooker; **~ podrida** Spanish stew.

ombligo [om'bliɣo] *nm* navel.

ominoso, a [omi'noso, a] *a* ominous.

omisión [omi'sjon] *nf* (*abstención*) omission; (*descuido*) neglect.

omiso, a [o'miso, a] *a*: **hacer caso ~ de** to ignore, pass over.

omitir [omi'tir] *vt* to omit.

omnipotente [omnipo'tente] *a* omnipotent.

omnívoro, a [om'niβoro, a] *a* omnivorous.

omóplato [o'moplato] *nm* shoulder blade.

O.M.S. *nf abr de* **Organización Mundial**

de la Salud W.H.O. (World Health Organization).

once ['onθe] num eleven; las ~ (fam) elevenses.

onda ['onda] nf wave; ~ corta/larga/media short/long/ medium wave; ~s acústicas/ hertzianas acoustic/Hertzian waves; ondear vt to wave // vi to wave; (tener ondas) to be wavy; (pelo) to flow; (agua) to ripple; ondearse vr to swing, sway.

ondulación [ondula'θjon] nf undulation; ondulado, a a wavy // nm wave; ondulante a undulating; (cartón, chapa) corrugated.

ondular [ondu'lar] vt (el pelo) to wave // vi, ~ se vr to undulate.

oneroso, a [one'roso, a] a onerous.

ONU nf abr de Organización de las Naciones Unidas UNO (United Nations Organization).

O.P. nfpl abr de Obras Públicas Public Works.

opaco, a [o'pako, a] a opaque; (fig) dull.

opalescente [opales'θente] a opalescent.

ópalo ['opalo] nm opal.

opción [op'θjon] nf (gen) option; (derecho) right, option.

ópera ['opera] nf opera; ~ bufa o cómica comic opera.

operación [opera'θjon] nf (gen) operation; (COM) transaction, deal.

operador, a [opera'ðor, a] nm/f operator; (en cine) projectionist; (de cine) camera operator.

operante [ope'rante] a operating.

operar [ope'rar] vt (producir) to produce, bring about; (MED) to operate on // vi (COM) to operate, deal; ~ se vr to occur; (MED) to have an operation.

opereta [ope'reta] nf operetta.

opinar [opi'nar] vt (estimar) to think // vi (enjuiciar) to give one's opinion; opinión nf (creencia) belief; (criterio) opinion.

opio ['opjo] nm opium.

oponente [opo'nente] nm/f opponent.

oponer [opo'ner] vt (resistencia) to put up, offer; (negativa) to raise; ~ se vr (objetar) to object; (estar frente a frente) to be opposed; (dos personas) to oppose each other; ~ A a B to set A against B; me opongo a pensar que... I refuse to believe or think that... .

oportunidad [oportuni'ðað] nf (ocasión) opportunity; (posibilidad) chance.

oportunismo [oportu'nismo] nm opportunism; oportunista nm/f opportunist.

oportuno, a [opor'tuno, a] a (apto) appropriate, suitable; (en su tiempo) opportune; (conveniente) convenient; en el momento ~ at the right moment.

oposición [oposi'θjon] nf opposition; oposiciones nfpl public examinations.

opositor, a [oposi'tor, a] nm/f (adversario) opponent; (concurrente) competitor.

opresión [opre'sjon] nf oppression;

opresivo, a a oppressive; opresor, a nm/f oppressor.

oprimir [opri'mir] vt to squeeze; (fig) to oppress.

oprobio [o'proβjo] nm (infamia) ignominy; (descrédito) shame.

optar [op'tar] vi (elegir) to choose; ~ a o por to opt for.

óptico, a ['optiko, a] a optic(al) // nm/f optician.

optimismo [opti'mismo] nm optimism; optimista nm/f optimist.

óptimo, a ['optimo, a] a (bueno) very good; (el mejor) very best.

opuesto, a [o'pwesto, a] a (contrario) opposite; (antagónico) opposing.

opugnar [opuɣ'nar] vt to attack.

opulencia [opu'lenθja] nf opulence; opulento, a a opulent.

oquedad [oke'ðað] nf (fig) void.

ora ['ora] ad: ~ tú ~ yo now you, now me.

oración [ora'θjon] nf (discurso) speech; (REL) prayer; (LING) sentence.

oráculo [o'rakulo] nm oracle.

orador, a [ora'ðor, a] nm/f (predicador) preacher; (conferenciante) speaker.

oral [o'ral] a oral.

orangután [orangu'tan] nm orang-utan.

orar [o'rar] vi (REL) to pray; (hablar) to make a speech.

oratoria [ora'torja] nf oratory.

órbita ['orβita] nf orbit.

orden ['orðen] nm (gen) order // nf (gen) order; ~ del día agenda; de primer ~ first-rate; en ~ de prioridad in order of priority.

ordenado, a [orðe'naðo, a] a (metódico) methodical; (arreglado) orderly.

ordenador [orðena'ðor] nm computer.

ordenanza [orðe'nanθa] nf ordinance.

ordenar [orðe'nar] vt (mandar) to order; (poner orden) to put in order, arrange; ~ se vr (REL) to be ordained.

ordeñadora [orðeɲa'ðora] nf milking machine.

ordeñar [orðe'ɲar] vt to milk.

ordinario, a [orði'narjo, a] a (común) ordinary, usual; (bajo) vulgar, common.

orégano [o'reɣano] nm oregano.

oreja [o'rexa] nf ear; (de zapatos) tongue; (MECÁNICA) lug, flange.

orfandad [orfan'dað] nf orphanhood.

orfebrería [orfeβre'ria] nf gold/silver work.

organillo [orɣa'niʎo] nm barrel organ.

organismo [orɣa'nismo] nm (BIO) organism; (POL) organization.

organista [orɣa'nista] nm/f organist.

organización [orɣaniθa'θjon] nf organization; organizar vt to organize.

órgano ['orɣano] nm organ.

orgasmo [or'ɣasmo] nm orgasm.

orgía [or'xia] nf orgy.

orgullo [or'ɣuʎo] nm (altanería) pride; (autorespeto) self-respect; orgulloso, a a *(gen)* proud; *(altanero)* haughty.

orientación [orjenta'θjon] *nf (posición)* position; *(dirección)* direction; *(entrenamiento)* training.

orientar [orjen'tar] *vt (situar)* to orientate; *(señalar)* to point; *(dirigir)* to direct; *(informar)* to guide; ~ **se** *vr* to get one's bearings; *(decidirse)* to decide on a course of action.

oriente [o'rjente] *nm* east; **Cercano/Medio/Lejano O~** Near/Middle/Far East.

origen [o'rixen] *nm (germen)* origin; *(nacimiento)* lineage, birth.

original [orixi'nal] *a (nuevo)* original; *(extraño)* odd, strange; **~idad** *nf* originality.

originar [orixi'nar] *vt* to originate; ~ **se** *vr* to originate; **~io, a** *a (nativo)* native; *(primordial)* original.

orilla [o'riʎa] *nf (borde)* border; *(de río)* bank; *(de bosque, tela)* edge; *(de taza etc)* rim, lip; *(de calle)* pavement; **orillar** *vt (bordear)* to skirt, go round; *(resolver)* to wind up; *(tocar: asunto)* to touch briefly on.

orín [o'rin] *nm* rust.

orina [o'rina] *nf* urine; **orinal** *nm (chamber)* pot; **orinar** *vi* to urinate; **orinarse** *vr* to wet o.s.; **orines** *nmpl* urine *sg.*

oriundo, a [o'rjundo, a] *a*: ~ **de** native of.

orlar [or'lar] *vt (adornar)* to adorn, decorate; *(encuadrar)* to frame.

ornamentar [ornamen'tar] *vt (adornar, ataviar)* to adorn; *(revestir)* to bedeck.

ornamento [orna'mento] *nm* ornament.

ornar [or'nar] *vt* to adorn.

oro ['oro] *nm* gold; **~s** *nmpl (NAIPES)* hearts.

oropel [oro'pel] *nm* tinsel.

orozuz [oro'θuθ] *nm* liquorice.

orquesta [or'kesta] *nf* orchestra; ~ **de cámara/sinfónica** chamber/symphony orchestra.

orquídea [or'kiðea] *nf* orchid.

ortiga [or'tixa] *nf* nettle.

ortodoxo, a [orto'ðokso, a] *a* orthodox.

ortografía [ortoxra'fia] *nf* spelling.

ortopedia [orto'peðja] *nf* orthopaedics *sg.*

oruga [o'ruxa] *nf* caterpillar; *(BOT)* rocket.

orzuelo [or'θwelo] *nm (MED)* stye.

os [os] *pron (gen)* you; *(a vosotros)* to you.

osa ['osa] *nf* (she-)bear; **O~ Mayor/Menor** Great/Little Bear.

osadía [osa'ðia] *nf* daring.

osar [o'sar] *vi* to dare.

oscilación [osθila'θjon] *nf (movimiento)* oscillation; *(fluctuación)* fluctuation; *(vacilación)* hesitation; *(columpio)* swinging, movement to and fro; **oscilar** *vi* to oscillate; to fluctuate; to hesitate.

ósculo ['oskulo] *nm* kiss.

oscurecer [oskure'θer] *vt* to darken // *vi* to grow dark; ~ **se** *vr* to grow *or* get dark.

oscuridad [oskuri'ðað] *nf* obscurity; *(tinieblas)* darkness.

oscuro, a [os'kuro, a] *a* dark; *(fig)* obscure; **a ~as** in the dark.

óseo, a ['oseo, a] *a* bony.

oso ['oso] *nm* bear; ~ **de peluche** teddy bear; ~ **hormiguero** anteater.

ostensible [osten'siβle] *a* obvious.

ostentación [ostenta'θjon] *nf (gen)* ostentation; *(acto)* display; **ostentar** *vt (gen)* to show; *(pey)* to flaunt, show off; *(poseer)* to have, possess; **ostentoso, a** *a* ostentatious, showy.

osteópata [oste'opata] *nm/f* osteopath.

ostra ['ostra] *nf* oyster.

ostracismo [ostra'θismo] *nm* ostracism.

osuno, a [o'suno, a] *a* bear-like.

OTAN ['otan] *nf abr de* **Organización del Tratado del Atlántico Norte** NATO (North Atlantic Treaty Organization).

otear [ote'ar] *vt* to observe; *(fig)* to look into.

otitis [o'titis] *nf* earache.

otoñal [oto'ñal] *a* autumnal.

otoño [o'toño] *nm* autumn.

otorgamiento [otorxa'mjento] *nm* conferring, granting; *(JUR)* execution.

otorgar [otor'xar] *vt (conceder)* to concede; *(dar)* to grant.

otro, a ['otro, a] *a (sg)* another; *(pl)* other // *pron* another one; ~ **s** others; ~ **a cosa** something else; **de ~a manera** otherwise; **en ~ tiempo** formerly, once; **ni uno ni ~** neither one nor the other; ~ **tanto** the same again.

ovación [oβa'θjon] *nf* ovation.

oval [o'βal], **ovalado, a** [oβa'laðo, a] *a* oval; **óvalo** *nm* oval.

oveja [o'βexa] *nf* sheep; **ovejuno, a** *a* sheep *cpd.*

overol [oβe'rol] *nm* overalls *pl.*

ovillar [oβi'ʎar] *vt* to wind (into a ball); ~ **se** *vr* to curl up into a ball.

OVNI ['oβni] *nm abr de* **objeto volante no identificado** UFO (unidentified flying object).

ovulación [oβula'θjon] *nf* ovulation; **óvulo** *nm* ovum.

oxidación [oksiða'θjon] *nf* rusting; **oxidar** *vt* to rust; **oxidarse** *vr* to become rusty.

óxido ['oksiðo] *nm* oxide.

oxigenado, a [oksixe'naðo, a] *a (QUÍMICA)* oxygenated; *(pelo)* bleached // *nm* peroxide.

oxígeno [ok'sixeno] *nm* oxygen.

oyente [o'jente] *nm/f* listener, hearer.

oyes, oyó *etc vb ver* **oír.**

P

P *abr de* **padre.**

pabellón [paβe'ʎon] *nm* bell tent; *(ARQ)* pavilion; *(de hospital etc)* block, section; *(bandera)* flag.

pábilo ['paβilo] *nm* wick.

pacer [pa'θer] *vi* to graze // *vt* to graze on.

paciencia [pa'θjenθja] *nf* patience.

paciente [pa'θjente] *a, nm/f* patient.

pacificación [paθifika'θjon] nf pacification; **pacificar** vt to pacify; (tranquilizar) to calm.

pacífico, a [pa'θifiko, a] a (persona) peace-loving; (existencia) pacific; **el (océano) P~** the Pacific (Ocean).

pacifismo [paθi'fismo] nm pacifism; **pacifista** nm/f pacifist.

pactar [pak'tar] vt to agree to, agree on // vi to come to an agreement.

pacto ['pakto] nm (tratado) pact; (acuerdo) agreement.

padecer [paðe'θer] vt (sufrir) to suffer; (soportar) to endure, put up with; (ser víctima de) to be a victim of; **padecimiento** nm suffering.

padrastro [pa'ðrastro] nm stepfather.

padre ['paðre] nm father // a (fam): **un éxito ~** a tremendous success; **~s** nmpl parents.

padrino [pa'ðrino] nm (REL) godfather; (fig) sponsor, patron; **~s** nmpl godparents; **~ de boda** best man.

padrón [pa'ðron] nm (censo) census, roll; (de socios) register; (TEC) pattern.

paella [pa'eʎa] nf paella, dish of rice with meat, shellfish etc.

paga ['paxa] nf (dinero pagado) payment; (sueldo) pay, wages pl.

pagadero, a [paxa'ðero, a] a payable; **~ a la entrega/a plazos** payable on delivery/in instalments.

pagador, a [paxa'ðor, a] nm/f (quien paga) payer; (cajero) cashier.

pagano, a [pa'xano, a] a, nm/f pagan, heathen.

pagar [pa'xar] vt (gen) to pay; (las compras, crimen) to pay for; (fig: favor) to repay // vi to pay; **~ al contado/a plazos** to pay (in) cash/in instalments; **~se** vr: **~se con algo** to be content with sth; **~se de sí mismo** to be conceited.

pagaré [paxa're] nm I.O.U.

página ['paxina] nf page.

pago ['paxo] nm (dinero) payment; (fig) return; (barrio) district; (AM) home region, home area; **estar ~** to be even or quits; **~ anticipado/a cuenta/a la entrega/en especie** advance payment/payment on account/cash on delivery/payment in kind.

país [pa'is] nm (gen) country; (región) land; (paisaje) landscape; **los P~es Bajos** the Low Countries; **el P~ Vasco** the Basque Country; **paisaje** nm countryside, scenery.

paisano, a [pai'sano, a] a of the same country // nm/f (compatriota) fellow countryman/woman; (campesino) peasant; **vestir de ~** (soldado) to be in civvies (fam); (guardia) to be in plain clothes.

paja ['paxa] nf straw; (fig) trash, rubbish.

pájara ['paxara] nf hen bird; (cometa) kite; (mujer) thief.

pájaro ['paxaro] nm bird.

pajita [pa'xita] nf (drinking) straw.

pala ['pala] nf (de mango largo) spade, (de mango corto) shovel; (raqueta etc) bat; (: de tenis) racquet; (CULIN) slice; **~ matamoscas** fly swat.

palabra [pa'laβra] nf (gen) word; (facultad) (power of) speech; (derecho de hablar) right to speak; **palabrota** nf swearword.

palacio [pa'laθjo] nm palace; (mansión) mansion, large house; **~ de justicia** courthouse; **~ municipal** town/city hall.

paladar [pala'ðar] nm (gen) palate; **paladear** vt to taste.

palanca [pa'lanka] nf lever; (fig) pull, influence.

palangana [palaŋ'gana] nf washbasin.

palco ['palko] nm box.

palenque [pa'lenke] nm (cerca) stockade, fence; (área) arena, enclosure; (de gallos) pit.

Palestina [pales'tina] nf Palestine.

paliar [pa'ljar] vt (mitigar) to mitigate; (disfrazar) to conceal; **paliativo** nm palliative.

palidecer [paliðe'θer] vi to turn pale; **palidez** nf paleness; **pálido, a** a pale.

palillo [pa'liʎo] nm small stick; (para dientes) toothpick.

paliza [pa'liθa] nf beating, thrashing.

palizada [pali'θaða] nf fence; (lugar cercado) enclosure.

palma ['palma] nf (ANAT) palm; (árbol) palm tree; **batir** o **dar ~s** to clap, applaud; **~da** nf slap; **~s** nfpl clapping sg, applause sg.

palmear [palme'ar] vi to clap.

palmo ['palmo] nm (medida) span; (fig) small amount; **~ a ~** inch by inch.

palmotear [palmote'ar] vi to clap, applaud; **palmoteo** nm clapping, applause; (palmada) slap.

palo ['palo] nm stick; (poste) post, pole; (mango) handle, shaft; (golpe) blow, hit; (de golf) club; (de béisbol) bat; (NAUT) mast; (NAIPES) suit; **~ de tienda** tent pole.

paloma [pa'loma] nf dove, pigeon.

palomilla [palo'miʎa] nf moth; (TEC: tuerca) wing nut; (: hierro) angle iron.

palomitas [palo'mitas] nfpl popcorn sg.

palpar [pal'par] vt to touch, feel; (acariciar) to caress, fondle; (caminar a tientas) to grope one's way along; (fig) to appreciate, understand; **~ a uno** to frisk sb.

palpitación [palpita'θjon] nf palpitation; **palpitante** a palpitating; (fig) burning; **palpitar** vi to palpitate; (latir) to beat.

palúdico, a [pa'luðiko, a] a marshy.

paludismo [palu'ðismo] nm malaria.

pampa ['pampa] nf (AM) pampa(s), prairie.

pan [pan] nm (en general) bread; (una barra) loaf; (trigo) wheat; **de ~ llevar** arable; **~ integral** wholemeal bread; **~ molido** breadcrumbs pl.

pana ['pana] nf corduroy.

panadería [panaðe'ria] nf baker's (shop); **panadero, a** nm/f baker.

Panamá [pana'ma] *nm* Panama; **panameño, a** a a Panamanian.
pancarta [pan'karta] *nf* placard, banner.
panda ['panda] *nf* panda.
pandereta [pande'reta] *nf* tambourine.
pandilla [pan'diʎa] *nf* set, group; (*de criminales*) gang; (*pey*) clique.
pando, a ['pando, a] a sagging.
panel [pa'nel] *nm* panel.
pánico ['paniko] *nm* panic.
panorama [pano'rama] *nm* panorama; (*vista*) view.
pantalones [panta'lones] *nmpl* trousers.
pantalla [pan'taʎa] *nf* (*de cine*) screen; (*cubre-luz*) lampshade.
pantano [pan'tano] *nm* (*ciénaga*) marsh, swamp; (*depósito: de agua*) reservoir; (*fig*) jam, fix, difficulty.
pantera [pan'tera] *nf* panther.
pantimedias [panti'meðjas] *nfpl* tights.
pantomima [panto'mima] *nf* pantomime.
pantorrilla [panto'rriʎa] *nf* calf (of the leg).
pantufla [pan'tufla] *nf* slipper.
panza ['panθa] *nf* belly, paunch; **panzudo, a, panzón, ona** a fat, potbellied.
pañal [pa'ɲal] *nm* nappy; ~**es** *nmpl* (*fig*) early stages, infancy *sg*.
pañería [paɲe'ria] *nf* drapery; **pañero, a** *nm/f* draper.
paño ['paɲo] *nm* (*tela*) cloth; (*pedazo de tela*) (piece of) cloth; (*trapo*) duster, rag; ~ **higiénico** sanitary towel; ~**s menores** underclothes.
pañuelo [pa'ɲwelo] *nm* handkerchief, hanky (*fam*); (*para la cabeza*) (head)scarf.
papa ['papa] *nf* (*AM*) potato // *nm*: **el P~** the Pope.
papá [pa'pa] (*pl* ~**s**) *nm* (*fam*) dad, daddy.
papagayo [papa'xajo] *nm* parrot.
papamoscas [papa'moskas] *nm inv* fly-catcher.
papanatas [papa'natas] *nm inv* (*fam*) sucker, simpleton.
papar [pa'par] *vt* to swallow, gulp (down).
paparrucha [papa'rrutʃa] *nf* (*tontería*) piece of nonsense; (*engaño*) hoax.
papaya [pa'paja] *nf* papaya.
papel [pa'pel] *nm* (*en general*) paper; (*hoja de papel*) sheet of paper; (*TEATRO*) part, role; ~ **de calcar/carbón/de cartas** tracing paper/carbon paper/stationery; ~ **de envolver/de empapelar** brown paper, wrapping paper/wallpaper; ~ **de estaño/higiénico** tinfoil/toilet paper; ~ **de lija** sandpaper; ~ **moneda** paper money; ~ **secante** blotting paper.
papeleo [pape'leo] *nm* red tape.
papelera [pape'lera] *nf* (*cesto*) wastepaper basket; (*escritorio*) desk.
papelería [papele'ria] *nf* (*papeles*) mass of papers; (*tienda*) stationer's (shop).
papeleta [pape'leta] *nf* (*pedazo de papel*) slip *or* bit of paper; (*tarjeta de archivo*) index card; (*POL*) ballot paper; (*ESCOL*) report.

paperas [pa'peras] *nfpl* mumps.
paquete [pa'kete] *nm* (*caja*) packet; (*bulto*) parcel; (*AM: fam*) nuisance, bore.
par [par] a (*igual*) like, equal; (*MAT*) even // *nm* equal; (*de guantes*) pair; (*de veces*) couple; (*dignidad*) peer; (*GOLF, COM*) par; **abrir de ~ en ~** to open wide.
para ['para] *prep* (*gen*) for; **no es ~ comer** it's not for eating; **decir ~ sí** to say to o.s.; **¿~ qué lo quieres?** what do you want it for?; **se casaron ~ separarse otra vez** they married only to separate again; **lo tendré ~ mañana** I'll have it for tomorrow; **ir ~ casa** to go home, head for home; ~ **profesor es muy estúpido** he's very stupid for a teacher; **¿quién es usted ~ gritar así?** who are you to shout like that?; **tengo bastante ~ vivir** I have enough to live on; **estoy ~ cantar** I'm about to sing.
parabién [para'βjen] *nm* congratulations *pl*.
parábola [pa'raβola] *nf* parable; (*MAT*) parabola.
parabrisas [para'βrisas] *nm inv* windscreen.
paracaídas [paraka'iðas] *nm inv* parachute; **paracaidista** *nm/f* parachutist; (*MIL*) paratrooper.
parachoques [para'tʃokes] *nm inv* bumper; (*en auto*) shock absorber.
parada [pa'raða] *nf ver* **parado.**
paradero [para'ðero] *nm* stopping-place; (*situación*) whereabouts; (*fin*) end.
parado, a [pa'raðo, a] a (*persona*) motionless, standing still; (*fábrica*) closed, at a standstill; (*coche*) stopped; (*AM*) standing (up); (*sin empleo*) unemployed, idle; (*confuso*) confused // *nf* (*gen*) stop; (*acto*) stopping; (*de industria*) shutdown, stoppage; (*de pagos*) suspension; (*lugar*) stopping-place; (*apuesta*) bet; ~**a de autobús** bus stop.
paradoja [para'ðoxa] *nf* paradox.
parador [para'ðor] *nm* (*luxury*) hotel.
paráfrasis [pa'rafrasis] *nm inv* paraphrase.
paragolpes [para'xolpes] *nm inv* bumper.
paraguas [pa'raɣwas] *nm inv* umbrella.
Paraguay [para'ɣwai] *nm*: **el ~** Paraguay.
paraíso [para'iso] *nm* paradise, heaven.
paraje [pa'raxe] *nm* place, spot.
paralelo, a [para'lelo, a] a parallel.
parálisis [pa'ralisis] *nf* paralysis; **paralítico, a** a *nm/f* paralytic; **paralizar** *vt* to paralyse; **paralizarse** *vr* to become paralysed; (*fig*) to come to a standstill.
paramilitar [paramili'tar] a para-military.
páramo ['paramo] *nm* bleak plateau.
parangón [paran'gon] *nm*: **sin ~** incomparable.
paranoico, a [para'noiko, a] *nm/f* paranoiac.
parapléjico, a [para'plexiko, a] a, *nm/f* paraplegic.

parar [pa'rar] *vt* to stop; (*golpe*) to ward off // *vi* to stop; ~**se** *vr* to stop; (*AM*) to stand up; **ha parado de llover** it has stopped raining; **van a ~ en la comisaría** they're going to end up in the police station; ~**se en** to pay attention to.

parásito, a [pa'rasito, a] *nm/f* parasite.

parasol [para'sol] *nm* parasol, sunshade.

parcela [par'θela] *nf* plot, piece of ground.

parcial [par'θjal] *a* (*pago*) part-; (*eclipse*) partial; (*juez*) prejudiced, biased; ~**idad** *nf* (*prejuicio*) prejudice, bias; (*partido, facción*) party, faction.

parco, a ['parko, a] *a* (*frugal*) frugal; (*mezquino*) mean; (*moderado*) moderate.

parche ['partʃe] *nm* (*MED*) sticking plaster; (*gen*) patch.

parear [pare'ar] *vt* (*juntar, hacer par*) to match, put together; (*calcetines*) to put into pairs; (*BIO*) to mate, pair.

parecer [pare'θer] *nm* (*opinión*) opinion, view; (*aspecto*) looks *pl* // *vi* (*tener apariencia*) to seem, look; (*asemejarse*) to look like, seem like; (*aparecer, llegar*) to appear; ~**se** *vr* to look alike, resemble each other; ~**se a** to look like, resemble; **según** *o* **a lo que parece** evidently, apparently; **me parece que** I think (that), it seems to me that; **parecido, a** *a* similar // *nm* similarity, likeness, resemblance; **bien parecido** good-looking, nice-looking.

pared [pa'reð] *nf* wall.

parejo, a [pa'rexo, a] *a* (*igual*) equal; (*liso*) smooth, even // *nf* (*dos*) pair; (: *de personas*) couple; (*el otro: de un par*) other one (of a pair); (: *persona*) partner.

parentela [paren'tela] *nf* relations *pl*.

parentesco [paren'tesko] *nm* relationship.

paréntesis [pa'rentesis] *nm inv* parenthesis; (*digresión*) digression; (*en escrito*) bracket.

parezco *etc vb ver* **parecer**.

pariente, a [pa'rjente, a] *nm/f* relative, relation.

parihuela [pari'wela] *nf* stretcher.

parir [pa'rir] *vt* to give birth to // *vi* (*mujer*) to give birth, have a baby.

París [pa'ris] *n* Paris.

parlamentar [parlamen'tar] *vi* (*hablar*) to talk, converse; (*negociar*) to parley.

parlamentario, a [parlamen'tarjo, a] *a* parliamentary // *nm/f* member of parliament.

parlamento [parla'mento] *nm* (*POL*) parliament; (*conversación*) parley.

parlanchín, ina [parlan'tʃin, ina] *a* loose-tongued, indiscreet // *nm/f* chatterbox.

parlar [par'lar] *vi* to chatter (away), talk (a lot); (*chismear*) to gossip; **parlero, a** *a* talkative; gossipy; (*pájaro*) singing.

paro ['paro] *nm* (*huelga*) stoppage (of work), strike; (*desempleo*) unemployment; **subsidio de ~** unemployment benefit; **hay ~ en la industria** work in the industry is at a standstill.

parodia [pa'roðja] *nf* parody; **parodiar** *vt* to parody.

parpadear [parpaðe'ar] *vi* (*los ojos*) to blink; (*luz*) to flicker.

párpado ['parpaðo] *nm* eyelid.

parque ['parke] *nm* (*lugar verde*) park; (*depósito*) depot; ~ **de atracciones/de estacionamiento/zoológico** fairground/car park/zoo.

parquímetro [par'kimetro] *nm* parking meter.

párrafo ['parrafo] *nm* paragraph; **echar un ~** (*fam*) to have a chat.

parranda [pa'rranda] *nf* (*fam*) spree, binge.

parrilla [pa'rriʎa] *nf* (*CULIN*) grill; (*de coche*) grille; (**carne de**) ~ barbecue; ~**da** *nf* barbecue.

párroco ['parroko] *nm* parish priest.

parroquia [pa'rrokja] *nf* parish; (*iglesia*) parish church; (*COM*) clientele, customers *pl*; ~**no, a** *nm/f* parishioner; client, customer.

parte ['parte] *nm* message; (*informe*) report // *nf* (*gen*) part; (*lado, cara*) side; (*de reparto*) share; (*JUR*) party; **en alguna ~ de Europa** somewhere in Europe; **en cualquier ~** anywhere; **en gran ~** to a large extent; **la mayor ~ de los españoles** most Spaniards; **de algún tiempo a esta ~** for some time past; **de ~ de alguien** on sb's behalf; **por ~ de** on the part of; **yo por mí ~** I for my part; **por otra ~** on the other hand; **dar ~** to inform; **tomar ~** to take part.

partera [par'tera] *nf* midwife.

partición [parti'θjon] *nf* division, sharing-out; (*POL*) partition.

participación [partiθipa'θjon] *nf* (*acto*) participation, taking part; (*parte, COM*) share; (*de lotería*) small prize; (*aviso*) notice, notification.

participante [partiθi'pante] *nm/f* participant; **participar** *vt* to notify, inform // *vi* to take part, participate; (*compartir*) to share.

partícipe [par'tiθipe] *nm/f* participant.

particular [partiku'lar] *a* (*especial*) particular, special; (*individual, personal*) private, personal // *nm* (*punto, asunto*) particular, point; (*individuo*) individual; **tiene coche ~** he has a car of his own; ~**izar** *vt* to distinguish; (*especificar*) to specify; (*detallar*) to give details about.

partida [par'tiða] *nf* (*salida*) departure; (*COM*) entry, item; (*juego*) game; (*apuesta*) bet; (*grupo, bando*) band, group; **mala ~** dirty trick; ~ **de nacimiento/matrimonio/defunción** birth/marriage/death certificate.

partidario, a [parti'ðarjo, a] *a* partisan // *nm/f* (*DEPORTE*) supporter; (*POL*) partisan.

partido [par'tiðo] *nm* (*POL*) party; (*encuentro*) game, match; (*apoyo*) support; (*equipo*) team; **sacar ~ de** to profit from, benefit from; **tomar ~** to take sides.

partir [par'tir] *vt* (*dividir*) to split, divide;

(*compartir, distribuir*) to share (out),
distribute; (*romper*) to break open, split
open; (*rebanada*) to cut (off) // vi (*tomar
camino*) to set off, set out; (*comenzar*) to
start (off or out); ~**se** vr to crack or split
or break (in two etc); **a ~ de** (starting)
from.

parto ['parto] nm birth; (*fig*) product,
creation; **estar de ~** to be in labour.

parvulario [parβu'larjo] nm nursery
school, kindergarten.

pasa ['pasa] nf raisin; ~ **de Corinto/de
Esmirna** currant/sultana.

pasada [pa'saδa] nf ver **pasado**.

pasadizo [pasa'δiθo] nm (*pasillo*) passage,
corridor; (*callejuela*) alley.

pasado, a [pa'saδo, a] a past; (*malo:
comida, fruta*) bad; (*muy cocido*) overdone;
(*anticuado*) out of date // nm past // nf
passing, passage; (*acción de pulir*) rub,
polish: ~**s** nmpl ancestors; ~ **mañana**
the day after tomorrow; **el mes ~** last
month; **de ~a** in passing, incidentally;
una mala ~a a dirty trick.

pasador [pasa'δor] nm (*gen*) bolt; (*de
pelo*) pin, grip; ~**es** nmpl cufflinks.

pasaje [pa'saxe] nm (*gen*) passage; (*pago
de viaje*) fare; (*los pasajeros*) passengers pl;
(*pasillo*) passageway.

pasajero, a [pasa'xero, a] a passing;
(*calle*) busy // nm/f passenger; (*viajero*)
traveller.

pasamanos [pasa'manos] nm rail,
handrail; (*de escalera*) banister.

pasaporte [pasa'porte] nm passport.

pasar [pa'sar] vt (*gen*) to pass; (*tiempo*) to
spend; (*durezas*) to suffer, endure; (*noticia*)
to give, pass on; (*río*) to cross; (*barrera*) to
pass through; (*falta*) to overlook, tolerate;
(*contrincante*) to surpass, do better than;
(*coche*) to overtake; (*enfermedad*) to give,
infect with // vi (*gen*) to pass; (*terminarse*)
to be over; (*ocurrir*) to happen; ~**se** vr
(*flores*) to fade; (*comida*) to go bad, go off;
(*fig*) to overdo it, go too far; ~ **de** to go
beyond, exceed; **¡pase!** come in!; ~**se al
enemigo** to go over to the enemy; **se me
pasó** I forgot; **no se le pasa nada**
nothing escapes him, he misses nothing;
pase lo que pase come what may.

pasarela [pasa'rela] nf footbridge; (*en
barco*) gangway.

pasatiempo [pasa'tjempo] nm pastime;
(*distracción*) amusement.

Pascua ['paskwa] nf: ~ (**de
Resurrección**) Easter; ~ **de Navidad**
Christmas; ~**s** nfpl Christmas time;
¡felices ~s! Merry Christmas.

pase ['pase] nm pass.

pasear [pase'ar] vt to take for a walk;
(*exhibir*) to parade, show off // vi, ~**se** vr
to walk, go for a walk; (*holgazanear*) to
idle, loaf about; ~ **en coche** to go for a
drive; **paseo** nm (*avenida*) avenue;
(*distancia corta*) short walk; **dar un paseo**
to go for a walk.

pasillo [pa'siλo] nm passage, corridor.

pasión [pa'sjon] nf passion.

pasivo, a [pa'siβo, a] a passive; (*inactivo*)
inactive // nm (*COM*) liabilities pl, debts pl.

pasmar [pas'mar] vt (*asombrar*) to amaze,
astonish; (*enfriar*) to chill (to the bone);
pasmo nm amazement, astonishment;
chill; (*fig*) wonder, marvel; **pasmoso, a** a
amazing, astonishing.

paso, a ['paso, a] a dried // nm (*gen*) step;
(*modo de andar*) walk; (*huella*) footprint;
(*rapidez*) speed, pace, rate; (*camino
accesible*) way through, passage; (*cruce*)
crossing; (*pasaje*) passing, passage; (*GEO*)
pass; (*estrecho*) strait; **a ese ~** (*fig*) at
that rate; **salir al ~ de** o a to waylay;
estar de ~ to be passing through; ~
elevado flyover; **prohibido el ~** no
entry; **ceda el ~** give way.

pasta ['pasta] nf (*gen*) paste; (*CULIN: masa*)
dough; (: de bizcochos etc) pastry; (*cartón*)
cardboard; (*fam*) money, dough (*fam*); ~**s**
nfpl (*bizcochos*) pastries, small cakes;
(*fideos, espaguetis etc*) noodles, spaghetti
sg etc; ~ **de dientes** o **dentífrica**
toothpaste; ~ **de madera** wood pulp.

pastar [pas'tar], **pastear** [paste'ar] vt, vi
to graze.

pastel [pas'tel] nm (*dulce*) cake; (*de carne*)
pie; (*pintura*) pastel; ~**ería** nf cake shop,
pastry shop.

pasteurizado, a [pasteuri'θaδo, a] a
pasteurized.

pastilla [pas'tiλa] nf (*de jabón, chocolate*)
cake, bar; (*píldora*) tablet, pill.

pasto ['pasto] nm (*hierba*) grass; (*lugar*)
pasture, field.

pastor, a [pas'tor, a] nm/f shepherd/ess //
nm clergyman, pastor.

pata ['pata] nf (*pierna*) leg; (*pie*) foot; (*de
muebles*) leg; ~**s arriba** upside down;
meter la ~ to put one's foot in it; (*TEC*):
~ **de cabra** crowbar; **tener
buena/mala ~** to be lucky/unlucky;
~**da** nf stamp; (*puntapié*) kick.

patalear [patale'ar] vi to stamp one's feet.

patata [pa'tata] nf potato; ~**s fritas** o **a
la española** chips, French fries; ~**s
inglesas** crisps.

patear [pate'ar] vt (*pisar*) to stamp on,
trample (on); (*pegar con el pie*) to kick //
vi to stamp (with rage), stamp one's foot.

patente [pa'tente] a obvious, evident;
(*COM*) patent // nf patent; **patentizar** vt to
show, reveal, make evident.

paternal [pater'nal] a fatherly, paternal;
paterno, a a paternal.

patético, a [pa'tetiko, a] a pathetic,
moving.

patillas [pa'tiλas] nfpl sideburns.

patín [pa'tin] nm skate; (*de tobogán*)
runner; **patinaje** nm skating; **patinar** vi
to skate; (*resbalarse*) to skid, slip; (*fam*) to
slip up, blunder.

patio ['patjo] nm (*de casa*) patio,
courtyard; ~ **de recreo** playground.

pato ['pato] nm duck; **pagar el ~** (*fam*) to
take the blame, carry the can.

patológico, a [pato'loxiko, a] *a* pathological.

patraña [pa'traɲa] *nf* story, fib.

patria ['patrja] *nf* native land, mother country.

patrimonio [patri'monjo] *nm* inheritance; (*fig*) heritage.

patriota [pa'trjota] *nm/f* patriot; **patriotismo** *nm* patriotism.

patrocinar [patroθi'nar] *vt* to sponsor; (*apoyar*) to back, support; **patrocinio** *nm* sponsorship; backing, support.

patrón, ona [pa'tron, ona] *nm/f* (*jefe*) boss, chief, master/mistress; (*propietario*) landlord/lady; (*REL*) patron saint // *nm* (*TEC, costura*) pattern; **patronal** *a*: **la clase patronal** management; **patronato** *nm* sponsorship; (*acto*) patronage; (*COM*) employers' association.

patrulla [pa'truʎa] *nf* patrol.

pausa ['pausa] *nf* pause; (*intervalo*) break; (*interrupción*) interruption.

pausado, a [pau'saðo, a] *a* slow, deliberate.

pauta ['pauta] *nf* line, guide line.

pavo ['paβo] *nm* turkey; ~ **real** peacock.

pavor [pa'βor] *nm* dread, terror.

payaso, a [pa'jaso, a] *nm/f* clown.

paz [paθ] *nf* peace; (*tranquilidad*) peacefulness, tranquillity; **hacer las paces** to make peace; (*fig*) to make up.

P.C.E. *abr de* **Partido Comunista Español.**

peaje [pe'axe] *nm* toll.

peatón [pea'ton] *nm* pedestrian.

peca ['peka] *nf* freckle.

pecado [pe'kaðo] *nm* sin; **pecador, a** *a* sinful // *nm/f* sinner.

pecaminoso, a [pekami'noso, a] *a* sinful.

pecar [pe'kar] *vi* (*REL*) to sin; (*fig*): **peca de generoso** he is too generous.

peculiar [peku'ljar] *a* special, peculiar; (*característico*) typical, characteristic; ~**idad** *nf* peculiarity; special feature, characteristic.

pecho ['petʃo] *nm* chest; (*de mujer*) breast(s) (*pl*), bosom; (*corazón*) heart, breast; (*valor*) courage, spirit; **dar el** ~ **a** to breast-feed; **tomar algo a** ~ to take sth to heart.

pechuga [pe'tʃuɣa] *nf* breast (of chicken *etc*).

pedal [pe'ðal] *nm* pedal; ~**ear** *vi* to pedal.

pedante [pe'ðante] *a* pedantic // *nm/f* pedant; ~**ría** *nf* pedantry.

pedazo [pe'ðaθo] *nm* piece, bit; **hacerse** ~**s** to fall to pieces; (*romperse*) to smash, shatter.

pedernal [peðer'nal] *nm* flint.

pediatra [pe'ðjatra] *nm/f* pediatrician.

pedicuro, a [peði'kuro, a] *nm/f* chiropodist.

pedido [pe'ðiðo] *nm* (*COM: mandado*) order; (*petición*) request.

pedir [pe'ðir] *vt* to ask for, request; (*comida, COM: mandar*) to order; (*exigir:*

precio) to ask; (*necesitar*) to need, demand, require // *vi* to ask; **me pidió que cerrara la puerta** he asked me to shut the door; **¿cuánto piden por el coche?** how much are they asking for the car?

pegadizo, a [peɣa'ðiθo, a] *a* sticky; (*MED*) infectious // *nm/f* sponger, hanger-on (*fam*).

pegajoso, a [peɣa'xoso, a] *a* sticky, adhesive; (*MED*) infectious.

pegamento [peɣa'mento] *nm* gum, sticky stuff.

pegar [pe'ɣar] *vt* (*papel, sellos*) to stick (on); (*cartel*) to post, stick up; (*coser*) to sew (on); (*unir: partes*) to join, fix together; (*MED*) to give, infect with; (*dar: golpe*) to give, deal // *vi* (*adherirse*) to stick, adhere; (*prender: fuego*) to catch; (*ir juntos: colores*) to match, go together; (*golpear*) to hit; (*quemar: el sol*) to strike hot, burn (*fig*); ~**se** *vr* (*gen*) to stick; (*dos personas*) to hit each other, fight; (*fam*): ~ **un grito** to let out a yell; ~ **un salto** to jump (with fright); ~ **en** to touch; ~**se un tiro** to shoot o.s.

peinado [pei'naðo] *nm* (*en peluquería*) hairdo; (*estilo*) hair style.

peinador, a [peina'ðor, a] *nm/f* hairdresser.

peinar [pei'nar] *vt* to comb; (*hacer estilo*) to style; ~**se** *vr* to comb one's hair.

peine ['peine] *nm* comb; ~**ta** *nf* ornamental comb.

Pekín [pe'kin] *n* Pekin(g).

pelado, a [pe'laðo, a] *a* (*cabeza*) shorn; (*fruta*) peeled; (*campo, fig*) bare // *nm* bare patch; (*fig*) wretch, poor devil.

pelaje [pe'laxe] *nm* (*ZOOL*) fur, coat; (*fig*) appearance.

pelambre [pe'lambre] *nm* (*pelo largo*) long hair, mop; (*piel de animal cortado*) fur; (: *de oveja*) fleece; (*parte sin piel*) bare patch.

pelar [pe'lar] *vt* (*cortar el pelo a*) to cut the hair of; (*quitar la piel: animal*) to skin; ~**se** *vr* (*la piel*) to peel off; (*persona*) to lose one's hair; **voy a** ~**me** I'm going to get my hair cut.

peldaño [pel'daɲo] *nm* step.

pelea [pe'lea] *nf* (*lucha*) fight; (*discusión*) quarrel, row; **pelear** *vi* to fight; **pelearse** *vr* to fight; (*reñirse*) to fall out, quarrel.

peletería [pelete'ria] *nf* furrier's, fur shop.

pelicano [peli'kano], **pelícano** [pe'likano] *nm* pelican.

pelicorto, a [peli'korto, a] *a* short-haired.

película [pe'likula] *nf* film; (*cobertura ligera*) thin covering; (*FOTO: rollo*) roll or reel of film.

peligro [pe'liɣro] *nm* danger; (*riesgo*) risk; **correr** ~ **de** to be in danger of; ~**so, a** *a* dangerous; risky.

pelirrojo, a [peli'rroxo, a] *a* red-haired, red-headed.

pelo ['pelo] *nm* (*cabellos*) hair; (*de barba, bigote*) whisker; (*de animal: pellejo*) fur, coat; (*de perro etc*) hair, coat; **al ~** just right; **venir al ~** to be exactly what one needs; **un hombre de ~ en pecho** a brave man; **por los ~s** by the skin of one's teeth; **no tener ~s en la lengua** to be outspoken, not mince words; **tomar el ~ a uno** to pull sb's leg.

pelón, ona [pe'lon, ona] *a* hairless, bald; (*fig*) broke, skint (*fam*).

pelota [pe'lota] *nf* ball; (*fam: cabeza*) nut (*fam*); **en ~ stark** naked; **~ vasca** pelota.

pelotón [pelo'ton] *nm* (*pelota*) big ball; (*muchedumbre*) crowd; (*MIL*) squad, detachment.

peluca [pe'luka] *nf* wig.

peluche [pe'lutʃe] *nm* felt.

peludo, a [pe'luðo, a] *a* hairy, shaggy.

peluquería [peluke'ria] *nf* hairdresser's; (*para hombres*) barber's (shop); **peluquero, a** *nm/f* hairdresser; barber.

pelleja [pe'ʎexa] *nf* skin, hide; (*fam*) whore.

pellejo [pe'ʎexo] *nm* (*de animal*) skin, hide; (*de fruta*) skin, peel.

pellizcar [peʎiθ'kar] *vt* to pinch, nip.

pena ['pena] *nf* (*congoja*) grief, sadness; (*ansia*) anxiety; (*remordimiento*) regret; (*dificultad*) trouble; (*dolor*) pain; **merecer o valer la ~** to be worthwhile; **a duras ~s** with great difficulty; **~ de muerte** death penalty; **~ pecuniaria** fine; **¡qué ~!** what a shame!

penal [pe'nal] *a* penal // *nm* (*cárcel*) prison; (*FÚTBOL*) penalty.

penalidad [penali'ðað] *nf* (*problema, dificultad*) trouble, hardship; (*JUR*) penalty, punishment.

penar [pe'nar] *vt* to penalize; (*castigar*) to punish // *vi* to suffer; **~se** *vr* to grieve, mourn.

pender [pen'der] *vi* (*colgar*) to hang; (*JUR*) to be pending.

pendiente [pen'djente] *a* (*colgante*) hanging; (*por resolver*) pending, unsettled // *nm* earring // *nf* hill, slope.

pene ['pene] *nm* penis.

penetración [penetra'θjon] *nf* (*acto*) penetration; (*agudeza*) sharpness, insight.

penetrante [pene'trante] *a* (*herida*) deep; (*persona, arma*) sharp; (*sonido*) penetrating, piercing; (*mirada*) searching; (*viento, ironía*) biting.

penetrar [pene'trar] *vt* to penetrate, pierce; (*entender*) to grasp // *vi* to penetrate, go in; (*líquido*) to soak in; (*emoción*) to pierce.

penicilina [peniθi'lina] *nf* penicillin.

península [pe'ninsula] *nf* peninsula; **peninsular** *a* peninsular.

penitencia [peni'tenθja] *nf* (*remordimiento*) penitence; (*castigo*) penance; **penitencial** *a* penitential; **~ría** *nf* prison, penitentiary.

penoso, a [pe'noso, a] *a* (*afligido*) painful, distressing; (*trabajoso*) laborious, difficult.

pensador, a [pensa'ðor, a] *nm/f* thinker.

pensamiento [pensa'mjento] *nm* (*gen*) thought; (*mente*) mind; (*idea*) idea; (*intento*) intention.

pensar [pen'sar] *vt* to think; (*considerar*) to think over, think out; (*proponerse*) to intend, plan, propose; (*imaginarse*) to think up, invent // *vi* to think; **~ en** to aim at, aspire to; **pensativo, a** *a* thoughtful, pensive.

pensión [pen'sjon] *nf* (*casa*) boarding house, guest house; (*dinero*) pension; (*cama y comida*) board and lodging; (*beca*) scholarship; **pensionista** *nm/f* (*jubilado*) (old-age) pensioner; (*quien vive en pensión*) lodger.

penúltimo, a [pe'nultimo, a] *a* penultimate, second last.

penumbra [pe'numbra] *nf* half-light, semi-darkness.

penuria [pe'nurja] *nf* shortage, want.

peña ['peɲa] *nf* (*roca*) rock; (*cuesta*) cliff, crag; (*grupo*) group, circle.

peñascal [peɲas'kal] *nm* rocky place; **peñasco** *nm* large rock, boulder.

peñón [pe'ɲon] *nm* mass of rock; **el P~** the Rock (of Gibraltar).

peón [pe'on] *nm* labourer; (*AM*) farm labourer, farmhand; (*eje*) spindle, shaft, axle; (*AJEDREZ*) pawn.

peor [pe'or] *a* (*comparativo*) worse; (*superlativo*) worst // *ad* worse; worst; **de mal en ~** from bad to worse.

pepino [pe'pino] *nm* cucumber; **(no) me importa un ~** I don't care two hoots.

pepita [pe'pita] *nf* (*BOT*) pip; (*MINERÍA*) nugget.

pequeñez [peke'ɲeθ] *nf* smallness, littleness; (*infancia*) infancy; (*trivialidad*) trifle, triviality.

pequeño, a [pe'keɲo, a] *a* small, little.

pera ['pera] *nf* pear; **peral** *nm* pear tree.

percance [per'kanθe] *nm* setback, misfortune.

percatarse [perka'tarse] *vr*: **~ de** to notice, take note of.

percepción [perθep'θjon] *nf* (*vista*) perception; (*idea*) notion, idea; (*colecta de fondos*) collection.

perceptible [perθep'tiβle] *a* perceptible, noticeable; (*COM*) payable, receivable.

percibir [perθi'βir] *vt* to perceive, notice; (*COM*) to earn, receive, get.

percusión [perku'sjon] *nf* percussion.

percha ['pertʃa] *nf* (*poste*) pole, support; (*ganchos*) coat stand; (*colgador*) coat hanger; (*de ave*) perch.

perdedor, a [perðe'ðor, a] *a* (*que pierde*) losing; (*olvidadizo*) forgetful // *nm/f* loser.

perder [per'ðer] *vt* (*gen*) to lose; (*tiempo, palabras*) to waste; (*oportunidad*) to lose, miss; (*tren*) to miss // *vi* to lose; **~se** *vr* (*extraviarse*) to get lost; (*desaparecer*) to disappear, be lost to view; (*arruinarse*) to be ruined; (*hundirse*) to sink; **echar a ~** (*comida*) to spoil, ruin; (*oportunidad*) to waste.

perdición [perði'θjon] *nf* perdition, ruin.

pérdida ['perðiða] nf (gen) loss; (de tiempo) waste; ~s nfpl (COM) losses.

perdido, a [per'ðiðo, a] a lost; (incorregible) incorrigible; ~so, a a (que pierde) losing; (fácilmente ~) easily lost.

perdiz [per'ðiθ] nf partridge.

perdón [per'ðon] nm (disculpa) pardon, forgiveness; (clemencia) mercy; ¡~! sorry!, I beg your pardon!; **perdonar** vt to pardon, forgive; (la vida) to spare; (excusar) to exempt, excuse.

perdurable [perðu'raβle] a lasting; (eterno) everlasting; **perdurar** vi (resistir) to last, endure; (seguir existiendo) to stand, still exist.

perecer [pere'θer] vi (morir) to perish, die; (objeto) to shatter.

peregrinación [pereɣrina'θjon] nf long tour, travels pl; (REL) pilgrimage; **peregrino, a** a travelling; (nuevo) newly-introduced // nm/f pilgrim.

perejil [pere'xil] nm parsley.

perenne [pe'renne] a everlasting, perennial.

perentorio, a [peren'torjo, a] a (urgente) urgent, peremptory; (fijo) set, fixed.

pereza [pe'reθa] nf (flojera) laziness; (lentitud) sloth, slowness; **perezoso, a** a lazy; slow, sluggish.

perfección [perfek'θjon] nf perfection; (acto) completion; **perfeccionar** vt to perfect; (acabar) to complete, finish.

perfecto, a [per'fekto, a] a perfect; (terminado) complete, finished.

perfidia [per'fiðja] nf perfidy, treachery.

perfil [per'fil] nm (parte lateral) profile; (silueta) silhouette, outline; (ARQ) (cross) section; ~es nmpl features; (fig) social graces; ~ado, a a (bien formado) well-shaped; (largo: cara) long; ~ar vt (trazar) to outline; (dar carácter a) to shape, give character to.

perforación [perfora'θjon] nf perforation; (con taladro) drilling; **perforadora** nf drill.

perforar [perfo'rar] vt to perforate; (agujero) to drill, bore; (papel) to punch a hole in // vi to drill, bore.

perfumado, a [perfu'maðo, a] a scented, perfumed.

perfume [per'fume] nm perfume, scent.

pericia [pe'riθja] nf skill, expertise.

periferia [peri'ferja] nf periphery; (de ciudad) outskirts pl.

perímetro [pe'rimetro] nm perimeter.

periódico, a [pe'rjoðiko, a] a periodic(al) // nm newspaper; **periodismo** nm journalism; **periodista** nm/f journalist.

periodo [pe'rjoðo], **período** [pe'rioðo] nm period.

perito, a [pe'rito, a] a (experto) expert; (diestro) skilled, skilful // nm/f expert; skilled worker; (técnico) technician.

perjudicar [perxuði'kar] vt (gen) to damage, harm; ese vestido le perjudica that dress doesn't suit her; **perjudicial** a damaging, harmful; (en detrimento) detri-

mental; **perjuicio** nm damage, harm; (pérdidas) financial loss.

perjurar [perxu'rar] vi to commit perjury.

perla ['perla] nf pearl; **me viene de ~** it suits me fine.

permanecer [permane'θer] vi (quedarse) to stay, remain; (seguir) to continue to be.

permanencia [perma'nenθja] nf (duración) permanence; (estancia) stay.

permanente [perma'nente] a (que queda) permanent; (constante) constant // nf perm.

permisible [permi'siβle] a permissible, allowable.

permiso [per'miso] nm permission; (licencia) permit, licence; **con ~** excuse me; **estar de ~** (MIL) to be on leave; **~ de conducir** o **conductor** driving licence.

permitir [permi'tir] vt to permit, allow.

pernicioso, a [perni'θjoso, a] a (maligno, MED) pernicious; (persona) wicked.

pernio ['pernjo] nm hinge.

perno ['perno] nm bolt.

pero ['pero] conj but; (aún) yet // nm (defecto) flaw, defect; (reparo) objection.

perorar [pero'rar] vi to make a speech.

perpendicular [perpendiku'lar] a perpendicular; **el camino es ~ al río** the road is at right angles to the river.

perpetrar [perpe'trar] vt to perpetrate.

perpetuamente [perpetwa'mente] ad perpetually; **perpetuar** vt to perpetuate; **perpetuo, a** a perpetual.

perplejo, a [per'plexo, a] a perplexed, bewildered.

perra ['perra] nf bitch; (fam) mania, crazy idea.

perrera [pe'rrera] nf kennel.

perrillo [pe'rriʎo] nm puppy.

perro ['perro] nm dog; **~ caliente** hot dog.

persa ['persa] a, nm/f Persian.

persecución [perseku'θjon] nf pursuit, hunt, chase; (REL, POL) persecution.

perseguir [perse'vir] vt to pursue, hunt; (cortejar) to chase after; (molestar) to pester, annoy; (REL, POL) to persecute.

perseverante [perseβe'rante] a persevering, persistent; **perseverar** vi to persevere, persist; **perseverar en** to persevere in, persist with.

persiana [per'sjana] nf (Venetian) blind.

persignarse [persiv'narse] vr to cross o.s.

persistente [persis'tente] a persistant; **persistir** vi to persist.

persona [per'sona] nf person; **10 ~s** 10 people.

personaje [perso'naxe] nm important person, celebrity; (TEATRO) character.

personal [perso'nal] a (particular) personal; (para una persona) single, for one person // nm personnel, staff; **~idad** nf personality.

personarse [perso'narse] vr to appear in person.

personificar [personifi'kar] *vt* to personify.

perspectiva [perspek'tiβa] *nf* perspective; (*vista, panorama*) view, panorama; (*posibilidad futura*) outlook, prospect.

perspicacia [perspi'kaθja] *nf* keen-sightedness; (*fig*) discernment, perspicacity.

perspicaz [perspi'kaθ] *a* (*agudo: de la vista*) keen; (*fig*) shrewd.

persuadir [perswa'ðir] *vt* (*gen*) to persuade; (*convencer*) to convince; ~**se** *vr* to become convinced; **persuasión** *nf* (*acto*) persuasion; (*estado de mente*) conviction; **persuasivo, a** *a* persuasive; convincing.

pertenecer [pertene'θer] *vi* to belong; (*fig*) to concern; **pertenencia** *nf* ownership; **pertenencias** *nfpl* possessions, property *sg*; **perteneciente a: perteneciente a** belonging to.

pertinaz [perti'naθ] *a* (*persistente*) persistent; (*terco*) obstinate.

pertinente [perti'nente] *a* relevant, pertinent; (*apropiado*) appropriate; ~ *a* concerning, relevant to.

perturbación [perturβa'θjon] *nf* (*POL*) disturbance; (*MED*) upset, disturbance.

perturbado, a [pertur'βaðo, a] *a* mentally unbalanced.

perturbador, a [perturβa'ðor, a] *a* (*que perturba*) perturbing, disturbing; (*subversivo*) subversive.

perturbar [pertur'βar] *vt* (*el orden*) to disturb; (*MED*) to upset, disturb; (*mentalmente*) to perturb.

Perú [pe'ru] *nm*: **el** ~ Peru; **peruano, a** *a, nm/f* Peruvian.

perversión [perβer'sjon] *nf* perversion; **perverso, a** *a* perverse; (*depravado*) depraved; **pervertido, a** *a* perverted // *nm/f* pervert; **pervertir** *vt* to pervert, corrupt; (*distorsionar*) to distort.

pesa ['pesa] *nf* weight; (*DEPORTE*) shot.

pesadez [pesa'ðeθ] *nf* (*calidad de pesado*) heaviness; (*lentitud*) slowness; (*aburrimiento*) tediousness.

pesadilla [pesa'ðiʎa] *nf* nightmare, bad dream.

pesado, a [pe'saðo, a] *a* (*gen*) heavy; (*lento*) slow; (*difícil, duro*) tough, hard; (*aburrido*) tedious, boring; (*bochornoso*) sultry.

pesadumbre [pesa'ðumbre] *nf* grief, sorrow.

pésame ['pesame] *nm* expression of condolence, message of sympathy.

pesar [pe'sar] *vt* to weigh // *vi* to weigh; (*ser pesado*) to weigh a lot, be heavy; (*fig: opinión*) to carry weight // *nm* (*sentimiento*) regret; (*pena*) grief, sorrow; **a** ~ **de** *o* **pese a (que)** in spite of, despite.

pesario [pe'sarjo] *nm* pessary.

pesca ['peska] *nf* (*acto*) fishing; (*cantidad de pescado*) catch; **ir de** ~ to go fishing.

pescadería [peskaðe'ria] *nf* fish shop.

pescado [pes'kaðo] *nm* fish.

pescador, a [peska'ðor, a] *nm/f* fisherman/woman.

pescar [pes'kar] *vt* (*coger*) to catch; (*tratar de coger*) to fish for; (*conseguir: trabajo*) to manage to get // *vi* to fish, go fishing; **viene a** ~ **un marido** she's come to get a husband.

pescuezo [pes'kweθo] *nm* neck.

pesebre [pe'seβre] *nm* manger.

peseta [pe'seta] *nf* peseta.

pesimista [pesi'mista] *a* pessimistic // *nm/f* pessimist.

pésimo, a ['pesimo, a] *a* abominable, vile.

peso ['peso] *nm* weight; (*balanza*) scales *pl*; (*moneda*) peso; ~ **bruto/neto** gross/net weight; **vender a** ~ to sell by weight.

pesquero, a [pes'kero, a] *a* fishing *cpd*.

pesquisa [pes'kisa] *nf* inquiry, investigation.

pestaña [pes'taɲa] *nf* (*ANAT*) eyelash; (*borde*) rim; **pestañear, pestañar** *vi* to blink.

peste ['peste] *nf* (*gen*) plague; (*mal olor*) stink, stench.

pesticida [pesti'θiða] *nm* pesticide.

pestilencia [pesti'lenθja] *nf* (*plaga*) pestilence, plague; (*mal olor*) stink, stench.

pétalo ['petalo] *nm* petal.

petardista [petar'ðista] *nm/f* (*tramposo*) cheat; (*rompehuelgas*) blackleg.

petición [peti'θjon] *nf* (*pedido*) request, plea; (*memorial*) petition; (*JUR*) plea.

petrificar [petrifi'kar] *vt* to petrify.

petróleo [pe'troleo] *nm* oil, petroleum; **petrolero, a** *a* petroleum *cpd* // *nm* (*COM*) oil man; (*extremista*) extremist, revolutionary; (*buque*) (oil) tanker.

peyorativo, a [pejora'tiβo, a] *a* pejorative.

pez [peθ] *nm* fish.

pezón [pe'θon] *nm* teat, nipple; (*MECÁNICA*) nipple, lubrication point.

piadoso, a [pja'ðoso, a] *a* (*devoto*) pious, devout; (*misericordioso*) kind, merciful.

pianista [pja'nista] *nm/f* pianist.

piano ['pjano] *nm* piano.

piar [pi'ar] *vi* to cheep.

picadillo [pika'ðiʎo] *nm* mince, minced meat.

picado, a [pi'kaðo, a] *a* pricked, punctured; (*mar*) choppy; (*diente*) bad; (*tabaco*) cut; (*enfadado*) cross // *nf* prick; (*de abeja*) sting; (*de mosquito*) bite.

picador [pika'ðor] *nm* (*TAUR*) picador; (*entrenador de caballos*) horse trainer; (*minero*) faceworker.

picadura [pika'ðura] *nf* (*diente*) bad tooth; (*pinchazo*) puncture; (*de abeja*) sting; (*de mosquito*) bite; (*tabaco picado*) cut tobacco.

picante [pi'kante] *a* hot; (*comentario*) racy, spicy.

picar [pi'kar] *vt* (*agujerear, perforar*) to prick, puncture; (*abeja*) to sting; (*mosquito, serpiente*) to bite; (*incitar*) to incite, goad; (*dañar, irritar*) to annoy, bother; (*quemar:*

lengua) to burn, sting // *vi* (*pez*) to bite, take the bait; (*el sol*) to burn, scorch; (*abeja*, MED) to sting; (*mosquito*) to bite; ~**se** *vr* (*decaer*) to decay; (*agriarse*) to turn sour, go off; (*ofenderse*) to take offence; ~ **en** (*fig*) to dabble in.

picardía [pikar'ðia] *nf* villainy; (*astucia*) slyness, craftiness; (*una* ~) dirty trick; (*palabra*) rude/bad word or expression.

pícaro, a ['pikaro, a] *a* (*malicioso*) villainous; (*travieso*) mischievous // *nm* (*ladrón*) crook; (*astuto*) sly sort; (*sinvergüenza*) rascal, scoundrel.

pico ['piko] *nm* (*de ave*) beak; (*punto agudo*) peak, sharp point; (TEC) pick, pickaxe; (GEO) peak, summit; **y** ~ **and a bit**.

picotear [pikote'ar] *vt* to peck // *vi* to nibble, pick; (*fam*) to chatter; ~**se** *vr* to squabble.

picudo, a [pi'kuðo, a] *a* pointed, with a point.

pichón [pi'tʃon] *nm* young pigeon.

pido, pidió *etc vb ver* **pedir**.

pie [pje] (*pl* ~**s**) *nm* (*gen*) foot; (*fig: motivo*) motive, basis; (: *fundamento*) foothold; **ir a** ~ to go on foot, walk; **estar de** ~ to be standing (up); **ponerse de** ~ to stand up; **al** ~ **de la letra** (*citar*) literally, verbatim; (*copiar*) exactly, word for word; **en** ~ **de guerra** on a war footing; **dar** ~ **a** to give cause for.

piedad [pje'ðað] *nf* (*lástima*) pity, compassion; (*clemencia*) mercy; (*devoción*) piety, devotion.

piedra ['pjeðra] *nf* stone; (*roca*) rock; (*de mechero*) flint; (METEOROLOGÍA) hailstone.

piel [pjel] *nf* (ANAT) skin; (ZOOL) skin, hide; (*de oso*) fur; (*cuero*) leather; (BOT) skin, peel; ~ **de ante o de Suecia** suede.

pienso *etc vb ver* **pensar**.

pierdo *etc vb ver* **perder**.

pierna ['pjerna] *nf* leg.

pieza ['pjeθa] *nf* piece; (*habitación*) room; ~ **de recambio o repuesto** spare (part).

pigmeo, a [piɣ'meo, a] *a, nm/f* pigmy.

pijama [pi'xama] *nm* pyjamas *pl*.

pila ['pila] *nf* (ELEC) battery; (*montón*) heap, pile; (*fuente*) sink.

píldora ['pildora] *nf* pill; **la** ~ (**anticonceptiva**) the pill.

pileta [pi'leta] *nf* basin, bowl; (AM) swimming pool.

pilón [pi'lon] *nm* pillar, post; (ELEC) pylon.

piloto [pi'loto] *nm* pilot; (*de aparato*) rear light, tail light; (AUTO) driver.

pillaje [pi'ʎaxe] *nm* pillage, plunder.

pillar [pi'ʎar] *vt* (*saquear*) to pillage, plunder; (*fam: coger*) to catch; (: *agarrar*) to grasp, seize; (: *entender*) to grasp, catch on to.

pillo, a ['piʎo, a] *a* villainous; (*astuto*) sly, crafty // *nm/f* rascal, rogue, scoundrel.

pimentón [pimen'ton] *nm* (*polvo*) paprika; (*pimiento*) red pepper.

pimienta [pi'mjenta] *nf* pepper.

pimiento [pi'mjento] *nm* pepper, pimiento.

pinacoteca [pinako'teka] *nf* art gallery.

pinar [pi'nar] *nm* pinewood.

pincel [pin'θel] *nm* paintbrush.

pinchar [pin'tʃar] *vt* (*perforar*) to prick, pierce; (*neumático*) to puncture; (*incitar*) to prod; (*herir*) to wound.

pinchazo [pin'tʃaθo] *nm* (*perforación*) prick; (*de llanta*) puncture; (*fig*) prod.

pinchitos [pin'tʃitos] *nmpl* bar snacks.

pingüino [pin'gwino] *nm* penguin.

pino ['pino] *nm* pine (tree); **en** ~ upright, vertical.

pinta ['pinta] *nf* spot; (*medida*) spot, drop; (*aspecto*) appearance, look(s) (*pl*); ~**do, a** a spotted; (*de muchos colores*) colourful.

pintar [pin'tar] *vt* to paint // *vi* to paint; (*fam*) to count, be important; ~**se** *vr* to put on make-up.

pintor, a [pin'tor, a] *nm/f* painter.

pintoresco, a [pinto'resko, a] *a* picturesque.

pintura [pin'tura] *nf* painting; ~ **a la acuarela** watercolour; ~ **al óleo** oil painting; ~ **rupestre** cave painting.

pinza ['pinθa] *nf* (ZOOL) claw; (*para colgar ropa*) clothes peg; (TEC) pincers *pl*; ~**s** *nfpl* (*para depilar*) tweezers *pl*.

piña ['piɲa] *nf* (*fruto del pino*) pine cone; (*fruta*) pineapple; (*fig*) group.

pío, a ['pio, a] *a* (*devoto*) pious, devout; (*misericordioso*) merciful // *nm* cheep, chirp.

piojo ['pjoxo] *nm* louse.

pionero, a [pjo'nero, a] *a* pioneering // *nm/f* pioneer.

pipa ['pipa] *nf* pipe; (BOT) edible sunflower seed.

pipí [pi'pi] *nm* (*fam*): **hacer** ~ to have a wee(wee).

pique ['pike] *nm* (*resentimiento*) pique, resentment; (*rivalidad*) rivalry, competition; **irse a** ~ to sink; (*familia*) to be ruined.

piquera [pi'kera] *nf* hole, vent.

piqueta [pi'keta] *nf* pick(axe).

piquete [pi'kete] *nm* (*herida*) prick, jab; (*agujerito*) small hole; (MIL) squad, party; (*de obreros*) picket.

piragua [pi'raɣwa] *nf* canoe; **piragüismo** *nm* (DEPORTE) canoeing.

pirámide [pi'ramiðe] *nf* pyramid.

pirata [pi'rata] *a, nm* pirate.

Pirineo(s) [piri'neo(s)] *nm(pl)* Pyrenees *pl*.

piropo [pi'ropo] *nm* compliment, (piece of) flattery.

pisada [pi'saða] *nf* (*paso*) footstep; (*huella*) footprint.

pisar [pi'sar] *vt* (*caminar sobre*) to walk on, tread on; (*apretar con el pie*) to press; (*fig*) to trample on, walk all over // *vi* to tread, step, walk.

piscina [pis'θina] *nf* swimming pool; (*para peces*) fishpond.

Piscis ['pisθis] *nm* Pisces.

piso ['piso] *nm* (*suelo, de edificio*) floor; (*apartamento*) flat, apartment.

pisotear [pisote'ar] *vt* to trample (on or underfoot).

pista ['pista] *nf* track, trail; (*indicio*) clue; ~ **de aterrizaje** runway; ~ **de baile** dance floor; ~ **de tenis** tennis court; ~ **de hielo** ice rink.

pistola [pis'tola] *nf* pistol; (*TEC*) spray-gun; **pistolero,** a *nm/f* gunman, gangster // *nf* holster.

pistón [pis'ton] *nm* (*TEC*) piston; (*MUS*) key.

pitar [pi'tar] *vt* (*hacer sonar*) to blow; (*rechiflar*) to whistle at, boo // *vi* to whistle; (*AUTO*) to sound *or* toot one's horn; (*AM*) to smoke.

pitillo [pi'tiʎo] *nm* cigarette.

pito ['pito] *nm* whistle; (*de coche*) horn.

pitón [pi'ton] *nm* (*ZOOL*) python; (*protuberancia*) bump, lump; (*de jarro*) spout.

pitonisa [pito'nisa] *nf* fortune-teller.

pizarra [pi'θarra] *nf* (*piedra*) slate; (*encerado*) blackboard.

pizca ['piθka] *nf* pinch, spot; (*fig*) spot, speck, trace; **ni** ~ not a bit.

placa ['plaka] *nf* plate; ~ **de matrícula** number plate.

placentero, a [plaθen'tero, a] *a* pleasant, agreeable.

placer [pla'θer] *nm* pleasure // *vt* to please.

plácido, a ['plaθiðo, a] *a* placid.

plaga ['plaɣa] *nf* pest; (*MED*) plague; (*abundancia*) abundance; **plagar** *vt* to infest, plague; (*llenar*) to fill.

plagio ['plaxjo] *nm* plagiarism.

plan [plan] *nm* (*esquema, proyecto*) plan; (*idea, intento*) idea, intention; **tener** ~ (*fam*) to have a date; **tener un** ~ (*fam*) to have an affair; **en** ~ **económico** (*fam*) on the cheap; **vamos en** ~ **de turismo** we're going as tourists; **si te pones en ese** ~... if that's your attitude... .

plana ['plana] *nf ver* **plano.**

plancha ['plantʃa] *nf* (*para planchar*) iron; (*rótulo*) plate, sheet; (*NAUT*) gangway; ~ **do** *nm* ironing; **planchar** *vt* to iron // *vi* to do the ironing.

planeador [planea'ðor] *nm* glider; ~ **a** *nf* bulldozer.

planear [plane'ar] *vt* to plan // *vi* to glide.

planeta [pla'neta] *nm* planet.

planicie [pla'niθje] *nf* plain.

planificación [planifika'θjon] *nf* planning; ~ **familiar** family planning.

plano, a ['plano, a] *a* flat, level, even // *nm* (*MAT, TEC, AVIAT*) plane; (*FOTO*) shot; (*ARQ*) plan; (*GEO*) map; (*de ciudad*) map, street plan // *nf* sheet (of paper), page; (*TEC*) trowel; **primer** ~ close-up; **caer de** ~ to fall flat; **en primera** ~**a** on the front page; ~ **a** mayor float.

planta ['planta] *nf* (*BOT, TEC*) plant; (*ANAT*) sole of the foot, foot; ~ **baja** ground floor.

plantación [planta'θjon] *nf* (*AGR*) plantation; (*acto*) planting.

plantar [plan'tar] *vt* (*BOT*) to plant; (*levantar*) to erect, set up; ~**se** *vr* to stand firm; ~ **a uno en la calle** to chuck sb out; **dejar plantado a uno** (*fam*) to stand sb up.

plantear [plante'ar] *vt* (*problema*) to pose; (*dificultad*) to raise; (*planificar*) to plan; (*institución*) to set up, establish; (*reforma*) to implant.

plantilla [plan'tiʎa] *nf* (*de zapato*) insole; (*de media*) sole; (*personal*) personnel; **ser de** ~ to be on the staff.

plantío [plan'tio] *nm* (*acto*) planting; (*lugar*) plot, bed, patch.

plantón [plan'ton] *nm* (*MIL*) guard, sentry; (*fam*) long wait; **dar** (**un**) ~ **a uno** to stand sb up.

plañidero, a [plaɲi'ðero, a] *a* mournful, plaintive.

plañir [pla'ɲir] *vi* to mourn.

plasmar [plas'mar] *vt* (*dar forma*) to mould, shape; (*representar*) to represent // *vi*: ~ **en** to take the form of.

plasticina [plasti'θina] *nf* plasticine.

plástico, a ['plastiko, a] *a* plastic // *nf* (art of) sculpture, modelling // *nm* plastic.

plata ['plata] *nf* (*metal*) silver; (*cosas hechas de plata*) silverware; (*AM*) money; **hablar en** ~ to speak bluntly *or* frankly.

plataforma [plata'forma] *nf* platform; ~ **de lanzamiento/perforación** launch(ing) pad/drilling rig.

platea [pla'tea] *nf* (*TEATRO*) pit.

plateado, a [plate'aðo, a] *a* silver; (*TEC*) silver-plated.

platería [plate'ria] *nf* silversmith's.

plática ['platika] *nf* talk, chat; **platicar** *vi* to talk, chat.

platillo [pla'tiʎo] *nm* saucer; ~**s** *nmpl* cymbals; ~ **volador** *o* **volante** flying saucer.

platino [pla'tino] *nm* platinum; ~**s** *nmpl* (*AUTO*) contact points.

plato ['plato] *nm* plate, dish; (*parte de comida*) course; (*guiso*) dish.

playa ['plaja] *nf* beach; (*lugar veraniego*) seaside resort; (*costa*) seaside; ~ **de estacionamiento** (*AM*) car park.

playera [pla'jera] *nf* T-shirt.

plaza ['plaθa] *nf* square; (*mercado*) market(place); (*sitio*) room, space; (*en vehículo*) seat, place; (*colocación*) post, job.

plazco *etc vb ver* **placer.**

plazo ['plaθo] *nm* (*lapso de tiempo*) time, period, term; (*fecha de vencimiento*) expiry date; (*pago parcial*) instalment; **a corto/largo** ~ short-/long-term; **comprar a** ~**s** to buy on hire purchase, pay for in instalments.

plazoleta [plaθo'leta], **plazuela** [pla-'θwela] *nf* small square.

pleamar [plea'mar] *nf* high tide.

plebe ['pleβe] *nf*: **la** ~ the common

people *pl*, the masses *pl*; (*pey*) the plebs *pl*; ~**yo**, **a** a plebeian; (*pey*) coarse, common.

plebiscito [pleˈβisˈθito] *nm* plebiscite.

plegable [pleˈɣaβle] **plegadizo, a** [pleɣaˈðiðo, a] *a* pliable; (*silla*) folding.

plegar [pleˈɣar] *vt* (*doblar*) to fold, bend; (*COSTURA*) to pleat; ~**se** *vr* to yield, submit.

pleito [ˈpleito] *nm* (*JUR*) lawsuit, case; (*fig*) dispute, feud.

plenilunio [pleniˈlunjo] *nm* full moon.

plenitud [pleniˈtuð] *nf* plenitude, fullness; (*abundancia*) abundance.

pleno, a [ˈpleno, a] *a* (*gen*) full; (*completo*) complete // *nm* plenum; **en ~ día** in broad daylight; **en ~ verano** at the height of summer; **en ~a cara** full in the face.

pleuresía [pleureˈsia] *nf* pleurisy.

plexiglás [pleksiˈɣlas] *nm* perspex.

pliego [ˈpljeɣo] *nm* (*hoja*) sheet (of paper); (*carta*) sealed letter/document; ~ **de condiciones** details *pl*, specifications *pl*.

pliegue [ˈpljeɣe] *nm* fold, crease; (*de vestido*) pleat.

plisado [pliˈsaðo] *nm* pleating; ~ **de acordeón** accordion pleats *pl*.

plomero [ploˈmero] *nm* plumber.

plomo [ˈplomo] *nm* (*metal*) lead; (*ELEC*) fuse.

pluma [ˈpluma] *nf* (*gen*) feather; (*para escribir*) pen.

plural [pluˈral] *a* plural; ~**idad** *nf* plurality; **una ~idad de votos** a majority of votes.

plus [plus] *nm* bonus.

plutocracia [plutoˈkraθja] *nf* plutocracy.

población [poβlaˈθjon] *nf* population; (*pueblo, ciudad*) town, city; **poblado, a** *a* inhabited // *nm* (*aldea*) village; (*pueblo*) (small) town; **densamente poblado** densely populated.

poblador, a [poβlaˈðor, a] *nm/f* settler, colonist; (*fundador*) founder.

poblar [poˈβlar] *vt* (*colonizar*) to colonize; (*fundar*) to found; (*habitar*) to inhabit.

pobre [ˈpoβre] *a* poor // *nm/f* poor person; **¡~!** poor thing!; ~**za** *nf* poverty.

pocilga [poˈθilɣa] *nf* pigsty.

poción [poˈθjon], **pócima** [ˈpoθima] *nf* potion.

poco, a [ˈpoko, a] *a* a little; ~**s** few // *ad* (*no mucho*) little, not much // *nm*: **un ~ a** little, a bit; **tener a uno en ~** to think little *or* not think much of sb; **por ~** almost, nearly; ~ **a ~** little by little, gradually; **dentro de ~** (+ *presente o futuro*) shortly; (+ *pasado*) soon after; **hace ~** a short time ago, not long ago.

podar [poˈðar] *vt* to prune.

podenco [poˈðenko] *nm* hound.

poder [poˈðer] *vi* can; (*sujeto: persona*) to be able to, can; (*permiso*) can, may; (*posibilidad, hipótesis*) may // *nm* (*gen*) power; (*autoridad*) authority; **puede que sea así** it may be, maybe; **¿se puede?** may I come in?; **¿puedes con eso?** can

you manage that?; **a más no ~** to the utmost; **no ~ menos de hacer algo** not to be able to help doing sth; **no ~ más** to have had enough; ~**ío** *nm* power; (*autoridad*) authority; ~**oso, a** *a* powerful.

podrido, a [poˈðriðo, a] *a* rotten, bad; (*fig*) rotten, corrupt.

podrir [poˈðrir] = **pudrir**.

poema [poˈema] *nm* poem.

poesía [poeˈsia] *nf* poetry.

poeta [poˈeta] *nm* poet; **poético, a** *a* poetic(al).

póker [ˈpoker] *nm* poker.

polaco, a [poˈlako, a] *a* Polish // *nm/f* Pole.

polar [poˈlar] *a* polar; ~**idad** *nf* polarity; ~**izarse** *vr* to polarize.

polea [poˈlea] *nf* pulley.

polémica [poˈlemika] *nf* (*gen*) polemics *sg*; (*una ~*) controversy.

policía [poliˈθia] *nm/f* policeman/woman // *nf* police; ~**co, a** *a* police *cpd*; **novela ~ca** detective story.

poligamia [poliˈɣamja] *nf* polygamy.

polilla [poˈliʎa] *nf* moth.

polio [ˈpoljo] *nf* polio.

politécnico [poliˈtekniko] *nm* polytechnic.

politene [poliˈtene], **politeno** [poliˈteno] *nm* polythene.

político, a [poˈlitiko, a] *a* political; (*discreto*) tactful; (*de familia*) in-law // *nm/f* politician // *nf* politics *sg*; (*económica, agraria*) policy; **padre ~** father-in-law; **politicastro** *nm* (*pey*) politician, politico.

póliza [ˈpoliθa] *nf* insurance policy.

polo [ˈpolo] *nm* (*GEO, ELEC*) pole; (*helado*) iced lolly; (*DEPORTE*) polo; (*suéter*) polo-neck; ~ **Norte/Sur** North/South Pole.

Polonia [poˈlonja] *nf* Poland.

poltrona [polˈtrona] *nf* reclining chair, easy chair.

polución [poluˈθjon] *nf* pollution.

polvera [polˈβera] *nf* powder compact, vanity case.

polvo [ˈpolβo] *nm* dust; (*QUÍMICA, CULIN, MED*) powder; ~**s** *nmpl* powder *sg*; ~ **de talco** talcum powder; **estar hecho ~** to be worn out *or* exhausted.

pólvora [ˈpolβora] *nf* gunpowder; (*fuegos artificiales*) fireworks *pl*.

polvoriento, a [polβoˈrjento, a] *a* (*superficie*) dusty; (*sustancia*) powdery.

pollería [poʎeˈria] *nf* poulterer's (shop).

pollo [ˈpoʎo] *nm* chicken.

pomada [poˈmaða] *nf* ointment.

pomelo [poˈmelo] *nm* grapefruit.

pómez [ˈpomeθ] *nf*: **piedra ~** pumice stone.

pompa [ˈpompa] *nf* (*burbuja*) bubble; (*bomba*) pump; (*esplendor*) pomp, splendour; **pomposo, a** *a* splendid, magnificent; (*pey*) pompous.

pómulo [ˈpomulo] *nm* cheekbone.

pon [pon] *vb ver* **poner**.

ponche [ˈpontʃe] *nm* punch.

poncho ['pontʃo] nm (AM) poncho, cape.

ponderado, a [ponde'raðo, a] a calm, steady, balanced.

ponderar [ponde'rar] vt (considerar) to weigh up, consider; (elogiar) to praise highly, speak in praise of.

pondré etc vb ver **poner.**

poner [po'ner] vt (gen) to put; (colocar) to place, set; (ropa) to put on; (problema, la mesa) to set; (telegrama) to send; (TELEC) to connect; (radio, TV) to switch on, turn on; (tienda) to open, set up; (nombre) to give; (añadir) to add; (TEATRO, CINE) to put on; (+ adjetivo) to make, turn; (suponer) to suppose // vi (ave) to lay (eggs); ~se vr to put or place o.s.; (ropa) to put on; (+ adjetivo) to turn, get, become; (el sol) to set; **póngame con el Señor X** get me Mr X, put me through to Mr X; ~**se de zapatero** to take a job as a shoemaker; ~**se a bien con uno** to get on good terms with sb; ~**se con uno** to quarrel with sb; ~**se rojo** to blush; ~**se a** to begin to.

pongo etc vb ver **poner.**

pontificado [pontifi'kaðo] nm papacy, pontificate; **pontífice** nm pope, pontiff.

pontón [pon'ton] nm pontoon.

ponzoña [pon'θoɲa] nf poison, venom; **ponzoñoso, a** a poisonous, venomous.

popa ['popa] nf stern.

popular [popu'lar] a popular; (del pueblo) of the people; ~**idad** nf popularity; ~**izarse** vr to become popular.

poquedad [poke'ðað] nf (escasez) scantiness; (una ~) small thing, trifle; (fig) timidity.

por [por] prep (con el fin de) in order to; (a favor de, hacia) for; (a causa de) out of, because of, from; (según) according to; (por agencia de) by; (a cambio de) for, in exchange for; (en lugar de) instead of, in place of; (durante) for; **10 ~ 10 son 100** 10 times 10 are 100; **será ~ poco tiempo** it won't be for long; ~ **correo/avión** by post/plane; ~ **centenares** by the hundred; **(el) 10 ~ ciento** 10 per cent; ~ **orden** in order; **ir a Bilbao ~ Santander** to go to Bilbao via Santander; **pasar ~ Madrid** to pass through Madrid; **camina ~ la izquierda** walk on the left; ~ **todo el país** throughout the country; **entra ~ delante/detrás** come/go in by the front/back (door); ~ **la calle** along the street; ~ **la mañana** in the morning; ~ **la noche** at night; **£2 ~ hora** £2 an hour; ~ **allí** over there; **está ~ el norte** it's somewhere in the north; ~ **mucho que quisiera, no puedo** much as I would like to, I can't; ~**que** because; **¿~ qué?** why?; ~ **(lo) tanto** so, therefore; ~ **cierto** (seguro) certainly; (a propósito) by the way; ~ **ejemplo** for example; ~ **favor** please; ~ **fuera/dentro** outside/inside; ~ **si (acaso)** just in case; ~ **sí mismo** o **sólo** by o.s.

porcelana [porθe'lana] nf porcelain; (china) china.

porcentaje [porθen'taxe] nm percentage.

porción [por'θjon] nf (parte) portion, share; (cantidad) quantity, amount.

pordiosear [porðjose'ar] vi to beg; **pordiosero, a** nm/f beggar.

porfía [por'fia] nf persistence; (terquedad) obstinacy; **porfiado, a** a persistent; obstinate; **porfiar** vi to persist, insist; (disputar) to argue stubbornly.

pormenor [porme'nor] nm detail, particular.

pornografía [pornoɣra'fia] nf pornography.

poro ['poro] nm pore; ~**so, a** a porous.

porque ['porke] conj (a causa de) because; (ya que) since; (con el fin de) so that, in order that.

porqué [por'ke] nm reason, cause.

porquería [porke'ria] nf (suciedad) filth, muck, dirt; (acción) dirty trick; (objeto) small thing, trifle; (fig) rubbish.

porro, a ['porro, a] a (fam) stupid // nf (arma) stick, club; (TEC) large hammer; (fam) bore.

porrón, ona [po'rron, ona] a slow, stupid // nm glass wine jar with a long spout.

portada [por'taða] nf (entrada) porch, doorway; (de revista) cover.

portador, a [porta'ðor, a] nm/f carrier, bearer.

portaequipajes [portaeki'paxes] nm inv boot; (arriba del coche) luggage rack.

portal [por'tal] nm (entrada) vestibule, hall; (portada) porch, doorway; (puerta de entrada) main door; (de ciudad) gate; (DEPORTE) goal.

portaligas [porta'liɣas] nm inv suspender belt.

portamaletas [portama'letas] nm inv boot.

portamonedas [portamo'neðas] nm inv purse.

portarse [por'tarse] vr to behave, conduct o.s.

portátil [por'tatil] a portable.

portaviones [porta'βjones] nm inv aircraft carrier.

portavoz [porta'βoθ] nm (megáfono) megaphone, loudhailer; (vocero) spokesman/woman.

portazo [por'taθo] nm: **dar un ~** to slam the door.

porte ['porte] nm (COM) transport; (precio) transport charges pl; (comportamiento) conduct, behaviour.

portento [por'tento] nm marvel, wonder; ~**so, a** a marvellous, extraordinary.

porteño, a [por'teɲo, a] a of or from Buenos Aires.

portería [porte'ria] nf (oficina) porter's office; (gol) goal.

portero, a [por'tero, a] nm/f porter; (conserje) caretaker; (ujier) doorman // nm goalkeeper.

pórtico ['portiko] *nm* (*patio*) portico, porch; (*fig*) gateway; (*arcada*) arcade.
portilla [por'tiʎa] *nf* porthole.
portillo [por'tiʎo] *nm* (*abertura*) gap, opening; (GEO) narrow pass.
portorriqueño, a [portorri'keɲo, a] *a* Puerto Rican.
Portugal [portu'ɣal] *nm* Portugal; **portugués, esa** *a, nm/f* Portuguese.
porvenir [porβe'nir] *nm* future.
pos [pos] *prep*: **en ~ de** after, in pursuit of.
posada [po'saða] *nf* (*refugio*) shelter, lodging; (*mesón*) guest house; **dar ~ a** to give shelter to, take in.
posaderas [posa'ðeras] *nfpl* backside *sg*, buttocks.
posar [po'sar] *vt* (*en el suelo*) to lay down, put down; (*la mano*) to place, put gently // *vi* to sit, pose; **~se** *vr* to settle; (*pájaro*) to perch ; (*avión*) to land, come down.
posdata [pos'ðata] *nf* postscript.
pose ['pose] *nf* pose.
poseedor, a [posee'ðor, a] *nm/f* owner, possessor; (*de récord, puesto*) holder.
poseer [pose'er] *vt* to have, possess, own; (*ventaja*) to enjoy; (*récord, puesto*) to hold; **poseído, a** *a* possessed; **posesión** *nf* possession; **posesionarse** *vr*: **posesionarse de** to take possession of, take over; **posesivo, a** *a* possessive.
posibilidad [posiβili'ðað] *nf* possibility; (*oportunidad*) chance; **posibilitar** *vt* to make possible, permit; (*hacer factible*) to make feasible.
posible [po'siβle] *a* possible; (*factible*) feasible; **de ser ~** if possible; **en lo ~ as** far as possible.
posición [posi'θjon] *nf* (*gen*) position; (*rango social*) status.
positivo, a [posi'tiβo, a] *a* positive // *nf* (FOTO) print.
poso ['poso] *nm* sediment.
posponer [pospo'ner] *vt* to put behind/below; (*aplazar*) to postpone.
posta ['posta] *nf* (*de caballos*) relay, team; (*pedazo*) slice // *nm* courier.
postal [pos'tal] *a* postal // *nf* postcard.
poste ['poste] *nm* (*de telégrafos*) post, pole; (*columna*) pillar; **dar ~ a uno** (*fam*) to keep sb hanging about.
postergar [poster'ɣar] *vt* (AM: *posponer*) to postpone, delay.
posteridad [posteri'ðað] *nf* posterity.
posterior [poste'rjor] *a* back, rear; (*siguiente*) following, subsequent; (*más tarde*) later; **~idad** *nf*: **con ~idad** later, subsequently.
postizo, a [pos'tiθo, a] *a* false, artificial // *nm* hairpiece.
postor, a [pos'tor, a] *nm/f* bidder.
postrado, a [pos'traðo, a] *a* prostrate; **postrar** *vt* (*derribar*) to cast down, overthrow; (*humillar*) to humble; (MED) to weaken, exhaust.
postre ['postre] *nm* sweet, dessert.
postremo, a [pos'tremo, a] **postrer,**

ero, a [pos'trer, ero, a] *a* (*último*) last; (*que viene detrás*) rear.
postulado [postu'laðo] *nm* postulate; **postular** *vt* (*empleo*) to apply for; (*pedir*) to seek, demand; (*proponer*) to postulate.
póstumo, a ['postumo, a] *a* posthumous.
postura [pos'tura] *nf* (*del cuerpo*) posture, position; (*fig*) attitude, position.
potable [po'taβle] *a* drinkable.
potaje [po'taxe] *nm* stew; **~s** *nmpl* mixed vegetables.
pote ['pote] *nm* pot, jar.
potencia [po'tenθja] *nf* power.
potencial [poten'θjal] *a, nm* potential.
potente [po'tente] *a* powerful.
pozo ['poθo] *nm* well; (*de río*) deep pool; (*de mina*) shaft.
práctica ['praktika] *nf* ver **práctico.**
practicable [prakti'kaβle] *a* practicable; (*camino*) passable, usable.
practicante [prakti'kante] *nm/f* (MED: *ayudante de doctor*) medical assistant; (: *enfermero*) male nurse; (*quien practica algo*) practitioner // *a* practising.
practicar [prakti'kar] *vt* to practise; (*deporte*) to go in for, play; (*realizar*) to carry out, perform.
práctico, a [a] [a] [a] [a] **práctico, a** [a] [a] **práctico, a** [a] **práctico, a** [a] **práctico, a** ['praktiko, a] *a* (*gen*) practical; (*conveniente*) handy; (*instruido*: *persona*) skilled, expert // *nf* practice; (*método*) method; (*arte, capacidad*) skill; **en la ~a** in practice.
pradera [pra'ðera] *nf* meadow; (*de Canadá*) prairie.
prado ['praðo] *nm* (*campo*) meadow, field; (*pastizal*) pasture.
Praga ['praɣa] *n* Prague.
pragmático, a [praɣ'matiko, a] *a* pragmatic.
preámbulo [pre'ambulo] *nm* preamble, introduction.
precario, a [pre'karjo, a] *a* precarious.
precaución [prekau'θjon] *nf* (*medida preventiva*) preventive measure, precaution; (*prudencia*) caution, wariness.
precaver [preka'βer] *vt* to guard against; (*impedir*) to forestall; **~se** *vr*: **~se de** *o* **contra algo** to be on one's guard against sth; **precavido, a** *a* cautious, wary.
precedencia [preθe'ðenθja] *nf* precedence; (*prioridad*) priority; (*superioridad*) greater importance, superiority; **precedente** *a* preceding; (*anterior*) former // *nm* precedent; **preceder** *vt, vi* to precede, go/come before.
precepto [pre'θepto] *nm* precept.
preciado, a [pre'θjaðo, a] *a* (*estimado*) esteemed, valuable; (*vanidoso*) presumptuous; **preciar** *vt* to esteem, value; **preciarse** *vr* to boast; **preciarse de** to pride o.s. on, boast of being.
precio ['preθjo] *nm* (*de mercado*) price; (*costo*) cost; (*valor*) value, worth; (*de viaje*) fare; **~ al contado/de coste/de**

oportunidad cash/cost/bargain price; ~ **tope** top price.

preciosidad [preθjosi'ðað] *nf* (*valor*) (high) value, (great) worth; (*encanto*) charm; (*cosa bonita*) beautiful thing; **es una** ~ it's lovely, it's really beautiful; **precioso, a** *a* precious; (*de mucho valor*) valuable; (*fam*) lovely, beautiful.

precipicio [preθi'piθjo] *nm* cliff, precipice; (*fig*) abyss.

precipitación [preθipita'θjon] *nf* haste; (*lluvia*) rainfall.

precipitado, a [preθipi'taðo, a] *a* hasty, rash; (*salida*) hasty, sudden.

precipitar [preθipi'tar] *vt* (*arrojar*) to hurl down, throw; (*apresurar*) to hasten; (*acelerar*) to speed up, accelerate; ~ **se** *vr* to throw o.s.; (*apresurarse*) to rush; (*actuar sin pensar*) to act rashly.

precipitoso, a [preθipi'toso, a] *a* (*escarpado*) steep, sheer; (*a la carrera, imprudente*) hasty, rash.

precisamente [preθisa'mente] *ad* precisely; (*justo*) precisely, exactly, just.

precisar [preθi'sar] *vt* (*necesitar*) to need, require; (*fijar*) to determine exactly, fix; (*especificar*) to specify // *vi* to be necessary.

precisión [preθi'sjon] *nf* (*exactitud*) precision; (*necesidad*) need, necessity.

preciso, a [pre'θiso, a] *a* (*exacto*) precise; (*necesario*) necessary, essential.

preconcebido, a [prekonθe'βiðo, a] *a* preconceived.

preconizar [prekoni'θar] *vt* (*aconsejar*) to advise; (*prever*) to foresee.

precoz [pre'koθ] *a* (*persona*) precocious; (*calvicie*) premature.

precursor, a [prekur'sor, a] *nm/f* precursor.

predecir [preðe'θir] *vt* to predict, foretell, forecast.

predestinado, a [preðesti'naðo, a] *a* predestined.

predeterminar [preðetermi'nar] *vt* to predetermine.

prédica ['preðika] *nf* sermon; **predicador, a** *nm/f* preacher; **predicar** *vt, vi* to preach.

predicción [preðik'θjon] *nf* prediction.

predilecto, a [preði'lekto, a] *a* favourite.

predio ['preðjo] *nm* property, estate.

predisponer [preðispo'ner] *vt* to predispose; (*pey*) to prejudice; **predisposición** *nf* predisposition, inclination; prejudice, bias.

predominante [preðomi'nante] *a* predominant.

predominar [preðomi'nar] *vt* to dominate // *vi* to predominate; (*prevalecer*) to prevail; **predominio** *nm* predominance; prevalence.

prefabricado, a [prefaβri'kaðo, a] *a* prefabricated.

prefacio [pre'faθjo] *nm* preface.

preferencia [prefe'renθja] *nf* preference; **de** ~ preferably, for preference;

preferible *a* preferable; **preferir** *vt* to prefer.

prefigurar [prefixu'rar] *vt* to foreshadow, prefigure.

pregonar [prexo'nar] *vt* to proclaim, announce.

pregunta [pre'xunta] *nf* question; **hacer una** ~ to ask *or* put a question.

preguntar [prexun'tar] *vt* to ask; (*cuestionar*) to question // *vi* to ask; ~ **se** *vr* to wonder; ~ **por alguien** to ask for sb; **preguntón, ona** *a* inquisitive.

prehistórico, a [preis'toriko, a] *a* prehistoric.

prejuicio [pre'xwiθjo] *nm* prejudgement; (*preconcepción*) preconception; (*pey*) prejudice, bias.

prelación [prela'θjon] *nf* priority.

preliminar [prelimi'nar] *a* preliminary.

preludio [pre'luðjo] *nm* prelude.

prematuro, a [prema'turo, a] *a* premature.

premeditación [premeðita'θjon] *nf* premeditation; **premeditar** *vt* to premeditate.

premiar [pre'mjar] *vt* to reward; (*en un concurso*) to give a prize to; **premio** *nm* reward; prize; (*com*) premium.

premonición [premoni'θjon] *nf* premonition.

premura [pre'mura] *nf* (*aprieto*) pressure; (*prisa*) haste, urgency.

prenatal [prena'tal] *a* antenatal, prenatal.

prenda ['prenda] *nf* (*ropa*) garment, article of clothing; (*garantía*) pledge; ~ **s** *nfpl* talents, gifts.

prendar [pren'dar] *vt* to captivate, enchant; ~ **se de uno** to fall in love with sb.

prendedor [prende'ðor] *nm* brooch.

prender [pren'der] *vt* (*captar*) to catch, capture; (*detener*) to arrest; (*coser*) to pin, attach; (*sujetar*) to fasten // *vi* to catch; (*arraigar*) to take root; ~ **se** *vr* (*encenderse*) to catch fire; (*engalanarse*) to dress up.

prensa ['prensa] *nf* press; **la P** ~ the press; **prensar** *vt* to press.

preñado, a [pre'ɲaðo, a] *a* (*mujer*) pregnant; ~ **de** pregnant with, full of; **preñez** *nf* pregnancy.

preocupación [preokupa'θjon] *nf* worry, concern; (*ansiedad*) anxiety; **preocupado, a** *a* worried, concerned; anxious.

preocupar [preoku'par] *vt* to worry; ~ **se** *vr* to worry; ~ **se de algo** (*hacerse cargo*) to worry about sth, take care of sth.

preparación [prepara'θjon] *nf* (*acto*) preparation; (*estado*) preparedness, readiness; (*entrenamiento*) training; **preparado, a** *a* (*dispuesto*) prepared; (*CULIN*) ready (to serve) // *nm* preparation.

preparador, a [prepara'ðor, a] *nm/f* trainer.

preparar [prepa'rar] *vt* (*disponer*) to prepare, get ready; (*TEC: tratar*) to

prepare, process, treat; (*entrenar*) to teach, train; ~**se** *vr*: ~**se a** *o* **para** to prepare to *or* for, get ready to *or* for;
preparativo, a *a* preparatory, preliminary; **preparativos** *nmpl* preparations; **preparatorio, a** *a* preparatory.

prerrogativa [prerroɣa'tiβa] *nf* prerogative, privilege.

presa ['presa] *nf* (*captura*) capture, seizure; (*cosa apresada*) catch; (*víctima*) victim; (*de animal*) prey; (*de agua*) dam.

presbítero [pres'βitero] *nm* priest.

prescindible [presθin'diβle] *a* dispensable.

prescindir [presθin'dir] *vi*: ~ **de** (*privarse de*) to do without, go without; (*descartar*) to dispense with.

prescribir [preskri'βir] *vt* to prescribe; **prescripción** *nf* prescription.

presencia [pre'senθja] *nf* presence; **presencial** *a*: **testigo presencial** eyewitness; **presenciar** *vt* to be present at; (*asistir a*) to attend; (*ver*) to see, witness.

presentación [presenta'θjon] *nf* presentation; (*introducción*) introduction.

presentador, a [presenta'ðor, a] *nm/f* compère.

presentar [presen'tar] *vt* to present; (*ofrecer*) to offer; (*mostrar*) to show, display; (*a una persona*) to introduce; ~**se** *vr* (*llegar inesperadamente*) to appear, turn up; (*ofrecerse: como candidato*) to run, stand; (*aparecer*) to show, appear; (*solicitar empleo*) to apply.

presente [pre'sente] *a* present // *nm* present; **hacer** ~ to state, declare; **tener** ~ to remember, bear in mind.

presentimiento [presenti'mjento] *nm* premonition, presentiment; **presentir** *vt* to have a premonition of.

preservación [preserβa'θjon] *nf* protection, preservation; **preservar** *vt* to protect, preserve; **preservativo** *nm* sheath, condom.

presidencia [presi'ðenθja] *nf* presidency; (*de comité*) chairmanship; **presidente** *nm/f* president; chairman/woman.

presidiario [presi'ðjarjo] *nm* convict; **presidio** *nm* (*penitenciaría*) prison, penitentiary; (*trabajo forzoso*) hard labour; (*MIL*) garrison.

presidir [presi'ðir] *vt* (*dirigir*) to preside at, preside over; (*: comité*) to take the chair at; (*dominar*) to dominate, rule // *vi* to preside; to take the chair.

presión [pre'sjon] *nf* pressure; **presionar** *vt* to press; (*fig*) to press, put pressure on // *vi*: **presionar para** *o* **por** to press for.

preso, a ['preso, a] *nm/f* prisoner; **tomar** *o* **llevar** ~ **a uno** to arrest sb, take sb prisoner.

prestado, a [pres'taðo, a] *a* on loan; **pedir** ~ to borrow.

prestamista [presta'mista] *nm/f* moneylender.

préstamo ['prestamo] *nm* loan.

prestar [pres'tar] *vt* to lend, loan; (*atención*) to pay; (*ayuda*) to give // *vi* to give, stretch.

prestatario, a [presta'tarjo, a] *nm/f* borrower.

presteza [pres'teθa] *nf* speed, promptness.

prestigio [pres'tixjo] *nm* prestige; ~**so, a** *a* (*honorable*) prestigious; (*famoso, renombrado*) renowned, famous.

presto, a ['presto, a] *a* (*rápido*) quick, prompt; (*dispuesto*) ready // *ad* at once, right away.

presumir [presu'mir] *vt* to presume // *vi* (*tener aires*) to be conceited; **según cabe** ~ as may be presumed, presumably; **presunción** *nf* presumption; **presunto, a** *a* (*supuesto*) supposed, presumed; (*así llamado*) so-called; **presuntuoso, a** *a* conceited, presumptuous.

presuponer [presupo'ner] *vt* to presuppose.

presupuesto [presu'pwesto] *nm* (*FINANZAS*) budget; (*estimación: de costo*) estimate.

presuroso, a [presu'roso, a] *a* (*rápido*) quick, speedy; (*que tiene prisa*) hasty.

pretencioso, a [preten'θjoso, a] *a* pretentious.

pretender [preten'der] *vt* (*intentar*) to try to, seek to; (*reivindicar*) to claim; (*buscar*) to seek, try for; (*cortejar*) to woo, court; ~ **que** to expect that; **pretendiente** *nm/f* (*candidato*) candidate, applicant; (*amante*) suitor; **pretensión** *nf* (*aspiración*) aspiration; (*reivindicación*) claim; (*orgullo*) pretension.

pretexto [pre'teksto] *nm* pretext; (*excusa*) excuse.

prevalecer [preβale'θer] *vi* to prevail; **prevaleciente** *a* prevailing, prevalent.

prevalerse [preβa'lerse] *vr*: ~ **de** to avail o.s. of.

prevención [preβen'θjon] *nf* (*preparación*) preparation; (*estado*) preparedness, readiness; (*el evitar*) prevention; (*previsión*) foresight, forethought; (*prejuicio*) bias, prejudice; (*precaución*) precaution.

prevenido, a [preβe'niðo, a] *a* prepared, ready; (*cauteloso*) cautious.

prevenir [preβe'nir] *vt* (*impedir*) to prevent; (*prever*) to foresee, anticipate; (*predisponer*) to prejudice, bias; (*avisar*) to warn; (*preparar*) to prepare, get ready; ~**se** *vr* to get ready, prepare; ~**se contra** to take precautions against; **preventivo, a** *a* preventive, precautionary.

prever [pre'βer] *vt* to foresee.

previo, a ['preβjo, a] *a* (*anterior*) previous; (*preliminar*) preliminary // *prep*: ~ **acuerdo de los otros** subject to the agreement of the others.

previsión [preβi'sjon] *nf* (*perspicacia*) foresight; (*predicción*) forecast; ~ **social** social security.

prieto, a ['prjeto, a] *a* (*oscuro*) dark; (*fig*) mean; (*comprimido*) tight, compressed.

prima ['prima] *nf ver* **primo**.
primacía [prima'θia] *nf* primacy.
primario, a [pri'marjo, a] *a* primary.
primavera [prima'ßera] *nf* (*temporada*) spring; (*período*) springtime.
primer, primero, a [pri'mer, pri'mero, a] *a* first; (*fig*) prime // *ad* first; (*más bien*) sooner, rather // *nf* (*AUTO*) first gear; (*FERRO*) first class; **de ~a** (*fam*) first-class, first-rate; **~a plana** front page.
primitivo, a [primi'tiβo, a] *a* primitive; (*original*) original.
primo, a ['primo, a] *nm/f* cousin; (*fam*) fool, dupe // *nf* (*COM*) bonus; **~ hermano** first cousin; **materias ~as** raw materials.
primogénito, a [primo'xenito, a] *a* first-born.
primordial [primor'ðjal] *a* basic, fundamental.
primoroso, a [primo'roso, a] *a* exquisite, delicate.
princesa [prin'θesa] *nf* princess.
principal [prinθi'pal] *a* principal, main // *nm* (*jefe*) chief, principal.
príncipe ['prinθipe] *nm* prince.
principiante [prinθi'pjante] *nm/f* beginner; **principiar** *vt* to begin.
principio [prin'θipjo] *nm* (*comienzo*) beginning, start; (*origen*) origin; (*primera etapa*) rudiment, basic idea; (*moral*) principle; **a ~s de** at the beginning of; **tener** *o* **tomar en ~** to start from, be based on.
pringue ['pringe] *nm* (*grasa*) grease, fat, dripping; (*mancha*) grease stain.
prioridad [priori'ðað] *nf* priority.
prisa ['prisa] *nf* (*apresuramiento*) hurry, haste; (*rapidez*) speed; (*urgencia*) (sense of) urgency; **a** *o* **de ~** quickly; **correr ~** to be urgent; **darse ~** to hurry up; **estar de** *o* **tener ~** to be in a hurry.
prisión [pri'sjon] *nf* (*cárcel*) prison; (*período de cárcel*) imprisonment; **prisionero, a** *nm/f* prisoner.
prismáticos [pris'matikos] *nmpl* binoculars.
privación [priβa'θjon] *nf* deprivation; (*falta*) want, privation.
privado, a [pri'ßaðo, a] *a* private.
privar [pri'ßar] *vt* to deprive; (*prohibir*) to forbid // *vi* (*gozar de favor*) to be in favour; (*prevalecer*) to prevail; **privativo, a** *a* exclusive.
privilegiado, a [prißile'xjaðo, a] *a* privileged; (*memoria*) very good; **privilegiar** *vt* to grant a privilege to; (*favorecer*) to favour.
privilegio [prißi'lexjo] *nm* privilege; (*concesión*) concession; **~ de invención** patent.
pro [pro] *nm o f* profit, advantage // *prep*: **asociación ~ ciegos** association for the blind // *pref*: **~ soviético/americano** pro-Soviet/American; **en ~ de** on behalf of, for; **los ~s y los contras** the pros and cons.

probabilidad [proßaßili'ðað] *nf* probability, likelihood; (*oportunidad, posibilidad*) chance, prospect; **probable** *a* probable, likely.
probanza [pro'ßanθa] *nf* proof, evidence.
probar [pro'ßar] *vt* (*demostrar*) to prove; (*someter a prueba*) to test, try; (*ropa*) to try on; (*comida*) to taste // *vi* to try; **~se un traje** to try on a suit.
probeta [pro'ßeta] *nf* test tube.
problema [pro'ßlema] *nm* problem.
procaz [pro'kaθ] *a* insolent, impudent.
procedente [proθe'ðente] *a* (*razonable*) reasonable; (*conforme a derecho*) proper, fitting; **~ de** coming from, originating in.
proceder [proθe'ðer] *vi* (*avanzar*) to proceed; (*actuar*) to act; (*ser correcto*) to be right (and proper), be fitting // *nm* (*acción*) course of action; (*comportamiento*) behaviour, conduct; **procedimiento** *nm* procedure; (*proceso*) process; (*método*) means, method.
procesado, a [proθe'saðo, a] *nm/f* accused (person); **procesar** *vt* to try, put on trial.
procesión [proθe'sjon] *nf* procession.
proceso [pro'θeso] *nm* process; (*JUR*) trial; (*lapso*) course (of time).
proclama [pro'klama] *nf* (*acto*) proclamation; (*cartel*) poster; **proclamar** *vt* to proclaim.
procreación [prokrea'θjon] *nf* procreation; **procrear** *vt, vi* to procreate.
procurador, a [prokura'ðor, a] *nm/f* attorney.
procurar [proku'rar] *vt* (*intentar*) to try, endeavour; (*conseguir*) to get, obtain; (*asegurar*) to secure; (*producir*) to produce.
prodigio [pro'ðixjo] *nm* prodigy; (*milagro*) wonder, marvel; **~so, a** *a* prodigious, marvellous.
pródigo, a ['proðixo, a] *a*: **hijo ~** prodigal son.
producción [proðuk'θjon] *nf* production; (*suma de productos*) output; (*producto*) product; **~ en serie** mass production.
producir [proðu'θir] *vt* to produce; (*generar*) to cause, bring about; **~se** *vr* (*gen*) to come about, happen; (*hacerse*) to be produced, be made; (*estallar*) to break out.
productividad [proðuktiβi'ðað] *nf* productivity; **productivo, a** *a* productive; (*provechoso*) profitable.
producto [pro'ðukto] *nm* product; (*producción*) production.
productor, a [proðuk'tor, a] *a* productive, producing // *nm/f* producer.
proeza [pro'eθa] *nf* exploit, feat.
profanar [profa'nar] *vt* to desecrate, profane; **profano, a** *a* profane // *nm/f* layman/woman.
profecía [profe'θia] *nf* prophecy.
proferir [profe'rir] *vt* (*palabra, sonido*) to utter; (*injuria*) to hurl, let fly.
profesar [profe'sar] *vt* (*declarar*) to profess; (*practicar*) to practise.

profesión [profe'sjon] *nf* profession; **profesional** *a* professional.
profesor, a [profe'sor, a] *nm/f* teacher; **~ado** *nm* teaching profession.
profeta [pro'feta] *nm/f* prophet; **profetizar** *vt, vi* to prophesy.
prófugo, a ['profuxo, a] *nm/f* fugitive; (*desertor*) deserter.
profundidad [profundi'ðað] *nf* depth; **profundizar** *vt* (*fig*) to go deeply into; **profundo, a** *a* deep; (*misterio, pensador*) profound.
progenie [pro'xenje] *nf* offspring.
progenitor [proxeni'tor] *nm* ancestor; **~es** *nmpl* (*fam*) parents.
programa [pro'xrama] *nm* programme; **~ción** *nf* programming; **~dor, a** *nm/f* programmer; **programar** *vt* to programme.
progresar [proxre'sar] *vi* to progress, make progress; **progresista** *a, nm/f* progressive; **progresivo, a** *a* progressive; (*gradual*) gradual; (*continuo*) continuous; **progreso** *nm* progress.
prohibición [proiði'θjon] *nf* prohibition, ban; **prohibir** *vt* to prohibit, ban, forbid; **se prohibe fumar** no smoking.
prohijar [proi'xar] *vt* to adopt.
prójimo, a ['proximo, a] *nm/f* fellow man, neighbour.
proletariado [proleta'rjaðo] *nm* proletariat; **proletario, a** *a, nm/f* proletarian.
proliferación [prolifera'θjon] *nf* proliferation; **proliferar** *vi* to proliferate; **prolífico, a** *a* prolific.
prolijo, a [pro'lixo, a] *a* long-winded, tedious.
prólogo ['proloxo] *nm* prologue.
prolongación [prolonga'θjon] *nf* extension; **prolongado, a** *a* (*largo*) long; (*alargado*) lengthy; **prolongar** *vt* (*gen*) to extend; (*en el tiempo*) to prolong; (*calle, tubo*) to make longer, extend.
promedio [pro'meðjo] *nm* average; (*de distancia*) middle, mid-point.
promesa [pro'mesa] *nf* promise.
prometer [prome'ter] *vt* to promise // *vi* to show promise; **~se** *vr* (*dos personas*) to get engaged; **prometido, a** *a* promised; engaged // *nm/f* fiancé/fiancée.
prominente [promi'nente] *a* prominent.
promiscuo, a [pro'miskwo, a] *a* (*mezclado*) mixed(-up), in disorder; (*ambiguo*) ambiguous.
promoción [promo'θjon] *nf* promotion.
promotor [promo'tor] *nm* promoter; (*instigador*) instigator.
promover [promo'ßer] *vt* to promote; (*causar*) to cause; (*instigar*) to instigate, stir up.
promulgar [promul'xar] *vt* to promulgate; (*fig*) to proclaim.
pronosticar [pronosti'kar] *vt* to predict, foretell, forecast; **pronóstico** *nm* prediction, forecast.
prontitud [pronti'tuð] *nf* speed, quickness;

(*de ingenio*) quickness, sharpness.
pronto, a ['pronto, a] *a* (*rápido*) prompt, quick; (*preparado*) ready; (*astuto*) quick, sharp // *ad* quickly, promptly; (*en seguida*) at once, right away; (*dentro de poco*) soon; (*temprano*) early // *nm:* **tener ~s de enojo** to be quick-tempered; **al ~** at first; **de ~** suddenly; **por lo ~** meanwhile, for the present.
pronunciación [pronunθja'θjon] *nf* pronunciation; **pronunciar** *vt* to pronounce; (*discurso*) to make, deliver; **pronunciarse** *vr* to revolt, rise, rebel; (*declararse*) to declare o.s.
propagación [propaxa'θjon] *nf* propagation.
propaganda [propa'xanda] *nf* (*política*) propaganda; (*comercial*) advertising.
propagar [propa'xar] *vt* to propagate.
propensión [propen'sjon] *nf* inclination, propensity; **propenso, a** *a* inclined to; **ser propenso a** to be inclined to, have a tendency to.
propiamente [propja'mente] *ad* properly; (*realmente*) really, exactly.
propicio, a [pro'piθjo, a] *a* favourable, propitious.
propiedad [propje'ðað] *nf* (*gen*) property; (*posesión*) possession, ownership; **~ industrial** patent rights *pl*; **~ literaria** copyright; **~ particular** private property.
propietario, a [propje'tarjo, a] *nm/f* owner, proprietor.
propina [pro'pina] *nf* tip.
propio, a ['propjo, a] *a* own, of one's own; (*característico*) characteristic, typical; (*conveniente*) proper; (*mismo*) selfsame, very; **el ~ ministro** the minister himself; **¿tienes casa ~a?** have you a house of your own?
proponer [propo'ner] *vt* to propose, put forward; (*problema*) to pose; **~se** *vr* to propose, plan, intend.
proporción [propor'θjon] *nf* proportion; (*MAT*) ratio; (*oportunidad*) chance, opportunity; **proporciones** *nfpl* dimensions; (*fig*) size *sg*; **proporcionado, a** *a* proportionate; (*regular*) medium, middling; (*justo*) just right; **proporcionar** *vt* (*dar*) to give, supply, provide; (*adaptar*) to adjust, adapt.
proposición [proposi'θjon] *nf* proposition; (*propuesta*) proposal.
propósito [pro'posito] *nm* purpose; (*intento*) aim, intention // *a:* **a ~** appropriate, suitable // *ad:* **a ~** by the way, incidentally; **a ~ de** about, with regard to; **de ~** on purpose, deliberately.
propuesta [pro'pwesta] *nf* proposal.
propulsar [propul'sar] *vt* to drive, propel; (*fig*) to promote, encourage; **propulsión** *nf* propulsion; **propulsión a chorro** *o* **por reacción** jet propulsion.
prórroga ['prorroxa] *nf* (*gen*) extension; (*JUR*) stay; (*COM*) deferment; **prorrogar** *vt*

(*período*) to extend; (*decisión*) to defer, postpone.

prorrumpir [prorrum'pir] *vi* to burst forth, break out.

prosa ['prosa] *nf* prose.

proscribir [proskri'βir] *vt* to prohibit, ban; (*desterrar*) to exile, banish; (*partido*) to proscribe; **proscripción** *nf* prohibition, ban; banishment; proscription.

prosecución [proseku'θjon] *nf* continuation; (*persecución*) pursuit.

proseguir [prose'xir] *vt* to continue, carry on, proceed with // *vi* to continue, go on.

prospección [prospek'θjon] *nf* exploration; (*del petróleo, del oro*) prospecting.

prospecto [pros'pekto] *nm* prospectus.

prosperar [prospe'rar] *vi* to prosper, thrive, flourish; **prosperidad** *nf* prosperity; (*éxito*) success; **próspero, a** *a* prosperous, thriving, flourishing; (*que tiene éxito*) successful.

prostíbulo [pros'tiβulo] *nm* brothel.

prostitución [prostitu'θjon] *nf* prostitution; **prostituir** *vt* to prostitute; **prostituirse** *vr* to prostitute o.s., become a prostitute; **prostituta** *nf* prostitute.

protagonista [protaɣo'nista] *nm/f* protagonist.

protección [protek'θjon] *nf* protection.

protector, a [protek'tor, a] *a* protective, protecting // *nm/f* protector.

proteger [prote'xer] *vt* to protect; **protegido, a** *nm/f* protégé / protégée.

proteína [prote'ina] *nf* protein.

protesta [pro'testa] *nf* protest; (*declaración*) protestation.

protestante [protes'tante] a Protestant.

protestar [protes'tar] *vt* to protest, declare; (*fé*) to protest // *vi* to protest.

protocolo [proto'kolo] *nm* protocol.

prototipo [proto'tipo] *nm* prototype.

provecho [pro'βetʃo] *nm* advantage, benefit; (*FINANZAS*) profit; **¡buen ~!** bon appétit!; **en ~ de** to the benefit of; **sacar ~ de** to benefit from, profit by.

proveer [proβe'er] *vt* to provide, supply; (*preparar*) to provide, get ready; (*vacante*) to fill; (*negocio*) to transact, dispatch // *vi*: **~ a** to provide for.

provenir [proβe'nir] *vi*: **~ de** to come from, stem from.

proverbio [pro'βerβjo] *nm* proverb.

providencia [proβi'ðenθja] *nf* providence; (*previsión*) foresight; **~s** *nfpl* measures, steps.

provincia [pro'βinθja] *nf* province; **~no, a** *a* provincial; (*del campo*) country *cpd*.

provisión [proβi'sjon] *nf* provision; (*abastecimiento*) provision, supply; (*medida*) measure, step.

provisional [proβisjo'nal] a provisional.

provocación [proβoka'θjon] *nf* provocation; **provocar** *vt* to provoke; (*alentar*) to tempt, invite; (*causar*) to bring about, lead to; (*promover*) to promote;

(*estimular*) to rouse, stir, stimulate; **provocativo, a** a provocative.

próximamente [proksima'mente] *ad* shortly, soon.

proximidad [proksimi'ðað] *nf* closeness, proximity; **próximo, a** a near, close; (*vecino*) neighbouring; (*el que viene*) next.

proyectar [projek'tar] *vt* (*objeto*) to hurl, throw; (*luz*) to cast, shed; (*CINE*) to screen, show; (*planear*) to plan.

proyectil [projek'til] *nm* projectile, missile; (*MIL*) missile.

proyecto [pro'jekto] *nm* plan; (*estimación de costo*) detailed estimate.

proyector [projek'tor] *nm* (*CINE*) projector; (*MIL*) searchlight; (*de teatro*) spotlight.

prudencia [pru'ðenθja] *nf* (*sabiduría*) wisdom, prudence; (*cautela*) care; **prudente** a sensible, wise, prudent; (*conductor*) careful.

prueba ['prweβa] *nf* proof; (*ensayo*) test, trial; (*saboreo*) testing, sampling; (*de ropa*) fitting; **~s** *nfpl* trials; **a ~** on trial; **a ~ de** proof against; **a ~ de agua/fuego** waterproof/fireproof; **sala de ~s** fitting room; **someter a ~** to put to the test.

prurito [pru'rito] *nm* itch; (*de bebé*) nappy rash.

psico... [siko] *pref* psycho...; **~análisis** *nm* psychoanalysis; **~logía** *nf* psychology; **~lógico, a** a psychological; **psicólogo, a** *nm/f* psychologist; **psicópata** *nm/f* psychopath; **~sis** *nf inv* psychosis.

psiquiatra [si'kjatra] *nm/f* psychiatrist; **psiquiátrico, a** a psychiatric.

psíquico, a ['sikiko, a] a psychic(al).

PSOE *abr de* **Partido Socialista Obrero Español.**

púa ['pua] *nf* sharp point; (*para guitarra*) plectrum; **alambre de ~** barbed wire.

pubertad [puβer'tað] *nf* puberty.

publicación [puβlika'θjon] *nf* publication; **publicar** *vt* (*editar*) to publish; (*hacer público*) to publicize; (*vulgarizar*) to make public, divulge.

publicidad [puβliθi'ðað] *nf* publicity; (*COM*) advertising; **publicitario, a** a publicity *cpd*; advertising *cpd*.

público, a ['puβliko, a] a public // *nm* public; (*TEATRO etc*) audience.

puchero [pu'tʃero] *nm* stew; **hacer ~s** to pout.

pude *etc vb ver* **poder.**

púdico, a ['puðiko, a] a modest.

pudiera *etc vb ver* **poder.**

pudor [pu'ðor] *nm* modesty.

pudrir [pu'ðrir] *vt* to rot; (*fam*) to upset, annoy; **~se** *vr* to rot, decay.

pueblo ['pweβlo] *nm* people; (*nación*) nation; (*aldea*) village.

puedo *etc vb ver* **poder.**

puente ['pwente] *nm* (*gen*) bridge; **~ aéreo** airlift; **~ colgante** suspension bridge; **hacer el ~** (*fam*) to take an extra day off work between 2 public holidays.

puerco, a ['pwerko, a] *nm/f* pig/sow // a

(sucio) dirty, filthy; (obsceno) disgusting; ~ de mar porpoise; ~ marino dolphin.

pueril [pwe'ril] a childish.

puerro ['pwerro] nm leek.

puerta ['pwerta] nf door; (de jardín) gate; (portal) doorway; (fig) gateway; (gol) goal; **a ~ cerrada** behind closed doors; ~ **giratoria** swing door, revolving door.

puertaventana [pwertaβen'tana] nf shutter.

puerto ['pwerto] nm port; (paso) pass; (fig) haven, refuge.

Puerto Rico [pwerto'riko] nm Puerto Rico; **puertorriqueño, a** a Puerto Rican.

pues [pwes] ad (entonces) then; (¡entonces!) well, well then; (así que) so // conj (ya que) since; ¡~! (sí) yes!, certainly!

puesto, a ['pwesto, a] pp de **poner** // a dressed // nm (lugar, posición) place; (trabajo) post, job; (COM) stall // conj: ~ **que** since, as // nf (apuesta) bet, stake; ~**a en marcha** starting; ~**a del sol** sunset.

púgil ['puxil] nm boxer.

pugna ['puxna] nf battle, conflict; ~**cidad** nf pugnacity, aggressiveness; **pugnar** vi (luchar) to struggle, fight; (pelear) to fight.

pulcro, a ['pulkro, a] a neat, tidy; (bello) exquisite.

pulga ['pulxa] nf flea.

pulgada [pul'xaða] nf inch.

pulgar [pul'xar] nm thumb.

pulir [pu'lir], **pulimentar** [pulimen'tar] vt to polish; (alisar) to smooth; (fig) to polish up, touch up.

pulmón [pul'mon] nm lung; **pulmonía** nf pneumonia.

pulpa ['pulpa] nf pulp; (de fruta) flesh, soft part.

púlpito ['pulpito] nm pulpit.

pulpo ['pulpo] nm octopus.

pulsación [pulsa'θjon] nf beat, pulsation; (ANAT) throb(bing).

pulsador [pulsa'ðor] nm button, push button.

pulsar [pul'sar] vt (tecla) to touch, tap; (MUS) to play; (botón) to press, push // vi to pulsate; (latir) to beat, throb; (MED): ~ **a uno** to take sb's pulse.

pulsera [pul'sera] nf bracelet.

pulso ['pulso] nm (ANAT) pulse; (: muñeca) wrist; (fuerza) strength; (firmeza) steadiness, steady hand; (tacto) tact, good sense.

pulverizador [pulβeriθa'ðor] nm spray, spray gun; **pulverizar** vt to pulverize; (líquido) to spray.

pulla ['puʎa] nf cutting remark; (expresión grosera) obscene remark.

pungir [pun'xir] vt to puncture, prick, pierce; (fig) to cause suffering to.

punición [puni'θjon] nf punishment; **punitivo, a** a punitive.

punta ['punta] nf point, tip; (extremidad) end; (fig) touch, trace; **horas ~s** peak hours, rush hours; **sacar ~ a** to sharpen; **estar de ~** to be edgy.

puntada [pun'taða] nf (COSTURA) stitch; (fam) hint; **no ha dado ~** he hasn't done a stroke.

puntal [pun'tal] nm prop, support.

puntapié [punta'pje] nm kick.

puntear [punte'ar] vt (marcar) to tick, mark; (coser) to stitch (up).

puntería [punte'ria] nf (de arma) aim, aiming; (destreza) marksmanship.

puntiagudo, a [puntja'xuðo, a] a sharp, pointed.

puntilla [pun'tiʎa] nf (de pluma) point, nib; (andar) **de ~s** (to walk) on tiptoe.

punto ['punto] nm (gen) point; (señal diminuta) spot, dot; (lugar) spot, place; (momento) point, moment; **a ~** ready; **estar a ~ de** to be on the point of or about to; **en ~** on the dot; ~ **de arranque** starting point; ~ **muerto** dead centre; (AUTO) neutral (gear); ~ **y coma** semicolon; ~ **de interrogación** question mark.

puntuación [puntwa'θjon] nf punctuation; (puntos: en examen) mark(s) (pl); (: DEPORTE) score.

puntual [pun'twal] a (a tiempo) punctual; (exacto) exact, accurate; (seguro) reliable; ~**idad** nf punctuality; exactness, accuracy; reliability; ~**izar** vt to fix, specify; (en la memoria) to fix in one's mind/memory.

punzante [pun'θante] a (dolor) shooting, sharp; (herramienta) sharp; **punzar** vt to prick, pierce // vi to shoot, stab.

puñado [pu'naðo] nm handful.

puñal [pu'nal] nm dagger; ~**ada** nf stab; ~**ada de misericordia** coup de grâce.

puñetazo [pune'taðo] nm punch.

puño ['puno] nm (ANAT) fist; (cantidad) fistful, handful; (COSTURA) cuff; (de herramienta) handle.

pupila [pu'pila] nf pupil.

pupitre [pu'pitre] nm desk.

puré [pu're] nm puree; (sopa) (thick) soup; ~ **de patatas** mashed potatoes.

pureza [pu'reθa] nf purity.

purga ['purxa] nf purge; **purgante** a, nm purgative; **purgar** vt to purge.

purgatorio [purxa'torjo] nm purgatory.

purificar [purifi'kar] vt to purify; (refinar) to refine.

puritano, a [puri'tano, a] a (actitud) puritanical; (iglesia, tradición) puritan // nm/f puritan.

puro, a ['puro, a] a pure; (cielo) clear; (verdad) simple, plain // ad: **de ~ cansado** out of sheer tiredness // nm cigar.

púrpura ['purpura] nf purple; **purpúreo, a** a purple.

puse, pusiera etc vb ver **poner.**

pústula ['pustula] nf pimple, sore.

puta ['puta] nf whore, prostitute.

putrefacción [putrefak'θjon] nf rotting, putrefaction.

pútrido, a ['putriðo, a] a rotten.

Q

q.e.p.d. *abr de* **que en paz descanse.**
q.e.s.m. *abr de* **que estrecha su mano.**
que [ke] *pron (sujeto)* who, that; (: *cosa*) which, that; (*complemento*) whom, that; (: *cosa*) which, that // *conj* that; **el momento en ~ llegó** the moment he arrived; **lo ~ digo** what I say; **dar ~ hablar** to give cause to talk, cause talk; **le ruego ~ se calle** I'm asking you to keep quiet; **te digo ~ sí** I'm telling you, I assure you; **yo ~ tú** if I were you.
qué [ke] *a* what?, which? // *pron* what?; ¡~ **divertido!** how funny!; ¿~ **edad tiene Ud?** how old are you?; ¿**de ~ me hablas?** what are you saying to me?; ¿~ **tal?** how are you?, how are things?; ¿~ **hay (de nuevo)?** what's new?
quebrada [ke'ßraða] *nf ver* **quebrado.**
quebradizo, a [keßra'ðiθo, a] *a* fragile; (*persona*) frail.
quebrado, a [ke'ßraðo, a] *a (roto)* broken; (*pálido*) pale; (*COM*) bankrupt // *nm/f* bankrupt // *nf* ravine.
quebradura [keßra'ðura] *nf (fisura)* fissure; (*GEO*) gorge; (*MED*) rupture.
quebrantadura [keßranta'ðura] *nf,* **quebrantamiento** [keßranta'mjento] *nm (acto)* breaking; (*estado*) exhaustion.
quebrantar [keßran'tar] *vt (romper)* to break; (*infringir*) to violate, transgress; **~se** *vr (persona)* to fail in health; (*deshacerse*) to break.
quebranto [ke'ßranto] *nm* damage, harm; (*decaimiento*) exhaustion; (*debilidad*) weakness; (*dolor*) grief, pain.
quebrar [ke'ßrar] *vt* to break, smash; (*interrumpir*) to interrupt // *vi* to go bankrupt; **~se** *vr* to break, get broken; (*MED*) to be ruptured.
quedar [ke'ðar] *vi (permanecer)* to stay; (*seguir siendo*) to remain; (*encontrarse*) to be; (*restar*) to remain, be left; **~se** *vr* to remain, stay (behind); **~se con** to keep; **~ en** (*acordar*) to agree on/to; (*acabar siendo*) to end up as; **~ por hacer** to be still to be done; **~ ciego/mudo** to be left blind/dumb; **no te queda bien ese vestido** that dress doesn't suit you; **quedamos a las seis** we agreed to meet at six.
quedo, a ['keðo, a] *a* still // *ad* softly, gently.
quehacer [kea'θer] *nm* task, job; (*doméstico*) chore.
queja ['kexa] *nf* complaint; **quejarse** *vr (enfermo)* to moan, groan; (*protestar*) to complain; **quejido** *nm* moan; **quejoso, a** *a* complaining.
quemado, a [ke'maðo, a] *a* burnt.
quemadura [kema'ðura] *nf* burn, scald.
quemar [ke'mar] *vt* to burn; (*fig*) to burn up, squander // *vi* to be burning hot; **~se** *vr* to burn (up); (*del sol*) to get sunburnt.

quemarropa [kema'rropa]: **a ~** *ad* point-blank.
quemazón [kema'θon] *nf* burn; (*calor*) intense heat; (*sensación*) itch.
quepo *etc vb ver* **caber.**
querella [ke'reʎa] *nf (JUR)* charge; (*disputa*) dispute.
querer [ke'rer] *vt (desear)* to want, wish; (*amar a*) to love; **~ hacer algo** to want to do sth; **querido, a** *a* dear // *nm/f* darling // *nf* mistress.
quesería [kese'ria] *nf* dairy, cheese factory.
queso ['keso] *nm* cheese; **~ crema** cream cheese; **~ helado** ice-cream brick.
quicio ['kiθjo] *nm* hinge; **sacar a uno de ~** to get on sb's nerves.
quiebra ['kjeßra] *nf* break, split; (*COM*) bankruptcy; (*ECON*) slump.
quiebro ['kjeßro] *nm (del cuerpo)* swerve.
quien [kjen] *pron* who; **hay ~ piensa que** there are those who think that; **no hay ~ lo haga** no-one will do it.
quién [kjen] *pron* who, whom; ¿~ **es?** who's there?
quienquiera [kjen'kjera] (*pl* **quienesquiera**) *pron* whoever.
quiero *etc vb ver* **querer.**
quieto, a ['kjeto, a] *a* still; (*carácter*) placid; **quietud** *nf* stillness.
quijada [ki'xaða] *nf* jaw, jawbone.
quilate [ki'late] *nm* carat.
quimera [ki'mera] *nf* chimera; **quimérico, a** *a* fantastic.
químico, a ['kimiko, a] *a* chemical // *nm/f* chemist // *nf* chemistry.
quincalla [kin'kaʎa] *nf* hardware, ironmongery.
quince ['kinθe] *num* fifteen; **~na** *nf* fortnight; (*pago*) fortnightly pay; **~nal** *a* fortnightly.
quiniela [ki'njela] *nf* pools coupon; **~s** *nfpl* football pools.
quinientos [ki'njentos] *num* five hundred.
quinina [ki'nina] *nf* quinine.
quinqui ['kinki] *nm* gangster.
quinto, a ['kinto, a] *a* fifth // *nf* country house; (*MIL*) call-up, draft.
quiosco ['kjosko] *nm (de música)* bandstand; (*de periódicos*) news stand.
quirúrgico, a [ki'rurxiko, a] *a* surgical.
quise, quisiera *etc vb ver* **querer.**
quisquilloso, a [kiski'ʎoso, a] *a* touchy; (*fam*) pernickety.
quiste ['kiste] *nm* cyst.
quita ['kita] *nf* remission of debt; **de ~ y pon** detachable.
quitaesmalte [kitaes'malte] *nm* nail-polish remover.
quitamanchas [kita'mantʃas] *nm inv* stain remover.
quitar [ki'tar] *vt* to remove, take away; (*ropa*) to take off; (*dolor*) to kill, stop; ¡**quita de ahí!** get away!; **~se** *vr* to

withdraw; **se quitó el sombrero** he took off his hat.

quitasol [kita'sol] *nm* sunshade.

quite ['kite] *nm* (*esgrima*) parry; (*evasión*) dodge.

quizá(s) [ki'θa(s)] *ad* perhaps, maybe.

R

rábano ['raβano] *nm* radish; **me importa un ~** I don't give a damn.

rabia ['raβja] *nf* (*MED*) rabies; (*fig*) fury, rage; **rabiar** *vi* to have rabies; to rage, be furious; **rabiar por algo** to be dying for *or* long for sth.

rabieta [ra'βjeta] *nf* tantrum, fit of temper.

rabino [ra'βino] *nm* rabbi.

rabioso, a [ra'βjoso, a] *a* rabid; (*fig*) furious.

rabo ['raβo] *nm* tail.

racial [ra'θjal] *a* racial, race *cpd*.

racimo [ra'θimo] *nm* bunch.

raciocinio [raθjo'θinjo] *nm* reason.

ración [ra'θjon] *nf* portion; **raciones** *nfpl* rations.

racional [raθjo'nal] *a* (*razonable*) reasonable; (*lógico*) rational; **~izar** *vt* to rationalize.

racionar [raθjo'nar] *vt* to ration (out).

racismo [ra'θismo] *nm* racialism, racism; **racista** *a, nm/f* racist.

racha ['ratʃa] *nf* gust of wind.

radar [ra'ðar] *nm* radar.

radiador [raðja'ðor] *nm* radiator.

radiante [ra'ðjante] *a* radiant.

radical [raði'kal] *a, nm/f* radical.

radicar [raði'kar] *vi* to take root; **~ en** to lie *or* consist in; **~se** *vr* to establish o.s., put down (one's) roots.

radio ['raðjo] *nf* radio; (*aparato*) radio (set) // *nm* (*MAT*) radius; (*QUÍMICA*) radium; **~activo, a** *a* radioactive; **~difusión** *nf* broadcasting; **~emisora** *nf* transmitter, radio station; **~escucha** *nm/f* listener; **~grafía** *nf* X-ray; **~grafiar** *vt* to X-ray; **~terapia** *nf* radiotherapy; **radioyente** *nm/f* listener.

raer [ra'er] *vt* to scrape (off).

ráfaga ['rafaxa] *nf* gust; (*de luz*) flash; (*de tiros*) burst.

raído, a [ra'iðo, a] *a* (*ropa*) threadbare; (*persona*) shameless.

raigambre [rai'xambre] *nf* (*BOT*) roots *pl*; (*fig*) tradition.

raíz [ra'iθ] (*pl* **raíces**) *nf* root; **~ cuadrada** square root; **a ~ de** as a result of.

raja ['raxa] *nf* (*de melón etc*) slice; (*grieta*) crack; **rajar** *vt* to split; (*fam*) to slash; (*fruta etc*) to slice; **rajarse** *vr* to split, crack; (*AM*) to quit.

rajatabla [raxa'taβla]: **a ~** *ad* (*estrictamente*) strictly, to the letter; (*cueste lo que cueste*) at all costs.

ralo, a ['ralo, a] *a* thin, sparse.

rallado, a [ra'ʎaðo, a] *a* grated; **rallador** *nm* grater; **rallar** *vt* to grate.

rama ['rama] *nf* branch; **~da** *nf*, **~je** *nm* branches *pl*, foliage; **ramal** *nm* (*de cuerda*) strand; (*FERRO*) branch line; (*AUTO*) branch (road).

rambla ['rambla] *nf* (*de agua*) stream; (*avenida*) avenue.

ramera [ra'mera] *nf* whore.

ramificación [ramifika'θjon] *nf* ramification; **ramificarse** *vr* to branch out.

ramillete [rami'ʎete] *nm* bouquet; (*fig*) select group.

ramo ['ramo] *nm* branch; (*COM*) department, section.

rampa ['rampa] *nf* (*MED*) cramp; (*plano*) ramp.

ramplón, ona [ram'plon, ona] *a* uncouth, coarse.

rana ['rana] *nf* frog; **~ toro** bullfrog; **salto de ~** leapfrog.

rancio, a ['ranθjo, a] *a* rancid; (*vino*) aged, mellow; (*fig*) ancient.

rancho ['rantʃo] *nm* grub (*fam*); (*AM*) farm.

rango ['rango] *nm* rank, standing.

ranura [ra'nura] *nf* groove; (*de teléfono*) slot.

rapacidad [rapaθi'ðað] *nf* rapacity.

rapar [ra'par] *vt* to shave; (*los cabellos*) to crop; (*fam*) to pinch, nick (*fam*).

rapaz [ra'paθ] *a* (*ladrón*) thieving; (*ZOOL*) predatory.

rapaz, a [ra'paθ, a] *nm/f* young boy/girl.

rape ['rape] *nm* quick shave; **al ~** cropped.

rapé [ra'pe] *nm* snuff.

rapidez [rapi'ðeθ] *nf* speed, rapidity; **rápido, a** *a* rapid, fast, quick // *ad* quickly // *nm* (*tren*) express; **rápidos** *nmpl* rapids.

rapiña [ra'piɲa] *nm* robbery; **ave de ~** bird of prey.

raptar [rap'tar] *vt* to kidnap; **rapto** *nm* kidnapping; (*impulso*) sudden impulse; (*éxtasis*) ecstasy, rapture.

raqueta [ra'keta] *nf* racquet.

raquítico, a [ra'kitiko, a] *a* stunted; (*fig*) poor, inadequate; **raquitismo** *nm* rickets *sg*.

rareza [ra'reθa] *nf* rarity; (*fig*) eccentricity.

raro, a ['raro, a] *a* (*poco común*) rare; (*extraño*) odd, strange; (*excepcional*) remarkable.

ras [ras] *nm*: **a ~ de** level with; **a ~ de tierra** at ground level.

rasar [ra'sar] *vt* (*igualar*) to level; (*frotar*) to graze.

rascacielos [raska'θjelos] *nm inv* skyscraper.

rascar [ras'kar] *vt* (*con las uñas*) to scratch; (*raspar*) to scrape; **~se** *vr* to scratch (o.s.).

rasgadura [rasxa'ðura] *nf* tear, rip; **rasgar** *vt* to tear, rip (up).

rasgo ['rasxo] *nm* stroke; **~s** *nmpl*

features, characteristics; **a grandes ~s** in outline, broadly.

rasguñar [rasɣuˈɲar] *vt* to scratch; **rasguño** *nm* scratch.

raso, a [ˈraso, a] *a* (*liso*) flat, level; (*a baja altura*) very low // *nm* satin; **cielo ~** clear sky; **soldado ~** private.

raspador [raspaˈðor] *nm* scraper.

raspadura [raspaˈðura] *nf* scrape; (*marca*) scratch; **~s** *nfpl* scrapings; **raspar** *vt* to scrape; (*arañar*) to scratch; (*limar*) to file.

rastra [ˈrastra] *nf* (*huella*) track; (AGR) rake; **a ~s** by dragging; (*fig*) unwillingly; **pescar a la ~** to trawl.

rastreador [rastreaˈðor] *nm* tracker; (NAUT) trawler; **~ de minas** minesweeper; **rastrear** *vt* to track; (*laguna, río*) to dredge, drag.

rastrero, a [rasˈtrero, a] *a* creeping; (*vestido*) trailing; (*fig*) despicable, mean.

rastrillar [rastriˈʎar] *vt* to rake; **rastrillo** *nm* rake.

rastro [ˈrastro] *nm* (AGR) rake; (*pista*) track, trail; (*curso*) course; (*vestigio*) trace; (*matadero*) slaughterhouse; **el R~** the Madrid fleamarket.

rastrojo [rasˈtroxo] *nm* stubble.

rasurador [rasuraˈðor] *nm*, **rasuradora** [rasuraˈðora] *nf* electric shaver; **rasurarse** *vr* to shave.

rata [ˈrata] *nf* rat.

ratear [rateˈar] *vt* (*robar*) to steal; (*distribuir*) to share out.

ratería [rateˈria] *nf* petty theft.

ratero, a [raˈtero, a] *a* light-fingered // *nm/f* pickpocket.

ratificar [ratifiˈkar] *vt* to ratify.

rato [ˈrato] *nm* while, short time; **a ~s** at times; **hay para ~** there's still a long way to go; **pasar el ~** to kill time; **pasar un buen/mal ~** to have a good/rough time.

ratón [raˈton] *nm* mouse; **ratonera** *nf* mousetrap.

raudal [rauˈðal] *nm* torrent; **a ~es** in abundance.

raya [ˈraja] *nf* line; (*marca*) scratch; (*en tela*) stripe; (*de pelo*) parting; (*límite*) boundary; **tener a ~** to keep in check; **rayar** *vt* to line; to scratch; (*talón*) to cross; (*subrayar*) to underline // *vi*: **rayar en o con** to border on.

rayo [ˈrajo] *nm* (*del sol*) ray, beam; (*de luz*) shaft; (*en una tormenta*) lightning, flash of lightning; **~s X** X-rays.

rayón [raˈjon] *nm* rayon.

raza [ˈraθa] *nf* race; **~ humana** human race.

razón [raˈθon] *nf* (*gen*) reason; (*justicia*) right, justice; (*razonamiento*) reasoning; (*motivo*) course; (MAT) ratio; **a ~ de 10 cada día** at the rate of 10 a day; **'~: ...'** "inquiries to ..."; **en ~ de** with regard to; **dar ~ a uno** to agree that sb is right; **tener ~** to be right; **~ directa/inversa** direct/inverse proportion; **~ de ser**

raison d'être; **razonable** *a* reasonable; (*justo, moderado*) fair; **razonamiento** *nm* (*juicio*) judgement; (*argumento*) reasoning; **razonar** *vt* to reason, argue; (*cuenta*) to itemize // *vi* to reason, argue.

reabastecer [reaβasteˈθer] *vt* to refuel.

reabrir [reaˈβrir] *vt* to reopen.

reacción [reakˈθjon] *nf* reaction; **avión a ~** jet plane; **~ en cadena** chain reaction; **reaccionar** *vi* to react; **reaccionario, a** *a* reactionary.

reacio, a [reˈaθjo, a] *a* stubborn.

reactor [reakˈtor] *nm* reactor.

readaptación [reaðaptaˈθjon] *nf*: **~ profesional** industrial retraining.

reafirmar [reafirˈmar] *vt* to reaffirm.

reagrupar [reaɣruˈpar] *vt* to regroup.

reajuste [reaˈxuste] *nm* readjustment.

real [reˈal] *a* real; (*del rey, fig*) royal.

realce [reˈalθe] *nm* (TEC) embossing; (*lustre, fig*) splendour; (ARTE) highlight; **poner de ~** to emphasize.

realidad [realiˈðað] *nf* reality, fact; (*verdad*) truth.

realista [reaˈlista] *nm/f* realist.

realización [realiθaˈθjon] *nf* fulfilment; (COM) sale, selling-up.

realizador, a [realiθaˈðor, a] *nm/f* (TV etc) producer.

realizar [realiˈθar] *vt* (*objetivo*) to achieve; (*plan*) to carry out; (*viaje*) to make, undertake; (COM) to sell up; **~se** *vr* to come about, come true.

realmente [realˈmente] *ad* really, actually.

realzar [realˈθar] *vt* (TEC) to raise; (*embellecer*) to enhance; (*acentuar*) to highlight.

reanimar [reaniˈmar] *vt* to revive; (*alentar*) to encourage; **~se** *vr* to revive.

reanudar [reanuˈðar] *vt* (*renovar*) to renew; (*retomar*) to resume.

reaparición [reapariˈθjon] *nf* reappearance.

rearme [reˈarme] *nm* rearmament.

reata [reˈata] *nf* rope, rein; **de ~** in single file.

rebaja [reˈβaxa] *nf* (COM) reduction; (*menoscabo*) lessening; **rebajar** *vt* (*bajar*) to lower; (*reducir*) to reduce; (*disminuir*) to lessen; (*humillar*) to humble.

rebanada [reβaˈnaða] *nf* slice.

rebaño [reˈβaɲo] *nm* herd; (*de ovejas*) flock.

rebasar [reβaˈsar] *vt* (*también ~ de*) to exceed; (AUTO) to overtake.

rebatir [reβaˈtir] *vt* to refute; (*descontar*) to deduct.

rebato [reˈβato] *nm* alarm; (*ataque*) surprise attack.

rebelarse [reβeˈlarse] *vr* to rebel, revolt.

rebelde [reˈβelde] *a* rebellious; (*indócil*) unruly // *nm/f* rebel; **rebeldía** *nf* rebelliousness; (*desobediencia*) disobedience; **rebelión** *nf* rebellion.

reblandecer [reβlandeˈθer] *vt* to soften.

rebosante [reβo'sante] *a* overflowing; **rebosar** *vi* to overflow; (*abundar*) to abound, be plentiful.

rebotar [reβo'tar] *vt* to bounce; (*rechazar*) to repel; ~**se** *vr* (*pelota*) to rebound; (*bala*) to ricochet; **rebote** *nm* rebound; **de rebote** on the rebound.

rebozar [reβo'θar] *vt* to wrap up; (*CULIN*) to fry in batter; **rebozo** *nm* muffler; (*AM*) shawl; **decir algo sin rebozo** to call a spade a spade.

rebuscado, a [reβus'kaðo, a] *a* affected.

rebuscar [reβus'kar] *vt* to search carefully; (*objeto*) to search for carefully.

rebuznar [reβuθ'nar] *vi* to bray.

recabar [reka'βar] *vt* to manage to get.

recado [re'kaðo] *nm* errand; (*mensaje*) message; **tomar un** ~ (*TELEC*) to take a message.

recaer [reka'er] *vi* to relapse; ~ **en** to fall to *or* on; **recaída** *nf* relapse.

recalcar [rekal'kar] *vt* (*fig*) to stress, emphasize.

recalcitrante [rekalθi'trante] *a* recalcitrant.

recalcitrar [rekalθi'trar] *vi* (*echarse atrás*) to step back; (*resistir*) to resist, be stubborn.

recalentar [rekalen'tar] *vt* (*volver a calentar*) to reheat; (*demasiado*) to overheat.

recambio [re'kambjo] *nm* spare; (*de pluma*) refill.

recapacitar [rekapaθi'tar] *vt* to think over // *vi* to reflect.

recargado, a [rekar'xaðo, a] *a* overloaded; **recargar** *vt* to overload; (*batería*) to recharge; **recargar los precios** to increase prices; **recargo** *nm* surcharge; (*aumento*) increase.

recatado, a [reka'taðo, a] *a* modest, demure; (*prudente*) cautious.

recatar [reka'tar] *vt* to hide; ~**se** *vr* to hide o.s.

recato [re'kato] *nm* modesty, demureness; (*cautela*) caution.

recaudación [rekauða'θjon] *nf* collection; (*suma*) takings *pl*; (*en deporte*) gate; **recaudador** *nm* tax collector.

recelar [reθe'lar] *vt*: ~ **que** (*sospechar*) to suspect that; (*temer*) to fear that // *vi*, ~**se** *vr*: ~**(se) de** to distrust; **recelo** *nm* distrust, suspicion; **receloso, a** *a* distrustful, suspicious.

recepción [reθep'θjon] *nf* reception; **recepcionista** *nm/f* receptionist.

receptáculo [reθep'takulo] *nm* receptacle.

receptivo, a [reθep'tiβo, a] *a* receptive.

receptor, a [reθep'tor, a] *nm/f* recipient // *nm* receiver.

recesión [reθe'sjon] *nf* recession.

receta [re'θeta] *nf* (*CULIN*) recipe; (*MED*) prescription.

recibidor, a [reθiβi'ðor, a] *nm/f* receiver, recipient.

recibimiento [reθiβi'mjento] *nm*

(*recepción*) reception; (*acogida*) welcome.

recibir [reθi'βir] *vt* (*gen*) to receive; (*dar la bienvenida*) to welcome // *vi* to entertain; ~**se** *vr*: ~**se de** to qualify as; **recibo** *nm* receipt.

reciedumbre [reθje'ðumbre] *nf* strength; (*vigor*) vigour.

recién [re'θjen] *ad* recently, newly; **el** ~ **llegado** the newcomer; **el** ~ **nacido** the newborn child.

reciente [re'θjente] *a* recent; (*fresco*) fresh.

recinto [re'θinto] *nm* (*gen*) enclosure; (*área*) area, place.

recio, a ['reθjo, a] *a* strong, tough; (*voz*) loud; (*tiempo*) harsh // *ad* hard; loud(ly).

recipiente [reθi'pjente] *nm* receptacle.

reciprocidad [reθiproθi'ðað] *nf* reciprocity; **recíproco, a** *a* reciprocal.

recital [reθi'tal] *nm* (*MUS*) recital; (*LITERATURA*) reading; **recitar** *vt* to recite.

reclamación [reklama'θjon] *nf* claim, demand; (*queja*) complaint.

reclamar [rekla'mar] *vt* to claim, demand // *vi*: ~ **contra** to complain about; ~ **en justicia** to take to court; **reclamo** *nm* (*anuncio*) advertisement; (*tentación*) attraction.

reclinar [rekli'nar] *vt* to recline, lean; ~**se** *vr* to lean back.

recluir [reklu'ir] *vt* to intern, confine.

reclusión [reklu'sjon] *nf* (*prisión*) prison; (*refugio*) seclusion; ~ **perpetua** life imprisonment.

recluta [re'kluta] *nm/f* recruit // *nf* recruitment.

reclutamiento [rekluta'mjento] *nm* recruitment.

recobrar [reko'βrar] *vt* (*recuperar*) to recover; (*rescatar*) to get back; ~**se** *vr* to recover.

recodo [re'koðo] *nm* (*de río, camino*) bend.

recogedor, a [rekoxe'ðor, a] *nm/f* picker, harvester.

recoger [reko'xer] *vt* (*gen*) to collect; (*AGR*) to harvest; (*levantar*) to pick up; (*juntar*) to gather; (*pasar a buscar*) to come for, fetch; (*dar asilo*) to give shelter to; (*faldas*) to gather up; (*pelo*) to put up; ~**se** *vr* (*retirarse*) to retire; **recogido, a** *a* (*lugar*) quiet, secluded; (*persona*) modest, retiring; (*pequeño*) small // *nf* (*del correo*) collection; (*AGR*) harvest.

recolección [rekolek'θjon] *nf* (*de las mieses*) harvesting; (*colecta*) collection.

recomendación [rekomenda'θjon] *nf* (*sugerencia*) suggestion, recommendation; (*elogio*) praise; **recomendar** *vt* to suggest, recommend; to praise; (*confiar*) to entrust.

recompensa [rekom'pensa] *nf* reward, recompense; **recompensar** *vt* to reward, recompense; (*por pérdidas*) to compensate.

recomponer [rekompo'ner] *vt* to mend; ~**se** *vr* (*fam*) to doll up.

reconciliación [rekonθilja'θjon] *nf* reconciliation; **reconciliar** *vt* to reconcile; **reconciliarse** *vr* to become reconciled.

reconfortar [rekonfor'tar] *vt* to comfort; ~**se** *vr*: ~**se con** to fortify o.s. with.

reconocer [rekono'θer] *vt* to recognize; (*registrar*) to search; (*MED*) to examine; **reconocido, a** *a* recognized; (*agradecido*) grateful; **reconocimiento** *nm* recognition; search; examination; gratitude; (*confesión*) admission.

reconquista [rekon'kista] *nf* reconquest.

reconstituyente [rekonstitu'jente] *nm* tonic.

reconstruir [rekonstru'ir] *vt* to reconstruct.

recopilación [rekopila'θjon] *nf* (*sumario*) summary; (*compendio*) compilation; **recopilar** *vt* to compile.

récord ['rekorð] *a inv, nm* record.

recordar [rekor'ðar] *vt* (*acordarse de*) to remember; (*acordar a otro*) to remind // *vi* to remember.

recorrer [reko'rrer] *vt* (*país*) to cross, travel through; (*distancia*) to cover; (*repasar*) to go over, look over; **recorrido** *nm* run, journey; **tren de largo recorrido** main-line train.

recortado, a [rekor'taðo, a] *a* uneven, irregular.

recortar [rekor'tar] *vt* to cut out; **recorte** *nm* (*acción*) cutting; (*de prensa*) cutting, clipping; (*de telas, chapas*) trimming.

recostado, a [rekos'taðo, a] *a* leaning; **estar** ~ to be lying down.

recostar [rekos'tar] *vt* to lean; ~**se** *vr* to lie down.

recoveco [reko'ßeko] *nm* bend; (*en casa*) cubby hole.

recreación [rekrea'θjon] *nf* recreation; (*TEATRO, CINE*) interval, intermission.

recrear [rekre'ar] *vt* (*entretener*) to entertain; (*volver a crear*) to recreate; **recreativo, a** *a* recreational; **recreo** *nm* recreation; (*ESCOL*) break, playtime.

recriminar [rekrimi'nar] *vt* to reproach // *vi* to recriminate; ~**se** *vr* to reproach each other.

recrudecer [rekruðe'θer] *vt, vi,* ~**se** *vr* to worsen.

recrudecimiento [rekruðeθi'mjento] *nm*, **recrudescencia** [rekruðes'θenðja] *nf* upsurge.

recta ['rekta] *nf ver* **recto**.

rectángulo, a [rek'tangulo, a] *a* rectangular // *nm* rectangle.

rectificar [rektifi'kar] *vt* to rectify; (*volverse recto*) to straighten // *vi* to correct o.s.

rectitud [rekti'tuð] *nf* (*exactitud*) correctness; (*fig*) rectitude.

recto, a [a 'rekto, a] *a* straight; (*persona*) honest, upright // *nm* rectum // *nf* straight line.

rector, a [rek'tor, a] *a* governing.

recua ['rekwa] *nf* mule train.

recuento [re'kwento] *nm* inventory; **hacer el** ~ **de** to count *or* reckon up.

recuerdo [re'kwerðo] *nm* souvenir; ~**s** *nmpl* memories; ¡~**s a tu madre!** give my regards to your mother.

recular [reku'lar] *vi* to fall back; (*fig*) to back down.

recuperable [rekupe'raßle] *a* recoverable; **recuperación** *nf* recovery.

recuperar [rekupe'rar] *vt* to recover; (*tiempo*) to make up; ~**se** *vr* to recuperate.

recurrir [reku'rrir] *vi* (*JUR*) to appeal; ~ **a** to resort to; (*persona*) to turn to; **recurso** *nm* resort; (*medios*) means *pl*, resources *pl*; (*JUR*) appeal.

recusar [reku'sar] *vt* to reject, refuse.

rechazar [retʃa'θar] *vt* to repel, drive back; (*idea*) to reject; (*oferta*) to turn down.

rechazo [re'tʃaðo] *nm* (*retroceso*) recoil; (*rebote*) rebound; (*negación*) rebuff.

rechifla [re'tʃifla] *nf* hissing, booing; (*fig*) derision; **rechiflar** *vt* to hiss, boo; **rechiflarse** *vr* to take things as a joke.

rechinar [retʃi'nar] *vi* to creak; (*gruñir*) to grumble; (*dientes*) to grind.

rechoncho, a [re'tʃontʃo, a] *a* (*fam*) chubby, thickset.

red [reð] *nf* net, mesh; (*de ferrocarriles etc*) network; (*trampa*) trap.

redacción [reðak'θjon] *nf* editing; (*oficina*) newspaper office; (*personal*) editorial staff.

redactar [reðak'tar] *vt* to draw up, draft; (*periódico*) to edit.

redada [re'ðaða] *nf*: ~ **policíaca** police raid, round-up.

rededor [reðe'ðor] *nm*: **al** *o* **en** ~ around, round about.

redención [reðen'θjon] *nf* redemption; **redentor, a** *a* redeeming.

redescubrir [reðesku'ßrir] *vt* to rediscover.

redicho, a [re'ðitʃo, a] *a* affected, stilted.

redil [re'ðil] *nm* sheepfold.

redimir [reði'mir] *vt* to redeem.

rédito ['reðito] *nm* interest, yield.

redoblar [reðo'ßlar] *vt* to redouble; (*plegar*) to fold back // *vi* (*tambor*) to play a roll on the drums.

redomado, a [reðo'maðo, a] *a* sly, crafty.

redonda [re'ðonda] *nf ver* **redondo**.

redondear [reðonde'ar] *vt* to round, round off; ~**se** *vr* to become wealthy.

redondel [reðon'del] *nm* (*círculo*) circle; (*TAUR*) bullring, arena.

redondo, a [re'ðondo, a] *a* (*circular*) round; (*directo*) straight; (*completo*) complete // *nf*: **a la** ~**a** around, round about.

reducción [reðuk'θjon] *nf* reduction; (*MED*) setting.

reducido, a [reðu'θiðo, a] *a* reduced; (*limitado*) limited; (*pequeño*) small; **reducir** *vt* to reduce; to limit; (*MED*) to set a bone; **reducirse** *vr* to diminish.

redundancia [reðun'danθja] *nf* redundancy.

reembolsar [reembol'sar] *vt* to reimburse; (*depósito*) to refund; **reembolso** *nm* reimbursement; refund.

reemplazar [reempla'θar] *vt* to replace; **reemplazo** *nm* replacement; **de reemplazo** (*MIL*) reserve.

refacción [refak'θjon] *nf* (*AM*) repair(s) (*pl*).

refajo [re'faxo] *nm* (*enagua*) flannel underskirt'; (*falda*) short skirt.

referencia [refe'renθja] *nf* reference; (*informe*) report; **con ~ a** with reference to.

referente [refe'rente] *a*: **~ a** concerning, relating to.

referir [refe'rir] *vt* (*contar*) to tell, recount; (*relacionar*) to refer, relate; **~se** *vr*: **~se a** to refer to.

refilón [refi'lon]: **de ~** *ad* obliquely, aslant.

refinado, a [refi'naðo, a] *a* refined; **refinamiento** *nm* refinement; **refinar** *vt* to refine; (*fig*) to perfect, polish.

reflejar [refle'xar] *vt* (*gen*) to reflect; **reflejo, a** *a* reflected; (*movimiento*) reflex // *nm* reflection; (*parte*) reflex.

reflexión [reflek'sjon] *nf* reflection; **reflexionar** *vt* to reflect on // *vi* to reflect; (*detenerse*) to pause (to think).

reflexivo, a [reflek'siβo, a] *a* thoughtful; (*LING, fig*) reflexive.

reflujo [re'fluxo] *nm* ebb.

refocilar [refoθi'lar] *vt* to cheer up.

reforma [re'forma] *nf* reform; (*ARQ etc*) repair; **~ agraria** agrarian reform.

reformar [refor'mar] *vt* (*modificar*) to change, alter; (*formar de nuevo*) to reform; (*ARQ*) to repair; **~se** *vr* to mend one's ways.

reformatorio [reforma'torjo] *nm* reformatory.

reforzar [refor'θar] *vt* (*gen*) to strengthen; (*ARQ*) to reinforce; (*fig*) to encourage.

refractario, a [refrak'tarjo, a] *a* stubborn; (*TEC*) heat-resistant.

refrán [re'fran] *nm* proverb, saying.

refregar [refre'xar] *vt* to scrub.

refrenar [refre'nar] *vt* to check, restrain.

refrendar [refren'dar] *vt* (*firma*) to endorse, countersign; (*pasaporte*) to stamp; (*ley*) to approve.

refrescar [refres'kar] *vt* (*gen*) to refresh // *vi* to cool down; **~se** *vr* to get cooler; (*tomar aire fresco*) to go out for a breath of fresh air.

refresco [re'fresko] *nm* soft drink, cool drink; "**~s**" "refreshments".

refriega [re'frjeʝa] *nf* scuffle, brawl.

refrigeración [refrixera'θjon] *nf* refrigeration; (*de casa*) air-conditioning; **refrigerador** *nm* refrigerator; **refrigerar** *vt* to refrigerate; to air-condition.

refuerzo [re'fwerθo] *nm* reinforcement; (*TEC*) support.

refugiado, a [refu'xjaðo, a] *nm/f* refugee; **refugiarse** *vr* to take refuge, shelter; **refugio** *nm* refuge; (*protección*) shelter.

refulgencia [reful'xenθja] *nf* brilliance; **refulgir** *vi* to shine, be dazzling.

refundición [refundi'θjon] *nf* recasting, revision; **refundir** *vt* to recast.

refunfuñar [refunfu'nar] *vi* to grunt, growl; (*quejarse*) to grumble.

refutación [refuta'θjon] *nf* refutation; **refutar** *vt* to refute.

regadera [reʝa'ðera] *nf* watering can.

regadío [reʝa'ðio] *nm* irrigated land.

regalado, a [reʝa'laðo, a] *a* comfortable, luxurious; (*gratis*) free, for nothing; (*pey*) soft.

regalar [reʝa'lar] *vt* (*dar*) to give, present; (*entregar*) to give away; (*mimar*) to pamper, make a fuss of.

regalía [reʝa'lia] *nf* privilege, prerogative; (*COM*) bonus; (*de autor*) royalty.

regaliz [reʝa'liθ] *nm*, **regaliza** [reʝa'liθa] *nf* liquorice.

regalo [re'ʝalo] *nm* (*obsequio*) gift, present; (*gusto*) pleasure; (*comodidad*) comfort.

regalón, ona [reʝa'lon, ona] *a* spoiled, pampered.

regañadientes [reʝaɲa'ðjentes]: **a ~** *ad* reluctantly.

regañar [reʝa'nar] *vt* to scold // *vi* to grumble; **regaño** *nm* scolding, telling-off; (*queja*) grumble; **regañón, ona** *a* grumbling; (*mujer*) nagging.

regar [re'ʝar] *vt* to water, irrigate; (*fig*) to scatter, sprinkle.

regatear [reʝate'ar] *vt* to bargain over; (*guardar*) to be mean with // *vi* to bargain, haggle; (*DEPORTE*) to dribble; **regateo** *nm* bargaining; dribbling; (*del cuerpo*) swerve, dodge.

regazo [re'ʝaθo] *nm* lap.

regeneración [rexenera'θjon] *nf* regeneration; **regenerar** *vt* to regenerate.

regentar [rexen'tar] *vt* to direct, manage; **regente** *nm* manager; (*POL*) regent.

régimen ['reximen] (*pl* **regímenes**) *nm* regime; (*MED*) diet.

regimiento [rexi'mjento] *nm* regiment; (*organización*) administration.

regio, a ['rexjo, a] *a* royal, regal; (*fig: suntuoso*) splendid.

región [re'xjon] *nf* region; **regionalista** *nm/f* regionalist.

regir [re'xir] *vt* to govern, rule; (*dirigir*) to manage, run // *vi* to apply, be in force.

registrador [rexistra'ðor] *nm* registrar, recorder.

registrar [rexis'trar] *vt* (*buscar en cajón*) to look through, search; (*inspeccionar*) to inspect; (*anotar*) to register, record; **~se** *vr* to register; (*ocurrir*) to happen.

registro [re'xistro] *nm* registration; (*MUS, libro*) register; (*inspección*) inspection, search; ~ **civil** registry office.

regla ['rexla] nf (ley) rule, regulation; (de medir) ruler, rule; **la ~** (MED) periods pl; **salir de ~** to step out of line.

reglamentación [rexlamenta'θjon] nf (acto) regulation; (lista) rules pl; **reglamentar** vt to regulate; **reglamentario, a** a statutory; **reglamento** nm rules pl, regulations pl.

reglar [re'xlar] vt (papel) to rule; (actos) to regulate.

regocijado, a [rexoθi'xaðo, a] a merry; **regocijar** vt to cheer up, gladden; **regocijarse** vr to have a good time, make merry; (alegrarse) to rejoice; **regocijo** nm joy, happiness.

regodearse [rexoðe'arse] vr to be glad, be delighted; **regodeo** nm delight.

regresar [rexre'sar] vi to come/go back, return; **regresivo, a** a backward; (fig) regressive; **regreso** nm return.

reguero [re'xero] nm irrigation ditch.

regulador [rexula'ðor] nm (gen) regulator; (de radio etc) knob, control.

regular [rexu'lar] a (gen) regular; (normal) normal, usual; (común) ordinary; (organizado) regular, orderly; (mediano) average; (fam) not bad, so-so // ad so-so, alright // vt (controlar) to control, regulate; (TEC) to adjust; **por lo ~** as a rule; **~idad** nf regularity; **~izar** vt to regularize.

regusto [re'xusto] nm aftertaste.

rehabilitación [reaβilita'θjon] nf rehabilitation; (ARQ) restoration; **rehabilitar** vt to rehabilitate; to restore; (reintegrar) to reinstate.

rehacer [rea'θer] vt (reparar) to mend, repair; (volver a hacer) to redo, repeat; **~se** vr (MED) to recover; (dominarse) to pull o.s. together.

rehén [re'en] nm hostage.

rehilete [rei'lete] nm (dardo) dart; (DEPORTE) badminton, shuttlecock.

rehuir [reu'ir] vt to avoid, shun.

rehusar [reu'sar] vt, vi to refuse.

reina ['reina] nf queen; **~do** nm reign; **reinante** a (fig) prevailing; **reinar** vi to reign.

reincidir [reinθi'ðir] vi to relapse.

reincorporarse [reinkorpo'rarse] vr: **~ a** to rejoin.

reino ['reino] nm kingdom; **el R~ Unido** the United Kingdom.

reintegrar [reinte'xrar] vt (reconstituir) to reconstruct; (persona) to reinstate; (dinero) to return, pay back; **~se** vr: **~se a** to return to.

reír [re'ir] vi, **~se** vr to laugh; **~se de** to laugh at.

reiterar [reite'rar] vt to reiterate.

reivindicación [reiβindika'θjon] nf (demanda) claim, demand; (justificación) vindication; **reivindicar** vt to claim; (restaurar) to restore.

reja ['rexa] nf (de ventana) grille, bars pl;

(en la calle) grating; (del arado) ploughshare.

rejilla [re'xiʎa] nf (de ventana) grille; (de silla) wickerwork; (de ventilación) vent; (de coche) luggage rack.

rejoneador [rexonea'ðor] nm mounted bullfighter.

rejuvenecer [rexuβene'θer] vt, vi to rejuvenate; **~se** vr to be rejuvenated.

relación [rela'θjon] nf relation, relationship; (MAT) ratio; (informe) report; **relaciones públicas** public relations; **con ~ a o en ~ con** in relation to; **relacionar** vt to relate, connect; **relacionarse** vr to be connected, be linked.

relajación [relaxa'θjon] nf relaxation; **relajado, a** a (disoluto) loose; (cómodo) relaxed; (MED) ruptured; **relajar** vt. **relajarse** vr to relax.

relamer [rela'mer] vt to lick (repeatedly); **~se** vr to lick one's lips.

relamido, a [rela'miðo, a] a (pulcro) overdressed; (afectado) affected.

relámpago [re'lampaxo] nm flash of lightning; **visita/huelga ~** lightning visit/strike; **relampaguear** vi to flash.

relatar [rela'tar] vt to tell, relate.

relativo, a [rela'tiβo, a] a relative; **en lo ~ a** concerning.

relato [re'lato] nm (narración) story, tale; (informe) report.

relegar [rele'xar] vt to relegate.

relevante [rele'ßante] a eminent, outstanding.

relevar [rele'ßar] vt (sustituir) to relieve; **~se** vr to relay; **~ a uno de un cargo** to relieve sb of his post.

relevo [re'leßo] nm relief; **carrera de ~s** relay race.

relieve [re'ljeße] nm (ARTE, TEC) relief; (fig) prominence, importance; **~s** nmpl left-overs; **bajo ~** bas-relief.

religión [reli'xjon] nf religion; **religiosidad** nf religiosity; **religioso, a** a religious // nm/f monk/nun // nm cleric.

relinchar [relin'tʃar] vi to neigh; **relincho** nm neigh; (acto) neighing.

reliquia [re'likja] nf relic; **~ de familia** family heirloom.

reloj [re'lo(x)] nm watch; (de iglesia etc) clock; **~ de pulsera** wristwatch; **~ despertador** alarm clock; **~ero, a** nm/f watchmaker; clockmaker.

reluciente [relu'θjente] a brilliant, shining; **relucir** vi to shine; (fig) to excel.

relumbrante [relum'brante] a dazzling; **relumbrar** vi to dazzle, shine brilliantly.

rellano [re'ʎano] nm (ARQ) landing.

rellenar [reʎe'nar] vt (llenar) to fill up; (CULIN) to stuff; (COSTURA) to pad; **relleno, a** a full up; stuffed // nm stuffing; (de tapicería) padding.

remachar [rema'tʃar] vt to rivet; (fig) to hammer home, drive home; **remache** nm rivet.

remanente [rema'nente] nm remainder;

(COM) balance; (de producto) surplus.

remanso [re'manso] nm pool; (fig) quiet place.

remar [re'mar] vi to row.

rematado, a [rema'taðo, a] a complete, utter.

rematar [rema'tar] vt to finish off; (COM) to sell off cheap // vi to end, finish off.

remate [re'mate] nm end, finish; (punta) tip; (DEPORTE) shot; (ARQ) top; (COM) auction sale; **de** o **para ~** to crown it all.

remedar [reme'ðar] vt to imitate.

remediar [reme'ðjar] vt (gen) to remedy; (subsanar) to make good, repair; (ayudar) to help; (evitar) to avoid.

remedio [re'meðjo] nm remedy; (alivio) relief, help; (JUR) recourse, remedy; **poner ~ a** to correct, stop; **no tener más ~** to have no alternative; **¡qué ~!** there's no choice; **sin ~** hopeless, incurable.

remedo [re'meðo] nm imitation; (pey) parody.

remendar [remen'dar] vt to repair; (con parche) to patch.

remesa [re'mesa] nf remittance; (COM) shipment; **remesar** vt to remit, send.

remiendo [re'mjendo] nm (gen) mend; (con parche) patch; (cosido) darn.

remilgado, a [remil'xaðo, a] a prim; (afectado) affected; **remilgo** nm primness; affectation.

reminiscencia [reminis'θenθja] nf reminiscence.

remisión [remi'sjon] nf (acto) sending, shipment.

remiso, a [re'miso, a] a remiss.

remitir [remi'tir] vt to remit, send; (perdonar) to pardon; (posponer) to postpone // vi to slacken; (en carta): **remite: X** sender: X; **remitente** nm/f sender.

remo ['remo] nm (de barco) oar; (deporte) rowing.

remoción [remo'θjon] nf removal.

remojar [remo'xar] vt to steep, soak; (galleta etc) to dip.

remojo [re'moxo] nm: **dejar la ropa a ~** to leave clothes to soak.

remolacha [remo'latʃa] nf beet, beetroot.

remolcador [remolka'ðor] nm (NAUT) tug; (AUTO) breakdown lorry.

remolinar [remoli'nar] vi to whirl, eddy; **remolino** nm (gen) eddy; (de agua) whirlpool; (de viento) whirlwind; (de gente) throng.

remolque [re'molke] nm tow, towing; (cuerda) towrope; **llevar a ~** to tow.

remontar [remon'tar] vt to mend; **~se** vr to soar; **~se a** (COM) to amount to; **~ el vuelo** to soar.

rémora ['remora] nf hindrance.

remorder [remor'ðer] vt to distress, disturb; **~se** vr to suffer remorse; **~se la conciencia** to have a troubled conscience; **remordimiento** nm remorse.

remoto, a [re'moto, a] a remote.

remover [remo'ßer] vt to stir; (tierra) to turn over; (objetos) to move around; (quitar) to remove.

remozar [remo'θar] vt to rejuvenate; **~se** vr to be rejuvenated, look younger.

remuneración [remunera'θjon] nf remuneration; **remunerar** vt to remunerate; (premiar) to reward.

renacer [rena'θer] vi to be reborn; (fig) to revive; **renacimiento** nm rebirth; **el Renacimiento** the Renaissance.

renal [re'nal] a renal, kidney cpd.

rencilla [ren'θiʎa] nf quarrel.

rencor [ren'kor] nm rancour, bitterness; **~oso, a** a spiteful.

rendición [rendi'θjon] nf surrender.

rendido, a [ren'diðo, a] a (sumiso) submissive; (cansado) worn-out.

rendimiento [rendi'mjento] nm (MIL) surrender; (producción) output; (agotamiento) exhaustion; (TEC, COM) efficiency.

rendir [ren'dir] vt (vencer) to defeat; (producir) to produce; (dar beneficio) to yield; (agotar) to exhaust; (dominar) to dominate // vi to pay; **~se vr** (someterse) to surrender; (cansarse) to wear o.s. out; **~ homenaje** o **culto a** to pay homage to.

renegado, a [rene'xaðo, a] a, nm/f renegade.

renegar [rene'xar] vi (renunciar) to renounce; (blasfemar) to blaspheme; (fam) to curse; (quejarse) to complain.

RENFE nf abr de **Red Nacional de los Ferrocarriles Españoles.**

renglón [ren'glon] nm (línea) line; (COM) item, article; **a ~ seguido** immediately after.

reniego [re'njexo] nm curse, oath; (queja) grumble, complaint.

renombrado, a [renom'braðo, a] a renowned; **renombre** nm renown.

renovación [renoßa'θjon] nf (de contrato) renewal; (ARQ) renovation; **renovar** vt to renew; to renovate.

renta ['renta] nf (ingresos) income; (beneficio) profit; (alquiler) rent; **~ vitalicia** annuity; **rentable** a profitable; **rentar** vt to produce, yield.

rentero, a [ren'tero, a] nm/f tenant farmer.

rentista [ren'tista] nm/f stockholder.

renuencia [re'nwenθja] nf reluctance; **renuente** a inv reluctant.

renuncia [re'nunθja] nf (gen) resignation.

renunciar [renun'θjar] vt to renounce // vi to resign; **~ a hacer algo** to give up doing sth.

reñido, a [re'niðo, a] a (batalla) bitter, hard-fought; **estar ~ con uno** to be on bad terms with sb.

reñir [re'nir] vt (regañar) to scold // vi (estar peleado) to quarrel, fall out; (combatir) to fight.

reo ['reo] nm/f culprit, offender; **~ de muerte** prisoner condemned to death.

reojo [re'oxo]: **de ~** ad out of the corner of one's eye; (fig) askance.

reorganizar [reorɣani'θar] *vt* to reorganize.

reorientar [reorjen'tar] *vt* to reorientate; (*reajustar*) to readjust.

reparación [repara'θjon] *nf* (*acto*) mending, repairing; (*TEC*) repair; (*fig*) amends, reparation; **reparar** *vt* to repair; to make amends for; (*suerte*) to retrieve; (*observar*) to observe // *vi*: **reparar en** (*darse cuenta de*) to notice; (*poner atención en*) to pay attention to.

reparo [re'paro] *nm* (*reparación*) repair; (*advertencia*) observation; (*duda*) doubt; (*dificultad*) difficulty; (*resguardo*) defence.

reparón, ona [repa'ron, ona] *a* carping.

repartición [reparti'θjon] *nf* distribution; (*división*) division; **repartidor, a** *nm/f* distributor.

repartir [repar'tir] *vt* to distribute, share out; (*correo*) to deliver; **reparto** *nm* distribution; delivery; (*TEATRO, CINE*) cast.

repasar [repa'sar] *vt* (*sitio*) to pass by again; (*lección*) to revise; (*MECÁNICA*) to check; **repaso** *nm* revision; overhaul, checkup; (*de ropa*) mending.

repatriar [repa'trjar] *vt* to repatriate.

repecho [re'petʃo] *nm* steep incline; **a ~** uphill.

repelente [repe'lente] *a* repellent, repulsive; **repeler** *vt* to repel.

repensar [repen'sar] *vt* to reconsider.

repente [re'pente] *nm*: **de ~** suddenly; **un ~ de ira** a fit of anger.

repentino, a [repen'tino, a] *a* sudden.

repercusión [reperku'sjon] *nf* repercussion.

repercutir [reperku'tir] *vi* to rebound; (*sonido*) to echo; **~se** *vr* to reverberate; **~ en** to have repercussions on.

repertorio [reper'torjo] *nm* list; (*TEATRO*) repertoire.

repetición [repeti'θjon] *nf* repetition; **repetir** *vt* to repeat; (*plato*) to have a second helping // *vi* to repeat; **repetirse** *vr* (*volver sobre tema*) to repeat o.s.; (*sabor*) to come back.

replicar [repi'kar] *vt* (*desmenuzar*) to chop up finely; (*campanas*) to ring; **~se** *vr* to boast.

repique [re'pike] *nm* pealing, ringing; **~teo** *nm* pealing; (*de tambor*) drumming.

repisa [re'pisa] *nf* ledge, shelf; **~ de chimenea** mantelpiece.

repito *etc vb ver* **repetir.**

replegar [reple'ɣar] *vt* to fold over; **~se** *vr* to fall back, retreat.

repleto, a [re'pleto, a] *a* replete, full up.

réplica ['replika] *nf* answer; (*ARTE*) replica.

replicar [repli'kar] *vi* to answer; (*objetar*) to argue, answer back.

repliegue [re'pljeɣe] *nm* (*MIL*) withdrawal.

repoblación [repoβla'θjon] *nf* repopulation; (*de río*) restocking; **~ forestal** reafforestation; **repoblar** *vt* to repopulate; to reafforest.

repollo [re'poʎo] *nm* cabbage.

reponer [repo'ner] *vt* to replace, put back; (*TEATRO*) to revive; **~se** *vr* to recover; **~ que** to reply that.

reportaje [repor'taxe] *nm* report, article.

reposacabezas [reposaka'βeθas] *nm inv* headrest.

reposado, a [repo'saðo, a] *a* (*descansado*) restful; (*tranquilo*) calm; **reposar** *vi* to rest, repose.

reposición [reposi'θjon] *nf* replacement; (*CINE*) remake.

repositorio [reposi'torjo] *nm* repository.

reposo [re'poso] *nm* rest.

repostar [repos'tar] *vt* to replenish; (*AUTO*) to fill up (with petrol).

repostería [reposte'ria] *nf* confectioner's (shop); (*depósito*) pantry, larder; **repostero, a** *nm/f* confectioner.

reprender [repren'der] *vt* to reprimand; **represión** *nf* rebuke, reprimand.

represa [re'presa] *nf* dam; (*lago artificial*) lake, pool.

represalia [repre'salja] *nf* reprisal.

representación [representa'θjon] *nf* representation; (*TEATRO*) performance; **representante** *nm/f* representative; performer.

representar [represen'tar] *vt* to represent; (*TEATRO*) to play; (*edad*) to look; **~se** *vr* to imagine; **representativo, a** *a* representative.

represión [repre'sjon] *nf* repression.

reprimir [repri'mir] *vt* to repress.

reprobar [repro'βar] *vt* to censure, reprove.

réprobo, a ['reproβo, a] *nm/f* reprobate.

reprochar [repro'tʃar] *vt* to reproach; **reproche** *nm* reproach.

reproducción [reproðuk'θjon] *nf* reproduction.

reproducir [reproðu'θir] *vt* to reproduce; **~se** *vr* to breed; (*situación*) to recur.

reptil [rep'til] *nm* reptile.

república [re'puβlika] *nf* republic; **republicano, a** *a, nm/f* republican.

repudiar [repu'ðjar] *vt* to repudiate; (*fe*) to renounce; **repudio** *nm* repudiation.

repuesto [re'pwesto] *nm* (*pieza de recambio*) spare (part); (*abastecimiento*) supply; **rueda de ~** spare wheel.

repugnancia [repuɣ'nanθja] *nf* repugnance; **repugnante** *a* repugnant, repulsive.

repugnar [repuɣ'nar] *vt* to disgust // *vi*, **~se** *vr* (*contradecirse*) to conflict; (*dar asco*) to be disgusting.

repujar [repu'xar] *vt* to emboss.

repulgar [repul'ɣar] *vt* to hem.

repulido, a [repu'liðo, a] *a* (*gen*) polished; (*persona*) dressed up, dolled up.

repulsa [re'pulsa] *nf* rebuff; (*fig*) reprimand.

repulsión [repul'sjon] *nf* repulsion, aversion; **repulsivo, a** *a* repulsive.

reputación [reputa'θjon] *nf* reputation.

reputar [repu'tar] vt to consider, deem.

requemado, a [reke'maðo, a] a (quemado) scorched; (bronceado) tanned.

requerimiento [rekeri'mjento] nm request; (JUR) summons.

requerir [reke'rir] vt (rogar) to ask, request; (exigir) to require; (llamar) to send for, summon.

requesón [reke'son] nm cottage cheese.

requete... [re'kete] pref extremely.

réquiem ['rekjem] nm requiem.

requisa [re'kisa] nf (inspección) survey, inspection; (MIL) requisition.

requisito [reki'sito] nm requirement, requisite.

res [res] nf beast, head of cattle.

resabio [re'saßjo] nm (maña) vice, bad habit; (dejo) aftertaste.

resaca [re'saka] nf (en el mar) undertow, undercurrent; (fig) backlash; (fam) hangover.

resalado, a [resa'laðo, a] a (fam) lively.

resaltar [resal'tar] vi to project, stick out; (persona) to stand out, be conspicuous.

resarcimiento [resarθi'mjento] nm compensation; **resarcir** vt to compensate; **resarcirse** vr to make up for.

resbaladero [resßala'ðero] nm (gen) slippery place; (en parque infantil) slide.

resbaladizo, a [resßala'ðiθo, a] a slippery.

resbalar [resßa'lar] vi, ~se vr to slip, slide; (fig) to slip (up).

rescatar [reska'tar] vt (heridos) to save, rescue; (objeto) to get back, recover; (cautivos) to ransom.

rescate [res'kate] nm rescue, recovery; **pagar un** ~ to pay a ransom.

rescindir [resθin'dir] vt to rescind.

rescisión [resθi'sjon] nf cancellation.

rescoldo [res'koldo] nm embers pl; (fig) scruple.

resecar [rese'kar] vt to dry thoroughly; (MED) to remove; ~se vr to dry up.

reseco, a [re'seko, a] a very dry; (fig) skinny.

resentido, a [resen'tiðo, a] a resentful; **resentimiento** nm resentment, bitterness.

resentirse [resen'tirse] vr (debilitarse: persona) to suffer; ~ con to resent; ~ de (consecuencias) to feel the effects of.

reseña [re'seɲa] nf (cuenta) account; (informe) report; (LITERATURA) review; **reseñar** vt to describe; to review.

reserva [re'serßa] nf (gen) reserve; (reservación) reservation; **a** ~ **de** except for; **con toda** ~ in strictest confidence.

reservado, a [reser'ßaðo, a] a reserved; (retraído) cold, distant // nm private room.

reservar [reser'ßar] vt (guardar) to keep; (habitación, entrada) to reserve; (callar) to keep to o.s.; ~se vr to save o.s.

resfriado [resfri'aðo] nm cold; **resfriarse** vr to cool; (MED) to catch (a) cold.

resguardar [resɣwar'ðar] vt to protect,

shield; ~se vr: ~se de to guard against; **resguardo** nm defence; (custodia) protection; (garantía) guarantee; (vale) voucher.

residencia [resi'ðenθja] nf residence.

residente [resi'ðente] a, nm/f resident.

residir [resi'ðir] vi to reside, live; ~ en to reside in, lie in.

residuo [re'siðwo] nm residue.

resignación [resiɣna'θjon] nf resignation; **resignar** vt to resign; **resignarse** vr: **resignarse a** o **con** to resign o.s. to, be resigned to.

resistencia [resis'tenθja] nf (dureza) endurance, strength; (oposición, eléctrica) resistance; **resistente** a strong, hardy, resistant.

resistir [resis'tir] vt (soportar) to bear; (oponerse a) to resist, oppose; (aguantar) to put up with // vi to resist; (aguantar) to last, endure; ~se vr: ~se a to refuse to, resist.

resma ['resma] nf ream.

resol [re'sol] nm glare of the sun.

resolución [resolu'θjon] nf (gen) resolution; (decisión) decision; **resoluto, a** a resolute.

resolver [resol'ßer] vt to resolve; (solucionar) to solve, resolve; (decidir) to decide, settle; ~se vr to make up one's mind.

resollar [reso'ʎar] vi to breathe noisily, wheeze.

resonancia [reso'nanθja] nf (del sonido) resonance; (repercusión) repercussion; **resonante** a resonant, resounding; (fig) tremendous; **resonar** vi to ring, echo.

resoplar [reso'plar] vi to snort; **resoplido** nm heavy breathing.

resorte [re'sorte] nm (pieza) spring; (elasticidad) elasticity; (fig) lever.

respaldar [respal'dar] vt to endorse; (fig) to back (up), support; ~se vr to lean back; ~se con o en to take one's stand on; **respaldo** nm (de cama) headboard; (de sillón) back; (fig) support, backing.

respectivo, a [respek'tißo, a] a respective; **en lo** ~ **a** with regard to.

respecto [res'pekto] nm: **al** ~ on this matter; **con** ~ **a**, ~ **de** with regard to, in relation to.

respetable [respe'taßle] a respectable; **respetar** vt to respect; **respeto** nm respect; (acatamiento) deference; **respetos** nmpl respects; **respetuoso, a** a respectful.

respingar [respin'gar] vi to shy; **respingo** nm start, jump; (fig) gesture of disgust.

respiración [respira'θjon] nf breathing; (MED) respiration; (ventilación) ventilation; **respirar** vi to breathe; (inhalar) to inhale; **respiratorio, a** a respiratory; **respiro** nm breathing; (fig) respite.

resplandecer [resplande'θer] vi to shine; **resplandeciente** a resplendent, shining;

resplandor *nm* brilliance, brightness; (*del fuego*) blaze.
responder [respon'der] *vt* to answer ; / *vi* to answer; (*fig*) to respond; (*pey*) to answer back; ~ **de** *o* **por** to answer for.
responsabilidad [responsaβili'ðað] *nf* responsibility; **responsable** *a* responsible.
respuesta [res'pwesta] *nf* answer, reply.
resquebrajar [reskeβra'xar] *vt*, ~**se** *vr* to crack, split.
resquemor [reske'mor] *nm* resentment.
resquicio [res'kiθjo] *nm* chink; (*hendedura*) crack.
restablecer [restaβle'θer] *vt* to re-establish, restore; ~**se** *vr* to recover.
restallar [resta'ʎar] *vi* to crack.
restante [res'tante] *a* remaining; **lo** ~ the remainder.
restar [res'tar] *vt* (*MAT*) to subtract; (*fig*) to take away // *vi* to remain, be left.
restauración [restaura'θjon] *nf* restoration.
restaurán [restau'ran], **restaurante** [restau'rante] *nm* restaurant.
restaurar [restau'rar] *vt* to restore.
restitución [restitu'θjon] *nf* return, restitution.
restituir [restitu'ir] *vt* (*devolver*) to return, give back; (*rehabilitar*) to restore; ~**se** *vr*: ~**se a** to rejoin.
resto ['resto] *nm* (*residuo*) rest, remainder; (*apuesta*) stake; ~**s** *nmpl* remains.
restregar [restre'xar] *vt* to scrub, rub.
restricción [restrik'θjon] *nf* restriction.
restrictivo, a [restrik'tiβo, a] *a* restrictive.
restringir [restrin'xir] *vt* to restrict, limit.
resucitar [resuθi'tar] *vt*, *vi* to resuscitate, revive.
resuelto, a [re'swelto, a] *pp de* **resolver** // *a* resolute, determined.
resuello [re'sweʎo] *nm* breath.
resultado [resul'taðo] *nm* (*conclusión*) outcome; (*consecuencia*) result, consequence; **resultante** *a* resulting, resultant.
resultar [resul'tar] *vi* (*llegar a ser*) to turn out to be; (*salir bien*) to turn out well; (*COM*) to amount to; ~ **de** to stem from; **me resulta difícil hacerlo** it's difficult for me to do it.
resumen [re'sumen] *nm* summary, résumé; **en** ~ in short.
resumir [resu'mir] *vt* to sum up; (*cortar*) to abridge, cut down.
retablo [re'taβlo] *nm* altarpiece.
retaguardia [reta'ɣwarðja] *nf* rearguard.
retahíla [reta'ila] *nf* series, string.
retal [re'tal] *nm* remnant.
retama [re'tama] *nf* (*AM*) broom.
retar [re'tar] *vt* (*gen*) to challenge; (*desafiar*) to defy, dare.
retardar [retar'ðar] *vt* (*demorar*) to delay; (*hacer más lento*) to slow down; (*retener*) to hold back; **retardo** *nm* delay.
retazo [re'taθo] *nm* snippet.

rete... ['rete] *pref* very, extremely.
retén [re'ten] *nm* (*TEC*) catch; (*reserva*) store, reserve.
retener [rete'ner] *vt* (*guardar*) to retain, keep; (*intereses*) to withhold.
retina [re'tina] *nf* retina.
retintín [retin'tin] *nm* jangle.
retirada [reti'raða] *nf* (*MIL*, *refugio*) retreat; (*de dinero*) withdrawal; (*de embajador*) recall; **retirado, a** *a* (*distante*) remote; (*tranquilo*) quiet; (*jubilado*) retired.
retirar [reti'rar] *vt* to withdraw; (*quitar*) to remove; (*jubilar*) to retire, pension off; ~**se** *vr* to retreat, withdraw; to retire; (*acostarse*) to retire, go to bed; **retiro** *nm* retreat; retirement; (*pago*) pension.
reto ['reto] *nm* dare, challenge.
retocar [reto'kar] *vt* (*fotografía*) to touch up, retouch.
retoño [re'toɲo] *nm* sprout, shoot; (*fig*) offspring, child.
retoque [re'toke] *nm* retouching; (*MED*) symptom.
retorcer [retor'θer] *vt* (*gen*) to twist; (*manos, lavado*) to wring; ~**se** *vr* to become twisted; (*mover el cuerpo*) to writhe.
retorcimiento [retorθi'mjento] *nm* twist, twisting; (*fig*) deviousness.
retórica [re'torika] *nf* rhetoric; (*fig*) affectedness.
retornar [retor'nar] *vt* to return, give back // *vi* to return, go/come back; **retorno** *nm* return.
retortijón [retorti'xon] *nm* twist, twisting.
retozar [reto'θar] *vi* (*juguetear*) to frolic, romp; (*saltar*) to gambol; **retozón, ona** *a* playful.
retracción [retrak'θjon], **retractación** [retrakta'θjon] *nf* retraction.
retractar [retrak'tar] *vt* to retract; ~**se** *vr* to retract; **me retracto** I take that back.
retraer [retra'er] *vt* to dissuade; ~**se** *vr* to retreat, withdraw; **retraído, a** *a* shy, retiring; **retraimiento** *nm* (*gen*) retirement; (*timidez*) shyness; (*lugar*) retreat.
retransmisión [retransmi'sjon] *nf* repeat (broadcast); **retransmitir** *vt* (*mensaje*) to relay; (*TV etc*) to retransmit; (: *en vivo*) to broadcast live.
retrasado, a [retra'saðo, a] *a* late; (*MED*) mentally retarded; (*país etc*) backward, underdeveloped; **retrasar** *vt* (*demorar*) to postpone, put off; (*retardar*) to slow down // *vi*, **retrasarse** *vr* (*atrasarse*) to be late; (*reloj*) to be slow; (*producción*) to fall (away); (*quedarse atrás*) to lag behind.
retraso [re'traso] *nm* (*demora*) delay; (*lentitud*) slowness; (*tardanza*) lateness; (*atraso*) backwardness; **llegar con** ~ to arrive late; ~ **mental** mental deficiency.
retratar [retra'tar] *vt* (*ARTE*) to paint the portrait of; (*fotografiar*) to photograph; (*fig*) to depict; ~**se** *vr* to have one's

portrait painted; **to have one's photograph taken**; **retrato** *nm* portrait; (*fig*) likeness; **retrato-robot** *nm* identikit picture.

retreta [re'treta] *nf* retreat.

retrete [re'trete] *nm* toilet, lavatory.

retribución [retriβu'θjon] *nf* (*recompensa*) reward; (*pago*) pay, payment; **retribuir** *vt* to reward; to pay.

retro... [retro] *pref* retro... .

retroactivo, a [retroak'tiβo, a] *a* retroactive, retrospective.

retroceder [retroθe'ðer] *vi* (*echarse atrás*) to move back(wards); (*tropas*) to fall back, retreat; (*arma de fuego*) to recoil; (*fig*) to back down.

retroceso [retro'θeso] *nm* backward movement; (*MIL*) withdrawal, retreat; (*MED*) relapse; (*fig*) backing down.

retrógrado, a [re'troxraðo, a] *a* (*atrasado*) retrograde; (*POL*) reactionary.

retropropulsión [retropropul'sjon] *nf* jet propulsion.

retrospectivo, a [retrospek'tiβo, a] *a* retrospective.

retrovisor [retroβi'sor] *nm* driving *or* rear-view mirror.

retumbante [retum'bante] *a* resounding; **retumbar** *vi* to echo, resound.

reuma ['reuma] *nm* rheumatism; **reumático, a** *a* rheumatic; **reumatismo** *nm* rheumatism.

reunificar [reunifi'kar] *vt* to reunify.

reunión [reu'njon] *nf* (*asamblea*) meeting; (*fiesta*) party; (*reencuentro*) reunion.

reunir [reu'nir] *vt* (*juntar*) to reunite, join; (*recoger*) to gather; (*personas*) to assemble; (*cualidades*) to combine; **~se** *vr* to meet, gather.

revalidar [reβali'ðar] *vt* to confirm, ratify.

revalorar [reβalo'rar] *vt* to revalue, reassess.

revancha [re'βantʃa] *nf* revenge.

revelación [reβela'θjon] *nf* revelation.

revelado [reβe'laðo] *nm* developing.

revelar [reβe'lar] *vt* to reveal; (*FOTO*) to develop.

revendedor, a [reβende'ðor, a] *nm/f* retailer; (*pey*) ticket tout.

reventar [reβen'tar] *vt* to burst, explode; (*fam*: *plan*) to ruin // *vi*, **~se** *vr* (*estallar*) to burst, explode; (*fam*: *morirse*) to kick the bucket (*fam*); **~ por** to be bursting to.

reventón [reβen'ton] *nm* burst, explosion; (*AUTO*) blow-out, puncture.

reverberación [reβerβera'θjon] *nf* reverberation; **reverberar** *vi* to reverberate; **reverbero** *nm* reverberation.

reverdecer [reβerðe'θer] *vi* (*fig*) to revive, come to life again.

reverencia [reβe'renθja] *nf* reverence; **reverenciar** *vt* to revere.

reverendo, a [reβe'rendo, a] *a* reverend; **reverente** *a* reverent.

reversión [reβer'sjon] *nf* reversion.

reverso [re'βerso] *nm* back, wrong side; (*de moneda*) reverse.

revertir [reβer'tir] *vi* to revert.

revés [re'βes] *nm* back, wrong side; (*fig*) reverse, setback; (*DEPORTE*) backhand; **hacer al ~** to do sth the wrong way round; **volver algo al ~** to turn sth round; (*ropa*) to turn sth inside out.

revestir [reβes'tir] *vt* to put on; (*cubrir*) to cover, coat; **~ con** *o* **de** to invest with.

revisar [reβi'sar] *vt* (*examinar*) to check; (*rever*) to revise; **revisión** *nf* revision.

revisor, a [reβi'sor, a] *nm/f* inspector; (*FERRO*) ticket collector.

revista [re'βista] *nf* magazine, review; (*TEATRO*) revue; (*inspección*) inspection; **pasar ~ a** to review, inspect.

revivir [reβi'βir] *vi* to revive.

revocación [reβoka'θjon] *nf* repeal; **revocar** *vt* to revoke.

revolcar [reβol'kar] *vt* to knock down, send flying; **~se** *vr* to roll about.

revolotear [reβolote'ar] *vi* to flutter; **revoloteo** *nm* fluttering.

revoltijo [reβol'tixo] *nm* mess, jumble.

revoltoso, a [reβol'toso, a] *a* (*travieso*) naughty, unruly; (*rebelde*) rebellious.

revolución [reβolu'θjon] *nf* revolution; **revolucionar** *vt* to revolutionize; **revolucionario, a** *a*, *nm/f* revolutionary.

revólver [re'βolβer] *nm* revolver.

revolver [reβol'βer] *vt* (*desordenar*) to disturb, mess up; (*mover*) to move about; (*poner al revés*) to turn over; (*investigar*) to look through; (*adentrarse en*) to go into; (*POL*) to stir up; (*hacer paquete*) to wrap up // *vi*: **~ en** to go through, rummage (about) in; **~se** *vr* to turn round; (*por dolor*) to writhe; (*volver contra*) to turn on *or* against.

revuelco [re'βwelko] *nm* fall, tumble.

revuelo [re'βwelo] *nm* fluttering; (*fig*) commotion.

revuelto, a [re'βwelto, a] *pp de* **revolver** // *a* (*mezclado*) mixed-up; (*huevos*) scrambled; (*descontento*) discontented; (*travieso*) mischievous // *nf* (*motín*) revolt; (*conmoción*) commotion.

revulsivo [reβul'siβo] *nm* enema.

rey [rei] *nm* king.

reyerta [re'jerta] *nf* quarrel, brawl.

rezagado, a [reθa'xaðo, a] *nm/f* straggler.

rezagar [reθa'xar] *vt* (*dejar atrás*) to leave behind; (*retrasar*) to delay, postpone.

rezar [re'θar] *vi* to pray; **~ con** (*fam*) to concern, have to do with; **rezo** *nm* prayer.

rezongar [reθon'gar] *vi* to grumble.

rezumar [reθu'mar] *vt* to ooze // *vi* to leak; **~se** *vr* to leak out.

ría ['ria] *nf* estuary.

riada [ri'aða] *nf* flood.

ribera [ri'βera] *nf* (*de río*) bank; (: *área*) riverside; (*del mar*) shore.

ribete [ri'βete] *nm* (*de vestido*) border; (*fig*) addition; **~ar** *vt* to edge, border.

rico, a ['riko, a] *a* (*gen*) rich; (*adinerado*)

wealthy; (*lujoso*) luxurious; (*comida*) tasty, delicious // *nm/f* rich person.

rictus ['riktus] *nm* (*mueca*) sneer, grin.

ridiculez [riðiku'leθ] *nf* absurdity; **ridiculizar** *vt* to ridicule.

ridículo, a [ri'ðikulo, a] *a* ridiculous; **hacer el** ~ to make o.s. ridiculous; **poner a uno en** ~ to ridicule sb.

riego ['rjeʋo] *nm* (*aspersión*) watering; (*irrigación*) irrigation.

riel [rjel] *nm* rail.

rienda ['rjenda] *nf* rein; **dar** ~ **suelta a** to give free rein to.

riente ['rjente] *a* laughing.

riesgo ['rjesʋo] *nm* risk; **correr el** ~ **de** to run the risk of.

rifa ['rifa] *nf* (*lotería*) raffle; (*disputa*) quarrel; **rifar** *vt* to raffle // *vi* to quarrel; **rifarse** *vr*: **rifarse algo** to fight over sth.

rifle ['rifle] *nm* rifle.

rigidez [rixi'ðeθ] *nf* rigidity, stiffness; (*fig*) strictness; **rígido, a** *a* rigid, stiff; strict, inflexible.

rigor [ri'ʋor] *nm* strictness, rigour; (*inclemencia*) harshness; **de** ~ **de rigueur**, essential; **riguroso, a** *a* rigorous; harsh; (*severo*) severe.

rimar [ri'mar] *vi* to rhyme.

rimbombante [rimbom'bante] *a* resounding; (*fig*) pompous.

rincón [rin'kon] *nm* (inside) corner.

rinoceronte [rinoθe'ronte] *nm* rhinoceros.

riña ['riɲa] *nf* (*disputa*) argument; (*pelea*) brawl.

riñón [ri'ɲon] *nm* (*gen*) kidney; **tener riñones** to have guts.

río *etc vb ver* **reír** // ['rio] *nm* river; (*fig*) torrent, stream; ~ **abajo/arriba** downstream/upstream.

rioplatense [riopla'tense] *a* of the River Plate region.

ripio ['ripjo] *nm* (*residuo*) refuse, waste; (*cascotes*) rubble, debris.

riqueza [ri'keθa] *nf* wealth, riches *pl*; (*cualidad*) richness.

risa ['risa] *nf* (*una* ~) laugh; (*gen*) laughter.

risco ['risko] *nm* crag, cliff; ~**so, a** *a* steep.

risible [ri'siβle] *a* (*ridículo*) ludicrous; (*jocoso*) laughable.

risotada [riso'taða] *nf* guffaw.

ristra ['ristra] *nf* string.

risueño, a [ri'sweɲo, a] *a* (*sonriente*) smiling; (*contento*) cheerful.

ritmo ['ritmo] *nm* rhythm; **a** ~ **lento** slowly; **trabajar a** ~ **lento** to go slow.

rito ['rito] *nm* rite.

ritual [ri'twal] *a*, *nm* ritual.

rival [ri'βal] *a*, *nm/f* rival; ~**idad** *nf* rivalry; ~**izar** *vi*: ~**izar con** to rival, vie with.

rizado, a [ri'θaðo, a] *a* curly // *nm* curls *pl*; **rizar** *vt* to curl; **rizarse** *vr* (*el pelo*) to

curl; (*el mar*) to ripple; **rizo** *nm* curl; ripple.

RNE *nf abr de* **Radio Nacional de España.**

robar [ro'βar] *vt* to rob; (*objeto*) to steal; (*casa etc*) to break into; (*NAIPES*) to draw.

roble ['roβle] *nm* oak; ~**do**, ~**dal** *nm* oakwood.

roblón [ro'βlon] *nm* rivet.

robo ['roβo] *nm* robbery, theft; ~ **relámpago** smash-and-grab raid.

robot [ro'βo(t)] *nm* robot.

robustecer [roβuste'θer] *vt* to strengthen.

robusto, a [ro'βusto, a] *a* robust, strong.

roca ['roka] *nf* rock.

rocalla [ro'kaʎa] *nf* pebbles *pl*.

roce ['roθe] *nm* (*caricia*) brush; (*TEC*) friction; (*en la piel*) graze; **tener** ~ **con** to be in close contact with.

rociada [ro'θjaða] *nf* (*aspersión*) sprinkling; (*fig*) hail, shower; **rociar** *vt* to spray.

rocín [ro'θin] *nm* nag, hack.

rocío [ro'θio] *nm* dew.

rocoso, a [ro'koso, a] *a* rocky.

rodado, a [ro'ðaðo, a] *a* (*con ruedas*) wheeled; (*redondo*) round // *nf* rut.

rodaja [ro'ðaxa] *nf* (*raja*) slice; (*rueda*) small wheel.

rodaje [ro'ðaxe] *nm* (*TEC*) wheels *pl*, set of wheels; (*CINE*) shooting, filming; (*AUTO*): **en** ~ running in.

rodar [ro'ðar] *vt* (*vehículo*) to wheel; (*escalera*) to roll down; (*viajar por*) to travel (over) // *vi* to roll; (*coche*) to go, run; (*CINE*) to shoot, film.

rodear [roðe'ar] *vt* to surround // *vi* to go round; ~**se** *vr*: ~**se de amigos** to surround o.s. with friends.

rodeo [ro'ðeo] *nm* (*ruta indirecta*) detour; (*evasión*) evasion; (*AM*) rodeo; **hablar sin** ~**s** to come to the point, speak plainly.

rodilla [ro'ðiʎa] *nf* knee; **de** ~**s** kneeling.

rodillo [ro'ðiʎo] *nm* roller; (*CULIN*) rolling-pin; ~ **apisonador** *o* **de vapor** steamroller.

rododendro [roðo'ðendro] *nm* rhododendron.

roedor, a [roe'ðor, a] *ε* gnawing // *nm* rodent.

roer [ro'er] *vt* (*masticar*) to gnaw; (*corroer*, *fig*) to corrode.

rogar [ro'ʋar] *vt*, *vi* (*pedir*) to ask for; (*suplicar*) to beg, plead; **se ruega no fumar** please do not smoke.

rojete [ro'xete] *nm* rouge.

rojizo, a [ro'xiθo, a] *a* reddish.

rojo, a ['roxo, a] *a*, *nm* red; **al** ~ **vivo** red-hot; ~ **de labios** lipstick.

rol [rol] *nm* list, roll; (*AM: papel*) role.

rollizo, a [ro'ʎiθo, a] *a* (*objeto*) cylindrical; (*persona*) plump.

rollo ['roʎo] *nm* (*gen*) roll; (*de cuerda*) coil; (*madera*) log; (*fam*) bore; **¡qué** ~**!** what a carry-on!

Roma ['roma] *n* Rome.

romance [ro'manθe] *nm* Romance language; (*LITERATURA*) ballad; **hablar en** ~ to speak plainly.

romántico, a [ro'mantiko, a] *a* romantic.

romería [rome'ria] *nf* (*REL*) pilgrimage; (*excursión*) trip, outing.

romero, a [ro'mero, a] *nm/f* pilgrim // *nm* rosemary.

romo, a ['romo, a] *a* blunt; (*fig*) dull.

rompecabezas [rompeka'βeθas] *nm inv* riddle, puzzle; (*juego*) jigsaw.

rompehuelgas [rompe'welɣas] *nm inv* strikebreaker, blackleg.

rompeolas [rompe'olas] *nm inv* breakwater.

romper [rom'per] *vt* (*gen*) to break; (*hacer pedazos*) to smash; (*papel etc*) to tear, rip // *vi* (*olas*) to break; (*sol, diente*) to break through; ~ **un contrato** to break a contract; ~ **a** to start (suddenly) to; ~ **en llanto** to burst into tears; ~ **con uno** to fall out with sb.

rompimiento [rompi'mjento] *nm* breaking; (*fig*) break; (*quiebra*) crack; ~ **de hostilidades** outbreak of hostilities.

ron [ron] *nm* rum.

roncar [ron'kar] *vi* to snore.

ronco, a ['ronko, a] *a* (*sin voz*) hoarse; (*áspero*) raucous.

roncha ['rontʃa] *nf* weal; (*contusión*) bruise.

ronda ['ronda] *nf* (*gen*) round; (*patrulla*) patrol; **rondar** *vt* to patrol // *vi* to patrol; (*fig*) to prowl round.

rondón [ron'don]: **de** ~ *ad* unexpectedly.

ronquear [ronke'ar] *vi* to be hoarse; **ronquedad** *nf* hoarseness.

ronquido [ron'kiðo] *nm* snore, snoring.

ronronear [ronrone'ar] *vi* to purr; **ronroneo** *nm* purr.

ronzal [ron'θal] *nm* halter.

roña ['roɲa] *nf* scab; (*mugre*) crust (of dirt).

roñoso, a [ro'ɲoso, a] *a* (*mugriento*) filthy; (*inútil*) useless; (*tacaño*) mean.

ropa ['ropa] *nf* clothes *pl*, clothing; ~ **blanca** linen; ~ **de cama** bed linen; ~ **interior** underwear; ~**je** *nm* gown, robes *pl*; ~**vejero, a** *nm/f* second-hand clothes dealer.

ropero [ro'pero] *nm* linen cupboard; (*guardarropa*) wardrobe.

roque ['roke] *nm* rook, castle.

roquedal [roke'ðal] *nm* rocky place.

rosa ['rosa] *a inv* pink // *nf* rose; (*ANAT*) red birthmark; ~ **de los vientos** the compass; ~**s** *nfpl* popcorn *sg*.

rosado, a [ro'saðo, a], **rosáceo, a** [ro'saθeo, a] *a* pink // *nm* rosé.

rosal [ro'sal] *nm* rosebush.

rosario [ro'sarjo] *nm* (*REL*) rosary; **rezar el** ~ to say the rosary.

rosca ['roska] *nf* (*de tornillo*) thread; (*de humo*) coil, spiral; (*pan, postre*) ring-shaped roll/pastry.

rosetón [rose'ton] *nm* rosette; (*ARQ*) rose

window; (*AUTO*) cloverleaf (junction).

rostro ['rostro] *nm* (*cara*) face.

rotación [rota'θjon] *nf* rotation; ~ **de cultivos** crop rotation.

rotativo, a [rota'tiβo, a] *a* rotary.

roto, a ['roto, a] *pp de* **romper** // *a* broken; (*disipado*) debauched.

rótula ['rotula] *nf* kneecap; (*TEC*) ball-and-socket joint.

rotular [rotu'lar] *vt* (*titular, encabezar*) to head, entitle; (*etiquetar*) to label; **rótulo** *nm* heading, title; label.

rotundo, a [ro'tundo, a] *a* round; (*enfático*) emphatic.

rotura [ro'tura] *nf* (*rompimiento*) breaking; (*quiebra*) crack; (*MED*) fracture.

roturar [rotu'rar] *vt* to plough.

rozado, a [ro'θaðo, a] *a* worn.

rozadura [roθa'ðura] *nf* abrasion, graze.

rozar [ro'θar] *vt* (*frotar*) to rub; (*arañar*) to scratch; (*arrugar*) to crumple; (*AGR*) to graze; (*tocar ligeramente*) to shave, touch lightly; ~**se** *vr* to rub (together); (*trabarse*) to trip over one's own feet; ~ **con** (*fam*) to rub shoulders with.

roznar [roθ'nar] *vi* to bray.

rte *abr de* **remite, remitente** sender.

rubí [ru'βi] *nm* ruby.

rubicundo, a [ruβi'kundo, a] *a* ruddy; (*de salud*) rosy with health.

rubio, a ['ruβjo, a] *a* fair-haired // *nm/f* blond/blonde; **tabaco** ~ Virginia tobacco.

rubor [ru'βor] *nm* (*timidez*) bashfulness; (*sonrojo*) blush; ~**izarse** *vr* to blush; ~**oso, a** *a* blushing.

rúbrica ['ruβrika] *nf* title, heading; (*de la firma*) flourish; **rubricar** *vt* (*firmar*) to sign with a flourish; (*concluir*) to sign and seal.

rucio, a ['ruθjo, a] *a* grey.

rudeza [ru'ðeθa] *nf* (*tosquedad*) coarseness; (*sencillez*) simplicity.

rudimento [ruði'mento] *nm* rudiment.

rudo, a ['ruðo, a] *a* (*sin pulir*) unpolished; (*tosco*) coarse; (*violento*) violent; (*vulgar*) common; (*estúpido*) stupid.

rueda ['rweða] *nf* (*gen*) wheel; (*círculo*) ring, circle; (*rodaja*) slice, round; ~ **delantera/trasera/de repuesto** front/back/spare wheel; ~ **de prensa** press conference.

ruedo ['rweðo] *nm* (*contorno*) edge, border; (*de vestido*) hem; (*círculo*) circle; (*TAUR*) arena, bullring.

ruego *etc vb ver* **rogar** // ['rweɣo] *nm* request.

rufián [ru'fjan] *nm* scoundrel.

rugby ['ruɣβi] *nm* rugby.

rugido [ru'xiðo] *nm* roar; **rugir** *vi* to roar.

rugoso, a [ru'ɣoso, a] *a* (*arrugado*) wrinkled; (*áspero*) rough; (*desigual*) ridged.

ruibarbo [rui'βarβo] *nm* rhubarb.

ruido ['rwiðo] *nm* (*gen*) noise; (*sonido*) sound; (*alboroto*) racket, row; (*escándalo*)

commotion, rumpus; ~**so, a** *a* noisy, loud; (*fig*) sensational.
ruin [ru'in] *a* contemptible, mean.
ruina ['rwina] *nf* (*gen*) ruin; (*colapso*) collapse; (*de persona*) ruin, downfall; (*de imperio*) decline.
ruindad [rwin'daθ] *nf* lowness, meanness; (*acto*) low *or* mean act.
ruinoso, a [rui'noso, a] *a* ruinous; (*destartalado*) dilapidated, tumbledown; (*COM*) disastrous.
ruiseñor [rwise'por] *nm* nightingale.
rula ['rula], **ruleta** [ru'leta] *nf* roulette.
Rumania [ru'manja] *nf* Rumania.
rumba ['rumba] *nf* rumba.
rumbo ['rumbo] *nm* (*ruta*) route, direction; (*ángulo de dirección*) course, bearing; (*fig*) course of events.
rumboso, a [rum'boso, a] *a* generous.
rumiante [ru'mjante] *nm* ruminant.
rumiar [rumi'nar] *vt* to chew; (*fig*) to chew over // *vi* to chew the cud.
rumor [ru'mor] *nm* (*ruido sordo*) low sound; (*murmuración*) murmur, buzz; ~**earse** *vr*: **se ~ea que** it is rumoured that; ~**eo** *nm* murmur.
rupestre [ru'pestre] *a* rock *cpd*.
ruptura [rup'tura] *nf* (*MED*) fracture; (*fig*) rupture.
rural [ru'ral] *a* rural.
Rusia ['rusja] *nf* Russia; **ruso, a** *a, nm/f* Russian.
rústico, a ['rustiko, a] *a* rustic; (*ordinario*) coarse, uncouth // *nm/f* yokel // *nf:* **libro en ~a** paperback.
ruta ['ruta] *nf* route.
rutina [ru'tina] *nf* routine; ~**rio, a** *a* routine.

S

S *abr de* **santo, a; sur.**
s. *abr de* **siglo; siguiente.**
sábado ['saβaðo] *nm* Saturday.
sábana ['saβana] *nf* sheet.
sabandija [saβan'dixa] *nf* bug, insect.
sabañón [saβa'ɲon] *nm* chilblain.
sabelotodo [saβelo'toðo] *nm/f inv* know-all.
saber [sa'βer] *vt* to know; (*llegar a conocer*) to find out, learn; (*tener capacidad de*) to know how to // *vi:* ~ **a** to taste of, taste like // *nm* knowledge, learning; **a** ~ namely; ¿**sabes nadar?** can you swim?; ¿**sabes ir?** do you know the way?
sabiduría [saβiðu'ria] *nf* (*conocimientos*) wisdom; (*instrucción*) knowledge, learning.
sabiendas [sa'βjendas]: **a** ~ *ad* knowingly.
sabio, a ['saβjo,a] *a* (*docto*) learned; (*prudente*) wise, sensible.
sabor [sa'βor] *nm* taste, flavour; ~**ear** *vt* to savour, relish; (*dar* ~ *a*) to flavour.
sabotaje [saβo'taxe] *nm* sabotage; **sabotear** *vt* to sabotage.
sabré *etc vb ver* **saber.**

sabroso, a [sa'βroso, a] *a* tasty; (*fig: fam*) racy, salty.
sacacorchos [saka'kortʃos] *nm inv* corkscrew.
sacapuntas [saka'puntas] *nm inv* pencil sharpener.
sacar [sa'kar] *vt* (*gen*) to take out; (*fig*) to get (out); (*quitar*) to remove, get out; (*hacer salir*) to bring out; (*conclusión*) to draw; (*novela etc*) to publish, bring out; (*ropa*) to take off; (*obra*) to make; (*FOTO*) to take; (*premio*) to receive; (*entradas*) to get; ~ **adelante** to bring up; ~ **a alguien a bailar** to get sb up to dance; ~ **apuntes** to take notes; ~ **la cara por alguien** to stick up for sb; ~ **la lengua** to stick out one's tongue.
sacarina [saka'rina] *nf* saccharin(e).
sacerdote [saθer'ðote] *nm* priest.
saco ['sako] *nm* (*gen*) bag; (*grande*) sack; (*su contenido*) bagful; (*AM*) jacket; ~ **de dormir** sleeping bag.
sacramento [sakra'mento] *nm* sacrament.
sacrificar [sakrifi'kar] *vt* to sacrifice; **sacrificio** *nm* sacrifice.
sacrilegio [sakri'lexjo] *nm* sacrilege; **sacrílego, a** *a* sacrilegious.
sacristía [sakris'tia] *nf* sacristy.
sacro, a ['sakro, a] *a* sacred.
sacudida [saku'ðiða] *nf* (*zarandeada*) shake, shaking; (*sacudimiento*) jolt, bump; ~ **eléctrica** electric shock; **sacudir** *vt* to shake; (*golpear*) to hit.
sádico, a ['saðiko, a] *a* sadistic; **sadismo** *nm* sadism.
saeta [sa'eta] *nf* (*flecha*) arrow; (*de reloj*) hand; (*brújula*) magnetic needle.
sagacidad [saɣaθi'ðaθ] *nf* shrewdness, cleverness; **sagaz** *a* shrewd, clever; (*astuto*) astute.
sagrado, a [sa'ɣraðo, a] *a* sacred, holy // *nm* sanctuary, asylum.
Sáhara ['saara] *nm:* **el** ~ the Sahara (desert).
sahumar [sau'mar] *vt* to fumigate.
sal [sal] *vb ver* **salir** // *nf* salt; ~ **de la Higuera** Epsom salts.
sala ['sala] *nf* (*cuarto grande*) large room; (~ *de estar*) living room; (*TEATRO*) house, auditorium; (*de hospital*) ward; ~ **de apelación** court; ~ **de espera** waiting room.
salado, a [sa'laðo, a] *a* salty; (*fig*) witty, amusing; **agua** ~**a** salt water; **salar** *vt* to salt, add salt to.
salario [sa'larjo] *nm* wage, pay.
salchicha [sal'tʃitʃa] *nf* pork sausage; **salchichón** *nm* (*salami-type*) sausage.
saldar [sal'dar] *vt* to pay; (*vender*) to sell off; (*fig*) to settle, resolve; **saldo** *nm* (*pago*) settlement; (*de una cuenta*) balance; (*lo restante*) remnant(s) (*pl*), remainder.
saldré *etc vb ver* **salir.**
salero [sa'lero] *nm* salt cellar.
salgo *etc vb ver* **salir.**

salida [sa'liða] *nf* exit, way out, (*acto*) leaving, going out; (*de tren, AVIAT*) departure; (*TEC*) output, production; (*fig*) way out; (*COM*) opening; (*GEO, válvula*) outlet; (*de gas, aire*) escape, leak; **calle sin ~ cul-de-sac; ~ de emergencia** emergency exit.

saliente [sa'ljente] *a* (*ARQ*) projecting; (*que se retira*) outgoing, retiring; (*el sol*) rising; (*fig*) outstanding.

salir [sa'lir] *vi* (*gen*) to come/go out; (*resultar*) to turn out; (*partir*) to leave, depart; (*aparecer*) to appear; (*sobresalir*) to project, jut out; **~se** *vr* (*vasija*) to leak; (*animal*) to escape, get out; **~ con** to go out with; **~ a la superficie** to come to the surface; **~ caro/barato** to work out expensive/cheap.

saliva [sa'liβa] *nf* saliva.

salmantino, a [salman'tino, a] *a* of Salamanca.

salmo ['salmo] *nm* psalm.

salmón [sal'mon] *nm* salmon.

salmuera [sal'mwera] *nf* pickle, brine.

salón [sa'lon] *nm* (*de casa*) living-room, lounge; (*muebles*) lounge suite; **~ de belleza** beauty parlour; **~ de pintura** art gallery; **~ de baile** dance hall.

salpicadero [salpika'ðero] *nm* dashboard.

salpicar [salpi'kar] *vt* (*rociar*) to sprinkle, spatter; (*esparcir*) to scatter.

salsa ['salsa] *nf* sauce; (*con carne asada*) gravy; (*fig*) spice.

saltamontes [salta'montes] *nm inv* grasshopper.

saltar [sal'tar] *vt* to jump (over), leap (over); (*dejar de lado*) to skip, miss out // *vi* to jump, leap; (*pelota*) to bounce; (*al aire*) to fly up; (*quebrarse*) to break; (*al agua*) to dive; (*fig*) to explode, blow up.

saltear [salte'ar] *vt* (*robar*) to rob (in a holdup); (*asaltar*) to assault, attack; (*CULIN*) to sauté.

saltimbanqui [saltim'banki] *nm/f* acrobat.

salto ['salto] *nm* jump, leap; (*al agua*) dive; (*DEPORTE*) jump; **~ de agua** waterfall.

saltón, ona [sal'ton, ona] *a* (*ojos*) bulging, popping; (*dientes*) protruding.

salubre [sa'luβre] *a* healthy, salubrious.

salud [sa'luð] *nf* health; **¡(a su ~)~!** good health!; **~able** *a* (*de buena ~*) healthy; (*provechoso*) good, beneficial.

saludar [salu'ðar] *vt* to greet; (*MIL*) to salute; **saludo** *nm* greeting; **saludos** (*en carta*) best wishes, regards, greetings.

salvación [salβa'θjon] *nf* (*gen*) salvation; (*rescate*) rescue.

salvaguardar [salβaxwar'ðar] *vt* to safeguard.

salvaje [sal'βaxe] *a* wild; (*tribú*) savage; **salvajismo** *nm*, **salvajez** *nf* savagery.

salvar [sal'βar] *vt* (*rescatar*) to save, rescue; (*resolver*) to overcome, resolve; (*cubrir distancias*) to cover, travel; (*hacer excepción*) to except, exclude; (*un barco*) to salvage.

salvavidas [salβa'βiðas] *nm inv* lifebelt // *a*: **bote/chaleco/cinturón ~** lifeboat/jacket/belt.

salvia ['salβja] *nf* sage.

salvo, a ['salβo, a] *a* safe // *ad* except (for), save; **a ~** out of danger; **~ que** unless; **~conducto** *nm* safe-conduct.

san [san] *a* saint; **~ Juan** St. John.

sanar [sa'nar] *vt* (*herida*) to heal; (*persona*) to cure // *vi* (*persona*) to get well, recover; (*herida*) to heal.

sanatorio [sana'torjo] *nm* sanatorium.

sanción [san'θjon] *nf* sanction; **sancionar** *vt* to sanction.

sandalia [san'dalja] *nf* sandal.

sandía [san'dia] *nf* watermelon.

sandwich ['sandwitʃ] *nm* sandwich.

saneamiento [sanea'mjento] *nm* sanitation; (*de la tierra*) drainage; (*indemnización*) compensation; (*fig*) remedy; **sanear** *vt* to drain; to compensate; to remedy, repair; (*garantizar*) to guarantee; (*asegurar*) to insure.

sangrar [san'grar] *vt, vi* to bleed; **sangre** *nf* blood.

sangría [san'gria] *nf* sangria, *sweetened drink of red wine with fruit.*

sangriento, a [san'grjento, a] *a* (*herido*) bleeding; (*batalla*) bloody.

sanguinario, a [san'gi'narjo, a] *a* bloodthirsty.

sanguíneo, a [san'gineo, a] *a* blood *cpd*.

sanidad [sani'ðað] *nf* sanitation; (*calidad de sano*) health, healthiness; **~ pública** public health.

sanitario, a [sani'tarjo, a] *a* sanitary; (*de la salud*) health *cpd*.

sano, a ['sano, a] *a* healthy; (*sin daños*) sound; (*comida*) good; (*entero*) whole, intact; **~ y salvo** safe and sound.

santidad [santi'ðað] *nf* holiness, sanctity; **santificar** *vt* to sanctify, make holy.

santiguar [santi'ɣwar] *vt* (*fig*) to slap, hit; **~se** *vr* to make the sign of the cross.

santo, a ['santo, a] *a* holy; (*fig*) wonderful, miraculous // *nm/f* saint // *nm* saint's day; **~ y seña** password.

santuario [san'twarjo] *nm* sanctuary, shrine.

saña ['saɲa] *nf* rage, fury.

sapo ['sapo] *nm* toad.

saque ['sake] *nm* (*TENIS*) service, serve; (*FUTBOL*) throw-in; **~ de esquina** corner (kick).

saquear [sake'ar] *vt* (*MIL*) to sack; (*robar*) to loot, plunder; (*fig*) to ransack; **saqueo** *nm* sacking; looting, plundering; ransacking.

sarampión [saram'pjon] *nm* measles *sg*.

sarcasmo [sar'kasmo] *nm* sarcasm; **sarcástico, a** *a* sarcastic.

sardina [sar'ðina] *nf* sardine.

sardónico, a [sar'ðoniko, a] *a* sardonic; (*irónico*) ironical, sarcastic.

sargento [sar'xento] *nm* sergeant.

sarna ['sarna] *nf* itch; (MED) scabies.
sartén [sar'ten] *nf* frying pan.
sastre ['sastre] *nm* tailor; ~**ría** *nf* (*arte*) tailoring; (*tienda*) tailor's (shop).
satélite [sa'telite] *nm* satellite.
sátira ['satira] *nf* satire.
satisfacción [satisfak'θjon] *nf* satisfaction; **satisfacer** *vt* to satisfy; (*gastos*) to meet; (*pérdida*) to make good; **satisfacerse** *vr* to satisfy o.s., be satisfied; (*vengarse*) to take revenge; **satisfecho, a** *a* satisfied; (*contento*) content(ed), happy; (*vanidoso*) self-satisfied, smug.
saturar [satu'rar] *vt* to saturate.
sauce ['sauθe] *nm* willow; ~ **llorón** weeping willow.
sauna ['sauna] *nf* sauna.
savia ['saβja] *nf* sap.
saxofón [sakso'fon], **saxófono** [sak-'sofono] *nm* saxophone.
sayo ['sajo] *nm* smock.
sazonado, a [saθo'naðo, a] *a* (*fruta*) ripe; (CULIN) flavoured, seasoned; **sazonar** *vt* to ripen; to flavour, season.
se [se] *pron reflexivo* oneself; (*sg: m*) himself; (: *f*) herself; (: *de una cosa*) itself; (: *de Ud*) yourself; (*pl*) themselves; (: *de Uds*) yourselves; (*de uno*) oneself; ~ **mira en el espejo** he looks at himself in the mirror; (*recíproco*) each other, one another; ~ **ayudan** they help each other; ~ **miraron (el uno al otro)** they looked at one another; (*uso impersonal*): ~ **compró hace 3 años** it was bought 3 years ago; **en esa parte** ~ **habla francés** in that area French is spoken *or* people speak French; (*dativo*): ~ **lo daré** I'll give it to him/her/you; **él** ~ **ha comprado un sombrero** he has bought himself a hat.
SE *abr de* **sudeste.**
sé *vb ver* **saber, ser.**
sea *etc vb ver* **ser.**
sebo ['seβo] *nm* fat, grease.
seca ['seka] *nf ver* **seco.**
secador [seka'ðor] *nm*: ~ **de cabello** *o* **para el pelo** hair-dryer.
secadora [seka'ðora] *nf* wringer; ~ **centrífuga** spin-dryer.
secar [se'kar] *vt* to dry; ~**se** *vr* to dry (off); (*río, planta*) to dry up.
sección [sek'θjon] *nf* section.
seco, a ['seko, a] *a* dry; (*carácter*) cold; (*respuesta*) sharp, curt; (*coñac*) straight // *nf* drought; **vivir a pan** ~ to live by bread alone; **habrá pan a** ~**as** there will be just bread; **decir algo a** ~**as** to say sth curtly; **parar en** ~ to stop dead.
secretaría [sekreta'ria] *nf* secretariat; **secretario, a** *nm/f* secretary.
secreto, a [se'kreto, a] *a* secret; (*persona*) secretive // *nm* secret; (*calidad*) secrecy.
secta ['sekta] *nf* sect; ~**rio, a** *a* sectarian.
sector [sek'tor] *nm* sector.
secuela [se'kwela] *nf* consequence.
secuestrar [sekwes'trar] *vt* to kidnap; (*bienes*) to seize, confiscate; **secuestro**

nm kidnapping; seizure, confiscation.
secular [seku'lar] *a* secular.
secundar [sekun'dar] *vt* to second, support.
secundario, a [sekun'darjo, a] *a* secondary.
sed [seð] *nf* thirst; **tener** ~ to be thirsty.
seda ['seða] *nf* silk.
sedal [se'ðal] *nm* fishing line.
sedante [se'ðante], **sedativo** [seða'tiβo] *nm* sedative.
sede ['seðe] *nf* (*de gobierno*) seat; (*de compañía*) headquarters *pl*; **Santa S**~ Holy See.
sediento, a [se'ðjento, a] *a* thirsty.
sedimentar [seðimen'tar] *vt* to deposit; ~**se** *vr* to settle; **sedimento** *nm* sediment.
seducción [seðuk'θjon] *nf* seduction; **seducir** *vt* to seduce; (*sobornar*) to bribe; (*cautivar*) to charm, fascinate; **seductor, a** *a* seductive; charming, fascinating; (*engañoso*) deceptive, misleading // *nm/f* seducer.
segadora-trilladora [seɣa'ðora triʎa-'ðora] *nf* combine harvester.
seglar [se'ɣlar] *a* secular, lay.
segregación [seɣreɣa'θjon] *nf* segregation; ~ **racial** racial segregation; **segregar** *vt* to segregate, separate.
seguido, a [se'ɣiðo, a] *a* (*continuo*) continuous, unbroken; (*recto*) straight; ~**s** consecutive, successive // *ad* (*directo*) straight (on); (*después*) after // *nf*: **en** ~**a** at once, right away; **5 días** ~**s** 5 days running, 5 days in a row.
seguimiento [seɣi'mjento] *nm* chase, pursuit; (*continuación*) continuation.
seguir [se'ɣir] *vt* (*gen*) to follow; (*venir después*) to follow on, come after; (*proseguir*) to continue; (*perseguir*) to chase, pursue // *vi* (*gen*) to follow; (*continuar*) to continue, carry *or* go on; ~**se** *vr* to follow; **sigo sin comprender** I still don't understand; **sigue lloviendo** it's still raining.
según [se'ɣun] *prep* according to // *ad* according to circumstances; ~ **y conforme** it all depends; ~ **esté el tiempo** depending on the weather.
segundo, a [se'ɣundo, a] *a* second // *nm* second // *nf* second meaning; **de** ~**a mano** second hand.
segur [se'ɣur] *nf* (*hacha*) axe; (*hoz*) sickle.
seguramente [seɣura'mente] *ad* surely; (*con certeza*) for sure, with certainty.
seguridad [seɣuri'ðað] *nf* (*gen*) safety; (*del estado, de casa etc*) security; (*certidumbre*) certainty; (*confianza*) confidence; (*estabilidad*) stability; ~ **social** social security.
seguro, a [se'ɣuro, a] *a* (*cierto*) sure, certain; (*fiel*) trustworthy; (*libre del peligro*) safe; (*bien defendido, firme*) secure // *ad* for sure, certainly // *nm* (COM) insurance; ~ **contra terceros/a todo riesgo** third party/comprehensive insurance; ~**s sociales** social security *sg*.

seis [seis] *num* six.

seismo ['seismo] *nm* tremor, earthquake.

selección [selek'θjon] *nf* selection; **seleccionar** *vt* to pick, choose, select; **selecto, a** *a* select, choice; (*escogido*) selected.

selva ['selβa] *nf* (*bosque*) forest, woods *pl*; (*jungla*) jungle.

sello ['seʎo] *nm* stamp; (*medicinal*) capsule, pill.

semáforo [se'maforo] *nm* (*AUTO*) traffic lights *pl*; (*FERRO*) signal.

semana [se'mana] *nf* week; **entre ~** during the week; **semanal, semanario, a** a weekly.

semblante [sem'blante] *nm* face; (*fig*) face, appearance.

sembrar [sem'brar] *vt* to sow; (*objetos*) to sprinkle, scatter about; (*noticias*) to spread.

semejante [seme'xante] *a* (*parecido*) similar; **~s** alike, similar // *nm* fellow man, fellow creature; **no he dicho cosa ~** I have not said any such thing; **semejanza** *nf* similarity, resemblance.

semejar [seme'xar] *vi* to seem like, resemble; **~se** *vr* to look alike, be similar.

semen ['semen] *nm* semen; **~tal** *nm* stud.

semestral [semes'tral] *a* half-yearly, bi-annual.

semicírculo [semi'θirkulo] *nm* semicircle.

semiconsciente [semikons'θjente] *a* semiconscious.

semilla [se'miʎa] *nf* seed.

seminario [semi'narjo] *nm* (*REL*) seminary; (*en universidad*) seminar.

sémola ['semola] *nf* semolina.

sempiterno, a [sempi'terno, a] *a* everlasting // *nf* evergreen.

Sena ['sena] *nm*: **el ~** the (river) Seine.

senado [se'naðo] *nm* senate; **senador, a** *nm/f* senator.

sencillez [senθi'ʎeθ] *nf* (*gen*) simplicity; (*naturalidad*) naturalness; **sencillo, a** a simple; natural, unaffected.

senda ['senda] *nf*, **sendero** [sen'dero] *nm* path, track.

sendos, as ['sendos, as] *apl*: **les dio ~ golpes** he hit both of them.

senil [se'nil] *a* senile.

seno ['seno] *nm* (*ANAT*) bosom, bust; (*fig*) bosom; (*vacío*) hollow; **~s** breasts.

sensación [sensa'θjon] *nf* (*gen*) sensation; (*sentido*) sense; (*sentimiento*) feeling.

sensato, a [sen'sato, a] *a* sensible.

sensible [sen'sible] *a* sensitive; (*apreciable*) perceptible, appreciable; (*pérdida*) considerable.

sensitivo, a [sensi'tiβo, a], **sensorio, a** [sen'sorjo, a], **sensorial** [senso'rjal] *a* sensory.

sensual [sen'swal] *a* sensual.

sentado, a [sen'taðo, a] *a* (*establecido*) settled; (*carácter*) sensible; **estar ~** to sit, be sitting (down) // *nf* sitting; **dar por ~** to take for granted, assume.

sentar [sen'tar] *vt* to sit, seat; (*fig*) to establish // *vi* (*vestido*) to suit; (*alimento*): **~ bien/mal a** to agree/disagree with; **~se** *vr* (*persona*) to sit, sit down; (*el tiempo*) to settle (down); (*los depósitos*) to settle.

sentencia [sen'tenθja] *nf* (*máxima*) maxim, saying; (*JUR*) sentence; **sentenciar** *vt* to sentence // *vi* to give one's opinion.

sentido, a [sen'tiðo, a] *a* (*pérdida*) regrettable; (*carácter*) sensitive // *nm* (*gen*) sense; (*sentimiento*) feeling; (*significado*) sense, meaning; (*dirección*) direction; **mi más ~ pésame** my deepest sympathy; **~ del humor** sense of humour; **~ único** one-way (street).

sentimental [sentimen'tal] *a* sentimental; **vida ~** love life.

sentimiento [senti'mjento] *nm* (*emoción*) feeling, emotion; (*sentido*) sense; (*pesar*) regret, sorrow.

sentir [sen'tir] *vt* (*gen*) to feel; (*percibir*) to perceive, sense; (*lamentar*) to regret, be sorry for // *vi* (*tener la sensación*) to feel; (*lamentarse*) to feel sorry // *nm* opinion, judgement; **~se** **bien/mal** to feel well/ill; **lo siento** I'm sorry.

seña ['seɲa] *nf* sign; (*MIL*) password; **~s** *nfpl* address *sg*; **~s personales** personal details.

señal [se'ɲal] *nf* (*gen*) sign; (*síntoma*) symptom; (*FERRO, TELEC*) signal; (*marca*) mark; (*COM*) deposit; **en ~ de** as a token of, as a sign of; **~ar** *vt* to mark; (*indicar*) to point out, indicate; (*fijar*) to fix, settle; **~arse** *vr* to make one's mark.

señor [se'ɲor] *nm* (*hombre*) man; (*caballero*) gentleman; (*dueño*) owner, master; (*trato: antes de nombre propio*) Mr; (: *directo*) sir; **muy ~ mío** Dear Sir; **el ~ alcalde/presidente** the mayor/president.

señora [se'ɲora] *nf* (*dama*) lady; (*trato*) Mrs; (*tratamiento de cortesía*) madam; (*fam*) wife; **Nuestra S~** Our Lady.

señorita [seɲo'rita] *nf* (*gen*) Miss; (*mujer joven*) young lady.

señuelo [se'ɲwelo] *nm* decoy.

sepa *etc vb ver* **saber.**

separación [separa'θjon] *nf* separation; (*división*) division; (*distancia*) gap, distance.

separar [sepa'rar] *vt* to separate; (*dividir*) to divide; **~se** *vr* (*parte*) to come away; (*partes*) to come apart; (*persona*) to leave, go away; (*matrimonio*) to separate; **separatismo** *nm* separatism.

sepia ['sepja] *nf* cuttlefish.

séptico, a ['septiko, a] *a* septic.

septiembre [sep'tjembre] *nm* September.

séptimo, a ['septimo, a] *a, nm* seventh.

sepultar [sepul'tar] *vt* to bury; **sepultura** *nf* (*acto*) burial; (*tumba*) grave, tomb; **sepulturero, a** *nm/f* gravedigger.

sequedad [seke'ðað] *nf* dryness; (*fig*) brusqueness, curtness.

sequía [se'kia] nf drought.

séquito ['sekito] nm followers pl, retinue.

ser [ser] vi (gen) to be; (devenir) to become // nm being; ~ **de** (origen) to be from, come from; (hecho de) to be (made) of; (pertenecer a) to belong to; **es la una** it is one o'clock; **es de esperar que** it is to be hoped that; **era de ver** it was worth seeing, you should have seen it; **a no ~ que** unless; **de no ~ así** if it were not so, were it not so; **o sea** that is to say; **sea como sea** be that as it may.

serenarse [sere'narse] vr to calm down.

sereno, a [se'reno, a] a (persona) calm, unruffled; (el tiempo) fine, settled; (ambiente) calm, peaceful // nm night watchman.

serie ['serje] nf series; (cadena) sequence, succession; **fuera de ~** out of order; **fabricación en ~** mass production.

seriedad [serje'ðað] nf seriousness; (formalidad) reliability; (de crisis) gravity, seriousness; **serio, a** a serious; reliable, dependable; grave, serious; **en serio** ad seriously.

sermón [ser'mon] nm (REL) sermon.

serpentear [serpente'ar] vi to wriggle; (fig) to wind, snake.

serpentina [serpen'tina] nf streamer.

serpiente [ser'pjente] nf snake; ~ **boa** boa constrictor; ~ **pitón** python; ~ **de cascabel** rattlesnake.

serranía [serra'nia] nf mountainous area; **serrano, a** a highland cpd, hill cpd // nm/f highlander.

serrar [se'rrar] vt = **aserrar.**

serrín [se'rrin] nm = **aserrín.**

serrucho [se'rrutʃo] nm saw.

servicio [ser'βiθjo] nm service; ~**s** toilet(s).

servidor, a [serβi'ðor, a] nm/f servant; **su seguro ~** (s.s.s.) yours faithfully; **servidumbre** nf (sujeción) servitude; (criados) servants pl, staff.

servil [ser'βil] a servile.

servilleta [serβi'ʎeta] nf serviette, napkin.

servir [ser'βir] vt to serve // vi to serve; (tener utilidad) to be of use, be useful; ~**se** vr to serve or help o.s.; ~**se de algo** to make use of sth, use sth; **sírvase pasar** please come in.

sesenta [se'senta] num sixty.

sesgado, a [ses'ɣaðo, a] a slanted, slanting; **sesgo** nm slant; (fig) slant, twist.

sesión [se'sjon] nf (POL) session, sitting; (CINE) showing.

seso ['seso] nm brain; **sesudo, a** a sensible, wise.

seta ['seta] nf mushroom.

setenta [se'tenta] num seventy.

seudo... ['seuðo] pref pseudo... .

seudónimo [seu'ðonimo] nm pseudonym.

severidad [seβeri'ðað] nf severity; **severo, a** a severe.

Sevilla [se'βiʎa] n Seville.

sexo ['sekso] nm sex.

sexto, a ['seksto, a] a, nm sixth.

sexual [sek'swal] a sexual; **vida ~ sex** life.

si [si] conj if; **me pregunto ~...** I wonder if or whether... .

sí [si] ad yes // pron (gen) oneself; (sg: m) himself; (: f) herself; (: de cosa) itself; (de usted) yourself; (pl) themselves; (de ustedes) yourselves; (recíproco) each other; **él no quiere pero yo ~** he doesn't want to but I do; **ella ~ vendrá** she will certainly come, she is sure to come; **claro que ~** of course; **creo que ~** I think so.

siderúrgico, a [siðe'rurxico, a] a iron and steel cpd // nf: **la ~a** the iron and steel industry.

sidra ['siðra] nf cider.

siembra ['sjembra] nf sowing.

siempre ['sjempre] ad (gen) always; (todo el tiempo) all the time; ~ **que** conj (cada vez) whenever; (dado que) provided that; **para ~** for ever.

sien [sjen] nf temple.

siento etc vb ver **sentar, sentir.**

sierra ['sjerra] nf (TEC) saw; (cadena de montañas) mountain range.

siervo, a ['sjerβo, a] nm/f slave.

siesta ['sjesta] nf siesta, nap.

siete ['sjete] num seven.

sífilis ['sifilis] nf syphilis.

sifón [si'fon] nm syphon; **whisky con ~** whisky and soda.

sigla ['siɣla] nf symbol.

siglo ['siɣlo] nm century; (fig) age.

significación [siɣnifika'θjon] nf significance.

significado [siɣnifi'kaðo] nm significance; (de palabra) meaning.

significar [siɣnifi'kar] vt to mean, signify; (notificar) to make known, express; ~**se** vr to become known, make a name for o.s.; **significativo, a** a significant.

signo ['siɣno] nm sign; ~ **de admiración** o **exclamación** exclamation mark; ~ **de interrogación** question mark.

sigo etc vb ver **seguir.**

siguiente [si'ɣjente] a next, following.

siguió etc vb ver **seguir.**

sílaba ['silaβa] nf syllable.

silbar [sil'βar] vt, vi to whistle; **silbato** nm whistle; **silbido** nm whistle, whistling.

silenciador [silenθja'ðor] nm silencer.

silenciar [silen'θjar] vt (persona) to silence; (escándalo) to hush up; **silencio** nm silence, quiet; **silencioso, a** a silent, quiet.

silicio [si'liθjo] nm silicon.

silueta [si'lweta] nf silhouette; (de edificio) outline; (figura) figure.

silvestre [sil'βestre] a rustic, rural; (salvaje) wild.

silla ['siʎa] nf (asiento) chair; (de jinete) saddle.

sillón [si'ʎon] *nm* armchair, easy chair; ~ **de ruedas** wheelchair.

simbólico, a [sim'boliko, a] *a* symbolic(al); **símbolo** *nm* symbol.

simetría [sime'tria] *nf* symmetry.

simiente [si'mjente] *nf* seed.

similar [simi'lar] *a* similar.

simio ['simjo] *nm* ape.

simpatía [simpa'tia] *nf* liking; (*afecto*) affection; (*amabilidad*) kindness; (*solidaridad*) mutual support, solidarity; **simpático, a** *a* nice, pleasant; kind; **simpatizante** *nm/f* sympathiser; **simpatizar** *vi*: **simpatizar con** to get on well with.

simple ['simple] *a* (*gen*) simple; (*elemental*) simple, easy; (*mero*) mere; (*puro*) pure, sheer // *nm/f* simpleton; ~**za** *nf* simpleness; (*necedad*) silly thing; **simplicidad** *nf* simplicity; **simplificar** *vt* to simplify.

simular [simu'lar] *vt* to simulate.

simultáneo, a [simul'taneo, a] *a* simultaneous.

sin [sin] *prep* without; **la ropa está** ~ **lavar** the clothes are unwashed; ~ **que** *conj* without; ~ **embargo** however, still.

sinagoga [sina'xoxa] *nf* synagogue.

sinceridad [sinθeri'ðað] *nf* sincerity; **sincero, a** *a* sincere.

sincronizar [sinkroni'θar] *vt* to synchronize.

sindical [sindi'kal] *a* union *cpd*, trade-union *cpd*; ~**ista** *nm/f* trade-unionist; **sindicato** *nm* (*de trabajadores*) trade(s) union; (*de negociantes*) syndicate.

sinfín [sin'fin] *nm*: **un** ~ **de** a great many, no end of.

sinfonía [sinfo'nia] *nf* symphony.

singular [singu'lar] *a* singular; (*fig*) outstanding, exceptional; (*pey*) peculiar, odd; ~**idad** *nf* singularity, peculiarity; ~**izar** *vt* to single out; ~**izarse** *vr* to distinguish o.s., stand out.

siniestro, a [si'njestro, a] *a* left; (*fig*) sinister.

sinnúmero [sin'numero] *nm* = **sinfín**.

sino ['sino] *nm* fate, destiny // *conj* (*pero*) but; (*salvo*) except, save.

sinónimo [si'nonimo] *nm* synonym.

sinrazón [sinra'θon] *nf* wrong, injustice.

síntesis ['sintesis] *nf* synthesis; **sintético, a** *a* synthetic; **sintetizar** *vt* to synthesize.

sintió *vb ver* **sentir**.

síntoma ['sintoma] *nm* symptom.

sinvergüenza [sinβer'ɣwenθa] *nm/f* shameless person.

sionismo [sjo'nismo] *nm* Zionism.

siquiera [si'kjera] *conj* even if, even though // *ad* at least; **ni** ~ not even.

sirena [si'rena] *nf* siren.

sirviente, a [sir'βjente, a] *nm/f* servant.

sirvo *etc vb ver* **servir**.

sisear [sise'ar] *vt, vi* to hiss.

sismógrafo [sis'moɣrafo] *nm* seismograph.

sistema [sis'tema] *nm* system; (*método*) method; **sistemático, a** *a* systematic.

sitiar [si'tjar] *vt* to beseige, lay seige to.

sitio ['sitjo] *nm* (*lugar*) place; (*espacio*) room, space; (*MIL*) siege.

situación [sitwa'θjon] *nf* situation, position; (*estatus*) position, standing.

situar [si'twar] *vt* to place, put; (*edificio*) to locate, situate.

slip [slip] *nm* pants *pl*, briefs *pl*.

smoking ['smokin] (*pl* ~**s**) *nm* dinner jacket.

so [so] *prep* under.

SO *abr de* **sudoeste**.

sobaco [so'βako] *nm* armpit.

soberanía [soβera'nia] *nf* sovereignty; **soberano, a** *a* sovereign; (*fig*) supreme // *nm/f* sovereign.

soberbio, a [so'βerβjo, a] *a* (*orgulloso*) proud; (*altivo*) haughty, arrogant; (*fig*) magnificent, superb // *nf* pride; haughtiness, arrogance; magnificence; (*cólera*) anger.

sobornar [soβor'nar] *vt* to bribe; **soborno** *nm* bribe.

sobra ['soβra] *nf* excess, surplus; ~**s** *nfpl* left-overs, scraps; **de** ~ surplus, extra; **tengo de** ~ I've more than enough; ~**do, a a** (*de* ~) more than enough; (*excesivo*) excessive // *ad* too, exceedingly; **sobrante** *a* remaining, extra // *nm* surplus, remainder; **sobrar** *vt* to exceed, surpass // *vi* (*tener de más*) to be more than enough; (*quedar*) to remain, be left (over).

sobre ['soβre] *prep* (*gen*) on; (*encima*) on (top of); (*por encima de, arriba de*) over, above; (*más que*) more than; (*además*) in addition to, besides; (*alrededor de, tratando de*) about // *nm* envelope.

sobrecama [soβre'kama] *nf* bedspread.

sobrecargar [soβrekar'var] *vt* (*camión*) to overload; (*COM*) to surcharge.

sobrehumano, a [soβreu'mano, a] *a* superhuman.

sobrellevar [soβreʎe'βar] *vt* (*fig*) to bear, endure.

sobremarcha [soβre'martʃa] *nf* (*AUTO*) overdrive.

sobrenatural [soβrenatu'ral] *a* supernatural.

sobrepasar [soβrepa'sar] *vt* to exceed, surpass.

sobreponer [soβrepo'ner] *vt* (*poner encima*) to put on top; (*añadir*) to add; ~**se** *vr*: ~**se a** to win through, pull through.

sobreprecio [soβre'preθjo] *nm* surcharge.

sobresaliente [soβresa'ljente] *a* projecting; (*fig*) outstanding, excellent; **sobresalir** *vi* to project, jut out; to stand out, excel.

sobresaltar [soβresal'tar] *vt* (*asustar*) to scare, frighten; (*sobrecoger*) to startle; **sobresalto** *nm* (*movimiento*) start; (*susto*) scare; (*turbación*) sudden shock; **de sobresalto** suddenly.

sobrescrito [soβres'krito] *nm* address.
sobretodo [soβre'toðo] *nm* overcoat.
sobreviviente [soβreβi'βjente] *a* surviving // *nm/f* survivor; **sobrevivir** *vi* to survive.
sobriedad [soβrje'ðað] *nf* sobriety, soberness; (*moderación*) moderation, restraint.
sobrino, a [so'βrino, a] *nm/f* nephew/niece.
sobrio, a ['soβrjo, a] *a* sober; (*moderado*) moderate, restrained.
socarrón, ona [soka'rron, ona] *a* (*sarcástico*) sarcastic, ironic(al); (*astuto*) crafty, cunning.
sociable [so'θjaβle] *a* (*persona*) sociable, friendly; (*animal*) social.
social [so'θjal] *a* social; (*COM*) company *cpd.*
socialdemócrata [soθjalde'mokrata] *nm/f* social democrat.
socialista [soθja'lista] *a, nm/f* socialist.
socializar [soθjali'θar] *vt* to socialize.
sociedad [soθje'ðað] *nf* (*gen*) society; (*COM*) company; ~ **anónima (SA)** limited company.
socio, a ['soθjo, a] *nm/f* (*miembro*) member; (*COM*) partner; ~ **comanditario** sleeping partner.
sociología [soθjolo'xia] *nf* sociology.
socorrer [soko'rrer] *vt* to help; **socorro** *nm* (*ayuda*) help, aid; (*MIL.*) relief; **¡socorro!** help!
soda ['soða] *nf* (*sosa*) soda; (*bebida*) soda water.
sofá [so'fa] (*pl* ~s) *nm* sofa, settee; ~-cama *nm* studio couch.
sofisticación [sofistika'θjon] *nf* sophistication.
sofocar [sofo'kar] *vt* to suffocate; (*apagar*) to smother, put out; ~se *vr* to suffocate; (*fig*) to blush, feel embarrassed; **sofoco** *nm* suffocation; embarrassment.
soga ['soɣa] *nf* rope.
sois *vb ver* **ser.**
sojuzgar [soxuθ'ɣar] *vt* to subdue, rule despotically.
sol [sol] *nm* sun; (*luz*) sunshine, sunlight; **hace** ~ it is sunny.
solamente [sola'mente] *ad* only, just.
solapa [so'lapa] *nf* (*de ropa*) lapel; (*de libro*) jacket.
solar [so'lar] *a* solar, sun *cpd.*
solaz [so'laθ] *nm* recreation, relaxation; (*alivio*) solace; ~**ar** *vt* (*divertir*) to amuse; (*aliviar*) to console.
soldada [sol'daða] *nf* pay.
soldado [sol'daðo] *nm* soldier.
soldador [solda'ðor] *nm* soldering iron; (*persona*) welder; **soldar** *vt* to solder, weld; (*unir*) to join, unite.
soledad [sole'ðað] *nf* solitude; (*estado infeliz*) loneliness; (*nostalgia*) grieving, mourning.
solemne [so'lemne] *a* solemn; **solemnidad** *nf* solemnity.

soler [so'ler] *vi* to be in the habit of, be accustomed to.
solfa ['solfa] *nf*, **solfeo** [sol'feo] *nm* solfa; (*conjunto de signos*) musical notation.
solicitación [soliθita'θjon] *nf* request; (*de votos*) canvassing; **solicitar** *vt* (*permiso*) to ask for, seek; (*puesto*) to apply for; (*votos*) to canvass; (*atención*) to attract; (*persona*) to pursue, chase after.
solícito, a [so'liθito, a] *a* (*diligente*) diligent; (*cuidadoso*) careful; **solicitud** *nf* (*calidad*) great care; (*petición*) request; (*memorial*) petition; (*a un puesto*) application.
solidaridad [soliðari'ðað] *nf* solidarity; **solidario, a** *a* (*participación*) joint, common; (*compromiso*) mutually binding.
solidez [soli'ðeθ] *nf* solidity; **sólido, a** *a* solid.
soliloquio [soli'lokjo] *nm* soliloquy, monologue.
solista [so'lista] *nm/f* soloist.
solitario, a [soli'tarjo, a] *a* lonely, solitary // *nm/f* recluse; (*en la sociedad*) loner // *nm* solitaire.
soliviar [soli'βjar] *vt* to lift.
solo, a ['solo, a] *a* (*único*) single, sole; (*sin compañía*) alone; (*solitario*) lonely; **hay una** ~**a dificultad** there is just one difficulty; **a** ~**as** alone, by o.s.
sólo ['solo] *ad* only, just.
solomillo [solo'miʎo] *nm* sirloin.
soltar [sol'tar] *vt* (*dejar ir*) to let go of; (*desprender*) to unfasten, loosen; (*librar*) to release, set free; (*estornudo, risa*) to let out.
soltero, a [sol'tero, a] *a* single, unmarried // *nm* bachelor // *nf* single woman, spinster.
soltura [sol'tura] *nf* looseness, slackness; (*de los miembros*) agility, ease of movement; (*en el hablar*) fluency, ease; (*MED*) diarrhoea.
soluble [so'luβle] *a* (*QUÍMICA*) soluble; (*problema*) solvable.
solución [solu'θjon] *nf* solution; **solucionar** *vt* (*problema*) to solve; (*asunto*) to settle.
solventar [solβen'tar] *vt* (*pagar*) to settle, pay; (*resolver*) to resolve.
sollozar [soʎo'θar] *vi* to sob; **sollozo** *nm* sob.
sombra ['sombra] *nf* shadow; (*como protección*) shade; ~**s** *nfpl* darkness *sg*; **tener buena/mala** ~ to be lucky/unlucky.
sombreador [sombrea'ðor] *nm*: ~ **de ojos** eyeshadow.
sombrero [som'brero] *nm* hat.
sombrilla [som'briʎa] *nf* parasol, sunshade.
sombrío, a [som'brio, a] *a* (*oscuro*) dark; (*sombreado*) shaded; (*fig*) sombre, sad; (*persona*) gloomy.
somero, a [so'mero, a] *a* superficial.
someter [some'ter] *vt* (*país*) to conquer; (*persona*) to subject to one's will; (*informe*) to present, submit; ~**se** *vr* to give in,

yield, submit; ~ **a** to subject to.
somnambulismo [somnambu'lismo] *nm*
sleepwalking; **somnámbulo, a** *nm/f*
sleepwalker.
somnífero [som'nifero] *nm* sleeping pill.
somos *vb ver* **ser.**
son [sɔn] *vb ver* **ser** // *nm* sound; **en ~ de
broma** as a joke.
sonar [so'nar] *vt* to ring // *vi* to sound;
(*hacer ruido*) to make a noise;
(*pronunciarse*) to be sounded, be
pronounced; (*ser conocido*) to sound
familiar; (*campana*) to ring; (*reloj*) to
strike, chime; ~**se** *vr*: ~**se (las narices)**
to blow one's nose; **me suena ese
nombre** that name rings a bell.
sonda ['sonda] *nf* (*NAUT*) sounding; (*TEC*)
bore, drill; (*MED*) probe; **sondear** *vt* to
sound; to bore (into), drill; to probe, sound;
(*fig*) to sound out; **sondeo** *nm* sounding;
boring, drilling; (*fig*) poll, enquiry.
sónico, a ['soniko, a] *a* sonic, sound *cpd*.
sonido [so'niðo] *nm* sound.
sonoro, a [so'noro, a] *a* sonorous;
(*resonante*) loud, resonant.
sonreír [sonre'ir] *vi*, ~**se** *vr* to smile;
sonriente a smiling; **sonrisa** *nf* smile.
sonrojo [son'roxo] *nm* blush.
soñador, a [soɲa'ðor, a] *nm/f* dreamer;
soñar *vt*, *vi* to dream; **soñar con** to
dream about, dream of.
soñoliento, a [soɲo'ljento, a] *a* sleepy,
drowsy.
sopa ['sopa] *nf* soup.
soplador ['sopla'ðor] *nm* fan, ventilator.
soplar [so'plar] *vt* (*polvo*) to blow away,
blow off; (*inflar*) to blow up; (*vela*) to blow
out // *vi* to blow; ~**se** *vr* (*fam: ufanarse*)
to get conceited; **soplo** *nm* blow, puff; (*de
viento*) gust.
soporífero [sopo'rifero] *nm* sleeping pill.
soportable [sopor'taβle] *a* bearable;
soportar *vt* to bear, carry; (*fig*) to bear,
put up with; **soporte** *nm* support; (*fig*)
pillar, support.
soprano [so'prano] *nf* soprano.
sorber [sor'βer] *vt* (*chupar*) to sip;
(*inhalar*) to inhale; (*tragar*) to swallow
(up); (*absorber*) to soak up, absorb.
sorbete [sor'βete] *nm* iced fruit drink.
sorbo ['sorβo] *nm* (*trago*) gulp, swallow;
(*chupada*) sip.
sordera [sor'ðera] *nf* deafness.
sórdido, a ['sorðiðo, a] *a* dirty, squalid;
(*palabra*) nasty, dirty; (*fig*) mean.
sordo, a ['sorðo, a] *a* (*persona*) deaf;
(*máquina*) quiet // *nm/f* deaf person; a
~**as** on the quiet; ~**mudo, a** *a* deaf and
dumb.
sorprendente [sorpren'dente] *a*
surprising; **sorprender** *vt* to surprise;
sorpresa *nf* surprise.
sortear [sorte'ar] *vt* to draw lots for;
(*objeto*) to raffle; (*dificultad*) to avoid;
sorteo *nm* drawing lots; raffle.
sosegado, a [sose'raðo, a] *a* quiet, calm;
sosegar *vt* to quieten, calm; (*el ánimo*) to

reassure // *vi* to rest; **sosiego** *nm*
quiet(ness), calm(ness).
soslayo [sos'lajo]: **al** *o* **de ~** *ad* obliquely,
sideways.
soso, a ['soso, a] *a* (*CULIN*) tasteless; (*fig*)
dull, uninteresting.
sospecha [sos'petʃa] *nf* suspicion;
sospechar *vt* to suspect; **sospechoso, a** *a*
suspicious; (*testimonio, opinión*) suspect //
nm/f suspect.
sostén [sos'ten] *nm* (*apoyo*) support;
(*prenda femenina*) bra, brassière;
(*alimentación*) sustenance, food.
sostener [soste'ner] *vt* to support;
(*mantener*) to keep up, maintain;
(*alimentar*) to sustain, keep going; ~**se** *vr*
to support o.s.; (*seguir*) to continue,
remain; **sostenido, a** *a* continuous,
sustained; (*prolongado*) prolonged.
sótano ['sotano] *nm* basement.
soterrar [sote'rrar] *vt* to bury.
soviético, a [so'βjetiko, a] *a* Soviet.
soy *vb ver* **ser.**
sport [sport] *nm* sport.
Sr *abr de* **Señor.**
Sra *abr de* **Señora.**
S.R.C. *abr de* **se ruega contestación**
R.S.V.P.
Sta *abr de* **Santa; Señorita.**
status ['status] *nm inv* status.
Sto *abr de* **Santo.**
su [su] *pron* (*de él*) his; (*de ella*) her; (*de una
cosa*) its; (*de ellos, ellas*) their; (*de usted,
ustedes*) your.
suave ['swaβe] *a* gentle; (*superficie*)
smooth; (*trabajo*) easy; (*música, voz*) soft,
sweet; **suavidad** *nf* gentleness,
smoothness; softness, sweetness; **suavizar**
vt to soften; (*quitar la aspereza*) to smooth
(out).
subalimentado, a [suβalimen'taðo, a] *a*
undernourished.
subasta [su'βasta] *nf* auction; **subastar** *vt*
to auction (off).
subconsciencia [suβkons'θjenθja] *nf*
subconscious; **subconsciente** *a*
subconscious.
subdesarrollado, a [suβðesarro'ʎaðo, a]
a underdeveloped; **subdesarrollo** *nm*
underdevelopment.
súbdito, a ['suβðito, a] *nm/f* subject.
subdividir [suβðiβi'ðir] *vt* to subdivide.
subestimar [suβesti'mar] *vt* to
underestimate, underrate; (*propiedad*) to
undervalue.
subexpuesto, a [suβeks'pwesto, a] *a*
underexposed.
subido, a [su'βiðo, a] *a* (*color*) bright,
strong; (*precio*) high // *nf* (*gen*) ascent,
climb; (*de precio*) rise, increase; (*camino*)
way up; (*pendiente*) slope, hill.
subir [su'βir] *vt* (*objeto*) to raise, lift up;
(*cuesta, calle*) to go up; (*montaña*) to climb;
(*precio*) to raise, put up // *vi* to go/come
up; (*a un coche*) to get in; (*a un autobús*) to
get on; (*precio*) to rise, go up; (*río*) to rise;
~**se** *vr* to get up, climb.

súbito, a ['suβito, a] *a* (*repentino*) sudden; (*imprevisto*) unexpected; (*precipitado*) hasty, rash // *ad*: (**de**) ~ suddenly.

sublevación [suβleβa'θjon] *nf* revolt, rising.

sublime [su'βlime] *a* sublime.

submarino, a [suβma'rino, a] *a* underwater // *nm* submarine.

subordinado, a [suβorðiˈnaðo, a] *a, nm/f* subordinate.

subrayar [suβra'jar] *vt* to underline.

subrepticio, a [suβrep'tiθjo, a] *a* surreptitious.

subsanar [suβsa'nar] *vt* (*reparar*) to make good; (*perdonar*) to excuse; (*sobreponerse a*) to overcome.

subscribir [suβskri'βir] *vt* = **suscribir.**

subsidiario, a [suβsi'ðjarjo, a] *a* subsidiary.

subsidio [suβ'siðjo] *nm* (*ayuda*) aid, financial help; (*subvención*) subsidy, grant; (*de enfermedad, paro etc*) benefit.

subsistencia [suβsis'tenθja] *nf* subsistence; **subsistir** *vi* (*gen*) to subsist; (*vivir*) to live; (*sobrevivir*) to survive, endure.

subterráneo, a [suβteˈrraneo, a] *a* underground, subterranean // *nm* underpass, underground passage.

suburbano, a [suβurˈβano, a] *a* suburban.

suburbio [su'βurβjo] *nm* (*barrio*) slum quarter; (*afueras*) suburbs *pl*.

subvencionar [suββenθjo'nar] *vt* to subsidize.

subversión [suββer'sjon] *nf* subversion; **subversivo, a** *a* subversive.

subyugar [suβju'xar] *vt* (*país*) to subjugate, subdue; (*enemigo*) to overpower; (*voluntad*) to dominate.

suceder [suθe'ðer] *vt, vi* to happen; (*seguir*) to succeed, follow; **lo que sucede es que...** the fact is that...; **sucesión** *nf* succession; (*serie*) sequence, series.

sucesivamente [suθesiβa'mente] *ad*: **y así** ~ and so on.

sucesivo, a [suθe'siβo, a] *a* successive, following; **en lo** ~ in future, from now on.

suceso [su'θeso] *nm* (*hecho*) event, happening; (*incidente*) incident; (*resultado*) outcome.

suciedad [suθje'ðað] *nf* (*estado*) dirtiness; (*mugre*) dirt, filth.

sucinto, a [su'θinto, a] *a* succinct, concise.

sucio, a ['suθjo, a] *a* dirty.

suculento, a [suku'lento, a] *a* succulent.

sucumbir [sukum'bir] *vi* to succumb.

sucursal [sukur'sal] *nf* branch (office).

sudamericano, a [suðameri'kano, a] *a* South American.

sudar [su'ðar] *vt, vi* to sweat.

sudeste [su'ðeste] *nm* south-east; **sudoeste** *nm* south-west.

sudor [su'ðor] *nm* sweat; ~**oso, a**, **sudoso, a**, ~**lento, a** *a* sweaty, sweating.

Suecia ['sweθja] *nf* Sweden; **sueco, a** *a* Swedish // *nm/f* Swede.

suegro, a ['sweɣro, a] *nm/f* father-/mother-in-law.

suela ['swela] *nf* sole.

sueldo ['sweldo] *nm* pay, wage(s) (*pl*); **el** ~ **mínimo** the minimum wage.

suele *etc vb ver* **soler.**

suelo ['swelo] *nm* (*tierra*) ground; (*de casa*) floor.

suelto, a ['swelto, a] *a* loose; (*libre*) free; (*separado*) detached, individual; (*ágil*) quick, agile; (*corriente*) fluent, flowing // *nm* (*loose*) change, small change.

sueño *etc vb ver* **soñar** // ['sweɲo] *nm* sleep; (*somnolencia*) sleepiness, drowsiness; (*lo soñado, fig*) dream; **tener** ~ to be sleepy.

suero ['swero] *nm* serum.

suerte ['swerte] *nf* (*fortuna*) luck; (*azar*) chance; (*destino*) fate, destiny; (*condición*) lot; (*género*) sort, kind; **tener** ~ to be lucky; **de otra** ~ otherwise, if not; **de** ~ **que** so that, in such a way that.

suéter ['sweter] *nm* sweater.

suficiente [sufi'θjente] *a* enough, sufficient; (*capaz*) capable.

sufragio [suˈfraxjo] *nm* (*voto*) vote; (*derecho de voto*) suffrage; (*ayuda*) help, aid.

sufrimiento [sufriˈmjento] *nm* (*dolor*) suffering; (*paciencia*) patience; (*tolerancia*) tolerance.

sufrir [su'frir] *vt* (*padecer*) to suffer; (*soportar*) to bear, stand, put up with; (*apoyar*) to hold up, support // *vi* to suffer.

sugerencia [suxe'renθja] *nf* suggestion; **sugerir** *vt* to suggest; (*sutilmente*) to hint.

sugestión [suxes'tjon] *nf* suggestion; (*sutil*) hint; **sugestionar** *vt* to influence.

sugestivo, a [suxes'tiβo, a] *a* stimulating; (*fascinante*) fascinating.

suicida [sui'θiða] *a* suicidal // *nm/f* suicidal person; (*muerto*) suicide, person who has committed suicide; **suicidio** *nm* suicide.

Suiza ['swiθa] *nf* Switzerland; **suizo, a** *a, nm/f* Swiss.

sujeción [suxe'θjon] *nf* subjection.

sujetador [suxeta'ðor] *nm* fastener, clip; (*de papeles*) paper clip.

sujetar [suxe'tar] *vt* (*fijar*) to fasten; (*detener*) to hold down; (*fig*) to subject, subjugate; ~**se** *vr* to subject o.s.; **sujeto, a** *a* fastened, secure // *nm* subject; (*individuo*) individual; **sujeto a** subject to.

suma ['suma] *nf* (*cantidad*) total, sum; (*de dinero*) sum; (*acto*) adding (up), addition; (*resumen*) summary; (*esencia*) essence; **en** ~ in short; ~**dora** *nf* adding machine.

sumamente [suma'mente] *ad* extremely, exceedingly.

sumar [su'mar] *vt* to add (up); (*reunir*) to collect, gather; (*abreviar*) to summarize, sum up // *vi* to add up.

sumario, a [su'marjo, a] *a* brief, concise // *nm* summary.

sumergir [sumer'xir] *vt* to submerge; (*hundir*) to sink; (*bañar*) to immerse, dip;

sumersión *nf* submersion; *(fig)* absorption.

sumidero [sumi'ðero] *nm* drain; *(TEC)* sump.

suministrador, a [suministra'ðor, a] *nm/f* supplier; **suministrar** *vt* to supply, provide; **suministro** *nm* supply; *(acto)* supplying, providing.

sumir [su'mir] *vt* to sink, submerge; *(fig)* to plunge.

sumisión [sumi'sjon] *nf (acto)* submission; *(calidad)* submissiveness, docility; **sumiso, a** a submissive, docile.

sumo, a ['sumo, a] a great, extreme; *(mayor)* highest, supreme.

supe *etc vb ver* **saber**.

super... [super] *pref* super..., over... // *nm* high-grade fuel.

superar [supe'rar] *vt (sobreponerse a)* to overcome; *(rebasar)* to surpass, do better than; *(pasar)* to go beyond; **~se** *vr* to excel o.s.

superávit [supe'raßit] *nm* surplus.

supercarburante [superkarßu'rante] *nm* high-grade fuel.

superestructura [superestruk'tura] *nf* superstructure.

superficial [superfi'θjal] a superficial; *(medida)* surface *cpd*, of the surface.

superficie [super'fiθje] *nf* surface; *(área)* area.

superfluo, a [su'perflwo, a] a superfluous.

superintendente [superinten'dente] *nm/f* supervisor, superintendent.

superior [supe'rjor] a *(piso, clase)* upper; *(temperatura, número, nivel)* higher; *(mejor: calidad, producto)* superior, better // *nm/f* superior; **~idad** *nf* superiority.

supermercado [supermer'kaðo] *nm* supermarket.

supersónico, a [super'soniko, a] a supersonic.

superstición [supersti'θjon] *nf* superstition; **supersticioso, a** a superstitious.

supervisor, a [superßi'sor, a] *nm/f* supervisor.

supervivencia [superßi'ßenθja] *nf* survival.

supiera *etc vb ver* **saber**.

suplementario, a [suplemen'tarjo, a] a supplementary; **suplemento** *nm* supplement.

suplente [su'plente] a, *nm/f* substitute.

súplica ['suplika] *nf* request; *(REL)* supplication.

suplicante [supli'kante] *nm/f* applicant.

suplicar [supli'kar] *vt (cosa)* to beg (for), plead for; *(persona)* to beg, plead with.

suplicio [su'pliθjo] *nm* torture.

suplir [su'plir] *vt (compensar)* to make good, make up for; *(reemplazar)* to replace, substitute // *vi*: **~ a o por** to take the place of, substitute for.

suponer [supo'ner] *vt* to suppose // *vi* to have authority; **suposición** *nf* supposition; *(autoridad)* authority.

supremacía [suprema'θia] *nf* supremacy.

supremo, a [su'premo, a] a supreme.

supresión [supre'sjon] *nf* suppression; *(de derecho)* abolition; *(de dificultad)* removal; *(de palabra)* deletion; *(de restricción)* cancellation, lifting.

suprimir [supri'mir] *vt* to suppress; *(derecho, costumbre)* to abolish; *(dificultad)* to remove; *(palabra)* to delete; *(restricción)* to cancel, lift.

supuesto, a [su'pwesto, a] a *(hipotético)* supposed; *(falso)* false // *nm* assumption, hypothesis; **~ que** *conj* since; **por ~** of course.

sur [sur] *nm* south.

surcar [sur'kar] *vt* to plough, furrow; *(superficie)* to cut, score; **surco** *nm* groove; *(AGR)* furrow.

surgir [sur'xir] *vi* to arise, emerge; *(dificultad)* to come up, crop up.

surtido, a [sur'tiðo, a] a mixed, assorted // *nm (gen)* selection, assortment; *(abastecimiento)* supply, stock.

surtir [sur'tir] *vt* to supply, provide // *vi* to spout, spurt.

susceptible [susθep'tißle] a susceptible; *(sensible)* sensitive; **~ de** capable of.

suscitar [susθi'tar] *vt* to cause, provoke; *(interés)* to arouse.

suscribir [suskri'ßir] *vt (firmar)* to sign; *(respaldar)* to subscribe to; endorse; **~se** *vr* to subscribe; **suscripción** *nf* subscription.

suspender [suspen'der] *vt (objeto)* to hang (up), suspend; *(trabajo)* to stop, suspend; *(a estudiante)* to fail; **suspensión** *nf* suspension; *(fig)* stoppage, suspension.

suspenso, a [su'spenso, a] a hanging, suspended; *(estudiante)* failed; *(admirado)* astonished, amazed // *nm*: **quedar o estar en ~** to be pending.

suspicacia [suspi'kaθja] *nf* suspicion, mistrust; **suspicaz** a suspicious, distrustful.

suspirar [suspi'rar] *vi* to sigh; **suspiro** *nm* sigh.

sustancia [sus'tanθja] *nf* substance.

sustentar [susten'tar] *vt (alimentar)* to sustain, nourish; *(objeto)* to hold up, support; *(idea, teoría)* to maintain, uphold; *(fig)* to sustain, keep going; **sustento** *nm* support; *(alimento)* sustenance, food.

sustituir [sustitu'ir] *vt* to substitute, replace; **sustituto** a *nm/f* substitute, replacement.

susto ['susto] *nm* fright, scare.

sustraer [sustra'er] *vt* to remove, take away; *(MAT)* to subtract; **~se** *vr (evitar)* to avoid; *(retirarse)* to withdraw.

susurrar [susu'rrar] *vi* to whisper; **susurro** *nm* whisper.

sutil [su'til] a subtle; *(tenue)* thin; **~eza** *nf* subtlety; thinness.

suyo, a ['sujo, a] a *(con artículo o después del verbo ser: de él)* his; *(: de ella)* hers; *(: de ellos, ellas)* theirs; *(: de Ud, Uds)* yours; *(después de un nombre: de él)* of his; *(: de* *ella*) of hers; (: *de ellos, ellas*) of theirs; (: *de Ud, Uds*) of yours.

T

t *abr de* **tonelada.**

taba ['taβa] *nf* (ANAT) ankle bone; (*juego*) jacks *sg.*

tabaco [ta'βako] *nm* tobacco; (*fam*) cigarettes *pl.*

taberna [ta'βerna] *nf* bar; **tabernero, a** *nm/f* (*encargado*) publican; (*camarero*) barman.

tabique [ta'βike] *nm* (*pared*) thin wall; (*para dividir*) partition.

tabla ['taβla] *nf* (*de madera*) plank; (*estante*) shelf; (*de anuncios*) board; (*lista, catálogo*) list; (*mostrador*) counter; (*de vestido*) pleat; (ARTE) panel; ~**s** (TAUR, TEATRO) boards; **hacer** ~**s** to draw; ~**do** *nm* (*plataforma*) platform; (*suelo*) plank floor; (TEATRO) stage.

tablero [ta'βlero] *nm* (*de madera*) plank, board; (*pizarra*) blackboard; (*de ajedrez, damas*) board; (AUTO) dashboard.

tablilla [ta'βliλa] *nf* small board; (MED) splint.

tablón [ta'βlon] *nm* (*de suelo*) plank; (*de techo*) beam; (*de anuncios*) notice board.

tabú [ta'βu] *nm* taboo.

tabular [taβu'lar] *vt* to tabulate.

taburete [taβu'rete] *nm* stool.

tacaño, a [ta'kaɲo, a] *a* (*avaro*) mean; (*astuto*) crafty.

tácito, a ['taθito, a] *a* tacit.

taciturno, a [taθi'turno, a] *a* (*callado*) silent; (*malhumorado*) sullen.

taco ['tako] *nm* (BILLAR) cue; (*libro de billetes*) book; (*manojo de billetes*) wad; (AM) heel; (*tarugo*) peg; (*fam: bocado*) snack; (: *palabrota*) swear word; (: *trago de vino*) swig.

tacón [ta'kon] *nm* heel; **de ~ alto** high heeled; **taconeo** *nm* (heel) stamping.

táctico, a ['taktiko, a] *a* tactical // *nf* tactics *pl.*

tacto ['takto] *nm* touch; (*acción*) touching.

tacha ['tatʃa] *nf* flaw; (TEC) stud; **poner** ~ **a** to find fault with; **tachar** *vt* (*borrar*) to cross out; (*corregir*) to correct; (*criticar*) to criticize; **tachar de** to accuse of.

tafetán [tafe'tan] *nm* taffeta; **tafetanes** *nmpl* (*fam*) frills; ~ **adhesivo** *o* **inglés** sticking plaster.

tafilete [tafi'lete] *nm* morocco leather.

tahona [ta'ona] *nf* (*panadería*) bakery; (*molino*) flourmill.

tahur [ta'ur] *nm* gambler; (*pey*) cheat.

taimado, a [tai'maðo, a] *a* (*astuto*) sly; (*resentido*) sullen.

taja ['taxa] *nf* (*corte*) cut; (*repartición*) division; ~**da** *nf* slice; ~**dera** *nf* (*instrumento*) chopper; (*madera*) chopping block; **tajante** *a* sharp.

tajar [ta'xar] *vt* to cut; **tajo** *nm* (*corte*) cut; (*filo*) cutting edge; (GEO) cleft.

tal [tal] *a* such; ~ **vez** perhaps // *pron* (*persona*) someone, such a one; (*cosa*) something, such a thing; ~ **como** such as; ~ **para cual** tit for tat; (*dos iguales*) two of a kind // *ad*: ~ **como** (*igual*) just as; ~ **cual** (*como es*) just as it is; ~ **el padre, cual el hijo** like father, like son; ¿**qué** ~? how are things?; ¿**qué** ~ **te gusta?** how do you like it? // *conj*: **con** ~ **de que** provided that.

talabartero [talaβar'tero] *nm* saddler.

taladrar [tala'ðrar] *vt* to drill; **taladro** *nm* (*gen*) drill; (*hoyo*) drill hole; **taladro neumático** pneumatic drill.

talante [ta'lante] *nm* (*humor*) mood; (*voluntad*) will, willingness.

talar [ta'lar] *vt* to fell, cut down; (*fig*) to devastate.

talco ['talko] *nm* (*polvos*) talcum powder; (MINEROLOGÍA) talc.

talego [ta'leɣo] *nm*, **talega** [ta'leɣa] *nf* sack.

talento [ta'lento] *nm* talent; (*capacidad*) ability; (*don*) gift.

talidomida [taliðo'miða] *nm* thalidomide.

talismán [talis'man] *nm* talisman.

talmente [tal'mente] *ad* (*de esta forma*) in such a way; (*hasta tal punto*) to such an extent; (*exactamente*) exactly.

talón [ta'lon] *nm* (*gen*) heel; (COM) counterfoil.

talonario [talo'narjo] *nm* (*de cheques*) chequebook; (*de billetes*) book of tickets; (*de recibos*) receipt book.

talud [ta'luð] *nm* slope.

talla ['taλa] *nf* (*estatura, fig, MED*) height, stature; (*palo*) measuring rod; (ARTE) carving.

tallado, a [ta'λaðo, a] *a* carved // *nm* carving; **tallar** *vt* (*trabajar*) to work, carve; (*grabar*) to engrave; (*medir*) to measure; (*repartir*) to deal // *vi* to deal.

tallarín [taλa'rin] *nm* noodle.

talle ['taλe] *nm* (ANAT) waist; (*medida*) size; (*física*) build; (: *de mujer*) figure; (*fig*) appearance.

taller [ta'λer] *nm* (TEC) workshop; (*de artista*) studio.

tallo ['taλo] *nm* (*de planta*) stem; (*de hierba*) blade; (*brote*) shoot; (*col*) cabbage; (CULIN) candied peel.

tamaño, a [ta'maɲo, a] *a* such a (*big/small*) // *nm* size; **de ~ natural** full-size.

tamarindo [tama'rindo] *nm* tamarind.

tambalearse [tambale'arse] *vr* (*persona*) to stagger; (*vehículo*) to sway.

también [tam'bjen] *ad* (*igualmente*) also, too, as well; (*además*) besides.

tambor [tam'bor] *nm* drum; (ANAT) eardrum; ~ **del freno** brake drum.

tamiz [ta'miθ] *nm* sieve; ~**ar** *vt* to sieve.

tamo ['tamo] *nm* fluff.

tampoco [tam'poko] *ad* nor, neither; **yo** ~ **lo compré** I didn't buy it either.

tampón [tam'pon] *nm* plug; (MED) tampon.

tan [tan] *ad* so; ~ **es así que** so much so that.

tanda ['tanda] nf (gen) series; (juego) set; (turno) shift; (grupo) gang.

tangente [tan'xente] nf tangent.

Tánger ['tanxer] n Tangier(s).

tangible [tan'xiβle] a tangible.

tanque ['tanke] nm (gen) tank; (AUTO, NAUT) tanker.

tantear [tante'ar] vt (calcular) to reckon (up); (medir) to take the measure of; (probar) to test, try out; (tomar la medida: persona) to take the measurements of; (considerar) to weigh up // vi (DEPORTE) to score; **tanteo** nm (cálculo) (rough) calculation; (prueba) test, trial; (DEPORTE) scoring; (adivinanzas) guesswork; **al tanteo** by trial and error.

tanto, a ['tanto, a] a (cantidad) so much, as much; ~s so many, as many; **20 y** ~s 20-odd // ad (cantidad) so much, as much; (tiempo) so long, as long; ~ **tú como yo** both you and I; ~ **como eso** it's not as bad as that; ~ **más ... cuanto que** it's all the more ... because; ~ **mejor/peor** so much the better/the worse; ~ **si viene como si va** whether he comes or whether he goes; ~ **es así que** so much so that; **por o por lo** ~ therefore; **me he vuelto ronco de o con** ~ **hablar** I have become hoarse with so much talking // conj: **con** ~ **que** provided (that); **en** ~ **que** while; **hasta** ~ **(que)** until such time as // nm (suma) certain amount; (proporción) so much; (punto) point; (gol) goal; **al** ~ up to date; **un** ~ **perezoso** somewhat lazy; **al** ~ **de** que because of the fact that // pron: **cada uno paga** ~ each one pays so much; **a** ~**s de agosto** on such and such a day in August.

tapar [ta'par] vt (cubrir) to cover; (envolver) to wrap or cover up; (la vista) to obstruct; (persona, falta) to conceal; (AM) to fill; ~**se** vr to wrap o.s. up.

taparrabo [tapa'rraβo] nm (bañador) (bathing or swimming) trunks pl.

tapete [ta'pete] nm table cover.

tapia ['tapja] nf (garden) wall; **tapiar** vt to wall in.

tapicería [tapiθe'ria] nf tapestry; (para muebles) upholstery; (tienda) upholsterer's (shop); **tapiz** nm (alfombra) carpet; (tela tejida) tapestry; **tapizar** vt (pared) to wallpaper; (suelo) to carpet; (muebles) to upholster.

tapón [ta'pon] nm (corcho) stopper; (TEC) plug; (MED) tampon; ~ **de rosca** o **de tuerca** screw-top.

taquigrafía [takixra'fia] nf shorthand; **taquígrafo, a** nm/f shorthand writer.

taquilla [ta'kiʎa] nf (donde se compra) booking office; (suma recogida) takings pl; **taquillero, a** a: **función taquillera** box office success // nm/f ticket clerk.

taquímetro [ta'kimetro] nm speedometer; (de control) tachymeter.

tara ['tara] nf (defecto) defect; (COM) tare.

tarántula [ta'rantula] nf tarantula.

tararear [tarare'ar] vi to hum.

tardanza [tar'ðanθa] nf (demora) delay; (lentitud) slowness.

tardar [tar'ðar] vi (tomar tiempo) to take a long time; (llegar tarde) to be late; (demorar) to delay; ¿**tarda mucho el tren?** does the train take long?; **a más** ~ at the latest; **no tardes en venir** come soon, come before long.

tarde ['tarðe] ad (hora) late; (después de tiempo) too late // nf (de día) afternoon; (al anochecer) evening; **de** ~ **en** ~ from time to time; ¡**buenas** ~**s!** (de día) good afternoon!; (de noche) good evening!; **a o por la** ~ in the afternoon; in the evening.

tardío, a [tar'ðio, a] a (retrasado) late; (lento) slow (to arrive).

tardo, a ['tarðo, a] a (lento) slow; (torpe) dull.

tarea [ta'rea] nf task; (ESCOL) homework; ~ **de ocasión** chore.

tarifa [ta'rifa] nf (lista de precios) price list; (COM) tariff; ~ **completa** all-in cost.

tarima [ta'rima] nf (plataforma) platform; (taburete) stool; (litera) bunk.

tarjeta [tar'xeta] nf card; ~ **postal/de crédito/de Navidad** postcard/credit card/Christmas card.

tarro ['tarro] nm jar, pot.

tarta ['tarta] nf (pastel) cake; (torta) tart.

tartamudear [tartamuðe'ar] vi to stammer; **tartamudo, a** a stammering // nm/f stammerer.

tartana [tar'tana] nf (barco) dinghy.

tartárico, a [tar'tariko, a] a: **ácido** ~ tartaric acid.

tártaro ['tartaro] a, nm Tartar.

tasa ['tasa] nf (precio) (fixed) price, rate; (valoración) valuation; (medida, norma) measure, standard; ~ **de interés** rate of interest; ~**ción** nf (gen) valuation; (de oro etc) appraisal; ~**dor** nm valuer.

tasajo [ta'saxo] nm dried beef.

tasar [ta'sar] vt (arreglar el precio) to fix a price for; (valorar) to value, assess; (limitar) to limit.

tasca ['taska] nf (fam) pub.

tatarabuelo [tatara'βwelo] nm great-great-grandfather.

tatuaje [ta'twaxe] nm (dibujo) tattoo; (acto) tattooing; **tatuar** vt to tattoo.

taumaturgo [tauma'turxo] nm miracleworker.

taurino, a [tau'rino, a] a bullfighting cpd.

Tauro ['tauro] nm Taurus.

tauromaquia [tauro'makja] nf tauromachy.

tautología [tautolo'xia] nf tautology.

taxi ['taksi] nm taxi.

taxidermia [taksi'ðermja] nf taxidermy.

taxista [tak'sista] nm/f taxi driver.

taza ['taθa] nf cup; (de retrete) bowl; ~ **para café** coffee cup; **tazón** nm (~ grande) large cup; (escudilla) basin.

te [te] pron (complemento de objeto) you; (complemento indirecto) (to) you; (reflexivo) (to) yourself; ¿~ **duele**

mucho el brazo? does your arm hurt a lot?; ~ equivocas you're wrong; ¡cálma~! calm yourself!

té [te] nm tea.

tea ['tea] nf torch.

teatral [tea'tral] a theatre cpd; (fig) theatrical; teatro nm (gen) theatre; (LITERATURA) plays pl, drama.

tebeo [te'βeo] nm children's comic.

tecla ['tekla] nf key; ~do nm keyboard; teclear vi to strum; (fam) to drum; tecleo nm (MUS: sonido) strumming; (forma de tocar) fingering; (fam) drumming.

técnico, a ['tekniko, a] a technical // nm technician; (experto) expert // nf (procedimientos) technique; (arte, oficio) craft.

tecnócrata [tek'nokrata] nm/f technocrat.

tecnología [teknolo'xia] nf technology; tecnológico, a a technological; tecnólogo nm technologist.

techo ['tetʃo] nm (externo) roof; (interno) ceiling; techumbre nf roof.

tedio ['teðjo] nm (aburrimiento) boredom; (apatía) apathy; (fastidio) depression; ~so, a a boring; (cansado) wearisome, tedious.

teja ['texa] nf (azulejo) tile; (BOT) lime (tree); ~do nm (tiled) roof.

tejanos [te'xanos] nmpl jeans.

tejemaneje [texema'nexe] nm (bullicio) bustle; (lío) fuss; (aspaviento) to-do; (intriga) intrigue.

tejer [te'xer] vt to weave; (AM) to knit; (fig) to fabricate; tejido nm fabric; (telaraña) web; (estofa, tela) (knitted) material; (ANAT) tissue; (textura) texture.

tel, teléf abr de teléfono.

tela ['tela] nf (material) material; (telaraña) web; (de fruta, en líquido) skin; (del ojo) film; telar nm (máquina) loom; (de teatro) gridiron; telares nmpl textile mill sg.

telaraña [tela'raɲa] nf cobweb.

tele ['tele] nf (fam) TV.

tele... [tele] pref tele...; ~comunicación nf telecommunication; ~control nm remote control; ~diario nm television news; ~difusión nf (television) broadcast; ~dirigido, a a remote-controlled; ~férico nm (tren) cable-railway; (de esquí) ski-lift; ~fonear vi to telephone; ~fónico, a a telephone cpd; ~fonista nm/f telephonist; teléfono nm telephone; ~foto nf telephoto; ~grafía nf telegraphy; telégrafo nm telegraph; (fam: persona) telegraph boy; ~grama nm telegram; ~impresor nm teleprinter; telémetro nm rangefinder; ~objetivo nm telephoto lens; ~pático, a a tele-pathic; ~scópico, a a telescopic; ~scopio nm telescope; ~silla nf chairlift; ~spectador, a nm/f viewer; ~squí nm ski-lift; ~tipista nm/f teletypist; ~tipo nm teletype; ~vidente nm/f viewer; ~visar vt to televise;

~visión nf television; ~visión en colores colour television; ~visor nm television set.

telex [te'leks] nm telex.

telón [te'lon] nm curtain; ~ de boca/seguridad front/safety curtain; ~ de acero (POL) iron curtain; ~ de fondo backcloth, background.

tema ['tema] nm (asunto) subject, topic; (MUS) theme // nf (obsesión) obsession; (manía) ill-will; tener ~ a uno to have a grudge against sb; temático, a a thematic.

tembladera [tembla'ðera] nf shaking; (AM) quagmire.

temblar [tem'blar] vi to shake, tremble; (de frío) to shiver; tembleque a shaking // nm = tembladera; temblón, ona a shaking; temblor nm trembling; (AM: de tierra) earthquake; tembloroso, a a trembling.

temer [te'mer] vt to fear // vi to be afraid; temo que llegue tarde I am afraid he may be late.

temerario, a [teme'rarjo, a] a (descuidado) reckless; (arbitrario) hasty; temeridad nf (imprudencia) rashness; (audacia) boldness.

temeroso, a [teme'roso, a] a (miedoso) fearful; (que inspira temor) frightful.

temible [te'miβle] a fearsome.

temor [te'mor] nm (miedo) fear; (duda) suspicion.

témpano ['tempano] nm (MUS) kettledrum; ~ de hielo ice-flow; ~ de tocino flitch of bacon.

temperamento [tempera'mento] nm temperament.

temperatura [tempera'tura] nf temperature.

temperie [tem'perje] nf state of the weather.

tempestad [tempes'taθ] nf storm; tempestuoso, a a stormy.

templado, a [tem'plaðo, a] a (moderado) moderate; (: en el comer) frugal; (: en el beber) abstemious; (agua) lukewarm; (clima) mild; (MUS) well-tuned; templanza nf moderation; abstemiousness; mildness.

templar [tem'plar] vt (moderar) to moderate; (furia) to restrain; (calor) to reduce; (solución) to dilute; (afinar) to tune (up); (acero) to temper; (tuerca) to tighten up // vi to moderate; ~se vr to be restrained; temple nm (humor) mood; (ajuste) tempering; (afinación) tuning; (clima) temperature; (pintura) tempera.

templete [tem'plete] nm bandstand.

templo ['templo] nm (iglesia) church; (pagano etc) temple.

temporada [tempo'raða] nf time, period; (estación) season.

temporal [tempo'ral] a (no permanente) temporary; (REL) temporal // nm storm.

tempranero, a [tempra'nero, a] a (BOT) early; (persona) early-rising.

temprano, a [tem'prano, a] a early;

(demasiado pronto) too soon, too early.

ten vb ver **tener.**

tenacidad [tenaθi'ðað] nf (gen) tenacity; (dureza) toughness; (terquedad) stubbornness.

tenacillas [tena'θiʎas] nfpl (gen) tongs; (para el pelo) curling tongs; (MED) forceps.

tenaz [te'naθ] a (material) tough; (persona) tenacious; (pegajoso) sticky; (terco) stubborn.

tenaza(s) [te'naθa(s)] nf(pl) (MED) forceps; (TEC) pliers; (ZOOL) pincers.

tendal [ten'dal] nm awning.

tendedero [tende'ðero] nm (para ropa) drying-place; (cuerda) clothes line.

tendencia [ten'denθja] nf tendency; (proceso) trend; **tener ~ a** to tend or have a tendency to; **tendencioso, a** a tendentious.

tender [ten'der] vt (extender) to spread out; (colgar) to hang out; (vía férrea, cable) to lay; (cuerda) to stretch // vi to tend; **~se** vr to lie down; (fig: dejarse llevar) to let o.s. go; (: dejar ir) to let things go; **~ la cama/la mesa** (AM) to make the bed/lay the table.

ténder ['tender] nm tender.

tenderete [tende'rete] nm (puesto) stall; (carretilla) barrow; (exposición) display of goods; (jaleo) mess.

tendero, a [ten'dero, a] nm/f shopkeeper.

tendido, a [ten'diðo, a] a (acostado) lying down, flat; (colgado) hanging // nm (ropa) washing; (TAUR) front rows of seats; (colocación) laying; (ARQ: enyesado) coat of plaster; **a galope ~** flat out.

tendón [ten'don] nm tendon.

tendré etc vb ver **tener.**

tenducho [ten'dutʃo] nm small dirty shop.

tenebroso, a [tene'ßroso, a] a (oscuro) dark; (fig) gloomy; (siniestro) sinister.

tenedor [tene'ðor] nm (CULIN) fork; (poseedor) holder; **~ de libros** book-keeper.

teneduría [teneðu'ria] nf keeping; **~ de libros** book-keeping.

tenencia [te'nenθja] nf (de casa) tenancy; (de oficio) tenure; (de propiedad) possession.

tener [te'ner] vt (poseer) to have; (en la mano) to hold; (caja) to hold, contain; (considerar) to consider; **~ suerte** to be lucky; **~ permiso** to have permission; **tiene 10 años** he is 10 years old; **¿cuántos años tienes?** how old are you?; **~ sed/hambre/frío/calor** to be thirsty/hungry/cold/hot; **~ ganas (de)** to want (to); **~ celos** to be jealous; **~ cuidado** to be careful; **~ razón** to be right; **~ un metro de ancho/de largo** to be one metre wide/long; **~ a bien** to see fit to; **~ en cuenta** to bear in mind, take into account; **~ a menos** to consider it beneath o.s.; **~ a uno en más (estima)** to think all the more of sb; **~ a uno por...** to think sb...; **~ por seguro** to be sure; **~ presente** to remember, bear in mind; **~**

que (obligación) to have to; **tiene que ser así** it has to be this way; **nos tiene preparada una sorpresa** he has prepared a surprise for us; **¿qué tiene?** what's the matter with him?; **¿ésas tenemos?** what's all this?; **tiene un mes de muerto** he has been dead for a month; **~se** vr (erguirse) to stand; (apoyarse) to lean (on); (fig) to control o.s.; (considerarse) to consider o.s.

tenería [tene'ria] nf tannery.

tengo etc vb ver **tener.**

tenia ['tenja] nf tapeworm.

teniente [te'njente] nm (rango) lieutenant; (ayudante) deputy.

tenis ['tenis] nm tennis; **~ta** nm/f tennis player.

tenor [te'nor] nm (tono) tone; (sentido) meaning; (MUS) tenor; **a ~ de** on the lines of.

tensar [ten'sar] vt to tauten; (arco) to draw.

tensión [ten'sjon] nf (gen) tension; (TEC) stress; (MED): **~ arterial** blood pressure; **tener la ~ alta** to have high blood pressure; **tenso, a** a tense.

tentación [tenta'θjon] nf temptation.

tentáculo [ten'takulo] nm tentacle.

tentador, a [tenta'ðor, a] a tempting // nm/f tempter/temptress.

tentar [ten'tar] vt (tocar) to touch, feel; (seducir) to tempt; (atraer) to attract; (probar) to try (out); (lanzarse a) to venture; (MED) to probe; **tentativa** nf attempt; **tentativa de asesinato** attempted murder.

tentempié [tentem'pje] nm (fam) snack.

tenue ['tenwe] a (delgado) thin, slender; (alambre) fine; (insustancial) tenuous; (sonido) faint; (neblina) light; (lazo, vínculo) slight; **tenuidad** nf thinness, fineness; (ligereza) lightness; (sencillez) simplicity.

teñir [te'ɲir] vt to dye; (fig) to tinge; **~se** vr to dye; **~se el pelo** to dye one's hair.

teología [teolo'xia] nf theology.

teorema [teo'rema] nm theorem.

teoría [teo'ria] nf theory; **en ~** in theory; **teóricamente** ad theoretically; **teórico, a** a theoretic(al) // nm/f theoretician, theorist; **teorizar** vi to theorize.

terapéutico, a [tera'peutiko, a] a therapeutic.

terapia [te'rapja] nf therapy; **~ laboral** occupational therapy.

tercer [ter'θer] a ver **tercero.**

tercería [terθe'ria] nf (mediación) mediation; (arbitraje) arbitration.

tercero, tercer a [ter'θero, ter'θer, a] a third // nm (árbitro) mediator; (JUR) third party.

terceto [ter'θeto] nm trio.

terciado, a [ter'θjaðo, a] a slanting; **azúcar ~** brown sugar.

terciar [ter'θjar] vt (MAT) to divide into three; (inclinarse) to slope; (llevar) to wear (across the shoulder) // vi (participar) to take part; (hacer de árbitro) to mediate;

~se vr to come up; **~ io, a** a tertiary.
tercio [ter'θjo] nm third.
terciopelo [terθjo'pelo] nm velvet.
terco, a ['terko, a] a obstinate; (material) tough.
tergiversación [terxiβersa'θjon] nf (deformación) distortion; (evasivas) prevarication; **tergiversar** vt to distort // vi to prevaricate.
termas ['termas] nfpl hot springs.
terminación [termina'θjon] nf (final) end; (conclusión) conclusion, ending; **terminal** a, nm, nf terminal; **terminante** a (final) final, · definitive; (tajante) categorical; **terminar** vt (completar) to complete, finish; (concluir) to end // vi (llegar a su fin) to end; (parar) to stop; (acabar) to finish; **terminarse** vr to come to an end; **terminar por hacer algo** to end up (by) doing sth; **término** nm end, conclusion; (parada) terminus; (límite) boundary; **término medio** average; (fig) middle way; **en último término** (a fin de cuentas) in the last analysis; (como último recurso) as a last resort; **en términos de** in terms of.
terminología [terminolo'xia] nf terminology.
termodinámico, a [termoði'namiko, a] a thermodynamic.
termómetro [ter'mometro] nm thermometer.
termonuclear [termonukle'ar] a thermonuclear.
termo(s) ['termo(s)] nm thermos.
termostato [termo'stato] nm thermostat.
ternero, a [ter'nero, a] nm/f (animal) calf // nf (carne) veal.
terneza [ter'neθa] nf tenderness.
terno ['terno] nm (traje) three-piece suit; (conjunto) set of three.
ternura [ter'nura] nf (trato) tenderness; (palabra) endearment; (cariño) fondness.
terquedad [terke'ðað] nf obstinacy; (dureza) harshness.
terrado [te'rraðo] nm terrace.
terraplén [terra'plen] nm (AGR) terrace; (FERRO) embankment; (MIL) rampart; (cuesta) slope.
terrateniente [terrate'njente] nm landowner.
terraza [te'rraθa] nf (balcón) balcony; (techo) flat roof; (AGR) terrace.
terremoto [terre'moto] nm earthquake.
terrenal [terre'nal] a earthly.
terreno [te'rreno] nm (tierra) land; (parcela) plot; (suelo) soil; (fig) field; **un ~** a piece of land.
terrero, a [te'rrero, a] a (de la tierra) earthy; (vuelo) low; (fig) humble.
terrestre [te'rrestre] a terrestrial; (ruta) land cpd.
terrible [te'rriβle] a (espantoso) terrible; (aterrador) dreadful; (tremendo) awful.
territorio [terri'torjo] nm territory.
terrón [te'rron] nm (de azúcar) lump; (de tierra) clod, lump; **terrones** nmpl land sg.

terror [te'rror] nm terror; **~ ífico, a** a terrifying; **~ ista** a, nm/f terrorist.
terroso, a [te'rroso, a] a earthy.
terruño [te'rruɲo] nm (pedazo) clod; (parcela) plot; (fig) native soil.
terso, a ['terso, a] a (liso) smooth; (pulido) polished; (fig: estilo) flowing; **tersura** nf smoothness; (brillo) shine.
tertulia [ter'tulja] nf (reunión informal) social gathering; (grupo) group, circle; (sala) clubroom.
tesar [te'sar] vt to tighten up.
tesis ['tesis] nf inv thesis.
tesón [te'son] nm (firmeza) firmness; (tenacidad) tenacity.
tesorero, a [teso'rero, a] nm/f treasurer; **tesoro** nm (gen) treasure; (FIN, POL) treasury.
testaferro [testa'ferro] nm figurehead.
testamentaría [testamenta'ria] nf execution of a will.
testamentario, a [testamen'tarjo, a] a testamentary // nm/f executor/executrix; **testamento** nm will; **testar** vi to make a will.
testarudo, a [testa'ruðo, a] a stubborn.
testero, a [tes'tero, a] nm/f (gen) front // nm (ARQ) front wall.
testes ['testes] nmpl testes.
testículo [tes'tikulo] nm testicle.
testificar [testifi'kar] vt to testify; (fig) to attest // vi to give evidence.
testigo [tes'tiɣo] nm/f witness; **~ de cargo/descargo** witness for the prosecution/defence; **~ ocular** eye witness.
testimoniar [testimo'njar] vt to testify to; (fig) to show; **testimonio** nm testimony.
teta ['teta] nf (de biberón) teat; (ANAT) nipple; (fam) breast.
tétanos ['tetanos] nm tetanus.
tetera [te'tera] nf teapot.
tetilla [te'tiʎa] nf (ANAT) nipple; (de biberón) teat.
tétrico, a ['tetriko, a] a gloomy, dismal.
textil [teks'til] a textile; **~ es** nmpl textiles.
texto ['teksto] nm text; **textual** a textual.
textura [teks'tura] nf (de tejido) texture; (de mineral) structure.
tez [teθ] nf (cutis) complexion; (color) colouring.
ti [ti] pron you; (reflexivo) yourself.
tía ['tia] nf (pariente) aunt; (mujer cualquiera) girl, bird (col); (fam: pej: vieja) old bag; (: prostituta) whore.
tibia ['tiβja] nf tibia.
tibieza [ti'βjeθa] nf (temperatura) tepidness; (fig) coolness; **tibio, a** a lukewarm.
tiburón [tiβu'ron] nm shark.
tic [tik] nm (ruido) click; (de reloj) tick; (MED): **~ nervioso** nervous tic.
tictac [tik'tak] nm (de reloj) tick tock.
tiempo ['tjempo] nm (gen) time; (época, período) age, period; (METEOROLOGÍA) weather; (LING) tense; (edad) age; (de

juego) half; **a ~ in** time; **a un *o* al mismo ~** at the same time; **al poco ~** very soon (after); **de ~ en ~** from time to time; **hace buen/mal ~** the weather is fine/bad; **estar a ~** to be in time; **hace ~** some time ago; **hacer ~** to while away the time; **motor de 2 ~s** two-stroke engine.

tienda ['tjenda] *nf* (*gen*) shop; (*más grande*) store; (*NAUT*) awning; **~ de campaña** tent.

tienes *etc vb ver* **tener**.

tienta ['tjenta] *nf* (*MED*) probe; (*fig*) tact; **andar a ~s** to grope one's way along.

tiento ['tjento] *nm* (*tacto*) touch; (*precaución*) wariness; (*pulso*) steady hand; (*ZOOL*) feeler; (*de ciego*) blind man's stick.

tierno, a ['tjerno, a] *a* (*blando, dulce*) tender; (*fresco*) fresh.

tierra ['tjerra] *nf* earth; (*suelo*) soil; (*mundo*) world; (*país*) country, land; **~ adentro** inland.

tieso, a ['tjeso, a] *a* (*rígido*) rigid; (*duro*) stiff; (*fig: testarudo*) stubborn; (*fam: orgulloso*) conceited // *ad* strongly.

tiesto ['tjesto] *nm* flowerpot; (*pedazo*) piece of pottery.

tiesura [tje'sura] *nf* rigidity; (*fig*) stubbornness; (*fam*) conceit.

tifo ['tifo] *nm* typhus.

tifoidea [tifoi'ðea] *nf* typhoid.

tifón [ti'fon] *nm* (*huracán*) typhoon; (*de mar*) tidal wave.

tifus ['tifus] *nm* typhus.

tigre ['tiɣre] *nm* tiger.

tijera [ti'xera] *nf* (*AM*) scissors *pl*; (*ZOOL*) claw; (*persona*) gossip; **de ~** folding; **~s** *nfpl* scissors; (*para plantas*) shears; **tijeretear** *vt* to snip // *vi* (*fig*) to meddle.

tildar [til'dar] *vt*: **~ de** to brand as.

tilde ['tilde] *nf* (*defecto*) defect; (*trivialidad*) triviality; (*TIPOGRAFÍA*) tilde.

tilín [ti'lin] *nm* tinkle.

tilo ['tilo] *nm* lime tree.

timar [ti'mar] *vt* (*robar*) to steal; (*estafar*) to swindle; **~se** *vr* (*fam*) to make eyes (*con uno* at sb).

timbal [tim'bal] *nm* small drum.

timbrar [tim'brar] *vt* to stamp.

timbre ['timbre] *nm* (*sello*) stamp; (*campanilla*) bell; (*tono*) timbre; (*COM*) stamp duty.

timidez [timi'ðeθ] *nf* shyness; **tímido, a** *a* shy.

timo ['timo] *nm* swindle.

timón [ti'mon] *nm* helm, rudder; **timonel** *nm* helmsman.

tímpano ['timpano] *nm* (*ANAT*) eardrum; (*MUS*) small drum.

tina ['tina] *nf* tub; (*baño*) bathtub; **tinaja** *nf* large jar.

tinglado [tin'glaðo] *nm* (*cobertizo*) shed; (*fig: truco*) trick; (*intriga*) intrigue.

tinieblas [ti'njeßlas] *nfpl* (*gen*) darkness *sg*; (*sombras*) shadows.

tino ['tino] *nm* (*habilidad*) skill; (*MIL*) marksmanship; (*juicio*) insight; (*moderación*) moderation.

tinta ['tinta] *nf* ink; (*TEC*) dye; (*ARTE*) colour.

tinte ['tinte] *nm* (*acto*) dyeing; (*carácter*) tinge; (*barniz*) veneer.

tinterillo [tinte'riʎo] *nm* penpusher.

tintero [tin'tero] *nm* inkwell.

tintinear [tintine'ar] *vt* to tinkle.

tinto, a ['tinto, a] *a* (*teñido*) dyed; (*manchado*) stained // *nm* red wine.

tintorera [tinto'rera] *nf* shark.

tintorería [tintore'ria] *nf* dry cleaner's.

tintura [tin'tura] *nf* (*acto*) dyeing; (*QUÍMICA*) dye; (*farmacéutico*) tincture.

tío ['tio] *nm* (*pariente*) uncle; (*fam: viejo*) old fellow; (: *individuo*) bloke, chap.

tiovivo [tio'ßißo] *nm* roundabout.

típico, a ['tipiko, a] *a* typical.

tiple ['tiple] *nm* soprano (voice) // *nf* soprano.

tipo ['tipo] *nm* (*clase*) type, kind; (*norma*) norm; (*patrón*) pattern; (*hombre*) fellow; (*ANAT*) build; (: *de mujer*) figure; (*IMPRENTA*) type; **~ bancario/de descuento/de interés/de cambio** bank/discount/interest/exchange rate.

tipografía [tipoɣra'fia] *nf* (*tipo*) printing; (*lugar*) printing press; **tipográfico, a** *a* printing; **tipógrafo, a** *nm/f* printer.

tiquismiquis [tikis'mikis] *nm* fussy person // *nmpl* (*querellas*) squabbling *sg*; (*escrúpulos*) silly scruples.

tira ['tira] *nf* strip; (*fig*) abundance; **~ y afloja** give and take.

tirabuzón [tiraßu'θon] *nm* corkscrew.

tirado, a [ti'raðo, a] *a* (*barato*) dirt-cheap; (*fam: fácil*) very easy // *nf* (*acto*) cast, throw; (*distancia*) distance; (*serie*) series; (*TIPOGRAFÍA*) printing, edition; **de una ~a** at one go.

tirador [tira'ðor] *nm* (*mango*) handle; (*ELEC*) flex.

tiranía [tira'nia] *nf* tyranny; **tirano, a** *a* tyrannical // *nm/f* tyrant.

tirante [ti'rante] *a* (*cuerda*) tight, taut; (*relaciones*) strained // *nm* (*ARQ*) brace; (*TEC*) stay; (*correa*) shoulder strap; **~s** *nmpl* braces; **tirantez** *nf* tightness; (*fig*) tension.

tirar [ti'rar] *vt* (*aventar*) to throw; (*dejar caer*) to drop; (*volcar*) to upset; (*derribar*) to knock down *or* over; (*jalar*) to pull; (*desechar*) to throw out *or* away; (*disipar*) to squander; (*imprimir*) to print; (*dar: golpe*) to deal // *vi* (*disparar*) to shoot; (*jalar*) to pull; (*fig*) to draw; (*fam: andar*) to go; (*tender a, buscar realizar*) to tend to; (*DEPORTE*) to shoot; **~se** *vr* to throw o.s.; (*fig*) to cheapen o.s.; **~ abajo** to bring down, destroy; **tira más a su padre** he takes more after his father; **ir tirando** to manage; **a todo ~** at the most.

tirita [ti'rita] *nf* (sticking) plaster.

tiritar [tiri'tar] *vi* to shiver.

tiro ['tiro] *nm* (*lanzamiento*) throw;

(*disparo*) shot; (*disparar*) shooting; (*DEPORTE*) drive; (*alcance*) range; (*de escalera*) flight (of stairs); (*golpe*) blow; (*engaño*) hoax; ~ **al blanco** target practice; **caballo de** ~ cart-horse; **andar de** ~**s largos** to be all dressed up; **al** ~ (*AM*) at once.

tirón [ti'ron] *nm* (*sacudida*) pull, tug; **de un** ~ in one go.

tirotear [tirote'ar] *vt* to shoot at; ~**se** *vr* to exchange shots; **tiroteo** *nm* exchange of shots, shooting.

tísico, a ['tisiko, a] *a* consumptive.

títere ['titere] *nm* puppet.

titilar [titi'lar] *vi* (*luz, estrella*) to twinkle; (*parpado*) to flutter.

titiritero, a [titiri'tero, a] *nm/f* puppeteer.

titubeante [tituβe'ante] *a* (*inestable*) shaky, tottering; (*farfullante*) stammering; (*dudoso*) hesitant; **titubear** *vi* to stagger; (*fig*) to hesitate; **titubeo** *nm* staggering; stammering; hesitation.

titulado, a [titu'laðo, a] *a* (*libro*) entitled; (*persona*) titled; **titular** *a* titular // *nm/f* occupant // *nm* headline // *vt* to title; **titularse** *vr* to be entitled; **título** *nm* (*gen*) title; (*de diario*) headline; (*certificado*) professional qualification; (*universitario*) university degree; (*fig*) right; **a título de** in the capacity of.

tiza ['tiθa] *nf* chalk.

tizna ['tiθna] *nf* grime; **tiznar** *vt* to blacken; (*fig*) to tarnish.

tizón [ti'θon], **tizo** ['tiθo] *nm* brand; (*fig*) stain.

toalla [to'aʎa] *nf* towel.

tobillo [to'βiʎo] *nm* ankle.

tobogán [toβo'ɣan] *nm* toboggan; (*montaña rusa*) switchback; (*resbaladilla*) chute, slide.

toca ['toka] *nf* headdress.

tocadiscos [toka'ðiskos] *nm inv* record player.

tocado, a [to'kaðo, a] *a* rotten; (*fam*) touched // *nm* headdress.

tocador [toka'ðor] *nm* (*mueble*) dressing table; (*cuarto*) boudoir; (*neceser*) toilet case; (*fam*) ladies' toilet.

tocante [to'kante]: ~ **a** *prep* with regard to.

tocar [to'kar] *vt* to touch; (*MUS*) to play; (*topar con*) to run into, strike; (*referirse a*) to allude to; (*padecer*) to suffer; (*el pelo*) to do // *vi* (*a la puerta*) to knock (on *or* at the door); (*ser de turno*) to fall to, be the turn of; (*ser hora*) to be due; (*barco, avión*) to call at; (*atañer*) to concern; ~**se** *vr* (*cubrirse la cabeza*) to cover one's head; (*tener contacto*) to touch (each other); **por lo que a mí me toca** as far as I am concerned; **esto toca en la locura** this verges on madness.

tocayo, a [to'kajo, a] *nm/f* namesake.

tocino [to'θino] *nm* bacon.

todavía [toða'βia] *ad* (*aun*) still; (*aún*) yet; ~ **más** yet more; ~ **no** not yet.

todo, a ['toðo, a] *a* all; (*cada*) every;

(*entero*) whole; (*sentido negativo*): **en** ~ **el día lo he visto** I haven't seen him all day; ~**as las semanas/**~**s los martes** every week/Tuesday // *ad* all, completely // *nm* everything // *pron*: ~**s/**~**as** everyone; **a** ~ **a velocidad** at full speed; **estaba** ~ **ojos** he was all eyes; **puede ser** ~ **lo honesto que quiera** he can be as honest as he likes; **ante** ~ above all; **en un** ~ as a whole; **corriendo y** ~, **no llegaron a tiempo** even though they ran, they still didn't arrive in time; **con** ~ still, even so; **del** ~ completely.

todopoderoso, a [toðopoðe'roso, a] *a* all powerful; (*REL*) almighty.

toga ['toɣa] *nf* toga; (*ESCOL*) gown.

Tokio ['tokjo] *n* Tokyo.

toldo ['toldo] *nm* (*para el sol*) sunshade; (*tienda*) marquee; (*fig*) pride.

tole ['tole] *nm* (*fam*) commotion.

tolerable [tole'raβle] *a* tolerable; **tolerancia** *nf* tolerance; **tolerar** *vt* to tolerate; (*resistir*) to endure.

toma ['toma] *nf* (*gen*) taking; (*MED*) dose.

tomar [to'mar] *vt* (*gen*) to take; (*aspecto*) to take on; (*beber*) to drink // *vi* to take; (*AM*) to drink; ~**se** *vr* to take; ~**se por** to consider o.s. to be; ~ **a bien/a mal** to take well/badly; ~ **en serio** to take seriously; ~ **el pelo a alguien** to pull sb's leg; ~**la con uno** to pick a quarrel with sb.

tomate [to'mate] *nm* tomato; ~**ra** *nf* tomato plant.

tomillo [to'miʎo] *nm* thyme.

tomo ['tomo] *nm* (*libro*) volume; (*tamaño*) size; (*fig*) importance.

ton [ton] *abr de* **tonelada** // *nm*: **sin** ~ **ni son** without rhyme or reason.

tonada [to'naða] *nf* tune.

tonalidad [tonali'ðað] *nf* tone.

tonel [to'nel] *nm* barrel.

tonelada [tone'laða] *nf* ton; **tonelaje** *nm* tonnage.

tonelero [tone'lero] *nm* cooper.

tónico, a ['toniko, a] *a* tonic // *nm* (*MED*) tonic // *nf* (*MUS*) tonic; (*fig*) keynote.

tonificar [tonifi'kar] *vt* to tone up.

tonillo [to'niʎo] *nm* monotonous voice.

tono ['tono] *nm* tone; **fuera de** ~ inappropriate; **darse** ~ to put on airs.

tontería [tonte'ria] *nf* (*estupidez*) foolishness; (*una* ~) stupid remark; ~**s** *nfpl* rubbish *sg*, nonsense *sg*.

tonto, a ['tonto, a] *a* stupid; (*sentimental*) silly // *nm/f* fool; (*payaso*) clown.

topacio [to'paθjo] *nm* topaz.

topar [to'par] *vt* (*tropezar*) to bump into; (*encontrar*) to find, come across; (*ZOOL*) to butt // *vi*: ~ **contra** *o* **en** to run into; ~ **con** to run up against; **el problema topa en eso** that's where the problem lies.

tope ['tope] *a* maximum // *nm* (*fin*) end; (*límite*) limit; (*riña*) quarrel; (*FERRO*) buffer; (*AUTO*) bumper; **al** ~ end to end.

tópico, a ['topiko, a] *a* topical // *nm* platitude.

topo ['topo] *nm* (*ZOOL*) mole; (*fig*) blunderer.

topografía [topoɤra'fia] *nf* topography; **topógrafo, a** *nm/f* topographer.

toque ['toke] *nm* touch; (*MUS*) beat; (*de campana*) peal; (*fig*) crux; **dar un ~ a** to test; **~ de queda** curfew; **~tear** *vt* to handle.

toquilla [to'kiʎa] *nf* (*bufanda*) headscarf; (*chal*) shawl.

torbellino [torbe'ʎino] *nm* whirlwind; (*fig*) whirl.

torcedura [torθe'ðura] *nf* twist; (*MED*) sprain.

torcer [tor'θer] *vt* to twist; (*la esquina*) to turn; (*MED*) to sprain; (*cuerda*) to plait; (*ropa, manos*) to wring; (*persona*) to corrupt // *vi* (*desviar*) to turn off; (*pelota*) to spin; **~se** *vr* (*ladearse*) to bend; (*desviarse*) to go astray; (*fracasar*) to go wrong; **torcido, a** *a* twisted; (*fig*) crooked // *nm* curl.

tordo, a ['torðo, a] *a* dappled // *nm* thrush.

torear [tore'ar] *vt* (*fig: evadir*) to avoid; (*jugar con*) to tease // *vi* to fight bulls; **toreo** *nm* bullfighting; **torero, a** *nm/f* bullfighter.

tormenta [tor'menta] *nf* storm; (*fig: confusión*) turmoil; (*desgracia*) misfortune.

tormento [tor'mento] *nm* torture; (*fig*) anguish.

tornar [tor'nar] *vt* (*devolver*) to return, give back; (*transformar*) to transform // *vi* to go back; **~se** *vr* (*ponerse*) to become; (*volver*) to return.

tornasol [torna'sol] *nm* (*BOT*) sunflower; **papel de ~** litmus paper; **~ado, a** *a* (*brillante*) iridescent; (*reluciente*) shimmering.

torneo [tor'neo] *nm* tournament.

tornero, a [tor'nero, a] *nm/f* machinist.

tornillo [tor'niʎo] *nm* screw.

torniquete [torni'kete] *nm* (*puerta*) turnstile; (*MED*) tourniquet.

torno ['torno] *nm* (*TEC*) winch; (*tambor*) drum; **en ~ (a)** round, about.

toro ['toro] *nm* bull; (*fam*) he-man; **los ~s** bullfighting.

toronja [to'ronxa] *nf* grapefruit.

torpe ['torpe] *a* (*poco hábil*) clumsy, awkward; (*necio*) dim; (*lento*) slow; (*indecente*) crude; (*no honrado*) dishonest.

torpedo [tor'peðo] *nm* torpedo.

torpeza [tor'peθa] *nf* (*falta de agilidad*) clumsiness; (*lentitud*) slowness; (*rigidez*) stiffness; (*error*) mistake; (*crudeza*) obscenity.

torre ['torre] *nf* tower; (*de petróleo*) derrick.

torrente [to'rrente] *nm* torrent.

tórrido, a ['torriðo, a] *a* torrid.

torrija [to'rrixa] *nf* fried bread; **~s** French toast *sg*.

torsión [tor'sjon] *nf* twisting.

torso ['torso] *nm* torso.

torta ['torta] *nf* cake; (*fam*) slap.

tortícolis [tor'tikolis] *nm* stiff neck.

tortilla [tor'tiʎa] *nf* omelette; (*AM*) maize pancake; **~ francesa/española** plain/potato omelette.

tórtola ['tortola] *nf* turtledove.

tortuga [tor'tuɤa] *nf* tortoise.

tortuoso, a [tor'twoso, a] *a* winding.

tortura [tor'tura] *nf* torture; **torturar** *vt* to torture.

tos [tos] *nf* cough; **~ ferina** whooping cough.

tosco, a ['tosko, a] *a* coarse.

toser [to'ser] *vi* to cough.

tostado, a [tos'taðo, a] *a* toasted; (*por el sol*) dark brown; (*piel*) tanned // *nf* tan; **tostador** *nm* toaster; **tostar** *vt* to toast; (*café*) to roast; (*al sol*) to tan; **tostarse** *vr* to get brown.

total [to'tal] *a* total // *ad* in short; (*al fin y al cabo*) when all is said and done // *nm* total; **~ que** to cut a long story short.

totalidad [totali'ðað] *nf* whole.

totalitario, a [totali'tarjo, a] *a* totalitarian.

tóxico, a ['toksiko, a] *a* toxic // *nm* poison.

tozudo, a [to'θuðo, a] *a* obstinate.

traba ['traβa] *nf* bond, tie; (*cadena*) fetter.

trabajador, a [traβaxa'ðor, a] *nm/f* worker // *a* hard-working.

trabajar [traβa'xar] *vt* to work; (*arar*) to till; (*empeñarse en*) to work at; (*empujar: persona*) to push; (*convencer*) to persuade // *vi* to work; (*esforzarse*) to strive; **trabajo** *nm* work; (*tarea*) task; (*POL*) labour; (*fig*) effort; **tomarse el trabajo de** to take the trouble to; **trabajo por turno/a destajo** shift work/ piecework; **trabajoso, a** *a* hard; (*MED*) pale.

trabalenguas [traβa'lengwas] *nm inv* tongue twister.

trabar [tra'βar] *vt* (*juntar*) to join, unite; (*atar*) to tie down, fetter; (*agarrar*) to seize; (*amistad*) to strike up; **~se** *vr* to become entangled; (*reñir*) to squabble; **trabazón** *nf* (*TEC*) joining, assembly; (*fig*) bond, link.

trabucar [traβu'kar] *vt* (*confundir*) to confuse, mix up; (*palabras*) to misplace.

tracción [trak'θjon] *nf* traction; **~ delantera/trasera** front-wheel/rear-wheel drive.

tractor [trak'tor] *nm* tractor.

tradición [traði'θjon] *nf* tradition; **tradicional** *a* traditional.

traducción [traðuk'θjon] *nf* translation; **traducir** *vt* to translate; **traductor, a** *nm/f* translator.

traer [tra'er] *vt* (*gen*) to bring; (*llevar*) to carry; (*ropa*) to wear; (*imán*) to draw; (*incluir*) to carry; (*fig*) to cause; **~se** *vr*: **~ se algo** to be up to sth; **~se bien/mal** to dress well/badly.

traficar [trafi'kar] *vi* to trade.

tráfico ['trafiko] *nm* (*COM*) trade; (*AUTO*) traffic.

tragaluz [traɤa'luθ] *nm* skylight.

tragamonedas [traɤamo'neðas] *nm inv*,

tragaperras [traɣa'perras] *nm inv* slot machine.

tragar [tra'ɣar] *vt* to swallow; (*devorar*) to devour, bolt down; ~**se** *vr* to swallow.

tragedia [tra'xeðja] *nf* tragedy; **trágico, a** a tragic.

trago ['traɣo] *nm* (*líquido*) drink; (*comido de golpe*) gulp; (*fam: de bebida*) swig; (*desgracia*) blow.

traición [trai'θjon] *nf* treachery; (*JUR*) treason; (*una* ~) act of treachery; **traicionar** *vt* to betray; **traidor, a, traicionero, a** a treacherous // *nm/f* traitor.

traigo *etc vb ver* **traer**.

traje ['traxe] *vb ver* **traer** //. *nm* (*gen*) dress; (*de hombre*) suit; (*vestimenta típica*) costume; (*fig*) garb; ~ **de baño** swimsuit; ~ **de luces** bullfighter's costume.

trajera *etc vb ver* **traer**.

trajín [tra'xin] *nm* haulage; (*fam: movimiento*) bustle; **trajines** *nmpl* goings-on; **trajinar** *vt* (*llevar*) to carry, transport // *vi* (*moverse*) to bustle about; (*viajar*) to travel around.

trama ['trama] *nf* (*fig*) link; (: *intriga*) plot; (*de tejido*) weft; **tramar** *vt* to plot; (*TEC*) to weave.

tramitar [trami'tar] *vt* (*asunto*) to transact; (*negociar*) to negotiate; (*manejar*) to handle; **trámite** *nm* (*paso*) step; (*JUR*) transaction; **trámites** *nmpl* (*burocracia*) paperwork *sg*, procedures; (*JUR*) proceedings.

tramo ['tramo] *nm* (*de tierra*) plot; (*de escalera*) flight; (*de vía*) section.

tramoya [tra'moja] *nf* (*TEATRO*) piece of stage machinery; (*fig*) trick; **tramoyista** *nm/f* scene shifter; (*fig*) trickster.

trampa ['trampa] *nf* (*gen*) trap; (*en el suelo*) trapdoor; (*prestidigitación*) conjuring trick; (*engaño*) trick; (*fam*) fiddle; (*de pantalón*) fly; **trampear** *vt, vi* to cheat; **trampista** *nm/f* = **tramposo**.

trampolín [trampo'lin] *nm* trampoline; (*de piscina etc*) diving board.

tramposo, a [tram'poso, a] a crooked, cheating // *nm/f* crook, cheat.

tranca ['tranka] *nf* (*palo*) stick; (*viga*) beam; (*de puerta, ventana*) bar; **trancar** *vt* to bar // *vi* to stride along.

trance ['tranθe] *nm* (*momento difícil*) difficult moment; (*situación crítica*) critical situation; (*estado hipnotizado*) trance.

tranco ['tranko] *nm* stride.

tranquilidad [trankili'ðað] *nf* (*calma*) calmness, stillness; (*paz*) peacefulness; **tranquilizar** *vt* (*calmar*) to calm (down); (*asegurar*) to reassure; **tranquilo, a** a (*calmado*) calm; (*apacible*) peaceful; (*mar*) calm; (*mente*) untroubled.

transacción [transak'θjon] *nf* transaction.

transar [tran'sar] *vt* = **transigir**.

transbordador [transβorða'ðor] *nm* ferry.

transbordar [transβor'ðar] *vt* to transfer; ~**se** *vr* to change; **transbordo** *nm*

transfer; **hacer transbordo** to change (trains).

transcurrir [transku'rrir] *vi* (*tiempo*) to pass; (*hecho*) to turn out.

transcurso [trans'kurso] *nm*: ~ **del tiempo** lapse (of time).

transeúnte [transe'unte] a transient // *nm/f* passer-by.

transferencia [transfe'renθja] *nf* transference; (*COM*) transfer; **transferir** *vt* to transfer; (*de tiempo*) to postpone.

transfigurar [transfiɣu'rar] *vt* to transfigure.

transformador [transforma'ðor] *nm* transformer.

transformar [transfor'mar] *vt* to transform; (*convertirse*) to convert.

tránsfuga ['transfuɣa] *nm/f* (*MIL*) deserter; (*POL*) turncoat.

transgresión [transɣre'sjon] *nf* transgression.

transición [transi'θjon] *nf* transition.

transido, a [tran'siðo, a] a overcome.

transigir [transi'xir] *vi* to compromise, make concessions.

transistor [transis'tor] *nm* transistor.

transitar [transi'tar] *vi* to go (from place to place); **tránsito** *nm* transit; (*AUTO*) traffic; (*parada*) stop; **transitorio, a** a transitory.

transmisión [transmi'sjon] *nf* (*TEC*) transmission; (*transferencia*) transfer; ~ **en directo/exterior** live/outside broadcast; **transmitir** *vt* (*gen*) to transmit; (*RADIO, TV*) to broadcast.

transparencia [transpa'renθja] *nf* transparency; (*claridad*) clearness, clarity; (*foto*) slide; **transparentar** *vt* to reveal // *vi* to be transparent; **transparente** a transparent; clear; (*ligero*) diaphanous // *nm* curtain.

transpirar [transpi'rar] *vi* to perspire; (*fig*) to transpire.

transponer [transpo'ner] *vt* to transpose; (*cambiar de sitio*) to change the place of // *vi* (*desaparecer*) to disappear; (*ir más allá*) to go beyond; ~**se** *vr* to change places; (*ocultarse*) to hide; (*sol*) to go down.

transportación [transporta'θjon] *nf* transportation; **transportar** *vt* to transport; (*llevar*) to carry; **transporte** *nm* transport; (*COM*) haulage.

tranvía [tran'βia] *nm* tram.

trapecio [tra'peθjo] *nm* trapeze; **trapecista** *nm/f* trapeze artist.

trapero, a [tra'pero, a] *nm/f* ragman.

trapicheos [trapi'tʃeos] *nmpl* (*fam*) schemes, fiddles.

trapisonda [trapi'sonda] *nf* (*jaleo*) row; (*estafa*) swindle.

trapo ['trapo] *nm* (*tela*) rag; (*de cocina*) cloth.

traqueteo [trake'teo] *nm* (*crujido*) crack; (*golpeteo*) rattling.

tras [tras] *prep* (*detrás*) behind; (*después*) after; ~ **de** besides.

trascendencia [trasθen'denθja] *nf*

(*importancia*) importance; (*filosofía*) transcendence; **trascendental** *a* important; transcendental; **trascender** *vi* (*oler*) to smell; (*evocar*) to evoke, suggest; (*noticias*) to come out; (*suceso*) to have a wide effect; **trascender a** to smack of.

trasegar [trase'var] *vt* (*moverse*) to move about; (*vino*) to decant.

trasero, a [tra'sero, a] *a* back // *nm* (ANAT) bottom; ~**s** *nmpl* ancestors.

trasfondo [tras'fondo] *nm* background.

trasgredir [trasxre'ðir] *vt* to contravene.

trashumante [trasu'mante] *a* migrating.

trasladar [trasla'ðar] *vt* (*gen*) to move; (*persona*) to transfer; (*postergar*) to postpone; (*copiar*) to copy; (*interpretar*) to interpret; **traslado** *nm* (*gen*) move; (*mudanza*) move, removal; (*copia*) copy.

traslucir [traslu'θir] *vt* to show; ~**se** *vr* to be translucent; (*fig*) to be revealed.

trasluz [tras'luθ] *nm* reflected light; **al ~** against *or* up to the light.

trasnochar [trasno'tʃar] *vi* (*acostarse tarde*) to stay up late; (*no dormir*) to have a sleepless night; (*pasar la noche*) to stay the night.

traspasar [traspa'sar] *vt* (*bala*) to pierce, go through; (*propiedad*) to sell, transfer; (*calle*) to cross over; (*límites*) to go beyond; (*ley*) to break; **traspaso** *nm* transfer; (*fig*) anguish.

traspié [tras'pje] *nm* (*caída*) stumble; (*tropezón*) trip; (*fig*) blunder.

trasplantar [trasplan'tar] *vt* to transplant.

traste [traste] *nm* (MUS) fret; **dar al ~ con algo** to ruin sth.

trastienda [tras'tjenda] *nf* backshop; **obtener algo por la ~** to get sth by underhand means.

trasto ['trasto] *nm* (*mueble*) piece of furniture; (*tarro viejo*) old pot; (*pey: cosa*) piece of junk; (: *persona*) dead loss; ~**s** *nmpl* (TEATRO) scenery *sg*.

trastornado, a [trastor'naðo, a] *a* (*loco*) mad; (*agitado*) crazy; **trastornar** *vt* to overturn, upset; (*fig: ideas*) to confuse; (: *nervios*) to shatter; (: *persona*) to drive crazy; **trastornarse** *vr* (*plan*) to fall through; **trastorno** *nm* (*acto*) overturning; (*confusión*) confusion.

trasunto [tra'sunto] *nm* copy.

tratable [tra'taβle] *a* friendly.

tratado [tra'taðo] *nm* (POL) treaty; (COM) agreement.

tratamiento [trata'mjento] *nm* treatment.

tratar [tra'tar] *vt* (*ocuparse de*) to treat; (*manejar*, TEC) to handle; (MED) to treat; (*dirigirse a: persona*) to address // *vi*: ~ **de** (*hablar sobre*) to deal with, be about; (*intentar*) to try to; ~ **con** (COM) to trade in; (*negociar*) to negotiate with; (*tener contactos*) to have dealings with; ~**se** *vr* to treat each other; **trato** *nm* dealings *pl*; (*relaciones*) relationship; (*comportamiento*)

manner; (COM) agreement; (*título*) (form of) address.

trauma ['trauma] *nm* trauma.

través [tra'βes] *nm* (*fig*) reverse; **al ~ ad** across, crossways; **a ~ de** *prep* across; (*sobre*) over; (*por*) through.

travesaño [traβe'saɲo] *nm* (ARQ) crossbeam; (DEPORTE) crossbar.

travesía [traβe'sia] *nf* (*calle*) cross-street; (NAUT) crossing.

travesura [traβe'sura] *nf* (*broma*) prank; (*ingenio*) wit; **travieso, a** (*niño*) naughty; (*adulto*) restless; (*ingenioso*) witty // *nf* crossing; (ARQ) crossbeam.

trayecto [tra'jekto] *nm* (*ruta*) road, way; (*viaje*) journey; (*tramo*) stretch; (*curso*) course; ~**ria** *nf* trajectory; (*fig*) path.

traza ['traβa] *nf* (ARQ) plan, design; (*aspecto*) looks *pl*; (*señal*) sign; (*engaño*) trick; (*habilidad*) skill; ~**do, a** *a*: **bien ~do** shapely, well-formed // *nm* (ARQ) plan, design; (*fig*) outline; **trazar** *vt* (ARQ) to plan; (ARTE) to sketch; (*fig*) to trace; (*plan*) to follow; **trazo** *nm* (*línea*) line; (*bosquejo*) sketch.

trébol ['treβol] *nm* (BOT) clover.

trece ['treθe] *num* thirteen.

trecho ['tretʃo] *nm* (*distancia*) distance; (*de tiempo*) while; (*fam*) piece; **de ~ en ~** at intervals.

tregua ['trewa] *nf* (MIL) truce; (*fig*) lull.

treinta ['treinta] *num* thirty.

tremendo, a [tre'mendo, a] *a* (*terrible*) terrible; (*imponente: cosa*) imposing; (*fam: fabuloso*) tremendous; (*divertido*) entertaining.

trémulo, a ['tremulo, a] *a* a quivering.

tren [tren] *nm* train; ~ **de aterrizaje** undercarriage.

trenza ['trenθa] *nf* (*de pelo*) plait; **trenzar** *vt* (*el pelo*) to plait // *vi* (*en baile*) to weave in and out; **trenzarse** *vr* (AM) to become involved with.

trepadora [trepa'ðora] *nf* (BOT) climber; **trepar** *vt, vi* to climb; (TEC) to drill.

trepidación [trepiða'θjon] *nf* shaking, vibration; **trepidar** *vi* to shake, vibrate.

tres [tres] *num* three.

tresillo [tre'siʎo] *nm* three-piece suite; (MUS) triplet.

treta ['treta] *nf* (COM *etc*) gimmick; (*fig*) trick.

triángulo ['trjangulo] *nm* triangle.

tribu ['triβu] *nf* tribe.

tribuna [tri'βuna] *nf* (*plataforma*) platform; (DEPORTE) stand; (*fig*) public speaking.

tribunal [triβu'nal] *nm* (*juicio*) court; (*comisión, fig*) tribunal.

tributar [triβu'tar] *vt* to pay; (*las gracias*) to give; (*cariño*) to show; **tributo** *nm* (COM) tax.

trigal [tri'val] *nm* wheat field; **trigo** *nm* wheat; **trigos** *nmpl* wheat field(s) (*pl*).

trigueño, a [tri'veɲo, a] *a* (*pelo*) corn-coloured; (*piel*) olive-skinned.

trillado, a [tri'ʎaðo, a] *a* a threshed; (*fig*)

trite, hackneyed; **trilladora** nf threshing machine; **trillar** vt (fig) to frequent; (AGR) to thresh.

trimestral [trimes'tral] a quarterly; (ESCOL) termly; **trimestre** nm (ESCOL) term.

trincar [trin'kar] vt (atar) to tie up; (NAUT) to lash; (agarrar) to pinion.

trinchar [trin'tʃar] vt to carve.

trinchera [trin'tʃera] nf (fosa) trench; (para vía) cutting; (impermeable) trench-coat.

trineo [tri'neo] nm sledge.

trinidad [trini'ðað] nf trio; (REL): **la T~** the Trinity.

trino ['trino] nm trill.

trinquete [trin'kete] nm (TEC) pawl; (NAUT) foremast.

tripa ['tripa] nf (ANAT) intestine; (fam) insides pl.

triple ['triple] a triple.

triplicado [tripli'kaðo] a: **por ~** in triplicate.

tripulación [tripula'θjon] nf crew; **tripulante** nm/f crewman/woman; **tripular** vt (barco) to man; (AUTO) to drive.

triquiñuela [triki'ɲwela] nf trick.

tris [tris] nm crack; **en un ~** in an instant.

triste ['triste] a (afligido) sad; (sombrío) melancholy, gloomy; (desolado) desolate; (lamentable) sorry, miserable; (viejo) old; **~za** nf (aflicción) sadness; (melancolía) melancholy.

triturar [tritu'rar] vt (moler) to grind; (mascar) to chew.

triunfar [trjun'far] vi (tener éxito) to triumph; (ganar) to win; **triunfo** nm triumph.

trivial [tri'βjal] a trivial; **~izar** vt to minimize, play down.

triza ['triθa] nf bit, piece; **hacer ~s** to smash to bits; **trizar** vt to smash to bits.

trocar [tro'kar] vt (COM) to exchange; (dinero, de lugar) to change; (palabras) to exchange; (confundir) to confuse; (vomitar) to vomit.

trocha ['trotʃa] nf (sendero) by-path; (atajo) short cut.

troche ['trotʃe] a: **~ y moche** ad helter-skelter, pell-mell.

trofeo [tro'feo] nm (premio) trophy; (éxito) success.

troj(e) ['trox(e)] nf granary.

tromba ['tromba] nf whirlwind.

trombón [trom'bon] nm trombone.

trombosis [trom'bosis] nf thrombosis.

trompa ['trompa] nf horn; (trompo) humming top; (hocico) snout; (fam): **cogerse una ~** to get tight.

trompeta [trom'peta] nf trumpet; (clarín) bugle.

trompo ['trompo] nm spinning top.

trompón [trom'pon] nm bump.

tronado, a [tro'naðo, a] a broken-down.

tronar [tro'nar] vt (AM) to shoot // vi to

thunder; (fig) to rage; (fam) to go broke.

tronco ['tronko] nm (de árbol, ANAT) trunk; (de planta) stem.

tronchar [tron'tʃar] vt (árbol) to chop down; (fig: vida) to cut short; (esperanza) to shatter; (persona) to tire out; **~se** vr to fall down.

tronera [tro'nera] nf (MIL) loophole; (ARQ) small window.

trono ['trono] nm throne.

tropa ['tropa] nf (MIL) troop; (soldados) soldiers pl; (gentío) mob.

tropel [tro'pel] nm (muchedumbre) crowd; (prisa) rush; (montón) throng.

tropelía [trope'lia] nm outrage.

tropezar [trope'θar] vi to trip, stumble; (fig) to slip up; **~ con** (encontrar) to run into; (topar con) to bump into; (reñir) to fall out with; **tropezón** nm trip; (fig) blunder.

tropical [tropi'kal] a tropical; **trópico** nm tropic.

tropiezo [tro'pjeθo] nm (error) slip, blunder; (desgracia) misfortune; (obstáculo) snag; (discusión) quarrel.

trotamundos [trota'mundos] nm inv globetrotter.

trotar [tro'tar] vi to trot; **trote** nm trot; (fam) travelling; **de mucho trote** hard-wearing.

trozo ['troθo] nm bit, piece.

truco ['truko] nm (habilidad) knack; (engaño) trick; **~s** nmpl billiards sg.

trucha ['trutʃa] nf (pez) trout; (TEC) crane.

trueno ['trweno] nm (gen) thunder; (estampido) boom; (de arma) bang.

trueque ['trweke] nm exchange; (COM) barter.

trufa ['trufa] nf (BOT) truffle; (fig: fam) fib.

truhán, ana [tru'an, ana] nm/f rogue.

truncado, a [trun'kaðo, a] a truncated; **truncar** vt (cortar) to truncate; (la vida etc) to cut short; (el desarrollo) to stunt.

tu [tu] a your.

tú [tu] pron you.

tubérculo [tu'βerkulo] nm (BOT) tuber.

tuberculosis [tußerku'losis] nf tuberculosis.

tubería [tuße'ria] nf pipes pl; (conducto) pipeline; **tubo** nm tube, pipe; **tubo de ensayo** test-tube; **tubo de escape** exhaust (pipe).

tuerca ['twerka] nf nut.

tuerto, a ['twerto, a] a (torcido) twisted; (ciego) blind in one eye // nm one-eyed person; (ofensa) wrong; a **~as** upside-down.

tuétano ['twetano] nm (gen) marrow; (BOT) pith.

tufo ['tufo] nm vapour; (fig: pey) stench.

tul [tul] nm tulle.

tulipán [tuli'pan] nm tulip.

tullido, a [tu'ʎiðo, a] a crippled; (cansado) exhausted.

tumba ['tumba] nf (sepultura) tomb; (sacudida) shake; (voltereta) somersault.

tumbar [tum'bar] *vt* to knock down; (*doblar*) to knock over; (*fam: suj: olor*) to overpower // *vi* to fall down; **~se** *vr* (*echarse*) to lie down; (*extenderse*) to stretch out.

tumbo ['tumbo] *nm* (*caída*) fall; (*de vehículo*) jolt; (*momento crítico*) critical moment.

tumido, a [tu'miðo, a] *a* swollen.

tumor [tu'mor] *nm* tumour.

tumulto [tu'multo] *nm* turmoil.

tuna ['tuna] *nf ver* **tuno**.

tunante [tu'nante] *a* rascally.

tunda ['tunda] *nf* (*de tela*) shearing; (*golpeo*) beating; **tundir** *vt* (*tela*) to shear; (*hierba*) to mow; (*fig*) to exhaust; (*fam: golpear*) to beat.

túnel ['tunel] *nm* tunnel.

Túnez ['tuneθ] *nm* Tunisia; (*ciudad*) Tunis.

tuno, a ['tuno, a] *nm/f* (*fam*) rogue // *nf* (*BOT*) prickly pear; (*MUS*) student music group.

tuntún [tun'tun]: **al ~** *ad* thoughtlessly.

tupido, a [tu'piðo, a] *a* (*denso*) dense; (*fig*) dim; (*tela*) close-woven.

turba ['turßa] *nf* crowd.

turbación [turßa'θjon] *nf* (*molestia*) disturbance; (*preocupación*) worry; **turbado, a** *a* (*molesto*) disturbed; (*preocupado*) worried; **turbar** *vt* (*molestar*) to disturb; (*incomodar*) to upset; **turbarse** *vr* to be disturbed.

turbina [tur'ßina] *nf* turbine.

turbio, a ['turßjo, a] *a* cloudy; (*lenguaje*) confused // *ad* indistinctly.

turbión [tur'ßjon] *nf* (*fig*) shower.

turbohélice [turßo'eliθe] *nm* turboprop.

turbulencia [turßu'lenθja] *nf* turbulence; (*fig*) restlessness; **turbulento, a** *a* turbulent; (*fig: intranquilo*) restless; (: *ruidoso*) noisy.

turco, a ['turko, a] *a* Turkish.

turismo [tu'rismo] *nm* tourism; (*coche*) saloon car; **turista** *nm/f* tourist; **turístico, a** *a* tourist *cpd*.

turnar [tur'nar] *vi*, **~se** *vr* to take (it in) turns; **turno** *nm* (*INDUSTRIA*) shift; (*oportunidad*, *orden de prioridad*) opportunity; (*DEPORTE etc*) turn.

turquesa [tur'kesa] *nf* turquoise.

Turquía [tur'kia] *nf* Turkey.

turrón [tu'rron] *nm* (*dulce*) nougat; (*fam*) sinecure.

tutear [tute'ar] *vt* to address as familiar 'tú'; **~se** *vr* to be on familiar terms.

tutela [tu'tela] *nf* (*legal*) guardianship; (*instrucción*) guidance; **tutelar** *a* tutelary // *vt* to protect.

tutor, a [tu'tor, a] *nm/f* (*legal*) guardian; (*ESCOL*) tutor.

tuve, tuviera *etc vb ver* **tener**.

tuyo, a ['tujo, a] *a* yours, of yours // *pron* yours; **los ~s** (*fam*) your relations, your family.

TVE *nf abr de* **Televisión Española**.

U

u [u] *conj* or.

ubérrimo, a [u'ßerrimo, a] *a* very rich, fertile.

ubicar [ußi'kar] *vt* (*AM*) to place, situate; (: *fig*) to install in a post; **~se** *vr* to lie, be located.

ubicuo, a [u'ßikwo, a] *a* ubiquitous.

ubre ['ußre] *nf* udder.

U.C.D. *abr de* **Unión del Centro Democrático.**

Ud(s) *abr de* **usted(es).**

ufanarse [ufa'narse] *vr* to boast; **~ de** to pride o.s. on; **ufano, a** *a* (*arrogante*) arrogant; (*presumido*) conceited.

U.G.T. *abr de* **Unión General de Trabajadores.**

ujier [u'xjer] *nm* usher; (*portero*) doorkeeper.

úlcera ['ulθera] *nf* ulcer; **ulcerar** *vt* to make sore; **ulcerarse** *vr* to ulcerate.

ulterior [ulte'rjor] *a* (*más allá*) farther, further; (*subsecuente*, *siguiente*) subsequent; **~mente** *ad* later, subsequently.

últimamente [ultima'mente] *ad* (*recientemente*) lately, recently; (*finalmente*) finally; (*como último recurso*) as a last resort.

ultimar [ulti'mar] *vt* to finish; (*finalizar*) to finalize; (*AM: rematar*) to finish off.

último, a ['ultimo, a] *a* last; (*más reciente*) latest, most recent; (*más bajo*) bottom; (*más alto*) top; (*fig*) final, extreme; **en las ~as** on one's last legs; **por ~** finally.

ultra ['ultra] *a* ultra // *nm/f* extreme right-winger.

ultrajar [ultra'xar] *vt* (*escandalizar*) to outrage; (*insultar*) to insult, abuse; **ultraje** *nm* outrage; insult.

ultramar [ultra'mar] *nm*: **de** *o* **en ~** abroad, overseas; **~ino, a** *a* overseas, foreign; **~inos** *nmpl* groceries; **tienda de ~inos** grocer's (shop).

ultranza [ul'tranθa]: **a ~** *ad* to the death; (*a todo trance*) at all costs; (*completo*) outright.

ultrasónico, a [ultra'soniko, a] *a* ultrasonic.

ulular [ulu'lar] *vi* to howl; (*búho*) to hoot.

umbral [um'bral] *nm* (*gen*) threshold.

umbroso, a [um'broso, a], **umbrío, a** [um'brio, a] *a* shady.

un, una [un, 'una] *det a* // *num* one; *ver* **uno.**

unánime [u'nanime] *a* unanimous; **unanimidad** *nf* unanimity.

unción [un'θjon] *nf* anointing; **extrema ~** Extreme Unction.

undécimo, a [un'deθimo, a] *a* eleventh.

undular [undu'lar] *vi ver* **ondular.**

ungir [un'xir] *vt* to rub with ointment; (*REL*) to anoint.

ungüento [un'gwento] *nm* ointment; (*fig*) salve, balm.

únicamente ['unikamente] *ad* solely; (*solamente*) only; **único, a** *a* only; (*solo*) sole, single; (*sin par*) unique.

unidad [uni'ðað] *nf* unity; (*TEC*) unit.

unido, a [u'niðo, a] *a* joined, linked; (*fig*) united.

unificar [unifi'kar] *vt* to unite, unify.

uniformar [unifor'mar] *vt* to make uniform, level up; (*persona*) to put into uniform; **uniforme** *a* uniform, equal; (*superficie*) even // *nm* uniform; **uniformidad** *nf* uniformity; (*llaneza*) levelness, evenness.

unilateral [unilate'ral] *a* unilateral.

unión [u'njon] *nf* (*gen*) union; (*acto*) uniting, joining; (*calidad*) unity; (*TEC*) joint; (*fig*) closeness, togetherness; **la U~** **Soviética** the Soviet Union.

unir [u'nir] *vt* (*juntar*) to join, unite; (*atar*) to tie, fasten; (*combinar*) to combine // *vi* to mix well; **~se** *vr* to join together, unite; (*empresas*) to merge.

unísono [u'nisono] *nm*: **al ~** in unison.

universal [uniβer'sal] *a* universal; (*mundial*) world *cpd*.

universidad [uniβersi'ðað] *nf* university.

universo [uni'βerso] *nm* universe.

uno ['uno] *num, det* one // *pron* one; (*alguien*) someone, somebody; **~s** some, a few; **~ a ~, ~ por ~** one by one; **cada ~** each *or* every one; **estar en ~** to be at one; **~ que otro** some, a few; **~s y otros** all of them; **~ y otro** both.

untar [un'tar] *vt* (*gen*) to rub; (*engrasar*) to grease, oil; (*MED*) to rub with ointment; (*fig*) to bribe; **~se** *vr* to be crooked; **unto** *nm* animal fat; (*MED*) ointment; (*fam*) slush fund.

uña ['uɲa] *nf* (*ANAT*) nail; (*garra*) claw; (*casco*) hoof; (*arrancaclavos*) claw.

uranio [u'ranjo] *nm* uranium.

urbanidad [urβani'ðað] *nf* courtesy, politeness.

urbanismo [urβa'nismo] *nm* town planning.

urbanización [urβaniθa'θjon] *nf* housing scheme.

urbano, a [ur'βano, a] *a* (*de ciudad*) urban; (*cortés*) courteous, polite.

urbe [ur'βe] *nf* large city.

urdimbre [ur'ðimbre] *nf* (*de tejido*) warp; (*intriga*) intrigue; **urdir** *vt* to warp; (*fig*) to plot, contrive.

urgencia [ur'xenθja] *nf* urgency; (*prisa*) haste, rush; **servicios de ~** emergency services; **urgente** *a* urgent; (*insistente*) insistent; **urgir** *vi* to be urgent.

urinario, a [uri'narjo, a] *a* urinary // *nm* urinal.

urna ['urna] *nf* urn; (*POL*) ballot box.

urraca [u'rraka] *nf* magpie.

URSS *nf*: **la ~** the USSR.

Uruguay [uru'rwai] *nm*: **el ~** Uruguay; **uruguayo, a** *a, nm/f* Uruguayan.

usado, a [u'saðo, a] *a* (*gen*) used; (*ropa etc*) worn.

usanza [u'sanθa] *nf* custom, usage.

usar [u'sar] *vt* to use; (*ropa*) to wear; (*tener costumbre*) to be in the habit of; **~se** *vr* to be used; **uso** *nm* use; wear; (*costumbre*) usage, custom; (*moda*) fashion; **al uso in** keeping with custom; **al uso de** in the style of.

usted [us'teð] *pron* you.

usual [u'swal] *a* usual.

usuario, a [usu'arjo, a] *nm/f* user.

usura [u'sura] *nf* usury; **usurero, a** *nm/f* usurer.

usurpar [usur'par] *vt* to usurp.

utensilio [uten'siljo] *nm* tool; (*CULIN*) utensil.

útero ['utero] *nm* uterus, womb.

útil ['util] *a* useful // *nm* tool; **utilidad** *nf* usefulness; (*COM*) profit; **utilizar** *vt* to use, utilize.

utopía [uto'pia] *nf* Utopia; **utópico, a** *a* Utopian.

uva ['uβa] *nf* grape.

V

v *abr de* **voltio.**

va *vb ver* **ir.**

vaca ['baka] *nf* (*animal*) cow; (*carne*) beef; (*cuero*) cowhide.

vacaciones [baka'θjones] *nfpl* holidays.

vacante [ba'kante] *a* vacant, empty // *nf* vacancy.

vacar [ba'kar] *vi* to fall vacant; **~ a** *o* **en** to devote o.s. to.

vaciado, a [ba'θjaðo, a] *a* (*hecho en molde*) cast in a mould; (*hueco*) hollow // *nm* cast.

vaciar [ba'θjar] *vt* to empty out; (*ahuecar*) to hollow out; (*moldear*) to cast // *vi* (*río*) to flow (into); **~se** *vr* to empty; (*fig*) to blab, spill the beans.

vaciedad [baθje'ðað] *nf* emptiness.

vacilación [baθila'θjon] *nf* hesitation; **vacilante** *a* unsteady; (*habla*) faltering; (*fig*) hesitant; **vacilar** *vi* to be unsteady; to falter; to hesitate, waver; (*persona*) to stagger, stumble; (*memoria*) to fail.

vacío, a [ba'θio, a] *a* empty; (*puesto*) vacant; (*desocupado*) idle; (*vano*) vain // *nm* emptiness; (*FÍSICA*) vacuum; (*un ~*) (empty) space.

vacuna [ba'kuna] *nf* vaccine; **vacunar** *vt* to vaccinate.

vacuno, a [ba'kuno, a] *a* bovine.

vacuo, a ['bakwo, a] *a* empty.

vadear [baðe'ar] *vt* (*río*) to ford; (*problema*) to overcome; (*persona*) to sound out; **vado** *nm* ford; (*solución*) solution; (*descanso*) respite.

vagabundo, a [baɣa'βundo, a] *a* wandering; (*pey*) vagrant // *nm* tramp.

vagamente [baɣa'mente] *ad* vaguely.

vagancia [ba'ɣanθja] *nf* vagrancy; **vagar** *vi* (*gen*) to wander; (*no hacer nada*) to idle // *nm* leisure.

vagido [ba'xiðo] *nm* wail.

vagina [ba'xina] *nf* vagina.

vago, a ['baxo, a] *a* vague; (*perezoso*) lazy; (*ambulante*) wandering // *nm/f* (*vagabundo*) tramp; (*flojo*) lazybones *sg*, idler.

vagón [ba'xon] *nm* (*de pasajeros*) carriage; (*de mercancías*) wagon.

vaguedad [baxe'ðað] *nf* vagueness.

vaho ['bao] *nm* (*vapor*) vapour, steam; (*olor*) smell; (*respiración*) breath.

vaina ['baina] *nf* sheath.

vainilla [bai'niʎa] *nf* vanilla.

vais *vb ver* **ir.**

vaivén [bai'ßen] *nm* to-and-fro movement; (*de tránsito*) coming and going; **vaivenes** *nmpl* (*fig*) ups and downs.

vajilla [ba'xiʎa] *nf* crockery, dishes *pl*.

val, valdré *etc vb ver* **valer.**

vale ['bale] *nm* voucher; (*recibo*) receipt; (*pagaré*) I.O.U.

valedero, a [bale'ðero, a] *a* valid.

valenciano, a [balen'θjano, a] *a* Valencian.

valentía [balen'tia] *nf* courage, bravery; (*pey*) boastfulness; (*acción*) heroic deed; **valentón, ona** *a* blustering.

valer [ba'ler] *vt* to aid, protect; (*MAT*) to equal // *vi* to be worth; (*costar*) to cost; (*ser útil*) to be useful; (*ser válido*) to be valid; ~**se** *vr* to defend o.s.; ~**se de** to make use of, take advantage of // *nm* worth, value; ~ **la pena** to be worthwhile; ¿**vale?** O. K.?

valgo *etc vb ver* **valer.**

validar [bali'ðar] *vt* to validate; **validez** *nf* validity; **válido, a** *a* valid.

valiente [ba'ljente] *a* brave, valiant; (*pey*) boastful // *nm* hero.

valija [ba'lixa] *nf* case; (*mochila*) satchel.

valioso, a [ba'ljoso, a] *a* valuable; (*rico*) wealthy.

valor [ba'lor] *nm* value, worth; (*precio*) price; (*valentía*) valour, courage; (*importancia*) importance; ~**es** *nmpl* (*COM*) securities; ~**ación** *nf* valuation; ~**ar** *vt* to value.

vals [bals] *nm* waltz.

válvula ['balßula] *nf* valve.

valla ['baʎa] *nf* fence; (*DEPORTE*) hurdle; (*fig*) barrier; **vallar** *vt* to fence in.

valle ['baʎe] *nm* valley, vale.

vamos *vb ver* **ir.**

vampiro, resa [bam'piro, i'resa] *nm/f* vampire.

van *vb ver* **ir.**

vanagloriarse [banaxlo'rjarse] *vr* to boast.

vándalo, a ['bandalo, a] *nm/f* vandal; **vandalismo** *nm* vandalism.

vanguardia [ban'gwardja] *nf* vanguard; (*ARTE*) avant-garde.

vanidad [bani'ðað] *nf* vanity; (*irrealidad*) unreality; **vanidoso, a** *a* vain, conceited.

vano, a ['bano, a] *a* (*irreal*) unreal; (*irracional*) unreasonable; (*inútil*) useless;

(*persona*) vain, conceited; (*frívolo*) frivolous.

vapor [ba'por] *nm* vapour; (*vaho*) steam; (*neblina*) mist; ~**es** *nmpl* (*MED*) hysterics; **al** ~ (*CULIN*) steamed; ~**izar** *vt* to vaporize; ~**oso, a** *a* vaporous; (*vahoso*) steamy.

vaquero, a [ba'kero, a] *a* cattle *cpd* // *nm* cowboy; ~**s** *nmpl* jeans.

vara ['bara] *nf* stick, wand; (*TEC*) rod.

varear [bare'ar] *vt* to hit, beat.

variable [ba'rjaßle] *a, nf* variable; **variación** *nf* variation; **variar** *vt* to vary; (*modificar*) to modify; (*cambiar de posición*) to switch around // *vi* to vary; **variedad** *nf* variety.

varilla [ba'riʎa] *nf* stick; (*BOT*) twig; (*TEC*) rod; (*de rueda*) spoke.

vario, a ['barjo, a] *a* (*variado*) varied; (*multicolor*) motley; (*cambiable*) changeable; ~**s** various, several.

varón [ba'ron] *nm* male, man; **varonil** *a* manly.

Varsovia [bar'soßja] *n* Warsaw.

vas *vb ver* **ir.**

vascongado, a [baskon'xaðo, a], **vascuence** [bas'kwenθe], **vasco, a** ['basko, a] *a* Basque; **las Vascongadas** the Basque Country.

vaselina [base'lina] *nf* vaseline.

vasija [ba'sixa] *nf* container, vessel.

vaso ['baso] *nm* glass, tumbler; (*ANAT*) vessel.

vástago ['bastaxo] *nm* (*BOT*) shoot; (*TEC*) rod; (*fig*) offspring.

vasto, a ['basto, a] *a* vast, huge.

Vaticano [bati'kano] *nm*: **el** ~ the Vatican.

vaticinio [bati'θinjo] *nm* prophecy.

vatio ['batjo] *nm* (*ELEC*) watt.

vaya *etc vb ver* **ir.**

Vd(s) *abr de* **usted(es).**

ve *vb ver* **ir, ver.**

vecindad [beθin'dað] *nf*, **vecindario** [beθin'darjo] *nm* neighbourhood; (*habitantes*) residents *pl*; **vecino, a** *a* neighbouring // *nm/f* neighbour; (*residente*) resident.

veda ['beða] *nf* prohibition.

vedado [be'ðaðo] *nm* preserve.

vedar [be'ðar] *vt* (*prohibir*) to ban, prohibit; (*impedir*) to stop, prevent.

vegetación [bexeta'θjon] *nf* vegetation.

vegetal [bexe'tal] *a, nm* vegetable.

vehemencia [bee'menθja] *nf* (*insistencia*) vehemence; (*pasión*) passion; (*fervor*) fervour; (*violencia*) violence; **vehemente** *a* vehement; passionate; fervent.

vehículo [be'ikulo] *nm* vehicle; (*MED*) carrier.

veía *etc vb ver* **ver.**

veinte ['beinte] *num* twenty.

vejación [bexa'θjon] *nf* vexation; (*humillación*) humiliation.

vejamen [be'xamen] *nm* satire.

vejar [be'xar] *vt* (*irritar*) to annoy, vex; (*humillar*) to humiliate.

vejez [be'xeθ] *nf* old age.

vejiga [be'xiɣa] *nf* (ANAT) bladder.

vela ['bela] *nf* (*de cera*) candle; (NAUT) sail; (*insomnio*) sleeplessness; (*vigilia*) vigil; (MIL) sentry duty; (*fam*) snot; **estar a dos ~s** (*fam*) to be skint (*fam*).

velado, a [be'laðo, a] *a* veiled; (*sonido*) muffled; (FOTO) blurred // *nf* soirée.

velador [bela'ðor] *nm* watchman; (*candelero*) candlestick.

velar [be'lar] *vt* (*hacer guardia*) to keep watch over; (*cubrir*) to veil // *vi* to stay awake; **~ por** to watch over, look after.

veleidad [belei'ðað] *nf* (*ligereza*) fickleness; (*capricho*) whim.

velero [be'lero] *nm* (NAUT) sailing ship; (AVIAT) glider.

veleta [be'leta] *nf* weather vane.

velo ['belo] *nm* veil.

velocidad [beloθi'ðað] *nf* speed; (TEC, AUTO) gear.

velocímetro [belo'θimetro] *nm* speedometer.

velódromo [be'loðromo] *nm* cycle track.

veloz [be'loθ] *a* fast.

vello ['beʎo] *nm* down, fuzz; **vellón** *nm* fleece; **~so, a** *a* fuzzy; **velludo, a** *a* shaggy // *nm* plush, velvet.

ven *vb ver* **venir**.

vena ['bena] *nf* vein.

venablo [be'naβlo] *nm* javelin.

venado [be'naðo] *nm* deer.

venal [be'nal] *a* (ANAT) venous; (*pey*) venal; **~idad** *nf* venality.

vencedor, a [benθe'ðor, a] *a* victorious // *nm/f* victor, winner.

vencer [ben'θer] *vt* (*dominar*) to defeat, beat; (*derrotar*) to vanquish; (*superar, controlar*) to overcome, master // *vi* (*triunfar*) to win (through), triumph; (*plazo*) to expire; **vencido, a** *a* (*derrotado*) defeated, beaten; (COM) due // *ad*: **pagar vencido** to pay in arrears; **vencimiento** *nm* collapse; (COM) maturity.

venda ['benda] *nf* bandage; **~je** *nm* bandage, dressing; **vendar** *vt* to bandage; **vendar los ojos** to blindfold.

vendaval [benda'βal] *nm* (*viento*) gale; (*huracán*) hurricane.

vendedor, a [bende'ðor, a] *nm/f* seller.

vender [ben'der] *vt* to sell; **~ al contado/al por mayor/al por menor** to sell for cash/wholesale/retail.

vendimia [ben'dimja] *nf* grape harvest.

vendré *etc vb ver* **venir**.

veneno [be'neno] *nm* poison, venom; **~so, a** *a* poisonous.

venerable [bene'raβle] *a* venerable; **veneración** *nf* veneration; **venerar** *vt* (*reconocer*) to venerate; (*adorar*) to worship.

venéreo, a [be'nereo, a] *a* venereal.

venero [be'nero] *nm* (*veta*) seam, lode; (*fuente*) spring.

venezolano, a [beneθo'lano, a] *a* Venezuelan.

Venezuela [beneˈθwela] *nf* Venezuela.

venganza [ben'ganθa] *nf* vengeance, revenge; **vengar** *vt* to avenge; **vengarse** *vr* to take revenge; **vengativo, a** *a* (*persona*) vindictive.

vengo *etc vb ver* **venir**.

venia ['benja] *nf* (*perdón*) pardon; (*permiso*) consent.

venial [be'njal] *a* venial.

venida [be'niða] *nf* (*llegada*) arrival; (*regreso*) return; (*fig*) rashness.

venidero, a [beni'ðero, a] *a* coming, future.

venir [be'nir] *vi* to come; (*llegar*) to arrive; (*fig*) to stem from; (*ocurrir*) to happen; **~ bien/mal** to be suitable/unsuitable; **el año que viene** next year; **~se abajo** to collapse.

venta ['benta] *nf* (COM) sale; **~ a plazos** hire purchase; **~ al contado/al por mayor/al por menor** *o* **al detalle** cash sale/wholesale/retail; **~ de liquidación** clearance sale.

ventaja [ben'taxa] *nf* advantage; **ventajoso, a** *a* advantageous.

ventana [ben'tana] *nf* window; **~ de guillotina/saial** sash/bay window; **ventanilla** *nf* (*de taquilla*) window (*of booking office etc*).

ventear [bente'ar] *vt* (*ropa*) to hang out to dry; (*oler*) to sniff // *vi* (*investigar*) to investigate; (*soplar*) to blow; **~se** *vr* (*romperse*) to crack; (ANAT) to break wind.

ventilación [bentila'θjon] *nf* ventilation; (*corriente*) draught; **ventilar** *vt* to ventilate; (*a secar*) to put out to dry; (*fig*) to air, discuss.

ventisca [ben'tiska] *nf*, **ventisquero** [bentis'kero] *nm* blizzard; (*nieve amontonada*) snowdrift.

ventosear [bentose'ar] *vi* to break wind.

ventoso, a [ben'toso, a] *a* windy.

ventrílocuo, a [ben'trilokwo, a] *nm/f* ventriloquist; **ventriloquia** *nf* ventriloquism.

ventura [ben'tura] *nf* (*felicidad*) happiness; (*buena suerte*) luck; (*destino*) fortune; **a la (buena) ~** at random; **venturoso, a** *a* happy; (*afortunado*) lucky, fortunate.

veo *etc vb ver* **ver**.

ver [ber] *vt, vi* to see; (*mirar*) to look at, watch; (*investigar*) to look into; **~se** *vr* (*encontrarse*) to meet; (*dejarse*) to be seen; (*hallarse: en un apuro*) to find o.s., be // *nm* looks *pl*, appearance; **a ~** let's see; **dejarse ~** to become apparent; **no tener nada que ~ con** to have nothing to do with; **a mi modo de ~** as I see it.

vera ['bera] *nf* edge, verge; (*de río*) bank.

veracidad [beraθi'ðað] *nf* truthfulness.

veranear [berane'ar] *vi* to spend the summer; **veraneo** *nm* summer holiday; **veraniego, a** *a* summer *cpd*; **verano** *nm* summer.

veras ['beras] *nfpl* truth *sg*; **de ~** really, truly.

veraz [be'raθ] *a* truthful.

verbal [ber'βal] *a* verbal.

verbena [ber'βena] *nf* street party.

verbigracia [berβi'xraθja] *ad* for example.

verbo ['berβo] *nm* verb; **~so, a** *a* verbose.

verdad [ber'ðað] *nf* (*lo verídico*) truth; (*fiabilidad*) reliability // *a* really; **de ~** *a* real, proper; **a decir ~** to tell the truth; **~ero, a** *a* (*veraz*) true, truthful; (*fiable*) reliable; (*fig*) real.

verde ['berðe] *a* green; (*sucio*) blue, dirty // *nm* green; **viejo ~** dirty old man; **~ar, ~cer** *vi* to turn green; **verdor** *nm* (*lo ~*) greenness; (*BOT*) verdure; (*fig*) youthful vigour.

verdugo [ber'ðuxo] *nm* executioner; (*BOT*) shoot; (*cardenal*) weal.

verdulero, a [berðu'lero, a] *nm/f* greengrocer.

verdura [ber'ðura] *nf* greenness; **~s** *nfpl* (*CULIN*) greens.

vereda [be'reða] *nf* path.

veredicto [bere'ðikto] *nm* verdict.

vergonzoso, a [berxon'θoso, a] *a* shameful; (*tímido*) timid, bashful.

vergüenza [ber'xwenθa] *nf* shame, sense of shame; (*timidez*) bashfulness; (*pudor*) modesty.

verídico, a [be'riðiko, a] *a* true, truthful.

verificar [berifi'kar] *vt* (*corroborar*) to verify; (*llevar a cabo*) to carry out; **~se** *vr* to occur, happen.

verja ['berxa] *nf* grating.

vermut [ber'mut] *nm* vermouth.

verosímil [bero'simil] *a* likely, probable; (*relato*) credible.

verruga [be'rruxa] *nf* wart.

versado, a [ber'saðo, a] *a*: **~ en** versed in.

versar [ber'sar] *vi* to go round, turn.

versátil [ber'satil] *a* versatile.

versión [ber'sjon] *nf* version; (*traducción*) translation.

verso ['berso] *nm* (*gen*) verse; **un ~** a line of poetry.

vértebra ['berteβra] *nf* vertebra.

verter [ber'ter] *vt* (*vaciar*) to empty, pour (out); (*tirar*) to dump // *vi* to flow.

vertical [berti'kal] *a* vertical.

vértice ['bertiθe] *nm* vertex, apex.

vertiente [ber'tjente] *nf* slope.

vertiginoso, a [bertixi'noso, a] *a* giddy, dizzy; **vértigo** *nm* vertigo; (*mareo*) dizziness.

vesícula [be'sikula] *nf* blister.

vespertino, a [besper'tino, a] *a* evening *cpd*.

vestíbulo [bes'tiβulo] *nm* hall; (*de teatro*) foyer.

vestido [bes'tiðo] *nm* (*ropa*) clothes *pl*, clothing; (*de mujer*) dress, frock.

vestigio [bes'tixjo] *nm* (*trazo*) trace; (*señal*) sign; **~s** *nmpl* remains.

vestimenta [besti'menta] *nf* clothing.

vestir [bes'tir] *vt* (*poner: ropa*) to put on; (*llevar: ropa*) to wear; (*cubrir*) to clothe, cover; (*pagar: la ropa*) to pay for the clothing of; (*sastre*) to make clothes for // *vi* (*ponerse: ropa*) to dress; (*verse bien*) to look good; **~se** *vr* to get dressed, dress o.s.

vestuario [bes'twarjo] *nm* clothes *pl*, wardrobe; (*TEATRO*) dressing room; (*DEPORTE*) changing room.

veta ['beta] *nf* (*vena*) vein, seam; (*raya*) streak; (*de madera*) grain.

vetar [be'tar] *vt* to veto.

veterano, a [bete'rano, a] *a, nm* veteran.

veterinario, a [beteri'narjo, a] *nm/f* vet(erinary surgeon) // *nf* veterinary science.

veto ['beto] *nm* veto.

vetusto, a [be'tusto, a] *a* ancient.

vez [beθ] *nf* time; (*turno*) turn; **a la ~ que** at the same time as; **a su ~** in its turn; **cada ~ más/menos** more and more/less and less; **una ~** once; **de una ~** in one go; **de una ~ para siempre** once and for all; **en ~ de** instead of; **a veces** sometimes; **una y otra ~** repeatedly; **de ~ en cuando** from time to time; **7 veces 9** 7 times 9; **hacer las veces de** to stand in for; **tal ~** perhaps.

v. g., v. gr. *abr de* **verbigracia.**

vía ['bia] *nf* track, route; (*FERRO*) line; (*fig*) way; (*ANAT*) passage, tube // *prep* via, by way of; **por ~ judicial** by legal means; **por ~ oficial** through official channels; **por ~ de** by way of; **en ~s de** in the process of; **~ aérea** airway.

viaducto [bja'ðukto] *nm* viaduct.

viajante [bja'xante] *nm* commercial traveller.

viajar [bja'xar] *vi* to travel; **viaje** *nm* journey; (*gira*) tour; (*NAUT*) voyage; **estar de viaje** to be on a journey; **viaje de ida y vuelta** round trip; **viaje de novios** honeymoon; **~ a a** *a* (*viajar*) travelling; (*ZOOL*) migratory // *nm/f* (*quien viaja*) traveller; (*pasajero*) passenger.

vial [bjal] *a* road *cpd*, traffic *cpd*.

víbora ['biβora] *nf* viper.

vibración [biβra'θjon] *nf* vibration; **vibrador** *nm* vibrator; **vibrante** *a* vibrant; **vibrar** *vt, vi* to vibrate.

vicario [bi'karjo] *nm* curate.

vicepresidente [biθepresi'ðente] *nm/f* vice president.

viciado, a [bi'θjaðo, a] *a* (*corrompido*) corrupt; (*contaminado*) foul, contaminated; **viciar** *vt* (*pervertir*) to pervert; (*adulterar*) to adulterate; (*falsificar*) to falsify; (*JUR*) to nullify; (*estropear*) to spoil; (*sentido*) to twist; **viciarse** *vr* to become corrupted.

vicio ['biθjo] *nm* (*libertinaje*) vice; (*mala costumbre*) bad habit; (*mimo*) spoiling; (*alabeo*) warp, warping; **~so, a** *a* (*muy malo*) vicious; (*corrompido*) depraved; (*mimado*) spoiled // *nm/f* depraved person.

vicisitud [biθisi'tuð] *nf* vicissitude.

víctima ['biktima] *nf* victim.

victoria [bik'torja] *nf* victory; **victorioso,**
a *a* victorious.

vicuña [bi'kuɲa] *nf* vicuna.

vid [bið] *nf* vine.

vida ['biða] *nf* (*gen*) life; (*duración*)
lifetime; **de por ~** for life; **en la/mi ~**
never; **estar con ~** to be still alive;
ganarse la ~ to earn one's living.

vidriero, a [bi'ðrjero, a] *nm/f* glazier // *nf*
(*ventana*) stained-glass window; (*puerta*)
glass door.

vidrio ['biðrjo] *nm* glass; **~so,** *a a* glassy;
(*frágil*) fragile, brittle; (*resbaladizo*)
slippery.

viejo, a ['bjexo, a] *a* old // *nm/f* old
man/woman.

vienes *etc vb ver* **venir.**

vienés, esa [bje'nes, esa] *a* Viennese.

viento ['bjento] *nm* wind; (*olfato*) scent.

vientre ['bjentre] *nm* belly; (*matriz*)
womb; **~s** *nmpl* bowels.

viernes ['bjernes] *nm inv* Friday.

Vietnam [bjet'nam] *nm*: **el ~** Vietnam;
vietnamita *a* Vietnamese.

viga ['biɣa] *nf* beam, rafter.

vigencia [bi'xenθja] *nf* validity; **estar en**
~ to be in force; **vigente** *a* valid, in force;
(*imperante*) prevailing.

vigésimo, a [bi'xesimo, a] *a* twentieth.

vigía [bi'xia] *nm* look-out // *nf* (*atalaya*)
watchtower; (*acción*) watching.

vigilancia [bixi'lanθja] *nf* vigilance;
vigilar *vt* to watch over // *vi* (*gen*) to be
vigilant; (*hacer guardia*) to keep watch.

vigilia [vi'xilja] *nf* wakefulness, being
awake; (*REL*) fast; **comer de ~** to fast.

vigor [bi'xor] *nm* vigour, vitality; **en ~** in
force; **entrar/poner en ~** to take/put
into effect; **~oso,** *a a* vigorous.

vil [bil] *a* vile, low; **~eza** *nf* vileness; (*acto*)
base deed.

vilipendiar [bilipen'djar] *vt* to vilify,
revile.

vilo ['bilo]: **en ~** *ad* in the air, suspended.

villa ['biʎa] *nf* (*pueblo*) small town;
(*municipalidad*) municipality.

villorrio [bi'ʎorrjo] *nm* one-horse town,
dump (*fam*).

vinagre [bi'naɣre] *nm* vinegar.

vinculación [binkula'θjon] *nf* (*lazo*) link,
bond; (*acción*) linking; **vincular** *vt* to link,
bind; **vínculo** *nm* link, bond.

vindicar [bindi'kar] *vt* to vindicate;
(*vengar*) to avenge; (*JUR*) to claim.

vine *etc vb ver* **venir.**

vinicultura [binikul'tura] *nf* wine
growing.

viniera *etc vb ver* **venir.**

vino ['bino] *nm* wine.

viña ['biɲa] *nf*, **viñedo** [bi'ɲeðo] *nm*
vineyard.

violación [bjola'θjon] *nf* violation; **~**
(**sexual**) rape; **violar** *vt* to violate; to
rape.

violencia [bjo'lenθja] *nf* (*fuerza*) violence,

force; (*embarazo*) embarrassment; (*acto*
injusto) unjust act; **violentar** *vt* to force;
(*casa*) to break into; (*agredir*) to assault;
(*violar*) to violate; **violento, a** *a* violent;
(*furioso*) furious; (*situación*) embarrassing;
(*acto*) forced, unnatural; (*difícil*) awkward.

violeta [bjo'leta] *nf* violet.

violín [bjo'lin] *nm* violin.

violón [bjo'lon] *nm* double bass.

viraje [bi'raxe] *nm* turn; (*de vehículo*)
swerve; (*de carretera*) bend; (*fig*) change
of direction; **virar** *vt*, *vi* to change
direction.

virgen ['birxen] *a*, *nf* virgin.

Virgo ['birxo] *nm* Virgo.

viril [bi'ril] *a* virile; **~idad** *nf* virility.

virtualmente [birtwal'mente] *ad*
virtually.

virtud [bir'tuð] *nf* virtue; **virtuoso, a** *a*
virtuous // *nm/f* virtuoso.

viruela [bi'rwela] *nf* smallpox; **~s** *nfpl*
pockmarks; **~s locas** chickenpox.

virulento, a [biru'lento, a] *a* virulent.

virus ['birus] *nm* virus.

visado [bi'saðo] *nm* visa.

viscoso, a [bis'koso, a] *a* viscous.

visera [bi'sera] *nf* visor.

visibilidad [bisiβili'ðað] *nf* visibility;
visible *a* visible; (*fig*) obvious.

visión [bi'sjon] *nf* (*ANAT*) vision, (eye)sight;
(*fantasía*) vision, fantasy; (*panorama*) view;
visionario, a *a* (*que preve*) visionary;
(*alucinado*) deluded // *nm/f* visionary;
(*chalado*) lunatic.

visita [bi'sita] *nf* call, visit; (*persona*)
visitor; **visitar** *vt* to visit, call on;
(*inspeccionar*) to inspect.

vislumbrar [bislum'brar] *vt* to glimpse,
catch a glimpse of; **vislumbre** *nf* glimpse;
(*centelleo*) gleam; (*idea vaga*) glimmer.

viso ['biso] *nm* (*del metal*) glint, gleam; (*de*
tela) sheen; (*aspecto*) appearance.

visón [bi'son] *nm* mink.

visor [bi'sor] *nm* (*FOTO*) viewfinder.

víspera ['bispera] *nf* eve, day before.

vista ['bista] *nf* sight, vision; (*capacidad de*
ver) (eye)sight; (*mirada*) look(s) (*pl*) // *nm*
customs officer; **a primera ~** at first
glance; **volver la ~** to look back; **está a la**
~ que it's obvious that; **en ~ de** in view
of; **en ~ de que** in view of the fact that;
¡hasta la ~! so long!, see you!; **con ~s a**
with a view to; **~zo** *nm* glance; **dar** *o*
echar un ~zo a to glance at.

visto *etc vb ver* **vestir.**

visto, a ['bisto, a] *pp de ver* // *a* seen;
(*considerado*) considered // *nm*: **~ bueno**
approval; **'~ bueno'** approved; **por lo ~**
evidently; **está ~ que** it's clear that; **está**
bien/mal ~ it's acceptable/unaccept-
able; **~ que** *conj* since, considering that.

vistoso, a [bis'toso, a] *a* colourful; (*alegre*)
gay; (*pey*) gaudy.

vital [bi'tal] *a* life *cpd*, living *cpd*; (*fig*) vital;
(*persona*) lively, vivacious; **~icio, a** *a* for
life.

vitamina [bita'mina] *nf* vitamin.
viticultor, a [bitikul'tor, a] *nm/f* vine grower; **viticultura** *nf* vine growing.
vitorear [bitore'ar] *vt* to cheer, acclaim.
vítreo, a ['bitreo, a] *a* vitreous.
vitrina [bi'trina] *nf* glass case.
vituperar [bitupe'rar] *vt* to condemn; **vituperio** *nm* (*condena*) condemnation; (*censura*) censure; (*insulto*) insult.
viudo, a ['bjuðo, a] *a* *nm/f* widower/widow; **viudez** *nf* widowhood.
vivacidad [biβaθi'ðað] *nf* (*vigor*) vigour; (*vida*) vivacity.
vivaracho, a [biβa'ratʃo, a] *a* jaunty, lively; (*ojos*) bright, twinkling.
vivaz [bi'βaθ] *a* (*que dura*) enduring; (*vigoroso*) vigorous; (*vivo*) lively.
víveres ['biβeres] *nmpl* provisions.
viveza [bi'βeθa] *nf* liveliness; (*agudeza*) sharpness.
vivienda [bi'βjenda] *nf* (*alojamiento*) housing; (*morada*) dwelling.
viviente [bi'βjente] *a* living.
vivificar [biβifi'kar] *vt* to give life to.
vivir [bi'βir] *vt, vi* to live // *nm* life, living.
vivo, a ['biβo, a] *a* living, live, alive; (*fig*) vivid; (*astuto*) smart, clever; **llegar a lo** ~ to cut to the quick.
vocablo [bo'kaβlo] *nm* (*palabra*) word; (*término*) term.
vocabulario [bokaβu'larjo] *nm* vocabulary.
vocación [boka'θjon] *nf* vocation.
vocal [bo'kal] *a* vocal // *nf* vowel; ~**izar** *vt* to vocalize.
vocear [boθe'ar] *vt* (*para vender*) to cry; (*aclamar*) to acclaim; (*fig*) to proclaim // *vi* to yell; **vocerío** *nm*, **vocería** *nf* shouting.
vocero [bo'θero] *nm/f* spokesman/woman.
vociferar [boθife'rar] *vt* to shout; (*jactarse*) to proclaim boastfully // *vi* to yell.
vociglero, a [boθin'glero, a] *a* vociferous; (*gárrulo*) garrulous; (*fig*) blatant.
vodka ['boðka] *nf* vodka.
vol *abr de* **volumen.**
volador, a [bola'ðor, a] *a* flying.
volante [bo'lante] *a* flying // *nm* (*de máquina, coche*) steering wheel; (*de reloj*) balance.
volar [bo'lar] *vt* (*demoler*) to blow up, demolish // *vi* to fly.
volátil [bo'latil] *a* volatile; (*fig*) changeable.
volcán [bol'kan] *nm* volcano; ~**ico, a** *a* volcanic.
volcar [bol'kar] *vt* to upset, overturn; (*tumbar, derribar*) to knock over; (*vaciar*) to empty out // *vi* to overturn; ~**se** *vr* to tip over.
volibol [boli'βol] *nm* volleyball.
volición [boli'θjon] *nf* volition.
voltaje [bol'taxe] *nm* voltage.
volteador, a [boltea'ðor, a] *nm/f* acrobat.

voltear [bolte'ar] *vt* to turn over; (*volcar*) to turn upside down; (*doblar*) to peal // *vi* to roll over.
voltio ['boltjo] *nm* volt.
voluble [bo'luβle] *a* fickle.
volumen [bo'lumen] *nm* volume; **voluminoso, a** *a* voluminous; (*enorme*) massive.
voluntad [bolun'tað] *nf* will, willpower; (*deseo*) desire, wish; (*afecto*) fondness.
voluntario, a [bolun'tarjo, a] *a* voluntary // *nm/f* volunteer.
voluntarioso, a [bolunta'rjoso, a] *a* headstrong.
voluptuoso, a [bolup'twoso, a] *a* voluptuous.
volver [bol'βer] *vt* (*gen*) to turn; (*dar vuelta*) to turn (over); (*voltear*) to turn round, turn upside down; (*poner al revés*) to turn inside out; (*devolver*) to return; (*transformar*) to change, transform // *vi* to return, go/come back; ~**se** *vr* to turn round; (*llegar a ser*) to become; ~ **la espalda** to turn one's back; ~ **bien por mal** to return good for evil; ~ **a hacer** to do again; ~ **en sí** to come to; ~**se loco** to go mad.
vomitar [bomi'tar] *vt, vi* to vomit; **vómito** *nm* (*acto*) vomiting; (*resultado*) vomit.
voraz [bo'raθ] *a* voracious; (*fig*) fierce.
vórtice ['bortiθe] *nm* whirlpool; (*de aire*) whirlwind.
vosotros [bo'sotros] *pron* you.
votación [bota'θjon] *nf* (*acto*) voting; (*voto*) vote; **votar** *vi* to vote; **voto** *nm* vote; (*promesa*) vow; (*maldición*) oath, curse; **votos** (good) wishes.
voy *vb ver* **ir.**
voz [boθ] *nf* voice; (*grito*) shout; (*chisme*) rumour; (*LING*) word; **dar voces** to shout, yell; **a media** ~ in a low voice; **a** ~ **en cuello o en grito** at the top of one's voice; **de viva** ~ verbally; **en** ~ **alta** aloud; ~ **de mando** command.
vuelco ['bwelko] *nm* spill, overturning; (*fig*) collapse.
vuelo ['bwelo] *vb ver* **voler** // *nm* flight; (*encaje*) lace, frill; (*fig*) importance; **coger al** ~ to catch in flight.
vuelta ['bwelta] *nf* (*gen*) turn; (*curva*) bend, curve; (*regreso*) return; (*revolución*) revolution; (*paseo*) stroll; (*circuito*) lap; (*de papel, tela*) reverse; (*cambio*) change; **V** ~ **de Francia** Tour de France; ~ **cerrada** hairpin bend; **a la** ~ on one's return; **a** ~ **de correo** by return of post; **dar** ~**s** to turn, revolve; **dar** ~**s a una idea** to turn over an idea (in one's head); **estar de** ~ (*fam*) to be back; **dar una** ~ to go for a walk.
vuelto *pp de* **volver.**
vuelvo *etc vb ver* **volver.**
vuestro, a ['bwestro, a] *a* your; **un amigo** ~ a friend of yours // *pron*: **el** ~/**la** ~**a**/**los** ~**s**/**las** ~**as** yours.
vulgar [bul'ʁar] *a* (*ordinario*) vulgar; (*común*) common; ~**idad** *nf* commonness; (*acto*) vulgarity; (*expresión*) coarse

expression; ~**idades** *nfpl* banalities; ~**izar** *vt* to popularize.
vulgo ['bulɣo] *nm* common people.
vulnerable [bulne'raβle] *a* vulnerable.
vulnerar [bulne'rar] *vt* to harm, damage.
vulpino, a [bul'pino, a] *a* vulpine; (*fig*) foxy.

W

wáter ['bater] *nm* lavatory.
wátman ['watman] *a inv* (*fam*) cool.
whisky ['wiski] *nm* whisky.

X

xenofobia [kseno'foβja] *nf* xenophobia.
xilófono [ksi'lofono] *nm* xylophone.

Y

y [i] *conj* and.
ya [ja] *ad* (*gen*) already; (*ahora*) now; (*en seguida*) at once; (*pronto*) soon // *excl* all right! // *conj* (*ahora que*) now that; ~ **lo sé** I know; ~ **dice que sí**, ~ **dice que no** first he says yes, then he says no; ~ **que** since.
yacer [ja'θer] *vi* to lie.
yacimiento [jaθi'mjento] *nm* bed, deposit.
yanqui ['janki] *a* Yankee.
yate ['jate] *nm* yacht.
yazco *etc vb ver* **yacer.**
yedra ['jeðra] *nf* ivy.
yegua ['jeɣwa] *nf* mare.
yema ['jema] *nf* (*del huevo*) yoke; (*BOT*) leaf bud; (*fig*) best part; ~ **del dedo** fingertip.
yergo *etc vb ver* **erguir.**
yermo, a ['jermo, a] *a* uninhabited // *nm* waste land.
yerno ['jerno] *nm* son-in-law.
yerro *etc vb ver* **errar.**
yerto, a ['jerto, a] *a* stiff.
yesca ['jeska] *nf* tinder.
yeso ['jeso] *nm* (*GEO*) gypsum; (*ARQ*) plaster.
yodo ['joðo] *nm* iodine.
yugo ['juɣo] *nm* yoke.
Yugoslavia [juɣos'laβja] *nf* Yugoslavia.
yugular [juɣu'lar] *a* jugular.
yunque ['junke] *nm* anvil.
yunta ['junta] *nf* yoke; **yuntero** *nm* ploughman.
yute ['jute] *nm* jute.
yuxtaponer [jukstapo'ner] *vt* to juxtapose; **yuxtaposición** *nf* juxtaposition.

Z

zafar [θa'far] *vt* (*soltar*) to untie; (*superficie*) to clear; ~**se** *vr* (*escaparse*) to escape; (*ocultarse*) to hide o.s. away; (*TEC*) to slip off.
zafio, a ['θafjo, a] *a* coarse.

zafiro [θa'firo] *nm* sapphire.
zaga ['θaɣa] *nf* rear; **a la** ~ behind, in the rear.
zagal, a [θa'ɣal, a] *nm/f* boy/girl, lad/lass.
zaguán [θa'ɣwan] *nm* hallway.
zahareño, a [θaa'reɲo, a] *a* (*salvaje*) wild; (*arisco*) unsociable.
zaherir [θae'rir] *vt* (*criticar*) to criticize; (*fig: herir*) to wound.
zahorí [θao'ri] *nm* clairvoyant.
zaino, a ['θaino, a] *a* (*color de caballo*) chestnut; (*pérfido*) treacherous; (*animal*) vicious.
zalamería [θala'merja] *nf* flattery; **zalamero, a** *a* flattering; (*relamido*) suave.
zamarra [θa'marra] *nf* (*piel*) sheepskin; (*saco*) sheepskin jacket.
zambra ['θambra] *nf* gypsy dance.
zambullirse [θambu'ʎirse] *vr* to dive; (*ocultarse*) to hide o.s.
zampar [θam'par] *vt* (*esconder*) to hide or put away (hurriedly); (*comer*) to gobble; (*arrojar*) to hurl // *vi* to eat voraciously; ~**se** *vr* (*chocar*) to bump; (*fig*) to gatecrash.
zanahoria [θana'orja] *nf* carrot.
zancada [θan'kaða] *nf* stride.
zancadilla [θanka'ðiʎa] *nf* trip; (*fig*) stratagem.
zancajo [θan'kaxo] *nm* (*ANAT*) heel; (*fig*) dwarf.
zanco ['θanko] *nm* stilt.
zancudo, a [θan'kuðo, a] *a* long-legged // *nm* (*AM*) mosquito.
zángano ['θangano] *nm* drone.
zanja ['θanxa] *nf* (*fosa*) ditch; (*tumba*) grave; **zanjar** *vt* (*fosa*) to ditch, trench; (*problema*) to surmount; (*conflicto*) to resolve.
zapapico [θapa'piko] *nm* pick, pickaxe.
zapata [θa'pata] *nf* half-boot; (*MECÁNICA*) shoe.
zapatear [θapate'ar] *vt* (*tocar*) to tap with one's foot; (*patear*) to kick; (*fam*) to ill-treat // *vi* to tap with one's feet.
zapatería [θapate'ria] *nf* (*oficio*) shoemaking; (*tienda*) shoe-shop; (*fábrica*) shoe factory; **zapatero, a** *nm/f* shoemaker.
zapatilla [θapa'tiʎa] *nf* slipper.
zapato [θa'pato] *nm* shoe.
zarabanda [θara'βanda] *nf* saraband; (*fig*) whirl.
zaranda [θa'randa] *nf* sieve; **zarandear** *vt* to sieve; (*fam*) to shake vigorously.
zarcillo [θar'θiʎo] *nm* earring.
zarpa ['θarpa] *nf* (*garra*) claw.
zarpar [θar'par] *vi* to weigh anchor.
zarza ['θarθa] *nf* (*BOT*) bramble; **zarzal** *nm* (*matorral*) bramble patch.
zarzamora [θarθa'mora] *nf* blackberry.
zarzuela [θar'θwela] *nf* Spanish light opera.
zigzag [θiɣ'θaɣ] *a* zigzag; **zigzaguear** *vi* to zigzag.

zinc [θink] nm zinc.
zócalo ['θokalo] nm (ARQ) plinth, base.
zona ['θona] nf zone; ~ fronteriza border area.
zoología [θoolo'xia] nf zoology; zoológico, a a zoological // nm zoo; zoólogo, a nm/f zoologist.
zopilote [θopi'lote] nm (AM) buzzard.
zoquete [θo'kete] nm (madera) block; (pan) crust; (fam) blockhead.
zorro, a ['θorro, a] a crafty // nm/f fox/vixen.
zozobra [θo'θoβra] nf (fig) anxiety; zozobrar vi (hundirse) to capsize; (fig) to fail.
zueco ['θweko] nm clog.

zumbar [θum'bar] vt (burlar) to tease; (golpear) to hit // vi to buzz; (fam) to be very close; ~se vr: ~se de to tease; zumbido nm buzzing; (fam) punch.
zumo ['θumo] nm juice; (ganancia) profit.
zurcir [θur'θir] vt (coser) to darn; (fig) to put together.
zurdo, a ['θurðo, a] a (mano) left; (persona) left-handed.
zurrar [θu'rrar] vt (TEC) to dress; (fam: pegar duro) to wallop; (: aplastar) to flatten; (: criticar) to criticize harshly.
zurriago [θu'rrjaɤo] nm whip, lash.
zurrón [θu'rron] nm pouch.
zutano, a [θu'tano, a] nm/f so-and-so.

ENGLISH - SPANISH
INGLÉS - ESPAÑOL

A

a, an [ei, ə, æn, ən, n] *det* un(a); **3 a day/week** 3 por día/semana; **10 km an hour** 10 km por hora.

A.A. *n abbr of* **Automobile Association; Alcoholics Anonymous.**

aback [ə'bæk] *ad*: **to be taken ~** quedar desconcertado.

abandon [ə'bændən] *vt* abandonar; (*renounce*) renunciar a // *n* abandono; (*wild behaviour*) desenfreno.

abashed [ə'bæʃt] *a* avergonzado, confuso.

abate [ə'beit] *vi* moderarse; (*lessen*) disminuir; (*calm down*) calmarse.

abattoir ['æbətwɑːʳ] *n* matadero.

abbey ['æbi] *n* monasterio.

abbot ['æbət] *n* abad *m*.

abbreviate [ə'briːvieit] *vt* abreviar; **abbreviation** [-'eiʃən] *n* (*short form*) abreviatura; (*act*) abreviación *f*.

abdicate ['æbdikeit] *vt, vi* abdicar; **abdication** [-'keiʃən] *n* abdicación *f*.

abdomen ['æbdəmən] *n* abdomen *m*.

abduct [æb'dʌkt] *vt* raptar, secuestrar; **~ion** [-'dʌkʃən] *n* rapto, secuestro.

aberration [æbə'reiʃən] *n* aberración *f*.

abet [ə'bet] *vt* (*incite*) incitar; (*aid*) ser cómplice de.

abeyance [ə'beiəns] *n*: **in ~** (*law*) en desuso; (*matter*) en suspenso.

abhor [əb'hɔːʳ] *vt* aborrecer, abominar (de); **~rent** *a* aborrecible, detestable.

abide [ə'baid], *pt, pp* **abode** *or* **abided** *vt* aguantar, soportar; **to ~ by** *vt fus* atenerse a.

ability [ə'biliti] *n* habilidad *f*, capacidad *f*; (*talent*) talento.

ablaze [ə'bleiz] *a* en llamas, ardiendo.

able ['eibl] *a* capaz; (*skilled*) hábil; **to be ~ to do sth** poder hacer algo; **~-bodied** *a* sano; **ably** *ad* hábilmente.

abnormal [æb'nɔːməl] *a* anormal; **~ity** [-'mæliti] *n* anormalidad *f*.

aboard [ə'bɔːd] *ad* a bordo // *prep* a bordo de.

abode [ə'bəud] *pt, pp of* **abide** // *n* domicilio.

abolish [ə'bɔliʃ] *vt* suprimir, abolir; **abolition** [æbəu'liʃən] *n* supresión *f*, abolición *f*.

abominable [ə'bɔminəbl] *a* abominable.

aborigine [æbə'ridʒini] *n* aborigen *m*.

abort [ə'bɔːt] *vt* abortar; **~ion** [ə'bɔːʃən] *n* aborto (provocado); **to have an ~ion** abortarse, hacerse abortar; **~ive** *a* fracasado.

abound [ə'baund] *vi* abundar.

about [ə'baut] *prep* (*subject*) acerca de, sobre; (*place*) alrededor de, por // *ad* casi, más o menos, a eso de; **to walk ~ the town** andar por la ciudad; **it takes ~ 10 hours** es cosa de 10 horas más o menos; **at ~ 2 o'clock** a eso de las 2; **to be ~ to** estar a punto de; **what** *or* **how ~ doing this?** ¿qué tal si hacemos esto?; **~ turn** *n* media vuelta.

above [ə'bʌv] *ad* encima, por encima, arriba // *prep* encima de; **mentioned ~** susodicho; **~ all** sobre todo; **~ board** *a* legítimo.

abrasion [ə'breiʒən] *n* (*on skin*) abrasión *f*; **abrasive** [ə'breiziv] *a* abrasivo.

abreast [ə'brest] *ad* de frente; **to keep ~ of** mantenerse al corriente de.

abridge [ə'bridʒ] *vt* abreviar.

abroad [ə'brɔːd] *ad* (*to be*) en el extranjero; (*to go*) al extranjero.

abrupt [ə'brʌpt] *a* (*sudden*) brusco; (*gruff*) áspero.

abscess ['æbsis] *n* absceso.

abscond [əb'skɔnd] *vi* fugarse.

absence ['æbsəns] *n* ausencia.

absent ['æbsənt] *a* ausente; **~ee** [-'tiː] *n* ausente *m/f*; **~eeism** [-'tiːizəm] *n* absentismo; **~-minded** *a* distraído.

absolute ['æbsəluːt] *a* absoluto; **~ly** [-'luːtli] *ad* absolutamente.

absolve [əb'zɔlv] *vt*: **to ~ sb (from)** absolver a alguien (de).

absorb [əb'zɔːb] *vt* absorber; **to be ~ed in a book** estar absorto en un libro; **~ent** *a* absorbente; **~ing** *a* absorbente.

abstain [əb'stein] *vi*: **to ~ (from)** abstenerse (de).

abstention [əb'stenʃən] *n* abstención *f*.

abstinence ['æbstinəns] *n* abstinencia.

abstract ['æbstrækt] *a* abstracto.

absurd [əb'sɔːd] *a* absurdo; **~ity** *n* absurdo.

abundance [ə'bʌndəns] *n* abundancia; **abundant** [-dənt] *a* abundante.

abuse [ə'bjuːs] *n* (*insults*) improperios *mpl*, injurias *fpl*; (*misuse*) abuso // *vt* [ə'bjuːz] (*ill-treat*) maltratar; (*take advantage of*) abusar de; **abusive** *a* ofensivo.

abysmal [ə'bizməl] *a* abismal; (*ignorance etc*) profundo.

abyss [ə'bis] *n* abismo.

academic [ækə'demik] *a* académico, universitario; (*pej: issue*) puramente teórico.

academy [ə'kædəmi] *n* (*learned body*) academia; (*school*) instituto, colegio.

accede [æk'siːd] *vi*: **to ~ to** (*request*) consentir en; (*throne*) subir a.

accelerate [æk'sɛləreɪt] *vt* acelerar // *vi* acelerarse; **acceleration** [-'reɪʃən] *n* aceleración *f*; **accelerator** *n* acelerador *m*.

accent ['æksɛnt] *n* acento.

accept [ək'sɛpt] *vt* aceptar; (*approve*) aprobar; (*permit*) admitir; **~able** *a* aceptable; admisible; **~ance** *n* aceptación *f*; aprobación *f*.

access ['æksɛs] *n* acceso; **to have ~ to** tener libre acceso a; **~ible** [-'sɛsəbl] *a* accesible.

accessory [æk'sɛsərɪ] *n* accesorio; **toilet accessories** *npl* artículos *mpl* de tocador.

accident ['æksɪdənt] *n* accidente *m*; (*chance*) casualidad *f*; **by ~** (*unintentionally*) sin querer; (*by coincidence*) por casualidad; **~al** [-'dɛntl] *a* accidental, fortuito; **~ally** [-'dɛntəlɪ] *ad* sin querer; por casualidad; **~-prone** *a* con tendencia a sufrir/causar accidentes.

acclaim [ə'kleɪm] *vt* aclamar, aplaudir // *n* aclamación *f*, aplausos *mpl*.

acclimatize [ə'klaɪmətaɪz] *vt*: **to become ~d** aclimatarse.

accommodate [ə'kɔmədeɪt] *vt* alojar, hospedar; (*reconcile*) componer; (*oblige, help*) complacer; (*adapt*): **to ~ one's plans to** acomodar sus proyectos a; **accommodating** *a* servicial, complaciente.

accommodation [əkɔmə'deɪʃən] *n* alojamiento; (*space*) sitio.

accompaniment [ə'kʌmpənɪmənt] *n* acompañamiento; **accompany** [-nɪ] *vt* acompañar.

accomplice [ə'kʌmplɪs] *n* cómplice *m/f*.

accomplish [ə'kʌmplɪʃ] *vt* (*finish*) acabar, alcanzar; (*achieve*) realizar, llevar a cabo; **~ed** *a* experto, hábil; **~ment** *n* (*ending*) conclusión *f*; (*bringing about*) realización *f*; (*skill*) talento.

accord [ə'kɔːd] *n* acuerdo // *vt* concordar; **of his own ~** espontáneamente; **~ance** *n*: **in ~ance with** de acuerdo con; **~ing to** *prep* según; (*in accordance with*) conforme a; **~ingly** *ad* (*thus*) por consiguiente.

accordion [ə'kɔːdɪən] *n* acordeón *m*.

accost [ə'kɔst] *vt* abordar, dirigirse a.

account [ə'kaunt] *n* (*COMM*) cuenta, factura; (*report*) informe *m*; **of little ~** de poca importancia; **on ~** a cuenta; **on no ~** de ninguna manera, bajo ningún concepto; **on ~ of** a causa de, por motivo de; **to take into ~, take ~ of** tomar o tener en cuenta; **to ~ for** *vt* (*answer for*) responder de; (*explain*) dar cuenta o razón de; **~able** *a* responsable.

accountancy [ə'kauntənsɪ] *n* contabilidad *f*; **accountant** [-tənt] *n* contador/a *m/f*.

accumulate [ə'kjuːmjuleɪt] *vt* acumular // *vi* acumularse; **accumulation** [-'leɪʃən] *n* acumulación *f*.

accuracy ['ækjurəsɪ] *n* exactitud *f*, precisión *f*; **accurate** [-rɪt] *a* (*number*) exacto; (*answer*) acertado; (*shot*) certero.

accusation [ækju'zeɪʃən] *n* acusación *f*; **accuse** [ə'kjuːz] *vt* acusar; (*blame*) echar la culpa a; **accused** [ə'kjuːzd] *n* acusado/a.

accustom [ə'kʌstəm] *vt* acostumbrar; **~ed** *a*: **~ed to** acostumbrado a.

ace [eɪs] *n* as *m*.

ache [eɪk] *n* dolor *m* // *vi* doler; **my head ~s** me duele la cabeza.

achieve [ə'tʃiːv] *vt* (*reach*) alcanzar; (*realize*) llevar a cabo; (*victory, success*) lograr, conseguir; **~ment** *n* (*completion*) realización *f*; (*success*) éxito.

acid ['æsɪd] *a* ácido; (*bitter*) agrio // *n* ácido; **~ity** [ə'sɪdɪtɪ] *n* acidez *f*; (*MED*) acedía.

acknowledge [ək'nɔlɪdʒ] *vt* (*letter*) acusar recibo de; (*fact*) reconocer; **~ment** *n* acuse *m* de recibo; reconocimiento.

acne ['æknɪ] *n* acné *m*.

acorn ['eɪkɔːn] *n* bellota.

acoustic [ə'kuːstɪk] *a* acústico; **~s** *n*, *npl* acústica *sg*.

acquaint [ə'kweɪnt] *vt*: **to ~ sb with sth** (*warn*) avisar a uno de algo; (*inform*) poner a uno al corriente de algo; **to be ~ed with** (*person*) conocer; (*fact*) estar al corriente de; **~ance** *n* conocimiento; (*person*) conocido/a.

acquiesce [ækwi'ɛs] *vi*: **to ~ in** consentir en, conformarse con.

acquire [ə'kwaɪə*] *vt* adquirir; (*achieve*) conseguir; **acquisition** [ækwɪ'zɪʃən] *n* adquisición *f*; **acquisitive** [ə'kwɪzɪtɪv] *a* codicioso.

acquit [ə'kwɪt] *vt* absolver, exculpar; **to ~ o.s. well** defenderse, salir con éxito; **~tal** *n* absolución *f*, exculpación *f*.

acre ['eɪkə*] *n* acre *m*.

acrimonious [ækrɪ'məunɪəs] *a* (*remark*) mordaz; (*argument*) reñido.

acrobat ['ækrəbæt] *n* acróbata *m/f*; **~ics** [ækrəu'bætɪks] *n*, *npl* acrobacia *sg*.

across [ə'krɔs] *prep* (*on the other side of*) al otro lado de, del otro lado de; (*crosswise*) a través de // *ad* de un lado a otro, de una parte a otra; a través, al través; **to run/swim ~** atravesar corriendo/nadando; **~ from** enfrente de.

act [ækt] *n* acto, acción *f*; (*THEATRE*) acto; (*in music-hall etc*) número; (*LAW*) decreto, ley *f* // *vi* (*machine*) funcionar, marchar; (*person*) actuar, comportarse; (*THEATRE*) actuar, trabajar; (*pretend*) fingir; (*take action*) obrar // *vt* (*part*) hacer el papel de, representar; **to ~ as** actuar o hacer de; **~ing** *a* suplente // *n*: **to do some ~ing** ser actor/actriz.

action ['ækʃən] *n* acción *f*, acto; (*MIL*) acción *f*, batalla; (*LAW*) proceso, demanda; **to take ~** tomar medidas.

activate ['æktɪveɪt] *vt* (*mechanism*) activar.

active ['æktɪv] *a* activo, enérgico; (*volcano*) en actividad; **activity** [-'tɪvɪtɪ] *n* actividad *f*.

actor ['æktɔ*] *n* actor *m*; **actress** [-trɪs] *n* actriz *f*.

actual ['æktjuəl] *a* verdadero, real; **~ly** *ad* realmente, en realidad.

acupuncture ['ækjupʌŋktʃɔ*] *n* acupuntura.

acute [ɔ'kjuːt] *a* (*gen*) agudo.

ad [æd] *n abbr of* **advertisement.**

A.D. *ad abbr of* **Anno Domini** A.C. (año de Cristo).

Adam ['ædɔm] *n* Adán; **~'s apple** *n* nuez *f* de la garganta.

adamant ['ædɔmɔnt] *a* firme, inflexible.

adapt [ɔ'dæpt] *vt* adaptar; (*reconcile*) acomodar // *vi*: **to ~ (to)** adaptarse (a), ajustarse (a); **~able** *a* (*device*) adaptable; (*person*) que se adapta; **~ation** [ædæp-'teɪʃən] *n* adaptación *f*; **~er** *n* (*ELEC*) adaptador *m*.

add [æd] *vt* añadir, agregar; (*figures: also:* **~ up**) sumar // *vi*: **to ~ to** (*increase*) aumentar, acrecentar; **it doesn't ~ up** no tiene sentido.

adder ['ædɔ*] *n* víbora.

addict ['ædɪkt] *n* (*enthusiast*) entusiasta *m/f*; (*to drugs etc*) adicto/a; **~ed** [ɔ'dɪktɪd] *a*: **to be ~ed to** ser aficionado de; ser adicto a; **addiction** [ɔ'dɪkʃən] *n* (*enthusiasm*) afición *f*; (*dependence*) hábito morboso.

adding machine ['ædɪŋmɔʃiːn] *n* calculadora.

addition [ɔ'dɪʃən] *n* (*adding up*) adición *f*; (*thing added*) añadidura, añadido; **in ~** además, por añadidura; **in ~ to** además de; **~al** *a* adicional.

additive ['ædɪtɪv] *n* aditivo.

address [ɔ'drɛs] *n* dirección *f*, señas *fpl*; (*speech*) discurso // *vt* (*letter*) dirigir; (*speak to*) dirigirse a, dirigir la palabra a; **~ee** [ædrɛ'siː] *n* destinatario/a.

adenoids ['ædɪnɔɪdz] *npl* vegetaciones *fpl* adenoideas.

adept ['ædɛpt] *a*: **~ at** experto *o* hábil en.

adequate ['ædɪkwɪt] *a* (*apt*) adecuado; (*enough*) suficiente.

adhere [ɔd'hɪɔ*] *vi*: **to ~ to** pegarse a; (*fig: abide by*) observar; (: *hold to*) adherirse a; **adherent** *n* partidario/a.

adhesive [ɔd'hiːzɪv] *a*, *n* adhesivo.

adjacent [ɔ'dʒeɪsɔnt] *a*: **~ to** contiguo a, inmediato a.

adjective ['ædʒɛktɪv] *n* adjetivo.

adjoining [ɔ'dʒɔɪnɪŋ] *a* contiguo, vecino.

adjourn [ɔ'dʒɔːn] *vt* aplazar; (*session*) suspender, levantar // *vi* suspenderse.

adjudicate [ɔ'dʒuːdɪkeɪt] *vi* sentenciar; **adjudicator** *n* juez *m*, árbitro.

adjust [ɔ'dʒʌst] *vt* (*change*) modificar; (*arrange*) arreglar; (*machine*) ajustar // *vi*: **to ~ (to)** adaptarse (a); **~able** *a* ajustable; **~ment** *n* modificación *f*; arreglo; (*of prices, wages*) ajuste *m*.

adjutant ['ædʒɔtɔnt] *n* ayudante *m*.

ad-lib [æd'lɪb] *vt*, *vi* improvisar; **ad lib** *ad a* voluntad, a discreción.

administer [ɔd'mɪnɪstɔ*] *vt* proporcionar; (*justice*) administrar; **administration** [-'treɪʃən] *n* administración *f*; (*government*) gobierno; **administrative** [-trɔtɪv] *a* administrativo; **administrator** [-treɪtɔ*] *n* administrador/a *m/f*.

admirable ['ædmɔrɔbl] *a* admirable.

admiral ['ædmɔrɔl] *n* almirante *m*; **A~ty** *n* Ministerio de Marina, Almirantazgo.

admiration [ædmɔ'reɪʃɔn] *n* admiración *f*.

admire [ɔd'maɪɔ*] *vt* admirar; **admirer** *n* admirador/a *m/f*; (*suitor*) pretendiente *m*.

admission [ɔd'mɪʃɔn] *n* (*entry*) entrada; (*enrolment*) ingreso; (*confession*) confesión *f*.

admit [ɔd'mɪt] *vt* dejar entrar, dar entrada a; (*permit*) admitir; (*acknowledge*) reconocer; (*accept*) aceptar; **to ~ to** confesarse culpable de; **~tance** *n* entrada; **~tedly** *ad* de acuerdo que.

admonish [ɔd'mɔnɪʃ] *vt* amonestar; (*advise*) aconsejar.

ado [ɔ'duː] *n*: **without (any) more ~** sin más (ni más).

adolescence [ædɔu'lɛsns] *n* adolescencia; **adolescent** [-'lɛsnt] *a*, *n* adolescente *m/f*.

adopt [ɔ'dɔpt] *vt* adoptar; **~ion** [ɔ'dɔpʃɔn] *n* adopción *f*; **~ed** *a* adoptivo.

adore [ɔ'dɔː*] *vt* adorar.

adorn [ɔ'dɔːn] *vt* adornar.

adrenalin [ɔ'drɛnɔlɪn] *n* adrenalina.

Adriatic [eɪdrɪ'ætɪk] *n*: **the ~ (Sea)** el (Mar) Adriático.

adrift [ɔ'drɪft] *ad* a la deriva; **to come ~** desprenderse.

adult ['ædʌlt] *n* (*gen*) adulto.

adulterate [ɔ'dʌltɔreɪt] *vt* adulterar.

adultery [ɔ'dʌltɔrɪ] *n* adulterio.

advance [ɔd'vɑːns] *n* (*gen*) adelanto, progreso; (*money*) anticipo, préstamo; (*MIL*) avance *m* // *vt* avanzar, adelantar; anticipar, prestar // *vi* avanzar, adelantarse; **in ~** por adelantado; **~d** *a* avanzado; (*SCOL: studies*) adelantado; **~d in years** entrado en años; **~ment** *n* progreso; (*in rank*) ascenso.

advantage [ɔd'vɑːntɪdʒ] *n* (*also TENNIS*) ventaja; **to take ~ of** (*use*) aprovecharse de; (*gain by*) sacar partido de; **~ous** [ædvɔn'teɪdʒɔs] *a* ventajoso, provechoso.

advent ['ædvɔnt] *n* advenimiento; **A~** Adviento.

adventure [ɔd'vɛntʃɔ*] *n* aventura; **adventurous** [-tʃɔrɔs] *a* aventurero.

adverb ['ædvɔːb] *n* adverbio.

adversary ['ædvɔsɔrɪ] *n* adversario, contrario.

adverse ['ædvɔːs] *a* adverso, contrario; **~ to** adverso a.

adversity [ɔd'vɔːsɪtɪ] *n* infortunio.

advert ['ædvɔːt] *n abbr of* **advertisement.**

advertise ['ædvɔtaɪz] *vi* hacer propaganda; (*in newspaper etc*) poner un anuncio // *vt* anunciar; **~ment** [ɔd-'vɔːtɪsmɔnt] *n* (*COMM*) anuncio; **advertising** *n* publicidad *f*, propaganda; anuncios *mpl*.

advice [əd'vaɪs] n consejo, consejos mpl; (notification) aviso; **to take legal ~** consultar a un abogado.

advisable [əd'vaɪzəbl] a aconsejable, conveniente.

advise [əd'vaɪz] vt aconsejar; (inform) avisar; **adviser** n consejero; (business adviser) asesor m; **advisory** a consultivo.

advocate ['ædvəkeɪt] vt (argue for) abogar por; (give support to) ser partidario de // n [-kɪt] abogado.

aerial ['cərɪəl] n antena // a aéreo.

aeroplane ['cərəpleɪn] n avión m.

aerosol ['cərəsɔl] n aerosol m.

aesthetic [iːs'θetɪk] a estético.

afar [ə'fɑ:*] ad: **from ~** desde lejos.

affable ['æfəbl] a afable.

affair [ə'fcə*] n asunto; (also: love ~) aventura o relación f (amorosa).

affect [ə'fckt] vt afectar, influir en; (move) conmover; **~ed** a afectado.

affection [ə'fckʃən] n afecto, cariño; **~ate** a afectuoso, cariñoso.

affiliated [ə'fɪlieɪtɪd] a afiliado.

affinity [ə'fɪnɪtɪ] n afinidad f.

affirmation [æfə'meɪʃən] n afirmación f.

affirmative [ə'fɔːmətɪv] a afirmativo.

affix [ə'fɪks] vt (signature) poner, añadir; (stamp) pegar.

afflict [ə'flɪkt] vt afligir; **~ion** [ə'flɪkʃən] n enfermedad f, aflicción f.

affluence ['æfluəns] n opulencia, riqueza; **affluent** [-ənt] a opulento, acaudalado.

afford [ə'fɔːd] vt (provide) dar, proporcionar; **can we ~ it?** ¿tenemos bastante dinero para comprarlo?

affront [ə'frʌnt] n afrenta, ofensa.

afield [ə'fiːld] ad: **far ~** muy lejos.

afloat [ə'fləut] ad (floating) a flote; (at sea) en el mar.

afoot [ə'fut] ad: **there is something ~** algo se está tramando.

aforesaid [ə'fɔːsɛd] a susodicho.

afraid [ə'freɪd] a: **to be ~ of** (person) tener miedo a; (thing) tener miedo de; **to be ~ to** tener miedo de, temer; **I am ~ that** me temo que.

afresh [ə'frɛʃ] ad de nuevo, otra vez.

Africa ['æfrɪkə] n África; **~n** a, n africano/a.

aft [ɑːft] ad (to be) en popa; (to go) a popa.

after ['ɑːftə*] prep (time) después de; (place, order) detrás de, tras // ad después // conj después (de) que; **what/who are you ~?** ¿qué/a quién busca Usted?; **to ask ~ sb** preguntar por alguien; **~ all** después de todo, al fin y al cabo; **you!** ¡pase Usted!; **~birth** n secundinas fpl; **~-effects** npl consecuencias fpl, efectos mpl; **~life** n vida futura; **~math** n consecuencias fpl, resultados mpl; **~noon** n tarde f; **~shave** (lotion) n loción f para después del afeitado; **~thought** n ocurrencia (tardía); **~wards** ad después, más tarde.

again [ə'gɛn] ad otra vez, de nuevo; **to do sth ~** volver a hacer algo; **~ and ~** una y otra vez; **now and ~** de vez en cuando.

against [ə'gɛnst] prep (opposed) contra, en contra de; (close to) contra, junto a.

age [eɪdʒ] n (gen) edad f; (old ~) vejez f; (period) época // vi envejecer(se) // vt envejecer; **to come of ~** llegar a la mayoría de edad; **it's been ~s since** hace muchísimo tiempo que; **~d** a ['eɪdʒd] viejo, anciano // a [eɪdʒd]: **~d 10** de 10 años de edad; **~ group** n: **to be in the same ~ group** tener la misma edad; **~less** a (eternal) eterno; (ever young) siempre joven; **~ limit** n edad mínima/máxima.

agency ['eɪdʒənsɪ] n agencia; **through or by the ~ of** por medio de.

agenda [ə'dʒɛndə] n orden m del día.

agent ['eɪdʒənt] n (gen) agente m/f; (representative) representante m/f, delegado/a.

aggravate ['ægrəveɪt] vt agravar; (annoy) irritar, exasperar; **aggravation** [-'veɪʃən] n agravación f.

aggregate ['ægrɪgeɪt] n (whole) conjunto; (collection) agregado.

aggression [ə'grɛʃən] n agresión f; **aggressive** [ə'grɛsɪv] a agresivo; (zealous) enérgico.

aggrieved [ə'griːvd] a ofendido, agraviado.

aghast [ə'gɑːst] a horrorizado; **to be ~** pasmarse.

agile ['ædʒaɪl] a ágil.

agitate ['ædʒɪteɪt] vt (shake) agitar; (trouble) inquietar; **to ~ for** hacer campaña pro o en favor de; **agitator** n agitador/a m/f.

ago [ə'gəu] ad: **2 days ~** hace 2 días; **not long ~** hace poco; **how long ~?** ¿hace cuánto tiempo?

agog [ə'gɔg] a (anxious) ansiado; (excited) emocionado.

agonizing ['ægənaɪzɪŋ] a (pain) atroz, agudo; (suspense) angustioso.

agony ['ægənɪ] n (pain) dolor m agudo; (distress) angustia; **to be in ~** sufrir atrozmente.

agree [ə'griː] vt (price) acordar, quedar en // vi (statements etc) coincidir, concordar; **to ~ (with)** (person) estar de acuerdo (con), ponerse de acuerdo (con); **to ~ to do** aceptar hacer; **to ~ to sth** consentir en algo; **to ~ that** (admit) estar de acuerdo en que; **garlic doesn't ~ with me** el ajo no me sienta bien; **~able** a agradable; (person) simpático; (willing) de acuerdo, conforme; **~d** a (time, place) convenido; **~ment** n acuerdo; (COMM) contrato; **in ~ment** de acuerdo, conforme.

agricultural [ægrɪ'kʌltʃərəl] a agrícola; **agriculture** ['ægrɪkʌltʃə*] n agricultura.

aground [ə'graund] ad: **to run ~** encallar, embarrancar.

ahead [ə'hɛd] ad delante; **~ of** delante de;

(*fig: schedule etc*) antes de; ~ **of time** antes de la hora; **to be** ~ **of sb** (*fig*) llevar la ventaja a alguien; **go right** *or* **straight** ~ ¡siga adelante!

aid [eɪd] *n* ayuda, auxilio // *vt* ayudar, auxiliar; **in** ~ **of** a beneficio de; **to** ~ **and abet** (*LAW*) ser cómplice de.

aide [eɪd] *n* (*person*) edecán *m*.

ailment ['eɪlmənt] *n* enfermedad *f*, achaque *m*.

aim [eɪm] *vt* (*gun, camera*) apuntar; (*missile, remark*) dirigir; (*blow*) asestar // *vi* (*also:* **take** ~) apuntar // *n* puntería; (*objective*) propósito, meta; **to** ~ **at** (*objective*) aspirar a, pretender; **to** ~ **to do** tener la intención de hacer; ~**less** *a* sin propósito, sin objeto; ~**lessly** *ad* a la ventura, a la deriva.

air [ɛə°] *n* aire *m*; (*appearance*) aspecto // *vt* ventilar; (*grievances, ideas*) airear // *cpd* (*currents, attack etc*) aéreo, aeronáutico; ~**borne** *a* (*in the air*) en el aire; (*MIL*) aerotransportado; ~**-conditioned** *a* con aire acondicionado; ~**conditioning** *n* aire acondicionado; ~**craft** *n, pl inv* avión *m*; ~**craft carrier** *n* porta(a)viones *m inv*; **A**~ **Force** *n* Fuerzas Aéreas *fpl*, aviación *f*; ~**gun** *n* escopeta de aire comprimido; ~ **hostess** *n* azafata; ~ **letter** *n* carta aérea; ~**lift** *n* puente *m* aéreo; ~**line** *n* línea aérea; ~**liner** *n* avión *m* de pasajeros; ~**lock** *n* esclusa de aire; ~**mail** *n*: **by** ~ **mail** por avión; ~**port** *n* aeropuerto; ~ **raid** *n* ataque *m* aéreo; ~**sick** *a*: **to be** ~**sick** marearse (en un avión); ~**strip** *n* pista de aterrizaje; ~**tight** *a* hermético; ~**y** *a* (*room*) bien ventilado; (*manners*) ligero.

aisle [aɪl] *n* (*of church*) nave *f*; (*of theatre*) pasillo.

ajar [ə'dʒɑː°] *a* entreabierto.

akin [ə'kɪn] *a*: ~ **to** relacionado con.

alarm [ə'lɑːm] *n* alarma; (*anxiety*) inquietud *f* // *vt* asustar, inquietar; ~ **clock** *n* despertador *m*.

Albania [æl'beɪnɪə] *n* Albania.

album ['ælbəm] *n* álbum *m*; (*L.P.*) elepé *m*.

alcohol ['ælkəhɔl] *n* alcohol *m*; ~**ic** [-'hɔlɪk] *a*, *n* alcohólico/a; ~**ism** *n* alcoholismo.

alcove ['ælkəuv] *n* nicho, hueco.

alderman ['ɔːldəmən] *n, pl* -**men** concejal *m*.

ale [eɪl] *n* cerveza.

alert [ə'lɜːt] *a* alerta; (*sharp*) despierto, despabilado // *n* alerta *m*, alarma // *vt* poner sobre aviso; **to be on the** ~ estar alerta *o* sobre aviso.

algebra ['ældʒɪbrə] *n* álgebra.

Algeria [æl'dʒɪərɪə] *n* Argelia; ~**n** *a*, *n* argelino/a.

alias ['eɪlɪəs] *ad* alias, por otro nombre // *n* alias *m*.

alibi ['ælɪbaɪ] *n* coartada.

alien ['eɪlɪən] *n* extranjero/a // *a*: ~ **to** distinto de, ajeno a; ~**ate** *vt* enajenar, alejar; ~**ation** [-'neɪʃən] *n* enajenación *f*.

alight [ə'laɪt] *a* ardiendo, quemando // *vi* apearse, bajar.

align [ə'laɪn] *vt* alinear; ~**ment** *n* alineación *f*.

alike [ə'laɪk] *a* semejantes, iguales // *ad* igualmente, del mismo modo; **to look** ~ parecerse.

alimony ['ælɪmənɪ] *n* (*payment*) alimentos *mpl*.

alive [ə'laɪv] *a* (*gen*) vivo; (*lively*) activo, enérgico.

alkali ['ælkəlaɪ] *n* álcali *m*.

all [ɔːl] *a* todo; (*pl*) todos(as) // *pron* todo; (*pl*) todos(as) // *ad* completamente, del todo; ~ **alone** completamente solo; **at** ~ en absoluto, del todo; ~ **the time/his life** todo el tiempo/toda su vida; ~ **five** todos los cinco; ~ **of them** todos (ellos); ~ **of us went** fuimos todos; **not as hard as** ~ **that** no tan difícil; ~ **in** ~ con todo, así y todo.

allay [ə'leɪ] *vt* (*fears*) aquietar; (*pain*) aliviar.

allegation [ælɪ'geɪʃən] *n* aseveración *f*, alegación *f*.

allege [ə'lɛdʒ] *vt* afirmar, pretender.

allegiance [ə'liːdʒəns] *n* lealtad *f*.

allegory ['ælɪgərɪ] *n* alegoría.

allergic [ə'lɜːdʒɪk] *a*: ~ **to** alérgico a; **allergy** ['ælədʒɪ] *n* alergia.

alleviate [ə'liːvɪeɪt] *vt* aliviar, mitigar.

alley ['ælɪ] *n* (*street*) callejuela; (*in garden*) paseo.

alliance [ə'laɪəns] *n* alianza *f*; **allied** ['ælaɪd] *a* aliado; (*related*) relacionado.

alligator ['ælɪgeɪtə°] *n* caimán *m*.

all-in ['ɔːlɪn] *a* (*also ad: charge*) todo incluido; ~ **wrestling** *n* lucha libre.

alliteration [əlɪtə'reɪʃən] *n* aliteración *f*.

all-night ['ɔːl'naɪt] *a* (*café*) abierto toda la noche; (*party*) que dura toda la noche.

allocate ['æləkeɪt] *vt* (*share out*) repartir, distribuir; (*devote*) asignar; **allocation** [-'keɪʃən] *n* (*of money*) ración *f*, cuota; (*distribution*) reparto.

allot [ə'lɔt] *vt* asignar; ~**ment** *n* ración *f*, porción *f*; (*garden*) parcela.

all-out ['ɔːlaut] *a* (*effort etc*) máximo; **all out** *ad* con todas sus fuerzas; (*speed*) a máxima velocidad.

allow [ə'lau] *vt* (*practice, behaviour*) permitir, dejar; (*sum to spend etc*) pagar, dar; (*a claim*) admitir; (*sum, time estimated*) dar, conceder; (*concede*): **to** ~ **that** reconocer que; **to** ~ **sb to do** permitir a alguien hacer; **to** ~ **for** *vt fus* tener en cuenta, tomar en consideración; ~**ance** *n* (*gen*) concesión *f*; (*payment*) subvención *f*, pensión *f*; (*discount*) descuento, rebaja; **family** ~**ance** subsidio familiar; **to make** ~**ances for** ser indulgente con; tener en cuenta.

alloy ['ælɔɪ] *n* (*mix*) mezcla.

all: ~ **right** *ad* (*well*) bien; (*correct*) correcto; (*as answer*) ¡conforme!, ¡está bien!; ~**-round** *a* (*gen*) completo; (*view*) amplio; (*person*) que hace de todo;

~-time a (record) de todos los tiempos.
allude [ə'lu:d] vi: to ~ to aludir a.
alluring [ə'ljuərıŋ] a seductor(a), atractivo.
allusion [ə'lu:ʒən] n referencia, alusión f.
ally ['ælaı] n aliado/a // vr [ə'laı]: to ~ o.s. with aliarse con.
almighty [ɔ:l'maıtı] a todopoderoso, omnipotente.
almond ['ɑ:mənd] n (fruit) almendra; (tree) almendro.
almost ['ɔ:lməust] ad casi, por poco.
alms [ɑ:mz] npl limosna sg.
aloft [ə'lɔft] ad arriba, en alto.
alone [ə'ləun] a solo // ad sólo, solamente; to leave sb ~ dejar a uno solo o en paz; to leave sth ~ no tocar algo, dejar algo sin tocar; let ~ sin hablar de.
along [ə'lɔŋ] prep a lo largo de, por // ad: is he coming ~ with us? ¿nos acompaña?; he was limping ~ iba cojeando; ~ with junto con, además de; ~side prep junto a, al lado de // ad (NAUT) al costado.
aloof [ə'lu:f] a reservado // ad: to stand ~ mantenerse a distancia.
aloud [ə'laud] ad en voz alta.
alphabet ['ælfəbet] n alfabeto; ~ical [-'betıkəl] a alfabético.
alpine ['ælpaın] a alpino, alpestre.
Alps [ælps] npl: the ~ los Alpes.
already [ɔ:l'redı] ad ya.
alright ['ɔ:l'raıt] ad = all right.
also ['ɔ:lsəu] ad también, además.
altar ['ɔltə*] n altar m.
alter ['ɔltə*] vt cambiar, modificar // vi cambiarse, mudarse; (worsen) alterarse; ~ation [ɔltə'reıʃən] n cambio, modificación f; alteración f.
alternate [ɔl'tə:nıt] a alterno, alternativo // vi ['ɔltə:neıt] alternarse; on ~ days un día si y otro no; ~ly ad alternativamente, por turno; **alternating** [-'neıtıŋ] a (current) alterno.
alternative [ɔl'tə:nətıv] a alternativo // n alternativa; ~ly ad: ~ly one could... por otra parte se podría... .
alternator ['ɔltə:neıtə*] n (AUT) alternador m.
although [ɔ:l'ðəu] conj aunque; (given that) si bien.
altitude ['æltıtju:d] n altitud f, altura.
alto ['æltəu] n (female) contralto f; (male) alto.
altogether [ɔ:ltə'geðə*] ad enteramente, del todo; (on the whole, in all) en total, en conjunto.
aluminium [ælju'mınıəm], **aluminum** [ə'lu:mınəm] (US) n aluminio.
always ['ɔ:lweız] ad siempre.
am [æm] vb see be.
a.m. ad abbr of ante meridiem de la mañana, antes de mediodía.
amalgamate [ə'mælgəmeıt] vi amalgamarse, unirse // vt amalgamar,

unir; **amalgamation** [-'meıʃən] n (COMM) amalgamación f, unión f.
amass [ə'mæs] vt amontonar, acumular.
amateur ['æmətə*] n aficionado/a, amateur m/f.
amaze [ə'meız] vt asombrar, pasmar; ~ment n asombro, sorpresa.
Amazon ['æməzən] n (GEO) Amazonas m.
ambassador [æm'bæsədə*] n embajador m.
amber ['æmbə*] n ámbar m; at ~ (AUT) en el amarillo.
ambidextrous [æmbı'dekstrəs] a ambidextro.
ambiguity [æmbı'gjuıtı] n ambigüedad f; (of meaning) doble sentido; **ambiguous** [-'bıgjuəs] a ambiguo.
ambition [æm'bıʃən] n ambición f; **ambitious** [-ʃəs] a ambicioso; (plan) grandioso.
ambivalent [æm'bıvələnt] a ambivalente; (pej) equívoco.
amble ['æmbl] vi (gen: ~ along) deambular, andar sin prisa.
ambulance ['æmbjuləns] n ambulancia.
ambush ['æmbuʃ] n emboscada // vt tender una emboscada a; (fig) coger por sorpresa.
amenable [ə'mi:nəbl] a: ~ to (advice etc) sensible a.
amend [ə'mend] vt (law, text) enmendar; (habits) corregir, mejorar; to make ~s compensar, dar satisfacción por; ~ment n enmienda.
amenities [ə'mi:nıtız] npl conveniencias fpl, comodidades fpl.
America [ə'merıkə] n Estados Unidos mpl; ~ n a, n norteamericano/a.
amiable ['eımıəbl] a (kind) amable, simpático; (hearty) bonachón(ona).
amicable ['æmıkəbl] a amistoso, amigable.
amid(st) [ə'mıd(st)] prep entre, en medio de.
amiss [ə'mıs] ad: to take sth ~ tomar algo a mal.
ammonia [ə'məunıə] n amoníaco.
ammunition [æmju'nıʃən] n municiones fpl.
amnesia [æm'ni:zıə] n amnesia.
amnesty ['æmnıstı] n amnistía.
amok [ə'mɔk] ad: to run ~ enloquecerse, desbocarse.
among(st) [ə'mʌŋ(st)] prep entre, en medio de.
amoral [æ'mɔrəl] a amoral.
amorous ['æmərəs] a amoroso; (in love) enamorado.
amount [ə'maunt] n (gen) cantidad f; (of bill etc) suma, importe m // vi: to ~ to (reach) alcanzar; (total) sumar; (be same as) equivaler a, significar.
amp(ere) ['æmp(ɛə*)] n amperio.
amphibian [æm'fıbıən] n anfibio; **amphibious** [-bıəs] a anfibio.
amphitheatre ['æmfıθıətə*] n anfiteatro.

ample ['æmpl] a (spacious) amplio, ancho; (abundant) abundante; (enough) bastante, suficiente.
amplifier ['æmplɪfaɪə*] n amplificador m.
amplify ['æmplɪfaɪ] vt amplificar, aumentar; (explain) explicar.
amputate ['æmpjuteɪt] vt amputar.
amuck [ə'mʌk] ad = **amok**.
amuse [ə'mjuːz] vt divertir; (distract) distraer, entretener; ~**ment** n diversión f; (pastime) pasatiempo; (laughter) risa.
an [æn, ən, n] det see **a**.
anaemia [ə'niːmɪə] n anemia; **anaemic** [-mɪk] a anémico; (fig) soso, insípido.
anaesthetic [ænɪs'θetɪk] n anestesia; **anaesthetist** [æ'niːsθɪtɪst] n anestesista m/f.
analgesic [ænæl'dʒiːsɪk] a, n analgésico.
analogy [ə'nælədʒɪ] n análogo.
analyse ['ænəlaɪz] vt analizar; **analysis** [ə'næləsɪs], pl -**ses** [-siːz] n análisis m inv; **analyst** [-lɪst] n (US) analista m/f; **analytic(al)** [-'lɪtɪk(əl)] a analítico.
anarchist ['ænəkɪst] a, n anarquista m/f; **anarchy** [-kɪ] n anarquía, desorden m.
anatomy [ə'nætəmɪ] n anatomía.
ancestor ['ænsɪstə*] n antepasado; **ancestry** [-trɪ] n ascendencia, abolengo.
anchor ['æŋkə*] n ancla, áncora // vi anclar // vt (fig) sujetar, asegurar; **to weigh** ~ levar anclas; ~**age** n ancladero.
anchovy ['æntʃəvɪ] n anchoa.
ancient ['eɪnʃənt] a antiguo.
and [ænd] conj y; (before i, hi) e; ~ **so on** etcétera, y así sucesivamente; **try** ~ **come** procure o intente venir; **better** ~ **better** cada vez mejor.
Andes ['ændiːz] npl: the ~ los Andes.
anecdote ['ænɪkdəʊt] n anécdota.
anew [ə'njuː] ad de nuevo, otra vez.
angel ['eɪndʒəl] n ángel m.
anger ['æŋgə*] n cólera, ira // vt enojar, provocar.
angina [æn'dʒaɪnə] n angina (de pecho).
angle ['æŋgl] n ángulo; **from their** ~ desde su punto de vista.
angler ['æŋglə*] n pescador/a m/f (de caña).
Anglican ['æŋglɪkən] a, n anglicano/a.
angling ['æŋglɪŋ] n pesca con caña.
Anglo- ['æŋgləʊ] pref anglo... .
angrily ['æŋgrɪlɪ] ad con enojo, airadamente.
angry ['æŋgrɪ] a enfadado, enojado; **to be** ~ **with sb/at sth** estar enfadado con alguien/por algo; **to get** ~ enfadarse, enojarse.
anguish ['æŋgwɪʃ] n (physical) dolor m agudo; (mental) angustia.
angular ['æŋgjulə*] a (shape) angular; (features) anguloso.
animal ['ænɪməl] n animal m, bestia; (insect) bicho // a animal.
animate ['ænɪmeɪt] vt (enliven) animar;

(encourage) estimular, alentar; ~**d** a vivo, animado.
animosity [ænɪ'mɔsɪtɪ] n animosidad f, rencor m.
aniseed ['ænɪsiːd] n anís m.
ankle ['æŋkl] n tobillo m.
annex ['æneks] n (also: **annexe**) (edificio) anexo, dependencia // vt [æ'neks] (territory) anexar; (document) adjuntar.
annihilate [ə'naɪəleɪt] vt aniquilar.
anniversary [ænɪ'vɜːsərɪ] n aniversario.
annotate ['ænəʊteɪt] vt anotar, comentar.
announce [ə'naʊns] vt comunicar, anunciar; ~**ment** n anuncio, aviso, declaración f; **announcer** n (RADIO, TV) locutor/a m/f.
annoy [ə'nɔɪ] vt molestar, fastidiar, irritar; **don't get** ~**ed!** ¡no se enfade!; ~**ance** n enojo; (thing) molestia; ~**ing** a molesto, fastidioso; (person) pesado.
annual ['ænjuəl] a anual // n (BOT) anual m; (book) anuario; ~**ly** ad anualmente, cada año.
annuity [ə'njuːɪtɪ] n renta o pensión f vitalicia.
annul [ə'nʌl] vt anular, cancelar; (law) revocar; ~**ment** n anulación f, cancelación f.
annum ['ænəm] n see **per**.
anoint [ə'nɔɪnt] vt untar.
anomaly [ə'nɔməlɪ] n anomalía.
anonymity [ænə'nɪmɪtɪ] n anonimato; **anonymous** [ə'nɔnɪməs] a anónimo.
anorak ['ænəræk] n anorak m.
anorexia [ænə'reksɪə] n (MED) anorexia.
another [ə'nʌðə*] a: ~ **book** (one more) otro libro; (a different one) un libro distinto // pron otro; see also **one**.
answer ['ɑːnsə*] n contestación f, respuesta; (to problem) solución f // vi contestar, responder // vt (reply to) contestar a, responder a; (problem) resolver; **to** ~ **the phone** contestar el teléfono; **in** ~ **to your letter** contestando o en contestación a su carta; **to** ~ **the bell** or **the door** acudir a la puerta; **to** ~ **back** vi replicar, ser respondón(ona); **to** ~ **for** vt fus responder de o por; **to** ~ **to** vt fus (description) corresponder a; (needs) satisfacer; ~**able** a: ~**able to sb for sth** responsable ante uno de algo.
ant [ænt] n hormiga.
antacid [ænt'æsɪd] a antiácido.
antagonist [æn'tægənɪst] n antagonista m/f, adversario/a; ~**ic** [-'nɪstɪk] a antagónico; (opposed) contrario, opuesto; **antagonize** [-naɪz] vt enemistarse con.
Antarctic [ænt'ɑːktɪk] n: **the** ~ el Antártico; ~**a** n Antártida.
antelope ['æntɪləʊp] n antílope m.
antenatal ['æntɪ'neɪtl] a antenatal, prenatal; ~ **clinic** n clínica prenatal.
antenna [æn'tenə], pl ~**e** [-niː] n antena.
anthem ['ænθəm] n: **national** ~ himno nacional.
anthology [æn'θɔlədʒɪ] n antología.

anthropologist [ænθrə'pɔlədʒɪst] n antropólogo; **anthropology** [-dʒɪ] n antropología.

anti... [æntɪ] pref anti...; ~**-aircraft** a antiaéreo.

antibiotic [æntɪbaɪ'ɔtɪk] a, n antibiótico.

anticipate [æn'tɪsɪpeɪt] vt (foresee) prever; (expect) esperar, contar con; (forestall) anticiparse a, adelantarse a; (look forward to) prometerse; **anticipation** [-'peɪʃən] n previsión f; esperanza; anticipación f, prevención f.

anticlimax [æntɪ'klaɪmæks] n decepción f.

anticlockwise [æntɪ'klɔkwaɪz] ad en dirección contraria a la de las agujas del reloj.

antics ['æntɪks] npl payasadas fpl; (of child) travesuras fpl.

anticyclone [æntɪ'saɪkləun] n anticiclón m.

antidote ['æntɪdəut] n antídoto.

antifreeze ['æntɪfri:z] n anticongelante m, solución f anticongelante.

antihistamine [æntɪ'hɪstəmi:n] n antihistamínico.

antiquated ['æntɪkweɪtɪd] a anticuado.

antique [æn'ti:k] n antigüedad f, antigualla // a antiguo, anticuado; ~ **dealer** n anticuario; ~ **shop** n tienda de antigüedades.

antiquity [æn'tɪkwɪtɪ] n antigüedad f.

antiseptic [æntɪ'sɛptɪk] a, n antiséptico.

antisocial [æntɪ'səuʃəl] a antisocial.

antlers ['æntləz] npl cuernas fpl.

anus ['eɪnəs] n ano.

anvil ['ænvɪl] n yunque m.

anxiety [æŋ'zaɪətɪ] n (worry) inquietud f; (eagerness) ansia, anhelo; (MED) ansiedad f.

anxious ['æŋkʃəs] a (worried) inquieto; (keen) deseoso; ~**ly** ad con inquietud, de manera angustiada.

any ['ɛnɪ] a (in negative and interrogative sentences = some) algún, alguno, alguna; (negative sense) ningún, ninguno, ninguna; (no matter which) cualquier(a); (each and every) todo; I **haven't** ~ **money/books** no tengo dinero/libros; **have you** ~ **butter/children?** ¿tiene mantequilla/hijos?; **at** ~ **moment** en cualquier momento; **in** ~ **case** de todas formas, de todas maneras; **at** ~ **rate** de todas formas, sea como sea // pron alguno; ninguno; (anybody) cualquiera; (in negative and interrogative sentences): I **haven't** ~ no tengo ninguno; **have you got** ~? ¿tiene algunos?; **can** ~ **of you sing?** ¿alguno de Ustedes sabe cantar? // ad (in negative sentences) nada; (in interrogative and conditional constructions) algo; I **can't hear him** ~ **more** no le oigo más; **do you want** ~ **more soup?** ¿quiere más sopa?; ~**body** pron cualquiera, cualquier persona; (in interrogative sentences) alguien; (in negative sentences): I **don't see** ~**body** no veo a nadie; ~**how** ad de todos modos, de todas maneras; (carelessly) de cualquier manera; ~**one** = ~**body**; ~**thing** pron (see ~**body**) algo, cualquier cosa; algo; (in negative sentences) nada; (everything) todo; ~**time** ad (at any moment) en cualquier momento, de un momento a otro; (whenever) no importa cuándo, cuando quiera; ~**way** ad de todas maneras; de cualquier modo; ~**where** ad (see ~**body**) dondequiera; en algún sitio; (negative sense) en ningún sitio; (everywhere) en or por todas partes; I **don't see him** ~**where** no le veo en ningún sitio.

apart [ə'pɑ:t] ad aparte, separadamente; **10 miles** ~ separados por 10 millas; ~ **from** prep aparte de.

apartheid [ə'pɑ:teɪt] n apartheid m.

apartment [ə'pɑ:tmənt] n (US) piso, apartamento; (room) cuarto.

apathetic [æpə'θɛtɪk] a apático, indiferente; **apathy** ['æpəθɪ] n apatía, indiferencia.

ape [eɪp] n mono // vt imitar, remedar.

aperitif [ə'pɛrɪtɪv] n aperitivo.

aperture ['æpətʃjuə*] n rendija, resquicio; (PHOT) abertura.

apex ['eɪpɛks] n ápice m; (fig) cumbre f.

aphrodisiac [æfrəu'dɪzɪæk] a, n afrodisíaco.

apiece [ə'pi:s] ad cada uno.

apologetic [əpɔlə'dʒɛtɪk] a (tone, letter) lleno de disculpas.

apologize [ə'pɔlədʒaɪz] vi: to ~ (for sth to sb) disculparse (con alguien de algo); **apology** [-dʒɪ] n disculpa, excusa.

apostle [ə'pɔsl] n apóstol m/f.

apostrophe [ə'pɔstrəfɪ] n apóstrofe m.

appal [ə'pɔ:l] vt horrorizar, espantar; ~**ling** a espantoso; (awful) pésimo.

apparatus [æpə'reɪtəs] n aparato.

apparent [ə'pærənt] a aparente; (obvious) manifiesto, claro; ~**ly** ad por lo visto, al parecer.

apparition [æpə'rɪʃən] n aparición f; (ghost) fantasma m.

appeal [ə'pi:l] vi (LAW) apelar // n (LAW) apelación f; (request) llamamiento; (plea) súplica, ruego; (charm) atractivo, encanto; to ~ **for** suplicar, reclamar; to ~ **to** (subj: person) rogar a, suplicar a; (subj: thing) atraer, interesar; to ~ **to sb for mercy** rogarle misericordia a alguien; **it doesn't** ~ **to me** no me atrae, no me llama la atención; ~**ing** a (nice) atrayente, atractivo; (touching) conmovedor(a), emocionante.

appear [ə'pɪə*] vi aparecer, presentarse; (LAW) comparecer; (publication) salir (a luz), publicarse; (seem) parecer; **it would** ~ **that** parecería que; ~**ance** n aparición f; (look, aspect) apariencia, aspecto.

appease [ə'pi:z] vt (pacify) apaciguar; (satisfy) satisfacer, saciar.

appendicitis [əpɛndɪ'saɪtɪs] n apendicitis f.

appendix [ə'pɛndɪks], pl -**dices** [-dɪsi:z] n apéndice m.

appetite ['æpɪtaɪt] n apetito; (fig) deseo, anhelo.

appetizing ['æpɪtaɪzɪŋ] a apetitoso.

applaud [ə'plɔːd] vt, vi aplaudir; **applause** [-ɔːz] n aplausos mpl.

apple ['æpl] n manzana; ~ **tree** n manzano.

appliance [ə'plaɪəns] n aparato.

applicable [ə'plɪkəbl] a aplicable, pertinente.

applicant ['æplɪkənt] n candidato/a, solicitante m/f.

application [æplɪ'keɪʃən] n aplicación f; (for a job, a grant etc) solicitud f, petición f; ~ **form** n formulario.

apply [ə'plaɪ] vt: **to** ~ **(to)** aplicar (a); (fig) emplear (para) // vi: **to** ~ **to** (ask) presentarse a, ser candidato a; (be suitable for) ser aplicable a; (be relevant to) tener que ver con; **to** ~ **for** (permit, grant, job) solicitar; **to** ~ **the brakes** aplicar los frenos; **to** ~ **o.s. to** aplicarse a, dedicarse a.

appoint [ə'pɔɪnt] vt (to post) nombrar; (date, place) fijar, señalar; ~**ment** n (engagement) cita; (date) compromiso; (act) nombramiento; (post) puesto.

apportion [ə'pɔːʃən] vt repartir, distribuir; (blame) dar.

appraisal [ə'preɪzl] n tasación f, valoración f.

appreciable [ə'priːʃəbl] a sensible.

appreciate [ə'priːʃɪeɪt] vt (like) apreciar, tener en mucho; (be grateful for) agradecer; (assess) valorar, apreciar; (be aware of) comprender, percibir // vi (COMM) aumentar(se) en valor, subir; **appreciation** [-'eɪʃən] n aprecio; reconocimiento, agradecimiento; aumento en valor.

appreciative [ə'priːʃɪətɪv] a (person) agradecido; (comment) elogioso.

apprehend [æprɪ'hɛnd] vt percibir, comprender; (arrest) detener.

apprehension [æprɪ'hɛnʃən] n (fear) recelo, aprensión f; **apprehensive** [-'hɛnsɪv] a aprensivo.

apprentice [ə'prɛntɪs] n aprendiz/a m/f; ~**ship** n aprendizaje m.

approach [ə'prəutʃ] vi acercarse // vt acercarse a; (be approximate) aproximarse a; (ask, apply to) dirigirse a // n acercamiento; aproximación f; (access) acceso; (proposal) proposición f; ~**able** a (person) abordable; (place) accesible.

appropriate [ə'prəuprɪeɪt] vt (take) apropiarse; (allot): **to** ~ **sth for** destinar algo a // a [-rɪɪt] (apt) apropiado, conveniente; (relevant) competente.

approval [ə'pruːvəl] n aprobación f, visto bueno; **on** ~ (COMM) a prueba.

approve [ə'pruːv] vt aprobar; ~**d school** n correccional m.

approximate [ə'prɔksɪmɪt] a aproximado // vt [-meɪt] aproximarse a, acercarse a;

approximation [-'meɪʃən] n aproximación f.

apricot ['eɪprɪkɔt] n albaricoque m.

April ['eɪprəl] n abril m; ~ **Fool's Day** n Día m de los Inocentes.

apron ['eɪprən] n delantal m.

apt [æpt] a (suitable) acertado, oportuno; (appropriate) conveniente; (likely): ~ **to do** con tendencia a hacer.

aptitude ['æptɪtjuːd] n aptitud f, capacidad f.

aqualung ['ækwəlʌŋ] n aparato de buceo autónomo.

aquarium [ə'kwɛərɪəm] n acuario.

Aquarius [ə'kwɛərɪəs] n Acuario.

aquatic [ə'kwætɪk] a acuático.

aqueduct ['ækwɪdʌkt] n acueducto.

Arab ['ærəb] n árabe m/f.

Arabia [ə'reɪbɪə] n Arabia; ~**n** a árabe.

Arabic ['ærəbɪk] n árabe m.

arable ['ærəbl] a cultivable.

arbitrary ['ɑːbɪtrərɪ] a arbitrario.

arbitrate ['ɑːbɪtreɪt] vi arbitrar; **arbitration** [-'treɪʃən] n arbitraje m; **arbitrator** n juez m árbitro.

arc [ɑːk] n arco.

arcade [ɑː'keɪd] n arcada; (round a square) soportales mpl; (passage with shops) galería, pasaje m.

arch [ɑːtʃ] n arco; (vault) bóveda; (of foot) empeine m // vt arquear.

archaeologist [ɑːkɪ'ɔlədʒɪst] n arqueólogo; **archaeology** [-dʒɪ] n arqueología.

archaic [ɑː'keɪɪk] a arcaico.

archbishop [ɑːtʃ'bɪʃəp] n arzobispo.

arch-enemy ['ɑːtʃ'ɛnɪmɪ] n enemigo jurado.

archer ['ɑːtʃə*] n arquero; ~**y** n tiro con arco.

archetype ['ɑːkɪtaɪp] n arquetipo.

archipelago [ɑːkɪ'pɛlɪgəu] n archipiélago.

architect ['ɑːkɪtɛkt] n arquitecto; ~**ural** [-'tɛktʃərəl] a arquitectónico; ~**ure** n arquitectura.

archives ['ɑːkaɪvz] npl archivo sg.

archway ['ɑːtʃweɪ] n arco, arcada.

Arctic ['ɑːktɪk] a ártico // n: **the** ~ el Ártico.

ardent ['ɑːdənt] a (passionate) ardiente, apasionado; (fervent) fervoroso; **ardour** ['ɑːdə*] n ardor m; fervor m.

arduous ['ɑːdjuəs] a (gen) arduo; (journey) penoso.

are [ɑː*] vb see **be**.

area ['ɛərɪə] n (gen) área; (MATH etc) superficie f, extensión f; (zone) región f, zona.

arena [ə'riːnə] n arena; (of circus) pista; (for bullfight) plaza, ruedo.

aren't [ɑːnt] = **are not**.

Argentina [ɑːdʒən'tiːnə] n Argentina; **Argentinian** [-'tɪnɪən] a, n argentino/a.

argue ['ɑːgjuː] vi (quarrel) discutir; (reason) argüir, discurrir; **to** ~ **that** sostener que; **argument** n (reasons) argumento; (*quarrel*) discusión f; (*debate*) debate m, disputa; **argumentative** [-mɛntətɪv] a discutidor(a).

aria ['ɑːrɪə] n (*MUS*) aria.

arid ['ærɪd] a árido.

Aries ['cɔrɪz] n Aries m.

arise [ə'raɪz], pt **arose**, pp **arisen** [ə'rɪzn] vi (*rise up*) levantarse, alzarse; (*emerge*) surgir, presentarse; to ~ from resultar de.

aristocracy [ærɪs'tɔkrəsɪ] n aristocracia; **aristocrat** ['ærɪstəkræt] n aristócrata m/f.

arithmetic [ə'rɪθmətɪk] n aritmética.

ark [ɑːk] n: Noah's A ~ Arca de Noé.

arm [ɑːm] n (*ANAT*) brazo; (*weapon, MIL*: *branch*) arma // vt armar; ~s npl (*weapons*) armas fpl; (*HERALDRY*) escudo sg; ~s race carrera de armamentos; ~ in ~ cogidos del brazo; ~band n brazalete m; ~chair n sillón m; ~ed a armado; ~ed robbery n robo a mano armada; ~ful n brazado, brazada.

armistice ['ɑːmɪstɪs] n armisticio.

armour ['ɑːmə*] n armadura; ~ed car n coche m blindado; ~y n armería, arsenal m.

armpit ['ɑːmpɪt] n sobaco, axila.

army ['ɑːmɪ] n ejército.

aroma [ə'rəumə] n aroma m, fragancia; ~tic [ærə'mætɪk] a aromático, fragante.

arose [ə'rəuz] pt of **arise**.

around [ə'raund] ad alrededor; (*in the area*) a la redonda // prep alrededor de, en torno de; (*fig*: *about*) alrededor de.

arouse [ə'rauz] vt despertar.

arrange [ə'reɪndʒ] vt arreglar, ordenar; (*programme*) organizar; ~ment n arreglo; (*agreement*) acuerdo; ~ments npl (*plans*) planes mpl, medidas fpl; (*preparations*) preparativos mpl.

arrears [ə'rɪəz] npl atrasos mpl; to be in ~ with one's rent atrasarse en el arriendo.

arrest [ə'rɛst] vt detener; (*sb's attention*) llamar // n detención f; under ~ detenido.

arrival [ə'raɪvl] n llegada; new ~ recién llegado.

arrive [ə'raɪv] vi llegar.

arrogance ['ærəgəns] n arrogancia; **arrogant** [-gənt] a arrogante.

arrow ['ærəu] n flecha.

arsenal ['ɑːsɪnl] n arsenal m.

arsenic ['ɑːsnɪk] n arsénico.

arson ['ɑːsn] n delito de incendiar.

art [ɑːt] n arte m; (*craft*) artes fpl y oficios mpl; (*skill*) destreza; (*technique*) técnica; A ~ s npl (*SCOL*) Letras fpl; ~ gallery n museo de bellas artes; (*small and private*) galería de arte.

artery ['ɑːtərɪ] n (*MED*) arteria; (*fig*) vía principal.

arthritis [ɑː'θraɪtɪs] n artritis f.

artichoke ['ɑːtɪtʃəuk] n alcachofa; Jerusalem ~ aguaturma.

article ['ɑːtɪkl] n artículo, objeto, cosa; (*in newspaper*) artículo; (*LAW*: *training*): ~s npl contrato sg de aprendizaje.

articulate [ɑː'tɪkjulɪt] a claro o distinto en el hablar // vt [-leɪt] articular; ~d lorry n camión m articulado.

artificial [ɑːtɪ'fɪʃəl] a artificial; (*teeth etc*) postizo; ~ respiration n respiración f artificial.

artillery [ɑː'tɪlərɪ] n artillería.

artisan ['ɑːtɪzæn] n artesano.

artist ['ɑːtɪst] n artista m/f; (*MUS*) intérprete m/f; ~ic [ɑː'tɪstɪk] a artístico; ~ry n arte m, habilidad f artística.

artless ['ɑːtlɪs] a (*innocent*) natural, sencillo; (*clumsy*) desmañado.

as [æz, əz] conj (*cause*) como, ya que; (*time*: *moment*) como, cuando; (: *duration*) mientras; (*manner*) como, lo mismo que, tal como; (*in the capacity of*) como; ~ big ~ tan grande como; twice ~ big ~ dos veces más grande que; ~ she said como ella dijo; ~ if o though como si; ~ for o to that en cuanto a eso, en lo que a eso se refiere; ~ or so long ~ conj mientras (que); ~ much/many ~ tanto(s)... como; ~ soon ~ conj tan pronto como; ~ such ad como tal; ~ well ad también, además; ~ well ~ conj así como; see also **such**.

asbestos [æz'bɛstəs] n asbesto, amianto.

ascend [ə'sɛnd] vt subir; ~ancy n ascendiente m, dominio.

ascent [ə'sɛnt] n subida; (*slope*) cuesta, pendiente m; (*promotion*) ascenso.

ascertain [æsə'teɪn] vt averiguar, determinar.

ascetic [ə'sɛtɪk] a ascético.

ascribe [ə'skraɪb] vt: to ~ sth to atribuir algo a.

ash [æʃ] n ceniza; (*tree*) fresno.

ashamed [ə'ʃeɪmd] a avergonzado; to be ~ of avergonzarse de.

ashen ['æʃn] a ceniciento, pálido.

ashore [ə'ʃɔː*] ad en tierra.

ashtray ['æʃtreɪ] n cenicero.

Asia ['eɪʃə] n Asia; ~n, ~tic [eɪsɪ'ætɪk] a, n asiático/a.

aside [ə'saɪd] ad aparte, a un lado.

ask [ɑːsk] vt (*question*) preguntar; (*demand*) pedir; (*invite*) invitar; to ~ sb sth/to do sth preguntar algo a alguien/pedir a alguien que haga algo; to ~ sb about sth preguntar algo a alguien; to ~ (sb) a question hacer una pregunta (a alguien); to ~ sb out to dinner invitar a comer a uno; to ~ for vt fus pedir.

askance [ə'skɑːns] ad: to look ~ at sb mirar con recelo a uno.

askew [ə'skjuː] ad sesgado, ladeado, oblicuamente.

asleep [ə'sliːp] a dormido; to fall ~ dormirse, quedarse dormido.

asparagus [əs'pærəgəs] n espárragos mpl.

aspect ['æspɛkt] n aspecto, apariencia; (*direction in which a building etc faces*) orientación f.

aspersions [əs'pəː∫ənz] npl: to cast ~ on difamar a, calumniar a.

asphalt ['æsfælt] n asfalto; (place) pista asfaltada.

asphyxiate [æs'fɪksɪeɪt] vt asfixiar // vi asfixiarse; **asphyxiation** [-'eɪ∫ən] n asfixia.

aspiration [æspə'reɪ∫ən] n (fig) anhelo, deseo, ambición f.

aspire [əs'paɪə*] vi: to ~ to aspirar a, ambicionar.

aspirin ['æsprɪn] n aspirina.

ass [æs] n asno, burro; (col) imbécil m.

assailant [ə'seɪlənt] n asaltador/a m/f, agresor/a m/f.

assassin [ə'sæsɪn] n asesino; **~ate** vt asesinar; **~ation** [-'neɪ∫ən] n asesinato.

assault [ə'sɔːlt] n (gen: attack) asalto, ataque m // vt asaltar, atacar; (sexually) violar.

assemble [ə'sɛmbl] vt reunir, juntar; (TECH) montar // vi reunirse, juntarse.

assembly [ə'sɛmblɪ] n (meeting) reunión f, asamblea; (people) concurrencia; (construction) montaje m; ~ **line** n línea de producción.

assent [ə'sɛnt] n asentimiento, aprobación f // vi consentir, asentir.

assert [ə'səːt] vt afirmar; (claim etc) hacer valer; **~ion** [ə'səː∫ən] n afirmación f.

assess [ə'sɛs] vt valorar, calcular; (tax, damages) fijar; (property etc: for tax) gravar; **~ment** n valoración f; gravamen m; **~or** n asesor/a m/f, (of tax) tasador/a m/f.

asset ['æsɛt] n posesión f; (quality) ventaja sg; **~s** npl (funds) activo sg, fondos mpl.

assiduous [ə'sɪdjuəs] a asiduo.

assign [ə'saɪn] vt (date) fijar; (task) asignar; (resources) destinar; (property) traspasar; **~ment** n asignación f; (task) tarea.

assimilate [ə'sɪmɪleɪt] vt asimilar.

assist [ə'sɪst] vt ayudar; (progress etc) fomentar; **~ance** n ayuda, auxilio; (welfare) subsidio; **~ant** n ayudante m/f, auxiliar m/f; (also: **shop** **~ant**) dependiente/a m/f.

assizes [ə'saɪzɪz] npl sesión f de un tribunal.

associate [ə'səu∫ɪt] a asociado // n asociado, colega m; (in crime) cómplice m/f; (member) miembro // (vb: [-∫ɪeɪt]) vt asociar, relacionar // vi: to ~ **with sb** tratar con alguien.

association [əsəusɪ'eɪ∫ən] n asociación f; (COMM) sociedad f.

assorted [ə'sɔːtɪd] a surtido, variado.

assortment [ə'sɔːtmənt] n surtido.

assume [ə'sjuːm] vt (suppose) suponer, dar por sentado; (responsibilities etc) asumir; (attitude, name) adoptar, tomar.

assumption [ə'sʌmp∫ən] n (supposition) suposición f, presunción f; (act) asunción f.

assurance [ə'∫uərəns] n garantía, promesa; (confidence) confianza, aplomo; (certainty) certeza; (insurance) seguro.

assure [ə'∫uə*] vt asegurar.

asterisk ['æstərɪsk] n asterisco.

astern [ə'stəːn] ad a popa, por la popa.

asteroid ['æstərɔɪd] n asteroide m.

asthma ['æsmə] n asma; **~tic** [æs'mætɪk] a, n asmático/a.

astonish [ə'stɔnɪ∫] vt asombrar, pasmar; **~ment** n asombro, sorpresa.

astound [ə'staund] vt asombrar, pasmar.

astray [ə'streɪ] ad: to go ~ extraviarse; **to lead** ~ llevar por mal camino.

astride [ə'straɪd] ad a horcajadas // prep a caballo o horcajadas sobre.

astrologer [əs'trɔlədʒə*] n astrólogo; **astrology** [-dʒɪ] n astrología.

astronaut ['æstrɔnɔːt] n astronauta m/f.

astronomer [əs'trɔnəmə*] n astrónomo; **astronomical** [æstrə'nɔmɪkəl] a astronómico; (fig) tremendo, enorme; **astronomy** [-mɪ] n astronomía.

astute [əs'tjuːt] a astuto.

asunder [ə'sʌndə*] ad: to tear ~ romper en dos, hacer pedazos.

asylum [ə'saɪləm] n (refuge) asilo; (hospital) manicomio.

at [æt] prep en, a; ~ **the top** en la cumbre; ~ **4 o'clock** a las cuatro; ~ **£1 a kilo** a libra el kilo; ~ **night** de noche, por la noche; ~ **a stroke** de un golpe; **two ~ a time** de dos en dos; ~ **times** a veces.

ate [eɪt] pt of **eat**.

atheist ['eɪθɪɪst] n ateo/a.

Athens ['æθɪnz] n Atenas f.

athlete ['æθliːt] n atleta m/f.

athletic [æθ'lɛtɪk] a atlético; **~s** n atletismo.

Atlantic [ət'læntɪk] n: the ~ (Ocean) el (Océano) Atlántico.

atlas ['ætləs] n atlas m.

atmosphere ['ætməsfɪə*] n atmósfera; (fig) ambiente m.

atom ['ætəm] n átomo; **~ic** [ə'tɔmɪk] a atómico; **~(ic) bomb** n bomba atómica; **~izer** ['ætəmaɪzə*] n atomizador m.

atone [ə'təun] vi: to ~ **for** expiar.

atrocious [ə'trəu∫əs] a (very bad) atroz; (fig) horrible, infame.

atrocity [ə'trɔsɪtɪ] n atrocidad f.

attach [ə'tæt∫] vt (gen) sujetar, pegar; (document, letter) adjuntar; **to be ~ed to sb/sth** (to like) tener cariño a alguien/algo.

attaché [ə'tæ∫eɪ] n agregado; ~ **case** n maletín m.

attachment [ə'tæt∫mənt] n (tool) accesorio; (love): ~ **(to)** cariño (a).

attack [ə'tæk] vt (MIL) atacar; (criminal) agredir, asaltar; (task etc) emprender // n ataque m, asalto; (on sb's life) atentado; **heart** ~ ataque al corazón o cardíaco; **~er** n agresor/a m/f, asaltante m/f.

attain [ə'teɪn] vt (also: ~ **to**) alcanzar; (achieve) lograr, conseguir; **~ments** npl dotes fpl, talento sg.

attempt [ə'tɛmpt] n tentativa, intento; (attack) atentado // vt intentar, tratar de.

attend [ə'tɛnd] vt asistir a; (patient)
atender; **to ~ to** vt fus (needs, affairs etc)
ocuparse de; (speech etc) prestar atención
a; (customer) atender a; **~ance** n
asistencia, presencia; (people present) concurrencia; **~ant** n sirviente/a m/f,
mozo/a; (THEATRE) acomodador/a m/f //
a concomitante.

attention [ə'tɛnʃən] n atención f // excl
(MIL) ¡firme(s)!; **for the ~ of...** (ADMIN)
atención... .

attentive [ə'tɛntɪv] a atento; (polite)
cortés.

attest [ə'tɛst] vi: **to ~ to** dar fe de.

attic ['ætɪk] n desván m, ático.

attitude ['ætɪtjuːd] n (gen) actitud f;
(disposition) disposición f.

attorney [ə'tɔːnɪ] n (lawyer) abogado;
(having proxy) apoderado; **A~ General** n
(Brit) fiscal m de la corona; (US)
procurador m general.

attract [ə'trækt] vt atraer; (attention)
llamar; **attraction** [ə'trækʃən] n (gen pl)
encantos mpl; (amusements) diversiones
fpl; (PHYSICS) atracción f; (fig: towards sth)
atractivo; **~ive** a atractivo; (interesting)
atrayente; (pretty) guapo, mono.

attribute ['ætrɪbjuːt] n atributo // vt
[ə'trɪbjuːt]: **to ~ sth to** atribuir o achacar
algo a.

aubergine ['əubəʒiːn] n berenjena.

auburn ['ɔːbən] a castaño rojizo.

auction ['ɔːkʃən] n (also: **sale by ~**)
subasta // vt subastar; **~eer** [-'nɪə*] n
subastador/a m/f.

audacious [ɔː'deɪʃəs] a audaz, atrevido;
(pej) descarado; **audacity** [ɔː'dæsɪtɪ] n
audacia, atrevimiento f; (pej) descaro.

audible ['ɔːdɪbl] a audible, que se puede
oír.

audience ['ɔːdɪəns] n auditorio, público;
(interview) audiencia.

audio-visual [ɔːdɪəu'vɪʒuəl] a audiovisual.

audit ['ɔːdɪt] vt revisar, intervenir.

audition [ɔː'dɪʃən] n audición f.

auditor ['ɔːdɪtə*] n interventor/a m/f,
censor/a m/f de cuentas.

auditorium [ɔːdɪ'tɔːrɪəm] n auditorio.

augment [ɔːg'mɛnt] vt aumentar // vi
aumentarse.

augur ['ɔːgə*] vi: **it ~s well** es de buen
agüero.

August ['ɔːgəst] n agosto.

aunt [ɑːnt] n tía; **~ie**, **~y** n diminutive of
aunt.

au pair ['əu'pɛə*] n (also: **~ girl**) au pair
f.

aura ['ɔːrə] n emanación f; (atmosphere)
ambiente m.

auspices ['ɔːspɪsɪz] npl: **under the ~ of**
bajo los auspicios de.

auspicious [ɔːs'pɪʃəs] a propicio, de buen
augurio.

austere [ɔs'tɪə*] a austero; (manner)
adusto; **austerity** [ɔ'stɛrɪtɪ] n austeridad f.

Australia [ɔs'treɪlɪə] n Australia; **~n** a, n
australiano/a.

Austria ['ɔstrɪə] n Austria; **~n** a, n
austríaco/a.

authentic [ɔː'θɛntɪk] a auténtico.

author ['ɔːθə] n autor/a m/f.

authoritarian [ɔːθɔrɪ'tɛərɪən] a
autoritario.

authoritative [ɔː'θɔrɪtətɪv] a autorizado;
(manner) autoritario.

authority [ɔː'θɔrɪtɪ] n autoridad f; **the
authorities** npl las autoridades.

authorize ['ɔːθəraɪz] vt autorizar.

auto ['ɔːtəu] n (US) coche m, automóvil m.

autobiography [ɔːtəbaɪ'ɔgrəfɪ] n
autobiografía.

autocratic [ɔːtə'krætɪk] a autocrático.

autograph ['ɔːtəgrɑːf] n autógrafo // vt
firmar; (photo etc) dedicar.

automatic [ɔːtə'mætɪk] a automático // n
(gun) pistola automática.

automation [ɔːtə'meɪʃən] n auto-
matización f.

automaton [ɔː'tɔmətən], pl **-mata** [-tə] n
autómata m/f.

automobile ['ɔːtəməbiːl] n (US) coche m,
automóvil m.

autonomous [ɔː'tɔnəməs] a autónomo.

autopsy ['ɔːtɔpsɪ] n autopsia.

autumn ['ɔːtəm] n otoño.

auxiliary [ɔːg'zɪlɪərɪ] a auxiliar.

Av. abbr of **avenue**.

avail [ə'veɪl] vt: **to ~ o.s. of**
aprovechar(se) de, valerse de // n: **to no
~ en vano, sin resultado.

availability [əveɪlə'bɪlɪtɪ] n disponibilidad
f.

available [ə'veɪləbl] a disponible; (usable)
asequible.

avalanche ['ævəlɑːnʃ] n alud m,
avalancha.

avant-garde ['ævãŋ'gɑːd] a de
vanguardia.

avaricious [ævə'rɪʃəs] a avaro, avariento.

Ave. abbr of **avenue**.

avenge [ə'vɛndʒ] vt vengar.

avenue ['ævənjuː] n avenida; (path)
camino.

average ['ævərɪdʒ] n promedio, término
medio // a (mean) medio, de término
medio; (ordinary) regular, corriente // vt
calcular el promedio de, prorratear; **on ~**
por regla general; **to ~ out** vi: **to ~ out
at** resultar por promedio, ser por regla
general.

averse [ə'vɜːs] a: **to be ~ to sth/doing**
sentir aversión o antipatía por algo/por
hacer; **aversion** [ə'vɜːʃən] n aversión f,
repugnancia.

avert [ə'vɜːt] vt prevenir; (blow) desviar;
(one's eyes) apartar.

aviary ['eɪvɪərɪ] n pajarera, avería.

aviation [eɪvɪ'eɪʃən] n aviación f.

avid ['ævɪd] a ávido, ansioso.

avocado [ævə'kɑːdəu] n (also: **~ pear**)
aguacate m.

avoid [ə'vɔɪd] vt evitar, eludir; **~able** a

evitable, eludible; ~ance n el evitar, evitación f.

await [ə'weit] vt esperar, aguardar.

awake [ə'weik] a despierto // (vb: pt **awoke**, pp **awoken** or **awaked**) vt despertar // vi despertarse; ~**ning** n el despertar.

award [ə'wɔːd] n (prize) premio, condecoración f; (LAW) fallo, sentencia; (act) concesión f // vt (prize) otorgar, conceder; (LAW: damages) adjudicar, decretar.

aware [ə'wɛə*] a consciente; (awake) despierto; (informed) enterado; to become ~ of darse cuenta de, enterarse de; ~ness n conciencia, conocimiento.

awash [ə'wɔʃ] a inundado.

away [ə'wei] ad (gen) fuera; (far ~) lejos; two kilometres ~ a dos kilómetros de distancia; two hours ~ by car a dos horas en coche; the holiday was two weeks ~ faltaba dos semanas para las vacaciones; ~ from lejos de, fuera de; he's ~ for a week estará ausente una semana; to take ~ vt llevar(se); to work/pedal ~ seguir trabajando/pedaleando; to fade ~ desvanecerse; (sound) apagarse; ~ match n (SPORT) partido de fuera.

awe [ɔː] n pavor m, respeto, temor m reverencial; ~**inspiring**, ~**some** a imponente, pasmoso; ~**struck** a pasmado.

awful ['ɔːfəl] a tremendo, terrible, pasmoso; ~**ly** ad (very) terriblemente.

awhile [ə'wail] ad durante un rato, un rato, algún tiempo.

awkward ['ɔːkwəd] a (clumsy) desmañado, torpe; (shape) incómodo; (problem) difícil; (embarrassing) delicado, desagradable.

awning ['ɔːniŋ] n (of shop) toldo; (of window etc) marquesina.

awoke [ə'wəuk], **awoken** [-kən] pt, pp of **awake**.

awry [ə'rai] ad: to be ~ estar de través o al sesgo; to go ~ salir mal, fracasar.

axe, ax (US) [æks] n hacha // vt (employee) despedir; (project etc) parar, cortar; (jobs) reducir.

axiom ['æksiəm] n axioma m.

axis ['æksis], pl **axes** [-siːz] n eje m.

axle ['æksl] n eje m, árbol m.

ay(e) [ai] excl (yes) sí; the **ayes** npl los que votan a favor.

Aztec ['æztɛk] n azteca m/f.

B

B.A. abbr of **Bachelor of Arts** licenciado en letras.

babble ['bæbl] vi barbullar.

baboon [bə'buːn] n mandril m.

baby ['beibi] n nene/a m/f; ~ **carriage** n (US) cochecito; ~**ish** a infantil; ~-**sit** vi hacer de canguro; ~-**sitter** n canguro m/f.

bachelor ['bætʃələ*] n soltero.

back [bæk] n (of person) espalda; (of animal) lomo; (of hand) dorso; (of house, car, train) parte f de atrás; (of chair) respaldo; (of page) reverso; (FOOTBALL) defensa m // vt (candidate: also: ~ up) respaldar, apoyar; (horse: at races) apostar a; (car) dar marcha atrás a o con // vi (car etc) dar marcha atrás // a (in compounds) tras; ~ **seats/wheels** (AUT) asientos mpl/ruedas fpl de atrás; ~ **payments** pagos mpl con efecto retroactivo; ~ **rent** renta atrasada // ad (not forward) (hacia) atrás; (returned): he's ~ está de vuelta, ha vuelto; he ran ~ retrocedió corriendo; (restitution): throw the ball ~ devuelve la pelota; can I have it ~? ¿me lo devuelve?; (again): he called ~ llamó de nuevo; to ~ **down** vi echarse atrás; to ~ **out** vi (of promise) volverse atrás.

back: ~**ache** n dolor m de espalda; ~**bencher** n miembro del parlamento sin portafolio; ~**biting** n murmuración f; ~**bone** n columna vertebral; ~-**cloth** n telón m de foro; ~**date** vt (letter) poner fecha atrasada a; ~**dated pay rise** alza de sueldo con efecto retroactivo; ~**er** n partidario; (COMM) promotor m; ~**fire** vi (AUT) petardear; (plans) fallar, salir al revés; ~**gammon** n backgammon m; ~**ground** n fondo; (of events) antecedentes mpl; (basic knowledge) bases fpl; (experience) conocimientos mpl, educación f; ~**ground music** m, antecedentes mpl; ~**hand** n (TENNIS: also: ~**hand stroke**) revés m; ~**handed** a (fig) ambiguo, equívoco; ~**hander** n (bribe) soborno; ~**ing** n (fig) apoyo, respaldo; ~**lash** n reacción f, resaca; ~**log** n: ~**log of work** atrasos mpl; ~ **number** n (of magazine etc) número atrasado; ~ **pay** n pago atrasado; ~**side** n (col) trasero, culo; ~**stage** ad entre bastidores; ~**stroke** n braza de espaldas; ~**ward** a (movement) hacia atrás; (person, country) atrasado; (shy) tímido; ~**wards** ad (move, go) hacia atrás; (read a list) al revés; (fall) de espaldas; ~**water** n (fig) lugar m atrasado o apartado; ~**yard** n traspatio.

bacon ['beikən] n tocino.

bacteria [bæk'tiəriə] npl bacteria sg.

bad [bæd] a malo; (serious) grave; (meat, food) podrido, pasado; to go ~ echarse a perder.

badge [bædʒ] n insignia; (of policeman) chapa, placa.

badger ['bædʒə*] n tejón m.

badly ['bædli] ad (work, dress etc) mal; ~ **wounded** gravemente herido; he needs it ~ le hace gran falta; to be ~ **off** (for money) andar mal de dinero.

badminton ['bædmintən] n badminton m.

bad-tempered ['bæd'tɛmpəd] a de mal genio o carácter; (temporary) de mal humor.

baffle ['bæfl] *vt* (*puzzle*) desconcertar, confundir.

bag [bæg] *n* bolsa, saco; (*handbag*) bolso; (*satchel*) mochila; (*case*) maleta; (*of hunter*) caza // *vt* (*col: take*) coger, pescar; **~ful** *n* saco (lleno); **~gage** *n* equipaje *m*; **~gy** *a* que hace bolsas; **~pipes** *npl* gaita *sg*.

bail [beil] *n* fianza, caución *f* // *vt* (*prisoner*: *gen*: **give ~ to**) poner en libertad bajo fianza; (*boat*: *also*: **~ out**) achicar; **to ~ sb out** obtener la libertad de uno bajo fianza; *see also* **bale.**

bailiff ['beilif] *n* alguacil *m*.

bait [beit] *n* cebo // *vt* cebar, poner el cebo en.

bake [beik] *vt* cocer (al horno) // *vi* (*cook*) cocerse; (*be hot*) hacer un calor terrible; **~d beans** *npl* judías *fpl* en salsa de tomate; **baker** *n* panadero; **~ry** *n* (*for bread*) panadería; (*for cakes*) pastelería; **baking** *n* (*act*) cocción *f*; (*batch*) hornada; **baking powder** *n* polvos *mpl* de levadura.

balaclava [bælə'klɑːvə] *n* (*also*: **~ helmet**) pasamontañas *m inv.*

balance ['bæləns] *n* equilibrio; (*COMM: sum*) balance *m*; (*remainder*) resto; (*scales*) balanza // *vt* equilibrar; (*budget*) nivelar; (*account*) saldar; (*compensate*) contrapesar; **~ of trade/payments** balanza de comercio/pagos; **~d** *a* (*personality, diet*) equilibrado; **~ sheet** *n* balance *m.*

balcony ['bælkəni] *n* (*open*) balcón *m*; (*closed*) galería.

bald [bɔːld] *a* calvo; **~ness** *n* calvicie *f.*

bale [beil] *n* (*AGR*) paca, fardo; **to ~ out** (*of a plane*) lanzarse en paracaídas; **to ~ sb out of a difficulty** sacar a uno de un problema.

baleful ['beilful] *a* (*look*) triste; (*sinister*) funesto, siniestro.

ball [bɔːl] *n* bola; (*football*) balón *m*; (*for tennis, golf*) pelota; (*dance*) baile *m.*

ballad ['bæləd] *n* balada, romance *m.*

ballast ['bæləst] *n* lastre *m.*

ballerina [bælə'riːnə] *n* bailarina.

ballet ['bælei] *n* ballet *m*, baile *m*; **~ dancer** *n* bailarín/ina *m/f.*

balloon [bə'luːn] *n* globo; **~ist** *n* ascensionista *m/f.*

ballot ['bælət] *n* votación *f*; **~ box** *n* urna (electoral); **~ paper** *n* papeleta.

ball-point pen ['bɔːlpɔint'-] *n* bolígrafo.

ballroom ['bɔːlrum] *n* salón *m* de baile.

balmy ['bɑːmi] *a* (*breeze, air*) suave, fragante; (*col*) = **barmy.**

Baltic ['bɔːltik] *n*: **the ~ (Sea)** el (Mar) Báltico.

balustrade ['bæləstreid] *n* barandilla.

bamboo [bæm'buː] *n* bambú *m.*

ban [bæn] *n* prohibición *f*, proscripción *f* // *vt* prohibir, proscribir; (*exclude*) excluir.

banal [bə'nɑːl] *a* banal, vulgar.

banana [bə'nɑːnə] *n* plátano.

band [bænd] *n* (*group*) banda; (*gang*) pandilla; (*strip*) faja, tira; (*at a dance*) orquesta; (*MIL*) banda; **to ~ together** *vi* juntarse, asociarse.

bandage ['bændidʒ] *n* venda, vendaje *m* // *vt* vendar.

bandit ['bændit] *n* bandido; **one-armed ~** máquina tragaperras.

bandstand ['bændstænd] *n* quiosco.

bandwagon ['bændwægən] *n*: **to jump on the ~** (*fig*) seguir la corriente o la moda.

bandy ['bændi] *vt* (*jokes, insults*) cambiar.

bandy-legged ['bændi'legd] *a* estevado.

bang [bæŋ] *n* estallido; (*of door*) portazo; (*blow*) golpe *m* // *vt* hacer estallar; (*door*) cerrar de golpe // *vi* estallar.

banger ['bæŋə*] *n* (*car: gen*: **old ~**) chatarra.

bangle ['bæŋgl] *n* ajorca.

banish ['bæniʃ] *vt* desterrar.

banister(s) ['bænistə(z)] *n(pl)* pasamanos *m inv.*

banjo ['bændʒəu], *pl* **~es** *or* **~s** *n* banjo.

bank [bæŋk] *n* (*COMM*) banco; (*of river, lake*) ribera, orilla; (*of earth*) terraplén *m* // *vi* (*AVIAT*) ladearse; **to ~ on** *vt fus* contar con; **to ~ with** tener la cuenta con; **~ account** *n* cuenta de banco; **~er** *n* banquero; **B~ holiday** *n* día *m* festivo; **~ing** *n* banca; **~note** *n* billete *m* de banco; **~ rate** *n* tipo de interés bancario.

bankrupt ['bæŋkrʌpt] *n* quebrado/a // *a* quebrado, insolvente; **to go ~** quebrar; **to be ~** estar en quiebra; **~cy** *n* quiebra; (*fraudulent*) bancarrota.

banner ['bænə*] *n* bandera; (*in demonstration*) pancarta.

banns [bænz] *npl* amonestaciones *fpl.*

banquet ['bæŋkwit] *n* banquete *m.*

baptism ['bæptizəm] *n* bautismo.

baptize [bæp'taiz] *vt* bautizar.

bar [bɑː*] *n* barra; (*of window etc*) tranca; (*of soap*) pastilla; (*fig: hindrance*) obstáculo; (*prohibition*) proscripción *f*; (*pub*) bar *m*; (*counter: in pub*) mostrador *m*; (*MUS*) barra // *vt* (*road*) obstruir; (*window*) atrancar; (*person*) excluir; (*activity*) prohibir; **behind ~s** en la cárcel; **the B~** (*LAW*) (*profession*) la abogacía; (*people*) el cuerpo de abogados; **~ none** sin excepción.

barbaric [bɑː'bærik] *a* bárbaro.

barbarous ['bɑːbərəs] *a* bárbaro.

barbecue ['bɑːbikjuː] *n* barbacoa.

barbed wire ['bɑːbd-] *n* alambre *m* de púas.

barber ['bɑːbə*] *n* peluquero, barbero.

barbiturate [bɑː'bitjurit] *n* barbitúrico.

bare [bɛə*] *a* desnudo; (*head*) descubierto // *vt* desnudar; **to ~ one's teeth** enseñar los dientes; **~back** *ad* sin montura; **~faced** *a* descarado; **~foot** *a, ad* descalzo; **~ly** *ad* apenas.

bargain ['bɑːgin] *n* pacto, negocio; (*good buy*) ganga // *vi* negociar; (*haggle*) regatear; **into the ~** además, por añadidura.

barge [bɑːdʒ] *n* barcaza; **to ~ in** *vi*

irrumpir, entrar sin permiso; to ~ into vt
fus dar contra.

baritone ['bærɪtəun] n barítono.

bark [baːk] n (of tree) corteza; (of dog)
ladrido // vi ladrar.

barley ['baːlɪ] n cebada.

barmaid ['baːmeɪd] n camarera.

barman ['baːmən] n camarero, barman m.

barmy ['baːmɪ] a (col) chiflado, lelo.

barn [baːn] n granero.

barnacle ['baːnəkl] n percebe m.

barometer [bə'rɒmɪtə°] n barómetro.

baron ['bærən] n barón m; ~ess n
baronesa.

barracks ['bærəks] npl cuartel m.

barrage ['bærɑːʒ] n (MIL) descarga,
bombardeo; (dam) presa.

barrel ['bærəl] n tonel m, barril m; (of gun)
cañón m.

barren ['bærən] a estéril, árido.

barricade [bærɪ'keɪd] n barricada // vt
levantar barricadas.

barrier ['bærɪə°] n barrera.

barring ['baːrɪŋ] prep excepto, salvo.

barrister ['bærɪstə°] n abogado m/f.

barrow ['bærəu] n (cart) carretilla (de
mano).

bartender ['baːtɛndə°] n (US) camarero,
barman m.

barter ['baːtə°] vt: to ~ sth for sth
trocar algo por algo.

base [beɪs] n base f // vt: to ~ sth on
basar o fundar algo en // a bajo, infame;
~ball n béisbol m; ~ment n sótano.

bash [bæʃ] vt (col) golpear.

bashful ['bæʃful] a tímido, vergonzoso.

bashing ['bæʃɪŋ] n (col) tunda.

basic ['beɪsɪk] a básico; ~ally ad
fundamentalmente, en el fondo.

basil ['bæzl] n albahaca.

basin ['beɪsn] n (vessel) cuenco, tazón m;
(GEO) cuenca; (also: wash~) palangana,
jofaina.

basis ['beɪsɪs] pl -ses [-siːz] n base f.

bask [baːsk] vi: to ~ in the sun tomar el
sol.

basket ['baːskɪt] n cesta, cesto; (with
handle) canasta; ~ball n baloncesto;
~work n cestería.

Basque [bæsk] a, n vasco/a; ~ Country
Euskadi m, País m Vasco.

bass [beɪs] n (MUS) contrabajo.

bassoon [bə'suːn] n bajón m.

bastard ['baːstəd] n bastardo.

baste [beɪst] vt (CULIN) pringar.

bastion ['bæstɪən] n baluarte m.

bat [bæt] n (ZOOL) murciélago; (for ball
games) palo; (for cricket, baseball) bate m;
(for table tennis) raqueta; he didn't ~ an
eyelid ni pestañeó.

batch [bætʃ] n (of bread) hornada; (of
papers) colección f, lote m.

bated ['beɪtɪd] a: with ~ breath sin
respiración.

bath [baːθ, pl baːðz] n (~ tub) baño, bañera;
(also: ~s pl) baño, piscina // vt bañar; to

have a ~ bañarse, tomar un baño;
~chair n silla de ruedas.

bathe [beɪð] vi bañarse // vt bañar; **bather**
n bañista m/f.

bathing ['beɪðɪŋ] n el bañarse; ~ cap n
gorro de baño; ~ costume n traje m de
baño; ~ trunks npl bañador m.

bath: ~mat n estera de baño; ~room n
(cuarto de) baño; ~s npl piscina sg; ~
towel n toalla de baño.

baton ['bætən] n (MUS) batuta.

battalion [bə'tælɪən] n batallón m.

batter ['bætə°] vt apalear, azotar // n
batido; ~ed a (hat, pan) estropeado.

battery ['bætərɪ] n batería; (of torch) pila.

battle ['bætl] n batalla; (fig) lucha // vi
luchar; ~field n campo m de batalla;
~ments npl almenas fpl; ~ship n
acorazado.

bawdy ['bɔːdɪ] a indecente; (joke) verde.

bawl [bɔːl] vi chillar, gritar.

bay [beɪ] n (GEO) bahía; (BOT) laurel m // vi
aullar; to hold sb at ~ mantener a
alguien a raya.

bayonet ['beɪənɪt] n bayoneta.

bay window ['beɪ-] n ventana salediza.

bazaar [bə'zaː°] n bazar m.

bazooka [bə'zuːkə] n bazuca.

b. & b., B. & B. abbr of bed and
breakfast cama y desayuno.

BBC n abbr of British Broadcasting
Corporation.

B.C. ad abbr of before Christ a. de J.C.
(antes de Jesucristo).

be [biː], pt was, were, pp been vi (of
state) ser; (of place, temporary condition)
estar; I am English soy inglés; I am
tired estoy cansado; how are you?
¿cómo está Usted?; who is it? ¿quién es?;
it is raining está lloviendo; I am warm
tengo calor; it is cold hace frío; how
much is it? ¿cuánto es o cuesta?; he is
four (years old) tiene cuatro años; 2 and
2 are 4 dos más dos son cuatro; where
have you been? ¿dónde has estado?, ¿de
dónde vienes?

beach [biːtʃ] n playa // vt varar.

beacon ['biːkən] n (lighthouse) faro;
(marker) guía.

bead [biːd] n cuenta, abalorio; (of sweat)
gota.

beak [biːk] n pico.

beaker ['biːkə°] n jarra.

beam [biːm] n (ARCH) viga, travesaño; (of
light) rayo, haz m de luz // vi brillar;
(smile) sonreír; ~ing a (sun, smile)
radiante.

bean [biːn] n judía; runner/broad ~
habichuela/haba; coffee ~ grano de
café.

bear [bɛə°] n oso // (vb: pt bore, pp borne)
vt (weight etc) llevar; (cost) pagar;
(responsibility) tener; (endure) soportar,
aguantar; (stand up to) resistir a; (children)
parir // vi: to ~ right/left torcer a la
derecha/izquierda; ~able a soportable.

beard [bɪəd] n barba; ~ed a barbado.

bearing ['bɛərɪŋ] *n* porte *m*, comportamiento; (*connection*) relación *f*; (*ball*) ~s *npl* cojinetes *mpl* a bolas; **to take a** ~ marcarse; **to find one's** ~s orientarse.

beast [biːst] *n* bestia; (*col*) bruto, salvaje *m*; ~**ly** *a* bestial; (*awful*) horrible.

beat [biːt] *n* (*of heart*) latido; (*MUS*) ritmo, compás *m*; (*of policeman*) ronda // (*vb: pt* **beat,** *pp* **beaten**) *vt* (*hit*) golpear; (*eggs*) batir; (*defeat*) vencer, derrotar; (*better*) sobrepasar; (*drum*) tocar; (*rhythm*) marcar // *vi* (*heart*) latir; **to** ~ **about the bush** ir por rodeos; **to** ~ **it** largarse; **to** ~ **off** *vt* rechazar; **to** ~ **up** *vt* (*col: person*) dar una paliza a; ~**er** *n* (*for eggs, cream*) batidora; ~**ing** *n* golpeo.

beautiful ['bjuːtɪful] *a* hermoso, bello; ~**ly** *ad* maravillosamente; **beautify** [-faɪ] *vt* embellecer.

beauty ['bjuːtɪ] *n* belleza, hermosura; (*person*) belleza; ~ **salon** *n* salón *m* de belleza; ~ **spot** *n* lunar *m* postizo; (*TOURISM*) lugar *m* de excepcional belleza.

beaver ['biːvə*] *n* castor *m*.

becalmed [bɪ'kɑːmd] *a* encalmado.

became [bɪ'keɪm] *pt of* **become.**

because [bɪ'kɔz] *conj* porque; ~ **of** *prep* debido a, a causa de.

beck [bɛk] *n*: **to be at the** ~ **and call of** estar a disposición de.

beckon ['bɛkən] *vt* (*also:* ~ **to**) llamar con señas.

become [bɪ'kʌm] (*irg: like* **come**) *vt* (*suit*) favorecer, sentar a // *vi* (+ *noun*) hacerse, llegar a ser; (+ *adj*) ponerse, volverse; **to** ~ **fat** engordarse.

becoming [bɪ'kʌmɪŋ] *a* (*behaviour*) decoroso; (*clothes*) favorecedor(a).

bed [bɛd] *n* cama; (*of flowers*) macizo; (*of coal, clay*) capa; **to go to** ~ acostarse; **single/double** ~ cama individual/matrimonial; ~**clothes** *npl* ropa *sg* de cama; ~**ding** *n* ropa de cama.

bedlam ['bɛdləm] *n* confusión *f.*

bedraggled [bɪ'drægld] *a* mojado, ensuciado.

bed: ~**ridden** *a* postrado (en cama); ~**room** *n* dormitorio, alcoba; ~**side** *n*: **at sb's** ~**side** a la cabecera de alguien; ~**sit(ter)** *n* apartamento // ~**spread** *n* sobrecama *m*, colcha.

bee [biː] *n* abeja.

beech [biːtʃ] *n* haya.

beef [biːf] *n* carne *f* de vaca; **roast** ~ rosbif *m*.

bee: ~**hive** *n* colmena; ~**line** *n*: **to make a** ~**line for** ir derecho a.

been [biːn] *pp of* **be.**

beer [bɪə*] *n* cerveza.

beetle ['biːtl] *n* escarabajo.

beetroot ['biːtruːt] *n* remolacha.

before [bɪ'fɔː*] *prep* (*of time*) antes de; (*of space*) delante de // *conj* antes (de) que // *ad* (*time*) antes, anteriormente; (*space*) delante, adelante; **the week** ~ la semana anterior; **I've never seen it** ~ no lo he visto nunca.

befriend [bɪ'frɛnd] *vt* ofrecer amistad a, ayudar.

beg [bɛg] *vi* pedir, rogar; (*as beggar*) pedir limosna // *vt* pedir, rogar; (*entreat*) suplicar.

began [bɪ'gæn] *pt of* **begin.**

beggar ['bɛgə*] *n* mendigo.

begin [bɪ'gɪn], *pt* **began,** *pp* **begun** *vt, vi* empezar, comenzar; ~**ner** *n* principiante *m/f*; ~**ning** *n* principio, comienzo.

begrudge [bɪ'grʌdʒ] *vt*: **to** ~ **sb sth** tenerle envidia a alguien por algo.

begun [bɪ'gʌn] *pp of* **begin.**

behalf [bɪ'hɑːf] *n*: **on** ~ **of** en nombre de, por.

behave [bɪ'heɪv] *vi* (*person*) portarse, comportarse; (*thing*) funcionar; (*well: also:* ~ **o.s.**) portarse bien; **behaviour, behavior** (*US*) *n* comportamiento, conducta.

behind [bɪ'haɪnd] *prep* detrás de // *ad* detrás, por detrás, atrás // *n* trasero; ~ **time** atrasado.

behold [bɪ'həʊld] (*irg: like* **hold**) *vt* contemplar.

beige [beɪʒ] *a* beige.

being ['biːɪŋ] *n* ser *m*; **to come into** ~ nacer, aparecer.

belated [bɪ'leɪtɪd] *a* atrasado, tardío.

belch [bɛltʃ] *vi* eructar // *vt* (*gen:* ~ **out:** *smoke etc*) arrojar.

belfry ['bɛlfrɪ] *n* campanario.

Belgian ['bɛldʒən] *a*, *n* belga *m/f.*

Belgium ['bɛldʒəm] *n* Bélgica.

belie [bɪ'laɪ] *vt* desmentir, contradecir.

belief [bɪ'liːf] *n* (*opinion*) opinión *f*; (*trust, faith*) fe *f*; (*acceptance as true*) creencia.

believable [bɪ'liːvəbl] *a* creíble.

believe [bɪ'liːv] *vt, vi* creer; ~**r** *n* creyente *m/f*, fiel *m/f*; (*POL*) partidario/a.

belittle [bɪ'lɪtl] *vt* minimizar, despreciar.

bell [bɛl] *n* campana; (*small*) campanilla; (*on door*) timbre *m*; (*animal's*) cencerro; (*on toy etc*) cascabel *m*.

belligerent [bɪ'lɪdʒərənt] *a* (*at war*) beligerante; (*fig*) agresivo.

bellow ['bɛləʊ] *vi* bramar; (*person*) rugir // *vt* (*orders*) gritar, vociferar.

bellows ['bɛləʊz] *npl* fuelle *m.*

belly ['bɛlɪ] *n* barriga, panza.

belong [bɪ'lɔŋ] *vi*: **to** ~ **to** pertenecer a; (*club etc*) ser socio de; ~**ings** *npl* pertenencias *fpl.*

beloved [bɪ'lʌvɪd] *a, n* querido/a, amado/a.

below [bɪ'ləʊ] *prep* bajo, debajo de // *ad* abajo, (por) debajo; **see** ~ véase más abajo.

belt [bɛlt] *n* cinturón *m*; (*MED*) faja; (*TECH*) correa, cinta // *vt* (*thrash*) golpear con correa.

bench [bɛntʃ] *n* banco; **the B**~ (*LAW*) tribunal *m*; (*people*) judicatura.

bend [bɛnd], *pt, pp* **bent** *vt* doblar, inclinar;

(leg, arm) torcer // *vi* doblarse, inclinarse // *n (in road)* recodo, vuelta; *(in pipe, river)* ángulo, curva; **to ~ down** *vi* inclinar, doblar; **to ~ over** *vi* inclinarse.

beneath [bɪ'ni:θ] *prep* bajo, debajo de; *(unworthy of)* indigno de // *ad* abajo, (por) debajo.

benefactor ['bɛnɪfæktə*] *n* bienhechor *m*.

beneficial [bɛnɪ'fɪʃəl] *a* provechoso, beneficioso.

benefit ['bɛnɪfɪt] *n* beneficio, provecho; *(profit)* utilidad *f*; *(money)* subsidio // *vt* beneficiar, aprovechar // *vi*: **he'll ~ from it** le sacará provecho.

Benelux ['bɛnɪlʌks] *n* Benelux *m*.

benevolent [bɪ'nɛvələnt] *a* benévolo.

bent [bɛnt] *pt, pp of* **bend** // *n* inclinación *f* // *a*: **to be ~ on** estar empeñado en.

bequeath [bɪ'kwi:ð] *vt* legar.

bequest [bɪ'kwɛst] *n* legado.

bereaved [bɪ'ri:vd] *n*: **the ~** los afligidos *mpl*; **bereavement** [-'ri:vmənt] *n* aflicción *f*.

beret ['bɛreɪ] *n* boina.

berry ['bɛrɪ] *n* baya.

berserk [bə'sɜ:k] *a*: **to go ~** perder los estribos.

berth [bɜ:θ] *n (bed)* litera; *(cabin)* camarote *m*; *(for ship)* amarradero // *vi* atracar, amarrar.

beseech [bɪ'si:tʃ], *pt, pp* **besought** [-'sɔt] *vt* suplicar.

beset [bɪ'sɛt], *pt, pp* **beset** *vt* rodear; *(person)* acosar.

beside [bɪ'saɪd] *prep* junto a, al lado de; **to be ~ o.s. (with anger)** estar fuera de sí.

besides [bɪ'saɪdz] *ad* además // *prep (as well as)* además de; *(except)* fuera de, excepto.

besiege [bɪ'si:dʒ] *vt (town)* sitiar; *(fig)* asediar.

best [bɛst] *a* (el/la) mejor // *ad* (lo) mejor; **the ~ part of** *(quantity)* la mayor parte de; **at ~** en el mejor de los casos; **to make the ~ of sth** sacar el mejor partido de algo; **to the ~ of my knowledge** que yo sepa; **to the ~ of my ability** como mejor puedo; **~ man** *n* padrino de boda.

bestow [bɪ'stəu] *vt* otorgar; *(affection)* ofrecer.

bestseller ['bɛst'sɛlə*] *n* éxito de librería, bestseller *m*.

bet [bɛt] *n* apuesta // *vt, vi, pt, pp* **bet** or **betted** apostar, jugar.

betray [bɪ'treɪ] *vt* traicionar; *(denounce)* delatar; **~al** *n* traición *f*.

better ['bɛtə*] *a* mejor // *ad* mejor // *vt* mejorar; *(go above)* superar // *n*: **to get the ~ of** quedar por encima de alguien; **you had ~ do it** más vale que lo haga; **he thought ~ of it** cambió de parecer; **to get ~** mejorar(se); *(MED)* reponerse; **~ off** a más acomodado.

betting ['bɛtɪŋ] *n* juego, el apostar; **~ shop** *n* agencia de apuestas.

between [bɪ'twi:n] *prep* entre // *ad* en medio.

beverage ['bɛvərɪdʒ] *n* bebida.

bevy ['bɛvɪ] *n*: **a ~ of** una bandada de.

beware [bɪ'wɛə*] *vi*: **to ~ (of)** precaverse de, tener cuidado con // *excl* ¡cuidado!

bewildered [bɪ'wɪldəd] *a* aturdido, perplejo.

bewitching [bɪ'wɪtʃɪŋ] *a* hechicero, encantador(a).

beyond [bɪ'jɔnd] *prep (in space)* más allá de; *(exceeding)* además de, fuera de; *(above)* superior a // *ad* más allá, más lejos; **~ doubt** fuera de toda duda; **~ repair** irreparable.

bias ['baɪəs] *n (prejudice)* prejuicio, pasión *f*; *(preference)* predisposición *f*; **~(s)ed** *a (against)* con prejuicios; *(towards)* partidario.

bib [bɪb] *n* babero.

Bible ['baɪbl] *n* Biblia.

bibliography [bɪblɪ'ɔgrəfɪ] *n* bibliografía.

bicker ['bɪkə*] *vi* reñir.

bicycle ['baɪsɪkl] *n* bicicleta.

bid [bɪd] *n (at auction)* oferta, postura; *(attempt)* tentativa, conato // *(vb: pt* **bade** [bæd] *or* **bid**, *pp* **bidden** ['bɪdn] *or* **bid**) *vi* hacer una oferta // *vt* mandar, ordenar; **to ~ sb good day** dar a uno los buenos días; **~der** *n*: **the highest ~der** el mejor postor; **~ding** *n (at auction)* ofertas *fpl*; *(order)* orden *f*, mandato.

bide [baɪd] *vt*: **to ~ one's time** esperar el momento adecuado.

bidet ['bi:deɪ] *n* bidet *m*.

bier [bɪə*] *n* féretro.

big [bɪg] *a* grande.

bigamy ['bɪgəmɪ] *n* bigamia.

bigheaded ['bɪg'hɛdɪd] *a* engreído.

bigot ['bɪgət] *n* fanático, intolerante *m/f*; **~ed** *a* fanático, intolerante; **~ry** *n* fanatismo, intolerancia.

bike [baɪk] *n* bici *f*.

bikini [bɪ'ki:nɪ] *n* bikini *m*.

bile [baɪl] *n* bilis *f*.

bilingual [baɪ'lɪŋgwəl] *a* bilingüe.

bill [bɪl] *n (account)* cuenta; *(invoice)* factura; *(POL)* proyecto de ley; *(US: banknote)* billete *m*; *(of bird)* pico; **stick no ~s** prohibido fijar carteles.

billet ['bɪlɪt] *n* alojamiento.

billfold ['bɪlfəuld] *n (US)* cartera.

billiards ['bɪlɪədz] *n* billar *m*.

billion ['bɪlɪən] *n (Brit)* billón *m*; *(US)* mil millones.

billy goat ['bɪlɪ-] *n* macho cabrío.

bin [bɪn] *n (gen)* cubo; **bread/litter ~** nasa/papelera.

bind [baɪnd], *pt, pp* **bound** *vt* atar, liar; *(wound)* vendar; *(book)* encuadernar; *(oblige)* obligar; **~ing** *a (contract)* obligatorio.

binge [bɪndʒ] *n* borrachera, juerga.

bingo ['bɪŋgəu] *n* bingo *m*.

binoculars [bɪ'nɔkjuləz] *npl* gemelos *mpl*, prismáticos *mpl*.

bio... [baɪɔ] pref: ~**chemistry** n bioquímica; ~**graphy** [baɪˈɔgrəfɪ] n biografía; ~**logical** a biológico; ~**logy** [baɪˈɔlədʒɪ] n biología.

birch [bəːtʃ] n abedul m; (cane) vara.

bird [bəːd] n ave f, pájaro; (col: girl) chica; ~**cage** n jaula; ~**'s eye view** n vista de pájaro; ~ **watcher** n ornitólogo.

birth [bəːθ] n nacimiento; (MED) parto; **to give** ~ **to** parir, dar a luz; ~ **certificate** n partida de nacimiento; ~ **control** n control m de natalidad; (methods) métodos mpl anticonceptivos; ~**day** n cumpleaños m; ~**place** n lugar m de nacimiento; ~ **rate** n (tasa de) natalidad f.

biscuit [ˈbɪskɪt] n galleta.

bisect [baɪˈsɛkt] vt bisecar.

bishop [ˈbɪʃəp] n obispo.

bit [bɪt] n trozo, pedazo, pedacito; (of horse) freno, bocado; **a** ~ **of** un poco de; **a** ~ **mad** algo loco; ~ **by** ~ poco a poco.

bitch [bɪtʃ] n (dog) perra.

bite [baɪt] pt **bit**, pp **bitten** vt, vi morder; (insect etc) picar // n mordedura; (insect ~) picadura; (mouthful) bocado; **let's have a** ~ **(to eat)** comamos algo.

biting [ˈbaɪtɪŋ] a penetrante, cortante; (sharp) mordaz.

bitten [ˈbɪtn] pp of **bite**.

bitter [ˈbɪtə*] a amargo; (wind, criticism) cortante, penetrante; (battle) encarnizado // n (beer) cerveza clara; ~**ness** n amargura; (anger) rencor m.

bizarre [bɪˈzɑː*] a raro, estrafalario.

blab [blæb] vi chismear, soplar // vt (also: ~ **out**) revelar, contar.

black [blæk] a (colour) negro; (dark) oscuro // n negro; (colour) color m negro // vt (shoes) lustrar; (INDUSTRY) boicotear; **to give sb a** ~ **eye** darle a uno una bofetada (en el ojo); ~ **and blue** a amoratado; ~**berry** n zarzamora; ~**bird** n mirlo; ~**board** n pizarra; ~**currant** n grosella negra; ~**en** vt ennegrecer; (fig) denigrar; ~**leg** n esquirol m, rompehuelgas m inv; ~**list** n lista negra; ~**mail** n chantaje m // vt chantajear; ~**mailer** n chantajista m/f; ~ **market** n mercado negro; ~**out** n apagón m; (fainting) desmayo, pérdida de conocimiento; ~**smith** n herrero.

bladder [ˈblædə*] n vejiga.

blade [bleɪd] n hoja; (cutting edge) filo; **a** ~ **of grass** una brizna de hierba.

blame [bleɪm] n culpa // vt: **to** ~ **sb for sth** echar a uno la culpa de algo; **to be to** ~ tener la culpa de; ~**less** a (person) inocente.

bland [blænd] a suave; (taste) soso.

blank [blæŋk] a en blanco; (shot) sin bala; (look) sin expresión // n blanco, espacio en blanco; cartucho sin bala o de fogueo.

blanket [ˈblæŋkɪt] n manta // vt envolver.

blare [blɛə*] vi (brass band, horns, radio) resonar.

blasé [ˈblɑːzeɪ] a hastiado.

blasphemy [ˈblæsfɪmɪ] n blasfemia.

blast [blɑːst] n (of wind) ráfaga, soplo; (of whistle) toque m; (of explosive) carga explosiva; (force) choque m // vt (blow up) volar; (blow open) abrir con carga explosiva; ~-**off** n (SPACE) lanzamiento.

blatant [ˈbleɪtənt] a descarado.

blaze [bleɪz] n (fire) fuego; (flames) llamarada; (fig) arranque m // vi (fire) arder en llamas; (fig) brillar // vt: **to** ~ **a trail** (fig) abrir (un) camino.

blazer [ˈbleɪzə*] n chaqueta ligera.

bleach [bliːtʃ] n (also: **household** ~) lejía // vt (linen) blanquear; ~**ed** a (hair) decolorado.

bleak [bliːk] a (countryside) desierto; (prospect) poco prometedor(a).

bleary-eyed [ˈblɪərɪˈaɪd] a de ojos legañosos.

bleat [bliːt] vi balar.

bleed [bliːd], pt, pp **bled** [blɛd] vt, vi sangrar.

blemish [ˈblɛmɪʃ] n mancha, tacha.

blend [blɛnd] n mezcla // vt mezclar // vi (colours etc) combinarse, mezclarse.

bless [blɛs], pt, pp **blessed** or **blest** [blɛst] vt bendecir; ~**ing** n bendición f; (advantage) beneficio, ventaja.

blew [bluː] pt of **blow**.

blight [blaɪt] vt (hopes etc) frustrar, arruinar.

blimey [ˈblaɪmɪ] excl (col) ¡caray!

blind [blaɪnd] a ciego // n (for window) persiana // vt cegar; (dazzle) deslumbrar; ~ **alley** n callejón m sin salida; ~ **corner** n esquina escondida; ~**fold** n venda // a, ad con los ojos vendados // vt vendar los ojos a; ~**ly** ad a ciegas, ciegamente; ~**ness** n ceguera; ~ **spot** n mácula.

blink [blɪŋk] vi parpadear, pestañear; (light) oscilar; ~**ers** npl anteojeras fpl.

blinking [ˈblɪŋkɪŋ] a (col): **this** ~... este condenado... .

bliss [blɪs] n felicidad f; (fig) éxtasis m.

blister [ˈblɪstə*] n (on skin) ampolla // vi (paint) ampollarse; ~**ing** a (heat) abrasador(a).

blithe [blaɪð] a alegre.

blithering [ˈblɪðərɪŋ] a (col): **this** ~ **idiot** este tonto perdido.

blitz [blɪts] n bombardeo aéreo.

blizzard [ˈblɪzəd] n ventisca.

bloated [ˈbləʊtɪd] a hinchado.

blob [blɔb] n (drop) gota; (stain, spot) mancha.

block [blɔk] n bloque m; (in pipes) obstáculo; (of buildings) manzana // vt (gen) obstruir, cerrar; (progress) estorbar; ~**ade** [-ˈkeɪd] n bloqueo // vt bloquear; ~**age** n estorbo, obstrucción f; ~ **of flats** n bloque m de pisos; ~ **letters** npl letras fpl de molde.

bloke [bləʊk] n (col) tipo, tío.

blond(e) [blɔnd] a, n rubio/a.

blood [blʌd] n sangre f; ~ **donor** n

donador/a *m/f* de sangre; ~ **group** *n* grupo sanguíneo; ~ **hound** *n* sabueso; ~ **pressure** *n* presión *f* sanguínea; ~**shed** *n* matanza; ~**shot** *a* inyectado en sangre; ~**stained** *a* manchado de sangre; ~**stream** *n* corriente *f* sanguínea; ~**thirsty** *a* sanguinario; ~ **transfusion** *n* transfusión *f* de sangre; ~**y** *a* sangriento; (*col!*): **this** ~**y...** este condenado/puñetero...; ~**y strong/ good** (*col!*) terriblemente fuerte/ bueno; ~**y-minded** *a* (*col*) malintencionado.

bloom [blu:m] *n* floración *f*; (*fig*) perfección *f*, plenitud *f* // *vi* florecer; ~**ing** *a* (*col*): **this** ~**ing...** este condenado... .

blossom ['blɔsəm] *n* flor *f* // *vi* florecer; (*fig*) desarrollarse.

blot [blɔt] *n* borrón *m* // *vt* secar; (*ink*) manchar; **to** ~ **out** *vt* (*view*) oscurecer, hacer desaparecer.

blotchy ['blɔtʃi] *a* (*complexion*) enrojecido, lleno de manchas.

blotting paper ['blɔtɪŋ-] *n* papel *m* secante.

blouse [blauz] *n* blusa.

blow [bləu] *n* golpe *m* // *vi* (*vb: pt* blew, *pp* blown) [bləun]) *vi* soplar // *vt* (*glass*) soplar; (*fuse*) quemar; (*instrument*) tocar; **to** ~ **one's nose** sonarse; **to** ~ **away** *vt* llevarse, arrancar; **to** ~ **down** *vt* derribar; **to** ~ **off** *vt* arrebatar; **to** ~ **out** *vi* apagarse; **to** ~ **over** *vi* pasar, quedar olvidado; **to** ~ **up** *vi* estallar // *vt* volar; (*tyre*) inflar; (*PHOT*) ampliar; ~**lamp** *n* soplete *m*, lámpara de soldar; ~**-out** *n* (*of tyre*) pinchazo.

blubber ['blʌbə*] *n* grasa de ballena // *vi* (*pej*) lloriquear.

blue [blu:] *a* azul; ~ **film/joke** film/chiste verde; **to have the** ~**s** estar melancólico; ~**bell** *n* campanilla, campánula azul; ~**bottle** *n* moscarda, mosca azul; ~ **jeans** *npl* bluejean *m inv*, vaqueros *mpl*; ~**print** *n* (*fig*) anteproyecto.

bluff [blʌf] *vi* hacer un bluff, farolear // *n* bluff *m*, farol *m*.

blunder ['blʌndə*] *n* error *m* garrafal, metedura de pata // *vi* cometer un error, meter la pata.

blunt [blʌnt] *a* embotado, desafilado; (*person*) franco, directo // *vt* embotar, desafilar; ~**ness** *n* (*of person*) franqueza, brusquedad *f*.

blur [blə:*] *n* aspecto borroso // *vt* hacer borroso, desdibujar.

blurt [blə:t]: ~ **out** *vt* (*say*) descolgarse con, dejar escapar.

blush [blʌʃ] *vi* ruborizarse, ponerse colorado // *n* rubor *m*.

blustering ['blʌstərɪŋ] *a* (*person*) fanfarrón(ona).

blustery ['blʌstəri] *a* (*weather*) tempestuoso, tormentoso.

board [bɔ:d] *n* tabla, tablero; (*on wall*) tablón *m*; (*for chess etc*) tablero; (*committee*) junta, consejo; (*in firm*) mesa *o* junta directiva // *vt* (*ship*) embarcarse en; (*train*) subir a; **full** ~ pensión *f* completa; **to go by the** ~ (*fig*) ser abandonado/olvidado; **to** ~ **up** *vt* (*door*) entablar, enmaderar; ~ **and lodging** *n* pensión *f*; ~**er** *n* huésped/a *m/f*; (*SCOL*) interno; ~**ing house** *n* casa de huéspedes; ~**ing school** *n* internado; ~ **room** *n* sala de juntas.

boast [bəust] *vi* jactarse, presumir // *vt* ostentar // *n* alarde *m*, baladronada; ~**ful** *a* presumido, jactancioso.

boat [bəut] *n* barco, buque *m*; (*small*) barca, bote *m*; ~**er** *n* (*hat*) sombrero de paja; ~**ing** *n* canotaje *m*; ~**man** *n* barquero; ~**swain** ['bəusn] *n* contramaestre *m*.

bob [bɔb] *vi* (*boat, cork on water: also:* ~ **up and down**) menearse, balancearse; **to** ~ **up** *vi* aparecer, levantarse // *n* (*col*) = **shilling.**

bobbin ['bɔbɪn] *n* (*of sewing machine*) carrete *m*, bobina.

bobby ['bɔbi] *n* (*col*) poli *m/f.*

bobsleigh ['bɔbsleɪ] *n* bob *m.*

bodice ['bɔdɪs] *n* corpiño.

bodily ['bɔdɪli] *a* corpóreo, corporal // *ad* (*in person*) en persona; (*lift*) en peso.

body ['bɔdi] *n* cuerpo; (*corpse*) cadáver *m*; (*of car*) caja, carrocería; (*fig: society*) conjunto; (*fig: quantity*) parte *f* principal; **in a** ~ en bloque, en conjunto; ~**guard** *n* guardaespaldas *m inv*; ~**work** *n* carrocería.

bog [bɔg] *n* pantano, ciénaga // *vt*: **to get** ~**ged down** (*fig*) empantanarse, atascarse.

boggle ['bɔgl] *vi*: **the mind** ~**s** le deja boquiabierto a uno.

bogus ['bəugəs] *a* falso, fraudulento; (*person*) fingido.

boil [bɔɪl] *vt* cocer; (*eggs*) pasar por agua // *vi* hervir // *n* (*MED*) furúnculo, divieso; **to come to the** ~ comenzar a hervir; **to** ~ **down to** (*fig*) reducirse a; ~**er** *n* caldera; ~**er suit** *n* mono; ~**ing point** *n* punto de ebullición *f.*

boisterous ['bɔɪstərəs] *a* (*noisy*) bullicioso; (*excitable*) exuberante; (*crowd*) tumultuoso.

bold [bəuld] *a* (*brave*) valiente, audaz; (*excessively*) atrevido; (*pej*) descarado; (*outline, colour*) fuerte; ~**ness** *n* valor *m*, audacia; (*cheek*) descaro.

Bolivia [bə'lɪvɪə] *n* Bolivia.

bollard ['bɔləd] *n* (*AUT*) poste *m.*

bolster ['bəulstə*] *n* travesero, cabezal *m*; **to** ~ **up** *vt* reforzar; (*fig*) alentar.

bolt [bəult] *n* (*lock*) cerrojo; (*with nut*) perno, tornillo // *vt* (*door*) echar el cerrojo a; (*food*) engullir // *vi* fugarse; (*horse*) desbocarse.

bomb [bɔm] *n* bomba // *vt* bombardear; ~**ard** [-'bɑ:d] *vt* bombardear; (*fig*) asediar; ~**ardment** [-'bɑ:dmənt] *n* bombardeo.

bombastic [bɔm'bæstɪk] a rimbombante; (person) farolero.

bomb: ~ disposal n desmontaje m de explosivos; ~er n (AVIAT) bombardero; ~shell n obús m, granada; (fig) bomba.

bona fide ['bəunə'faɪdɪ] a genuino, auténtico.

bond [bɔnd] n (binding promise) fianza; (FINANCE) bono; (link) vínculo, lazo.

bondage [bɔndɪdʒ] n esclavitud f.

bone [bəun] n hueso; (of fish) espina // vt deshuesar; quitar las espinas a; ~-dry a completamente seco; ~ idle a gandul.

bonfire ['bɔnfaɪə*] n hoguera, fogata.

bonnet ['bɔnɪt] n gorra; (Brit: of car) capó m.

bonus ['bəunəs] n sobrepaga, prima.

bony ['bəunɪ] a (arm, face, MED. tissue) huesudo; (meat) lleno de huesos; (fish) lleno de espinas.

boo [bu:] vt abuchear, rechiflar.

booby trap ['bu:bɪ-] n trampa explosiva.

book [buk] n libro; (notebook) libreta; (of stamps etc) librito; (COMM): ~s las cuentas, el balance // vt (ticket) sacar; (seat, room) reservar; (driver) fichar; ~case n librería, estante m para libros; ~ing office n (RAIL) despacho de billetes; (THEATRE) taquilla; ~keeping n teneduría de libros; ~let n folleto; ~maker n corredor m de apuestas; ~seller n librero; ~shop n librería; ~stall n quiosco de libros.

boom [bu:m] n (noise) trueno, estampido; (in prices etc) alza rápida; (ECON) boom m, prosperidad f repentina.

boomerang ['bu:məræŋ] n bumerang m.

boon [bu:n] n favor m, beneficio.

boost [bu:st] n estímulo, empuje m // vt estimular, empujar; ~er n (MED) reinyección f.

boot [bu:t] n bota; (Brit: of car) maleta, maletero // vt dar un puntapié a; to ~ (in addition) además, por añadidura.

booth [bu:ð] n (at fair) barraca; (telephone ~, voting ~) cabina.

booty ['bu:tɪ] n botín m.

booze [bu:z] (col) n bebida, trago // vi emborracharse.

border ['bɔ:də*] n borde m, margen m, orilla; (of a country) frontera // a fronterizo; the B~s región fronteriza entre Escocia e Inglaterra; to ~ on vt fus lindar con; (fig) rayar en; ~line n (fig) frontera.

bore [bɔ:*] pt of bear // vt (hole) taladrar, agujerear; (person) aburrir // n (person) pelmazo, pesado; (of gun) calibre m; ~dom n aburrimiento.

boring ['bɔ:rɪŋ] a aburrido.

born [bɔ:n] a: to be ~ nacer; I was ~ in 1960 nací en 1960.

borne [bɔ:n] pp of bear.

borough ['bʌrə] n municipio.

borrow ['bɔrəu] vt: to ~ sth (from sb) pedir algo prestado a alguien.

borstal ['bɔ:stl] n reformatorio (de menores).

bosom ['buzəm] n pecho; (fig) seno; ~ friend n amigo del alma o íntimo.

boss [bɔs] n jefe m; (employer) patrón/ona m/f; (political boss) cacique m // vt regentar, dar órdenes a; ~y a mandón(ona).

bosun ['bəusn] n contramaestre m.

botanist ['bɔtənɪst] n botanista m/f; botany [-nɪ] n botánica.

botch [bɔtʃ] vt (also: ~ up) arruinar, estropear.

both [bəuθ] a, pron ambos(as), los dos; ~ of us went, we ~ went fuimos los dos, ambos fuimos // ad: ~ A and B tanto A como B.

bother ['bɔðə*] vt (worry) preocupar; (disturb) molestar, fastidiar // vi (gen: ~ o.s.) molestarse; to ~ doing tomarse la molestia de hacer // n: what a ~! ¡qué lata!

bottle ['bɔtl] n botella; (small) frasco; (baby's) biberón m // vt embotellar; to ~ up vt embotellar, contener; ~neck n embotellamiento; ~-opener n destapador m, abrebotellas m inv.

bottom ['bɔtəm] n (of box, sea) fondo; (buttocks) trasero, culo; (of page, list) pie m // a (low) inferior, más bajo; (last) último; ~less a sin fondo, insondable.

bough [bau] n rama.

bought [bɔ:t] pt, pp of buy.

boulder ['bəuldə*] n canto rodado.

bounce [bauns] vi (ball) (re)botar; (cheque) ser rechazado o incobrable // vt hacer (re)botar // n (rebound) (re)bote m.

bound [baund] pt, pp of bind // n (leap) salto; (gen pl: limit) límite m // vi (leap) saltar // a: ~ by (limited by) rodeado de, confinado con; to be ~ to do sth (obliged) tener el deber de hacer algo; (likely) estar seguro de hacer algo; out of ~s prohibido el paso; ~ for con destino a.

boundary ['baundrɪ] n límite m, lindero.

boundless ['baundlɪs] a ilimitado.

bouquet ['bukeɪ] n (of flowers) ramo; (of wine) aroma m.

bout [baut] n (of malaria etc) ataque m; (BOXING etc) combate m, encuentro.

bow [bəu] n (knot) lazo; (weapon, MUS) arco // n [bau] (of the head) reverencia; (NAUT) proa // vi [bau] inclinarse, hacer una reverencia; (yield): to ~ to or before ceder ante, someterse a.

bowels [bauəlz] npl intestinos mpl, vientre m.

bowl [bəul] n tazón m, cuenco; (for washing) palangana, jofaina; (ball) bola // vi (CRICKET) arrojar la pelota; ~s n juego de las bochas, bolos mpl.

bow-legged ['bəulegɪd] a estevado.

bowler ['bəulə*] n (CRICKET) lanzador m (de la pelota); (also: ~ hat) hongo, bombín m.

bowling ['bəulɪŋ] n (game) bochas fpl, bolos mpl; ~ alley n bolera; ~ green n pista para bochas.

bow tie ['bəʊ-] n corbata de lazo.

box [bɒks] n (also: **cardboard ~**) caja, cajón m; (for jewels) estuche m; (for money) cofre m; (THEATRE) palco // vt encajonar // vi (SPORT) boxear; **~er** n (person) boxeador m; (dog) boxer m; **~ing** n (SPORT) boxeo; **B~ing Day** n Día de San Esteban, 26 de diciembre; **~ing gloves** npl guantes mpl de boxeo; **~ing ring** n ring m, cuadrilátero; **~ office** n taquilla; **~room** n trastero.

boy [bɔɪ] n (young) niño; (older) muchacho; (servant) criado.

boycott ['bɔɪkɒt] n boicot m // vt boicotear.

boyfriend ['bɔɪfrɛnd] n novio.

boyish ['bɔɪɪʃ] a muchachil.

B.R. abbr of **British Rail**.

bra [brɑː] n sostén m.

brace [breɪs] n refuerzo, abrazadera; (on teeth) aparato; (tool) berbiquí m // vt asegurar, reforzar; **~s** npl tirantes mpl; to **~ o.s.** (fig) fortalecer el ánimo.

bracelet ['breɪslɪt] n pulsera, brazalete m.

bracing ['breɪsɪŋ] a vigorizante, tónico.

bracken ['brækən] n helecho.

bracket ['brækɪt] n (TECH) soporte m, puntal m; (group) clase f, categoría; (also: **brace ~**) soporte m, abrazadera; (also: **round ~**) paréntesis m inv; (gen: **square ~**) corchete m // vt (group) agrupar.

brag [bræg] vi jactarse.

braid [breɪd] n (trimming) galón m; (of hair) trenza.

Braille [breɪl] n Braille m.

brain [breɪn] n cerebro; **~s** npl sesos mpl; **~child** n parto del ingenio; **~wash** vt lavar el cerebro a; **~wave** n idea luminosa; **~y** a muy listo o inteligente.

braise [breɪz] vt cocer a fuego lento.

brake [breɪk] n (on vehicle) freno // vt, vi frenar; **~ drum** n tambor de freno; **~ fluid** n líquido para freno.

bramble ['bræmbl] n zarza.

branch [brɑːntʃ] n rama; (fig) ramo; (road) ramal m; (COMM) sucursal f // vi (also: **~ out**) ramificarse; (: fig) extenderse.

brand [brænd] n marca; (iron) hierro de marcar // vt (cattle) marcar con hierro candente.

brandish ['brændɪʃ] vt blandir.

brand-new ['brænd'njuː] a flamante, completamente nuevo.

brandy ['brændɪ] n coñac m, brandy m.

brash [bræʃ] a (rough) tosco; (cheeky) descarado.

brass [brɑːs] n latón m; **~ band** n banda de metal.

brassière ['bræsɪə*] n sostén m.

brat [bræt] n (pej) mocoso.

bravado [brə'vɑːdəʊ] n baladronada.

brave [breɪv] a valiente, valeroso // n valiente m // vt (challenge) desafiar; (resist) aguantar; **~ry** n valor m, valentía.

brawl [brɔːl] n pendencia, reyerta // vi pelearse.

brawn [brɔːn] n fuerza; (meat) carne f en gelatina; **~y** a fornido, musculoso.

bray [breɪ] n rebuzno // vi rebuznar.

brazen ['breɪzn] a descarado, cínico // vt: to **~ it out** defenderse con descaro.

brazier ['breɪzɪə*] n brasero.

Brazil [brə'zɪl] n (el) Brasil; **~ian** a, n brasileño/a.

breach [briːtʃ] vt abrir brecha en // n (gap) brecha; (breaking): **~ of contract** infracción f de contrato; **~ of the peace** perturbación f del orden público.

bread [brɛd] n pan m; **~ and butter** n pan m con mantequilla; (fig) pan (de cada día) // a común y corriente; **~crumbs** npl migajas fpl; (CULIN) pan molido.

breadth [brɛtθ] n anchura; (fig) amplitud f.

breadwinner ['brɛdwɪnə*] n sostén m de la familia.

break [breɪk], pt **broke**, pp **broken** (gen) romper; (promise) faltar a; (fall) amortiguar; (journey) interrumpir; (law) violar, infringir; (record) batir; (news) comunicar // vi romperse, quebrarse; (storm) estallar // n (gap) abertura; (crack) grieta; (fracture) fractura; (breakdown) ruptura, rompimiento; (rest) descanso; (time) intervalo; (: at school) (período de) recreo; (chance) oportunidad f; (escape) evasión f, fuga; to **~ down** vt (figures, data) analizar, descomponer; (undermine) acabar con // vi estropearse; (MED) sufrir un colapso; (AUT) averiarse; (person) romper a llorar; to **~ even** vi salir sin ganar ni perder; to **~ free or loose** vi abrirse paso; to **~ in** vt (horse etc) domar // vi (burglar) forzar una entrada; to **~ into** vt fus (house) forzar; to **~ off** vi (speaker) pararse, detenerse; (branch) partir; to **~ open** vt (door etc) abrir por la fuerza, forzar; to **~ out** vi estallar; to **~ out in spots** salir a uno granos; to **~ up** vi romperse // vt romper, intervenir en; **~able** a quebradizo; **~age** n rotura; **~down** n (AUT) avería; (in communications) interrupción f; (MED: also: **nervous ~down**) colapso, crisis f nerviosa; **~down lorry** n grúa, camión m grúa; **~er** n rompiente m, ola grande.

breakfast ['brɛkfəst] n desayuno.

break: **~through** n ruptura; (fig) avance m, adelanto; **~water** n rompeolas m inv.

breast [brɛst] n (of woman) pecho, seno; (chest) pecho; (of bird) pechuga; **~stroke** n braza de pecho.

breath [brɛθ] n aliento, respiración f; **out of ~** sin aliento, sofocado; **~alyser** n prueba de alcohol por el aliento.

breathe [briːð] vt, vi respirar; (noisily) resollar; **breather** n respiro.

breath: **~less** a sin aliento, jadeante; **~taking** a imponente, pasmoso.

breed [briːd], pt, pp **bred** [brɛd] vt criar, engendrar // vi reproducirse, procrear // n raza, casta; **~er** n (person) criador/a m/f; **~ing** n (of person) educación f.

breeze [bri:z] n brisa.

breezy ['bri:zi] a de mucho viento, ventoso; (person) despreocupado.

brevity ['brɛvɪtɪ] n brevedad f.

brew [bru:] vt (tea) hacer; (beer) elaborar // vi hacerse, prepararse; (fig) amenazar; ~**er** n cervecero; ~**ery** n fábrica de cerveza.

bribe [braɪb] n soborno // vt sobornar, cohechar; ~**ry** n soborno, cohecho.

brick [brɪk] n ladrillo; ~**layer** n albañil m; ~**works** n ladrillar m.

bridal ['braɪdl] a nupcial.

bride [braɪd] n novia; ~**groom** n novio; **bridesmaid** n dama de honor.

bridge [brɪdʒ] n puente m; (NAUT) puente m de mando; (of nose) caballete m; (CARDS) bridge m // vt (river) tender un puente sobre; ~**head** n cabeza de puente.

bridle ['braɪdl] n brida, freno // vt poner la brida a; (fig) reprimir, refrenar; ~ **path** n camino de herradura.

brief [bri:f] a breve, corto // n (LAW) escrito // vt (inform) informar; (instruct) dar órdenes a; ~**s** npl (for men) calzoncillos mpl; (for women) bragas fpl; ~**case** n cartera; ~**ing** n (PRESS) informe m.

brigade [brɪ'geɪd] n (MIL) brigada.

brigadier [brɪgə'dɪə°] n general m de brigada.

bright [braɪt] a claro, luminoso; (weather) de sol; (person: clever) listo, inteligente; (: lively) alegre, animado; (colour) vivo; ~**en** vt (room) hacer más alegre // vi (weather) despejarse; (person: gen: ~**en up**) animarse, alegrarse.

brilliance ['brɪljəns] n brillo, brillantez f; **brilliant** [-ənt] a brillante; (clever) genial.

brim [brɪm] n borde m; (of hat) ala; ~**ful** a lleno hasta el borde; (fig) rebosante (de).

brine [braɪn] n (CULIN) salmuera.

bring [brɪŋ], pt, pp **brought** vt (thing) traer; (person) conducir; to ~ **about** vt ocasionar, producir; to ~ **back** vt volver a traer; (return) devolver; to ~ **down** vt bajar; (price) rebajar; to ~ **forward** vt adelantar; to ~ **in** vt (harvest) recoger; to ~ **off** vt (task, plan) lograr, conseguir; to ~ **out** vt (object) sacar; to ~ **round** vt (unconscious person) hacer volver en sí; (convince) convencer, ganar; to ~ **up** vt (person) educar, criar; (carry up) subir; (question) sacar a colación.

brink [brɪŋk] n borde m.

brisk [brɪsk] a enérgico, vigoroso; (speedy) rápido; (trade) activo.

brisket ['brɪskɪt] n carne f de vaca para asar.

bristle ['brɪsl] n cerda // vi erizarse.

Britain ['brɪtən] n Gran Bretaña.

British ['brɪtɪʃ] a británico; the ~ npl los británicos; the ~ **Isles** npl las Islas Británicas.

Briton ['brɪtən] n británico/a.

brittle ['brɪtl] a quebradizo, frágil.

broach [brəʊtʃ] vt (subject) abordar.

broad [brɔːd] a ancho, amplio; (accent) cerrado; **in** ~ **daylight** en pleno día; ~**cast** n emisión f // (vb: pt, pp ~**cast**) vt (RADIO) emitir; (TV) transmitir; (TV) vi hablar o tocar por la radio; ~**casting** n radiodifusión f, difusión f; ~**en** vt ensanchar // vi ensancharse; ~**ly** ad en general; ~**minded** a tolerante, liberal.

brochure ['brəʊʃjuə°] n folleto.

broke [brəʊk] pt of **break** // a (col) pelado, sin blanca.

broken ['brəʊkən] pp of **break** // a: ~ **leg** pierna rota; **in** ~ **English** en un inglés imperfecto; ~**-hearted** con el corazón partido.

broker ['brəʊkə°] n agente m/f, bolsista m/f.

bronchitis [brɒŋ'kaɪtɪs] n bronquitis f.

bronze [brɒnz] n bronce m.

brooch [brəʊtʃ] n prendedor m.

brood [bru:d] n camada, cría; (children) progenie f; (: pej) prole f // vi (hen) empollar; (obsessively) darle vueltas (a).

brook [bruk] n arroyo.

broom [brum] n escoba; (BOT) retama; ~**stick** n palo de escoba.

Bros. abbr of **Brothers**.

broth [brɒθ] n caldo.

brothel ['brɒθl] n burdel m.

brother ['brʌðə°] n hermano; ~**-in-law** n cuñado.

brought [brɔːt] pt, pp of **bring**.

brow [brau] n ceja; (forehead) frente m; (of hill) cumbre f.

brown [braun] a moreno; (hair) castaño; (tanned) bronceado // n (colour) color m moreno o pardo // vt poner moreno; (tan) broncear; (CULIN) dorar; ~**ie** n niña Girl Guide.

browse [brauz] vi (among books) hojear libros.

bruise [bru:z] n cardenal m, contusión f // vt magullar.

brunette [bru:'nɛt] n morena.

brunt [brʌnt] n: **the** ~ **of** lo más fuerte de, lo peor de.

brush [brʌʃ] n cepillo; (large) escoba; (for painting, shaving etc) brocha; (artist's) pincel m; (BOT) maleza; (quarrel) escaramuza, encuentro // vt cepillar; (gen: ~ **past**, ~ **against**) rozar al pasar; to ~ **aside** vt rechazar, no hacer caso a; to ~ **up** vt (knowledge) repasar, refrescar; ~**wood** n (bushes) maleza; (sticks) leña.

brusque [bru:sk] a brusco, áspero.

Brussels ['brʌslz] n Bruselas; ~ **sprout** n colecilla de Bruselas.

brutal ['bru:tl] a brutal; ~**ity** [-'tælɪtɪ] n brutalidad f.

brute [bru:t] n bruto; (person) bestia.

B.Sc. abbr of **Bachelor of Science** licenciado en ciencias.

bubble ['bʌbl] n burbuja, ampolla // vi burbujear, borbotar; ~ **gum** n chicle m de globo.

buck [bʌk] n macho; (US: col) dólar m // vi

corcovear; **to pass the ~ (to sb)** echar (a uno) el muerto; **to ~ up** vi (cheer up) animarse, cobrar ánimo.

bucket ['bʌkɪt] n cubo, balde m.

buckle ['bʌkl] n hebilla // vt abrochar con hebilla // vi torcerse, combarse.

bud [bʌd] n brote m, yema; (of flower) capullo // vi brotar, echar brotes; (fig) florecer.

Buddhism ['budɪzm] n Budismo.

budding ['bʌdɪŋ] a en ciernes, en embrión.

buddy ['bʌdɪ] n (US) compañero, compinche m.

budge [bʌdʒ] vt mover; (fig) hacer ceder // vi moverse.

budgerigar ['bʌdʒərɪgɑ:*] n periquito.

budget ['bʌdʒɪt] n presupuesto.

budgie ['bʌdʒɪ] n = **budgerigar**.

buff [bʌf] a (colour) color m de ante // n (enthusiast) entusiasta m/f.

buffalo ['bʌfələu], pl ~ or ~es n búfalo.

buffer ['bʌfə*] n amortiguador m.

buffet n ['bufeɪ] n (bar) bar m, cafetería; (food) buffet m // vt ['bʌfɪt] (strike) abofetear; (wind etc) golpear; ~ car n coche-comedor m.

buffoon [bə'fu:n] n bufón m.

bug [bʌg] n (insect) chinche m; (: gen) bicho, sabandija; (: fig: germ) microbio, bacilo; (spy device) micrófono oculto; (tap) intervención f; (machine for tapping) aparato de intervención // vt (fam) fastidiar; (spy on) poner micrófono oculto en.

bugle ['bju:gl] n corneta, clarín m.

build [bɪld] n (of person) talle m, tipo // vt, pt, pp built construir, edificar; ~er n constructor m; (contractor) contratista m/f; ~ing n (act of) construcción f; (habitation, offices) edificio; ~ing society n sociedad f inmobiliaria, cooperativa de construcciones; **to ~ up** vt (MED) fortalecer; (stocks) acumular.

built [bɪlt] pt, pp of build // a: ~-in (cupboard) empotrado; (device) interior, incorporado; ~-up (area) urbanizado.

bulb [bʌlb] n (BOT) bulbo; (ELEC) bombilla.

Bulgaria [bʌl'gɛərɪə] n Bulgaria; ~n a, n búlgaro/a.

bulge [bʌldʒ] n bombeo, pandeo // vi bombearse, pandearse; (pocket etc) hacer bulto.

bulk [bʌlk] n (mass) bulto, volumen m; (major part) grueso; **in ~** (COMM) a granel; **the ~ of** la mayor parte de; ~head n mamparo; ~y a voluminoso, abultado.

bull [bul] n toro; ~dog n dogo.

bulldozer ['buldəuzə*] n aplanadora, motoniveladora.

bullet ['bulɪt] n bala; ~proof a a prueba de balas; ~ wound n balazo.

bulletin ['bulɪtɪn] n anuncio, parte m.

bullfight ['bulfaɪt] n corrida de toros; ~er n torero; ~ing n los toros mpl, el toreo; (art of ~ing) tauromaquia.

bullion ['buljən] n oro o plata en barras.

bullock ['bulək] n novillo.

bull's-eye ['bulzaɪ] n centro del blanco.

bully ['bulɪ] n valentón m, matón m // vt intimidar, tiranizar.

bum [bʌm] n (col: backside) culo, trasero; (tramp) vagabundo.

bumblebee ['bʌmblbi:] n (zool) abejorro.

bump [bʌmp] n (blow) tope m, choque m; (jolt) sacudida; (on road etc, on head) bollo, abolladura // vt (strike) chocar contra, topetar // vi dar sacudidas; **to ~ into** vt fus chocar contra, tropezar con; (person) topar; ~er n (Brit) parachoques m inv // a: ~er crop/harvest cosecha abundante.

bumpy ['bʌmpɪ] a (road) lleno de baches; (journey) zarandeado.

bun [bʌn] n bollo; (of hair) moño.

bunch [bʌntʃ] n (of flowers) ramo; (of keys) manojo; (of bananas) piña; (of people) grupo; (pej) pandilla.

bundle ['bʌndl] n (gen) bulto, fardo; (of sticks) haz f; (of papers) legajo // vt (also: ~ up) atar, envolver; (put): **to ~ sth/sb into** meter algo/a alguien precipitadamente en.

bung [bʌŋ] n tapón m, bitoque m // vt (throw: gen: ~ into) arrojar.

bungalow ['bʌŋgələu] n bungalow m, chalé m.

bungle ['bʌŋgl] vt chapucear.

bunion ['bʌnjən] n juanete m.

bunk [bʌŋk] n tonterías fpl; ~ beds npl literas fpl.

bunker ['bʌŋkə*] n (coal store) carbonera; (MIL) refugio; (GOLF) bunker m.

bunny ['bʌnɪ] n (also: ~ rabbit) conejito.

bunting ['bʌntɪŋ] n empavesada, banderas fpl.

buoy [bɔɪ] n boya; **to ~ up** vt mantener a flote; (fig) animar; ~ant a boyante.

burden ['bə:dn] n carga // vt cargar.

bureau [bjuə'rəu] pl ~x [-z] n (furniture) escritorio, buró m; (office) oficina, agencia.

bureaucracy [bjuə'rɔkrəsɪ] n burocracia; **bureaucrat** ['bjuərəkræt] n burócrata m/f.

burglar ['bə:glə*] n ladrón/ona m/f; ~ alarm n alarma f de ladrones; ~y n robo con allanamiento, robo de una casa; **burgle** ['bə:gl] vt robar (con allanamiento).

burial ['berɪəl] n entierro; ~ ground n cementerio.

burlesque [bə:'lesk] n parodia.

burly ['bə:lɪ] a fornido, membrudo.

Burma ['bə:mə] n Birmania.

burn [bə:n], pt, pp burned or burnt vt quemar; (house) incendiar // vi quemarse, arder; incendiarse; (sting) escocer // n quemadura; **to ~ down** vt incendiar; ~er n (gas) quemador m, fuego; ~ing a ardiente.

burp [bə:p] (col) n eructo // vi eructar.

burrow ['bʌrəu] n madriguera // vt hacer una madriguera.

bursar ['bɔ:sɔ°] n tesorero; (student) becario; ~ y n beca.

burst [bɔ:st], pt, pp burst vt (balloon, pipe) reventar; (banks etc) romper // vi reventarse; romperse; (tyre) pincharse; (bomb) estallar // n (gen) reventón m; (explosion) estallido; (shots) ráfaga de tiros; a ~ of energy una explosión f de energía; to ~ into flames estallar en llamas; to ~ into laughter soltar la carcajada; to ~ into tears deshacerse en lágrimas; to be ~ing with reventar por o de; to ~ into vt fus (room etc) irrumpir en; to ~ open vi abrirse de golpe.

bury ['bɛrɪ] vt enterrar; (body) enterrar, sepultar.

bus [bʌs] n autobús m.

bush [buʃ] n arbusto; (scrub land) monte m; to beat about the ~ ir por rodeos; ~ y a (thick) espeso, poblado.

busily ['bɪzɪlɪ] ad atareadamente, afanosamente.

business ['bɪznɪs] n (matter) negocio; (trading) comercio, negocios mpl; (firm) empresa, casa; (occupation) oficio; (affair) asunto; it's my ~ to... me toca o corresponde...; it's none of my ~ yo no tengo nada que ver; he means ~ habla en serio; ~like a formal, metódico; ~man n hombre m de negocios.

bus-stop ['bʌsstɔp] n parada de autobús.

bust [bʌst] n (ANAT) pecho / a (broken) roto, estropeado; to go ~ quebrarse.

bustle ['bʌsl] n bullicio, movimiento // vi menearse, apresurarse; bustling a (town) animado, bullicioso.

busy ['bɪzɪ] a ocupado, atareado; (shop, street) concurrido, animado // vr: to ~ o.s. with ocuparse en; ~body n entrometido.

but [bʌt] conj pero // prep excepto, menos; nothing ~ nada más que; ~ for a no ser por, si no fuera por; all ~ finished casi terminado.

butane ['bju:teɪn] n butano.

butcher ['butʃɔ°] n carnicero // vt hacer una carnicería con; (cattle etc for meat) matar; ~'s (shop) n carnicería.

butler ['bʌtlɔ°] n mayordomo.

butt [bʌt] n (cask) tonel m; (for rain) tina; (thick end) cabo, extremo; (of gun) culata; (of cigarette) colilla; (fig: target) blanco // vt dar cabezadas contra, topetar.

butter ['bʌtɔ°] n mantequilla // vt untar con mantequilla; ~ bean n judía blanca; ~cup n ranúnculo.

butterfly ['bʌtɔflaɪ] n mariposa.

buttocks ['bʌtɔks] npl nalgas fpl.

button ['bʌtn] n botón m // vt abotonar, abrochar // vi abrocharse; ~hole n ojal m; (flower) flor f que se lleva en el ojal // vt obligar a escuchar.

buttress ['bʌtrɪs] n contrafuerte m; (fig) apoyo, sostén m.

buxom ['bʌksɔm] a (baby) rollizo; (woman) frescachona.

buy [baɪ], pt, pp bought vt comprar // n compra; to ~ sb sth/sth from sb comprar algo para alguien/comprarle algo a alguien; ~er n comprador/a m/f.

buzz [bʌz] n zumbido; (col: phone call) llamada (por teléfono) // vi zumbar.

buzzard ['bʌzɔd] n águila ratonera.

buzzer ['bʌzɔ°] n zumbador m, vibrador m.

by [baɪ] prep por; (beside) junto a, cerca de; (according to) según, de acuerdo con; (before): ~ 4 o'clock para las cuatro // ad see pass, go etc; ~ bus/car en autobús/coche; paid ~ the hour pagado por horas; ~ night/day de noche/día; (all) ~ oneself (completamente) solo; ~ the way a propósito, por cierto; ~ and large en general; ~ and ~ luego, más tarde.

bye(-bye) ['baɪ'baɪ] excl adiós, hasta luego.

by(e)-law ['baɪlɔ:] n ordenanza municipal.

by-election ['baɪɪlekʃɔn] n elección f parcial.

bygone ['baɪgɔn] a pasado, del pasado // n: let ~s be ~s lo pasado, pasado está.

bypass ['baɪpɑ:s] n carretera de circunvalación // vt evitar.

by-product ['baɪprɔdʌkt] n subproducto, derivado.

bystander ['baɪstændɔ°] n espectador/a m/f.

byword ['baɪwɔːd] n: to be a ~ for ser conocidísimo por.

C

C. abbr of centigrade.

C.A. abbr of chartered accountant.

cab [kæb] n taxi m; (of truck) cabina.

cabaret ['kæbəreɪ] n cabaret m.

cabbage ['kæbɪdʒ] n col m, berza.

cabin ['kæbɪn] n cabaña; (on ship) camarote m; ~ cruiser n yate m de motor.

cabinet ['kæbɪnɪt] n (POL) consejo de ministros; (furniture) armario; (also: display ~) vitrina; ~-maker n ebanista m.

cable ['keɪbl] n cable m // vt cablegrafiar; ~-car n coche m de teleférico, tren m aéreo.

cackle ['kækl] vi cacarear.

cactus ['kæktəs], pl -ti [-taɪ] n cacto.

caddie ['kædɪ] n cadi m.

cadet [kə'dɛt] n (MIL) cadete m.

cadge [kædʒ] vt gorronear; cadger n gorrón/ona m/f.

Caesarean (section) [si:'zɛərɪən] n cesárea.

café ['kæfeɪ], cafeteria [kæfɪ'tɪərɪə] n café m.

caffein(e) ['kæfi:n] n cafeína.

cage [keɪdʒ] n jaula // vt enjaular.

cagey ['keɪdʒɪ] a (col) cauteloso, reservado.

Cairo ['kaɪərəu] n el Cairo.

cajole [kə'dʒəul] vt engatusar.
cake [keɪk] n (large) pastel m; (small) pasta, bizcocho; (of soap) pastilla; ~d with cubierto de.
calamitous [kə'læmɪtəs] a calamitoso; **calamity** [-ɪtɪ] n calamidad f.
calcium ['kælsɪəm] n calcio.
calculate ['kælkjuleɪt] vt calcular; **calculating** a (clever) astuto; (devious) calculador(a); **calculation** [-'leɪʃən] n cálculo, cómputo; **calculator** n calculadora.
calculus ['kælkjuləs] n cálculo.
calendar ['kæləndə*] n calendario; ~ month/year mes m/año civil.
calf [kɑ:f], pl **calves** n (of cow) ternero, becerro; (of other animals) cría; (also: ~skin) piel m de becerro; (ANAT) pantorrilla.
calibre, caliber (US) ['kælɪbə*] n calibre m.
call [kɔ:l] vt (gen, also TEL) llamar // vi (shout) llamar; (telephone) llamar por teléfono; (visit: also: ~ in, ~ round) hacer una visita // n (shout, TEL) llamada; (of bird) canto; (appeal) llamamiento; to ~ for vt fus (demand) pedir, exigir; (fetch) venir por; to ~ off vt suspender; (cancel) cancelar; to ~ on vt fus (visit) visitar; (turn to) acudir a; to ~ out vi gritar, dar voces; to ~ up vt (MIL) llamar al servicio militar; ~box n cabina telefónica; ~er n visita m/f; (TEL) usuario; ~ girl n prostituta; ~ing n vocación f, profesión f.
callous ['kæləs] a insensible, cruel.
calm [kɑ:m] n calma, tranquilidad f // vt calmar, tranquilizar // a (gen) tranquilo; (sea) liso, en calma; ~ly ad tranquilamente, con calma; ~ness n calma; to ~ down vi calmarse, tranquilizarse // vt calmar, tranquilizar.
calorie ['kælɔrɪ] n caloría.
calve [kɑ:v] vi parir.
calves [kɑ:vz] pl of **calf**.
camber ['kæmbə*] n (of road) combadura, comba.
Cambodia [kæm'bəudjə] n Camboya.
came [keɪm] pt of **come**.
camel ['kæməl] n camello.
cameo ['kæmɪəu] n camafeo.
camera ['kæmərə] n máquina fotográfica; (CINEMA, TV) cámara; **in** ~ en secreto; ~ man n cámaraman m, cámara m/f.
camouflage ['kæməflɑ:ʒ] n camuflaje m // vt camuflar.
camp [kæmp] n campo, campamento // vi acampar // a afectado, afeminado.
campaign [kæm'peɪn] n (MIL, POL etc) campaña // vi hacer campaña.
camp: ~bed n cama de campaña; ~er n campista m/f; (vehicle) caravana; ~ing n camping m; to go ~ing hacer camping; ~site n camping m.
campus ['kæmpəs] n ciudad f universitaria.
can [kæn] auxiliary vb (gen) poder; (know how to) saber; **I** ~ **swim** sé nadar // n (of oil, water) lata, bote m // vt enlatar; (preserve) conservar en lata.
Canada ['kænədə] n el Canadá; **Canadian** [kə'neɪdɪən] a, n canadiense m/f.
canal [kə'næl] n canal m.
canary [kə'nɛərɪ] n canario; **C~ Islands** npl las (Islas) Canarias fpl.
cancel ['kænsəl] vt cancelar; (train) suprimir; (appointment) anular; (cross out) tachar, borrar; ~**lation** [-'leɪʃən] n cancelación f; supresión f.
cancer ['kænsə*] n cáncer m; **C~** (ASTRO) Cáncer m.
candid ['kændɪd] a franco, abierto.
candidate ['kændɪdeɪt] n candidato.
candle ['kændl] n vela; (in church) cirio; ~**stick** n (also: ~ **holder**) (single) candelero; (low) palmatoria; (bigger, ornate) candelabro.
candour ['kændə*] n franqueza.
candy ['kændɪ] n azúcar m cande; (US) dulce m, caramelo.
cane [keɪn] n (BOT) caña; (stick) vara, palmeta // vt (SCOL) castigar (con palmeta).
canine ['kænaɪn] a canino.
canister ['kænɪstə*] n bote m, lata.
cannabis ['kænəbɪs] n cáñamo, marijuana.
canned [kænd] a en lata, de lata.
cannibal ['kænɪbəl] n caníbal m/f; ~**ism** n canibalismo.
cannon ['kænən], pl ~ or ~**s** n cañón m; ~**ball** n bala (de cañón).
cannot ['kænɔt] = **can not.**
canny ['kænɪ] a astuto.
canoe [kə'nu:] n canoa; (SPORT) piragua; ~**ing** n (SPORT) piragüismo; ~**ist** n piragüista m/f.
canon ['kænən] n (clergyman) canónigo; (standard) canon m.
canonize ['kænənaɪz] vt canonizar.
can opener ['kænəupnə*] n abrelatas m inv.
canopy ['kænəpɪ] n dosel m, toldo; (ARCH) baldaquín m.
can't [kænt] = **can not.**
cantankerous [kæn'tæŋkərəs] a arisco, malhumorado.
canteen [kæn'ti:n] n cantina; (bottle) cantimplora; (of cutlery) juego (de cubiertos).
canter ['kæntə*] n medio galope // vi ir a medio galope.
canvas ['kænvəs] n (gen) lona; (painting) lienzo; (NAUT) velas fpl; **under** ~ (camping) bajo lona.
canvass ['kænvəs] vt (POL) solicitar votos de.
canyon ['kænjən] n cañón m.
cap [kæp] n gorra; (of pen) capuchón m; (of bottle) tapa, cápsula; (MED) diafragma m // vt coronar, poner remate a; (outdo) superar; (FOOTBALL) seleccionar (para el equipo nacional).

capability [keɪpə'bɪlɪtɪ] n capacidad f; **capable** ['keɪpəbl] a capaz.
capacity [kə'pæsɪtɪ] n capacidad f; (position) calidad f.
cape [keɪp] n capa; (GEO) cabo.
caper ['keɪpəˀ] n (CULIN. gen: ~s) alcaparra; (prank) travesura.
capital ['kæpɪtl] n (also: ~ city) capital f; (money) capital m; (also: ~ letter) mayúscula; ~**ism** n capitalismo; ~**ist** a, n capitalista m/f; ~ **punishment** n pena de muerte.
capitulate [kə'pɪtjuleɪt] vi capitular, rendirse; **capitulation** [-'leɪʃən] n capitulación f, rendición f.
capricious [kə'prɪʃəs] a caprichoso.
Capricorn ['kæprɪkɔːn] n Capricornio.
capsize [kæp'saɪz] vt volcar, hacer zozobrar // vi volcarse, zozobrar.
capstan ['kæpstən] n cabrestante m.
capsule ['kæpsjuːl] n cápsula.
captain ['kæptɪn] n capitán m // vt capitanear, ser el capitán de.
caption ['kæpʃən] n (heading) título; (to picture) leyenda.
captivate ['kæptɪveɪt] vt cautivar, encantar.
captive ['kæptɪv] a, n cautivo/a; **captivity** [-'tɪvɪtɪ] n cautiverio.
capture ['kæptʃəˀ] vt prender, apresar; (place) tomar; (attention) captar, llamar // n apresamiento; toma; (thing taken) presa.
car [kɑːˀ] n coche m, automóvil m; (RAIL) vagón m.
carafe [kə'ræf] n garrafa.
caramel ['kærəməl] n caramelo.
carat ['kærət] n quilate m.
caravan ['kærəvæn] n caravana, rulota; (of camels) caravana.
caraway ['kærəweɪ] n: ~ **seed** carvi m.
carbohydrate [kɑːbəu'haɪdreɪt] n hidrato de carbono; (food) fécula.
carbon ['kɑːbən] n carbono; ~ **copy** n copia al carbón; ~ **paper** n papel m carbón.
carburettor [kɑːbju'rɛtəˀ] n carburador m.
carcass ['kɑːkəs] n cadáver m de animal.
card [kɑːd] n carta, naipe m; (visiting ~, post~ etc) tarjeta; ~**board** n cartón m, cartulina; ~ **game** n juego de naipes.
cardiac ['kɑːdɪæk] a cardiaco.
cardigan ['kɑːdɪgən] n rebeca.
cardinal ['kɑːdɪnl] a cardinal // n cardenal m.
card index n fichero.
care [kɛəˀ] n (gen) cuidado; (worry) inquietud f, solicitud f; (charge) cargo, custodia // vi: to ~ **about** preocuparse de, tener interés en; **in sb's** ~ a cargo de alguien; **to take** ~ **to** cuidarse o tener cuidado de; **to take** ~ **of** cuidar; **to** ~ **for** vt fus cuidar a; (like) querer; **I don't** ~ no me importa.
career [kə'rɪəˀ] n carrera // vi (also: ~

along) correr a toda velocidad.
carefree ['kɛəfriː] a despreocupado.
careful ['kɛəful] a cuidadoso; (cautious) cauteloso; **(be)** ~**!** ¡tenga cuidado!; ~**ly** ad con cuidado, cuidadosamente.
careless ['kɛəlɪs] a descuidado; (heedless) poco atento; ~**ly** ad sin cuidado, a la ligera; ~**ness** n descuido, falta de atención.
caress [kə'rɛs] n caricia // vt acariciar.
caretaker ['kɛəteɪkəˀ] n portero, conserje m/f.
car-ferry ['kɑːfɛrɪ] n transbordador m para coches.
cargo ['kɑːgəu], pl ~**es** n cargamento, carga.
Caribbean [kærɪ'biːən] n: **the** ~ **(Sea)** el Caribe.
caricature ['kærɪkətjuəˀ] n caricatura.
carnal ['kɑːnl] a carnal.
carnation [kɑː'neɪʃən] n clavel m.
carnival ['kɑːnɪvəl] n fiesta, feria, carnaval m.
carnivore ['kɑːnɪvɔːˀ] n carnívoro.
carol ['kærəl] n: **(Christmas)** ~ villancico.
carp [kɑːp] n (fish) carpa; **to** ~ **at** vt fus quejarse de.
car park n aparcamiento, parking m.
carpenter ['kɑːpɪntəˀ] n carpintero; **carpentry** [-trɪ] n carpintería.
carpet ['kɑːpɪt] n alfombra // vt alfombrar; ~ **slippers** npl zapatillas fpl.
carriage ['kærɪdʒ] n coche m; (RAIL) vagón m; (for goods) transporte m; (bearing) porte m; ~**way** n (part of road) carretera; **dual** ~**way** carretera de doble calzada.
carrier ['kærɪəˀ] n trajinista m/f; (company) empresa de transportes; ~ **bag** n bolsa (de papel).
carrot ['kærət] n zanahoria.
carry ['kærɪ] vt (gen) llevar; (transport) transportar; (a motion, bill) aprobar; (involve: responsibilities etc) entrañar, implicar // vi (sound) oírse; **to** ~ **on** vi (continue) seguir (adelante), continuar; (fam: complain) quejarse, protestar // vt proseguir, continuar; **to** ~ **out** vt (orders) cumplir; (investigation) llevar a cabo, realizar.
cart [kɑːt] n carro, carreta // vt acarrear, llevar (en carro).
cartilage ['kɑːtɪlɪdʒ] n cartílago.
cartographer [kɑː'tɔgrəfəˀ] n cartógrafo.
carton ['kɑːtən] n (box) caja (de cartón); (of yogurt) pote m.
cartoon [kɑː'tuːn] n (PRESS) caricatura; (comic strip) tira cómica; (film) dibujos mpl animados; ~**ist** n caricaturista m/f; dibujante m/f.
cartridge ['kɑːtrɪdʒ] n cartucho.
carve [kɑːv] vt (meat) trinchar; (wood, stone) cincelar, esculpir; (on tree) grabar; **to** ~ **up** dividir, repartir; **carving** n (in wood etc) escultura, (obra de) talla; **carving knife** n trinchante m.

car wash n lavado de coches.

cascade [kæs'keɪd] n salto de agua, cascada; (fig) chorro // vi caer a chorros o en forma de cascada.

case [keɪs] n (container) caja; (MED) caso; (for jewels etc) estuche m; (LAW) causa, proceso; (also: suit~) maleta; **in ~ (of)** en caso de (que), por si; **in any ~** en todo caso; **just in ~** por si acaso; **to make a good ~** tener buenos argumentos.

cash [kæʃ] n (dinero en) efectivo, dinero contante // vt cobrar, hacer efectivo; **to pay (in) ~** pagar al contado; **~ on delivery** cóbrese al entregar; **~book** n libro de caja; **~desk** n caja.

cashew [kæ'ʃu:] n (also: ~ **nut**) anacardo.

cashier [kæ'ʃɪə*] n cajero.

cashmere [kæʃ'mɪə*] n casimir m, cachemira.

cash register n caja.

casing ['keɪsɪŋ] n envoltura; (of boiler etc) revestimiento.

casino [kə'si:nəu] n casino.

cask [kɑ:sk] n tonel m, barril m.

casket ['kɑ:skɪt] n cofre m, estuche m; (US: coffin) ataúd m.

casserole ['kæsərəul] n cacerola; (food) cazuela.

cassette [kæ'sɛt] n cassette m; ~ **player** n tocacassettes m inv.

cassock ['kæsək] n sotana.

cast [kɑ:st], pt, pp **cast** vt (throw) echar, arrojar, lanzar; (skin) mudar, perder; (metal) fundir; (THEATRE) hacer el reparto de // vi (FISHING) lanzar // n (THEATRE) reparto; (mould) forma, molde m; (also: plaster ~) vaciado; **to ~ away** vt desechar; **to ~ down** vt derribar; **to ~ loose** soltar; **to ~ one's vote** dar el voto; **to ~ off** vi (NAUT) desamarrar.

castanets [kæstə'nɛts] npl castañuelas fpl.

castaway ['kɑ:stəwəɪ] n náufrago.

caste [kɑ:st] n casta.

casting vote ['kɑ:stɪŋ-] n voto decisivo.

cast iron n hierro fundido.

castle ['kɑ:sl] n castillo; (CHESS) torre f.

castor ['kɑ:stə*] n (wheel) ruedecilla; ~ **oil** n aceite m de ricino; ~ **sugar** n azúcar m extrafino.

castrate [kæs'treɪt] vt castrar.

casual ['kæʒjul] a (by chance) fortuito; (irregular: work etc) eventual, temporero; (unconcerned) despreocupado; (informal: clothes) de sport; ~**ly** ad por casualidad; de manera despreocupada.

casualty ['kæʒjultɪ] n víctima m/f, herido; (dead) muerto; (MIL) baja; **casualties** npl pérdidas fpl.

cat [kæt] n gato.

Catalan ['kætələn] a, n Catalán/ana m/f.

catalogue, catalog (US) ['kætələg] n catálogo // vt catalogar.

Catalonia [kætə'ləunɪə] n Cataluña.

catalyst ['kætəlɪst] n catalizador m.

catapult ['kætəpʌlt] n tirador m.

cataract ['kætərækt] n (also MED) catarata.

catarrh [kə'tɑ:*] n catarro.

catastrophe [kə'tæstrəfɪ] n catástrofe m; **catastrophic** [kætə'strɔfɪk] a catastrófico.

catch [kætʃ], pt, pp **caught** vt (gen) coger; (arrest) detener; (grasp) asir; (breath) suspender; (person: by surprise) sorprender; (attract: attention) ganar; (MED) contagiarse de, coger; (also: ~ **up**) alcanzar // vi (fire) encenderse; (in branches etc) enredarse // n (fish etc) pesca; (act of catching) cogida; (trick) trampa; (of lock) pestillo, cerradura; **to ~ on** vi (understand) caer en la cuenta; (grow popular) hacerse popular; **to ~ sight of** divisar; **to ~ up** vi (fig) ponerse al día.

catch: ~**ing** a (MED) contagioso; ~**ment area** n zona de captación; ~ **phrase** n lema m, slogan m; ~**y** a (tune) pegadizo.

catechism ['kætɪkɪzəm] n (REL) catequismo.

categoric(al) [kætɪ'gɔrɪk(əl)] a categórico, terminante.

categorize ['kætɪgəraɪz] vt clasificar; **category** [-rɪ] n categoría, clase f.

cater ['keɪtə*] vi: **to ~ for** abastecer a; (needs) atender a; (consumers) proveer a; ~**er** n abastecedor m, proveedor m; ~**ing** n servicio de comidas; (trade) abastecimiento.

caterpillar ['kætəpɪlə*] n oruga, gusano; ~ **track** n rodado de oruga.

cathedral [kə'θi:drəl] n catedral f.

catholic ['kæθəlɪk] a católico; **C~** a, n (REL) católico/a.

cattle ['kætl] npl ganado sg.

catty ['kætɪ] a malicioso, rencoroso.

Caucasus ['kɔ:kəsəs] n Cáucaso.

caught [kɔ:t] pt, pp of **catch**.

cauliflower ['kɔlɪflauə*] n coliflor f.

cause [kɔ:z] n causa, motivo, razón f // vt causar; (provoke) provocar.

causeway ['kɔ:zweɪ] n (road) carretera elevada; (embankment) terraplén m.

caustic ['kɔ:stɪk] a cáustico; (fig) mordaz.

caution ['kɔ:ʃən] n cautela, prudencia; (warning) advertencia, amonestación f // vt amonestar.

cautious ['kɔ:ʃəs] a cauteloso, prudente, precavido; ~**ly** ad con cautela; ~**ness** n cautela.

cavalier [kævə'lɪə*] a arrogante, desdeñoso.

cavalry ['kævəlrɪ] n caballería.

cave [keɪv] n cueva, caverna; **to ~ in** vi (roof etc) derrumbarse, hundirse; ~**man** n cavernícola m/f, troglodita m/f.

cavern ['kævən] n caverna.

caviar(e) ['kævɪɑ:*] n caviar m.

cavity ['kævɪtɪ] n hueco, cavidad f.

cavort [kə'vɔ:t] vi dar cabrioladas.

caw [kɔ:] vi graznar.

CBI n abbr of **Confederation of British Industries.**

cc *abbr of* **cubic centimetres; carbon copy.**

cease [si:s] *vt, vi* cesar; **~fire** *n* cese *m* de hostilidades *o* fuego; **~less** *a* incesante; **~lessly** *ad* sin cesar.

cedar ['si:də*] *n* cedro.

cede [si:d] *vt* ceder.

ceiling ['si:lɪŋ] *n* techo; (*fig*) límite *m*.

celebrate ['selibreit] *vt* celebrar; (*marriage*) solemnizar // *vi* divertirse; **~d** *a* célebre; **celebration** [-'breiʃən] *n* fiesta, celebración *f*.

celebrity [si'lebriti] *n* celebridad *f*.

celery ['seləri] *n* apio.

celestial [si'lestiəl] *a* (*of sky*) celeste; (*divine*) celestial.

celibacy ['selibəsi] *n* celibato.

cell [sel] *n* celda; (*BIOL*) célula; (*ELEC*) elemento.

cellar ['selə*] *n* sótano; (*for wine*) bodega.

'cello ['tʃeləu] *n* violoncelo.

cellophane ['seləfein] *n* celofán *m*.

cellular ['seljulə*] *a* celular.

cellulose ['seljuləus] *n* celulosa.

Celt [kelt, selt] *a, n* celta *m/f*; **~ic** *a* celta.

cement [sə'ment] *n* cemento // *vt* cementar; (*fig*) cimentar, fortalecer.

cemetery ['semitri] *n* cementerio.

cenotaph ['senətɑ:f] *n* cenotafio.

censor ['sensə*] *n* censor // *vt* (*cut*) tachar, suprimir; **~ship** *n* censura.

censure ['senʃə*] *vt* censurar.

census ['sensəs] *n* censo.

cent [sent] *n* (*US: coin*) centavo, céntimo; *see also* **per.**

centenary [sen'ti:nəri] *n* centenario.

centi... [senti] *pref:* **~grade** *a* centígrado; **~litre** *n* centilitro; **~metre** *n* centímetro; **~pede** *n* ciempiés *m*.

central ['sentrəl] *a* central; (*of town*) céntrico; **C~** **American** *a* centroamericano; **~ heating** *n* calefacción *f* central; **~ ize** *vt* centralizar.

centre ['sentə*] *n* centro; **~- forward** *n* (*SPORT*) delantero centro; **~-half** *n* (*SPORT*) medio centro.

century ['sentjuri] *n* siglo; **20th ~** siglo veinte.

ceramic [si'ræmik] *a* cerámico; **~s** *n* cerámica

cereal ['si:riəl] *n* cereal *m*.

ceremony ['seriməni] *n* ceremonia.

certain ['sə:tən] *a* (*gen*) seguro; (*correct*) cierto; (*person*) seguro; (*a particular*) cierto; **for ~** a ciencia cierta; **~ly** *ad* desde luego, por cierto; **~ty** *n* certeza, certidumbre *f*, seguridad *f*.

certificate [sə'tifikit] *n* certificado.

certify ['sə:tifai] *vt* certificar.

cervix ['sə:viks] *n* cerviz *f*.

cessation [sə'seiʃən] *n* cesación *f*, suspensión *f*.

cf. *abbr* = **compare** cfr.

chafe [tʃeif] *vt* (*rub*) rozar; (*wear*) desgastar; (*irritate*) irritar.

chaffinch ['tʃæfintʃ] *n* pinzón *m* vulgar.

chagrin ['ʃægrin] *n* disgusto, desazón *f*.

chain [tʃein] *n* (*gen*) cadena // *vt* (*also:* **~ up**) encadenar; **~ reaction** *n* reacción *f* en cadena; **~ store** *n* tienda de una cadena.

chair [tʃeə*] *n* silla; (*armchair*) sillón *m*; (*of university*) cátedra // *vt* (*meeting*) presidir; **~lift** *n* telesilla; **~man** *n* presidente *m*.

chalet ['ʃælei] *n* chalet *m*.

chalice ['tʃælis] *n* cáliz *m*.

chalk [tʃɔ:k] *n* (*GEO*) creta; (*for writing*) tiza.

challenge ['tʃælindʒ] *n* desafío, reto // *vt* desafiar, retar; (*statement, right*) poner en duda, cuestionar; **to ~ sb to do sth** retar a uno a que haga algo; **challenger** *n* (*SPORT*) contrincante *m/f*; **challenging** *a* desafiante; (*tone*) de desafío.

chamber ['tʃeimbə*] *n* cámara, sala; **~ of commerce** cámara de comercio; **~maid** *n* camarera; **~ music** *n* música de cámara.

chamois ['ʃæmwɑ:] *n* gamuza.

champagne [ʃæm'pein] *n* champaña *m*, champán *m*.

champion ['tʃæmpiən] *n* campeón/ona *m/f*; **~ship** *n* campeonato.

chance [tʃɑ:ns] *n* (*luck*) casualidad *f*, suerte *f*; (*fate*) azar *m*; (*opportunity*) ocasión *f*, oportunidad *f*; (*likelihood*) posibilidad *f*; (*risk*) riesgo // *vt* arriesgar, probar // *a* fortuito, casual; **to ~ it** aventurarse, arriesgarse; **to take a ~** arriesgarse; **by ~** por casualidad.

chancel ['tʃɑ:nsəl] *n* coro y presbiterio.

chancellor ['tʃɑ:nsələ*] *n* canciller *m*; **C~ of the Exchequer** *n* Ministro de Hacienda.

chandelier [ʃændə'liə*] *n* araña (de luces).

change [tʃeindʒ] *vt* (*gen*) cambiar; (*replace*) reemplazar; (*gear, clothes, house*) cambiar de, mudar de; (*exchange*) trocar; (*transform*) transformar // *vi* (*gen*) cambiar(se), mudar; (*trains*) hacer transbordo; **to ~ into** transformarse en // *n* cambio, modificación *f*, transformación *f*; (*coins*) moneda suelta, suelto; (*money returned*) vuelta; **for a ~** para variar; **~able** *a* (*weather*) cambiable, mudable; **~less** *a* inmutable; **~over** *n* (*to new system*) cambio.

changing ['tʃeindʒiŋ] *a* cambiante; **~ room** *n* vestuario.

channel ['tʃænl] *n* (*TV*) canal *m*; (*of river*) cauce *m*; (*of sea*) estrecho; (*groove, fig: medium*) conducto, medio // *vt* canalizar, encauzar; **the (English) C~** el Canal (de la Mancha); **the C~ Islands** las Islas Normandas *fpl*.

chant [tʃɑ:nt] *n* canto // *vt* cantar; (*fig*) recitar en tono monótono.

chaos ['keiɔs] *n* caos *m*; **chaotic** [kei'ɔtik] *a* caótico, desordenado.

chap [tʃæp] *n* (*col: man*) tío, tipo // *vi* (*skin*) agrietarse.

chapel ['tʃæpəl] n capilla.
chaperon ['ʃæpərəun] n carabina.
chaplain ['tʃæplɪn] n capellán m.
chapter ['tʃæptəˠ] n capítulo.
char [tʃɑ:ˠ] vt (burn) carbonizar, chamuscar // n = **charlady**.
character ['kærɪktəˠ] n carácter m, naturaleza, índole f, calidad f; (in novel, film) personaje m; (role) papel m; ~**istic** [-'rɪstɪk] a característico // n característica; ~**ize** vt caracterizar.
charade [ʃəˈrɑ:d] n charada.
charcoal ['tʃɑ:kəul] n carbón m vegetal; (ART) carboncillo.
charge [tʃɑ:dʒ] n carga; (LAW) cargo, acusación f; (cost) precio, coste m; (responsibility) cargo; (task) encargo // vt (LAW) acusar (with de); (gun, battery, MIL: enemy) cargar; (price) pedir; (customer) cobrar; (sb with task) encargar // vi cargar, precipitarse; (make pay) cobrar; ~**s** npl: bank ~**s** suplemento cobrado por el banco; free of ~ gratis; to reverse the ~**s** (TEL) poner una conferencia por cobrar; to take ~ of hacerse cargo de, encargarse de; to be in ~ of estar a cargo de o encargado de; how much do you ~? ¿cuánto cobra Usted?; to ~ an expense (up) to sb's account cargar algo a cuenta de alguien.
charitable ['tʃærɪtəbl] a caritativo.
charity ['tʃærɪtɪ] n (gen) caridad f; (sympathy) compasión f; (organization) sociedad f benéfica.
charlady ['tʃɑ:leɪdɪ] n mujer f de la limpieza.
charm [tʃɑ:m] n encanto, atractivo; (spell) hechizo; (object) amuleto // vt encantar; hechizar; ~**ing** a encantador(a), simpático.
chart [tʃɑ:t] n cuadro; (graph) gráfica; (map) carta de navegación // vt (course) trazar.
charter ['tʃɑ:təˠ] vt (plane) alquilar; (ship) fletar // n (document) carta; ~**ed accountant** n perito contable; ~ **flight** n vuelo charter.
charwoman ['tʃɑ:wumən] n = **charlady**.
chase [tʃeɪs] vt (follow) perseguir; (hunt) cazar // n persecución f; caza; to ~ after correr tras.
chasm ['kæzəm] n abismo.
chassis ['ʃæsɪ] n chasis m.
chaste [tʃeɪst] a casto; **chastity** ['tʃæstɪtɪ] n castidad f.
chat [tʃæt] vi (also: **have a** ~) charlar // n charla.
chatter ['tʃætəˠ] vi (person) charlar; (teeth) castañetear // n (of birds) parloteo; (of people) charla, cháchara; ~**box** n parlanchín/ina m/f.
chatty ['tʃætɪ] a (style) familiar; (person) hablador(a), locuaz.
chauffeur ['ʃəufəˠ] n chófer m.
cheap [tʃi:p] a barato; (trick) malo; (poor quality) barato, de poca calidad // ad barato; ~**en** vt rebajar el precio,

abaratar; to ~**en o.s.** rebajarse; ~**ly** ad barato, a bajo precio.
cheat [tʃi:t] vi hacer trampa // vt defraudar, timar // n trampa, fraude m; (person) tramposo; ~**ing** n trampa, fraude m.
check [tʃek] vt (examine) controlar; (facts) comprobar; (count) contar; (halt) parar, detener; (restrain) refrenar, restringir // n (inspection) control m, inspección f; (curb) freno; (bill) nota, cuenta; (obstacle) impedimento, estorbo; (token) ficha; (pattern: gen pl) cuadro; to ~ **in** vi (in hotel, airport) registrarse // vt (luggage) facturar; to ~ **out** vi (of hotel) pagar la cuenta y marcharse; to ~ **up** vi: to ~ **up on sth** comprobar algo; to ~ **up on sb** investigar a una persona; ~**mate** n jaque m mate; ~**out** n caja; ~**point** n (punto de) control m; ~**up** n (MED) reconocimiento general; (of machine) repaso.
cheek [tʃi:k] n mejilla; (impudence) descaro; ~**bone** n pómulo; ~**y** a fresco, descarado.
cheer [tʃɪəˠ] vt vitorear, aplaudir; (gladden) alegrar, animar // vi aplaudir, gritar con entusiasmo // n grito (de entusiasmo); ~**s** npl aplausos mpl; ~**s!** ¡salud!; to ~ **up** vi animarse, cobrar ánimos // vt alegrar, animar; ~**ful** a alegre; ~**fulness** n alegría; **cheerio** excl ¡hasta luego!; ~**less** a triste, sombrío.
cheese [tʃi:z] n queso.
chef [ʃef] n jefe/a m/f de cocina.
chemical ['kemɪkəl] a químico // n elemento químico.
chemist ['kemɪst] n farmacéutico; (scientist) químico; ~**ry** n química; ~**'s (shop)** n farmacia.
cheque [tʃek] n cheque m; ~**book** n libro de cheques, chequera.
chequered ['tʃekəd] a (fig) variado, accidentado.
cherish ['tʃerɪʃ] vt (love) querer, apreciar; (protect) cuidar; (hope etc) abrigar.
cherry ['tʃerɪ] n cereza.
chess [tʃes] n ajedrez m; ~**board** n tablero (de ajedrez); ~**man** n pieza, trebejo.
chest [tʃest] n (ANAT) pecho; (box) cofre m, cajón m; ~ **of drawers** n cómoda.
chestnut ['tʃesnʌt] n castaña; ~ **(tree)** n castaño.
chew [tʃu:] vt mascar, masticar; ~**ing gum** n chicle m.
chic [ʃi:k] a elegante.
chick [tʃɪk] n pollito, polluelo; (fam) chica.
chicken ['tʃɪkɪn] n gallina, pollo; (food) pollo; ~**pox** n varicela.
chickpea ['tʃɪkpi:] n garbanzo.
chicory ['tʃɪkərɪ] n (for coffee) achicoria; (salad) escarola.
chief [tʃi:f] n jefe/a m/f // a principal; ~**ly** ad principalmente.
chiffon ['ʃɪfən] n gasa.
chilblain ['tʃɪlbleɪn] n sabañón m.

child [tʃaɪld], *pl* ~ **ren** ['tʃɪldrən] *n* niño/a; (*offspring*) hijo/a; ~ **birth** *n* parto; ~ **hood** *n* niñez *f*, infancia; ~ **ish** *a* pueril, aniñado; ~ **like** *a* como (de) niño; ~ **minder** *n* cuidadora de niños.

Chile ['tʃɪlɪ] *n* Chile *m*; ~ **an** *a, n* chileno/a.

chill [tʃɪl] *n* frío; (MED) escalofrío, resfriado // *vt* enfriar; (CULIN) congelar; ~ **y** *a* frío.

chime [tʃaɪm] *n* (*peal*) repique *m*, campanada // *vi* repicar, sonar.

chimney ['tʃɪmnɪ] *n* chimenea; ~ **sweep** *n* deshollinador *m*.

chimpanzee [tʃɪmpæn'zi:] *n* chimpancé *m*.

chin [tʃɪn] *n* barba, barbilla.

china ['tʃaɪnə] *n* porcelana; (*gen*) loza.

China ['tʃaɪnə] *n* China; **Chinese** [tʃaɪ'ni:z] *a* chino // *n* chino/a; (LING) el chino.

chink [tʃɪŋk] *n* (*opening*) grieta, hendedura; (*noise*) tintineo.

chip [tʃɪp] *n* (*gen pl*: CULIN) patata frita; (*of wood*) astilla; (*of glass, stone*) lasca; (*at poker*) ficha // *vt* (*cup, plate*) astillar; **to** ~ **in** *vi* interrumpir, (*contribute*) compartir los gastos.

chiropodist [kɪ'rɔpədɪst] *n* pedicuro.

chirp [tʃə:p] *vi* gorjear, piar; (*cricket*) chirriar.

chisel ['tʃɪzl] *n* (*for wood*) formón *m*; (*for stone*) cincel *m*.

chit [tʃɪt] *n* nota.

chitchat ['tʃɪttʃæt] *n* chismes *mpl*, habladurías *fpl*.

chivalrous ['ʃɪvəlrəs] *a* caballeroso; **chivalry** [-rɪ] *n* caballerosidad *f*.

chives [tʃaɪvz] *npl* cebollino *sg*.

chlorine ['klɔ:ri:n] *n* cloro.

chock [tʃɔk]: ~ **-a-block**, ~ **-full** *a* de bote en bote, atestado.

chocolate ['tʃɔklɪt] *n* chocolate *m*.

choice [tʃɔɪs] *n* elección *f*, selección *f*; (*preference*) preferencia // *a* selecto, elegido.

choir ['kwaɪə*] *n* coro; ~ **boy** *n* corista *m*.

choke [tʃəuk] *vi* sofocarse; (*on food*) atragantarse // *vt* ahogar, sofocar; (*block*) obstruir // *n* (AUT) estrangulador *m*; **choker** *n* (*necklace*) gargantilla.

cholera ['kɔlərə] *n* cólera *m*.

choose [tʃu:z], *pt* **chose**, *pp* **chosen** *vt* escoger, elegir; (*team*) seleccionar.

chop [tʃɔp] *vt* (*wood*) cortar, tajar; (CULIN: *also*: ~ **up**) desmenuzar; (*meat*) picar // *n* golpe *m* cortante; (CULIN) chuleta; ~ **s** *npl* (*jaws*) boca *sg*, labios *mpl*; ~ **py** *a* (*sea*) picado, agitado; ~ **sticks** *npl* palillos *mpl*.

choral ['kɔ:rəl] *a* coral.

chord [kɔ:d] *n* (MUS) acorde *m*.

chore [tʃɔ:*] *n* faena, tarea; (*routine task*) trabajo rutinario.

choreographer [kɔrɪ'ɔgrəfə*] *n* coreógrafo.

chorister ['kɔrɪstə*] *n* corista *m/f*.

chortle ['tʃɔ:tl] *vi* reír entre dientes.

chorus ['kɔ:rəs] *n* coro; (*repeated part of song*) estribillo.

chose [tʃəuz], **chosen** ['tʃəuzn] *pt, pp of* **choose**.

Christ [kraɪst] *n* Cristo.

christen ['krɪsn] *vt* bautizar; ~ **ing** *n* bautizo.

Christian ['krɪstɪən] *a, n* cristiano/a; ~ **ity** [-'ænɪtɪ] *n* cristianismo; ~ **name** *n* nombre *m* de pila.

Christmas ['krɪsməs] *n* Navidad *f*; **Merry** ~! ¡Felices Pascuas!; ~ **Eve** *n* Nochebuena.

chrome [krəum], **chromium** ['krəumɪəm] *n* cromo.

chromosome ['krəuməsəum] *n* cromosoma *m*.

chronic ['krɔnɪk] *a* crónico.

chronicle ['krɔnɪkl] *n* crónica.

chronological [krɔnə'lɔdʒɪkəl] *a* cronológico.

chrysanthemum [krɪ'sænθəməm] *n* crisantemo.

chubby ['tʃʌbɪ] *a* rechoncho.

chuck [tʃʌk] *vt* lanzar, arrojar; **to** ~ **out** *vt* echar (fuera), tirar; **to** ~ (**up**) *vt* abandonar.

chuckle ['tʃʌkl] *vi* reírse entre dientes.

chug [tʃʌg] *vi* resoplar; **to** ~ **along** *vi* (*fig*) ir tirando.

chum [tʃʌm] *n* compinche *m*, compañero.

chunk [tʃʌŋk] *n* pedazo, trozo.

church [tʃə:tʃ] *n* iglesia; ~ **yard** *n* campo santo.

churlish ['tʃə:lɪʃ] *a* grosero, hosco.

churn [tʃə:n] *n* (*for butter*) mantequera; (*for milk*) lechera // *vt* revolver, agitar.

chute [ʃu:t] *n* (*also*: **rubbish** ~) vertedero; (*children's slide*) tobogán *m*.

chutney ['tʃʌtnɪ] *n* salsa picante.

CID *n abbr of* **Criminal Investigation Department** B.I.C. (Brigada de Investigación Criminal).

cider ['saɪdə*] *n* sidra.

cigar [sɪ'gɑ:*] *n* puro.

cigarette [sɪgə'ret] *n* cigarrillo; (*fam*) pitillo; ~ **case** *n* pitillera; ~ **end** *n* colilla; ~ **holder** *n* boquilla.

Cinderella [sɪndə'relə] *n* la Cenicienta.

cinders ['sɪndəz] *npl* cenizas *fpl*.

cine [sɪnɪ]: ~ **-camera** *n* cámara cinematográfica; ~ **-film** *n* película cinematográfica.

cinema ['sɪnəmə] *n* cine *m*.

cinnamon ['sɪnəmən] *n* canela.

cipher ['saɪfə*] *n* cifra.

circle ['sə:kl] *n* círculo; (*in cinema*) anfiteatro // *vi* dar vueltas // *vt* (*surround*) rodear, cercar; (*move round*) dar la vuelta a.

circuit ['sə:kɪt] *n* circuito; (*tour*) gira; (*track*) pista; (*lap*) vuelta; ~ **ous** [sə:'kjuɪtəs] *a* tortuoso, indirecto.

circular ['sə:kjulə*] *a* circular // *n* circular *f*.

circulate ['sə:kjuleɪt] *vi* circular // *vt* poner en circulación, hacer circular;

circulation [-'leɪʃən] n circulación f; (of newspaper) tirada.

circumcise ['səːkəmsaɪz] vt circuncidar.

circumference [səˈkʌmfərəns] n circunferencia.

circumspect ['səːkəmspekt] a circunspecto, prudente.

circumstances ['səːkəmstənsɪz] npl circunstancias fpl; (financial condition) situación f económica.

circus ['səːkəs] n circo; (roundabout) glorieta.

cistern ['sɪstən] n tanque m, depósito; (in toilet) cisterna.

cite [saɪt] vt citar.

citizen ['sɪtɪzn] n (POL) ciudadano/a; (resident) vecino/a, habitante m/f; ~ship n ciudadanía.

citrus fruit ['sɪtrəs-] n agrios mpl.

city ['sɪtɪ] n ciudad f; the C~ centro financiero de Londres.

civic ['sɪvɪk] a cívico, municipal.

civil ['sɪvɪl] a civil; (polite) atento, cortés; (defence) pasivo; (well-bred) educado; ~ engineer n ingeniero civil; C~ Service administración f pública; ~ian [sɪˈvɪlɪən] a civil, de paisano // n civil m/f, paisano.

civilization [sɪvɪlaɪˈzeɪʃən] n civilización f.

civilized ['sɪvɪlaɪzd] a civilizado.

claim [kleɪm] vt exigir, reclamar; (rights etc) reivindicar; (assert) pretender // vi (for insurance) reclamar // n reclamación f; (LAW) demanda; (pretension) pretensión f; ~ant n (ADMIN, LAW) demandante m/f.

clairvoyant [kleəˈvɔɪənt] n clarividente m/f.

clam [klæm] n almeja.

clamber ['klæmbəʳ] vi subir gateando, trepar.

clammy ['klæmɪ] a (cold) frío y húmedo; (sticky) pegajoso.

clamp [klæmp] n abrazadera, grapa // vt afianzar (con abrazadera); to ~ down on vt fus suprimir, restringir.

clan [klæn] n clan m.

clang [klæŋ] n sonido metálico // vi sonar, hacer estruendo.

clap [klæp] vi aplaudir // vt (hands) batir; (put) poner // n (of hands) palmada; (of thunder) estampido (de trueno); ~ping n aplausos mpl.

claret ['klærət] n clarete m.

clarification [klærɪfɪˈkeɪʃən] n aclaración f; clarify ['klærɪfaɪ] vt aclarar.

clarinet [klærɪˈnet] n clarinete m.

clarity ['klærɪtɪ] n claridad f.

clash [klæʃ] n estruendo; (fig) choque m // vi (meet) encontrarse; (battle) chocar; (disagree) estar en desacuerdo.

clasp [klɑːsp] n broche m; (on jewels) cierre m // vt abrochar; (hand) apretar, estrechar; (embrace) abrazar.

class [klɑːs] n (gen) clase f // a clasista, de clase // vt clasificar.

classic ['klæsɪk] a clásico // n (work) obra clásica; ~al a clásico.

classification [klæsɪfɪˈkeɪʃən] n clasificación f; classify ['klæsɪfaɪ] vt clasificar.

class: ~mate n compañero de clase; ~room n aula.

clatter ['klætəʳ] n ruido, estruendo; (of hooves) trápala // vi hacer ruido o estruendo.

clause [klɔːz] n cláusula; (LING) oración f.

claustrophobia [klɔːstrəˈfəʊbɪə] n claustrofobia.

claw [klɔː] n (of cat) uña; (of bird of prey) garra; (of lobster) pinza; (TECH) garfio // vt: to ~ at arañar; (tear) desgarrar.

clay [kleɪ] n arcilla.

clean [kliːn] a limpio; (clear) neto, bien definido // vt limpiar; to ~ out vt limpiar; to ~ up vt limpiar, asear; ~-cut a (person) de buen parecer; (clear) nítido; ~er n (person) asistenta; ~ing n (gen) limpieza; (clothes) limpieza en seco; ~liness ['klenlɪnɪs] n limpieza; ~-shaven a sin barba, lampiño.

cleanse [klenz] vt limpiar; cleanser n agente m de limpieza; (for face) desmaquillador m; cleansing department n departamento de limpieza.

clear [klɪəʳ] a claro; (road, way) limpio, libre; (complete) completo // vi (space) despejar, limpiar; (LAW. suspect) absolver; (obstacle) salvar, saltar por encima de; (debt) liquidar // vi (gen) aclararse; (fog etc) despejarse // ad: ~ of a distancia de; to ~ up vt limpiar; (mystery) aclarar, resolver; ~ance n (removal) despeje m; (permission) acreditación f; ~-cut a bien definido, nítido; ~ing n (in wood) claro; ~ing bank n cámara de compensación; ~ly ad claramente; ~way n (Brit) carretera donde no se puede aparcar.

cleaver ['kliːvəʳ] n cuchilla (de carnicero).

clef [klef] n (MUS) clave f.

clemency ['klemənsɪ] n clemencia.

clench [klentʃ] vt apretar, cerrar.

clergy ['kləːdʒɪ] n clero; ~man n clérigo.

clerical ['klerɪkəl] a oficinista; (REL) clerical.

clerk [klɑːk, (US) klɜːrk] n empleado, oficinista m/f.

clever ['klevəʳ] a (mentally) inteligente, listo; (deft, crafty) hábil; (device, arrangement) ingenioso.

cliché ['kliːʃeɪ] n cliché m, frase f hecha.

click [klɪk] vt (tongue) chasquear; (heels) taconear.

client ['klaɪənt] n cliente m/f; ~ele [kliːɑːnˈtel] n clientela.

cliff [klɪf] n acantilado.

climate ['klaɪmɪt] n clima m; (fig) ambiente m.

climax ['klaɪmæks] n colmo, punto culminante; (sexual) clímax m.

climb [klaɪm] vi subir, trepar // vt (stairs) subir; (tree) trepar a; (hill) escalar // n subida; ~er n alpinista m/f, montañista m/f; ~ing n alpinismo.

clinch [klɪntʃ] vt (deal) cerrar; (argument) remachar.

cling [klɪŋ], pt, pp **clung** [klʌŋ] vi: **to ~ to** pegarse a, quedar pegado a; (of clothes) ajustarse a.

clinic ['klɪnɪk] n clínica; **~al** a clínico.

clink [klɪŋk] vi tintinar.

clip [klɪp] n (for hair) prendido; (also: **paper ~**) sujetapapeles m inv; (clamp) grapa // vt (cut) cortar; (shorten) acortar; (clamp) sujetar; **~pers** npl (for gardening) tijeras fpl; (for hair) maquinilla sg; (for nails) cortauñas m inv; **~ping** n recorte m.

clique [kli:k] n camarilla, pandilla.

cloak [kləuk] n capa, manto // vt (fig) encubrir, disimular; **~room** n guardarropa; (in station) consigna; (WC) lavabo, aseos mpl.

clock [klɔk] n reloj m; (in taxi) taxímetro; (fam) cara; **~wise** ad en el sentido de las agujas del reloj; **~work** n aparato de relojería // a de cuerda.

clog [klɔg] n zueco, chanclo // vt atascar // vi atascarse.

cloister ['klɔɪstə*] n claustro.

close a, ad and derivatives [kləus] a cercano, próximo; (print, weave) tupido, compacto; (friend) íntimo; (connection) estrecho; (examination) detallado, minucioso; (weather) bochornoso; (atmosphere) sofocante; (room) mal ventilado // ad cerca // vb and derivatives [kləuz] vt (shut) cerrar; (end) concluir, terminar // vi (shop etc) cerrarse; (end) concluirse, terminarse // n (end) fin m, final m, conclusión f; **to ~ down** vi cerrarse definitivamente; **to ~ up** vi (crowd) arrimarse; **~d** a (shop etc) cerrado; **~d shop** n acuerdo de emplear sólo trabajadores sindicados; **~ly** ad (exactly) fielmente; (carefully) atentamente.

closet ['klɔzɪt] n (cupboard) armario; (WC) lavabo.

close-up ['kləusʌp] n primer plano.

closure ['kləuʒə*] n (close-down) cierre m, clausura; (end) fin m.

clot [klɔt] n (gen: **blood ~**) embolia; (fam: idiot) imbécil m/f // vi (blood) cuajarse, coagularse.

cloth [klɔθ] n (material) tela, paño; (rag) trapo.

clothe [kləuð] vt vestir; (fig) revestir; **~s** npl ropa sg; **~s brush** n cepillo (para la ropa); **~s line** n cuerda (para tender la ropa); **~s peg** n pinza; **clothing** n = **clothes**.

cloud [klaud] n nube f; (storm ~) nubarrón m; **~burst** n chaparrón m; **~y** a nublado, nubloso; (liquid) turbio.

clout [klaut] vt dar un tortazo a.

clove [kləuv] n clavo; **~ of garlic** diente m de ajo.

clover ['kləuvə*] n trébol m.

clown [klaun] n payaso // vi (also: **~ about, ~ around**) hacer el payaso.

club [klʌb] n (society) club m; (weapon)

porra, cachiporra; (also: **golf ~**) palo // vt aporrear // vi: **to ~ together** hacer una colecta; **~s** npl (CARDS) tréboles mpl; **~ house** n sala de reunión.

cluck [klʌk] vi cloquear.

clue [klu:] n pista; (in crosswords) indicación f; **I haven't a ~** no tengo idea.

clump [klʌmp] n (of trees) grupo.

clumsy ['klʌmzɪ] a (person) torpe, desmañado; (movement) pesado.

cluster ['klʌstə*] n grupo; (BOT) racimo // vi agruparse, apiñarse.

clutch [klʌtʃ] n (grip, grasp) apretón m, agarro; (AUT) embrague m; (pedal) pedal m de embrague // vt sujetar, empuñar.

clutter ['klʌtə*] vt atestar, llenar desordenadamente.

Co. abbr of **county; company.**

c/o abbr of **care of** c/a (en casa de), a/c (a cuidado de).

coach [kəutʃ] n (bus) autocar m; (horse-drawn) coche m; (of train) vagón m, coche m; (SPORT) entrenador m, instructor m // vt (SPORT) entrenar; (student) preparar, enseñar.

coagulate [kəu'ægjuleɪt] vi coagularse.

coal [kəul] n carbón m; **~ face** n frente m de carbón; **~ field** n yacimiento de carbón.

coalition [kəuə'lɪʃən] n coalición f.

coal: ~man, ~ merchant n carbonero; **~mine** n mina de carbón.

coarse [kɔːs] a basto, burdo; (vulgar) grosero, ordinario.

coast [kəust] n costa, litoral m // vi (AUT) ir en punto muerto; **~al** a costero, costanero; **~er** n buque m costero, barco de cabotaje; **~guard** n guardacostas m inv; **~line** n litoral m.

coat [kəut] n (jacket) chaqueta; (overcoat) abrigo; (of animal) pelo, lana; (of paint) mano f, capa // vt cubrir, revestir; **~ of arms** n escudo de armas; **~ hanger** n percha; **~ing** n capa, baño.

coax [kəuks] vt engatusar.

cob [kɔb] n see **corn.**

cobbler ['kɔblə*] n zapatero remendón.

cobbles ['kɔblz], **cobblestones** ['kɔblstəunz] npl guijarros mpl.

cobra ['kəubrə] n cobra.

cobweb ['kɔbwɛb] n telaraña.

cocaine [kə'keɪn] n cocaína.

cock [kɔk] n (rooster) gallo; (male bird) macho // vt (gun) amartillar; **~atoo** n cacatúa; **~erel** n gallito.

cockle ['kɔkl] n berberecho.

cockney ['kɔknɪ] n habitante m/f de ciertos barrios bajos de Londres.

cockpit ['kɔkpɪt] n (in aircraft) carlinga, cabina.

cockroach ['kɔkrəutʃ] n cucaracha.

cocktail ['kɔkteɪl] n combinado, coctel m; **~ cabinet** n mueble-bar m; **~ party** n coctel m, cóctel m.

cocoa ['kəukəu] n cacao; (drink) chocolate m.

coconut ['kəukənʌt] n coco.

cocoon [kə'ku:n] n capullo.

cod [kɔd] n bacalao.

code [kəud] n código; (cipher) clave f;
codify vt codificar.

coerce [kəu'ɔ:s] vt forzar, obligar;
coercion [-'ɔ:ʃən] n coacción f.

coexistence [ˌkəuɪg'zɪstəns] n
coexistencia.

coffee ['kɔfi] n café m; ~ bean n grano de
café; ~ grounds npl heces fpl de café;
~pot n cafetera.

coffin ['kɔfin] n ataúd m.

cog [kɔg] n diente m; ~wheel n rueda
dentada.

cognac ['kɔnjæk] n coñac m.

coherent [kəu'hɪərənt] a coherente.

coil [kɔil] n rollo; (rope) adujada; (ELEC)
bobina, carrete m; (contraceptive) espiral f
// vi enrollarse, arrollarse.

coin [kɔin] n moneda // vt (word) inventar,
idear; ~age n moneda; ~-box n caja
recaudadora.

coincide [kəuɪn'said] vi coincidir; (agree)
estar de acuerdo; coincidence [kəu-
'ɪnsɪdəns] n casualidad f.

coke [kəuk] n (coal) coque m.

Coke ® [kəuk] n (drink) Coca-Cola f.

colander ['kɔləndə*] n colador m,
escurridor m.

cold [kəuld] a frío // n frío; (MED) resfriado;
it's ~ hace frío; to be ~ tener frío; to
catch ~ resfriarse, acatarrarse; to
~-shoulder tratar con frialdad; ~ly a
fríamente; ~ sore n herpes m labial.

coleslaw ['kəulslɔ:] n ensalada de col.

colic ['kɔlik] n cólico.

collaborate [kə'læbəreit] vi colaborar;
collaboration [-'reiʃən] n colaboración f.

collage [kɔ'lɑ:ʒ] n collage m.

collapse [kə'læps] vi (gen) hundirse,
derrumbarse; (MED) sufrir colapso // n
(gen) hundimiento; (MED) colapso;
collapsible a plegable.

collar ['kɔlə*] n (of coat, shirt) cuello;
~bone n clavícula.

collate [kɔ'leit] vt cotejar.

colleague ['kɔli:g] n colega m/f.

collect [kə'lekt] vt reunir; (as a hobby)
coleccionar; (call and pick up) recoger;
(wages) cobrar; (debts) recaudar;
(donations, subscriptions) colectar // vi
reunirse; coleccionar; ~ion [kə'lekʃən]
n colección f, cobro; (of people) grupo; (of
donations) recaudación f; (of post)
recogida.

collective [kə'lektiv] a colectivo.

collector [kə'lektə*] n coleccionista m/f;
(of taxes etc) recaudador m.

college ['kɔlidʒ] n colegio.

collide [kə'laid] vi chocar.

collie ['kɔli] n perro pastor.

collision [kə'liʒən] n choque m.

colloquial [kə'ləukwiəl] a familiar,
coloquial.

colon ['kəulən] n (sign) dos puntos; (MED)
colón m.

colonel ['kə:nl] n coronel m.

colonial [kə'ləuniəl] a colonial.

colonize ['kɔlənaiz] vt colonizar.

colony ['kɔləni] n colonia.

colossal [kə'lɔsl] a colosal.

colour, color (US) ['kʌlə*] n color m // vt
color(e)ar; (with crayons) pintar; (dye)
teñir // vi (blush) sonrojarse; ~s npl (of
party, club) colores mpl; ~-blind a
daltoniano; ~ed a de color; (photo) a
colores; ~eds npl gente f de color; ~
film n película en colores; ~ful a lleno de
color; (personality) animado; ~ing n
colorido; ~less a incoloro, sin color; ~
scheme n combinación f de colores; ~
television n televisión f en color(es).

colt [kəult] n potro.

column ['kɔləm] n columna; ~ist
['kɔləmnist] n columnista m/f.

coma ['kəumə] n coma m.

comb [kəum] n peine m; (ornamental)
peineta // vt (hair) peinar; (area)
registrar.

combat ['kɔmbæt] n combate m // vt
combatir.

combination [kɔmbi'neiʃən] n (gen)
combinación f.

combine [kəm'bain] vt combinar;
(qualities) reunir // vi combinarse // n
['kɔmbain] (ECON) asociación f; (pej)
monopolio; ~ (harvester) n
cosechadora.

combustion [kəm'bʌstʃən] n combustión f.

come [kʌm], pt came, pp come vi venir;
to ~ about vi suceder, ocurrir; to ~
across vt fus (person) topar; (thing) dar
con; to ~ away vi marcharse; to ~ back
vi volver; to ~ by vt fus (acquire)
conseguir; to ~ down vi bajar; (plane)
aterrizarse; (crash) estrellarse; (buildings)
desplomarse; to ~ forward vi
presentarse; to ~ in vi entrar; (train)
llegar; (fashion) ponerse de moda; to ~ in
for vt fus (criticism etc) merecer; to ~
into vt fus (money) heredar; to ~ off vi
(button) soltarse, desprenderse; (attempt)
tener lugar; to ~ on vi (pupil, undertaking)
crecer, desarrollarse // vt (find)
encontrar; ~ on! ¡vamos!; to ~ out vi
salir, aparecer; (be revealed) salir a luz; to
~ out for/against declararse
por/contra; to ~ to vi volver en sí; (total)
sumar; to ~ up vi subir; (sun) salir;
(problem) surgir; to ~ up against vt fus
(resistance, difficulties) tropezar con; to ~
up with vt fus (idea) sugerir, proponer; to
~ upon vt fus dar o topar con; ~back n
(THEATRE) reaparición f.

comedian [kə'mi:diən] n cómico;
comedienne [-'en] n cómica.

comedown ['kʌmdaun] n (fam) revés m,
bajón m.

comedy ['kɔmidi] n comedia.

comet ['kɔmit] n cometa m.

comfort ['kʌmfət] n comodidad f, confort

m; (*well-being*) bienestar *m*; (*solace*) consuelo; (*relief*) alivio // *vt* consolar; aliviar; ~ **able** *a* cómodo.

comic ['kɔmɪk] *a* (*also*: ~ **al**) cómico // *n* (*magazine*) tebeo; ~ **strip** *n* tira cómica.

coming ['kʌmɪŋ] *n* venida, llegada // *a* que viene; ~(**s**) **and going(s)** *n*(*pl*) ir y venir *m*, ajetreo.

comma ['kɔmə] *n* coma.

command [kə'mɑ:nd] *n* orden *f*, mandato; (*MIL*: *authority*) mando; (*mastery*) dominio // *vt* (*troops*) mandar; (*give orders to*) mandar, ordenar; (*dispose of*) disponer de; (*deserve*) merecer; ~ **eer** [kɔmən'dɪəˈ] *vt* requisar; ~ **er** *n* (*MIL*) comandante *m/f*, jefe/a *m/f*.

commando [kə'mɑ:ndəu] *n* comando.

commemorate [kə'mɛməreɪt] *vt* conmemorar; **commemoration** [-'reɪʃən] *n* conmemoración *f*; **commemorative** [-rətɪv] *a* conmemorativo.

commence [kə'mɛns] *vt*, *vi* comenzar, empezar.

commend [kə'mɛnd] *vt* (*praise*) elogiar, alabar; (*recommend*) recomendar; (*entrust*) encomendar; ~ **ation** [kɔmɛn-'deɪʃən] *n* elogio, encomio; recomendación *f*.

commensurate [kə'mɛnʃərɪt] *a* equivalente (*with* a).

comment ['kɔmɛnt] *n* comentario // *vi* hacer comentarios; ~ **ary** ['kɔməntərɪ] *n* comentario; ~ **ator** ['kɔməntertəˈ] *n* comentador *m*.

commerce ['kɔmə:s] *n* comercio.

commercial [kə'mə:ʃəl] *a* comercial // *n* (*TV*) anuncio (comercial); ~ **break** *n* emisión *f* publicitaria; ~ **ize** *vt* comercializar.

commiserate [kə'mɪzəreɪt] *vi*: to ~ **with** compadecerse de, condolerse de.

commission [kə'mɪʃən] *n* (*fee*) comisión *f*; (*act*) perpetración *f* // *vt* (*MIL*) nombrar; (*work of art*) encargar; **out of** ~ inutilizado; ~ **aire** [kəmɪʃə'nɛəˈ] *n* portero; ~ **er** *n* comisario; (*POLICE*) jefe/a *m/f* de policía.

commit [kə'mɪt] *vt* (*act*) cometer; (*to sb's care*) entregar; **to** ~ **o.s. (to do)** comprometerse (a hacer); **to** ~ **suicide** suicidarse; ~ **ment** *n* compromiso.

committee [kə'mɪtɪ] *n* comité *m*.

commodity [kə'mɔdɪtɪ] *n* mercancía.

common ['kɔmən] *a* (*gen*) común; (*pej*) ordinario // *n* campo común; **the C~s** *npl* (la Cámara de) los Comunes; **in** ~ en común; ~ **er** *n* plebeyo; ~ **law** *n* ley *f* consuetudinaria; ~ **ly** *ad* comúnmente; **C~ Market** *n* Mercado Común; ~ **place** *a* vulgar, trivial; ~ **room** *n* salón *m* común; ~ **sense** *n* sentido común; **the C~wealth** *n* la Mancomunidad.

commotion [kə'məuʃən] *n* tumulto, confusión *f*.

communal ['kɔmju:nl] *a* comunal.

commune ['kɔmju:n] *n* (*group*) comuna // *vi* [kə'mju:n]: **to** ~ **with** comulgar o conversar con.

communicate [kə'mju:nɪkeɪt] *vt* comunicar // *vi*: **to** ~ **(with)** comunicarse (con).

communication [kəmju:nɪ'keɪʃən] *n* comunicación *f*; ~ **cord** *n* timbre *m* de alarma.

communion [kə'mju:nɪən] *n* (*also*: **Holy C~**) comunión *f*.

communiqué [kə'mju:nɪkeɪ] *n* comunicado, parte *m*.

communism ['kɔmjunɪzəm] *n* comunismo; **communist** *a*, *n* comunista *m/f*.

community [kə'mju:nɪtɪ] *n* comunidad *f*; (*large group*) colectividad *f*; (*locals*) vecindario; ~ **centre** *n* centro social.

commute [kə'mju:t] *vi* viajar a diario // *vt* conmutar; **commuter** *n* persona que viaja a menudo.

compact [kəm'pækt] *a* compacto; (*style*) conciso; (*packed*) apretado // *n* ['kɔmpækt] (*pact*) pacto; (*for powder*) polvera.

companion [kəm'pænɪən] *n* compañero; ~ **ship** *n* compañerismo.

company ['kʌmpənɪ] *n* (*gen*) compañía; (*COMM*) sociedad *f*, compañía; **to keep sb** ~ acompañar a uno; **limited** ~ sociedad *f* anónima.

comparable ['kɔmpərəbl] *a* comparable.

comparative [kəm'pærətɪv] *a* relativo.

compare [kəm'pɛəˈ] *vt* comparar; (*set side by side*) cotejar // *vi*: **to** ~ **(with)** compararse (con); **comparison** [-'pærɪsn] *n* comparación *f*; cotejo; **in comparison (with)** en comparación (con).

compartment [kəm'pɑ:tmənt] *n* (*also RAIL*) departamento.

compass ['kʌmpəs] *n* brújula; ~ **es** *npl* compás *m*.

compassion [kəm'pæʃən] *n* compasión *f*; ~ **ate** *a* compasivo.

compatible [kəm'pætɪbl] *a* compatible.

compel [kəm'pɛl] *vt* obligar; ~ **ling** *a* (*fig*: *argument*) convincente.

compendium [kəm'pɛndɪəm] *n* compendio.

compensate ['kɔmpənseɪt] *vt* compensar // *vi*: **to** ~ **for** compensar; **compensation** [-'seɪʃən] *n* (*for loss*) indemnización *f*.

compère ['kɔmpɛəˈ] *n* presentador *m*.

compete [kəm'pi:t] *vi* (*take part*) tomar parte, concurrir; (*vie with*) competir, hacer competencia.

competence ['kɔmpɪtəns] *n* capacidad *f*, aptitud *f*; **competent** [-ənt] *a* competente, capaz.

competition [kɔmpɪ'tɪʃən] *n* (*contest*) concurso; (*ECON*) competencia; (*rivalry*) competencia.

competitive [kəm'pɛtɪtɪv] *a* (*ECON*) competitivo; (*spirit*) competidor(a), de competencia.

competitor [kəm'pɛtɪtəˈ] *n* (*rival*)

competidor/a *m/f*; (*participant*)
concursante *m/f*.
compile [kəm'paɪl] *vt* recopilar, compilar.
complacency [kəm'pleɪsnsɪ] *n*
satisfacción *f* de sí mismo; **complacent**
[-sənt] *a* complacido.
complain [kəm'pleɪn] *vi* (*gen*) quejarse;
~**t** *n* (*gen*) queja; (*JUR*) demanda,
querella; (*MED*) enfermedad *f*.
complement ['kɒmplɪmənt] *n*
complemento; (*esp ship's crew*) dotación *f*;
~**ary** [kɒmplɪ'mɛntərɪ] *a* complementario.
complete [kəm'pliːt] *a* (*full*) completo;
(*finished*) acabado // *vt* (*fulfil*) completar;
(*finish*) acabar; (*a form*) llenar; ~**ly** *ad*
completamente; **completion** *n* (*gen*)
conclusión *f*, terminación *f*; (*of contract
etc*) realización *f*.
complex ['kɒmplɛks] *a* complejo // *n*
(*gen*) complejo.
complexion [kəm'plɛkʃən] *n* (*of face*) tez
f, cutis *m*; (*fig*) aspecto.
complexity [kəm'plɛksɪtɪ] *n* complejidad
f.
compliance [kəm'plaɪəns] *n* (*submission*)
sumisión *f*; (*agreement*) conformidad *f*; **in
~ with** de acuerdo con; **compliant** [-ənt]
a sumiso; conforme.
complicate ['kɒmplɪkeɪt] *vt* complicar;
~**d** *a* complicado; **complication**
[-'keɪʃən] *n* complicación *f*.
compliment *n* ['kɒmplɪmənt] (*formal*)
cumplido; (*lovers'*) piropo; ~**s** *npl* saludos
mpl; **to pay sb a** ~ (*amorously*) piropear,
echar piropos a alguien; ~**ary** [-'mɛntərɪ]
a lisonjero; (*free*) de favor.
comply [kəm'plaɪ] *vi*: **to** ~ **with** cumplir
con.
component [kəm'pəunənt] *a* componente
// *n* (*TECH*) pieza.
compose [kəm'pəuz] *vt* componer; **to be
~d of** componerse de, constar de; **to** ~
o.s. tranquilizarse; ~**d** *a* sosegado;
composer *n* (*MUS*) compositor *m*.
composite ['kɒmpəzɪt] *a* compuesto.
composition [kɒmpə'zɪʃən] *n* composición
f.
compost ['kɒmpɒst] *n* abono compuesto.
composure [kəm'pəuʒə*] *n* serenidad *f*,
calma.
compound ['kɒmpaund] *n* (*CHEM, LING*)
compuesto; (*enclosure*) recinto // *a* (*gen*)
compuesto; (*fracture*) complicado.
comprehend [kɒmprɪ'hɛnd] *vt*
comprender; **comprehension** [-'hɛnʃən] *n*
comprensión *f*.
comprehensive [kɒmprɪ'hɛnsɪv] *a*
(*broad*) extenso; (*general*) de conjunto;
(*INSURANCE*) contra todo riesgo; ~
(**school**) *n* integrado.
compress [kəm'prɛs] *vt* comprimir // *n*
['kɒmprɛs] (*MED*) compresa; ~**ion**
[-'prɛʃən] *n* compresión *f*.
comprise [kəm'praɪz] *vt* (*also*: **be** ~**d of**)
comprender, constar de.
compromise ['kɒmprəmaɪz]

(*agreement*) componenda, arreglo;
(*midpoint*) término medio // *vt*
comprometer // *vi* transigir.
compulsion [kəm'pʌlʃən] *n* obligación *f*.
compulsive [kəm'pʌlsɪv] *a* compulsivo;
(*PSYCH*) empedernido.
compulsory [kəm'pʌlsərɪ] *a* obligatorio.
computer [kəm'pjuːtə*] *n* ordenador *m*,
computador *m*, computadora; ~**ize** *vt*
computerizar; ~ **programmer** *n*
programador/a *m/f*; ~ **programming** *n*
programación *f*; ~ **science** *n* ciencia de
computadoras.
comrade ['kɒmrɪd] *n* camarada *m/f*;
~**ship** *n* camaradería, compañerismo.
con [kɒn] *vt* estafar // *n* estafa.
concave ['kɒnkeɪv] *a* cóncavo.
conceal [kən'siːl] *vt* ocultar.
concede [kən'siːd] *vt* conceder // *vi* ceder,
darse por vencido.
conceit [kən'siːt] *n* presunción *f*; ~**ed** *a*
presumido.
conceivable [kən'siːvəbl] *a* concebible.
conceive [kən'siːv] *vt, vi* concebir.
concentrate ['kɒnsəntreɪt] *vi*
concentrarse // *vt* concentrar.
concentration [kɒnsən'treɪʃən] *n*
concentración *f*; ~ **camp** *n* campo de
concentración.
concept ['kɒnsɛpt] *n* concepto.
conception [kən'sɛpʃən] *n* (*idea*)
concepto, idea; (*BIOL*) concepción *f*.
concern [kən'sɜːn] *n* (*matter*) asunto;
(*COMM*) empresa; (*anxiety*) preocupación *f*
// *vt* tener que ver con; **to be** ~**ed**
(**about**) interesarse (por), preocuparse
(por); ~**ing** *prep* sobre, acerca de.
concert ['kɒnsət] *n* concierto; ~ **hall** *n*
sala de conciertos.
concertina [kɒnsə'tiːnə] *n* concertina.
concerto [kən'tʃɛːtəu] *n* concierto.
concession [kən'sɛʃən] *n* concesión *f*; **tax
~** privilegio fiscal.
conciliation [kənsɪlɪ'eɪʃən] *n* conciliación
f; **conciliatory** [-'sɪlɪətrɪ] *a* conciliador(a).
concise [kən'saɪs] *a* conciso.
conclude [kən'kluːd] *vt* (*finish*) concluir;
(*treaty etc*) firmar; (*agreement*) llegar a;
(*decide*) llegar a la conclusión de;
conclusion [-'kluːʒən] *n* conclusión *f*;
conclusive [-'kluːsɪv] *a* decisivo,
concluyente.
concoct [kən'kɒkt] *vt* (*gen*) confeccionar;
(*plot*) tramar.
concrete ['kɒnkriːt] *n* hormigón *m* // *a*
concreto.
concur [kən'kɜː*] *vi* estar de acuerdo,
asentir.
concurrently [kən'kʌrntlɪ] *ad* al mismo
tiempo.
concussion [kən'kʌʃən] *n* conmoción *f*
cerebral.
condemn [kən'dɛm] *vt* condenar; ~**ation**
[kɒndɛm'neɪʃən] *n* (*gen*) condenación *f*;
(*blame*) censura.

condensation [kɔndɛn'seɪʃən] n condensación f.

condense [kən'dɛns] vi condensarse // vt condensar, abreviar; ~d milk n leche f condensada.

condescend [kɔndɪ'sɛnd] vi condescender, dignarse; ~ing a condescendiente.

condition [kən'dɪʃən] n condición f // vt condicionar; on ~ that a condición (de) que.

condolences [kən'dəulənsɪz] npl pésame m.

condone [kən'dəun] vt condonar.

conducive [kən'djuːsɪv] a: ~ to conducente a.

conduct ['kɔndʌkt] n conducta, comportamiento // [kən'dʌkt] (lead) conducir; (manage) llevar, dirigir; (MUS) dirigir // vi (MUS) llevar la batuta; to ~ o.s. comportarse; ~or n (of orchestra) director m; (on bus) cobrador m; (ELEC) conductor m; ~ress n (on bus) cobradora.

cone [kəun] n cono; (for ice-cream) barquillo.

confectioner [kən'fɛkʃənəº] n pastelero; ~'s (shop) n pastelería; (sweet shop) confitería; ~y n (cakes) pasteles mpl; (sweets) dulces mpl.

confederation [kənfɛdə'reɪʃən] n confederación f.

confer [kən'fɔːº] vt otorgar (on a) // vi conferenciar.

conference ['kɔnfərns] n (meeting) congreso.

confess [kən'fɛs] vt confesar // vi confesarse; ~ion [-'fɛʃən] n confesión f; ~ional [-'fɛʃənl] n confesionario; ~or n confesor m.

confetti [kən'fɛtɪ] n confeti m.

confide [kən'faɪd] vi: to ~ in confiar en, fiarse de.

confidence ['kɔnfɪdns] n (gen) confianza; (secret) confidencia; ~ trick n timo; **confident** a seguro de sí mismo; **confidential** [kɔnfɪ'dɛnʃəl] a confidencial; (secretary) de confianza.

confine [kən'faɪn] vt (limit) limitar; (shut up) encerrar; ~d a (space) reducido; ~ment n (prison) prisión f; (enclosure) encierro; (MED) parto, sobreparto; ~s ['kɔnfaɪnz] npl confines mpl.

confirm [kən'fɜːm] vt confirmar; ~ation [kɔnfə'meɪʃən] n confirmación f, ~ed a empedernido.

confiscate ['kɔnfɪskeɪt] vt confiscar; **confiscation** [-'keɪʃən] n incautación f.

conflict ['kɔnflɪkt] n conflicto // vi [kən-'flɪkt] (opinions) chocar; ~ing a contrario.

conform [kən'fɔːm] vi conformarse; to ~ to ajustarse a, cuadrar con; ~ist n conformista m/f.

confound [kən'faund] vt confundir; ~ed a condenado.

confront [kən'frʌnt] vt (problems) encararse con; (enemy, danger)

enfrentarse con; ~ation [kɔnfrən'teɪʃən] n enfrentamiento.

confuse [kən'fjuːz] vt (perplex) aturdir, desconcertar; (mix up) confundir; ~d a confuso; (person) perplejo, despistado; **confusing** a confuso; **confusion** [-'fjuːʒən] n confusión f.

congeal [kən'dʒiːl] vi (freeze) congelarse; (coagulate) coagularse.

congenial [kən'dʒiːnɪəl] a simpático, agradable.

congenital [kən'dʒɛnɪtl] a congénito.

congested [kən'dʒɛstɪd] a (gen) lleno; (area) superpoblado; **congestion** [-'dʒɛstʃən] n congestión f.

conglomeration [kənglɔmə'reɪʃən] n conglomeración f.

congratulate [kən'grætjuleɪt] vt felicitar; **congratulations** [-'leɪʃənz] npl felicidades fpl.

congregate ['kɔngrɪgeɪt] vi congregarse; **congregation** [-'geɪʃən] n (in church) fieles mpl; (assembly) reunión f.

congress ['kɔngrɛs] n congreso; ~man n (US) diputado.

conical ['kɔnɪkl] a cónico.

conifer ['kɔnɪfəº] n conífera; ~ous [kə'nɪfərəs] a (forest) conífero.

conjecture [kən'dʒɛktʃəº] n conjetura.

conjugal ['kɔndʒugl] a conyugal.

conjugate ['kɔndʒugeɪt] vt conjugar.

conjunction [kən'dʒʌŋkʃən] n conjunción f.

conjure ['kʌndʒəº] vi hacer juegos de manos; to ~ up vt (ghost, spirit) hacer aparecer; (memories) evocar; **conjurer** n ilusionista m/f; **conjuring trick** n ilusionismo, juego de manos.

conk [kɔŋk]: ~ out vi (col) estropearse.

con man ['kɔn-] n timador m.

connect [kə'nɛkt] vt juntar, unir; (ELEC) conectar; (fig) relacionar, asociar // vi: to ~ with (train) enlazar con; ~ion [-ʃən] n juntura, unión f; (ELEC) conexión f; (RAIL) correspondencia; (TEL) comunicación f; (fig) relación f.

connive [kə'naɪv] vi: to ~ at hacer la vista gorda a.

connoisseur [kɔnɪ'sɜːº] n experto, entendido.

connotation [kɔnə'teɪʃən] n connotación f.

conquer ['kɔŋkəº] vt (gen) conquistar; (enemy) vencer; (feelings) dominar; ~or n conquistador m.

conquest ['kɔŋkwɛst] n conquista.

cons [kɔnz] npl see pro.

conscience ['kɔnʃəns] n conciencia.

conscientious [kɔnʃɪ'ɛnʃəs] a concienzudo; (objection) de conciencia.

conscious ['kɔnʃəs] a consciente; ~ness n conciencia; (MED) conocimiento.

conscript ['kɔnskrɪpt] n recluto m/f; ~ion [kən'skrɪpʃən] n servicio militar (obligatorio).

consecrate ['kɔnsɪkreɪt] vt consagrar.

consecutive [kən'sɛkjutɪv] *a* sucesivo, seguido.

consensus [kən'sɛnsəs] *n* consenso.

consent [kən'sɛnt] *n* consentimiento // *vi*: **to ~ to** consentir en.

consequence ['kɔnsɪkwəns] *n* consecuencia.

consequently ['kɔnsɪkwəntlɪ] *ad* por consiguiente.

conservation [kɔnsə'veɪʃən] *n* conservación *f*.

conservative [kən'sɔːvətɪv] *a* conservador(a); (*cautious*) cauteloso; **C~** *a*, *n* conservador/a *m/f*.

conservatory [kən'sɔːvətrɪ] *n* (*greenhouse*) invernadero.

conserve [kən'sɔːv] *vt* conservar // *n* conserva.

consider [kən'sɪdə*] *vt* (*gen*) considerar; (*take into account*) tomar en cuenta; (*study*) estudiar, examinar; **~able** *a* considerable; (*sum*) importante.

considerate [kən'sɪdərɪt] *a* considerado; **consideration** [-'reɪʃən] *n* consideración *f*; (*reward*) retribución *f*.

considering [kən'sɪdərɪŋ] *prep* en consideración a.

consign [kən'saɪn] *vt* consignar; **~ment** *n* envío.

consist [kən'sɪst] *vi*: **to ~ of** consistir en.

consistency [kən'sɪstənsɪ] *n* (*of person etc*) consecuencia; (*thickness*) consistencia.

consistent [kən'sɪstənt] *a* (*person*) consecuente; (*even*) constante.

consolation [kɔnsə'leɪʃən] *n* consuelo.

console [kən'səʊl] *vt* consolar // *n* ['kɔnsəʊl] consola.

consolidate [kən'sɔlɪdeɪt] *vt* consolidar.

consommé [kən'sɔmeɪ] *n* consomé *m*, caldo.

consonant ['kɔnsənənt] *n* consonante *f*.

consortium [kən'sɔːtɪəm] *n* consorcio.

conspicuous [kən'spɪkjuəs] *a* (*visible*) visible; (*garish etc*) llamativo; (*outstanding*) notable.

conspiracy [kən'spɪrəsɪ] *n* conjura, complot *m*.

conspire [kən'spaɪə*] *vi* conspirar.

constable ['kʌnstəbl] *n* policía *m/f*; **chief ~** jefe *m* de policía.

constabulary [kən'stæbjulərɪ] *n* policía.

constant ['kɔnstənt] *a* (*gen*) constante; (*loyal*) leal, fiel.

constellation [kɔnstə'leɪʃən] *n* constelación *f*.

consternation [kɔnstə'neɪʃən] *n* consternación *f*.

constipated ['kɔnstɪpeɪtəd] *a* estreñido.

constituency [kən'stɪtjuənsɪ] *n* (*POL*) distrito electoral; **constituent** [-ənt] *n* (*POL*) elector/a *m/f*; (*part*) componente *m*.

constitute ['kɔnstɪtjuːt] *vt* constituir.

constitution [kɔnstɪ'tjuːʃən] *n* constitución *f*; **~al** *a* constitucional.

constrain [kən'streɪn] *vt* obligar; **~ed** *a*:

to feel ~ed to... sentirse en la necesidad de...; **~t** *n* (*force*) fuerza; (*confinement*) encierro; (*shyness*) reserva.

constrict [kən'strɪkt] *vt* apretar, estrechar.

construct [kən'strʌkt] *vt* construir; **~ion** [-ʃən] *n* construcción *f*; **~ive** *a* constructivo.

construe [kən'struː] *vt* interpretar.

consul ['kɔnsl] *n* cónsul *m/f*; **~ate** ['kɔnsjulɪt] *n* consulado.

consult [kən'sʌlt] *vt*, *vi* consultar; **~ant** *n* (*MED*) especialista *m/f*; (*other specialist*) asesor *m*; **~ation** [kɔnsəl'teɪʃən] *n* consulta; **~ing room** *n* consultorio.

consume [kən'sjuːm] *vt* (*eat*) comerse; (*drink*) beberse; (*fire etc, COMM*) consumir; **consumer** *n* consumidor/a *m/f*; **consumer goods** *npl* bienes *mpl* de consumo; **consumer society** *n* sociedad *f* de consumo.

consummate ['kɔnsʌmeɪt] *vt* consumar.

consumption [kən'sʌmpʃən] *n* consumo.

cont. *abbr of* **continued.**

contact ['kɔntækt] *n* contacto; (*pej*) enchufe *m* // *vt* ponerse en contacto con; **he has good ~s** tiene buenas relaciones; **~ lenses** *npl* lentes *fpl* de contacto, microlentillas *fpl*.

contagious [kən'teɪdʒəs] *a* contagioso.

contain [kən'teɪn] *vt* contener; **to ~ o.s.** contenerse; **~er** *n* recipiente *m*; (*for shipping etc*) contenedor *m*.

contaminate [kən'tæmɪneɪt] *vt* contaminar; **contamination** [-'neɪʃən] *n* contaminación *f*.

cont'd *abbr of* **continued.**

contemplate ['kɔntəmpleɪt] *vt* (*gen*) contemplar; (*expect*) contar con; (*intend*) pensar; **contemplation** [-'pleɪʃən] *n* contemplación *f*.

contemporary [kən'tɛmpərərɪ] *a*, *n* contemporáneo/a.

contempt [kən'tɛmpt] *n* desprecio; **~ible** *a* despreciable; **~uous** *a* despectivo, desdeñoso.

contend [kən'tɛnd] *vt* (*argue*) afirmar // *vi* (*struggle*) luchar; **~er** *n* contendiente *m/f*.

content [kən'tɛnt] *a* (*happy*) contento; (*satisfied*) satisfecho // *vt* contentar; satisfacer // *n* ['kɔntɛnt] contento; satisfacción *f*; **~s** *npl* contenido *sg*; **~ed** *a* contento; satisfecho.

contention [kən'tɛnʃən] *n* contienda; (*argument*) argumento.

contentment [kən'tɛntmənt] *n* contento.

contest ['kɔntɛst] *n* contienda; (*competition*) concurso // *vt* [kən'tɛst] (*dispute*) impugnar; (*legal case*) defender; (*POL*) ser candidato en; **~ant** [kən'tɛstənt] *n* concursante *m/f*; (*in fight*) contendiente *m/f*.

context ['kɔntɛkst] *n* contexto.

continent ['kɔntɪnənt] *n* continente *m*; **the C~** el continente europeo; **~al** [-'nɛntl] *a* continental.

contingency [kən'tɪndʒənsɪ] n
contingencia; **contingent** [-ənt] n
contingente m.
continual [kən'tɪnjuəl] a continuo; ~ly ad
constantemente.
continuation [kəntɪnju'eɪʃən] n
prolongación f; (after interruption)
continuación f.
continue [kən'tɪnju:] vi seguir, continuar
// vt seguir, continuar; (start again)
proseguir.
continuity [kɔntɪ'njuɪtɪ] n continuidad f.
continuous [kən'tɪnjuəs] a continuo.
contort [kən'tɔːt] vt retorcer; ~ion
[-'tɔːʃən] n contorsión f; ~ionist
[-'tɔːʃənɪst] n contorsionista m/f.
contour ['kɔntuə*] n contorno f; (also: ~
line) curva de nivel.
contraband ['kɔntrəbænd] n contrabando.
contraception [kɔntrə'sɛpʃən] n
contracepción f; **contraceptive** [-'sɛptɪv]
a, n anticonceptivo.
contract ['kɔntrækt] n contrato // (vb:
[kən'trækt]) vi (COMM): to ~ to do sth
comprometerse por contrato a hacer algo;
(become smaller) contraerse, encogerse //
vt contraer; ~ion [-ʃən] n contracción f;
~or n contratista m/f.
contradict [kɔntrə'dɪkt] vt (deny)
desmentir; (be contrary to) contradecir;
~ion [-ʃən] n contradicción f.
contralto [kən'træltəu] n contralto.
contraption [kən'træpʃən] n (pej)
armatoste m.
contrary ['kɔntrərɪ] a, n contrario.
contrast ['kɔntrɑːst] n contraste m // vt
[kən'trɑːst] comparar; ~ing a opuesto.
contravene [kɔntrə'viːn] vt oponerse a;
(law) contravenir.
contribute [kən'trɪbjuːt] vi contribuir //
vt: to ~ to (gen) contribuir a; (newspaper)
escribir para; **contribution**
[kɔntrɪ'bjuːʃən] n (money) aportación f; (to
debate) intervención f; (to journal)
colaboración f; **contributor** n (to
newspaper) colaborador m.
contrive [kən'traɪv] vt (invent) idear;
(carry out) efectuar; (plot) tramar // vi: to
~ to do lograr hacer.
control [kən'trəul] vt (gen) controlar;
(traffic etc) dirigir; (machinery) regular;
(temper) dominar // n (command) control
m; (of car) conducción f; (check) freno;
~s npl mando sg; ~ **panel** n tablero de
instrumentos; ~ **room** n sala de mando;
~ **tower** n (AVIAT) torre f de control.
controversial [kɔntrə'vəːʃl] a discutible;
controversy ['kɔntrəvəːsɪ] n controversia.
convalesce [kɔnvə'lɛs] vi convalecer;
convalescence n convalecencia;
convalescent a, n convaleciente m/f.
convector [kən'vɛktə*] n (heater)
calentador m de convección.
convene [kən'viːn] vt convocar // vi
reunirse.
convenience [kən'viːnɪəns] n (comfort)
comodidad f; (advantage) ventaja; at your

~ cuando le sea conveniente; **public** ~
aseos públicos mpl; **convenient** [-ənt] a
cómodo; (useful) útil; (place) accesible;
(time) oportuno, conveniente.
convent ['kɔnvənt] n convento; ~ **school**
n colegio de monjas.
convention [kən'vɛnʃən] n convención f;
(meeting) asamblea; ~al a convencional.
converge [kən'vəːdʒ] vi converger.
conversant [kən'vəːsnt] a: **to be** ~ **with**
ser enterado de.
conversation [kɔnvə'seɪʃən] n
conversación f; ~al a (familiar) familiar;
(talkative) locuaz.
converse [kən'vəːs] n inversa // vi [kən-
'vəːs] conversar; ~ly [-'vəːslɪ] ad a la
inversa.
conversion [kən'vəːʃən] n conversión f; ~
table n tabla de conversión.
convert [kən'vəːt] vt (REL, COMM)
convertir; (alter) transformar //
['kɔnvəːt] converso/a; ~ible a
convertible // n descapotable m.
convex ['kɔn'vɛks] a convexo.
convey [kən'veɪ] vt (gen) llevar; (thanks)
comunicar; (idea) expresar; ~or **belt** n
cinta transportadora.
convict [kən'vɪkt] vt (gen) condenar;
(sentence) declarar culpable // n
['kɔnvɪkt] presidiario; ~ion [-ʃən] n
condena; (belief) creencia, convicción f.
convince [kən'vɪns] vt convencer;
convincing a convincente.
convoy ['kɔnvɔɪ] n convoy m.
convulse [kən'vʌls] vt convulsionar;
(laughter) hacer morir de la risa;
convulsion [-'vʌlʃən] n convulsión f;
(laughter) paroxismo.
coo [ku:] vi arrullar.
cook [kuk] vt (gen) cocinar; (stew etc)
guisar; (meal) preparar // vi cocer;
(person) cocinar // n cocinero; ~er n
cocina; ~ery n (dishes) cocina; (art) arte
m de cocinar; ~ery **book** n libro de
cocina; ~ie n (US) bizcocho; ~ing n
cocina.
cool [ku:l] a fresco; (not hot) tibio; (not
afraid) tranquilo; (unfriendly) frío // vt
enfriar // vi enfriarse; ~ness n frescura;
tranquilidad f; (hostility) frialdad f; (indifference) falta de entusiasmo.
coop [ku:p] n gallinero // vt: to ~ **up** (fig)
encerrar.
co-op ['kəuɔp] n abbr of **Cooperative
(Society)**.
cooperate [kəu'ɔpəreɪt] vi cooperar,
colaborar; **cooperation** [-'reɪʃən] n
cooperación f, colaboración f;
cooperative [-rətɪv] a cooperativo // n
cooperativa.
coordinate [kəu'ɔːdɪneɪt] vt coordinar;
coordination [-'neɪʃən] n coordinación f.
cop [kɔp] n (col) poli m.
cope [kəup] vi: to ~ **with** poder con;
(problem) hacer frente a.
co-pilot ['kəu'paɪlət] n copiloto.
copious ['kəupɪəs] a copioso, abundante.

copper ['kɔpə*] n (metal) cobre m; (col: policeman) poli m; ~s npl monedas fpl de poco valor.

coppice ['kɔpɪs], **copse** [kɔps] n bosquecillo.

copulate ['kɔpjuleɪt] vi copularse; **copulation** [-'leɪʃən] n cópula.

copy ['kɔpɪ] n copia; (of book etc) ejemplar m; (of writing) original m // vt copiar; ~**right** n derechos mpl de autor.

coral ['kɔrəl] n coral m; ~ **reef** n arrecife m (de coral).

cord [kɔːd] n cuerda; (ELEC) cordón m; (fabric) pana.

cordial ['kɔːdɪəl] a afectuoso // n cordial m.

cordon ['kɔːdn] n cordón m; **to** ~ **off** vt acordonar.

corduroy ['kɔːdərɔɪ] n pana.

core [kɔː*] n (gen) centro, núcleo; (of fruit) corazón m // vt quitar el corazón de.

coriander [kɔrɪ'ændə*] n culantro.

cork [kɔːk] n corcho; (tree) alcornoque m; ~**screw** n sacacorchos m inv.

cormorant ['kɔːmərnt] n cormorán m grande.

corn [kɔːn] n (wheat) trigo; (US: maize) maíz m; (cereals) granos mpl; (on foot) callo; ~ **on the cob** (CULIN) maíz en la mazorca.

corned beef ['kɔːnd-] n carne f de vaca acecinada.

corner ['kɔːnə*] n (gen) ángulo; (outside) esquina; (inside) rincón m; (in road) curva; (FOOTBALL) córner m // vt (trap) arrinconar; (COMM) acaparar // vi (in car) tomar una curva; ~**stone** n piedra angular.

cornet ['kɔːnɪt] n (MUS) corneta; (of ice-cream) barquillo.

cornflour ['kɔːnflauə*] n harina de maíz.

Cornwall ['kɔːnwəl] n Cornualles m.

corny ['kɔːnɪ] a (col) viejo, gastado.

corollary [kə'rɔlərɪ] n corolario.

coronary ['kɔrənərɪ] n: ~ **(thrombosis)** trombosis f coronaria.

coronation [kɔrə'neɪʃən] n coronación f.

coroner ['kɔrənə*] n juez m de primera instancia.

coronet ['kɔrənɪt] n corona.

corporal ['kɔːpərl] n cabo // a corporal.

corporate ['kɔːpərɪt] a corporativo.

corporation [kɔːpə'reɪʃən] n (of town) ayuntamiento; (COMM) corporación f.

corps [kɔː*], pl **corps** [kɔːz] n cuerpo.

corpse [kɔːps] n cadáver m.

corpuscle ['kɔːpʌsl] n corpúsculo.

corral [kə'rɑːl] n corral m.

correct [kə'rɛkt] a (accurate) justo, exacto; (proper) correcto // vt corregir; (exam) calificar; ~**ion** [-ʃən] n rectificación f; (erasure) tachadura.

correlate ['kɔrɪleɪt] vt correlacionar.

correspond [kɔrɪs'pɔnd] vi (write) escribirse; (be equal to) corresponder; ~**ence** n correspondencia; ~**ence** course n curso por correspondencia; ~**ent** n corresponsal m/f; ~**ing** a correspondiente.

corridor ['kɔrɪdɔː*] n pasillo.

corroborate [kə'rɔbəreɪt] vt corroborar.

corrode [kə'rəud] vt corroer // vi corroerse; **corrosion** [-'rəuʒən] n corrosión f.

corrugated ['kɔrəgeɪtɪd] a ondulado; ~ **iron** n chapa ondulada.

corrupt [kə'rʌpt] a corrompido; (person) venal // vt corromper; (bribe) sobornar; ~**ion** [-ʃən] n corrupción f.

corset ['kɔːsɪt] n faja.

Corsica ['kɔːsɪkə] n Córcega.

cortège [kɔː'teːʒ] n cortejo, desfile m.

cortisone ['kɔːtɪzəun] n cortisona.

cosh [kɔʃ] n cachiporra.

cosiness ['kəuzɪnɪs] n comodidad f; (atmosphere) lo holgado.

cos lettuce [kɔs-] n lechuga cos.

cosmetic [kɔz'mɛtɪk] n cosmético.

cosmic ['kɔzmɪk] a cósmico.

cosmonaut ['kɔzmənɔːt] n cosmonauta m/f.

cosmopolitan [kɔzmə'pɔlɪtn] a cosmopolita.

cosmos ['kɔzmɔs] n cosmos m.

cost [kɔst] n (gen) coste m, costo; (price) precio; ~**s** npl costes mpl // vi, pt, pp **cost** costar, valer // vt preparar el presupuesto de; **at the** ~ **of** a costa de; **how much does it** ~? ¿cuánto cuesta?

co-star ['kəustɑː*] n colega m/f de reparto.

Costa Rican ['kɔstə'riːkən] a costarriqueño.

costly ['kɔstlɪ] a (expensive) costoso; (valuable) suntuoso.

cost price n precio de coste.

costume ['kɔstjuːm] n traje m; (also: swimming ~) traje de baño.

cosy ['kəuzɪ] a cómodo; (atmosphere) acogedor(a); (life) holgado.

cot [kɔt] n (child's) cuna.

cottage ['kɔtɪdʒ] n casita de campo; (rustic) barraca; ~ **cheese** n requesón m.

cotton ['kɔtn] n algodón m; (thread) hilo; **to** ~ **on to** vt (col) caer en la cuenta de; ~ **wool** n algodón m (hidrófilo).

couch [kautʃ] n sofá m.

cough [kɔf] vi toser // n tos f; **to** ~ **up** vt escupir; ~ **drop** n pastilla para la tos.

could [kud] pt of **can**; ~**n't** = **could not**.

council ['kaunsl] n consejo; **city** or **town** ~ consejo municipal; ~ **estate** n polígono de renta limitada; ~ **house** n vivienda de renta limitada; ~**lor** n concejal m/f.

counsel ['kaunsl] n (advice) consejo; (lawyer) abogado // vt aconsejar; ~**lor** n consejero.

count [kaunt] vt (gen) contar; (include) incluir // vi contar // n (gen) cuenta; (of votes) escrutinio; (nobleman) condé m; (sum) total m, suma; **to** ~ **on** vt fus contar con; **that doesn't** ~! ¡eso no vale!;

~down n cuenta hacia atrás.
counter ['kauntə°] n (in shop) mostrador m; (in games) ficha // vt contrarrestar; (blow) parar; (attack) contestar a // ad: ~ to contrario a; ~act vt contrarrestar; ~attack n contrataque m // vi contratacar; ~balance n contrapeso; ~-espionage n contraespionaje m.
counterfeit ['kauntəfɪt] n moneda falsa // vt falsificar // a falso, falsificado.
counterfoil ['kauntəfɔɪl] n talón m.
counterpart ['kauntəpɑ:t] n (of person) colega m/f.
counter-revolution [kauntərevə'lu:ʃən] n contrarrevolución f.
countersign ['kauntəsaɪn] vt refrendar.
countess ['kauntɪs] n condesa.
countless ['kauntlɪs] a incontable.
country ['kʌntrɪ] n país m; (native land) patria; (as opposed to town) campo; (region) región f, tierra; ~ dancing n baile m regional; ~ house n quinta, finca; ~side n campo.
county ['kauntɪ] n condado; ~ town n cabeza de partido.
coup [ku:], pl ~s [-z] n golpe m; ~ d'état/de grâce golpe de estado/de gracia.
coupé ['ku:peɪ] n cupé m.
couple ['kʌpl] n (of things) par m; (of people) pareja; (married ~) matrimonio // vt (ideas, names) unir, juntar; (machinery) acoplar; a ~ of un par de.
coupling ['kʌplɪŋ] n (RAIL) enganche m.
coupon ['ku:pɔn] n cupón m; (pools ~) boleto.
courage ['kʌrɪdʒ] n valor m, valentía; ~ous [kə'reɪdʒəs] a valiente.
courier ['kurɪə°] n estafeta; (diplomatic) correo; (for tourists) agente m/f de turismo.
course [kɔ:s] n (direction) dirección f; (of river, ESCOL) curso; (of ship) rumbo, derrota; (of bullet) trayectoria; (fig) proceder m; (GOLF) campo; (part of meal) plato; of ~ ad desde luego, naturalmente; of ~! ¡claro!; in due ~ en el momento oportuno.
court [kɔ:t] n (royal) corte m; (LAW) tribunal m, juzgado; (TENNIS) pista, cancha // vt (woman) cortejar, hacer la corte a; (danger etc) buscar; to take to ~ demandar.
courteous ['kɔ:tɪəs] a cortés.
courtesan [kɔ:tɪ'zæn] n cortesana.
courtesy ['kɔ:təsɪ] n cortesía; by ~ of con permiso de.
court-house ['kɔ:thaus] n (US) palacio de justicia.
courtier ['kɔ:tɪə°] n cortesano.
court: ~-martial, pl ~s-martial n consejo de guerra // vt someter a consejo de guerra; ~room n sala de justicia; ~yard n patio.
cousin ['kʌzn] n primo/a; first ~ primo carnal.
cove [kəuv] n cala, ensenada.

covenant ['kʌvənənt] n convenio.
cover ['kʌvə°] vt (gen) cubrir; (with lid) tapar; (chairs etc) revestir; (distance) recorrer; (include) abarcar; (protect) abrigar; (journalist) investigar; (issues) tratar // n (gen) cubierta; (lid) tapa; (for chair etc) funda; (for bed) cobertor m; (envelope) sobre m; (for book) forro; (of magazine) portada; (shelter) abrigo; (insurance) cobertura; under ~ (indoors) bajo techo; under ~ of al abrigo de; (fig) so capa de; to ~ up for sb encubrir a uno; ~age n alcance m; ~ charge n precio del cubierto; ~ing n cubierta, envoltura; ~ing letter n carta explicatoria.
covet ['kʌvɪt] vt codiciar.
cow [kau] n vaca // vt intimidar.
coward ['kauəd] n cobarde m/f; ~ice [-ɪs] n cobardía; ~ly a cobarde.
cowboy ['kaubɔɪ] n vaquero.
cower ['kauə°] vi encogerse (de miedo).
cowshed ['kauʃed] n establo.
coxswain ['kɔksn] n (abbr: cox) timonel m/f.
coy [kɔɪ] a tímido.
coyote [kɔɪ'əutɪ] n coyote m.
crab [kræb] n cangrejo; ~ apple n manzana silvestre.
crack [kræk] n grieta; (noise) crujido; (: of whip) chasquido; (fam) chiste m // vt agrietar, romper; (nut) cascar; (safe) forzar; (whip etc) chasquear; (knuckles) crujir; (joke) contar // a (expert) experto; to ~ up vi (MED) sufrir un colapso nervioso; ~er n (biscuit) cracker m; (Christmas cracker) sorpresa.
crackle ['krækl] vi crepitar; crackling n (of fire) crepitación f; (of leaves etc) crujido; (of pork) chicharrón m.
cradle ['kreɪdl] n cuna.
craft [krɑ:ft] n (skill) arte m; (trade) oficio; (cunning) astucia; (boat) barco.
craftsman ['krɑ:ftsmən] n artesano; ~ship n artesanía.
crafty ['krɑ:ftɪ] a astuto.
crag [kræg] n peñasco; ~gy a escarpado.
cram [kræm] vt (fill) llenar, henchir; ~med a atestado.
cramp [kræmp] n (MED) calambre m; (TECH) grapa // vt (limit) restringir; (annoy) estorbar; ~ed a apretado, estrecho.
crampon ['kræmpən] n crampón m.
cranberry ['krænbərɪ] n arándano agrio.
crane [kreɪn] n (TECH) grúa; (bird) grulla.
crank [kræŋk] n manivela; (person) chiflado; ~shaft n eje m del cigüeñal.
cranky ['kræŋkɪ] a (eccentric) maniático; (bad-tempered) irritable.
cranny ['krænɪ] n see nook.
crash [kræʃ] n (noise) estruendo; (of cars etc) choque m; (of plane) accidente m de avión; (COMM) quiebra // vt (plane) estrellar // vi (plane) estrellarse; (two cars) chocar; (fall noisily) caer con estrépito; ~ course n curso acelerado; ~

helmet n casco (protector); ~ **landing** n aterrizaje m forzoso.

crate [kreɪt] n cajón m de embalaje; (fam) armatoste m.

crater ['kreɪtə*] n cráter m.

cravat(e) [krə'væt] n pañuelo.

crave [kreɪv] vt: **to** ~ **for** ansiar, anhelar; **craving** n (of pregnant woman) antojo.

crawl [krɔːl] vi (gen) arrastrarse; (child) andar a gatas, gatear; (vehicle) avanzar a paso de tortuga // n (swimming) crol m.

crayfish ['kreɪfɪʃ] n, pl inv langostino.

crayon ['kreɪən] n pastel m, lápiz m de color.

craze [kreɪz] n manía; (fashion) moda.

crazy ['kreɪzɪ] a (person) loco; (idea) disparatado.

creak [kriːk] vi chirriar, rechinar; (door etc) crujir.

cream [kriːm] n (of milk) nata; (gen) crema; (fig) flor y nata // a (colour) color m (de) crema; ~ **cake** n pastel m de nata; ~ **cheese** n queso de nata; ~y a cremoso.

crease [kriːs] n (fold) pliegue m; (in trousers) raya; (wrinkle) arruga // vt (fold) doblar, plegar; (wrinkle) arrugar // vi (wrinkle up) arrugarse.

create [kriːˈeɪt] vt crear; **creation** [-ʃən] n creación f; **creative** a creador(a); **creator** n creador m.

creature ['kriːtʃə*] n (animal) animal m, bicho; (living thing) criatura.

crèche, creche [krɛʃ] n guardería infantil.

credentials [krɪˈdɛnʃlz] npl credenciales fpl.

credibility [krɛdɪˈbɪlɪtɪ] n credibilidad f.

credible ['krɛdɪbl] a creíble.

credit ['krɛdɪt] n (gen) crédito; (merit) honor m, mérito // vt (comm) abonar; (believe) creer, prestar fe a // a crediticio; ~s npl (cinema) fichas técnicas; ~**able** a estimable, digno de elogio; ~ **card** n tarjeta de crédito; ~**or** n acreedor m.

credulity [krɪˈdjuːlɪtɪ] n credulidad f.

creed [kriːd] n credo.

creek [kriːk] n cala, ensenada; (US) riachuelo.

creep [kriːp] pt, pp **crept** vi (animal) deslizarse; (gen) arrastrarse; (plant) trepar; ~**er** n enredadera; ~y a (frightening) horripilante.

cremate [krɪˈmeɪt] vt incinerar; **cremation** [-ʃən] n incineración f.

crematorium [krɛməˈtɔːrɪəm] pl **-ria** [-rɪə] n (horno) crematorio.

creosote ['krɪəsəut] n creosota.

crêpe [kreɪp] n (fabric) crespón m; (rubber) crepé m; ~ **bandage** n venda de crepé.

crept [krɛpt] pt, pp of **creep**.

crescent ['krɛsnt] n media luna; (street) calle f en semicírculo.

cress [krɛs] n mastuerzo.

crest [krɛst] n (of bird) cresta; (of hill)

cima, cumbre f; (of helmet) cimera; (of coat of arms) blasón m; ~**fallen** a alicaído.

Crete [kriːt] n Creta.

crevasse [krɪˈvæs] n grieta.

crevice ['krɛvɪs] n grieta, hendedura.

crew [kruː] n (of ship etc) tripulación f; (gang) banda; (mil) dotación f; ~-**cut** n corte m al rape; ~-**neck** n cuello plano.

crib [krɪb] n pesebre m // vt (col) plagiar.

crick [krɪk] n (in neck) tortícolis m.

cricket ['krɪkɪt] n (insect) grillo; (game) críquet m.

crime [kraɪm] n crimen m; (less serious) delito; **criminal** ['krɪmɪnl] n criminal m, delincuente m // a criminal, delictivo; (law) penal; **the Criminal Investigation Department (CID)** Brigada de Investigación Criminal (B.I.C.).

crimson ['krɪmzn] a carmesí.

cringe [krɪndʒ] vi agacharse, encogerse.

crinkle ['krɪŋkl] vt arrugar.

cripple ['krɪpl] n lisiado, mutilado // vt lisiar, tullir.

crisis ['kraɪsɪs] pl **-ses** [-siːz] n crisis f.

crisp [krɪsp] a fresco; (cooked) tostado; (hair) crespo; (manner) seco; ~s npl papas fritas fpl.

criss-cross ['krɪskrɔs] a entrelazado.

criterion [kraɪˈtɪərɪən] pl **-ria** [-rɪə] n criterio.

critic ['krɪtɪk] n (gen) criticón/ona m/f; (paper) crítico; ~**al** a (gen) crítico; (illness) grave; ~**ally** ad (ill) gravemente; ~**ism** ['krɪtɪsɪzm] n crítica; ~**ize** ['krɪtɪsaɪz] vt criticar.

croak [krəuk] vi (frog) croar; (raven) graznar // n graznido.

crochet ['krəuʃeɪ] n ganchillo.

crockery ['krɔkərɪ] n loza, vajilla.

crocodile ['krɔkədaɪl] n cocodrilo.

crocus ['krəukəs] n azafrán m.

croft [krɔft] n granja pequeña; ~**er** n pequeño granjero.

croissant ['krwasã] n croissant m, medialuna.

crone [krəun] n bruja.

crony ['krəunɪ] n compinche m/f.

crook [kruk] n (fam) maleante m/f; (of shepherd) cayado; (of arm) pliegue m; ~**ed** ['krukɪd] a torcido; (path) tortuoso; (action) poco limpio.

crop [krɔp] n (species) cultivo; (quantity) cosecha // vt cortar, recortar; **to** ~ **up** vi surgir, presentarse.

croquet ['krəukeɪ] n croquet m.

croquette [krəˈkɛt] n croqueta.

cross [krɔs] n cruz f // vt (street etc) cruzar, atravesar // a de mal humor, malhumorado; **to** ~ **o.s.** santiguarse; **to** ~ **out** vt tachar; **to** ~ **over** vi cruzar; ~**bar** n travesaño; (sport) larguero; ~**country** (race) n carrera a campo traviesa, cross m; ~-**examination** n repregunta, interrogatorio; ~-**examine** vt repreguntar; ~-**eyed** a bizco; ~**ing** n (road) cruce m; (rail) paso a nivel; (sea-passage) travesía; (also: **pedestrian** ~ing) paso para peatones; ~ **purposes** npl: **to be at** ~ **purposes** malentenderse uno a otro; ~**-reference** n contra-rreferencia; ~**roads** n cruce m, encrucijada; ~ **section** n corte m transversal; (of population) sección f representativa; ~**wind** n viento de costado; ~ **word** n crucigrama m.

crotch [krɔtʃ] n (of garment) entrepierna.

crotchet ['krɔtʃɪt] n (MUS) negra.

crotchety ['krɔtʃɪti] a (person) arisco.

crouch [krautʃ] vi agacharse, acurrucarse.

croupier ['kru:pɪə] n crupier m/f.

crow [krəu] n (bird) cuervo; (of cock) canto, cacareo // vi (cock) cantar, cacarear.

crowbar ['krəubɑ:*] n palanca.

crowd [kraud] n muchedumbre f; (SPORT) público; (unruly) tropel m; (common herd) vulgo // vt (gather) amontonar; (fill) llenar // vi (gather) reunirse; (pile up) amontonarse; ~**ed** a (full) atestado; (well-attended) concurrido.

crown [kraun] n corona; (of head) coronilla; (of hat) copa; (of hill) cumbre f // vt coronar; ~ **jewels** npl joyas fpl reales; ~ **prince** n príncipe m heredero.

crucial ['kru:ʃl] a decisivo.

crucifix ['kru:sɪfɪks] n crucifijo; ~**ion** [-'fɪkʃən] n crucifixión f; **crucify** [-faɪ] vt crucificar.

crude [kru:d] a (materials) bruto; (fig: basic) tosco; (: vulgar) ordinario; ~ **(oil)** n aceite m crudo.

cruel ['kruəl] a cruel; ~**ty** n crueldad f.

cruet ['kru:ɪt] angarillas fpl.

cruise [kru:z] n crucero, viaje m por mar // vi (ship) hacer un crucero; (car) circular lentamente; **cruiser** n crucero.

crumb [krʌm] n miga, migaja.

crumble ['krʌmbl] vt desmenuzar // vi (gen) desmenuzarse; (building) desmoro-narse; **crumbly** a desmenuzable.

crumpet ['krʌmpɪt] n bollo blando.

crumple ['krʌmpl] vt (paper) estrujar; (material) arrugar.

crunch [krʌntʃ] vt (food etc) mascar; (underfoot) hacer crujir // n (fig) crisis f; ~**y** a crujiente.

crusade [kru:'seɪd] n cruzada.

crush [krʌʃ] n (people) agolpamiento; (crowd) aglomeración f; (drink): **lemon** ~ limonada // vt (gen) aplastar; (paper) estrujar; (cloth) arrugar; (fruit) exprimir; ~**ing** a aplastante; (burden) agobiador(a).

crust [krʌst] n corteza; (MED) costra.

crutch [krʌtʃ] n muleta.

crux [krʌks] n lo esencial.

cry [kraɪ] vi llorar; (shout) gritar // n grito.

crypt [krɪpt] n cripta.

cryptic ['krɪptɪk] a enigmático, secreto.

crystal ['krɪstl] n cristal m; ~**-clear** a transparente, claro como el agua; **crystallize** vt cristalizar // vi cristalizarse.

cub [kʌb] n cachorro.

Cuba ['kju:bə] n Cuba; ~**n** a, n cubano/a.

cubbyhole ['kʌbɪhəul] n chiribitil m.

cube [kju:b] n cubo; (of sugar) terrón m // vt (MATH) cubicar; ~ **root** n raíz f cúbica; **cubic** a cúbico.

cubicle ['kju:bɪkl] n (at pool) caseta; (for bed) camarilla.

cuckoo ['kuku:] n cuco; ~ **clock** n reloj m de cuclillo.

cucumber ['kju:kʌmbə*] n pepino.

cuddle ['kʌdl] vt abrazar amorosamente // vi abrazarse; **cuddly** a mimoso.

cue [kju:] n (snooker) taco; (THEATRE etc) entrada, apunte m.

cuff [kʌf] n (of shirt, coat etc) puño; (blow) bofetada; **off the** ~ ad de improviso; ~**links** npl gemelos mpl.

cuisine [kwɪ'zi:n] n cocina.

cul-de-sac ['kʌldəsæk] n callejón m sin salida.

culinary ['kʌlɪnərɪ] a culinario.

cull [kʌl] vt (flowers) coger; (select) entresacar.

culminate ['kʌlmɪneɪt] vi: **to** ~ **in** terminar en; **culmination** [-'neɪʃən] n culminación f, colmo.

culpable ['kʌlpəbl] a culpable.

culprit ['kʌlprɪt] n (persona) culpable, delincuente m/f.

cult [kʌlt] n culto.

cultivate ['kʌltɪveɪt] vt (also fig) cultivar; **cultivation** [-'veɪʃən] n cultivo; (fig) cultura.

cultural ['kʌltʃərəl] a cultural.

culture ['kʌltʃə*] n (also fig) cultura; ~**d** a culto.

cumbersome ['kʌmbəsəm] a molesto, incómodo.

cumulative ['kju:mjulətɪv] a cumulativo.

cunning ['kʌnɪŋ] n astucia // a astuto.

cup [kʌp] n taza; (prize, event) copa.

cupboard ['kʌbəd] n armario; (on wall) alacena.

Cupid ['kju:pɪd] n Cupido.

cupola ['kju:pələ] n cúpula.

cup-tie ['kʌptaɪ] n partido de copa.

cur [kɜ:] n perro de mala raza; (person) canalla m/f.

curable ['kjuərəbl] a curable.

curate ['kjuərɪt] n cura m.

curator [kjuə'reɪtə*] n director m.

curb [kɜ:b] vt refrenar // n freno.

curdle ['kɜ:dl] vi cuajarse.

curds [kɜ:dz] npl requesón m.

cure [kjuə*] vt curar // n cura, curación f.

curfew ['kɜ:fju:] n toque m de queda.

curio ['kjuərɪəu] n curiosidad f.

curiosity [kjuərɪ'ɔsɪtɪ] n curiosidad f; **curious** ['kjuərɪəs] a curioso.

curl [kɜ:l] n rizo, bucle m // vt (hair) rizar; (paper) arrollar; (lip) truncir // vi rizarse; arrollarse; **to** ~ **up** vi arrollarse; (person) hacer un ovillo; (fam) morirse de risa; ~**er** n bigudí m, chincho; ~**y** a rizado.

currant ['kʌrnt] *n* pasa; (*black, red*) grosella.

currency ['kʌrnsi] *n* moneda.

current ['kʌrnt] *n* corriente *f* // *a* corriente, actual; ~ **account** *n* cuenta corriente; ~ **affairs** *npl* actualidades *fpl*; ~**ly** *ad* actualmente.

curriculum [kə'rikjuləm], *pl* ~**s** or **-la** [-lə] *n* plan *m* de estudios; ~ **vitae** *n* currículum *m*.

curry ['kʌri] *n* curry *m* // *vt*: **to** ~ **favour with** buscar favores con; ~ **powder** *n* polvos *mpl* de curry.

curse [kə:s] *vi* echar pestes // *vt* maldecir, echar pestes de // *n* maldición *f*; (*swearword*) palabrota.

cursory ['kə:səri] *a* rápido, superficial.

curt [kə:t] *a* corto, seco.

curtail [kə:'teil] *vt* (*visit etc*) acortar; (*expenses etc*) restringir.

curtain ['kə:tn] *n* cortina; (*THEATRE*) telón *m*; ~ **ring** *n* anilla.

curts(e)y ['kə:tsi] *n* reverencia // *vi* hacer una reverencia.

curve [kə:v] *n* curva // *vt* encorvar, torcer // *vi* encorvarse, torcerse; (*road*) hacer (una) curva.

cushion ['kuʃən] *n* cojín *m*; (*SNOOKER*) banda // *vt* (*seat*) acolchar; (*shock*) amortiguar.

custard ['kʌstəd] *n* (*for pouring*) natilla.

custodian [kʌs'təudiən] *n* custodio.

custody ['kʌstədi] *n* custodia; **to take into** ~ detener.

custom ['kʌstəm] *n* costumbre *f*; (*COMM*) clientela; ~**ary** *a* acostumbrado.

customer ['kʌstəmə°] *n* cliente *m/f*.

custom-made ['kʌstəm'meid] *a* hecho a la medida.

customs ['kʌstəmz] *npl* aduana *sg*; ~ **duty** *n* derechos *mpl* de aduana; ~ **officer** *n* aduanero.

cut [kʌt], *pt, pp* **cut** *vt* cortar; (*price*) rebajar; (*record*) grabar; (*reduce*) reducir // *vi* cortar; (*intersect*) cruzarse // *n* (*gen*) corte *m*; (*in skin*) cortadura; (*with sword*) tajo; (*of knife*) cuchillada; (*in salary etc*) rebaja; (*of meat*) tajada; **power** ~ apagón *m*; **to** ~ **a tooth** salirle a uno un diente; **to** ~ **down** *vt* (*tree*) derribar; (*reduce*) reducir; **to** ~ **off** *vt* (*gen*) cortar; (*retreat*) impedir; (*troops*) cercar; **to** ~ **out** *vt* (*shape*) recortar; (*delete*) suprimir; **to** ~ **through** *vi* abrirse camino; ~**back** *n* reducción *f*.

cute [kju:t] *a* lindo; (*shrewd*) listo.

cuticle ['kju:tikl] *n* cutícula.

cutlery ['kʌtləri] *n* cubiertos *mpl*.

cutlet ['kʌtlit] *n* chuleta.

cut: ~**out** *n* recortable *m*; ~**-price** *a* a precio reducido; ~**throat** *n* asesino // *a* intenso.

cutting ['kʌtiŋ] *a* (*gen*) cortante; (*remark*) mordaz // *n* (*PRESS*) recorte *m*; (*RAIL*) desmonte *m*.

cwt *abbr of* **hundredweight(s)**.

cyanide ['saiənaid] *n* cianuro.

cyclamen ['sikləmən] *n* ciclamen *m*.

cycle ['saikl] *n* ciclo; (*bicycle*) bicicleta // *vi* ir en bicicleta; **cycling** *n* ciclismo; **cyclist** *n* ciclista *m/f*.

cyclone ['saikləun] *n* ciclón *m*.

cygnet ['signit] *n* pollo de cisne.

cylinder ['silində°] *n* cilindro; ~ **block** *n* bloque *m* de cilindros; ~ **capacity** *n* cilindrada; ~ **head** *n* culata de cilindro; ~**-head gasket** *n* junta de culata.

cymbals ['simblz] *npl* platillos *mpl*.

cynic ['sinik] *n* cínico; ~**al** *a* cínico; ~**ism** ['sinisizəm] *n* cinismo.

cypress ['saipris] *n* ciprés *m*.

Cypriot ['sipriət] *a*, *n* chipriota *m/f*.

Cyprus ['saiprəs] *n* Chipre *f*.

cyst [sist] *n* quiste *m*; ~**itis** *n* cistitis *f*.

czar [zɑ:°] *n* zar *m*.

Czech [tʃek] *a*, *n* checo/a.

Czechoslovakia [tʃekəslə'vækiə] *n* Checoslovaquia.

D

dab [dæb] *vt* (*eyes, wound*) tocar (ligeramente); (*paint, cream*) mojar ligeramente // *n* (*of paint*) brochazo; (*of liquid*) gota; (*amount*) pequeña cantidad *f*.

dabble ['dæbl] *vi*: **to** ~ **in** interesarse por.

dad [dæd], **daddy** ['dædi] *n* papá *m*; **daddy-long-legs** *n* típula.

daffodil ['dæfədil] *n* narciso trompón.

daft [dɑ:ft] *a* estúpido, tonto.

dagger ['dægə°] *n* puñal *m*, daga; **to look** ~**s at sb** apuñalar a alguien con la mirada.

daily ['deili] *a* diario, cotidiano // *n* (*paper*) diario; (*domestic help*) asistenta // *ad* a diario, cada día.

dainty ['deinti] *a* delicado; (*tasteful*) elegante, primoroso.

dairy ['dɛəri] *n* (*shop*) lechería; (*on farm*) vaquería // *a* lechero; ~ **farm** *n* granja; ~ **produce** *n* productos *mpl* lácteos.

daisy ['deizi] *n* margarita.

dale [deil] *n* valle *m*.

dam [dæm] *n* presa *f* // *vt* represar.

damage ['dæmidʒ] *n* daño, perjuicio; (*to machine*) avería // *vt* dañar, perjudicar; averiar; ~**s** *npl* (*LAW*) daños y perjuicios.

damn [dæm] *vt* condenar; (*curse*) maldecir // *n* (*col*): **I don't give a** ~ me trae sin cuidado // *a* (*col*) maldito; ~ (**it**)! ¡mecachis!; ~**ing** *a* (*evidence*) irrecusable.

damp [dæmp] *a* húmedo, mojado // *n* humedad *f* // *vt* (*also*: ~**en**) (*cloth, rag*) mojar; (*enthusiasm etc*) desalentar; ~**ness** *n* humedad *f*.

damson ['dæmzən] *n* ciruela damascena.

dance [dɑ:ns] *n* baile *m* // *vi* bailar; ~ **hall** *n* salón *m* de baile; **dancer** *n* bailador/a *m/f*; (*professional*) bailarín/ina *m/f*; **dancing** *n* baile *m*.

dandelion ['dændilaiən] *n* diente *m* de león.

dandruff ['dændrəf] n caspa.
Dane [deɪn] n danés/esa m/f.
danger ['deɪndʒə°] n peligro; (risk) riesgo;
  ~! (on sign) ¡peligro de muerte!; **to be in**
  ~ **of** correr riesgo de; ~**ous** a peligroso;
  ~**ously** ad peligrosamente.
dangle ['dæŋgl] vt colgar // vi pender,
  estar colgado.
Danish ['deɪnɪʃ] a, n danés/esa m/f.
dare [dɛə°] vt: **to** ~ **sb to do** desafiar a
  uno a hacer algo // vi: **to** ~ (**to**) **do sth**
  atreverse a hacer algo; ~**devil** n
  temerario, atrevido; **daring** a atrevido,
  osado // n atrevimiento, osadía.
dark [dɑ:k] a (gen) oscuro; (hair,
  complexion) moreno; (cheerless) triste,
  sombrío; (fig) secreto, escondido // n
  (gen) oscuridad f; (night) tinieblas fpl; **to**
  be left in the ~ **about** (fig) quedar sin
  saber nada de; **after** ~ después del
  anochecer; ~**en** vt oscurecer; (colour)
  hacer más oscuro // vi oscurecerse; (sky)
  anublarse; ~ **glasses** npl gafas fpl
  oscuras; ~**ness** n oscuridad f, tinieblas
  fpl; ~ **room** n cuarto oscuro.
darling ['dɑ:lɪŋ] a, n querido/a.
darn [dɑ:n] vt zurcir.
dart [dɑ:t] n dardo; (in game) rehilete m;
  (in sewing) sisa // vi precipitarse; **to** ~
  away/along irse/seguir precipitado;
  ~**board** n blanco; ~**s** n juego de
  rehiletes.
dash [dæʃ] n (sign) guión m; (: long) raya;
  (rush) carrera // vt (break) romper,
  estrellar; (hopes) defraudar // vi
  precipitarse, ir de prisa; **to** ~ **away** or **off**
  vi marcharse apresuradamente; ~**board**
  n tablero de instrumentos; ~**ing** a
  gallardo.
data ['deɪtə] npl datos mpl; ~ **processing**
  n procesamiento de datos.
date [deɪt] n (day) fecha; (with friend) cita;
  (fruit) dátil m; (tree) palmera // vt fichar;
  citar; **to** ~ ad hasta la fecha; **out of** ~
  fuera de moda; **up to** ~ moderno, al día;
  ~**d** a anticuado.
daub [dɔ:b] vt manchar.
daughter ['dɔ:tə°] n hija; ~**-in-law** n
  nuera, hija política.
daunting ['dɔ:ntɪŋ] a desalentador(a).
dawdle ['dɔ:dl] vi (waste time) perder el
  tiempo; (go slow) andar muy despacio.
dawn [dɔ:n] n alba, amanecer m // vi
  (day) amanecer; (fig): **it** ~**ed on him**
  that... cayó en la cuenta de que... .
day [deɪ] n día m; (working ~) jornada; **the**
  ~ **before** el día anterior; **the following**
  ~ el día siguiente; **by** ~ de día; ~**break**
  n amanecer m; ~**dream** n ensueño // vi
  soñar despierto; ~**light** n luz f (del día);
  ~**time** n día m // a de día.
daze [deɪz] vt (stun) aturdir // n: **in a** ~
  aturdido.
dazzle ['dæzl] vt deslumbrar; **dazzling** a
  deslumbrante.
dead [dɛd] a (gen) muerto; (deceased)
  difunto; (telephone) cortado; (ELEC) sin

corriente // ad (gen) totalmente; (exactly)
  justo; ~ **tired** muerto de cansancio; **to**
  stop ~ parar en seco; **the** ~ los
  muertos; ~**en** vt (blow, sound)
  amortiguar; (make numb) calmar, aliviar;
  ~ **end** n callejón m sin salida; ~ **heat** n
  (SPORT) empate m; ~**line** n fecha o hora
  tope; ~**lock** n punto muerto; ~**ly** a
  mortal, fatal; ~**pan** a sin expresión.
deaf [dɛf] a sordo; ~**-aid** n audífono; ~**en**
  vt ensordecer; ~**ening** a
  ensordecedor(a); ~**ness** n sordera;
  ~**-mute** n sordomudo/a.
deal [di:l] n (agreement) pacto, convenio;
  (business) negocio, trato; (CARDS) reparto
  // vt, pt, pp **dealt** [dɛlt] (gen) dar; **a great**
  ~ (**of**) bastante, mucho; **to** ~ **in** tratar
  en, comerciar en; **to** ~ **with** vt fus
  (people) tratar con; (problem) ocuparse
  de; (subject) tratar de; (punish) castigar;
  ~**er** n comerciante m, tratante m; (CARDS)
  mano f; ~**ings** npl transacciones fpl;
  (relations) relaciones fpl.
dear [dɪə°] a querido; (expensive) caro //
  n: **my** ~ mi querido/a // excl: ~ **me!**
  ¡Dios mío!; **D**~ **Sir/Madam** (in letter)
  Muy Señor Mío, estimado Señor/estimada
  Señora; ~**ly** ad (love) tiernamente; (pay)
  caro.
death [dɛθ] n muerte f; ~**bed** n lecho de
  muerte; ~ **certificate** n partida de
  defunción; ~ **duties** npl (Brit) derechos
  mpl de herencia; ~**ly** a mortal; (silence)
  profundo; ~ **penalty** n pena de muerte;
  ~ **rate** n mortalidad f.
debar [dɪ'bɑ:°] vt (exclude) excluir.
debase [dɪ'beɪs] vt degradar.
debate [dɪ'beɪt] n debate m // vt discutir.
debauchery [dɪ'bɔ:tʃərɪ] n libertinaje m.
debit ['dɛbɪt] n debe m // vt: **to** ~ **a sum**
  to sb or **to sb's account** cargar una suma
  en cuenta a alguien.
debris ['dɛbri:] n escombros mpl.
debt [dɛt] n deuda; **to be in** ~ tener
  deudas; ~**or** n deudor/a m/f.
début ['deɪbju:] n presentación f.
decade ['dɛkeɪd] n decenio.
decadence ['dɛkədəns] n decadencia.
decay [dɪ'keɪ] n decadencia; (of building)
  desmoronamiento; (fig) deterioro;
  (rotting) pudrición f; (of tooth) caries f //
  vi (rot) pudrirse; (fig) decaer.
deceased [dɪ'si:st] a difunto.
deceit [dɪ'si:t] n engaño; ~**ful** a engañoso.
deceive [dɪ'si:v] vt engañar.
decelerate [di:'sɛləreɪt] vt moderar la
  marcha de // vi decelerar.
December [dɪ'sɛmbə°] n diciembre m.
decency ['di:sənsɪ] n decencia.
decent ['di:sənt] a (proper) decente;
  (person) amable, bueno.
decentralize [di:'sɛntrəlaɪz] vt
  descentralizar.
deception [dɪ'sɛpʃən] n engaño;
  deceptive [-tɪv] a engañoso.
decibel ['dɛsɪbɛl] n decibel(io) m.
decide [dɪ'saɪd] vt (person) decidir;

(*question, argument*) resolver // *vi* decidir; to ~ on sth decidir por algo; ~d a (*resolute*) decidido; (*clear, definite*) indudable; ~dly [-dɪdlɪ] *ad* decididamente.
deciduous [dɪˈsɪdjuəs] a de hoja caduca.
decimal [ˈdɛsɪməl] a decimal // n decimal f; ~ point n coma de decimales.
decimate [ˈdɛsɪmeɪt] *vt* diezmar.
decipher [dɪˈsaɪfə*] *vt* descifrar.
decision [dɪˈsɪʒən] n decisión f.
decisive [dɪˈsaɪsɪv] a decisivo; (*conclusive*) terminante; (*manner*) tajante.
deck [dɛk] n (NAUT) cubierta; (*of bus*) piso; (*of cards*) baraja; ~chair n tumbona, hamaca.
declaration [dɛkləˈreɪʃən] n declaración f; **declare** [dɪˈklɛə*] *vt* (*gen*) declarar.
decline [dɪˈklaɪn] n decaimiento, decadencia; (*lessening*) disminución f // vt rehusar // vi decaer; disminuir; (*fall*) bajar.
declutch [ˈdiːˈklʌtʃ] *vi* desembragar.
decode [diːˈkəud] *vt* descifrar.
decompose [diːkəmˈpəuz] *vi* descomponerse; **decomposition** [diːkɔmpəˈzɪʃən] n descomposición f.
decontaminate [diːkənˈtæmɪneɪt] *vt* descontaminar.
décor [ˈdeɪkɔː*] n decoración f; (THEATRE) decorado.
decorate [ˈdɛkəreɪt] *vt* adornar, decorar; (*paint*) pintar; (*paper*) empapelar; **decoration** [-ˈreɪʃən] n adorno; (*act*) decoración f; (*medal*) condecoración f; **decorator** n (*painter*) pintor m.
decoy [ˈdiːkɔɪ] n señuelo.
decrease [ˈdiːkriːs] n disminución f // (*vb*: [diːˈkriːs]) *vt* disminuir, reducir // vi reducirse.
decree [dɪˈkriː] n decreto; ~ nisi n orden f provisional de divorcio.
decrepit [dɪˈkrɛpɪt] a decrépito.
dedicate [ˈdɛdɪkeɪt] *vt* dedicar; **dedication** [-ˈkeɪʃən] n (*devotion*) dedicación f; (*in book*) dedicatoria.
deduce [dɪˈdjuːs] *vt* deducir.
deduct [dɪˈdʌkt] *vt* restar; (*from wage etc*) descontar; ~ion [dɪˈdʌkʃən] n descuento; (*conclusion*) deducción f, conclusión f.
deed [diːd] n hecho, acto; (*feat*) hazaña; (LAW) escritura.
deem [diːm] *vt* juzgar.
deep [diːp] a (*gen*) profundo; (*voice*) bajo; (*breath*) profundo, a pleno pulmón; (*person*) insondable // ad: the spectators stood 20 ~ los espectadores se formaron de 20 en fondo; to be 4 metres ~ tener 4 metros de profundo; ~en *vt* ahondar, profundizar // vi (*darkness*) intensificarse; ~-freeze n congeladora; ~-fry *vt* freír en aceite abundante; ~-sea diving n buceo de altura; ~-seated a (*beliefs*) (profundamente) arraigado; ~-set a (*eyes*) hundido.
deer [dɪə*] n, pl inv ciervo; ~skin n gamuza, piel f de ciervo.
deface [dɪˈfeɪs] *vt* desfigurar, mutilar.

defamation [dɛfəˈmeɪʃən] n difamación f.
default [dɪˈfɔːlt] *vi* no pagar; (SPORT) dejar de presentarse // n: by ~ (LAW) en rebeldía; (SPORT) por no presentarse el adversario; ~er n (*in debt*) moroso/a.
defeat [dɪˈfiːt] n derrota // *vt* derrotar, vencer; (*fig: efforts*) frustrar; ~ist a, n derrotista m/f.
defect [ˈdiːfɛkt] n defecto // vi [dɪˈfɛkt] desertar; ~ive [dɪˈfɛktɪv] a (*gen*) defectuoso; (*person*) anormal.
defence [dɪˈfɛns] n defensa; ~less a indefenso.
defend [dɪˈfɛnd] *vt* defender; ~ant n acusado/a; (*in civil case*) demandado/a; ~er n defensor m.
defensive [dɪˈfɛnsɪv] a defensivo; on the ~ a la defensiva.
defer [dɪˈfɜː*] *vt* (*postpone*) aplazar; to ~ to diferir a; ~ence [ˈdɛfərəns] n deferencia, respeto.
defiance [dɪˈfaɪəns] n desafío; in ~ of en contra de; **defiant** [-ənt] a (*insolent*) insolente; (*challenging*) retador(a).
deficiency [dɪˈfɪʃənsɪ] n (*lack*) falta; (*defect*) defecto; **deficient** [-ənt] a (*lacking*) insuficiente; (*incomplete*) incompleto; (*defective*) defectuoso; (*mentally*) anormal; **deficient in** falto de.
deficit [ˈdɛfɪsɪt] n déficit m.
defile [dɪˈfaɪl] *vt* manchar, deshonrar.
define [dɪˈfaɪn] *vt* definir.
definite [ˈdɛfɪnɪt] a (*fixed*) determinado; (*clear, obvious*) claro, categórico; he was ~ about it no dejó lugar a dudas (sobre ello); ~ly ad claramente.
definition [dɛfɪˈnɪʃən] n definición f.
definitive [dɪˈfɪnɪtɪv] a definitivo.
deflate [diːˈfleɪt] *vt* (*gen*) desinflar; (*person*) quitar los humos a.
deflect [dɪˈflɛkt] *vt* desviar.
deform [dɪˈfɔːm] *vt* deformar; ~ed a deformado; ~ity n deformación f.
defraud [dɪˈfrɔːd] *vt* estafar; to ~ sb of sth estafar algo a uno.
defrost [diːˈfrɔst] *vt* (*fridge*) deshelar, descongelar.
deft [dɛft] a diestro, hábil.
defunct [dɪˈfʌŋkt] a difunto.
defuse [diːˈfjuːz] *vt* quitar el fusible a.
defy [dɪˈfaɪ] *vt* (*resist*) oponerse resueltamente a; (*challenge*) desafiar; (*order*) contravenir.
degenerate [dɪˈdʒɛnəreɪt] *vi* degenerar // a [dɪˈdʒɛnərɪt] degenerado.
degradation [dɛgrəˈdeɪʃən] n degradación f; **degrading** [dɪˈgreɪdɪŋ] a degradante.
degree [dɪˈgriː] n grado; (SCOL) título; ~ in maths licencia en matemáticas.
dehydrated [diːhaɪˈdreɪtɪd] a deshidratado; (*milk*) en polvo.
de-ice [diːˈaɪs] *vt* (*windscreen*) deshelar.
deign [deɪn] vi: to ~ to do dignarse hacer.
deity [ˈdiːɪtɪ] n deidad f, divinidad f.
dejected [dɪˈdʒɛktɪd] a abatido,

desanimado; (*face*) cariacontecido; **dejection** [-ʃən] *n* abatimiento.

delay [dɪ'leɪ] *vt* demorar, aplazar; (*person*) entretener; (*trains*) retrasar // *vi* tardar // *n* (*gen*) dilación *f*; (a ~) demora, retraso; **without ~** en seguida, sin tardar.

delegate ['dɛlɪgɪt] *n* delegado/a // *vt* ['dɛlɪgeɪt] delegar; **delegation** [-'geɪʃən] *n* delegación *f*.

delete [dɪ'li:t] *vt* suprimir, tachar.

deliberate [dɪ'lɪbərɪt] *a* (*intentional*) intencionado; (*slow*) pausado, lento // *vi* [dɪ'lɪbəreɪt] deliberar; **~ly** *ad* (*on purpose*) a propósito; (*slowly*) pausadamente.

delicacy ['dɛlɪkəsɪ] *n* delicadeza; (*choice food*) golosina.

delicate ['dɛlɪkɪt] *a* (*gen*) delicado; (*fragile*) frágil; (*skilled*) fino.

delicatessen [dɛlɪkə'tɛsn] *n* tienda especializada en comida exótica.

delicious [dɪ'lɪʃəs] *a* delicioso, rico.

delight [dɪ'laɪt] *n* (*feeling*) placer *m*, deleite *m*; (*object*) encanto, delicia // *vt* encantar, deleitar; **to take ~ in** deleitarse con; **~ful** *a* encantador(a), delicioso.

delinquency [dɪ'lɪŋkwənsɪ] *n* delincuencia; **delinquent** [-ənt] *a, n* delincuente *m/f*.

delirious [dɪ'lɪrɪəs] *a* delirante; **delirium** [-ɪəm] *n* delirio.

deliver [dɪ'lɪvə*] *vt* (*distribute*) repartir; (*hand over*) entregar; (*message*) comunicar; (*speech*) pronunciar; (*blow*) lanzar, dar; (*MED*): **to be ~ed** dar a luz; **~y** *n* reparto; entrega; (*distribution*) distribución *f*; (*of speaker*) modo de expresarse; (*MED*) parto, alumbramiento; (*saving*) liberación *f*; **to take ~y of** recibir.

delta ['dɛltə] *n* delta *m*.

delude [dɪ'lu:d] *vt* engañar.

deluge ['dɛlju:dʒ] *n* diluvio // *vt* inundar.

delusion [dɪ'lu:ʒən] *n* ilusión *f*, engaño.

de luxe [də'lʌks] *a* de lujo.

delve [dɛlv] *vi*: **to ~ into** ahondar en.

demand [dɪ'mɑ:nd] *vt* (*gen*) exigir; (*rights*) reclamar // *n* (*gen*) exigencia; (*claim*) reclamación *f*; (*ECON*) demanda; **to be in ~** ser muy solicitado; **on ~** a solicitud; **~ing** *a* (*boss*) exigente; (*work*) absorbente.

demarcation [di:mɑ:'keɪʃən] *n* demarcación *f*.

demean [dɪ'mi:n] *vt*: **to ~ o.s.** rebajarse.

demeanour [dɪ'mi:nə*] *n* porte *m*, conducta.

demented [dɪ'mɛntɪd] *a* demente.

demister [di:'mɪstə*] *n* (*AUT*) de(s)fuminador *m* de vapores.

democracy [dɪ'mɔkrəsɪ] *n* democracia; **democrat** ['dɛməkræt] *n* demócrata *m/f*; **democratic** [dɛmə'krætɪk] *a* democrático.

demolish [dɪ'mɔlɪʃ] *vt* derribar, demoler; **demolition** [dɛmə'lɪʃən] *n* derribo, demolición *f*.

demonstrate ['dɛmənstreɪt] *vt* demostrar

// *vi* manifestarse; **demonstration** [-'streɪʃən] *n* (*POL*) manifestación *f*; (*proof*) prueba, demostración *f*; **demonstrator** *n* (*POL*) manifestante *m/f*.

demoralize [dɪ'mɔrəlaɪz] *vt* desmoralizar.

demote [dɪ'məut] *vt* degradar.

demure [dɪ'mjuə*] *a* recatado.

den [dɛn] *n* (*of animal*) guarida; (*study*) estudio.

denial [dɪ'naɪəl] *n* (*refusal*) negativa; (*of report etc*) desmentimiento; **self-~** abnegación *f*.

denim ['dɛnɪm] *n* dril *m*; **~s** *npl* vaqueros *mpl*.

Denmark ['dɛnmɑ:k] *n* Dinamarca.

denomination [dɪnɔmɪ'neɪʃən] *n* valor *m*; (*REL*) confesión *f*.

denominator [dɪ'nɔmɪneɪtə*] *n* denominador *m*.

denote [dɪ'nəut] *vt* indicar, significar.

denounce [dɪ'nauns] *vt* denunciar.

dense [dɛns] *a* (*thick*) espeso; (: *foliage etc*) tupido; (*stupid*) torpe, duro de mollera; **~ly** *ad*: **~ly populated** con gran densidad de población.

density ['dɛnsɪtɪ] *n* densidad *f*.

dent [dɛnt] *n* abolladura // *vt* (*also*: **make a ~ in**) abollar.

dental ['dɛntl] *a* dental; **~ surgeon** *n* odontólogo.

dentist ['dɛntɪst] *n* dentista *m/f*; **~ry** *n* odontología.

dentures ['dɛntʃəz] *npl* dentadura *sg* (postiza).

deny [dɪ'naɪ] *vt* (*gen*) negar; (*charge*) rechazar; (*report*) desmentir; **to ~ o.s.** privarse de).

deodorant [di:'əudərənt] *n* desodorante *m*.

depart [dɪ'pɑ:t] *vi* irse, marcharse; (*train*) salir; **to ~ from** (*fig*: *differ from*) apartarse de.

department [dɪ'pɑ:tmənt] *n* (*COMM*) sección *f*; (*SCOL*) ramo; (*POL*) ministerio; **~ store** *n* gran almacén *m*.

departure [dɪ'pɑ:tʃə*] *n* partida, ida; (*of train*) salida; **a new ~** un nuevo rumbo.

depend [dɪ'pɛnd] *vi*: **to ~ on** depender de; (*rely on*) contar con; **it ~s** ¡depende!, ¡según!; **~able** *a* (*person*) formal, serio; **~ence** *n* dependencia; **~ant, ~ent** *n* dependiente *m/f*.

depict [dɪ'pɪkt] *vt* (*in picture*) pintar; (*describe*) representar.

depleted [dɪ'pli:tɪd] *a* reducido.

deplorable [dɪ'plɔ:rəbl] *a* lamentable, deplorable; **deplore** [dɪ'plɔ:*] *vt* lamentar, deplorar.

deploy [dɪ'plɔɪ] *vt* desplegar.

depopulation ['di:pɔpju'leɪʃən] *n* despoblación *f*.

deport [dɪ'pɔ:t] *vt* deportar; **~ation** [-'teɪʃən] *n* deportación *f*; **~ment** *n* comportamiento.

depose [dɪ'pəuz] *vt* deponer.

deposit [dɪ'pɔzɪt] *n* (*gen*) depósito; (*CHEM*) sedimento; (*of ore, oil*) yacimiento // *vt* (*gen*) depositar; ~ **account** *n* cuenta de ahorros; ~**or** *n* cuentacorrentista *m/f.*

depot ['dɛpəu] *n* (*storehouse*) depósito; (*for vehicles*) parque *m*.

depraved [dɪ'preɪvd] *a* depravado, vicioso; **depravity** [-'prævɪtɪ] *n* depravación *f*, vicio.

depreciate [dɪ'priːʃɪeɪt] *vi* depreciarse, perder valor; **depreciation** [-'eɪʃən] *n* depreciación *f.*

depress [dɪ'prɛs] *vt* deprimir; (*press down*) presionar; ~**ed** *a* deprimido; ~**ing** *a* deprimente; ~**ion** [dɪ'prɛʃən] *n* depresión *f.*

deprivation [dɛprɪ'veɪʃən] *n* privación *f*; (*loss*) pérdida.

deprive [dɪ'praɪv] *vt*: to ~ sb of privar a alguien de; ~**d** *a* pobre.

depth [dɛpθ] *n* (*gen*) profundidad *f*; (*of room etc*) fondo; **in the** ~**s of** en lo más hondo de.

deputation [dɛpju'teɪʃən] *n* delegación *f.*

deputize ['dɛpjutaɪz] *vi*: to ~ **for sb** sustituir por uno.

deputy ['dɛpjutɪ] *a*: ~ **head** subdirector/a *m/f* // *n* sustituto/a, suplente *m*; (*POL*) diputado; (*agent*) representante *m*.

derail [dɪ'reɪl] *vt*: to **be** ~**ed** descarrilarse; ~**ment** *n* descarrilamiento.

deranged [dɪ'reɪndʒd] *a* (*person*) vuelto loco, trastornado (mentalmente).

derelict ['dɛrɪlɪkt] *a* abandonado.

deride [dɪ'raɪd] *vt* ridiculizar, mofarse de; **derision** [-'rɪʒən] *n* irrisión *f*, mofas *fpl.*

derivative [dɪ'rɪvətɪv] *n* derivado // *a* derivado; (*work*) poco original.

derive [dɪ'raɪv] *vt* derivar // *vi*: to ~ **from** derivarse de.

dermatitis [dəːmə'taɪtɪs] *n* dermatitis *f*; **dermatology** [-'tɒlədʒɪ] *n* dermatología *f.*

derogatory [dɪ'rɒɡətərɪ] *a* despectivo.

derrick ['dɛrɪk] *n* torre *f* de perforación.

descend [dɪ'sɛnd] *vt*, *vi* descender, bajar; to ~ **from** descender de; ~**ant** *n* descendiente *m/f.*

descent [dɪ'sɛnt] *n* descenso; (*GEO*) pendiente *m*, declive *m*; (*origin*) descendencia.

describe [dɪs'kraɪb] *vt* describir; **description** [-'krɪpʃən] *n* descripción *f*; (*sort*) clase *f*, género; **descriptive** [-'krɪptɪv] *a* descriptivo.

desecrate ['dɛsɪkreɪt] *vt* profanar.

desert ['dɛzət] *n* desierto // (*vb*: [dɪ'zəːt]) *vt* abandonar, desamparar // *vi* (*MIL*) desertar; ~**er** *n* desertor *m*; ~**ion** [dɪ'zəːʃən] *n* deserción *f.*

deserve [dɪ'zəːv] *vt* merecer, ser digno de; **deserving** *a* (*person*) digno; (*action, cause*) meritorio.

design [dɪ'zaɪn] *n* (*sketch*) bosquejo; (*layout, shape*) diseño; (*pattern*) dibujo; (*intention*) propósito, intención *f* // *vt* (*gen*) diseñar; (*plan*) proyectar.

designate ['dɛzɪɡneɪt] *vt* (*point to*) señalar; (*appoint*) nombrar; (*destine*)

designar // *a* ['dɛzɪɡnɪt] designado; **designation** [-'neɪʃən] *n* (*appointment*) nombramiento; (*name*) denominación *f.*

designer [dɪ'zaɪnə*] *n* (*ART*) dibujante *m*; (*TECH*) diseñador *m*; (*fashion* ~) modista *m/f.*

desirable [dɪ'zaɪərəbl] *a* (*proper*) deseable; (*attractive*) atractivo.

desire [dɪ'zaɪə*] *n* deseo // *vt* desear.

desk [dɛsk] *n* (*in office*) escritorio; (*for pupil*) pupitre *m*; (*in hotel, at airport*) recepción *f.*

desolate ['dɛsəlɪt] *a* (*place*) desierto; (*person*) afligido; **desolation** [-'leɪʃən] *n* (*of place*) desolación *f*; (*of person*) aflicción *f.*

despair [dɪs'pɛə*] *n* desesperación *f* // *vi*: to ~ **of** desesperarse de.

despatch [dɪs'pætʃ] *n*, *vt* = **dispatch.**

desperate ['dɛspərɪt] *a* desesperado; (*fugitive*) peligroso; ~**ly** *ad* desesperadamente; (*very*) terriblemente, gravemente.

desperation [dɛspə'reɪʃən] *n* desesperación *f*; **in** ~ desesperado.

despicable [dɪs'pɪkəbl] *a* vil, despreciable.

despise [dɪs'paɪz] *vt* despreciar.

despite [dɪs'paɪt] *prep* a pesar de, pese a.

despondent [dɪs'pɒndənt] *a* deprimido, abatido.

dessert [dɪ'zəːt] *n* postre *m*; ~**spoon** *n* cuchara (de postre).

destination [dɛstɪ'neɪʃən] *n* destino.

destiny ['dɛstɪnɪ] *n* destino.

destitute ['dɛstɪtjuːt] *a* desamparado, indigente.

destroy [dɪs'trɔɪ] *vt* (*gen*) destruir; (*finish*) acabar con; ~**er** *n* (*NAUT*) destructor *m.*

destruction [dɪs'trʌkʃən] *n* destrucción *f*; (*fig*) ruina; **destructive** [-tɪv] *a* destructivo, destructor(a).

detach [dɪ'tætʃ] *vt* separar; (*unstick*) despegar; ~**able** *a* separable; (*TECH*) desmontable; ~**ed** *a* (*attitude*) objetivo, imparcial; (*house*) independiente, solo; ~**ment** *n* (*gen*) separación *f*; (*MIL*) destacamento; (*fig*) objetividad *f*, imparcialidad *f.*

detail ['diːteɪl] *n* detalle *m* // *vt* (*gen*) detallar; (*MIL*) destacar; **in** ~ en detalle; ~**ed** *a* detallado.

detain [dɪ'teɪn] *vt* retener; (*in captivity*) detener.

detect [dɪ'tɛkt] *vt* (*gen*) descubrir; (*MED, POLICE*) identificar; (*MIL, RADAR, TECH*) detectar; ~**ion** [dɪ'tɛkʃən] *n* descubrimiento; identificación *f*; ~**ive** *n* detective *m*; ~**ive story** *n* novela policíaca; ~**or** *n* detector *m.*

détente [deɪ'tɑːnt] *n* detente *f.*

detention [dɪ'tɛnʃən] *n* detención *f*, arresto.

deter [dɪ'təː*] *vt* (*discourage*) desalentar; (*dissuade*) disuadir; (*prevent*) impedir.

detergent [dɪ'təːdʒənt] *n* detergente.

deteriorate [dɪ'tɪərɪəreɪt] *vi* deteriorarse; **deterioration** [-'reɪʃən] *n* deterioro.

determination [dɪtəːmɪ'neɪʃən] *n* (*gen*)

determinación f; (*resolve*) resolución f.

determine [dɪˈtɜːmɪn] vt (*gen*) determinar; (*limits etc*) definir; (*dispute*) resolver; ~**d** a (*person*) resuelto.

deterrent [dɪˈtɛrənt] n fuerza de disuasión.

detest [dɪˈtɛst] vt aborrecer; ~**able** a aborrecible.

detonate [ˈdɛtəneɪt] vi estallar // vt hacer detonar; **detonator** n detonador m, fulminante m.

detour [ˈdiːtuə*] n rodeo.

detract [dɪˈtrækt] vt: **to** ~ **from** quitar mérito a, desvirtuar.

detriment [ˈdɛtrɪmənt] n: **to the** ~ **of** en perjuicio de; ~**al** [dɛtrɪˈmɛntl] a perjudicial (*to* a).

devaluation [diːvæljuˈeɪʃən] n devaluación f; **devalue** [-ˈvæljuː] vt devaluar.

devastate [ˈdɛvəsteɪt] vt devastar; **he was** ~**d by the news** las noticias le dejaron desolado; **devastating** a devastador(a); (*fig*) arrollador(a).

develop [dɪˈvɛləp] vt (*gen*) desarrollar; (*PHOT*) revelar; (*disease*) coger; (*engine trouble*) empezar a tener // vi desarrollarse; (*advance*) progresar; (*appear*) aparecer; ~**ing country país m** en desarrollo; ~**ment** n desarrollo; (*advance*) progreso; (*of affair, case*) desenvolvimiento; (*of land*) urbanización f.

deviate [ˈdiːvɪeɪt] vi desviarse; **deviation** [-ˈeɪʃən] n desviación f.

device [dɪˈvaɪs] n (*scheme*) estratagema f, recurso; (*apparatus*) aparato, mecanismo.

devil [ˈdɛvl] n diablo, demonio; ~**ish** a diabólico.

devious [ˈdiːvɪəs] a intricado, enrevesado; (*person*) taimado.

devise [dɪˈvaɪz] vt idear, inventar.

devoid [dɪˈvɔɪd] a: ~ **of** desprovisto de.

devote [dɪˈvəut] vt: **to** ~ **sth to** dedicar algo a; ~**d** a (*loyal*) leal, fiel; **the book is** ~**d to** el libro trata de la política; **devotee** [dɛvəuˈtiː] n devoto/a.

devotion [dɪˈvəuʃən] n dedicación f; (*REL*) devoción f.

devour [dɪˈvauə*] vt devorar.

devout [dɪˈvaut] a devoto.

dew [djuː] n rocío.

dexterity [dɛksˈtɛrɪtɪ] n destreza.

diabetes [daɪəˈbiːtiːz] n diabetes f; **diabetic** [-ˈbɛtɪk] a, n diabético/a.

diagnose [daɪəgˈnəuz] vt diagnosticar; **diagnosis** [-ˈnəusɪs], pl **-ses** [-ˈnəusiːz] n diagnóstico.

diagonal [daɪˈægənl] a diagonal // n diagonal f.

diagram [ˈdaɪəgræm] n diagrama m, esquema m.

dial [ˈdaɪəl] n esfera, cuadrante m // vt (*number*) marcar; ~**ling tone** n tono de marcar.

dialect [ˈdaɪəlɛkt] n dialecto.

dialogue [ˈdaɪəlɔg] n diálogo.

diameter [daɪˈæmɪtə*] n diámetro.

diamond [ˈdaɪəmənd] n diamante m; ~**s** npl (*CARDS*) oros mpl.

diaper [ˈdaɪəpə*] n (*US*) pañal m.

diaphragm [ˈdaɪəfræm] n diafragma m.

diarrhoea, diarrhea (*US*) [daɪəˈriːə] n diarrea.

diary [ˈdaɪərɪ] n (*daily account*) diario; (*book*) agenda m.

dice [daɪs] n, pl inv dados mpl // vt (*CULIN*) cortar en cuadritos.

dictate [dɪkˈteɪt] vt dictar; ~**s** [ˈdɪkteɪts] npl dictados mpl; **dictation** [-ˈteɪʃən] n dictado.

dictator [dɪkˈteɪtə*] n dictador m; ~**ship** n dictadura.

diction [ˈdɪkʃən] n dicción f.

dictionary [ˈdɪkʃənrɪ] n diccionario.

did [dɪd] pt of **do**.

die [daɪ] vi morir; **to** ~ **away** vi (*sound, light*) extinguirse lentamente; **to** ~ **down** vi (*gen*) apagarse; (*wind*) amainar; **to** ~ **out** vi desaparecer, extinguirse.

diesel [ˈdiːzəl]: ~ **engine** n motor m Diesel; ~ **(oil)** n gas-oil m.

diet [ˈdaɪət] n dieta; (*restricted food*) régimen m // vi (*also*: **be on a** ~) estar a dieta, hacer régimen.

differ [ˈdɪfə*] vi (*be different*) ser distinto, diferenciarse; (*disagree*) discrepar; ~**ence** n diferencia; (*quarrel*) desacuerdo; ~**ent** a diferente, distinto; ~**entiate** [-ˈrɛnʃɪeɪt] vt distinguir // vi diferenciarse; **to** ~**entiate between** distinguir entre; ~**ently** ad de otro modo, en forma distinta.

difficult [ˈdɪfɪkəlt] a difícil; ~**y** n dificultad f.

diffidence [ˈdɪfɪdəns] n timidez f; **diffident** [-ənt] a tímido.

diffuse [dɪˈfjuːs] a difuso // vt [dɪˈfjuːz] difundir.

dig [dɪg] pt, pp **dug** vt (*hole*) cavar; (*garden*) cultivar; (*coal*) extraer; (*nails etc*) hincar // n (*prod*) empujón m; (*archaeological*) excavación f; (*remark*) indirecta; **to** ~ **in** vi atrincherarse; **to** ~ **into** vt (*savings*) consumir; **to** ~ **out** vt (*hole*) excavar; (*fig*) sacar; **to** ~ **up** vt desenterrar; (*plant*) desarraigar.

digest [daɪˈdʒɛst] vt (*food*) digerir; (*facts*) asimilar // n [ˈdaɪdʒɛst] resumen m; ~**ion** [dɪˈdʒɛstʃən] n digestión f.

digital [ˈdɪdʒɪtəl] a digital.

dignified [ˈdɪgnɪfaɪd] a grave, solemne; (*action*) decoroso.

dignity [ˈdɪgnɪtɪ] n dignidad f.

digress [daɪˈgrɛs] vi: **to** ~ **from** apartarse de; ~**ion** [daɪˈgrɛʃən] n digresión f.

digs [dɪgz] npl (*Brit: col*) pensión f, alojamiento.

dilapidated [dɪˈlæpɪdeɪtɪd] a desmoronado, ruinoso.

dilate [daɪˈleɪt] vt dilatar // vi dilatarse.

dilemma [daɪˈlɛmə] n dilema m.

diligent [ˈdɪlɪdʒənt] a diligente.

dilute [daɪˈluːt] vt diluir // a diluido.

dim [dɪm] a (*light*) débil; (*sight*) turbio; (*outline*) indistinto; (*stupid*) lerdo; (*room*) oscuro // vt (*light*) bajar; (*AUT*) poner a media luz.

dime [daɪm] n (*us*) moneda de diez centavos.

dimension [dɪ'mɛnʃən] n dimensión f.

diminish [dɪ'mɪnɪʃ] vi disminuirse.

diminutive [dɪ'mɪnjutɪv] a diminuto // n (*LING*) diminutivo.

dimly ['dɪmlɪ] ad débilmente; (*not clearly*) indistintamente.

dimple ['dɪmpl] n hoyuelo.

din [dɪn] n estruendo, estrépito.

dine [daɪn] vi cenar; **diner** n (*person*) comensal m/f; (*RAIL*) = dining car.

dinghy ['dɪŋgɪ] n bote m; **rubber ~** lancha (neumática).

dingy ['dɪndʒɪ] a (*room*) sombrío; (*dirty*) sucio; (*dull*) deslucido.

dining ['daɪnɪŋ] ~ **car** n coche-comedor m; ~ **room** n comedor m.

dinner ['dɪnə*] n (*evening meal*) cena; (*lunch*) comida; (*public*) cena, banquete m; ~ **jacket** n smoking m; ~ **party** n cena; ~ **time** n hora de cenar o comer.

diocese ['daɪəsɪs] n diócesis f.

dip [dɪp] n (*slope*) pendiente m; (*in sea*) baño // vt (*in water*) mojar; (*ladle etc*) meter; (*AUT: lights*) poner a media luz // vi inclinarse hacia abajo.

diphtheria [dɪf'θɪərɪə] n difteria.

diploma [dɪ'pləumə] n diploma m.

diplomacy [dɪ'pləuməsɪ] n diplomacia; **diplomat** ['dɪpləmæt] n diplomático; **diplomatic** [dɪplə'mætɪk] a diplomático.

dipstick ['dɪpstɪk] n (*AUT*) varilla graduada, indicador m de nivel (del aceite).

dire [daɪə*] a calamitoso.

direct [daɪ'rɛkt] a (*gen*) directo // vt dirigir; **can you ~ me to...?** ¿puede indicarme dónde está...?

direction [dɪ'rɛkʃən] n dirección f; ~**s** npl (*advice*) órdenes fpl, instrucciones fpl; ~**s for use** modo de empleo.

directly [dɪ'rɛktlɪ] ad (*in straight line*) directamente; (*at once*) en seguida.

director [dɪ'rɛktə*] n director m; **managing ~** director gerente.

directory [dɪ'rɛktərɪ] n (*TEL*) guía (telefónica).

dirt [dɜːt] n suciedad f; ~**-cheap** a tirado, muy barato; ~**y** a sucio; (*joke*) verde // vt ensuciar; (*stain*) manchar; ~**y trick** n juego sucio.

disability [dɪsə'bɪlɪtɪ] n incapacidad f; **disabled** [dɪs'eɪbld] a disminuido, minusválido.

disadvantage [dɪsəd'vɑːntɪdʒ] n desventaja, inconveniente m.

disagree [dɪsə'griː] vi (*differ*) discrepar; (*be against, think otherwise*): **to ~ (with)** no estar de acuerdo (con); ~**able** a desagradable; ~**ment** n (*gen*) desacuerdo; (*quarrel*) riña.

disallow ['dɪsə'lau] vt (*goal*) anular.

disappear [dɪsə'pɪə*] vi desaparecer; ~**ance** n desaparición f.

disappoint [dɪsə'pɔɪnt] vt decepcionar; (*hopes*) defraudar; ~**ing** a decepcionante; ~**ment** n decepción f.

disapproval [dɪsə'pruːvəl] n desaprobación f.

disapprove [dɪsə'pruːv] vi: **to ~ of** desaprobar.

disarm [dɪs'ɑːm] vt desarmar; ~**ament** n desarme m; ~**ing** a encantador(a).

disaster [dɪ'zɑːstə*] n desastre m; **disastrous** a desastroso.

disband [dɪs'bænd] vt disolver // vi desbandarse.

disbelief [dɪsbə'liːf] n incredulidad f.

disc [dɪsk] n disco.

discard [dɪs'kɑːd] vt (*old things*) tirar; (*fig*) descartar.

discern [dɪ'sɜːn] vt percibir, discernir; ~**ing** a perspicaz.

discharge [dɪs'tʃɑːdʒ] vt (*duties*) cumplir, desempeñar; (*ship etc*) descargar; (*patient*) dar de alta; (*employee*) despedir; (*soldier*) licenciar; (*defendant*) poner en libertad // n ['dɪstʃɑːdʒ] (*ELEC*) descarga; (*dismissal*) despedida; (*of duty*) desempeño; (*of debt*) pago, descargo.

disciple [dɪ'saɪpl] n discípulo.

discipline ['dɪsɪplɪn] n disciplina // vt disciplinar.

disclaim [dɪs'kleɪm] vt negar.

disclose [dɪs'kləuz] vt revelar; **disclosure** [-'kləuʒə*] n revelación f.

disco ['dɪskəu] n abbr of **discothèque**.

discoloured [dɪs'kʌləd] a descolorado.

discomfort [dɪs'kʌmfət] n incomodidad f; (*unease*) inquietud f; (*physical*) malestar m.

disconcert [dɪskən'sɜːt] vt desconcertar.

disconnect [dɪskə'nɛkt] vt (*gen*) separar; (*ELEC etc*) desconectar.

discontent [dɪskən'tɛnt] n descontento; ~**ed** a descontento.

discontinue [dɪskən'tɪnjuː] vt interrumpir; (*payments*) suspender.

discord ['dɪskɔːd] n discordia; (*MUS*) disonancia; ~**ant** [dɪs'kɔːdənt] a disonante.

discothèque ['dɪskəutɛk] n discoteca.

discount ['dɪskaunt] n descuento // vt [dɪs'kaunt] descontar.

discourage [dɪs'kʌrɪdʒ] vt desalentar; (*oppose*) oponerse a; **discouraging** a desalentador(a).

discourteous [dɪs'kɜːtɪəs] a descortés.

discover [dɪs'kʌvə*] vt descubrir; ~**y** n descubrimiento.

discredit [dɪs'krɛdɪt] vt desacreditar.

discreet [dɪs'kriːt] a (*tactful*) discreto; (*careful*) circunspecto, prudente; ~**ly** ad discretamente.

discrepancy [dɪ'skrɛpənsɪ] n (*difference*) diferencia; (*disagreement*) discrepancia.

discretion [dɪ'skrɛʃən] n (*tact*) discreción f; (*care*) prudencia, circunspección f.

discriminate [dɪ'skrɪmɪneɪt] *vi*: to ~ between distinguir entre; to ~ against discriminar contra; **discriminating** *a* perspicaz; **discrimination** [-'neɪʃən] *n* (*discernment*) perspicacia; (*bias*) discriminación *f*.

discuss [dɪ'skʌs] *vt* (*gen*) discutir; (*a theme*) tratar; ~ion [dɪ'skʌʃən] *n* discusión *f*.

disdain [dɪs'deɪn] *n* desdén *m* // *vt* desdeñar.

disease [dɪ'zi:z] *n* enfermedad *f*.

disembark [dɪsɪm'bɑːk] *vt*, *vi* desembarcar.

disengage [dɪsɪn'geɪdʒ] *vt* soltar; (*clutch*) desembragar.

disentangle [dɪsɪn'tæŋgl] *vt* desenredar.

disfigure [dɪs'fɪgə*] *vt* desfigurar.

disgrace [dɪs'greɪs] *n* ignominia; (*downfall*) caída; (*shame*) vergüenza, escándalo // *vt* deshonrar; ~ful *a* vergonzoso; (*behaviour*) escandaloso.

disgruntled [dɪs'grʌntld] *a* disgustado, malhumorado.

disguise [dɪs'gaɪz] *n* disfraz *m* // *vt* disfrazar; in ~ disfrazado.

disgust [dɪs'gʌst] *n* repugnancia // *vt* repugnar, dar asco a; ~ing *a* repugnante, asqueroso.

dish [dɪʃ] *n* (*gen*) plato; to do *or* wash the ~es fregar los platos; to ~ up *vt* servir; to ~ out *vt* repartir; ~cloth *n* paño de cocina, bayeta.

dishearten [dɪs'hɑːtn] *vt* desalentar.

dishevelled [dɪ'ʃevəld] *a* despeinado, desmelenado.

dishonest [dɪs'ɒnɪst] *a* (*person*) poco honrado, tramposo; (*means*) fraudulento; ~y *n* falta de honradez.

dishonour [dɪs'ɒnə*] *n* deshonra; ~able *a* deshonroso.

dishwasher ['dɪʃwɒʃə*] *n* lavaplatos *m inv*; (*person*) friegaplatos *m/f inv*.

disillusion [dɪsɪ'luːʒən] *vt* desilusionar.

disinfect [dɪsɪn'fekt] *vt* desinfectar; ~ant *n* desinfectante *m*.

disintegrate [dɪs'ɪntɪgreɪt] *vi* disgregarse, desintegrarse.

disinterested [dɪs'ɪntrəstɪd] *a* desinteresado.

disjointed [dɪs'dʒɔɪntɪd] *a* inconexo.

disk [dɪsk] *n* = **disc**.

dislike [dɪs'laɪk] *n* antipatía, aversión *f* // *vt* tener antipatía a.

dislocate ['dɪsləkeɪt] *vt* dislocar.

dislodge [dɪs'lɒdʒ] *vt* sacar; (*enemy*) desalojar.

disloyal [dɪs'lɔɪəl] *a* desleal.

dismal ['dɪzml] *a* (*dark*) sombrío; (*depressing*) triste; (*depressed*) abatido; (*very bad*) fatal.

dismantle [dɪs'mæntl] *vt* desmontar, desarmar.

dismay [dɪs'meɪ] *n* consternación *f* // *vt* consternar.

dismiss [dɪs'mɪs] *vt* (*worker*) despedir; (*official*) destituir; (*idea*, *LAW*) rechazar; (*possibility*) descartar // *vi* (*MIL*) romper filas; ~al *n* despedida; destitución *f*.

dismount [dɪs'maunt] *vi* apearse.

disobedience [dɪsə'biːdɪəns] *n* desobediencia; **disobedient** [-ənt] *a* desobediente.

disobey [dɪsə'beɪ] *vt* desobedecer.

disorder [dɪs'ɔːdə*] *n* desorden *m*; (*rioting*) disturbio; (*MED*) trastorno; (*disease*) enfermedad *f*; ~ly *a* (*untidy*) desordenado; (*meeting*) alborotado; (*conduct*) escandaloso.

disorganized [dɪs'ɔːgənaɪzd] *a* desorganizado.

disorientated [dɪs'ɔːrɪenteɪtəd] *a* desorientado.

disown [dɪs'əun] *vt* desconocer.

disparaging [dɪs'pærɪdʒɪŋ] *a* despreciativo.

disparity [dɪs'pærɪtɪ] *n* disparidad *f*.

dispatch [dɪs'pætʃ] *vt* enviar; (*kill*) despachar // *n* (*sending*) envío; (*speed*) prontitud *f*; (*PRESS*) informe *m*; (*MIL*) parte *m*.

dispel [dɪs'pel] *vt* disipar, dispersar.

dispensary [dɪs'pensərɪ] *n* dispensario, farmacia.

dispense [dɪs'pens] *vt* dispensar, repartir; to ~ with *vt fus* prescindir de; **dispenser** *n* (*container*) distribuidor *m* automático; **dispensing chemist** *n* farmacéutico.

dispersal [dɪs'pɔːsl] *n* dispersión *f*; **disperse** [-'pɔːs] *vt* dispersar // *vi* dispersarse.

displace [dɪs'pleɪs] *vt* (*shift*) sacar de su sitio; ~d person *n* (*POL*) desplazado/a; ~ment *n* cambio de sitio.

display [dɪs'pleɪ] *n* (*exhibition*) exposición *f*; (*MIL*) alarde *m*; (*of feeling*) manifestación *f*; (*pej*) aparato, pompa // *vt* exponer; manifestar; (*ostentatiously*) lucir.

displease [dɪs'pliːz] *vt* (*offend*) ofender; (*annoy*) enojar, enfadar; (*be unpleasant to*) desagradar; ~d with disgustado con; **displeasure** [-'pleʒə*] *n* disgusto.

disposable [dɪs'pəuzəbl] *a* para (usar y) tirar.

disposal [dɪs'pəuzl] *n* (*sale*) venta; (*of house*) traspaso; (*arrangement*) colocación *f*; (*of rubbish*) destrucción *f*; at one's ~ a disposición de uno.

dispose [dɪs'pəuz] *vt*: to ~ of (*time*, *money*) disponer de; (*unwanted goods*) deshacerse de; (*throw away*) tirar; ~d *a*: ~d to do dispuesto a hacer; **disposition** [-'zɪʃən] *n* disposición *f*.

disproportionate [dɪsprə'pɔːʃənət] *a* desproporcionado.

disprove [dɪs'pruːv] *vt* refutar.

dispute [dɪs'pjuːt] *n* disputa; (*verbal*) discusión *f*; (*also*: industrial ~) conflicto (laboral) // *vt* (*argue*) disputar; (*question*) cuestionar.

disqualification [dɪskwɒlɪfɪ'keɪʃən] *n*

inhabilitación *f*; (*SPORT, from driving*) descalificación *f*.

disqualify [dɪs'kwɔlɪfaɪ] *vt* (*SPORT*) descalificar; **to ~ sb for sth/from doing sth** inhabilitar a alguien para algo/hacer algo.

disregard [dɪsrɪ'gɑːd] *vt* desatender; (*ignore*) no hacer caso de.

disrepair [dɪsrɪ'pɛə°] *n*: **to fall into ~** desmoronarse.

disreputable [dɪs'rɛpjutəbl] *a* (*person*) de mala fama; (*behaviour*) vergonzoso.

disrespectful [dɪsrɪ'spɛktful] *a* irrespetuoso.

disrupt [dɪs'rʌpt] *vt* (*plans*) desbaratar; (*conversation*) interrumpir; **~ion** [-'rʌpʃən] *n* trastorno; desbaratamiento; interrupción *f*.

dissatisfaction [dɪssætɪs'fækʃən] *n* disgusto, descontento; **dissatisfied** [-'sætɪsfaɪd] *a* insatisfecho.

dissect [dɪ'sɛkt] *vt* disecar.

dissent [dɪ'sɛnt] *n* disensión *f*.

disservice [dɪs'sɜːvɪs] *n*: **to do sb a ~** perjudicar a alguien.

dissident ['dɪsɪdnt] *a*, *n* disidente *m/f*.

dissipate ['dɪsɪpeɪt] *vt* disipar; (*waste*) desperdiciar.

dissociate [dɪ'səuʃɪeɪt] *vt* disociar.

dissolute ['dɪsəluːt] *a* disoluto.

dissolve [dɪ'zɔlv] *vt* disolver // *vi* disolverse.

dissuade [dɪ'sweɪd] *vt*: **to ~ sb (from)** disuadir a alguien (de).

distance ['dɪstns] *n* distancia; **in the ~** a lo lejos.

distant ['dɪstnt] *a* lejano; (*manner*) reservado, frío.

distaste [dɪs'teɪst] *n* repugnancia; **~ful** *a* repugnante, desagradable.

distil [dɪs'tɪl] *vt* destilar; **~lery** *n* destilería.

distinct [dɪs'tɪŋkt] *a* (*different*) distinto; (*clear*) claro; (*unmistakeable*) inequívoco; **as ~ from** a diferencia de; **~ion** [dɪs-'tɪŋkʃən] *n* distinción *f*; (*in exam*) sobresaliente *m*; **~ive** *a* distintivo; **~ly** *ad* claramente.

distinguish [dɪs'tɪŋgwɪʃ] *vt* distinguir; **~ed** *a* (*eminent*) distinguido; **~ing** *a* (*feature*) distintivo.

distort [dɪs'tɔːt] *vt* torcer, retorcer; **~ion** [dɪs'tɔːʃən] *n* deformación *f*; (*of sound*) distorsión *f*.

distract [dɪs'trækt] *vt* distraer; (*attention*) apartar; (*bewilder*) aturdir; **~ed** *a* distraído; **~ion** [dɪs'trækʃən] *n* distracción *f*; (*confusion*) aturdimiento; (*amusement*) diversión *f*.

distraught [dɪs'trɔːt] *a* turbado, enloquecido.

distress [dɪs'trɛs] *n* (*anguish*) angustia; (*misfortune*) desgracia; (*want*) miseria; (*pain*) dolor *m*; (*danger*) peligro // *vt* (*cause anguish*) apenar, afligir; (*pain*) doler; **~ing** *a* doloroso; **~ signal** *n* señal *f* de socorro.

distribute [dɪs'trɪbjuːt] *vt* (*gen*) distribuir; (*share out*) repartir; **distribution** [-'bjuːʃən] *n* distribución *f*; **distributor** *n* (*AUT*) distribuidor *m*; (*COMM*) distribuidora.

district ['dɪstrɪkt] *n* (*of country*) zona, región *f*; (*of town*) barrio; (*ADMIN*) distrito; **~ attorney** *n* (*US*) fiscal *m/f*; **~ nurse** *n* (*Brit*) enfermera que asiste a domicilio.

distrust [dɪs'trʌst] *n* desconfianza // *vt* desconfiar de.

disturb [dɪs'tɜːb] *vt* (*gen*) perturbar; (*bother*) molestar; (*interrupt*) interrumpir; (*upset*) trastornar; (*disorganize*) desordenar; **~ance** *n* (*gen*) perturbación *f*; (*political etc*) disturbio; (*violence*) alboroto; (*of mind*) trastorno; **~ing** *a* inquietante, perturbador(a).

disuse [dɪs'juːs] *n*: **to fall into ~** caer en desuso.

disused [dɪs'juːzd] *a* abandonado.

ditch [dɪtʃ] *n* zanja; (*irrigation ~*) acequia // *vt* (*col*) deshacerse de.

dither ['dɪðə°] *vi* vacilar.

ditto ['dɪtəu] *ad* ídem, lo mismo.

divan [dɪ'væn] *n* diván *m*.

dive [daɪv] *n* (*from board*) salto; (*underwater*) buceo; (*of submarine*) sumersión *f*; (*AVIAT*) picada // *vi* saltar; bucear; sumergirse; picar; **diver** *n* (*SPORT*) saltador/a *m/f*; (*underwater*) buzo.

diverge [daɪ'vɜːdʒ] *vi* divergir.

diverse [daɪ'vɜːs] *a* diversos(as), varios(as).

diversify [daɪ'vɜːsɪfaɪ] *vt* diversificar.

diversion [daɪ'vɜːʃən] *n* (*AUT*) desviación *f*; (*distraction, MIL*) diversión *f*.

diversity [daɪ'vɜːsɪtɪ] *n* diversidad *f*.

divert [daɪ'vɜːt] *vt* (*turn aside*) desviar; (*amuse*) divertir.

divest [daɪ'vɛst] *vt*: **to ~ sb of sth** despojar a alguien de algo.

divide [dɪ'vaɪd] *vt* dividir; (*separate*) separar // *vi* dividirse; (*road*) bifurcarse.

dividend ['dɪvɪdɛnd] *n* dividendo; (*fig*) beneficio.

divine [dɪ'vaɪn] *a* divino.

diving ['daɪvɪŋ] *n* (*SPORT*) salto; (*underwater*) buceo; **~ board** *n* trampolín *m*; **~ suit** *n* escafandra.

divinity [dɪ'vɪnɪtɪ] *n* divinidad *f*; (*SCOL*) teología.

division [dɪ'vɪʒən] *n* división *f*; (*sharing out*) repartimiento; (*disagreement*) discordia; (*POL*) votación *f*.

divorce [dɪ'vɔːs] *n* divorcio // *vt* divorciarse de; **~d** *a* divorciado; **divorcee** [-'siː] *n* divorciado/a.

divulge [daɪ'vʌldʒ] *vt* divulgar, revelar.

D.I.Y. *a*, *n abbr of* **do-it-yourself.**

dizziness ['dɪzɪnɪs] *n* vértigo.

dizzy ['dɪzɪ] *a* (*person*) mareado; (*height*) vertiginoso; **to feel ~** marearse, estar mareado.

DJ *n abbr of* **disc jockey.**

do [duː], *pt* **did**, *pp* **done** *vt*, *vi* (*gen*) hacer; (*speed*) ir a; (*THEATRE*) representar // *n* (col) fiesta; **he didn't laugh no se rió; she swims better than I** ~ nada mejor que yo; **he laughed, didn't he?** se rió ¿no?; **that will** ~! ¡basta!; **to make** ~ **with** contentarse con; ~ **you agree?** ¿está Usted de acuerdo?; **to** ~ **one's hair** (comb) peinarse; (style) arreglarse el pelo; **will it** ~? ¿sirve?, ¿conviene?; **to** ~ **well** prosperar, tener éxito; **to** ~ **without sth** prescindir de algo; **to** ~ **away with** vt fus (kill) exterminar; (suppress) suprimir; **to** ~ **up** vt (laces) liar, atar; (room) renovar.

docile ['dəusaıl] a dócil.

dock [dɔk] n (NAUT) muelle m; (LAW) banquillo (de los acusados); ~**s** npl muelles mpl, puerto // vi (arrive) llegar; (enter ~) atracar el muelle; (pay etc) rebajar; ~**er** n trabajador m portuario, estibador m; ~**yard** n astillero.

doctor ['dɔktə°] n médico; (Ph.D. etc) doctor/a m/f // vt (fig) arreglar, falsificar; (drink etc) adulterar.

doctrine ['dɔktrın] n doctrina.

document ['dɔkjumənt] n documento; ~**ary** [-'mentərı] a documental // n documental m; ~**ation** [-'teıʃən] n documentación f.

dodge [dɔdʒ] n (of body) regate m; (fig) truco // vt (gen) evadir; (blow) esquivar.

dodgems ['dɔdʒəmz] npl coches mpl de choque.

dog [dɔg] n perro // vt seguir los pasos de; ~ **biscuits** npl galletas fpl de perro; ~ **collar** n collar m de perro; (fig) cuello de cura.

dogged ['dɔgıd] a tenaz, obstinado.

dogma ['dɔgmə] n dogma m; ~**tic** [-'mætık] a dogmático.

doings ['duıŋz] npl (events) sucesos mpl; (acts) hechos mpl.

do-it-yourself [du:ıtjɔː'self] n bricolaje m.

doldrums ['dɔldrəmz] npl: **to be in the** ~ (person) estar abatido; (business) estar encalmado.

dole [dəul] n (Brit) (payment) subsidio de paro; **on the** ~ parado; **to** ~ **out** vt repartir.

doleful ['dəulful] a triste, lúgubre.

doll [dɔl] n muñeca; **to** ~ **o.s. up** ataviarse.

dollar ['dɔlə°] n dólar m.

dolphin ['dɔlfın] n delfín m.

domain [də'meın] n campo, competencia; (empire) dominio.

dome [dəum] n (ARCH) cúpula; (shape) bóveda.

domestic [də'mestık] a (gen) doméstico; (national) nacional; (home-loving) hogareño; (internal: trade) interior; (: strife) interno; ~**ated** a domesticado; (home-loving) casero, hogareño.

dominant ['dɔmınənt] a dominante.

dominate ['dɔmıneıt] vt dominar; **domination** [-'neıʃən] n dominación f.

domineering [dɔmı'nıərıŋ] a dominante.

dominion [də'mınıən] n dominio.

domino ['dɔmınəu], pl ~**es** n ficha de dominó; ~**es** n (game) dominó.

donate [də'neıt] vt donar; **donation** [də'neıʃən] n donativo.

done [dʌn] pp of **do**.

donkey ['dɔŋkı] n burro.

donor ['dəunə°] n donante m/f.

don't [dəunt] = **do not**.

doom [du:m] n (fate) suerte f; (death) muerte f // vt: **to be** ~**ed to failure** ser condenado al fracaso.

door [dɔː°] n puerta; (entry) entrada; **next** ~ en la casa de al lado; ~**bell** n timbre m; ~ **handle** n tirador m; (of car) manija; ~ **knocker** n aldaba; ~**man** n (in hotel) portero; ~**mat** n felpudo, estera; ~**step** n peldaño.

dope [dəup] n (col: person) imbécil m/f // vt (horse etc) drogar.

dopey ['dəupı] a (dizzy) mareado.

dormant ['dɔːmənt] a inactivo; (latent) latente.

dormitory ['dɔːmıtrı] n dormitorio.

dormouse ['dɔːmaus], pl -**mice** [-maıs] n lirón m.

dosage ['dəusıdʒ] n dósis f inv.

dose [dəus] n dósis f inv // vt: **to** ~ **o.s.** medicinarse.

doss house ['dɔss-] n pensión f de mala muerte.

dot [dɔt] n punto; ~**ted with** salpicado de; **on the** ~ en punto.

dote [dəut]: **to** ~ **on** vt fus adorar, idolatrar.

double ['dʌbl] a doble // ad (twice): **to cost** ~ costar el doble // n (gen) doble m // vt doblar; (efforts) redoblar // vi doblarse; **at the** ~, **on the** ~ corriendo; ~**s** n (TENNIS) juego de dobles; ~ **bass** n contrabajo; ~ **bed** n cama matrimonial; ~ **bend** n doble curva; ~**-breasted** a cruzado; ~**-cross** vt (trick) engañar; (betray) traicionar; ~**-decker** n autobús m de dos pisos; ~ **room** n cuarto para dos; **doubly** ad doblemente.

doubt [daut] n duda // vt dudar; (suspect) dudar de; **to** ~ **that** dudar que; **there is no** ~ **that** no cabe duda de que; ~**ful** a dudoso; (person) sospechoso; ~**less** ad sin duda.

dough [dəu] n masa, pasta; ~**nut** n buñuelo.

dove [dʌv] n paloma; ~**tail** vi (fig) encajar.

dowdy ['daudı] a desaliñado; (inelegant) poco elegante.

down [daun] n (fluff) pelusa; (feathers) plumón m, flojel m // ad (~wards) abajo, hacia abajo; (on the ground) por/en tierra // prep abajo // vt (col: drink) beberse; (: food) devorar; **the D~s** zona de colinas del sur de Inglaterra; ~ **with X!** ¡abajo X!; ~**-at-heel** a venido a menos; (appearance) desaliñado; ~**cast** a abatido; ~**fall** n caída, ruina; ~**hearted** a desanimado; ~**hill** ad: **to go** ~**hill** ir cuesta abajo; ~ **payment** n enganche m, pago al contado; **~pour** n aguacero; **~right** a (clear) manifiesto; (out-and-out) terminante, definitivo; **~stairs** ad (below) (en la casa) de abajo; (~wards) escaleras abajo; **~stream** ad aguas o río abajo; **~-to-earth** a práctico; **~town** ad en el centro de la ciudad; **~ward** a, ad, **~wards** ad hacia abajo.

dowry ['daurɪ] n dote f.

doz. abbr of **dozen.**

doze [dəuz] vi dormitar; **to ~ off** vi quedarse medio dormido.

dozen ['dʌzn] n docena.

Dr. abbr of **doctor; drive.**

drab [dræb] a gris, monótono.

draft [drɑ:ft] n (first copy) borrador m; (COMM) giro; (US: call-up) quinta // vt (plan) redactar; (send) mandar; (conscript) quintar; (write roughly) hacer un borrador de; see also **draught.**

drag [dræg] vt arrastrar; (river) dragar, rastrear // vi arrastrarse por el suelo // n (col) lata; **to ~ on** vi ser interminable.

dragonfly ['drægɔnflaɪ] n libélula.

drain [dreɪn] n desaguadero; (in street) sumidero; (source of loss) desagüe m; (loss) pérdida; (on resources) sumidero // vt (land, marshes) desaguar; (MED) drenar; (reservoir) desecar; (fig) agotar // vi escurrirse; **~age** n (act) desagüe m; (MED, AGR) drenaje m; (sewage) alcantarillado; **~ing board, ~board** (US) n escurridera, escurridor m; **~pipe** n tubo de desagüe.

dram [dræm] n (drink) trago.

drama ['drɑ:mə] n (art) teatro; (play) drama m; (~tic [drə'mætɪk] a dramático; **~tist** ['dræmətɪst] n dramaturgo.

drank [dræŋk] pt of **drink.**

drape [dreɪp] vt cubrir; **~s** npl (US) cortinas fpl; **draper** n pañero.

drastic ['dræstɪk] a (measure) severo; (change) radical; (forceful) enérgico.

draught [drɑ:ft] n (of air) corriente f; (drink) trago; (NAUT) calado; **~s** n juego de damas; **on ~** (beer) de barril; **~board** n tablero de damas.

draughtsman ['drɑ:ftsmən] n proyectista m, delineante m.

draw [drɔ:], pt **drew,** pp **drawn** vt (pull) tirar; (take out) sacar; (attract) atraer; (picture) dibujar; (money) retirar // vi (SPORT) empatar // n (SPORT) empate m; (lottery) sorteo; (attraction) atracción f; **to ~ near** vi acercarse; **to ~ out** vi (lengthen) alargar; **to ~ up** vi (stop) pararse // vt (document) redactar; **~back** n inconveniente m, desventaja; **~bridge** n puente m levadizo.

drawer [drɔ:*] n cajón m.

drawing ['drɔ:ɪŋ] n dibujo; **~ board** n tablero (de dibujante); **~ pin** n chinche m; **~ room** n salón m.

drawl [drɔ:l] n habla lenta y cansina.

drawn [drɔ:n] pp of **draw.**

dread [drɛd] n pavor m, terror m // vt temer, tener miedo o pavor a; **~ful** a espantoso.

dream [dri:m] n sueño // vt, vi, pt, pp **dreamed** or **dreamt** [drɛmt] soñar; **~er** n soñador/a m/f; **~y** a (distracted) soñador(a), distraído; (music) de sueño.

dreary ['drɪərɪ] a monótono, aburrido.

dredge [drɛdʒ] vt dragar; **dredger** n (ship) draga; (also: **sugar dredger**) espolvoreador n.

dregs [drɛgz] npl heces fpl.

drench [drɛntʃ] vt empapar; **to get ~ed** mojarse hasta los huesos.

dress [drɛs] n vestido; (clothing) ropa // vt vestir; (wound) vendar; (CULIN) aliñar // vi vestirse; **to ~ up** vi vestirse de etiqueta; (in fancy dress) disfrazarse; **~ circle** n principal m; **~er** n (furniture) aparador m; (: US) cómoda con espejo; **~ing** n (MED) vendaje m; (CULIN) aliño; **~ing gown** n bata; **~ing room** n (THEATRE) camarín m; (SPORT) vestidor m; **~ing table** n tocador m; **~maker** n modista, costurera; **~making** n costura; **~ rehearsal** n ensayo general; **~ shirt** n camisa de frac.

drew [dru:] pt of **draw.**

dribble ['drɪbl] vi gotear, caer gota a gota; (baby) babear // vt (ball) regatear.

dried [draɪd] a (gen) seco; (fruit) paso; (milk) en polvo.

drift [drɪft] n (of current etc) velocidad f; (of sand etc) montón m; (distance off course) deriva; (meaning) significado // vi (boat) ir a la deriva; (sand, snow) amontonarse; **~wood** n madera de deriva.

drill [drɪl] n taladro; (bit) broca; (of dentist) fresa; (for mining etc) perforadora, barrena; (MIL) instrucción f // vt perforar, taladrar // vi (for oil) perforar.

drink [drɪŋk] n bebida // vt, vi, pt **drank,** pp **drunk** beber; **to have a ~** tomar; **~er** n bebedor/a m/f; **~ing water** n agua potable.

drip [drɪp] n (act) goteo; (one ~) gota; (MED) gota a gota // vi gotear, caer gota a gota; **~-dry** a (shirt) de lava y pon; **~ping** n pringue m; **~ping wet** a calado.

drive [draɪv] n paseo o vuelta en coche; (journey) viaje m; (also: **~way**) entrada; (energy) energía, vigor m; (PSYCH) impulso; (SPORT) ataque m // (vb: pt **drove,** pp **driven** ['drɪvn]) vt (car) conducir; (urge) hacer trabajar; (by power) mover; (nail) clavar; (push) empujar; (TECH: motor) impulsar // vi (AUT: at controls) conducir; (: travel) pasearse en coche; **left-/right-hand ~** conducción f a la izquierda/derecha.

driver ['draɪvə*] n conductor m; (of taxi, bus) chofer m; **~'s license** n (US) permiso de conducir.

driving ['draɪvɪŋ] n el conducir, automovilismo; **~ instructor** n instructor m de conducción; **~ lesson** n clase f de conducción; **~ licence** n (Brit) permiso

de conducir; ~ **mirror** *n* retrovisor *m*; ~ **school** *n* autoescuela; ~ **test** *n* examen *m* de conducción.
drizzle ['drɪzl] *n* llovizna // *vi* lloviznar.
drone [drəun] *n* zumbido; (*male bee*) zángano.
drool [druːl] *vi* babear; **to** ~ **over sth** extasiarse ante algo.
droop [druːp] *vi* colgar; (*fig*) decaer, desanimarse.
drop [drɔp] *n* (*of water*) gota; (*lessening*) baja; (*fall*) caída; (*of cliff*) pendiente *m*, declive *m* // *vt* (*allow to fall*) dejar caer; (*voice, eyes, price*) bajar; (*set down from car*) dejar; (*omit*) omitir // *vi* caer; (*price, temperature*) bajar; (*wind*) amainar; **to** ~ **off** *vi* (*sleep*) dormirse // *vt* (*passenger*) bajar; **to** ~ **out** *vi* (*withdraw*) retirarse; ~**out** *n* marginado; ~**per** *n* cuentagotas *m inv*; ~**pings** *npl* excremento *sg* (de animal).
drought [draut] *n* sequía.
drove [drəuv] *pt of* **drive**.
drown [draun] *vt* ahogar // *vi* ahogarse.
drowsy ['drauzɪ] *a* soñoliento; **to be** ~ tener sueño.
drudgery ['drʌdʒərɪ] *n* trabajo monótono.
drug [drʌg] *n* medicamento; (*narcotic*) droga // *vt* drogar; ~ **addict** *n* drogadicto/a; ~**gist** *n* (*US*) farmacéutico; ~**store** *n* (*US*) farmacia.
drum [drʌm] *n* tambor *m*; (*large*) bombo; (*for oil, petrol*) bidón *m*; ~**s** *npl* batería *sg* // *vi* tocar el tambor; (*with fingers*) tamborilear; ~**mer** *n* tambor *m*; ~**stick** *n* (*MUS*) palillo; (*of chicken*) muslo.
drunk [drʌŋk] *pp of* **drink** // *a* borracho // *n* (*also*: ~**ard**) borracho/a; ~**en** *a* borracho; ~**enness** *n* embriaguez *f*.
dry [draɪ] *a* seco; (*day*) sin lluvia; (*climate*) árido, seco // *vt* secar; (*tears*) enjuagar // *vi* secarse; **to** ~ **up** *vi* agotarse; (*in speech*) atascarse; ~**-cleaner's** *n* tintorería; ~**-cleaning** *n* lavado en seco; ~**er** *n* lavadora; ~**ness** *n* sequedad *f*; ~ **rot** *n* putrefacción *f* fungoide.
dual ['djuəl] *a* doble; ~**-control** *a* de doble mando; ~ **nationality** *n* doble nacionalidad *f*; ~**-purpose** *a* de doble uso.
dubbed [dʌbd] *a* (*CINEMA*) doblado.
dubious ['djuːbɪəs] *a* dudoso; (*reputation, company*) sospechoso.
duchess ['dʌtʃɪs] *n* duquesa.
duck [dʌk] *n* pato // *vi* agacharse; ~**ling** *n* patito.
duct [dʌkt] *n* conducto, canal *m*.
dud [dʌd] *n* (*shell*) obús *m* que no estalla; (*object, tool*): **it's a** ~ es una filfa // *a*: ~ **cheque** cheque *m* sin fondos.
due [djuː] *a* (*proper*) debido; (*expected*) esperado; (*fitting*) conveniente, oportuno // *n* (*debt*) deuda; (*desert*) lo que merece uno // *ad*: ~ **north** derecho al norte; ~**s** *npl* (*for club, union*) cuota *sg*; (*in harbour*) derechos *mpl*; **in** ~ **course** a su debido tiempo; ~ **to** debido a.

duel ['djuəl] *n* duelo.
duet [djuː'ɛt] *n* dúo.
dug [dʌg] *pt, pp of* **dig**.
duke [djuːk] *n* duque *m*.
dull [dʌl] *a* (*light*) apagado; (*slow*) torpe; (*boring*) pesado; (*sound, pain*) sordo; (*weather, day*) gris // *vt* (*pain, grief*) aliviar; (*mind, senses*) entorpecer.
duly ['djuːlɪ] *ad* debidamente; (*on time*) a su debido tiempo.
dumb [dʌm] *a* mudo; (*stupid*) estúpido; ~**founded** [dʌm'faundɪd] *a* pasmado.
dummy ['dʌmɪ] *n* (*tailor's model*) maniquí *m*; (*for baby*) chupete *m* // *a* falso, postizo.
dump [dʌmp] *n* (*heap*) montón *m*; (*place*) basurero, vaciadero; (*col*) casucha; (*MIL*) depósito // *vt* (*put down*) verter, vaciar; (*get rid of*) deshacerse de; (*goods*) inundar el mercado con; ~**ing** *n* (*ECON*) dumping *m*; (*of rubbish*): **'no** ~**ing'** 'prohibido verter basura'.
dumpling ['dʌmplɪŋ] *n* bola de masa hervida.
dunce [dʌns] *n* zopenco.
dune [djuːn] *n* duna.
dung [dʌŋ] *n* estiércol *m*.
dungarees [dʌŋgə'riːz] *npl* mono *sg*.
dungeon ['dʌndʒən] *n* calabozo.
dupe [djuːp] *n* (*victim*) víctima // *vt* engañar.
duplicate ['djuːplɪkət] *n* duplicado // *vt* ['djuːplɪkeɪt] duplicar; (*on machine*) multicopiar; **in** ~ por duplicado; **duplicator** *n* multicopista *m*.
durable ['djuərəbl] *a* duradero.
duration [djuə'reɪʃən] *n* duración *f*.
duress [djuə'rɛs] *n*: **under** ~ por compulsión.
during ['djuərɪŋ] *prep* durante.
dusk [dʌsk] *n* crepúsculo, anochecer *m*.
dust [dʌst] *n* polvo // *vt* (*furniture*) desempolvorar; (*cake etc*): **to** ~ **with** espolvorear de; ~**bin** *n* (*Brit*) cubo de la basura; ~**er** *n* paño, trapo, bayeta; (*feather* ~) plumero; ~ **jacket** *n* sobrecubierta; ~**man** *n* (*Brit*) basurero; ~**y** *a* polvoriento.
Dutch [dʌtʃ] *a* holandés(esa) // *n* (*LING*) holandés *m*; ~**man/woman** *n* holandés/esa *m/f*.
duty ['djuːtɪ] *n* deber *m*; (*tax*) derechos *mpl* de aduana; **on** ~ de servicio; (*at night etc*) de guardia; **off** ~ libre (de servicio); ~**-free** *a* libre de derechos de aduana.
dwarf [dwɔːf], *pl* **dwarves** [dwɔːvz] *n* enano // *vt* empequeñecer.
dwell [dwɛl] *pt, pp* **dwelt** [dwɛlt] *vi* morar; **to** ~ **on** *vt fus* explayarse en; ~**ing** *n* vivienda.
dwindle ['dwɪndl] *vi* menguar, disminuir.
dye [daɪ] *n* tinte *m* // *vt* teñir.
dying ['daɪɪŋ] *a* moribundo, agonizante; (*moments*) final; (*words*) último.
dynamic [daɪ'næmɪk] *a* dinámico; ~**s** *n*, *npl* dinámica *sg*.
dynamite ['daɪnəmaɪt] *n* dinamita.

dynamo ['daɪnəməʊ] n dinamo f.
dynasty ['dɪnəstɪ] n dinastía.

E

each [iːtʃ] det cada inv // pron cada uno; ~ other el uno al otro; **they hate** ~ **other** se odian (entre ellos o mutuamente); **they have 2 books** ~ tiene 2 libros por persona.
eager ['iːgəʳ] a (gen) impaciente; (hopeful) ilusionado; (ambitious) ambicioso; **to be** ~ **to do sth** ansiar hacer algo, impacientarse por hacer algo; **to be** ~ **for** ansiar, anhelar.
eagle ['iːgl] n águila f.
ear [ɪəʳ] n oreja; (MUS) oído; (of corn) espiga; ~**ache** n dolor m de oídos; ~**drum** n tímpano.
earl [əːl] n conde m.
early ['əːlɪ] ad (gen) temprano; (before time) con tiempo, con anticipación // a (gen) temprano; (reply) pronto; (first) primero; (work) juvenil; **have an** ~ **night** acuéstate temprano; **in the** ~ **or** ~ **in the spring/19th century** a principios de primavera/del siglo diez y nueve; **as** ~ **as possible** cuánto antes, lo más pronto posible.
earmark ['ɪəmɑːk] vt reservar (for para), destinar (for a).
earn [əːn] vt (gen) ganar; (salary) percibir; (interest) devengar; (praise) merecerse.
earnest ['əːnɪst] a serio, formal; **in** ~ ad en serio.
earnings ['əːnɪŋz] npl (personal) sueldo, ingresos mpl; (company) ganancias fpl.
ear: ~**phones** npl auriculares mpl; ~**ring** n pendiente m, arete m; ~**shot** n: **within** ~**shot** al alcance del oído.
earth [əːθ] n (gen) tierra; (ELEC) cable m de toma de tierra // vt (ELEC) conectar a tierra; ~**enware** n loza de barro; ~**quake** n terremoto; ~**y** a (fig: vulgar) grosero; (: sensual) sensual.
earwig ['ɪəwɪg] n tijereta.
ease [iːz] n (gen) facilidad f; (relief) alivio; (calm) tranquilidad f; (relaxed state) comodidad f // vt facilitar, aliviar; tranquilizar; (loosen) soltar; (relieve: pressure) aflojar; (weight) aligerar; (help pass): **to** ~ **sth in/out** meter/sacar con cuidado; **at** ~! (MIL) ¡descanso!; **to** ~ **off** or **up** vi suavizarse; (at work) dejar de trabajar tanto; (wind) amainar; (rain) moderarse.
easel ['iːzl] n caballete m.
east [iːst] n este m, oriente m // a del este, oriental // ad al este, hacia el este; **the E**~ el Oriente.
Easter ['iːstəʳ] n Pascua (de Resurrección).
easterly ['iːstəlɪ] a (to the east) al este; (from the east) del este.
eastern ['iːstən] a del este, oriental.
East Germany n Alemania Oriental.
eastward(s) ['iːstwəd(z)] ad hacia el este.

easy ['iːzɪ] a (gen) fácil; (simple) sencillo; (slow) lento, pausado; (comfortable) holgado, cómodo; (relaxed) natural, llano // ad: **to take it** or **things** ~ (not worry) tomarlo con calma; (go slowly) ir despacio; (rest) descansar; ~ **chair** n sillón m; ~ **going** a acomodadizo.
eat [iːt] pt **ate**, pp **eaten** ['iːtn] vt (gen) comer; (supper) cenar; **to** ~ **into, to** ~ **away at** vt fus corroer; ~**able** a comestible.
eau de Cologne [əʊdəkə'ləʊn] n (agua de) Colonia.
eaves [iːvz] npl alero sg.
eavesdrop ['iːvzdrɔp] vi escuchar a escondidas (on sb a uno).
ebb [ɛb] n reflujo // vi bajar; (fig: also: ~ away) decaer; ~ **tide** n marea menguante.
ebony ['ɛbənɪ] n ébano.
eccentric [ɪk'sɛntrɪk] a, n excéntrico/a.
ecclesiastical [ɪkliːzɪ'æstɪkəl] a eclesiástica.
echo ['ɛkəʊ], pl ~**es** n eco m // vt (sound) repetir // vi resonar, hacer eco.
eclipse [ɪ'klɪps] n eclipse m // vt eclipsar.
ecology [ɪ'kɔlədʒɪ] n ecología.
economic [iːkə'nɔmɪk] a económico; (business etc) rentable; ~**al** a económico; ~**s** n (la) economía; **economist** [ɪ'kɔnəmɪst] n economista m/f.
economize [ɪ'kɔnəmaɪz] vi economizar, ahorrar.
economy [ɪ'kɔnəmɪ] n economía.
ecstasy ['ɛkstəsɪ] n éxtasis m; **ecstatic** [-'tætɪk] a extático.
ecumenical [iːkju'mɛnɪkl] a ecuménico.
eczema ['ɛksɪmə] n eczema m.
edge [ɛdʒ] n (of knife etc) filo; (of object) borde m; (of lake etc) orilla // vt (SEWING) ribetear; **on** ~ (fig) = **edgy**; **to** ~ **away from** alejarse poco a poco; ~**ways** ad: **he couldn't get a word in** ~**ways** no pudo meter baza; **edging** n (SEWING) ribete m; (of path) borde m.
edgy ['ɛdʒɪ] a nervioso, inquieto.
edible ['ɛdɪbl] a comestible.
edict ['iːdɪkt] n edicto.
edifice ['ɛdɪfɪs] n edificio.
edit ['ɛdɪt] vt (be editor of) dirigir; (cut) cortar; ~**ion** [ɪ'dɪʃən] n (gen) edición f; (number printed) tirada; ~**or** n (of newspaper) director m; (of book) autor m de la edición; ~**orial** [-'tɔːrɪəl] a editorial, de la dirección // n editorial m.
educate ['ɛdjukeɪt] vt (gen) educar; (instruct) instruir.
education [ɛdju'keɪʃən] n educación f; (schooling) enseñanza; (ESCOL) pedagogía; ~**al** a (policy etc) educacional; (teaching) docente; (instructive) educativo.
EEC n abbr of **European Economic Community** CEE (Comunidad Económica Europea).
eel [iːl] n anguila.
eerie ['ɪərɪ] a (strange) extraño; (mysterious) misterioso.

effect [ɪ'fɛkt] n efecto // vt efectuar, llevar a cabo; ~s npl efectos mpl; to take ~ (drug) surtir efecto; **in** ~ en realidad; ~**ive** a (gen) eficaz; (striking) impresionante; (real) efectivo; **to become** ~**ive** entrar en vigor; ~**iveness** n eficacia.

effeminate [ɪ'fɛmɪnɪt] a afeminado.

effervescent [ɛfə'vɛsnt] a efervescente.

efficiency [ɪ'fɪʃənsɪ] n (gen) eficiencia; (of machine) rendimiento.

efficient [ɪ'fɪʃnt] a eficiente.

effigy ['ɛfɪdʒɪ] n efigie f.

effort ['ɛfət] n esfuerzo; **to make an** ~ **to** esforzarse por; ~**less** a sin esfuerzo (alguno).

effrontery [ɪ'frʌntərɪ] n descaro.

effusive [ɪ'fjuːsɪv] a efusivo.

e.g. ad abbr of exempli gratia p. ej. (por ejemplo).

egg [ɛg] n huevo; **hard-boiled/poached/soft-boiled** ~ huevo duro/escalfado/pasado por agua; **scrambled** ~**s** huevos revueltos; **to** ~ **on** vt incitar; ~**cup** n huevera; ~**shell** n cáscara de huevo.

ego ['iːgəu] n ego; ~**ism** n egoísmo; ~**ist** n egoísta m/f.

Egypt ['iːdʒɪpt] n Egipto; ~**ian** [ɪ'dʒɪpʃən] a, n egipcio/a.

eiderdown ['aɪdədaun] n edredón m.

eight [eɪt] num ocho; ~**een** num diez y ocho, dieciocho; **eighth** a, n octavo; ~**y** num ochenta.

Eire ['ɛərə] n Eire m.

either ['aɪðə°] det cualquier ... de los dos; (both, each) uno u otro; **on** ~ **side** en ambos lados // pron: ~ (of them) cualquiera de los dos; **I don't like** ~ no me gusta ni uno ni otro // ad tampoco; **no, I don't** ~ no, yo tampoco // conj: ~ **yes or no** o sí o no.

eject [ɪ'dʒɛkt] vt echar; (tenant) desahuciar; ~**or seat** n asiento proyectable.

eke [iːk]: **to** ~ **out** vt (make last) escatimar; (add to) suplir las deficiencias de.

elaborate [ɪ'læbərɪt] a complicado; (decorated) rebuscado // (vb: [ɪ'læbəreɪt]) vt elaborar // vi explicarse con muchos detalles.

elapse [ɪ'læps] vi transcurrir.

elastic [ɪ'læstɪk] a, n elástico; ~ **band** n gomita.

elated [ɪ'leɪtɪd] a: **to be** ~ regocijarse; **elation** [ɪ'leɪʃən] n regocijo.

elbow ['ɛlbəu] n codo.

elder ['ɛldə°] a mayor // n (tree) saúco; (person) mayor; (of tribe) anciano; ~**ly** a de edad, mayor // n: **the** ~**ly** la gente mayor.

eldest ['ɛldɪst] a, n el/la mayor.

elect [ɪ'lɛkt] vt elegir; **to** ~ **to do** optar por hacer // a: **the president** ~ el presidente electo; ~**ion** [ɪ'lɛkʃən] n elección f; ~**ioneering** [ɪlɛkʃə'nɪərɪŋ] n campaña electoral; ~**or** n elector/a m/f;

~**oral** a electoral; ~**orate** n electorado.

electric [ɪ'lɛktrɪk] a eléctrico; ~**al** a eléctrico; ~ **blanket** n manta eléctrica; ~ **chair** n silla eléctrica; ~ **cooker** n cocina eléctrica; ~ **fire** n estufa eléctrica.

electrician [ɪlɛk'trɪʃən] n electricista m/f.

electricity [ɪlɛk'trɪsɪtɪ] n electricidad f.

electrify [ɪ'lɛktrɪfaɪ] vt (RAIL) electrificar; (audience) electrizar.

electro... [ɪlɛktrəu] pref: ~**cute** [-kjuːt] vt electrocutar; **electrode** [ɪ'lɛktrəud] n electrodo; ~**magnetic** a electromagnético.

electron [ɪ'lɛktrɔn] n electrón m.

electronic [ɪlɛk'trɔnɪk] a electrónico; ~**s** n electrónica.

elegance ['ɛlɪgəns] n elegancia; **elegant** [-gənt] a elegante.

element ['ɛlɪmənt] n (gen) elemento; **to brave the** ~**s** salir a la intemperie; ~**ary** [-'mɛntərɪ] a (gen) elemental; (primitive) rudimentario; (school, education) de primera enseñanza.

elephant ['ɛlɪfənt] n elefante m.

elevate ['ɛlɪveɪt] vt (gen) elevar; (in rank) ascender.

elevation [ɛlɪ'veɪʃən] n elevación f; (rank) ascenso; (height) altura.

elevator ['ɛlɪveɪtə°] n (US) ascensor m.

eleven [ɪ'lɛvn] num once; ~**ses** npl las once; ~**th** a undécimo.

elf [ɛlf], pl **elves** [ɛlvz] n duende m.

elicit [ɪ'lɪsɪt] vt: **to** ~ (**from**) sacar (de).

eligible ['ɛlɪdʒəbl] a elegible; **to be** ~ **for** sth llenar los requisitos para algo.

eliminate [ɪ'lɪmɪneɪt] vt eliminar; (strike out) suprimir; (suspect) descartar; **elimination** [-'neɪʃən] n eliminación f; supresión f.

élite [eɪ'liːt] n élite f.

elm [ɛlm] n olmo.

elocution [ɛlə'kjuːʃən] n elocución f.

elongated ['iːlɔŋgeɪtɪd] a alargado, estirado.

elope [ɪ'ləup] vi fugarse con su amante; ~**ment** n fuga.

eloquence ['ɛləkwəns] n elocuencia; **eloquent** [-wənt] a elocuente.

else [ɛls] ad lo(s) demás; **something** ~ otra cosa; **somewhere** ~ en otra parte; **everywhere** ~ en todas partes (menos aquí); **where** ~? ¿dónde más? ¿en qué otra parte?; **there was little** ~ **to do** apenas quedaba otra cosa que hacer; **nobody** ~ **spoke** no habló nadie más; ~**where** ad (be) en otra parte; (go) a otra parte.

elucidate [ɪ'luːsɪdeɪt] vt aclarar, elucidar.

elude [ɪ'luːd] vt (gen) eludir; (blow) esquivar; (pursuer) escaparse de, zafarse de.

elusive [ɪ'luːsɪv] a esquivo; (answer) difícil de encontrar.

emaciated [ɪ'meɪsɪeɪtɪd] a demacrado.

emanate ['ɛməneɪt] vi emanar, proceder.

emancipate [ɪ'mænsɪpeɪt] vt emancipar; ~**d** a liberado; **emancipation** [-'peɪʃən] n emancipación f, liberación f.
embalm [ɪm'bɑːm] vt embalsamar.
embankment [ɪm'bæŋkmənt] n terraplén m; (riverside) dique m.
embargo [ɪm'bɑːgəu], pl ~**es** n prohibición f.
embark [ɪm'bɑːk] vi embarcarse // vt embarcar; **to** ~ **on** (fig) emprender, lanzarse a; ~**ation** [embɑː'keɪʃən] n (people) embarco; (goods) embarque m.
embarrass [ɪm'bærəs] vt desconcertar, azorar; (financially etc) poner en un aprieto; ~**ing** a embarazoso; ~**ment** n desconcierto, azoramiento; (financial) apuros mpl.
embassy ['embəsɪ] n embajada f.
embed [ɪm'bed] vt (gen) empotrar; (teeth etc) clavar.
embellish [ɪm'belɪʃ] vt embellecer; (fig) adornar.
embers ['embəz] npl rescoldo sg, ascua sg.
embezzle [ɪm'bezl] vt desfalcar, malversar; ~**ment** n desfalco, malversación f.
embitter [ɪm'bɪtə*] vt amargar; (fig) envenenar; ~**ed** a resentido, amargado.
emblem ['embləm] n emblema m.
embody [ɪm'bɒdɪ] vt (features) encarnar; (ideas) expresar.
embossed [ɪm'bɒst] a realzado; ~ **with** con grabado en relieve.
embrace [ɪm'breɪs] vt abrazar, dar un abrazo a; (include) abarcar; (adopt: idea) adherirse a // vi abrazarse // n abrazo.
embroider [ɪm'brɔɪdə*] vt bordar; (fig: story) adornar, embellecer; ~**y** n bordado.
embryo ['embrɪəu] n (also fig) embrión m.
emerald ['emərəld] n esmeralda f.
emerge [ɪ'mɜːdʒ] vi (gen) salir, aparecer; (arise) surgir; **emergence** n salida, aparición f; surgimiento.
emergency [ɪ'mɜːdʒənsɪ] n (event) emergencia; (crisis) crisis f; (need) necesidad f urgente; **in an** ~ en caso de urgencia; **state of** ~ estado de emergencia; ~ **exit** n salida de emergencia; ~ **landing** n aterrizaje m forzoso; ~ **meeting** n reunión f extraordinaria.
emery ['emərɪ]: ~ **board** n lima de uñas; ~ **paper** n papel m de esmeril.
emetic [ɪ'metɪk] n emético.
emigrant ['emɪgrənt] n emigrante m/f.
emigrate ['emɪgreɪt] vi emigrarse; **emigration** [-'greɪʃən] n emigración f.
eminence ['emɪnəns] n eminencia f.
eminent [-ənt] a eminente.
emission [ɪ'mɪʃən] n emisión f.
emit [ɪ'mɪt] vt (gen) emitir; (smoke) arrojar; (smell) despedir; (sound) producir.
emotion [ɪ'məuʃən] n emoción f; ~**al** a (person) sentimental; (scene) conmovedor(a), emocionante; ~**ally** ad con emoción.

emotive [ɪ'məutɪv] a emotivo.
emperor ['empərə*] n emperador m.
emphasis ['emfəsɪs], pl -**ses** [-siːz] n énfasis m inv.
emphasize ['emfəsaɪz] vt (word, point) subrayar, recalcar; (feature) hacer resaltar.
emphatic [em'fætɪk] a (strong) enérgico; (unambiguous, clear) enfático; ~**ally** ad con énfasis.
empire ['empaɪə*] n imperio.
empirical [em'pɪrɪkl] a empírico.
employ [ɪm'plɔɪ] vt emplear; ~**ee** [-'iː] n empleado/a; ~**er** n patrón/ona m/f, empresario; ~**ment** n (gen) empleo; (work) trabajo; **full** ~**ment** pleno empleo; ~**ment agency** n agencia de colocaciones; ~**ment exchange** n bolsa de trabajo.
empower [ɪm'pauə*] vt: **to** ~ **sb to do sth** autorizar a uno a hacer algo.
empress ['emprɪs] n emperatriz f.
emptiness ['emptɪnɪs] n (gen) vacío; (of life etc) vaciedad f.
empty ['emptɪ] a vacío; (place) desierto; (house) desocupado; (threat) vano // n (bottle) envase m // vt vaciar; (place) dejar vacío // vi vaciarse; (house) quedar desocupado; (place) quedar desierto; ~-**handed** a con las manos vacías.
emulate ['emjuleɪt] vt emular.
emulsion [ɪ'mʌlʃən] n emulsión f.
enable [ɪ'neɪbl] vt: **to** ~ **sb to do sth** (allow) permitir a uno hacer algo; (prepare) capacitar a uno para hacer algo.
enact [ɪn'ækt] vt (law) promulgar; (play) representar; (role) hacer.
enamel [ɪ'næməl] n esmalte m.
enamoured [ɪ'næməd] a: **to be** ~ **of** (person) estar enamorado de; (activity etc) tener gran afición a; (idea) aferrarse a.
encased [ɪn'keɪst] a: ~ **in** (enclosed) encerrado en; (covered) revestido de.
enchant [ɪn'tʃɑːnt] vt encantar; ~**ing** a encantador(a).
encircle [ɪn'sɜːkl] vt (gen) rodear; (waist) ceñir.
encl. abbr of **enclosed** adj. (adjunto).
enclose [ɪn'kləuz] vt (land) cercar; (with letter etc) adjuntar; (in receptacle) encerrar; **please find** ~**d** le adjunto.
enclosure [ɪn'kləuʒə*] n cercado, recinto; (COMM) carta adjunta.
encore [ɔŋ'kɔː*] excl ¡otra!, ¡bis! // n bis m.
encounter [ɪn'kauntə*] n encuentro // vt encontrar, encontrarse con; (difficulty) tropezar con.
encourage [ɪn'kʌrɪdʒ] vt alentar, animar; (growth) estimular; ~**ment** n estímulo; (of industry) fomento.
encroach [ɪn'krəutʃ] vi: **to** ~ (**up**)**on** (gen) invadir; (time) ocupar.
encrusted [ɪn'krʌstəd] a: ~ **with** incrustado de.
encumber [ɪn'kʌmbə*] vt: **to be** ~**ed with** (carry) tener que cargar con; (debts) estar gravado de.

encyclop(a)edia [ensaɪkləu'piːdɪə] *n* enciclopedia.

end [end] *n* (*gen, also aim*) fin *m*; (*of table*) extremo; (*of street*) final *m*; (*SPORT*) lado // *vt* terminar, acabar; (*also*: **bring to an ~, put an ~ to**) acabar con // *vi* terminar, acabar; **in the ~** al fin, por fin, finalmente; **on ~** (*object*) de punta, de cabeza; **to stand on ~** (*hair*) erizarse; **for hours on ~** horas seguidas; **to ~ up** *vi*: **to ~ up in** terminar en; (*place*) ir a parar en.

endanger [ɪn'deɪndʒə*] *vt* poner en peligro.

endear [ɪn'dɪə*] *vr*: **to ~ o.s. to** hacerse querer de; **~ing** *a* simpático, atractivo; **~ment** *n* cariño, palabra cariñosa.

endeavour [ɪn'devə*] *n* esfuerzo; (*attempt*) tentativa; (*striving*) empeño // *vi*: **to ~ to do** esforzarse por hacer; (*try*) procurar hacer.

ending ['endɪŋ] *n* fin *m*, conclusión *f*; (*of book*) desenlace *m*; (*LING*) terminación *f*.

endless ['endlɪs] *a* interminable, inacabable.

endorse [ɪn'dɔːs] *vt* (*cheque*) endosar; (*approve*) aprobar; **~ment** *n* (*on driving licence*) nota de inhabilitación.

endow [ɪn'dau] *vt* (*provide with money*) dotar; (: *institution*) fundar; **to be ~ed with** estar dotado de.

endurance [ɪn'djuərəns] *n* resistencia; **endure** *vt* (*bear*) aguantar, soportar; (*resist*) resistir // *vi* (*last*) durar; (*resist*) resistir.

enemy ['enəmɪ] *a, n* enemigo/a.

energetic [enə'dʒetɪk] *a* enérgico.

energy ['enədʒɪ] *n* energía.

enforce [ɪn'fɔːs] *vt* (*LAW*) hacer cumplir; **~d** *a* forzoso, forzado.

engage [ɪn'geɪdʒ] *vt* (*attention*) llamar; (*in conversation*) abordar; (*worker*) contratar; (*taxi*) alquilar; (*clutch*) embragar // *vi* (*TECH*) engranar con; **to ~ in** dedicarse a, ocuparse en; **~d** *a* (*busy, in use*) ocupado; (*betrothed*) prometido; **to get ~d** prometerse; **he is ~d in research** se dedica a la investigación; **~d tone** *n* señal *f* de comunicando; **~ment** *n* (*appointment*) compromiso, cita; (*battle*) combate *m*; (*to marry*) compromiso; (*period*) noviazgo; **~ment ring** *n* alianza, anillo de prometida.

engaging [ɪn'geɪdʒɪŋ] *a* atractivo, simpático.

engender [ɪn'dʒendə*] *vt* engendrar.

engine ['endʒɪn] *n* (*AUT*) motor *m*; (*RAIL*) locomotora; **~ driver** *n* maquinista *m*.

engineer [endʒɪ'nɪə*] *n* ingeniero; (*US: RAIL*) maquinista *m*; **~ing** *n* ingeniería.

England ['ɪŋglənd] *n* Inglaterra.

English ['ɪŋglɪʃ] *a* inglés(esa) // *n* (*LING*) el inglés; **the ~** los ingleses; **~man/woman** *n* inglés/esa *m/f*.

engrave [ɪn'greɪv] *vt* grabar; **engraving** *n* grabado.

engrossed [ɪn'grəust] *a*: **~ in** absorto en.

engulf [ɪn'gʌlf] *vt* sumergir, hundir.

enhance [ɪn'hɑːns] *vt* (*gen*) intensificar, aumentar; (*beauty*) realzar.

enigma [ɪ'nɪgmə] *n* enigma *m*; **~tic** [enɪg-'mætɪk] *a* enigmático.

enjoy [ɪn'dʒɔɪ] *vt* (*possess*) poseer; (*have: health, fortune*) disfrutar de, gozar de; (*food*) comer con gusto; **to ~ o.s.** divertirse, pasarlo bien; **~able** *a* (*pleasant*) agradable; (*amusing*) divertido; **~ment** *n* (*use*) disfrute *m*; (*joy*) placer *m*.

enlarge [ɪn'lɑːdʒ] *vt* aumentar; (*broaden*) extender; (*PHOT*) ampliar // *vi*: **to ~ on** (*subject*) tratar con más detalles; **~ment** *n* (*PHOT*) ampliación *f*.

enlighten [ɪn'laɪtn] *vt* (*inform*) informar, instruir; **~ed** *a* (*cultured*) culto; (*knowledgeable*) bien informado; (*tolerant*) comprensivo; **~ment** *n* (*HISTORY*): **the E~ment** la Ilustración, el Siglo de las Luces.

enlist [ɪn'lɪst] *vt* alistar; (*support*) conseguir // *vi* alistarse.

enmity ['enmɪtɪ] *n* enemistad *f*.

enormity [ɪ'nɔːmɪtɪ] *n* enormidad *f*; **enormous** [-məs] *a* enorme.

enough [ɪ'nʌf] *a*: **~ time/books** bastante tiempo/bastantes libros // *n*: **have you got ~?** ¿tiene Usted bastante? // *ad*: **big ~** bastante grande; **he has not worked ~** no ha trabajado bastante; **~!** ¡basta ya!; **that's ~, thanks** con eso basta, gracias; **I've had ~ of him** estoy harto de él; ... **which, funnily ~ ...** lo que, por extraño que parezca...

enquire [ɪn'kwaɪə*] *vt, vi* = **inquire**.

enrage [ɪn'reɪdʒ] *vt* enfurecer, hacer rabiar.

enrich [ɪn'rɪtʃ] *vt* enriquecer.

enrol [ɪn'rəul] *vt* inscribir; (*SCOL*) matricular // *vi* inscribirse; matricularse; **~ment** *n* inscripción *f*; matriculación *f*.

en route [ɔn'ruːt] *ad* (*on the way to*) camino de; (*on the way*) en camino.

ensign ['ensaɪn] *n* (*flag*) bandera; (*MIL*) alférez *m*.

enslave [ɪn'sleɪv] *vt* esclavizar.

ensue [ɪn'sjuː] *vi* seguirse; (*result*) resultar; (*happen*) sobrevenir.

ensure [ɪn'ʃuə*] *vt* asegurar.

entail [ɪn'teɪl] *vt* (*imply*) suponer; (*result in*) acarrear.

entangle [ɪn'tæŋgl] *vt* enredar, enmarañar; **~ment** *n* enredo.

enter ['entə*] *vt* (*room*) entrar en; (*club*) hacerse socio de; (*army*) alistarse en; (*sb for a competition*) inscribir; (*write down*) anotar, apuntar // *vi* entrar; **to ~ for** *vt fus* presentarse para; **to ~ into** *vt fus* (*relations*) establecer; (*plans*) formar parte de; (*debate*) tomar parte en; (*agreement*) llegar a, firmar; **to ~ (up)on** *vt fus* (*career*) emprender.

enteritis [entə'raɪtɪs] *n* enteritis *f*.

enterprise ['entəpraɪz] *n* empresa; (*spirit*) iniciativa; **free ~** la libre empresa; **private ~** la iniciativa privada;

enterprising a emprendedor(a).
entertain [ɛntə'teɪn] vt (amuse) divertir; (receive: guest) recibir (en casa); (idea) abrigar; (plan) estudiar; ~**er** n artista m/f; ~**ing** a divertido, entretenido; ~**ment** n (amusement) diversión f; (show) espectáculo; (party) fiesta.
enthralled [ɪn'θrɔ:ld] a encantado, cautivado.
enthusiasm [ɪn'θu:zɪæzəm] n entusiasmo.
enthusiast [ɪn'θu:zɪæst] n entusiasta m/f; ~**ic** [-'æstɪk] a entusiasta inv; to be ~**ic** about entusiasmarse por.
entice [ɪn'taɪs] vt tentar; (seduce) seducir; **enticing** a atractivo, tentador(a).
entire [ɪn'taɪə*] a entero, completo; (in total) total, todo; ~**ly** ad totalmente; ~**ty** [ɪn'taɪərətɪ] n: **in its** ~**ty** en su totalidad.
entitle [ɪn'taɪtl] vt: to ~ **sb** to sth dar a uno derecho a algo; ~**d** a (book) que se titula; to be ~**d** to do tener derecho a hacer.
entourage [ɔntu'rɑ:ʒ] n séquito.
entrails ['ɛntreɪlz] npl entrañas fpl.
entrance ['ɛntrəns] n entrada // vt [ɪn'trɑ:ns] encantar, hechizar; to gain ~ to (university etc) ingresar en; ~ **examination** n examen m de ingreso; ~ **fee** n cuota.
entrant ['ɛntrənt] n participante m/f.
entreat [ɛn'tri:t] vt rogar, suplicar; ~**y** n ruego, súplica.
entrée ['ɔntreɪ] n (CULIN) entrada.
entrenched [ɛn'trɛntʃd] a atrincherado.
entrepreneur [ɔntrəprə'nə:] n empresario; (of works) contratista m/f.
entrust [ɪn'trʌst] vt: to ~ **sth to sb** confiar algo a uno.
entry ['ɛntrɪ] n entrada; (permission to enter) acceso; (in register) apunte m; (in account) partida; ~ **form** n boleto de inscripción; **no** ~ prohibido el paso; (AUT) dirección prohibida.
enumerate [ɪ'nju:məreɪt] vt enumerar.
enunciate [ɪ'nʌnsɪeɪt] vt pronunciar; (principle etc) enunciar.
envelop [ɪn'vɛləp] vt envolver.
envelope ['ɛnvələup] n sobre m.
envious ['ɛnvɪəs] a envidioso; (look) de envidia.
environment [ɪn'vaɪərnmənt] n medio ambiente; ~**al** [-'mɛntl] a ambiental.
envisage [ɪn'vɪzɪdʒ] vt (foresee) prever; (imagine) concebir, representarse.
envoy ['ɛnvɔɪ] n enviado.
envy ['ɛnvɪ] n envidia // vt tener envidia a; to ~ **sb sth** envidiar algo a uno.
enzyme ['ɛnzaɪm] n enzima.
ephemeral [ɪ'fɛmərl] a efímero.
epic ['ɛpɪk] n épica // a épico.
epidemic [ɛpɪ'dɛmɪk] n epidemia.
epilepsy ['ɛpɪlɛpsɪ] n epilepsia; **epileptic** [-'lɛptɪk] a, n epiléptico/a.
episode ['ɛpɪsəud] n episodio.
epistle [ɪ'pɪsl] n epístola.
epitaph ['ɛpɪtɑːf] n epitafio.

epitome [ɪ'pɪtəmɪ] n epítome m; **epitomize** vt epitomar, resumir.
epoch ['i:pɔk] n época.
equable ['ɛkwəbl] a uniforme, igual; (character) tranquilo, afable.
equal ['i:kwl] a (gen) igual; (treatment) equitativo // n igual m/f // vt ser igual a; to be ~ to (task) estar a la altura de; ~**ity** [i:'kwɔlɪtɪ] n igualdad f; ~**ize** vt, vi igualar; (SPORT) lograr el empate; ~**izer** n igualada; ~**ly** ad igualmente; (share etc) por igual.
equanimity [ɛkwə'nɪmɪtɪ] n ecuanimidad f.
equate [ɪ'kweɪt] vt: to ~ **sth with** considerar algo equivalente a; **equation** [ɪ'kweɪʃən] n (MATH) ecuación f.
equator [ɪ'kweɪtə*] n ecuador m; ~**ial** [ɛkwə'tɔ:rɪəl] a ecuatorial.
equilibrium [i:kwɪ'lɪbrɪəm] n equilibrio.
equinox ['i:kwɪnɔks] n equinoccio.
equip [ɪ'kwɪp] vt (gen) equipar; (person) proveer; to be well ~**ped** estar bien dotado; ~**ment** n equipo; (tools) avíos mpl.
equitable ['ɛkwɪtəbl] a equitativo.
equivalent [ɪ'kwɪvəlnt] a equivalente; to be ~ to equivaler a // n equivalente m.
equivocal [ɪ'kwɪvəkl] a equívoco; (open to suspicion) ambiguo.
era ['ɪərə] n era, época.
eradicate [ɪ'rædɪkeɪt] vt erradicar, extirpar.
erase [ɪ'reɪz] vt borrar; **eraser** n goma de borrar.
erect [ɪ'rɛkt] a erguido // vt erigir, levantar; (assemble) montar.
erection [ɪ'rɛkʃən] n construcción f; (assembly) montaje m; (structure) edificio; (MED) erección f.
ermine ['ə:mɪn] n armiño.
erode [ɪ'rəud] vt (GEO) erosionar; (metal) corroer, desgastar; **erosion** [ɪ'rəuʒən] n erosión f; desgaste m.
erotic [ɪ'rɔtɪk] a erótico; ~**ism** [ɪ'rɔtɪsɪzm] n erotismo.
err [ə:*] vi errar, equivocarse; (REL) pecar.
errand ['ɛrnd] n recado, mandado; ~ **boy** n recadero.
erratic [ɪ'rætɪk] a irregular; (uneven) desigual, poco uniforme.
erroneous [ɪ'rəunɪəs] a erróneo.
error ['ɛrə*] n error m, equivocación f.
erupt [ɪ'rʌpt] vi estar en erupción; (MED) hacer erupción; (fig) estallar; ~**ion** [ɪ'rʌpʃən] n erupción f; (fig) explosión f.
escalate ['ɛskəleɪt] vi extenderse, intensificarse; **escalation** [-'leɪʃən] n escalamiento, intensificación f.
escalator ['ɛskəleɪtə*] n escalera móvil.
escapade [ɛskə'peɪd] n travesura.
escape [ɪ'skeɪp] n (gen) fuga; (from duties) escapatoria; (from chase) fuga, evasión f // vi (gen) escaparse; (flee) huir, evadirse; (leak) fugarse // vt evitar, eludir; (consequences) escapar a; to ~ **from**

(*place*) escaparse de; (*person*) escaparse a; (*clutches*) librarse de; **escapism** *n* escapismo.

escort ['eskɔːt] *n* acompañante *m/f*; (*MIL*) escolta; (*NAUT*) convoy *m* // *vt* [ɪ'skɔːt] acompañar; (*MIL, NAUT*) escoltar.

Eskimo ['eskɪməu] *n* esquimal *m/f*.

especially [ɪ'speʃlɪ] *ad* (*gen*) especialmente; (*above all*) sobre todo; (*particularly*) en particular.

espionage ['espɪɒnɑːʒ] *n* espionaje *m*.

esplanade [esplə'neɪd] *n* (*by sea*) paseo marítimo.

espouse [ɪ'spauz] *vt* adherirse a.

Esquire [ɪ'skwaɪə] *n* (*abbr* **Esq.**): **J. Brown, ~ Sr.** Don J. Brown.

essay ['eseɪ] *n* (*SCOL*) ensayo.

essence ['esns] *n* esencia.

essential [ɪ'senʃl] *a* (*necessary*) imprescindible; (*basic*) esencial; **~ly** *ad* esencialmente.

establish [ɪ'stæblɪʃ] *vt* establecer; (*facts*) verificar; (*proof*) demostrar; (*relations*) entablar; **~ed** *a* (*business*) de buena reputación; (*staff*) de plantilla; **~ment** *n* establecimiento; **the E~ment** la clase dirigente.

estate [ɪ'steɪt] *n* (*land*) finca, hacienda; (*property*) propiedad *f*; (*inheritance*) herencia; (*POL*) estado; **housing ~** urbanización *f*; **industrial ~** polígono industrial; **~ agent** *n* agente *m/f* inmobiliario; **~ car** *n* (*Brit*) furgoneta.

esteem [ɪ'stiːm] *n*: **to hold sb in high ~** estimar en mucho a uno // *vt* estimar.

estimate ['estɪmət] *n* estimación *f*, apreciación *f*; (*assessment*) tasa, cálculo; (*COMM*) presupuesto // *vt* [-meɪt] estimar; tasar, calcular; **estimation** [-'meɪʃən] *n* opinión *f*, juicio; (*esteem*) aprecio.

estrange [ɪ'streɪndʒ] *vt* enajenar.

estuary ['estjuərɪ] *n* estuario, ría.

etching ['etʃɪŋ] *n* aguafuerte *f*.

eternal [ɪ'tɜːnl] *a* eterno.

eternity [ɪ'tɜːnɪtɪ] *n* eternidad *f*.

ether ['iːθə] *n* éter *m*.

ethical ['eθɪkl] *a* ético; (*honest*) honrado; **ethics** ['eθɪks] *n* ética // *npl* moralidad *f*.

ethnic ['eθnɪk] *a* étnico.

etiquette ['etɪket] *n* etiqueta.

eucalyptus [juːkə'lɪptəs] *n* eucalipto.

euphemism ['juːfəmɪzm] *n* eufemismo.

euphoria [juː'fɔːrɪə] *n* euforia.

Europe ['juərəp] *n* Europa; **European** [-'piːən] *a*, *n* europeo/a.

euthanasia [juːθə'neɪzɪə] *n* eutanasia.

evacuate [ɪ'vækjueɪt] *vt* desocupar; **evacuation** [-'eɪʃən] *n* evacuación *f*.

evade [ɪ'veɪd] *vt* evadir, eludir.

evaluate [ɪ'væljueɪt] *vt* evaluar; (*value*) tasar; (*evidence*) interpretar.

evangelist [ɪ'vændʒəlɪst] *n* evangelizador *m*, evangelista *m/f*.

evaporate [ɪ'væpəreɪt] *vi* evaporarse, desvanecerse // *vt* evaporar; **~d milk** *n*

leche *f* evaporada; **evaporation** [-'reɪʃən] *n* evaporación *f*.

evasion [ɪ'veɪʒən] *n* evasiva, evasión *f*; **evasive** [-sɪv] *a* evasivo.

eve [iːv] *n*: **on the ~ of** en vísperas de.

even ['iːvn] *a* (*level*) llano; (*smooth*) liso; (*speed, temperature*) uniforme; (*number*) par; (*nature*) ecuánime; (*SPORT*) igual(es) // *ad* hasta, aun, siquiera; **~ more** aun más; **~ so** aun así; **not ~** ni siquiera; **he was there** hasta él estuvo allí; **~ on Sundays** incluso los domingos; **to ~ out** *vi* nivelarse; **to get ~ with sb** ajustar cuentas con uno.

evening ['iːvnɪŋ] *n* tarde *f*; (*dusk*) atardecer *m*; (*night*) noche *f*; (*event*) velada; **in the ~** por la tarde; **~ class** *n* clase *f* nocturna; **~ dress** *n* (*man's*) traje *m* de etiqueta; (*woman's*) traje *m* de noche.

event [ɪ'vent] *n* suceso, acontecimiento; (*SPORT*) prueba; **in the ~ of** en caso de (que); **~ful** *a* accidentado; (*game etc*) lleno de emoción.

eventual [ɪ'ventʃuəl] *a* (*last*) final; (*resulting*) consiguiente; **~ity** [-'ælɪtɪ] *n* eventualidad *f*; **~ly** *ad* (*finally*) finalmente, al fin y al cabo; (*in time*) a la larga.

ever ['evə*] *ad* nunca, jamás; (*at all times*) alguna vez; **the best ~** el/la mejor que se ha visto jamás; **have you ~ seen it?** ¿lo ha visto Usted jamás?; **better than ~** mejor que nunca; **~ since** *ad* desde entonces // *conj* después de que; **~green** *n* árbol *m* de hoja perenne; **~lasting** *a* eterno, perpetuo.

every ['evrɪ] *det* (*each*) cada; (*all*) todo; **~ day** cada día; **~ other car** cada dos coches; **~ now and then** de vez en cuando; **~body** *pron* todos *pl*, todo el mundo; **~day** *a* (*daily*) diario, cotidiano; (*usual*) corriente; (*common*) vulgar; (*routine*) rutinario; **~one = ~body**; **~thing** *pron* todo; **~where** *ad* (*be*) en todas partes; (*go*) a *o* por todas partes.

evict [ɪ'vɪkt] *vt* desahuciar; **~ion** [ɪ'vɪkʃən] *n* desahucio.

evidence ['evɪdəns] *n* (*proof*) prueba; (*of witness*) testimonio; (*facts*) datos *mpl*, hechos *mpl*; **to give ~** prestar declaración, dar testimonio.

evident ['evɪdənt] *a* evidente, manifiesto; **~ly** *ad* naturalmente.

evil ['iːvl] *a* malo; (*influence*) funesto; (*smell*) horrible // *n* mal *m*, maldad *f*; **~doer** *n* malhechor/a *m/f*.

evocative [ɪ'vɒkətɪv] *a* sugestivo, evocador(a).

evoke [ɪ'vəuk] *vt* evocar.

evolution [iːvə'luːʃən] *n* evolución *f*, desarrollo.

evolve [ɪ'vɒlv] *vt* desarrollar // *vi* evolucionar, desarrollarse.

ewe [juː] *n* oveja.

ex-... [eks] *pref* ex.

exact [ɪg'zækt] *a* exacto // *vt*: **to ~ sth**

(**from**) exigir algo (de); **~ing** *a* exigente; (*conditions*) arduo; **~itude** *n* exactitud *f*; **~ly** *ad* exactamente; (*time*) en punto.

exaggerate [ɪgˈzædʒəreɪt] *vt, vi* exagerar; **exaggeration** [-ˈreɪʃən] *n* exageración *f*.

exalted [ɪgˈzɔːltɪd] *a* exaltado, elevado.

exam [ɪgˈzæm] *n abbr of* **examination**.

examination [ɪgzæmɪˈneɪʃən] *n* (*gen*) examen *m*; (*LAW*) interrogación *f*; (*inquiry*) investigación *f*.

examine [ɪgˈzæmɪn] *vt* (*gen*) examinar; (*inspect*) inspeccionar, escudriñar; (*SCOL, LAW: person*) interrogar; (*at customs: luggage*) registrar; **examiner** *n* inspector *m*.

example [ɪgˈzɑːmpl] *n* ejemplo; (*copy*) ejemplar *m*; **for ~** por ejemplo.

exasperate [ɪgˈzɑːspəreɪt] *vt* exasperar, irritar; **exasperating** *a* irritante.

excavate [ˈɛkskəveɪt] *vt* excavar; **excavation** [-ˈveɪʃən] *n* excavación *f*.

exceed [ɪkˈsiːd] *vt* exceder; (*number*) pasar de; (*speed limit*) sobrepasar; (*limits*) rebasar; (*powers*) excederse en; (*hopes*) superar; **~ingly** *ad* sumamente, sobremanera.

excel [ɪkˈsɛl] *vi* sobresalir.

excellence [ˈɛksələns] *n* excelencia.

Excellency [ˈɛksələnsɪ] *n*: **His ~** Su Excelencia.

excellent [ˈɛksələnt] *a* excelente.

except [ɪkˈsɛpt] *prep* (*also:* **~ for, ~ing**) excepto, salvo, con excepción de // *vt* exceptuar, excluir; **~ if/when** excepto si/cuando; **~ that** salvo que; **~ion** [ɪkˈsɛpʃən] *n* excepción *f*; **to take ~ion to** ofenderse por; **~ional** [ɪkˈsɛpʃənl] *a* excepcional.

excerpt [ˈɛksəːpt] *n* extracto.

excess [ɪkˈsɛs] *n* exceso; (*COMM*) excedente *m*; **~ baggage** *n* exceso de equipaje; **~ fare** *n* suplemento; **~ive** *a* excesivo.

exchange [ɪksˈtʃeɪndʒ] *n* cambio; (*of goods*) canje *m*; (*of ideas*) intercambio; (*also:* **telephone ~**) central *f* (telefónica) // *vt* cambiar; canjear.

exchequer [ɪksˈtʃɛkəʳ] *n* hacienda.

excise [ˈɛksaɪz] *n* impuestos *mpl* sobre el comercio exterior // *vt* [ɛkˈsaɪz] suprimir.

excite [ɪkˈsaɪt] *vt* (*stimulate*) excitar; (*awaken*) despertar; (*move*) entusiasmar; **to get ~d** emocionarse; **~ment** *n* emoción *f*; (*anticipation*) ilusión *f*; (*agitation*) agitación *f*; **exciting** *a* emocionante.

exclaim [ɪkˈskleɪm] *vi* exclamar; **exclamation** [ɛksklɔˈmeɪʃən] *n* exclamación *f*; **exclamation mark** *n* punto de admiración.

exclude [ɪkˈskluːd] *vt* excluir; (*except*) exceptuar; **exclusion** [ɪkˈskluːʒən] *n* exclusión *f*.

exclusive [ɪkˈskluːsɪv] *a* exclusivo; (*club, district*) selecto; **~ of tax** excluyendo impuestos; **~ly** *ad* únicamente.

excommunicate [ɛkskəˈmjuːnɪkeɪt] *vt* excomulgar.

excrement [ˈɛkskrəmənt] *n* excremento.

excrete [ɪkˈskriːt] *vi* excretar.

excruciating [ɪkˈskruːʃɪeɪtɪŋ] *a* agudísimo, atroz.

excursion [ɪkˈskəːʃən] *n* excursión *f*.

excusable [ɪkˈskjuːzəbl] *a* perdonable.

excuse [ɪkˈskjuːs] *n* disculpa, excusa; (*evasion*) pretexto // *vt* [ɪkˈskjuːz] disculpar, perdonar; **to ~ sb from doing sth** dispensar a uno de hacer algo; **~ me!** ¡perdón!; **if you will ~ me** con su permiso.

execute [ˈɛksɪkjuːt] *vt* (*plan*) realizar; (*order*) cumplir; (*person*) ajusticiar, ejecutar; **execution** *n* realización *f*; cumplimiento; ejecución *f*; **executioner** *n* verdugo.

executive [ɪgˈzɛkjutɪv] *n* (*COMM, POL*) ejecutivo // *a* ejecutivo.

executor [ɪgˈzɛkjutəʳ] *n* albacea *m*, testamentario.

exemplary [ɪgˈzɛmplərɪ] *a* ejemplar.

exemplify [ɪgˈzɛmplɪfaɪ] *vt* ejemplificar.

exempt [ɪgˈzɛmpt] *a*: **~ from** exento de // *vt*: **to ~ sb from** eximir a uno de; **~ion** [ɪgˈzɛmpʃən] *n* exención *f*; (*immunity*) inmunidad *f*.

exercise [ˈɛksəsaɪz] *n* ejercicio // *vt* ejercer; (*right*) valerse de; (*dog*) llevar de paseo // *vi* hacer ejercicio(s); **~ book** *n* cuaderno.

exert [ɪgˈzəːt] *vt* ejercer; **to ~ o.s.** esforzarse, afanarse; (*overdo things*) trabajar demasiado; **~ion** *n* esfuerzo.

exhaust [ɪgˈzɔːst] *n* (*pipe*) escape *m*; (*fumes*) gases *mpl* de escape // *vt* agotar; **~ion** [ɪgˈzɔːstʃən] *n* agotamiento; **nervous ~ion** postración *f* nerviosa; **~ive** *a* exhaustivo.

exhibit [ɪgˈzɪbɪt] *n* (*ART*) obra expuesta; (*LAW*) objeto expuesto // *vt* (*show*) manifestar; (*emotion*) acusar; (*film*) presentar; (*paintings*) exponer; **~ion** [ɛksɪˈbɪʃən] *n* exposición *f*; **~ionist** [ɛksɪˈbɪʃənɪst] *n* exhibicionista *m/f*.

exhilarating [ɪgˈzɪləreɪtɪŋ] *a* estimulante, tónico.

exhort [ɪgˈzɔːt] *vt* exhortar.

exile [ˈɛksaɪl] *n* exilio; (*person*) exiliado/a // *vt* desterrar, exiliar.

exist [ɪgˈzɪst] *vi* existir; (*live*) vivir; **~ence** *n* existencia; (*life*) vida; **~ing** *a* existente, actual.

exit [ˈɛksɪt] *n* salida.

exonerate [ɪgˈzɔnəreɪt] *vt*: **to ~ from** exculpar de.

exorcize [ˈɛksɔːsaɪz] *vt* exorcizar.

exotic [ɪgˈzɔtɪk] *a* exótico.

expand [ɪkˈspænd] *vt* (*widen*) ensanchar; (*number*) aumentar // *vi* (*trade etc*) expandirse; (*gas, metal*) dilatarse.

expanse [ɪkˈspæns] *n* extensión *f*; (*of wings*) envergadura.

expansion [ɪkˈspænʃən] *n* (*of town*) ensanche *m*; (*of trade*) expansión *f*.

expatriate [ɛksˈpætrɪət] *n* expatriado/a.

expect [ɪkˈspɛkt] *vt* (*gen*) esperar; (*count*

on) contar con; (suppose) suponer // vi: to
be ~ing estar encinta; ~ant mother n
mujer f encinta; ~ation [ɛkspek'teɪʃən] n
esperanza, expectativa.
expedience [ɛk'spi:dɪəns], **expediency**
[ɛk'spi:dɪənsɪ] n conveniencia; **expedient**
a conveniente, oportuno // n recurso,
expediente m.
expedition [ɛkspə'dɪʃən] n expedición f.
expel [ɪk'spɛl] vt arrojar; (SCOL) expulsar.
expend [ɪk'spɛnd] vt gastar, (use up)
consumir; ~able a prescindible; ~iture
n gastos mpl, desembolso.
expense [ɪk'spɛns] n gasto, gastos mpl;
(high cost) costa; ~s npl (COMM) gastos
mpl; **at the ~ of** a costa o expensas de;
~ **account** n cuenta de gastos.
expensive [ɪk'spɛnsɪv] a caro, costoso.
experience [ɪk'spɪərɪəns] n experiencia //
vt experimentar; (suffer) sufrir; ~d a
experimentado.
experiment [ɪk'spɛrɪmənt] n experimento
// vi hacer experimentos; ~al [-'mɛntl] a
experimental.
expert ['ɛkspə:t] a experto, perito // n
experto, perito; (specialist) especialista
m/f; ~ise [-'ti:z] n pericia.
expire [ɪk'spaɪə*] vi (gen) expirar; (end)
terminar; (run out) caducar, vencerse;
expiry n expiración f; terminación f;
vencimiento.
explain [ɪk'spleɪn] vt explicar; (clarify)
aclarar; (demonstrate) exponer;
explanation [ɛksplə'neɪʃən] n explicación
f; aclaración f; **explanatory** [ɪk'splænətrɪ]
a explicativo; aclaratorio.
explicit [ɪk'splɪsɪt] a explícito.
explode [ɪk'spləud] vi estallar, explotar;
(with anger) reventar // vt volar, explotar.
exploit ['ɛksplɔɪt] n hazaña // vt [ɪk'splɔɪt]
explotar; ~ation [-'teɪʃən] n explotación f.
exploration [ɛksplə'reɪʃən] n exploración
f; **exploratory** [ɪk'splɔrətrɪ] a (fig: talks)
exploratorio, de sondaje.
explore [ɪk'splɔ:*] vt explorar; (fig)
examinar, sondar; **explorer** n explorador
m.
explosion [ɪk'spləuʒən] n explosión f;
explosive [-sɪv] a, n explosivo.
exponent [ɪk'spəunənt] n exponente m/f,
intérprete m/f.
export [ɛk'spɔ:t] vt exportar // n ['ɛkspɔ:t]
exportación f // cpd de exportación;
~ation [-'teɪʃən] n exportación f; ~er n
exportador m.
expose [ɪk'spəuz] vt exponer; (unmask)
desenmascarar; ~d a expuesto; (position)
desabrigado.
exposure [ɪk'spəuʒə*] n exposición f;
(PHOT) revelación f; (: shot) fotografía; **to
die from ~** (MED) morir de frío; ~
meter n fotómetro.
expound [ɪk'spaund] vt exponer, explicar.
express [ɪk'sprɛs] a (definite) expreso,
explícito; (letter etc) urgente // n (train)
rápido // ad (send) por carta urgente // vt
expresar; (squeeze) exprimir; ~ion [ɪk-

'sprɛʃən] n expresión f; ~ive a expresivo;
~ly ad expresamente.
expulsion [ɪk'spʌlʃən] n expulsión f.
exquisite [ɛk'skwɪzɪt] a exquisito.
extend [ɪk'stɛnd] vt (visit, street)
prolongar; (building) ensanchar; (offer)
ofrecer // vi (land) extenderse.
extension [ɪk'stɛnʃən] n extensión f;
(building) ampliación f; (TEL: line) línea
derivada; (: telephone) extensión f; (of
deadline) prórroga.
extensive [ɪk'stɛnsɪv] a (gen) extenso;
(broad) vasto, ancho; (frequent) general,
común; **he's travelled ~ly** ha viajado
por muchos países.
extent [ɪk'stɛnt] n (breadth) extensión f;
(scope) alcance m; **to some ~** hasta
cierto punto; **to the ~ of...** hasta el punto
de...; **to such an ~ that...** hasta tal punto
que...; **to what ~?** ¿hasta qué punto?
exterior [ɛk'stɪərɪə*] a exterior, externo
// n exterior m; (appearance) aspecto.
exterminate [ɪk'stə:mɪneɪt] vt
exterminar; **extermination** [-'neɪʃən] n
exterminación f.
external [ɛk'stə:nl] a externo, exterior;
~ly ad por fuera.
extinct [ɪk'stɪŋkt] a extinto; ~ion [ɪk-
'stɪŋkʃən] n extinción f.
extinguish [ɪk'stɪŋgwɪʃ] vt extinguir,
apagar; ~er n extintor m.
extort [ɪk'stɔ:t] vt sacar a la fuerza (from
sb de uno); ~ion [ɪk'stɔ:ʃən] n exacción f;
~ionate [ɪk'stɔ:ʃnət] a excesivo,
exorbitante.
extra ['ɛkstrə] a adicional; (excessive) de
más, de sobra; (bonus: payment)
extraordinario // ad (in addition)
especialmente // n (addition) extra m,
suplemento; (THEATRE) extra m/f,
comparsa m/f; (newspaper) edición f
extraordinaria.
extra... [ɛkstrə] pref extra... .
extract [ɪk'strækt] vt sacar, extraer;
(confession) arrancar, obtener // n
['ɛkstrækt] extracto.
extradite ['ɛkstrədaɪt] vt (from country)
conceder la extradición de; (to country)
obtener la extradición de; **extradition**
[-'dɪʃən] n extradición f.
extramarital [ɛkstrə'mærɪtl] a extra-
matrimonial.
extramural [ɛkstrə'mjuərl] a de
extramuros.
extraordinary [ɪk'strɔ:dnrɪ] a extraordinario; (odd) raro.
extravagant [ɪk'strævəgənt] a (lavish)
pródigo; (wasteful) derrochador(a); (price)
exorbitante; (praise) excesivo; (odd) raro.
extreme [ɪk'stri:m] a extremo; (poverty
etc) extremado; (case) excepcional // n
extremo, extremidad f; ~ly ad
sumamente, extremadamente; **extremist**
a, n extremista m/f.
extremity [ɪk'strɛmətɪ] n extremidad f,
punta; (need) apuro, necesidad f.
extricate ['ɛkstrɪkeɪt] vt librar.

extrovert ['ɛkstrəvəːt] n extrovertido/a.
exuberant [ɪg'zjuːbərnt] a (person) eufórico; (style) exuberante.
exude [ɪg'zjuːd] vt rezumar, sudar.
exult [ɪg'zʌlt] vi regocijarse.
eye [aɪ] n ojo // vt mirar de soslayo, ojear; **to keep an ~ on** vigilar, estar pendiente de; **~ball** n globo del ojo; **~bath** n ojera; **~brow** n ceja; **~brow pencil** n lápiz m de cejas; **~-catching** a llamativo; **~drops** npl gotas fpl para los ojos; **~lash** n pestaña; **~lid** n párpado; **~-opener** n revelación f, gran sorpresa; **~shadow** n sombreador m de ojos; **~sight** n vista; **~sore** n monstruosidad f; **~wash** n (fig) disparates mpl, tonterías fpl; **~witness** n testigo m/f presencial.
eyrie ['ɪərɪ] n aguilera.

F

F. abbr of **Fahrenheit.**
fable ['feɪbl] n fábula.
fabric ['fæbrɪk] n tejido, tela.
fabrication [fæbrɪ'keɪʃən] n invención f.
fabulous ['fæbjuləs] a fabuloso.
façade [fə'sɑːd] n fachada.
face [feɪs] n cara, rostro; (of clock) esfera; (side, surface) superficie f // vt (person) encararse con; (building) dar a; **to lose ~** desprestigiarse; **in the ~ of** (difficulties etc) en vista de; **on the ~ of it** a primera vista; **~ to ~** cara a cara; **to ~ up to** vt fus hacer frente a, arrostrar; **~ cloth** n paño; **~ cream** n crema (de belleza); **~ lift** n cirugía estética; **~ powder** n polvos mpl; **~-saving** a para salvar las apariencias.
facet ['fæsɪt] n faceta.
facetious [fə'siːʃəs] a chistoso.
face value ['feɪs'væljuː] n (of stamp) valor m nominal; **to take sth at ~** (fig) tomar algo en sentido literal, aceptar las apariencias de algo.
facial ['feɪʃəl] a de la cara.
facile ['fæsaɪl] a superficial, ligero.
facilitate [fə'sɪlɪteɪt] vt facilitar.
facilities [fə'sɪlɪtɪz] npl facilidades fpl.
facing ['feɪsɪŋ] prep frente a // a de enfrente.
fact [fækt] n hecho; **in ~** en realidad.
faction ['fækʃən] n facción f.
factor ['fæktə] n factor m.
factory ['fæktərɪ] n fábrica.
factual ['fæktjuəl] a objetivo.
faculty ['fækəltɪ] n facultad f; (US: teaching staff) profesorado.
fade [feɪd] vi desteñirse; (sound, hope) desvanecerse; (light) apagarse; (flower) marchitarse.
fag [fæg] n (col: cigarette) pitillo; **~ end** n colilla; **~ged out** a (col) agotado.
fail [feɪl] vt (candidate) suspender; (exam) no aprobar // vi acabarse; (engine) fallar; (voice) desfallecer; (patient) debilitarse; **to ~ to do sth** (neglect) dejar de hacer algo;

(be unable) no poder hacer algo; **without ~** sin falta; **~ing** n falta, defecto // prep a falta de; **~ure** ['feɪljə] n fracaso; (person) fracasado/a; (mechanical etc) fallo.
faint [feɪnt] a débil; (recollection) vago; (mark) apenas visible // n desmayo // vi desmayarse; **to feel ~** estar mareado, marearse; **~-hearted** a pusilánime; **~ly** ad débilmente; vagamente; **~ness** n debilidad f.
fair [fɛə] a justo; (colour) rubio; (weather) bueno; (good enough) suficiente; (sizeable) considerable // ad (play) limpio // n feria; (funfair) parque m de atracciones; **~ly** ad (justly) con justicia; (equally) equitativamente; (quite) bastante; **~ness** n justicia; (impartiality) imparcialidad f.
fairy ['fɛərɪ] n hada; **~ tale** n cuento de hadas.
faith [feɪθ] n fe f; (trust) confianza; (sect) religión f; **~ful** a fiel; **~fully** ad fielmente; **yours ~fully** le saluda atentamente.
fake [feɪk] n (painting etc) falsificación f; (person) impostor m // a falso // vt fingir; (painting etc) falsificar; **his illness is a ~** su enfermedad es una invención.
falcon ['fɔːlkən] n halcón m.
fall [fɔːl] n caída; (US: autumn) otoño // vi, pt **fell**, pp **fallen** ['fɔːlən] caer, caerse; (price) bajar; **~s** npl (waterfall) cascada, salto de agua; **to ~ flat** vi (on one's face) caerse (boca abajo); (plan) fracasar; **to ~ back** vi retroceder; **to ~ back on** vt fus (remedy etc) recurrir a; **to ~ backwards** vi caer de espaldas; **to ~ behind** vi quedarse atrás; **to ~ down** vi (person) caerse; (building, hopes) derrumbarse; **to ~ for** vt fus (trick) dejarse engañar por; (person) enamorarse de; **to ~ in** vi (roof) hundirse; (MIL) alinearse; **to ~ off** vi caerse; (diminish) disminuir; **to ~ out** vi (friends etc) reñir; (MIL) romper filas; **to ~ through** vi (plan, project) fracasar.
fallacy ['fæləsɪ] n (error) error m; (lie) mentira.
fallible ['fæləbl] a falible.
fallout ['fɔːlaut] n lluvia radioactiva; **~ shelter** n refugio contra ataques nucleares.
false [fɔːls] a (gen) falso; (hair, teeth etc) postizo; (disloyal) desleal, traidor(a); **under ~ pretences** con engaños; **~hood** n (lie) mentira; (falseness) falsedad f; **~ly** ad (accuse) falsamente; **~ teeth** npl dentadura postiza sg.
falter ['fɔːltə] vi vacilar.
fame [feɪm] n fama.
familiar [fə'mɪlɪə] a familiar; (well-known) conocido; (tone) de confianza; **to be ~ with** (subject) estar enterado de; **~ity** [fəmɪlɪ'ærɪtɪ] n familiaridad f; **~ize** [fə'mɪlɪəraɪz] vr: **to ~ize o.s. with** familiarizarse con.
family ['fæmɪlɪ] n familia; **~ business** n

negocio familiar; ~ **doctor** n médico de cabecera.

famine ['fæmɪn] n hambre f.

famished ['fæmɪʃt] a hambriento.

famous ['feɪməs] a famoso, célebre; ~**ly** ad (get on) estupendamente.

fan [fæn] n abanico; (ELEC) ventilador m; (person) aficionado/a // vt abanicar; (fire, quarrel) atizar; **to ~ out** vi desparramarse.

fanatic [fə'nætɪk] n fanático/a; ~**al** a fanático.

fan belt ['fænbɛlt] n correa de ventilador.

fanciful ['fænsɪful] a (gen) fantástico; (imaginary) imaginario.

fancy ['fænsɪ] n (whim) capricho, antojo; (taste) afición f, gusto; (imagination) imaginación f; (delusion) quimera // a (decorative) hermoso; (luxury) de lujo; (as decoration) de adorno // vt (feel like, want) tener ganas de; (imagine) imaginarse; (think) creer; **to take a ~ to** encapricharse por, tomar afición a; **it took** or **caught my ~** me cayó en gracia; **to ~ that...** imaginarse que...; **he fancies her** le gusta (ella); ~ **dress** n disfraz m; ~**-dress ball** n baile m de disfraces.

fang [fæŋ] n colmillo.

fantastic [fæn'tæstɪk] a fantástico.

fantasy ['fæntəzɪ] n fantasía.

far [fɑː] a (distant) lejano // ad lejos; ~ **away**, ~ **off** (a lo) lejos; ~ **better** mucho mejor; ~ **from** lejos de; **by** ~ con mucho; **go as** ~ **as the farm** vaya hasta la granja; **as** ~ **as I know** que yo sepa; **how** ~? ¿hasta dónde?; (fig) ¿hasta qué punto?; **the F~ East** el Extremo Oriente; ~**away** a remoto.

farce [fɑːs] n farsa; **farcical** a absurdo.

fare [fɛə] n (on trains, buses) precio (del billete); (in taxi: cost) tarifa; (: passenger) pasajero; (food) comida.

farewell [fɛə'wɛl] excl, n adiós m.

farm [fɑːm] n granja, finca, estancia (AM) // vt cultivar; ~**er** n granjero, estanciero (AM); ~**hand** n peón m; ~**house** n casa de labranza; ~**ing** n (gen) agricultura; (tilling) cultivo; ~**land** n tierra de cultivo; ~ **worker** n = ~**hand**; ~**yard** n corral m.

far-sighted ['fɑː'saɪtɪd] a previsor(a).

fart [fɑːt] (col!) n pedo // vi tirarse un pedo.

farther ['fɑːðə] ad más lejos, más allá.

farthest ['fɑːðɪst] superlative of **far**.

fascinate ['fæsɪneɪt] vt fascinar; **fascination** [-'neɪʃən] n fascinación f.

fascism ['fæʃɪzəm] n fascismo; **fascist** [-ɪst] a, n fascista m/f.

fashion ['fæʃən] n moda; (manner) manera // vt formar; **in** ~ a la moda; **out of** ~ pasado de moda; ~**able** a de moda; ~ **show** n desfile m de modelos.

fast [fɑːst] a rápido; (dye, colour) sólido; (clock): **to be** ~ estar adelantado // ad rápidamente, de prisa; (stuck, held) firmemente // n ayuno // vi ayunar; ~

asleep profundamente dormido.

fasten ['fɑːsn] vt asegurar, sujetar; (coat, belt) abrochar // vi cerrarse; ~**er**, ~**ing** n (gen) cierre m; (of door etc) cerrojo; **zip** ~**er** cremallera.

fastidious [fæs'tɪdɪəs] a (fussy) delicado; (demanding) exigente.

fat [fæt] a gordo; (meat) con mucha grasa; (greasy) grasiento // n grasa; (on person) carnes fpl; (lard) manteca.

fatal ['feɪtl] a (gen) fatal; (injury) mortal; (consequence) funesto; ~**ism** n fatalismo; ~**ity** [fə'tælɪtɪ] n (road death etc) víctima m/f; ~**ly** ad: ~**ly injured** herido a muerte.

fate [feɪt] n destino; (of person) suerte f; ~**ful** a fatídico.

father ['fɑːðə] n padre m; ~**hood** n paternidad f; ~**-in-law** n suegro; ~**ly** a paternal.

fathom ['fæðəm] n braza // vt (NAUT) sondear; (unravel) desentrañar; (understand) lograr comprender.

fatigue [fə'tiːg] n fatiga, cansancio.

fatten ['fætn] vt, vi engordar.

fatty ['fætɪ] a (food) graso // n (fam) gordito/a, gordinflón/ona m/f.

faucet ['fɔːsɪt] n (US) grifo.

fault [fɔːlt] n (error) falta; (blame) culpa; (defect: in character) defecto; (in manufacture) desperfecto; (GEO) falla // vt tachar; **it's my** ~ es culpa mía; **to find** ~ **with** criticar, poner peros a; **at** ~ culpable; ~**less** a (action) intachable; (person) sin defectos; ~**y** a defectuoso.

fauna ['fɔːnə] n fauna.

faux pas ['fəu'pɑː] n paso en falso; (gaffe) plancha.

favour, favor (US) ['feɪvə] n favor m; (support) apoyo; (approval) aprobación f // vt (proposition) estar a favor de, aprobar; (person etc) favorecer; (assist) ser propicio a; **to ask a** ~ **of** pedir un favor a; **to do sb a** ~ hacer un favor a uno; **to find** ~ **with** caer en gracia de; **in** ~ **of** a favor de; ~**able** a favorable; ~**ite** [-rɪt] a, n favorito, preferido; ~**itism** n favoritismo.

fawn [fɔːn] n cervato // a (also: ~**-coloured**) color de cervato, leonado.

fear [fɪə] n miedo, temor m // vt tener miedo a o de, temer; **for** ~ **of** por temor a; ~**ful** a temeroso, miedoso; (cowardly) tímido; (awful) terrible; ~**less** a (gen) sin miedo o temor; (bold) audaz.

feasible ['fiːzəbl] a factible.

feast [fiːst] n banquete m; (REL: also: ~ **day**) fiesta // vt, vi banquetear.

feat [fiːt] n hazaña.

feather ['fɛðə] n pluma; ~**-weight** n (BOXING) peso pluma.

feature ['fiːtʃə] n (gen) característica; (ANAT) rasgo; (article) crónica // vt (subj: film) presentar // vi figurar; ~**s** npl (of face) facciones fpl; ~ **film** n película (de largo metraje).

February ['fɛbruərɪ] n febrero.

fed [fɛd] pt, pp of **feed.**

federal ['fɛdərəl] a federal; **federation** [-'reɪʃən] n federación f.

fed-up [fɛd'ʌp] a: **to be ~** estar harto.

fee [fiː] n derechos mpl, honorarios mpl; (of school) matrícula; (of club) cuota.

feeble ['fiːbl] a débil; **~-minded** a imbécil.

feed [fiːd] n (gen) comida; (of baby) alimento infantil; (of animal) pienso // vt, pt, pp **fed** (gen) alimentar; (baby: breastfeed) dar el pecho a; (animal) dar de comer a; (data, information): **to ~ into** suministrar a; **to ~ on** vt fus alimentarse de; **~ing bottle** n biberón m.

feel [fiːl] n (sensation) sensación f; (sense of touch) tacto // vt, pt, pp **felt** tocar, palpar; (cold, pain etc) sentir; (think, believe) creer; **to ~ hungry/cold** tener hambre/frío; **to ~ lonely/better** sentirse solo/mejor; **it ~s soft** es suave al tacto; **to ~ like** (want) tener ganas de; **to ~ about** or **around** tantear; **~er** n (of insect) antena; **to put out ~ers** (fig) sondear; **~ing** n (gen) sensación f; (foreboding) presentimiento; (opinion) opinión f; (emotion) sentimiento.

feet [fiːt] pl of **foot.**

feign [feɪn] vt fingir.

feline ['fiːlaɪn] a felino.

fell [fɛl] pt of **fall** // vt (tree) talar.

fellow ['fɛləu] n (gen) tipo; (fam) tío; (of learned society) socio; **~ students** compañeros mpl de curso, condiscípulos mpl; **~ citizen** n conciudadano; **~ countryman** n compatriota m/f; **~ men** npl semejantes mpl; **~ship** n compañerismo; (grant) beca.

felony ['fɛlənɪ] n crimen m.

felt [fɛlt] pt, pp of **feel** // n fieltro; **~-tip pen** n rotulador m.

female ['fiːmeɪl] n (woman) mujer f; (zooL) hembra // a femenino.

feminine ['fɛmɪnɪn] a femenino.

feminist ['fɛmɪnɪst] n feminista.

fence [fɛns] n valla, cerca // vt (also: **~ in**) cercar // vi hacer esgrima; **fencing** n esgrima.

fend [fɛnd] vi: **to ~ for o.s.** arreglárselas por su cuenta.

fender ['fɛndə*] n guardafuego; (US: AUT) parachoques m inv; (: RAIL) trompa.

ferment [fə'mɛnt] vi fermentar // n ['fɔːmɛnt] (fig) agitación f; **~ation** [-'teɪʃən] n fermentación f.

fern [fɔːn] n helecho.

ferocious [fə'rəuʃəs] a feroz; **ferocity** [-'rɔsɪtɪ] n ferocidad f.

ferret ['fɛrɪt] n hurón m // vt: **to ~ out** descubrir.

ferry ['fɛrɪ] n (small) barca (de pasaje), balsa; (large: also: **~boat**) transbordador m // vt transportar.

fertile ['fɔːtaɪl] a fértil; (BIOL) fecundo; **fertility** [fə'tɪlɪtɪ] n fertilidad f; fecundidad f; **fertilize** ['fɔːtɪlaɪz] vt fertilizar;

fecundar; (AGR) abonar; **fertilizer** n fertilizante m.

fervent ['fɔːvənt] a ardiente, apasionado.

fester ['fɛstə*] vi ulcerarse.

festival ['fɛstɪvəl] n (REL) fiesta; (ART, MUS) festival m.

festive ['fɛstɪv] a festivo; **the ~ season** (Christmas) las Navidades.

festivities [fɛs'tɪvɪtɪz] npl fiestas fpl.

fetch [fɛtʃ] vt ir a buscar; (sell for) venderse por.

fetching ['fɛtʃɪŋ] a atractivo.

fête [feɪt] n fiesta.

fetish ['fɛtɪʃ] n fetiche m.

fetters ['fɛtəz] npl grillos mpl.

feud [fjuːd] n (hostility) enemistad f; (quarrel) disputa.

feudal ['fjuːdl] a feudal; **~ism** n feudalismo.

fever ['fiːvə*] n fiebre f; **~ish** a febril.

few [fjuː] a (not many) pocos; (some) algunos, unos; **a ~** a unos pocos // pron algunos; **~er** a menos; **~est** a los/las menos.

fiancé [fɪ'ɑ̃ːŋseɪ] n novio, prometido; **~e** n novia, prometida.

fiasco [fɪ'æskəu] n fiasco.

fibre, fiber (US) ['faɪbə*] n fibra; **~-glass** n fibra de vidrio.

fickle ['fɪkl] a inconstante.

fiction ['fɪkʃən] n (gen) ficción f; **~al** a novelesco; **fictitious** [fɪk'tɪʃəs] a ficticio.

fiddle ['fɪdl] n (MUS) violín m; (cheating) trampa; (swindle) estafa // vt (accounts) falsificar; **to ~ with** vt fus jugar con; **fiddler** n violinista m/f.

fidelity [fɪ'dɛlɪtɪ] n fidelidad f.

fidget ['fɪdʒɪt] vi moverse nerviosamente; **~y** a nervioso.

field [fiːld] n campo; (ELEC) prado; (fig) esfera, especialidad f; (competitors) competidores mpl; (entrants) concurrentes mpl; **~ glasses** npl gemelos mpl; **~ marshal** n mariscal m; **~work** n trabajo de campo.

fiend [fiːnd] n demonio; **~ish** a diabólico.

fierce [fɪəs] a feroz; (wind, attack) violento; (heat) intenso; (fighting, enemy) encarnizado.

fiery ['faɪərɪ] a (burning) ardiente; (temperament) apasionado.

fifteen [fɪf'tiːn] num quince.

fifth [fɪfθ] a, n quinto.

fiftieth ['fɪftɪɪθ] a quincuagésimo.

fifty ['fɪftɪ] num cincuenta.

fig [fɪg] n higo.

fight [faɪt] n (gen) pelea; (MIL) combate m; (struggle) lucha // vt, pt, pp **fought** vt luchar contra; (cancer, alcoholism) combatir // vi pelear, luchar; **~er** n combatiente m/f; (fig) luchador/a m/f; (plane) caza; **~ing** n (gen) el luchar; (battle) combate m.

figment ['fɪgmənt] n: **a ~ of the imagination** una quimera.

figurative ['fɪgjurətɪv] a figurado.

figure 260 **fit**

figure ['fɪgə*] n (DRAWING, GEOM) figura, dibujo; (number, cipher) cifra; (body, outline) talle m, tipo // vt (esp US) imaginar // vi (appear) figurar; **to ~ out** vt (understand) comprender; **~head** n mascarón m de proa; **~ skating** n patinaje m de figuras.

file [faɪl] n (tool) lima; (dossier) expediente m; (folder) carpeta; (row) fila // vt limar; (papers) clasificar; (LAW. claim) presentar; (store) archivar; **to ~ in/out** vi entrar/salir en fila; **to ~ past** vt fus desfilar ante; **filing** n el archivar; **filing cabinet** n fichero, archivo.

fill [fɪl] vt llenar // n: **to eat one's ~** llenarse; **to ~ in** vt rellenar; **to ~ up** vt llenar (hasta el borde) // vi (AUT) poner gasolina.

fillet ['fɪlɪt] n filete m.

filling ['fɪlɪŋ] n (CULIN) relleno; (for tooth) empaste m; **~ station** n estación f de servicio.

film [fɪlm] n película // vt (scene) filmar // vi rodar (una película); **~ star** n astro, estrella de cine; **~strip** n tira de película.

filter ['fɪltə*] n filtro // vt filtrar; **~ tip** n boquilla.

filth [fɪlθ] n suciedad f; **~y** a sucio; (language) obsceno.

fin [fɪn] n (gen) aleta.

final ['faɪnl] a (last) final, último; (definitive) definitivo, terminante // n (SPORT) final f; **~s** npl (SCOL) exámenes mpl finales.

finale [fɪ'nɑːlɪ] n final m.

final: ~ist n (SPORT) finalista m/f; **~ize** vt concluir, completar; **~ly** ad (lastly) por último, finalmente; (eventually) por fin; (irrevocably) de modo definitivo.

finance [faɪ'næns] n (money) fondos mpl; **~s** npl finanzas fpl // vt financiar; **financial** [-'nænʃəl] a financiero; (economic) económico; **financier** n (gen) financiero; (investor) inversionista m/f.

find [faɪnd], pt, pp **found** vt (gen) encontrar, hallar; (come upon) descubrir // n hallazgo; descubrimiento; **to ~ sb guilty** (LAW) declarar culpable a uno; **to ~ out** vt averiguar; (truth, secret) descubrir; **to ~ out about** (by chance) enterarse de; **~ings** npl (LAW) veredicto sg, fallo sg; (of report) recomendaciones fpl.

fine [faɪn] a (delicate) fino; (good) bueno; (beautiful) bonito // ad (well) bien; (small) delgado // n (LAW) multa // vt (LAW) multar; **to be ~** (weather) hacer buen tiempo; **~ arts** npl bellas artes fpl.

finery ['faɪnərɪ] n adornos mpl.

finesse [fɪ'nɛs] n sutileza.

finger ['fɪŋgə*] n dedo // vt (touch) manosear; (MUS) tocar (distraídamente); **little/index ~** dedo meñique/índice; **~nail** n uña; **~print** n huella dactilar; **~tip** n yema del dedo.

finicky ['fɪnɪkɪ] a (fussy) delicado.

finish ['fɪnɪʃ] n (end) fin m; (goal) meta; (polish etc) acabado // vt, vi terminar; **to ~ off** vt acabar, terminar; (kill) acabar con; **to ~ third** llegar el tercero; **~ing line** n línea de llegada o meta.

finite ['faɪnaɪt] a finito.

Finland ['fɪnlənd] n Finlandia.

Finn [fɪn] n finlandés/esa m/f; **~ish** a finlandés(esa) // n (LING) finlandés m.

fiord [fjɔːd] n fiordo.

fir [fəː*] n abeto.

fire ['faɪə*] n (gen) fuego; (accidental) incendio // vt (gun) disparar; (set fire to) incendiar; (excite) exaltar; (interest) despertar; (dismiss) despedir // vi encenderse; **on ~** ardiendo, en llamas; **~ alarm** n alarma de incendios; **~arm** n arma de fuego; **~ brigade** n (cuerpo de) bomberos mpl; **~ engine** n coche m de bomberos; **~ escape** n escalera de incendios; **~ extinguisher** n extintor m (de fuego); **~man** n bombero; **~place** n chimenea; **~proof** a a prueba de fuego; **~side** n hogar m; **~ station** n parque m de bomberos; **~wood** n leña; **~works** npl fuegos mpl artificiales.

firing ['faɪərɪŋ] n (MIL) disparos mpl, tiroteo; **~ squad** n pelotón m de ejecución.

firm [fəːm] a firme // n firma; **~ly** ad firmemente; **~ness** n firmeza.

first [fəːst] a primero // ad (before others) primero; (when listing reasons etc) en primer lugar, primeramente // n (person: in race) primero; (AUT) primera; **at ~** al principio; **~ of all** ante todo; **~-aid kit** n botiquín m; **~-class** a de primera clase; **~-hand** a de primera mano; **~ly** ad en primer lugar; **~ name** n nombre m de pila; **~-rate** a de primera clase.

fir tree n abeto.

fiscal ['fɪskəl] a fiscal.

fish [fɪʃ] n, pl inv pez m; (food) pescado // vt, vi pescar; **to go ~ing** ir de pesca; **~erman** n pescador m; **~ery** n pesquería; **~ fingers** npl dedos mpl de pescado; **~ing boat** n barca de pesca; **~ing line** n sedal m; **~ing rod** n caña (de pescar); **~ing tackle** n aparejo (de pescar); **~ market** n mercado de pescado; **~monger** n pescadero; **~monger's (shop)** n pescadería; **~y** a (fig) sospechoso.

fission ['fɪʃən] n fisión f.

fissure ['fɪʃə*] n fisura.

fist [fɪst] n puño.

fit [fɪt] a (MED, SPORT) en (buena) forma; (proper) adecuado, apropiado // vt (clothes) sentar bien a; (try on: clothes) probar; (facts) cuadrar o corresponder con; (accommodate) ajustar, adaptar; (correspond exactly) encajar en // vi (clothes) entallar; (in space, gap) caber; (correspond) corresponder // n (MED) ataque m; **~ to** apto para; **~ for** apropiado para; **this dress is a good ~** este vestido me sienta bien; **to ~ in** vi (gen) encajarse; (fig: person) llevarse bien (con todos); **to ~ out** (also: **~ up**) vt equipar; **~ful** a espasmódico, intermitente; **~ment** n mueble m; **~ness** n (MED) salud f; (of remark) conveniencia; **~ter** n ajustador m; **~ting** a apropiado // n (of dress) prueba; **~tings** npl instalaciones fpl.

five [faɪv] num cinco; **fiver** n (Brit: col) billete m de cinco libras.

fix [fɪks] vt (secure) fijar, asegurar; (mend) arreglar // n: **to be in a ~** estar en un aprieto; **~ed** [fɪkst] a (prices etc) fijo; **~ture** ['fɪkstʃə*] n cosa fija; (furniture) mueble m fijo; (SPORT) partido.

fizz [fɪz] vi hacer efervescencia.

fizzle ['fɪzl]: **~ out** vi apagarse.

fizzy ['fɪzɪ] a (drink) gaseoso; (gen) efervescente.

fjord [fjɔːd] = **fiord**.

flabbergasted ['flæbəgɑːstɪd] a pasmado.

flabby ['flæbɪ] a flojo; (fat) gordo.

flag [flæg] n bandera; (stone) losa // vi acabarse, decaer; **to ~ sb down** hacer signos a uno para que se detenga; **~pole** n asta de bandera.

flagrant ['fleɪgrənt] a flagrante.

flair [flɛə*] n aptitud f especial.

flake [fleɪk] n (of rust, paint) escama; (of snow, soap powder) copo // vi (also: **~ off**) desprenderse en escamas.

flamboyant [flæm'bɔɪənt] a (dress) vistoso; (person) extravagante.

flame [fleɪm] n llama.

flamingo [flə'mɪŋɡəu] n flamenco.

flammable ['flæməbl] a inflamable.

flan [flæn] n tarta.

flank [flæŋk] n flanco; (of person) costado // vt flanquear.

flannel ['flænl] n (also: **face ~**) paño; (fabric) franela; (col) coba; **~s** npl pantalones mpl de franela.

flap [flæp] n (of pocket) cartera; (of envelope) solapa; (of table) hoja (plegadiza); (wing movement) aletazo // vt (wings) aletear // vi (sail, flag) ondear.

flare [flɛə*] n llamarada; (MIL) bengala; (in skirt etc) vuelo; **to ~ up** vi encenderse; (fig: person) encolerizarse; (: revolt) estallar.

flash [flæʃ] n relámpago; (also: **news ~**) noticias fpl de última hora; (PHOT) flash m // vt (light, headlights) encender y apagar (la luz); (torch) encender // vi brillar, relampaguear; **in a ~** en un instante; **he ~ed by** or **past** pasó como un rayo; **~back** n flashback m; **~ bulb** n bombilla fusible; **~er** n (AUT) intermitente m.

flashy ['flæʃɪ] a (pej) ostentoso.

flask [flɑːsk] n frasco; (also: **vacuum ~**) termo.

flat [flæt] a llano; (smooth) liso; (tyre) desinflado; (beer) muerto; (MUS) desafinado // n (apartment) piso, apartamento; (MUS) bemol m; (AUT) pinchazo; **~ly** ad terminantemente, de plano; **~ness** n (of land) llanura, lo llano; **~ten** vt (also: **~ten out**) allanar;

(smooth out) alisar; (demolish) aplastar.

flatter ['flætə*] vt adular, halagar; **~er** n adulador/a m/f; **~ing** a halagüeño; **~y** n adulación f.

flatulence ['flætjuləns] n flatulencia.

flaunt [flɔːnt] vt ostentar, lucir.

flavour, flavor (US) ['fleɪvə*] n sabor m, gusto // vt sazonar, condimentar; **~ed with** con sabor a; **~ing** n condimento.

flaw [flɔː] n defecto; **~less** a intachable.

flax [flæks] n lino; **~en** a rubio.

flea [fliː] n pulga; **~pit** n cine m de baja categoría.

flee [fliː], pt, pp **fled** [flɛd] vt huir de, abandonar // vi huir, fugarse.

fleece [fliːs] n vellón m; (wool) lana // vt (col) pelar.

fleet [fliːt] n (gen) flota; (of lorries etc) escuadra.

fleeting ['fliːtɪŋ] a fugaz.

Flemish ['flɛmɪʃ] a flamenco.

flesh [flɛʃ] n carne f; (of fruit) pulpa; **of ~ and blood** de carne y hueso.

flew [fluː] pt of **fly**.

flex [flɛks] n cordón m // vt (muscles) tensar; **~ibility** [-ɪ'bɪlɪtɪ] n flexibilidad f; **~ible** a flexible.

flick [flɪk] n golpecito; (with finger) capirotazo; (with whip) chasquido // vt dar un golpecito a; **to ~ through** vt fus hojear.

flicker ['flɪkə*] vi (light) parpadear; (flame) vacilar // n parpadeo.

flier ['flaɪə*] n aviador/a m/f.

flight [flaɪt] n vuelo; (escape) huida, fuga; (also: **~ of steps**) tramo (de escaleras); **to take ~** huir, darse a la fuga; **to put to ~** ahuyentar; **~ deck** n (AVIAT) cabina.

flimsy ['flɪmzɪ] a (thin) muy ligero; (weak) débil.

flinch [flɪntʃ] vi acobardarse.

fling [flɪŋ], pt, pp **flung** vt arrojar.

flint [flɪnt] n pedernal m; (in lighter) piedra.

flip [flɪp] vt dar la vuelta a; (coin) echar a cara o cruz.

flippant ['flɪpənt] a poco serio.

flirt [flɜːt] vi coquetear, flirtear // n coqueta m/f; **~ation** [-'teɪʃən] n coqueteo, flirteo.

flit [flɪt] vi revolotear.

float [fləut] n flotador m; (in procession) carroza // vi flotar; (swimmer) hacer la plancha // vt (gen) hacer flotar; (company) lanzar.

flock [flɔk] n (of sheep) rebaño; (of birds) bandada; (of people) multitud f.

flog [flɔɡ] vt azotar; (col) vender.

flood [flʌd] n inundación f; (of words, tears etc) torrente m // vt inundar; **~ing** n inundación f; **~light** n foco.

floor [flɔː*] n suelo; (storey) piso; (of sea) fondo; (dance ~) pista // vt (fig) dejar sin respuesta; **ground ~** (Brit), **first ~** (US) planta baja; **first ~** (Brit), **second ~**

(*US*) primer piso; **~board** *n* tabla; **~show** *n* cabaret *m*.

flop [flɔp] *n* fracaso // *vi* (*fail*) fracasar.

floppy ['flɔpɪ] *a* flojo.

flora ['flɔːrə] *n* flora; **floral** ['flɔːrl] *a* floral.

florid ['flɔrɪd] *a* (*style*) florido.

florist ['flɔrɪst] *n* florista *m/f*; **~'s (shop)** *n* florería.

flounce [flauns] *n* volante *m*; **to ~ out** *vi* salir enfadado.

flounder ['flaundəʳ] *vi* tropezar.

flour ['flauəʳ] *n* harina.

flourish ['flʌrɪʃ] *vi* florecer; **~ing** *a* floreciente.

flout [flaut] *vt* burlarse de.

flow [fləu] *n* (*movement*) flujo; (*direction*) curso; (*tide*) corriente *f* // *vi* correr, fluir; (*blood*) derramarse.

flower ['flauəʳ] *n* flor *f* // *vi* florecer; **~bed** *n* macizo; **~pot** *n* tiesto; **~y** *a* florido.

flown [fləun] *pp of* **fly**.

flu [fluː] *n* gripe *f*.

fluctuate ['flʌktjueɪt] *vi* fluctuar; **fluctuation** [-'eɪʃən] *n* fluctuación *f*.

fluent ['fluːənt] *a* (*speech*) elocuente; he **speaks ~ French**, he's **~ in French** domina el francés; **~ly** *ad* con fluidez.

fluff [flʌf] *n* pelusa; **~y** *a* velloso.

fluid ['fluːɪd] *a, n* fluido, líquido.

fluke [fluːk] *n* (*col*) chiripa.

flung [flʌŋ] *pt, pp of* **fling**.

fluorescent [fluəˈrɛsnt] *a* fluorescente.

fluoride ['fluəraɪd] *n* fluoruro.

flurry ['flʌrɪ] *n* (*of snow*) ráfago; (*haste*) agitación *f*; **~ of activity** frenesí *m* de actividad.

flush [flʌʃ] *n* (*on face*) rubor *m*; (*plenty*) plenitud *f*, abundancia // *vt* limpiar con agua // *vi* ruborizarse // *a*: **~ with** a ras de; **to ~ the toilet** hacer funcionar el WC; **~ed** *a* ruborizado.

flustered ['flʌstəd] *a* aturdido.

flute [fluːt] *n* flauta.

flutter ['flʌtəʳ] *n* emoción *f*; (*of wings*) revoloteo, aleteo; (*fam: bet*) apuesta // *vi* revolotear.

flux [flʌks] *n* flujo; **in a state of ~** cambiando continuamente.

fly [flaɪ] *n* (*insect*) mosca; (*on trousers: also:* **flies**) bragueta // (*vb: pt* **flew**, *pp* **flown**) *vt* (*gen*) hacer volar; (*plane*) pilot(e)ar; (*cargo*) transportar (en avión); (*distances*) recorrer (en avión) // *vi* volar; (*passengers*) ir o subir en avión; (*escape*) evadirse; (*flag*) ondear; **to let ~** desahogarse; **~ing** *n* (*activity*) (el) volar // *a*: **~ing visit** visita relámpago; **with ~ing colours** con lucimiento; **~ing saucer** *n* platillo volante; **~over** *n* (*Brit: bridge*) paso a desnivel o superior; **~past** *n* desfile *m* aéreo; **~sheet** *n* (*for tent*) doble techo.

foal [fəul] *n* potro.

foam [fəum] *n* espuma // *vi* echar espuma; **~ rubber** *n* espuma de caucho.

fob [fɔb] *vt*: **to ~ sb off** deshacerse de alguien con excusas.

focal ['fəukəl] *a* focal.

focus ['fəukəs], *pl* **~es** *n* foco // *vt* (*field glasses etc*) enfocar; **to ~ on** enfocar a; **in/out of ~** enfocado/desenfocado.

fodder ['fɔdəʳ] *n* pienso.

foe [fəu] *n* enemigo.

foetus ['fiːtəs] *n* feto.

fog [fɔg] *n* niebla; **~gy** *a*: **it's ~gy** hay niebla, está brumoso.

foil [fɔɪl] *vt* frustrar // *n* hoja; (*also:* **kitchen ~**) papel *m* (de) aluminio; (*FENCING*) florete *m*.

fold [fəuld] *n* (*bend, crease*) pliegue *m*; (*of skin*) arruga; (*AGR*) redil *m* // *vt* doblar; **to ~ up** *vi* (*map etc*) plegarse, doblarse; (*business*) quebrar // *vt* (*map etc*) plegar; **~er** *n* (*for papers*) carpeta; (*brochure*) folleto; **~ing** *a* (*chair, bed*) plegable.

foliage ['fəulɪdʒ] *n* follaje *m*.

folk [fəuk] *npl* gente *f* // *a* popular, folklórico; **~s** *npl* familia, parientes *mpl*; **~lore** ['fəuklɔːʳ] *n* folklore *m*; **~song** *n* canción *f* popular o folklórica.

follow ['fɔləu] *vt* seguir // *vi* seguir; (*result*) resultar; he **~ed suit** hizo lo mismo; **to ~ up** *vt* (*letter, offer*) responder a; (*case*) investigar; **~er** *n* seguidor/a *m/f*, (*POL*) partidario/a; **~ing** *a* siguiente // *n* afición *f*, partidarios *mpl*.

folly ['fɔlɪ] *n* locura.

fond [fɔnd] *a* (*loving*) cariñoso; **to be ~ of** tener cariño a.

fondle ['fɔndl] *vt* acariciar.

fondness ['fɔndnɪs] *n* (*for things*) gusto; (*for people*) cariño.

font [fɔnt] *n* pila bautismal.

food [fuːd] *n* comida; **~ mixer** *n* batidora; **~ poisoning** *n* botulismo; **~stuffs** *npl* comestibles *mpl*.

fool [fuːl] *n* tonto/a; (*CULIN*) puré *m* de frutas con nata // *vt* engañar // *vi* (*gen*: **~ around**) bromear; (*waste time*) perder el tiempo; **~hardy** *a* temerario; **~ish** *a* tonto; (*stupid*) estúpido; (*careless*) imprudente; **~proof** *a* (*plan etc*) infalible.

foot [fut], *pl* **feet** *n* pie *m*; (*measure*) pie *m* (= 304 *mm*); (*of animal*) pata // *vt* (*bill*) pagar; **on ~** a pie; **~ball** *n* balón *m*; (*game*) fútbol *m*; **~baller** *n* futbolista *m*; **~brake** *n* freno de pie; **~bridge** *n* puente *m* para peatones; **~hills** *npl* estribaciones *fpl*; **~hold** *n* pie *m* firme; **~ing** *n* (*fig*) posición *f*; **to lose one's ~ing** perder el pie; **on an equal ~ing** en pie de igualdad; **~lights** *npl* candilejas *fpl*; **~man** *n* lacayo; **~note** *n* nota de pie; **~path** *n* sendero; (*pavement*) acera; **~sore** *a* con los pies adoloridos; **~step** *n* paso; **~wear** *n* calzado.

for [fɔːʳ] *prep* (*gen*) para; (*as, in exchange for, because of*) por; (*during*) durante; (*in spite of*) a pesar de // *conj* pues, ya que; **it was sold ~ 100 pesetas** se vendió por 100 pesetas; **what ~?** ¿para qué?; **what's it ~?** ¿para qué sirve?; he **was away ~**

2 years estuvo fuera 2 años; **he went ~ the paper** fue a buscar el periódico; **~ sale** se vende.

forage ['fɔrɪdʒ] n forraje m.

foray ['fɔreɪ] n incursión f.

forbid [fə'bɪd], pt **forbad(e)** [fə'bæd], pp **forbidden** [fə'bɪdn] vt prohibir; **~ding** a (gloomy) lúgubre; (severe) severo.

force [fɔːs] n fuerza // vt forzar; **to ~ o.s.** to hacer un esfuerzo por; **the F~s** npl las Fuerzas Armadas; **in ~** en vigor; **~d** [fɔːst] a forzado; **~ful** a enérgico.

forceps ['fɔːseps] npl fórceps m inv.

forcibly ['fɔːsəblɪ] ad a la fuerza.

ford [fɔːd] n vado // vt vadear.

forearm ['fɔːrɑːm] n antebrazo.

foreboding [fɔː'bəʊdɪŋ] n presagio.

forecast ['fɔːkɑːst] n pronóstico // vt (irg: like cast) pronosticar.

forefathers ['fɔːfɑːðəz] npl antepasados mpl.

forefinger ['fɔːfɪŋgə*] n (dedo) índice m.

forego = **forgo.**

foregone ['fɔːgɒn] a: **it's a ~ conclusion** es una conclusión inevitable.

foreground ['fɔːgraʊnd] n primer plano.

forehead ['fɔrɪd] n frente f.

foreign ['fɔrɪn] a extranjero; (trade) exterior; **~er** n extranjero; **~ exchange** n divisas fpl; **F~ Minister** n Ministro de Asuntos Exteriores; **F~ Office** n Ministerio de Asuntos Exteriores.

foreleg ['fɔːleg] n pata delantera.

foreman ['fɔːmən] n capataz m; (in construction) maestro de obras.

foremost ['fɔːməʊst] a principal.

forensic [fə'rensɪk] a forense.

forerunner ['fɔːrʌnə*] n precursor/a m/f.

foresee [fɔː'siː] (irg: like see) vt prever; **~able** a previsible.

foresight ['fɔːsaɪt] n previsión f.

forest ['fɒrɪst] n bosque m.

forestall [fɔː'stɔːl] vt prevenir.

forestry ['fɒrɪstrɪ] n silvicultura.

foretaste ['fɔːteɪst] n (gen) anticipo; (sample) muestra.

foretell [fɔː'tel] (irg: like tell) vt predecir, pronosticar.

forever [fə'revə*] ad para siempre.

foreword ['fɔːwɜːd] n prefacio.

forfeit ['fɔːfɪt] n pérdida; (fine) multa // vt perder (derecho a).

forgave [fə'geɪv] pt of **forgive.**

forge [fɔːdʒ] n fragua; (smithy) herrería // vt (signature, money) falsificar; (metal) forjar; **to ~ ahead** vi avanzar constantemente; **forger** n falsificador/a m/f; **~ry** n falsificación f.

forget [fə'get], pt **forgot**, pp **forgotten** vt olvidar // vi olvidarse; **~ful** a olvidadizo; **~fulness** n (gen) olvido; (thoughtlessness) descuido; (oblivion) falta de memoria.

forgive [fə'gɪv], pt **forgave**, pp **forgiven** vt perdonar; **to ~ sb for sth** perdonar algo a uno; **~ness** n perdón m.

forgo [fɔː'gəʊ] (irg: like go) vt (give up)

renunciar a; (go without) privarse de.

forgot [fə'gɒt] pt of **forget.**

forgotten [fə'gɒtn] pp of **forget.**

fork [fɔːk] n (for eating) tenedor m; (for gardening) horca; (of roads) bifurcación f; (in tree) horcadura // vi (road) bifurcarse; **to ~ out** vt (col: pay) desembolsar; **~ed** [fɔːkt] a (lightning) en zigzag; **~lift truck** n elevadora-transportadora de horquilla.

form [fɔːm] n forma; (SCOL) clase f; (questionnaire) formulario // vt formar; **in top ~** en plena forma.

formal ['fɔːməl] a (offer, receipt) oficial; (person etc) ceremonioso; (occasion, dinner) oficial, protocolario; (dress) de etiqueta; **~ity** [-'mælɪtɪ] n ceremonia; **~ities** npl formalidades fpl; **~ly** ad oficialmente.

format ['fɔːmæt] n formato.

formation [fɔː'meɪʃən] n formación f.

formative ['fɔːmətɪv] a (years) formativo.

former ['fɔːmə*] a anterior; (earlier) antiguo; (ex) ex; **the ~ ... the latter ...** aquél ... éste ...; **~ly** ad antiguamente.

formidable ['fɔːmɪdəbl] a formidable.

formula ['fɔːmjʊlə] n fórmula.

formulate ['fɔːmjʊleɪt] vt formular.

forsake [fə'seɪk], pt **forsook** [fə'sʊk], pp **forsaken** [fə'seɪkən] vt (gen) abandonar; (plan) renunciar a.

fort [fɔːt] n fuerte m.

forte ['fɔːtɪ] n fuerte m.

forth [fɔːθ] ad en adelante; **back and ~** de acá para allá; **and so ~** y así sucesivamente; **~coming** a próximo, venidero; (character) comunicativo; **~right** a franco.

fortieth ['fɔːtɪɪθ] a cuadragésimo.

fortification [fɔːtɪfɪ'keɪʃən] n fortificación f; **fortify** ['fɔːtɪfaɪ] vt fortalecer.

fortitude ['fɔːtɪtjuːd] n fortaleza.

fortnight ['fɔːtnaɪt] n quincena; **~ly** a quincenal // ad quincenalmente.

fortress ['fɔːtrɪs] n fortaleza.

fortuitous [fɔː'tjuːɪtəs] a fortuito.

fortunate ['fɔːtʃənɪt] a: **to be ~** tener suerte; **it is ~ that...** es afortunado que...; **~ly** ad afortunadamente.

fortune ['fɔːtʃən] n suerte f; (wealth) fortuna; **~-teller** n adivina.

forty ['fɔːtɪ] num cuarenta.

forum ['fɔːrəm] n foro.

forward ['fɔːwəd] a (movement, position) avanzado; (front) delantero; (not shy) atrevido // n (SPORT) delantero // vt (letter) remitir; (career) progresar; **to move ~** avanzar; **~(s)** ad (hacia) adelante.

fossil ['fɒsl] n fósil m.

foster ['fɒstə*] vt fomentar; **~ brother** n hermano de leche; **~ child** n hijo adoptivo; **~ mother** n madre f adoptiva.

fought [fɔːt] pt, pp of **fight.**

foul [faʊl] a (gen) sucio, puerco; (weather) horrible; (smell etc) asqueroso // n (FOOTBALL) falta (en contra) // vt (dirty) ensuciar; (*block*) atascar; (*football player*) cometer una falta contra; ~ **play** n (*SPORT*) mala jugada; (*LAW*) muerte f violenta.

found [faund] *pt, pp of* **find** // *vt* (*establish*) fundar; ~**ation** [-'deɪʃən] n (*act*) fundación f; (*basis*) base f; (*also*: ~**ation cream**) crema base; ~**ations** npl (*of building*) cimientos mpl.

founder ['faundə*] n fundador/a m/f // vi hundirse.

foundry ['faundrɪ] n fundición f.

fountain ['fauntɪn] n fuente f; ~ **pen** n pluma-fuente f.

four [fɔ:*] num cuatro; **on all** ~**s** a gatas; ~**-poster** n cama a columnas; ~**some** ['fɔ:səm] n grupo de cuatro personas; ~**teen** num catorce; ~**teenth** a décimocuarto; ~**th** a cuarto.

fowl [faul] n ave f (de corral).

fox [fɔks] n zorro // vt confundir; ~ **trot** n fox m.

foyer ['fɔɪeɪ] n vestíbulo.

fracas ['fræka:] n gresca, riña.

fraction ['frækʃən] n fracción f.

fracture ['fræktʃə*] n fractura // vt fracturar.

fragile ['frædʒaɪl] a frágil.

fragment ['frægmənt] n fragmento; ~**ary** a fragmentario.

fragrance ['freɪgrəns] n fragancia; **fragrant** [-ənt] a fragante, oloroso.

frail [freɪl] a (*fragile*) frágil, quebradizo; (*weak*) delicado.

frame [freɪm] n (*gen*) estructura f; (*body*) talle m; (*TECH*) armazón m; (*of picture, door etc*) marco m; (*of spectacles: also*: ~**s**) montura // vt encuadrar; (*reply*) formular; (*fam*) incriminar; ~ **of mind** n estado de ánimo; ~**work** n marco m.

France [frɑ:ns] n Francia.

franchise ['fræntʃaɪz] n (*POL*) derecho de votar, sufragio.

frank [fræŋk] a franco // vt (*letter*) franquear; ~**ly** ad francamente; ~**ness** n franqueza.

frantic ['fræntɪk] a frenético.

fraternal [frə'tə:nl] a fraterno; **fraternity** [-nɪtɪ] n (*club*) fraternidad f; (*US*) club m de estudiantes; (*guild*) cofradía; **fraternize** ['frætənaɪz] vi confraternizar.

fraud [frɔ:d] n fraude m; (*person*) impostor m; ~**ulent** a fraudulento.

fraught [frɔ:t] a: ~ **with** cargado de.

fray [freɪ] n combate m, lucha // vi deshilacharse; **tempers were** ~**ed** tenían los nervios a punto.

freak [fri:k] n (*person*) fenómeno; (*event*) suceso anormal; (*thing*) cosa insólita.

freckle ['frɛkl] n peca.

free [fri:] a (*gen*) libre; (*not fixed*) suelto; (*gratis*) gratuito; (*unoccupied*) desocupado; (*liberal*) generoso // vt (*prisoner etc*) poner en libertad; (*jammed object*) soltar; ~ (**of charge**) ad gratis; ~**dom** ['fri:dəm] n libertad f; ~**-for-all** n riña general; ~ **kick** n tiro libre; ~**lance** a

independiente; ~**ly** ad libremente; generosamente; ~**mason** n francmasón m; ~ **trade** n libre comercio; ~**way** n (*US*) autopista; ~**wheel** vi ir en punto muerto; ~ **will** n libre albedrío; **of one's own** ~ **will** por su propia voluntad.

freeze [fri:z] pt **froze**, pp **frozen** vi helarse, congelarse // vt helar; (*prices, food, salaries*) congelar // n helada; congelación f; **freezer** n congelador m.

freezing ['fri:zɪŋ] a helado; ~ **point** n punto de congelación; **3 degrees below** ~ tres grados bajo cero.

freight [freɪt] n (*goods*) carga; (*money charged*) flete m; ~ **car** n (*US*) vagón m de mercancías.

French [frɛntʃ] a francés(esa) // n (*LING*) francés m; **the** ~ los franceses; ~ **fried** (**potatoes**) npl patatas fpl fritas; ~**man/woman** n francés/esa m/f; ~ **window** n puertaventana.

frenzy ['frɛnzɪ] n frenesí m.

frequency ['fri:kwənsɪ] n frecuencia; **frequent** [-ənt] a frecuente // vt [frɪ'kwɛnt] frecuentar; **frequently** [-əntlɪ] ad frecuentemente, a menudo.

fresco ['frɛskəu] n fresco.

fresh [frɛʃ] a (*gen*) fresco; (*new*) nuevo; (*water*) dulce; ~**en** vi (*wind, air*) soplar más recio; **to** ~**en up** vi (*person*) lavarse, arreglarse; ~**ly** ad (*newly*) nuevamente; (*recently*) recientemente; ~**ness** n frescura.

fret [frɛt] vi inquietarse.

friar ['fraɪə*] n fraile m; (*before name*) fray.

friction ['frɪkʃən] n fricción f.

Friday ['fraɪdɪ] n viernes m.

fridge [frɪdʒ] n nevera.

friend [frɛnd] n amigo/a; ~**liness** n simpatía; ~**ly** a simpático; ~**ship** n amistad f.

frieze [fri:z] n friso.

frigate ['frɪgɪt] n fragata.

fright [fraɪt] n susto; **to take** ~ asustarse; ~**en** vt asustar; ~**ening** a espantoso; ~**ful** a espantoso, horrible; ~**fully** ad terriblemente.

frigid ['frɪdʒɪd] a (*MED*) frígido, frío; ~**ity** [frɪ'dʒɪdɪtɪ] n frialdad f; (*MED*) frigidez f.

frill [frɪl] n volante m.

fringe [frɪndʒ] n flequillo; (*edge: of forest etc*) borde m, margen m; ~ **benefits** npl ventajas fpl supletorias.

frisky ['frɪskɪ] a juguetón(ona), fogoso.

fritter ['frɪtə*] n buñuelo; **to** ~ **away** vt desperdiciar.

frivolous ['frɪvələs] a frívolo.

frizzy ['frɪzɪ] a rizado.

fro [frəu] see **to**.

frock [frɔk] n vestido.

frog [frɔg] n rana; ~**man** n hombre-rana m.

frolic ['frɔlɪk] vi juguetear.

from [frɔm] prep de; ~ **January** (**on**) a partir de enero; ~ **what he says** por lo que dice.

front [frʌnt] n (foremost part) parte f delantera; (of house) fachada; (promenade: also: sea ~) paseo marítimo; (MIL. POL. METEOROLOGY) frente m; (fig: appearances) apariencias fpl // a delantero, primero; in ~ (of) delante (de); ~al a frontal; ~ door n puerta principal; ~ier ['frʌntɪə*] n frontera; ~ page n primera plana; ~ room n (Brit) salón m, sala; ~-wheel drive n tracción f delantera.

frost [frɔst] n (gen) helada; (visible) escarcha; ~bite n congelación f; ~ed a (glass) deslustrado; ~y a (window) cubierto de escarcha; (welcome) glacial.

froth [frɔθ] n espuma.

frown [fraun] n ceño // vi fruncir el ceño.

froze [frəuz] pt of freeze.

frozen ['frəuzn] pp of freeze.

frugal ['fru:gəl] a frugal.

fruit [fru:t] n, pl inv fruta; ~erer n frutero; ~erer's (shop) n frutería; ~ful a provechoso; ~ion [fru:'ɪʃən] n: to come to ~ion realizarse; ~ machine n máquina tragaperras.

frustrate [frʌs'treɪt] vt frustrar; ~d a frustrado; **frustration** [-'treɪʃən] n frustración f.

fry [fraɪ], pt, pp fried vt freír; **small** ~ gente f menuda; ~ing pan n sartén f.

ft. abbr of foot, feet.

fuchsia ['fju:ʃə] n fucsia.

fudge [fʌdʒ] n (CULIN) dulce m de azúcar, manjar m.

fuel [fjuəl] n (for heating) combustible m; (coal) carbón m; (wood) leña; (for propelling) carburante m; ~ oil n aceite m combustible; ~ tank n depósito de combustible.

fugitive ['fju:dʒɪtɪv] n fugitivo.

fulfil [ful'fɪl] vt (function) cumplir con; (condition) satisfacer; (wish, desire) realizar; ~ment n satisfacción f; realización f.

full [ful] a lleno; (fig) pleno; (complete) completo; (information) detallado // ad: ~ well perfectamente; I'm ~ estoy lleno; ~ employment pleno empleo; ~ fare pasaje m completo; a ~ two hours dos horas completas; at ~ speed a máxima velocidad; in ~ (reproduce, quote) íntegramente; ~-length a (portrait) de cuerpo entero; ~ moon n luna llena; ~-sized a (portrait etc) de tamaño natural; ~ stop n punto; ~-time a (work) de tiempo completo // n (SPORT) final m; ~y ad completamente; ~y-fledged a (teacher, barrister) diplomado.

fumble ['fʌmbl]: to ~ with vt fus revolver, manosear.

fume [fju:m] vi humear, echar humo; ~s npl humo sg, gases mpl.

fumigate ['fju:mɪgeɪt] vt fumigar.

fun [fʌn] n (amusement) diversión f; (joy) alegría; to have ~ divertirse; for ~ en broma; to make ~ of vt fus burlarse de.

function ['fʌŋkʃən] n función f // vi funcionar; ~al a funcional.

fund [fʌnd] n fondo; (source, store) fuente f; ~s npl fondos mpl.

fundamental [fʌndə'mɛntl] a fundamental.

funeral ['fju:nərəl] n (burial) entierro; (ceremony) funerales mpl; ~ service n misa de difuntos.

funfair ['fʌnfɛə*] n parque m de atracciones.

fungus ['fʌngəs], pl -gi [-gaɪ] n hongo.

funnel ['fʌnl] n embudo; (of ship) chimenea.

funnily ['fʌnɪlɪ] ad de modo divertido.

funny ['fʌnɪ] a gracioso, divertido; (strange) curioso, raro.

fur [fə:*] n piel f; (in kettle etc) sarro; ~ coat n abrigo de pieles.

furious ['fjuərɪəs] a furioso; (effort) violento; ~ly ad con furia.

furlong ['fə:lɔŋ] n octava parte de una milla.

furlough ['fə:ləu] n (US) licencia.

furnace ['fə:nɪs] n horno.

furnish ['fə:nɪʃ] vt amueblar; (supply) suministrar; ~ings npl muebles mpl.

furniture ['fə:nɪtʃə*] n muebles mpl; **piece of** ~ mueble m; ~ polish n cera de lustrar.

furrier ['fʌrɪə*] n peletero.

furrow ['fʌrəu] n surco.

furry ['fə:rɪ] a peludo.

further ['fə:ðə*] a (new) nuevo, adicional; (place) más lejano // ad más lejos; (more) más; (moreover) además // vt promover, adelantar; ~ education n educación f superior; ~more [fə:ðə'mɔ:*] ad además.

furthest ['fə:ðɪst] superlative of far.

furtive ['fə:tɪv] a furtivo.

fury ['fjuərɪ] n furia.

fuse, fuze (US) [fju:z] n fusible m; (for bomb etc) mecha // vt (metal) fundir; (fig) fusionar // vi fundirse; fusionarse; (ELEC): to ~ the lights fundir los plomos; ~ box n caja de fusibles.

fuselage ['fju:zəlɑ:ʒ] n fuselaje m.

fusion ['fju:ʒən] n fusión f.

fuss [fʌs] n (noise) bulla; (dispute) lío; (complaining) protesta; (ceremony) ceremonias fpl; to make a ~ armar un lío o jaleo; ~y a (person) exigente.

futile ['fju:taɪl] a vano; **futility** [-'tɪlɪtɪ] n inutilidad f.

future ['fju:tʃə*] a (gen) futuro; (coming) venidero // n futuro; **futuristic** [-'rɪstɪk] a futurístico.

fuzzy ['fʌzɪ] a (PHOT) borroso; (hair) muy rizado.

G

gabble ['gæbl] vi hablar atropelladamente; (gossip) cotorrear.

gable ['geɪbl] n aguilón m.

gadget ['gædʒɪt] n aparato.

Gaelic ['geɪlɪk] n (LING) gaélico.

gag [gæg] n (joke) chiste m // vt amordazar.

gaiety ['geɪɪtɪ] n alegría.

gaily ['geɪlɪ] ad alegremente.

gain [geɪn] n ganancia // vt ganar // vi (watch) adelantarse; to ~ by sth sacar provecho de algo; to ~ on sb ir ganando terreno a uno.

gait [geɪt] n modo de andar.

gala ['gɑːlə] n fiesta.

galaxy ['gæləksɪ] n galaxia.

gale [geɪl] n (wind) vendaval m.

gallant ['gælənt] a valiente; (towards ladies) atento; ~ry n valentía; (courtesy) cortesía.

gall-bladder ['gɔːlblædə*] n vesícula biliar.

gallery ['gælərɪ] n galería; (also: art ~) museo.

galley ['gælɪ] n (ship's kitchen) cocina; (ship) galera.

gallon ['gæln] n galón m (4.543 litros).

gallop ['gæləp] n galope m // vi galopar.

gallows ['gæləuz] n horca.

gallstone ['gɔːlstəun] n cálculo biliario.

gamble ['gæmbl] n (risk) riesgo; (bet) apuesta // vt: to ~ on apostar a; (fig) confiar en que // vi jugar; (COMM) especular; **gambler** n jugador/a m/f; **gambling** n el juego.

game [geɪm] n (gen) juego; (match) partido; (of cards) partida; (HUNTING) caza // a valiente; (ready): **to be ~ for** anything atreverse a todo; ~ **bird** n ave f de caza; ~**keeper** n guardabosques m inv.

gammon ['gæmən] n (bacon) tocino ahumado; (ham) jamón m ahumado.

gang [gæŋ] n pandilla; (of workmen) brigada // vi: to ~ **up on sb** conspirar contra uno.

gangrene ['gæŋgriːn] n gangrena.

gangster ['gæŋstə*] n gángster m.

gangway ['gæŋweɪ] n (in theatre etc) pasillo; (on ship) pasarela; (on dock) pasadera.

gaol [dʒeɪl] = **jail.**

gap [gæp] n vacío, hueco; (in trees, traffic) claro; (in time) intervalo.

gape [geɪp] vi estar o quedarse boquiabierto; **gaping** a (hole) muy abierto.

garage ['gærɑːʒ] n garaje m.

garbage ['gɑːbɪdʒ] n basura; ~ **can** n (US) cubo de la basura.

garbled ['gɑːbld] a (distorted) falsificado, amañado.

garden ['gɑːdn] n jardín m; ~**er** n jardinero; ~**ing** n jardinería.

gargle ['gɑːgl] vi hacer gárgaras.

gargoyle ['gɑːgɔɪl] n gárgola.

garish ['gɛərɪʃ] a chillón(ona).

garland ['gɑːlənd] n guirnalda.

garlic ['gɑːlɪk] n ajo.

garment ['gɑːmənt] n prenda (de vestir).

garnish ['gɑːnɪʃ] vt adornar; (CULIN) aderezar.

garrison ['gærɪsn] n guarnición f // vt guarnecer.

garrulous ['gærjuləs] a gárrulo.

garter ['gɑːtə*] n liga; ~ **belt** portaligas m inv.

gas [gæs] n gas m; (US: gasoline) gasolina // vt asfixiar con gas; ~ **cooker** n cocina de gas; ~ **cylinder** n bombona de gas; ~ **fire** n estufa de gas.

gash [gæʃ] n raja; (on face) cuchillada // vt (gen) rajar; (with knife) acuchillar.

gasket ['gæskɪt] n (AUT) junta.

gas: ~**mask** n careta antigás; ~ **meter** n contador m de gas.

gasoline ['gæsəliːn] n (US) gasolina.

gasp [gɑːsp] n grito sofocado // vi (pant) jadear; to ~ **out** vt (say) decir con voz entrecortada.

gas: ~ **ring** n hornillo de gas; ~ **stove** n cocina de gas; ~**sy** a gaseoso; ~ **tap** n llave f del gas.

gastric ['gæstrɪk] a gástrico; ~ **ulcer** n úlcera gástrica.

gate [geɪt] n puerta; (RAIL) barrera; ~**crash** vt colarse de gorra en; ~**way** n puerta.

gather ['gæðə*] vt (flowers, fruit) coger; (assemble) reunir; (pick up) recoger; (SEWING) fruncir; (understand) entender // vi (assemble) reunirse; ~**ing** n reunión f, asamblea.

gauche [gəuʃ] a torpe.

gaudy ['gɔːdɪ] a chillón(ona).

gauge [geɪdʒ] n medida; (RAIL) entrevía; (instrument) indicador m // vt medir.

gaunt [gɔːnt] a descarnado; (grim, desolate) desolado.

gauntlet ['gɔːntlɪt] n (fig): **to run the ~** correr baquetas; **to throw down the ~** arrojar el guante.

gauze [gɔːz] n gasa.

gave [geɪv] pt of **give.**

gay [geɪ] a (person) alegre; (colour) vistoso, vivo; (homosexual) gay.

gaze [geɪz] n mirada fija; to ~ **at sth** mirar algo con fijeza.

gazelle [gə'zɛl] n gacela.

gazetteer [gæzə'tɪə*] n diccionario geográfico.

G.B. abbr of **Great Britain.**

G.C.E. n abbr of **General Certificate of Education.**

gear [gɪə*] n equipo, herramientas fpl; (TECH) engranaje m; (AUT) velocidad f, marcha; **top/low** ~ tercera (o cuarta)/primera velocidad; **in** ~ en marcha; ~ **box** n caja de cambios; ~ **lever,** ~ **shift** (US) n palanca de velocidades; ~ **wheel** n rueda dentada.

geese [giːs] pl of **goose.**

gelatin(e) ['dʒɛlətiːn] n gelatina.

gelignite ['dʒɛlɪgnaɪt] n gelignita.

gem [dʒɛm] n joya.

Gemini ['dʒɛmɪnaɪ] n Géminis m, Gemelos mpl.

gender ['dʒɛndə*] n género.

general ['dʒenərl] n general m // a general; **in ~** en general; **~ election** n elecciones fpl generales; **~ization** [-aɪ'zeɪʃən] n generalización f; **~ize** vi generalizar; **~ly** ad generalmente, en general; **~ practitioner (G.P.)** n médico general.

generate ['dʒenəreɪt] vt (ELEC) generar; (fig) producir.

generation [dʒenə'reɪʃən] n generación f.

generator ['dʒenəreɪtə*] n generador m.

generosity [dʒenə'rɔsɪtɪ] n generosidad f; **generous** ['dʒenərəs] a generoso; (helping etc) abundante.

genetics [dʒɪ'netɪks] n genética.

Geneva [dʒɪ'niːvə] n Ginebra.

genial ['dʒiːnɪəl] a afable, simpático.

genitals ['dʒenɪtlz] npl órganos mpl genitales.

genius ['dʒiːnɪəs] n genio.

genocide ['dʒenəusaɪd] n genocidio.

gent [dʒent] n abbr of **gentleman**.

genteel [dʒen'tiːl] a fino, elegante.

gentle ['dʒentl] a (sweet) amable, dulce; (touch etc) ligero, suave; (animal) manso.

gentleman ['dʒentlmən] n señor m; (well-bred man) caballero.

gentleness ['dʒentlnɪs] n dulzura; (of touch) suavidad f; (of animal) mansedumbre f.

gently ['dʒentlɪ] ad suavemente.

gentry ['dʒentrɪ] n alta burguesía.

gents [dʒents] n (aseos de) caballeros mpl.

genuine ['dʒenjuɪn] a auténtico; (person) sincero.

geographic(al) [dʒɪə'græfɪk(l)] a geográfico; **geography** [dʒɪ'ɔgrəfɪ] n geografía.

geological [dʒɪə'lɒdʒɪkl] a geológico; **geologist** [dʒɪ'ɔlədʒɪst] n geólogo; **geology** [dʒɪ'ɔlədʒɪ] n geología.

geometric(al) [dʒɪə'metrɪk(l)] a geométrico; **geometry** [dʒɪ'ɔmətrɪ] n geometría.

geranium [dʒɪ'reɪnjəm] n geranio.

germ [dʒəːm] n (gen) microbio, bacteria; (BIO, fig) germen m.

German ['dʒəːmən] a alemán(ana) // n alemán/ana m/f; (LING) alemán m; **~ measles** n rubéola.

Germany ['dʒəːmənɪ] n Alemania.

germination [dʒəːmɪ'neɪʃən] n germinación f.

gesticulate [dʒes'tɪkjuleɪt] vi gesticular.

gesture ['dʒestjə*] n gesto.

get [get], pt, pp **got**, pp **gotten** (US) vt (obtain) obtener; (receive) recibir; (achieve) conseguir; (find) encontrar; (catch) coger; (fetch) traer, ir a buscar; (understand) entender // vi (become) hacerse, volverse; **to ~ old** hacerse viejo, envejecer; **to ~ to** (place) llegar a; **he got under the fence** pasó por debajo de la barrera; **to ~ ready/washed** prepararse/lavarse; **to ~ sb to do sth** hacer que alguien haga algo; **to ~ sth**

out of sth sacar algo de algo; **to ~ about** vi salir mucho, viajar mucho; (news) divulgarse; **to ~ along** vi (agree) entenderse; (depart) marcharse; (manage) = **to get by**; **to ~ at** vt fus (attack) atacar; (reach) llegar a; (the truth) descubrir; **to ~ away** vi marcharse; (on holiday) irse de vacaciones; (escape) escaparse; **to ~ away with** vt fus hacer impunemente; **to ~ back** vi (return) volver // vt recobrar; **to ~ by** vi (pass) lograr pasar; (manage) arreglárselas; **to ~ down** vi bajarse // vt (object) bajar; (depress) deprimir; **to ~ down to** vt fus (work) ponerse a (hacer); **to ~ in** vi (train) llegar; (arrive home) volver a casa, regresar; **to ~ off** vi (from train etc) bajar; (depart: person, car) marcharse // vt fus (train, bus) bajar de; **to ~ on** vi (at exam etc) tener éxito; (agree) entenderse // vt (horse) subir; **to ~ out** vi salir; (of vehicle) bajarse // vt saberse // vt (take out) sacar; **to ~ out of** vt fus (duty etc) escaparse de; **to ~ over** vt (illness) recobrarse de; (put across) hacer comprender; **to ~ round** vt fus rodear; (fig: person) engatusar a; **to ~ through to** vt fus (TEL) comunicar con; **to ~ together** vi reunirse; **to ~ up** vi (rise) levantarse // vt fus levantar; **to ~ up to** vt fus (reach) llegar a; (prank etc) hacer; **~away** n fuga, escape m.

geyser ['giːzə*] n calentador m de agua; (GEO) géiser m.

Ghana ['gɑːnə] n Ghana.

ghastly ['gɑːstlɪ] a horrible; (pale) pálido.

gherkin ['gəːkɪn] n pepinillo.

ghetto ['getəu] n ghetto.

ghost [gəust] n fantasma m; **~ly** a fantasmal.

giant ['dʒaɪənt] n gigante m // a gigantesco, gigante.

gibberish ['dʒɪbərɪʃ] n galimatías m.

gibe [dʒaɪb] n pulla.

giblets ['dʒɪblɪts] npl menudillos mpl.

giddiness ['gɪdɪnɪs] n vértigo; **giddy** a (dizzy) mareado; (speed) vertiginoso; (frivolous) atolondrado; **it makes me giddy** me marea.

gift [gɪft] n (gen) regalo; (offering) obsequio; (ability) talento; **~ed** a dotado.

gigantic [dʒaɪ'gæntɪk] a gigantesco.

giggle ['gɪgl] vi reírse con risa tonta // n risilla tonta.

gill [dʒɪl] n (measure) = 0.14 l // n [gɪl] (of fish) agalla, branquia.

gilt [gɪlt] a, n dorado; **~-edged** a (COMM) del Estado.

gimmick ['gɪmɪk] n truco.

gin [dʒɪn] n (liquor) ginebra.

ginger ['dʒɪndʒə*] n jengibre m; **~ ale** n cerveza de jengibre; **~bread** n pan m de jengibre; **~-haired** a pelirrojo.

gingerly ['dʒɪndʒəlɪ] ad con pies de plomo.

gipsy ['dʒɪpsɪ] n gitano/a.

giraffe [dʒɪ'rɑːf] n jirafa.

girder ['gəːdə*] n viga.

girdle ['gɔːdl] n (corset) faja // vt ceñir.

girl [gɜːl] n (small) niña; (young woman) chica, joven f, muchacha; **an English ~** una (chica) inglesa; **~friend** n (of girl) amiga; (of boy) novia; **~ish** a de niña.

girth [gɜːθ] n circunferencia; (stoutness) gordura.

gist [dʒɪst] n lo esencial.

give [gɪv], pt **gave**, pp **given** vt (gen) dar; (deliver) entregar; (as gift) regalar // vi (break) romperse; (stretch: fabric) dar de sí; **to ~ sb sth, ~ sth to sb** dar algo a uno; **to ~ away** vt (give free) regalar; (betray) traicionar; (disclose) revelar; **to ~ back** vt devolver; **to ~ in** vi ceder // vt entregar; **to ~ off** vt despedir; **to ~ out** vt distribuir; **to ~ up** vi renunciar, darse por vencido // vt renunciar a; **to ~ up smoking** dejar de fumar; **to ~ way** vi ceder; (AUT) ceder el paso.

glacier ['glæsɪə*] n glaciar m.

glad [glæd] a contento; **~den** vt alegrar.

gladioli [glædɪˈəʊlaɪ] npl gladíolos mpl.

gladly ['glædlɪ] ad con mucho gusto.

glamorous ['glæmərəs] a encantador(a), atractivo; **glamour** n encanto, atractivo.

glance [glɑːns] n ojeada, mirada // vi: **to ~ at** echar una ojeada a; **to ~ off** (bullet) rebotar; **glancing** a (blow) oblicuo.

gland [glænd] n glándula.

glare [glɛə*] n luz f deslumbradora, brillo // vi deslumbrar; **to ~ at** mirar ferozmente a; **glaring** a (mistake) notorio.

glass [glɑːs] n vidrio, cristal m; (for drinking) vaso; (: with stem) copa; (also: **looking ~**) espejo; **~es** npl gafas fpl; **~house** n invernadero; **~ware** n cristalería; **~y a** (eyes) vidrioso.

glaze [gleɪz] vt (door) poner cristal a; (pottery) barnizar // n barniz m; **~d** a (eye) vidrioso; (pottery) barnizado.

glazier ['gleɪzɪə*] n vidriero.

gleam [gliːm] n destello // vi brillar; **~ing** a reluciente.

glee [gliː] n alegría, regocijo.

glen [glɛn] n cañada, valle m estrecho.

glib [glɪb] a de mucha labia; **~ness** n labia.

glide [glaɪd] vi deslizarse; (AVIAT, birds) planear // n deslizamiento; (AVIAT) vuelo sin motor; **glider** n (AVIAT) planeador m; **gliding** n (AVIAT) vuelo sin motor.

glimmer ['glɪmə*] n luz f trémula.

glimpse [glɪmps] n vista momentánea, vislumbre m // vt vislumbrar, entrever.

glint [glɪnt] n destello; (in the eye) chispa // vi centellear.

glisten ['glɪsn] vi relucir, brillar.

glitter ['glɪtə*] vi relucir, brillar // n brillo.

gloat [gləʊt] vi: **to ~ (over)** recrearse en, saborear.

global ['gləʊbl] a mundial; (sum) global.

globe [gləʊb] n globo, esfera.

gloom [gluːm] n tinieblas fpl, oscuridad f; (sadness) tristeza, melancolía; **~y a**

(dark) oscuro; (sad) triste; (pessimistic) pesimista.

glorify ['glɔːrɪfaɪ] vt glorificar; (praise) alabar.

glorious ['glɔːrɪəs] a glorioso; **glory** n gloria.

gloss [glɔs] n (shine) brillo; (paint) pintura brillante o esmalte; **to ~ over** vt fus encubrir.

glossary ['glɔsərɪ] n glosario.

glossy ['glɔsɪ] a lustroso.

glove [glʌv] n guante m; **~ compartment** n (AUT) guantera.

glow [gləʊ] vi (shine) brillar; (fire) arder // n brillo.

glower ['glaʊə*] vi: **to ~ at** mirar con ceño.

glucose ['gluːkəʊs] n glucosa.

glue [gluː] n goma (de pegar) // vt pegar.

glum [glʌm] a (mood) abatido; (person, tone) melancólico.

glut [glʌt] n superabundancia.

glutton ['glʌtn] n glotón/ona m/f; **a ~ for work** un trabajador incansable; **~y n** gula, glotonería.

glycerin(e) ['glɪsəriːn] n glicerina.

gnarled [nɑːld] a nudoso.

gnat [næt] n mosquito.

gnaw [nɔː] vt roer.

gnome [nəʊm] n gnomo.

go [gəʊ], pt **went**, pp **gone** vi ir; (travel) viajar; (depart) irse, marcharse; (work) funcionar, marchar; (be sold) venderse; (time) pasar; (fit, suit): **to ~ with** hacer juego con; (become) ponerse; (break etc) estropearse, romperse // n, pl **~es:** **to have a ~ (at)** probar suerte (con); **to be on the ~** moverse, estar trabajando; **whose ~ is it?** ¿a quién le toca?; **he's going to do it** va a hacerlo; **to ~ for a walk** ir de paseo; **to ~ dancing** ir a bailar; **how did it ~?** ¿qué tal salió o resultó?; ¿cómo ha ido?; **to ~ about** vi (rumour) propagarse // vt fus: **how do I ~ about this?** ¿cómo me las arreglo para hacer esto?; **to ~ ahead** vi (make progress) avanzar; (get going) seguir; **to ~ along** vi ir // vt fus bordear; **to ~ along with** estar de acuerdo con; **to ~ away** vi irse, marcharse; **to ~ back** vi volver; (fall back) retroceder; **to ~ back on** vt fus (promise) faltar a; **to ~ by** vi (years, time) pasar // vt fus guiarse por; **to ~ down** vi bajar; (ship) hundirse; (sun) ponerse // vt fus bajar por; **to ~ for** vt fus (fetch) ir por; (like) gustar; (attack) atacar; **to ~ in** vi entrar; **to ~ in for** vt fus (competition) presentarse a; **to ~ into** vt fus entrar en; (investigate) investigar; (embark on) embarcarse en; **to ~ off** vi irse, marcharse; (food) pasarse; (explode) estallar; (event) realizarse // vt fus dejar de gustar; **to ~ on** vi seguir, continuar; (happen) pasar, ocurrir; **to ~ on doing sth** seguir haciendo algo; **to ~ out** vi salir; (fire, light) apagarse; **to ~ over** vi (ship) zozobrar // vt fus (check) revisar; **to**

~ through vt fus (town etc) atravesar; **to ~ up** vi subir; **to ~ without** vt fus pasarse sin.

goad [gəud] vt aguijonear.

go-ahead ['gəuəhɛd] a emprendedor(a) // n luz f verde.

goal [gəul] n meta; (score) gol m; **~keeper** n portero; **~-post** n poste m de la portería.

goat [gəut] n cabrío, cabra m/f.

gobble ['gɔbl] vt (also: **~ down**, **~ up**) engullirse (ávidamente).

goblet ['gɔblit] n copa.

goblin ['gɔblin] n duende m.

go-cart ['gəukɑ:t] n go-cart m.

god [gɔd] n dios m; **G~** n Dios m; **~child** n ahijado/a; **~dess** n diosa; **~father** n padrino; **~-forsaken** a dejado de la mano de Dios; **~mother** n madrina; **~send** n don m del cielo; **~son** n ahijado.

goggles ['gɔglz] npl gafas fpl submarinas.

going ['gəuiŋ] n (conditions) estado del terreno // a: **the ~ rate** la tarifa corriente o en vigor.

gold [gəuld] n oro // a (made of ~) de oro; (~ in colour) dorado; **~fish** n pez m de colores; **~ mine** n mina de oro.

golf [gɔlf] n golf m; **~ club** n club m de golf; (stick) palo (de golf); **~ course** n campo de golf; **~er** n jugador/a m/f de golf.

gondola ['gɔndələ] n góndola.

gone [gɔn] pp of **go**.

gong [gɔŋ] n gong m.

gonorrhea [gɔnə'riə] n gonorrea.

good [gud] a (gen) bueno; (kind) bueno, amable; (well-behaved) educado; (useful) útil // n bien m, provecho; **~s** npl bienes mpl; (COMM) mercancías fpl; **to be ~ at** tener aptitud para; **to be ~ for** servir para; **it's ~ for you** te hace bien; **would you be ~ enough to...?** ¿podría hacerme el favor de...?; ¿sería tan amable de...?; a **~ deal (of)** mucho; a **~ many** muchos; **to make ~** reparar; **for ~** para siempre, definitivamente; **~ morning/afternoon!** ¡buenos días/buenas tardes!; **~ evening!** ¡buenas noches!; **~ night!** ¡buenas noches!; **~bye!** ¡adiós!; **to say ~bye** despedirse; **G~ Friday** n Viernes m Santo; **~-looking** a guapo; **~ness** n (of person) bondad f; **for ~ness sake!** ¡Por Dios!; **~ness gracious!** ¡Dios mío!; **~will** n buena voluntad f.

goose [gu:s], pl **geese** [gi:s] n ganso, oca.

gooseberry ['guzbəri] n grosella espinosa.

gooseflesh ['gu:sfleʃ] n, **goose pimples** npl carne f de gallina.

gore [gɔ:*] vt cornear // n sangre f.

gorge [gɔ:dʒ] n barranco // vr: **to ~ o.s. (on)** atracarse (de).

gorgeous ['gɔ:dʒəs] a magnífico, maravilloso.

gorilla [gə'rilə] n gorila m.

gorse [gɔ:s] n aulaga.

gory ['gɔ:ri] a sangriento.

go-slow ['gəu'sləu] n huelga de trabajo lento.

gospel ['gɔspl] n evangelio.

gossip ['gɔsip] n (scandal) chismorreo, chismes mpl; (chat) charla; (scandalmonger) chismoso/a; (talker) hablador/a m/f // vi cotillear.

got [gɔt] pt, pp of **get**; **~ten** (US) pp of **get**.

gout [gaut] n gota.

govern ['gʌvn] vt (gen) gobernar; (dominate) dominar.

governess ['gʌvənis] n institutriz f.

government ['gʌvnmənt] n gobierno; **~al** [-'mɛntl] a gubernamental.

governor ['gʌvənə*] n gobernador m; (of jail) director/a m/f.

gown [gaun] n traje m; (of teacher, judge) toga.

G.P. n abbr of **general practitioner.**

GPO n abbr of **General Post Office.**

grab [græb] vt coger, arrebatar.

grace [greis] n (REL) gracia; (gracefulness) elegancia, finura // vt (favour) honrar; (adorn) adornar; **5 days' ~** un plazo de 5 días; **to say ~** bendecir la mesa; **~ful** a elegante, gracioso; **gracious** ['greiʃəs] a amable.

grade [greid] n (quality) clase f, calidad f; (degree) grado; (US SCOL) clase f // vt clasificar.

gradient ['greidiənt] n pendiente f.

gradual ['grædjuəl] a paulatino; **~ly** ad paulatinamente.

graduate ['grædjuit] n graduado, licenciado // vi ['grædjueit] graduarse, licenciarse; **graduation** [-'eiʃən] n graduación f.

graft [grɑ:ft] n (AGR, MED) injerto; (bribery) corrupción f // vt injertar.

grain [grein] n grano; (corn) granos mpl, cereales mpl; (in wood) fibra.

gram [græm] n gramo.

grammar ['græmə*] n gramática; **grammatical** [grə'mætikl] a gramatical.

gramme [græm] n = **gram.**

gramophone ['græməfəun] n tocadiscos m inv.

granary ['grænəri] n granero, troj f.

grand [grænd] a magnífico, imponente; **~children** npl nietos mpl; **~dad** n yayo, abuelito; **~daughter** n nieta; **~eur** ['grændjə*] n magnificencia, lo grandioso; **~father** n abuelo; **~iose** ['grændiəuz] a grandioso; (pej) pomposo; **~ma** n yaya, abuelita; **~mother** n abuela; **~pa** n = **~dad**; **~ piano** n piano de cola; **~son** n nieto; **~stand** n (SPORT) tribuna.

granite ['grænit] n granito.

granny ['græni] n abuelita, yaya.

grant [grɑ:nt] vt (concede) conceder; (admit) asentir // n (SCOL) beca; **to take sth for ~ed** dar algo por sentado.

granulated sugar ['grænjuleitid-] n azúcar m granulado.

granule ['grænju:l] n gránulo.

grape [greip] n uva; **sour ~s** (fig) envidia.

grapefruit ['greipfru:t] n pomelo, toronja (AM).

graph [gra:f] n gráfica; **~ic** a gráfico.

grapple ['græpl] vi: **to ~ with sth** esforzarse por resolver algo.

grasp [gra:sp] vt agarrar, asir; (understand) comprender // n (grip) asimiento; (reach) alcance m; (understanding) comprensión f; **~ing** a avaro.

grass [gra:s] n hierba; (lawn) césped m; **~hopper** n saltamontes m inv; **~land** n pradera; **~-roots** a popular; **~ snake** n culebra; **~y** a cubierto de hierba.

grate [greit] n (fireplace) chimenea; (of iron) parrilla // vi rechinar // vt (CULIN) rallar.

grateful ['greitful] a agradecido.

grater ['greitə*] n rallador m.

gratify ['grætifai] vt complacer; (whim) satisfacer; **~ing** a grato.

grating ['greitiŋ] n (iron bars) rejilla // a (noise) áspero.

gratitude ['grætitju:d] n agradecimiento.

gratuity [grə'tju:iti] n gratificación f.

grave [greiv] n tumba // a serio, grave; **~digger** n sepulturero.

gravel ['grævl] n grava.

grave: ~stone n lápida; **~yard** n cementerio, camposanto.

gravity ['græviti] n gravedad f; (seriousness) seriedad f.

gravy ['greivi] n salsa.

gray [grei] a = **grey**.

graze [greiz] vi pacer // vt (touch lightly) rozar; (scrape) raspar // n (MED) rasguño.

grease [gri:s] n (fat) grasa; (lubricant) lubricante m // vt engrasar; **~proof** a a prueba de grasa; (paper) apergaminado; **greasy** a grasiento.

great [greit] a grande; (col) magnífico, estupendo; **G~ Britain** n Gran Bretaña; **~-grandfather/mother** n bisabuelo/a; **~ly** ad sumamente, mucho, muy; **~ness** n grandeza.

Greece [gri:s] n Grecia.

greed [gri:d] n (also: **~iness**) codicia, avaricia; (for food) gula; **~ily** ad con avidez; **~y** a avaro; (for food) glotón(ona).

Greek [gri:k] a griego // n griego/a; (LING) griego.

green [gri:n] a verde; (inexperienced) novato // n verde m; (stretch of grass) césped m; **~s** npl verduras fpl; **~gage** n claudia; **~grocer** n verdulero; **~house** n invernadero; **~ish** a verdoso.

Greenland ['gri:nlənd] n Groenlandia.

greet [gri:t] vt saludar; (welcome) dar la bienvenida a; **~ing** n (gen) saludo; (welcome) bienvenida.

gregarious [grə'gɛəriəs] a gregario.

grenade [grə'neid] n granada.

grew [gru:] pt of **grow**.

grey [grei] a gris; **~-haired** a canoso; **~hound** n galgo.

grid [grid] n reja; (ELEC) red f.

grief [gri:f] n dolor m, pena.

grievance ['gri:vəns] n motivo de queja, agravio.

grieve [gri:v] vi afligirse, acongojarse // vt dar pena a; **to ~ for** llorar por.

grievous ['gri:vəs] a penoso.

grill [gril] n (on cooker) parrilla // vt asar a la parrilla; (question) interrogar duramente.

grille [gril] n reja; (AUT) rejilla.

grim [grim] a siniestro; (fam) horrible.

grimace [gri'meis] n mueca // vi hacer muecas.

grime [graim] n mugre f; **grimy** a mugriento.

grin [grin] n sonrisa abierta // vi sonreír abiertamente.

grind [graind] pt, pp **ground** vt (coffee, pepper etc) moler; (make sharp) afilar // n (work) trabajo pesado y aburrido; **to ~ one's teeth** rechinar los dientes.

grip [grip] n (hold) asimiento; (of hands) apretón m; (handle) asidero; (of racquet etc) mango; (holdall) maletín m; (understanding) comprensión f // vt agarrar; **to come to ~s with** luchar a brazo partido con; **~ping** a absorbente.

grisly ['grizli] a horripilante, horrible.

gristle ['grisl] n cartílago.

grit [grit] n gravilla; (courage) valor m // vt (road) poner gravilla en; **to ~ one's teeth** apretar los dientes.

groan [grəun] n gemido, quejido // vi gemir, quejarse.

grocer ['grəusə*] n tendero de ultramarinos; **~ies** npl comestibles mpl; **~'s (shop)** n tienda de ultramarinos.

groggy ['grɔgi] a aturdido; (BOXING) grogui.

groin [grɔin] n ingle f.

groom [gru:m] n mozo de caballos; (also: **bride~**) novio // vt (horse) cuidar; **well-~ed** acicalado.

groove [gru:v] n ranura, surco.

grope [grəup] vi ir a tientas; **to ~ for** vt fus buscar a tientas.

gross [grəus] a grueso; (COMM) bruto; **~ly** ad (greatly) enormemente.

grotesque [grə'tɛsk] a grotesco.

grotto ['grɔtəu] n gruta.

ground [graund] pt, pp of **grind** // n suelo, tierra; (SPORT) campo, terreno; (reason: gen pl) causa, razón f // vt (plane) mantener en tierra; (US. ELEC) conectar con tierra // vi (ship) varar, encallar; **~s** npl (of coffee etc) poso sg; (gardens etc) jardines mpl, parque m; **on the ~** en el suelo; **to the ~** al suelo; **~ floor** n planta baja; **~ing** n (in education) conocimientos mpl básicos; **~less** a infundado; **~sheet** n tela impermeable; **~ staff** n personal m de tierra; **~ work** n preparación f.

group [gru:p] n grupo; (musical) conjunto

// (vb: also: ~ **together**) vt agrupar // vi agruparse.
grouse [graus] n, pl inv (bird) urogallo // vi (complain) quejarse.
grove [grəuv] n arboleda.
grovel ['grɔvl] vi (fig) humillarse.
grow [grəu], pt **grew**, pp **grown** vi (gen) crecer; (plants) cultivarse; (increase) aumentarse; (spread) extenderse, desarrollarse; (become) volverse; to ~ **rich/weak** enriquecerse/debilitarse // vt cultivar, dejar crecer; to ~ **up** vi crecer, hacerse hombre/mujer; ~**er** n cultivador/a m/f, productor/a m/f; ~**ing** a creciente.
growl [graul] vi gruñir.
grown [grəun] pp of grow; ~**-up** n adulto, persona mayor.
growth [grəuθ] n crecimiento, desarrollo; (what has grown) brote m; (MED) acceso, tumor m.
grub [grʌb] n gusano; (col: food) comida.
grubby ['grʌbɪ] a sucio, mugriento.
grudge [grʌdʒ] n motivo de rencor // vt: to ~ **sb sth** dar algo a uno de mala gana, escatimar algo a uno; to **bear sb a** ~ guardar rencor a uno; he ~**s (giving) the money** da el dinero de mala gana.
gruelling ['gruəlɪŋ] a penoso, duro.
gruesome ['gru:səm] a horrible.
gruff [grʌf] a (voice) bronco; (manner) brusco.
grumble ['grʌmbl] vi refunfuñar, quejarse.
grumpy ['grʌmpɪ] a gruñón(ona).
grunt [grʌnt] vi gruñir // n gruñido.
guarantee [gærən'ti:] n garantía // vt garantizar.
guarantor [gærən'tɔ:*] n garante m/f, fiador/a m/f.
guard [gɑ:d] n guardia; (RAIL) jefe m de tren // vt guardar; ~**ed** a (fig) cauteloso; ~**ian** n guardián/ana m/f; (of minor) tutor/a m/f; ~**'s van** n (RAIL) furgón m.
guerrilla [gə'rɪlə] n guerrillero; ~ **warfare** n guerra de guerrillas.
guess [gɛs] vi, vt (gen) adivinar; (suppose) suponer // n suposición f, conjetura; to **take** or **have a** ~ tratar de adivinar; ~**work** n conjeturas fpl.
guest [gɛst] n invitado/a; (in hotel) huésped/a m/f; ~**-house** n casa de huéspedes, pensión f; ~ **room** n cuarto de huéspedes.
guffaw [gʌ'fɔ:] n carcajada // vi reírse a carcajadas.
guidance ['gaɪdəns] n (gen) dirección f; (advice) consejos mpl.
guide [gaɪd] n (person) guía m/f; (book, fig) guía f // vt guiar; (girl) ~ n exploradora; ~ **book** n guía; ~ **dog** n perro guía; ~ **lines** npl (fig) principios mpl generales.
guild [gɪld] n gremio; ~ **hall** n (Brit) ayuntamiento.
guile [gaɪl] n astucia; ~**less** a cándido.
guillotine ['gɪlətiːn] n guillotina.
guilt [gɪlt] n culpabilidad f; ~**y** a culpable.

guinea pig ['gɪnɪpɪg] n conejillo de Indias.
guise [gaɪz] n: **in** or **under the** ~ **of** so capa de.
guitar [gɪ'tɑ:*] n guitarra; ~**ist** n guitarrista m/f.
gulf [gʌlf] n golfo; (abyss) abismo.
gull [gʌl] n gaviota.
gullet ['gʌlɪt] n esófago; (fam) garganta.
gullible ['gʌlɪbl] a crédulo.
gully ['gʌlɪ] n barranco.
gulp [gʌlp] vi tragar saliva // vt (also: ~ **down**) tragarse // n: **at one** ~ de un trago.
gum [gʌm] n (ANAT) encía; (glue) goma; (sweet) caramelo de goma; (also: **chewing-**~) chiclé m // vt engomar, pegar con goma; ~**boots** npl botas fpl de goma.
gun [gʌn] n (gen) arma de fuego; (small) pistola; (shotgun) escopeta; (rifle) fusil m; (cannon) cañón m; ~**boat** n cañonero; ~**fire** n fuego, disparos mpl; ~**man** n pistolero; ~**ner** n artillero; **at** ~**point** bajo la amenaza de un arma; ~**powder** n pólvora; ~**shot** n escopetazo, cañonazo; ~**smith** n armero.
gurgle ['gə:gl] vi gorgotear.
gush [gʌʃ] vi chorrear; (fig) deshacerse en efusiones.
gusset ['gʌsɪt] n escudete m.
gust [gʌst] n (of wind) ráfaga.
gusto ['gʌstəu] n entusiasmo.
gut [gʌt] n intestino, tripa; (MUS etc) cuerda de tripa; ~**s** npl (courage) valor m.
gutter ['gʌtə*] n (of roof) canalón m; (in street) arroyo.
guttural ['gʌtərl] a gutural.
guy [gaɪ] n (also: ~**rope**) cuerda; (col: man) tío, tipo.
guzzle ['gʌzl] vi tragar // vt engullir.
gym [dʒɪm] n (also: **gymnasium**) gimnasio; (also: **gymnastics**) gimnasia; ~**nast** n gimnasta m/f; ~**nastics** n gimnasia; ~ **shoes** npl zapatillas fpl de gimnasia; ~ **slip** n túnica de colegiala.
gynaecologist, gynecologist (US) [gaɪnɪ'kɔlədʒɪst] n ginecólogo; **gynaecology, gynecology** (US) [-nə'kɔlədʒɪ] n ginecología.
gypsy ['dʒɪpsɪ] n = **gipsy**.
gyrate [dʒaɪ'reɪt] vi girar.

H

haberdashery ['hæbə'dæʃərɪ] n mercería.
habit ['hæbɪt] n hábito, costumbre f; (costume) hábito.
habitable ['hæbɪtəbl] a habitable.
habitual [hə'bɪtjuəl] a acostumbrado, habitual; (drinker, liar) empedernido; ~**ly** ad por costumbre.
hack [hæk] vt (cut) cortar; (slice) tajar // n corte m; (axe blow) hachazo.
hackneyed ['hæknɪd] a trillado, gastado.
had [hæd] pt, pp of **have**.

haddock ['hædək], pl ~ or ~s n especie de merluza.

hadn't ['hædnt] = had not.

haemorrhage, hemorrhage (US) ['heməridʒ] n hemorragia.

haemorrhoids, hemorrhoids (US) ['hemərɔidz] npl hemorroides fpl.

haggard ['hægəd] a ojeroso.

haggle ['hægl] vi (argue) discutir; (bargain) regatear.

Hague [heig] n: The ~ La Haya.

hail [heil] n (weather) granizo // vt saludar; (call) llamar a // vi granizar; ~**stone** n (piedra de) granizo.

hair [hɛə*] n (gen) pelo, cabellos mpl; (one ~) pelo, cabello; (head of ~) cabellera; (on legs) vello; **grey** ~ canas fpl; ~**brush** n cepillo (del pelo); ~**cut** n corte m de pelo; ~**do** n peinado; ~**dresser** n peluquero; ~**dresser's** n peluquería; ~**drier** n secador m de pelo; ~**net** n redecilla; ~**piece** n trenza postiza; ~**pin** n horquilla; ~**pin bend** n curva de horquilla; ~**raising** a espeluznante; ~ **remover** n depilador m; (cream) crema depilatoria; ~ **spray** n laca; ~**style** n peinado; ~**y** a peludo; velludo.

half [hɑːf], pl **halves** n mitad f // a medio // ad medio, a medias; ~**-an-hour** media hora; **two and a** ~ dos y media; ~ **a pound** media libra; **to cut sth in** ~ cortar algo por la mitad; ~ **asleep** medio dormido; ~**-price** a mitad de precio; ~**-back** n (SPORT) medio; ~**-breed**, ~**-caste** n mestizo; ~**-hearted** a indiferente, poco entusiasta; ~**-hour** n media hora; ~**-penny** ['heipni] n medio penique; ~**-time** n medio tiempo; ~**way** ad a medio camino.

halibut ['hælibət] n, pl inv halibut m.

hall [hɔːl] n (for concerts) sala; (entrance way) hall m, vestíbulo; **town** ~ palacio municipal; ~ **of residence** n residencia (universitaria).

hallmark ['hɔːlmɑːk] n (mark) marca; (seal) sello.

hallo [hə'ləu] excl = **hello**.

hallucination [həluːsi'neiʃən] n alucinación f.

halo ['heiləu] n (of saint) aureola.

halt [hɔːlt] n (stop) alto, parada; (RAIL) apeadero // vt parar // vi pararse; (process) interrumpirse.

halve [hɑːv] vt partir por la mitad.

halves [hɑːvz] pl of **half**.

ham [hæm] n jamón m (cocido); (actor) comicastro.

hamburger ['hæmbɔːgə*] n hamburguesa.

hamlet ['hæmlit] n aldea.

hammer ['hæmə*] n martillo // vt amartillar // vi (on door) golpear.

hammock ['hæmək] n hamaca.

hamper ['hæmpə*] vt estorbar // n cesto.

hand [hænd] n mano f; (of clock) manecilla; (writing) letra; (applause) aplausos mpl; (worker) obrero; (measure) palmo // vt

(give) dar, pasar; (deliver) entregar; **to give sb a** ~ dar una mano a uno, ayudar a uno; **at** ~ a la mano; **in** ~ entre manos; **on the one** ~ ..., **on the other** ~ ... por una parte ... por otra (parte) ...; **to** ~ **in** vt entregar; **to** ~ **out** vt distribuir; **to** ~ **over** vt (deliver) entregar; (surrender) ceder; ~**bag** n bolso; ~**basin** n lavabo; ~**book** n manual m; ~**brake** n freno de mano; ~**cuffs** npl esposas fpl; ~**ful** n puñado.

handicap ['hændikæp] n handicap m, desventaja // vt estorbar; **mentally/physically** ~**ped** incapacitado mentalmente/físicamente.

handicraft ['hændikrɑːft] n artesanía.

handkerchief ['hæŋkətʃif] n pañuelo.

handle ['hændl] n (of door etc) tirador m, manija; (of cup etc) asa; (of knife etc) mango; (for winding) manivela; (fam: name) título // vt (touch) tocar; (deal with) encargarse de; (treat: people) manejar; '~ **with care'** 'tratar con cuidado'; **to fly off the** ~ perder los estribos; ~**bar(s)** n(pl) manillar m.

hand-luggage ['hændlʌgidʒ] n equipaje m de mano.

handmade ['hændmeid] a hecho a mano.

handout ['hændaut] n (distribution) repartición f; (charity) limosna; (leaflet) folleto.

handshake ['hændʃeik] n apretón m de manos.

handsome ['hænsəm] a guapo.

handwriting ['hændraitiŋ] n letra.

handy ['hændi] a (close at hand) a mano; (convenient) práctico; (skilful) hábil, diestro; ~**man** n (hombre) mañoso.

hang [hæŋ], pt, pp **hung** vt colgar; (criminal: pt, pp **hanged**) ahorcar; (head) bajar // vi colgar; **to** ~ **about** vi haraganear; **to** ~ **on** vi (wait) esperar; **to** ~ **up** vi (TEL) colgar.

hangar ['hæŋə*] n hangar m.

hanger ['hæŋə*] n percha; ~**-on** n parásito.

hangover ['hæŋəuvə*] n (after drinking) resaca.

hang-up ['hæŋʌp] n complejo.

hanker ['hæŋkə*] vi: **to** ~ **after** (miss) echar de menos; (long for) añorar.

hankie, hanky ['hæŋki] n abbr of **handkerchief**.

haphazard [hæp'hæzəd] a fortuito.

happen ['hæpən] vi suceder, ocurrir; (take place) tener lugar, realizarse; **to** ~ **upon** tropezar con; ~**ing** n suceso, acontecimiento.

happily ['hæpili] ad (luckily) afortunadamente; (cheerfully) alegremente.

happiness ['hæpinis] n (gen) felicidad f; (joy) alegría.

happy ['hæpi] a feliz, alegre; **to be** ~ (with) estar contento (con); **to be** ~ **ser** feliz.

harass ['hærəs] vt acosar, hostigar;

~**ment** n persecución f; (worry) preocupación f.

harbour, harbor (US) ['hɑːbə°] n puerto // vt (hope etc) abrigar; (hide) esconder.

hard [hɑːd] a (gen) duro; (difficult) difícil; (work) arduo; (person) severo // ad (work) mucho, duro, duramente; (think, try) seriamente; **to look** ~ mirar fijo o fijamente; **no** ~ **feelings!** sin rencor; **to be** ~ **of hearing** ser duro de oído; **to be** ~ **done by** ser tratado injustamente; ~**back** n libro encuadernado; ~**board** n chapa de madera; ~**en** vt endurecer; (fig) curtir // vi endurecerse; ~**headed** a poco sentimental, práctico; ~ **labour** n trabajos mpl forzados.

hardly ['hɑːdlɪ] ad (scarcely) apenas; **that can** ~ **be true** difícilmente puede ser cierto; ~ **ever** casi nunca.

hardness ['hɑːdnɪs] n dureza.

hardship ['hɑːdʃɪp] n (troubles) penas fpl; (financial) apuro.

hard-up [hɑːd'ʌp] a (col) pelado.

hardware ['hɑːdwɛə°] n ferretería; (COMPUTERS) material m; ~ **shop** n ferretería.

hard-wearing [hɑːd'wɛərɪŋ] a resistente, duradero.

hard-working [hɑːd'wɜːkɪŋ] a trabajador(a).

hardy ['hɑːdɪ] a fuerte; (plant) resistente.

hare [hɛə°] n liebre f; ~-**brained** a casquivano.

harem [hɑːˈriːm] n harén m.

haricot (bean) ['hærɪkəʊ] n alubia.

harm [hɑːm] n daño, mal m // vt (person) hacer daño a, perjudicar; (thing) dañar; **out of** ~'**s way** a salvo; ~**ful** a perjudicial; (pest) dañino; ~**less** a inofensivo.

harmonica [hɑːˈmɒnɪkə] n armónica.

harmonious [hɑːˈməʊnɪəs] a armonioso; **harmonize** ['hɑːmənaɪz] vt, vi armonizar; **harmony** ['hɑːmənɪ] n armonía.

harness ['hɑːnɪs] n arreos mpl // vt (horse) enjaezar; (resources) aprovechar.

harp [hɑːp] n arpa // vi: **to** ~ **on about** hablar constantemente de; ~**ist** n arpista m/f.

harpoon [hɑːˈpuːn] n arpón m.

harrowing ['hærəʊɪŋ] a horroroso.

harsh [hɑːʃ] a (hard) duro, cruel; (severe) severo; (unpleasant) desagradable; (: colour) chillón(ona); (contrast) violento; ~**ness** n dureza.

harvest ['hɑːvɪst] n cosecha; (of grapes) vendimia // vt, vi cosechar; ~**er** n (machine) cosechadora.

has [hæz] vb see **have**.

hash [hæʃ] n (CULIN) picadillo; (fig: mess) lío.

hashish ['hæʃɪʃ] n hachís m, hachich m.

hasn't ['hæznt] = **has not**.

hassle ['hæsl] n pelea // vt molestar a.

haste [heɪst] n prisa; **hasten** ['heɪsn] vt acelerar // vi darse prisa; **hastily** ad de prisa; **hasty** a apresurado.

hat [hæt] n sombrero.

hatch [hætʃ] n (NAUT. also: ~**way**) escotilla // vi salir del cascarón // vt incubar; (plot) tramar.

hatchback ['hætʃbæk] n (AUT) coche m con puerta trasera.

hatchet ['hætʃɪt] n hacha.

hate [heɪt] vt odiar, aborrecer // n odio; ~**ful** a odioso; **hatred** n odio.

hat trick ['hættrɪk] n (SPORT, also fig) tres triunfos seguidos.

haughty ['hɔːtɪ] a altanero, arrogante.

haul [hɔːl] vt tirar; (by lorry) transportar // n (of fish) redada; (of stolen goods etc) botín m; ~**age** n transporte m; (costs) gastos mpl de transporte; ~**ier** n contratista m de transportes.

haunch [hɔːntʃ] n anca; (of meat) pierna.

haunt [hɔːnt] vt (subj: ghost) aparecer en; (frequent) frecuentar; (obsess) obsesionar // n guarida; ~**ed house** casa de fantasmas.

have [hæv], pt, pp **had** vt (gen) tener; (possess) poseer; (meal, shower) tomar; **to** ~ **sth done** hacer hacer algo; **she has to do it** tiene que hacerlo; **I had better leave** más vale que me marche; **I won't** ~ **it** no lo tolero; **he has gone se ha ido**; **to** ~ **it out with sb** ajustar cuentas con alguien; **to** ~ **a baby** parir, dar a luz.

haven ['heɪvn] n puerto; (fig) refugio.

haven't ['hævnt] = **have not**.

haversack ['hævəsæk] n mochila.

havoc ['hævək] n estragos mpl.

hawk [hɔːk] n halcón m.

hay [heɪ] n heno; ~ **fever** n fiebre f del heno; ~**stack** n almiar m.

haywire ['heɪwaɪə°] a (col): **to go** ~ (person) volverse loco; (plan) embarullarse.

hazard ['hæzəd] n riesgo // vt aventurar; ~**ous** a (dangerous) peligroso; (risky) arriesgado.

haze [heɪz] n neblina.

hazelnut ['heɪzlnʌt] n avellana.

hazy ['heɪzɪ] a brumoso; (idea) vago.

he [hiː] pron él; ~ **who...** él que..., quien...; ~-**man** n macho.

head [hɛd] n cabeza; (leader) jefe/a m/f // vt (list) encabezar; (group) capitanear; ~**s (or tails)** cara (o cruz); ~ **first** de cabeza; ~ **over heels** patas arriba; **to** ~ **the ball** cabecear (la pelota); **to** ~ **for** vt fus dirigirse a; ~**ache** n dolor m de cabeza; ~**ing** n título; ~**lamp** n faro; ~**land** n promontorio; ~**light** = ~**lamp**; ~**line** n titular m; ~**long** ad (fall) de cabeza; (rush) precipitadamente; ~**master/ mistress** n director/a m/f (de escuela); ~ **office** n oficina central, central f; ~-**on** a (collision) de frente; ~**phones** npl auriculares mpl; ~**quarters (HQ)** npl sede f central; (MIL) cuartel m general; ~-**rest** n reposacabezas m inv; ~**room** n (in car) espacio para la cabeza; (under bridge) luz f; ~**scarf** n pañuelo (de cabeza); ~**stone** n lápida mortuoria; ~**strong** a voluntarioso; ~ **waiter** n jefe m de camareros; ~**way** n progreso; **to make** ~**way** avanzar; ~**wind** n viento contrario.

heal [hi:l] vt curar // vi cicatrizarse.

health [hɛlθ] n salud f; **good** ~! ¡salud y pesetas!; ~ **food** n comida natural; H~ **Service** n Seguro de Enfermedad; ~**y** a (gen) sano.

heap [hi:p] n montón m // vt amontonar; (plate) colmar.

hear [hɪə*], pt, pp **heard** [hɜ:d] vt oír; (perceive) sentir; (listen to) escuchar; (lecture) asistir a // vi oír; **to** ~ **about** oír hablar de; **to** ~ **from sb** tener noticias de alguien; ~**ing** n (sense) oído; (LAW) vista; ~**ing aid** n audífono; ~**say** n rumores mpl, hablillas fpl.

hearse [hɜ:s] n coche m fúnebre.

heart [ha:t] n corazón m; ~**s** npl (CARDS) corazones mpl; **at** ~ en el fondo; **by** ~ (learn, know) de memoria; ~ **attack** n ataque m cardíaco; ~**beat** n latido (del corazón); ~**breaking** a desgarrador(a); **to be** ~**broken** estar angustiado; ~**burn** n acedía; ~ **failure** n fallo cardíaco; ~**felt** a (cordial) cordial; (deeply felt) más sentido.

hearth [ha:θ] n (gen) hogar m; (fireplace) chimenea.

heartily ['ha:tɪlɪ] ad sinceramente, cordialmente; (laugh) a carcajadas; (eat) con buen apetito.

heartless ['ha:tlɪs] a cruel.

hearty ['ha:tɪ] a cordial.

heat [hi:t] n (gen) calor m; (ardour) ardor m; (SPORT. also: **qualifying** ~) prueba eliminatoria // vt calentar; (fig) acalorar; **to** ~ **up** vi (gen) calentarse; ~**ed** a caliente; (fig) acalorado; ~**er** n calentador m.

heath [hi:θ] n (Brit) brezal m.

heathen ['hi:ðn] a, n pagano/a.

heather ['hɛðə*] n brezo.

heating ['hi:tɪŋ] n calefacción f.

heatstroke ['hi:tstrəuk] n insolación f.

heatwave ['hi:tweɪv] n ola de calor.

heave [hi:v] vt (pull) tirar de; (push) empujar con esfuerzo; (lift) levantar (con esfuerzo) // vi (water) agitarse // n tirón m; empujón m; (effort) esfuerzo; (throw) echada.

heaven ['hɛvn] n cielo; (REL) paraíso; ~**ly** a celestial; (REL) divino.

heavily ['hɛvɪlɪ] ad pesadamente, (drink, smoke) con exceso; (sleep, sigh) profundamente.

heavy ['hɛvɪ] a pesado; (work) duro; (sea, rain, meal) fuerte; (drinker, smoker) gran; (eater) comilón(ona); ~**weight** n (SPORT) peso pesado.

Hebrew ['hi:bru:] a hebreo.

heckle ['hɛkl] vt interrumpir.

hectic ['hɛktɪk] a febril, agitado.

he'd [hi:d] = **he would; he had.**

hedge [hɛdʒ] n seto // vt cercar (con un seto) // vi contestar con evasivas; **to** ~ **one's bets** (fig) cubrirse.

hedgehog ['hɛdʒhɔg] n erizo.

heed [hi:d] vt (also: **take** ~ **of**) (attend to) hacer caso de; (bear in mind) tener en cuenta; ~**less** a desatento.

heel [hi:l] n talón m // vt (shoe) poner tacón a.

hefty ['hɛftɪ] a (person) fornido; (piece) grande; (price) gordo.

heifer ['hɛfə*] n novilla, ternera.

height [haɪt] n (of person) talle m; (of building) altura; (high ground) cerro; (altitude) altitud f; ~**en** vt elevar; (fig) aumentar.

heir [ɛə*] n heredero; ~**ess** n heredera; ~**loom** n reliquia de familia.

held [hɛld] pt, pp of **hold.**

helicopter ['hɛlɪkɔptə*] n helicóptero.

hell [hɛl] n infierno; ~**!** ¡demonios!

he'll [hi:l] = **he will, he shall.**

hellish ['hɛlɪʃ] a infernal; (fam) horrible.

hello [hə'ləu] excl ¡hola!; (surprise) ¡caramba!

helm [hɛlm] n (NAUT) timón m.

helmet ['hɛlmɪt] n casco.

help [hɛlp] n ayuda; (charwoman) criada, asistenta; (assistant etc) empleado // vt ayudar; (¡socorro!; ~ **yourself** sírvete; **he can't** ~ **it** no es culpa suya; ~**er** n ayudante m/f; ~**ful** a útil, servicial; ~**ing** n ración f; ~**less** a (incapable) incapaz; (defenceless) indefenso.

hem [hɛm] n dobladillo; **to** ~ **in** vt cercar.

hemisphere ['hɛmɪsfɪə*] n hemisferio.

hen [hɛn] n gallina.

hence [hɛns] ad (therefore) por lo tanto; **2 years** ~ de aquí a 2 años; ~**forth** ad de hoy en adelante.

henchman ['hɛntʃmən] n (pej) secuaz m.

henpecked ['hɛnpɛkt] a dominado por su mujer.

her [hɜ:*] pron (direct) la; (indirect) le; (stressed, after prep) ella // a su.

herald ['hɛrəld] n (forerunner) precursor/a m/f // vt anunciar.

heraldry ['hɛrəldrɪ] n heráldica.

herb [hɜ:b] n hierba.

herd [hɜ:d] n rebaño.

here [hɪə*] ad aquí; ~**!** (present) presente; ~ **she is** aquí está; ~**after** ad en el futuro // n: **the** ~**after** (la vida de) ultratumba; ~**by** ad (in letter) por la presente.

hereditary [hɪ'rɛdɪtrɪ] a hereditario; **heredity** [-tɪ] n herencia.

heresy ['hɛrəsɪ] n herejía.

heretic ['hɛrətɪk] n hereje m/f; ~**al** [hɪ'rɛtɪkl] a herético.

heritage ['hɛrɪtɪdʒ] n (gen) herencia; (fig) patrimonio.

hermit ['hɜ:mɪt] n ermitaño.

hernia ['hɜ:nɪə] n hernia.

hero ['hɪərəu], pl ~**es** n héroe m; (in book, film) protagonista m; ~**ic** [hɪ'rəuɪk] a heroico.

heroin ['herəuin] n heroína.
heroine ['herəuin] n heroína; (in book, film) protagonista.
heroism ['herəuizm] n heroísmo.
heron ['herən] n garza.
herring ['heriŋ] n arenque m.
hers [hə:z] pron (el) suyo/(la) suya etc.
herself [hə:'self] pron (reflexive) se; (emphatic) ella misma; (after prep) sí (misma).
he's [hi:z] = **he is; he has.**
hesitant ['hezitənt] a vacilante, dudoso.
hesitate ['heziteit] vi dudar, vacilar; **hesitation** ['·teiʃən] n indecisión f.
hew [hju:] vt cortar con hacha.
hexagon ['heksəgən] n hexágono; **~al** [-'sægənl] a hexagonal.
hi [hai] excl ¡oye!, ¡hola!
hibernate ['haibəneit] vi invernar.
hiccough, hiccup ['hikʌp] vi hipar; **~s** npl hipo sg.
hid [hid] pt of **hide.**
hidden ['hidn] pp of **hide.**
hide [haid] n (skin) piel f // (vb: pt **hid,** pp **hidden**) vt esconder, ocultar // vi: **to ~ (from sb)** esconderse o ocultarse (de alguien); **~-and-seek** n escondite m; **~away** n escondite m.
hideous ['hidiəs] a horrible.
hiding ['haidiŋ] n (beating) paliza; **to be in ~** (concealed) estar escondido; **~ place** n escondrijo.
hierarchy ['haiəra:ki] n jerarquía.
high [hai] a (gen) alto; (speed, number) grande; (price) elevado; (wind) fuerte; (voice) agudo // ad alto, a gran altura; **it is 20 m ~** tiene 20 m de altura; **~ in the air** en las alturas; **~brow** a, n culto; **~chair** n silla alta; **~-handed** a despótico; **~-heeled** a de tacón alto; **~jack = hijack; ~ jump** n (SPORT) salto de altura; **~light** n (fig: of event) punto culminante // vt subrayar; **~ly** ad sumamente; **~ly strung** a hipertenso; **H~ Mass** n misa mayor; **~ness** n altura; **Her H~ness** Su Alteza; **~-pitched** a agudo; **~-rise block** n torre f de pisos; **~ school** n colegio de segunda enseñanza, Instituto; **~ street** n calle f mayor; **~way** n carretera.
hijack ['haidʒæk] vt secuestrar; **~er** n secuestrador/a m/f.
hike [haik] vi (go walking) ir de excursión; (tramp) caminar // n caminata; **hiker** n excursionista m/f.
hilarious [hi'lɛəriəs] a (behaviour, event) regocijante.
hill [hil] n colina; (high) montaña; (slope) cuesta; **~side** n ladera; **~y** a montañoso; (uneven) accidentada.
hilt [hilt] n (of sword) empuñadura; **to the ~** completamente.
him [him] pron (direct) le, lo; (indirect) le; (stressed, after prep) él; **~self** pron (reflexive) se; (emphatic) él mismo; (after prep) sí (mismo).
hind [haind] a posterior // n cierva.

hinder ['hində*] vt estorbar, impedir; **hindrance** ['hindrəns] n estorbo, obstáculo.
Hindu ['hindu:] n hindú m/f.
hinge [hindʒ] n bisagra, gozne m // vi (fig): **to ~ on** depender de.
hint [hint] n indirecta; (advice) consejo // vt: **to ~ that** insinuar que // vi soltar indirectas; **to ~ at** hacer una alusión a.
hip [hip] n cadera; **~ pocket** n bolsillo de atrás.
hippopotamus [hipə'pɒtəməs], pl **~es** or **-mi** [-mai] n hipopótamo.
hire ['haiə*] vt (car, equipment) alquilar; (worker) contratar // n alquiler m; (of person) salario; **for ~** se alquila; (taxi) libre; **~ purchase (H.P.)** n compra a plazos.
his [hiz] pron (el) suyo/(la) suya etc // a su.
Hispanic [his'pænik] a hispánico.
hiss [his] vi silbar, sisear // n silbido, siseo.
historian [hi'stɔ:riən] n historiador/a m/f.
historic(al) [hi'stɔrik(l)] a histórico.
history ['histəri] n historia.
hit [hit], pt, pp **hit** vt (strike) golpear, pegar; (reach: target) alcanzar; (collide with: car) chocar contra // n golpe m; (success) éxito, sensación f; **to ~ it off with sb** hacer buenas migas con alguien.
hitch [hitʃ] vt (fasten) atar, amarrar; (also: **~ up**) alzar // n (difficulty) dificultad f; **to ~ a lift** hacer autostop.
hitch-hike ['hitʃhaik] vi hacer autostop; **hitch-hiker** n autostopista m/f.
hive [haiv] n colmena.
hoard [hɔ:d] n acumulación f // vt acumular; **~ing** n acumulación f; (for posters) cartelera.
hoarfrost ['hɔ:frɒst] n escarcha.
hoarse [hɔ:s] a ronco.
hoax [həuks] n trampa.
hobble ['hɔbl] vi cojear // vt (horse) manear.
hobby ['hɔbi] n pasatiempo, afición f; **~-horse** n (fig) tema, manía.
hobo ['həubəu] n (US) vagabundo.
hockey ['hɔki] n hockey m.
hoe [həu] n azadón m // vt azadonar.
hog [hɔg] n cerdo, puerco // vt (fig) acaparar; **to go the whole ~** liarse la manta a la cabeza.
hoist [hɔist] n (lift) montacargas m inv; (crane) grúa.
hold [həuld], pt, pp **held** vt tener; (contain) contener; (keep back) retener; (believe) sostener; (take ~ of) coger; (take weight) soportar; (meeting) celebrar // vi (withstand pressure) resistir; (be valid) valer; (stick) pegarse // n (handle) asidero; (grasp) asimiento; (fig) dominio; (WRESTLING) presa; (NAUT) bodega; **~ the line!** (TEL) no cuelgue; **to ~ one's own** (fig) defenderse; **to catch** or **get (a) ~ of** agarrarse, asirse de; **to ~ back** vt retenerse; (secret) guardarse; **to ~ down** vt (person) sujetar; (job) conservar; **to ~ off** vt (enemy) rechazar; **to ~ on** vi

agarrarse bien; (*wait*) esperar; ~ on!
(*TEL*) no cuelgue; **to ~ on to** *vt tus*
agarrarse a; (*keep*) guardar; **to ~ out** *vt*
alargar // *vi* (*resist*) resistir; **to ~ up** *vt*
(*raise*) levantar; (*support*) apoyar; (*delay*)
atrasar; (*rob*) asaltar; **~all** *n* funda,
neceser *m*; **~er** *n* (*of ticket, record*)
poseedor/a *m/f*; (*of office, title etc*) titular
m/f; **~ing** *n* (*share*) interés *m*; **~up** *n*
(*robbery*) atraco; (*delay*) parada; (*in
traffic*) embotellamiento.
hole [həul] *n* agujero // *vt* agujerear.
holiday ['hɔlɪdɪ] *n* vacaciones *fpl*; (*day off*)
(día de) fiesta, feriado; **~-maker** *n*
veraneante *m/f*; ~ **resort** *n* punto de
veraneo.
holiness ['həulɪnɪs] *n* santidad *f*.
Holland ['hɔlənd] *n* Holanda.
hollow ['hɔləu] *a* hueco, vacío; (*eyes*)
hundido; (*sound*) sordo; (*doctrine*) falso //
n (*gen*) hueco; (*in ground*) hoyo // *vt*: **to
~ out** ahuecar.
holly ['hɔlɪ] *n* acebo; **~hock** *n* malva loca.
holster ['həulstə*] *n* pistolera.
holy ['həulɪ] *a* (*gen*) santo, sagrado;
(*water*) bendito; **H~ Ghost** *or* **Spirit** *n*
Espíritu *m* Santo.
homage ['hɔmɪdʒ] *n* homenaje *m*; **to pay
~ to** rendir homenaje a.
home [həum] *n* casa; (*country*) patria;
(*institution*) asilo // *a* (*domestic*) casero, de
casa; (*ECON, POL*) nacional // *ad* (*direction*)
a casa; **at ~** en casa; **to go/come ~**
ir/volver a casa; **make yourself at ~**
¡estás en tu casa!; **~ address** *n* señas *fpl*;
~land *n* tierra natal; **~less** *a* sin hogar,
sin casa; **~ly** *a* (*domestic*) casero;
(*simple*) sencillo; **~-made** *a* hecho en
casa; ~ **rule** *n* autonomía; **H~
Secretary** *n* (*Brit*) Ministro del Interior;
~ sick *a*: **to be ~sick** tener morriña,
tener nostalgia; ~ **town** *n* ciudad *f* natal;
~ward ['həumwəd] *a* (*journey*) hacia
casa; ~ **work** *n* tarea.
homicide ['hɔmɪsaɪd] *n* (*US*) homicidio.
homosexual [hɔməu'sɛksjuəl] *a*, *n*
homosexual *m*.
honest ['ɔnɪst] *a* honrado; (*sincere*) franco,
sincero; **~ly** *ad* honradamente;
francamente; **~y** *n* honradez *f*.
honey ['hʌnɪ] *n* miel *f*; **~comb** *n* panal *m*;
(*pattern*) nido de abejas; **~moon** *n* luna
de miel; (*trip*) viaje *m* de novios.
honk [hɔŋk] *vi* (*AUT*) tocar la bocina.
honorary ['ɔnərərɪ] *a* no remunerado;
(*duty, title*) honorario.
honour, honor (*US*) ['ɔnə*] *vt* honrar // *n*
honor *m*, honra; **~able** *a* honorable; **~s
degree** *n* (*SCOL*) título universitario.
hood [hud] *n* capucha; (*Brit*: *AUT*) capota;
(*US*: *AUT*) capó *n*.
hoodlum ['huːdləm] *n* matón *m*.
hoof [huːf], *pl* **hooves** *n* pezuña.
hook [huk] *n* gancho; (*on dress*) corchete
m, broche *m*; (*for fishing*) anzuelo // *vt*
enganchar.
hooligan ['huːlɪgən] *n* gamberro.

hoop [huːp] *n* aro.
hoot [huːt] *vi* (*AUT*) tocar la bocina; (*siren*)
tocar la sirena // *n* bocinazo; toque *m* de
sirena; **to ~ with laughter** morirse de
risa; **~er** *n* (*AUT*) bocina; (*NAUT*) sirena.
hooves [huːvz] *pl* of **hoof**.
hop [hɔp] *vi* saltar, brincar; (*on one foot*)
saltar con un pie // *n* salto, brinco.
hope [həup] *vt, vi* esperar // *n* esperanza; **I
~ so/not** espero que sí/no; **~ful** *a*
(*person*) optimista, lleno de esperanzas;
(*situation*) prometedor(a); **~fully** *ad* con
optimismo, con esperanza; **~less** *a*
desesperado.
hops [hɔps] *npl* lúpulo *sg*.
horde [hɔːd] *n* horda.
horizon [hə'raɪzn] *n* horizonte *m*; **~tal**
[hɔrɪ'zɔntl] *a* horizontal.
hormone ['hɔːməun] *n* hormona.
horn [hɔːn] *n* cuerno; (*MUS*) trompa; (*AUT*)
bocina; **~-rimmed** *a* de concha; **~ed** *a*
(*animal*) con cuernos.
hornet ['hɔːnɪt] *n* avispón *m*.
horny ['hɔːnɪ] *a* (*material*) córneo; (*hands*)
calloso.
horoscope ['hɔrəskəup] *n* horóscopo.
horrible ['hɔrɪbl] *a* horrible.
horrid ['hɔrɪd] *a* horrible, horroroso.
horrify ['hɔrɪfaɪ] *vt* horrorizar.
horror ['hɔrə*] *n* horror *m*; ~ **film** *n*
película de horror.
hors d'œuvre [ɔː'dəːvrə] *n* entremeses
mpl.
horse [hɔːs] *n* caballo; **on ~back** *a*
caballo; **~man/woman** *n* jinete
m/amazona; **~power (h.p.)** *n* caballo (de
fuerza); **~-racing** *n* carreras *fpl* de
caballos; **~radish** *n* rábano picante;
~shoe *n* herradura.
horticulture ['hɔːtɪkʌltʃə*] *n* horticultura.
hose [həuz] *n* (*also*: **~pipe**) manga.
hosiery ['həuzɪərɪ] *n* calcetería.
hospitable ['hɔspɪtəbl] *a* hospitalario.
hospital ['hɔspɪtl] *n* hospital *m*.
hospitality [hɔspɪ'tælɪtɪ] *n* hospitalidad *f*.
host [həust] *n* anfitrión *m*; (*in hotel etc*)
huésped *m*; (*large number*): **a ~ of**
multitud de; (*REL*) hostia.
hostage ['hɔstɪdʒ] *n* rehén *m*.
hostel ['hɔstl] *n* hostal *m*; **youth ~** *n*
albergue *m* de juventud.
hostess ['həustɪs] *n* anfitriona; (*air ~*)
azafata; (*in night-club*) cabaretera.
hostile ['hɔstaɪl] *a* hostil; **hostility** [-'stɪlɪtɪ]
n hostilidad *f*.
hot [hɔt] *a* caliente; (*weather*) caluroso, de
calor; (*as opposed to only warm*) muy
caliente; (*spicy*) picante; (*fig*) ardiente,
acalorado; ~ **dog** *n* perro caliente.
hotel [həu'tɛl] *n* hotel *m*; **~ier** *n* hotelero.
hot: **~headed** *a* exaltado; **~house** *n*
invernadero; **~ly** *ad* con pasión,
apasionadamente; **~-water bottle** *n*
bolsa de agua caliente.
hound [haund] *vt* acosar // *n* perro de
caza.

hour ['auə*] n hora; ~**ly** ad cada hora.
house [haus, pl: 'hauzız] n (also: firm) casa; (POL) cámara; (THEATRE) sala // vt [hauz] (person) alojar; **on the ~** (fig) la casa invita; ~ **arrest** n arresto domiciliario; ~**boat** n casa flotante; ~**breaking** n robo (en una casa); ~**coat** n bata; ~**hold** n familia; ~**keeper** n ama de llaves; ~**keeping** n (work) trabajos domésticos mpl; ~**keeping (money)** dinero para gastos domésticos; ~-**warming party** n fiesta de estreno de casa; ~**wife** n ama de casa; ~ **work** n faenas fpl (de la casa).
housing ['hauzıŋ] n (act) alojamiento; (houses) viviendas fpl; ~ **estate** n bloque m de viviendas.
hovel ['hɔvl] n pocilga.
hover ['hɔvə*] vi flotar (en el aire); ~**craft** n hidroala m, aerodeslizador m.
how [hau] ad cómo; ~ **are you?** ¿cómo está Vd?, ¿cómo estás?; ~ **long have you been here?** ¿cuánto tiempo hace que estás aquí?; ~ **lovely!** ¡qué bonito!; ~ **many/much?** ¿cuántos/cuánto?; ~ **old are you?** ¿cuántos años tienes?; ~**ever** ad de cualquier manera; (+ adjective) por muy ... que; (in questions) cómo // conj sin embargo, no obstante.
howl [haul] n aullido // vi aullar.
h.p., H.P. abbr of **hire purchase; horse power.**
HQ abbr of **headquarters.**
hub [hʌb] n (of wheel) centro.
hubbub ['hʌbʌb] n barahúnda, barullo.
hubcap ['hʌbkæp] n tapacubo.
huddle ['hʌdl] vi: **to ~ together** amontonarse.
hue [hju:] n color m, matiz m; ~ **and cry** n alarma.
huff [hʌf] n: **in a ~** con rabieta.
hug [hʌg] vt abrazar // n abrazo.
huge [hju:dʒ] a enorme.
hulk [hʌlk] n (wreck) barco viejo; (hull) casco.
hull [hʌl] n (of ship) casco.
hullo [hə'ləu] excl = **hello.**
hum [hʌm] vt tararear, canturrear // vi tararear, canturrear; (insect) zumbar // n zumbido.
human ['hju:mən] a, n humano.
humane [hju:'meın] a humano, humanitario.
humanity [hju:'mænıtı] n humanidad f.
humble ['hʌmbl] a humilde // vt humillar; **humbly** ad humildemente.
humbug ['hʌmbʌg] n embustes mpl; (sweet) caramelo de menta.
humdrum ['hʌmdrʌm] a (boring) monótono, aburrido; (routine) rutinario.
humid ['hju:mıd] a húmedo; ~**ity** [-'mıdıtı] n humedad f.
humiliate [hju:'mılıeıt] vt humillar; **humiliation** [-'eıʃən] n humillación f.
humility [hju:'mılıtı] n humildad f.
humorist ['hju:mərıst] n humorista m/f.

humorous ['hju:mərəs] a gracioso, divertido.
humour, humor (US) ['hju:mə*] n humorismo, sentido del humor; (mood) humor m // vt (person) complacer.
hump [hʌmp] n (in ground) montículo; (camel's) giba.
hunch [hʌntʃ] n (premonition) presentimiento; ~**back** n joroba; ~**ed** a jorobado.
hundred ['hʌndrəd] num ciento; (before n) cien; ~**weight** n (Brit) = 50.8 kg; 112 lb; (US) = 45.3 kg; 100 lb.
hung [hʌŋ] pt, pp of **hang.**
Hungarian [hʌŋ'geərıən] a, n húngaro/a.
Hungary ['hʌŋgərı] n Hungría.
hunger ['hʌŋgə*] n hambre f // vi: **to ~ for** (gen) tener hambre de; (desire) anhelar; ~ **strike** n huelga de hambre; **hungrily** [-grəlı] ad ávidamente, con ganas; **hungry** [-grı] a hambriento; **to be hungry** tener hambre.
hunt [hʌnt] vt (seek) buscar; (SPORT) cazar // vi cazar // n caza, cacería; ~**er** n cazador m; ~**ing** n caza.
hurdle ['hə:dl] n (SPORT) valla; (fig) obstáculo.
hurl [hə:l] vt lanzar, arrojar.
hurrah [hu'rɑ:], **hurray** [hu'reı] n ¡viva!, ¡vítor!
hurricane ['hʌrıkən] n huracán m.
hurried ['hʌrıd] a (fast) apresurado; (rushed) hecho de prisa; ~**ly** ad con prisa, apresuradamente.
hurry ['hʌrı] n prisa // vi apresurarse, darse prisa // vt (person) dar prisa a; (work) apresurar; **to be in a ~** tener prisa.
hurt [hə:t], pt, pp **hurt** vt hacer daño a // vi doler // a lastimado; ~**ful** a (gen) dañoso; (remark) hiriente.
hurtle ['hə:tl] vi: **to ~ past** pasar como un rayo; **to ~ down** caer con violencia.
husband ['hʌzbənd] n marido.
hush [hʌʃ] n silencio // vt hacer callar; (cover up) encubrir; ~**! ** ¡chitón!, ¡cállate!
husk [hʌsk] n (of wheat) cáscara.
husky ['hʌskı] a ronco; (burly) fornido // n perro esquimal.
hustle ['hʌsl] vt (push) empujar; (hurry) dar prisa a // n bullicio, actividad f febril; ~ **and bustle** n vaivén m.
hut [hʌt] n cabaña; (shed) cobertizo.
hutch [hʌtʃ] n conejera.
hyacinth ['haıəsınθ] n jacinto.
hybrid ['haıbrıd] a, n híbrido.
hydrant ['haıdrənt] n (also: **fire ~**) boca de incendios.
hydraulic [haı'drɔ:lık] a hidráulico.
hydroelectric [haıdrəu'lektrık] a hidroeléctrico.
hydrogen ['haıdrədʒən] n hidrógeno.
hyena [haı'i:nə] n hiena.
hygiene ['haıdʒi:n] n higiene f; **hygienic** [-'dʒi:nık] a higiénico.
hymn [hım] n himno.

hyphen ['haɪfn] *n* guión *m*.
hypnosis [hɪp'nəusɪs] *n* hipnosis *f*; **hypnotic** [-'nɔtɪk] *a* hipnótico; **hypnotism** ['hɪpnətɪzm] *n* hipnotismo; **hypnotist** ['hɪpnətɪst] *n* hipnotista *m/f*; **hypnotize** ['hɪpnətaɪz] *vt* hipnotizar.
hypocrisy [hɪ'pɔkrɪsɪ] *n* hipocresía; **hypocrite** ['hɪpəkrɪt] *n* hipócrita *m/f*; **hypocritical** [hɪpə'krɪtɪkl] *a* hipócrita.
hypothesis [haɪ'pɔθɪsɪs], *pl* **-ses** [-siːz] *n* hipótesis *f*; **hypothetic(al)** [-pəu'θetɪk(l)] *a* hipotético.
hysteria [hɪ'stɪərɪə] *n* histeria; **hysterical** [-'sterɪkl] *a* histérico; **hysterics** [-'sterɪks] *npl* histeria *sg*, histerismo *sg*.

I

I [aɪ] *pron* yo.
ice [aɪs] *n* hielo // *vt* (*cake*) alcorzar; (*drink*) helar // *vi* (*also*: ~ **over**, ~ **up**) helarse; ~ **age** *n* período glacial; ~ **axe** *n* piolet *m*; ~**berg** *n* iceberg *m*; ~**box** *n* (*US*) nevera; ~**-cold** *a* helado; ~ **cream** *n* helado; ~ **cube** *n* cubito de hielo; ~ **hockey** *n* hockey *m* sobre hielo.
Iceland ['aɪslənd] *n* Islandia; ~**er** *n* islandés/esa *m/f*; ~**ic** [-'lændɪk] *a* islandés(esa).
ice: ~ **rink** *n* pista de hielo; ~ **skating** *n* patinaje *m* sobre hielo.
icicle ['aɪsɪkl] *n* carámbano.
icing ['aɪsɪŋ] *n* (*CULIN*) alcorza, garapiña; (*AVIAT etc*) formación *f* de hielo; ~ **sugar** *n* azúcar *m* de alcorza.
icon ['aɪkɔn] *n* icono.
icy ['aɪsɪ] *a* (*road*) helado; (*fig*) glacial.
I'd [aɪd] = **I would**; **I had**.
idea [aɪ'dɪə] *n* idea.
ideal [aɪ'dɪəl] *n* idea! *m* // *a* ideal; ~**ist** *n* idealista *m/f*.
identical [aɪ'dentɪkl] *a* idéntico.
identification [aɪdentɪfɪ'keɪʃən] *n* identificación *f*; **means of** ~ documentos *mpl* personales.
identify [aɪ'dentɪfaɪ] *vt* identificar.
identikit picture [aɪ'dentɪkɪt-] *n* retrato-robot *m*.
identity [aɪ'dentɪtɪ] *n* identidad *f*.
ideological [aɪdɪə'lɔdʒɪkəl] *a* ideológico; **ideology** [-dɪ'ɔlədʒɪ] *n* ideología.
idiocy ['ɪdɪəsɪ] *n* idiotez *f*; (*stupid act*) estupidez *f*.
idiom ['ɪdɪəm] *n* modismo; (*style of speaking*) lenguaje *m*.
idiosyncrasy [ɪdɪəu'sɪŋkrəsɪ] *n* idiosincrasia.
idiot ['ɪdɪət] *n* (*gen*) idiota *m/f*; (*fool*) tonto/a; ~**ic** [-'ɔtɪk] *a* idiota; tonto.
idle ['aɪdl] *a* (*gen*) ocioso; (*lazy*) holgazán(ana); (*unemployed*) desocupado; (*pointless*) inútil // *vi* (*machine*) marchar en vacío // *vt*: **to** ~ **away the time** malgastar el tiempo; ~**ness** *n* ociosidad *f*; holgazanería; desocupación *f*.
idol ['aɪdl] *n* ídolo; ~**ize** *vt* idolatrar.

if [ɪf] *conj* si.
igloo ['ɪgluː] *n* iglú *m*.
ignite [ɪg'naɪt] *vt* encender; (*set fire to*) incendiar // *vi* encenderse.
ignition [ɪg'nɪʃən] *n* (*AUT*) encendido; **to switch on/off the** ~ encender/apagar el motor; ~ **key** *n* (*AUT*) llave *f* de contacto.
ignorance ['ɪgnərəns] *n* ignorancia; **ignorant** [-ənt] *a* ignorante; **to be ignorant of** ignorar.
ignore [ɪg'nɔː*] *vt* (*person*) no hacer caso de; (*fact*) pasar por alto.
I'll [aɪl] = **I will**; **I shall**.
ill [ɪl] *a* enfermo, malo; (*bad*) malo // *n* mal *m*; (*fig*) infortunio // *ad* mal; **to take** *or* **be taken** ~ ponerse enfermo, enfermar; ~**-advised** *a* poco recomendable; (*misled*) mal aconsejado; ~**-at-ease** *a* incómodo.
illegal [ɪ'liːgl] *a* ilegal.
illegible [ɪ'ledʒɪbl] *a* ilegible.
illegitimate [ɪlɪ'dʒɪtɪmət] *a* ilegítimo.
ill: ~**-fated** *a* malogrado; ~ **feeling** *n* rencor *m*.
illicit [ɪ'lɪsɪt] *a* ilícito.
illiterate [ɪ'lɪtərət] *a* analfabeto.
ill-mannered [ɪl'mænəd] *a* mal educado.
illness ['ɪlnɪs] *n* enfermedad *f*.
illogical [ɪ'lɔdʒɪkl] *a* ilógico.
ill-treat [ɪl'triːt] *vt* maltratar.
illuminate [ɪ'luːmɪneɪt] *vt* (*room, street*) iluminar, alumbrar; (*subject*) aclarar; **illumination** [-'neɪʃən] *n* alumbrado; **illuminations** *npl* luminarias *fpl*.
illusion [ɪ'luːʒən] *n* ilusión *f*; **to be under the** ~ **that...** estar bajo la ilusión de que...; **illusory** [-sərɪ] *a* ilusorio.
illustrate ['ɪləstreɪt] *vt* (*gen*) ilustrar; (*subject*) aclarar; (*point*) poner ejemplos a; **illustration** [-'streɪʃən] *n* (*example*) ejemplo; (*explanation*) aclaración *f*; (*in book*) lámina.
illustrious [ɪ'lʌstrɪəs] *a* ilustre.
ill will [ɪl'wɪl] *n* rencor *m*.
I'm [aɪm] = **I am**.
image ['ɪmɪdʒ] *n* imagen *f*.
imaginary [ɪ'mædʒɪnərɪ] *a* imaginario; **imagination** [-'neɪʃən] *n* imaginación *f*; (*inventiveness*) inventiva; (*illusion*) fantasía; **imaginative** [-nətɪv] *a* imaginativo; **imagine** *vt* imaginarse; (*delude o.s.*) hacerse la ilusión (de que).
imbalance [ɪm'bæləns] *n* (*gen*) desequilibrio; (*inequality*) falta de correspondencia.
imbecile ['ɪmbəsiːl] *n* imbécil *m/f*.
imbue [ɪm'bjuː] *vt*: **to** ~ **sth with** imbuir algo de.
imitate ['ɪmɪteɪt] *vt* imitar; **imitation** [-'teɪʃən] *n* imitación *f*; (*copy*) copia; (*mimicry*) mímica.
immaculate [ɪ'mækjulət] *a* perfectamente limpio; (*REL*) inmaculado.
immaterial [ɪmə'tɪərɪəl] *a* incorpóreo; **it is** ~ **whether...** no importa si... .

immature [ɪmə'tjuə*] *a* (*person*) poco maduro; (*of one's youth*) juvenil.

immediate [ɪ'miːdɪət] *a* inmediato; (*pressing*) urgente, apremiante; ~ly *ad* (*at once*) en seguida; ~ly **next to** muy junto a.

immense [ɪ'mɛns] *a* inmenso, enorme.

immerse [ɪ'məːs] *vt* (*submerge*) sumergir; (*sink*) hundir; **to be** ~**d in** (*fig*) estar absorto en.

immersion heater [ɪ'məːʃn-] *n* calentador *m* de inmersión.

immigrant ['ɪmɪgrənt] *n* inmigrante *m/f*; **immigrate** [-greɪt] *vi* inmigrar; **immigration** [-'greɪʃən] *n* inmigración *f.*

imminent ['ɪmɪnənt] *a* inminente.

immobile [ɪ'məubaɪl] *a* inmóvil; **immobilize** [-bɪlaɪz] *vt* inmovilizar.

immoral [ɪ'mɔrl] *a* inmoral; ~**ity** [-'rælɪtɪ] *n* inmoralidad *f.*

immortal [ɪ'mɔːtl] *a* inmortal; ~**ize** *vt* inmortalizar.

immune [ɪ'mjuːn] *a*: ~ (**to**) inmune (contra); **immunity** *n* (*MED*) inmunidad *f*; (*COMM*) exención *f.*

immunization [ɪmjunaɪ'zeɪʃən] *n* inmunización *f*; **immunize** ['ɪmjunaɪz] *vt* inmunizar.

imp [ɪmp] *n* diablillo.

impact ['ɪmpækt] *n* (*gen*) impacto.

impair [ɪm'pɛə*] *vt* perjudicar.

impale [ɪm'peɪl] *vt* atravesar.

impart [ɪm'pɑːt] *vt* comunicar.

impartial [ɪm'pɑːʃl] *a* imparcial; ~**ity** [ɪmpɑːʃɪ'ælɪtɪ] *n* imparcialidad *f.*

impassable [ɪm'pɑːsəbl] *a* (*barrier*) infranqueable; (*river*) invadeable; (*road*) intransitable.

impatience [ɪm'peɪʃəns] *n* impaciencia; **impatient** [-ənt] *a* impaciente; **to get** *or* **grow impatient** impacientarse.

impeccable [ɪm'pɛkəbl] *a* impecable.

impede [ɪm'piːd] *vt* estorbar, dificultar.

impediment [ɪm'pɛdɪmənt] *n* obstáculo, estorbo; (*also*: **speech** ~) defecto (del habla).

impending [ɪm'pɛndɪŋ] *a* (*near*) próximo.

impenetrable [ɪm'pɛnɪtrəbl] *a* (*gen*) impenetrable; (*unfathomable*) insondable.

imperative [ɪm'pɛrətɪv] *a* (*tone*) imperioso; (*necessary*) indispensable; (*pressing*) urgente // *n* (*LING*) imperativo.

imperceptible [ɪmpə'sɛptɪbl] *a* imperceptible, insensible.

imperfect [ɪm'pəːfɪkt] *a* imperfecto; (*goods etc*) defectuoso; ~**ion** [-'fɛkʃən] *n* (*blemish*) desperfecto; (*state*) imperfección *f.*

imperial [ɪm'pɪərɪəl] *a* imperial; ~**ism** *n* imperialismo.

imperil [ɪm'pɛrɪl] *vt* arriesgar, poner en peligro.

impersonal [ɪm'pəːsənl] *a* impersonal.

impersonate [ɪm'pəːsəneɪt] *vt* hacerse pasar por; (*THEATRE*) imitar.

impertinent [ɪm'pəːtɪnənt] *a* impertinente, insolente.

impervious [ɪm'pəːvɪəs] *a* impermeable; (*fig*): ~ **to** insensible a.

impetuous [ɪm'pɛtjuəs] *a* impetuoso, irreflexivo.

impetus ['ɪmpətəs] *n* ímpetu *m*; (*fig*) impulso.

impinge [ɪm'pɪndʒ]: **to** ~ **on** *vt fus* invadir, abusar de; (*affect*) afectar a.

implausible [ɪm'plɔːzɪbl] *a* inverosímil.

implement ['ɪmplɪmənt] *n* instrumento, herramienta // *vt* ['ɪmplɪmənt] hacer efectivo; (*carry out*) realizar.

implicate ['ɪmplɪkeɪt] *vt* (*compromise*) comprometer; (*involve*) enredar; **implication** [-'keɪʃən] *n* consecuencia, implicancia (*AM*).

implicit [ɪm'plɪsɪt] *a* (*gen*) implícito; (*complete*) absoluto.

implore [ɪm'plɔː*] *vt* (*person*) suplicar.

imply [ɪm'plaɪ] *vt* (*involve*) implicar; (*mean*) significar; (*hint*) dar a entender que; **it is implied** se sobreentiende.

impolite [ɪmpə'laɪt] *a* mal educado.

import [ɪm'pɔːt] *vt* importar // *n* ['ɪmpɔːt] (*COMM*) importación *f*; (: *article*) artículo importado; (*meaning*) significado, sentido.

importance [ɪm'pɔːtəns] *n* importancia; **important** [-ənt] *a* importante; **it's not important** no importa, no tiene importancia.

importer [ɪm'pɔːtə*] *n* importador/a *m/f.*

impose [ɪm'pəuz] *vt* imponer // *vi*: **to** ~ **on sb** abusar de uno; **imposing** *a* imponente, impresionante.

impossible [ɪm'pɔsɪbl] *a* imposible; (*person*) insoportable.

impostor [ɪm'pɔstə*] *n* impostor/a *m/f.*

impotence ['ɪmpətəns] *n* impotencia; **impotent** [-ənt] *a* impotente.

impound [ɪm'paund] *vt* embargar.

impoverished [ɪm'pɔvərɪʃt] *a* necesitado; (*land*) agotado.

impracticable [ɪm'præktɪkəbl] *a* no factible, irrealizable.

impractical [ɪm'præktɪkl] *a* (*person*) poco práctico.

imprecise [ɪmprɪ'saɪs] *a* impreciso.

impregnable [ɪm'prɛgnəbl] *a* invulnerable; (*castle*) inexpugnable.

impregnate ['ɪmprɛgneɪt] *vt* (*gen*) impregnar; (*soak*) empapar; (*fertilize*) fecundar.

impresario [ɪmprɪ'sɑːrɪəu] *n* empresario.

impress [ɪm'prɛs] *vt* impresionar; (*mark*) estampar // *vi* hacer buena impresión; **to** ~ **sth on sb** convencer a uno de algo; **it** ~**ed itself on me** se me grabó (en la memoria).

impression [ɪm'prɛʃən] *n* impresión *f*; (*footprint etc*) huella; (*print run*) edición *f*; **to be under the** ~ **that** tener la impresión de que; ~**able** *a* influenciable; (*sensitive*) sensible; ~**ist** *n* impresionista *m/f.*

impressive [ɪm'prɛsɪv] *a* impresionante.

imprint ['ɪmprɪnt] n impresión f, huella.
imprison [ɪm'prɪzn] vt encarcelar;
~**ment** n encarcelamiento, cárcel f.
improbable [ɪm'prɔbəbl] a improbable,
inverosímil.
impromptu [ɪm'prɔmptjuː] a improvisado
// ad de improviso.
improper [ɪm'prɔpə*] a (incorrect)
impropio; (unseemly) indecoroso;
(indecent) indecente.
impropriety [ɪmprə'praɪətɪ] n falta de
decoro; (indecency) indecencia; (of
language) impropiedad f.
improve [ɪm'pruːv] vt mejorar // vi
mejorarse; (become perfect) per-
feccionarse; (pupils) hacer progresos;
~**ment** n mejoramiento; perfección f;
progreso.
improvise ['ɪmprəvaɪz] vt, vi improvisar.
imprudent [ɪm'pruːdnt] a imprudente.
impudent ['ɪmpjudnt] a descarado,
insolente.
impulse ['ɪmpʌls] n impulso; **to act on** ~
obrar sin reflexión; **impulsive** [-'pʌlsɪv] a
irreflexivo.
impunity [ɪm'pjuːnɪtɪ] n: **with** ~
impunemente.
impure [ɪm'pjuə*] a (adulterated)
adulterado; (not pure) impuro; **impurity** n
(gen) impureza.
in [ɪn] prep en; (within) dentro de; (with
time: during, within): ~ **2 days** en 2 días;
(: after): ~ **2 weeks** dentro de 2
semanas; (with town, country): **it's** ~
France está en Francia // ad dentro,
adentro; (fashionable) de moda; **is he** ~?
¿está en casa?; ~ **the country** en el
campo; ~ **the distance** a lo lejos; ~
town en el centro (de la ciudad); ~ **the
sun** al sol, bajo el sol; ~ **the rain** bajo la
lluvia; ~ **French** en francés; **1** ~ **10** uno
sobre 10, uno de cada 10; ~ **hundreds**
por centenares; **the best pupil** ~ **the
class** el mejor alumno de la clase; ~
written ~ **pencil** escrito con lápiz; ~
saying this al decir esto; **their party is**
~ su partido ha llegado al poder; **to ask
sb** ~ invitar a uno a entrar; **to run/limp**
~ entrar corriendo/cojeando; **the** ~**s
and outs** los recovecos.
in., **ins** abbr of **inch(es)**.
inability [ɪnə'bɪlɪtɪ] n incapacidad f.
inaccessible [ɪnæk'sɛsɪbl] a inaccesible.
inaccuracy [ɪn'ækjurəsɪ] n inexactitud f;
inaccurate [-rət] a inexacto, incorrecto.
inactivity [ɪnæk'tɪvɪtɪ] n inactividad f.
inadequate [ɪn'ædɪkwət] a (insufficient)
insuficiente; (unsuitable) inadecuado;
(person) incapaz.
inadvertently [ɪnəd'vəːtntlɪ] ad por
equivocación o descuido.
inadvisable [ɪnəd'vaɪzəbl] a no
aconsejable.
inane [ɪ'neɪn] a necio, fatuo.
inanimate [ɪn'ænɪmət] a inanimado.
inapplicable [ɪn'æplɪkəbl] a inaplicable.
inappropriate [ɪnə'prəuprɪət] a

inoportuno, inconveniente; (word,
expression) impropio.
inapt [ɪn'æpt] a impropio; ~**itude** n
incapacidad f.
inarticulate [ɪnɑː'tɪkjulət] a (person)
incapaz de expresarse; (speech)
inarticulado.
inasmuch as [ɪnəz'mʌtʃæz] ad (given that)
puesto que; (since) ya que.
inattentive [ɪnə'tɛntɪv] a distraído.
inaudible [ɪn'ɔːdɪbl] a inaudible.
inaugural [ɪ'nɔːɡjurəl] a (speech) de
apertura; **inaugurate** [-reɪt] vt inaugurar;
inauguration [-'reɪʃən] n ceremonia de
apertura.
in-between [ɪnbɪ'twiːn] a intermedio, de
entre medio.
inborn [ɪn'bɔːn] a (feeling) innato.
inbred [ɪn'brɛd] a innato; (family)
engendrado por endogamia.
incalculable [ɪn'kælkjuləbl] a
incalculable.
incapable [ɪn'keɪpəbl] a incapaz.
incapacitate [ɪnkə'pæsɪteɪt] vt: **to** ~ **sb**
incapacitar a uno.
incapacity [ɪnkə'pæsɪtɪ] n (inability)
incapacidad f.
incarcerate [ɪn'kɑːsəreɪt] vt encarcelar.
incarnate [ɪn'kɑːnɪt] a en persona // vt
['ɪnkɑːneɪt] encarnar; **incarnation**
[-'neɪʃən] n encarnación f.
incendiary [ɪn'sɛndɪərɪ] a incendiario.
incense ['ɪnsɛns] n incienso // vt [ɪn'sɛns]
(anger) indignar, encolerizar.
incentive [ɪn'sɛntɪv] n incentivo, estímulo.
incessant [ɪn'sɛsnt] a incesante, contínuo;
~**ly** ad constantemente.
incest ['ɪnsɛst] n incesto.
inch [ɪntʃ] n pulgada; **to be within an** ~
of estar a dos dedos de; **he didn't give an**
~ no dio concesión alguna; **to** ~
forward avanzar palmo a palmo.
incidence ['ɪnsɪdns] n (of crime, disease)
frecuencia.
incident ['ɪnsɪdnt] n incidente m, suceso;
(in book) episodio.
incidental [ɪnsɪ'dɛntl] a no esencial,
accesorio; (unplanned) fortuito; ~ **to** al
margen de; ~**ly** [-'dɛntəlɪ] ad (by the way)
a propósito.
incinerator [ɪn'sɪnəreɪtə*] n incinerador
m.
incipient [ɪn'sɪpɪənt] a incipiente.
incision [ɪn'sɪʒən] n corte m.
incisive [ɪn'saɪsɪv] a (mind) penetrante;
(tone) mordaz; (remark etc) tajante.
incite [ɪn'saɪt] vt provocar.
inclination [ɪnklɪ'neɪʃən] n (tendency)
tendencia, inclinación f.
incline ['ɪnklaɪn] n pendiente m, cuesta //
(vb: [ɪn'klaɪn]) vt (slope) inclinar; (head)
poner de lado // vi inclinarse; **to be** ~**d**
to (tend) ser propenso a; (be willing) estar
dispuesto a.
include [ɪn'kluːd] vt incluir, comprender;

(*in letter*) adjuntar; **including** *prep* incluso, inclusive.

inclusion [ɪnˈkluːʒən] *n* inclusión *f*; **inclusive** [-sɪv] *a* inclusivo // *ad* inclusive.

incognito [ɪnkɔgˈniːtəu] *ad* de incógnito.

incoherent [ɪnkəuˈhɪərənt] *a* incoherente.

income [ˈɪŋkʌm] *n* (*personal*) ingresos *mpl*; (*from property etc*) renta; (*profit*) rédito; ~ **tax** *n* impuesto sobre la renta; ~ **tax inspector** *n* inspector/a *m/f* fiscal; ~ **tax return** *n* registro fiscal.

incoming [ˈɪnkʌmɪŋ] *a*: ~ **flight** vuelo entrante.

incomparable [ɪnˈkɔmpərəbl] *a* incomparable, sin par.

incompatible [ɪnkəmˈpætɪbl] *a* incompatible.

incompetence [ɪnˈkɔmpɪtəns] *n* incompetencia; **incompetent** [-ənt] *a* incompetente.

incomplete [ɪnkəmˈpliːt] *a* incompleto; (*unfinished*) sin terminar.

incomprehensible [ɪnkɔmprɪˈhɛnsɪbl] *a* incomprensible.

inconceivable [ɪnkənˈsiːvəbl] *a* inconcebible.

inconclusive [ɪnkənˈkluːsɪv] *a* sin resultado (definitivo); (*argument*) poco convincente.

incongruous [ɪnˈkɔŋgruəs] *a* (*foolish*) absurdo, estrafalario; (*remark, act*) disonante, nada lógico.

inconsiderate [ɪnkənˈsɪdərət] *a* desconsiderado; **how** ~ **of him!** ¡qué falta de consideración (de su parte)!

inconsistent [ɪnkənˈsɪstnt] *a* inconsecuente; ~ **with** (que) no concuerda con.

inconspicuous [ɪnkənˈspɪkjuəs] *a* poco llamativo, modesto; **to make o.s.** ~ no llamar la atención.

inconstant [ɪnˈkɔnstnt] *a* inconstante.

incontinent [ɪnˈkɔntɪnənt] *a* incontinente.

inconvenience [ɪnkənˈviːnjəns] *n* (*gen*) inconvenientes *mpl*; (*trouble*) molestia, incomodidad *f* // *vt* incomodar; **inconvenient** [-ənt] *a* incómodo, poco práctico; (*time, place*) inoportuno.

incorporate [ɪnˈkɔːpəreɪt] *vt* incorporar; (*contain*) comprender; (*add*) agregar; ~**d** *a*: ~**d company** (*US: abbr* **Inc.**) Sociedad Anónima (S.A.).

incorrect [ɪnkəˈrɛkt] *a* incorrecto.

incorruptible [ɪnkəˈrʌptɪbl] *a* (*gen*) incorruptible; (*not open to bribes*) insobornable.

increase [ˈɪnkriːs] *n* aumento // *vi* [ɪnˈkriːs] aumentarse; (*grow*) crecer; (*price*) subir; **increasing** *a* (*number*) creciente, en aumento; **increasingly** *ad* de más en más, cada vez más.

incredible [ɪnˈkrɛdɪbl] *a* increíble.

incredulous [ɪnˈkrɛdjuləs] *a* incrédulo.

increment [ˈɪnkrɪmənt] *n* aumento, incremento.

incriminate [ɪnˈkrɪmɪneɪt] *vt* incriminar.

incubation [ɪnkjuˈbeɪʃən] *n* incubación *f*;

incubator [ˈɪnkjubeɪtə*] *n* incubadora.

incumbent [ɪnˈkʌmbənt] *n* ocupante *m/f* // *a*: **it is** ~ **on him to...** le incumbe... .

incur [ɪnˈkəː*] *vt* (*expenses*) contraer; (*gen*) incurrir en.

incurable [ɪnˈkjuərəbl] *a* incurable; (*fig*) irremediable.

incursion [ɪnˈkəːʃən] *n* incursión *f*.

indebted [ɪnˈdɛtɪd] *a*: **to be** ~ **to sb** estar en deuda con uno.

indecent [ɪnˈdiːsnt] *a* indecente; ~ **assault** *n* atentado contra el pudor; ~ **exposure** *n* exhibicionismo.

indecisive [ɪndɪˈsaɪsɪv] *a* indeciso; (*discussion*) no resuelto, inconcluyente.

indeed [ɪnˈdiːd] *ad* de hecho, realmente; **yes** ~! claro que sí.

indefinite [ɪnˈdɛfɪnɪt] *a* indefinido; (*uncertain*) incierto; ~**ly** *ad* (*wait*) indefinidamente.

indelible [ɪnˈdɛlɪbl] *a* imborrable.

indemnify [ɪnˈdɛmnɪfaɪ] *vt* indemnizar, resarcir.

indentation [ɪndɛnˈteɪʃən] *n* mella; (*TYP*) sangría.

independence [ɪndɪˈpɛndns] *n* independencia; **independent** [-ənt] *a* independiente; **to become independent** independizarse.

index [ˈɪndɛks] *n* (*pl*: ~**es**: *in book*) índice *m*; (: *in library etc*) catálogo; (*pl*: **indices** [ˈɪndɪsiːz]: *ratio, sign*) exponente *m*; ~ **card** *n* ficha; ~ **finger** *n* índice *m*; ~**-linked** *a* vinculado al índice del coste de la vida.

India [ˈɪndɪə] *n* la India; ~**n** *a, n* indio/a; **Red** ~**n** piel roja *m/f*.

indicate [ˈɪndɪkeɪt] *vt* indicar; **indication** [-ˈkeɪʃən] *n* indicio, señal *f*; **indicator** *n* (*gen*) indicador *m*.

indices [ˈɪndɪsiːz] *pl of* **index**.

indict [ɪnˈdaɪt] *vt* acusar; ~**ment** *n* acusación *f*.

indifference [ɪnˈdɪfrəns] *n* indiferencia; **indifferent** [-ənt] *a* indiferente; (*poor*) regular.

indigenous [ɪnˈdɪdʒɪnəs] *a* indígena *inv*.

indigestion [ɪndɪˈdʒɛstʃən] *n* indigestión *f*, empacho.

indignant [ɪnˈdɪgnənt] *a*: **to be** ~ **about sth** indignarse por algo; **indignation** [-ˈneɪʃən] *n* indignación *f*.

indignity [ɪnˈdɪgnɪtɪ] *n* indignidad *f*; (*insult*) ultraje *m*, afrenta.

indigo [ˈɪndɪgəu] *a* color de añil // *n* añil *m*.

indirect [ɪndɪˈrɛkt] *a* indirecto; ~**ly** *ad* indirectamente.

indiscreet [ɪndɪˈskriːt] *a* indiscreto; (*rash*) imprudente; **indiscretion** [-ˈskrɛʃən] *n* indiscreción *f*; imprudencia.

indiscriminate [ɪndɪˈskrɪmɪnət] *a* indistinto.

indispensable [ɪndɪˈspɛnsəbl] *a* indispensable, imprescindible.

indisposed [ɪndɪˈspəuzd] *a* (*unwell*) indispuesto.

indisputable [ɪndɪˈspjuːtəbl] *a* incontestable.
indistinct [ɪndɪˈstɪŋkt] *a* indistinto; (*memory, noise*) confuso.
individual [ɪndɪˈvɪdjuəl] *n* individuo // *a* individual; (*personal*) personal; (*for/of one only*) particular; ~**ist** *n* individualista *m/f*; ~**ity** [-ˈælɪtɪ] *n* individualidad *f*; ~**ly** *ad* individualmente; particularmente.
indoctrinate [ɪnˈdɒktrɪneɪt] *vt* adoctrinar; **indoctrination** [-ˈneɪʃən] *n* adoctrinamiento.
indolent [ˈɪndələnt] *a* indolente, perezoso.
indoor [ˈɪndɔː*] *a* (*inner*) interior; (*household*) de casa; (*inside*) de puertas adentro; (*swimming-pool*) cubierto; (*games*) de salón; (*sport*) bajo cubierta; ~**s** [ɪnˈdɔːz] *ad* dentro; (*at home*) en casa.
induce [ɪnˈdjuːs] *vt* inducir; (*bring about*) producir; (*provoke*) provocar; ~**ment** *n* (*incentive*) incentivo, aliciente *m*.
induction [ɪnˈdʌkʃən] *n* (MED: *of birth*) inducción *f*; ~ **course** *n* curso de inducción.
indulge [ɪnˈdʌldʒ] *vt* (*desire*) dar rienda suelta a; (*whim*) condescender con; (*person*) complacer; (*child*) consentir // *vi*: ~ **in** darse el lujo de; **indulgence** *n* (*of desire*) gratificación *f*; (*leniency*) complacencia; **indulgent** *a* indulgente.
industrial [ɪnˈdʌstrɪəl] *a* industrial; ~ **action** *n* huelga; ~ **estate** *n* zona industrial; ~**ist** *n* industrial *m/f*; ~**ize** *vt* industrializar.
industrious [ɪnˈdʌstrɪəs] *a* (*gen*) trabajador(a); (*student*) aplicado.
industry [ˈɪndəstrɪ] *n* industria; (*diligence*) aplicación *f*.
inebriated [ɪˈniːbrɪeɪtɪd] *a* borracho.
inedible [ɪnˈɛdɪbl] *a* incomible; (*plant etc*) no comestible.
ineffective [ɪnɪˈfɛktɪv] *a* ineficaz, inútil.
inefficiency [ɪnɪˈfɪʃənsɪ] *n* ineficacia; **inefficient** [-ənt] *a* ineficaz, ineficiente.
ineligible [ɪnˈɛlɪdʒɪbl] *a* (*candidate*) inelegible; **to be** ~ **for sth** no tener derecho a algo.
inept [ɪˈnɛpt] *a* incompetente, incapaz.
inequality [ɪnɪˈkwɒlɪtɪ] *n* desigualdad *f*.
inert [ɪˈnɜːt] *a* inerte, inactivo; (*immobile*) inmóvil; ~**ia** [ɪˈnɜːʃə] *n* inercia; (*laziness*) pereza.
inescapable [ɪnɪˈskeɪpəbl] *a* ineludible.
inestimable [ɪnˈɛstɪməbl] *a* inestimable.
inevitable [ɪnˈɛvɪtəbl] *a* inevitable; (*necessary*) forzoso.
inexcusable [ɪnɪksˈkjuːzəbl] *a* imperdonable.
inexhaustible [ɪnɪgˈzɔːstɪbl] *a* inagotable.
inexorable [ɪnˈɛksərəbl] *a* inexorable, implacable.
inexpensive [ɪnɪkˈspɛnsɪv] *a* económico.
inexperience [ɪnɪkˈspɪərɪəns] *n* falta de experiencia; ~**d** *a* inexperto.
inexplicable [ɪnɪkˈsplɪkəbl] *a* inexplicable.
inextricable [ɪnɪkˈstrɪkəbl] *a* inextricable.

infallible [ɪnˈfælɪbl] *a* infalible.
infamous [ˈɪnfəməs] *a* infame; **infamy** [-mɪ] *n* infamia.
infancy [ˈɪnfənsɪ] *n* infancia.
infant [ˈɪnfənt] *n* (*baby*) criatura; (*young child*) niño/a; ~**ile** *a* infantil; (*pej*) aniñado; ~ **school** *n* escuela de párvulos.
infantry [ˈɪnfəntrɪ] *n* infantería; ~**man** *n* soldado (de infantería).
infatuated [ɪnˈfætjueɪtɪd] *a*: ~ **with** (*gen*) encaprichado por; (*in love*) enamorado de; **infatuation** [-ˈeɪʃən] *n* encaprichamiento; enamoramiento.
infect [ɪnˈfɛkt] *vt* (*wound*) infectar; (*person*) contagiar; (*fig: pej*) corromper; ~**ed with** (*illness*) contagiado de; ~**ion** [ɪnˈfɛkʃən] *n* infección *f*; (*fig*) contagio; ~**ious** [ɪnˈfɛkʃəs] *a* contagioso; (*also: fig*) infeccioso.
infer [ɪnˈfɜː*] *vt* deducir, inferir; ~**ence** [ˈɪnfərəns] *n* deducción *f*, inferencia.
inferior [ɪnˈfɪərɪə*] *a*, *n* inferior *m/f*; ~**ity** [-rɪˈɔrɪtɪ] *n* inferioridad *f*; ~**ity complex** *n* complejo de inferioridad.
infernal [ɪnˈfɜːnl] *a* infernal.
inferno [ɪnˈfɜːnəu] *n* infierno; (*fig*) hoguera.
infertile [ɪnˈfɜːtaɪl] *a* estéril, infecundo; **infertility** [-ˈtɪlɪtɪ] *n* esterilidad *f*, infecundidad *f*.
infested [ɪnˈfɛstɪd] *a*: ~ **(with)** plagado (de).
infidelity [ɪnfɪˈdɛlɪtɪ] *n* infidelidad *f*.
in-fighting [ˈɪnfaɪtɪŋ] *n* (*fig*) luchas *fpl* internas.
infiltrate [ˈɪnfɪltreɪt] *vt* (*troops etc*) infiltrarse en // *vi* infiltrarse.
infinite [ˈɪnfɪnɪt] *a* infinito.
infinitive [ɪnˈfɪnɪtɪv] *n* infinitivo.
infinity [ɪnˈfɪnɪtɪ] *n* (*also* MATH) infinito; (*an* ~) infinidad *f*.
infirm [ɪnˈfɜːm] *a* enfermo, débil; ~**ary** *n* hospital *m*; ~**ity** *n* debilidad *f*; (*illness*) enfermedad *f*, achaque *m*.
inflame [ɪnˈfleɪm] *vt* inflamar.
inflammable [ɪnˈflæməbl] *a* inflamable; (*explosive*) explosivo.
inflammation [ɪnfləˈmeɪʃən] *n* inflamación *f*.
inflate [ɪnˈfleɪt] *vt* (*tyre, balloon*) inflar; (*fig*) hinchar; ~**d** *a* (*style*) exagerado; (*value*) excesivo; **inflation** [ɪnˈfleɪʃən] *n* (ECON) inflación *f*; **inflationary** [ɪnˈfleɪʃnərɪ] *a* inflacionario.
inflexible [ɪnˈflɛksɪbl] *a* inflexible.
inflict [ɪnˈflɪkt] *vt*: **to** ~ **on** infligir en; (*tax etc*) imponer a; ~**ion** [ɪnˈflɪkʃən] *n* imposición *f*.
inflow [ˈɪnfləu] *n* afluencia.
influence [ˈɪnfluəns] *n* influencia // *vt* influir en, influenciar; (*persuade*) sugestionar; **under the** ~ **of alcohol** en estado de embriaguez; **influential** [-ˈɛnʃl] *a* influyente.
influenza [ɪnfluˈɛnzə] *n* gripe *f*.
influx [ˈɪnflʌks] *n* afluencia.

inform [ɪnˈfɔːm] vt: **to ~ sb of sth** informar a uno sobre o de algo; (warn) avisar a uno de algo; (communicate) comunicar algo a uno // vi soplar; **to ~ on sb** delatar a uno.

informal [ɪnˈfɔːml] a (person, manner) desenvuelto; (tone) familiar; (visit, discussion) extraoficial; (intimate) de confianza; **~ity** [-ˈmælɪtɪ] n falta de ceremonia; (intimacy) intimidad f; (familiarity) familiaridad f; (ease) afabilidad f.

information [ɪnfəˈmeɪʃən] n información f, informes mpl; (news) noticias fpl; (knowledge) conocimientos mpl; (LAW) delatación f; **a piece of ~** un dato.

informative [ɪnˈfɔːmətɪv] a informativo.

informer [ɪnˈfɔːmə*] n delator/a m/f; (also: **police ~**) soplón/ona m/f.

infra-red [ɪnfrəˈrɛd] a infrarrojo.

infrequent [ɪnˈfriːkwənt] a infrecuente.

infringe [ɪnˈfrɪndʒ] vt infringir, violar // vi: **to ~ on** invadir, abusar de; **~ment** n infracción f; (of rights) invasión f; (SPORT) falta.

infuriate [ɪnˈfjuərɪeɪt] vt enfurecer; **infuriating** a enloquecedor(a).

ingenious [ɪnˈdʒiːnjəs] a ingenioso; **ingenuity** [-dʒɪˈnjuːɪtɪ] n ingeniosidad f.

ingenuous [ɪnˈdʒɛnjuəs] a ingenuo.

ingot [ˈɪŋgət] n lingote m, barra.

ingrained [ɪnˈgreɪnd] a arraigado.

ingratiate [ɪnˈgreɪʃɪeɪt] vt: **to ~ o.s. with** congraciarse con.

ingratitude [ɪnˈgrætɪtjuːd] n ingratitud f.

ingredient [ɪnˈgriːdɪənt] n ingrediente m.

inhabit [ɪnˈhæbɪt] vt habitar, vivir en; (occupy) ocupar; **~ant** n habitante m/f.

inhale [ɪnˈheɪl] vt inhalar // vi (in smoking) aspirar.

inherent [ɪnˈhɪərənt] a: **~ in or to** inherente a.

inherit [ɪnˈhɛrɪt] vt heredar; **~ance** n herencia; (fig) patrimonio.

inhibit [ɪnˈhɪbɪt] vt inhibir, impedir; **to ~ sb from doing sth** impedir a uno hacer algo; **~ion** [-ˈbɪʃən] n inhibición f.

inhospitable [ɪnhəsˈpɪtəbl] a (person) inhospitalario; (place) inhóspito.

inhuman [ɪnˈhjuːmən] a inhumano.

inimitable [ɪˈnɪmɪtəbl] a inimitable.

iniquity [ɪˈnɪkwɪtɪ] n inicuidad f; (injustice) injusticia.

initial [ɪˈnɪʃl] a inicial; (first) primero // n inicial f // vt firmar con las iniciales; **~s** npl iniciales fpl; (abbreviation) siglas fpl; **~ly** ad al principio, en primer lugar.

initiate [ɪˈnɪʃɪeɪt] vt (start) iniciar, dar comienzo a; **to ~ sb into a secret** iniciar a uno en un secreto; **to ~ proceedings against sb** (LAW) entablar proceso contra uno; **initiation** [-ˈeɪʃən] n (into secret etc) iniciación f; (beginning) comienzo.

initiative [ɪˈnɪʃɪətɪv] n iniciativa.

inject [ɪnˈdʒɛkt] vt (liquid) inyectar; (fig) injertar; **~ion** [ɪnˈdʒɛkʃən] n inyección f.

injunction [ɪnˈdʒʌŋkʃən] n interdicto.

injure [ˈɪndʒə*] vt herir, lastimar; (fig) perjudicar; (offend) ofender; **injury** n herida, lesión f; (wrong) perjuicio, daño; **injury time** n (SPORT) descuento.

injustice [ɪnˈdʒʌstɪs] n injusticia.

ink [ɪŋk] n tinta.

inkling [ˈɪŋklɪŋ] n sospecha; (idea) idea, atisbo.

inlaid [ˈɪnleɪd] a taraceado, entarimado.

inland [ˈɪnlənd] a interior, del interior // ad [ɪnˈlænd] tierra adentro; **I~ Revenue** n (Brit) el fisco.

in-laws [ˈɪnlɔːz] npl parientes mpl políticos.

inlet [ˈɪnlɛt] n (GEO) ensenada, cala; (TECH) admisión f, entrada.

inmate [ˈɪnmeɪt] n (in prison) presidiario; (in asylum) internado/a.

inn [ɪn] n posada, mesón m.

innate [ɪˈneɪt] a innato.

inner [ˈɪnə*] a interior, interno; **~ city** n centro de la ciudad; **~ tube** n (of tyre) cámara.

innocence [ˈɪnəsns] n inocencia; **innocent** [-nt] a inocente.

innocuous [ɪˈnɒkjuəs] a innocuo.

innovation [ɪnəuˈveɪʃən] n novedad f.

innuendo [ɪnjuˈɛndəu] pl **~es** n indirecta.

innumerable [ɪˈnjuːmrəbl] a innumerable.

inoculation [ɪnɒkjuˈleɪʃən] n inoculación f.

inopportune [ɪnˈɒpətjuːn] a inoportuno.

inordinately [ɪˈnɔːdɪnɪtlɪ] ad desmesuradamente.

inorganic [ɪnɔːˈgænɪk] a inorgánico.

in-patient [ˈɪnpeɪʃənt] n paciente m/f interno/a.

input [ˈɪnput] n (ELEC) entrada; (COMM) inversión f.

inquest [ˈɪnkwɛst] n pesquisa judicial; (coroner's) encuesta judicial.

inquire [ɪnˈkwaɪə*] vi pedir informes // vt (ask) preguntar; (seek information about) pedir informes sobre; **to ~ about** vt fus (person) preguntar por; (fact) informarse de; **to ~ into** vt fus investigar, indagar; **inquiring** a (mind) penetrante; (look) interrogativo; **inquiry** n pregunta; (LAW) investigación f, pesquisa; (commission) comisión f investigadora; **inquiry office** n oficina de informaciones.

inquisitive [ɪnˈkwɪzɪtɪv] a (curious) activo, inquiridor(a); (prying) preguntón(ona), fisgón(ona).

inroad [ˈɪnrəud] n incursión f; (fig) invasión f.

insane [ɪnˈseɪn] a loco; (MED) demente.

insanitary [ɪnˈsænɪtərɪ] a insalubre.

insanity [ɪnˈsænɪtɪ] n demencia, locura.

insatiable [ɪnˈseɪʃəbl] a insaciable.

inscribe [ɪnˈskraɪb] vt inscribir; (book etc): **to ~ (to sb)** dedicar (a uno).

inscription [ɪnˈskrɪpʃən] n (gen) inscripción f; (in book) dedicatoria.

inscrutable [ɪnˈskruːtəbl] a inescrutable, insondable.

insect ['ɪnsɛkt] n insecto; ~icide [ɪn-'sɛktɪsaɪd] n insecticida m.

insecure [ɪnsɪ'kjuə*] a inseguro; insecurity n inseguridad f.

insensible [ɪn'sɛnsɪbl] a impasible, insensible; (unconscious) inconsciente.

insensitive [ɪn'sɛnsɪtɪv] a insensible.

inseparable [ɪn'sɛprəbl] a inseparable; they were ~ friends les unía una estrecha amistad.

insert [ɪn'sɜːt] vt (between things) intercalar; (into sth) introducir; (in paper) publicar; (: advert) poner // n [ɪn'sɜːt] hoja suelta (intercalada); ~ion [ɪn'sɜːʃən] n inserción f; (publication) publicación f; (of pages) materia añadida.

inshore [ɪn'ʃɔː*] a cercano a la orilla o costa // ad (be) cerca de la orilla; (move) hacia la orilla.

inside ['ɪn'saɪd] n interior m; (lining) forro // a interior, interno; (secret) secreto // ad (within) (por) dentro; (with movement) hacia dentro; (fam: in prison) en la cárcel // prep dentro de; (of time): ~ 10 minutes en menos de 10 minutos; ~s npl (col) tripas fpl; ~ forward n (SPORT) delantero interior; ~ lane n (AUT. in Britain) el lado o carril izquierdo; ~ out ad (turn) al revés; (know) a fondo.

insidious [ɪn'sɪdɪəs] a insidioso; (underground) clandestino.

insight ['ɪnsaɪt] n perspicacia.

insignificant [ɪnsɪg'nɪfɪknt] a insignificante.

insincere [ɪnsɪn'sɪə*] a poco sincero; insincerity [-'sɛrɪtɪ] n falta de sinceridad, doblez f.

insinuate [ɪn'sɪnjueɪt] vt insinuar; insinuation [-'eɪʃən] n insinuación f; (hint) indirecta.

insipid [ɪn'sɪpɪd] a soso, insulso.

insist [ɪn'sɪst] vi insistir; to ~ on doing empeñarse en hacer; to ~ that insistir en que; (claim) exigir que; ~ence n insistencia; (stubbornness) empeño; ~ent a insistente; empeñado.

insole ['ɪnsəul] n plantilla.

insolence ['ɪnsələns] n insolencia, descaro; insolent [-ənt] a insolente, descarado.

insoluble [ɪn'sɔljubl] a insoluble.

insolvent [ɪn'sɔlvənt] a insolvente.

insomnia [ɪn'sɔmnɪə] n insomnio.

inspect [ɪn'spɛkt] vt inspeccionar, examinar; (troops) pasar revista a; ~ion [ɪn'spɛkʃən] n inspección f, examen m; ~or n inspector/a m/f; (RAIL) revisor m.

inspiration [ɪnspə'reɪʃən] n inspiración f; inspire [ɪn'spaɪə*] vt inspirar.

instability [ɪnstə'bɪlɪtɪ] n inestabilidad f.

install [ɪn'stɔːl] vt instalar; ~ation [ɪnstə'leɪʃən] n instalación f.

instalment, installment (US) [ɪn-'stɔːlmənt] n plazo; (of story) entrega; (of TV serial etc) episodio.

instance ['ɪnstəns] n ejemplo, caso; for ~

por ejemplo; in the first ~ en primer lugar.

instant ['ɪnstənt] n instante m, momento // a instantáneo, inmediato; (coffee) en polvo; ~ly ad en seguida.

instead [ɪn'stɛd] ad en cambio; ~ of en lugar de, en vez de.

instep ['ɪnstɛp] n empeine m.

instigation [ɪnstɪ'geɪʃən] n instigación f.

instil [ɪn'stɪl] vt: to ~ into infundir a, inculcar en.

instinct ['ɪnstɪŋkt] n instinto; ~ive [-'stɪŋktɪv] a instintivo; ~ively [-'stɪŋktɪvlɪ] ad por instinto.

institute ['ɪnstɪtjuːt] n instituto; (professional body) colegio // vt (inquiry) iniciar, empezar; (proceedings) entablar.

institution [ɪnstɪ'tjuːʃən] n (gen) institución f; (beginning) iniciación f; (organization) instituto; (MED. home) asilo; (asylum) manicomio; (custom) costumbre f.

instruct [ɪn'strʌkt] vt: to ~ sb in sth instruir a uno en o sobre algo; to ~ sb to do sth dar instrucciones a uno de hacer algo; ~ion [ɪn'strʌkʃən] n (teaching) instrucción f; ~ions npl órdenes fpl; ~ions (for use) modo sg de empleo; ~ive a aleccionador(a); ~or a m/f. instructor/a m/f.

instrument ['ɪnstrumənt] n instrumento; ~al [-'mɛntl] a (MUS) instrumental; to be ~al in contribuir materialmente a; ~ panel n tablero (de instrumentos).

insubordinate [ɪnsə'bɔːdənɪt] a insubordinado; insubordination [-'neɪʃən] n insubordinación f; (disobedience) desobediencia.

insufferable [ɪn'sʌfrəbl] a insufrible.

insufficient [ɪnsə'fɪʃənt] a insuficiente.

insular ['ɪnsjulə*] a insular; (outlook) de miras estrechas.

insulate ['ɪnsjuleɪt] vt aislar; insulating tape n cinta aislante; insulation [-'leɪʃən] n aislamiento.

insulin ['ɪnsjulɪn] n insulina.

insult ['ɪnsʌlt] n insulto; (offence) ofensa // vt [ɪn'sʌlt] insultar, injuriar; ofender; ~ing a insultante; ofensivo.

insuperable [ɪn'sjuːprəbl] a insuperable.

insurance [ɪn'ʃuərəns] n seguro; fire/life ~ seguro sobre la vida/contra incendios; ~ agent n agente m/f de seguros; ~ policy n póliza (de seguros).

insure [ɪn'ʃuə*] vt asegurar.

insurrection [ɪnsə'rɛkʃən] n insurrección f.

intact [ɪn'tækt] a íntegro; (unharmed) ileso, sano.

intake ['ɪnteɪk] n (TECH) entrada, toma; (: pipe) tubo de admisión; (of food) cantidad admitida; (SCOL): an ~ of 200 a year 200 matriculados al año.

intangible [ɪn'tændʒɪbl] a intangible.

integral ['ɪntɪgrəl] a (whole) íntegro; (part) integrante.

integrate ['ɪntɪgreɪt] vt integrar // vi integrarse.

integrity [ɪn'tɛgrɪtɪ] n honradez f, rectitud f.

intellect ['ɪntəlɛkt] n intelecto; ~ual [-'lɛktjuəl] a, n intelectual m/f.

intelligence [ɪn'tɛlɪdʒəns] n inteligencia; (MIL etc) informes mpl; I~ Service n Servicio de Inteligencia; **intelligent** [-ənt] a inteligente.

intelligible [ɪn'tɛlɪdʒɪbl] a inteligible, comprensible.

intend [ɪn'tɛnd] vt (gift etc): to ~ sth for destinar algo a; to ~ to do sth tener intención de o proponerse hacer algo; ~ed a (effect) deseado /// n prometido/a.

intense [ɪn'tɛns] a intenso; (person) nervioso; ~ly ad intensamente; (very) sumamente.

intensify [ɪn'tɛnsɪfaɪ] vt intensificar; (increase) aumentar.

intensity [ɪn'tɛnsɪtɪ] n intensidad f; (strength) fuerza.

intensive [ɪn'tɛnsɪv] a intensivo; ~ care unit n centro de cuidados intensivos.

intent [ɪn'tɛnt] n propósito // a (absorbed) absorto; (attentive) atento; to all ~s and purposes prácticamente; to be ~ on doing sth estar resuelto a hacer algo.

intention [ɪn'tɛnʃən] n intento, propósito; (plan) proyecto; ~al a intencional, deliberado; ~ally ad a propósito.

intently [ɪn'tɛntlɪ] ad atentamente, fijamente.

inter [ɪn'tɜ:ˀ] vt enterrar.

interact [ɪntər'ækt] vi influirse mutuamente; ~ion [-'ækʃən] n influencia mútua, acción f recíproca.

intercede [ɪntə'si:d] vi: to ~ (with) interceder (con).

intercept [ɪntə'sɛpt] vt interceptar; (stop) detener; ~ion [-'sɛpʃən] n interceptación f; detención f.

interchange ['ɪntətʃeɪndʒ] n intercambio; (exchange) canje m; (on motorway) paso a desnivel // vt [ɪntə'tʃeɪndʒ] intercambiar; canjear; ~able a intercambiable.

intercom ['ɪntəkɔm] n sistema m de intercomunicación.

interconnect [ɪntəkə'nɛkt] vi (rooms) conectarse.

intercourse ['ɪntəkɔ:s] n (sexual) relaciones fpl; (social) trato.

interest ['ɪntrɪst] n (also COMM) interés m; (profit) provecho // vt interesar; to be ~ed in interesarse por; ~ing a interesante.

interfere [ɪntə'fɪəˀ] vi: to ~ in (quarrel, other people's business) entrometerse o mezclarse en; to ~ with (hinder) estorbar; (damage) estropear; (radio) interferir con.

interference [ɪntə'fɪərəns] n (gen) intromisión f; (RADIO, TV) interferencia.

interim ['ɪntərɪm] n: in the ~ entretanto, en el interino.

interior [ɪn'tɪərɪəˀ] n interior m // a interior.

interject [ɪntə'dʒɛkt] vt interponerse; ~ion [-'dʒɛkʃən] n interyección f.

interlock [ɪntə'lɔk] vi entrelazarse; (wheels etc) endentarse.

interloper ['ɪntələupəˀ] n intruso.

interlude ['ɪntəlu:d] n intervalo; (rest) descanso; (THEATRE) intermedio.

intermarry [ɪntə'mærɪ] vi casarse (parientes).

intermediary [ɪntə'mi:dɪərɪ] n intermediario.

intermediate [ɪntə'mi:dɪət] a intermedio, medio.

intermission [ɪntə'mɪʃən] n (THEATRE) descanso.

intermittent [ɪntə'mɪtnt] a intermitente.

intern [ɪn'tɜ:n] vt internar; (enclose) encerrar // n ['ɪntə:n] (US) interno.

internal [ɪn'tɜ:nl] a interno, interior; ~ly ad interiormente; 'not to be taken ~ly' 'uso externo'; ~ revenue n (US) rentas fpl públicas.

international [ɪntə'næʃənl] a internacional; ~ game partido internacional; ~ player jugador/a m/f internacional.

interplay ['ɪntəpleɪ] n interacción f.

interpret [ɪn'tɜ:prɪt] vt interpretar; (translate) traducir; (understand) entender // vi hacer de intérprete; ~ation [-'teɪʃən] n interpretación f; traducción f; entendimiento; ~er n intérprete m/f.

interrelated [ɪntərɪ'leɪtɪd] a interrelacionado.

interrogate [ɪn'tɛrəugeɪt] vt interrogar; **interrogation** [-'geɪʃən] n interrogatorio; **interrogative** [ɪntə'rɔgətɪv] a interrogativo.

interrupt [ɪntə'rʌpt] vt, vi interrumpir; ~ion [-'rʌpʃən] n interrupción f.

intersect [ɪntə'sɛkt] vt cruzar // vi (roads) cruzarse; ~ion [-'sɛkʃən] n intersección f; (of roads) cruce m.

intersperse [ɪntə'spə:s] vt esparcir, entremezclar.

intertwine [ɪntə'twaɪn] vt entrelazar // vi entrelazarse.

interval ['ɪntəvl] n intérvalo; (SCOL) recreo; (THEATRE, SPORT) descanso; at ~s a ratos, de vez en cuando.

intervene [ɪntə'vi:n] vi (gen) intervenir; (take part) participar; (occur) sobrevenir; **intervention** [-'vɛnʃən] n intervención f.

interview ['ɪntəvju:] n (RADIO, TV etc) entrevista // vt entrevistarse con; ~ee [-'i:] n entrevistado/a; ~er n entrevistador/a m/f.

intestine [ɪn'tɛstɪn] n: **large/small** ~ intestino grueso/delgado.

intimacy ['ɪntɪməsɪ] n intimidad f; (relations) relaciones fpl íntimas.

intimate ['ɪntɪmət] a íntimo; (friendship) estrecho; (knowledge) profundo // vt ['ɪntɪmeɪt] (announce) dar a entender.

intimidate [ɪn'tɪmɪdeɪt] vt intimidar,

amedrentar; **intimidation** [-'deɪʃən] *n* intimidación *f*.

into ['ɪntu] *prep* (*gen*) en; (*towards*) a; (*inside*) hacia el interior de; **~ 3 pieces/French** en 3 pedazos/ francés.

intolerable [ɪn'tɔlərəbl] *a* intolerable, insufrible; **intolerance** [-rəns] *n* intolerancia; **intolerant** [-rənt] *a*: **intolerant of** intolerante con *o* para.

intonation [ɪntəʊ'neɪʃən] *n* entonación *f*.

intoxicate [ɪn'tɔksɪkeɪt] *vt* embriagar; **~d** *a* embriagado; **intoxication** [-'keɪʃən] *n* embriaguez *f*.

intractable [ɪn'træktəbl] *a* (*child*) intratable; (*material*) difícil de trabajar; (*problem*) espinoso.

intransigent [ɪn'trænsɪdʒənt] *a* intransigente.

intransitive [ɪn'trænsɪtɪv] *a* intransitivo.

intravenous [ɪntrə'viːnəs] *a* intravenoso.

intrepid [ɪn'trepɪd] *a* intrépido.

intricate ['ɪntrɪkət] *a* intrincado; (*complex*) complejo.

intrigue [ɪn'triːg] *n* intriga // *vt* interesar, fascinar // *vi* andar en intrigas; **intriguing** *a* intrigante.

intrinsic [ɪn'trɪnsɪk] *a* intrínseco.

introduce [ɪntrə'djuːs] *vt* introducir, meter; **to ~ sb (to sb)** presentar uno (a otro); **to ~ sb to** (*pastime, technique*) introducir a uno a; **introduction** [-'dʌkʃən] *n* introducción *f*; (*of person*) presentación *f*; **introductory** [-'dʌktərɪ] *a* preliminar.

introspective [ɪntrəʊ'spektɪv] *a* introspectivo.

introvert ['ɪntrəʊvɜːt] *a*, *n* introvertido/a.

intrude [ɪn'truːd] *vi* (*person*) entrometerse; **to ~ on** *or* **into** estorbar; **intruder** *n* intruso/a; **intrusion** [-ʒən] *n* invasión *f*; **intrusive** [-sɪv] *a* intruso.

intuition [ɪntjuː'ɪʃən] *n* intuición *f*; **intuitive** [-'tjuːɪtɪv] *a* intuitivo.

inundate ['ɪnʌndeɪt] *vt*: **to ~ with** inundar de.

invade [ɪn'veɪd] *vt* invadir; **invader** *n* invasor/a *m/f*.

invalid ['ɪnvəlɪd] *n* inválido/a // *a* [ɪn-'vælɪd] (*not valid*) inválido, nulo; **~ate** [ɪn-'vælɪdeɪt] *vt* invalidar, anular.

invaluable [ɪn'væljuəbl] *a* inestimable.

invariable [ɪn'vɛərɪəbl] *a* invariable.

invasion [ɪn'veɪʒən] *n* invasión *f*.

invent [ɪn'vent] *vt* inventar; **~ion** [ɪn-'venʃən] *n* invento; (*inventiveness*) inventiva; (*lie*) ficción *f*, mentira; **~ive** *a* ingenioso; **~iveness** *n* ingenio, inventiva; **~or** *n* inventor/a *m/f*.

inventory ['ɪnvəntrɪ] *n* inventario.

inverse [ɪn'vɜːs] *a*, *n* inverso; **~ly** *ad* a la inversa.

invert [ɪn'vɜːt] *vt* invertir, volver al revés; **~ed commas** *npl* comillas *fpl*.

invertebrate [ɪn'vɜːtɪbrət] *n* invertebrado.

invest [ɪn'vest] *vt*, *vi* invertir.

investigate [ɪn'vestɪgeɪt] *vt* investigar; (*study*) estudiar, examinar; **investigation**

[-'geɪʃən] *n* investigación *f*, pesquisa; examen *m*; **investigator** *n* investigador/a *m/f*.

investiture [ɪn'vestɪtʃə*] *n* investidura.

investment [ɪn'vestmənt] *n* inversión *f*.

investor [ɪn'vestə*] *n* inversionista *m/f*.

inveterate [ɪn'vetərət] *a* empedernido.

invigorating [ɪn'vɪgəreɪtɪŋ] *a* vigorizante.

invincible [ɪn'vɪnsɪbl] *a* invencible.

inviolate [ɪn'vaɪələt] *a* inviolado.

invisible [ɪn'vɪzɪbl] *a* invisible; **~ ink** *n* tinta simpática.

invitation [ɪnvɪ'teɪʃən] *n* invitación *f*.

invite [ɪn'vaɪt] *vt* (*gen*) invitar; (*to drink, food*) convidar; (*opinions etc*) solicitar, pedir; (*trouble*) buscarse; **inviting** *a* atractivo; (*look*) incitante; (*food*) apetitoso.

invoice ['ɪnvɔɪs] *n* factura // *vt* facturar.

invoke [ɪn'vəʊk] *vt* invocar; (*aid*) implorar; (*law*) recurrir a.

involuntary [ɪn'vɔləntrɪ] *a* involuntario.

involve [ɪn'vɔlv] *vt* (*entail*) suponer, implicar; **to ~ sb (in)** comprometer a uno (con); **~d** *a* complicado; **~ment** *n* (*gen*) enredo; (*obligation*) compromiso; (*difficulty*) apuro.

invulnerable [ɪn'vʌlnərəbl] *a* invulnerable.

inward ['ɪnwəd] *a* (*movement*) interior, interno; (*thought, feeling*) íntimo; **~ly** *ad* (*feel, think etc*) para sí, para dentro; **~(s)** *ad* hacia dentro.

iodine ['aɪəʊdiːn] *n* yodo.

iota [aɪ'əʊtə] *n* (*fig*) jota, ápice *m*.

IOU *n abbr of* **I owe you** pagaré *m*.

IQ *n abbr of* **intelligence quotient** cociente *m* intelectual.

Iran [ɪ'rɑːn] *n* Irán *m*; **~ian** [ɪ'reɪnɪən] *a*, *n* iraní *m/f*.

Iraq [ɪ'rɑːk] *n* El Irak; **~i** *a*, *n* irakí *m/f*.

irascible [ɪ'ræsɪbl] *a* irascible.

irate [aɪ'reɪt] *a* enojado, indignado.

Ireland ['aɪələnd] *n* Irlanda.

iris ['aɪrɪs], *pl* **~es** *n* (*ANAT*) iris *m*; (*BOT*) lirio.

Irish ['aɪrɪʃ] *a* irlandés(esa) // *npl*: **the ~** los irlandeses; **~man/ woman** *n* irlandés/esa *m/f*.

irk [ɜːk] *vt* fastidiar; **~some** *a* fastidioso.

iron ['aɪən] *n* hierro; (*for clothes*) plancha // *a* de hierro // *vt* (*clothes*) planchar; **~s** *npl* (*chains*) grillos *mpl*; **to ~ out** (*crease*) quitar; (*fig*) allanar.

ironic(al) [aɪ'rɔnɪk(l)] *a* irónico.

ironing ['aɪənɪŋ] *n* (*act*) planchado; (*ironed clothes*) ropa planchada; (*to be ironed*) ropa por planchar; **~ board** *n* tabla de planchar.

ironmonger ['aɪənmʌŋgə*] *n* ferretero; **~'s (shop)** *n* ferretería, quincallería.

iron ore ['aɪən'ɔː*] *n* mineral *m* de hierro.

irony ['aɪrənɪ] *n* ironía; **the ~ of it is that...** lo irónico es que...

irrational [ɪ'ræʃənl] *a* irracional.

irreconcilable [ɪrɛkən'saɪləbl] *a*

inconciliable, irreconcilable.
irrefutable [ırı'fju:təbl] *a* irrefutable.
irregular [ı'rɛgjulə°] *a* irregular; (*surface*) desigual; (*illegal*) ilegal; ~**ity** [-'lærıtı] *n* irregularidad *f*; desigualdad *f*.
irrelevant [ı'rɛləvənt] *a* fuera de lugar, inoportuno.
irreparable [ı'rɛprəbl] *a* irreparable.
irreplaceable [ırı'pleısəbl] *a* irremplazable.
irrepressible [ırı'prɛsəbl] *a* irrefrenable.
irreproachable [ırı'prəutʃəbl] *a* irreprochable.
irresistible [ırı'zıstıbl] *a* irresistible.
irresolute [ı'rɛzəlu:t] *a* indeciso.
irrespective [ırı'spɛktıv]: ~ **of** *prep* sin tener en cuenta, no importa.
irresponsible [ırı'spɔnsıbl] *a* (*act*) irresponsable; (*person*) poco serio.
irreverent [ı'rɛvərnt] *a* irreverente, irrespetuoso.
irrevocable [ı'rɛvəkəbl] *a* irrevocable.
irrigate ['ırıgeıt] *vt* regar; **irrigation** [-'geıʃən] *n* riego.
irritable ['ırıtəbl] *a* irritable; (*mood*) de mal humor.
irritate ['ırıteıt] *vt* irritar; (*MED*) picar; **irritation** [-'teıʃən] *n* irritación *f*, enojo; picazón *m*, picor *m*.
is [ız] *vb see* **be**.
Islam ['ızlɑːm] *n* Islam *m*.
island ['aılənd] *n* isla; (*also:* **traffic** ~) refugio; ~**er** *n* isleño/a.
isle [aıl] *n* isla.
isn't ['ıznt] = **is not**.
isolate ['aısəleıt] *vt* aislar; ~**d** *a* aislado; **isolation** [-'leıʃən] *n* aislamiento.
isotope ['aısəutəup] *n* isótopo.
Israel ['ızreıl] *n* Israel *m*; ~**i** [ız'reılı] *a*, *n* israelí *m/f*.
issue ['ısju:] *n* cuestión *f*, asunto; (*outcome*) resultado; (*of banknotes etc*) emisión *f*; (*of newspaper etc*) número; (*offspring*) sucesión *f*, descendencia // *vt* (*rations, equipment*) distribuir, repartir; (*orders*) dar; (*certificate*) expedir; (*decree*) promulgar; (*book*) publicar; (*cheques*) extender; (*banknotes, stamps*) emitir.
isthmus ['ısməs] *n* istmo.
it [ıt] *pron* (*subject*) él/ella; (*direct object*) lo/la; (*indirect object*) le; (*impersonal*) ello; (*after prep*) él/ella/ello; ~**'s raining** llueve, está lloviendo; **where is** ~? ¿dónde está?; **he's proud of** ~ le enorgullece; **he agreed to** ~ está de acuerdo (con ello).
Italian [ı'tæljən] *a* italiano // *n* italiano/a; (*LING*) el italiano.
italic [ı'tælık] *a* cursivo; ~**s** *npl* cursiva *sg*.
Italy ['ıtəlı] *n* Italia.
itch [ıtʃ] *n* comezón *m*; (*fig*) prurito // *vi* (*person*) sentir o tener comezón; (*part of body*) picar; **I'm** ~**ing to do sth** rabio por hacer algo; ~**ing** *n* comezón *m*; ~**y** *a*: **to be** ~**y** picar.
it'd ['ıtd] = **it would; it had**.

item ['aıtəm] *n* (*gen*) artículo; (*detail*) detalle *m*; (*on agenda*) asunto a tratar; (*in programme*) número; (*also:* **news** ~) noticia; ~**ize** *vt* detallar.
itinerant [ı'tınərənt] *a* ambulante.
itinerary [aı'tınərərı] *n* itinerario.
it'll ['ıtl] = **it will, it shall**.
its [ıts] *a* su // *pron* (el) suyo/(la) suya.
it's [ıts] = **it is; it has**.
itself [ıt'sɛlf] *pron* (*reflexive*) sí mismo/a; (*emphatic*) él mismo/ella misma.
ITV *n abbr of* **Independent Television**.
I.U.D. *n abbr of* **intra-uterine device** DIU.
I've [aıv] = **I have**.
ivory ['aıvərı] *n* marfil *m*; ~ **tower** *n* (*fig*) torre *f* de marfil.
ivy ['aıvı] *n* hiedra.

J

jab [dʒæb] *vt* (*elbow*) dar un codazo a; (*punch*) dar un golpe rápido a; **to** ~ **sth into sth** clavar algo en algo // *n* codazo; golpe *m* (rápido); (*MED: col*) pinchazo.
jabber ['dʒæbə°] *vt, vi* farfullar.
jack [dʒæk] *n* (*AUT*) gato; (*BOWLS*) boliche *m*; (*CARDS*) sota; **to** ~ **up** *vt* (*AUT*) alzar con gato.
jackdaw ['dʒækdɔ:] *n* grajilla.
jacket ['dʒækıt] *n* chaqueta, americana; (*of boiler etc*) camisa; (*of book*) sobrecubierta; **potatoes in their** ~**s** patatas con su piel.
jack-knife ['dʒæknaıf] *n* navaja.
jackpot ['dʒækpɔt] *n* premio gordo.
jade [dʒeıd] *n* (*stone*) jade *m*.
jaded ['dʒeıdıd] *a* (*tired*) cansado; (*fed-up*) hastiado.
jagged ['dʒægıd] *a* dentado.
jail [dʒeıl] *n* cárcel *f*; ~**break** *n* fuga o evasión *f* (de la cárcel); ~**er** *n* carcelero.
jam [dʒæm] *n* mermelada; (*also:* **traffic** ~) embotellamiento; (*difficulty*) apuro // *vt* (*passage etc*) obstruir, cerrar; (*mechanism, drawer etc*) atascar; (*RADIO*) interferir // *vi* atascarse, trabarse; **to** ~ **sth into sth** meter algo por la fuerza en algo.
Jamaica [dʒə'meıkə] *n* Jamaica.
jangle ['dʒæŋgl] *vi* sonar (de manera) discordante.
janitor ['dʒænıtə°] *n* (*caretaker*) portero, conserje *m*.
January ['dʒænjuərı] *n* enero.
Japan [dʒə'pæn] *n* (el) Japón; ~**ese** [dʒæpə'ni:z] *a* japonés/esa // *n, pl inv* japonés/esa *m/f*; (*LING*) japonés *m*.
jar [dʒɑ:°] *n* (*glass: large*) jarra; (*: small*) tarro // *vi* (*sound*) chirriar; (*colours*) desentonar.
jargon ['dʒɑ:gən] *n* jerga.
jasmin(e) ['dʒæzmın] *n* jazmín *m*.
jaundice ['dʒɔ:ndıs] *n* ictericia; ~**d** *a* (*fig: embittered*) amargado; (*: disillusioned*) desilusionado.

jaunt [dʒɔ:nt] n excursión f; ~y a alegre.
javelin ['dʒævlɪn] n jabalina.
jaw [dʒɔ:] n mandíbula.
jaywalker ['dʒeɪwɔ:kə°] n peatón m imprudente.
jazz [dʒæz] n jazz m; **to ~ up** vt (liven up) animar, avivar; ~y a de colores llamativos.
jealous ['dʒeləs] a (gen) celoso; (envious) envidioso; **to be ~** tener celos; ~y n celos mpl; envidia.
jeans [dʒi:nz] npl (pantalones) vaqueros o tejanos mpl.
jeep [dʒi:p] n jeep m.
jeer [dʒɪə°] vi: **to ~ (at)** (boo) abuchear; (mock) mofarse (de).
jelly ['dʒelɪ] n jalea, gelatina; ~**fish** n medusa.
jeopardize ['dʒepədaɪz] vt arriesgar, poner en peligro; **jeopardy** [-dɪ] n: **to be in jeopardy** estar en peligro o a riesgo.
jerk [dʒə:k] n (jolt) sacudida; (wrench) tirón m // vt dar una sacudida a // vi (vehicle) traquetear.
jerkin ['dʒə:kɪn] n cazadora.
jerky ['dʒə:kɪ] a espasmódico.
jersey ['dʒə:zɪ] n jersey m.
jest [dʒest] n broma.
jet [dʒet] n (of gas, liquid) chorro; (AVIAT) avión m a reacción; ~**-black** a de azabache; ~ **engine** n motor m a reacción.
jettison ['dʒetɪsn] vt desechar.
jetty ['dʒetɪ] n muelle m, embarcadero.
Jew [dʒu:] n judío; ~**ess** n judía.
jewel ['dʒu:əl] n joya; (in watch) rubí m; ~**ler** n joyero; ~**ler's (shop)** n joyería; ~**lery** n joyas fpl, alhajas fpl.
Jewish ['dʒu:ɪʃ] a judío.
jibe [dʒaɪb] n pulla.
jiffy ['dʒɪfɪ] n (col): **in a ~** en un instante.
jig [dʒɪg] n jiga.
jigsaw ['dʒɪgsɔ:] n (also: ~ **puzzle**) rompecabezas m inv.
jilt [dʒɪlt] vt dar calabazas a.
jingle ['dʒɪŋgl] n (advert) estribillo // vi tintinear.
jinx [dʒɪŋks] n (col) gafe m, maldición f.
jitters ['dʒɪtəz] npl (col): **to get the ~** ponerse nervioso.
job [dʒɔb] n (gen) trabajo; (task) tarea, (duty) deber m; (post) empleo; (fam: difficulty) dificultad f; **it's a good ~ that...** menos mal que...; **just the ~!** ¡estupendo!; ~**less** a sin trabajo.
jockey ['dʒɔkɪ] n jockey m // vi: **to ~ for position** maniobrar para conseguir una posición.
jocular ['dʒɔkjulə°] a (humorous) jocoso; (merry) alegre.
jog [dʒɔg] vt empujar (ligeramente) // vi (run) hacer footing; **to ~ along** ir tirando; **to ~ sb's memory** refrescar la memoria a uno; ~**ging** n footing m.
join [dʒɔɪn] vt (things) juntar, unir; (become member of) inscribirse en, afiliarse a;

(meet: people) reunirse o encontrarse con // vi (roads, rivers) confluir // n juntura; **to ~ up** vi unirse; (MIL) alistarse.
joiner ['dʒɔɪnə°] n carpintero; ~**y** n carpintería.
joint [dʒɔɪnt] n (TECH) junta, unión f; (wood) ensambladura; (ANAT) articulación f; (CULIN) asado; (col: place) garito // a (common) común; (combined) combinado; (committee) mixto; **by ~ agreement** por común acuerdo; ~**ly** ad (gen) mutuamente, en común; (collectively) colectivamente; (together) conjuntamente.
joke [dʒəuk] n chiste m; (also: **practical ~**) broma // vi bromear; **to play a ~ on** gastar una broma a; **joker** n chistoso/a, bromista m/f; (CARDS) comodín m.
jolly ['dʒɔlɪ] a (merry) alegre; (enjoyable) divertido // ad (col) muy, terriblemente.
jolt [dʒəult] n (shake) sacudida; (blow) golpe m; (shock) susto // vt sacudir; asustar.
Jordan ['dʒɔ:dən] n Jordania.
jostle ['dʒɔsl] vt dar empellones a, codear.
jot [dʒɔt] n: **not one ~** ni jota, ni pizca; **to ~ down** vt apuntar; ~**ter** n bloc m; (SCOL) cuaderno.
journal ['dʒə:nl] n (paper) periódico; (magazine) revista; (diary) diario; ~**ese** [-'li:z] n (pej) lenguaje m periodístico; ~**ism** n periodismo; ~**ist** n periodista m/f.
journey ['dʒə:nɪ] n viaje m; (distance covered) trayecto // vi viajar; **return ~** viaje de regreso.
joy [dʒɔɪ] n alegría; ~**ful**, ~**ous** a alegre; ~ **ride** n paseo en coche; (illegal) paseo en coche robado.
J.P. n abbr of **Justice of the Peace.**
Jr, Jun., Junr abbr of **junior.**
jubilant ['dʒu:bɪlnt] a jubiloso; **jubilation** [-'leɪʃən] n júbilo.
jubilee ['dʒu:bɪli:] n aniversario.
judge [dʒʌdʒ] n juez m // vt (gen) juzgar; (estimate) considerar; **judg(e)ment** n juicio; (punishment) sentencia, fallo.
judicial [dʒu:'dɪʃl] a judicial.
judicious [dʒu:'dɪʃəs] a juicioso.
judo ['dʒu:dəu] n judo.
jug [dʒʌg] n jarro.
juggernaut ['dʒʌgənɔ:t] n (huge truck) mastodonte m.
juggle ['dʒʌgl] vi hacer juegos malabares; **juggler** n malabarista m/f.
Jugoslav ['ju:gəu'slɑ:v] a, n = **Yugoslav.**
juice [dʒu:s] n zumo, jugo; **juicy** a jugoso.
jukebox ['dʒu:kbɔks] n rocola.
July [dʒu:'laɪ] n julio.
jumble ['dʒʌmbl] n revoltijo // vt (also: ~ **up**: mix up) revolver; (: disarrange) mezclar; ~ **sale** n (Brit) venta de objetos usados.
jumbo (jet) ['dʒʌmbəu] n jumbo-jet m.
jump [dʒʌmp] vi saltar, dar saltos; (start) asustarse, sobresaltarse; (increase) aumentar // vt saltar // n salto; aumento; **to ~ the queue** colarse.

jumper ['dʒʌmpə*] n suéter m, jersey m.
jumpy ['dʒʌmpɪ] a nervioso.
junction ['dʒʌŋkʃən] n (of roads) cruce m; (RAIL) empalme m.
juncture ['dʒʌŋktʃə*] n: **at this ~** en este momento, en esta coyuntura.
June [dʒu:n] n junio.
jungle ['dʒʌŋgl] n selva, jungla.
junior ['dʒu:nɪə*] a (in age) menor, más joven; (competition) juvenil; (position) subalterno // n menor m/f, joven m/f; **~ school** n escuela primaria.
junk [dʒʌŋk] n (cheap goods) baratijas fpl; (lumber) trastos viejos mpl; (rubbish) basura; (ship) junco; **~shop** n tienda de objetos usados.
jurisdiction [dʒuərɪs'dɪkʃən] n jurisdicción f.
jurisprudence [dʒuərɪs'pru:dəns] n jurisprudencia.
jury ['dʒuərɪ] n jurado.
just [dʒʌst] a justo // ad (exactly) exactamente; (only) sólo, solamente; **he's ~ done it/left** acaba de hacerlo/irse; **~ right** perfecto, perfectamente; **~ two o'clock** las dos en punto; **~ as well that...** menos mal que...; **~ as he was leaving** en el momento en que se marchaba; **~ before/enough** justo antes/lo suficiente; **~ here** aquí mismo; **he ~ missed** ha fallado por poco; **~ listen** escucha (solamente).
justice ['dʒʌstɪs] n justicia; **J~ of the Peace (J.P.)** n juez m de paz.
justifiable [dʒʌstɪ'faɪəbl] a justificable; **justifiably** ad justificadamente.
justification [dʒʌstɪfɪ'keɪʃən] n justificación f; **justify** ['dʒʌstɪfaɪ] vt justificar.
justly ['dʒʌstlɪ] ad (gen) justamente; (with reason) con razón.
justness ['dʒʌstnɪs] n justicia.
jut [dʒʌt] vi (also: **~ out**) sobresalir.
juvenile ['dʒu:vənaɪl] a juvenil; (court) de menores; (books) para jóvenes // n joven m/f, menor m/f de edad.
juxtapose ['dʒʌkstəpəuz] vt yuxtaponer.

K

kaleidoscope [kə'laɪdəskəup] n calidoscopio.
kangaroo [kæŋgə'ru:] n canguro.
keel [ki:l] n quilla; **on an even ~** (fig) en equilibrio.
keen [ki:n] a (interest, desire) grande, vivo; (eye, intelligence) agudo; (competition) intenso; (edge) afilado; (eager) entusiasta inv; **to be ~** to do o/ or on doing sth tener muchas ganas de hacer algo; **to be ~ on sth/sb** interesarse por algo/alguien; **~ness** n (eagerness) entusiasmo, interés m.
keep [ki:p] n, pt, pp **kept** vt (retain, preserve) guardar; (hold back) quedarse con; (shop, diary) llevar; (feed: family etc) mantener; (promise) cumplir; (chickens, bees etc)

criar // vi (food) conservarse; (remain) seguir, continuar // n (of castle) torreón m; (food etc) comida, subsistencia; **to ~ doing sth** seguir haciendo algo; **to ~ sb from doing sth** impedir a alguien hacer algo; **to ~ sth from happening** impedir que algo ocurra; **to ~ sb happy** hacer a alguien feliz; **to ~ a place tidy** mantener un lugar limpio; **to ~ sth to o.s.** guardar algo para sí mismo; **to ~ sth (back) from sb** ocultar algo a alguien; **to ~ time** (clock) mantener la hora exacta; **to ~ on** vi seguir, continuar; **to ~ out** vi (stay out) permanecer fuera; **'~ out'** prohibida la entrada; **to ~ up** vt mantener, conservar // vi no retrasarse; **to ~ up with** (pace) ir al paso de; (level) mantenerse a la altura de; **~er** n guardián m; **~ing** n (care) cuidado; **in ~ing with** de acuerdo con; **~sake** n recuerdo.
keg [keg] n barrilete m, barril m.
kennel ['kenl] n perrera; **~s** npl criadero sg de perros.
Kenya ['kenjə] n Kenia.
kept [kept] pt, pp of **keep.**
kerb [kə:b] n bordillo.
kernel ['kə:nl] n almendra.
kerosene ['kerəsi:n] n keroseno.
ketchup ['ketʃəp] n salsa de tomate, catsup m.
kettle ['ketl] n hervidor m, olla.
key [ki:] n (gen) llave f; (MUS) tono; (of piano, typewriter) tecla; **~board** n teclado; **~hole** n ojo (de la cerradura); **~note** n (MUS) tónica; **~ring** n llavero; **~stone** n piedra clave.
khaki ['kɑ:kɪ] n caqui.
kick [kɪk] vt (person) dar una patada a; (ball) dar un puntapié a // vi (horse) dar coces // n patada; puntapié m; (of rifle) culetazo; (thrill): **he does it for ~s** lo hace para divertirse; **to ~ off** vi (SPORT) hacer el saque inicial; **~-off** n (SPORT) saque m inicial.
kid [kɪd] n (child) chiquillo; (animal) cabrito; (leather) cabritilla // vi (col) bromear.
kidnap ['kɪdnæp] vt secuestrar; **~per** n secuestrador/a m/f; **~ping** n secuestro.
kidney ['kɪdnɪ] n riñón m.
kill [kɪl] vt (gen) matar; (murder) asesinar; (destroy) destruir; (finish off) acabar con // n acto de matar; **~er** n asesino; **~ing** n (one) asesinato; (several) matanza // a (funny) divertido.
kiln [kɪln] n horno.
kilo ['ki:ləu] n kilo; **~gram(me)** ['kɪləugræm] n kilo, kilogramo; **~metre, ~meter** (US) ['kɪləmi:tə*] n kilómetro; **~watt** ['kɪləuwɔt] n kilovatio.
kilt [kɪlt] n falda escocesa.
kimono [kɪ'məunəu] n quimono.
kin [kɪn] n parientes mpl.
kind [kaɪnd] a (generous) bondadoso; (good) bueno, amable // n clase f, especie f; (species) género; **in ~** (COMM) en

especie; **a ~ of** una especie de; **two of a ~** dos de la misma especie.

kindergarten ['kɪndəgɑːtn] n jardín m de infancia.

kind-hearted [kaɪnd'hɑːtɪd] a bondadoso, de buen corazón.

kindle ['kɪndl] vt encender.

kindly ['kaɪndlɪ] a (gen) bondadoso; (good) bueno; (gentle) cariñoso // ad bondadosamente, amablemente; **will you ~...** sea Usted tan amable de... .

kindness ['kaɪndnɪs] n bondad f, amabilidad f.

kindred ['kɪndrɪd] n familia, parientes mpl // a: **~ spirit** espíritu m afín.

king [kɪŋ] n rey m; **~dom** n reino; **~fisher** n martín m pescador; **~-size** a de tamaño extra.

kink [kɪŋk] n (of rope) enroscadura.

kinky ['kɪŋkɪ] a (odd) excéntrico; (pej) pervertido.

kiosk ['kiːɔsk] n quiosco; (TEL) cabina.

kipper ['kɪpə*] n arenque m ahumado.

kiss [kɪs] n beso // vt besar; **to ~ (each other)** besarse.

kit [kɪt] n (gen) avíos mpl; (equipment) equipo; (set of tools etc) (caja de) herramientas fpl; (for assembly) mecano.

kitchen ['kɪtʃɪn] n cocina; **~ garden** n huerto; **~ sink** n fregadero; **~ware** n batería de cocina.

kite [kaɪt] n (toy) cometa.

kitten ['kɪtn] n gatito.

kitty ['kɪtɪ] n (pool of money) fondo común; (CARDS) polla.

kleptomaniac [klɛptəu'meɪnɪæk] n cleptómano/a.

knack [næk] n: **to have the ~ of doing sth** tener el don de hacer algo.

knapsack ['næpsæk] n mochila.

knead [niːd] vt amasar.

knee [niː] n rodilla; **~cap** n rótula.

kneel [niːl], pt, pp knelt vi arrodillarse.

knell [nɛl] n toque m de difuntos.

knelt [nɛlt] pt, pp of kneel.

knew [njuː] pt of know.

knickers ['nɪkəz] npl bragas fpl.

knife [naɪf], pl knives n cuchillo // vt acuchillar.

knight [naɪt] n caballero; (CHESS) caballo; **~hood** n caballería; (title): **to get a ~hood** recibir el título de sir.

knit [nɪt] vt hacer a punto; (brows) fruncir // vi hacer punto; (bones) soldarse; **to ~ together** (fig) unir, juntar; **~ting** n labor f de punto; **~ting machine** n máquina de tricotar; **~ting needle** n aguja de hacer punto; **~wear** n géneros mpl de punto.

knives [naɪvz] pl of knife.

knob [nɔb] n (of door) tirador m; (of stick) puño; (lump) bulto; (fig): **a ~ of butter** una porción de mantequilla.

knock [nɔk] vt (strike) golpear; (bump into) chocar contra; (fig: col) denigrar // n golpe m; (on door) llamada; **to ~ at or on the door** llamar a la puerta; **to ~ down**

vt atropellar; **to ~ off** vi (col: finish) despachar // vt (col: steal) birlar; **to ~ out** vt dejar sin sentido; (BOXING) poner fuera de combate, dejar K.O.; **~er** n (on door) aldaba; **~-kneed** a patizambo; **~out** n (BOXING) K.O. m, knockout m.

knot [nɔt] n (gen) nudo // vt anudar; **~ty** a (fig) complicado.

know [nəu], pt knew, pp known vt (gen) saber; (person, author, place) conocer; **to ~ that...** saber que...; **to ~ how to swim** saber nadar; **~-all** n sabelotodo m/f; **~-how** n habilidad f; **~ing** a (look: of complicity) de complicidad; (: spiteful) malicioso; **~ingly** ad (purposely) adrede; (spitefully) maliciosamente.

knowledge ['nɔlɪdʒ] n (gen) conocimiento; (range of learning) saber m, conocimientos mpl; (learning) erudición f, ciencia; **~able** a entendido, erudito.

known [nəun] pp of know.

knuckle ['nʌkl] n nudillo.

K.O. n abbr of knockout.

Koran [kɔ'rɑːn] n Corán m.

L

l. abbr of litre.

lab [læb] n abbr of laboratory.

label ['leɪbl] n etiqueta; (brand: of record) marca // vt poner etiqueta a.

laboratory [lə'bɔrətərɪ] n laboratorio.

laborious [lə'bɔːrɪəs] a penoso.

labour, labor (US) ['leɪbə*] n (task) trabajo; (~ force) mano f de obra; (workers) trabajadores mpl; (MED) (dolores mpl del) parto // vi: **to ~ (at)** trabajar (en) // vt insistir en; **in ~** (MED) de parto; **L~**, **the L~ party** el partido laborista; **hard ~** trabajos mpl forzados; **~ed** a (movement) penoso; (style) pesado; **~er** n peón m; (on farm) peón m, bracero; (day ~er) jornalero.

labyrinth ['læbɪrɪnθ] n laberinto.

lace [leɪs] n encaje m; (of shoe etc) cordón m // vt (shoe) atar.

lack [læk] n (absence) falta; (scarcity) escasez f // vt no tener, carecer de; **through or for ~ of** por falta de; **to be ~ing** faltar, no haber.

lackadaisical [lækə'deɪzɪkl] a (careless) descuidado; (indifferent) indiferente.

laconic [lə'kɔnɪk] a lacónico.

lacquer ['lækə*] n laca.

lad [læd] n muchacho, chico; (in stable etc) mozo.

ladder ['lædə*] n escalera (de mano); (in tights) carrera // vt (tights) hacer una carrera en.

laden ['leɪdn] a: **~ (with)** cargado (de).

ladle ['leɪdl] n cucharón m.

lady ['leɪdɪ] n señora; (distinguished, noble) dama; **young ~** señorita; **'ladies' (toilets)** 'señoras'; **~bird**, **~bug** (US) n mariquita; **~-in-waiting** n dama de honor; **~like** a fino.

lag [læg] vi (also: **~ behind**) retrasarse,

quedarse atrás // vt (*pipes*) calorifugar.
lager ['lɑːgəʳ] n cerveza (rubia).
lagging ['læɡɪŋ] n revestimiento.
lagoon [ləˈɡuːn] n laguna.
laid [leɪd] pt, pp of **lay.**
lain [leɪn] pp of **lie.**
lair [lɛəʳ] n guarida.
lake [leɪk] n lago.
lamb [læm] n cordero; (*meat*) carne f de
cordero; ~ **chop** n chuleta de cordero;
lambswool n lana de cordero.
lame [leɪm] a cojo; (*weak*) débil, poco
convincente.
lament [ləˈment] n lamento // vt
lamentarse de; ~**able** ['læməntəbl] a
lamentable.
laminated ['læmɪneɪtɪd] a laminado.
lamp [læmp] n lámpara.
lampoon [læmˈpuːn] vt satirizar.
lamp: ~**post** n farol m; ~**shade** n
pantalla.
lance [lɑːns] n lanza // vt (MED) abrir con
lanzeta; ~ **corporal** n soldado de
primera clase.
lancet ['lɑːnsɪt] n lanceta.
land [lænd] n (gen) tierra; (*country*) país
m; (*piece of* ~) terreno; (*estate*) tierras fpl,
finca; (AGR) campo // vi (*from ship*)
desembarcar; (AVIAT) aterrizar; (*fig: fall*)
caer, terminar // vt (*obtain*) conseguir;
(*passengers, goods*) desembarcar; **to** ~ **up**
in/at ir a parar a/en; ~**ing** n
desembarco; aterrizaje m; (*of staircase*)
rellano; ~**ing craft** n barca de
desembarco; ~**ing gear** n tren m de
aterrizaje; ~**ing stage** n
desembarcadero; ~**ing strip** n pista de
aterrizaje; ~**lady** n (*of boarding house*)
patrona; (*owner*) dueña; ~**locked** a
cercado de tierra; ~**lord** n propietario;
(*of pub etc*) patrón m; ~**lubber** n hombre
m de tierra; ~**mark** n lugar m conocido;
to be a ~**mark** (*fig*) hacer época;
~**owner** n terrateniente m/f.
landscape ['lænskeɪp] n paisaje m; ~**d** a
reformado artísticamente.
landslide ['lændslaɪd] n (GEO) corrimiento
de tierras; (*fig: POL*) victoria arrolladora.
lane [leɪn] n (*in country*) vereda; (*in town*)
callejón m; (AUT) carril m; (*in race*) calle f;
(*for air or sea traffic*) ruta.
language ['læŋɡwɪdʒ] n lenguaje m;
(*national tongue*) idioma m, lengua; **bad** ~
lenguaje indecente.
languid ['læŋɡwɪd] a lánguido.
languish ['læŋɡwɪʃ] vi languidecer.
lank [læŋk] a (*hair*) lacio.
lanky ['læŋkɪ] a larguirucho.
lantern ['læntən] n linterna; (NAUT) farol m.
lap [læp] n (*of track*) vuelta; (*of body*): **to**
sit on sb's ~ sentarse en las rodillas de
uno // vt (*also:* ~ **up**) lamer // vi (*waves*)
chapotear; ~**dog** n perro faldero.
lapel [ləˈpel] n solapa.
Lapland ['læplænd] n Laponia; **Lapp** [læp]
a, n lapón/ona m/f.
lapse [læps] n error m, equivocación f;

(*moral*) desliz m // vi (*expire*) caducar;
(LAW) equivocarse; (*morally*) caer en un
desliz; (*time*) pasar, transcurrir; **to** ~
into bad habits volver a las andadas; ~
of time lapso, período.
larceny ['lɑːsənɪ] n latrocinio; **petty** ~
robo de menor cuantía.
lard [lɑːd] n manteca (de cerdo).
larder ['lɑːdəʳ] n despensa.
large [lɑːdʒ] a (gen) grande; (*fat*) gordo; **at**
~ (*free*) en libertad; (*generally*) en
general; ~**ly** ad en gran parte; ~**-scale** a
(*map*) en gran escala; (*fig*) importante.
lark [lɑːk] n (*bird*) alondra; (*joke*)
travesura, broma; **to** ~ **about** vi
bromear, divertirse tontamente.
larva ['lɑːvə], pl ~**vae** [-viː] n larva.
laryngitis [lærɪnˈdʒaɪtɪs] n laringitis f.
larynx ['lærɪŋks] n laringe f.
lascivious [ləˈsɪvɪəs] a lascivo.
laser ['leɪzəʳ] n laser m.
lash [læʃ] n latigazo; (*punishment*) azote m;
(*gen: eyelash*) pestaña // vt azotar; (*tie*)
atar; **to** ~ **out** vi: **to** ~ **out at** or **against**
sb atacar violentamente a alguien; **to** ~
out (*col: spend*) gastar generosamente.
lass [læs] n chica.
lasso [læˈsuː] n lazo // vt coger con lazo.
last [lɑːst] a (gen) último; (*final*) último,
final // ad por último // vi (*endure*) durar;
(*continue*) continuar, seguir; ~ **week** la
semana pasada; ~ **night** anoche; **at** ~
por fin, ~ **but one** penúltimo; ~**ing** a
duradero; ~**-minute** a de última hora.
latch [lætʃ] n picaporte m, pestillo; ~**key** n
llavín m.
late [leɪt] a (*not on time*) tarde, atrasado;
(*far on in day etc*) tardío; (*hour*) avanzado;
(*recent*) reciente; (*former*) antiguo, ex;
(*dead*) fallecido // ad tarde; (*behind time,
schedule*) con retraso; **of** ~ últimamente;
in ~ **May** hacia fines de mayo; **the** ~
Mr X el difunto Sr X; ~**comer** n recién
llegado; ~**ly** ad últimamente; ~**ness** n
(*of person*) retraso; (*of event*) lo tardío.
latent ['leɪtnt] a latente.
later ['leɪtəʳ] a (*date etc*) posterior;
(*version etc*) más reciente // ad más tarde,
después.
lateral ['lætərl] a lateral.
latest ['leɪtɪst] a último; **at the** ~ a más
tardar.
lathe [leɪð] n torno.
lather ['lɑːðəʳ] n espuma (de jabón) // vt
enjabonar // vi hacer espuma.
Latin ['lætɪn] n latín m // a latino; ~
America n América latina; ~**-American**
a latinoamericano.
latitude ['lætɪtjuːd] n latitud f.
latrine [ləˈtriːn] n letrina.
latter ['lætəʳ] a último; (*of two*) segundo //
n: **the** ~ el último, éste; ~**ly** ad
últimamente.
lattice ['lætɪs] n enrejado; (*on window*)
reja.
laudable ['lɔːdəbl] a loable.
laugh [lɑːf] n risa; (*loud*) carcajada // vi

reírse, reír; reírse a carcajadas; to ~ at
vt fus reírse de; to ~ off vt tomar algo a
risa; ~able a risible, ridículo; to be the
~ing stock of the town ser el
hazmerreír de la ciudad; ~ter n risa.
launch [lɔːntʃ] n (boat) lancha; see also
~ing // vt (ship, rocket, plan) lanzar;
~ing n (of rocket etc) lanzamiento;
(inauguration) estreno; ~(ing) pad n
plataforma de lanzamiento.
launder ['lɔːndə*] vt lavar.
launderette [lɔːn'drɛt] n lavandería
(automática).
laundry ['lɔːndrɪ] n lavandería; (clothes)
ropa sucia; to do the ~ hacer la colada.
laureate ['lɔːrɪət] a see poet.
laurel ['lɔrl] n laurel m.
lava ['lɑːvə] n lava.
lavatory ['lævətərɪ] n lavabo; **lavatories**
npl servicios mpl, aseos mpl.
lavender ['lævəndə*] n lavanda.
lavish ['lævɪʃ] a abundante; (giving freely):
~ with pródigo en // vt: to ~ sth on sb
colmar a uno de algo.
law [lɔː] n ley f; (study) derecho; (of game)
regla; ~-**abiding** a que cumple la ley; ~
and order n órden m público; ~**breaker**
n infractor m (de la ley); ~ **court** n
tribunal m (de justicia); ~**ful** a legítimo,
lícito; ~**fully** ad legalmente; ~**less** a
(act) ilegal; (person) rebelde; (country)
desordenado.
lawn [lɔːn] n césped m; ~**mower** n
cortacésped m; ~ **tennis** [-'tɛnɪs] n tenis
m.
law-: ~ **school** n facultad f de derecho; ~
student n estudiante m/f de derecho.
lawsuit ['lɔːsuːt] n pleito.
lawyer ['lɔːjə*] n abogado; (for sales, wills
etc) notario.
lax [læks] a flojo; (negligent) negligente.
laxative ['læksətɪv] n laxante m.
laxity ['læksɪtɪ] n flojedad f; (moral)
relajamiento; (negligence) negligencia.
lay [leɪ] pt of **lie** // a laico; (not expert)
profano // vt, pt, pp **laid** (place) colocar;
(eggs, table) poner; (trap) tender; to ~
aside or **by** vt dejar a un lado; to ~ **down**
vt (pen etc) dejar; (~ flat) acostar; (arms)
rendir; (policy) asentar; to ~ **down** the
law imponer la ley; to ~ **off** vt (workers)
despedir, poner en paro; to ~ **on** vt
(water, gas) instalar; (provide) proveer; to
~ **out** vt (design) diseñar; (display)
disponer; (spend) gastar; to ~ **up** vt
(store) guardar; (ship) desarmar; (subj:
illness) obligar a guardar cama; ~**about**
n vago/a; ~**-by** n apartadero.
layer ['leɪə*] n capa.
layette [leɪ'ɛt] n canastilla, ajuar m (de
niño).
layman ['leɪmən] n persona no experta;
(REL) lego.
layout ['leɪaut] n (design) plan m, trazado;
(disposition) disposición f; (PRESS)
composición f.
laze [leɪz] vi no hacer nada; (pej)

holgazanear; **laziness** n pereza; **lazy** a
perezoso, vago.
lb. abbr of **pound** (weight).
lead [liːd] n (front position) delantera;
(SPORT) liderato; (distance, time ahead)
ventaja; (clue) pista; (ELEC) cable m; (for
dog) correa; (THEATRE) papel m principal
// n [lɛd] plomo; (in pencil) mina // (vb: pt,
pp **led**) vt conducir; (induce) llevar; (be
leader of) dirigir; (SPORT) ir en cabeza de
// vi ir primero; to ~ **to** llevar a, salir a;
to ~ **astray** vt llevar por mal camino; to
~ **away** vt llevar; to ~ **back** vt hacer
volver; to ~ **on** vt (tease) coquetear con;
to ~ **on to** vt (induce) incitar a; to ~ **up**
to conducir a.
leader ['liːdə*] n (gen) jefe m, líder m; (of
union etc) dirigente m/f; (of gang)
cabecilla m; (guide) guía m/f; (of
newspaper) artículo de fondo; ~**ship** n
dirección f; (quality) dotes fpl de mando.
leading ['liːdɪŋ] a (main) principal;
(outstanding) destacado; (first) primero;
(front) delantero; ~ **lady** n (THEATRE)
primera actriz f; ~ **light** n (person)
figura principal.
leaf [liːf], pl **leaves** n hoja // vi: to ~
through hojear; to turn over a new ~
reformarse.
leaflet ['liːflɪt] n folleto.
league [liːg] n sociedad f; (FOOTBALL) liga;
to be in ~ **with** estar de manga con.
leak [liːk] n (of liquid, gas) escape m, fuga;
(hole) agujero; (in roof) gotera; (of money)
filtración f // vi (shoes, ship) hacer agua;
(pipe) tener (un) escape; (roof) gotear;
(container) salirse; (gas) escaparse; (fig:
news) filtrarse // vt (gas) dejar escapar;
(exude) rezumar; **the information was**
~**ed to the enemy** las informaciones se
pasaron al enemigo; **the news** ~**ed out**
trascendió la noticia.
lean [liːn] a (thin) flaco; (meat) magro //
(vb: pt, pp **leaned** or **leant** [lɛnt]) vt: to ~
sth on apoyar algo en // vi (slope)
inclinarse; (rest): to ~ **against** apoyarse
contra; to ~ **on** apoyarse en; (fig: rely on)
contar con (el apoyo de); to ~
back/forward vi inclinarse hacia
atrás/hacia adelante; to ~ **over** vi
ladearse; ~**ing** a inclinado // n: ~**ing**
(**towards**) inclinación f (hacia); ~**-to** n
colgadizo.
leap [liːp] n salto // vi, pt, pp **leaped** or
leapt [lɛpt] saltar; ~**frog** n pídola; ~
year n año bisiesto.
learn [lɜːn], pt, pp **learned** or **learnt** vt
(gen) aprender; (come to know of)
enterarse de // vi aprender; to ~ **how to**
do sth aprender a hacer algo; ~**ed**
['lɜːnɪd] a erudito; ~**er** n principiante m/f;
~**ing** n el saber m, conocimientos mpl.
lease [liːs] n arriendo // vt arrendar.
leash [liːʃ] n cuerda.
least [liːst] a (slightest) menor; (smallest)
más pequeño; (smallest amount of) mínimo
// ad menos // n: **the** ~ lo menos; **the** ~

possible **effort** el mínimo de esfuerzo posible; **at ~** por lo menos, al menos; **not in the ~** en absoluto.

leather ['leðə*] n cuero.

leave [li:v], pt, pp **left** vt dejar; (go away from) abandonar // vi irse; (train) salir // n permiso; **to be left** quedar, sobrar; **there's some milk left over** sobra o queda algo de leche; **on ~** de permiso; **to take one's ~ of** despedirse de; **to ~ out** vt omitir.

leaves [li:vz] pl of **leaf**.

Lebanon ['lebənən] n Líbano.

lecherous ['letʃərəs] a lascivo.

lecture ['lektʃə*] n conferencia; (SCOL) clase f // vi dar una clase // vt (scold) sermonear; **to give a ~ on** dar una conferencia sobre; **lecturer** n conferenciante m/f; (at university) profesor adjunto/profesora adjunta m/f.

led [led] pt, pp of **lead**.

ledge [ledʒ] n (of window, on wall) repisa, reborde m; (of mountain) plataforma.

ledger ['ledʒə*] n libro mayor.

lee [li:] n sotavento.

leek [li:k] n puerro.

leer [liə*] vi: **to ~ at sb** mirar impúdicamente a alguien.

leeway ['li:wei] n (fig): **to have some ~** tener cierta libertad de acción.

left [left] pt, pp of **leave** // a izquierdo; (POL) de izquierda // n izquierda // ad a la izquierda; **the L~** (POL) la izquierda; **~-handed** a zurdo; **the ~-hand side** n la izquierda; **~-luggage (office)** n consigna; **~-overs** npl sobras fpl; **~-wing** a (POL) de izquierdas, izquierdista.

leg [leg] n pierna; (of animal) pata; (of chair) pie m; (CULIN: of meat) pierna; (of journey) etapa; **1st/2nd ~** (SPORT) partido de ida/de vuelta; **to pull sb's ~** bromear con uno.

legacy ['legəsi] n legado.

legal ['li:gl] a (gen) lícito; (of law) legal; (enquiry etc) jurídico; **~ize** vt legalizar; **~ly** ad legalmente; **~ tender** n moneda corriente.

legend ['ledʒənd] n leyenda; **~ary** a legendario.

legible ['ledʒəbl] a legible.

legion ['li:dʒən] n legión f.

legislate ['ledʒisleit] vi legislar; **legislation** [-'leiʃən] n legislación f; **legislative** [-lətiv] a legislativo; **legislature** [-lətʃə*] n cuerpo legislativo.

legitimacy [li'dʒitiməsi] n legitimidad f; **legitimate** [-mət] a legítimo.

leg-room ['legru:m] n espacio para las piernas.

leisure ['leʒə*] n ocio, tiempo libre; **at ~** con tranquilidad; **~ centre** n centro de diversiones; **~ly** a pausado, lento.

lemon ['lemən] n limón m; **~ade** [-'neid] n (fruit juice) limonada; (fizzy) gaseosa.

lend [lend] pt, pp **lent** vt: **to ~ sth to sb** prestar algo a alguien; **~er** n prestador/a

m/f; **~ing library** n biblioteca circulante.

length [leŋθ] n largo, longitud f; (section: of road, pipe etc) tramo; **at ~** (at last) por fin, finalmente; (lengthily) largamente; **~en** vt alargar // vi alargarse; **~ways** ad de largo; **~y** a largo, extenso; (meeting) prolongado.

leniency ['li:niənsi] n indulgencia; **lenient** [-ənt] a indulgente.

lens [lenz] n (of spectacles) lente f; (of camera) objetivo.

lent [lent] pt, pp of **lend**.

Lent [lent] n Cuaresma.

lentil ['lentl] n lenteja.

Leo ['li:əu] n Leo.

leopard ['lepəd] n leopardo.

leotard ['li:əta:d] n leotardo.

leper ['lepə*] n leproso/a; **leprosy** [-prəsi] n lepra.

lesbian ['lezbiən] n lesbiana.

less [les] det a (in size, degree etc) menor; (in quantity) menos // pron, ad menos; **~ than half** menos de la mitad; **~ and ~** cada vez menos; **the ~ he works...** cuanto menos trabaja... .

lessen ['lesn] vi disminuir, menguar // vt disminuir, reducir.

lesson ['lesn] n lección f; **a maths ~** una clase o una lección de matemáticas.

lest [lest] conj: **~ it happen** para que no pase.

let [let] pt, pp **let** vt (allow) dejar, permitir; (lease) alquilar; **~'s go** ¡vamos!; **~ him come** que venga; '**to ~**' 'se alquila'; **to ~ down** vt (lower) bajar; (dress) alargar; (tyre) desinflar; (hair) soltar; (disappoint) defraudar; **to ~ go** vi soltar; (fig) dejarse ir // vt abandonar; **to ~ in** vt dejar entrar; (visitor etc) hacer pasar; **to ~ off** vt dejar libre; (firework etc) disparar; (smell etc) despedir; **to ~ on** vt (col) divulgar (that que); **to ~ out** vt dejar salir; (dress) ensanchar; **to ~ up** vi amainar, disminuir.

lethal ['li:θl] a mortífero; (wound) mortal.

lethargic [le'θɑ:dʒik] a letárgico; **lethargy** ['leθədʒi] n letargo.

letter ['letə*] n (of alphabet) letra; (correspondence) carta; **~ bomb** n carta con bomba explosiva; **~box** n buzón m; **~ing** n letras fpl.

lettuce ['letis] n lechuga.

let-up ['letʌp] n descanso, tregua.

leukaemia, leukemia (US) [lu:'ki:miə] n leucemia.

level ['levl] a (flat) llano; (flattened) nivelado; (uniform) igual // ad a nivel // n nivel m; (flat place) llano // vt nivelar, allanar; **to be ~ with** estar a nivel de; **'A' ~s** npl Bachillerato Superior, B.U.P.; **'O' ~s** npl bachillerato elemental, octavo de básica; **on the ~** (fig: honest) en serio; **to ~ off o out** vi (prices etc) estabilizarse; **~ crossing** n paso a nivel; **~-headed** a sensato.

lever ['li:və*] n palanca // vt: **to ~ up**

alzar con palanca; ~**age** n (fig: influence) influencia.

levity ['levɪtɪ] n frivolidad f, informalidad f.

levy ['levɪ] n impuesto // vt exigir, recaudar.

lewd [luːd] a impúdico, obsceno.

liability [laɪə'bɪlɪtɪ] n responsabilidad f; (handicap) desventaja; (risk) riesgo; **liabilities** npl obligaciones fpl; (COMM) deudas fpl, pasivo sg.

liable ['laɪəbl] a (subject): ~ **to** sujeto a; **to be** ~ **for** ser responsable de; **to be** ~ **to** (likely) tener tendencia a.

liaison [liː'eɪzɔn] n (coordination) enlace m; (affair) relaciones fpl amorosas.

liar ['laɪə*] n mentiroso/a.

libel ['laɪbl] n calumnia // vt calumniar.

liberal ['lɪbərl] a (gen) liberal; (generous): ~ **with** generoso con.

liberate ['lɪbəreɪt] vt liberar; **liberation** [-'reɪʃən] n liberación f.

liberty ['lɪbətɪ] n libertad f; **to be at** ~ **to** tener permiso para; **to take the** ~ **of doing sth** tomarse la libertad de hacer algo.

Libra ['liːbrə] n Libra.

librarian [laɪ'brεərɪən] n bibliotecario/a; **library** ['laɪbrərɪ] n biblioteca.

libretto [lɪ'brεtəʊ] n libreto.

Libya ['lɪbɪə] n Libia; ~**n** a, n libio/a.

lice [laɪs] pl of **louse**.

licence, license (US) ['laɪsns] n (gen) licencia; (permit) permiso; (also: driving ~) carnet m de conducir; (excessive freedom) libertinaje m; ~ **number** n matrícula; ~ **plate** n placa (de matrícula).

license ['laɪsns] n (US) = **licence** // vt autorizar, licenciar; ~**d** a (for alcohol) autorizado para la venta de bebidas alcohólicas.

licensee [laɪsən'siː] n (in a pub) patrón/ona m/f.

licentious [laɪ'sεnʃəs] a licencioso.

lichen ['laɪkən] n liquen m.

lick [lɪk] vt lamer // n lamedura; **a** ~ **of paint** una mano de pintura.

licorice ['lɪkərɪs] n = **liquorice**.

lid [lɪd] n (of box, case) tapa; (of pan) cobertera.

lido ['laɪdəʊ] n piscina.

lie [laɪ] n mentira // vi mentir // vi, pt **lay**, pp **lain** (act) echarse; (state) estar echado, estar acostado; (of object: be situated) estar, encontrarse; **to** ~ **low** (fig) esconderse; **to** ~ **about** vi (things) estar en desorden; (people) gandulear; **to have a** ~-**down** echarse una siesta); **to have a** ~-**in** quedarse pegado a las sábanas.

lieu [luː]: **in** ~ **of** prep en lugar de.

lieutenant [lεf'tεnənt] n lugarteniente m; (MIL) teniente m.

life [laɪf], pl **lives** n (gen) vida; (way of ~) modo de vivir; (of licence etc) vigencia; ~ **assurance** n seguro de vida; ~**belt** n cinturón m salvavidas; ~**boat** n bote m salvavidas; ~**guard** n vigilante m; ~**jacket** n chaleco salvavidas; ~**less** a sin vida; (dull) soso; ~**like** a natural; ~**line** n cuerda salvavidas; ~**long** a de toda la vida; ~-**saver** n bañero, socorrista m/f; ~ **sentence** n condena perpetua; ~-**sized** a de tamaño natural; ~ **span** n vida; ~ **support system** n (MED) respirador m artificial; ~**time** n: **in his** ~ **time** durante su vida; **once in a** ~ **time** una vez en la vida.

lift [lɪft] vt levantar; (steal) robar // vi (fog) levantarse, disiparse // n (elevator) ascensor m; **to give sb a** ~ llevar a uno en el coche; ~-**off** n despegue m.

ligament ['lɪgəmənt] n ligamento.

light [laɪt] n (gen) luz f; (flame) lumbre f; (lamp) luz f, lámpara; (daylight) luz del día; (headlight) faro; (rear ~) luz trasera; (for cigarette etc): **have you got a** ~? ¿tiene fuego? // vt, pt, pp **lighted** or **lit** (candle, cigarette, fire) encender; (room) alumbrar // a (colour) claro; (not heavy, also fig) ligero; (room) alumbrado; **to** ~ **up** vi (smoke) encender un cigarrillo; (face) iluminarse // vt (illuminate) iluminar, alumbrar; ~ **bulb** n bombilla; ~**en** vi (grow ~) clarear // vt (give light to) iluminar; (make lighter) aclarar; (make less heavy) aligerar; ~**er** n (also: cigarette ~**er**) encendedor m, mechero; ~-**headed** a (dizzy) mareado; (excited) exaltado; (by nature) casquivano; ~-**hearted** a alegre; ~**house** n faro; ~**ing** n (act) iluminación f; (system) alumbrado; ~**ly** ad (touch) ligeramente; (thoughtlessly) a la ligera; (slightly) levemente; (not seriously) con poca seriedad; **to get off** ~**ly** ser castigado con poca severidad; ~ **meter** n (PHOT) fotómetro; ~**ness** n claridad f; (in weight) ligereza.

lightning ['laɪtnɪŋ] n relámpago, rayo; ~ **conductor** n pararrayos m inv.

light: ~**weight** a (suit) ligero // n (BOXING) peso ligero; ~ **year** n año luz.

like [laɪk] vt (person) querer, tener cariño a; (things) gustarle a uno // prep como // a parecido, semejante // n: **the** ~ semejante m/f; **his** ~**s and dislikes** sus gustos y aversiones; **I would** ~, **I'd** ~ me gustaría; (for purchase) quisiera; **would you** ~ **a coffee?** ¿te apetece un café?; **to be** or **look** ~ **sb/sth** parecerse a alguien/algo; **that's just** ~ **him** es muy de él, es característico de él; **it is nothing** ~... no tiene parecido alguno con...; ~**able** a simpático, agradable.

likelihood ['laɪklɪhʊd] n probabilidad f; **likely** [-lɪ] a probable; **he's likely to leave** es probable que se vaya.

like-minded [laɪk'maɪndɪd] a de la misma opinión.

liken ['laɪkən] vt: **to** ~ **sth to sth** comparar algo con algo.

likewise ['laɪkwaɪz] ad igualmente.

liking ['laɪkɪŋ] n: **to his** ~ para su gusto.

lilac ['laɪlək] n lila // a (colour) de color lila.

lily ['lɪlɪ] n lirio, azucena; ~ **of the valley** n lirio de los valles.

limb [lɪm] n miembro.

limber ['lɪmbə*]: **to ~ up** vi (fig) entrenarse; (SPORT) desentumecerse.

limbo ['lɪmbəʊ] n: **to be in ~** (fig) caer en el olvido.

lime [laɪm] n (tree) limero; (fruit) lima; (GEO) cal f.

limelight ['laɪmlaɪt] n: **to be in the ~** (fig) ser el centro de atención.

limerick ['lɪmərɪk] n quintilla humorística.

limestone ['laɪmstəʊn] n piedra caliza.

limit ['lɪmɪt] n límite m // vt limitar; ~**ation** [-'teɪʃən] n limitación f; ~**ed** a limitado; **to be ~ed to** limitarse a; ~**ed (liability) company (Ltd)** n sociedad f anónima; ~**less** a sin límites.

limousine ['lɪməzi:n] n limusina.

limp [lɪmp] n: **to have a ~** tener cojera // vi cojear // a flojo.

limpet ['lɪmpɪt] n lapa.

limpid ['lɪmpɪd] a límpido, cristalino.

line [laɪn] n (gen) línea; (straight ~) raya; (rope) cuerda; (for fishing) sedal m; (wire) hilo; (row, series) fila, hilera; (of writing) renglón m; (on face) arruga; (specialty) rama // vt (SEWING) forrar (with de); **to ~ the streets** ocupar las aceras; **in ~ with** de acuerdo con; **to ~ up** vi hacer cola // vt alinear, poner en fila; ~**d** a (face) arrugado; (paper) rayado.

linear ['lɪnɪə*] a lineal.

linen ['lɪnɪn] n ropa blanca; (cloth) lino.

liner ['laɪnə*] n vapor m de línea, transatlántico.

linesman ['laɪnzmən] n (SPORT) juez m de línea.

line-up ['laɪnʌp] n alineación f.

linger ['lɪŋgə*] vi retrasarse, tardar en marcharse; (smell, tradition) persistir.

lingerie ['lænʒəri:] n ropa interior (de mujer).

lingering ['lɪŋgərɪŋ] a persistente; (death) lento.

lingo ['lɪŋgəʊ], pl ~**es** n (pej) jerga.

linguist ['lɪŋgwɪst] n lingüista m/f; ~**ic** a lingüístico; ~**ics** n lingüística.

lining ['laɪnɪŋ] n forro.

link [lɪŋk] n (of a chain) eslabón m; (connection) conexión f; (bond) vínculo, lazo // vt vincular, unir; ~**s** npl campo sg de golf; **to ~ up** vt acoplar // vi unirse; ~**-up** n (gen) unión f; (in space) acoplamiento.

lino ['laɪnəʊ], **linoleum** [lɪ'nəʊlɪəm] n linóleo.

lintel ['lɪntl] n dintel m.

lion ['laɪən] n león m; ~**ess** n leona.

lip [lɪp] n labio; (of jug) pico; (of cup etc) borde m; ~**read** vi leer los labios; ~ **service** n: **to pay ~ service to sth** alabar algo pero sin hacer nada; ~**stick**

n lápiz m labial, barra de labios.

liquefy ['lɪkwɪfaɪ] vt liquidar.

liqueur [lɪ'kjuə*] n licor m.

liquid ['lɪkwɪd] a, n líquido.

liquidate ['lɪkwɪdeɪt] vt liquidar; **liquidation** [-'deɪʃən] n liquidación f; **liquidator** n liquidador/a m/f.

liquidize ['lɪkwɪdaɪz] vt (CULIN) licuar.

liquor ['lɪkə*] n licor m, bebidas alcohólicas fpl.

liquorice ['lɪkərɪs] n regaliz m.

lisp [lɪsp] n ceceo.

list [lɪst] n lista; (of ship) inclinación f // vt (write down) hacer una lista de; (enumerate) catalogar // vi (ship) inclinarse.

listen ['lɪsn] vi escuchar, oír; (pay attention) atender; ~**er** n oyente m/f.

listless ['lɪstlɪs] a apático, indiferente.

lit [lɪt] pt, pp of **light**.

litany ['lɪtənɪ] n letanía.

literacy ['lɪtərəsɪ] n capacidad f de leer y escribir; ~ **campaign** campaña de alfabetización.

literal ['lɪtərl] a literal; ~**ly** ad literalmente.

literary ['lɪtərərɪ] a literario.

literate ['lɪtərət] a que sabe leer y escribir; (fig) culto.

literature ['lɪtərɪtʃə*] n literatura; (brochures etc) folletos mpl.

lithe [laɪð] a ágil.

litigation [lɪtɪ'geɪʃən] n litigio.

litre, liter (US) ['li:tə*] n litro.

litter ['lɪtə*] n (rubbish) basura; (paper) papel m tirado; (young animals) camada, cría; (stretcher) camilla; ~ **bin** n papelera; ~**ed** a: ~**ed with** (scattered) esparcido con; (covered with) lleno de.

little ['lɪtl] a (small) pequeño; (not much) poco; often translated by suffix: eg ~ **house** casita // ad poco; **a ~** un poco (de); ~ **by** ~ poco a poco.

liturgy ['lɪtədʒɪ] n liturgia.

live [lɪv] vi vivir // vt (a life) llevar; (experience) vivir // a [laɪv] (animal) vivo; (wire) conectado; (broadcast) en directo; (shell) cargado; **to ~ down** vt hacer olvidar; **to ~ on** vt fus (food) vivirse de, alimentarse de; **to ~ up to** vt fus (fulfil) cumplir con; (justify) justificar.

livelihood ['laɪvlɪhud] n sustento.

lively ['laɪvlɪ] a (gen) vivo; (talk) animado; (pace) rápido; (party, tune) alegre.

liver ['lɪvə*] n (ANAT) hígado; ~**ish** a (fig) rezongón(ona).

livery ['lɪvərɪ] n librea.

lives [laɪvz] pl of **life**.

livestock ['laɪvstɔk] n ganado.

livid ['lɪvɪd] a lívido; (furious) furioso.

living ['lɪvɪŋ] a (alive) vivo // n: **to earn** or **make a ~** ganarse la vida; ~ **conditions** npl condiciones fpl de vida; ~ **room** n sala (de estar); ~ **standards** npl nivel m de vida; ~ **wage** n sueldo suficiente para vivir.

lizard ['lɪzəd] *n* lagartija.

llama ['lɑ:mə] *n* llama.

load [ləud] *n* (*gen*) carga; (*weight*) peso // *vt*: to ~ (**with**) cargar (con); (*fig*) colmar (de); **a ~ of, ~s of** (*fig*) (gran) cantidad de, montones de; **~ed** *a* (*dice*) cargado; (*question, word*) intencionado; (*col: rich*) forrado (de dinero); (*: drunk*) trompa.

loaf [ləuf], *pl* **loaves** *n* (barra de) pan *m* // *vi* (*also*: ~ **about**, ~ **around**) holgazanear.

loan [ləun] *n* préstamo; (*COMM*) empréstito // *vt* prestar; **on** ~ prestado.

loath [ləuθ] *a*: to be ~ to do sth estar poco dispuesto a hacer algo.

loathe [ləuð] *vt* aborrecer; (*person*) odiar; **loathing** *n* aversión *f*, odio; **it fills me with loathing** me da asco.

loaves [ləuvz] *pl of* **loaf**.

lobby ['lɒbɪ] *n* vestíbulo, sala de espera; (*POL: pressure group*) grupo de presión // *vt* presionar.

lobe [ləub] *n* lóbulo.

lobster ['lɒbstə*] *n* langosta; (*large*) bogavante *m*.

local ['ləukl] *a* local // *n* (*pub*) bar *m*; **the ~s** *npl* los vecinos, los del lugar; **~ity** [-'kælɪtɪ] *n* localidad *f*; **~ly** [-kəlɪ] *ad* en la vecindad.

locate [ləu'keɪt] *vt* (*find*) localizar; (*situate*) colocar.

location [ləu'keɪʃən] *n* situación *f*; **on ~** (*CINEMA*) en exteriores, fuera del estudio.

loch [lɒx] *n* lago.

lock [lɒk] *n* (*of door, box*) cerradura; (*of canal*) esclusa; (*stop*) tope *m*; (*of hair*) mechón *m* // *vt* (*with key*) cerrar con llave; (*immobilize*) inmovilizar // *vi* (*door etc*) cerrarse con llave; (*wheels*) bloquearse, trabarse.

locker ['lɒkə*] *n* casillero.

locket ['lɒkɪt] *n* medallón *m*.

lockout ['lɒkaut] *n* paro patronal, lockout *m*.

locomotive [ləukə'məutɪv] *n* locomotora.

locum ['ləukəm] *n* (*MED*) (médico) interino.

locust ['ləukəst] *n* langosta.

lodge [lɒdʒ] *n* casa del guarda; (*porter's*) portería; (*FREEMASONRY*) logia // *vi* (*person*): to ~ (**with**) alojarse (en casa de) // *vt* (*complaint*) presentar; **lodger** *n* huésped/a *m/f*.

lodgings ['lɒdʒɪŋz] *npl* alojamiento *sg*; (*house*) casa *sg* de huéspedes.

loft [lɒft] *n* desván *m*.

lofty ['lɒftɪ] *a* alto; (*haughty*) orgulloso.

log [lɒg] *n* (*of wood*) leño, tronco; (*book*) = **logbook**.

logarithm ['lɒgərɪðəm] *n* logaritmo.

logbook ['lɒgbuk] *n* (*NAUT*) diario de a bordo; (*AVIAT*) libro de vuelo; (*of car*) documentación *f* (del coche).

loggerheads ['lɒgəhedz] *npl*: at ~ (**with**) de pique (con).

logic ['lɒdʒɪk] *n* lógica; **~al** *a* lógico.

logistics [lɒ'dʒɪstɪks] *n* logística.

loin [lɔɪn] *n* (*CULIN*) lomo, solomillo; **~s** *npl* lomos *mpl*; **~ cloth** *n* taparrabo.

loiter ['lɔɪtə*] *vi* perder el tiempo; (*pej*) merodear.

loll [lɒl] *vi* (*also*: ~ **about**) repantigarse.

lollipop ['lɒlɪpɒp] *n* pirulí *m*; (*iced*) polo; **~ man/lady** *n* persona encargada de ayudar a los niños a cruzar la calle.

London ['lʌndən] *n* Londres; **~er** *n* londinense *m/f*.

lone [ləun] *a* solitario.

loneliness ['ləunlɪnɪs] *n* soledad *f*, aislamiento; **lonely** [-lɪ] *a* solitario, solo.

loner ['ləunə*] *n* solitario.

long [lɒŋ] *a* largo // *ad* mucho tiempo, largamente // *vi*: to ~ **for** sth anhelar *o* suspirar por algo; **in the** ~ **run** a la larga; **so** *or* **as** ~ **as** mientras, con tal que; **don't be** ~! ¡no tardes!, ¡vuelve pronto!; **how** ~ **is the street?** ¿cuánto tiene la calle de largo?; **how** ~ **is the lesson?** ¿cuánto dura la lección?; **6 metres** ~ que mide 6 metros, de 6 metros de largo; **6 months** ~ que dura 6 meses, de 6 meses de duración; **all night** ~ toda la noche; ~ **before** mucho antes; **before** ~ (+ *future*) dentro de poco; (+ *past*) poco tiempo después; **at** ~ **las**t al fin, por fin; ~-**distance** *a* (*race*) de larga distancia; (*call*) interurbano; ~-**haired** *a* de pelo largo; ~-**hand** *n* escritura (corriente); ~-**ing** *n* anhelo, ansia; (*nostalgia*) nostalgia // *a* anhelante.

longitude ['lɒŋgɪtju:d] *n* longitud *f*.

long: ~ **jump** *n* salto de longitud; ~-**lost** *a* desaparecido hace mucho tiempo; ~-**playing record (L.P.)** *n* elepé *m*, disco de larga duración; ~-**range** *a* de gran alcance; ~-**sighted** *a* (*fig*) previsor(a); ~-**standing** *a* de mucho tiempo; ~-**suffering** *a* sufrido; ~-**term** *a* a largo plazo; ~ **wave** *a* de onda larga; ~-**winded** *a* prolijo.

loo [lu:] *n* (*col*) wáter *m*.

loofah ['lu:fə] *n* esponja de lufa.

look [luk] *vi* mirar; (*seem*) parecer; (*building etc*): to ~ **south/on to the sea** dar al sur/al mar // *n* mirada; (*glance*) vistazo; (*appearance*) aire *m*, aspecto; ~**s** *npl* físico, apariencia; to ~ **like sb** parecerse a alguien; to ~ **after** *vt fus* cuidar a; to ~ **at** *vt fus* mirar; (*consider*) considerar; to ~ **back** *vi* mirar hacia atrás; to ~ **down on** *vt fus* (*fig*) despreciar, mirar con desprecio; to ~ **for** *vt fus* buscar; to ~ **forward to** *vt fus* esperar con ilusión; to ~ **into** *vt fus* investigar; to ~ **on** *vi* mirar (como espectador); to ~ **out** *vi* (*beware*): to ~ **out (for)** tener cuidado (de); to ~ **out for** *vt fus* (*seek*) buscar; (*await*) esperar; to ~ **round** *vi* volver la cabeza; to ~ **to** *vt fus* ocuparse de; (*rely on*) contar con; to ~ **up** *vi* mirar hacia arriba; (*improve*) mejorar // *vt* (*word*) buscar; (*friend*) visitar; to ~ **up to** *vt fus* admirar; ~-**out**

n (*tower etc*) puesto de observación; (*person*) vigía m; **to be on the ~-out for sth** estar al acecho de algo.
loom [lu:m] n telar m // vi asomarse; (*threaten*) amenazar.
loony ['lu:nɪ] n (*col*) loco/a; ~ **bin** n (*col*) manicomio.
loop [lu:p] n lazo; (*bend*) vuelta, recodo; (*contraceptive*) espiral f; **~hole** n escapatoria.
loose [lu:s] a (*gen*) suelto; (*not tight*) flojo; (*wobbly etc*) movedizo; (*clothes*) ancho; (*morals, discipline*) relajado; **to be at a ~ end** no saber qué hacer; **~ly** ad libremente, aproximadamente; **loosen** vt (*free*) soltar; (*untie*) desatar; (*slacken*) aflojar.
loot [lu:t] n botín m // vt saquear; **~ing** n pillaje m.
lop [lɔp]: **to ~ off** vt cortar; (*branches*) podar.
lop-sided ['lɔp'saɪdɪd] a desequilibrado.
lord [lɔ:d] n señor m; **L~ Smith** Lord Smith; **the L~** el Señor; **the (House of) L~s** la Cámara de los Lores; **~ly** a señorial; (*arrogant*) arrogante; **~ship** n: **your L~ship** su señoría.
lore [lɔ:*] n saber m popular, tradiciones fpl.
lorry ['lɔrɪ] n camión m; ~ **driver** n camionero.
lose [lu:z], pt, pp **lost** vt perder // vi perder, ser vencido; **to ~ (time)** (*clock*) atrasarse; **loser** n perdedor/a m/f.
loss [lɔs] n pérdida; **to be at a ~** no saber qué hacer; **to be a dead ~** ser completamente inútil.
lost [lɔst] pt, pp of **lose** // a perdido; ~ **property** n objetos mpl perdidos.
lot [lɔt] n (*at auctions*) lote m; (*destiny*) suerte f; **the ~** el todo, todos; **a ~ mucho, bastante; **a ~ of, ~s of** mucho(s) (pl); **to draw ~s (for sth)** echar suertes (para decidir algo); **I read a ~** leo bastante.
lotion ['ləuʃən] n loción f.
lottery ['lɔtərɪ] n lotería.
loud [laud] a (*voice*) alto; (*shout*) fuerte; (*noisy*) estrepitoso; (*gaudy*) chillón(ona) // ad (*speak etc*) en alta voz; **~hailer** n megáfono; **~ly** ad (*noisily*) ruidosamente; (*aloud*) en alta voz; **~speaker** n altavoz m.
lounge [laundʒ] n salón m, sala (de estar) // vi reposar, holgazanear; ~ **suit** n traje m de calle.
louse [laus], pl **lice** n piojo.
lousy ['lauzɪ] a (*fig*) vil, asqueroso.
lout [laut] n gamberro.
lovable ['lʌvəbl] a amable, simpático.
love [lʌv] n amor m // vt amar, querer; **to ~ to do** gustar(le a uno) mucho hacer; **to be in ~ with** estar enamorado de; **to make ~** hacer el amor; **for the ~ of** por amor de; **'15 ~'** (*TENNIS*) 15 a cero; **I ~ paella** me gusta mucho la paella; **'with ~'** con cariño; ~ **affair** n aventura

sentimental; ~ **letter** n carta de amor; ~ **life** n vida sentimental.
lovely ['lʌvlɪ] a (*delightful*) precioso, encantador(a); (*beautiful*) hermoso.
lover ['lʌvə*] n amante m/f; (*amateur*): **a ~ of** un aficionado a o un amante de.
lovesong ['lʌvsɔŋ] n canción f de amor.
loving ['lʌvɪŋ] a amoroso, cariñoso.
low [ləu] a, ad bajo // n (*METEOROLOGY*) área de baja presión // vi (*cow*) mugir; **to feel ~** sentirse deprimido; **to turn (down) ~** vt bajar; **~-cut** a (*dress*) escotado.
lower ['ləuə*] vt bajar; (*reduce*) reducir // vr: **to ~ o.s.** to (*fig*) rebajarse a.
low: **~-grade** a de baja calidad; **~ly** a humilde; **~-lying** a de bajo nivel.
loyal ['lɔɪəl] a leal; **~ty** n lealtad f.
lozenge ['lɔzɪndʒ] n (*MED*) pastilla.
L.P. n abbr of **long-playing record.**
L-plates ['ɛlpleɪts] npl placa de aprendiz de conductor.
Ltd abbr of **limited company** S.A.
lubricant ['lu:brɪkənt] n lubricante m; **lubricate** [-keɪt] vt lubricar, engrasar.
lucid ['lu:sɪd] a lúcido; **~ity** [-'sɪdɪtɪ] n lucidez f.
luck [lʌk] n suerte f; **bad ~** mala suerte; **good ~!** ¡que tengas suerte!, ¡suerte!; **~ily** ad afortunadamente; **~y** a afortunado.
lucrative ['lu:krətɪv] a lucrativo.
ludicrous ['lu:dɪkrəs] a absurdo.
ludo ['lu:dəu] n parchís m.
lug [lʌg] vt (*drag*) arrastrar; (*pull*) tirar de.
luggage ['lʌgɪdʒ] n equipaje m; ~ **rack** n (*in train*) rejilla, redecilla; (*on car*) vaca, portaequipajes m inv.
lukewarm ['lu:kwɔ:m] a tibio, templado.
lull [lʌl] n tregua // vt (*child*) acunar; (*person, fear*) calmar.
lullaby ['lʌləbaɪ] n canción f de cuna.
lumbago [lʌm'beɪgəu] n lumbago.
lumber ['lʌmbə*] n (*junk*) trastos viejos mpl; (*wood*) maderos mpl; **~jack** n maderero.
luminous ['lu:mɪnəs] a luminoso.
lump [lʌmp] n terrón m; (*fragment*) trozo; (*in sauce*) grumo; (*in throat*) nudo; (*swelling*) bulto // vt (*also:* **~ together**) amontonar; **a ~ sum** suma global; **~y** a (*sauce*) lleno de grumos.
lunacy ['lu:nəsɪ] n locura.
lunar ['lu:nə*] a lunar.
lunatic ['lu:nətɪk] a, n loco/a; ~ **asylum** n manicomio.
lunch [lʌntʃ] n almuerzo, comida // vi almorzar; ~ **time** n hora del almuerzo o de comer.
luncheon ['lʌntʃən] n almuerzo; ~ **meat** n pastel m de carne.
lung [lʌŋ] n pulmón m; ~ **cancer** n cáncer m de pulmón.
lunge [lʌndʒ] vi (*also:* ~ **forward**) abalanzarse; **to ~ at** arremeter contra.
lurch [lə:tʃ] vi dar sacudidas // n sacudida;

to leave sb in the ~ dejar a uno plantado.

lure [luɔ°] n (*bait*) cebo; (*decoy*) señuelo // vt atraer, seducir.

lurid ['luɔrɪd] a (*light*) misterioso; (*dress*) chillón(ona); (*account*) sensacional; (*detail*) horrible.

lurk [lɔ:k] vi (*hide*) esconderse; (*wait*) estar al acecho.

luscious ['lʌʃɔs] a delicioso.

lush [lʌʃ] a exuberante.

lust [lʌst] n lujuria; (*greed*) codicia; to ~ after vt fus codiciar; ~ful a lascivo, lujurioso.

lustre, luster (*US*) ['lʌstɔ°] n lustre m, brillo.

lusty ['lʌstɪ] a robusto, fuerte.

lute [lu:t] n laúd m.

Luxembourg   ['lʌksɔmbɔːg]   n Luxemburgo.

luxuriant [lʌg'zjuɔrɪɔnt] a exuberante.

luxurious [lʌg'zjuɔrɪɔs] a lujoso; **luxury** ['lʌkʃɔrɪ] n lujo // cpd de lujo.

lying ['laɪɪŋ] n mentiras fpl // a mentiroso.

lynch [lɪntʃ] vt linchar; ~ing n linchamiento.

lynx [lɪnks] n lince m.

lyre ['laɪɔ°] n lira.

lyric ['lɪrɪk] a lírico; ~s npl (*of song*) letra sg; ~al a lírico.

M

m. abbr of metre; mile; million.

M.A. abbr of Master of Arts licenciado en letras.

mac [mæk] n impermeable m.

macaroni [mækɔ'rɔunɪ] n macarrones mpl.

mace [meɪs] n (*BOT*) macis f.

machine [mɔ'ʃi:n] n máquina // vt (*dress etc*) coser a máquina; ~ gun n ametralladora; ~ry n maquinaria; (*fig*) mecanismo; **machinist** n operario (de máquina).

mackerel ['mækrl] n, pl inv caballa.

mackintosh ['mækɪntɔʃ] n impermeable m.

mad [mæd] a (*gen*) loco; (*crazed*) demente; (*angry*) furioso.

madam ['mædɔm] n señora.

madden ['mædn] vt volver loco.

made [meɪd] pt, pp of make; ~-to-measure a hecho a la medida.

madly ['mædlɪ] ad locamente.

madman ['mædmɔn] n loco.

madness ['mædnɪs] n locura.

magazine [mægɔ'zi:n] n revista; (*MIL: store*) almacén m; (*of firearm*) recámara.

maggot ['mægɔt] n gusano.

magic ['mædʒɪk] n magia // a mágico; ~al a mágico; ~ian [mɔ'dʒɪʃɔn] n mago; (*conjurer*) prestidigitador m.

magistrate ['mædʒɪstreɪt] n juez m/f (municipal).

magnanimous [mæg'nænɪmɔs] a magnánimo.

magnate ['mægneɪt] n magnate m.

magnet ['mægnɪt] n imán m; ~ic [-'nɛtɪk] a magnético; ~ism n magnetismo.

magnification [mægnɪfɪ'keɪʃɔn] n aumento.

magnificence [mæg'nɪfɪsns] n magnificencia; **magnificent** [-nt] a magnífico.

magnify ['mægnɪfaɪ] vt aumentar; (*fig*) exagerar; ~ing glass n lupa.

magnitude ['mægnɪtju:d] n magnitud f.

magnolia [mæg'nɔulɪɔ] n magnolia.

magpie ['mægpaɪ] n urraca.

mahogany [mɔ'hɔgɔnɪ] n caoba // cpd de caoba.

maid [meɪd] n criada; old ~ (*pej*) solterona.

maiden ['meɪdn] n doncella // a (*aunt etc*) solterona; (*speech, voyage*) inaugural; ~ name n nombre m de soltera.

mail [meɪl] n correo; (*letters*) cartas fpl // vt (*post*) echar al correo; (*send*) mandar por correo; ~box n (*US*) buzón m; ~-order n pedido postal; (*business*) venta por correo.

maim [meɪm] vt mutilar, lisiar.

main [meɪn] a principal, mayor // n (*pipe*) cañería maestra; the ~s (*ELEC*) la red eléctrica; in the ~ en general; ~land n continente m; ~stay n (*fig*) pilar m; ~stream n corriente f principal.

maintain [meɪn'teɪn] vt mantener; (*keep up*) conservar (en buen estado); (*affirm*) sostener; **maintenance** ['meɪntɔnɔns] n mantenimiento.

maisonette [meɪzɔ'nɛt] n apartamento de dos pisos.

maize [meɪz] n maíz m.

majestic [mɔ'dʒɛstɪk] a majestuoso; **majesty** ['mædʒɪstɪ] n majestad f.

major ['meɪdʒɔ°] n (*MIL*) comandante m // a principal; (*MUS*) mayor.

Majorca [mɔ'jɔ:kɔ] n Mallorca.

majority [mɔ'dʒɔrɪtɪ] n mayoría.

make [meɪk] pt, pp **made** vt hacer; (*manufacture*) hacer, fabricar; (*cause to be*): to ~ sb sad hacer o poner triste a alguien; (*force*): to ~ sb do sth obligar a uno a hacer algo; (*equal*): 2 and 2 ~ 4 2 y 2 son 4 // n marca; to ~ do with contentarse con; to ~ for vt fus (*place*) dirigirse a; to ~ out vt (*decipher*) descifrar; (*understand*) entender; (*see*) distinguir; to ~ up vt (*invent*) inventar; (*parcel*) envolver // vi reconciliarse; (*with cosmetics*) maquillarse; to ~ up for vt fus compensar; ~-believe a fingido; **maker** n fabricante m/f; ~shift a improvisado; ~-up n maquillaje m.

making ['meɪkɪŋ] n (*fig*): in the ~ en vías de formación.

malaise [mæ'leɪz] n malestar m.

malaria [mɔ'lɛɔrɪɔ] n malaria.

Malay [mɔ'leɪ] a, n malayo/a.

Malaysia [mɔ'leɪzɪɔ] n Malaysia.

male [meɪl] n (BIOL, ELEC) macho // a (sex, attitude) masculino; (child etc) varón.
malevolent [mə'levələnt] a malévolo.
malfunction [mæl'fʌŋkʃən] n funcionamiento defectuoso.
malice ['mælɪs] n (ill will) malevolencia; (rancour) rencor m; **malicious** [mə'lɪʃəs] a malévolo; rencoroso.
malign [mə'laɪn] vt difamar, calumniar // a maligno.
malignant [mə'lɪɡnənt] a (MED) maligno.
malingerer [mə'lɪŋɡərə*] n enfermo fingido.
malleable ['mælɪəbl] a maleable.
mallet ['mælɪt] n mazo.
malnutrition [mælnju:'trɪʃən] n desnutrición f.
malpractice [mæl'præktɪs] n falta profesional.
malt [mɔːlt] n malta.
Malta ['mɔːltə] n Malta; **Maltese** [-'tiːz] a, n, pl inv maltés/esa m/f.
maltreat [mæl'triːt] vt maltratar.
mammal ['mæml] n mamífero.
mammoth ['mæməθ] n mamut m // a gigantesco.
man [mæn], pl **men** n hombre m; (CHESS) pieza // vt (NAUT) tripular; (MIL) guarnecer; **an old** ~ un viejo; ~ **and wife** marido y mujer.
manacle ['mænəkl] n manilla; ~**s** npl grillos mpl.
manage ['mænɪdʒ] vi arreglárselas, ir tirando // vt (be in charge of) dirigir; (person etc) manejar; ~**able** a manejable; ~**ment** n dirección f, administración f; ~**manager/ess** n director/a m/f; (SPORT) entrenador/a m/f; **managerial** [-ə'dʒɪərɪəl] a directivo; **managing director** n director m general.
mandarin ['mændərɪn] n (also: ~ **orange**) mandarina; (person) mandarín m.
mandate ['mændeɪt] n mandato.
mandatory ['mændətərɪ] a obligatorio.
mandolin(e) ['mændəlɪn] n mandolina.
mane [meɪn] n (of horse) crin f; (of lion) melena.
manfully ['mænfəlɪ] ad violentemente.
mangle ['mæŋɡl] vt mutilar, magullar // n rodillo.
mango ['mæŋɡəʊ], pl ~**es** n mango.
mangy ['meɪndʒɪ] a roñoso, sarnoso.
manhandle ['mænhændl] vt maltratar.
manhole ['mænhəʊl] n pozo de visita.
manhood ['mænhʊd] n edad f viril.
man-hour ['mæn'aʊə*] n hora-hombre f.
manhunt ['mænhʌnt] n caza de hombre.
mania ['meɪnɪə] n manía; **maniac** ['meɪnɪæk] n maníaco; (fig) maniático.
manicure ['mænɪkjʊə*] n manicura // vt (person) hacer la manicura a; ~ **set** n estuche m de manicura.
manifest ['mænɪfest] vt manifestar, mostrar // a manifiesto; ~**ation** [-'teɪʃən] n manifestación f.

manifesto [mænɪ'festəʊ] n manifiesto.
manipulate [mə'nɪpjʊleɪt] vt manipular, manejar.
mankind [mæn'kaɪnd] n la humanidad, el género humano.
manly ['mænlɪ] a varonil.
man-made ['mæn'meɪd] a artificial.
manner ['mænə*] n manera, modo; (behaviour) conducta, manera de ser; (type) clase f; ~**s** npl modales mpl, educación f; **bad** ~**s** mala educación; ~**ism** n hábito, peculiaridad f.
manoeuvre, maneuver (US) [mə'nuːvə*] vt, vi maniobrar // n maniobra.
manor ['mænə*] n (also: ~ **house**) casa solariega.
manpower ['mænpaʊə*] n mano f de obra.
mansion ['mænʃən] n palacio, casa grande.
manslaughter ['mænslɔːtə*] n homicidio no premeditado.
mantelpiece ['mæntlpiːs] n repisa, chimenea.
mantle ['mæntl] n manto; (fig) capa.
manual ['mænjʊəl] a manual // n manual m; (MUS) teclado.
manufacture [mænju'fæktʃə*] vt fabricar // n fabricación f; **manufacturer** n fabricante m/f.
manure [mə'njʊə*] n estiércol m, abono.
manuscript ['mænjuskrɪpt] n manuscrito.
Manx [mæŋks] a de la Isla de Man.
many ['menɪ] det muchos(as) // pron muchos/as; **a great** ~ muchísimos, buen número de; ~ **a time** muchas veces.
map [mæp] n mapa m // vt trazar el mapa de; **to** ~ **out** vt proyectar.
maple ['meɪpl] n arce m.
mar [mɑː*] vt estropear.
marathon ['mærəθən] n maratón m.
marauder [mə'rɔːdə*] n merodeador m; (intruder) intruso.
marble ['mɑːbl] n mármol m; (toy) canica.
March [mɑːtʃ] n marzo.
march [mɑːtʃ] vi (MIL) marchar; (fig) caminar con resolución // n marcha; (demonstration) manifestación f, marcha; ~**-past** n desfile m.
mare [mɛə*] n yegua.
margarine [mɑːdʒə'riːn] n margarina.
margin ['mɑːdʒɪn] n margen m; ~**al** a marginal.
marigold ['mærɪɡəʊld] n caléndula.
marijuana [mærɪ'wɑːnə] n marijuana.
marina [mə'riːnə] n marina.
marine [mə'riːn] a marino // n soldado de marina.
marital ['mærɪtl] a matrimonial; ~ **status** estado civil.
maritime ['mærɪtaɪm] a marítimo.
marjoram ['mɑːdʒərəm] n orégano.
mark [mɑːk] n marca, señal f; (imprint) huella; (stain) mancha; (SCOL) puntuación f, nota; (currency) marco // vt marcar;

manchar; (SCOL) calificar; **to ~ time**
marcar el paso; **to ~ out** vt trazar; **~ed**
a marcado, acusado; **~er** n (sign)
marcador m; (bookmark) registro.

market ['mɑːkɪt] n mercado // vt (COMM)
vender; **black ~** mercado negro;
Common M~ Mercado Común; **~ day** n
día de mercado; **~ garden** n (Brit)
huerto; **~ing** n márketing m.
mercadotecnia; **~-place** n mercado; **~
research** n análisis m inv de mercados.

marksman ['mɑːksmən] n tirador m;
~ship n puntería.

marmalade ['mɑːməleɪd] n mermelada
(de naranjas).

maroon [mə'ruːn] vt (fig): **to be ~ed**
(shipwrecked) naufragarse; (fig) quedar
abandonado // a marrón.

marquee [mɑː'kiː] n entoldado.

marquess, marquis ['mɑːkwɪs] n
marqués m.

marriage ['mærɪdʒ] n (state) matrimonio;
(wedding) boda; (act) casamiento; **~
bureau** n agencia matrimonial; **~
certificate** n partida de casamiento.

married ['mærɪd] a casado; (life, love)
conyugal.

marrow ['mærəu] n médula; (vegetable)
calabacín m.

marry ['mærɪ] vt casarse con; (subj: father,
priest etc) casar // vi (also: **get married**)
casarse.

marsh [mɑːʃ] n pantano; (salt ~) marisma.

marshal ['mɑːʃl] n (MIL) mariscal m; (at
sports meeting etc) oficial m // vt (facts)
ordenar; (soldiers) formar.

marshmallow [mɑːʃ'mæləu] n
malvavisco.

marshy ['mɑːʃɪ] a pantanoso.

martial ['mɑːʃl] a marcial; **~ law** n ley f
marcial.

martyr ['mɑːtə*] n mártir m/f // vt
martirizar; **~dom** n martirio.

marvel ['mɑːvl] n maravilla, prodigio //
vi: **to ~ (at)** maravillarse (de); **~lous,
~ous** (US) a maravilloso.

Marxism ['mɑːksɪzəm] n marxismo;
Marxist [-sɪst] a, n marxista m/f.

marzipan ['mɑːzɪpæn] n mazapán m.

mascara [mæs'kɑːrə] n rímel m.

mascot ['mæskət] n mascota.

masculine ['mæskjulɪn] a masculino;
masculinity [-'lɪnɪtɪ] n masculinidad f.

mash [mæʃ] n (mix) mezcla; (pulp)
amasijo; **~ed potatoes** puré m de
patatas.

mask [mɑːsk] n máscara // vt enmascarar.

masochist ['mæsəukɪst] n masoquista m/f.

mason ['meɪsn] n (also: **stone~**) albañil
m; (also: **free~**) masón m; **~ic**
[mə'sɔnɪk] a masónico; **~ry** n masonería;
(building) mampostería.

masquerade [mæskə'reɪd] n baile m de
máscaras; (fig) farsa // vi: **to ~ as**
disfrazarse de, hacerse pasar por.

mass [mæs] n (people) muchedumbre f;
(PHYSICS) masa; (REL) misa; (great quantity)

montón m // vi reunirse; (MIL)
concentrarse; **the ~es** las masas.

massacre ['mæsəkə*] n masacre f // vt
masacrar.

massage ['mæsɑːʒ] n masaje m // vt dar
masaje a.

masseur [mæ'səː*] n masajista m;
masseuse [-'səːz] n masajista f.

massive ['mæsɪv] a (solid) sólido; (head
etc) grande; (support, intervention) masivo.

mass media ['mæs'miːdɪə] npl medios mpl
de comunicación masiva.

mass-production ['mæsprə'dʌkʃən] n
fabricación f en serie.

mast [mɑːst] n (NAUT) mástil m; (RADIO etc)
torre f.

master ['mɑːstə*] n maestro; (landowner)
señor m, amo; (in secondary school)
profesor m; (title for boys): **M~ X**
Señorito X // vt dominar; (learn) aprender
a fondo; **~ key** n llave f maestra; **~ly** a
magistral; **~mind** n inteligencia superior
// vt dirigir, planear; **M~ of Arts** n
Licenciado en Letras; **~piece** n obra
maestra; **~ plan** n plan m rector; **~
stroke** n golpe m maestro; **~y** n
maestría.

masturbate ['mæstəbeɪt] vi masturbarse;
masturbation [-'beɪʃən] n masturbación f.

mat [mæt] n estera; (also: **door~**) felpudo
// a = **matt**.

match [mætʃ] n cerilla; (game) partido;
(fig) igual m/f // vt emparejar; (go well
with) hacer juego con; (equal) igualar, ser
igual a // vi hacer juego; **to be a good ~**
hacer una buena pareja; **~box** n caja de
cerillas; **~ing** a que hace juego; **~less** a
sin par, incomparable.

mate [meɪt] n compañero; (assistant)
ayudante m/f; (CHESS) mate m; (in
merchant navy) segundo de a bordo // vi
acoplarse, parearse // vt acoplar, parear.

material [mə'tɪərɪəl] n (substance)
materia; (equipment) material m; (cloth)
tela, tejido; (data) datos mpl // a (material;
(important) importante; **~s** npl materiales
mpl; **~istic** [-'lɪstɪk] a materialista;
~ize vi materializarse.

maternal [mə'təːnl] a maternal.

maternity [mə'təːnɪtɪ] n maternidad f; **~
dress** n vestido premamá; **~ hospital** n
hospital m de maternidad.

mathematical [mæθə'mætɪkl] a
matemático; **mathematician** [-mə'tɪʃən] n
matemático; **mathematics** [-tɪks], **maths**
[mæθs] n matemáticas fpl.

matinée ['mætɪneɪ] n función f de tarde.

mating ['meɪtɪŋ] n apareamiento; **~ call**
n llamada del macho; **~ season** n época
de celo.

matriarchal [meɪtrɪ'ɑːkl] a matriarcal.

matrices ['meɪtrɪsiːz] pl of **matrix**.

matrimonial [mætrɪ'məunɪəl] a
matrimonial.

matrimony ['mætrɪmənɪ] n matrimonio.

matrix ['meɪtrɪks], pl **matrices** n matriz
f.

matron ['meɪtrən] *n* (*in hospital*) enfermera jefe; (*in school*) ama de llaves; ~ly *a* de matrona; (*fig: figure*) corpulento.

matt [mæt] *a* mate.

matted ['mætɪd] *a* enmarañado.

matter ['mætə*] *n* cuestión *f*, asunto; (*PHYSICS*) sustancia, materia; (*content*) contenido; (*MED: pus*) pus *m* // *vi* importar; it doesn't ~ no importa; what's the ~? ¿qué pasa?; no ~ what pase lo que pase; as a ~ of course por rutina; as a ~ of fact de hecho; ~-of-fact *a* prosaico, práctico.

mattress ['mætrɪs] *n* colchón *m*.

mature [mə'tjuə*] *a* maduro // *vi* madurar; **maturity** *n* madurez *f*.

maudlin ['mɔ:dlɪn] *a* llorón(ona).

maul [mɔ:l] *vt* magullar.

mausoleum [mɔ:sə'lɪəm] *n* mausoleo.

mauve [məuv] *a* de color malva.

maxim ['mæksɪm] *n* máxima.

maxima ['mæksɪmə] *pl of* **maximum**.

maximum ['mæksɪməm] *a* máximo // *n*, *pl* **maxima** máximo.

May [meɪ] *n* mayo.

may [meɪ] *vi* (*conditional*: **might**) (*indicating possibility*): he ~ come puede que venga; (*be allowed to*): ~ I smoke? ¿puedo fumar?; (*wishes*): ~ God bless you! que Dios le bendiga.

maybe ['meɪbi:] *ad* quizá(s).

mayday ['meɪdeɪ] *n* S.O.S. *m* (*llamada de socorro internacional*).

mayhem ['meɪhɛm] *n* mutilación *f* criminal.

mayonnaise [meɪə'neɪz] *n* mayonesa.

mayor [mɛə*] *n* alcalde *m*; ~ess *n* alcaldesa.

maypole ['meɪpəul] *n* mayo.

maze [meɪz] *n* laberinto.

M.D. *abbr of* **Doctor of Medicine.**

me [mi:] *pron* me; (*stressed, after prep*) mí; with ~ conmigo; it's ~ soy yo.

meadow ['mɛdəu] *n* prado, pradera.

meagre, meager (*US*) ['mi:gə*] *a* escaso, pobre.

meal [mi:l] *n* comida; (*flour*) harina; ~ time *n* hora de comer.

mean [mi:n] *a* (*with money*) tacaño; (*unkind*) mezquino, malo; (*shabby*) humilde, vil; (*of poor quality*) inferior; (*average*) medio // *vt, pt, pp* **meant** (*signify*) querer decir, significar; (*intend*): to ~ to do sth pensar *o* pretender hacer algo // *n* medio, término medio; ~s *npl* medio *sg*, manera *sg*; (*resource*) recursos *mpl*, medios *mpl*; by ~s of mediante, por medio de; by all ~s! ¡naturalmente!, ¡claro que sí!; do you ~ it? ¿lo dices en serio?; what do you ~? ¿qué quiere decir?

meander [mɪ'ændə*] *vi* (*river*) serpentear; (*person*) vagar.

meaning ['mi:nɪŋ] *n* significado, sentido; ~ful *a* significativo; ~less *a* sin sentido.

meanness ['mi:nnɪs] *n* (*with money*) tacañería; (*shabbiness*) vileza, bajeza; (*unkindness*) maldad *f*, mezquindad *f*.

meant [mɛnt] *pt, pp of* **mean.**

meantime ['mi:ntaɪm], **meanwhile** ['mi:nwaɪl] *ad* (*also*: in the ~) mientras tanto.

measles ['mi:zlz] *n* sarampión *m*; German ~ rubéola.

measly ['mi:zlɪ] *a* (*col*) miserable.

measure ['mɛʒə*] *vt* medir; (*for clothes etc*) tomar las medidas a; (*consider*) pesar // *vi* medir // *n* medida; (*ruler*) regla; ~d *a* moderado; (*tone*) mesurado; ~ments *npl* medidas *fpl*.

meat [mi:t] *n* carne *f*; cold ~ fiambre *m*; ~ball *n* albóndiga; ~ pie *n* pastel *m* de carne; ~y *a* carnoso; (*fig*) sustancioso.

mechanic [mɪ'kænɪk] *n* mecánico; ~s *n* mecánica // *npl* mecanismo *sg*; ~al *a* mecánico.

mechanism ['mɛkənɪzəm] *n* mecanismo.

mechanization [mɛkənaɪ'zeɪʃən] *n* mecanización *f*.

medal ['mɛdl] *n* medalla; ~lion [mɪ'dælɪən] *n* medallón *m*; ~list, ~ist (*US*) *n* (*SPORT*) ganador/a *m/f*.

meddle ['mɛdl] *vi*: to ~ in entrometerse en; to ~ with sth manosear algo; ~some *a* entrometido.

media ['mi:dɪə] *npl* medios *mpl* de comunicación.

mediaeval [mɛdɪ'i:vl] *a* = **medieval.**

mediate ['mi:dɪeɪt] *vi* mediar; **mediation** [-'eɪʃən] *n* mediación *f*; **mediator** *n* intermediario, mediador/a *m/f*.

medical ['mɛdɪkl] *a* médico // *n* reconocimiento médico.

medicated ['mɛdɪkeɪtɪd] *a* medicinal.

medicinal [mɛ'dɪsɪnl] *a* medicinal.

medicine ['mɛdsɪn] *n* medicina; (*drug*) medicamento; ~ chest *n* botiquín *m*.

medieval [mɛdɪ'i:vl] *a* medieval.

mediocre [mi:dɪ'əukə*] *a* mediocre; **mediocrity** [-'ɔkrɪtɪ] *n* mediocridad *f*.

meditate ['mɛdɪteɪt] *vi* meditar; **meditation** [-'teɪʃən] *n* meditación *f*.

Mediterranean [mɛdɪtə'reɪnɪən] *a* mediterráneo; the ~ (Sea) el (Mar) Mediterráneo.

medium ['mi:dɪəm] *a* mediano, regular // *n* (*pl* **media: means**) medio; (*pl* **mediums**: *person*) médium *m/f*.

medley ['mɛdlɪ] *n* mezcla; (*MUS*) popurrí *m*.

meek [mi:k] *a* manso, dócil.

meet [mi:t] *pt, pp* **met** *vt* (*gen*) encontrar; (*accidentally*) encontrarse con, tropezar con; (*by arrangement*) reunirse con; (*for the first time*) conocer; (*go and fetch*) ir a buscar; (*opponent*) enfrentarse con; (*obligations*) cumplir // *vi* encontrarse; (*in session*) reunirse; (*join: objects*) unirse; (*get to know*) conocerse; to ~ with *vt fus* reunirse con; (*face: difficulty*) tropezar con; ~ing *n* encuentro; (*session: of club etc*) reunión *f*; (*interview*) entrevista; (*COMM*) junta, sesión *f*; (*POL*) mítin *m*.

megalomaniac [mɛgələu'meɪnɪæk] a, n megalómano/a.

megaphone ['mɛgəfəun] n megáfono.

melancholy ['mɛlənkəlɪ] n melancolía // a melancólico.

melee ['mɛleɪ] n refriega.

mellow ['mɛləu] a (sound) dulce; (colour) suave; (fruit) maduro // vi (person) madurar.

melodious [mɪ'ləudɪəs] a melodioso.

melodrama ['mɛləudrɑːmə] n melodrama m.

melody ['mɛlədɪ] n melodía.

melon ['mɛlən] n melón m.

melt [mɛlt] vi (metal) fundirse; (snow) derretirse; (fig) ablandarse // vt (also: ~ down) fundir; to ~ away vi desvanecerse; ~ing point n punto de fusión; ~ing pot n (fig) crisol m.

member ['mɛmbə*] n (gen) miembro; (of club) socio; M~ of Parliament (M.P.) diputado; ~ship n (members) número de miembros; to seek ~ship of pedir el ingreso a; ~ship card carnet m de socio.

membrane ['mɛmbreɪn] n membrana.

memento [mə'mɛntəu] n recuerdo.

memo ['mɛməu] n apunte m, nota.

memoirs ['mɛmwɑːz] npl memorias fpl.

memorable ['mɛmərəbl] a memorable.

memorandum [mɛmə'rændəm], pl -da [-də] n apunte m, nota; (POL) memorándum m.

memorial [mɪ'mɔːrɪəl] n monumento conmemorativo // a conmemorativo.

memorize ['mɛməraɪz] vt aprender de memoria.

memory ['mɛmərɪ] n memoria; (recollection) recuerdo.

men [mɛn] pl of **man**.

menace ['mɛnəs] n amenaza // vt amenazar; **menacing** a amenazador(a).

menagerie [mɪ'nædʒərɪ] n casa de fieras.

mend [mɛnd] vt reparar, arreglar; (darn) zurcir // vi reponerse // n (gen) remiendo; (darn) zurcido; **to be on the ~** ir mejorando; ~ing n reparación f; (clothes) ropa por remendar.

menial ['miːnɪəl] a doméstico; (pej) bajo // n criado.

meningitis [mɛnɪn'dʒaɪtɪs] n meningitis f.

menopause ['mɛnəupɔːz] n menopausia.

menstruate ['mɛnstrueɪt] vi menstruar; **menstruation** [-'eɪʃən] n menstruación f.

mental ['mɛntl] a mental; ~ity [-'tælɪtɪ] n mentalidad f.

mention ['mɛnʃən] n mención f // vt mencionar; (speak of) hablar de; **don't ~ it!** ¡de nada!

menu ['mɛnjuː] n (set ~) menú m; (printed) carta.

mercenary ['mɜːsɪnərɪ] a, n mercenario.

merchandise ['mɜːtʃəndaɪz] n mercancías fpl.

merchant ['mɜːtʃənt] n comerciante m/f; ~ **bank** n banco comercial; ~ **navy** n marina mercante.

merciful ['mɜːsɪful] a compasivo; (fortunate) afortunado.

merciless ['mɜːsɪlɪs] a despiadado.

mercury ['mɜːkjurɪ] n mercurio.

mercy ['mɜːsɪ] n compasión f; (REL) misericordia; **at the ~ of** a la merced de.

mere [mɪə*] a simple, mero; ~ly ad simplemente, sólo.

merge [mɜːdʒ] vt (join) unir; (mix) mezclar; (fuse) fundir // vi unirse; (COMM) fusionarse; **merger** n (COMM) fusión f.

meridian [mə'rɪdɪən] n meridiano.

meringue [mə'ræŋ] n merengue m.

merit ['mɛrɪt] n mérito // vt merecer.

mermaid ['mɜːmeɪd] n sirena.

merriment ['mɛrɪmənt] n alegría.

merry ['mɛrɪ]38 a alegre; ~-go-round n tiovivo.

mesh [mɛʃ] n malla; (TECH) engranaje m // vi (gears) engranar.

mesmerize ['mɛzməraɪz] vt hipnotizar.

mess [mɛs] n (gen) confusión f; (of objects) revoltijo; (tangle) lío; (MIL) comedor m; **to ~ about** vi (col) perder el tiempo; (pass the time) entretenerse; **to ~ about with** vt fus (col) (play with) divertirse con; (handle) manosear; **to ~ up** vt (disarrange) desordenar; (spoil) estropear; (dirty) ensuciar.

message ['mɛsɪdʒ] n recado, mensaje m.

messenger ['mɛsɪndʒə*] n mensajero/a.

messy ['mɛsɪ] a (dirty) sucio; (untidy) desordenado.

met [mɛt] pt, pp of **meet**.

metabolism [mɛ'tæbəlɪzəm] n metabolismo.

metal ['mɛtl] n metal m; ~lic [-'tælɪk] a metálico; ~lurgy [-'tælədʒɪ] n metalurgia.

metamorphosis [mɛtə'mɔːfəsɪs], pl -ses [-siːz] n metamorfosis f inv.

metaphor ['mɛtəfə*] n metáfora.

metaphysics [mɛtə'fɪzɪks] n metafísica.

mete [miːt]: **to ~ out** vt fus (gen) repartir; (punishment) imponer.

meteor ['miːtɪə*] n meteoro.

meteorological [miːtɪərə'lɔdʒɪkl] a meteorológico; **meteorology** [-'rɔlədʒɪ] n meteorología.

meter ['miːtə*] n (instrument) contador m; (US) = **metre**.

method ['mɛθəd] n método; ~ical [mɪ'θɔdɪkl] a metódico.

Methodist ['mɛθədɪst] a, n metodista m/f.

meths [mɛθs], **methylated spirit** ['mɛθɪleɪtɪd-] n alcohol m metilado o desnaturalizado.

meticulous [mɛ'tɪkjuləs] a meticuloso.

metre, meter (US) ['miːtə*] n metro.

metric ['mɛtrɪk] a métrico.

metronome ['mɛtrənəum] n metrónomo.

metropolis [mɪ'trɔpəlɪs] n metrópoli f.

mettle ['mɛtl] n (spirit) valor m, ánimo; (tone) temple m.

mew [mjuː] vi (cat) maullar.

mews [mjuːz] n: ~ **cottage** casa

acondicionada en antiguos establos o cocheras.

Mexican ['mɛksɪkən] a, n mejicano/a, mexicano/a (AM).

Mexico ['mɛksɪkəu] n Méjico, México (AM).

mezzanine ['mɛtsəniːn] n entresuelo.

miaow [miːˈau] vi maullar.

mice [maɪs] pl of **mouse.**

microbe ['maɪkrəub] n microbio.

micro... [maɪkrəu] pref micro...; **~film** n microfilm m; **~phone** n micrófono; **~processor** n microprocesador m; **~scope** n microscopio; **~scopic** [-'skɔpɪk] a microscópico; **~wave** a de microonda.

mid [mɪd] a: **in ~ May** a mediados de mayo; **in ~ afternoon** a media tarde; **in ~ air** en el aire; **~day** n mediodía m.

middle ['mɪdl] n medio, centro; (half) mitad f; (waist) cintura // a medio; (quantity, size) mediano; **~-aged** a de mediana edad; **the M~ Ages** npl la Edad Media; **~-class** a de clase media; **M~ East** n Oriente m Medio; **~man** n intermediario; **~ name** n segundo nombre.

middling ['mɪdlɪŋ] a mediano.

midge [mɪdʒ] n mosca.

midget ['mɪdʒɪt] a enano // a minúsculo.

Midlands ['mɪdləndz] npl la región central de Inglaterra.

midnight ['mɪdnaɪt] n medianoche f.

midriff ['mɪdrɪf] n diafragma m.

midst [mɪdst] n: **in the ~ of** entre, en medio de.

midsummer [mɪd'sʌmə°] n: **a ~ day** un día de pleno verano.

midway [mɪd'weɪ] a, ad: **~ (between)** a mitad de camino, a medio camino (entre).

midweek [mɪd'wiːk] ad entre semana.

midwife ['mɪdwaɪf], pl **-wives** [-waɪvz] n comadrona, partera; **~ry** [-wɪfərɪ] n partería.

midwinter [mɪd'wɪntə°] n: **in ~** en pleno invierno.

might [maɪt] vb: **he ~ be there** podría estar allí, puede que está allí; **I ~ as well go** más vale que vaya; **you ~ like to try** podría intentar // n fuerza, poder m; **~y** a fuerte, poderoso.

migraine ['miːgreɪn] n jaqueca.

migrant ['maɪgrənt] n (bird) ave f migratoria; (person) emigrante m/f; (fig) nómada m/f // a migratorio; (worker) emigrante.

migrate [maɪ'greɪt] vi emigrar; **migration** [-'greɪʃən] n emigración f.

mike [maɪk] n abbr of **microphone** micro.

mild [maɪld] a (character) pacífico; (climate) templado; (slight) ligero; (taste) suave; (illness) benigno, leve.

mildew ['mɪldjuː] n moho.

mildness ['maɪldnɪs] n (softness) suavidad f; (gentleness) dulzura f; (quiet character) apacibilidad f.

mile [maɪl] n milla; **~age** n número de

millas; (AUT) kilometraje m; **~stone** n mojón m.

milieu ['miːljəː] n medio, medio ambiente.

militant ['mɪlɪtnt] a, n militante m/f.

military ['mɪlɪtərɪ] a militar.

militate ['mɪlɪteɪt] vi: **to ~ against** militar contra.

militia [mɪ'lɪʃə] n milicia.

milk [mɪlk] n leche f // vt (cow) ordeñar; (fig) chupar; **~man** n lechero; **~ shake** n batido de leche; **~y** a lechoso; **M~y Way** n Vía Láctea.

mill [mɪl] n (windmill etc) molino; (coffee ~) molinillo; (factory) fábrica; (spinning ~) hilandería // vt moler // vi (also: ~ about) moverse por todas partes, apiñarse.

millennium [mɪ'lɛnɪəm], pl **~s** or **-ia** [-nɪə] n milenio, milenario.

miller ['mɪlə°] n molinero.

millet ['mɪlɪt] n mijo.

milli... ['mɪlɪ] pref: **~gram(me)** n miligramo; **~litre** n mililitro; **~metre** n milímetro.

milliner ['mɪlɪnə°] n modista de sombreros; **~y** n sombrerería.

million ['mɪljən] n millón m; **a ~ times** un millón de veces; **~aire** n millonario.

millstone ['mɪlstəun] n piedra de molino.

milometer [maɪ'lɔmɪtə°] n cuenta-kilómetros m inv.

mime [maɪm] n mímica; (actor) mimo // vt remedar // vi actuar de mimo.

mimic ['mɪmɪk] n imitador/a m/f // a mímico // vt remedar, imitar; **~ry** n imitación f.

min. abbr of **minute(s); minimum.**

minaret [mɪnə'rɛt] n alminar m.

mince [mɪns] vt picar // vi (in walking) andar con pasos menudos // n (CULIN) carne f picada, picadillo; **~meat** n conserva de fruta picada; **~ pie** n empanadilla rellena de fruta picada; **mincer** n máquina de picar carne.

mind [maɪnd] n (gen) mente f; (intellect) inteligencia; (contrasted with matter) espíritu // vt (attend to, look after) ocuparse de, cuidar; (be careful of) tener cuidado con; (object to): **I don't ~ the noise** no me importa el ruido; **it is on my ~** me preocupa; **to my ~** en mi opinión; **to be out of one's ~** estar fuera de juicio; **never ~!** ¡es igual!, ¡no importa!; (don't worry) ¡no se preocupe!; **to bear sth in ~** tomar o tener algo en cuenta; **to make up one's ~** decidirse; **'~ the step'** cuidado con el escalón; **~ful** a: **~ful of** consciente de; **~less** a estúpido.

mine [maɪn] pron (el) mío/(la) mía etc // a: **this book is ~** este libro es mío // n mina // vt (coal) extraer, explotar; (ship, beach) minar; **~field** n campo de minas; **miner** n minero.

mineral ['mɪnərəl] a mineral // n mineral m; **~s** npl (soft drinks) aguas fpl minerales, gaseosa sg.

minesweeper ['maɪnswiːpə*] n dragaminas m inv.

mingle ['mɪŋgl] vi: **to ~ with** mezclarse con.

mingy ['mɪndʒɪ] a (col) tacaño.

miniature ['mɪnɪtʃə*] a (en) miniatura // n miniatura.

minibus ['mɪnɪbʌs] n microbús m.

minicab ['mɪnɪkæb] n microtaxi m.

minim ['mɪnɪm] n (mus) blanca.

minimal ['mɪnɪml] a mínimo.

minimize ['mɪnɪmaɪz] vt minimizar.

minimum ['mɪnɪməm] n, pl **minima** ['mɪnɪmə] mínimo // a mínimo.

mining ['maɪnɪŋ] n explotación f minera // a minero.

miniskirt ['mɪnɪskəːt] n minifalda.

minister ['mɪnɪstə*] n (pol) ministro; (rel) pastor m // vi atender; **~ial** [-'tɪərɪəl] a (pol) ministerial.

ministry ['mɪnɪstrɪ] n ministerio.

mink [mɪŋk] n visón m; **~ coat** n abrigo de visón.

minnow ['mɪnəu] n pececillo (de agua dulce).

minor ['maɪnə*] a menor; (unimportant) sin importancia; (inferior) secundario; (mus) menor // n (law) menor m/f de edad.

minority [maɪ'nɔrɪtɪ] n minoría; (age) minoridad f.

minster ['mɪnstə*] n catedral f.

minstrel ['mɪnstrəl] n juglar m.

mint [mɪnt] n (plant) menta, herbabuena; (sweet) caramelo de menta // vt (coins) acuñar; **the (Royal) M~** la (Real) Casa de la Moneda; **in ~ condition** en perfecto estado.

minuet [mɪnjuˈet] n minué m.

minus ['maɪnəs] n (also: **~ sign**) signo de menos // prep menos.

minute ['mɪnɪt] n minuto; (fig) momento; **~s** npl actas fpl // a [maɪˈnjuːt] diminuto; (search) minucioso; **at the last ~** a última hora.

miracle ['mɪrəkl] n milagro; **miraculous** [mɪˈrækjuləs] a milagroso.

mirage ['mɪrɑːʒ] n espejismo.

mirror ['mɪrə*] n espejo; (in car) retrovisor m // vt reflejar.

mirth [məːθ] n alegría; (laughter) risa, risas fpl.

misadventure [mɪsədˈventʃə*] n desgracia, accidente m.

misanthropist [mɪˈzænθrəpɪst] n misántropo.

misapprehension ['mɪsæprɪˈhenʃən] n equivocación f.

misbehave [mɪsbɪˈheɪv] vi portarse mal; **misbehaviour** n mala conducta.

miscalculate [mɪsˈkælkjuleɪt] vt calcular mal; **miscalculation** [-ˈleɪʃən] n error m (de cálculo).

miscarriage ['mɪskærɪdʒ] n (med) aborto; (failure) fracaso; **~ of justice** error m judicial.

miscellaneous [mɪsɪˈleɪnɪəs] a vario(s), diverso(s).

mischance [mɪsˈtʃɑːns] n desgracia, mala suerte f.

mischief ['mɪstʃɪf] n (naughtiness) travesura; (harm) mal m, daño; (maliciousness) malicia; **mischievous** [-ʃɪvəs] a travieso; dañoso; (playful) malicioso.

misconception ['mɪskənˈsepʃən] n concepto erróneo, equivocación f.

misconduct [mɪsˈkɔndʌkt] n mala conducta; **professional ~** falta profesional.

miscount [mɪsˈkaunt] vt, vi contar mal.

misdeed [mɪsˈdiːd] n delito.

misdemeanour, misdemeanor (us) [mɪsdɪˈmiːnə*] n delito, ofensa.

misdirect [mɪsdɪˈrekt] vt (person) informar mal; (letter) poner señas incorrectas en.

miser ['maɪzə*] n avaro/a.

miserable ['mɪzərəbl] a (unhappy) triste, desgraciado; (wretched) miserable; (despicable) despreciable.

miserly ['maɪzəlɪ] a avariento, tacaño.

misery ['mɪzərɪ] n (unhappiness) tristeza, sufrimiento; (wretchedness) miseria, desdicha.

misfire [mɪsˈfaɪə*] vi fallar.

misfit ['mɪsfɪt] n (person) inadaptado/a, desplazado/a.

misfortune [mɪsˈfɔːtʃən] n desgracia.

misgiving(s) [mɪsˈgɪvɪŋ(z)] n(pl) (mistrust) recelo; (apprehension) presentimiento.

misguided [mɪsˈgaɪdɪd] a equivocado.

mishandle [mɪsˈhændl] vt (treat roughly) maltratar; (mismanage) manejar mal.

mishap ['mɪshæp] n desgracia, contratiempo.

mishear [mɪsˈhɪə*] (irg: like **hear**) vt oír mal.

misinform [mɪsɪnˈfɔːm] vt informar mal.

misinterpret [mɪsɪnˈtəːprɪt] vt interpretar mal.

misjudge [mɪsˈdʒʌdʒ] vt juzgar mal.

mislay [mɪsˈleɪ] (irg: like **lay**) vt extraviar, perder.

mislead [mɪsˈliːd] (irg: like **lead**) vt llevar a conclusiones erróneas; **~ing** a engañoso, erróneo.

mismanage [mɪsˈmænɪdʒ] vt administrar mal; **~ment** n mala administración f.

misnomer [mɪsˈnəumə*] n nombre m inapropiado o equivocado.

misogynist [mɪˈsɔdʒɪnɪst] n misógino.

misplace [mɪsˈpleɪs] vt (lose) extraviar, perder.

misprint ['mɪsprɪnt] n errata, error m de imprenta.

mispronounce [mɪsprəˈnauns] vt pronunciar mal.

misread [mɪsˈriːd] (irg: like **read**) vt leer mal.

misrepresent [mɪsreprɪ'zɛnt] vt falsificar.

miss [mɪs] vt (train etc) perder; (fail to hit) errar, fallar; (regret the absence of): **I ~ him** (yo) le echo de menos o a faltar // vi fallar // n (shot) tiro fallido o perdido; (fig): **that was a near ~** (near accident) faltó poco para que chocáramos; **to ~ out** vt omitir.

Miss [mɪs] n Señorita.

missal ['mɪsl] n misal m.

misshapen [mɪs'ʃeɪpən] a deforme.

missile ['mɪsaɪl] n (AVIAT) mísil m; (object thrown) proyectil m.

missing ['mɪsɪŋ] a (pupil) ausente; (thing) perdido; (MIL) desaparecido; **to go ~** desaparecer.

mission ['mɪʃən] n misión f; **~ary** n misionero.

misspent ['mɪs'spɛnt] a: **his ~ youth** su juventud disipada.

mist [mɪst] n (light) neblina; (heavy) niebla; (at sea) bruma // vi (also: ~ over, ~ up) empañarse.

mistake [mɪs'teɪk] n error m // vt (irg: like **take**) entender mal, equivocarse sobre; **to ~ A for B** confundir A con B; **mistaken** a (idea etc) equivocado; **to be mistaken** equivocarse, engañarse.

mister ['mɪstə*] n (col) señor m; see **Mr.**

mistletoe ['mɪsltəu] n muérdago.

mistook [mɪs'tuk] pt of **mistake**.

mistreat [mɪs'triːt] vt maltratar; **~ment** n maltrato.

mistress ['mɪstrɪs] n (lover) amante f; (of house) señora (de la casa); (in primary school) maestra; (in secondary school) profesora; see **Mrs.**

mistrust [mɪs'trʌst] vt desconfiar de, dudar de.

misty ['mɪstɪ] a nebuloso, brumoso; (day) de niebla; (glasses) empañado.

misunderstand [mɪsʌndə'stænd] (irg: like **understand**) vt, vi entender mal; **~ing** n malentendido.

misuse [mɪs'juːs] n mal uso; (of power) abuso // vt [mɪs'juːz] abusar de; (funds) malversar.

mitigate ['mɪtɪgeɪt] vt mitigar.

mitre, miter (US) ['maɪtə*] n mitra; (CARPENTRY) inglete m.

mitt(en) ['mɪt(n)] n mitón m.

mix [mɪks] vt (gen) mezclar; (combine) unir // vi mezclarse; (people) llevarse bien // n mezcla; **to ~ up** vt mezclar; (confuse) confundir; **~ed** a (assorted) variado, surtido; (school etc) mixto; **~ed-up** a (confused) confuso, revuelto; **~er** n (for food) licuadora; (person) persona sociable; **~ture** n mezcla; **~-up** n confusión f.

moan [məun] n gemido // vi gemir; (col: complain): **to ~ (about)** quejarse (de).

moat [məut] n foso.

mob [mɔb] n multitud f; (pej): **the ~** el populacho // vt acosar.

mobile ['məubaɪl] a móvil // n móvil m; **~ home** n caravana.

mobility [məu'bɪlɪtɪ] n movilidad f.

mobilize ['məubɪlaɪz] vt movilizar.

moccasin ['mɔkəsɪn] n mocasín m.

mock [mɔk] vt (make ridiculous) ridiculizar; (laugh at) burlarse de // a fingido; **~ery** n burla; **~ing** a burlón(ona); **~-up** n maqueta.

mode [məud] n modo; (fashion) moda.

model ['mɔdl] n (gen) modelo; (ARCH) maqueta; (person: for fashion, ART) modelo m/f // a modelo // vt modelar // vi servir de modelo; **~ railway** ferrocarril m de juguete; **to ~ clothes** pasar modelos, ser modelo.

moderate ['mɔdərət] a, n moderado/a // (vb: [-reɪt]) vi moderarse, calmarse // vt moderar; **moderation** [-'reɪʃən] n moderación f.

modern ['mɔdən] a moderno; **~ize** vt modernizar.

modest ['mɔdɪst] a modesto; **~y** n modestia.

modicum ['mɔdɪkəm] n: **a ~ of** un mínimo de.

modification [mɔdɪfɪ'keɪʃən] n modificación f; **modify** ['mɔdɪfaɪ] vt modificar.

modulation [mɔdju'leɪʃən] n modulación f.

mohair ['məuhɛə*] n moer m.

moist [mɔɪst] a húmedo; **~en** ['mɔɪsn] vt humedecer; **~ure** ['mɔɪstʃə*] n humedad f; **~urizer** ['mɔɪstʃəraɪzə*] n crema hidratante.

molar ['məulə*] n muela.

molasses [məu'læsɪz] n melaza.

mole [məul] n (animal) topo; (spot) lunar m.

molecule ['mɔlɪkjuːl] n molécula.

molehill ['məulhɪl] n topera.

molest [məu'lɛst] vt importunar.

mollusc ['mɔləsk] n molusco.

mollycoddle ['mɔlɪkɔdl] vt mimar.

molten ['məultən] a fundido; (lava) líquido.

moment ['məumənt] n momento; **~ary** a momentáneo; **~ous** [-'mɛntəs] a trascendental, importante.

momentum [məu'mɛntəm] n momento; (fig) ímpetu m; **to gather ~** cobrar velocidad.

monarch ['mɔnək] n monarca m/f; **~y** n monarquía.

monastery ['mɔnəstərɪ] n monasterio.

monastic [mə'næstɪk] a monástico.

Monday ['mʌndɪ] n lunes m.

monetary ['mʌnɪtərɪ] a monetario.

money ['mʌnɪ] n dinero; **to make ~** ganar dinero; **~lender** n prestamista m/f; **~ order** n giro.

mongol ['mɔŋgəl] a, n (MED) mongólico.

mongrel ['mʌŋgrəl] n (dog) perro cruzado.

monitor ['mɔnɪtə*] n (SCOL) monitor m; (also: **television ~**) receptor m de control // vt controlar.

monk [mʌŋk] n monje m.

monkey ['mʌŋkɪ] n mono; **~ nut** n

cacahuete m; ~ **wrench** n llave f inglesa.
mono... [ˈmɔnəu] pref: ~**chrome** a monocromo.
monocle [ˈmɔnəkl] n monóculo.
monogram [ˈmɔnəgræm] n monograma m.
monologue [ˈmɔnələg] n monólogo.
monopoly [məˈnɔpəlɪ] n monopolio.
monorail [ˈmɔnəureɪl] n monorriel m.
monosyllabic [mɔnəusɪˈlæbɪk] a monosilábico.
monotone [ˈmɔnətəun] n monotonía; **to speak in a** ~ hablar en un solo tono.
monotonous [məˈnɔtənəs] a monótono; **monotony** [-nɪ] n monotonía.
monsoon [mɔnˈsuːn] n monzón m/f.
monster [ˈmɔnstə*] n monstruo.
monstrosity [mɔnsˈtrɔsɪtɪ] n monstruosidad f.
monstrous [ˈmɔnstrəs] a (huge) enorme; (atrocious) monstruoso.
montage [mɔnˈtɑːʒ] n montaje m.
month [mʌnθ] n mes m; ~**ly** a mensual // ad mensualmente // n (magazine) revista mensual.
monument [ˈmɔnjumənt] n monumento; ~**al** [-ˈmɛntl] a monumental.
moo [muː] vi mugir.
mood [muːd] n humor m; **to be in a good/bad** ~ estar de buen/mal humor; ~**y** a (variable) de humor variable; (sullen) melancólico.
moon [muːn] n luna; ~**beam** n rayo de luna; ~**light** n luz f de la luna; ~**lit** a: a ~**lit night** una noche de luna.
moor [muə*] n páramo // vt (ship) amarrar // vi echar las amarras.
Moor [muə*] n moro/a.
moorings [ˈmuərɪŋz] npl (chains) amarras fpl; (place) amarradero sg.
Moorish [ˈmuərɪʃ] a moro; (architecture) árabe, morisco.
moorland [ˈmuələnd] n páramo, brezal m.
moose [muːs] n, pl inv alce m.
mop [mɔp] n fregona; (of hair) greña, melena // vt fregar; **to** ~ **up** vt limpiar.
mope [məup] vi estar o andar deprimido.
moped [ˈməupɛd] n (Brit) ciclomotor m.
moral [ˈmɔrl] a moral // n moraleja; ~**s** npl moralidad f, moral f.
morale [mɔˈrɑːl] n moral f.
morality [məˈrælɪtɪ] n moralidad f.
morass [məˈræs] n pantano.
morbid [ˈmɔːbɪd] a (depressed) melancólico; (MED) mórbido; **don't be** ~! ¡no seas morboso!
more [mɔː*] det, ad más; **once** ~ otra vez, una vez más; **I want** ~ quiero más; ~ **dangerous than** más peligroso que; ~ **or less** más o menos; ~ **than ever** más que nunca.
moreover [mɔːˈrəuvə*] ad además, por otra parte.
morgue [mɔːg] n depósito de cadáveres.
moribund [ˈmɔrɪbʌnd] a moribundo.
Mormon [ˈmɔːmən] n mormón/ona m/f.

morning [ˈmɔːnɪŋ] n (gen) mañana; (early ~) madrugada; **good** ~ buenos días; **in the** ~ por la mañana; **7 o'clock in the** ~ las 7 de la mañana; **tomorrow** ~ mañana por la mañana.
Moroccan [məˈrɔkən] a, n marroquí m/f.
Morocco [məˈrɔkəu] n Marruecos m.
moron [ˈmɔːrɔn] n imbécil m/f; ~**ic** [məˈrɔnɪk] a imbécil.
morose [məˈrəus] a hosco, malhumorado.
morphine [ˈmɔːfiːn] n morfina.
Morse [mɔːs] n (also: ~ **code**) (alfabeto) morse.
morsel [ˈmɔːsl] n (of food) bocado.
mortal [ˈmɔːtl] a, n mortal m/f; ~**ity** [-ˈtælɪt] n mortalidad f.
mortar [ˈmɔːtə*] n argamasa; (dish) mortero.
mortgage [ˈmɔːgɪdʒ] n hipoteca // vt hipotecar.
mortify [ˈmɔːtɪfaɪ] vt mortificar, humillar.
mortuary [ˈmɔːtjuərɪ] n depósito de cadáveres.
mosaic [məuˈzeɪɪk] n mosaico.
Moscow [ˈmɔskəu] n Moscú m.
Moslem [ˈmɔzləm] a, n = **Muslim.**
mosque [mɔsk] n mezquita.
mosquito [mɔsˈkiːtəu] pl ~**es** n mosquito.
moss [mɔs] n musgo.
most [məust] det la mayor parte de, la mayoría de // pron la mayor parte, la mayoría // ad el más; (very) muy; **the** ~ (also: + adjective) el más; ~ **of them** la mayor parte de ellos; **I saw the** ~ yo vi el que más; **at the** (very) ~ a lo sumo, todo lo más; **to make the** ~ **of** aprovechar (al máximo); ~**ly** ad en su mayor parte, principalmente; **a** ~ **interesting book** un libro interesantísimo.
MOT n abbr of **Ministry of Transport: the** ~ (**test**) inspección (anual) obligatoria de coches y camiones.
motel [məuˈtɛl] n motel m.
moth [mɔθ] n mariposa nocturna; (clothes ~) polilla; ~**ball** n bola de naftalina; ~**-eaten** a apolillado.
mother [ˈmʌðə*] n madre f // a materno // vt (care for) cuidar (como una madre); ~**hood** n maternidad f; ~**-in-law** n suegra; ~**ly** a maternal; ~**-of-pearl** n nácar m; ~**-to-be** n futura madre; ~ **tongue** n lengua materna.
motif [məuˈtiːf] n motivo; (theme) tema m.
motion [ˈməuʃən] n movimiento; (gesture) ademán m, señal f; (at meeting) moción f // vt, vi: **to** ~ (**to**) **sb to do sth** hacer señas a uno para que haga algo; ~**less** a inmóvil; ~ **picture** n película.
motivated [ˈməutɪveɪtɪd] a motivado; **motivation** [-ˈveɪʃən] n motivación f.
motive [ˈməutɪv] n motivo // a motor (f: motora, motriz).
motley [ˈmɔtlɪ] a variado.
motor [ˈməutə*] n motor m; (col: vehicle) coche m, automóvil m // a motor (f:

motora, motriz); **~bike** n moto f; **~boat** n lancha motora; **~car** n coche m, automóvil m; **~cycle** n motocicleta; **~cyclist** n motorista m/f; **~ing** n automovilismo; **~ist** n conductor/a m/f, automovilista m/f; **~ oil** n aceite m de coche; **~ racing** n carreras fpl de coches, automovilismo; **~ scooter** n moto f; **~ vehicle** n automóvil m; **~way** n (Brit) autopista.

mottled ['mɔtld] a abigarrado, multicolor.

motto ['mɔtəu], pl **~es** n lema m; (watchword) consigna.

mould, mold (US) [məuld] n molde m; (mildew) moho // vt moldear; (fig) formar; **~er** vi (decay) decaer; **~ing** n moldura; **~y** a enmohecido.

moult, molt (US) [məult] vi mudar (la piel/la pluma).

mound [maund] n montón m, montículo.

mount [maunt] n monte m; (horse) montura; (for jewel etc) engaste m; (for picture) marco // vt montar, subir a // vi (also: **~ up**) subirse, montarse.

mountain ['mauntin] n montaña // cpd de montaña; **~eer** [-'nɪə*] n alpinista m/f, montañero/a; **~eering** [-'nɪərɪŋ] n alpinismo, montañismo; **to go ~eering** hacer alpinismo; **~ous** a montañoso; **~side** n ladera de la montaña.

mourn [mɔːn] vt llorar, lamentar // vi: **to ~ for** llorar la muerte de, lamentarse por; **~er** n pariente m/f/amigo del difunto; **~ful** a triste, lúgubre; **~ing** n luto // cpd (dress) de luto; **in ~ing** de luto.

mouse [maus], pl **mice** n ratón m; **~trap** n ratonera.

moustache [məs'tɑːʃ] n bigote m.

mousy ['mausı] a (person) tímido; (hair) pardusco.

mouth [mauθ], pl **~s** [-ŏz] n boca; (of river) desembocadura; **~ful** n bocado; **~organ** n armónica; **~piece** n (of musical instrument) boquilla; (spokesman) portavoz m; **~wash** n enjuague m; **~watering** a apetitoso.

movable ['muːvəbl] a movible.

move [muːv] n (movement) movimiento; (in game) jugada; (: turn to play) turno; (change of house) mudanza // vt mover; (emotionally) conmover; (POL: resolution etc) proponer // vi (gen) moverse; (traffic) circular; (also: **~ house**) trasladarse, mudarse; **to ~ sb to do sth** mover a uno a hacer algo; **to get a ~ on** darse prisa; **to ~ about** vi ir de acá para allá; (travel) viajar; **to ~ along** vi avanzar, adelantarse; **to ~ away** vi alejarse; **to ~ back** vi retroceder; **to ~ forward** vi avanzar // vt adelantar; **to ~ in** vi (to a house) instalarse (en una casa); **to ~ on** vi ponerse en camino; **to ~ out** vi (of house) abandonar una casa); **to ~ up** vi subir; (employee) ser ascendido.

movement ['muːvmənt] n movimiento; (TECH) mecanismo.

movie ['muːvɪ] n película; **to go to the ~s** ir al cine; **~ camera** n cámara cinematográfica.

moving ['muːvɪŋ] a (emotional) conmovedor(a); (that moves) móvil.

mow [məu], pt **mowed**, pp **mowed** or **mown** vt (grass) cortar; (corn: also: **~ down**) segar; **~er** n segadora; (for lawn) cortacéspedes m inv.

M.P. n abbr of **Member of Parliament**.

m.p.h. abbr of miles per hour.

Mr ['mɪstə*] n: **~ Smith** (el) Sr. Smith.

Mrs ['mɪsɪz] n: **~ Smith** (la) Sra. Smith.

Ms [mɪz] n = Miss or Mrs: **~ Smith** (la) Sa. Smith.

M.Sc. abbr of **Master of Science**.

much [mʌtʃ] det mucho // ad, n or pron mucho; (before pp) muy; **how ~ is it?** ¿cuánto es?, ¿cuánto cuesta?; **too ~** demasiado; **it's not ~** no es mucho; **as ~ as** tanto como; **however ~ he tries** por mucho que se esfuerce.

muck [mʌk] n (dirt) suciedad f; (fig) porquería; **to ~ about** vi (col) perder el tiempo; (enjoy o.s.) entretenerse; **to ~ up** vt (col: ruin) arruinar, estropear; **~y** a (dirty) sucio.

mucus ['mjuːkəs] n moco.

mud [mʌd] n barro, lodo.

muddle ['mʌdl] n desorden m, confusión f; (mix-up) embrollo, lío // vt (also: **~ up**) embrollar, confundir; **to ~ through** vi salir del paso sin saber cómo.

mud: **~dy** a fangoso, cubierto de lodo; **~guard** n guardabarros m inv; **~pack** n mascarilla (de belleza); **~-slinging** n injurias fpl, difamación f.

muff [mʌf] n manguito // vt (chance) desperdiciar; (lines) estropear.

muffin ['mʌfɪn] n mollete m.

muffle ['mʌfl] vt (sound) amortiguar; (against cold) embozar; **~d** a sordo, apagado.

mufti ['mʌftɪ] n: **in ~** vestido de paisano.

mug [mʌg] n (cup) taza (alta, sin platillo); (: for beer) jarra; (col: face) jeta; (: fool) bobo // vt (assault) asaltar; **~ging** n asalto.

muggy ['mʌgɪ] a bochornoso.

mule [mjuːl] n mula.

mull [mʌl]: **to ~ over** vt meditar sobre.

mulled [mʌld] a: **~ wine** vino calentado y con especias.

multi... [mʌltɪ] pref multi...; **~coloured**, **~colored** (US) a multicolor.

multifarious [mʌltɪ'fɛərɪəs] a múltiple.

multiple ['mʌltɪpl] a, n múltiplo; **~ sclerosis** n esclerosis f múltiple; **~ store** n (cadena de) grandes almacenes.

multiplication [mʌltɪplɪ'keɪʃən] n multiplicación f; **multiply** ['mʌltɪplaɪ] vt multiplicar // vi multiplicarse.

multitude ['mʌltɪtjuːd] n multitud f.

mum [mʌm] n mamá // a: **to keep ~** callarse.

mumble ['mʌmbl] *vt, vi* hablar entre dientes, refunfuñar.

mummy ['mʌmi] *n* (*mother*) mamá; (*embalmed*) momia.

mumps [mʌmps] *n* paperas *fpl*.

munch [mʌntʃ] *vt, vi* mascar.

mundane [mʌn'deɪn] *a* mundano.

municipal [mju:'nɪsɪpl] *a* municipal; **~ity** [-'pælɪtɪ] *n* municipio.

munitions [mju:'nɪʃənz] *npl* municiones *fpl*.

mural ['mjuərl] *n* (pintura) mural *m*.

murder ['mɔ:də°] *n* asesinato; (*in law*) homicidio // *vt* asesinar, matar; (*spoil*) estropear; **~er** *n* asesino; **~ess** *n* asesina; **~ous** *a* homicida.

murky ['mɔ:kɪ] *a* oscuro; (*fig*) tenebroso.

murmur ['mɔ:mə°] *n* murmullo // *vt, vi* murmurar.

muscle ['mʌsl] *n* músculo; (*fig: strength*) fuerza (muscular); **to ~ in** *vi* introducirse por fuerza; **muscular** ['mʌskjulə°] *a* muscular; (*person*) musculoso.

muse [mju:z] *vi* meditar // *n* musa.

museum [mju:'zɪəm] *n* museo.

mushroom ['mʌʃrum] *n* (*gen*) seta, hongo; (*food*) champiñón *m* // *vi* (*fig*) crecer de la noche a la mañana.

mushy ['mʌʃɪ] *a* triturado; (*pej*) sensiblero.

music ['mju:zɪk] *n* música; **~al** *a* melodioso; (*person*) musical // *n* (*show*) (comedia) musical; **~al instrument** *n* instrumento musical; **~ hall** *n* teatro de variedades; **~ian** [-'zɪʃən] *n* músico/a.

musket ['mʌskɪt] *n* mosquete *m*.

Muslim ['mʌzlɪm] *a, n* musulmán/ana *m/f*.

muslin ['mʌzlɪn] *n* muselina.

mussel ['mʌsl] *n* mejillón *m*.

must [mʌst] *auxiliary vb* (*obligation*): **I ~ do it** debo hacerlo, tengo que hacerlo; (*probability*): **he ~ be there by now** ya debe estar allí // *n* necesidad *f*; **it's a ~** es imprescindible.

mustard ['mʌstəd] *n* mostaza.

muster ['mʌstə°] *vt* juntar, reunir.

mustn't ['mʌsnt] = **must not.**

musty ['mʌstɪ] *a* mohoso, que huele a humedad.

mute [mju:t] *a, n* mudo/a.

muted ['mju:tɪd] *a* callado; (*MUS*) apagado.

mutilate ['mju:tɪleɪt] *vt* mutilar; **mutilation** [-'leɪʃən] *n* mutilación *f*.

mutinous ['mju:tɪnəs] *a* (*troops*) amotinado; (*attitude*) rebelde.

mutiny ['mju:tɪnɪ] *n* motín *m* // *vi* amotinarse.

mutter ['mʌtə°] *vt, vi* murmurar, hablar entre dientes.

mutton ['mʌtn] *n* carne *f* de cordero.

mutual ['mju:tʃuəl] *a* mutuo; (*gen: shared*) común; **~ly** *ad* mutuamente.

muzzle ['mʌzl] *n* hocico; (*protective device*) bozal *m*; (*of gun*) boca // *vt* amordazar; (*dog*) poner un bozal a.

my [maɪ] *a* mi // *interj*: **~!** ¡caramba!

mynah bird ['maɪnə°] *n* mainat *m*.

myopic [maɪ'ɔpɪk] *a* miope.

myself [maɪ'sɛlf] *pron* (*reflexive*) me; (*emphatic*) yo mismo; (*after prep*) mí (mismo).

mysterious [mɪs'tɪərɪəs] *a* misterioso; **mystery** ['mɪstərɪ] *n* misterio.

mystic ['mɪstɪk] *a, n* místico/a; **~al** *a* místico.

mystify ['mɪstɪfaɪ] *vt* (*perplex*) dejar perplejo; (*disconcert*) desconcertar.

myth [mɪθ] *n* mito; **~ical** *a* mítico; **~ological** [mɪθə'lɔdʒɪkl] *a* mitológico; **~ology** [mɪ'θɔlədʒɪ] *n* mitología.

N

nab [næb] *vt* (*col: grab*) coger; (: *catch out*) pillar.

nag [næg] *n* (*pej: horse*) rocín *m* // *vt* (*scold*) regañar; (*annoy*) fastidiar; **~ging** *a* (*doubt*) persistente; (*pain*) continuo // *n* quejas *fpl*.

nail [neɪl] *n* (*human*) uña; (*metal*) clavo // *vt* clavar; (*fig: catch*) coger, pillar; **to ~ sb down to doing sth** comprometer a uno a que haga algo; **~brush** *n* cepillo para las uñas; **~file** *n* lima para las uñas; **~ polish** *n* esmalte *m* o laca para las uñas; **~ scissors** *npl* tijeras *fpl* para las uñas.

naïve [naɪ'i:v] *a* ingenuo; (*simple*) sencillo.

naked ['neɪkɪd] *a* (*nude*) desnudo; (*fig*) inerme, indefenso; (*flame*) expuesto al aire; **~ness** *n* desnudez *f*.

name [neɪm] *n* (*gen*) nombre *m*; (*surname*) apellido; (*reputation*) fama, renombre *m* // *vt* (*child*) poner nombre a; (*criminal*) dar el nombre de; (*appoint*) nombrar; **by ~ de nombre; maiden ~** nombre de soltera; **in the ~ of** en nombre de; **what's your ~?** ¿cómo se llama?; **to give one's ~ and address** dar las señas; **~less** *a* anónimo, sin nombre; **~ly** *ad* a saber; **~sake** *n* tocayo/a.

nanny ['nænɪ] *n* niñera; **~ goat** *n* cabra.

nap [næp] *n* (*sleep*) sueñecito, siesta.

napalm ['neɪpa:m] *n* nápalm *m*.

nape [neɪp] *n*: **the ~ of the neck** la nuca, el cogote.

napkin ['næpkɪn] *n* (*also*: **table ~**) servilleta; (*Brit: for baby*) pañal *m*.

nappy ['næpɪ] *n* pañal *m*; **~ liner** *n* gasa; **~ rash** *n* prurito.

narcissus [na:'sɪsəs] *pl* **-si** [-saɪ] *n* narciso.

narcotic [na:'kɔtɪk] *a, n* narcótico.

narrate [nə'reɪt] *vt* narrar, contar; **narrative** ['nærətɪv] *n* narrativa // *a* narrativo; **narrator** *n* narrador/a *m/f*.

narrow ['nærəu] *a* estrecho, angosto; (*fig*) de miras estrechas, intolerante // *vi* estrecharse, angostarse; (*diminish*) reducirse; **to ~ down the possibilities** to reducir las posibilidades a; **~ly** *ad* (*miss*) por poco; **~-minded** *a* de miras estrechas.

nasal ['neɪzl] *a* nasal.

nastiness ['na:stɪnɪs] *n* (*malice*)

malevolencia; (*rudeness*) grosería.

nasty ['nɑːstɪ] *a* (*unpleasant*: *remark*) feo, horrible; (: *person*) antipático; (*malicious*) rencoroso; (*rude*) grosero; (*revolting*: *taste, smell*) asqueroso, repugnante; (*wound, disease etc*) peligroso, grave.

nation ['neɪʃən] *n* nación *f*.

national ['næʃənl] *a, n* nacional *m/f*; ~**ism** *n* nacionalismo; ~**ist** *a, n* nacionalista *m/f*; ~**ity** [-'nælɪtɪ] *n* nacionalidad *f*; ~**ization** [-aɪ'zeɪʃən] *n* nacionalización *f*; ~**ize** *vt* nacionalizar; ~**ly** *ad* (*nationwide*) en escala nacional; (*as a nation*) nacionalmente, como nación.

nationwide ['neɪʃənwaɪd] *a* en escala o a nivel nacional.

native ['neɪtɪv] *n* (*local inhabitant*) natural *m/f*, nacional *m/f*; (*in colonies*) indígena *m/f*, nativo/a // *a* (*indigenous*) indígena; (*of one's birth*) natal; (*innate*) natural, innato.

NATO ['neɪtəu] *n abbr of* **North Atlantic Treaty Organization** OTAN (Organización del Tratado del Atlántico del Norte).

natter ['nætə*] *vi* charlar.

natural ['nætʃrəl] *a* natural; (*unaffected*: *manner*) inafectado, sin afectación; ~**ist** *n* naturalista *m/f*; ~**ize** *vt*: **to become** ~**ized** (*person*) naturalizarse; (*plant*) aclimatarse; ~**ly** *ad* naturalmente; (*of course*) desde luego, por supuesto; (*instinctively*) por instinto, por naturaleza; ~**ness** *n* naturalidad *f*.

nature ['neɪtʃə*] *n* naturaleza; (*group, sort*) género, clase *f*; (*character*) carácter *m*, genio; **by** ~ por *o* de naturaleza.

naughty ['nɔːtɪ] *a* (*child*) travieso; (*story, film*) verde, escabroso.

nausea ['nɔːsɪə] *n* náusea; **nauseate** [-sɪeɪt] *vt* dar náuseas a; (*fig*) dar asco a; **nauseating** [-sɪeɪtɪŋ] *a* nauseabundo; (*fig*) asqueroso.

nautical ['nɔːtɪkl] *a* náutico, marítimo; (*mile*) marino.

naval ['neɪvl] *a* naval, de marina; ~ **officer** *n* oficial *m/f* de marina.

nave [neɪv] *n* nave *f*.

navel ['neɪvl] *n* ombligo.

navigable ['nævɪgəbl] *a* navegable.

navigate ['nævɪgeɪt] *vt* (*guide*) gobernar; (*sail along*) navegar por; (*fig*) guiar // *vi* navegar; **navigation** [-'geɪʃən] *n* (*action*) navegación *f*; (*science*) náutica; **navigator** *n* navegador/a *m/f*, navegante *m/f*.

navvy ['nævɪ] *n* peón *m* caminero.

navy ['neɪvɪ] *n* marina de guerra; (*ships*) armada, flota; ~**(-blue)** *a* azul marino.

Nazi ['nɑːtsɪ] *n* nazi *m/f*; **nazism** *n* nazismo.

neap tide [niːp-] *n* marea muerta.

near [nɪə*] *a* (*place*) cercano, vecino; (*time*) próximo; (*relation*) estrecho, íntimo // *ad* cerca // *prep* (*also*: ~ **to**) (*space*) cerca de, junto a; (*time*) cerca de, casi // *vt* acercarse a, aproximarse a; ~**by**

[nɪə'baɪ] *a* cercano, próximo // *ad* cerca; **N~ East** *n* Cercano Oriente *m*; ~**ly** *ad* casi, por poco; **I** ~**ly fell** por poco me caigo; ~ **miss** *n* tiro cercano; ~**ness** *n* proximidad *f*, cercanía; (*relationship*) intimidad *f*; ~ **side** *n* (AUT. *in Britain*) lado izquierdo; (: *in Spain*) lado derecho; ~**-sighted** *a* miope, corto de vista.

neat [niːt] *a* (*place*) bien arreglado *o* cuidado; (*person*) pulcro, esmerado; (*skilful*) diestro; (: *plan*) hábil, ingenioso; (*spirits*) solo.

nebulous ['nebjuləs] *a* nebuloso; (*fig*) vago, confuso.

necessarily ['nesɪsrɪlɪ] *ad* necesariamente.

necessary ['nesɪsrɪ] *a* necesario, preciso; **he did all that was** ~ hizo todo lo necesario.

necessitate [nɪ'sesɪteɪt] *vt* necesitar, exigir.

necessity [nɪ'sesɪtɪ] *n* (*thing needed*) necesidad *f*, requisito; (*compelling circumstances*) la necesidad; **necessities** *npl* artículos *mpl* de primera necesidad.

neck [nɛk] *n* (ANAT.) cuello; (*of animal*) pescuezo // *vi* besuquearse, abrazarse; ~ **and** ~ parejos; **to stick one's** ~ **out** arriesgarse.

necklace ['nɛklɪs] *n* collar *m*.

neckline ['nɛklaɪn] *n* escote *m*.

necktie ['nɛktaɪ] *n* corbata.

née [neɪ] *a*: ~ **Scott** de soltera Scott.

need [niːd] *n* (*lack*) escasez *f*, falta; (*necessity*) necesidad *f*; (*thing needed*) requisito, necesidad *f* // *vt* (*require*) necesitar; **I** ~ **to do it** tengo que *o* debo hacerlo, hay que hacerlo; **you don't** ~ **to go** no hace falta que vayas.

needle ['niːdl] *n* aguja // *vt* (*fig*: *fam*) picar, fastidiar.

needless ['niːdlɪs] *a* innecesario, inútil; ~ **to say** huelga decir que.

needlework ['niːdlwəːk] *n* (*activity*) costura, labor *f* de aguja.

needy ['niːdɪ] *a* necesitado.

negation [nɪ'geɪʃən] *n* negación *f*.

negative ['negətɪv] *n* (PHOT.) negativo; (*answer*) negativa // *a* negativo.

neglect [nɪ'glɛkt] *vt* (*one's duty*) faltar a, no cumplir con; (*child*) descuidar, desatender // *n* (*gen*) negligencia, abandono; (*personal*) dejadez *f*; (*of duty*) incumplimiento.

negligee ['neglɪʒeɪ] *n* (*nightdress*) salto de cama; (*housecoat*) bata.

negligence ['neglɪdʒəns] *n* negligencia, descuido; **negligent** [-ənt] *a* (*careless*) descuidado, negligente; (*forgetful*) olvidadizo.

negligible ['neglɪdʒɪbl] *a* insignificante, despreciable.

negotiable [nɪ'gəuʃɪəbl] *a* (*cheque*) negociable; (*road*) transitable.

negotiate [nɪ'gəuʃɪeɪt] *vi* negociar // *vt* (*treaty*) negociar; (*transaction*) gestionar, tramitar; (*obstacle*) franquear;

negotiation [-'eɪʃən] n negociación f, gestión f; negotiator n negociador/a m/f.

Negress ['niːgrɪs] n negra.

Negro ['niːgrəu] a, n negro.

neigh [neɪ] n relincho // vi relinchar.

neighbour, neighbor (US) ['neɪbə*] n vecino/a; ~hood n (place) vecindad f, barrio; (people) vecindario; ~ing a vecino; ~ly a amistoso, de buen vecino.

neither ['naɪðə*] a ni // conj: I didn't move and ~ did John no me he movido, ni Juan tampoco // pron ninguno // ad: ~ good nor bad ni bueno ni malo.

neo... [niːəu] pref neo-.

neon ['niːɔn] n neón m; ~ light n lámpara de neón.

nephew ['nɛvjuː] n sobrino.

nerve [nɜːv] n (ANAT) nervio; (courage) valor m; (impudence) descaro, frescura; ~-racking a que crispa los nervios; ~s npl (fig: anxiety) nerviosidad f, nerviosismo.

nervous ['nɜːvəs] a (anxious, ANAT) nervioso; (timid) tímido, miedoso; ~ breakdown n crisis f nerviosa; ~ly ad nerviosamente; tímidamente; ~ness n nerviosidad f, nerviosismo; timidez f.

nest [nɛst] n (of bird) nido; (of wasp) avispero // vi anidar.

nestle ['nɛsl] vi: to ~ up to sb arrimarse a uno.

net [nɛt] n (gen) red f; (fig) trampa // a (COMM) neto, líquido // vt coger con red; (SPORT) marcar; ~ball n básquet m.

Netherlands ['nɛðələndz] npl: the ~ los Países Bajos.

nett [nɛt] a = net.

netting ['nɛtɪŋ] n red f, redes fpl.

nettle ['nɛtl] n ortiga.

network ['nɛtwɜːk] n red f.

neurosis [njuə'rəusɪs] pl -ses [-siːz] n neurosis f; neurotic [-'rɔtɪk] a, n neurótico/a.

neuter ['njuːtə*] a (sexless) castrado, sin sexo; (LING) neutro // vt castrar, capar.

neutral ['njuːtrəl] a (person) neutral; (colour etc, ELEC) neutro // n (AUT) punto muerto; ~ity [-'trælɪtɪ] n neutralidad f.

neutron ['njuːtrɔn] n neutrón m; ~ bomb n bomba de neutrones.

never ['nɛvə*] ad nunca, jamás; I ~ went no fui nunca; ~ in my life jamás en la vida; ~-ending a interminable, sin fin; ~theless [nɛvəðə'lɛs] ad sin embargo, no obstante.

new [njuː] a (brand ~) nuevo; (recent) reciente; (different) nuevo, distinto; (inexperienced) tierno, nuevo; ~-born a recién nacido; ~comer ['njuːkʌmə*] n recién venido o llegado; ~ly ad nuevamente, recién; ~ moon n luna nueva; ~ness n novedad f; (fig) inexperiencia.

news [njuːz] n noticias fpl; a piece of ~ una noticia; the ~ (RADIO, TV) las noticias fpl, telediario; ~ agency n agencia de noticias; ~agent n vendedor/a m/f de periódicos; ~caster n presentador/a m/f

de noticias; ~ flash n noticia de última hora; ~letter n hoja informativa, boletín m; ~paper n periódico, diario; ~reel n noticiario; ~ stand n quiosco o puesto de periódicos.

New Year ['njuː'jɪə*] n Año Nuevo; ~'s Day n Día m de Año Nuevo; ~'s Eve n Nochevieja.

New York ['njuː'jɔːk] n Nueva York.

New Zealand [njuː'ziːlənd] n Nueva Zelanda.

next [nɛkst] a (in space) próximo, vecino; (in time) próximo, siguiente // ad (place) después; (time) después, luego; ~ time la próxima vez; ~ year el año próximo o que viene; ~ door ad en la casa de al lado // a vecino, de al lado; ~-of-kin n pariente(s) m(pl) cercano(s); ~ to prep junto a, al lado de.

N.H.S. n abbr of **National Health Service.**

nib [nɪb] n plumilla.

nibble ['nɪbl] vt mordisquear, mordiscar; (ZOOL) roer.

nice [naɪs] a (likeable) simpático, majo; (kind) amable; (pleasant) agradable; (attractive) bonito, mono; (subtle) fino, preciso; ~-looking a atractivo, guapo; ~ly ad amablemente, bien.

niche [niːʃ] n nicho.

nick [nɪk] n (wound) rasguño; (cut, indentation) mella, muesca // vt (col) birlar, robar; in the ~ of time a última hora.

nickel ['nɪkl] n níquel m.

nickname ['nɪkneɪm] n apodo, mote m // vt apodar.

nicotine ['nɪkətiːn] n nicotina.

niece [niːs] n sobrina.

Nigeria [naɪ'dʒɪərɪə] n Nigeria; ~n a, n nigeriano/a.

niggardly ['nɪgədlɪ] a (person) avaro, tacaño; (amount) miserable.

niggling ['nɪglɪŋ] a (trifling) nimio, insignificante; (annoying) molesto.

night [naɪt] n (gen) noche f; (evening) tarde f; last ~ anoche; the ~ before last anteanoche; good ~! ¡buenas noches!; at or by ~ de noche, por la noche; ~cap n (drink) resopón m; ~ club n cabaret m; ~dress n camisón m; ~fall n anochecer m; ~ie ['naɪtɪ] n camisón m.

nightingale ['naɪtɪŋgeɪl] n ruiseñor m.

nightly ['naɪtlɪ] a de noche, nocturno // ad todas las noches, cada noche.

night: ~mare n pesadilla; ~ school n clase(s) f(pl) nocturna(s); ~ shift n turno nocturno o de noche; ~-time n noche f; ~ watchman n sereno.

nil [nɪl] n cero, nada.

nimble ['nɪmbl] a (agile) ágil, ligero; (skilful) diestro.

nine [naɪn] num nueve; ~teen num diecinueve, diez y nueve; ~ty num noventa.

ninth [naɪnθ] a noveno.

nip [nɪp] vt (*pinch*) pellizcar; (*bite*) morder // n (*drink*) trago, gota.

nipple ['nɪpl] n (ANAT) pezón m; (*of bottle*) tetilla; (TECH) boquilla, manguito.

nippy ['nɪpɪ] a (*person*) ágil, rápido; (*taste*) picante.

nitrate ['naɪtreɪt] n nitrato.

nitrogen ['naɪtrədʒən] n nitrógeno.

no [nəu] ad no // a ninguno, no ... alguno // n no.

nobility [nəu'bɪlɪtɪ] n nobleza.

noble ['nəubl] a (*person*) noble; (*title*) de nobleza; (*generous*) noble; ~**man** n noble m, aristócrata m.

nobody ['nəubədɪ] pron nadie.

nod [nɒd] vi saludar con la cabeza; (*in agreement*) decir que sí con la cabeza; (*doze*) cabecear // vt inclinar // n inclinación f de cabeza; **to** ~ **off** vi cabecear.

noise [nɔɪz] n ruido; (*din*) escándalo, estrépito; **noisily** ad ruidosamente; **noisy** a (*gen*) ruidoso; (*child*) escandaloso.

nomad ['nəumæd] n nómada m/f; ~**ic** [-'mædɪk] a nómada.

nominal ['nɒmɪnl] a nominal.

nominate ['nɒmɪneɪt] vt (*propose*) proponer; (*appoint*) nombrar; **nomination** [-'neɪʃən] n propuesta; nombramiento.

nominee [nɒmɪ'niː] n candidato/a.

non... [nɒn] pref no, des..., in...; ~**-alcoholic** no alcohólico; ~**-aligned** a no alineado; ~**-committal** ['nɒnkə'mɪtl] a (*reserved*) reservado; (*uncommitted*) evasivo; ~ **conformist** a no conformista; ~**descript** ['nɒndɪskrɪpt] a indeterminado; (*pej*) mediocre.

none [nʌn] pron (*person*) nadie; (*thing*) ninguno, nada // ad de ninguna manera.

nonentity [nɒ'nentɪtɪ] n cero a la izquierda, nulidad f.

nonetheless [nʌnðə'les] ad sin embargo, no obstante.

non: ~**-fiction** n literatura no novelesca; ~**plussed** a perplejo.

nonsense ['nɒnsəns] n tonterías fpl, disparates fpl.

non-stop ['nɒn'stɒp] a continuo; (RAIL) directo // ad sin parar.

noodles ['nuːdlz] npl tallarines mpl.

nook [nuk] n rincón m; ~**s and crannies** escondrijos mpl.

noon [nuːn] n mediodía m.

no-one ['nəuwʌn] pron = **nobody.**

noose [nuːs] n lazo corredizo; (*hangman's*) dogal m.

nor [nɔː*] conj = **neither** // ad see **neither.**

norm [nɔːm] n norma.

normal ['nɔːml] a (*usual*) normal; (*ordinary*) corriente, regular; ~**ly** ad normalmente.

north [nɔːθ] n norte m // a del norte, norteño // ad al o hacia el norte; **N**~ **America** n América del Norte; ~**-east** n nor(d)este m; ~**ern** ['nɔːðən] a norteño,

del norte; **N**~**ern Ireland** n Irlanda del Norte; **N**~ **Pole** n Polo Norte; **N**~ **Sea** n Mar m del Norte; ~**ward(s)** ['nɔːθwəd(z)] ad hacia el norte; ~**-west** n nor(d)oeste m.

Norway ['nɔːweɪ] n Noruega; **Norwegian** [-'wiːdʒən] a, n noruego/a.

nose [nəuz] n (ANAT) nariz f; (ZOOL) hocico; (*sense of smell*) olfato // vi: **to** ~ **about** curiosear; ~**bleed** n hemorragia nasal; ~**-dive** n (*deliberate*) picado vertical; (*involuntary*) caída de narices; ~**y** a curioso, fisgón(ona).

nostalgia [nɒs'tældʒɪə] n nostalgia; **nostalgic** a nostálgico.

nostril ['nɒstrɪl] n ventana de la nariz; ~**s** npl narices fpl.

nosy ['nəuzɪ] a = **nosey.**

not [nɒt] ad no; ~ **at all** no ... en absoluto; ~ **that...** no es que...; ~ **yet** todavía no; ~ **now** ahora no; **why** ~? ¿por qué no?

notable ['nəutəbl] a notable.

notary ['nəutərɪ] n notario.

notch [nɒtʃ] n muesca, corte m.

note [nəut] n (MUS) nota; (*banknote*) billete m; (*letter*) nota, carta; (*record*) nota, apunte m; (*fame*) importancia, renombre m; (*tone*) tono // vt (*observe*) notar, observar; (*write down*) apuntar, anotar; ~**book** n libreta, cuaderno; ~**case** n cartera, billetero; ~**d** ['nəutɪd] a célebre, conocido; ~**paper** n papel m para cartas.

nothing ['nʌθɪŋ] n nada; (*zero*) cero; **for** ~ (*free*) gratis, sin pago; (*in vain*) en balde.

notice ['nəutɪs] n (*announcement*) anuncio; (*attention*) atención f, interés m; (*warning*) aviso; (*dismissal*) despido; (*resignation*) dimisión f; (*period of time*) plazo // vt (*observe*) notar, observar; **to take** ~ **of** tomar nota de, prestar atención a; **at short** ~ a corto plazo, con poca anticipación; **until further** ~ hasta nuevo aviso; ~**able** a evidente, obvio; ~**board** n (*Brit*) tablón m de anuncios.

notification [nəutɪfɪ'keɪʃən] n aviso; **notify** ['nəutɪfaɪ] vt avisar, notificar.

notion ['nəuʃən] n noción f, concepto; (*opinion*) opinión f.

notorious [nəu'tɔːrɪəs] a notorio, célebre.

notwithstanding [nɒtwɪθ'stændɪŋ] ad no obstante, sin embargo; ~ **this** a pesar de esto.

nougat ['nuːgɑː] n turrón m.

nought [nɔːt] n cero.

noun [naun] n nombre m, sustantivo.

nourish ['nʌrɪʃ] vt nutrir, alimentar; (*fig*) fomentar, nutrir; ~**ing** a nutritivo, rico; ~**ment** n alimento, sustento.

novel ['nɒvl] n novela // a (*new*) nuevo, original; (*unexpected*) insólito; ~**ist** n novelista m/f; ~**ty** n novedad f.

November [nəu'vembə*] n noviembre m.

novice ['nɒvɪs] n principiante m/f, novato/a; (REL) novicio/a.

now [nau] ad (*at the present time*) ahora; (*these days*) actualmente, hoy día; **right**

~ ahora mismo; ~ **and then,** ~ **and again** de vez en cuando; **from** ~ **on** de ahora en adelante; ~**adays** ['nauɔdeɪz] *ad* hoy (en) día, actualmente.

nowhere ['nɔuwɛɔ°] *ad* (*direction*) a ninguna parte; (*location*) en ninguna parte.

nozzle ['nɔzl] *n* (*gen*) boquilla; (*TECH*) tobera, inyector *m*.

nuance ['nju:ɑ:ns] *n* matiz *m*.

nuclear ['nju:klɪɔ°] *a* nuclear.

nucleus ['nju:klɪɔs], *pl* **-lei** [-lɪaɪ] *n* núcleo.

nude [nju:d] *a, n* desnudo/a; **in the** ~ desnudo.

nudge [nʌdʒ] *vt* dar un codazo a.

nudist ['nju:dɪst] *n* nudista *m/f*.

nudity ['nju:dɪtɪ] *n* desnudez *f*.

nuisance ['nju:sns] *n* molestia, fastidio; (*person*) pesado, latoso; **what a** ~! ¡qué lata!

null [nʌl] *a*: ~ **and void** nulo y sin efecto; ~**ify** ['nʌlɪfaɪ] *vt* anular, invalidar.

numb [nʌm] *a* entumecido; (*fig*) insensible // *vt* entumecer, entorpecer.

number ['nʌmbɔ°] *n* número; (*numeral*) número, cifra // *vt* (*pages etc*) numerar, poner número a; (*amount to*) sumar, ascender a; **to be** ~**ed among** figurar entre; **a** ~ **of** varios, algunos; **they were ten in** ~ eran diez; ~ **plate** *n* placa de matrícula.

numbness ['nʌmnɪs] *n* entumecimiento; (*fig*) insensibilidad *f*.

numeral ['nju:mɔrɔl] *n* número, cifra.

numerical ['nju:'mɛrɪkl] *a* numérico.

numerous ['nju:mɔrɔs] *a* numeroso, muchos.

nun [nʌn] *n* monja, religiosa.

nurse [nɔ:s] *n* enfermero/a; (*nanny*) niñera // *vt* (*patient*) cuidar, atender; (*baby*) criar, amamantar; (*fig*) guardar; **wet** ~ nodriza.

nursery ['nɔ:sɔrɪ] *n* (*institution*) guardería infantil; (*room*) cuarto de los niños; (*for plants*) criadero, semillero; ~ **rhyme** *n* canción *f* infantil; ~ **school** *n* parvulario, escuela de párvulos; ~ **slope** *n* (*SKI*) cuesta para principiantes.

nursing ['nɔ:sɪŋ] *n* (*profession*) profesión *f* de enfermera; (*care*) asistencia, cuidado; ~ **home** *n* clínica de reposo.

nut [nʌt] *n* (*TECH*) tuerca; (*BOT*) nuez *f*; ~**s** *a* (*col*) loco; ~**case** *n* (*col*) loco/a, chalado/a; ~**crackers** *npl* cascanueces *m inv*; ~**meg** ['nʌtmɛg] *n* nuez *f* moscada.

nutrient ['nju:trɪɔnt] *n* nutrimento.

nutrition [nju:'trɪʃɔn] *n* nutrición *f*, alimentación *f*; **nutritious** [-ʃɔs] *a* nutritivo, rico.

nutshell ['nʌtʃɛl] *n* cáscara de nuez; **in a** ~ en resumidas cuentas.

nylon ['naɪlɔn] *n* nilón *m* // *a* de nilón; ~**s** *npl* medias *fpl* (de nilón).

nymph [nɪmf] *n* ninfa.

O

oaf [ɔuf] *n* zoquete *m*.

oak [ɔuk] *n* roble *m* // *a* de roble.

O.A.P. *abbr of* **old-age pensioner.**

oar [ɔ:°] *n* remo; **oarsman** *n* remero.

oasis [ɔu'eɪsɪs], *pl* **-ses** [-si:z] *n* oasis *m*.

oath [ɔuθ] *n* juramento; (*swear word*) palabrota; **on** ~ bajo juramento.

oatmeal ['ɔutmi:l] *n* harina de avena.

oats [ɔuts] *n* avena.

obedience [ɔ'bi:dɪɔns] *n* obediencia; **in** ~ **to** de acuerdo con; **obedient** [-ɔnt] *a* obediente.

obesity [ɔu'bi:sɪtɪ] *n* obesidad *f*.

obey [ɔ'beɪ] *vt* obedecer; (*instructions, regulations*) cumplir.

obituary [ɔ'bɪtjuɔrɪ] *n* necrología.

object ['ɔbdʒɪkt] *n* (*gen*) objeto; (*purpose*) objeto, propósito; (*LING*) complemento // *vi* [ɔb'dʒɛkt]: **to** ~ **to** (*attitude*) protestar contra; (*proposal*) oponerse a; **I** ~! ¡yo protesto!; ~**ion** [ɔb'dʒɛkʃɔn] *n* protesta; **I have no** ~**ion to...** no tengo inconveniente en que...; ~**ionable** [ɔb-'dʒɛkʃɔnɔbl] *a* (*gen*) desagradable; (*conduct*) censurable; ~**ive** *a, n* objetivo; ~**ivity** [ɔbdʒɪk'tɪvɪtɪ] *n* objetividad *f*; ~**or** *n* objetor/a *m/f*.

obligation [ɔblɪ'geɪʃɔn] *n* obligación *f*; (*debt*) deber *m*; **without** ~ sin compromiso.

obligatory [ɔ'blɪgɔtɔrɪ] *a* obligatorio.

oblige [ɔ'blaɪdʒ] *vt* (*force*): **to** ~ **sb to do sth** forzar o obligar a uno a hacer algo; (*do a favour for*) complacer, hacer un favor a; **I should be** ~**d if...** le agradecería que...; **obliging** *a* servicial, atento.

oblique [ɔ'bli:k] *a* oblicuo; (*allusion*) indirecto.

obliterate [ɔ'blɪtɔreɪt] *vt* borrar.

oblivion [ɔ'blɪvɪɔn] *n* olvido; **oblivious** [-ɪɔs] *a*: **oblivious of** inconsciente de.

oblong ['ɔblɔŋ] *a* rectangular // *n* rectángulo.

obnoxious [ɔb'nɔkʃɔs] *a* odioso, detestable; (*smell*) nauseabundo.

oboe ['ɔubɔu] *n* oboe *m*.

obscene [ɔb'si:n] *a* obsceno; **obscenity** [-'sɛnɪtɪ] *n* obscenidad *f*.

obscure [ɔb'skjuɔ°] *a* oscuro // *vt* oscurecer; (*hide: sun*) esconder; **obscurity** *n* oscuridad *f*.

obsequious [ɔb'si:kwɪɔs] *a* obsequioso.

observance [ɔb'zɔ:vns] *n* observancia, cumplimiento; (*ritual*) práctica.

observant [ɔb'zɔ:vnt] *a* observador(a).

observation [ɔbzɔ'veɪʃɔn] *n* observación *f*; (*by police etc*) vigilancia; (*MED*) examen *m*.

observatory [ɔb'zɔ:vɔtrɪ] *n* observatorio.

observe [ɔb'zɔ:v] *vt* (*gen*) observar; (*rule*) cumplir; **observer** *n* observador/a *m/f*.

obsess [ɔb'sɛs] *vt* obsesionar; ~**ion** [ɔb-

'sɛʃən] n obsesión f, idea fija; ~ive a obsesivo, obsesionante.

obsolescence [ɔbsə'lɛsns] n caída en desuso; **obsolete** ['ɔbsəli:t] a (que está) en desuso.

obstacle ['ɔbstəkl] n obstáculo; (nuisance) estorbo; ~ **race** n carrera de obstáculos.

obstetrician [ɔbstə'trɪʃən] n obstétrico; **obstetrics** [-'stɛtrɪks] n obstetricia.

obstinate ['ɔbstɪnɪt] a terco, porfiado; (determined) tenaz.

obstruct [əb'strʌkt] vt (block) obstruir; (hinder) estorbar, obstaculizar; ~**ion** [əb-'strʌkʃən] n obstrucción f; estorbo, obstáculo.

obtain [əb'teɪn] vt (get) obtener; (achieve) conseguir; ~**able** a asequible.

obtrusive [əb'tru:sɪv] a (person) importuno, entrometido; (building etc) demasiado visible.

obvious ['ɔbvɪəs] a (clear) obvio, evidente; (unsubtle) poco sutil; ~**ly** ad evidentemente, naturalmente.

occasion [ə'keɪʒən] n (gen) oportunidad f, ocasión f; (reason) motivo; (time) ocasión f, vez f; (event) acontecimiento // vt ocasionar, causar; ~**ally** ad de vez en cuando.

occult [ɔ'kʌlt] a (gen) oculto.

occupant ['ɔkjupənt] n (of house) inquilino/a; (of car) ocupante m/f.

occupation [ɔkju'peɪʃən] n (of house) tenencia; (job) trabajo; (: calling) oficio; **unfit for** ~ (house) inhabitable; ~**al hazard** n riesgo profesional.

occupier ['ɔkjupaɪə*] n inquilino/a.

occupy ['ɔkjupaɪ] vt (gen) ocupar; (house) habitar, vivir en; (time) emplear, pasar; (attention) entretener; **to** ~ **o.s. with** or **by doing** (as job) dedicarse a hacer; (to pass time) pasar el tiempo haciendo.

occur [ə'kə:*] vi pasar, suceder; **to** ~ **to sb** ocurrírsele a uno; **it** ~**s to me that...** se me ocurre que...; ~**rence** n (event) acontecimiento; (existence) existencia.

ocean ['əuʃən] n océano; ~-**going** a de alta mar; ~ **liner** n transatlántico.

o'clock [ə'klɔk] ad: **it is 5** ~ son las 5.

octagonal [ɔk'tægənl] a octagonal.

octane ['ɔkteɪn] n octano.

octave ['ɔktɪv] n octava.

October [ɔk'təubə*] n octubre m.

octopus ['ɔktəpəs] n pulpo.

odd [ɔd] a (strange) extraño, raro; (number) impar; (left over) sobrante, suelto; **60**~ 60 y pico; **at** ~ **times** de vez en cuando; **to be the** ~ **one out** estar de más; ~**ity** n rareza; (person) excéntrico; ~-**job man** n hombre m que hace de todo; ~ **jobs** npl bricolaje m; ~**ly** ad curiosamente, extrañamente; ~**ments** npl (COMM) retales mpl; ~**s** npl (in betting) puntos mpl de ventaja; **it makes no** ~**s** no importa, lo mismo da; **at** ~**s** reñidos(as).

ode [əud] n oda.

odious ['əudɪəs] a odioso.

odour, odor (US) ['əudə*] n olor m; (perfume) perfume m; ~**less** a inodoro.

of [ɔv, əv] prep de; **a friend** ~ **ours** un amigo nuestro; **3** ~ **them** 3 de ellos; **the 5th** ~ **July** el 5 de julio; **a boy** ~ **10** un niño de 10 años; **made** ~ **wood** hecho de madera.

off [ɔf] a, ad (engine) desconectado; (light) apagado; (tap) cerrado; (food: bad) pasado, malo; (milk) cortado; (cancelled) anulado // prep de; **to be** ~ (to leave) irse, marcharse; **to be 5 km** ~ estar a 5 kilómetros; **a day** ~ un día libre o sin trabajar; **to have an** ~ **day** tener un día malo; **he had his coat** ~ se había quitado el abrigo; **10%**~ (COMM) (con el) 10% de descuento; **5 km** ~ **(the road)** a 5 km (de la carretera); ~ **the coast** frente a la costa; **on the** ~ **chance** por si acaso.

offal ['ɔfl] n (CULIN) menudencias fpl.

off-colour ['ɔf'kʌlə*] a (ill) indispuesto.

offence, offense (US) [ə'fɛns] n (crime) delito; (insult) ofensa; **to take** ~ **at** ofenderse por.

offend [ə'fɛnd] vt (person) ofender; ~**er** n delincuente m/f; (against regulations) infractor/a m/f.

offensive [ə'fɛnsɪv] a ofensivo; (smell etc) repugnante // n (MIL) ofensiva.

offer ['ɔfə*] n (gen) oferta, ofrecimiento; (proposal) propuesta // vt ofrecer; (opportunity) facilitar; **'on** ~' (COMM) 'en oferta'; ~**ing** n ofrenda; ~**tory** n (REL) ofertorio.

offhand [ɔf'hænd] a informal // ad de improviso.

office ['ɔfɪs] n (place) oficina; (room) despacho; (position) carga, oficio; **to take** ~ entrar en funciones; ~ **block** n bloque m de oficinas; ~ **boy** n mozo (de oficina); **officer** n (MIL etc) oficial m; (of organization) director m; (also: **police officer**) agente m/f de policía; ~ **worker** n oficinista m/f.

official [ə'fɪʃl] a (authorized) oficial, autorizado // n funcionario, oficial m; ~**dom** n burocracia.

officious [ə'fɪʃəs] a oficioso.

offing ['ɔfɪŋ] n: **in the** ~ (fig) en perspectiva.

off: ~-**licence** n (Brit: shop) bodega, tienda de vinos y bebidas alcohólicas; ~-**peak** a de temporada de poca actividad; ~-**putting** a que desanima; ~-**season** a, ad fuera de temporada.

offset ['ɔfsɛt] (irg: like set) vt (counteract) contrarrestar, compensar // n (also: ~ **printing**) offset m.

offshore [ɔf'ʃɔ:*] a (que está) cerca de la costa.

offside ['ɔf'saɪd] a (SPORT) fuera de juego.

offspring ['ɔfsprɪŋ] n descendencia, descendientes mpl or fpl.

off: ~-**stage** ad entre bastidores; ~-**the-peg** ad confeccionado; ~-**white** a blanco grisáceo.

often ['ɔfn] ad a menudo, con frecuencia.

ogle ['əugl] vt echar miradas a.

oil [ɔil] n aceite m; (petroleum) petróleo // vt (machine) engrasar; ~can n lata de aceite; ~field n campo petrolífero; ~-fired a que quema aceite combustible; ~ painting n pintura de óleo; ~ refinery n refinería de petróleo; ~ rig n torre f de perforación; ~skins npl impermeables mpl de hule, chubasquero sg; ~ tanker n petrolero; ~ well n pozo (de petróleo); ~y a aceitoso; (food) grasiento.

ointment ['ɔintmənt] n ungüento.

O.K., okay ['əu'kei] excl O.K., ¡está bien!, ¡vale! // a bien // vt dar el visto bueno a.

old [əuld] a viejo; (former) antiguo; how ~ are you? ¿cuántos años tienes?, ¿qué edad tienes?; he's 10 years ~ tiene 10 años; ~er brother hermano mayor; ~ age n la vejez; ~-age pensioner (O.A.P.) n jubilado/a; ~-fashioned a anticuado, pasado de moda.

olive ['ɔliv] n (fruit) aceituna; (tree) olivo // a (also: ~-green) verde oliva; ~ oil n aceite m de oliva.

Olympic [əu'limpik] a olímpico; the ~ Games, the ~s los Juegos Olímpicos.

omelet(te) ['ɔmlit] n tortilla (de huevo).

omen ['əumən] n presagio.

ominous ['ɔminəs] a de mal agüero, amenazador(a).

omission [əu'miʃən] n omisión f; (error) descuido.

omit [əu'mit] vt omitir; (by mistake) olvidar, descuidar.

on [ɔn] prep en, sobre // ad (machine) conectado; (light, radio) encendido; (tap) abierto; is the meeting still ~? ¿todavía hay reunión?; when is this film ~? ¿cuándo van a poner esta película?; ~ the wall en la pared, colgado de la pared; ~ television en la televisión; ~ horseback a caballo; ~ seeing this al ver esto; ~ arrival al llegar; ~ the left a la izquierda; ~ Friday el viernes; a week ~ Friday el viernes en ocho días; to have one's coat ~ tener el abrigo puesto; to go ~ seguir adelante; it's not ~! ¡eso no se hace!

once [wʌns] ad una vez; (formerly) antiguamente // conj una vez que; at ~ en seguida, inmediatamente; (simultaneously) a la vez; ~ a week una vez por semana; ~ more otra vez; ~ and for all de una vez por todas; ~ upon a time érase una vez.

oncoming ['ɔnkʌmiŋ] a (traffic) que viene de frente.

one [wʌn] det, num un, uno, una // pron uno; (impersonal) se // a (sole) único; (same) mismo; this ~ éste/a; that ~ ése/a, aquél/aquella; ~ by ~ uno por uno; ~ never knows nunca se sabe; ~ another el uno al otro; ~-man a (business) individual; ~-man band n un hombre-orquesta; ~self pron uno mismo; (after

prep, also emphatic) sí (mismo/a); '~-way' 'dirección única'.

ongoing ['ɔngəuiŋ] a continuo.

onion ['ʌnjən] n cebolla.

onlooker ['ɔnlukə*] n espectador/a m/f.

only ['əunli] ad solamente, sólo // a único, solo // conj solamente que, pero; an ~ child un hijo único; not ~ ... but also ~ no sólo ... sino también... .

onset ['ɔnset] n (beginning) comienzo; (attack) ataque m.

onslaught ['ɔnslɔːt] n ataque m, embestida.

onto ['ɔntu] prep = on to.

onus ['əunəs] n responsabilidad f.

onward(s) ['ɔnwəd(z)] ad (move) (hacia) adelante; from this time ~ de ahora en adelante.

onyx ['ɔniks] n ónice m, onyx m.

ooze [uːz] vi rezumar.

opal ['əupl] n ópalo.

opaque [əu'peik] a opaco.

open ['əupn] a abierto; (car) descubierto; (road, view) despejado; (meeting) público; (admiration) manifiesto // vt abrir // vi (flower, eyes, door, debate) abrirse; (book etc: commence) comenzar; to ~ on to vt fus (subj: room, door) dar a; to ~ up vt abrir; (blocked road) despejar // vi abrirse, empezar; in the ~ (air) al aire libre; ~ing n abertura, comienzo; (opportunity) oportunidad f; (job) puesto vacante, vacante f; ~ly ad abiertamente; ~-minded a imparcial; ~-necked a sin corbata.

opera ['ɔpərə] n ópera; ~ glasses npl gemelos mpl; ~ house n teatro de la ópera.

operate ['ɔpəreit] vt (machine) hacer funcionar; (company) dirigir // vi funcionar; (drug) hacer efecto; to ~ on sb (MED) operar a uno.

operatic [ɔpə'rætik] a de ópera.

operating ['ɔpəreitiŋ] ~ table n mesa de operaciones; ~ theatre n sala de operaciones.

operation [ɔpə'reiʃən] n (gen) operación f; (of machine) funcionamiento; to be in ~ estar en funcionamiento o funcionando; ~al a operacional, en buen estado.

operative ['ɔpərətiv] a (measure) en vigor.

operator ['ɔpəreitə*] n (of machine) maquinista m/f; operario; (TEL) operador/a m/f, telefonista m/f.

operetta [ɔpə'retə] n opereta; (in Spain) zarzuela.

ophthalmic [ɔf'θælmik] a oftálmico.

opinion [ə'piniən] n (gen) opinión f; (point of view) parecer m, juicio; ~ated a testarudo; ~ poll n encuesta, sondeo.

opium ['əupiəm] n opio.

opponent [ə'pəunənt] n adversario/a, contrincante m/f.

opportune ['ɔpətjuːn] a oportuno; opportunist [-'tjuːnist] n oportunista m/f.

opportunity [ɔpə'tjuːniti] n oportunidad f.

oppose [ə'pəuz] vt oponerse a; **to be ~d to sth** oponerse a algo, resistirse a aceptar algo; **opposing** a (side) opuesto, contrario.

opposite ['ɔpəzit] a opuesto; (house etc) de enfrente // ad en frente // prep en frente de, frente a // n lo contrario.

opposition [ɔpə'zi∫ən] n oposición f.

oppress [ə'prɛs] vt oprimir; **~ion** [ə'prɛ∫ən] n opresión f; **~ive** a opresivo.

opt [ɔpt] vi: **to ~ for** elegir; **to ~ to do** optar por hacer; **to ~ out of** optar por no hacer.

optical ['ɔptikl] a óptico.

optician [ɔp'ti∫ən] n óptico.

optimism ['ɔptimizəm] n optimismo.

optimist ['ɔptimist] n optimista m/f; **~ic** [-'mistik] a optimista.

optimum ['ɔptiməm] a óptimo.

option ['ɔp∫ən] n opción f; **to keep one's ~s open** (fig) mantener las opciones abiertas; **~al** a facultativo, discrecional.

opulent ['ɔpjulənt] a opulento.

or [ɔː*] conj o; (before o, ho) u; (with negative): **he hasn't seen ~ heard anything** no ha visto ni oído nada; **~ else** si no.

oracle ['ɔrəkl] n oráculo.

oral ['ɔːrəl] a oral // n examen m oral.

orange ['ɔrindʒ] n (fruit) naranja // a color naranja.

oration [ɔː'rei∫ən] n oración f; **orator** ['ɔrətə*] n orador/a m/f.

orbit ['ɔːbit] n órbita // vt, vi orbitar.

orchard ['ɔːt∫əd] n huerto.

orchestra ['ɔːkistrə] n orquesta; **orchestral** [-'kɛstrəl] a orquestral.

orchid ['ɔːkid] n orquídea.

ordain [ɔː'dein] vt (REL) ordenar, decretar; (decide) mandar.

ordeal [ɔː'diːl] n experiencia penosa.

order ['ɔːdə*] n orden m; (command) orden f; (type, kind) clase f; (state) estado; (COMM) pedido, encargo // vt (also: **put in ~**) arreglar, poner en orden; (COMM) encargar, pedir; (command) mandar, ordenar; **in ~** (of document) en regla; **in ~ to do** para hacer; **to ~ sb to do sth** mandar a uno hacer algo; **~ly** n (MIL) ordenanza m; (MED) enfermero (auxiliar) // a (room) en orden, ordenado; (person) ordenado.

ordinary ['ɔːdnri] a corriente, normal; (pej) ordinario, vulgar; **out of the ~** fuera de lo común.

ordnance ['ɔːdnəns] n (MIL: unit) artillería; **O~ Survey** n servicio oficial de topografía y cartografía.

ore [ɔː*] n mineral m.

organ ['ɔːgən] n órgano; **~ic** [ɔː'gænik] a orgánico.

organism ['ɔːgənizəm] n organismo.

organist ['ɔːgənist] n organista m/f.

organization [ɔːgənai'zei∫ən] n organización f; **organize** ['ɔːgənaiz] vt organizar; **organizer** ['ɔːgənaizə*] n organizador/a m/f.

orgasm ['ɔːgæzəm] n orgasmo.

orgy ['ɔːdʒi] n orgía.

Orient ['ɔːriənt] n Oriente m; **oriental** [-'ɛntl] a oriental.

orientate ['ɔːriənteit] vt orientar.

origin ['ɔridʒin] n origen m; (point of departure) procedencia.

original [ə'ridʒinl] a original; (first) primero; (earlier) primitivo // n original m; **~ity** [-'næliti] n originalidad f; **~ly** ad (at first) al principio; (with originality) con originalidad.

originate [ə'ridʒineit] vi: **to ~ from or in** surgir de, tener su origen en.

ornament ['ɔːnəmənt] n adorno; (trinket) chuchería; **~al** [-'mɛntl] a decorativo, de adorno.

ornate [ɔː'neit] a muy ornado, vistoso.

ornithologist [ɔːni'θɔlədʒist] n ornitólogo; **ornithology** [-dʒi] n ornitología.

orphan ['ɔːfn] n huérfano // vt: **to be ~ed** quedar huérfano; **~age** n orfelinato.

orthodox ['ɔːθədɔks] a ortodoxo; **~y** n ortodoxia.

orthopaedic, orthopedic (US) [ɔːθə'piːdik] a ortopédico; **~s** n ortopedia.

oscillate ['ɔsileit] vi oscilar; (person) vacilar.

ostensibly [ɔs'tɛnsibli] ad aparentemente.

ostentatious [ɔstɛn'tei∫əs] a pretencioso, aparatoso; (person) ostentativo.

osteopath ['ɔstiəpæθ] n osteópata m/f.

ostracize ['ɔstrəsaiz] vt condenar al ostracismo.

ostrich ['ɔstrit∫] n avestruz m.

other ['ʌðə*] a otro; **~ than** (in another way) de otra manera que; (apart from) aparte de; **~wise** ad, conj de otra manera; (if not) si no.

otter ['ɔtə*] n nutria.

ought [ɔːt], pt **ought** auxiliary vb: **I ~ to do it** debería hacerlo; **this ~ to have been corrected** esto debiera de haberse corregido; **he ~ to win** (probability) debe o debiera ganar.

ounce [auns] n onza (28.35g).

our ['auə*] a nuestro; **~s** pron (el) nuestro/(la) nuestra etc; **~selves** pron pl (reflexive, after prep) nosotros; (emphatic) nosotros mismos.

oust [aust] vt desalojar.

out [aut] ad fuera, afuera; (not at home) fuera (de casa); (light, fire) apagado; **~ there** allí, allí fuera; **he's ~** (absent) no está, ha salido; **to be ~ in one's calculations** equivocarse (en sus cálculos); **to run ~** salir corriendo; **~ loud** en alta voz; **~ of** (outside) fuera de; (because of: anger etc) por; **~ of petrol** sin gasolina; **"~ of order"** "no funciona"; **~-of-the-way** (fig) insólito.

outback ['autbæk] n interior m.

outboard ['autbɔːd] a: **~ motor** motor m de fuera de borda.

outbreak ['autbreik] n (of war) comienzo;

(of disease) epidemia; (of violence etc) arranque m.

outburst ['autbɔːst] n explosión f, arranque m.

outcast ['autkɑːst] n paria m/f.

outcome ['autkʌm] n resultado.

outcry ['autkraɪ] n protesta ruidosa.

outdated [aut'deɪtɪd] a anticuado, fuera de moda.

outdo [aut'duː] (irg: like do) vt exceder.

outdoor [aut'dɔː*] a, ~s ad al aire libre.

outer ['autə*] a exterior, externo; ~ space n el espacio.

outfit ['autfɪt] n equipo; (clothes) traje m; ~ter's n camisería.

outgoing ['autgəuɪŋ] a (character) extrovertido; ~s npl gastos mpl.

outgrow [aut'grəu] (irg: like grow) vt: he has ~n his clothes su ropa le queda pequeña ya.

outing ['autɪŋ] n excursión f, paseo.

outlandish [aut'lændɪʃ] a estrafalario.

outlaw ['autlɔː] n proscrito // vt (person) declarar fuera de la ley; (practice) declarar ilegal.

outlay ['autleɪ] n inversión f.

outlet ['autlɛt] n salida; (of pipe) desagüe m; (for emotion) desahogo; (also: retail ~) lugar m de venta.

outline ['autlaɪn] n (shape) contorno, perfil m; (of plan) trazado; (sketch) esbozo, idea general.

outlive [aut'lɪv] vt sobrevivir.

outlook ['autluk] n perspectiva; (opinion) punto de vista.

outlying ['autlaɪɪŋ] a remoto, aislado.

outmoded [aut'məudɪd] a anticuado, pasado de moda.

outnumber [aut'nʌmbə*] vt exceder en número.

outpatient ['autpeɪʃənt] n paciente m/f de consulta externa.

outpost ['autpəust] n puesto avanzado.

output ['autput] n (volumen m de) producción f, rendimiento.

outrage ['autreɪdʒ] n (scandal) escándalo; (atrocity) atrocidad f // vt ultrajar; ~ous [-'reɪdʒəs] a monstruoso.

outright [aut'raɪt] ad completamente // a ['autraɪt] completo.

outset ['autsɛt] n principio.

outside ['aut'saɪd] n exterior m; (surface) superficie f; (aspect) aspecto // a exterior, externo // ad fuera // prep fuera de; (beyond) más allá de; at the ~ (fig) a lo sumo; ~ lane n (AUT: in Britain) carril m de la derecha; ~-left n (FOOTBALL) extremo izquierdo; **outsider** n (stranger) extraño, forastero.

outsize ['autsaɪz] a (clothes) de talla grande.

outskirts ['autskɔːts] npl alrededores mpl, afueras fpl.

outspoken [aut'spəukən] a muy franco.

outstanding [aut'stændɪŋ] a excepcional, destacado; (unfinished) pendiente.

outstay [aut'steɪ] vt: to ~ one's welcome quedarse más tiempo de lo indicado.

outstretched [aut'strɛtʃt] a (hand) extendido.

outward ['autwəd] a (sign, appearances) externo; (journey) de ida; ~ly ad por fuera.

outweigh [aut'weɪ] vt pesar más que.

outwit [aut'wɪt] vt ser más listo que, burlar.

oval ['əuvl] a ovalado // n óvalo.

ovary ['əuvərɪ] n ovario.

ovation [əu'veɪʃən] n ovación f.

oven ['ʌvn] n horno; ~proof a refractario.

over ['əuvə*] ad encima, por encima // a (or ad) (finished) terminado // prep (por) encima de; (above) sobre; (on the other side of) al otro lado de; (more than) más de; (during) durante; ~ here (por) aquí; ~ there (por) allí o allá; all ~ (everywhere) por todas partes; ~ and ~ (again) una y otra vez; ~ and above más de; to ask sb ~ invitar a uno; to bend ~ inclinarse.

over... ['əuvə*] pref sobre..., super...; ~abundant a superabundante.

overall ['əuvərɔːl] a (length) total; (study) de conjunto // ad [əuvər'ɔːl] en conjunto; ~s npl mono sg o bata sg (de trabajo).

overbalance [əuvə'bæləns] vi perder el equilibrio.

overbearing [əuvə'bɛərɪŋ] a autoritario, imperioso.

overboard ['əuvəbɔːd] ad (NAUT) por la borda; man ~! ¡hombre al agua!

overcast ['əuvəkɑːst] a encapotado.

overcharge [əuvə'tʃɑːdʒ] vt: to ~ sb cobrar un precio excesivo a uno.

overcoat ['əuvəkəut] n abrigo, sobretodo.

overcome [əuvə'kʌm] (irg: like come) vt (gen) vencer; (difficulty) superar.

overcrowded [əuvə'kraudɪd] a atestado de gente; (country) superpoblado.

overdo [əuvə'duː] (irg: like do) vt exagerar; (overcook) cocer demasiado.

overdose ['əuvədəus] n dosis f excesiva.

overdraft ['əuvədrɑːft] n saldo deudor.

overdrawn [əuvə'drɔːn] a (account) en descubierto.

overdue [əuvə'djuː] a retrasado; (recognition) tardío.

overestimate [əuvər'ɛstɪmeɪt] vt sobreestimar.

overexcited [əuvərɪk'saɪtɪd] a sobreexcitado.

overexpose [əuvərɪk'spəuz] vt (PHOT) sobreexponer.

overflow [əuvə'fləu] vi desbordarse // n ['əuvəfləu] (excess) exceso; (of river) desbordamiento; (also: ~ pipe) (cañería de) desagüe m.

overgrown [əuvə'grəun] a (garden) cubierto de hierba.

overhaul [əuvə'hɔːl] vt revisar, repasar // n ['əuvəhɔːl] revisión f.

overhead [əuvə'hɛd] ad por lo alto // a

['ɔuvəhɛd] de arriba; (*railway*) elevado, aéreo; ~s npl gastos mpl generales.

overhear [ɔuvə'hɪə*] (*irg: like hear*) vt oír por casualidad.

overjoyed [ɔuvə'dʒɔɪd] a encantado, lleno de alegría.

overland ['ɔuvəlænd] a, ad por tierra.

overlap [ɔuvə'læp] vi traslaparse // n ['ɔuvəlæp] traslapo.

overleaf [ɔuvə'liːf] ad al dorso.

overload [ɔuvə'ləud] vt sobrecargar.

overlook [ɔuvə'luk] vt (*have view on*) dar a, tener vistas a; (*miss: by mistake*) pasar por alto; (: *deliberately*) no hacerse caso de; (*forgive*) perdonar.

overnight [ɔuvə'naɪt] ad durante la noche; (*fig*) de la noche a la mañana // a de noche; to stay ~ pasar la noche.

overpass ['ɔuvəpɑːs] n paso superior.

overpower [ɔuvə'pauə*] vt dominar; ~ing a (*heat, stench*) abrumador(a).

overrate [ɔuvə'reɪt] vt sobreestimar.

override [ɔuvə'raɪd] (*irg: like ride*) vt (*order, objection*) no hacer caso de; **overriding** a predominante.

overrule [ɔuvə'ruːl] vt (*decision*) anular; (*claim*) denegar.

overseas [ɔuvə'siːz] ad en ultramar; (*abroad*) en el extranjero // a (*trade*) exterior; (*visitor*) extranjero.

overseer ['ɔuvəsiə*] n (*in factory*) superintendente m/f; (*foreman*) capataz m.

overshadow [ɔuvə'ʃædəu] vt (*fig*) eclipsar.

overshoot [ɔuvə'ʃuːt] (*irg: like shoot*) vt excederse.

oversight ['ɔuvəsaɪt] n descuido.

oversleep [ɔuvə'sliːp] (*irg: like sleep*) vi despertarse (muy) tarde.

overspend [ɔuvə'spɛnd] (*irg: like spend*) vi gastar demasiado.

overspill ['ɔuvəspɪl] n exceso de población.

overstate [ɔuvə'steɪt] vt exagerar; ~ment n exageración f.

overt [əu'vəːt] a abierto.

overtake [ɔuvə'teɪk] (*irg: like take*) vt sobrepasar; (AUT) adelantar; **overtaking** n (AUT) adelantamiento.

overthrow [ɔuvə'θrəu] (*irg: like throw*) vt (*government*) derrocar.

overtime ['ɔuvətaɪm] n horas fpl extraordinarias.

overtone ['ɔuvətəun] n (*fig*) sugestión f, alusión f.

overture ['ɔuvətʃuə*] n (MUS) obertura; (*fig*) propuesta.

overturn [ɔuvə'təːn] vt, vi volcar.

overweight [ɔuvə'weɪt] a demasiado gordo o pesado.

overwhelm [ɔuvə'wɛlm] vt aplastar; ~ing a (*victory, defeat*) arrollador(a); (*desire*) irresistible.

overwork [ɔuvə'wəːk] n trabajo excesivo // vt hacer trabajar demasiado // vi trabajar demasiado.

overwrought [ɔuvə'rɔːt] a sobreexcitado.

owe [əu] vt deber; to ~ sb sth, to ~ sth to sb deber algo a uno; **owing to** prep debido a, por causa de.

owl [aul] n búho, lechuza.

own [əun] vt tener, poseer // a propio; **a room of my** ~ una habitación propia; **to get one's** ~ **back** tomar revancha; **on one's** ~ solo, a solas; to ~ **up** vi confesar; ~er n dueño; ~ership n posesión f.

ox [ɔks], pl ~en ['ɔksn] n buey m.

oxide ['ɔksaɪd] n óxido.

oxtail ['ɔksteɪl] n: ~ **soup** sopa de rabo de buey.

oxygen ['ɔksɪdʒən] n oxígeno; ~ **mask/tent** máscara/tienda de oxígeno.

oyster ['ɔɪstə*] n ostra.

oz. abbr of **ounce(s)**.

ozone ['əuzəun] n ozono.

P

p [piː] abbr of **penny, pence**.

p.a. abbr of **per annum**.

pa [pɑː] n (*col*) papá m.

pace [peɪs] n paso; (*rhythm*) ritmo // vi: to ~ **up and down** pasarse de un lado a otro; **to keep** ~ **with** llevar el mismo paso que; (*events*) mantenerse a la altura de o al corriente de; ~**maker** n (MED) regulador m cardíaco, marcapasos m inv.

pacific [pə'sɪfɪk] a pacífico // n: **the P**~ (Ocean) el (Océano) Pacífico.

pacifist ['pæsɪfɪst] n pacifista m/f.

pacify ['pæsɪfaɪ] vt (*soothe*) apaciguar; (*country*) pacificar.

pack [pæk] n (*gen*) paquete m; (*of hounds*) jauría; (*of thieves etc*) manada, bando; (*of cards*) baraja; (*bundle*) fardo; (*back* ~) mochila // vt (*wrap*) empaquetar; (*fill*) llenar; (*in suitcase etc*) meter o poner (en maleta); (*cram*) llenar, atestar; (*fig: meeting etc*) llenar- de partidarios; to ~ **sb off** despachar a uno; ~ **it in!** (*col*) ¡déjalo!; to ~ **one's case** hacerse la maleta.

package ['pækɪdʒ] n paquete m; (*bulky*) bulto; (*also:* ~ **deal**) acuerdo global; ~ **tour** n viaje m todo incluido.

packet ['pækɪt] n paquete m; (NAUT) paquebote m.

packing ['pækɪŋ] n embalaje m; (*external*) envase m; (*internal*) relleno; ~ **case** n cajón m de embalaje.

pact [pækt] n pacto.

pad [pæd] n (*of paper*) bloc m; (*cushion*) cojinete m; (*launching* ~) plataforma (de lanzamiento); (*foot*) pata; (*col: flat*) casa // vi andar (sin hacer ruido); ~**ding** n relleno; (*fig*) paja.

paddle ['pædl] n (*oar*) canalete m // vt impulsar con canalete // vi (*with feet*) chapotear; ~ **steamer** n vapor m de ruedas; **paddling pool** n estanque m de juegos.

paddock ['pædək] n corral m.

paddy field ['pædi-] n arrozal m.
padlock ['pædlɔk] n candado // vt cerrar con candado.
padre ['pɑːdrɪ] n capellán m.
paediatrics, pediatrics (US) [piːdɪ'ætrɪks] n pediatría.
pagan ['peɪɡən] a, n pagano/a.
page [peɪdʒ] n (of book) página; (of newspaper) plana; (also: ~ boy) paje m // vt (in hotel etc) buscar (a uno) llamando su nombre.
pageant ['pædʒənt] n (procession) desfile m; (show) espectáculo; ~ry n pompa.
pagoda [pə'ɡəudə] n pagoda.
paid [peɪd] pt, pp of **pay** // a (work) remunerado; (official) asalariado; to put ~ to acabar con.
pail [peɪl] n cubo, balde m.
pain [peɪn] n dolor m; to be in ~ sufrir; on ~ of death so pena de muerte; to take ~s to do sth tomarse trabajo en hacer algo; ~ed a (expression) afligido; ~ful a doloroso; (difficult) penoso; (disagreeable) desagradable; ~fully ad (fig: very) terriblemente; ~killer n calmante m; ~less a que no causa dolor; **painstaking** ['peɪnzteɪkɪŋ] a (person) concienzudo, esmerado.
paint [peɪnt] n pintura // vt pintar; to ~ one's face pintarse (la cara); to ~ the door blue pintar la puerta de azul; ~brush n (artist's) pincel m; (decorator's) brocha; ~er n pintor/a m/f; ~ing n pintura.
pair [pɛə*] n (of shoes, gloves etc) par m; (of people) pareja; a ~ of scissors unas tijeras; a ~ of trousers unos pantalones, un pantalón.
pajamas [pɪ'dʒɑːməz] npl (US) pijama m.
Pakistan [pɑːkɪ'stɑːn] n Paquistán m; ~i a, n paquistaní.
pal [pæl] n (col) compinche m/f, compañero/a.
palace ['pæləs] n palacio.
palatable ['pælɪtəbl] a sabroso; (acceptable) aceptable.
palate ['pælɪt] n paladar m.
palaver [pə'lɑːvə*] n (fuss) lío; (hindrances) molestias fpl.
pale [peɪl] a (gen) pálido; (colour) claro; to grow ~ palidecer; to be beyond the ~ estar excluido; ~ness n palidez f.
Palestine ['pælɪstaɪn] n Palestina; **Palestinian** [-'tɪnɪən] a, n palestino/a.
palette ['pælɪt] n paleta.
paling ['peɪlɪŋ] n (stake) estaca; (fence) valla.
palisade [pælɪ'seɪd] n palizada.
pall [pɔːl] n (of smoke) capa (de humo) // vi perder el sabor.
pallid ['pælɪd] a pálido.
palm [pɑːm] n (gen) palma; (also: ~ tree) palmera, palma // vt: to ~ sth off on sb (col) encajar algo a uno; ~ist n quiromántico/a; P~ Sunday n Domingo de Ramos.
palpable ['pælpəbl] a palpable.

palpitation [pælpɪ'teɪʃən] n palpitación f; to have ~s tener vahídos.
paltry ['pɔːltrɪ] a (insignificant) baladí; (miserable) vil.
pamper ['pæmpə*] vt mimar.
pamphlet ['pæmflət] n folleto.
pan [pæn] n (also: **saucepan**~) cacerola, cazuela; (also: **frying** ~) sartén m; (of lavatory) taza // vi (CINEMA) tomar una vista panorámica.
panacea [pænə'sɪə] n panacea.
Panama ['pænəmɑː] n Panamá m.
pancake ['pænkeɪk] n canapé m.
panda ['pændə] n panda m/f; ~ car n coche m de la policía.
pandemonium [pændɪ'məunɪəm] n (noise) estruendo; (mess) caos m.
pander ['pændə*] vi: to ~ to complacer a.
pane [peɪn] n cristal m.
panel ['pænl] n (of wood) panel m; (of cloth) paño; (RADIO, TV) tablero; ~ling, ~ing (US) n paneles mpl, entrepaños mpl.
pang [pæŋ] n: ~s of conscience remordimiento sg; ~s of hunger dolores mpl del hambre.
panic ['pænɪk] n (terror) pánico // vi aterrarse; ~ky a (person) asustadizo; ~-stricken a preso de pánico.
pannier ['pænɪə*] n (on bicycle) cartera; (on mule etc) alforja.
panorama [pænə'rɑːmə] n panorama m.
pansy ['pænzɪ] n (BOT) pensamiento; (col) maricón m.
pant [pænt] vi jadear.
panther ['pænθə*] n pantera.
panties ['pæntɪz] npl bragas fpl, pantis mpl.
pantomime ['pæntəmaɪm] n revista musical representada en Navidad, basada en cuentos de hadas.
pantry ['pæntrɪ] n despensa.
pants [pænts] n (woman's) bragas fpl; (man's) calzoncillos mpl; (US: trousers) pantalones mpl.
papal ['peɪpəl] a papal.
paper ['peɪpə*] n papel m; (also: **news**~) periódico, diario; (study, article) artículo; (exam) examen m // a de papel // vt empapelar; (identity) ~s npl papeles mpl, documentos mpl; ~back n libro de bolsillo; ~ bag n saco de papel; ~ clip n grapa; ~ hankie n pañuelo de papel; ~ money n papel moneda; ~weight n pisapapeles m inv; ~work n trabajo administrativo; (pej) papeleo.
papier-mâché ['pæpɪeɪ'mæʃeɪ] n cartón m piedra.
paprika ['pæprɪkə] n pimienta húngara o roja.
par [pɑː*] n par f; (GOLF) par m; to be on a ~ with correr parejas con.
parable ['pærəbl] n parábola.
parachute ['pærəʃuːt] n paracaídas m inv // vi lanzarse en paracaídas; ~ jump n salto en paracaídas.
parade [pə'reɪd] n desfile m // vt (gen)

recorrer, desfilar por; (*show off*) hacer
alarde de // *vi* desfilar; (*MIL*) pasar
revista.
paradise ['pærədaɪs] *n* paraíso.
paradox ['pærədɔks] *n* paradoja; ~**ical**
[-'dɔksɪkl] *a* paradójico.
paraffin ['pærəfɪn] *n*: ~ (**oil**) petróleo.
paragraph ['pærəgrɑ:f] *n* párrafo.
parallel ['pærəlɛl] *a* en paralelo; (*fig*)
semejante // *n* (*line*) paralela; (*fig, GEO*)
paralelo.
paralysis [pə'rælɪsɪs] *n* parálisis *f*;
paralyze ['pærəlaɪz] *vt* paralizar.
paramount ['pærəmaunt] *a*: **of** ~
importance de la mayor importancia,
primordial.
paranoia [pærə'nɔɪə] *n* paranoia;
paranoiac *a* paranoico.
paraphernalia [pærəfə'neɪlɪə] *n* (*gear*)
avíos *mpl*.
paraplegic [pærə'pli:dʒɪk] *n* parapléjico.
parasite ['pærəsaɪt] *n* parásito.
parasol [pærə'sɔl] *n* sombrilla, quitasol *m*.
paratrooper ['pærətru:pə*] *n* paracaidista
m/f.
parcel ['pɑ:sl] *n* paquete *m* // *vt* (*also*: ~
up) empaquetar, embalar.
parch [pɑ:tʃ] *vt* secar, resecar; ~**ed** *a*
(*person*) muerto de sed.
parchment ['pɑ:tʃmənt] *n* pergamino.
pardon ['pɑ:dn] *n* perdón *m*; (*LAW*) indulto
// *vt* perdonar; indultar; ~**!** ¡perdone!; ~
me!, I beg your ~**!** ¡perdone Usted!; (**I**
beg your) ~? ¿cómo?
parent ['pɛərənt] *n* padre *m*/madre *f*; ~**s**
npl padres *mpl*; ~**al** [pə'rɛntl] *a*
paternal/maternal.
parenthesis [pə'rɛnθɪsɪs], *pl* -**theses**
[-θɪsi:z] *n* paréntesis *m inv*.
Paris ['pærɪs] *n* París.
parish ['pærɪʃ] *n* parroquia; ~**ioner**
[pə'rɪʃənə*] *n* feligrés/esa *m/f*.
Parisian [pə'rɪzɪən] *a, n* parisino/a,
parisiense *m/f*.
parity ['pærɪtɪ] *n* paridad *f*, igualdad *f*.
park [pɑ:k] *n* parque *m* // *vt* estacionar //
vi aparcar, estacionarse; ~**ing** *n*
aparcamiento, estacionamiento; **'no**
~**ing'** 'prohibido estacionarse'; ~**ing lot**
n (*US*) parking *m*; ~**ing meter** *n*
parquímetro.
parliament ['pɑ:ləmənt] *n* parlamento;
(*Spanish*) Cortes *mpl*; ~**ary** [-'mɛntərɪ] *a*
parlamentario.
parlour, parlor (*US*) ['pɑ:lə*] *n* sala de
recibo, salón *m*.
parochial [pə'rəukɪəl] *a* parroquial; (*pej*)
de miras estrechas.
parody ['pærədɪ] *n* parodia // *vt* parodiar.
parole [pə'rəul] *n*: **on** ~ libre bajo
palabra.
parquet ['pɑ:keɪ] *n*: ~ **floor(ing)** parquet
m.
parrot ['pærət] *n* loro, papagayo; ~
fashion *ad* mecánicamente.
parry ['pærɪ] *vt* parar.

parsimonious [pɑ:sɪ'məunɪəs] *a* parco.
parsley ['pɑ:slɪ] *n* perejil *m*.
parsnip ['pɑ:snɪp] *n* chirivía.
parson ['pɑ:sn] *n* (*parish*) párroco; (*gen*)
cura *m*.
part [pɑ:t] *n* (*gen, MUS*) parte *f*; (*bit*) trozo;
(*of machine*) pieza; (*THEATRE etc*) papel *m*;
(*of serial*) entrega // *ad* = **partly** // *vt*
dividir; (*break*) partir // *vi* (*people*)
separarse; (*roads*) bifurcarse; (*crowd*)
apartarse; (*break*) romperse; **to take** ~
in participar *o* tomar parte en; **to take**
sth in good ~ tomar algo en buena
parte; **to take sb's** ~ defender a uno; **for**
my ~ por mi parte; **for the most** ~ en
la mayor parte; **to** ~ **with** *vt fus* ceder,
entregar; (*money*) pagar; (*get rid of*)
deshacerse de; **in** ~ **exchange** como
parte del pago; **spare** ~ pieza de
recambio.
partial ['pɑ:ʃl] *a* parcial; **to be** ~ **to** ser
aficionado a; ~**ly** *ad* en parte.
participant [pɑ:'tɪsɪpənt] *n* (*in*
competition) concursante *m/f*; **par-**
ticipate [-peɪt] *vi*: **to participate in**
participar en; **participation** [-'peɪʃən] *n*
participación *f*.
participle ['pɑ:tɪsɪpl] *n* participio.
particle ['pɑ:tɪkl] *n* partícula; (*of dust*)
grano; (*fig*) pizca.
particular [pə'tɪkjulə*] *a* (*special*)
particular; (*concrete*) concreto; (*given*)
determinado; (*detailed*) detallado,
minucioso; (*fussy*) quisquilloso, exigente;
~**s** *npl* (*information*) datos *mpl*, detalles
mpl; (*details*) pormenores *mpl*; ~**ly** *ad*
especialmente, en particular.
parting ['pɑ:tɪŋ] *n* (*act of*) separación *f*;
(*farewell*) despedida; (*in hair*) raya // *a* de
despedida.
partisan [pɑ:tɪ'zæn] *a, n* partidario/a.
partition [pɑ:'tɪʃən] *n* (*POL*) división *f*;
(*wall*) tabique *m* // *vt* dividir; dividir con
tabique.
partly ['pɑ:tlɪ] *ad* en parte.
partner ['pɑ:tnə*] *n* (*COMM*) socio/a;
(*SPORT, at dance*) pareja; (*spouse*) cónyuge
m/f; (*friend etc*) compañero/a // *vt*
acompañar; ~**ship** *n* (*gen*) asociación *f*;
(*COMM*) sociedad *f*.
partridge ['pɑ:trɪdʒ] *n* perdiz *f*.
part-time ['pɑ:t'taɪm] *a, ad* de medio
tiempo *o* media jornada.
party ['pɑ:tɪ] *n* (*POL*) partido; (*celebration*)
fiesta; (*group*) grupo; (*LAW*) parte *f*,
interesado *o* (*a POL*) de partido; (*dress*
etc) de fiesta, de gala.
pass [pɑ:s] *vt* (*time, object*) pasar; (*place*)
pasar por; (*exam*) aprobar; (*overtake,*
surpass) rebasar; (*approve*) aprobar // *vi*
pasar; (*SCOL*) aprobar, ser aprobado // *n*
(*permit*) permiso; (*membership card*)
carnet *m*; (*in mountains*) puerto,
desfiladero; (*SPORT*) pase *m*; (*SCOL: also*: ~
mark): **to get a** ~ **in** aprobar en; **to** ~
sth through sth pasar algo por algo; **to**
~ **away** *vi* fallecer; **to** ~ **by** *vi* pasar //

vt (*ignore*) pasar por alto; **to ~ for** pasar por; **to ~ out** *vi* desmayarse; **to ~ up** *vt* renunciar a; **~able** *a* (*road*) transitable; (*work*) pasable.

passage ['pæsɪdʒ] *n* (*also:* **~way**) pasillo; (*act of passing*) tránsito; (*fare, in book*) pasaje *m*; (*by boat*) travesía; (*MECH, MED*) tubo.

passenger ['pæsɪndʒə*] *n* pasajero, viajero.

passer-by [pɑːsə'baɪ] *n* transeúnte *m/f*.

passing ['pɑːsɪŋ] *a* (*fleeting*) pasajero; **in ~** de paso.

passion ['pæʃən] *n* pasión *f*; (*anger*) cólera; **~ate** *a* apasionado; colérico.

passive ['pæsɪv] *a* (*also LING*) pasivo.

Passover ['pɑːsəuvə*] *n* Pascua (de los judíos).

passport ['pɑːspɔːt] *n* pasaporte *m*.

password ['pɑːswɜːd] *n* santo y seña.

past [pɑːst] *prep* (*further than*) más allá de; (*later than*) después de // *a* pasado; (*president etc*) ex, antiguo // *n* el pasado; (*antecedents*) antecedentes *mpl*; **he's ~ forty** tiene más de cuarenta años; **for the ~ few/3 days** durante los últimos/3 días; **to run ~** pasar a la carrera por.

pasta ['pæstə] *n* pastas *fpl*.

paste [peɪst] *n* (*gen*) pasta; (*glue*) engrudo // *vt* (*stick*) pegar; (*glue*) engomar.

pastel ['pæstl] *a* pastel; (*painting*) al pastel.

pasteurized ['pæstəraɪzd] *a* pasteurizado.

pastille ['pæstl] *n* pastilla.

pastime ['pɑːstaɪm] *n* pasatiempo.

pastor ['pɑːstə*] *n* pastor *m*.

pastoral ['pɑːstərl] *a* pastoral.

pastry ['peɪstrɪ] *n* pasta; (*cakes*) pastas *fpl*. pasteles *mpl*.

pasture ['pɑːstʃə*] *n* (*grass*) pasto; (*land*) prado, pasto.

pasty ['pæstɪ] *n* empanada // *a* ['peɪstɪ] pastoso; (*complexion*) pálido.

pat [pæt] *vt* dar una palmadita a; (*dog etc*) acariciar // *n* (*of butter*) pastelillo; **to give sb a ~ on the back** felicitar a uno.

patch [pætʃ] *n* (*of material*) parche *m*; (*piece*) pedazo; (*mend*) remiendo; (*of land*) terreno // *vt* (*clothes*) remendar; **to ~ up** *vt* (*mend temporarily*) componer de modo provisional; (*quarrel*) hacer las paces con; **~work** *n* labor *m* de retazos; **~y** *a* desigual.

pâté ['pæteɪ] *n* pastel *m* de carne.

patent ['peɪtnt] *n* patente *f* // *vt* patentar // *a* patente, evidente; **~ leather** *n* charol *m*.

paternal [pə'tɜːnl] *a* paternal; (*relation*) paterno; **paternity** [-nɪtɪ] *n* paternidad *f*.

path [pɑːθ] *n* senda, sendero; (*trail, track*) pista; (*of missile*) trayectoria.

pathetic [pə'θetɪk] *a* (*pitiful*) patético, lastimoso; (*very bad*) malísimo; (*moving*) conmovedor(a).

pathologist [pə'θɒlədʒɪst] *n* patólogo; **pathology** [-dʒɪ] *n* patología.

pathos ['peɪθɒs] *n* patetismo, lo patético.

pathway ['pɑːθweɪ] *n* sendero, vereda.

patience ['peɪʃns] *n* paciencia; (*CARDS*) solitario.

patient ['peɪʃnt] *n* paciente *m/f* // *a* paciente, sufrido.

patio ['pætɪəu] *n* patio.

patriot ['peɪtrɪət] *n* patriota *m/f*; **~ic** [pætrɪ'ɒtɪk] *a* patriótico.

patrol [pə'trəul] *n* patrulla // *vt* patrullar por; **~ car** *n* coche *m* patrulla; **~ man** *n* (*US*) policía *m*.

patron ['peɪtrən] *n* (*in shop*) cliente *m/f*; (*of charity*) patrocinador/a *m/f*; **~ of the arts** mecenas *m*; **~age** ['pætrənɪdʒ] *n* mecenazgo, protección *f*; **~ize** ['pætrənaɪz] *vt* (*shop*) ser cliente de; (*business*) patrocinar; (*look down on*) tratar con condescendencia; **~ saint** *n* patrono.

patter ['pætə*] *n* golpeteo; (*of feet*) pasos *mpl* ligeros; (*sales talk*) jerga // *vi* andar con pasos ligeros; (*rain*) tamborilear.

pattern ['pætən] *n* modelo; (*SEWING*) patrón *m*; (*design*) dibujo; (*sample*) muestra.

paunch [pɔːntʃ] *n* panza, barriga.

pauper ['pɔːpə*] *n* pobre *m/f*.

pause [pɔːz] *n* pausa; (*interval*) intérvalo // *vi* hacer una pausa.

pave [peɪv] *vt* pavimentar; **to ~ the way for** preparar el terreno para.

pavement ['peɪvmənt] *n* (*Brit*) acera.

pavilion [pə'vɪlɪən] *n* pabellón *m*; (*for band etc*) quiosco; (*SPORT*) caseta.

paving ['peɪvɪŋ] *n* pavimento, enlosado; **~ stone** *n* losa.

paw [pɔː] *n* pata; (*of cat*) garra // *vt* tocar con la pata; (*touch*) tocar, manosear; (*amorously*) sobar.

pawn [pɔːn] *n* (*CHESS*) peón *m*; (*fig*) instrumento // *vt* empeñar; **~broker** *n* prestamista *m/f*; **~shop** *n* monte *m* de piedad.

pay [peɪ] *n* paga; (*wage etc*) sueldo // (*vb: pt, pp* **paid**) *vt* pagar; (*debt*) liquidar; (*visit*) hacer; (*respect*) ofrecer // *vi* pagar; (*be profitable*) rendir; **to ~ attention (to)** prestar atención (a); **to ~ back** *vt* (*money*) devolver; (*person*) pagar; **to ~ for** *vt* pagar por; **to ~ in** *vt* ingresar; **to ~ off** *vt* liquidar; **to ~ up** *vt* pagar (de mala gana); **~able** *a* pagadero; **~ day** *n* día *m* de paga; **~ee** *n* portador/a *m/f*; **~ing** *a* provechoso; **~ment** *n* pago; **advance ~ment** anticipo; **monthly ~ment** mensualidad *f*; **~ packet** *n* sobre *m* de paga; **~roll** *n* nómina; **~ slip** *n* hoja de paga.

p.c. *abbr of* **per cent.**

pea [piː] *n* guisante *m*; **sweet ~** guisante de olor.

peace [piːs] *n* paz *f*; (*calm*) paz *f*, tranquilidad *f*; **~able** *a* pacífico; **~ful** *a* (*gentle*) pacífico; (*calm*) tranquilo, sosegado; **~keeping** *n* pacificación *f*; **~ offering** *n* prenda de paz.

peach [piːtʃ] *n* melocotón *m*, durazno (*AM*).

peacock ['piːkɔk] *n* pavo real.

peak [pi:k] n (of mountain: top) cumbre f, cima; (: point) pico; (of cap) visera; (fig) cumbre f; ~ **hours** npl horas fpl punta.

peal [pi:l] n (of bells) repique m, toque m de campanas; ~ **of laughter** carcajada.

peanut ['pi:nʌt] n cacahuete m, maní m (AM); ~ **butter** n manteca de cacahuete.

pear [pɛə°] n pera; ~ **tree** n peral m.

pearl [pɜ:l] n perla; **mother-of-~** n nácar m.

peasant ['pɛznt] n campesino/a.

peat [pi:t] n turba.

pebble ['pɛbl] n guijarro.

peck [pɛk] vt (also: ~ **at**) picotear; (food) comer sin ganas // n picotazo; (kiss) beso ligero; ~**ing order** n orden m de jerarquía; ~**ish** a (col) con hambre.

peculiar [pɪ'kju:lɪə°] a (odd) extraño, raro; (typical) propio, característico; (marked) especial; ~ **to** propio de; ~**ity** [pɪkju:lɪ'ærɪtɪ] n peculiaridad f; (feature) característica; (oddity) rareza, singularidad f.

pedal ['pɛdl] n pedal m // vi pedalear.

pedantic [pɪ'dæntɪk] a pedante.

peddle ['pɛdl] vt vender (de puerta en puerta); **peddler** n vendedor/a m/f ambulante.

pedestal ['pɛdəstl] n pedestal m.

pedestrian [pɪ'dɛstrɪən] n peatón m // a pedestre; ~ **crossing** n paso de peatones.

pedigree ['pɛdɪgri:] n genealogía; (of animal) raza // cpd (animal) de raza, de casta.

peek [pi:k] vi mirar a hurtadillas.

peel [pi:l] n piel f; (of orange, lemon) peladuras fpl // vt pelar // vi (paint etc) desconcharse; (wallpaper) despegarse, desprenderse.

peep [pi:p] n (look) mirada furtiva; (sound) pío // vi piar; **to ~ out** vi asomar la cabeza; ~**hole** n mirilla.

peer [pɪə°] vi: **to ~ at** mirar con ojos de miope // n (noble) par m; (equal) igual m; ~**age** n nobleza; ~**less** a sin par.

peeved [pi:vd] a enojado.

peevish ['pi:vɪʃ] a malhumorado.

peg [pɛg] n clavija; (for coat etc) gancho, colgadero; (also: **clothes** ~) pinza; (tent ~) estaca // vt (prices) fijar; **off the** ~ ad de confección.

pejorative [pɪ'dʒɔrətɪv] a peyorativo.

pekingese [pi:kɪ'ni:z] n pequinés/esa m/f.

pelican ['pɛlɪkən] n pelícano.

pellet ['pɛlɪt] n bolita; (bullet) perdigón m.

pelmet ['pɛlmɪt] n galería.

pelt [pɛlt] vt: **to ~ sb with sth** tirar algo a uno // vi (rain) llover a cántaros // n pellejo.

pelvis ['pɛlvɪs] n pelvis f.

pen [pɛn] n pluma; (for sheep) redil m; **play~** parque m de niño; ~ **name** n seudónimo.

penal ['pi:nl] a penal; ~**ize** vt penar; (SPORT) castigar.

penalty ['pɛnltɪ] n (gen) pena; (fine) multa; (SPORT) castigo; ~ **(kick)** n (FOOTBALL) penalty m.

penance ['pɛnəns] n penitencia.

pence [pɛns] pl of **penny.**

pencil ['pɛnsl] n lápiz m; (for eyebrows) lápiz de cejas; **propelling** ~ lapicero; ~ **sharpener** n sacapuntas m inv.

pendant ['pɛndnt] n pendiente m.

pending ['pɛndɪŋ] prep antes de // a pendiente.

pendulum ['pɛndjuləm] n péndulo.

penetrate ['pɛnɪtreɪt] vt penetrar; **penetrating** a penetrante; **penetration** [-'treɪʃən] n penetración f.

penfriend ['pɛnfrɛnd] n amigo/a por correspondencia.

penguin ['pɛŋgwɪn] n pingüino.

penicillin [pɛnɪ'sɪlɪn] n penicilina.

peninsula [pə'nɪnsjulə] n península.

penis ['pi:nɪs] n pene m.

penitence ['pɛnɪtns] n penitencia; **penitent** [-nt] a (gen) arrepentido; (REL) penitente.

penitentiary [pɛnɪ'tɛnʃərɪ] n (US) cárcel f, presidio.

penknife ['pɛnnaɪf] n navaja.

pennant ['pɛnənt] n banderola.

penniless ['pɛnɪlɪs] a sin dinero.

penny ['pɛnɪ], pl **pennies** ['pɛnɪz] or **pence** [pɛns] n penique m.

pension ['pɛnʃən] n (gen) pensión f; (old-age) jubilación f; (MIL) retiro; ~**er** n jubilado; ~ **fund** n caja de jubilaciones.

pensive ['pɛnsɪv] a pensativo; (withdrawn) preocupado.

pentagon ['pɛntəgən] n pentágono.

Pentecost ['pɛntɪkɔst] n Pentecostés m.

penthouse ['pɛnthaus] n ático.

pent-up ['pɛntʌp] a (feelings) reprimido.

penultimate [pɛ'nʌltɪmət] a penúltimo.

people ['pi:pl] npl gente f; (citizens) pueblo sg, ciudadanos mpl // n (nation, race) pueblo, nación f // vt poblar; **several** ~ **came** vinieron varias personas; ~ **say that...** dice la gente que... .

pep [pɛp] n (col) energía; **to ~ up** vt animar.

pepper ['pɛpə°] n pimienta; (vegetable) pimiento // vt (fig) salpicar; ~**mint** n menta; (sweet) pastilla de menta.

peptalk ['pɛptɔ:k] n (col) palabras fpl para levantar los ánimos.

per [pə:°] prep por; ~ **day/person** por día/persona; ~ **cent** por ciento; ~ **annum** al año.

perceive [pə'si:v] vt percibir; (realize) darse cuenta de.

percentage [pə'sɛntɪdʒ] n porcentaje m.

perception [pə'sɛpʃən] n percepción f; (insight) perspicacia; **perceptive** [-'sɛptɪv] a perspicaz.

perch [pə:tʃ] n (fish) perca; (for bird) percha // vi posarse.

percolator ['pə:kəleɪtə°] n cafetera filtradora.

percussion [pə'kʌʃən] n percusión f.

peremptory [pə'rɛmptərɪ] a perentorio; (person: imperious) imperioso.
perennial [pə'rɛnɪəl] a perenne.
perfect ['pɜ:fɪkt] a perfecto // n (also: ~ tense) perfecto // vt [pə'fɛkt] perfeccionar; ~**ion** [-'fɛkʃən] n perfección f; ~**ionist** n perfeccionista m/f.
perforate ['pɜ:fəreɪt] vt perforar; ~**d** a (stamp) dentado; **perforation** [-'reɪʃən] n perforación f.
perform [pə'fɔ:m] vt (carry out) realizar, cumplir; (concert etc) representar; (piece of music) interpretar // vi (animal) hacer trucos; (THEATRE) actuar; (TECH) funcionar; ~**ance** n (of task) cumplimiento, realización f; (of an artist) representación f; (of player etc) actuación f; (of car, engine) funcionamiento; (of function) desempeño; ~**er** n (actor) actor/actriz m/f; (MUS) intérprete m/f; ~**ing** a (animal) amaestrado.
perfume ['pɜ:fju:m] n perfume m // vt perfumar.
perhaps [pə'hæps] ad quizá(s), tal vez.
peril ['pɛrɪl] n peligro, riesgo.
perimeter [pə'rɪmɪtə*] n perímetro.
period ['pɪərɪəd] n período; (HISTORY) época; (time limit) plazo; (SCOL) clase f; (full stop) punto; (MED) regla, reglas fpl // a (costume, furniture) de época; ~**ic** [-'ɔdɪk] a periódico; ~**ical** [-'ɔdɪkl] n periódico; ~**ically** [-'ɔdɪklɪ] ad de vez en cuando, cada cierto tiempo.
peripheral [pə'rɪfərəl] a periférico; **periphery** [-rɪ] n periferia.
periscope ['pɛrɪskəup] n periscopio.
perish ['pɛrɪʃ] vi perecer; (decay) echarse a perder, deteriorar(se); ~**able** a perecedero; ~**ing** a (col: cold) helado, glacial.
perjure ['pɜ:dʒə*] vt: to ~ o.s. perjurarse; **perjury** n (LAW) perjurio.
perk [pɜ:k] n pago encima del sueldo; to ~ up vi (cheer up) animarse; (in health) sentirse mejor; ~**y** a (cheerful) alegre, despabilado.
perm [pɜ:m] n permanente f.
permanent ['pɜ:mənənt] a permanente.
permissible [pə'mɪsɪbl] a permisible, lícito.
permission [pə'mɪʃən] n permiso; (authorization) licencia.
permissive [pə'mɪsɪv] a permisivo.
permit ['pɜ:mɪt] n permiso, licencia // vt [pə'mɪt] permitir; (authorize) autorizar; (accept) tolerar.
permutation [pɜ:mju'teɪʃən] n permutación f.
pernicious [pɜ:'nɪʃəs] a nocivo, (MED) pernicioso.
perpendicular [pɜ:pən'dɪkjulə*] a perpendicular.
perpetrate ['pɜ:pɪtreɪt] vt cometer.
perpetual [pə'pɛtjuəl] a perpetuo.
perpetuate [pə'pɛtjueɪt] vt perpetuar.
perplex [pə'plɛks] vt dejar perplejo.
persecute ['pɜ:sɪkju:t] vt (pursue) perseguir; (harass) acosar; **persecution** [-'kju:ʃən] n persecución f.
persevere [pɜ:sɪ'vɪə*] vi persistir.
Persian ['pɜ:ʃən] a, n persa m/f.
persist [pə'sɪst] vi: to ~ (in doing sth) persistir (en hacer algo); ~**ence** n empeño; (of disease) pertinacia; ~**ent** a persistente; (determined) porfiado; (disease) pertinaz.
person ['pɜ:sn] n persona; ~**able** a atractivo; ~**al** a personal; (private) particular; (visit) en persona; (TEL) persona a persona; (column) de anuncios personales; ~**ality** [-'nælɪtɪ] n personalidad f; ~**ally** ad personalmente; ~**ify** [-'sɔnɪfaɪ] vt encarnar.
personnel [pɜ:sə'nɛl] n personal m.
perspective [pə'spɛktɪv] n perspectiva.
perspex ['pɜ:spɛks] n plexiglás m.
perspiration [pɜ:spɪ'reɪʃən] n transpiración f, sudor m; **perspire** [-'spaɪə*] vi transpirar, sudar.
persuade [pə'sweɪd] vt persuadir; **persuasion** [-'sweɪʒən] n persuasión f; (persuasiveness) persuasiva; (creed) creencia; **persuasive** [-'sweɪsɪv] a persuasivo.
pert [pɜ:t] a impertinente, fresco.
pertaining [pɜ:'teɪnɪŋ]: ~ to prep relacionado con.
pertinent ['pɜ:tɪnənt] a pertinente, a propósito.
perturb [pə'tɜ:b] vt perturbar.
Peru [pə'ru:] n el Perú.
peruse [pə'ru:z] vt leer con detención, examinar.
Peruvian [pə'ru:vjən] a, n peruano/a.
pervade [pə'veɪd] vt impregnar, saturar.
perverse [pə'vɜ:s] a perverso; (stubborn) terco; (wayward) travieso; **perversion** [-'vɜ:ʃən] n perversión f.
pervert ['pɜ:vɜ:t] n pervertido/a // vt [pə'vɜ:t] pervertir.
pessary ['pɛsərɪ] n pesario.
pessimism ['pɛsɪmɪzəm] n pesimismo; **pessimist** [-mɪst] n pesimista m/f; **pessimistic** [-'mɪstɪk] a pesimista.
pest [pɛst] n plaga; (insect) insecto nocivo; (fig) lata, molestia.
pester ['pɛstə*] vt molestar, acosar.
pesticide ['pɛstɪsaɪd] n pesticida m.
pet [pɛt] n animal doméstico; (favourite) favorito // vt acariciar // vi (col) besuquearse, sobarse.
petal ['pɛtl] n pétalo.
peter ['pi:tə*]: to ~ out vi agotarse, acabarse.
petite [pə'ti:t] a chiquita.
petition [pə'tɪʃən] n petición f.
petrified ['pɛtrɪfaɪd] a (fig) pasmado, horrorizado; **petrify** vt petrificar; (frighten) pasmar.
petrol ['pɛtrəl] n (Brit) gasolina; (for lighter) bencina.
petroleum [pə'trəulɪəm] n petróleo.
petrol: ~ **pump** n (in car) bomba de

gasolina; (in garage) surtidor m de gasolina; ~ **station** n gasolinera; ~ **tank** n depósito de gasolina.

petticoat ['petɪkəut] n enagua; (slip) combinación f.

pettiness ['petɪnɪs] n mezquindad f.

petty ['petɪ] a (mean) mezquino; (unimportant) nimio; ~ **cash** n dinero suelto; ~ **officer** n contramaestre m.

petulant ['petjulənt] a malhumorado.

pew [pju:] n banco.

pewter ['pju:tə*] n peltre m.

phallic ['fælɪk] a fálico.

phantom ['fæntəm] n fantasma m.

Pharaoh ['fɛərəu] n Faraón m.

pharmacist ['fɑ:məsɪst] n farmacéutico; **pharmacy** [-sɪ] n farmacia.

phase [feɪz] n fase f // vt: to ~ sth in/out introducir/reducir algo por etapas.

Ph.D. abbr of **Doctor of Philosophy.**

pheasant ['feznt] n faisán m.

phenomenon [fə'nɔmɪnən], pl **-mena** [-mɪnə] n fenómeno.

phial ['faɪəl] n ampolla.

philanthropist [fɪ'lænθrəpɪst] n filántropo/a.

philately [fɪ'lætəlɪ] n filatelia.

Philippines ['fɪlɪpi:nz] npl (also: **Philippine Islands**) (Islas) Filipinas fpl.

philosopher [fɪ'lɔsəfə*] n filósofo; **philosophical** [fɪlə'sɔfɪkl] a filosófico; **philosophy** [-fɪ] n filosofía.

phlegm [flem] n flema; ~**atic** [fleg-'mætɪk] a flemático.

phobia ['fəubjə] n fobia.

phone [fəun] n teléfono // vt telefonear, llamar (por teléfono); **to be on the** ~ tener teléfono; (be calling) estar llamando; **to** ~ **back** vt, vi devolver la llamada.

phonetics [fə'netɪks] n fonética.

phoney ['fəunɪ] a falso; (person) insincero // n (person) farsante m/f.

phosphate ['fɔsfeɪt] n fosfato.

phosphorus ['fɔsfərəs] n fósforo.

photo ['fəutəu] n fotografía.

photo... [fəutəu] pref: ~**copier** n fotocopiador m; ~**copy** n fotocopia // vt fotocopiar; ~**genic** [-'dʒenɪk] a fotogénico; ~**graph** n fotografía // vt fotografiar; ~**grapher** [fə'tɔgrəfə*] n fotógrafo; ~**graphic** [-'græfɪk] a fotográfico; ~**graphy** [fə'tɔgrəfɪ] n fotografía; ~**stat** ['fəutəustæt] n fotóstato.

phrase [freɪz] n frase f // vt expresar; ~ **book** n libro de frases.

physical ['fɪzɪkl] a físico.

physician [fɪ'zɪʃən] n médico.

physicist ['fɪzɪsɪst] n físico.

physics ['fɪzɪks] n física.

physiology [fɪzɪ'ɔlədʒɪ] n fisiología.

physiotherapy [fɪzɪəu'θerəpɪ] n fisioterapia.

physique [fɪ'zi:k] n físico.

pianist ['pi:ənɪst] n pianista m/f.

piano [pɪ'ænəu] n piano; **grand** ~ piano de cola.

pick [pɪk] n (tool: also: ~-**axe**) pico, piqueta // vt (select) elegir, escoger; (gather) recoger; (lock) forzar; **take your** ~ escoja lo que quiera; **the** ~ **of** lo mejor de; **to** ~ **one's teeth** limpiarse los dientes; **to** ~ **pockets** ratear, ser carterista; **to** ~ **off** vt (kill) matar de un tiro; **to** ~ **on** vt fus (person) meterse con; **to** ~ **out** vt escoger; (distinguish) lograr ver; **to** ~ **up** vi (improve) reponerse // vt (from floor) recoger; (telephone) descolgar; (buy) comprar; (find) encontrar; (learn) aprender; **to** ~ **up speed** acelerarse; **to** ~ **o.s. up** levantarse.

picket ['pɪkɪt] n (in strike) guardia, piquete m // vt piquetear; ~ **line** n línea de huelgistas.

pickle ['pɪkl] n (also: ~**s**: as condiment) escabeche m; (fig: mess) apuro // vt encurtir; (in vinegar) conservar en vinagre.

pickpocket ['pɪkpɔkɪt] n carterista m/f.

pickup ['pɪkʌp] n (on record player) pickup m; (small truck) furgoneta.

picnic ['pɪknɪk] n picnic m, merienda de campo // vi merendar en el campo.

pictorial [pɪk'tɔ:rɪəl] a pictórico; (magazine etc) ilustrado.

picture ['pɪktʃə*] n cuadro; (painting) pintura; (photograph) fotografía; (film) película // vt pintar; **the** ~**s** el cine; ~ **book** n libro de imágenes.

picturesque [pɪktʃə'resk] a pintoresco.

pidgin ['pɪdʒɪn] a: ~ **English** el inglés macarrónico.

pie [paɪ] n pastel m; (open) tarta; (of meat) empanada.

piebald ['paɪbɔ:ld] a pío.

piece [pi:s] n pedazo, trozo; (of land) terreno; (of cake) porción f; (item): **a** ~ **of furniture/advice** un mueble/un consejo // vt: **to** ~ **together** juntar; (TECH) montar; **to take to** ~**s** desmontar; ~**meal** ad poco a poco; ~**work** n trabajo a destajo.

pier [pɪə*] n muelle m; (jetty) embarcadero, malecón m.

pierce [pɪəs] vt penetrar, atravesar; (puncture) pinchar.

piercing ['pɪəsɪŋ] a (cry) penetrante.

piety ['paɪətɪ] n piedad f.

pig [pɪg] n cerdo, puerco; (fig) cochino.

pigeon ['pɪdʒən] n paloma; (as food) pichón m; ~**hole** n casilla.

piggy bank ['pɪgɪbæŋk] n hucha en forma de cerdito.

pigheaded ['pɪg'hedɪd] a terco, testarudo.

pigment ['pɪgmənt] n pigmento; ~**ation** [-'teɪʃən] n pigmentación f.

pigmy ['pɪgmɪ] n = **pygmy**.

pigsty ['pɪgstaɪ] n pocilga.

pigtail ['pɪgteɪl] n (girl's) trenza; (Chinese) coleta.

pike [paɪk] n (spear) pica; (fish) lucio.

pilchard ['pɪltʃəd] n sardina arenque.

pile [paɪl] n (heap) montón m; (of carpet)

pelo; (of cloth) pelillo // (vb: also: ~ **up**) vt amontonar; (fig) acumular // vi amontonarse.

piles [paɪlz] npl (MED) almorranas fpl, hemorroides mpl.

pile-up ['paɪlʌp] n (AUT) accidente m múltiple.

pilfer ['pɪlfə*] vt ratear; ~**ing** n ratería.

pilgrim ['pɪlgrɪm] n peregrino/a; ~**age** n peregrinaje m, romería.

pill [pɪl] n píldora; **the** ~ la píldora.

pillage ['pɪlɪdʒ] n saqueo, pillaje m.

pillar ['pɪlə*] n (gen) pilar m; (concrete) columna; ~ **box** n (Brit) buzón m.

pillion ['pɪljən] n (of motor cycle) asiento de atrás.

pillory ['pɪlərɪ] vt poner en ridículo.

pillow ['pɪləu] n almohada; ~**case** n funda.

pilot ['paɪlət] n piloto // a (scheme etc) piloto // vt pilotar; (fig) guiar, conducir; ~ **light** n piloto.

pimp [pɪmp] n alcahuete m, chulo.

pimple ['pɪmpl] n grano.

pin [pɪn] n alfiler m; (TECH) perno; (: wooden) clavija // vt prender (con alfiler); sujetar con perno; ~**s and needles** hormigueo sg; **rolling/ safety** ~ rodillo/imperdible m; **to** ~ **sb down** (fig) hacer que uno concrete; **to** ~ **sth on sb** (fig) acusar (falsamente) a uno de algo.

pinafore ['pɪnəfɔ:*] n delantal m; ~ **dress** n mandil m.

pinball ['pɪnbɔ:l] n billar m automático.

pincers ['pɪnsəz] npl pinzas fpl, tenazas fpl.

pinch [pɪntʃ] n pellizco; (of salt etc) pizca // vt pellizcar; (col: steal) birlar; (: arrest) coger, pescar // vi (shoe) apretar; **to feel the** ~ pasar apuros.

pincushion ['pɪnkuʃən] n acerico.

pine [paɪn] n (also: ~ **tree**) pino // vi: **to** ~ **for** suspirar por; **to** ~ **away** languidecer.

pineapple ['paɪnæpl] n piña, ananás m.

ping [pɪŋ] n (noise) tintineo; (of bullet through air) subido; ~-**pong** n pingpong m.

pink [pɪŋk] a rosado, color de rosa // n (colour) color m de rosa; (BOT) clavel m, clavellina.

pinnacle ['pɪnəkl] n cumbre f.

pinpoint ['pɪnpɔɪnt] vt poner el dedo en.

pint [paɪnt] n pinta (0.57 litros); **to go for a** ~ ir a tomar una cerveza.

pin-up ['pɪnʌp] n fotografía de mujer bonita.

pioneer [paɪə'nɪə*] n pionero.

pious ['paɪəs] a piadoso, devoto.

pip [pɪp] n (seed) pepita; (time signal on radio) señal f.

pipe [paɪp] n tubo, caño; (for smoking) pipa // vt conducir en cañerías; ~**s** npl (gen) cañería sg; (also: **bag**~**s**) gaita sg; **to** ~ **down** vi (col) callarse; ~ **dream** n sueño imposible; ~**line** n tubería, cañería; (for oil) oleoducto; (for gas) gasoducto; **piper** n

(gen) flautista m/f; (with bagpipes) gaitero.

piping ['paɪpɪŋ] ad: ~ **hot** bien caliente.

piquant ['pi:kənt] a picante.

pique [pi:k] n pique m, resentimiento.

pirate ['paɪərət] n pirata m; ~ **radio** n emisora ilegal.

pirouette [pɪru'ɛt] n pirueta // vi piruetear.

Pisces ['paɪsi:z] n Piscis m.

piss [pɪs] vi (col) mear; ~**ed** a (col: drunk) trompa.

pistol ['pɪstl] n pistola.

piston ['pɪstən] n pistón m, émbolo.

pit [pɪt] n hoyo; (also: **coal** ~) mina; (in garage) foso de inspección; (also: **orchestra** ~) platea; (quarry) cantera // vt: **to** ~ **A against B** oponer A a B; ~**s** npl (AUT) box m.

pitch [pɪtʃ] n (throw) lanzamiento; (MUS) tono; (SPORT) campo, terreno; (tar) brea; (in market etc) puesto // vt (throw) arrojar, lanzar // vi (fall) caer(se); (NAUT) cabecear; **to** ~ **a tent** armar una tienda (de campaña); ~-**black** a negro como boca de lobo; ~**ed battle** n batalla campal.

pitcher ['pɪtʃə*] n cántaro, jarro.

pitchfork ['pɪtʃfɔ:k] n horca.

piteous ['pɪtɪəs] a lastimoso.

pitfall ['pɪtfɔ:l] n escollo, peligro.

pith [pɪθ] n (of orange) médula; (fig) meollo.

pithy ['pɪθɪ] a jugoso.

pitiable ['pɪtɪəbl] a lastimoso.

pitiful ['pɪtɪful] a (touching) lastimoso, conmovedor(a); (contemptible) lamentable, miserable.

pitiless ['pɪtɪlɪs] a despiadado.

pittance ['pɪtns] n miseria.

pity ['pɪtɪ] n (compassion) compasión f, piedad f; (shame) lástima // vt tener lástima a, compadecer(se de); **what a** ~! ¡qué lástima!

pivot ['pɪvət] n eje m // vi: **to** ~ **on** girar sobre; (fig) depender de.

pixie ['pɪksɪ] n duende m.

placard ['plækɑ:d] n (sign) letrero; (in march etc) pancarta.

placate [plə'keɪt] vt apaciguar.

place [pleɪs] n lugar m, sitio; (rank) rango; (seat) plaza, asiento; (post) puesto; (home): **at/to his** ~ en/a su casa // vt (object) poner, colocar; (identify) reconocer, ubicar; (find a post for) dar un puesto a, colocar; **to take** ~ tener lugar; **to be** ~**d** (in race, exam) colocarse; **out of** ~ (not suitable) fuera de lugar; **in the first** ~ en primer lugar; **to change** ~**s with sb** trocarse con uno.

placid ['plæsɪd] a apacible.

plagiarism ['pleɪdʒjərɪzm] n plagio.

plague [pleɪg] n plaga; (MED) peste f // vt (fig) acosar, atormentar; **to** ~ **sb** fastidiar a uno.

plaice [pleɪs] n, pl inv platija.

plaid [plæd] n (*material*) tela a cuadros; (*pattern*) plaid m.

plain [pleɪn] a (*clear*) claro, evidente; (*simple*) sencillo, llano; (*frank*) franco, abierto; (*not handsome*) sin atractivo; (*pure*) natural, puro // ad claro, claramente // n llano, llanura; **in ~ clothes** (*police*) de paisano; **~ly** ad claramente, evidentemente; (*frankly*) francamente, con franqueza; **~ness** n claridad f; sencillez f; franqueza.

plaintiff ['pleɪntɪf] n demandante m/f.

plait [plæt] n trenza // vt trenzar.

plan [plæn] n (*drawing*) plano; (*scheme*) plan m, proyecto; (*schedule*) programa m // vt (*think in advance*) proyectar; (*prepare*) planear, planificar // vi hacer proyectos; **to ~ to do** proponerse hacer.

plane [pleɪn] n (AVIAT) avión m; (*tree*) plátano; (*tool*) cepillo; (MATH) plano.

planet ['plænɪt] n planeta m; **~arium** [-'tɛərɪəm] n planetario.

plank [plæŋk] n tabla; (POL) punto.

planner ['plænə*] n planificador/a m/f.

planning ['plænɪŋ] n planificación f; **family ~** planificación familiar.

plant [plɑ:nt] n planta; (*machinery*) maquinaria; (*factory*) fábrica // vt plantar; (*field*) sembrar; (*bomb*) colocar; (*fam*) colocar a escondidas.

plantation [plæn'teɪʃən] n plantación f; (*estate*) hacienda.

plaque [plæk] n placa.

plasma ['plæzmə] n plasma m.

plaster ['plɑ:stə*] n (*for walls*) yeso; (*also:* **sticking ~**) curitas m inv, parche m // vt enyesar; (*cover*): **to ~ with** llenar o cubrir de; **~ed** a (*col*) trompa; **~er** n yesero.

plastic ['plæstɪk] n plástico // a de plástico.

plasticine ['plæstɪsi:n] n plasticina.

plastic surgery ['plæstɪk'sə:dʒərɪ] n cirujía plástica.

plate [pleɪt] n (*dish*) plato; (*metal, in book*) lámina; (PHOT, *dental*) placa.

plateau ['plætəʊ], pl **~s** or **~x** [-z] n meseta, altiplanicie f.

plateful ['pleɪtful] n plato.

plate glass [pleɪt'glɑ:s] n vidrio cilindrado.

platform ['plætfɔ:m] n (RAIL) andén m; (*stage*) plataforma; (*at meeting*) tribuna; (POL) programa m electoral; **~ ticket** n billete m de andén.

platinum ['plætɪnəm] n platino.

platitude ['plætɪtju:d] n lugar m común, tópico.

platoon [plə'tu:n] n pelotón m.

platter ['plætə*] n fuente f, platón m.

plausible ['plɔ:zɪbl] a verosímil, admisible; (*person*) convincente.

play [pleɪ] n (*gen*) juego; (*also:* **~time**) recreo; (THEATRE) obra, comedia // vt (*game*) jugar; (*instrument*) tocar; (THEATRE) representar; (: *part*) hacer (el papel de); (*fig*) desempeñar // vi jugar;

(*amuse o.s.*) divertirse; (*frolic*) juguetear; **to ~ down** vt quitar importancia a; **to ~ up** vt (*cause trouble to*) fastidiar a; **~-acting** n teatro; **~er** n jugador/a m/f; (THEATRE) actor/actriz m/f; (MUS) músico/a; **~ful** a juguetón(ona); **~ground** n (*in park*) parque m de juegos; (*in school*) patio de recreo; **~group** n jardín m de niños; **~ing card** n naipe m, carta; **~ing field** n campo de deportes; **~mate** n compañero de juego; **~-off** n (SPORT) partido de desempate; **~pen** n corral m; **~thing** n juguete m; **~wright** n dramaturgo.

plea [pli:] n (*request*) súplica, petición f; (*excuse*) pretexto, disculpa; (LAW) alegato, defensa.

plead [pli:d] vt (LAW) interceder; (*give as excuse*) poner como pretexto // vi (LAW) declarar; (*beg*): **to ~ with sb** suplicar o rogar a uno.

pleasant ['plɛznt] a agradable; (*surprise*) grato; (*person*) simpático; **~ness** n (*of person*) simpatía, amabilidad f; (*of place*) lo agradable; **~ries** npl (*polite remarks*) cortesías fpl.

please [pli:z] vt (*give pleasure to*) dar gusto a, agradar; (*get on well with*) caer en gracia a // vi (*think fit*): **do as you ~** haga lo que quiera o (lo que le da la gana); **~!** ¡por favor!; **~ yourself!** ¡como Usted guste!, ¡como quiera!; **~d** a (*happy*) alegre, contento; **~d (with)** satisfecho (de); **pleasing** a (*gen*) agradable; (*surprise*) grato; (*flattering*) halagüeño.

pleasure ['plɛʒə*] n placer m, gusto; (*will*) voluntad f // cpd de recreo; **'it's a ~'** el gusto es mío; **it's a ~ to see him** da gusto verle.

pleat [pli:t] n pliegue m.

plebs [plɛbz] npl (*pej*) la plebe.

plectrum ['plɛktrəm] n plectro.

pledge [plɛdʒ] n (*object*) prenda; (*promise*) promesa, voto // vt (*pawn*) empeñar; (*promise*) prometer.

plentiful ['plɛntɪful] a copioso, abundante.

plenty ['plɛntɪ] n abundancia; **~ of** (*enough*) bastante; (*many*) muchos.

pleurisy ['pluərɪsɪ] n pleuresía.

pliable ['plaɪəbl] a flexible; (*fig*) manejable.

pliers ['plaɪəz] npl alicates mpl, tenazas fpl.

plight [plaɪt] n condición f, situación f difícil.

plimsolls ['plɪmsəlz] npl zapatos mpl de tenis.

plod [plɔd] vi caminar penosamente; (*fig*) trabajar laboriosamente; **~der** n empollón/ona m/f; **~ding** a laborioso.

plonk [plɔŋk] (*col*) n (*wine*) vino corriente // vt: **to ~ sth down** dejar caer algo (pesadamente).

plot [plɔt] n (*scheme*) complot m, conjura; (*of story, play*) argumento; (*of land*) terreno // vt (*mark out*) trazar; (*conspire*) tramar, urdir // vi conspirar; **~ter** n conspirador/a m/f.

plough, plow (US) [plau] n arado // vt
(earth) arar; to ~ **back** vt (COMM)
reinvertir; to ~ **through** vt fus (crowd)
abrirse paso por la fuerza.
ploy [plɔɪ] n truco, estratagema.
pluck [plʌk] vt (fruit) coger; (musical
instrument) puntear; (bird) desplumar // n
valor m, ánimo; to ~ **up courage** hacer
de tripas corazón; ~**y** a valiente,
valeroso.
plug [plʌg] n tapón m; (ELEC) enchufe m,
clavija; (AUT: also: **sparking** ~) bujía //
vt (hole) tapar; (col: advertise) dar
publicidad a.
plum [plʌm] n (fruit) ciruela // a (col: job)
breva, chollo.
plumage ['plu:mɪdʒ] n plumaje m.
plumb [plʌm] ad (exactly) exactamente,
en punto // vt sondar, sondear.
plumber ['plʌmə*] n fontanero; **plumbing**
[-mɪŋ] n (trade) fontanería; (piping)
instalación f de cañerías.
plume [plu:m] n (gen) pluma; (on helmet)
penacho.
plummet ['plʌmɪt] vi: to ~ (down) caer
a plomo.
plump [plʌmp] a rechoncho, rollizo // vt:
to ~ sth (down) on dejar caer algo en;
to ~ for (col: choose) optar por.
plunder ['plʌndə*] n pillaje m; (loot) botín
m // vt pillar, saquear; (tomb) robar.
plunge [plʌndʒ] n (dive) salto;
(submersion) zambullida; (bath) baño // vt
sumergir, hundir // vi (fall) caer; (dive)
saltar; (person) arrojarse; (sink) hundirse;
to take the ~ resolverse; **plunger** n
émbolo; **plunging** a (neckline) escotado.
pluperfect [plu:'pə:fɪkt] n pluscuam-
perfecto.
plural ['pluərl] n plural m.
plus [plʌs] n (also: ~ **sign**) signo más //
prep más, y, además de; **ten/twenty** ~
diez/veinte y pico.
plush [plʌʃ] a de felpa.
ply [plaɪ] vt (a trade) ejercer // vi (ship) ir
y venir; (for hire) ofrecerse (para
alquilar); **three** ~ (wool) de tres
cordones; to ~ **sb with drink** ofrecer
bebidas a alguien muchas veces; ~**wood**
n madera contrachapada.
P.M. abbr of **Prime Minister.**
p.m. ad abbr of **post meridiem** de la tarde
o noche.
pneumatic [nju:'mætɪk] a neumático.
pneumonia [nju:'məʊnɪə] n pulmonía.
poach [pəʊtʃ] vt (cook) escalfar; (steal)
cazar en vedado // vi cazar/pescar en
finca ajena; ~**ed** a (egg) escalfado; ~**er**
n cazador m furtivo; ~**ing** n caza/pesca
furtiva.
pocket ['pɒkɪt] n bolsillo; (of air, GEO, fig)
bolsa; (BILLIARDS) tronera // vt meter en el
bolsillo; (steal) embolsar; (BILLIARDS)
entronerar; **to be out of** ~ salir
perdiendo; ~**book** n (US: wallet) cartera;
~ **knife** n navaja; ~ **money** n dinero
para gastos personales.

pod [pɒd] n vaina.
podgy ['pɒdʒɪ] a gordinflón(ona).
poem ['pəʊɪm] n poema m.
poet ['pəʊɪt] n poeta m/f; ~**ess** n poetisa;
~**ic** [-'ɪtɪk] a poético; ~ **laureate** n poeta
laureado; ~**ry** n poesía.
poignant ['pɔɪnjənt] a conmovedor(a);
(sharp) agudo.
point [pɔɪnt] n (gen) punto; (tip) punta;
(purpose) fin m, finalidad f; (use) utilidad f;
(significant part) lo significativo;
(characteristic) rasgo; (also: **decimal** ~):
2 ~ **3** (2.3) dos punto tres // vt (show)
subrayar; (gun etc): to ~ **sth at sb**
apuntar algo a uno // vi señalar con el
dedo; ~**s** npl (AUT) contactos mpl; (RAIL)
agujas fpl; **to make a** ~ **of** no dejar de; to
get the ~ comprender; **to come to the**
~ ir al grano; **there's no** ~ **(in doing)**
no hay para qué (hacer); to ~ **out** vt
señalar; to ~ **to** indicar con el dedo; (fig)
indicar, señalar; ~-**blank** ad (also: at
~-**blank range**) a quemarropa; ~**ed** a
(shape) puntiagudo, afilado; (remark)
directo, enfático; ~**edly** ad directamente,
con énfasis; ~**er** n (stick) puntero;
(needle) aguja, indicador m; ~**less** a
(useless) inútil; (senseless) sin sentido;
(motiveless) sin motivo; ~ **of view** n
punto de vista.
poise [pɔɪz] n (balance) equilibrio; (of head,
body) aire m, porte m; (calmness)
confianza.
poison ['pɔɪzn] n veneno // vt envenenar;
~**ing** n envenenamiento; ~**ous** a
venenoso; (fumes etc) tóxico; (fig)
pernicioso.
poke [pəʊk] vt (fire) hurgar, atizar; (jab
with finger, stick etc) empujar; (put): to ~
sth in(to) introducir algo en // n (to fire)
hurgonada; (push) empujón m; (with
elbow) codazo; to ~ **about** vi fisgar.
poker ['pəʊkə*] n badila, atizador m;
(CARDS) póker m; ~-**faced** a de cara
impasible.
poky ['pəʊkɪ] a estrecho.
Poland ['pəʊlənd] n Polonia.
polar ['pəʊlə*] a polar; ~ **bear** n oso
polar.
polarize ['pəʊləraɪz] vt polarizar.
pole [pəʊl] n palo; (GEO) polo; (TEL) poste
m; (flag~) asta; (tent ~) mástil m.
Pole [pəʊl] n polaco/a.
pole vault ['pəʊlvɔ:lt] n salto con pértiga.
police [pə'li:s] n policía // vt mantener el
orden en; ~ **car** n coche-patrulla m;
~**man** n policía m, guardia m; ~ **state** n
estado policíaco; ~ **station** n comisaría;
~**woman** n mujer f policía.
policy ['pɒlɪsɪ] n política; (also: **insurance**
~) póliza.
polio ['pəʊlɪəʊ] n polio f.
Polish ['pəʊlɪʃ] a, n polaco.
polish ['pɒlɪʃ] n (for shoes) betún m; (for
floor) cera (de lustrar); (for nails) esmalte
m; (shine) brillo, lustre m; (fig: refinement)
cultura, urbanidad f // vt (shoes) limpiar;

(*make shiny*) pulir, sacar brillo a; (*fig*: *improve*) refinar, repasar; **to ~ off** *vt* (*work*) terminar; (*food*) despachar; **~ed a** (*fig*: *person*) culto; (: *manners*) fino.
polite [pə'laɪt] *a* cortés, atento; (*formal*) correcto; **~ness** *n* cortesía.
politic ['pɔlɪtɪk] *a* prudente; **~al** [pə'lɪtɪkl] *a* político; **~ian** [-'tɪʃən] *n* político; **~s** *npl* política *sg*.
polka ['pɔlkə] *n* polca; **~ dot** *n* punto.
poll [pəul] *n* (*votes*) votación *f*, votos *mpl*; (*also*: **opinion ~**) sondeo, encuesta // *vt* (*votes*) recibir, obtener.
pollen ['pɔlən] *n* polen *m*.
pollination [pɔlɪ'neɪʃən] *n* polinización *f*.
polling ['pəulɪŋ]: **~ booth** *n* cabina de votar; **~ day** *n* día *m* de elecciones; **~ station** *n* centro electoral.
pollute [pə'luːt] *vt* contaminar; **pollution** [-'luːʃən] *n* polución *f*, contaminación *f*.
polo ['pəuləu] *n* (*sport*) polo; **~-neck** *a* de cuello vuelto.
polyester [pɔlɪ'estə*] *n* poliester *m*.
polygamy [pə'lɪgəmɪ] *n* poligamia.
Polynesia [pɔlɪ'niːzɪə] *n* Polinesia.
polytechnic [pɔlɪ'tɛknɪk] *n* politécnico, escuela de formación profesional.
polythene ['pɔlɪθiːn] *n* politeno.
pomegranate ['pɔmɪgrænɪt] *n* granada.
pommel ['pɔmɪ] *n* pomo // *vt* dar de puñetazos.
pomp [pɔmp] *n* pompa.
pompous ['pɔmpəs] *a* pomposo.
pond [pɔnd] *n* (*natural*) charca; (*artificial*) estanque *m*.
ponder ['pɔndə*] *vt* meditar; **~ous** *a* pesado.
pontiff ['pɔntɪf] *n* pontífice *m*.
pontificate [pɔn'tɪfɪkeɪt] *vi* (*fig*): **to ~** (*about*) pontificar (sobre).
pontoon [pɔn'tuːn] *n* pontón *m*; (*card game*) veintiuna.
pony ['pəunɪ] *n* poney *m*, jaca; **~tail** *n* cola de caballo; **~ trekking** *n* excursión *f* a caballo.
poodle ['puːdl] *n* perro de lanas.
pool [puːl] *n* (*of rain*) charca; (*pond*) estanque *m*; (*also*: **swimming ~**) piscina; (*billiards*) trucos *mpl* // *vt* juntar; (*football*) **~s** quinielas *fpl*.
poor [puə*] *a* pobre; (*bad*) de baja calidad // *npl*: **the ~** los pobres; **~ly** *a* mal, enfermo.
pop [pɔp] *n* ¡pum!; (*sound*) ruido seco; (*MUS*) pop *m*; (*US*: *col*: *father*) papá *m*; (*lemonade*) gaseosa // *vt* (*put*) poner // *vi* reventar; (*cork*) saltar; **to ~ in** *vi* entrar de sopetón; **to ~ out** *vi* salir un momento; **to ~ up** *vi* aparecer inesperadamente; **~ concert** *n* concierto pop; **~corn** *n* palomitas *fpl*.
pope [pəup] *n* papa *m*.
poplar ['pɔplə*] *n* álamo.
poplin ['pɔplɪn] *n* popelina.
poppy ['pɔpɪ] *n* amapola.
populace ['pɔpjuləs] *n* pueblo, plebe *f*.

popular ['pɔpjulə*] *a* popular; (*fashionable*) de moda; **~ity** [-'lærɪtɪ] *n* popularidad *f*; **~ize** *vt* popularizar; (*disseminate*) vulgarizar.
populate ['pɔpjuleɪt] *vt* poblar; **population** [-'leɪʃən] *n* población *f*.
populous ['pɔpjuləs] *a* populoso.
porcelain ['pɔːslɪn] *n* porcelana.
porch [pɔːtʃ] *n* pórtico, entrada.
porcupine ['pɔːkjupaɪn] *n* puerco espín.
pore [pɔː*] *n* poro // *vi*: **to ~ over** estar absorto en.
pork [pɔːk] *n* carne *f* de cerdo.
pornographic [pɔːnə'græfɪk] *a* pornográfico; **pornography** [-'nɔgrəfɪ] *n* pornografía.
porous ['pɔːrəs] *a* poroso.
porpoise ['pɔːpəs] *n* marsopa.
porridge ['pɔrɪdʒ] *n* avena.
port [pɔːt] *n* (*harbour*) puerto; (*NAUT*: *left side*) babor *m*; (*wine*) (vino de) oporto.
portable ['pɔːtəbl] *a* portátil.
portend [pɔː'tɛnd] *vt* presagiar, anunciar; **portent** ['pɔːtɛnt] *n* presagio, augurio.
porter ['pɔːtə*] *n* (*for luggage*) mozo; (*doorkeeper*) portero, conserje *m*.
porthole ['pɔːthəul] *n* portilla.
portion ['pɔːʃən] *n* porción *f*; (*helping*) ración *f*.
portly ['pɔːtlɪ] *a* corpulento.
portrait ['pɔːtreɪt] *n* retrato.
portray [pɔː'treɪ] *vt* retratar; (*in writing*) describir, representar; **~al** *n* representación *f*.
Portugal ['pɔːtjugl] *n* Portugal *m*.
Portuguese [pɔːtju'giːz] *a* portugués(esa) // *n*, *pl inv* portugués/esa *m/f*; (*LING*) portugués *m*.
pose [pəuz] *n* postura, actitud *f*; (*pej*) afectación *f*, pose *f* // *vi* posar; (*pretend*): **to ~ as** darse tono de // *vt* (*question*) plantear.
posh [pɔʃ] *a* (*col*) elegante, de lujo.
position [pə'zɪʃən] *n* posición *f*; (*job*) puesto // *vt* colocar.
positive ['pɔzɪtɪv] *a* positivo; (*certain*) seguro; (*definite*) definitivo.
posse ['pɔsɪ] *n* (*US*) pelotón *m*.
possess [pə'zɛs] *vt* poseer; **~ion** [pə'zɛʃən] *n* posesión *f*; **~ive a** posesivo.
possibility [pɔsɪ'bɪlɪtɪ] *n* posibilidad *f*; **possible** ['pɔsɪbl] *a* posible; **as big as possible** lo más grande posible; **possibly** ['pɔsɪblɪ] *ad* (*perhaps*) posiblemente, tal vez; **I cannot possibly come** me es imposible venir.
post [pəust] *n* (*letters, delivery*) correo; (*job, situation*) puesto; (*pole*) poste *m* // *vt* (*send by post*) echar al correo; (*MIL*) apostar; (*bills*) fijar, pegar; (*appoint*): **to ~ to** enviar a; **~age** *n* porte *m*, franqueo; **~al** *a* postal, de correos; **~al order** *n* giro postal; **~box** *n* buzón *m*; **~card** *n* tarjeta postal.
postdate [pəust'deɪt] *vt* (*cheque*) poner fecha adelantada a.

poster ['pəustə*] n cartel m.
posterior [pɔs'tiəriə*] n (col) culo, trasero.
posterity [pɔs'tɛriti] n posteridad f.
postgraduate ['pəust'grædjuət] n postgraduado.
posthumous ['pɔstjuməs] a póstumo.
post: ~**man** n cartero; ~**mark** n matasellos m inv; ~**master** n administrador/a m/f de correos.
post-mortem [pəust'mɔːtəm] n autopsia.
post office ['pəustɔfis] n (building) correos f; (organization) Administración General de Correos; ~ **box (P.O. box)** n apartado postal.
postpone [pəs'pəun] vt aplazar; ~**ment** n aplazamiento.
postscript ['pəustskript] n posdata.
postulate ['pɔstjuleit] vt postular.
posture ['pɔstʃə*] n postura, actitud f.
postwar [pəust'wɔː*] a de posguerra.
posy ['pəuzi] n ramillete m (de flores).
pot [pɔt] n (for cooking) olla; (for flowers) maceta; (for jam) tarro, pote m; (col: marijuana) mota // vt (plant) poner en tiesto; (conserve) conservar.
potato [pə'teitəu], pl ~**es** n patata, papa (AM).
potent ['pəutnt] a potente, poderoso; (drink) fuerte.
potential [pə'tɛnʃl] a potencial, en potencial // n potencial m, potencialidad f.
pothole ['pɔthəul] n (in road) bache m; (underground) caverna; **potholer** n espeleólogo; **potholing** n: **to go potholing** dedicarse a la espeleología.
potion ['pəuʃən] n poción f, pócima.
potluck [pɔt'lʌk] n: **to take** ~ contentarse con lo que haya.
potshot ['pɔtʃɔt] n: **to take a** ~ **at sth** tirar a algo sin apuntar.
potted ['pɔtid] a (food) en conserva; (plant) en tiesto o maceta.
potter ['pɔtə*] n (artistic) ceramista m/f; (artisan) alfarero // vi: **to** ~ **around**, ~ **about** ocuparse en fruslerías; ~**y** n cerámica; alfarería.
potty ['pɔti] a (col: mad) chiflado // n orinal m de niño.
pouch [pautʃ] n (ZOOL) bolsa; (for tobacco) petaca.
pouf(fe) [puːf] n pouf m.
poultice ['pəultis] n cataplasma, emplasto.
poultry ['pəultri] n aves fpl de corral; (dead) pollos mpl; ~ **farm** n granja avícola.
pounce [pauns] vi: **to** ~ **on** precipitarse sobre // n salto, ataque m.
pound [paund] n (gen) libra; (for dogs) corral m; (for cars) depósito // vt (beat) golpear; (crush) machacar // vi (beat) dar golpes; ~ **sterling** n (libra) esterlina.
pour [pɔː*] vt echar; (tea) servir // vi correr, fluir; (rain) llover a cántaros; **to** ~ **away** or **off** vt vaciar, verter; **to** ~ **in** vi (people) entrar en tropel; **to** ~ **out** vi (people) salir en tropel // vt (drink) echar, servir; ~**ing** a: ~**ing rain** lluvia torrencial.
pout [paut] vi hacer pucheros.
poverty ['pɔvəti] n pobreza, miseria; (fig) falta, escasez f; ~-**stricken** a necesitado.
powder ['paudə*] n polvo; (face ~) polvos mpl; (gun ~) pólvora // vt polvorear; **to** ~ **one's face** empolvarse; ~ **compact** n polvera; ~ **room** n aseos mpl; ~**y** a polvoriento.
power ['pauə*] n (gen) poder m; (strength) fuerza; (nation) potencia; (ability, POL: of party, leader) poder m, poderío; (drive) empuje m; (TECH) potencia; (ELEC) fuerza, energía // vt impulsar; ~ **cut** n apagón m; ~**ed** a: ~**ed by** impulsado por; ~**ful** a poderoso; (engine) potente; (build) fuerte; (emotion) intenso; ~**less** a impotente, ineficaz; ~ **line** n línea de conducción eléctrica; ~ **point** n enchufe m; ~ **station** n central f eléctrica.
p.p. abbr of **per procurationem:** ~ **J. Smith** p.p. (por poder de) J. Smith.
practicable ['præktikəbl] a (scheme) factible.
practical ['præktikl] a práctico; ~ **joke** n broma pesada; ~**ly** ad (almost) prácticamente.
practice ['præktis] n (habit) costumbre f; (exercise) práctica, ejercicio; (training) adiestramiento; (MED) clientela // vt, vi (US) = **practise;** **in** ~ (in reality) en la práctica; **out of** ~ desentrenado.
practise, practice (US) ['præktis] vt (carry out) practicar; (be in the habit of) tener por costumbre; (profession) ejercer; (train at) hacer ejercicios de // vi ejercer (profesión); (train) entrenarse, adiestrarse; **practising** a (Christian etc) practicante; (lawyer) que ejerce.
practitioner [præk'tiʃənə*] n practicante m/f; (MED) médico/a.
pragmatic [præg'mætik] a pragmático.
prairie ['prɛəri] n pradera, pampa.
praise [preiz] n alabanza, elogio, alabanzas fpl, elogios mpl; ~-**worthy** a loable, digno de elogios.
pram [præm] n cochecito de niño.
prance [prɑːns] vi (horse) hacer cabriolas.
prank [præŋk] n travesura.
prattle ['prætl] vi parlotear; (child) balbucear.
prawn [prɔːn] n gamba; (small) quisquilla.
pray [prei] vi rezar; ~**er** n oración f, rezo; (entreaty) ruego, súplica; ~**er book** n devocionario, misal m.
preach [priːtʃ] vi predicar; ~**er** n predicador/a m/f; (US) pastor m.
preamble [pri'æmbl] n preámbulo.
prearranged [priːə'reindʒd] a arreglado de antemano.
precarious [pri'kɛəriəs] a precario.
precaution [pri'kɔːʃən] n precaución f.
precede [pri'siːd] vt, vi preceder.
precedence ['prɛsidəns] n precedencia;

(*priority*) prioridad *f*; **precedent** [-ɔnt] *n* precedente *m*.

preceding [prɪ'si:dɪŋ] *a* precedente.

precept ['pri:sɛpt] *n* precepto.

precinct ['pri:sɪŋkt] *n* recinto; **~s** *npl* contornos *mpl*; **pedestrian ~** zona reservada para peatones; **shopping ~** zona comercial.

precious ['prɛʃəs] *a* precioso; (*stylized*) afectado.

precipice ['prɛsɪpɪs] *n* precipicio, despeñadero.

precipitate [prɪ'sɪpɪtɪt] *a* (*hasty*) precipitado, apresurado // *vt* [prɪ'sɪpɪteɪt] (*hasten*) acelerar; (*bring about*) causar; **precipitation** [-'teɪʃən] *n* precipitación *f*.

precipitous [prɪ'sɪpɪtəs] *a* (*steep*) escarpado.

precise [prɪ'saɪs] *a* preciso, exacto; (*person*) escrupuloso; **~ly** *ad* exactamente, precisamente; **precision** [-'sɪʒən] *n* precisión *f*.

preclude [prɪ'klu:d] *vt* excluir.

precocious [prɪ'kəuʃəs] *a* precoz.

preconceived [pri:kən'si:vd] *a* (*idea*) preconcebido.

precursor [pri:'kə:sə*] *n* precursor/a *m/f*.

predator ['prɛdətə*] *n* animal *m* de rapiña; **~y** *a* rapaz, de rapiña.

predecessor ['pri:dɪsɛsə*] *n* antecesor/a *m/f*.

predestination [pri:dɛstɪ'neɪʃən] *n* predestinación *f*.

predetermine [pri:dɪ'tə:mɪn] *vt* predeterminar.

predicament [prɪ'dɪkəmənt] *n* apuro.

predict [prɪ'dɪkt] *vt* pronosticar; **~ion** [-'dɪkʃən] *n* pronóstico.

predominant [prɪ'dɔmɪnənt] *a* predominante; **predominate** [-neɪt] *vi* predominar.

pre-eminent [pri:'ɛmɪnənt] *a* preeminente.

pre-empt [pri:'ɛmt] *vt* apropiarse de antemano.

preen [pri:n] *vt*: **to ~ itself** (*bird*) limpiarse (las plumas); **to ~ o.s.** pavonearse.

prefab ['pri:fæb] *n* casa prefabricada.

prefabricated [pri:'fæbrikeɪtɪd] *a* prefabricado.

preface ['prɛfəs] *n* prefacio.

prefect ['pri:fɛkt] *n* (*Brit: in school*) tutor *m*, monitor *m*.

prefer [prɪ'fə:*] *vt* preferir; **~able** ['prɛfrəbl] *a* preferible; **~ably** ['prɛfrəblɪ] *ad* de preferencia; **~ence** ['prɛfrəns] *n* preferencia, prioridad *f*; **~ential** [prɛfə'rɛnʃəl] *a* preferente.

prefix ['pri:fɪks] *n* prefijo.

pregnancy ['prɛgnənsɪ] *n* embarazo; **pregnant** [-ənt] *a* embarazada; **to be pregnant** estar encinta; **pregnant with** preñado de.

prehistoric ['pri:hɪs'tɔrɪk] *a* prehistórico.

prejudge [pri:'dʒʌdʒ] *vt* prejuzgar.

prejudice ['prɛdʒudɪs] *n* (*bias*) prejuicio; (*harm*) perjuicio // *vt* (*predispose*) predisponer; (*harm*) perjudicar; **~d** *a* (*person*) predispuesto, con prejuicios; (*view*) parcial, interesado.

prelate ['prɛlət] *n* prelado.

preliminary [prɪ'lɪmɪnərɪ] *a* preliminar.

prelude ['prɛlju:d] *n* preludio.

premarital ['pri:'mærɪtl] *a* premarital.

premature ['prɛmətʃuə*] *a* prematuro.

premeditated [pri:'mɛdɪteɪtɪd] *a* premeditado.

premier ['prɛmɪə*] *a* primero, principal // *n* (*POL*) primer ministro.

première ['prɛmɪɛə*] *n* estreno.

premise ['prɛmɪs] *n* premisa; **~s** *npl* local *m*; (*house*) casa *sg*; (*shop*) tienda *sg*; **on the ~s** en el local.

premium ['pri:mɪəm] *n* premio; (*COMM*) prima; **to be at a ~** ser muy solicitado.

premonition [prɛmə'nɪʃən] *n* presentimiento.

preoccupation [pri:ɔkju'peɪʃən] *n* preocupación *f*; **preoccupied** [-'ɔkjupaɪd] *a* (*worried*) preocupado; (*absorbed*) absorto.

prep [prɛp] *n* (*SCOL: study*) deberes *mpl*; **~ school** *n* = **preparatory school.**

prepaid [pri:'peɪd] *a* con porte pagado.

preparation [prɛpə'reɪʃən] *n* preparación *f*; **~s** *npl* preparativos *mpl*.

preparatory [prɪ'pærətərɪ] *a* preparatorio, preliminar; **~ to** con miras a; **~ school** *n* escuela preparatoria.

prepare [prɪ'pɛə*] *vt* preparar, disponer // *vi*: **to ~ for** prepararse o disponerse para; (*make preparations*) hacer preparativos para; **~d to** dispuesto a.

preponderance [prɪ'pɔndərns] *n* preponderancia, predominio.

preposition [prɛpə'zɪʃən] *n* preposición *f*.

preposterous [prɪ'pɔstərəs] *a* absurdo, ridículo.

prerequisite [pri:'rɛkwɪzɪt] *n* requisito (*previo*).

prerogative [prɪ'rɔgətɪv] *n* prerrogativa.

presbyterian [prɛzbɪ'tɪərɪən] *a, n* presbiteriano/a.

preschool ['pri:'sku:l] *a* preescolar.

prescribe [prɪ'skraɪb] *vt* prescribir; (*MED*) recetar.

prescription [prɪ'skrɪpʃən] *n* prescripción *f*; (*MED*) receta.

presence ['prɛzns] *n* presencia; (*attendance*) asistencia; **~ of mind** *n* presencia de ánimo.

present ['prɛznt] *a* (*in attendance*) presente; (*current*) actual // *n* (*gift*) regalo; (*actuality*) actualidad *f*, presente *m* // *vt* [prɪ'zɛnt] (*introduce*) presentar; (*expound*) exponer; (*give*) presentar, dar, ofrecer; (*THEATRE*) representar; **at ~** actualmente; **~able** [prɪ'zɛntəbl] *a* presentable; **~ation** [-'teɪʃən] *n* presentación *f*; (*gift*) obsequio; (*of case*) exposición *f*; (*THEATRE*) representación *f*;

~**-day** a actual; ~**ly** ad (*soon*) dentro de poco.

preservation [prɛzə'veɪʃən] n conservación f.

preservative [prɪ'zɜ:vətɪv] n preservativo.

preserve [prɪ'zɜ:v] vt (*keep safe*) preservar, proteger; (*maintain*) conservar; (*food*) hacer una conserva de; (*in salt*) salar // n (*for game*) coto, vedado; (*often pl*: *jam*) conserva, confitura.

preside [prɪ'zaɪd] vi presidir.

presidency ['prɛzɪdənsɪ] n presidencia; **president** [-ənt] n presidente m/f; **presidential** [-'dɛnʃl] a presidencial.

press [prɛs] n (*tool, machine, newspapers*) prensa; (*printer's*) imprenta; (*crowd*) apiñamiento, agolpamiento; (*of hand*) apretón m // vt (*push*) empujar; (*squeeze*) apretar; (*clothes*: *iron*) planchar; (*TECH*) prensar; (*harry*) acosar; (*insist*): **to ~ sth on sb** insistir en que uno acepte algo // vi (*squeeze*) apretar; (*pressurize*) ejercer presión; **we are ~ed for time** tenemos poco tiempo; **to ~ on** vi avanzar; (*hurry*) apretar el paso; ~ **agency** n agencia de prensa; ~ **conference** n conferencia de prensa; ~ **cutting** n recorte m (de periódico); ~**ing** a apremiante; ~ **stud** n botón m de presión.

pressure ['prɛʃə*] n presión f; (*urgency*) apremio, urgencia; (*influence*) influencia; (*MED*) tensión f nerviosa; ~ **cooker** n olla a presión; ~ **gauge** n manómetro; ~ **group** n grupo de presión; **pressurized** a a presión.

prestige [prɛs'ti:ʒ] n prestigio; **prestigious** [-'tɪdʒəs] a prestigioso.

presumably [prɪ'zju:məblɪ] ad se supone que, cabe presumir que.

presume [prɪ'zju:m] vt presumir, suponer; **to ~ to do** (*dare*) atreverse a; (*set out to*) pretender.

presumption [prɪ'zʌmpʃən] n suposición f; (*pretension*) pretensión f; (*boldness*) atrevimiento.

presuppose [pri:sə'pəʊz] vt presuponer.

pretence, pretense (*US*) [prɪ'tɛns] n (*claim*) pretensión f; (*display*) ostentación f; (*pretext*) pretexto; (*make-believe*) fingimiento; **on the ~ of** so pretexto de.

pretend [prɪ'tɛnd] vt (*feign*) fingir // vi (*feign*) fingir; (*claim*): **to ~ to sth** pretender a algo.

pretension [prɪ'tɛnʃən] n (*presumption*) presunción f; (*claim*) pretensión f.

pretentious [prɪ'tɛnʃəs] a presumido; (*ostentacious*) ostenso, aparatoso.

pretext ['pri:tɛkst] n pretexto.

pretty ['prɪtɪ] a (*gen*) hermoso; (*person*) guapo; (*dress*) bonito; (*sum*) importante // ad (*quite*) bastante; (*nearly*) casi.

prevail [prɪ'veɪl] vi (*win*) imponerse; (*be current*) imperar; (*be in fashion*) estar de moda; (*be usual*) prevalecer; (*persuade*): **to ~ (up)on sb to do sth** persuadir a uno a hacer algo; ~**ing** a (*dominant*)

imperante; (*usual*) corriente.

prevalent ['prɛvələnt] a (*dominant*) predominante; (*usual*) corriente; (*fashionable*) en boga; (*present-day*) actual.

prevent [prɪ'vɛnt] vt: **to ~ (sb) from doing sth** impedir (a uno) hacer algo; ~**able** a evitable; ~**ative** a preventivo; ~**ion** [-'vɛnʃən] n prevención f; ~**ive** a preventivo.

preview ['pri:vju:] n (*of film*) preestreno; (*fig*) anticipo.

previous ['pri:vɪəs] a previo, anterior; (*hasty*) prematuro; ~**ly** ad previamente, con anticipación; (*in earlier times*) antes.

prewar [pri:'wɔ:*] a de preguerra, prebélico.

prey [preɪ] n presa // vi: **to ~ on** vivir a costa de; (*feed on*) alimentarse de; (*plunder*) robar, pillar; **it was ~ing on his mind** le agobiaba, le preocupaba.

price [praɪs] n precio // vt (*goods*) fijar el precio de; ~**less** a inapreciable.

prick [prɪk] n pinchazo; (*with pin*) alfilerazo; (*sting*) picadura // vt pinchar; picar; **to ~ up one's ears** aguzar el oído.

prickle ['prɪkl] n (*sensation*) escozor m; (*BOT*) espina; (*ZOOL*) púa; **prickly** a espinoso; (*fig*: *person*) malhumorado; (: *touchy*) quisquilloso.

pride [praɪd] n orgullo; (*pej*) soberbia // vt: **to ~ o.s. on** enorgullecerse de, ufanarse de.

priest [pri:st] n sacerdote m; ~**ess** n sacerdotisa; ~**hood** n (*practice*) sacerdocio; (*priests*) clero.

prig [prɪg] n presumido/a, pedante m/f.

prim [prɪm] a (*formal*) estirado; (*affected*) remilgado; (*prudish*) gazmoño.

primarily ['praɪmərɪlɪ] ad (*above all*) ante todo; (*firstly*) en primer lugar.

primary ['praɪmərɪ] a primario; (*first in importance*) principal; ~ **school** n escuela primaria.

primate ['praɪmɪt] n (*REL*) primado // n ['praɪmeɪt] (*ZOOL*) primate m.

prime [praɪm] a primero, principal; (*basic*) fundamental; (*excellent*) selecto, de primera clase // vt (*gun, pump*) cebar; (*fig*) preparar, aprestar; **in the ~ of life** en la flor de la vida; ~ **minister** n primer ministro; **primer** n (*book*) libro de texto; (*paint*) pintura de base.

primitive ['prɪmɪtɪv] a primitivo; (*crude*) rudimentario; (*uncivilized*) inculto.

primrose ['prɪmrəʊz] n primavera, prímula.

primus (stove) ['praɪməs] n hornillo de campaña a presión.

prince [prɪns] n príncipe m.

princess [prɪn'sɛs] n princesa.

principal ['prɪnsɪpl] a principal, mayor // n director/a m/f.

principality [prɪnsɪ'pælɪtɪ] n principado.

principle ['prɪnsɪpl] n principio.

print [prɪnt] n (*impression*) marca, impresión f; (*letters*) letra de molde; (*fabric*) estampado; (*ART*) estampa,

grabado; (PHOT) positiva // vt (gen)
imprimir; (on mind) grabar; (write in
capitals) escribir en letras de molde; out
of ~ agotado; ~ed matter n impresos
mpl; ~er n impresor/a m/f; ~ing n (art)
imprenta; (act) impresión f; (quantity)
tirada; ~ing press n (prensa de)
imprenta.

prior ['praɪə*] a anterior, previo // n prior
m; ~ to doing antes de o hasta hacer.

priority [praɪ'ɔrɪtɪ] n prioridad f.

prise [praɪz] vt: to ~ open abrir con
palanca.

prism ['prɪzəm] n prisma m.

prison ['prɪzn] n cárcel f, prisión f // a
carcelario; ~er n (in prison) preso; (under
arrest) detenido; (in dock) acusado.

privacy ['prɪvəsɪ] n (seclusion)
aislamiento, soledad f; (intimacy)
intimidad f.

private ['praɪvɪt] a (personal) particular;
(confidential) secreto, reservado;
(intimate) privado, íntimo; (sitting etc) a
puertas cerradas // n soldado raso; '~'
(on envelope) 'privado'; (on door) 'uso
particular o privado'; in ~ en privado; ~
enterprise n la empresa privada; ~ eye
n detective m privado; ~ly ad en privado;
(in o.s.) en el fondo.

privet ['prɪvɪt] n alheña.

privilege ['prɪvɪlɪdʒ] n privilegio;
(prerogative) prerrogativa; ~d a
privilegiado.

privy ['prɪvɪ] a: to be ~ to estar enterado
de; P~ Council n Consejo Privado.

prize [praɪz] n premio // a premiado; (first
class) de primera clase // vt apreciar,
estimar; ~-giving n distribución f de
premios; ~-winner n premiado/a.

pro [prəu] n (SPORT) profesional m/f; the
~s and cons los pros y los contras.

probability [prɔbə'bɪlɪtɪ] n probabilidad f;
probable ['prɔbəbl] a probable; (plausible)
verosímil; probably ['prɔbəblɪ] ad proba-
blemente.

probation [prə'beɪʃən] n: on ~
(employee) de prueba; (LAW) en libertad
condicional.

probe [prəub] n (MED, SPACE) sonda;
(enquiry) encuesta, sondeo // vt sondar;
(investigate) indagar.

problem ['prɔbləm] n problema m; ~atic
[-'mætɪk] a problemático.

procedure [prə'si:dʒə*] n (ADMIN, LAW)
procedimiento; (method) proceder m;
(bureaucratic) trámites mpl.

proceed [prə'si:d] vi proceder; (continue):
to ~ (with) continuar o seguir (con);
~ings npl acto sg, actos mpl; (LAW)
medidas fpl; (meeting) función f; (records)
actas fpl; ~s ['prəusi:dz] npl ganancias fpl,
ingresos mpl.

process ['prəuses] n proceso; (method)
método, sistema m; (proceeding)
procedimiento // vt tratar, elaborar; in ~
en curso; ~ing n elaboración f.

procession [prə'seʃən] n desfile m;
funeral ~ cortejo fúnebre.

proclaim [prə'kleɪm] vt proclamar;
(announce) anunciar; proclamation
[prɔklə'meɪʃən] n proclamación f; (written)
proclama.

procreation [prəukrɪ'eɪʃən] n procreación
f.

procure [prə'kjuə*] vt conseguir, obtener.

prod [prɔd] vt (push) empujar; (with elbow)
dar un codazo a; (jab) pinchar // n empuje
m; codazo; pinchazo.

prodigal ['prɔdɪgl] a pródigo.

prodigious [prə'dɪdʒəs] a prodigioso.

prodigy ['prɔdɪdʒɪ] n prodigio.

produce ['prɔdju:s] n (AGR) productos mpl
agrícolas // [prə'dju:s] (gen) producir;
(profit) rendir; (show) presentar, mostrar;
(THEATRE) presentar, poner en escena;
(offspring) dar a luz; producer n
(THEATRE) director/a m/f; (AGR, CINEMA)
productor/a m/f.

product ['prɔdʌkt] n (thing) producto;
(result) fruto, resultado.

production [prə'dʌkʃən] n (act)
producción f; (thing) producto; (THEATRE)
representación f, obra; ~ line n línea o
cadena de montaje.

productive [prə'dʌktɪv] a productivo;
productivity [prɔdʌk'tɪvɪtɪ] n
productividad f.

profane [prə'feɪn] a profano; (language
etc) fuerte.

profess [prə'fes] vt profesar; (regret)
manifestar.

profession [prə'feʃən] n profesión f; ~al
n profesional m/f; (expert) perito // a
profesional; perito, experto; (by profession)
de oficio.

professor [prə'fesə*] n catedrático/a.

proficiency [prə'fɪʃənsɪ] n pericia,
habilidad f; proficient [-ənt] a perito,
hábil.

profile ['prəufaɪl] n perfil m.

profit ['prɔfɪt] n (COMM) ganancia; (fig)
provecho // vi: to ~ by or from
aprovechar o sacar provecho de;
~ability [-ə'bɪlɪtɪ] n rentabilidad f;
~able a (ECON) rentable; (useful)
provechoso; ~eering [-'tɪərɪŋ] n (pej)
ganancias fpl excesivas.

profound [prə'faund] a profundo.

profuse [prə'fju:s] a profuso, pródigo; ~ly
ad profusamente, pródigamente;
profusion [-'fju:ʒən] n profusión f,
abundancia.

progeny ['prɔdʒɪnɪ] n progenie f, prole f.

programme, program (US)
['prəugræm] n programa m // vt
programar; programming, programing
(US) n programación f.

progress ['prəugres] n progreso;
(development) desarrollo // vi [prə'gres]
progresar, avanzar; desarrollarse; in ~
en marcha; ~ion [-'greʃən] n progresión f;
~ive [-'gresɪv] a progresivo; (person)
progresista m/f.

prohibit [prə'hɪbɪt] *vt* prohibir; **to ~ sb from doing sth** prohibir a uno hacer algo; **~ion** [prəʊɪ'bɪʃən] *n* (*US*) prohibicionismo; **~ive** *a* (*price etc*) excesivo.

project ['prɔdʒɛkt] *n* proyecto // (*vb*: [prə'dʒɛkt]) *vt* proyectar // *vi* (*stick out*) salir, sobresalir.

projectile [prə'dʒɛktaɪl] *n* proyectil *m*.

projection [prə'dʒɛkʃən] *n* proyección *f*; (*overhang*) saliente *m*.

projector [prə'dʒɛktə*] *n* proyector *m*.

proletarian [prəʊlɪ'tɛərɪən] *a*, *n* proletario/a; **proletariat** [-rɪət] *n* proletariado.

proliferate [prə'lɪfəreɪt] *vi* proliferar, multiplicarse; **proliferation** [-'reɪʃən] *n* proliferación *f*.

prolific [prə'lɪfɪk] *a* prolífico.

prologue ['prəʊlɔg] *n* prólogo.

prolong [prə'lɔŋ] *vt* prolongar, extender.

prom [prɔm] *n abbr of* **promenade** baile *m* de gala.

promenade [prɔmə'naːd] *n* (*by sea*) paseo marítimo; **~ concert** *n* concierto (en que parte del público permanece de pie).

prominence ['prɔmɪnəns] *n* (*fig*) eminencia, importancia; **prominent** [-ənt] *a* (*standing out*) saliente; (*important*) eminente, importante.

promiscuous [prə'mɪskjuəs] *a* (*sexually*) libertino.

promise ['prɔmɪs] *n* promesa // *vt*, *vi* prometer; **promising** *a* prometedor(a).

promontory ['prɔməntrɪ] *n* promontorio.

promote [prə'məʊt] *vt* (*gen*) promover; (*new product*) hacer propaganda por; (*MIL*) ascender; **promoter** *n* (*of sporting event*) promotor/a *m/f*; **promotion** [-'məʊʃən] *n* (*gen*) promoción *f*; (*MIL*) ascenso.

prompt [prɔmpt] *a* pronto // *ad* (*punctually*) puntualmente // *vt* (*urge*) mover, incitar; (*THEATRE*) apuntar; **to ~ sb to do sth** mover a uno a hacer algo; **~er** *n* (*THEATRE*) apuntador/a *m/f*; **~ly** *ad* (*punctually*) puntualmente; (*rapidly*) rápidamente; **~ness** *n* puntualidad *f*; rapidez *f*.

prone [prəʊn] *a* (*lying*) postrado; **~ to** propenso a.

prong [prɔŋ] *n* diente *m*, púa.

pronoun ['prəʊnaʊn] *n* pronombre *m*.

pronounce [prə'naʊns] *vt* pronunciar; (*declare*) declarar // *vi*: **to ~ (up)on** pronunciarse sobre; **~d** *a* (*marked*) marcado; **~ment** *n* declaración *f*.

pronunciation [prənʌnsɪ'eɪʃən] *n* pronunciación *f*.

proof [pruːf] *n* prueba; (*of alcohol*) graduación *f* normal // *a*: **~ against** a prueba de; **~reader** *n* corrector/a *m/f* de pruebas.

prop [prɔp] *n* apoyo *m*, (*fig*) sostén *m* // *vt* (*also*: **~ up**) apoyar; (*lean*): **to ~ sth against** apoyar algo contra.

propaganda [prɔpə'gændə] *n* propaganda.

propagate ['prɔpəgeɪt] *vt* propagar.

propel [prə'pɛl] *vt* impulsar, propulsar; **~ler** *n* hélice *f*; **~ling pencil** *n* lapicero.

proper ['prɔpə*] *a* (*suited, right*) propio; (*exact*) justo; (*apt*) apropiado, conveniente; (*timely*) oportuno; (*seemly*) correcto, decente; (*authentic*) verdadero; (*col: real*) auténtico.

property ['prɔpətɪ] *n* (*gen*) propiedad *f*; (*goods*) bienes *mpl*; (*estate*) hacienda; **it's their ~** es suyo, les pertenece.

prophecy ['prɔfɪsɪ] *n* profecía; **prophesy** [-saɪ] *vt* profetizar; (*fig*) predecir.

prophet ['prɔfɪt] *n* profeta *m/f*; **~ic** [prə'fɛtɪk] *a* profético.

proportion [prə'pɔːʃən] *n* proporción *f*; (*share*) parte *f*, porción *f*; **~al** *a* proporcional; **~ate** *a* proporcionado.

proposal [prə'pəʊzl] *n* propuesta; (*offer*) oferta; (*plan*) proyecto; (*of marriage*) declaración *f*; (*suggestion*) sugerencia.

propose [prə'pəʊz] *vt* proponer; (*offer*) ofrecer // *vi* declararse; **to ~ to do** proponerse hacer.

proposition [prɔpə'zɪʃən] *n* propuesta, proposición *f*.

proprietor [prə'praɪətə*] *n* propietario, dueño.

propulsion [prə'pʌlʃən] *n* propulsión *f*.

pro rata [prəʊ'raːtə] *ad* a prorrateo.

prosaic [prəʊ'zeɪɪk] *a* prosaico.

prose [prəʊz] *n* prosa.

prosecute ['prɔsɪkjuːt] *vt* (*LAW*) procesar; **prosecution** [-'kjuːʃən] *n* proceso, causa; (*accusing side*) parte *f* actora; **prosecutor** *n* acusador/a *m/f*; (*also*: **public prosecutor**) fiscal *m*.

prospect ['prɔspɛkt] *n* (*view*) vista; (*chance*) posibilidad *f*; (*outlook*) perspectiva; (*hope*) esperanza // (*vb*: [prə'spɛkt]) *vt* explorar // *vi* buscar; **~s** *npl* (*for work etc*) perspectivas *fpl*; **~ing** *n* prospección *f*; **~ive** *a* (*possible*) probable, esperado; (*certain*) futuro; (*heir*) presunto; (*legislation*) en perspectiva; **~or** *n* explorador/a *m/f*.

prospectus [prə'spɛktəs] *n* prospecto.

prosper ['prɔspə*] *vi* prosperar; **~ity** [-'spɛrɪtɪ] *n* prosperidad *f*; **~ous** *a* próspero.

prostitute ['prɔstɪtjuːt] *n* prostituta.

prostrate ['prɔstreɪt] *a* postrado; (*fig*) abatido.

protagonist [prə'tægənɪst] *n* protagonista *m/f*.

protect [prə'tɛkt] *vt* proteger; **~ion** *n* protección *f*; **~ive** *a* protector(a); **~or** *n* protector/a *m/f*.

protégé ['prəʊtɛʒeɪ] *n* protegido.

protein ['prəʊtiːn] *n* proteína.

protest ['prəʊtɛst] *n* protesta // (*vb*: [prə'tɛst]) *vi* protestar // *vt* (*affirm*) afirmar, declarar.

Protestant ['prɔtɪstənt] *a*, *n* protestante *m/f*.

protocol ['prəʊtəkɔl] *n* protocolo.

prototype ['prəʊtətaɪp] *n* prototipo.

protracted [prə'træktɪd] *a* prolongado.

protrude [prə'truːd] *vi* salir fuera, sobresalir.

proud [praud] *a* orgulloso; (*pej*) soberbio, altanero; (*imposing*) imponente.

prove [pruːv] *vt* probar; (*verify*) comprobar; (*show*) demostrar // *vi*: **to ~ correct** resultar correcto; **to ~ o.s.** ponerse a prueba.

proverb ['prɔvəːb] *n* refrán *m*; **~ial** [prə'vəːbiəl] *a* proverbial.

provide [prə'vaid] *vt* proporcionar, dar; **to ~ sb with sth** proveer a uno de algo; **to ~ for** *vt* (*person*) mantener a; (*emergency*) prevenir; **~d (that)** *conj* con tal que, siempre que.

providing [prə'vaidiŋ] *conj* a condición de que, siempre que.

province ['prɔvins] *n* provincia; (*fig*) esfera; **provincial** [prə'vinʃəl] *a* de provincia; (*pej*) provinciano.

provision [prə'viʒən] *n* (*gen*) provisión *f*; (*supply*) suministro; (*supplying*) abastecimiento; **~s** *npl* (*food*) comestibles *mpl*; **~al** *a* provisional; (*temporary*) interino.

proviso [prə'vaizəu] *n* condición *f*, estipulación *f*.

provocation [prɔvə'keiʃən] *n* provocación *f*.

provocative [prə'vɔkətiv] *a* provocativo; (*stimulating*) sugestivo.

provoke [prə'vəuk] *vt* (*arouse*) provocar, incitar; (*cause*) causar, producir; (*anger*) irritar.

prow [prau] *n* proa.

prowess ['prauis] *n* (*skill*) destreza, habilidad *f*; (*courage*) valor *m*.

prowl [praul] *vi* (*also:* **~ about, ~ around**) rondar // *n*: **on the ~** de ronda; **~er** *n* rondador/a *m/f*; (*thief*) ladrón/ona *m/f*.

proximity [prɔk'simiti] *n* proximidad *f*.

proxy ['prɔksi] *n* poder *m*; (*person*) apoderado/a; **by ~** por poder *o* poderes.

prudence ['pruːdns] *n* prudencia; **prudent** [-ənt] *a* prudente.

prudish ['pruːdiʃ] *a* gazmoño.

prune [pruːn] *n* ciruela pasa // *vt* podar.

pry [prai] *vi*: **to ~ into** entrometerse en.

psalm [sɑːm] *n* salmo.

pseudo- [sjuːdəu] *pref* seudo...; **~nym** *n* seudónimo.

psychiatric [saiki'ætrik] *a* psiquiátrico; **psychiatrist** [-'kaiətrist] *n* psiquiatra *m/f*; **psychiatry** [-'kaiətri] *n* psiquiatría.

psychic ['saikik] *a* (*also:* **~al**) psíquico // *n* medium *m/f*.

psychoanalyse [saikəu'ænəlaiz] *vt* psicoanalizar; **psychoanalysis** [-kəuə'nælisis] *n* psicoanálisis *m inv*; **psychoanalyst** [-'ænəlist] *n* psicoanalista *m/f*.

psychological [saikə'lɔdʒikl] *a* psicológico.

psychologist [sai'kɔlədʒist] *n* psicólogo; **psychology** [-dʒi] *n* psicología.

psychopath ['saikəupæθ] *n* psicópata *m/f*.

psychosomatic ['saikəusə'mætik] *a* psicosomático.

psychotic [sai'kɔtik] *a*, *n* psicótico.

pub [pʌb] *n abbr of* **public house** pub *m*, taberna.

puberty ['pjuːbəti] *n* pubertad *f*.

public ['pʌblik] *a*, *n* público.

publican ['pʌblikən] *n* tabernero.

publication [pʌbli'keiʃən] *n* publicación *f*.

public: **~ convenience** *n* aseos *mpl* públicos; **~ house** *n* bar *m*, pub *m*.

publicity [pʌb'lisiti] *n* publicidad *f*.

publicly ['pʌblikli] *ad* públicamente, en público.

public: **~ opinion** *n* opinión *f* pública; **~ relations** *n* relaciones *fpl* públicas; **~ school** *n* (*Brit*) escuela privada; **~-spirited** *a* de buen ciudadano.

publish ['pʌbliʃ] *vt* publicar; **~er** *n* editor/a *m/f*; **~ing** *n* (*industry*) la industria editorial.

puce [pjuːs] *a* de color pardo rojizo.

pucker ['pʌkə*] *vt* (*pleat*) arrugar; (*brow etc*) fruncir.

pudding ['pudiŋ] *n* pudín *m*; (*sweet*) postre *m*; **black ~** morcilla.

puddle ['pʌdl] *n* charco.

puff [pʌf] *n* soplo; (*from mouth*) bocanada; (*sound*) resoplido; (*also:* **powder ~**) borla // *vt*: **to ~ one's pipe** chupar la pipa // *vi* (*gen*) soplar; (*pant*) jadear; **to ~ out smoke** echar humo; **to ~ up** *vt* hinchar, inflar; **~ed** *a* (*col: out of breath*) sin aliento.

puffin ['pʌfin] *n* frailecillo.

puffy ['pʌfi] *a* hinchado.

pull [pul] *n* (*tug*): **to give sth a ~** dar un tirón a algo; (*fig: advantage*) ventaja; (*: influence*) influencia // *vt* tirar de; (*tug*) jalar; (*muscle*) torcerse; (*haul*) tirar, arrastrar // *vi* tirar, dar un tirón; **to ~ a face** hacer muecas; **to ~ to pieces** hacer pedazos; **to ~ one's punches** no emplear toda la fuerza; **to ~ one's weight** hacer su parte; **to ~ o.s. together** serenarse; **to ~ sb's leg** tomarle el pelo a uno; **to ~ apart** *vt* (*break*) romper (en dos); **to ~ down** *vt* (*house*) derribar; **to ~ in** *vi* (*AUT: at the kerb*) parar (junto a la acera); (*RAIL*) llegar (al andén); **to ~ off** *vt* (*deal etc*) cerrar, concluir con éxito; **to ~ out** *vi* irse, marcharse; (*AUT: from kerb*) salir // *vt* sacar, arrancar; **to ~ through** *vi* salir (de un apuro); (*MED*) recobrar la salud; **to ~ up** *vi* (*stop*) parar // *vt* (*uproot*) arrancar, desarraigar; (*stop*) parar.

pulley ['puli] *n* polea.

pullover ['puləuvə*] *n* jersey *m*.

pulp [pʌlp] *n* (*of fruit*) pulpa; (*for paper*) pasta.

pulpit ['pulpit] *n* púlpito.

pulsate [pʌl'seit] *vi* pulsar, latir.

pulse [pʌls] *n* (*ANAT*) pulso; (*of music, engine*) pulsación *f*; (*BOT*) legumbre *f*.

pulverize ['pʌlvəraiz] *vt* pulverizar; (*fig*) hacer polvo.

puma ['pju:mə] n puma.
pummel ['pʌml] vt dar de puñetazos.
pump [pʌmp] n bomba; (shoe) zapato de tenis // vt sacar con una bomba; (fig: col) sonsacar; to ~ up vt inflar.
pumpkin ['pʌmpkin] n calabaza.
pun [pʌn] n juego de palabras.
punch [pʌntʃ] n (blow) golpe m, puñetazo; (tool) punzón m; (for tickets) taladro; (drink) ponche m // vt (hit): to ~ sb/sth dar un puñetazo o golpear a uno/algo; (make a hole in) punzar; ~card n tarjeta perforada; ~line n palabras que rematan un chiste; ~-up n (col) riña.
punctual ['pʌŋktjuəl] a puntual; ~ity [-'ælɪtɪ] n puntualidad f.
punctuate ['pʌŋktjueɪt] vt interrumpir; **punctuation** [-'eɪʃən] n puntuación f.
puncture ['pʌŋktʃə°] n pinchazo // vt pinchar.
pundit ['pʌndɪt] n sabio.
pungent ['pʌndʒənt] a acre.
punish ['pʌnɪʃ] vt castigar; ~ment n castigo.
punt [pʌnt] n (boat) batea.
punter ['pʌntə°] n (gambler) jugador/a m/f.
puny ['pju:nɪ] a débil.
pup [pʌp] n cachorro.
pupil ['pju:pl] n alumno/a.
puppet ['pʌpɪt] n títere m.
puppy ['pʌpɪ] n cachorro, perrito.
purchase ['pɜ:tʃɪs] n compra; (grip) pie m firme // vt comprar; **purchaser** n comprador/a m/f.
pure [pjuə°] a puro.
purée ['pjuəreɪ] n puré m.
purge [pɜ:dʒ] n (MED) purgante m; (POL) purga // vt purgar.
purification [pjuərɪfɪ'keɪʃən] n purificación f, depuración f; **purify** ['pjuərɪfaɪ] vt purificar, depurar.
purist ['pjuərɪst] n purista m/f.
puritan ['pjuərɪtən] n puritano/a; ~ical [-'tænɪkl] a puritano.
purity ['pjuərɪtɪ] n pureza.
purl [pɜ:l] n punto del revés.
purple ['pɜ:pl] a purpúreo; (bruise) morado.
purport [pɜ:'pɔ:t] vi: to ~ to be/do dar a entender que es/hace.
purpose ['pɜ:pəs] n propósito; on ~ a propósito, adrede; ~ful a resuelto, determinado.
purr [pɜ:°] n ronroneo // vi ronronear.
purse [pɜ:s] n monedero; (bag) bolsa // vt fruncir.
purser ['pɜ:sə°] n (NAUT) contador m de navío.
pursue [pə'sju:] vt seguir, perseguir; (profession) ejercer; **pursuer** n perseguidor/a m/f.
pursuit [pə'sju:t] n (chase) caza; (persecution) persecución f; (occupation) carrera; (pastime) pasatiempo.
purveyor [pə'veɪə°] n proveedor/a m/f.

pus [pʌs] n pus m.
push [puʃ] n (gen) empuje m; (shove) empujón m; (attack) ataque m; (advance) avance m // vt empujar; (button) apretar; (promote) promover; (thrust): to ~ sth (into) meter algo a la fuerza (en) // vi empujar; (fig) hacer esfuerzos; to ~ aside vt apartar con la mano; to ~ off vi (col) largarse; to ~ on vi (continue) seguir adelante; to ~ through vt (measure) despachar; to ~ up vt (total, prices) hacer subir; ~chair n sillita de ruedas; ~ing a emprendedor(a), enérgico; ~over n (col): it's a ~over está tirado; ~y a (col): (pej) agresivo.
puss [pus], **pussy(-cat)** ['pusɪ(kæt)] n minino.
put [put], pt, pp put vt (place) poner, colocar; (~ into) meter; (say) declarar, expresar; (a question) hacer; (estimate) calcular; to ~ about vi (NAUT) virar // vt (rumour) diseminar; to ~ across vt (ideas etc) comunicar; to ~ away vt (store) guardar; to ~ back vt (replace) devolver a su lugar; (postpone) posponer; to ~ by vt (money) guardar; to ~ down vt (on ground) poner en el suelo; (animal) sacrificar; (in writing) apuntar; (suppress: revolt etc) sofocar; (attribute) atribuir; to ~ forward vt (ideas) presentar, proponer; (date) adelantar; to ~ in vt (application, complaint) presentar; to ~ off vt (postpone) aplazar; (discourage) desanimar; to ~ on vt (clothes, lipstick etc) ponerse; (light etc) encender; (play etc) presentar; (weight) ganar; (brake) echar; (attitude) adoptar postura de; to ~ out vt (fire, light) apagar; (one's hand) alargar; (news, rumour) sacar a luz, diseminar; (tongue etc) sacar; (person: inconvenience) molestar, fastidiar; to ~ up vt (raise) levantar, alzar; (hang) colgar; (build) construir; (increase) aumentar; (accommodate) alojar; to ~ up with vt fus aguantar.
putrid ['pju:trɪd] a podrido.
putt [pʌt] vt golpear con poca fuerza // n put m, golpe m corto; ~er n (GOLF) putter m; ~ing green n campo de golf en miniatura.
putty ['pʌtɪ] n masilla.
puzzle ['pʌzl] n (riddle) acertijo; (jigsaw) rompecabezas m inv; (crossword) crucigrama m; (mystery) misterio, problema m // vt dejar perplejo, confundir // vi devanarse los sesos; **puzzling** a misterioso, enigmático.
pygmy ['pɪgmɪ] n pigmeo.
pyjamas [pɪ'dʒɑ:məz] npl pijama m.
pylon ['paɪlən] n pilón m, poste m.
pyramid ['pɪrəmɪd] n pirámide m.
python ['paɪθən] n pitón m.

Q

quack [kwæk] n (of duck) graznido; (pej: doctor) curandero // vi graznar.

quad [kwɔd] abbr of **quadrangle**; **quadruple**.

quadrangle ['kwɔdræŋgl] n (courtyard: abbr: quad) patio.

quadruple [kwɔ'druːpl] a cuádruple // n cuádruplo // vt, vi cuadruplicar.

quadruplets [kwɔ'druːplɪts] npl cuatrillizos mpl.

quagmire ['kwægmaɪə*] n lodazal m, cenegal m.

quail [kweɪl] n (bird) codorniz f // vi amedrentarse.

quaint [kweɪnt] a curioso; (picturesque) pintoresco.

quake [kweɪk] vi temblar // n abbr of **earthquake**.

Quaker ['kweɪkə*] n cuáquero/a.

qualification [kwɔlɪfɪ'keɪʃən] n (reservation) reserva; (modification) modificación f; (act) calificación f; (degree) título; **qualified** ['kwɔlɪfaɪd] a (trained) cualificado; (fit) apto, competente; (limited) limitado; (professionally) con título.

qualify ['kwɔlɪfaɪ] vt calificar; (capacitate) capacitar; (modify) modificar; (limit) moderar // vi (SPORT) clasificarse; **to ~ (as)** calificarse (de), graduarse (en); **to ~ (for)** reunir los requisitos (para).

quality ['kwɔlɪtɪ] n calidad f; (moral) cualidad f.

qualm [kwɑːm] n escrúpulo.

quandary ['kwɔndrɪ] n: **to be in a ~** estar en un dilema.

quantity ['kwɔntɪtɪ] n cantidad f.

quarantine ['kwɔrəntiːn] n cuarentena.

quarrel ['kwɔrl] n (argument) riña; (fight) pelea // vi reñir; pelearse; **~some** a pendenciero.

quarry ['kwɔrɪ] n (for stone) cantera; (animal) presa.

quart [kwɔːt] n cuarto de galón = 1.136 litros.

quarter ['kwɔːtə*] n cuarto, cuarta parte f; (of year) trimestre m; (district) barrio // vt dividir en cuartos; (MIL: lodge) alojar; **~s** npl (barracks) cuartel m; (living ~s) alojamiento sg; **a ~ of an hour** un cuarto de hora; **~ final** n cuarto de final; **~ly** a trimestral // ad cada 3 meses, trimestralmente; **~master** n (MIL) comisario, intendente m militar.

quartet(te) [kwɔː'tɛt] n cuarteto.

quartz [kwɔːts] n cuarzo.

quash [kwɔʃ] vt (verdict) anular.

quasi- ['kweɪzaɪ] pref cuasi.

quaver ['kweɪvə*] n (MUS) corchea // vi temblar.

quay [kiː] n (also: ~side) muelle m.

queasy ['kwiːzɪ] a (sickly) delicado.

queen [kwiːn] n (gen) reina; (CARDS etc)

dama; **~ mother** n reina madre.

queer [kwɪə*] a (odd) raro, extraño; (suspect) sospechoso // n (col) maricón m.

quell [kwɛl] vt calmar; (put down) sofocar.

quench [kwɛntʃ] vt apagar.

query ['kwɪərɪ] n (question) pregunta; (doubt) duda; (fig) interrogante f // vt preguntar; poner en duda.

quest [kwɛst] n busca, búsqueda.

question ['kwɛstʃən] n pregunta; (matter) asunto, cuestión f // vt (gen) preguntar; (doubt) dudar de; (interrogate) interrogar, hacer preguntas a; **beyond ~** fuera de toda duda; **out of the ~** imposible, ni hablar; **~able** a discutible; (doubtful) dudoso; **~ mark** n punto de interrogación; **~naire** [-'nɛə*] n cuestionario.

queue [kjuː] n cola // vi hacer cola.

quibble ['kwɪbl] vi sutilizar.

quick [kwɪk] a rápido; (temper) vivo; (agile) ágil; (mind) listo; (eye) agudo; (ear) fino; **be ~!** ¡date prisa!; **~en** vt apresurar // vi apresurarse, darse prisa; **~ly** ad rápidamente, de prisa; **~ness** n rapidez f; agilidad f; (liveliness) viveza; **~sand** n arenas fpl movedizas; **~step** n (dance) fox-trot m, quickstep m; **~-witted** a perspicaz.

quid [kwɪd] n, pl inv (Brit: col) libra.

quiet ['kwaɪət] a tranquilo; (silent) callado; (ceremony) discreto // n silencio, tranquilidad f; **keep ~!** ¡cállate!, ¡silencio!; **~en** (also: **~en down**) vi (grow calm) calmarse; (grow silent) callarse // vt calmar; hacer callar; **~ly** ad (gen) tranquilamente; (silently) silenciosamente; **~ness** n (silence) silencio; (calm) tranquilidad f.

quilt [kwɪlt] n edredón m; (continental) **~** n edredón m.

quin [kwɪn] abbr of **quintuplet**.

quinine [kwɪ'niːn] n quinina.

quintet(te) [kwɪn'tɛt] n quinteto.

quintuplets [kwɪn'tjuːplɪts] npl quintillizos mpl.

quip [kwɪp] n pulla.

quirk [kwɜːk] n peculiaridad f.

quit [kwɪt] pt, pp **quit** or **quitted** vt dejar, abandonar; (premises) desocupar // vi (give up) retirarse; (go away) irse; (resign) dimitir; (stop work) abandonar (una empresa).

quite [kwaɪt] ad (rather) bastante; (entirely) completamente; **~ a few of them** un buen número de ellos; **~ (so)!** ¡así es!, ¡exactamente!

quits [kwɪts] a: **~ (with)** en paz (con).

quiver ['kwɪvə*] vi estremecerse // n (for arrows) carcaj m.

quiz [kwɪz] n (game) concurso; (questioning) interrogatorio // vt interrogar; **~zical** a burlón(ona).

quoits [kwɔɪts] npl juego de aros.

quorum ['kwɔːrəm] n quórum m.

quota ['kwəutə] n cuota.

quotation [kwəu'teɪʃən] n cita; (estimate)

presupuesto; ~ **marks** *npl* comillas *fpl*.
quote [kwəut] *n* cita // *vt* (*sentence*) citar;
(*price*) fijar // *vi*: **to** ~ **from** citar de.
quotient ['kwəuʃənt] *n* cociente *m*.

R

rabbi ['ræbaɪ] *n* rabino.
rabbit ['ræbɪt] *n* conejo; ~ **hole** *n* hura
(de conejos); ~ **hutch** *n* conejera.
rabble ['ræbl] *n* (*pej*) chusma, populacho.
rabies ['reɪbi:z] *n* rabia.
RAC *n abbr of* **Royal Automobile Club.**
raccoon [rə'ku:n] *n* mapache *m*.
race [reɪs] *n* (*gen*) carrera; (*species*) raza,
estirpe *f* // *vt* (*horse*) presentar (en
carrera); (*engine*) acelerar // *vi* (*compete*)
competir; (*run*) correr; (*pulse*) latir a
ritmo acelerado; ~ **course** *n* hipódromo;
~ **horse** *n* caballo de carreras; ~ **track** *n*
hipódromo; (*for cars*) autódromo.
racial ['reɪʃl] *a* racial; ~ **ism** *n* racismo;
~ **ist** *a*, *n* racista *m/f*.
racing ['reɪsɪŋ] *n* carreras *fpl*; ~ **car** *n*
coche *m* de carreras; ~ **driver** *n*
corredor/a *m/f* de coches.
racist ['reɪsɪst] *a*, *n* (*pej*) racista *m/f*.
rack [ræk] *n* (*also*: **luggage** ~) rejilla;
(*shelf*) estante *m*; (*also*: **roof** ~) baca,
portaequipajes *m inv*; (*clothes* ~) percha
// *vt* (*cause pain to*) atormentar.
racket ['rækɪt] *n* (*for tennis*) raqueta;
(*noise*) ruido, estrépito; (*swindle*) estafa,
timo.
racoon [rə'ku:n] *n* = **raccoon.**
racquet ['rækɪt] *n* raqueta.
racy ['reɪsɪ] *a* picante, salado.
radar ['reɪda:*] *n* radar *m*.
radiance ['reɪdɪəns] *n* brillantez *f*,
resplandor *m*; **radiant** [-ənt] *a* brillante,
resplandeciente.
radiate ['reɪdɪeɪt] *vt* (*heat*) radiar,
irradiar // *vi* (*lines*) extenderse.
radiation [reɪdɪ'eɪʃən] *n* radiación *f*.
radiator ['reɪdɪeɪtə*] *n* radiador *m*; ~
cap *n* tapón *m* de radiador.
radical ['rædɪkl] *a* radical.
radio ['reɪdɪəu] *n* radio *f*; **on the** ~ por
radio; ~ **station** *n* emisora.
radio... [reɪdɪəu] *pref*: ~ **active** *a*
radioactivo; ~ **activity** *n* radioactividad *f*;
~ **-controlled** *a* teledirigido; ~ **graphy**
[-'ɔgrəfɪ] *n* radiografía; ~ **logy** [-'ɔlədʒɪ] *n*
radiología; ~ **telephone** *n* radioteléfono;
~ **therapy** *n* radioterapia.
radish ['rædɪʃ] *n* rábano.
radius ['reɪdɪəs], *pl* **radii** [-ɪaɪ] *n* radio.
raffia ['ræfɪə] *n* rafia.
raffle ['ræfl] *n* rifa, sorteo // *vt* rifar.
raft [rɑ:ft] *n* (*also*: **life** ~) balsa.
rafter ['rɑ:ftə*] *n* viga.
rag [ræg] *n* (*piece of cloth*) trapo; (*torn
cloth*) harapo; (*pej*: *newspaper*)
periodicucho; (*for charity*) actividades
estudiantiles benéficas // *vt* tomar el pelo
a; ~ **s** *npl* harapos *mpl*; ~ **-and-bone man**

n trapero; ~ **doll** *n* muñeca de trapo.
rage [reɪdʒ] *n* (*fury*) rabia, furor *m*;
(*fashion*) boga // *vi* (*person*) rabiar, estar
furioso; (*storm*) bramar.
ragged ['rægɪd] *a* (*edge*) desigual,
mellado; (*cuff*) roto; (*appearance*)
andrajoso, harapiento; (*coastline*)
accidentado.
raid [reɪd] *n* (*MIL*) incursión *f*; (*criminal*)
asalto; (*attack*) ataque *m*; (*by police*)
redada // *vt* invadir, atacar; asaltar; ~ **er**
n invasor/a *m/f*; (*criminal*) asaltante *m/f*.
rail [reɪl] *n* (*on stair*) barandilla,
pasamanos *m inv*; (*on bridge, balcony*)
pretil *m*; (*of ship*) borda; (*for train*) riel *m*,
carril *m*; ~ **s** *npl* vía *sg*; **by** ~ por
ferrocarril; ~ **ing(s)** *n(pl)* verja *sg*,
enrejado *sg*; ~ **road** (*US*), ~ **way** *n*
ferrocarril *m*, vía férrea; ~ **wayman** *n*
ferroviario; ~ **way station** *n* estación *f* de
ferrocarril.
rain [reɪn] *n* lluvia // *vi* llover; **in the** ~
bajo la lluvia; **it's** ~ **ing** llueve, está
lloviendo; ~ **bow** *n* arco iris; ~ **coat** *n*
impermeable *m*; ~ **drop** *n* gota de lluvia;
~ **fall** *n* lluvia; ~ **y** *a* lluvioso.
raise [reɪz] *n* aumento // *vt* (*lift*) levantar;
(*build*) erigir, edificar; (*increase*)
aumentar; (*doubts*) suscitar; (*a question*)
plantear; (*cattle, family*) criar; (*crop*)
cultivar; (*army*) reclutar; (*funds*) reunir;
(*loan*) obtener; **to** ~ **one's voice** alzar la
voz.
raisin ['reɪzn] *n* paso de Corinto.
rake [reɪk] *n* (*tool*) rastrillo; (*person*)
libertino // *vt* (*garden*) rastrillar; (*fire*)
hurgar; (*with machine gun*) barrer.
rakish ['reɪkɪʃ] *a* (*suave*) gallardo; **at a** ~
angle echado al lado.
rally ['rælɪ] *n* (*POL etc*) reunión *f*, mitin *m*;
(*AUT*) rallye *m*; (*TENNIS*) peloteo // *vt*
reunir; (*encourage*) reanimar // *vi*
reunirse; (*sick person, Stock Exchange*)
recuperarse; **to** ~ **round** *vt fus* (*fig*) dar
apoyo a.
ram [ræm] *n* carnero; (*TECH*) pisón *m* // *vt*
(*crash into*) dar contra, chocar con; (*tread
down*) apisonar.
ramble ['ræmbl] *n* caminata, excursión *f*
en el campo // *vi* (*pej*: *also*: ~ **on**)
divagar; **rambler** *n* excursionista *m/f*;
(*BOT*) trepadora; **rambling** *a* (*speech*)
divagador(a); (*BOT*) trepador(a) // *n* excursionismo.
ramp [ræmp] *n* rampa.
rampage [ræm'peɪdʒ] *n*: **to be on the** ~
desbocarse // *vi*: **they went rampaging
through the town** corrieron como locos
por la ciudad.
rampant ['ræmpənt] *a* (*disease etc*)
violento.
rampart ['ræmpɑ:t] *n* terraplén *m*; (*wall*)
muralla.
ramshackle ['ræmʃækl] *a* destartalado.
ran [ræn] *pt of* **run.**
ranch [rɑ:ntʃ] *n* hacienda, estancia; ~ **er** *n*
ganadero.

rancid ['rænsɪd] a rancio.

rancour, rancor (US) ['ræŋkə*] n rencor m.

random ['rændəm] a fortuito, sin orden // n: **at ~** al azar.

randy ['rændɪ] a (col) cachondo.

rang [ræŋ] pt of **ring.**

range [reɪndʒ] n (of mountains) cadena, cordillera; (of missile) alcance m; (of voice) extensión f; (series) serie f; (of products) surtido; (MIL: also: **shooting ~**) campo de tiro; (also: **kitchen ~**) fogón m // vt (place) colocar; (arrange) arreglar // vi: **to ~ over** (wander) recorrer; (extend) extenderse por; **to ~ from ... to...** oscilar entre ... y...; **ranger** n guardabosques m inv.

rank [ræŋk] n (row) fila; (MIL) rango; (status) categoría; (also: **taxi ~**) parada // vi: **to ~ among** figurar entre // a (stinking) fétido, rancio; **the ~ and file** (fig) la base.

rankle ['ræŋkl] vi (insult) doler.

ransack ['rænsæk] vt (search) registrar; (plunder) saquear.

ransom ['rænsəm] n rescate m; **to hold sb to ~** (fig) poner a uno entre la espada y la pared.

rant [rænt] vi divagar, desvariar; **~ing** n lenguaje m declamatorio.

rap [ræp] n golpecito, golpe m seco // vt tocar, dar un golpecito en.

rape [reɪp] n violación f // vt violar.

rapid ['ræpɪd] a rápido; **~s** npl (GEO) rápidos mpl; **~ity** [rə'pɪdɪtɪ] n rapidez f.

rapist ['reɪpɪst] n violador m.

rapport [ræ'pɔ:*] n armonía, relación f amistosa.

rapture ['ræptʃə*] n éxtasis m, rapto; **rapturous** a extático; (applause) entusiasta.

rare [rɛə*] a raro, poco común; (CULIN: steak) poco hecho.

rarely ['rɛəlɪ] ad rara vez.

rarity ['rɛərɪtɪ] n rareza.

rascal ['rɑːskl] n pillo, pícaro.

rash [ræʃ] a imprudente, precipitado // n (MED) salpullido, erupción f (cutánea).

rasher ['ræʃə*] n lonja.

rasp [rɑːsp] n (tool) escofina.

raspberry ['rɑːzbərɪ] n frambuesa; **~ bush** n frambueso.

rasping ['rɑːspɪŋ] a: **a ~ noise** un ruido áspero.

rat [ræt] n rata.

ratchet ['rætʃɪt] n (TECH) trinquete m.

rate [reɪt] n (ratio) razón f; (percentage) tanto por ciento; (price) precio; (: of hotel) tarifa; (of interest) tipo; (speed) velocidad f // vt (value) tasar; (estimate) estimar; **to ~ as** ser considerado como; **~s** npl (Brit) impuesto sg municipal; (fees) tarifa sg; **~able** value n valor m impuesto; **~payer** n contribuyente m/f.

rather ['rɑːðə*] ad antes, más bien; (in speech) mejor dicho; **it's ~ expensive** es algo caro; (too much) es demasiado caro;

there's ~ a lot hay bastante; **I would** or **I'd ~ go** preferiría ir.

ratify ['rætɪfaɪ] vt ratificar.

rating ['reɪtɪŋ] n (valuation) tasación f; (value) valor m; (standing) posición f; (NAUT: category) clase f; (: sailor) marinero.

ratio ['reɪʃɪəʊ] n razón f; **in the ~ of 100 to 1** a razón de 100 a 1.

ration ['ræʃən] n ración f; **~s** npl víveres mpl // vt racionar.

rational ['ræʃənl] a racional, (solution, reasoning) lógico, razonable; (person) cuerdo, sensato; **rationale** [-'nɑːl] n razón f fundamental; **~ize** vt organizar lógicamente, racionalizar; **~ly** ad racionalmente; (logically) lógicamente.

rationing ['ræʃnɪŋ] n racionamiento.

rattle ['rætl] n golpeteo; (of train etc) traqueteo; (of hail) tamborileo; (object: of baby) sonaja, sonajero; (: of sports fan) matraca; (of snake) cascabel m // vi sonar, golpear; traquetear; tamborilear; (small objects) castañetear // vt agitar, sacudir; **~snake** n serpiente f de cascabel.

raucous ['rɔːkəs] a estridente, ronco.

ravage ['rævɪdʒ] vt hacer estragos, destrozar; **~s** npl estragos mpl.

rave [reɪv] vi (in anger) encolerizarse; (with enthusiasm) entusiasmarse; (MED) delirar, desvariar.

raven ['reɪvən] n cuervo.

ravenous ['rævənəs] a hambriento, famélico.

ravine [rə'viːn] n barranco.

raving ['reɪvɪŋ] a: **~ lunatic** loco de atar.

ravioli [rævɪ'əʊlɪ] n raviolis mpl.

ravish ['rævɪʃ] vt encantar; **~ing** a encantador(a).

raw [rɔː] a (uncooked) crudo; (not processed) bruto; (sore) vivo; (inexperienced) novato, inexperto; **~ material** n materia prima.

ray [reɪ] n rayo; **~ of hope** (rayo de) esperanza.

rayon ['reɪɔn] n rayón m.

raze [reɪz] vt arrasar.

razor ['reɪzə*] n (open) navaja; (safety ~) máquina de afeitar; **~ blade** n hoja de afeitar.

Rd abbr of **road.**

re [riː] prep con referencia a.

reach [riːtʃ] n alcance m; (BOXING) envergadura; (of river etc) extensión f entre dos recodos // vt alcanzar, llegar a; (achieve) lograr; (stretch out) alargar, extender // vi alcanzar, extenderse; **within ~** (object) al alcance (de la mano); **out of ~** fuera del alcance; **to ~ out for sth** alargar o tender la mano para tomar algo.

react [riː'ækt] vi reaccionar; **~ion** [-'ækʃən] n reacción f; **~ionary** [-'ækʃənrɪ] a, n reaccionario/a.

reactor [riː'æktə*] n reactor m.

read [riːd], pt, pp **read** [rɛd] vi leer // vt

leer; (*understand*) entender; (*study*) estudiar; **to** ~ **out** *vi* leer en alta voz; ~**able** *a* (*writing*) legible; (*book*) que merece leerse; ~**er** *n* lector/a *m/f*; (*book*) libro de lecturas; (*at university*) profesor/a *m/f*; ~**ership** *n* (*of paper etc*) número de lectores.

readily ['rɛdɪlɪ] *ad* (*willingly*) de buena gana; (*easily*) fácilmente; (*quickly*) en seguida.

readiness ['rɛdɪnɪs] *n* buena voluntad; (*preparedness*) preparación *f*; **in** ~ (*prepared*) listo, preparado.

reading ['riːdɪŋ] *n* lectura; (*understanding*) comprensión *f*; (*on instrument*) indicación *f*.

readjust [riːə'dʒʌst] *vt* reajustar // *vi* (*person*): **to** ~ **to** reorientarse a.

ready ['rɛdɪ] *a* listo, preparado; (*willing*) dispuesto; (*available*) disponible // *ad*: ~-**cooked** listo para comer // *n*: **at the** ~ (*MIL*) listo para tirar; ~-**made** *a* confeccionado; ~ **reckoner** *n* libro de cálculos hechos.

reaffirm [riːə'fəːm] *vt* reafirmar.

real [rɪəl] *a* verdadero, auténtico; **in** ~ **terms** en términos reales; ~ **estate** *n* bienes *mpl* raíces; ~-**ism** *n* (*also ART*) realismo; ~-**ist** *n* realista *m/f*; ~-**istic** [-'lɪstɪk] *a* realista.

reality [riː'ælɪtɪ] *n* realidad *f*; **in** ~ en realidad.

realization [rɪəlaɪ'zeɪʃən] *n* comprensión *f*; (*COMM*) realización *f*.

realize ['rɪəlaɪz] *vt* (*understand*) darse cuenta de; (*a project, COMM: asset*) realizar.

really ['rɪəlɪ] *ad* verdaderamente, realmente; ~? ¿de veras?

realm [rɛlm] *n* reino; (*fig*) esfera.

reap [riːp] *vt* segar; (*fig*) cosechar, recoger; ~**er** *n* segadora.

reappear [riːə'pɪə*] *vi* reaparecer; ~**ance** *n* reaparición *f*.

reapply [riːə'plaɪ] *vi*: **to** ~ **for** aplicar de nuevo.

rear [rɪə*] *a* trasero // *n* parte *f* trasera // *vt* (*cattle, family*) criar // *vi* (*also*: ~ **up**) (*animal*) encabritarse; ~-**engined** *a* (*AUT*) con motor trasero; ~-**guard** *n* retaguardia.

rearm [riː'ɑːm] *vt, vi* rearmar; ~**ament** *n* rearme *m*.

rearrange [riːə'reɪndʒ] *vt* ordenar o arreglar de nuevo.

rear-view ['rɪəvjuː] *a*: ~ **mirror** (*AUT*) espejo retrovisor.

reason ['riːzn] *n* (*gen*) razón *f*; (*cause*) motivo, causa; (*sense*) sensatez *f* // *vi*: **to** ~ **with sb** alegar razones para convencer a uno; **it stands to** ~ **that** es lógico que; ~**able** *a* razonable; (*sensible*) sensato; ~**ably** *ad* razonablemente; ~**ed** *a* (*argument*) razonado; ~**ing** *n* razonamiento, argumentos *mpl*.

reassemble [riːə'sɛmbl] *vt* (*machine*) montar de nuevo // *vi* reunirse de nuevo.

reassure [riːə'ʃuə*] *vt* tranquilizar,

alentar; **to** ~ **sb of** tranquilizar a uno diciendo que; **reassuring** *a* alentador(a).

rebate ['riːbeɪt] *n* (*on product*) rebaja; (*on tax etc*) descuento.

rebel ['rɛbl] *n* rebelde *m/f* // *vi* [rɪ'bɛl] rebelarse, sublevarse; ~**lion** *n* rebelión *f*, sublevación *f*; ~**lious** *a* rebelde; (*child*) revoltoso.

rebirth [riː'bəːθ] *n* renacimiento.

rebound [rɪ'baund] *vi* (*ball*) rebotar // *n* ['riːbaund] rebote *m*.

rebuff [rɪ'bʌf] *n* desaire *m*, rechazo // *vt* rechazar.

rebuild [riː'bɪld] (*irg: like* **build**) *vt* reconstruir.

rebuke [rɪ'bjuːk] *n* reprimenda // *vt* reprender.

recalcitrant [rɪ'kælsɪtrənt] *a* reacio.

recall [rɪ'kɔːl] *vt* (*remember*) recordar; (*ambassador etc*) retirar // *n* aviso, llamada.

recant [rɪ'kænt] *vi* retractarse.

recap ['riːkæp] *vt, vi* recapitular.

recapture [riː'kæptʃə*] *vt* (*town*) reconquistar; (*atmosphere*) hacer revivir.

recede [rɪ'siːd] *vi* retroceder; **receding** *a* (*forehead, chin*) huidizo.

receipt [rɪ'siːt] *n* (*document*) recibo; (*act of receiving*) recepción *f*; ~**s** *npl* (*COMM*) ingresos *mpl*.

receive [rɪ'siːv] *vt* recibir; (*guest*) acoger; (*wound*) sufrir; **receiver** *n* (*TEL*) auricular *m*; (*of stolen goods*) receptador/a *m/f*; (*COMM*) recibidor/a *m/f*.

recent ['riːsnt] *a* reciente; ~**ly** *ad* recién, recientemente.

receptacle [rɪ'sɛptɪkl] *n* receptáculo.

reception [rɪ'sɛpʃən] *n* (*gen*) recepción *f*; (*welcome*) acogida; ~ **desk** *n* recepción *f*; ~**ist** *n* recepcionista *m/f*.

receptive [rɪ'sɛptɪv] *a* receptivo.

recess [rɪ'sɛs] *n* (*in room*) hueco; (*for bed*) nicho; (*secret place*) escondrijo; (*POL etc*: *holiday*) vacaciones *fpl*; ~**ion** *n* recesión *f*.

recharge [riː'tʃɑːdʒ] *vt* (*battery*) recargar.

recipe ['rɛsɪpɪ] *n* receta.

recipient [rɪ'sɪpɪənt] *n* recibidor/a *m/f*; (*of letter*) destinatario/a.

reciprocal [rɪ'sɪprəkl] *a* recíproco.

recital [rɪ'saɪtl] *n* recital *m*.

recite [rɪ'saɪt] *vt* (*poem*) recitar; (*complaints etc*) enumerar.

reckless ['rɛkləs] *a* temerario, imprudente; (*speed*) excesivo, peligroso; ~**ly** *ad* imprudentemente; de modo peligroso.

reckon ['rɛkən] *vt* (*count*) contar; (*consider*) considerar; (*think*): **I** ~ **that...** me parece que...; ~**ing** *n* (*calculation*) cálculo; **the day of** ~**ing** el día del juicio (final).

reclaim [rɪ'kleɪm] *vt* (*land*) recuperar; (: *from sea*) rescatar; (*demand back*) reclamar; **reclamation** [rɛklə'meɪʃən] *n* recuperación *f*; rescate *m*.

recline [rɪ'klaɪn] *vi* reclinarse; (*lean*) apoyarse; **reclining** *a* (*seat*) reclinable.

recluse [rɪˈkluːs] n recluso.
recognition [rɛkəgˈnɪʃən] n reconocimiento; **transformed beyond ~ tan** transformado que resulta irreconocible.
recognizable [ˈrɛkəgnaɪzəbl] a: ~ **(by)** reconocible (por).
recognize [ˈrɛkəgnaɪz] vt reconocer, conocer; **to ~ by/as** reconocer de/por.
recoil [rɪˈkɔɪl] vi (gun) retroceder; (person): **to ~ from doing sth** sentir repugnancia por hacer algo.
recollect [rɛkəˈlɛkt] vt recordar, acordarse de; **~ion** [-ˈlɛkʃən] n recuerdo.
recommend [rɛkəˈmɛnd] vt recomendar; **~ation** [-ˈdeɪʃən] n recomendación f.
recompense [ˈrɛkəmpɛns] vt recompensar // n recompensa.
reconcile [ˈrɛkənsaɪl] vt (two people) reconciliar; (two facts) conciliar; **to ~ o.s. to sth** resignarse a algo, conformarse a algo; **reconciliation** [-sɪlɪˈeɪʃən] n reconciliación f.
reconnaissance [rɪˈkɔnɪsns] n (MIL) reconocimiento.
reconnoitre, reconnoiter (US) [rɛkəˈnɔɪtə*] vt, vi (MIL) reconocer.
reconsider [riːkənˈsɪdə*] vt repensar.
reconstitute [riːˈkɔnstɪtjuːt] vt reconstituir.
reconstruct [riːkənˈstrʌkt] vt reconstruir; **~ion** [-kʃən] n reconstrucción f.
record [ˈrɛkɔːd] n (MUS) disco; (of meeting etc) relación f; (register) registro, partida; (file) archivo; (also: **police ~**) antecedentes mpl; (written) expediente m; (SPORT) récord m // vt [rɪˈkɔːd] (set down) registrar; (relate) hacer constar; (MUS: song etc) grabar; **in ~ time** en un tiempo récord; **off the ~** a no oficial // ad confidencialmente; **~ card** n (in file) ficha; **~er** n (MUS) flauta de pico; (TECH) contador m; **~ holder** n (SPORT) recordman m; **~ing** n (MUS) grabación f; **~ player** n tocadiscos m inv.
recount [rɪˈkaunt] vt contar.
re-count [ˈriːkaunt] n (POL: of votes) segundo escrutinio // vt [riːˈkaunt] volver a contar.
recoup [rɪˈkuːp] vt: **to ~ one's losses** recuperar las pérdidas.
recourse [rɪˈkɔːs] n recurso; **to have ~ to** recurrir a.
recover [rɪˈkʌvə*] vt recobrar, recuperar; (rescue) rescatar // vi (from illness) reponerse; (from shock) sobreponerse; **~y** n recuperación f; rescate m; (MED) mejora.
recreate [riːkrɪˈeɪt] vt recrear.
recreation [rɛkrɪˈeɪʃən] n recreación f; (play) recreo; **~al** a de recreo.
recrimination [rɪkrɪmɪˈneɪʃən] n recriminación f.
recruit [rɪˈkruːt] n recluta m/f // vt reclutar; **~ment** n reclutamiento.
rectangle [ˈrɛktæŋgl] n rectángulo; **rectangular** [-ˈtæŋgjulə*] a rectangular.
rectify [ˈrɛktɪfaɪ] vt rectificar.

rector [ˈrɛktə*] n (REL) párroco; (SCOL) rector/a m/f; (of parish) párroco.
recuperate [rɪˈkuːpəreɪt] vi reponerse, restablecerse.
recur [rɪˈkɜː*] vi repetirse; (opportunity) producirse de nuevo; **~rence** n repetición f; **~rent** a repetido.
red [rɛd] n rojo // a rojo; **to be in the ~** deber dinero; **R~ Cross** n Cruz f Roja; **~currant** n grosella; **~den** vt enrojecer // vi enrojecerse; **~dish** a (hair) rojizo.
redecorate [riːˈdɛkəreɪt] vt decorar de nuevo; **redecoration** [-ˈreɪʃən] n renovación f.
redeem [rɪˈdiːm] vt (gen) redimir; (sth in pawn) desempeñar; (fig, also REL) rescatar; **~ing** a: **~ing feature** rasgo bueno o favorable.
redeploy [riːdɪˈplɔɪ] vt (resources) disponer de nuevo.
red: **~-haired** a pelirrojo; **~-handed** a: **to be caught ~-handed** cogerse con las manos en la masa; **~head** n pelirrojo/a; **~-hot** a candente.
redirect [riːdaɪˈrɛkt] vt (mail) reexpedir.
redness [ˈrɛdnɪs] n lo rojo; (of hair) rojez f.
redo [riːˈduː] (irg: like do) vt rehacer.
redouble [riːˈdʌbl] vt: **to ~ one's efforts** intensificar los esfuerzos.
redress [rɪˈdrɛs] n reparación f // vt reajustar.
red tape n (fig) trámites mpl, papeleo.
reduce [rɪˈdjuːs] vt reducir; (lower) rebajar; **'~ speed now'** (AUT) 'reduzca la velocidad'; **at a ~d price** (of goods) (a precio) rebajado; **reduction** [rɪˈdʌkʃən] n reducción f; (of price) rebaja; (discount) descuento.
redundancy [rɪˈdʌndənsɪ] n desempleo.
redundant [rɪˈdʌndnt] a (worker) parado, sin trabajo; (detail, object) superfluo; **to be made ~** quedarse sin trabajo.
reed [riːd] n (BOT) junco, caña; (MUS: of clarinet etc) lengüeta.
reef [riːf] n (at sea) arrecife m.
reek [riːk] vi: **to ~ (of)** oler o heder a.
reel [riːl] n (gen) carrete m, bobina; (of film) rollo, película // vt (TECH) devanar; (also: **~ in**) cobrar // vi (sway) tambalear.
re-election [riːɪˈlɛkʃən] n reelección f.
re-enter [riːˈɛntə*] vt reingresar en; **re-entry** n reingreso.
ref [rɛf] n (col) abbr of **referee**.
refectory [rɪˈfɛktərɪ] n refectorio, comedor m.
refer [rɪˈfɜː*] vt (send) remitir; (ascribe) referir a, relacionar con // vi: **to ~ to** (allude to) referirse a, aludir a; (apply to) relacionarse con; (consult) remitirse a.
referee [rɛfəˈriː] n árbitro; (for job application) persona que recomienda a otro // vt arbitrar.
reference [ˈrɛfrəns] n (mention) referencia; (sending) remisión f; (relevance) relación f; (for job application: letter) referencia, carta de

recomendación; **with ～ to** con referencia a; (*COMM: in letter*) me remito a; **～ book** *n* libro de consulta.

referendum [refə'rendəm], *pl* **-da** [-də] *n* referéndum *m*.

refill [ri:'fil] *vt* rellenar // *n* ['ri:fil] repuesto, recambio.

refine [rɪ'faɪn] *vt* (*sugar, oil*) refinar; **～d** *a* (*person, taste*) refinado, culto; **～ment** *n* (*of person*) cultura, educación *f*; **～ry** *n* refinería.

reflect [rɪ'flekt] *vt* (*light, image*) reflejar // *vi* (*think*) reflexionar, pensar; **it ～s badly/well on him** le perjudica/le hace honor; **～ion** [-'flekʃən] *n* (*act*) reflexión *f*; (*image*) reflejo; (*criticism*) reproche *m*, crítica; **on ～ion** pensándolo bien; **～or** *n* (*also AUT*) captafaros *m inv*, reflector *m*.

reflex ['ri:fleks] *a*, *n* reflejo; **～ive** [rɪ'fleksɪv] *a* (*LING*) reflexivo.

reform [rɪ'fɔ:m] *n* reforma // *vt* reformar; **the R～ation** [refə'meɪʃən] *n* la Reforma; **～er** *n* reformador/a *m/f*; **～ist** *n* reformista *m/f*.

refrain [rɪ'freɪn] *vi*: **to ～ from doing** abstenerse de hacer // *n* estribillo.

refresh [rɪ'freʃ] *vt* refrescar; **～er course** *n* curso de repaso; **～ments** *npl* (*drinks*) refrescos *mpl*.

refrigeration [rɪfrɪdʒə'reɪʃən] *n* refrigeración *f*; **refrigerator** [-'frɪdʒəreɪtə*] *n* refrigeradora, nevera.

refuel [ri:'fjuəl] *vi* repostar combustible.

refuge ['refju:dʒ] *n* refugio, asilo; **to take ～ in** refugiarse en.

refugee [refju'dʒi:] *n* refugiado/a.

refund ['ri:fʌnd] *n* reembolso // *vt* [rɪ'fʌnd] devolver, reembolsar.

refurbish [ri:'fɔ:bɪʃ] *vt* restaurar, renovar.

refusal [rɪ'fju:zəl] *n* negativa; **first ～** primera opción.

refuse ['refju:s] *n* basura // (*vb*: [rɪ'fju:z]) *vt* (*reject*) rehusar; (*say no to*) negarse a // *vi* negarse; (*horse*) rehusar; **～ bin** *n* cubo de la basura; **～ tip** *n* vertedero.

refute [rɪ'fju:t] *vt* refutar, rebatir.

regain [rɪ'geɪn] *vt* recobrar, recuperar.

regal ['ri:gl] *a* regio, real.

regalia [rɪ'geɪlɪə] *n*, *npl* insignias *fpl* reales.

regard [rɪ'ɡɑ:d] *n* (*gaze*) mirada; (*aspect*) respecto; (*attention*) atención *f*; (*esteem*) respeto, consideración *f* // *vt* (*consider*) considerar; (*look at*) mirar; **'with kindest ～s'** con muchos recuerdos; **～ing, as ～s, with ～ to** con respecto a, en cuanto a; **～less** *ad* a pesar de todo.

regatta [rɪ'ɡætə] *n* regata.

regent ['ri:dʒənt] *n* regente *m/f*.

régime [reɪ'ʒi:m] *n* régimen *m*.

regiment ['redʒɪmənt] *n* regimiento // *vt* reglamentar; **～al** [-'mentl] *a* militar; **～ation** [-'teɪʃən] *n* regimentación *f*.

region ['ri:dʒən] *n* región *f*; **in the ～ of** (*fig*) alrededor de; **～al** *a* regional.

register ['redʒɪstə*] *n* (*gen*) registro; (*list*) lista // *vt* registrar; (*birth*) declarar; (*letter*) certificar; (*subj: instrument*) marcar, indicar // *vi* (*at hotel*) registrarse; (*sign on*) inscribirse; (*make impression*) producir impresión; **～ed** *a* (*design*) registrado; (*letter*) certificado.

registrar ['redʒɪstrɑ:*] *n* secretario (del registro civil).

registration [redʒɪs'treɪʃən] *n* (*act*) inscripción *f*; (*AUT: also*: **～ number**) matrícula.

registry ['redʒɪstrɪ] *n* registro, archivo; **～ office** *n* registro civil; **to get married in a ～ office** casarse por lo civil.

regret [rɪ'ɡret] *n* sentimiento, pesar *m*; (*remorse*) remordimiento // *vt* sentir, lamentar; (*repent of*) arrepentirse de; **～fully** *ad* con pesar, sentidamente; **～table** *a* lamentable; (*loss*) sensible.

regroup [ri:'ɡru:p] *vt* reagrupar // *vi* reagruparse.

regular ['reɡjulə*] *a* (*gen*) regular; (*usual*) corriente, normal; (*soldier*) de línea; (*intensive*) verdadero // *n* (*client etc*) cliente *m/f* habitual; **～ity** [-'lærɪtɪ] *n* regularidad *f*; **～ly** *ad* con regularidad.

regulate ['reɡjuleɪt] *vt* regular; (*TECH*) arreglar, ajustar; **regulation** [-'leɪʃən] *n* (*rule*) regla, reglamento; (*adjustment*) ajuste *m*.

rehabilitation ['ri:həbɪlɪ'teɪʃən] *n* rehabilitación *f*.

rehearsal [rɪ'hə:səl] *n* ensayo; **rehearse** *vt* ensayar.

reign [reɪn] *n* reinado; (*fig*) dominio // *vi* reinar; (*fig*) imperar; **～ing** *a* (*monarch*) reinante, actual; (*predominant*) imperante.

reimburse [ri:ɪm'bə:s] *vt* reembolsar; **～ment** *n* reembolso.

rein [reɪn] *n* (*for horse*) rienda; **to give ～ to** dar rienda suelta a.

reincarnation [ri:ɪnkɑ:'neɪʃən] *n* reencarnación *f*.

reindeer ['reɪndɪə*] *n*, *pl inv* reno.

reinforce [ri:ɪn'fɔ:s] *vt* reforzar; **～d** *a* (*concrete*) armado; **～ment** *n* (*action*) reforzamiento; **～ments** *npl* (*MIL*) refuerzos *mpl*.

reinstate [ri:ɪn'steɪt] *vt* (*worker*) reintegrar a su puesto.

reiterate [ri:'ɪtəreɪt] *vt* reiterar, repetir.

reject ['ri:dʒekt] *n* (*COMM*) artículo defectuoso // *vt* [rɪ'dʒekt] rechazar; (*plan*) desechar; (*solution*) descartar; **～ion** [rɪ'dʒekʃən] *n* rechazo.

rejoice [rɪ'dʒɔɪs] *vi*: **to ～ at** *or* **over** regocijarse o alegrarse de.

rejuvenate [rɪ'dʒu:vəneɪt] *vt* rejuvenecer.

rekindle [ri:'kɪndl] *vt* reencender; (*fig*) despertar.

relapse [rɪ'læps] *n* (*MED*) recaída; (*into crime*) reincidencia.

relate [rɪ'leɪt] *vt* (*tell*) contar, relatar; (*connect*) relacionar // *vi* relacionarse; **～d** *a* afín, conexio; (*person*) emparentado; **～d to** con referencia a, relacionado con; **relating to** *prep* acerca de.

relation [rɪ'leɪʃən] *n* (*person*) pariente *m/f*; (*link*) relación *f*; **～ship** *n* relación *f*;

(*personal ties*) relaciones *fpl*; (*also:* **family ~ship**) parentesco.

relative ['rɛlətɪv] *n* pariente *m/f*, familiar *m/f* // *a* relativo.

relax [rɪ'læks] *vi* descansar; (*person: unwind*) relajarse // *vt* relajar; (*mind, person*) descansar; **~ation** [riːlæk'seɪʃən] *n* (*rest*) descanso; (*ease*) relajación *f*, relax *m*; (*amusement*) recreo; (*entertainment*) diversión *f*; **~ed** *a* relajado; (*tranquil*) tranquilo; **~ing** *a* enervante.

relay ['riːleɪ] *n* (*race*) carrera de relevos // *vt* (*message*) retransmitir.

release [rɪ'liːs] *n* (*from prison, obligation*) liberación *f*, libertad *f*; (*of shot*) disparo; (*of gas etc*) escape *m*; (*of film etc*) estreno // *vt* (*prisoner*) poner en libertad; (*book, film*) estrenar; (*report, news*) publicar; (*gas etc*) despedir, arrojar; (*free: from wreckage etc*) soltar; (*TECH. catch, spring etc*) desenganchar; (*let go*) soltar, aflojar.

relegate ['rɛləgeɪt] *vt* relegar; (*SPORT*): **to be ~d** descender.

relent [rɪ'lɛnt] *vi* ablandarse, ceder; **~less** *a* implacable.

relevance ['rɛləvəns] *n* relación *f*; **relevant** [-ənt] *a* relacionado; (*fact*) pertinente; (*apt*) oportuno.

reliable [rɪ'laɪəbl] *a* (*person, firm*) de confianza, de fiar; (*method, machine*) seguro; (*news*) fidedigno; **reliably** *ad*: **to be reliably informed that...** saber de fuente fidedigna que... .

reliance [rɪ'laɪəns] *n*: **~ (on)** dependencia (de).

relic ['rɛlɪk] *n* (*REL*) reliquia; (*of the past*) vestigio.

relief [rɪ'liːf] *n* (*from pain, anxiety*) alivio, desahogo; (*help, supplies*) socorro, ayuda; (*ART, GEO*) relieve *m*.

relieve [rɪ'liːv] *vt* (*pain, patient*) aliviar; (*bring help to*) ayudar, socorrer; (*burden*) aligerar; (*take over from: gen*) sustituir a; (: *guard*) relevar; **to ~ sb of sth** quitar algo a uno; **to ~ o.s.** hacer sus necesidades.

religion [rɪ'lɪdʒən] *n* religión *f*; **religious** *a* religioso.

relinquish [rɪ'lɪŋkwɪʃ] *vt* abandonar; (*plan, habit*) renunciar a.

relish ['rɛlɪʃ] *n* (*CULIN*) salsa, condimento; (*enjoyment*) entusiasmo; (*flavour*) sabor *m*, gusto // *vt* (*food etc*) saborear; **to ~ doing** gustar de hacer.

reload [riː'ləud] *vt* recargar.

reluctance [rɪ'lʌktəns] *n* renuencia; **reluctant** [-ənt] *a* renuente; **reluctantly** [-əntlɪ] *ad* con renuencia.

rely [rɪ'laɪ]: **to ~ on** *vt fus* confiar en, fiarse de; (*be dependent on*) depender de.

remain [rɪ'meɪn] *vi* (*survive*) quedar; (*be left*) sobrar; (*continue*) quedar(se), permanecer; **~der** *n* resto; **~ing** *a* sobrante; **~s** *npl* restos *mpl*; (*leftovers*) desperdicios *mpl*.

remand [rɪ'mɑːnd] *n*: **on ~** detenido (en espera del juicio) // *vt*: **to ~ in custody** reencarcelar, mantener bajo custodia; **~ home** *n* reformatorio.

remark [rɪ'mɑːk] *n* comentario // *vt* comentar; (*notice*) observar, notar; **~able** *a* notable; (*outstanding*) extraordinario.

remarry [riː'mærɪ] *vi* casarse por segunda vez.

remedial [rɪ'miːdɪəl] *a* (*tuition, classes*) de niños atrasados.

remedy ['rɛmədɪ] *n* remedio // *vt* remediar, curar.

remember [rɪ'mɛmbə*] *vt* recordar, acordarse de; (*bear in mind*) tener presente; **remembrance** *n* (*memory*) memoria; (*souvenir*) recuerdo.

remind [rɪ'maɪnd] *vt*: **to ~ sb to do sth** recordar a uno que haga algo; **to ~ sb of sth** recordar algo a uno; **she ~s me of her mother** me recuerda a su madre; **~er** *n* advertencia; (*souvenir*) recuerdo.

reminisce [rɛmɪ'nɪs] *vi* recordar viejas historias; **reminiscent** *a*: **to be reminiscent of sth** recordar algo.

remiss [rɪ'mɪs] *a* descuidado; **it was ~ of him** fue un descuido suyo.

remission [rɪ'mɪʃən] *n* remisión *f*; (*of debt, sentence*) perdón *m*.

remit [rɪ'mɪt] *vt* (*send: money*) remitir, enviar; **~tance** *n* remesa, envío.

remnant ['rɛmnənt] *n* resto; (*of cloth*) retazo.

remorse [rɪ'mɔːs] *n* remordimientos *mpl*; **~ful** *a* arrepentido; **~less** *a* (*fig*) implacable, despiadado.

remote [rɪ'məut] *a* (*distant*) lejano; (*person*) distante; **~ control** *n* telecontrol *m*; **~ly** *ad* remotamente; (*slightly*) levemente; **~ness** *n* alejamiento; distancia.

remould ['riːməuld] *vt* (*tyre*) recauchutar.

removable [rɪ'muːvəbl] *a* (*detachable*) amovible, separable.

removal [rɪ'muːvəl] *n* (*taking away*) el quitar; (*from house*) mudanza; (*from office: sacking*) destitución *f*; (*MED*) extirpación *f*; **~ van** *n* camión *m* de mudanzas.

remove [rɪ'muːv] *vt* quitar; (*employee*) destituir; (*name: from list*) tachar, borrar; (*doubt, abuse*) disipar; (*TECH*) retirar, separar; (*MED*) extirpar; **removers** *npl* (*company*) agencia de mudanzas.

remuneration [rɪmjuːnə'reɪʃən] *n* remuneración *f*.

rend [rɛnd], *pt, pp* **rent** *vt* rasgar, desgarrar.

render ['rɛndə*] *vt* (*give*) dar, prestar; (*hand over*) entregar; (*reproduce*) reproducir; (*make*) hacer, volver; (*return*) devolver; **~ing** *n* (*MUS etc*) interpretación *f*.

rendez-vous ['rɔndɪvuː] *n* cita.

renegade ['rɛnɪgeɪd] *n* renegado.

renew [rɪ'njuː] *vt* renovar; (*resume*) reanudar; (*loan etc*) prorrogar; (*negotiations*) volver a; (*acquaintance*) entablar de nuevo; ~al n renovación f; reanudación f; prórroga.

renounce [rɪ'naʊns] vt renunciar a; (disown) renunciar.

renovate ['rɛnəʊveɪt] vt renovar; **renovation** [-'veɪʃən] n renovación f.

renown [rɪ'naʊn] n renombre m; ~ed a renombrado.

rent [rɛnt] pt, pp of **rend** // n alquiler m, arriendo // vt alquilar; ~al n (for television, car) alquiler m.

renunciation [rɪnʌnsɪ'eɪʃən] n renuncia.

reorganize [riː'ɔːɡənaɪz] vt reorganizar.

rep [rɛp] n abbr of **representative**; **repertory**.

repair [rɪ'pɛə*] n reparación f, compostura; (patch) remiendo // vt reparar, componer; (shoes) remendar; in good/bad ~ en buen/mal estado; ~ kit n caja de herramientas para reparaciones.

repartee [rɛpɑː'tiː] n dimes y diretes.

repay [riː'peɪ] (irg: like **pay**) vt (money) devolver, reembolsar; (person) pagar; (debt) liquidar; (sb's efforts) devolver, corresponder a; ~ment n reembolso, devolución f; (of debt) pago.

repeal [rɪ'piːl] n (of law) abrogación f; (of sentence) anulación f // vt abrogar, revocar.

repeat [rɪ'piːt] n (RADIO, TV) retransmisión f // vt repetir // vi repetirse; ~edly ad repetidas veces.

repel [rɪ'pɛl] vt (lit, fig) repugnar; ~lent a repugnante // n: **insect** ~lent crema/loción f anti-insectos.

repent [rɪ'pɛnt] vi: to ~ (of) arrepentirse (de); ~ance n arrepentimiento.

repercussion [riːpə'kʌʃən] n (consequence) repercusión f; to have ~s repercutir.

repertoire ['rɛpətwɑː*] n repertorio.

repertory ['rɛpətərɪ] n (also: ~ theatre) teatro de repertorio.

repetition [rɛpɪ'tɪʃən] n repetición f.

repetitive [rɪ'pɛtɪtɪv] a (movement, work) reiterativo; (speech) lleno de repeticiones.

replace [rɪ'pleɪs] vt (put back) devolver a su sitio; (take the place of) reemplazar, sustituir; ~ment n (gen) reemplazo; (act) reposición f; (person) suplente m/f.

replenish [rɪ'plɛnɪʃ] vt (glass) rellenar; (stock etc) reponer; (with fuel) repostar.

replete [rɪ'pliːt] a repleto; (well-fed) lleno.

replica ['rɛplɪkə] n copia, reproducción f.

reply [rɪ'plaɪ] n respuesta, contestación f // vi contestar, responder.

report [rɪ'pɔːt] n informe m; (PRESS etc) reportaje m; (also: **school** ~) nota; (of gun) estallido // vt informar sobre; (PRESS etc) hacer un reportaje sobre; (bring to notice: occurrence) dar cuenta de // vi (make a report) presentar un informe; (present o.s.): to ~ (to sb) presentarse (ante uno); ~er n periodista m/f.

reprehensible [rɛprɪ'hɛnsɪbl] a reprensible, censurable.

represent [rɛprɪ'zɛnt] vt representar; (fig) hablar en nombre de; (COMM) ser agente de; ~ation [-'teɪʃən] n representación f; (petition) petición f; ~ations npl (protest) quejas fpl; ~ative n representante m/f // a representativo.

repress [rɪ'prɛs] vt reprimir; ~ion [-'prɛʃən] n represión f; ~ive a represivo.

reprieve [rɪ'priːv] n (LAW) indulto; (fig) alivio // vt indultar, suspender la pena de.

reprimand ['rɛprɪmɑːnd] n reprimenda // vt reprender.

reprint ['riːprɪnt] n reimpresión f // vt [riː'prɪnt] reimprimir.

reprisal [rɪ'praɪzl] n represalia.

reproach [rɪ'prəʊtʃ] n reproche m // vt: to ~ sb with sth reprochar algo a uno; beyond ~ intachable; ~ful a lleno de reproches.

reproduce [riːprə'djuːs] vt reproducir // vi reproducirse; **reproduction** [-'dʌkʃən] n reproducción f; **reproductive** [-'dʌktɪv] a reproductor(a).

reprove [rɪ'pruːv] vt: to ~ sb for sth reprender algo a uno.

reptile ['rɛptaɪl] n reptil m.

republic [rɪ'pʌblɪk] n república; ~an a, n republicano/a.

repudiate [rɪ'pjuːdɪeɪt] vt (accusation) rechazar; (friend) repudiar; (obligation) desconocer.

repugnant [rɪ'pʌɡnənt] a repugnante.

repulse [rɪ'pʌls] vt rechazar, repulsar; **repulsive** a repulsivo.

reputable ['rɛpjʊtəbl] a (make etc) de toda confianza; (person) formal.

reputation [rɛpjʊ'teɪʃən] n reputación f.

repute [rɪ'pjuːt] n reputación f, fama; ~d a supuesto; ~dly ad según dicen o se dice.

request [rɪ'kwɛst] n petición f; (formal) solicitud f // vt: to ~ sth of or from sb pedir algo a uno; (formally) solicitar algo a uno.

requiem ['rɛkwɪəm] n réquiem m.

require [rɪ'kwaɪə*] vt (need: subj: person) necesitar, tener necesidad de; (: thing, situation) exigir; (want) pedir; (order) insistir en que; ~ment n requisito; (need) necesidad f.

requisite ['rɛkwɪzɪt] n requisito // a preciso, imprescindible; **toilet** ~s artículos mpl de aseo personal.

requisition [rɛkwɪ'zɪʃən] n: ~ (for) solicitud f (de) // vt (MIL) requisar.

reroute [riː'ruːt] vt (train etc) desviar.

resale [riː'seɪl] n reventa.

rescue ['rɛskjuː] n rescate m // vt rescatar; to ~ from librar de; ~ party n expedición f de salvamento; **rescuer** n salvador/a m/f.

research [rɪ'sɜːtʃ] n investigaciones fpl // vt investigar; ~er n investigador/a m/f; ~ work n investigación f.

resell [riː'sɛl] vt revender.

resemblance [rɪ'zɛmbləns] n parecido; to

bear a ~ to parecerse a; **resemble** vt parecerse a.
resent [rɪ'zɛnt] vt resentirse de; **~ful** a resentido; **~ment** n resentimiento.
reservation [rɛzə'veɪʃən] n (gen) reserva; (on road: also: **central ~**) faja intermedia.
reserve [rɪ'zəːv] n reserva; (SPORT) suplente m/f; (game **~**) coto // vt (seats etc) reservar; **~s** npl (MIL) reserva sg; **in ~ de** reserva; **~d** a reservado.
reservoir ['rɛzəvwɑː*] n (large) embalse m; (small) depósito.
reshape [riː'ʃeɪp] vt (policy) reformar, rehacer.
reshuffle [riː'ʃʌfl] n: **Cabinet ~** (POL) reconstrucción f del gabinete.
reside [rɪ'zaɪd] vi residir, vivir.
residence ['rɛzɪdəns] n residencia; (formal: home) domicilio; (length of stay) permanencia; **resident** [-ənt] n vecino, (in hotel) huésped/a m/f // a (population) permanente; (doctor) interno; **residential** [-'dɛnʃəl] a residencial.
residue ['rɛzɪdjuː] n resto, residuo; (COMM) saldo.
resign [rɪ'zaɪn] vt (one's post) renunciar a // vi dimitir; **to ~ o.s. to** (endure) resignarse a; **~ation** [rɛzɪg'neɪʃən] n renuncia; (state of mind) resignación f; **~ed** a resignado.
resilience [rɪ'zɪlɪəns] n (of material) elasticidad f; (of person) resistencia; **resilient** [-ənt] a (person) resistente.
resin ['rɛzɪn] n resina.
resist [rɪ'zɪst] vt resistir, oponerse a; **~ance** n resistencia.
resolute ['rɛzəluːt] a resuelto.
resolution [rɛzə'luːʃən] n (gen) resolución f; (purpose) propósito.
resolve [rɪ'zɔlv] n resolución f; (purpose) propósito // vt resolver // vi resolverse; **to ~ to do** resolver hacer; **~d** a resuelto.
resonant ['rɛzənənt] a resonante.
resort [rɪ'zɔːt] n (town) centro de turismo; (recourse) recurso // vi: **to ~ to** recurrir a; **in the last ~** en último caso.
resound [rɪ'zaund] vi resonar, retumbar; **the room ~ed with shouts** los gritos resonaron en el cuarto; **~ing** a sonoro; (fig) clamoroso.
resource [rɪ'sɔːs] n recurso; **~s** npl recursos mpl; **~ful** a inventivo, ingenioso.
respect [rɪs'pɛkt] n (consideration) respeto; (relation) respecto; **~s** npl recuerdos mpl, saludos mpl // vt respetar; **with ~ to** con respecto a; **in this ~** en cuanto a eso; **~ability** [-ə'bɪlɪtɪ] a respetabilidad f; **~able** a respetable; (large) apreciable; (passable) tolerable; **~ful** a respetuoso.
respective [rɪs'pɛktɪv] a respectivo; **~ly** ad respectivamente.
respiration [rɛspɪ'reɪʃən] n respiración f.
respiratory [rɛs'pɪrətərɪ] a respiratorio.
respite ['rɛspaɪt] n respiro; (LAW) prórroga.

resplendent [rɪs'plɛndənt] a resplandeciente.
respond [rɪs'pɔnd] vi responder; (react) reaccionar; **response** [-'pɔns] n respuesta; reacción f.
responsibility [rɪspɔnsɪ'bɪlɪtɪ] n responsabilidad f.
responsible [rɪs'pɔnsɪbl] a (liable): **~ (for)** responsable (de); (character) serio, formal; (job) de confianza.
responsive [rɪs'pɔnsɪv] a sensible.
rest [rɛst] n descanso, reposo; (MUS) pausa, silencio; (support) apoyo; (remainder) resto // vi descansar; (be supported): **to ~ on** posar(se) en // vt (lean): **to ~ sth on/against** apoyar algo en o sobre/contra.
restart [riː'stɑːt] vt (engine) volver a arrancar; (work) volver a empezar.
restaurant ['rɛstərɔŋ] n restorán m, restaurante m; **~ car** n coche-comedor m.
restful ['rɛstful] a descansado, reposado.
rest home n residencia para jubilados.
restitution [rɛstɪ'tjuːʃən] n: **to make ~ to sb for sth** indemnizar a uno por algo.
restive ['rɛstɪv] a inquieto; (horse) rebelón(ona).
restless ['rɛstlɪs] a inquieto; **~ly** ad inquietamente.
restoration [rɛstə'reɪʃən] n restauración f; **restore** [rɪ'stɔː*] vt (building) restaurar; (sth stolen) devolver; (health) restablecer.
restrain [rɪs'treɪn] vt (feeling) contener, refrenar; (person): **to ~ (from doing)** disuadir (de hacer); **~ed** a (style) moderado; **~t** n (restriction) freno, control m; (moderation) moderación f; (of style) reserva.
restrict [rɪs'trɪkt] vt restringir, limitar; **~ion** [-kʃən] n restricción f, limitación f; **~ive** a restrictivo.
rest room n (US) aseos mpl.
result [rɪ'zʌlt] n resultado // vi: **to ~ in** terminar en, dar por resultado; **as a ~ of** a consecuencia de.
resume [rɪ'zjuːm] vt, vi (work, journey) reanudar.
résumé ['reɪzjuːmeɪ] n resumen m.
resumption [rɪ'zʌmpʃən] n reanudación f.
resurgence [rɪ'səːdʒəns] n resurgimiento.
resurrection [rɛzə'rɛkʃən] n resurrección f.
resuscitate [rɪ'sʌsɪteɪt] vt (MED) resucitar; **resuscitation** [-'teɪʃn] n resucitación f.
retail ['riːteɪl] n venta al por menor // cpd al por menor // vt vender al por menor o al detalle; **~er** n detallista m/f.
retain [rɪ'teɪn] vt (keep) retener, conservar; (employ) contratar; **~er** n (servant) criado; (fee) anticipo.
retaliate [rɪ'tælɪeɪt] vi: **to ~ (against)** tomar represalias (contra); **retaliation** [-'eɪʃən] n represalias fpl.
retarded [rɪ'tɑːdɪd] a retrasado.
retch [rɛtʃ] vi dar arcadas.

retentive [rɪ'tɛntɪv] a (*memory*) retentivo.
reticent ['rɛtɪsnt] a reservado.
retina ['rɛtɪnə] n retina.
retinue ['rɛtɪnjuː] n séquito, comitiva.
retire [rɪ'taɪə*] vi (*give up work*) jubilarse; (*withdraw*) retirarse; (*go to bed*) (ir a) acostarse; ~**d** a (*person*) jubilado; ~**ment** n (*state*) retiro; (*act*) jubilación f; **retiring** a (*leaving*) saliente; (*shy*) retraído.
retort [rɪ'tɔːt] n (*reply*) réplica // vi contestar.
retrace [riː'treɪs] vt: **to ~ one's steps** volver sobre sus pasos, desandar lo andado.
retract [rɪ'trækt] vt (*statement*) retirar; (*claws*) retraer; (*undercarriage, aerial*) replegar // vi retractarse; ~**able** a replegable.
retrain [riː'treɪn] vt reeducar; ~**ing** n readaptación f profesional.
retreat [rɪ'triːt] n (*place*) retiro; (*act*) retraimiento; (MIL) retirada // vi retirarse; (*flood*) bajar.
retribution [rɛtrɪ'bjuːʃən] n desquite m.
retrieve [rɪ'triːv] vt (*gen*) recobrar; (*situation, honour*) salvar; (*error, loss*) recuperar; **retriever** n perro cobrador, perdiguero.
retrospect ['rɛtrəspɛkt] n: **in ~** retrospectivamente, mirando hacia atrás; ~**ive** [-'spɛktɪv] a (*law*) retroactivo.
return [rɪ'tɜːn] n (*going or coming back*) vuelta, regreso; (*of sth stolen etc*) devolución f; (*recompense*) recompensa; (FINANCE: *from land, shares*) ganancia, ingresos mpl; (*report*) informe m // cpd (*journey*) de regreso; (*ticket*) de ida y vuelta; (*match*) de vuelta // vi (*person etc: come or go back*) volver, regresar; (*symptoms etc*) reaparecer // vt devolver; (*favour, love etc*) corresponder a; (*verdict*) declarar; (POL: *candidate*) elegir; ~**s** npl (COMM) ingresos mpl; **in ~** en cambio; **many happy ~s (of the day)!** ¡muchas felicidades!, ¡feliz cumpleaños!
reunion [riː'juːnɪən] n reunión f.
reunite [riːjuː'naɪt] vt reunir; (*reconcile*) reconciliar.
rev [rɛv] n abbr of **revolution** (AUT) // (vb: also: ~ **up**) vt girar (el motor de) // vi acelerarse.
reveal [rɪ'viːl] vt (*make known*) revelar; ~**ing** a revelador(a).
reveille [rɪ'vælɪ] n (MIL) diana.
revel ['rɛvl] vi: **to ~ in sth/in doing sth** deleitarse en algo/en hacer algo.
revelation [rɛvə'leɪʃən] n revelación f.
reveller ['rɛvlə*] n jaranero, juergista m/f; **revelry** [-rɪ] n jarana, juerga.
revenge [rɪ'vɛndʒ] n venganza; (*in sport*) revancha; **to take ~ on** vengarse de.
revenue ['rɛvənjuː] n ingresos mpl, renta; (*on investment*) rédito; (*profit*) ganancia.
reverberate [rɪ'vɜːbəreɪt] vi (*sound*) resonar, retumbar; **reverberation** [-'reɪʃən] n retumbo, eco.
revere [rɪ'vɪə*] vt reverenciar, venerar;

reverence ['rɛvərəns] n reverencia; **reverent** ['rɛvərənt] a reverente.
reverie ['rɛvərɪ] n ensueño.
reversal [rɪ'vɜːsl] n (*of order*) inversión f; (*of direction*) cambio completo; (*of decision*) revocación f.
reverse [rɪ'vɜːs] n (*opposite*) contrario; (*back: of cloth*) revés m; (: *of coin*) reverso; (: *of paper*) dorso; (AUT: also: ~ **gear**) marcha atrás, contramarcha // a (*order*) inverso; (*direction*) contrario // vt (*turn over*) volver al revés; (*invert*) invertir; (*change: opinion*) cambiar (completamente) de // vi (AUT) poner en marcha atrás.
revert [rɪ'vɜːt] vi: **to ~ to** volver a.
review [rɪ'vjuː] n (*magazine, MIL*) revista; (*of book, film*) reseña; (*examination*) repaso, examen m // vt repasar, examinar; (MIL) pasar revista a; (*book, film*) reseñar; ~**er** n crítico/a.
revile [rɪ'vaɪl] vt injuriar, vilipendiar.
revise [rɪ'vaɪz] vt (*manuscript*) corregir; (*opinion*) modificar; (*study: subject*) repasar; (*look over*) revisar; **revision** [rɪ'vɪʒən] n corrección f; modificación f; repaso; revisión f.
revitalize [riː'vaɪtəlaɪz] vt revivificar.
revival [rɪ'vaɪvəl] n (*recovery*) restablecimiento; (*of interest*) renacimiento; (THEATRE) reestreno m; (*of faith*) despertar m.
revive [rɪ'vaɪv] vt (*gen*) resucitar; (*custom*) restablecer; (*hope, courage*) reanimar; (*play*) reestrenar // vi (*person*) volver en sí, restablecerse; (*from faint*) revivir; (*activity*) recobrarse.
revoke [rɪ'vəuk] vt revocar.
revolt [rɪ'vəult] n rebelión f, sublevación f // vi rebelarse, sublevarse // vt dar asco a, repugnar; ~**ing** a asqueroso, repugnante.
revolution [rɛvə'luːʃən] n revolución f; ~**ary** a, n revolucionario/a; ~**ize** vt revolucionar.
revolve [rɪ'vɔlv] vi dar vueltas, girar.
revolver [rɪ'vɔlvə*] n revólver m.
revolving [rɪ'vɔlvɪŋ] a (*chair etc*) giratorio; ~ **door** n puerta giratoria.
revue [rɪ'vjuː] n (THEATRE) revista.
revulsion [rɪ'vʌlʃən] n asco, repugnancia.
reward [rɪ'wɔːd] n premio, recompensa // vt: **to ~ (for)** recompensar o premiar (por); ~**ing** a (*fig*) provechoso, valioso.
rewire [riː'waɪə*] vt (*house*) renovar el alambrado de.
reword [riː'wɔːd] vt expresar en otras palabras.
rewrite [riː'raɪt] (*irg: like* **write**) vt volver a escribir o redactar.
rhapsody ['ræpsədɪ] n (MUS) rapsodia; (*fig*) transporte m (de admiración).
rhetoric ['rɛtərɪk] n retórica; ~**al** [rɪ'tɔrɪkl] a retórico.
rheumatic [ruː'mætɪk] a reumático; **rheumatism** ['ruːmətɪzəm] n reumatismo, reúma.

Rhine [raɪn] *n*: the ~ el (río) Rin.
rhinoceros [raɪ'nɔsərəs] *n* rinoceronte *m*.
rhododendron [rəudə'dɛndrn] *n* rododendro.
Rhone [rəun] *n*: the ~ el (río) Ródano.
rhubarb ['ruːbɑːb] *n* ruibarbo.
rhyme [raɪm] *n* rima; (*verse*) poesía.
rhythm ['rɪðm] *n* ritmo; ~ **method** método de Ojino; ~**ic(al)** *a* rítmico.
rib [rɪb] *n* (ANAT) costilla // *vt* (*mock*) tomar el pelo a.
ribald ['rɪbəld] *a* escabroso.
ribbon ['rɪbən] *n* cinta; **in** ~**s** (*torn*) hecho trizas.
rice [raɪs] *n* arroz *m*; ~**field** *n* arrozal *m*; ~ **pudding** *n* arroz *m* con leche.
rich [rɪtʃ] *a* rico; (*banquet*) suntuoso; (*soil*) fértil; (*food*) fuerte; (: *sweet*) empalagoso; **the** ~ los ricos; ~**es** *npl* riqueza *sg*; ~**ness** *n* riqueza; suntuosidad *f*; fertilidad *f*.
rickets ['rɪkɪts] *n* raquitismo.
rickety ['rɪkɪtɪ] *a* desvencijado; (*shaky*) tambaleante.
rickshaw ['rɪkʃɔː] *n* rikisha.
ricochet ['rɪkəʃeɪ] *n* rebote *m* // *vi* rebotar.
rid [rɪd] *pt*, *pp* **rid** *vt*: to ~ **sb of sth** librar a uno de algo; to **get** ~ **of** deshacerse *o* desembarazarse de.
ridden ['rɪdn] *pp of* **ride**.
riddle ['rɪdl] *n* (*conundrum*) acertijo; (*mystery*) enigma *m*, misterio; (*sieve*) criba // *vt*: to **be** ~**d with** ser lleno *o* plagado de.
ride [raɪd] *n* (*gen*) paseo; (*on horse*) cabalgata; (*distance covered*) viaje *m*, recorrido // (*vb: pt* **rode**, *pp* **ridden**) *vi* (*as sport*) montar; (*go somewhere: on horse, bicycle*) dar un paseo, pasearse; (*journey: on bicycle, motor cycle, bus*) viajar // *vt* (*a horse*) montar a; (*distance*) viajar; to ~ **a bicycle** ir en bicicleta; to ~ **at anchor** (NAUT) estar al ancla; to **take sb for a** ~ (*fig*) engañar a uno; **rider** *n* (*on horse*) jinete *m*; (*on bicycle*) ciclista *m/f*; (*on motorcycle*) motociclista *m/f*.
ridge [rɪdʒ] *n* (*of hill*) cresta; (*of roof*) caballete *m*; (*wrinkle*) arruga.
ridicule ['rɪdɪkjuːl] *n* irrisión *f*, mofa // *vt* poner en ridículo, mofarse de; **ridiculous** [-'dɪkjuləs] *a* ridículo.
riding ['raɪdɪŋ] *n* montar *m* a caballo; ~ **school** *n* escuela de equitación.
rife [raɪf] *a*: to **be** ~ ser muy común; to **be** ~ **with** abundar en.
riffraff ['rɪfræf] *n* gentuza.
rifle ['raɪfl] *n* rifle *m*, fusil *m* // *vt* saquear; ~ **range** *n* campo de tiro; (*at fair*) tiro al blanco.
rift [rɪft] *n* (*fig: disagreement: between friends*) desavenencia; (: *in party*) escisión *f*.
rig [rɪg] *n* (*also*: **oil** ~) torre *f* de perforación // *vt* (*election etc*) falsificar los resultados de; to ~ **out** *vt* ataviar de;

to ~ **up** *vt* armar; ~**ging** *n* (NAUT) aparejo.
right [raɪt] *a* (*true, correct*) correcto, exacto; (*suitable*) indicado, debido; (*proper*) apropiado, propio; (*just*) justo; (*morally good*) bueno; (*not left*) derecho // *n* (*title, claim*) derecho; (*not left*) derecha // *ad* (*correctly*) bien, correctamente; (*straight*) derecho, directamente; (*not on the left*) a la derecha; (*to the* ~) hacia la derecha // *vt* enderezar // *excl* ¡bueno!, ¡está bien!; to **be** ~ (*person*) tener razón; **all** ~**!** ¡está bien!; (*enough*) ¡basta!; ~ **now** ahora mismo; ~ **in the middle** justo en medio, en pleno centro; ~ **away** en seguida; **by** ~**s** en justicia; **on the** ~ a la derecha; ~ **angle** *n* ángulo recto; ~**eous** ['raɪtʃəs] *a* justado, honrado; (*anger*) justificado; ~**eousness** ['raɪtʃəsnɪs] *n* justicia; ~**ful** *a* (*heir*) legítimo; ~**-hand** *a* por la derecha; ~**-handed** *a* (*person*) que usa la mano derecha; ~**ly** *ad* correctamente, debidamente; (*with reason*) con razón; ~**-wing** *a* (POL) derechista.
rigid ['rɪdʒɪd] *a* rígido; (*principle*) inflexible; ~**ity** [rɪ'dʒɪdɪtɪ] *n* rigidez *f*, inflexibilidad *f*.
rigmarole ['rɪgmərəul] *n* galimatías *m*.
rigorous ['rɪgərəs] *a* riguroso.
rigour, rigor (US) ['rɪgə°] *n* rigor *m*, severidad *f*.
rig-out ['rɪgaut] *n* (*col*) atuendo.
rile [raɪl] *vt* irritar.
rim [rɪm] *n* borde *m*; (*of spectacles*) aro; (*of wheel*) aro, llanta.
rind [raɪnd] *n* (*of bacon*) piel *f*; (*of lemon etc*) cáscara; (*of cheese*) costra.
ring [rɪŋ] *n* (*of metal*) aro; (*on finger*) anillo; (*of people, objects*) círculo, grupo; (*of spies*) camarilla; (*for boxing*) cuadrilátero; (*of circus*) pista; (*bull*~) ruedo, plaza; (*sound of bell*) toque *m*; (*telephone call*) llamada // (*vb: pt* **rang**, *pp* **rung**) *vi* (*on telephone*) llamar por teléfono; (*large bell*) repicar; (*also*: ~ **out**: *voice, words*) sonar; (*ears*) zumbar // *vt* (TEL: *also*: ~ **up**) llamar; (*bell etc*) hacer sonar; (*doorbell*) tocar; to ~ **back** *vt, vi* (TEL) devolver la llamada; to ~ **off** *vi* (TEL) colgar, cortar la comunicación; ~**ing** *n* (*of large bell*) repique *m*; (*in ears*) zumbido; ~**leader** *n* (*of gang*) cabecilla *m/f*.
ringlets ['rɪŋlɪts] *npl* rizos *mpl*, tirabuzones *mpl*.
ring road *n* carretera periférica *o* de circunvalación.
rink [rɪŋk] *n* (*also*: **ice** ~) pista.
rinse [rɪns] *n* (*of dishes*) enjuague *m*; (*of hair*) reflejo // *vt* enjuagar; dar reflejos a.
riot ['raɪət] *n* motín *m*, disturbio // *vi* amotinarse; to **run** ~ desmandarse; ~**er** *n* amotinado/a; ~**ous** *a* (*gen*) alborotado; (*party*) bullicioso; (*uncontrolled*) desenfrenado.
rip [rɪp] *n* rasgón *m*, rasgadura // *vt*

rasgar, desgarrar // vi correr; ~cord n cabo de desgarre.

ripe [raɪp] a (fruit) maduro; (ready) listo; ~n vt madurar // vi madurarse; ~ness n madurez f.

ripple ['rɪpl] n onda, rizo; (sound) murmullo // vi rizarse // vt rizar.

rise [raɪz] n (slope) cuesta, pendiente m; (hill) altura; (increase: in wages) aumento; (: in prices, temperature) subida, alza; (fig: to power etc) ascenso // vi, pt **rose**, pp **risen** ['rɪzn] (gen) elevarse; (prices) subir; (waters) crecer; (river) nacer; (sun) salir; (person: from bed etc) levantarse; (also: ~ up: rebel) sublevarse; (in rank) ascender; to give ~ to dar lugar o origen a; to ~ to the occasion ponerse a la altura de las circunstancias.

risk [rɪsk] n riesgo, peligro // vt (gen) arriesgar; (dare) atreverse a; to take or run the ~ of doing correr el riesgo de hacer; at ~ en peligro; at one's own ~ bajo su propia responsabilidad; ~y a arriesgado, peligroso.

risqué ['riːskeɪ] a (joke) subido de color.

rissole ['rɪsəʊl] n croqueta.

rite [raɪt] n rito; funeral ~s exequias fpl.

ritual ['rɪtjʊəl] a ritual // n ritual m, rito.

rival ['raɪvl] n rival m/f; (in business) competidor/a m/f // a rival, opuesto // vt competir con; ~ry n rivalidad f, competencia.

river ['rɪvəʳ] n río; up/down ~ río arriba/abajo; ~bank n orilla (del río); ~bed n lecho, cauce m; ~side n ribera, orilla // cpd (port, traffic) de río, del río.

rivet ['rɪvɪt] n roblón m, remache m // vt remachar; (fig) clavar.

Riviera [rɪvɪ'eərə] n: the (French) ~ la Costa Azul (Francesa).

road [rəʊd] n (gen) camino; (motorway etc) carretera; (in town) calle f; ~block n barricada; ~hog n loco del volante; ~map n mapa m de carreteras; ~side n borde m (del camino) // cpd al lado de la carretera; ~sign n señal f (de carretera o calle); ~user n usuario de la vía pública; ~way n calzada; ~worthy a (car) listo para conducir.

roam [rəʊm] vi vagar // vt vagar por.

roar [rɔːʳ] n (of animal) rugido, bramido; (of crowd) rugido; (of vehicle, storm) estruendo; (of laughter) carcajada // vi rugir, bramar; hacer estruendo; to ~ with laughter reírse a carcajadas; to do a ~ing trade hacer buen negocio.

roast [rəʊst] n carne f asada, asado // vt (meat) asar; (coffee) tostar.

rob [rɔb] vt robar; to ~ sb of sth robar algo a uno; (fig: deprive) quitarle algo a uno; ~ber n ladrón/ona m/f; ~bery n robo.

robe [rəʊb] n (for ceremony etc) toga; (also: bath ~) bata.

robin ['rɔbɪn] n petirrojo.

robot ['rəʊbɔt] n robot m.

robust [rəʊ'bʌst] a robusto, fuerte.

rock [rɔk] n (gen) roca; (boulder) peña, peñasco; (sweet) piruli // vt (swing gently: cradle) balancear, mecer; (: child) arrullar; (shake) sacudir // vi mecerse, balancearse; sacudirse; on the ~s (drink) sobre las rocas; (marriage etc) en ruinas; to ~ the boat (fig) causar perturbaciones; ~ and roll n rocanrol m; ~-bottom a (fig) por los suelos; ~ery n cuadro alpino.

rocket ['rɔkɪt] n cohete m.

rocking ['rɔkɪŋ]: ~ chair n mecedora; ~ horse n caballo de balancín.

rocky ['rɔkɪ] a (gen) rocoso; (unsteady: table) débil.

rod [rɔd] n vara, varilla; (TECH) barra; (also: fishing ~) caña.

rode [rəʊd] pt of **ride**.

rodent ['rəʊdnt] n roedor m.

rodeo ['rəʊdɪəʊ] n rodeo.

roe [rəʊ] n (species: also: ~ deer) corzo; (of fish): hard/soft ~ hueva/lecha.

rogue [rəʊg] n pícaro, pillo; **roguish** a pícaro.

role [rəʊl] n papel m, rol m.

roll [rəʊl] n rollo; (of banknotes) fajo; (also: bread ~) panecillo, bollo; (register) lista, nómina; (sound: of drums etc) redoble m; (movement: of ship) balanceo // vt hacer rodar; (also: ~ up: string) enrollar; (: sleeves) arremangar; (cigarettes) liar; (also: ~ out: pastry) aplanar // vi (gen) rodar; (drum) redoblar; (in walking) bambolearse; (ship) balancearse; to ~ by vi (time) pasar; to ~ in vi (mail, cash) entrar a raudales; to ~ over vi dar una vuelta; to ~ up vi (col: arrive) presentarse, aparecer // vt (carpet) arrollar; ~ call n acto de pasar lista; ~er n rodillo; (wheel) rueda; ~er skates npl patines mpl de rueda.

rollicking ['rɔlɪkɪŋ] a alegre, divertido.

rolling ['rəʊlɪŋ] a (landscape) ondulado; ~ pin n rodillo (de cocina); ~ stock n (RAIL) material m rodante.

Roman ['rəʊmən] a, n romano/a; ~ Catholic a, n católico/a (romano).

romance [rə'mæns] n (love affair) amoríos mpl, aventura sentimental; (charm) lo romántico.

Romanesque [rəʊmə'nɛsk] a románico.

Romania [rəʊ'meɪnɪə] n = **Rumania**.

romantic [rə'mæntɪk] a romántico; **romanticism** [-tɪsɪzəm] n romanticismo.

romp [rɔmp] n retozo, juego // vi (also: ~ about) jugar, brincar.

rompers ['rɔmpəz] npl pelele m.

roof [ruːf], pl ~s n (gen) techo; (of house) techo, tejado; (of car) baca // vt techar, poner techo a; the ~ of the mouth el paladar, el cielo de la boca; ~ing n techumbre f; ~ rack n (AUT) baca, portaequipajes m inv.

rook [rʊk] n (bird) graja; (CHESS) torre f.

room [ruːm] n (in house) cuarto, habitación f, pieza; (also: bed~) dormitorio; (in school etc) sala; (space) sitio, cabida; ~s npl (*lodging*) alojamiento sg; '**~s to let**' '**se alquilan pisos o cuartos**'; **single/double** ~ habitación individual/doble o para dos personas; **~mate** n compañero/a de cuarto; ~ **service** n servicio de habitaciones; **~y** a espacioso.

roost [ru:st] n percha // vi pasar la noche.

rooster ['ru:stə°] a gallo.

root [ru:t] n (*BOT, MATH*) raíz f // vi (*plant, belief*) arriesgarse; **to** ~ **about** vi (*fig*) andar buscando; **to** ~ **for** vt fus apoyar a; **to** ~ **out** vt desarraigar.

rope [rəup] n cuerda; (*NAUT*) cable m // vt (*box*) atar o amarrar con (una) cuerda; (*climbers: also:* ~ **together**) encordarse; **to** ~ **sb in** (*fig*) persuadir a uno a tomar parte; **to know the ~s** (*fig*) conocer un negocio a fondo; ~ **ladder** n escala de cuerda.

rosary ['rəuzəri] n rosario.

rose [rəuz] pt of **rise** // n rosa; (*also:* ~**bush**) rosal m; (*on watering can*) roseta // a color de rosa.

rosé ['rəuzei] n vino rosado, clarete m.

rose: ~**bed** n rosaleda; ~**bud** n capullo de rosa; ~**bush** n rosal m.

rosemary ['rəuzməri] n romero.

rosette [rəu'zet] n rosetón m.

roster ['rɔstə°] n: **duty** ~ lista de deberes.

rostrum ['rɔstrəm] n tribuna.

rosy ['rəuzi] a rosado, sonrosado; **a** ~ **future** un futuro prometedor.

rot [rɔt] n (*decay*) putrefacción f, podredumbre f; (*fig: pej*) decadencia // vt, vi pudrirse, corromperse.

rota ['rəutə] n lista (de tandas).

rotary ['rəutəri] a rotativo.

rotate [rəu'teit] vt (*revolve*) hacer girar, dar vueltas a; (*change round: crops*) cultivar en rotación; (: *jobs*) alternar // vi (*revolve*) girar, dar vueltas; **rotating** a (*movement*) rotativo; **rotation** [-'teiʃən] n rotación f; **in rotation** por turno.

rotor ['rəutə°] n rotor m.

rotten ['rɔtn] a (*decayed*) podrido; (: *wood*) carcomido; (*fig*) corrompido; (*col: bad*) vil, miserable; **to feel** ~ (*ill*) sentirse muy mal.

rotting ['rɔtiŋ] a podrido.

rotund [rəu'tʌnd] a rotundo.

rouble, ruble (*US*) ['ru:bl] n rublo.

rouge [ru:ʒ] n colorete m.

rough [rʌf] a (*skin, surface*) áspero; (*terrain*) quebrado; (*road*) desigual; (*voice*) bronco; (*person, manner: coarse*) tosco, grosero; (*weather*) borrascoso; (*treatment*) brutal; (*sea*) bravo; (*cloth*) basto; (*plan*) preliminar; (*guess*) aproximado; (*violent*) violento // n (*person*) matón m; (*GOLF*): **in the** ~ en las hierbas altas; **to** ~ **it** vivir sin comodidades; **to sleep** ~ pasar la noche al raso; ~**-and-ready** a improvisado; ~**en** vt (*a surface*) poner áspero; ~**ly** ad (*handle*) torpemente; (*make*) toscamente; (*approximately*)

aproximadamente; ~**ness** n aspereza; tosquedad f; brutalidad f.

roulette [ru:'let] n ruleta.

Roumania [ru:'meiniə] n = **Rumania**.

round [raund] a redondo // n círculo; (*of toast*) rodaja; (*of policeman*) ronda; (*of milkman*) recorrido; (*of doctor*) visitas fpl; (*game: of cards, in competition*) partida; (*of ammunition*) cartucho; (*BOXING*) asalto; (*of talks*) ronda // vt (*corner*) doblar // prep alrededor de // ad: **all** ~ por todos lados; **the long way** ~ el camino menos directo; **all the year** ~ durante todo el año; **it's just** ~ **the corner** (*fig*) está a la vuelta de la esquina; **to go** ~ **to sb's** (*house*) ir a casa de uno; **to go** ~ **the back** pasar por atrás; **to go** ~ **a house** visitar una casa; **to go the** ~**s** (*story*) divulgarse; **to** ~ **off** vt (*speech etc*) acabar, poner término a; **to** ~ **up** vt (*cattle*) acorralar; (*people*) reunir; (*prices*) redondear; ~**about** n (*AUT*) glorieta, redondel m; (*at fair*) tiovivo // a (*route, means*) indirecto; **a** ~ **of applause** una salva de aplausos; **a** ~ **of drinks** una ronda de bebidas; ~**ed** a redondeado; (*style*) expresivo; ~**ly** ad (*fig*) rotundamente; ~**-shouldered** a cargado de espaldas; ~ **trip** n viaje m de ida y vuelta; ~**up** n rodeo; (*of criminals*) redada.

rouse [rauz] vt (*wake up*) despertar; (*stir up*) suscitar; **rousing** a emocionado, entusiasta.

rout [raut] n (*MIL*) derrota; (*flight*) fuga // vt derrotar.

route [ru:t] n ruta, camino; (*of bus*) recorrido; (*of shipping*) rumba, derrota; ~ **map** n (*for journey*) mapa m de carreteras.

routine [ru:'ti:n] a (*work*) rutinario // n rutina; (*THEATRE*) número.

roving ['rəuviŋ] a (*wandering*) errante; (*salesman*) ambulante.

row [rəu] n (*line*) fila, hilera; (*KNITTING*) pasada // n [rau] (*noise*) estrépito, estruendo; (*racket*) escándalo; (*dispute*) bronca, pelea; (*fuss*) jaleo, follón m; (*scolding*) regaño // vi (*in boat*) remar // vi [rau] reñir(se) // vt (*boat*) conducir remando.

rowdy ['raudi] a (*person: noisy*) ruidoso; (: *quarrelsome*) pendenciero; (*occasion*) alborotado // n pendenciero.

rowing ['rəuiŋ] n remo; ~ **boat** n bote m de remos.

royal ['rɔiəl] a real; ~**ist** a, n monárquico/a; ~**ty** n (~ *persons*) familia real; (*payment to author*) derechos mpl de autor.

R.S.V.P. abbr of **répondez s'il vous plaît** SRC (Se Ruega Contestación).

rub [rʌb] vt (*gen*) frotar; (*hard*) restregar; (*polish*) sacar brillo a // n (*gen*) frotamiento; (*touch*) roce m; **to** ~ **sb up the wrong way** coger a uno a contrapelo;

to ~ **off** vi borrarse; **to ~ off on** influir en; **to ~ out** vt borrar.

rubber ['rʌbə*] n caucho, goma; (Brit: eraser) goma de borrar; ~ **band** n goma, gomita; ~ **plant** n árbol m del caucho, gomero; ~**y** a elástico.

rubbish ['rʌbɪʃ] n (from household) basura; (waste) desperdicios mpl; (fig: pej) tonterías fpl; (trash) pacotilla; ~ **bin** n cubo de la basura; ~ **dump** n (in town) vertedero, basurero.

rubble ['rʌbl] n escombros mpl.

ruby ['ru:bɪ] n rubí m.

rucksack ['rʌksæk] n mochila.

ructions ['rʌkʃənz] npl lío sg, jaleo sg.

rudder ['rʌdə*] n timón m.

ruddy ['rʌdɪ] a (face) rubicundo, frescote; (col: damned) condenado.

rude [ru:d] a (impolite: person) grosero; (: word, manners) rudo, grosero; (sudden) repentino; (shocking) verde, indecente; ~**ly** ad groseramente, toscamente; repentinamente; ~**ness** n grosería, tosquedad f.

rudiment ['ru:dɪmənt] n rudimento; ~**ary** [-'mentərɪ] a rudimentario.

rue [ru:] vt arrepentirse de; ~**ful** a arrepentido.

ruffian ['rʌfɪən] n matón m, criminal m.

ruffle ['rʌfl] vt (hair) despeinar; (clothes) arrugar; (fig: person) agitar.

rug [rʌg] n alfombra; (for knees) manta.

rugby ['rʌgbɪ] n (also: ~ **football**) rugby m.

rugged ['rʌgɪd] a (landscape) accidentado; (features, character) fuerte.

rugger ['rʌgə*] n (col) rugby m.

ruin ['ru:ɪn] n ruina // vt arruinar; (spoil) estropear; ~**s** npl ruinas fpl, restos mpl; ~**ous** a ruinoso.

rule [ru:l] n (norm) norma, costumbre f; (regulation) regla; (government) dominio; (ruler) metro // vt (country, person) gobernar; (decide) disponer; (draw) trazar // vi regir; (LAW) fallar; **to ~ out** excluir; **as a ~** por regla general; ~**d** a (paper) rayado; **ruler** n (sovereign) soberano; (for measuring) regla; **ruling** a (party) gobernante; (class) dirigente // n (LAW) fallo, decisión f.

rum [rʌm] n ron m.

Rumania [ru:'meɪnɪə] n Rumanía; ~**n** a, n rumano/a.

rumble ['rʌmbl] n retumbo, ruido sordo; (of thunder) redoble m // vi retumbar, hacer un ruido sordo; (stomach, pipe) sonar.

rummage ['rʌmɪdʒ] vi revolverlo todo.

rumour, rumor (US) ['ru:mə*] n rumor m // vt: **it is ~ed that...** se rumorea que... .

rump [rʌmp] n (of animal) ancas fpl, grupa; ~ **steak** n filete m de lomo.

rumpus ['rʌmpəs] n (col) lío, jaleo; (quarrel) pelea, riña.

run [rʌn] n carrera; (outing) paseo, excursión f; (distance travelled) trayecto; (series) serie f; (THEATRE) temporada; (SKI) pista // (vb: pt **ran**, pp **run**) vt

(operate: business) dirigir; (: competition, course) organizar; (: hotel, house) administrar, llevar; (to pass: hand) pasar; (water, bath) abrir el grifo (del baño) // vi (gen) correr; (work: machine) funcionar, marchar; (bus, train: operate) circular, ir; (: travel) ir; (continue: play) seguir; (: contract) ser válido; (flow: river, bath) fluir; (colours, washing) desteñirse; (in election) ser candidato; **there was a ~ on** (meat, tickets) hubo mucha demanda de; **in the long ~** a la larga, a largo plazo; **on the ~** en fuga; **I'll ~ you to the station** te llevaré a la estación en coche; **to ~ a risk** correr un riesgo; **to ~ about** vi (children) correr por todos lados; **to ~ across** vt fus (find) dar con, toparse con; **to ~ away** vi huir; **to ~ down** vi (clock) parar // vt (AUT) atropellar; (criticize) criticar; **to be ~ down** estar debilitado; **to ~ off** vt (water) dejar correr // vi huir corriendo; **to ~ out** vi (person) salir corriendo; (liquid) irse; (lease) caducar, vencer; (money) acabarse; **to ~ out of** vt fus quedar sin; **to ~ over** vt sep (AUT) atropellar // vt fus (revise) repasar; **to ~ through** vt fus (instructions) repasar; **to ~ up** vt (debt) incurrir en; **to ~ up against** (difficulties) tropezar con; ~**away** a (horse) desbocado; (truck) sin frenos; (person) fugitivo.

rung [rʌŋ] pp of **ring** // n (of ladder) escalón m, peldaño.

runner ['rʌnə*] n (in race: person) corredor/a m/f; (: horse) caballo; (on sledge) patín m; (on curtain) anillo; (wheel) ruedecilla; ~ **bean** n (BOT) judía escarlata; ~-**up** n subcampeón/ona m/f.

running ['rʌnɪŋ] n (sport) atletismo; (race) carrera // a (water) corriente; (commentary) continuo; **6 days ~** 6 días seguidos; ~ **board** n estribo.

runny ['rʌnɪ] a derretido.

run-of-the-mill ['rʌnəvðə'mɪl] a común y corriente.

runt [rʌnt] n (also: pej) redrojo, enano.

runway ['rʌnweɪ] n (AVIAT) pista de aterrizaje.

rupee [ru:'pi:] n rupia.

rupture ['rʌptʃə*] n (MED) hernia // vt: **to ~ o.s.** causarse una hernia, quebrarse.

rural ['ruərl] a rural.

ruse [ru:z] n ardid m.

rush [rʌʃ] n ímpetu m; (hurry) prisa; (COMM) demanda repentina; (BOT) junco; (current) corriente f fuerte, ráfaga // vt apresurar; (work) hacer de prisa; (attack: town etc) asaltar // vi correr, precipitarse; ~ **hour** n horas fpl punta.

rusk [rʌsk] n bizcocho tostado.

Russia ['rʌʃə] n Rusia; ~**n** a, n ruso/a.

rust [rʌst] n herrumbre f, moho // vi oxidarse.

rustic ['rʌstɪk] a rústico.

rustle ['rʌsl] vi susurrar // vt (paper) hacer crujir; (US: cattle) hurtar, robar.

rustproof ['rʌstpruːf] a inoxidable, a prueba de herrumbre.
rusty ['rʌstɪ] a oxidado, mohoso.
rut [rʌt] n rodera, carril m; (ZOOL) celo; **to be in a ~** ir encarrilado.
ruthless ['ruːθlɪs] a despiadado; **~ness** n crueldad f, implacabilidad f.
rye [raɪ] n centeno; **~ bread** n pan de centeno.

S

sabbath ['sæbəθ] n domingo; (Jewish) sábado.
sabbatical [sə'bætɪkl] a: **~ year** año de licencia.
sabotage ['sæbɑːtɑːʒ] n sabotaje m // vt sabotear.
saccharin(e) ['sækərɪn] n sacarina.
sack [sæk] n (bag) saco, costal m // vt (dismiss) despedir; (plunder) saquear; **to get the ~** ser despedido; **~ing** n (material) harpillera.
sacrament ['sækrəmənt] n sacramento.
sacred ['seɪkrɪd] a sagrado, santo.
sacrifice ['sækrɪfaɪs] n sacrificio // vt sacrificar.
sacrilege ['sækrɪlɪdʒ] n sacrilegio.
sacrosanct ['sækrəʊsæŋkt] a sacrosanto.
sad [sæd] a (unhappy) triste; (deplorable) lamentable; **~den** vt entristecer.
saddle ['sædl] n silla (de montar); (of cycle) sillín m // vt (horse) ensillar; **to be ~d with sth** (col) quedar cargado con algo; **~bag** n alforja.
sadism ['seɪdɪzm] n sadismo; **sadist** n sadista m/f; **sadistic** [sə'dɪstɪk] a sádico.
sadly ['sædlɪ] ad tristemente; **~ lacking (in)** muy deficiente (en).
sadness ['sædnɪs] n tristeza.
safari [sə'fɑːrɪ] n safari m.
safe [seɪf] a (out of danger) fuera de peligro; (not dangerous, sure) seguro; (unharmed) a salvo, ileso; (trustworthy) digno de confianza // n caja de caudales, caja fuerte; **~ and sound** sano y salvo; (just) **to be on the ~ side** por mayor seguridad; **~guard** n protección f, garantía // vt proteger, defender; **~keeping** n custodia; **~ly** ad seguramente, con seguridad; (without mishap) sin peligro.
safety ['seɪftɪ] n seguridad f // a de seguridad; **~ first!** ¡precaución!; **~ belt** n cinturón m (de seguridad); **~ pin** n imperdible m.
saffron ['sæfrən] n azafrán m.
sag [sæg] vi aflojarse.
sage [seɪdʒ] n (herb) salvia; (man) sabio.
Sagittarius [sædʒɪ'tɛərɪəs] n Sagitario.
sago ['seɪgəʊ] n sagú m.
said [sed] pt, pp of **say**.
sail [seɪl] n (on boat) vela; (trip): **to go for a ~** tomar un paseo en barco // vt (boat) gobernar // vi (travel: ship) navegar; (: passenger) pasear en barco; (set off)

zarpar; **they ~ed into Copenhagen** llegaron a Copenhague; **to ~ through** vi, vt fus (fig) hacer con facilidad; **~boat** n (US) velero, barco de vela; **~ing** n (SPORT) balandrismo; **to go ~ing** salir en balandro; **~ing ship** n barco de vela; **~or** n marinero, marino.
saint [seɪnt] n santo; **S~ John** San Juan; **~ly** a santo.
sake [seɪk] n: **for the ~ of** por (motivo de).
salad ['sæləd] n ensalada; **~ bowl** n ensaladera; **~ cream** n mayonesa; **~ dressing** n aliño; **~ oil** n aceite m para ensaladas.
salami [sə'lɑːmɪ] n salami m.
salary ['sælərɪ] n sueldo.
sale [seɪl] n venta; (at reduced prices) liquidación f, saldo; **"grand ~"** grandes rebajas; **"for ~"** "se vende"; **on ~** en venta; **~room** n sala de subastas; **salesman/woman** n vendedor/a m/f; (in shop) dependiente/a m/f; (representative) viajante m/f; **salesmanship** n arte m de vender.
saliva [sə'laɪvə] n saliva.
sallow ['sæləʊ] a cetrino.
salmon ['sæmən] n, pl inv salmón m.
saloon [sə'luːn] n (US) bar m, taberna; (AUT) (coche m de) turismo; (ship's lounge) cámara, salón m.
salt [sɔːlt] n sal f // vt salar; (put ~ on) poner sal en; **~ cellar** n salero; **~water** a de agua salada; **~y** a salado.
salutary ['sæljʊtərɪ] a saludable.
salute [sə'luːt] n saludo; (of guns) salva // vt saludar.
salvage ['sælvɪdʒ] n (saving) salvamento, recuperación f; (things saved) objetos mpl salvados // vt salvar.
salvation [sæl'veɪʃən] n salvación f; **S~ Army** n Ejército de Salvación.
salve [sælv] n (cream etc) ungüento, bálsamo.
salver ['sælvə*] n bandeja.
same [seɪm] a mismo // ad de la misma forma, igual // pron: **the ~** el mismo/la misma; **the ~ book** as el mismo libro que; **all** or **just the ~** sin embargo, aun así; **to do the ~** (as sb) hacer lo mismo (que otro); **the ~ to you!** ¡igualmente!
sample ['sɑːmpl] n muestra // vt (food, wine) probar.
sanatorium [sænə'tɔːrɪəm], pl **-ria** [-rɪə] n sanatorio.
sanctify ['sæŋktɪfaɪ] vt santificar.
sanctimonious [sæŋktɪ'məʊnɪəs] a santurrón(ona).
sanction ['sæŋkʃən] n sanción f // vt sancionar.
sanctity ['sæŋktɪtɪ] n (gen) santidad f; (inviolability) inviolabilidad f.
sanctuary ['sæŋktjʊərɪ] n (gen) santuario; (refuge) asilo, refugio.
sand [sænd] n arena; (beach) playa // vt enarenar.
sandal ['sændl] n sandalia; (wood) sándalo.

sand: ~**bag** n saco de arena; ~**bank** n banco de arena; ~**castle** n castillo de arena; ~ **dune** n duna; ~**paper** n papel m de lija; ~**pit** n (for children) cajón m de arena; ~**stone** n piedra arenisca.

sandwich ['sændwɪtʃ] n bocadillo, sándwich m // vt (also: ~ **in**) intercalar; ~**ed between** apretujado entre; **cheese/ham** ~ sándwich de queso/jamón; ~ **board** n cartelón m; ~ **course** n curso de medio tiempo.

sandy ['sændɪ] a arenoso; (colour) rojizo.

sane [seɪn] a cuerdo, sensato; (sensible) prudente.

sang [sæŋ] pt of **sing**.

sanitarium [sænɪ'tɛərɪəm] (US) = **sanatorium**.

sanitary ['sænɪtərɪ] a (system, arrangements) sanitario; (clean) higiénico; ~ **towel**, ~ **napkin** (US) n paño higiénico, compresa higiénica.

sanitation [sænɪ'teɪʃən] n (in house) saneamiento; (in town) sanidad f, higiene f.

sanity ['sænɪtɪ] n cordura; (common sense) juicio, sentido común.

sank [sæŋk] pt of **sink**.

Santa Claus [sæntə'klɔːz] n San Nicolás, Papá Noel.

sap [sæp] n (of plants) savia // vt (strength) minar, agotar.

sapling ['sæplɪŋ] n árbol nuevo o joven.

sapphire ['sæfaɪə*] n zafiro.

sarcasm ['sɑːkæzm] n sarcasmo; **sarcastic** [-'kæstɪk] a sarcástico.

sardine [sɑː'diːn] n sardina.

Sardinia [sɑː'dɪnɪə] n Cerdeña.

sari ['sɑːrɪ] n sari m.

sash [sæʃ] n faja.

sat [sæt] pt, pp of **sit**.

Satan ['seɪtn] n Satanás m.

satchel ['sætʃl] n bolsa; (child's) cartera.

satellite ['sætəlaɪt] a satélite m.

satin ['sætɪn] n raso // a de raso.

satire ['sætaɪə*] n sátira; **satirical** [sə'tɪrɪkl] a satírico; **satirize** ['sætɪraɪz] vt satirizar.

satisfaction [sætɪs'fækʃən] n satisfacción f; (of debt) liquidación f; **satisfactory** [-'fæktərɪ] a satisfactorio.

satisfy ['sætɪsfaɪ] vt satisfacer; (pay) liquidar; (convince) convencer; ~**ing** a satisfactorio.

saturate ['sætʃəreɪt] vt: to ~ (with) empapar o saturar (de); **saturation** [-'reɪʃən] n saturación f.

Saturday ['sætədɪ] n sábado.

sauce [sɔːs] n salsa; (sweet) crema; (fig: cheek) frescura; ~**pan** n perola.

saucer ['sɔːsə*] n platillo.

saucy ['sɔːsɪ] a fresco, descarado; (flirtatious) coqueta.

sauna ['sɔːnə] n sauna.

saunter ['sɔːntə*] vi deambular.

sausage ['sɔsɪdʒ] n salchicha; (cold meat) embutido; ~ **roll** n empanadita.

sauté ['səʊteɪ] a salteado.

savage ['sævɪdʒ] a (cruel, fierce) feroz, furioso; (primitive) salvaje // a salvaje m/f // vt (attack) embestir; ~**ry** n ferocidad f; salvajismo.

save [seɪv] vt (rescue) salvar, rescatar; (money, time) ahorrar; (put by) guardar; (avoid: trouble) evitar // vi (also: ~ **up**) ahorrar // n (SPORT) parada // prep salvo, excepto.

saving ['seɪvɪŋ] n (on price etc) economía // a: **the** ~ **grace of** el único mérito de; ~**s** npl ahorros mpl; ~**s bank** n caja de ahorros.

saviour ['seɪvjə*] n salvador/a m/f.

savour, savor (US) ['seɪvə*] n sabor m, gusto // vt saborear; ~**y** a sabroso; (dish: not sweet) no dulce; (: salted) salado.

saw [sɔː] pt of **see** // n (tool) sierra // vt, pt **sawed**, pp **sawed** or **sawn** serrar; ~**dust** n (a)serrín m; ~**mill** n aserradero.

saxophone ['sæksəfəʊn] n saxófono.

say [seɪ] n: **to have one's** ~ expresar su opinión; **to have a** o **some** ~ **in sth** tener voz o tener que ver en algo // vt, pt, pp **said** decir; **to** ~ **yes/no** decir que sí/no; **that is to** ~ es decir; **that goes without** ~**ing** eso va sin decir; ~**ing** n dicho, refrán m.

scab [skæb] n costra; (pej) esquirol/a m/f; ~**by** a costroso, lleno de costras.

scaffold ['skæfəʊld] n (for execution) cadalso, patíbulo; ~**ing** n andamios mpl, andamiaje m.

scald [skɔːld] n escaldadura // vt escaldar; ~**ing** a (hot) hirviendo.

scale [skeɪl] n (gen, MUS) escala; (of fish) escama; (of salaries, fees etc) escalafón m; (of map, also size, extent) escala // vt (mountain) escalar; (tree) trepar; ~**s** npl (small) balanza sg; (large) báscula sg; **on a large** ~ a gran escala; ~ **of charges** tarifa, lista de precios; **social** ~ escala social; ~ **drawing** n dibujo a escala; ~ **model** n modelo a escala.

scallop ['skɔləp] n (ZOOL) venera; (SEWING) festón m.

scalp [skælp] n cabellera // vt escalpar.

scalpel ['skælpl] n escalpelo.

scamp [skæmp] n diablillo, travieso.

scamper ['skæmpə*] vi: to ~ **away**, ~ **off** irse corriendo.

scan [skæn] vt (examine) escudriñar; (glance at quickly) dar un vistazo a; (TV, RADAR) explorar, registrar.

scandal ['skændl] n escándalo; (gossip) chismes mpl; ~**ize** vt escandalizar; ~**ous** a escandaloso; (libellous) calumnioso.

Scandinavia [skændɪ'neɪvɪə] n Escandinavia; ~**n** a escandinavo.

scant [skænt] a escaso; ~**y** a escaso.

scapegoat ['skeɪpgəʊt] n cabeza de turco, chivo expiatorio.

scar [skɑː] n cicatriz f // vt marcar con una cicatriz // vi cicatrizarse.

scarce [skɛəs] a escaso; ~**ly** ad apenas; **scarcity** n escasez f; (shortage) carestía.

scare [skɛə*] n susto, sobresalto; (panic)

pánico // vt asustar, espantar; **to ~ sb
stiff** dejar muerto de miedo a uno; **bomb
~** amenaza de bomba; **~crow** n
espantapájaros m inv; **~d** a: **to be ~d**
asustarse, estar asustado.

scarf [skɑ:f], pl **scarves** n (long) bufanda;
(square) pañuelo.

scarlet ['skɑ:lɪt] a escarlata; **~ fever** n
escarlatina.

scarves [skɑ:vz] pl of **scarf**.

scary ['skɛərɪ] a (col) de miedo.

scathing ['skeɪðɪŋ] a mordaz.

scatter ['skætə*] vt (spread) esparcir,
desparramar; (put to flight) dispersar // vi
desparramarse; dispersarse; **~brained** a
ligero de cascos; (forgetful) olvidadizo.

scavenger ['skævəndʒə*] n (refuse
collector) basurero; (zool) animal m/ave f
que se alimenta de la carroña.

scene [si:n] n (THEATRE, fig etc) escena; (of
crime, accident) escenario; (sight, view)
vista, perspectiva; (fuss) escándalo; **~ry**
n (THEATRE) decorado; (landscape) paisaje
m; **scenic** a (picturesque) pintoresco.

scent [sɛnt] n perfume m, olor m; (fig:
track) rastro, pista; (sense of smell) olfato
// vt perfumar; (smell) oler; (sniff out)
husmear; (suspect) sospechar.

sceptic, skeptic (US) ['skɛptɪk] n
escéptico/a; **~al** a escéptico; **~ism**
['skɛptɪsɪzm] n escepticismo.

sceptre, scepter (US) ['sɛptə*] n cetro.

schedule ['ʃɛdju:l] n (of trains) horario; (of
events) programa m; (plan) plan m; (list)
lista // vt (timetable) establecer el horario
de; (list) cataloger; (visit) fijar la hora de;
on ~ a la hora, sin retraso; **to be ahead
of/behind ~** estar adelantado/en
retraso.

scheme [ski:m] n (plan) plan m, proyecto;
(method) esquema m; (plot) intriga; (trick)
ardid m; (arrangement) disposición f // vi
proyectar // vi (plan) hacer proyectos;
(intrigue) intrigar; **scheming** a intrigante.

schism ['skɪzəm] n cisma m.

schizophrenia [skɪtsəu'fri:nɪə] n
esquizofrenia; **schizophrenic** [-sə'frɛnɪk]
a esquizofrénico.

scholar ['skɒlə*] n (pupil) alumno/a,
estudiante m/f; (learned person) sabio,
erudito; **~ly** a erudito; **~ship** n erudición
f; (grant) beca.

school [sku:l] n (gen) escuela, colegio; (in
university) facultad f // vt (animal)
amaestrar; **~ age** n edad f escolar;
~book n libro de texto; **~boy** n alumno;
~days npl años mpl del colegio; **~girl** n
alumna; **~ing** n enseñanza;
~master/mistress n (primary)
maestro/a; (secondary) profesor/a m/f;
~room n clase f; **~teacher** n
maestro/a.

schooner ['sku:nə*] n (ship) goleta; (glass)
jarra.

sciatica [saɪ'ætɪkə] n ciática.

science ['saɪəns] n ciencia; **~ fiction** n
ciencia-ficción f; **scientific** [-'tɪfɪk] a

científico; **scientist** n científico.

scimitar ['sɪmɪtə*] n cimitarra.

scintillating ['sɪntɪleɪtɪŋ] a brillante,
ingenioso.

scissors ['sɪzəz] npl tijeras fpl; **a pair of
~** unas tijeras.

scoff [skɒf] vt (col: eat) engullir // vi: **to ~
(at)** (mock) mofarse (de).

scold [skəuld] vt regañar.

scone [skɒn] n panecillo.

scoop [sku:p] n cucharón m; (for flour etc)
pala; (PRESS) exclusiva; **to ~ out** vt
excavar; **to ~ up** vt recoger.

scooter ['sku:tə*] n (motor cycle) moto f;
(toy) patinete m.

scope [skəup] n (of plan, undertaking)
ámbito; (reach) alcance m; (of person)
competencia; (opportunity) campo (de
acción).

scorch [skɔ:tʃ] vt (clothes) chamuscar;
(earth, grass) quemar, secar; **~er** n (col:
hot day) día m abrasador; **~ing** a
abrasador(a).

score [skɔ:*] n (points etc) puntuación f;
(MUS) partitura; (reckoning) cuenta;
(twenty) veinte m, veintena // vt (goal,
point) ganar; (mark) rayar // vi marcar un
tanto; (FOOTBALL) marcar (un) gol; (keep
score) llevar el tanteo; **on that ~** en lo
que se refiere a eso; **to ~ 6 out of 10**
obtener una puntuación de 6 sobre 10;
~board n marcador m; **~card** n (SPORT)
tanteador m; **scorer** n marcador m; (keeping score) tanteador m.

scorn [skɔ:n] n desprecio // vt despreciar;
~ful a desdeñoso, despreciativo.

Scorpio ['skɔ:pɪəu] n Escorpión m.

scorpion ['skɔ:pɪən] n escorpión m.

Scot [skɒt] n escocés/esa m/f.

scotch [skɒtʃ] vt (rumour) desmentir;
(plan) abandonar; **S~** n whisky m
escocés.

Scotland ['skɒtlənd] n Escocia.

Scots [skɒts] a escocés(esa);
~man/woman n escocés/esa m/f;
Scottish ['skɒtɪʃ] a escocés(esa).

scoundrel ['skaundrl] n canalla m/f,
sinvergüenza m/f.

scour ['skauə*] vt (clean) fregar, estregar;
(search) recorrer, registrar; **~er** n
estropajo.

scourge [skɜ:dʒ] n azote m.

scout [skaut] n (MIL, also: **boy ~**)
explorador m; **to ~ around** reconocer el
terreno.

scowl [skaul] vi fruncir el ceño; **to ~ at**
sb mirar con ceño a uno.

scraggy ['skrægɪ] a flaco, descarnado.

scram [skræm] vi (col) largarse.

scramble ['skræmbl] n (climb) subida
(difícil); (struggle) pelea // vi: **to ~
out/through** salir/abrirse paso con
dificultad; **to ~ for** pelear por; **~d eggs**
npl huevos mpl revueltos.

scrap [skræp] n (bit) pedacito; (fig) pizca;
(fight) riña, bronca; (also: **~ iron**)
chatarra, hierro viejo // vt reducir a

chatarra; (*discard*) desechar, descartar // vi reñir, armar (una) bronca; ~**s** *npl* (*waste*) sobras *fpl*, desperdicios *mpl*; ~ **book** *n* álbum *m* de recortes.

scrape [skreɪp] *n* (*fig*) lío, apuro // vt raspar; (*skin etc*) rasguñar; (~ *against*) rozar // vi: **to** ~ **through** pasar con dificultad; **scraper** *n* raspador *m*.

scrap: ~ **heap** *n* (*fig*): **on the** ~ **heap** desperdiciado; ~ **merchant** *n* chatarrero; ~ **paper** *n* pedazos *mpl* de papel; ~**py** *a* (*poor*) pobre; (*speech*) inconexo; (*bitty*) fragmentario.

scratch [skrætʃ] *n* rasguño; (*from claw*) arañazo // a: ~ **team** equipo improvisado // vt (*record*) rayar; (*with claw, nail*) rasguñar, arañar // vi rascarse; **to start from** ~ partir de cero, empezar desde el principio; **to be up to** ~ estar a la altura (de las circunstancias).

scrawl [skrɔːl] *n* garabatos *mpl* // vi hacer garabatos.

scream [skriːm] *n* chillido // vi chillar.

screech [skriːtʃ] vi chirriar.

screen [skriːn] *n* (*CINEMA, TV*) pantalla; (*movable*) biombo; (*wall*) tabique *m*; (*also*: **wind**~) parabrisas *m inv*; (*fig*) cortina // vt (*conceal*) tapar; (*from the wind etc*) proteger; (*film*) proyectar; (*candidates etc*) investigar a; ~**ing** *n* (*MED*) investigación *f* médica; ~ **test** *n* prueba de pantalla.

screw [skruː] *n* tornillo; (*propeller*) hélice *f* // vt atornillar; (*also*: ~ **in**) apretar; ~**driver** *n* destornillador *m*; ~**y** *a* (*col*) chiflado.

scribble ['skrɪbl] *n* garabatos *mpl* // vt escribir con prisa.

script [skrɪpt] *n* (*CINEMA etc*) guión *m*; (*writing*) escritura, letra.

Scripture ['skrɪptʃə*] *n* Sagrada Escritura.

scriptwriter ['skrɪptraɪtə*] *n* guionista *m/f*.

scroll [skrəul] *n* rollo.

scrounge [skraundʒ] vt (*col*): **to** ~ **sth off** *or* **from sb** obtener algo de otro por gorronería // vi: **to** ~ **on sb** vivir a costa de uno; **scrounger** *n* gorrón/ona *m/f*.

scrub [skrʌb] *n* (*clean*) fregado; (*land*) maleza // vt fregar, restregar; (*reject*) cancelar, anular.

scruff [skrʌf] *n*: **by the** ~ **of the neck** por el pescuezo.

scruffy ['skrʌfɪ] *a* desaliñado, piojoso.

scruple ['skruːpl] *n* escrúpulo; **scrupulous** *a* escrupuloso.

scrutinize ['skruːtɪnaɪz] vt escudriñar; (*votes*) escrutar; **scrutiny** [-nɪ] *n* escrutinio, examen *m*.

scuff [skʌf] vt desgastar, restregar.

scuffle ['skʌfl] *n* refriega.

scullery ['skʌlərɪ] *n* fregadero, trascocina.

sculptor ['skʌlptə*] *n* escultor *m*; **sculpture** [-tʃə*] *n* escultura.

scum [skʌm] *n* (*on liquid*) nata; (*pej*: *people*) canalla; (*fig*) heces *fpl*.

scurry ['skʌrɪ] vi: **to** ~ **off** escabullirse.

scurvy ['skɜːvɪ] *n* escorbuto.

scuttle ['skʌtl] *n* (*also*: **coal** ~) cubo, carbonera // vt (*ship*) barrenar // vi (*scamper*): **to** ~ **away,** ~ **off** escabullirse.

scythe [saɪð] *n* guadaña.

sea [siː] *n* mar *m or f*; **on the** ~ (*boat*) en el mar; (*town*) junto al mar; **to be all at** ~ (*fig*) estar despistado; **out to** *or* **at** ~ en alta mar; ~ **bird** *n* ave *f* marina; ~**board** *n* litoral *m*; ~ **breeze** *n* brisa de mar; ~**farer** *n* marinero; ~**food** *n* mariscos *mpl*; ~ **front** *n* (*beach*) playa; (*prom*) paseo marítimo; ~**going** *a* (*ship*) de alta mar; ~ **gull** *n* gaviota.

seal [siːl] *n* (*animal*) foca; (*stamp*) sello // vt (*close*) cerrar; (: *with* ~) sellar; **to** ~ **off** obturar; **it** ~**ed his fate** decidió su destino.

sea level ['siːlevl] *n* nivel *m* del mar.

sealing wax ['siːlɪŋwæks] *n* lacre *m*.

sea lion ['siːlaɪən] *n* león *m* marino.

seam [siːm] *n* costura; (*of metal*) juntura; (*of coal*) veta, filón *m*.

seaman ['siːmən] *n* marinero.

seamless ['siːmlɪs] *a* sin costura.

seamstress ['sɛmstrɪs] *n* costurera.

seance ['seɪɔns] *n* sesión *f* de espiritismo.

sea: ~**plane** *n* hidroavión *m*; ~**port** *n* puerto de mar.

search [sɜːtʃ] *n* (*for person, thing*) busca, búsqueda; (*of drawer, pockets*) registro; (*inspection*) reconocimiento // vt (*look in*) buscar en; (*examine*) examinar; (*person, place*) registrar // vi: **to** ~ **for** buscar; **to** ~ **through** vt fus registrar; **in** ~ **of** en busca de; ~**ing** *a* penetrante; ~**light** *n* reflector *m*; ~ **party** *n* pelotón *m* de salvamento; ~ **warrant** *n* mandamiento (judicial).

sea: ~**shore** *n* playa, orilla del mar; ~**sick** *a* mareado; ~**side** *n* playa, orilla del mar; ~**side resort** *n* playa.

season ['siːzn] *n* (*of year*) estación *f*; (*sporting etc*) temporada; (*gen*) época, período // vt (*food*) sazonar; ~**al** *a* estacional; ~**ing** *n* condimento, aderezo; ~ **ticket** *n* billete *m* de abono.

seat [siːt] *n* (*in bus, train*: *place*) asiento; (*chair*) silla; (*PARLIAMENT*) escaño; (*buttocks*) culo, trasero; (*of government*) sede *f* // vt sentar; (*have room for*) tener asientos para; **to be** ~**ed** sentarse; ~ **belt** *n* cinturón *m* de seguridad.

sea: ~ **water** *n* agua *m* del mar; ~**weed** *n* alga marina; ~ **worthy** *a* marinero, en condiciones de navegar.

sec. *abbr of* **second(s)**.

secede [sɪˈsiːd] vi separarse.

secluded [sɪˈkluːdɪd] *a* retirado; **seclusion** [-ˈkluːʒən] *n* retiro.

second ['sɛkənd] *a* segundo // ad (*in race etc*) en segundo lugar // *n* (*gen*) segundo; (*AUT*: *also*: ~ **gear**) segunda; (*COMM*) artículo con algún desperfecto // vt (*motion*) apoyar; ~**ary** *a* secundario; ~**ary school** *n* escuela secundaria; ~-**class** *a* de segunda clase; ~**hand** *a* de segunda

mano, usado; ~ **hand** n (on clock)
segundero; ~**ly** ad en segundo lugar;
~**ment** [sɪ'kɔndmənt] n traslado
temporal; ~**rate** a de segunda categoría.
secrecy ['siːkrəsɪ] n secreto; **secret** [-krɪt]
a, n secreto.
secretarial [sckrɪ'tɛərɪəl] a de
secretario/a.
secretariat [sckrɪ'tɛərɪət] n secretaría.
secretary ['sckrətərɪ] n secretario/a; **S~**
of State (Brit: POL) Ministro (con cartera).
secretive ['siːkrətɪv] a reservado, sigiloso.
sect [sckt] n secta; ~**arian** [-'tɛərɪən] a
sectario.
section ['sckʃən] n sección f; (part) parte f;
(of document) artículo; (of opinion) sector
m; ~**al** a (drawing) en corte.
sector ['scktə°] n sector m.
secular ['sckjulə°] a secular, seglar.
secure [sɪ'kjuə°] a (free from anxiety)
seguro; (firmly fixed) firme, fijo // vt (fix)
asegurar, afianzar; (get) conseguir.
security [sɪ'kjurɪtɪ] n seguridad f; (for
loan) fianza; (: object) prenda.
sedate [sɪ'deɪt] a (calm) tranquilo;
(formal) serio, formal // vt tratar con
calmantes.
sedation [sɪ'deɪʃən] n (MED) sedación f.
sedative ['scdɪtɪv] n sedante m, sedativo.
sedentary ['scdntrɪ] a sedentario.
sediment ['scdɪmənt] n sedimento.
seduce [sɪ'djuːs] vt (gen) seducir;
seduction [-'dʌkʃən] n seducción f;
seductive [-'dʌktɪv] a seductor(a).
see [siː], pt **saw**, pp **seen** vt (gen) ver;
(accompany): to ~ **sb to the door**
acompañar a uno a la puerta; (understand)
ver, comprender; (look at) mirar // vi ver
// n sede f; to ~ **that** (ensure) asegurar
que; to ~ **about** vi atender a, encargarse
de; to ~ **off** vt despedirse de; to ~
through vt penetrar (con la vista) // vt fus
llevar a cabo; to ~ **to** vt fus atender a,
encargarse de.
seed [siːd] n semilla; (in fruit) pepita;
(sperm) semen m, simiente f; (fig) germen
m; (TENNIS) preseleccionado/a; ~**ling** n
planta de semillero; ~**y** a (shabby) desaseado, raído.
seeing ['siːɪŋ] conj: ~ (that) visto que, en
vista de que.
seek [siːk], pt, pp **sought** vt (gen) buscar;
(post) solicitar.
seem [siːm] vi parecer; ~**ingly** ad
aparentemente, según parece.
seen [siːn] pp of **see**.
seep [siːp] vi filtrarse.
seesaw ['siːsɔː] n balancín m, columpio.
seethe [siːð] vi hervir; to ~ **with anger**
enfurecerse.
segment ['scgmənt] n segmento.
segregate ['scgrɪgeɪt] vt segregar;
segregation [-'geɪʃən] n segregación f.
seismic ['saɪzmɪk] a sísmico.
seize [siːz] vt (grasp) agarrar, asir; (take
possession of) secuestrar; (: territory)
apoderarse de; (opportunity) aprovecharse

de; to ~ (up)on vt fus valerse de; to ~
up vi (TECH) agarrotarse.
seizure ['siːʒə°] n (MED) ataque m; (LAW)
incautación f.
seldom ['scldəm] ad rara vez.
select [sɪ'lckt] a selecto, escogido // vt
escoger, elegir; (SPORT) seleccionar; ~**ion**
[-'lckʃən] n selección f, elección f; (COMM)
surtido; ~**ive** a selectivo; ~**or** n (person)
seleccionador/a m/f.
self [sclf] pron se; (after prep) sí mismo //
n, pl **selves** uno mismo; **him~/her~** él
mismo/ella misma; **the** ~ el yo.
self... pref auto...; ~**-appointed** a
autonombrado; ~**-assured** a seguro de sí
mismo; ~**-catering** a sin pensión;
~**-centred** a egocéntrico; ~**-coloured** a
de color natural; (of one colour) de un
color; ~**-confidence** n confianza en sí
mismo; ~**-conscious** a cohibido;
~**-contained** a (gen) independiente;
(flat) con entrada particular; ~**-control** n
autodominio; ~**-defence** n defensa
propia; ~**-discipline** n autodisciplina;
~**-employed** a que trabaja por cuenta
propia; ~**-evident** a patente;
~**-governing** a autónomo; ~**-important**
a presumido; ~**-indulgent** a inmoderado;
~**-interest** n egoísmo; ~**-ish** a egoísta;
~**-ishness** n egoísmo; ~**-lessly** ad
desinteresadamente; ~**-pity** n
autocompasión f; ~**-portrait** n
autorretrato; ~**-possessed** a sereno,
dueño de sí mismo; ~**-preservation** n
propia conservación f; ~**-reliant** a
independiente, seguro de sí mismo;
~**-respect** n amor m propio;
~**-righteous** a santurrón(ona);
~**-sacrifice** n abnegación f; ~**-satisfied**
a satisfecho de sí mismo; ~**-service** a de
autoservicio; ~**-sufficient** a auto-
suficiente; ~**-taught** a autodidacta.
sell [scl], pt, pp **sold** vt vender // vi
venderse; to ~ **at** or **for £10** vender a 10
libros; to ~ **off** vi liquidar; to ~ **out** vi
transigir, transar (AM); ~**er** n vendedor/a
m/f; ~**ing price** n precio de venta.
sellotape ['scləteɪp] n celo.
sellout ['sclaut] n traición f; (of tickets): **it**
was a ~ fue un éxito de taquilla.
selves [sclvz] pl of **self**.
semaphore ['scməfɔː°] n semáforo.
semen ['siːmən] n semen m.
semi... [scmɪ] pref semi..., medio...;
~**circle** n semicírculo; ~**colon** n punto y
coma; ~**conscious** a semiconsciente;
~**detached** (house) n (casa)
semiseparada; ~**final** n semi-final m.
seminar ['scmɪnɑː°] n seminario.
semitone ['scmɪtəun] n (MUS) semitono.
semolina [scmə'liːnə] n sémola.
senate ['scnɪt] n senado; **senator** n
senador/a m/f.
send [scnd], pt, pp **sent** vt mandar, enviar;
(dispatch) despachar; (telegram) poner; to
~ **away** vt (letter, goods) despachar; to
~ **away for** vt fus despachar por; to ~

back vt devolver; **to ~ for** vt fus mandar traer; **to ~ off** vt (goods) despachar; (SPORT. player) expulsar; **to ~ out** vt (invitation) mandar; (signal) emitir; **to ~ up** vt (person, price) hacer subir; (parody) parodiar; **~er** n remitente m/f; **~-off** n: **a good ~-off** una buena despedida.

senile ['siːnaɪl] a senil; **senility** [sɪ'nɪlɪtɪ] n senilidad f.

senior ['siːnɪəʳ] a (older) mayor, más viejo; (: on staff) más antiguo; (of higher rank) superior // n mayor m; (in service) miembro más antiguo; **~ity** [-'ɔrɪtɪ] n antigüedad f.

sensation [sɛn'seɪʃən] n sensación f; **~al** a sensacional; **~alism** n sensacionalismo.

sense [sɛns] n sentido; (feeling) sensación f; (good ~) sentido común, juicio; (sentiment) opinión f // vt sentir, percibir; **it makes ~** tiene sentido; **~less** a estúpido, insensato; (unconscious) sin sentido.

sensibility [sɛnsɪ'bɪlɪtɪ] n sensibilidad f; **sensibilities** npl delicadeza sg.

sensible ['sɛnsɪbl] a sensato, juicio; (cautious) prudente; (reasonable) razonable, lógico; (perceptible) apreciable.

sensitive ['sɛnsɪtɪv] a sensible; (touchy) susceptible; **sensitivity** [-'tɪvɪtɪ] n sensibilidad f; susceptibilidad f.

sensual ['sɛnsjuəl] a sensual.

sensuous ['sɛnsjuəs] a sensual.

sent [sɛnt] pt, pp of **send**.

sentence ['sɛntns] n (LING) frase f, oración f; (LAW) sentencia, fallo // vt: **to ~ sb to death/to 5 years** condenar a uno a muerte/a 5 años de cárcel.

sentiment ['sɛntɪmənt] n sentimiento; (opinion) opinión f; **~al** [-'mɛntl] a sentimental; **~ality** [-'tælɪtɪ] n sentimentalismo.

sentry ['sɛntrɪ] n centinela m.

separate ['sɛprɪt] a separado; (distinct) distinto // (vb: ['sɛpəreɪt]) vt separar; (part) dividir // vi separarse; **~ly** ad por separado; **~s** npl (clothes) coordinados mpl; **separation** [-'reɪʃən] n separación f.

September [sɛp'tɛmbəʳ] n se(p)tiembre m.

septic ['sɛptɪk] a séptico.

sequel ['siːkwl] n consecuencia, resultado; (of story) continuación f.

sequence ['siːkwəns] n sucesión f, serie f; (CINEMA) secuencia.

sequin ['siːkwɪn] n lentejuela.

serenade [sɛrə'neɪd] n serenata // vt dar serenata a.

serene [sɪ'riːn] a sereno, tranquilo; **serenity** [sə'rɛnɪtɪ] n serenidad f, tranquilidad f.

sergeant ['sɑːdʒənt] n sargento.

serial ['sɪərɪəl] n novela por entregas; **~ize** vt publicar por entregas; **~ number** n número de serie.

series ['sɪərɪːs] n serie f.

serious ['sɪərɪəs] a serio; (grave) grave;

~ly ad en serio; gravemente; **~ness** n seriedad f, gravedad f.

sermon ['sɜːmən] n sermón m.

serrated [sɪ'reɪtɪd] a serrado, dentellado.

serum ['sɪərəm] n suero.

servant ['sɜːvənt] n (gen) servidor/a m/f; (house ~) criado/a; **civil ~** funcionario.

serve [sɜːv] vt (gen) servir; (in shop: goods) servir, despachar; (: customer) atender; (subj: train) pasar por; (treat) tratar; (apprenticeship) hacer; (prison term) cumplir // vi (also TENNIS) sacar; (be useful): **to ~ as/for/to do** servir de/para/para hacer // n (TENNIS) saque m; **to ~ out, ~ up** vt (food) servir.

service ['sɜːvɪs] n (gen) servicio; (REL) misa; (AUT) mantenimiento; (of dishes) vajilla, juego // vt (car, washing machine) mantener; (: repair) reparar; **the S~s** las fuerzas armadas; **to be of ~ to sb** ser útil a uno; **~able** a servible, utilizable; **~ area** n (on motorway) servicios mpl; **~man** n militar m; **~ station** n estación f de servicio.

serviette [sɜːvɪ'ɛt] n servilleta.

servile ['sɜːvaɪl] a servil.

session ['sɛʃən] n (sitting) sesión f; **to be in ~** estar celebrando sesión.

set [sɛt] n juego; (RADIO) aparato; (TV) televisor m; (of utensils) batería; (of cutlery) cubierto; (of books) colección f; (TENNIS) set m; (group of people) grupo; (CINEMA) plató m; (THEATRE) decorado; (HAIRDRESSING) marcado // a (fixed) fijo; (ready) listo; (resolved) resuelto, decidido // (vb: pt, pp set) vt (place) poner, colocar; (fix) fijar; (: a time) señalar; (adjust) ajustar, arreglar; (decide: rules etc) establecer, decidir // vi (sun) ponerse; (jam, jelly) cuajarse; (concrete) fraguar; **to be ~ on doing sth** estar empeñado en hacer algo; **to ~ to music** poner música a; **to ~ on fire** incendiar, poner fuego a; **to ~ free** poner en libertad; **to ~ sth going** poner algo en marcha; **to ~ sail** zarpar, hacerse a la vela; **to ~ about** vt fus (task) ponerse a; **to ~ aside** vt poner aparte, dejar de lado; **to ~ back** vt (in time): **to ~ back (by)** retrasar (por); **to ~ off** vi partir // vt (bomb) hacer estallar; (cause to start) poner en marcha; (show up well) hacer resaltar; **to ~ out** vi: **to ~ out to do sth** ponerse a hacer algo // vt (arrange) disponer; (state) exponer; **to ~ up** vt (organization, record) establecer; **to ~ up shop** (fig) establecerse; **~back** n (hitch) revés m, contratiempo.

settee [sɛ'tiː] n sofá m.

setting ['sɛtɪŋ] n (frame) marco; (placing) colocación f; (of sun) puesta; (of jewel) engaste m, montadura.

settle ['sɛtl] vt (argument, matter) componer; (accounts) ajustar, liquidar; (land) colonizar; (MED: calm) calmar, sosegar // vi (dust etc) depositarse; (weather) serenarse; (also: **~ down**) instalarse, establecerse; to ~ **for sth** convenir en aceptar algo; to ~ **in** vi instalarse; to ~ **on** sth quedar en algo; to ~ **up with sb** ajustar cuentas con uno; ~**ment** n (payment) liquidación f; (agreement) acuerdo, convenio; (village etc) pueblo; **settler** n colono/a, colonizador/a m/f.

setup ['sɛtʌp] n (arrangement) plan m; (situation) situación f.

seven ['sɛvn] num siete; ~**teen** num diez y siete, diecisiete; ~**th** a séptimo; ~**ty** num setenta.

sever ['sɛvəʳ] vt cortar; (relations) romper.

several ['sɛvərl] a, pron varios mpl, algunos mpl; ~ **of us** varios de nosotros.

severance ['sɛvərəns] n (of relations) ruptura; ~ **pay** n pago de despedida.

severe [sɪ'vɪəʳ] a severo; (serious) grave; (hard) duro; (pain) intenso; **severity** [sɪ'vɛrɪtɪ] n severidad f; gravedad f; intensidad f.

sew [səu], pt **sewed**, pp **sewn** vt, vi coser; to ~ **up** vt coser, zurcir.

sewage ['suːɪdʒ] n (effluence) aguas fpl residuales; (system) alcantarillado.

sewer ['suːəʳ] n alcantarilla, cloaca.

sewing ['səuɪŋ] n costura; ~ **machine** n máquina de coser.

sewn [səun] pp of **sew**.

sex [sɛks] n sexo; to have ~ **with sb** tener sexo con alguien; ~ **act** n acto sexual.

sextet [sɛks'tɛt] n sexteto.

sexual ['sɛksjuəl] a sexual.

sexy ['sɛksɪ] a sexy.

shabby ['ʃæbɪ] a (person) desharrapado; (clothes) raído, gastado.

shack [ʃæk] n choza, chabola.

shackles ['ʃæklz] npl grillos mpl, grilletes mpl.

shade [ʃeɪd] n sombra; (for lamp) pantalla; (for eyes) visera; (of colour) matiz m, tonalidad f // vt dar sombra a; **in the** ~ en la sombra.

shadow ['ʃædəu] n sombra // vt (follow) seguir y vigilar; ~ **cabinet** n (POL) gabinete paralelo formado por el partido de oposición; ~**y** a oscuro; (dim) indistinto.

shady ['ʃeɪdɪ] a sombreado; (fig: dishonest) sospechoso; (: deal) turbio.

shaft [ʃɑːft] n (of arrow, spear) astil m; (AUT, TECH) eje m, árbol m; (of mine) pozo; (of lift) hueco, caja; (of light) rayo.

shaggy ['ʃægɪ] a peludo.

shake [ʃeɪk], pt **shook**, pp **shaken** vt sacudir; (building) hacer temblar; (perturb) inquietar, perturbar; (weaken) debilitar; (surprise) sorprender, pasmar // vi estremecerse; (tremble) temblar // n (movement) sacudida; to ~ **hands with sb** estrechar la mano con uno; to ~ **off** vt sacudirse; (fig) deshacerse de; to ~ **up** vt agitar; **shaky** a (hand, voice) trémulo; (building) inestable.

shall [ʃæl] auxiliary vb: **I** ~ **go** iré.

shallot [ʃə'lɔt] n chalote m.

shallow ['ʃæləu] a poco profundo; (fig) superficial.

sham [ʃæm] n fraude m, engaño // a falso, fingido // vt fingir, simular.

shambles ['ʃæmblz] n confusión f.

shame [ʃeɪm] n vergüenza; (pity) lástima // vt avergonzar; **it is a** ~ **that/to do es** una lástima que/hacer; **what a** ~**!** ¡qué lástima!; ~**faced** a avergonzado; ~**ful** a vergonzoso; ~**less** a descarado; (immodest) impúdico.

shampoo [ʃæm'puː] n champú m // vt lavar el pelo (con champú).

shamrock ['ʃæmrɔk] n trébol m.

shandy ['ʃændɪ] n mezcla de cerveza con gaseosa.

shan't [ʃɑːnt] = **shall not**.

shanty town ['ʃæntɪ-] n barrio de chabolas.

shape [ʃeɪp] n forma // vt formar, dar forma a; (sb's ideas) formar; (sb's life) determinar // vi (also: ~ **up**) (events) desarrollarse; (person) formarse; to **take** ~ tomar forma; **-shaped** suff: **heart-shaped** en forma de corazón; ~**less** a informe, sin forma definida; ~**ly** a bien formado o proporcionado.

share [ʃɛəʳ] n (part) parte f, porción f; (contribution) cuota; (COMM) acción f // vt dividir; (have in common) compartir; to ~ **out** (among or between) repartir (entre); ~**holder** n accionista m/f.

shark [ʃɑːk] n tiburón m.

sharp [ʃɑːp] a (razor, knife) afilado; (point) puntiagudo; (outline) definido; (pain) intenso; (MUS) desafinado; (contrast) marcado; (voice) agudo; (person: quick-witted) astuto; (dishonest) poco escrupuloso // n (MUS) sostenido // ad: **at 2 o'clock** ~ a las 2 en punto; ~**en** vt afilar; (pencil) sacar punta a; (fig) agudizar; ~**ener** n (also: **pencil** ~**ener**) afilador m; ~**-eyed** a de vista aguda; ~**-witted** a listo, perspicaz.

shatter ['ʃætəʳ] vt hacer añicos o pedazos; (fig: ruin) destruir, acabar con // vi hacerse añicos.

shave [ʃeɪv] vt afeitar, rasurar // vi afeitarse // n: to have a ~ afeitarse; **shaver** n (also: **electric shaver**) máquina de afeitar (eléctrica).

shaving ['ʃeɪvɪŋ] n (action) el afeitarse, rasurado; ~**s** npl (of wood etc) virutas fpl; ~ **brush** n brocha (de afeitar); ~ **cream** n crema (de afeitar).

shawl [ʃɔːl] n chal m.

she [ʃiː] pron ella; ~**-cat** n gata; NB: for ships, countries follow the gender of your translation.

sheaf [ʃiːf], pl **sheaves** n (of corn) gavilla; (of arrows) haz m; (of papers) fajo.

shear [ʃɪəʳ], pt **sheared**, pp **sheared** or **shorn** vt (sheep) esquilar, trasquilar; to ~ **off** vt cercenar; ~**s** npl (for hedge) tijeras fpl de jardín.

sheath [ʃiːθ] n vaina; (contraceptive) preservativo.

sheaves [ʃiːvz] pl of **sheaf**.

shed [ʃed] n cobertizo // vt, pt, pp shed (gen) desprenderse de; (skin) mudar; (tears) derramar.

she'd [ʃiːd] = **she had; she would**.

sheep [ʃiːp] n, pl inv oveja; ~dog n perro pastor; ~ish a tímido, vergonzoso; ~skin n piel f de carnero.

sheer [ʃɪə*] a (utter) puro, completo; (steep) escarpado; (almost transparent) diáfano // ad verticalmente.

sheet [ʃiːt] n (on bed) sábana; (of paper) hoja; (of glass, metal) lámina.

sheik(h) [ʃeɪk] n jeque m.

shelf [ʃelf], pl **shelves** n estante m.

shell [ʃel] n (on beach) concha; (of egg, nut etc) cáscara; (explosive) proyectil m, obús m; (of building) armazón m // vt (peas) desenvainar; (MIL) bombardear.

she'll [ʃiːl] = **she will; she shall**.

shellfish [ʃelfɪʃ] n, pl inv crustáceo; (pl: as food) mariscos mpl.

shelter [ʃeltə*] n abrigo, refugio // vt (aid) amparar, proteger; (give lodging to) abrigar; (hide) esconder // vi abrigarse, refugiarse; ~ed a (life) protegido; (spot) abrigado.

shelve [ʃelv] vt (fig) aplazar; ~s pl of shelf.

shepherd [ʃepəd] n pastor m // vt (guide) guiar, conducir; ~ess n pastora f; ~'s pie n pastel m de carne y patatas.

sheriff [ʃerɪf] n sheriff m.

sherry [ʃerɪ] n jerez m.

she's [ʃiːz] = **she is; she has**.

shield [ʃiːld] n escudo; (TECH) blindaje m // vt: to ~ (from) proteger (contra).

shift [ʃɪft] n (change) cambio; (of place) traslado; (of workers) turno // vt trasladar; (remove) quitar // vi moverse; (change place) cambiar de sitio; ~ work n trabajo por turno; ~y a tramposo; (eyes) furtivo.

shilling [ʃɪlɪŋ] n chelín m.

shimmer [ʃɪmə*] n reflejo trémulo // vi relucir.

shin [ʃɪn] n espinilla.

shine [ʃaɪn] n brillo, lustre m // (vb: pt, pp shone) vi brillar, relucir // vt (shoes) lustrar, sacar brillo a; to ~ a torch on sth dirigir una linterna hacia algo.

shingle [ʃɪŋgl] n (on beach) guijarras fpl; ~s n (MED) herpes mpl or fpl.

shiny [ʃaɪnɪ] a brillante, lustroso.

ship [ʃɪp] n buque m, barco // vt (goods) embarcar; (oars) desarmar; (send) transportar o enviar (por vía marítima); ~building n construcción f de barcos; ~ment n (act) embarque m/f; (goods) envío; ~per n exportador/a m/f; ~ping n (act) embarque m; (traffic) buques mpl; ~shape a en regla; ~wreck n naufragio; ~yard n astillero.

shire [ʃaɪə*] n condado.

shirk [ʃəːk] vt eludir, esquivar; (obligations) faltar a.

shirt [ʃəːt] n camisa; in ~ sleeves en mangas de camisa.

shiver [ʃɪvə*] n temblor m, estremecimiento // vi temblar, estremecerse.

shoal [ʃəul] n (of fish) banco.

shock [ʃɔk] n (impact) choque m; (ELEC) descarga (eléctrica); (emotional) conmoción f; (start) sobresalto, susto; (MED) postración f nerviosa // vt dar un susto a; (offend) escandalizar; ~ absorber n amortiguador m; ~ing a (awful) espantoso; (improper) escandaloso; ~proof a a prueba de choques.

shod [ʃɔd] pt, pp of shoe // a calzado.

shoddy [ʃɔdɪ] a de pacotilla, de bajísima calidad.

shoe [ʃuː] n zapato; (for horse) herradura; (brake ~) zapata // vt, pt, pp shod (horse) herrar; ~brush n cepillo para zapatos; ~horn n calzador m; ~lace n cordón m; ~maker n zapatero; ~ polish n betún m; ~shop n zapatería.

shone [ʃɔn] pt, pp of shine.

shook [ʃuk] pt of shake.

shoot [ʃuːt] n (on branch, seedling) retoño, vástago // (vb: pt, pp shot) vt disparar; (kill) matar (con arma de fuego); (wound) herir (con arma de fuego); (execute) fusilar; (film) rodar, filmar // vi (with gun, bow): to ~ (at) tirar (a); (FOOTBALL) chutar; to ~ down vt (plane) derribar; to ~ in/out vi entrar corriendo/salir disparado; to ~ up vi (fig) subir (vertiginosamente); ~ing n (shots) tiros mpl; (HUNTING) caza con escopeta; ~ing star n estrella fugaz.

shop [ʃɔp] n tienda; (workshop) taller m // vi (also: go ~ping) ir de compras; ~ assistant n dependiente/a m/f; ~ floor a (fig) de la base; ~keeper n tendero/a; ~lifter n mechero/a; ~lifting n mechería; ~per n comprador/a m/f; ~ping n (goods) compras fpl; ~ping bag n bolsa (de compras); ~ping centre, ~ping center (US) n zona comercial o de tiendas; ~-soiled a usado; ~ steward n (INDUSTRY) enlace m/f; ~ window n escaparate m.

shore [ʃɔː*] n (of sea, lake) orilla // vt: to ~ (up) reforzar.

shorn [ʃɔːn] pp of shear.

short [ʃɔːt] a (not long) corto; (in time) breve, de corta duración; (person) bajo; (curt) brusco, seco; (insufficient) insuficiente // vi (ELEC) ponerse en cortocircuito // n (also: ~ film) cortometraje m; (a pair of) ~s (unos) pantalones mpl cortos; to be ~ of sth estar falto de algo; in ~ en pocas palabras; it is ~ for es la forma abreviada de; to cut ~ (speech, visit) interrumpir, terminar inesperadamente; to fall ~ of resultar (ser) insuficiente; to stop ~ parar en seco; to stop ~ of detenerse antes de; ~age n escasez f, falta; ~bread n torta seca y quebradiza; ~-circuit n cortocircuito // vt poner en cortocircuito // vi ponerse en cortocircuito; **~coming** n defecto, deficiencia; **~(crust) pastry** n pasta quebradiza; **~cut** n atajo; **~en** vt acortar; (visit) interrumpir; **~hand** n taquigrafía; **~hand typist** n taquimecanógrafo/a; **~ list** n (for job) lista de candidatos escogidos; **~lived** a efímero; **~ly** ad en breve, dentro de poco; **~ ness** n (of distance) cortedad f; (of time) brevedad f; (manner) brusquedad f; **~-sighted** a corto de vista, miope; (fig) imprudente; **~ story** n cuento; **~-tempered** a enojadizo; **~-term** a (effect) a corto plazo; **~wave** n (RADIO) onda corta.

shot [ʃɔt] pt, pp of **shoot** // n (sound) tiro, disparo; (person) tirador/a m/f; (try) tentativa; (injection) inyección f; (PHOT) toma, fotografía; **~gun** n escopeta.

should [ʃud] auxiliary vb: I **~** go now debo irme ahora; he **~** be there now debe de haber llegado (ya); I **~** go if I were you yo en tu lugar me iría; I **~** like to me gustaría.

shoulder ['ʃəuldəʳ] n hombro; (of road): **hard ~** andén m // vt (fig) cargar con; **~ blade** n omóplato.

shouldn't ['ʃudnt] = **should not.**

shout [ʃaut] n grito // vt gritar // vi gritar, dar voces; **to ~ down** vt hundir a gritos; **~ing** n gritería.

shove [ʃʌv] n empujón m // vt empujar; (col: put): **to ~ sth in** meter algo; **to ~ off** vi (NAUT) alejarse del muelle; (fig: col) largarse.

shovel ['ʃʌvl] n pala; (mechanical) excavadora // vt mover con pala.

show [ʃəu] n (of emotion) demostración f; (semblance) apariencia; (exhibition) exposición f; (THEATRE) función f, espectáculo f; (vb: pt showed, pp shown) vt mostrar, enseñar; (courage etc) mostrar, manifestar; (exhibit) exponer; (film) proyectar // vi mostrarse; (appear) aparecer; **to ~ sb in** hacer pasar a uno; **to ~ off** vi (pej) presumir // vt (display) lucir; (pej) hacer gala de; **to ~ sb out** acompañar a uno a la puerta; **to ~ up** vi (stand out) destacar; (col: turn up) presentarse // vt descubrir; (unmask) desenmascarar; **~ business** n el mundo del espectáculo; **~down** n crisis f, momento decisivo.

shower ['ʃauəʳ] n (rain) chaparrón m, chubasco; (of stones etc) lluvia; (also: **~bath**) ducha // vi llover // vt: **to ~ sb with sth** colmar a uno de algo; **~proof** a impermeable; **~y** a (weather) lluvioso.

showing ['ʃəuɪŋ] n (of film) proyección f.

show jumping ['ʃəudʒʌmpɪŋ] n hipismo.

shown [ʃəun] pp of **show.**

show: ~-off n (col: person) presumido; **~piece** n (of exhibition etc) obra más importante o central; **~room** n sala de muestras.

shrank [ʃræŋk] pt of **shrink.**

shrapnel ['ʃræpnl] n metralla.

shred [ʃrɛd] n (gen pl) triza, jirón m // vt hacer trizas; (CULIN) desmenuzar.

shrewd [ʃruːd] a astuto; **~ness** n astucia.

shriek [ʃriːk] n chillido // vt, vi chillar.

shrill [ʃrɪl] a agudo, estridente.

shrimp [ʃrɪmp] n camarón m.

shrine [ʃraɪn] n santuario, sepulcro.

shrink [ʃrɪŋk], pt **shrank**, pp **shrunk** vi encogerse; (be reduced) reducirse // vt encoger; **to ~ from doing sth** no atreverse a hacer algo; **~age** n encogimiento; reducción f.

shrivel ['ʃrɪvl] (also: **~ up**) vt (dry) secar; (crease) arrugar // vi secarse; arrugarse.

shroud [ʃraud] n sudario // vt: **~ed in mystery** envuelto en el misterio.

Shrove Tuesday ['ʃrəuv'tjuːzdi] n martes m de carnaval.

shrub [ʃrʌb] n arbusto; **~bery** n arbustos mpl.

shrug [ʃrʌg] n encogimiento de hombros // vt, vi: **to ~ (one's shoulders)** encogerse de hombros; **to ~ off** vt negar importancia a.

shrunk [ʃrʌŋk] pp of **shrink.**

shudder ['ʃʌdəʳ] n estremecimiento, escalofrío // vi estremecerse.

shuffle ['ʃʌfl] vt (cards) barajar; **to ~ (one's feet)** arrastrar los pies.

shun [ʃʌn] vt rehuir, esquivar.

shunt [ʃʌnt] vt (RAIL) maniobrar // vi: **to ~ to and fro** mandar de aquí para allá.

shut [ʃʌt], pt, pp **shut** vt cerrar // vi cerrarse; **to ~ down** vt, vi cerrarse, parar; **to ~ off** vt (supply etc) interrumpir, cortar; **to ~ up** vi (col: keep quiet) callarse // vt (close) cerrar; (silence) callar; **~ter** n contraventana; (PHOT) obturador m.

shuttle ['ʃʌtl] n lanzadera; (also: **~ service**) servicio de transporte entre dos estaciones.

shuttlecock ['ʃʌtlkɔk] n volante m.

shy [ʃaɪ] a tímido; (reserved) reservado, cohibido; (unsociable) huraño; **~ness** n timidez f; reserva; lo huraño.

Siamese [saɪə'miːz] a: **~ cat** gato siamés.

Sicily ['sɪsɪlɪ] n Sicilia.

sick [sɪk] a (ill) enfermo; (nauseated) mareado; (humour) negro; (vomiting): **to be ~** vomitar; **to feel ~** estar mareado; **to be ~ of** (fig) estar harto de; **~ bay** n enfermería; **~en** vt dar asco a // vi enfermar; **~ening** a (fig) asqueroso.

sickle ['sɪkl] n hoz f.

sick: ~ leave n baja por enfermedad; **~ly** a enfermizo; (causing nausea) nauseabundo; **~ness** n enfermedad f, mal m; (vomiting) náuseas fpl; **~ pay** n subsidio de enfermedad.

side [saɪd] n (gen) lado; (of body) costado; (of lake) orilla; (aspect) aspecto; (team) equipo; (of hill) ladera // a (door, entrance) accesorio // vi: **to ~ with sb** tomar el partido de uno; **by the ~ of** al lado de; **~ by ~** juntos(as), lado a lado; **from all ~s** de todos lados; **to take ~s (with)**

tomar partido (con); **~board** n aparador m; **~boards**, **~burns** npl patillas fpl; **~ effect** n efecto secundario; **~light** n (AUT) luz f lateral; **~line** n (SPORT) línea lateral; (fig) empleo suplementario; **~long** a de soslayo; **~ road** n calle f lateral; **~saddle** ad a mujeriegas, a la inglesa; **~ show** n (stall) caseta; (fig) atracción f secundaria; **~step** vt (fig) esquivar; **~track** vt (fig) desviar (de su propósito); **~walk** n (US) acera; **~ways** ad de lado.

siding ['saɪdɪŋ] n (RAIL) apartadero, vía muerta.

sidle ['saɪdl] vi: to ~ up (to) acercarse furtivamente (a).

siege [siːdʒ] n cerco, sitio.

sieve [sɪv] n coladera // vt cribar.

sift [sɪft] vt cribar; (fig: information) escudriñar.

sigh [saɪ] n suspiro // vi suspirar.

sight [saɪt] n (faculty) vista, visión f; (spectacle) espectáculo; (on gun) mira, alza // vt ver, divisar; **in ~** a la vista; **out of ~** fuera de (la) vista; **~seeing** n excursionismo, turismo; **to go ~seeing** visitar monumentos.

sign [saɪn] n (with hand) señal f, seña; (indication) indicio; (trace) huella, rastro; (notice) letrero; (written) signo // vt firmar; **to ~ sth over to sb** firmar el traspaso de algo a uno; **to ~ up** vi (MIL) alistarse // vt (contract) contratar.

signal ['sɪgnl] n señal f // vi (AUT) señalizar // vt (person) hacer señas a uno; (message) transmitir.

signature ['sɪgnətʃə*] n firma.

signet ring ['sɪgnətrɪŋ] n anillo de sello.

significance [sɪg'nɪfɪkəns] n significado; (importance) trascendencia; **significant** [-ənt] a significativo; trascendente.

signify ['sɪgnɪfaɪ] vt significar.

sign: **~ language** n la mímica, lenguaje m por señas o de señas; **~post** n indicador m.

silence ['saɪlns] n silencio // vt hacer callar; (guns) reducir al silencio; **silencer** n (on gun, AUT) silenciador m.

silent ['saɪlnt] a (gen) silencioso; (not speaking) callado; (film) mudo; **to remain ~** guardar silencio.

silhouette [sɪluː'et] n silueta; **~d against** destacado sobre o contra.

silicon chip ['sɪlɪkən'tʃɪp] n plata de silicio, astilla de silicona.

silk [sɪlk] n seda // a de seda; **~y** a sedoso.

silly ['sɪlɪ] a (person) tonto; (idea) absurdo.

silt [sɪlt] n sedimento.

silver ['sɪlvə*] n plata; (money) moneda suelta // a de plata, plateado; **~ paper** n papel m de plata; **~plated** a plateado; **~smith** n platero; **~y** a plateado.

similar ['sɪmɪlə*] a: **~ to** parecido o semejante a; **~ity** [-'lærɪtɪ] n parecido, semejanza; **~ly** ad del mismo modo.

simmer ['sɪmə*] vi hervir a fuego lento.

simpering ['sɪmpərɪŋ] a afectado; (foolish) bobo.

simple ['sɪmpl] a (easy) sencillo; (foolish, COMM) simple; **~ton** n inocentón/ona m/f; **simplicity** [-'plɪsɪtɪ] n sencillez f; (foolishness) ingenuidad f; **simplify** ['sɪmplɪfaɪ] vt simplificar.

simulate ['sɪmjuleɪt] vt simular; **simulation** [-'leɪʃən] n simulación f.

simultaneous [sɪməl'teɪnɪəs] a simultáneo; **~ly** ad simultáneamente.

sin [sɪn] n pecado // vi pecar.

since [sɪns] ad desde entonces, después // prep desde // conj (time) desde que; (because) ya que, puesto que; **~ then** desde entonces.

sincere [sɪn'sɪə*] a sincero; **yours ~ly le saluda** (afectuosamente); **sincerity** [-'serɪtɪ] n sinceridad f.

sinful ['sɪnful] a (thought) pecaminoso; (person) pecador(a).

sing [sɪŋ], pt **sang**, pp **sung** vt cantar // vi (gen) cantar; (bird) trinar; (ears) zumbar.

singe [sɪndʒ] vt chamuscar.

singer ['sɪŋə*] n cantante m/f.

singing ['sɪŋɪŋ] n (gen) canto; (songs) canciones fpl; (in the ears) zumbido.

single ['sɪŋgl] a único, solo; (unmarried) soltero; (not double) simple, sencillo; (bed, room) individual // n (also: ~ ticket) billete m sencillo; (record) single m; **~s** npl (TENNIS) individual m; **to ~ out** vt (choose) escoger; (point out) singularizar; **~ bed** n cama individual; **in ~ file** en fila de uno; **~-handed** ad sin ayuda; **~-minded** a resuelto, firme; **~ room** n cuarto individual.

singular ['sɪŋgjulə*] a (odd) raro, extraño; (LING) singular // n (LING) singular m.

sinister ['sɪnɪstə*] a siniestro.

sink [sɪŋk] n fregadero // (vb: pt **sank**, pp **sunk**) vt (ship) hundir, echar a pique; (foundations) excavar; (piles etc): **to ~ sth** fijar algo bajo tierra // vi (gen) hundirse; **to ~ in** vi (fig) penetrar, calar; **a ~ing feeling** un sentimiento de que toda se acaba.

sinner ['sɪnə*] n pecador/a m/f.

sinus ['saɪnəs] n (ANAT) seno.

sip [sɪp] n sorbo // vt sorber, beber a sorbitos.

siphon ['saɪfən] n sifón m; **to ~ off** vt quitar poco a poco.

sir [sə*] n señor m; **S~ John Smith** el Señor John Smith; **yes ~** sí, señor.

siren ['saɪərn] n sirena.

sirloin ['səːlɔɪn] n solomillo.

sister ['sɪstə*] n hermana; (nurse) enfermera jefe; **~-in-law** n cuñada.

sit [sɪt], pt, pp **sat** vi sentarse; (be sitting) estar sentado; (assembly) reunirse // vt (exam) presentarse a; **to ~ down** vi sentarse; **to ~ in on** asistir a; **to ~ up** vi incorporarse; (not go to bed) velar.

site [saɪt] n sitio; (also: building ~) solar m // vt situar.

sit-in ['sɪtɪn] n (demonstration)

manifestación f de brazos caídos.

sitting ['sɪtɪŋ] n (of assembly etc) sesión f; (in canteen) turno; ~ **room** n sala de estar.

situated ['sɪtjueɪtɪd] a situado.

situation [sɪtju'eɪʃən] n situación f.

six [sɪks] num seis; ~**teen** num diez y seis, dieciséis; ~**th** a sexto; ~**ty** num sesenta.

size [saɪz] n (gen) tamaño; (extent) extensión f; (of clothing) talla; (of shoes) número; (glue) cola, apresto; **to** ~ **up** vt formarse una idea de; ~**able** a importante, considerable.

sizzle ['sɪzl] vi crepitar.

skate [skeɪt] n patín m; (fish: pl inv) raya // vi patinar; ~**board** n skateboard m; **skater** n patinador/a m/f; **skating** n patinaje m; **skating rink** n pista de patinaje.

skeleton ['skɛlɪtn] n esqueleto; (TECH) armazón m; (outline) esquema m; ~ **key** n llave f maestra; ~ **staff** n personal m reducido.

sketch [skɛtʃ] n (drawing) dibujo; (outline) esbozo, bosquejo; (THEATRE) pieza corta // vt dibujar; esbozar; ~ **book** n libro de dibujos; ~ **pad** n bloc m de dibujo; ~**y** a incompleto.

skewer ['skju:ə*] n broqueta.

ski [ski:] n esquí m // vi esquiar; ~ **boot** n bota de esquí.

skid [skɪd] n patinazo // vi patinar; ~ **mark** n huella de patinazo.

ski: ~**er** n esquiador/a m/f; ~**ing** n esquí m; ~ **jump** n pista para salto de esquí.

skilful ['skɪlful] a diestro, experto.

ski lift n telesilla.

skill [skɪl] n destreza, pericia; ~**ed** a hábil, diestro; (worker) cualificado.

skim [skɪm] vt (milk) desnatar; (glide over) rozar, rasar // vi: **to** ~ **through** (book) hojear.

skimp [skɪmp] vt (work) chapucear; (cloth etc) escatimar; ~**y** a (meagre) escaso; (skirt) muy corto.

skin [skɪn] n (gen) piel f; (complexion) cutis m // vt (fruit etc) pelar; (animal) despellejar; ~-**deep** a superficial; ~-**diving** n natación f submarina; ~**ny** a flaco, magro; ~**tight** a (dress etc) muy ajustado.

skip [skɪp] n brinco, salto; (container) cuba // vi brincar; (with rope) saltar a la comba // vt (pass over) omitir, saltar.

ski pants npl pantalones mpl de esquí.

skipper ['skɪpə*] n (NAUT, SPORT) capitán m.

skipping rope ['skɪpɪŋ-] n cuerda (de saltar).

skirmish ['skɔ:mɪʃ] n escaramuza.

skirt [skɔ:t] n falda // vt (surround) ceñir, rodear; (go round) ladear; ~**ing board** n rodapié m.

skit [skɪt] n sátira, parodia.

skittle ['skɪtl] n bolo; ~**s** n (game) boliche m.

skive [skaɪv] vi (Brit: col) gandulear.

skull [skʌl] n calavera; (ANAT) cráneo.

skunk [skʌŋk] n mofeta; (fig: person) canalla m/f.

sky [skaɪ] n cielo; ~-**blue** a azul celeste; ~**light** n tragaluz m, claraboya; ~**scraper** n rascacielos m inv.

slab [slæb] n (stone) bloque m; (flat) losa; (of cake) porción f gruesa.

slack [slæk] a (loose) flojo; (slow) de poca actividad; (careless) descuidado; ~**s** npl pantalones mpl; ~**en** (also: ~**en off**) vi aflojarse // vt aflojar; (speed) disminuir.

slag [slæg] n escoria, escombros mpl; ~ **heap** n escorial m, escombrera.

slalom ['slɑ:ləm] n slalom m.

slam [slæm] vt (door) cerrar de golpe; (throw) arrojar (violentamente); (criticize) hablar mal de // vi cerrarse de golpe.

slander ['slɑ:ndə*] n calumnia, difamación f // vt calumniar, difamar; ~**ous** a calumnioso, difamatorio.

slang [slæŋ] n argot m; (jargon) jerga; (private language) caló.

slant [slɑ:nt] n sesgo, inclinación f; (fig) punto de vista; ~**ed**, ~**ing** a inclinado.

slap [slæp] n palmada; (in face) bofetada; (fig) palmetazo // vt dar una palmada/bofetada a // ad (directly) exactamente, directamente; ~**dash** a descuidado; ~**stick** n (comedy) payasadas fpl.

slash [slæʃ] vt acuchillar; (fig: prices) quemar.

slate [sleɪt] n pizarra // vt (fig: criticize) criticar duramente.

slaughter ['slɔ:tə*] n (of animals) matanza; (of people) carnicería // vt matar; ~**house** n matadero.

Slav [slɑ:v] a eslavo.

slave [sleɪv] n esclavo // vi (also: ~ **away**) sudar tinta; ~**ry** n esclavitud f; **slavish** a servil.

Slavonic [slə'vɔnɪk] a eslavo.

slay [sleɪ] vt matar.

sleazy ['sli:zɪ] a (fig: place) de mala fama.

sledge [slɛdʒ] n trineo; ~**hammer** n mazo.

sleek [sli:k] a (gen) lustroso; (neat) pulcro.

sleep [sli:p] n sueño // vi, pt, pp **slept** dormir; **to go to** ~ dormirse; **to** ~ **in** vi (oversleep) dormir tarde; ~ **in** (person) durmiente m/f; (RAIL: on track) traviesa; (: train) coche-cama m; ~**ily** ad soñolientamente; ~**ing bag** n saco de dormir; ~**ing car** n coche-cama m; ~**ing pill** n somnífero; ~**lessness** n insomnio; ~**walker** n sonámbulo/a; ~**y** a soñoliento.

sleet [sli:t] n nevisca.

sleeve [sli:v] n manga; (TECH) manguito; ~**less** a (garment) sin mangas.

sleigh [sleɪ] n trineo.

sleight [slaɪt] n: ~ **of hand** escamoteo.

slender ['slɛndə*] a delgado; (means) escaso.

slept [slɛpt] pt, pp of **sleep**.

slice [slaɪs] n (of meat) tajada; (of bread)

rebanada; (*of lemon*) rodaja; (*utensil*) pala // *vt* cortar, tajar; rebanar.

slick [slɪk] *a* (*skilful*) hábil, diestro; (*quick*) rápido; (*astute*) astuto // *n* (*also:* **oil ~**) masa flotante.

slid [slɪd] *pt, pp of* **slide.**

slide [slaɪd] *n* (*in playground*) tobogán *m*; (*PHOT*) diapositiva; (*also:* **hair ~**) pasador *m* // (*vb: pt, pp* **slid**) *vt* correr, deslizar // *vi* (*slip*) resbalarse; (*glide*) deslizarse; **sliding** *a* (*door*) corredizo.

slight [slaɪt] *a* (*slim*) delgado; (*frail*) delicado; (*pain etc*) leve; (*trifling*) sin importancia; (*small*) pequeño // *n* desaire *m* // *vt* (*offend*) ofender, desairar; **not in the ~est** (ni) en lo más mínimo, en absoluto; **~ly** *ad* ligeramente, un poco.

slim [slɪm] *a* delgado, esbelto // *vi* adelgazar.

slime [slaɪm] *n* limo, cieno; **slimy** *a* limoso.

slimming ['slɪmɪŋ] *n* adelgazamiento; *a* **~ diet** un régimen.

sling [slɪŋ] *n* (*MED*) cabestrillo; (*weapon*) honda // *vt, pt, pp* **slung** tirar, arrojar.

slip [slɪp] *n* (*slide*) resbalón *m*; (*fall*) tropezón *m*; (*mistake*) descuido; (*underskirt*) combinación *f*; (*of paper*) trozo // *vt* (*slide*) deslizar // *vi* (*slide*) deslizarse; (*stumble*) resbalar(se); (*decline*) decaer; **to give sb the ~** eludir *o* escaparse de uno; **to ~ away** *vi* escabullirse; **to ~ in** *vt* meter // *vi* meterse; **to ~ out** *vi* (*go out*) salir (un momento).

slipper ['slɪpə°] *n* zapatilla.

slippery ['slɪpərɪ] *a* resbaladizo.

slip: ~ road *n* carretera de acceso; **~shod** *a* descuidado; **~-up** *n* (*error*) equivocación *f*; (*by neglect*) descuido; **~way** *n* grada, gradas *fpl*.

slit [slɪt] *n* raja; (*cut*) corte *m* // *vt, pt, pp* **slit** rajar, cortar.

slither ['slɪðə°] *vi* deslizarse.

slob [slɔb] *n* (*col*) patán *m*.

slog [slɔg] *vi* sudar tinta; **it was a ~** costó trabajo (hacerlo).

slogan ['sləʊgən] *n* slogan *m*, lema *m*.

slop [slɔp] *vi* (*also:* **~ over**) derramarse, desbordarse // *vt* derramar, verter.

slope [sləʊp] *n* (*gen*) cuesta, pendiente *m*; (*down*) declive *m*; (*side of mountain*) falda, vertiente *m* // *vi*: **to ~ down** estar en declive; **to ~ up** inclinarse; **sloping** *a* en pendiente; en declive.

sloppy ['slɔpɪ] *a* (*work*) descuidado; (*appearance*) desaliñado.

slot [slɔt] *n* ranura // *vt*: **to ~ into** encajar en; **~ machine** *n* máquina tragaperras.

slouch [slaʊtʃ] *vi*: **to ~ about** (*laze*) gandulear.

slovenly ['slʌvənlɪ] *a* (*dirty*) desaliñado, desaseado; (*careless*) descuidado.

slow [sləʊ] *a* lento; (*watch*): **to be ~** atrasarse // *ad* lentamente, despacio // *vt, vi* (*also:* **~ down, ~ up**) retardar; **'~'** (*road sign*) 'disminuir velocidad'; **~ly** *ad*

lentamente, despacio; **in ~ motion** a cámara lenta; **~ness** *n* lentitud *f*.

sludge [slʌdʒ] *n* lodo, fango.

slug [slʌg] *n* babosa; (*bullet*) posta; **~gish** *a* (*slow*) lento; (*lazy*) perezoso.

sluice [sluːs] *n* (*gate*) esclusa; (*channel*) canal *m*.

slum [slʌm] *n* (*area*) tugurios *mpl*; (*house*) casucha.

slumber ['slʌmbə°] *n* sueño.

slump [slʌmp] *n* (*economic*) depresión *f* // *vi* hundirse.

slung [slʌŋ] *pt, pp of* **sling.**

slur [slɜ°] *n* calumnia // *vt* calumniar, difamar; (*word*) pronunciar indistintamente.

slush [slʌʃ] *n* nieve *f* a medio derretir; **~y** *a* (*snow*) a medio derretir; (*street*) fangoso; (*fig*) sentimental, sensiblero.

slut [slʌt] *n* marrana.

sly [slaɪ] *a* (*clever*) astuto; (*nasty*) malicioso.

smack [smæk] *n* (*slap*) manotada; (*blow*) golpe *m* // *vt* dar una manotada a, golpear con la mano // *vi*: **to ~ of** saber a, oler a.

small [smɔːl] *a* pequeño; **~holder** *n* granjero, parcelero; **~ish** *a* más bien pequeño; **~pox** *n* viruela; **~ talk** *n* cháchara.

smart [smɑːt] *a* elegante; (*clever*) listo, inteligente; (*quick*) rápido, vivo // *vi* escocer, picar; **to ~en up** *vi* arreglarse // *vt* arreglar.

smash [smæʃ] *n* (*also:* **~-up**) choque *m* // *vt* (*break*) hacer pedazos; (*car etc*) estrellar; (*SPORT: record*) romper // *vi* (*collide*) chocar; (*against wall etc*) estrellarse; **~ing** *a* (*col*) cojonudo.

smattering ['smætərɪŋ] *n*: **a ~ of** ligeros conocimientos *mpl* de.

smear [smɪə°] *n* mancha; (*MED*) citología // *vt* untar; (*fig*) calumniar, difamar.

smell [smɛl] *n* olor *m*; (*sense*) olfato // (*vb: pt, pp* **smelt** *or* **smelled**) *vt, vi* oler; **it ~s good/of garlic** huele bien/a ajo; **~y** *a* que huele mal.

smile [smaɪl] *n* sonrisa // *vi* sonreír; **smiling** *a* sonriente.

smirk [smɜːk] *n* sonrisa falsa *o* afectada.

smith [smɪθ] *n* herrero; **~y** ['smɪðɪ] *n* herrería.

smock [smɔk] *n* blusa; (*children's*) delantal *m*.

smoke [sməʊk] *n* humo // *vi* fumar; (*chimney*) echar humo // *vt* (*cigarettes*) fumar; **~d** *a* (*bacon, glass*) ahumado; **smoker** *n* (*person*) fumador/a *m/f*; (*RAIL*) coche *m* fumador; **~ screen** *n* cortina de humo; **smoking** *n*: **'no smoking'** (*sign*) 'prohibido fumar'; **smoky** *a* (*gen*) humeante; (*room*) lleno de humo.

smooth [smuːð] *a* (*gen*) liso; (*sea*) tranquilo; (*flat*) llano; (*flavour, movement*) suave; (*person*) culto, refinado; (: *pej*) meloso // *vt* alisar; (*also:* **~ out**) (*creases, difficulties*) allanar.

smother ['smʌðə°] vt sofocar; (repress) ahogar.

smoulder ['sməuldə°] vi arder sin llama.

smudge [smʌdʒ] n mancha // vt manchar.

smug [smʌg] a presumido.

smuggle ['smʌgl] vt pasar de contrabando; **smuggler** n contrabandista m/f; **smuggling** n contrabando.

smutty ['smʌtı] a (fig) verde, obsceno.

snack [snæk] n bocado; ~ **bar** n cafetería.

snag [snæg] n dificultad f, pero.

snail [sneɪl] n caracol m.

snake [sneɪk] n (gen) serpiente f; (harmless) culebra; (poisonous) víbora.

snap [snæp] n (sound) castañetazo; (of whip) chasquido; (click) golpe m seco; (photograph) foto f // a repentino // vt (fingers etc) castañetear; (whip) chasquear; (break) quebrar; (photograph) tomar una foto de // vi (break) quebrarse; (fig: person) contestar bruscamente; (sound) hacer un ruido seco; to ~ **shut** cerrarse de golpe; to ~ **at** vt fus (subj: dog) intentar morder; to ~ **off** vi (break) romperse (y separarse); to ~ **up** vt aprovecharse de, agarrar; ~**shot** n foto f (instantánea).

snare [snɛə°] n trampa // vt cazar con trampa; (fig) engañar.

snarl [snɑ:l] n gruñido // vi gruñir.

snatch [snætʃ] n (fig) robo; (small amount): ~ **es** de trocitos mpl de // vt (~ away) arrebatar; (grasp) coger, agarrar.

sneak [sni:k] vi: to ~ **in/out** entrar/salir a hurtadillas // n (fam) soplón/ona m/f; ~**y** a furtivo.

sneer [snɪə°] n sonrisa de desprecio // vi sonreír con desprecio; (mock) mofarse.

sneeze [sni:z] n estornudo // vi estornudar.

sniff [snɪf] n (of dog) husmeo; (of person) sorbo (por las narices) // vi sorber (por la nariz) // vt husmear, oler.

snigger ['snɪgə°] n risa disimulada // vi reírse con disimulo.

snip [snɪp] n tijeretazo; (piece) recorte m; (bargain) ganga // vt tijeretear.

sniper ['snaɪpə°] n francotirador/a m/f.

snippet ['snɪpɪt] n retazo.

snivelling ['snɪvlɪŋ] a (whimpering) llorón(ona).

snob [snɔb] n snob m/f; ~**bery** n snobismo; ~**bish** a snob.

snooker ['snu:kə°] n especie de billar.

snoop [snu:p] vi: to ~ **about** fisgonear; ~**er** n fisgón/ona m/f.

snooty ['snu:tı] a presumido.

snooze [snu:z] n siesta // vi echar una siesta.

snore [snɔ:°] vi roncar // n ronquido.

snorkel ['snɔ:kl] n tubo snorkel.

snort [snɔ:t] n bufido // vi bufar.

snout [snaut] n hocico, morro.

snow [snəu] n nieve // vi nevar; ~ **ball** n bola de nieve // vi acumularse; ~**bound** a bloqueado por la nieve; ~**drift** n ventisquero; ~**drop** n campanilla; ~**fall**

n nevada; ~**flake** n copo de nieve; ~**man** n figura de nieve; ~**plough**, ~**plow** (US) n quitanieves m inv; ~**storm** n nevada, nevasca; S~ **White** n Blanca Nieves.

snub [snʌb] vt rechazar con desdén // n desaire m, repulsa.

snuff [snʌf] n rapé m.

snug [snʌg] a (sheltered) abrigado; (fitted) ajustado.

snuggle ['snʌgl] vi: to ~ **up to sb** arrimarse a uno.

so [səu] ad (degree) tan; (manner: thus) así, de este modo // conj así que, por tanto; ~ **that** (purpose) para que, a fin de que; (result) de modo que; ~ **do I** yo también; **if** ~ de ser así, si es así; **I hope** ~ espero que sí; **10 or** ~ 10 más o menos; ~ **far** hasta aquí; ~ **long!** ¡hasta luego!; ~ **many** tantos(as); ~ **much** ad, det tanto; ~ **and** ~ n Fulano.

soak [səuk] vt (drench) empapar; (put in water) remojar // vi remojarse, estar a remojo; to ~ **in** vi penetrar; to ~ **up** vt absorber.

soap [səup] n jabón m; ~**flakes** npl escamas fpl de jabón; ~ **powder** n jabón en polvo; ~ **y** a jabonoso.

soar [sɔ:°] vi (on wings) remontarse; (building etc) elevarse.

sob [sɔb] n sollozo // vi sollozar.

sober ['səubə°] a (serious) serio; (sensible) sensato; (moderate) moderado; (not drunk) sobrio; (colour, style) discreto; to ~ **up** vi pasársele a uno la borrachera.

Soc. abbr of **society**.

so-called ['səu'kɔ:ld] a llamado.

soccer ['sɔkə°] n fútbol m.

sociable ['səuʃəbl] a sociable.

social ['səuʃl] a (gen) social; (sociable) sociable; ~ n velada, fiesta; ~ **climber** n arribista m/f; ~ **club** n club m; ~**ism** n socialismo; ~**ist** a, n socialista m/f; ~**ly** ad socialmente; ~ **science** n ciencias fpl sociales; ~ **security** n seguridad f social; ~ **work** n asistencia social; ~ **worker** n asistente/a m/f social.

society [sə'saɪətɪ] n sociedad f; (club) asociación f; (also: **high** ~) buena sociedad.

sociologist [səusɪ'ɔlədʒɪst] n sociólogo; **sociology** [-dʒɪ] n sociología.

sock [sɔk] n calcetín m.

socket ['sɔkɪt] n (ELEC) enchufe m.

sod [sɔd] n (of earth) césped m; (col!) cabrón/ona m/f.

soda ['səudə] n (CHEM) sosa; (also: ~ **water**) sifón m.

sodden ['sɔdn] a empapado.

sodium ['səudɪəm] n sodio.

sofa ['səufə] n sofá m.

soft [sɔft] a (gen) blando; (gentle, not loud) suave; (kind) tierno, compasivo; (weak) débil; (stupid) tonto; ~ **drink** n bebida no alcohólica; ~**en** ['sɔfn] vt ablandar; suavizar; debilitar // vi ablandarse; suavizarse; debilitarse; ~**-hearted** a

compasivo, bondadoso; ~ly *ad*
suavemente; (*gently*) delicadamente, con
delicadeza; ~ness *n* blandura; suavidad *f*;
(*sweetness*) dulzura; (*tenderness*) ternura.

soggy ['sɔgɪ] *a* empapado.

soil [sɔɪl] *n* (*earth*) tierra, suelo // *vt*
ensuciar; ~ed *a* sucio.

solace ['sɔlɪs] *n* consuelo.

solar ['səuləᵉ] *a* solar.

sold [səuld] *pt, pp of* **sell**; ~ **out** (*COMM*)
agotado.

solder ['səuldəᵉ] *vt* soldar // *n* soldadura.

soldier ['səuldʒəᵉ] *n* (*gen*) soldado; (*army
man*) militar *m*.

sole [səul] *n* (*of foot*) planta; (*of shoe*) suela;
(*fish: pl inv*) lenguado // *a* único; ~ly *ad*
únicamente, sólo, solamente.

solemn ['sɔləm] *a* solemne.

solicitor [sə'lɪsɪtəᵉ] *n* (*for wills etc*)
notario; (*in court*) abogado.

solid ['sɔlɪd] *a* (*not hollow*) sólido; (*gold etc*)
macizo; (*person*) serio // *n* sólido.

solidarity [sɔlɪ'dærɪtɪ] *n* solidaridad *f*.

solidify [sə'lɪdɪfaɪ] *vi* solidificarse.

solitaire [sɔlɪ'tɛəᵉ] *n* (*game, gem*)
solitario.

solitary ['sɔlɪtərɪ] *a* solitario, solo;
(*isolated*) apartado, aislado; (*only*) único;
~ **confinement** *n* incomunicación *f*.

solitude ['sɔlɪtjuːd] *n* soledad *f*.

solo ['səuləu] *n* solo; ~ist *n* solista *m/f*.

soluble ['sɔljubl] *a* soluble.

solution [sə'luːʃən] *n* solución *f*.

solve [sɔlv] *vt* resolver, solucionar.

solvent ['sɔlvənt] *a* (*COMM*) solvente // *n*
(*CHEM*) solvente *m*.

sombre, somber (*US*) ['sɔmbəᵉ] *a*
sombrío.

some [sʌm] *det* (*a few*) algunos(as);
(*certain*) algún/una; (*a certain number or
amount*) *see phrases below*; (*unspecified*)
algo de // *pron* algunos/as; (*a bit*) algo //
ad: ~ **10 people** unas 10 personas; ~
children came vinieron algunos niños;
have ~ tea tome té; **there's ~ milk in
the fridge** hay leche en la refrigeradora;
~ **was left** quedaba algo; **I've got ~**
(*books etc*) tengo algunos; (*milk, money
etc*) tengo algo; ~**body** *pron* alguien; ~
day *ad* algún día; ~**how** *ad* de alguna
manera; (*for some reason*) por una u otra
razón; ~**one** *pron* = ~**body**.

somersault ['sʌməsɔːlt] *n* (*deliberate*)
salto mortal; (*accidental*) vuelco // *vi* dar
un salto mortal; dar vuelcos.

something ['sʌmθɪŋ] *pron* algo.

sometime ['sʌmtaɪm] *ad* (*in future*) algún
día, en algún momento; (*in past*): ~ **last
month** durante el mes pasado.

sometimes ['sʌmtaɪmz] *ad* a veces.

somewhat ['sʌmwɔt] *ad* algo.

somewhere ['sʌmwɛəᵉ] *ad* (*be*) en alguna
parte; (*go*) a alguna parte; ~ **else** (*be*) en
otra parte; (*go*) a otra parte.

son [sʌn] *n* hijo.

song [sɔŋ] *n* canción *f*; ~**writer** *n*

compositor/a *m/f* de canciones.

sonic ['sɔnɪk] *a* (*boom*) sónico.

son-in-law ['sʌnɪnlɔː] *n* yerno.

sonnet ['sɔnɪt] *n* soneto.

soon [suːn] *ad* pronto, dentro de poco;
(*early*) temprano; ~ **afterwards** poco
después; *see also* **as**; ~**er** *ad* (*time*) antes,
más temprano; (*preference*): **I would**
~**er do that** preferiría hacer eso; ~**er
or later** tarde o temprano.

soot [sut] *n* hollín *m*.

soothe [suːð] *vt* tranquilizar; (*pain*) aliviar.

sophisticated [sə'fɪstɪkeɪtɪd] *a* sofisticado.

soporific [sɔpə'rɪfɪk] *a* soporífero.

sopping ['sɔpɪŋ] *a*: ~ **wet** totalmente
empapado.

soppy ['sɔpɪ] *a* (*pej*) bobo, tonto.

soprano [sə'prɑːnəu] *n* soprano *f*.

sorcerer ['sɔːsərəᵉ] *n* hechicero.

sordid ['sɔːdɪd] *a* (*dirty*) sucio, asqueroso;
(*wretched*) miserable.

sore [sɔːᵉ] *a* (*painful*) doloroso, que duele;
(*offended*) resentido // *n* llaga; ~ly *ad*: **I
am** ~ly **tempted** casi estoy por.

sorrow ['sɔrəu] *n* pena, dolor *m*; ~**ful** *a*
afligido, triste.

sorry ['sɔrɪ] *a* (*regretful*) arrepentido;
(*condition, excuse*) lastimoso; ~! **¡lo
siento!, ¡perdón!, ¡perdone!; to feel** ~ **for
sb** sentir lástima por uno; **I feel** ~ **for
him** me da lástima.

sort [sɔːt] *n* clase *f*, género, tipo // *vt* (*also:
~ **out**: *papers*) clasificar; (: *problems*)
arreglar, solucionar; ~**ing office** *n*
oficina de distribución de correos.

SOS *n abbr of* **save our souls**.

so-so ['səusəu] *ad* regular, así-así.

soufflé ['suːfleɪ] *n* suflé *m*.

sought [sɔːt] *pt, pp of* **seek**.

soul [səul] *n* alma *m*; ~**-destroying** *a*
embrutecedor(a); ~**ful** *a* lleno de
sentimiento; ~**less** *a* desalmado.

sound [saund] *a* (*healthy*) sano; (*safe, not
damaged*) firme, sólido; (*secure*) seguro;
(*reliable, not superficial*) formal, digno de
confianza; (*sensible*) sensato, razonable //
ad: ~ **asleep** profundamente dormido //
n (*noise*) sonido, ruido; (*GEO*) estrecho //
vt (*alarm*) sonar; (*also*: ~ **out**: *opinions*)
consultar, sondear // *vi* sonar, resonar;
(*fig: seem*) parecer; **to** ~ **like** sonar a; ~
barrier *n* barrera del sonido; ~ **effects**
npl efectos *mpl* sonoros; ~**ing** *n* (*NAUT etc*)
sondeo; ~**ly** *ad* (*sleep*) profundamente;
(*beat*) completamente; ~**proof** *a* a
prueba de sonidos; ~**track** *n* (*of film*)
banda sonora.

soup [suːp] *n* (*thick*) sopa; (*thin*) caldo; **in
the** ~ (*fig*) en apuros; ~**spoon** *n* cuchara
sopera.

sour ['sauəᵉ] *a* agrio; (*milk*) cortado; (*fig*)
desabrido, acre.

source [sɔːs] *n* fuente *f*.

south [sauθ] *n* sur *m* // *a* del sur // *ad* al
sur, hacia el sur; S~ **Africa** *n* África del
Sur; S~ **African** *a, n* sudafricano/a; S~
America *n* América (del Sur); S~

American a, n sudamericano/a; **~-east** n sudeste m; **~erly** ['sʌðəlɪ] a sur; (from the ~) del sur; **~ern** ['sʌðən] a del sur, meridional; **S~ Pole** n Polo Sur; **~ward(s)** ad hacia el sur; **~-west** n suroeste m.

souvenir [su:və'nɪə*] n recuerdo.

sovereign ['sɔvrɪn] a, n soberano; **~ty** n soberanía.

soviet ['sɔuvɪət] a soviético; **the S~ Union** la Unión Soviética.

sow [sau] n cerda, puerca // vt [səu], pt **sowed**, pp **sown** [səun] (gen) sembrar; (spread) esparcir.

soy [sɔɪ] n: **~ sauce** salsa de soja.

soya bean ['sɔɪbiːn] n semilla de soja.

spa [spɑː] n (spring) baños mpl térmicos; (town) balneario.

space [speɪs] n (gen) espacio; (room) sitio // vt (also: **~ out**) espaciar; **~craft** n nave f espacial; **~man/woman** n astronauta m/f, cosmonauta m/f; **spacing** n espaciamiento.

spacious ['speɪʃəs] a amplio.

spade [speɪd] n (tool) pala, laya; **~s** npl (CARDS: British) picos mpl; (: Spanish) espadas fpl.

spaghetti [spə'gɛtɪ] n espaguetis mpl, fideos mpl.

Spain [speɪn] n España.

span [spæn] n (of bird, plane) envergadura; (of hand) palmo; (of arch) luz f; (in time) lapso // vt extenderse sobre, cruzar; (fig) abarcar.

Spaniard ['spænjəd] n español/a m/f.

spaniel ['spænjəl] n perro de aguas.

Spanish ['spænɪʃ] a español(a) // n (LING) español m, castellano.

spank [spæŋk] vt zurrar.

spanner ['spænə*] n llave f (inglesa).

spar [spɑː*] n palo, verga // vi (BOXING) entrenarse.

spare [spɛə*] a (free) desocupado; (surplus) sobrante, de más; (available) disponible // n (part) pieza de repuesto // vt (do without) pasarse sin; (afford to give) tener de sobra; (refrain from hurting) perdonar, (be grudging with) escatimar; **~ part** n pieza de repuesto; **~ time** n ratos mpl de ocio, tiempo libre.

sparing ['spɛərɪŋ] a: **to be ~ with** ser parco en; **~ly** ad escasamente.

spark [spɑːk] n chispa; (fig) chispazo; **~(ing) plug** n bujía.

sparkle ['spɑːkl] n centelleo, destello // vi centellear; (shine) relucir, brillar; **sparkling** a centelleante; (wine) espumoso.

sparrow ['spærəu] n gorrión m.

sparse [spɑːs] a esparcido, escaso.

spasm ['spæzəm] n (MED) espasmo; (fig) arranque m, acceso; **~odic** [-'mɔdɪk] a espasmódico.

spastic ['spæstɪk] n espástico/a.

spat [spæt] pt, pp of **spit**.

spate [speɪt] n (fig): **~ of** torrente m de; **in ~** (river) crecido.

spatter ['spætə*] vt salpicar, rociar.

spatula ['spætjulə] n espátula.

spawn [spɔːn] vi desovar, frezar // n huevas fpl.

speak [spiːk], pt **spoke**, pp **spoken** vt (language) hablar; (truth) decir // vi hablar; (make a speech) intervenir; **to ~ to sb/of** or **about sth** hablar con uno/de o sobre algo; **~ up!** ¡habla fuerte!; **~er** n (in public) orador a m/f; (also: **loud~er**) altavoz m, parlante m; (POL): **the S~er** el Presidente del Congreso.

spear [spɪə*] n lanza; (for fishing) arpón m // vt alancear; arponear; **~head** n punta de lanza.

special ['spɛʃl] a especial; (edition etc) extraordinario; (delivery) urgente; **take ~ care** ponga un cuidado especial; **~ist** n especialista m/f; **~ity** [spɛʃɪ'ælɪtɪ] n especialidad f; **~ize** vi: **to ~ize (in)** especializarse en; **~ly** ad sobre todo, en particular.

species ['spiːʃiːz] n especie f.

specific [spə'sɪfɪk] a específico; **~ally** ad específicamente.

specification [spɛsɪfɪ'keɪʃən] n especificación f; **~s** npl presupuesto; **specify** ['spɛsɪfaɪ] vt, vi especificar, precisar.

specimen ['spɛsɪmən] n ejemplar m, espécimen m.

speck [spɛk] n grano, mota.

speckled ['spɛkld] a moteado.

specs [spɛks] npl (col) gafas fpl.

spectacle ['spɛktəkl] n espectáculo; **~s** npl gafas fpl, anteojos mpl; **spectacular** [-'tækjulə*] a espectacular; (success) impresionante.

spectator [spɛk'teɪtə*] n espectador a m/f.

spectre, specter (US) ['spɛktə*] n espectro, fantasma m.

spectrum ['spɛktrəm], pl **-tra** [-trə] n espectro.

speculate ['spɛkjuleɪt] vi especular; (try to guess): **to ~ about** especular sobre; **speculation** [-'leɪʃən] n especulación f.

speech [spiːtʃ] n (faculty) habla, palabra; (formal talk) discurso; (talk) palabras fpl; (language) idioma m, lenguaje m; **~less** a mudo, estupefacto.

speed [spiːd] n velocidad f, rapidez f; (haste) prisa; (promptness) prontitud f; **at full** or **top ~** a máxima velocidad; **to ~ up** vi acelerarse // vt acelerar; **~boat** n lancha motora; **~ily** ad rápido, rápidamente; **~ing** n (AUT) exceso de velocidad; **~ limit** n límite m de velocidad, velocidad f máxima; **~ometer** [spɪ'dɔmɪtə*] n velocímetro; **~way** n (SPORT) carreras fpl de moto; **~y** a (fast) veloz, rápido; (prompt) pronto.

spell [spɛl] n (also: **magic ~**) encanto, hechizo; (period of time) rato, período; (turn) turno // vt, pt, pp **spelt** or **spelled** (also: **~ out**) deletrear; (fig) anunciar, presagiar; **to cast a ~ on sb** hechizar a uno; **he can't ~** no sabe escribir bien, sabe poco de ortografía; **~bound** *a* embelesado, hechizado; **~ing** *n* ortografía.

spend [spɛnd], *pt, pp* **spent** [spɛnt] *vt* (*money*) gastar; (*time*) pasar; (*life*) dedicar; **~thrift** *n* derrochador/a *m/f*, pródigo/a.

sperm [spɔːm] *n* esperma; **~ whale** *n* cachalote *m*.

spew [spjuː] *vt* vomitar, arrojar.

sphere [sfɪə*] *n* esfera; **spherical** ['sfɛrɪkl] *a* esférico.

sphinx [sfɪŋks] *n* esfinge *f*.

spice [spaɪs] *n* especia // *vt* especiar; **spicy** *a* especiado; (*fig*) picante.

spider ['spaɪdə*] *n* araña.

spike [spaɪk] *n* (*point*) punta; (*zool*) pincho, púa; (*bot*) espiga.

spill [spɪl], *pt, pp* **spilt** *or* **spilled** *vt* derramar, verter // *vi* derramarse; **to ~ over** desbordarse.

spin [spɪn] *n* (*revolution of wheel*) vuelta, revolución *f*; (*aviat*) barrena; (*trip in car*) paseo (en coche) // (*vb: pt, pp* **spun**) *vt* (*wool etc*) hilar; (*wheel*) girar // *vi* girar, dar vueltas; **to ~ out** *vt* alargar, prolongar.

spinach ['spɪnɪtʃ] *n* espinaca; (*as food*) espinacas *fpl*.

spinal ['spaɪnl] *a* espinal; **~ cord** *n* columna vertebral.

spindly ['spɪndlɪ] *a* zanquivano.

spin-drier [spɪn'draɪə*] *n* secador *m* centrífugo.

spine [spaɪn] *n* espinazo, columna vertebral; (*thorn*) espina; **~less** *a* (*fig*) débil, flojo.

spinning ['spɪnɪŋ] *n* (*of thread*) hilado; (*art*) hilandería; **~ top** *n* peonza; **~ wheel** *n* rueca, torno de hilar.

spinster ['spɪnstə*] *n* soltera; (*pej*) solterona.

spiral ['spaɪərl] *n* espiral *m* // *a* en espiral; **~ staircase** *n* escalera de caracol.

spire ['spaɪə*] *n* aguja, chapitel *m*.

spirit ['spɪrɪt] *n* (*gen*) espíritu *m*; (*soul*) alma *m*; (*ghost*) fantasma *m*; (*humour*) humor *m*; (*courage*) valor *m*, ánimo; **~s** *npl* (*drink*) alcohol *m*, bebidas *fpl* alcohólicas; **in good ~s** alegre, de buen ánimo; **~ed** *a* enérgico, vigoroso; **~ level** *n* nivel *m* de aire.

spiritual ['spɪrɪtjuəl] *a* espiritual // *n* (*also*: **Negro ~**) canción *f* religiosa, espiritual *m*; **~ism** *n* espiritualismo.

spit [spɪt] *n* (*for roasting*) asador *m*, espetón *m* // *vi*, *pt*, *pp* **spat** escupir; (*sound*) chisporrotear.

spite [spaɪt] *n* rencor *m*, ojeriza // *vt* causar pena a, mortificar; **in ~ of** a pesar de, pese a; **~ful** *a* rencoroso, malévolo.

spittle ['spɪtl] *n* saliva, baba.

splash [splæʃ] *n* (*sound*) chapoteo; (*of colour*) mancha // *vt* salpicar de // *vi* (*also*: **~ about**) chapotear.

spleen [spliːn] *n* (*anat*) bazo.

splendid ['splɛndɪd] *a* espléndido; **splendour, splendor** (*us*) [-də*] *n* esplendor *m*; (*of achievement*) brillo, gloria.

splint [splɪnt] *n* tablilla.

splinter ['splɪntə*] *n* (*of wood*) astilla; (*in finger*) espigón *m* // *vi* astillarse, hacer astillas.

split [splɪt] *n* hendedura, raja; (*fig*) división *f*; (*pol*) escisión *f* // (*vb: pt, pp* **split**) *vt* partir, rajar; (*party*) dividir; (*work, profits*) repartir // *vi* (*divide*) dividirse, escindirse; **to ~ up** *vi* (*couple*) separarse; (*meeting*) acabarse.

splutter ['splʌtə*] *vi* chisporrotear; (*person*) balbucear.

spoil [spɔɪl], *pt, pp* **spoilt** *or* **spoiled** *vt* (*damage*) dañar; (*mar*) estropear, echar a perder; (*child*) mimar, consentir; **~s** *npl* despojo *sg*, botín *m*; **~sport** *n* aguafiestas *m inv*.

spoke [spəʊk] *pt of* **speak** // *n* rayo, radio.

spoken ['spəʊkn] *pp of* **speak.**

spokesman ['spəʊksmən] *n* vocero, portavoz *m*.

sponge [spʌndʒ] *n* esponja; (*cake*) pastel *m* // *vt* lavar con esponja // *vi*: **to ~ on sb** vivir a costa de uno; **~ bag** *n* esponjera; **~ cake** *n* bizcocho, pastel *m*; **spongy** *a* esponjoso.

sponsor ['spɒnsə*] *n* (*radio*, *tv*) patrocinador/a *m/f*; (*for membership*) padrino; (*comm*) fiador/a *m/f* // *vt* patrocinar; apadrinar; (*idea etc*) presentar, promover; **~ship** *n* patrocinio.

spontaneous [spɒn'teɪnɪəs] *a* espontáneo.

spool [spuːl] *n* carrete *m*; (*of sewing machine*) canilla.

spoon [spuːn] *n* cuchara; **~-feed** *vt* dar de comer con cuchara; (*fig*) tratar como un niño; **~ful** *n* cucharada.

sporadic [spə'rædɪk] *a* esporádico.

sport [spɔːt] *n* deporte *m*; (*person*) buen perdedor *m*; **~ing** *a* deportivo; **~s car** *n* coche *m* sport; **~s jacket** *n* chaqueta sport; **sportsman** *n* deportista *m*; **sportsmanship** *n* deportividad *f*; **sportswear** *n* trajes *mpl* de deporte o sport; **sportswoman** *n* deportista *f*; **~y** *a* deportivo.

spot [spɒt] *n* sitio, lugar *m*; (*dot: on pattern*) punto, mancha; (*pimple*) grano; (*freckle*) peca; (*small amount*): **a ~ of** un poquito de // *vt* (*notice*) notar, observar; **on the ~** en el acto, acto seguido; (*in difficulty*) en un aprieto; **~ check** *n* reconocimiento rápido; **~less** *a* nítido, perfectamente limpio; **~light** *n* foco, reflector *m*; **~ted** *a* (*pattern*) de puntos; **~ty** *a* (*face*) con granos.

spouse [spauz] *n* cónyuge *m/f*.

spout [spaut] *n* (*of jug*) pico; (*pipe*) caño // *vi* chorrear.

sprain [spreɪn] *n* torcedura // *vt*: **to ~ one's ankle** torcerse el tobillo.

sprang [spræŋ] *pt of* **spring.**

sprawl [sprɔ:l] vi tumbarse.

spray [spreɪ] n rociada; (of sea) espuma; (container) atomizador m; (of paint) pistola rociadora; (of flowers) ramita // vt rociar; (crops) regar.

spread [sprɛd] n extensión f; (distribution) diseminación f, propagación f; (col: food) comilona f // (vb: pt, pp **spread**) vt extender; diseminar; (butter) untar; (wings, sails) desplegar; (scatter) esparcir // vi extenderse; diseminarse; untarse; desplegarse; esparcirse.

spree [spri:] n: to go on a ~ ir de juerga.

sprightly ['spraɪtlɪ] a vivo, enérgico.

spring [sprɪŋ] n (leap) salto, brinco; (coiled metal) resorte m; (season) primavera; (of water) fuente f, manantial f // vi, pt **sprang**, pp **sprung** (arise) brotar, nacer; (leap) saltar, brincar; **to ~ up** vi nacer de repente, aparecer repentinamente; **~board** n trampolín m; **~-clean** n (also: **~-cleaning**) limpieza general; **~time** n primavera; **~y** a elástico; (grass) muelle.

sprinkle ['sprɪŋkl] vt (pour) rociar; **to ~ water on, ~ with water** rociar o salpicar de agua; **~d with** (fig) sembrado o salpicado de.

sprint [sprɪnt] n sprint m // vi (gen) correr a toda velocidad; (SPORT) sprintar; **~er** n sprinter m/f, corredor/a m/f.

sprite [spraɪt] n duende m.

sprout [spraʊt] vi brotar, retoñar; (Brussels) **~s** npl colecillos mpl de Bruselas.

spruce [spru:s] n (BOT) pícea // a aseado, pulcro.

sprung [sprʌŋ] pp of **spring**.

spry [spraɪ] a ágil, activo.

spun [spʌn] pt, pp of **spin**.

spur [spə:°] n espuela; (fig) estímulo, aguijón m // vt (also: ~ **on**) estimular, incitar; **on the ~ of the moment** de improviso.

spurn [spə:n] vt desdeñar, rechazar.

spurt [spə:t] n esfuerzo supremo; (of energy) arrebato // vi hacer un esfuerzo supremo.

spy [spaɪ] n espía m/f // vi: **to ~ on** espiar a // vt (see) divisar, lograr ver; **~ing** n espionaje m.

sq. abbr of **square**.

squabble ['skwɔbl] n riña, pelea // vi reñir, pelear.

squad [skwɔd] n (MIL, POLICE) pelotón m, escuadra.

squadron ['skwɔdrn] n (MIL) escuadrón m; (AVIAT, NAUT) escuadra.

squalid ['skwɔlɪd] a vil, miserable, escuálido.

squall [skwɔ:l] n (storm) chubasco; (wind) ráfaga.

squalor ['skwɔlə°] n miseria.

squander ['skwɔndə°] vt (money) derrochar, despilfarrar; (chances) desperdiciar.

square [skwɛə°] n cuadro; (in town) plaza // a cuadrado; (col: ideas, tastes) pasota //

vt (arrange) arreglar; (MATH) cuadrar; **all ~ igual(es)**; **a ~ meal** una comida abundante; **2 metres ~** 2 metros en cuadro; **1 ~ metre** un metro cuadrado; **~ly** ad en cuadro; (fully) de lleno.

squash [skwɔʃ] n (drink): **lemon/orange ~** zumo de limón/naranja; (SPORT) squash m, frontenis m // vt aplastar; **to ~ together** apiñar.

squat [skwɔt] a achaparrado // vi agacharse, sentarse en cuclillas; **~ter** n persona que ocupa ilegalmente una casa.

squawk [skwɔ:k] vi graznar.

squeak [skwi:k] n chirrido, rechinamiento; (of shoe) crujido; (of mouse) chillido // vi chirriar, rechinar; crujir; chillar.

squeal [skwi:l] vi chillar, dar gritos agudos.

squeamish ['skwi:mɪʃ] a delicado, remilgado.

squeeze [skwi:z] n (gen) estrujón m; (of hand) apretón m; (in bus etc) apiñamiento // vt estrujar, apretar; (hand, arm) apretar; **to ~ out** vt exprimir; (fig) excluir; **to ~ through** abrirse paso con esfuerzos.

squelch [skwɛltʃ] vi aplastar, despachurrar.

squid [skwɪd] n calamar m.

squint [skwɪnt] vi bizquear, ser bizco // n (MED) estrabismo; **to ~ at sth** mirar algo de soslayo.

squirm [skwə:m] vi retorcerse, revolverse.

squirrel ['skwɪrəl] n ardilla.

squirt [skwə:t] vi salir a chorros.

Sr abbr of **senior**.

St abbr of **saint; street**.

stab [stæb] n (with knife etc) puñalada; (of pain) pinchazo; (col: try): **to have a ~ at (doing) sth** intentar (hacer) algo // vt apuñalar.

stability [stə'bɪlɪtɪ] n estabilidad f; **stabilize** ['steɪbəlaɪz] vt estabilizar // vi estabilizarse; **stable** ['steɪbl] a estable // n cuadra, caballeriza.

stack [stæk] n montón m, pila // vt amontonar, apilar.

stadium ['steɪdɪəm] n estadio.

staff [stɑ:f] n (work force) personal m, plantilla; (stick) bastón m // vt proveer de personal.

stag [stæg] n ciervo, venado.

stage [steɪdʒ] n escena; (profession): **the ~** el escenario, el teatro; (point) etapa; (platform) plataforma // vt (play) poner en escena, representar; (demonstration) montar, organizar; (fig: perform: recovery etc) llevar a cabo; **~coach** n diligencia; **~ door** n entrada de artistas; **~ manager** n director/a m/f de escena.

stagger ['stægə°] vi tambalear // vt (amaze) asombrar; (hours, holidays) escalonar; **~ing** a (amazing) asombroso, pasmoso.

stagnant ['stægnənt] a estancado; **stagnate** [-'neɪt] vi estancarse.

stag party n fiesta de solteros.

staid [steɪd] a serio, formal.

stain [steɪn] n mancha; (colouring) tintura // vt manchar; (wood) teñir; **~ed glass window** n vidriera de colores; **~less** a (steel) inoxidable.

stair [stɛə°] n (step) peldaño, escalón m; **~s** npl escaleras fpl; **~case**, **~way** n escalera.

stake [steɪk] n estaca, poste m; (BETTING) apuesta // vt apostar; **to be at ~** estar en juego.

stalactite ['stæləktaɪt] n estalactita.

stalagmite ['stæləgmaɪt] n estalagmita.

stale [steɪl] a (bread) duro; (food) no fresco, pasado.

stalemate ['steɪlmeɪt] n tablas fpl (por ahogado); (fig) estancamiento.

stalk [stɔːk] n tallo, caña // vt acechar, cazar al acecho; **to ~ off** irse con paso airado.

stall [stɔːl] n (in market) puesto; (in stable) casilla (de establo) // vt (AUT) parar // vi (AUT) pararse; (fig) buscar evasivas; **~s** npl (in cinema, theatre) butacas fpl.

stallion ['stælɪən] n caballo padre, semental m.

stalwart ['stɔːlwət] n (in build) fornido; (in spirit) valiente.

stamina ['stæmɪnə] n resistencia.

stammer ['stæmə°] n tartamudeo, balbuceo // vi tartamudear, balbucir.

stamp [stæmp] n sello, estampilla; (mark, also fig) marca, huella; (on document) timbre m // vi patear // vt patear, golpear con el pie; (in dance) zapatear; (letter) poner sellos en; (with rubber ~) marcar con estampilla; **~ album** n álbum m para sellos; **~ collecting** n filatelia.

stampede [stæm'piːd] n estampida.

stance [stæns] n postura.

stand [stænd] n (position) posición f, postura; (for taxis) parada; (hall ~) perchero; (music ~) atril m; (SPORT) tribuna; (news ~) quiosco // (vb: pt, pp stood) vi (be) estar, encontrarse; (be on foot) estar de pie, (rise) levantarse; (remain) quedar en pie // vt (place) poner, colocar; (tolerate, withstand) aguantar, soportar; (cost) pagar; (invite) invitar; **to make a ~** resistir; (fig) aferrarse a un principio; **to ~ for parliament** presentarse como candidato al parlamento; **to ~ by** vi (be ready) estar listo // vt fus (opinion) aferrarse a; **to ~ for** vt fus (defend) apoyar; (signify) significar; (tolerate) aguantar, permitir; **to ~ in for** vt fus suplir a; **to ~ out** vi (be prominent) destacarse; **to ~ up** vi (rise) levantarse, ponerse de pie; **to ~ up for** vt fus defender; **to ~ up to** vt fus hacer frente a.

standard ['stændəd] n patrón m, norma; (flag) estandarte m; (degree) grado // a (size etc) normal, corriente, stándard; **~s** npl (morals) valores mpl morales; **~ize** vt estandarizar; **~ lamp** n lámpara de pie; **~ of living** n nivel m de vida.

stand-by ['stændbaɪ] n (alert) alerta, aviso; **to be on ~** estar sobre aviso; **~ ticket** n (AVIAT) billete m standby.

stand-in ['stændɪn] n suplente m/f; (CINEMA) doble m/f.

standing ['stændɪŋ] a (upright) derecho; (on foot) de pie, en pie // n reputación f; **of many years'** ~ que lleva muchos años; **~ order** n (at bank) giro bancario; **~ orders** npl (MIL) reglamento sg general; **~ room** n sitio para estar de pie.

stand: **~-offish** a reservado, poco afable; **~point** n punto de vista; **~still** n: **at a ~still** paralizado, en paro; **to come to a ~still** pararse, quedar paralizado.

stank [stæŋk] pt of **stink.**

staple ['steɪpl] n (for papers) grapa // a (food etc) corriente // vt unir con grapa, engrapar; **stapler** n grapadora.

star [stɑː°] n estrella; (celebrity) estrella, astro // vi: **to ~ in** ser la estrella o el astro de.

starboard ['stɑːbəd] n estribor m.

starch [stɑːtʃ] n almidón m; **~ed** a (collar) almidonado; **~y** a feculento.

stardom ['stɑːdəm] n estrellato, calidad f de estrella.

stare [stɛə°] n mirada fija // vi: **to ~ at** mirar fijo.

starfish ['stɑːfɪʃ] n estrella de mar.

stark [stɑːk] a (bleak) severo, escueto // ad: **~ naked** en cueros, en pelota.

starlight ['stɑːlaɪt] n: **by ~** a la luz de las estrellas.

starling ['stɑːlɪŋ] n estornino.

starry ['stɑːrɪ] a estrellado; **~-eyed** a (innocent) inocentón(ona), ingenuo.

start [stɑːt] n (beginning) principio, comienzo; (departure) salida; (sudden movement) salto, sobresalto; (advantage) ventaja // vt empezar, comenzar; (cause) causar; (found) fundar; (engine) poner en marcha // vi (begin) comenzar, empezar; (with fright) asustarse, sobresaltarse; (train etc) salir; **to ~ off** vi empezar, comenzar; (leave) salir, ponerse en camino; **to ~ up** vi comenzar; (car) ponerse en marcha // vt comenzar; (car) poner en marcha; **~er** n (AUT) botón m de arranque; (SPORT. official) juez m/f de salida; (: runner) corredor/a m/f; (CULIN) entrada; **~ing point** n punto de partida.

startle ['stɑːtl] vt asustar, sobrecoger; **startling** a alarmante.

starvation [stɑː'veɪʃən] n hambre f; (MED) inanición f; **starve** vi pasar hambre; (to death) morir de hambre // vt hacer pasar hambre; (fig) privar; **I'm starving** estoy muerto de hambre.

state [steɪt] n estado // vt (say, declare) afirmar; (a case) presentar, exponer; **the S~s** los Estados Unidos; **to be in a ~** estar agitado; **~ly** a majestuoso, imponente; **~ment** n afirmación f; (LAW) declaración f; **statesman** n estadista m.

static ['stætɪk] n (RADIO) parásitos mpl // a estático; **~ electricity** n estática.

station ['steɪʃən] n (gen) estación f; (place) puesto, sitio; (RADIO) emisora; (rank) posición f social // vt colocar, situar; (MIL) apostar.

stationary ['steɪʃnərɪ] a estacionario, fijo.

stationer's (shop) ['steɪʃənəz] n papelería; **stationery** [-nərɪ] n papel m de escribir.

station master n (RAIL) jefe m de estación.

station wagon n (US) break m.

statistic [stə'tɪstɪk] n estadística; ~s npl (science) estadística sg; ~al a estadístico.

statue ['stætjuː] n estatua.

stature ['stætʃə°] n estatura; (fig) talla.

status ['steɪtəs] n condición f, estado; (reputation) reputación f, status m; the ~ quo el statu quo; ~ symbol n símbolo de prestigio.

statute ['stætjuːt] n estatuto, ley f; **statutory** a estatutario.

staunch [stɔːntʃ] a firme, incondicional.

stave [steɪv] vt: to ~ off (attack) rechazar; (threat) evitar.

stay [steɪ] n (period of time) estancia // vi (remain) quedar, quedarse; (as guest) hospedarse; (spend some time) pasar (un) tiempo; to ~ put seguir en el mismo sitio; to ~ the night pasar la noche; to ~ behind vi quedar atrás; to ~ in vi (at home) quedarse en casa; to ~ on vi quedarse; to ~ out vi (of house) no volver a casa; to ~ up vi (at night) velar, no acostarse; ~ing power n resistencia.

steadfast ['stɛdfɑːst] a firme, resuelto.

steadily ['stɛdɪlɪ] ad (firmly) firmemente; (unceasingly) sin parar; (fixedly) fijamente; (walk) normalmente; (drive) a velocidad constante.

steady ['stɛdɪ] a (constant) constante, fijo; (unswerving) firme; (regular) regular; (person, character) sensato, juicioso; (diligent) trabajador; (calm) sereno // vt (hold) mantener firme; (stabilize) estabilizar; (nerves) calmar; to ~ o.s. on or against sth afirmarse en algo.

steak [steɪk] n (gen) filete m; (beef) bistec m.

steal [stiːl] n, pt stole, pp stolen vt, vi robar.

stealth [stɛlθ] n: by ~ a escondidas, sigilosamente; ~y a cauteloso, sigiloso.

steam [stiːm] n vapor m; (mist) vaho, humo // vt empañar; (CULIN) cocer al vapor // vi echar vapor; (ship): to ~ along avanzar, ir avanzando; ~ engine n máquina de vapor; ~er n vapor m; ~roller n apisonadora; ~y a vaporoso; (room) lleno de vapor; (window) empañado.

steel [stiːl] n acero // a de acero; ~works n (fábrica) siderúrgica.

steep [stiːp] a escarpado, abrupto; (stair) empinado; (price) exorbitante, excesivo // vt empapar, remojar.

steeple ['stiːpl] n aguja, campanario; ~chase n carrera de obstáculos; ~jack

n reparador m de chimeneas.

steer [stɪə°] vt conducir, dirigir // vi conducir; ~ing n (AUT) dirección f; ~ing wheel n volante m.

stellar ['stɛlə°] a estelar.

stem [stɛm] n (of plant) tallo; (of glass) pie m; (of pipe) cañón m // vt detener; (blood) restañar; to ~ from vt fus proceder de.

stench [stɛntʃ] n hedor m.

stencil ['stɛnsl] n (typed) cliché m, clisé m; (lettering) plantilla // vt hacer un cliché de.

step [stɛp] n paso; (sound) paso, pisada; (stair) peldaño, escalón m // vi: to ~ forward dar un paso adelante; ~s npl = ~ladder; to ~ down vi (fig) retirarse; to ~ off vt fus bajar de; to ~ on vt fus pisar; to ~ over vt fus pasar por encima de; to ~ up vt (increase) aumentar; ~brother n hermanastro; ~daughter n hijastra; ~father n padrastro; ~ladder n escalera de tijera o doble; ~mother n madrastra; ~ping stone n pasadera; ~sister n hermanastra; ~son n hijastro.

stereo ['stɛrɪəu] n estereo // a (also: ~phonic) estereo(fónico).

stereotype ['stɪərɪətaɪp] n estereotipo // vt estereotipar.

sterile ['stɛraɪl] a estéril; **sterility** [-'rɪlɪtɪ] n esterilidad f; **sterilization** [-'zeɪʃən] n esterilización f; **sterilize** ['stɛrɪlaɪz] vt esterilizar.

sterling ['stɜːlɪŋ] a esterlina; (silver) de ley; (fig) auténtico.

stern [stɜːn] a severo, austero // n (NAUT) popa.

stethoscope ['stɛθəskəup] n estetoscopio.

stew [stjuː] n cocido, estofado; (fig: mess) apuro // vt, vi estofar, guisar; (fruit) cocer.

steward ['stjuːəd] n (gen) camarero; ~ess n azafata.

stick [stɪk] n palo; (as weapon) porra; (walking ~) bastón m // (vb: pt, pp stuck) vt (glue) pegar; (thrust): to ~ sth into clavar o hincar algo en; (col: put) meter; (col: tolerate) aguantar, soportar // vi pegar, pegarse; (come to a stop) quedarse parado; (in mind etc) atascarse; (pin etc) clavarse; to ~ out, to ~ up vi sobresalir; to ~ up for vt fus defender; ~er n etiqueta engomada.

stickler ['stɪklə°] n: to be a ~ for dar mucha importancia a.

stick-up ['stɪkʌp] n asalto, atraco.

sticky ['stɪkɪ] a pegajoso; (label) engomado; (fig) difícil.

stiff [stɪf] a rígido, tieso; (hard) duro; (difficult) difícil; (person) inflexible; (price) exorbitante; ~en vt hacer más rígido; (limb) entumecer // vi endurecerse; (grow stronger) fortalecerse; ~ness n rigidez f, tiesura; difícultad f; (character) frialdad f.

stifle ['staɪfl] vt ahogar, sofocar; **stifling** a (heat) sofocante, bochornoso.

stigma ['stɪgmə], pl (BOT, MED, REL) ~ta [-tə], (fig) ~s n estigma m.

stile [stail] n escalera para pasar una cerca.

stiletto [stɪ'lɛtəu] n (also: ~ **heel**) tacón m de aguja.

still [stɪl] a inmóvil, quieto // ad (up to this time) todavía; (even) aún; (nonetheless) sin embargo, aun así; ~**born** a nacido muerto; ~ **life** n naturaleza muerta.

stilt [stɪlt] n zanco; (pile) pilar m, soporte m.

stilted ['stɪltɪd] a afectado.

stimulant ['stɪmjulənt] n estimulante m.

stimulate ['stɪmjuleɪt] vt estimular; **stimulating** a estimulante; **stimulation** [-'leɪʃən] n estímulo.

stimulus ['stɪmjuləs], pl **-li** [-laɪ] n estímulo, incentivo.

sting [stɪŋ] n (wound) picadura; (pain) escozor m, picazón m; (organ) aguijón m // (vb: pt, pp **stung**) vt picar // vi picar, escocer.

stingy ['stɪndʒɪ] a tacaño.

stink [stɪŋk] n hedor m, tufo // vi, pt **stank**, pp **stunk** heder, apestar; ~**ing** a hediondo, fétido.

stint [stɪnt] n tarea, destajo; **to do one's ~** hacer su parte // vi: **to ~ on** escatimar.

stipend ['staɪpɛnd] n (of vicar etc) estipendio, sueldo.

stipulate ['stɪpjuleɪt] vt estipular, poner como condición; **stipulation** [-'leɪʃən] n estipulación f, condición f.

stir [stə:*] n (fig: agitation) conmoción f // vt (tea etc) remover; (fire) atizar; (move) mover; (fig: emotions) conmover // vi moverse, menearse; **to ~ up** vt excitar; (trouble) fomentar; ~**ring** a conmovedor(a).

stirrup ['stɪrəp] n estribo.

stitch [stɪtʃ] n (SEWING) puntada; (KNITTING) punto; (MED) punto (de sutura); (pain) punzada // vt coser; (MED) suturar.

stoat [stəut] n armiño.

stock [stɔk] n (COMM: reserves) existencias fpl, stock m; (: selection) surtido; (AGR) ganado, ganadería; (CULIN) caldo; (fig: lineage) estirpe f; (FINANCE) capital m; (: shares) acciones fpl // a (fig: reply etc) clásico, acostumbrado // vt (have in ~) tener (en existencia o almacén); (supply) proveer, abastecer; **to take ~ of** (fig) asesorar, examinar; **to ~ up with** vt abastecerse de; ~**s** npl cepo sg; ~**s and shares** acciones y valores.

stockade [stɔ'keɪd] n estacada.

stockbroker ['stɔkbrəukə*] n agente m/f o corredor/a m/f de bolsa.

stock exchange n bolsa.

stocking ['stɔkɪŋ] n media.

stock market n bolsa (de valores).

stockpile ['stɔkpaɪl] n reserva // vt acumular, almacenar.

stocktaking ['stɔkteɪkɪŋ] n (COMM) inventario, balance m.

stocky ['stɔkɪ] a (strong) robusto; (short) achaparrado.

stodgy ['stɔdʒɪ] a indigesto, pesado.

stoical ['stəuɪkəl] a estoico.

stoke [stəuk] vt cargar, cebar.

stole [stəul] pt of **steal** // n estola.

stolen ['stəuln] pp of **steal**.

stomach ['stʌmək] n (ANAT) estómago; (belly) vientre m; (appetite) apetito // vt tragar, aguantar; ~ **ache** n dolor m de estómago.

stone [stəun] n piedra; (in fruit) hueso; (weight) medida de peso (6.348kg) // a de piedra // vt apedrear; ~**-cold** a helado; ~**-deaf** a totalmente sordo; ~**work** n (art) cantería; (stones) piedras fpl; **stony** a pedregoso; (glance) glacial.

stood [stud] pt, pp of **stand**.

stool [stu:l] n taburete m.

stoop [stu:p] vi (also: **have a ~**) ser cargado de espaldas; (bend) inclinarse, encorvarse.

stop [stɔp] n parada, alto; (in punctuation) punto // vt parar, detener; (break off) suspender; (block) tapar, cerrar; (also: **put a ~ to**) terminar, poner término a // vi pararse, detenerse; (end) acabarse; **to ~ doing sth** dejar de hacer algo; **to ~ dead** vi pararse en seco; **to ~ off** vi interrumpir el viaje; **to ~ up** vt (hole) tapar; ~**gap** n recurso (temporal); ~**lights** npl (AUT) luces fpl de detención; ~**over** n parada intermedia.

stoppage ['stɔpɪdʒ] n (strike) paro; (temporary stop) interrupción f; (of pay) suspensión f; (blockage) obstrucción f.

stopper ['stɔpə*] n tapón m.

stopwatch ['stɔpwɔtʃ] n cronómetro.

storage ['stɔ:rɪdʒ] n almacenaje m.

store [stɔ:*] n (stock) provisión f; (depot, large shop) almacén m; (reserve) reserva, repuesto; ~**s** npl víveres mpl // vt almacenar; (keep) guardar; **to ~ up** vt acumular; ~**room** n despensa.

storey, story (US) ['stɔ:rɪ] n piso.

stork [stɔ:k] n cigüeña.

storm [stɔ:m] n tormenta; (wind) vendaval m; (fig) tempestad f // vi (fig) rabiar // vt tomar por asalto, asaltar; ~ **cloud** n nubarrón m; ~**y** a tempestuoso.

story ['stɔ:rɪ] n historia, relato; (joke) cuento, chiste m; (plot) argumento; (lie) cuento, embuste m; (US) = **storey**; ~**book** n libro de cuentos; ~**teller** n cuentista m/f.

stout [staut] a (strong) sólido, macizo; (fat) gordo, corpulento // n cerveza negra.

stove [stəuv] n (for cooking) cocina; (for heating) estufa.

stow [stəu] vt meter, poner; (NAUT) estibar; ~**away** n polizón/ona m/f.

straddle ['strædl] vt montar a horcajadas.

straggle ['strægl] vi (wander) vagar en desorden; (lag behind) rezagarse; **straggler** n rezagado; **straggling**, **straggly** a (hair) desordenado.

straight [streɪt] a recto, derecho; (honest) honrado; (frank) franco, directo; (simple) sencillo; (in order) en orden // ad derecho, directamente; (drink) sin mezcla; **to put**

or get sth ~ dejar algo en claro; ~ **away**, ~ **off** *(at once)* en seguida; ~**en** *vt* *(also:* ~**en out)** enderezar, poner derecho; ~**-faced** *a* solemne, sin expresión; ~**forward** *a* *(simple)* sencillo; *(honest)* honrado, franco.

strain [streɪn] *n* *(gen)* tensión *f;* *(TECH)* esfuerzo; *(MED)* torcedura; *(breed)* raza // *vt* *(back etc)* torcerse; *(tire)* cansar; *(stretch)* estirar; *(filter)* filtrar // *vi* esforzarse; ~**s** *npl* *(MUS)* son *m;* ~**ed** *a* *(muscle)* torcido; *(laugh)* forzado; *(relations)* tenso; ~**er** *n* colador *m.*

strait [streɪt] *n* *(GEO)* estrecho; ~**-jacket** *n* camisa de fuerza; ~**-laced** *a* mojigato, gazmoño.

strand [strænd] *n* *(of thread)* hebra; *(of hair)* trenza; *(of rope)* ramal *m;* ~**ed** *a* abandonado *(sin recursos),* desamparado.

strange [streɪndʒ] *a* *(not known)* desconocido; *(odd)* extraño, raro; **stranger** *n* desconocido/a; *(from another area)* forastero/a.

strangle ['stræŋgl] *vt* estrangular; *(sobs etc)* ahogar; ~**hold** *n* *(fig)* dominio completo; **strangulation** [-'leɪʃən] *n* estrangulación *f.*

strap [stræp] *n* correa; *(of slip, dress)* tirante *m* // *vt* atar con correa; *(punish)* azotar.

strapping ['stræpɪŋ] *a* robusto, fornido.

strata ['strɑːtə] *pl of* **stratum.**

stratagem ['strætɪdʒəm] *n* estratagema.

strategic [strə'tiːdʒɪk] *a* estratégico.

strategy ['strætɪdʒɪ] *n* estrategia.

stratum ['strɑːtəm], *pl* **-ta** *n* estrato.

straw [strɔː] *n* paja; *(drinking* ~) caña, pajita.

strawberry ['strɔːbərɪ] *n* fresa.

stray [streɪ] *a* *(animal)* extraviado; *(bullet)* perdido; *(scattered)* disperso // *vi* extraviarse, perderse.

streak [striːk] *n* raya; *(fig: of madness etc)* vena // *vt* rayar // *vi:* **to** ~ **past** pasar como un rayo; ~**y** *a* rayado.

stream [striːm] *n* riachuelo, arroyo; *(jet)* chorro; *(current)* corriente *f;* *(of people)* oleada // *vt* *(SCOL)* dividir en grupos por habilidad // *vi* correr, fluir; **to** ~ **in/out** *(people)* entrar/salir en tropel.

streamer ['striːmə*] *n* serpentina.

streamlined ['striːmlaɪnd] *a* aerodinámico.

street [striːt] *n* calle *f* // *a* callejero; ~**car** *n* *(US)* tranvía; ~ **lamp** *n* farol *m.*

strength [streŋθ] *n* fuerza; *(of girder, knot etc)* resistencia; ~**en** *vt* fortalecer, reforzar.

strenuous ['strenjuəs] *a* *(tough)* arduo; *(energetic)* enérgico; *(determined)* tenaz.

stress [stres] *n* *(force, pressure)* presión *f;* *(mental strain)* tensión *f,* *(accent)* énfasis *m,* acento; *(TECH)* tensión *f,* carga // *vt* subrayar, recalcar.

stretch [stretʃ] *n* *(of sand etc)* trecho, tramo // *vi* estirarse; *(extend):* **to** ~ **to or as far as** extenderse hasta // *vt* extender,

estirar; *(make demands of)* exigir el máximo esfuerzo a; **to** ~ **out** *vi* tenderse // *vt* *(arm etc)* extender; *(spread)* estirar.

stretcher ['stretʃə*] *n* camilla.

strewn [struːn] *a:* ~ **with** cubierto *o* sembrado de.

stricken ['strɪkən] *a* *(wounded)* herido; *(ill)* enfermo.

strict [strɪkt] *a* *(person)* severo, riguroso; *(precise)* estricto, exacto; ~**ly** *ad* *(exactly)* estrictamente; *(totally)* terminantemente; *(severely)* rigurosamente; ~**ness** *n* exactitud *f;* rigor *m,* severidad *f.*

stride [straɪd] *n* zancada, tranco // *vi, pt* **strode,** *pp* **stridden** ['strɪdn] dar zancadas, andar a trancos.

strident ['straɪdnt] *a* estridente; *(colour)* chillón(ona).

strife [straɪf] *n* lucha.

strike [straɪk] *n* huelga; *(of oil etc)* descubrimiento; *(attack)* ataque *m;* *(SPORT)* golpe *m* // *(vb: pt, pp* **struck)** *vt* golpear, pegar; *(oil etc)* descubrir; *(obstacle)* topar con // *vi* declarar la huelga; *(attack)* atacar; *(clock)* dar la hora; **to** ~ **a match** encender un fósforo; **to** ~ **down** *vt* derribar; **to** ~ **out** *vt* borrar, tachar; **to** ~ **up** *vt* *(MUS)* empezar a tocar; *(conversation)* entablar; *(friendship)* trabar; ~**breaker** *n* rompehuelgas *m/f inv;* **striker** *n* huelgista *m/f;* *(SPORT)* delantero; **striking** *a* impresionante; *(nasty)* chocante; *(colour)* llamativo.

string [strɪŋ] *n* *(gen)* cuerda; *(row)* hilera // *vt, pt, pp* **strung: to** ~ **together** ensartar // *vi:* **to** ~ **out** extenderse; **the** ~**s** *npl* *(MUS)* los instrumentos de cuerda; **to pull** ~**s** *(fig)* mover palancas; ~ **bean** *n* judía verde, habichuela; ~**(ed) instrument** *n* *(MUS)* instrumento de cuerda.

stringent ['strɪndʒənt] *a* riguroso, severo.

strip [strɪp] *n* tira; *(of land)* franja; *(of metal)* cinta, lámina // *vt* desnudar; *(also:* ~ **down:** *machine)* desmontar // *vi* desnudarse; ~ **cartoon** *n* tira cómica.

stripe [straɪp] *n* raya; *(MIL)* galón *m;* ~**d** *a* a rayas, rayado.

stripper ['strɪpə*] *n* artista de striptease.

striptease ['strɪptiːz] *n* striptease *m.*

strive [straɪv], *pt* **strove,** *pp* **striven** ['strɪvn] *vi:* **to** ~ **to** do sth esforzarse *o* luchar por hacer algo.

strode [strəud] *pt of* **stride.**

stroke [strəuk] *n* *(blow)* golpe *m;* *(MED)* ataque *m* fulminante; *(caress)* caricia; *(of pen)* trazo // *vt* acariciar, frotar suavemente; **at a** ~ de golpe.

stroll [strəul] *n* paseo, vuelta // *vi* dar un paseo *o* una vuelta.

strong [strɔŋ] *a* fuerte; **they are 50** ~ son 50; ~**box** *n* caja fuerte; ~**hold** *n* fortaleza; *(fig)* baluarte *m;* ~**ly** *ad* fuertemente, con fuerza; *(believe)*

firmemente; **~room** n cámara
acorazada.
strove [strəuv] pt of **strive**.
struck [strʌk] pt, pp of **strike**.
structural ['strʌktʃərəl] a estructural;
structure n estructura; (building)
construcción f.
struggle ['strʌgl] n lucha // vi luchar.
strum [strʌm] vt (guitar) rasguear.
strung [strʌŋ] pt, pp of **string**.
strut [strʌt] n puntal m // vi pavonearse.
stub [stʌb] n (of ticket etc) talón m; (of
cigarette) colilla; **to ~ out** vt apagar; **to
~ one's toe** dar con el dedo contra algo.
stubble ['stʌbl] n rastrojo; (on chin) barba
(de pocos días).
stubborn ['stʌbən] a terco, testarudo.
stuck [stʌk] pt, pp of **stick** // a (jammed)
atascado; **~-up** a engreído, presumido.
stud [stʌd] n (shirt ~) botón m; (of boot)
taco; (of horses) caballeriza; (also: ~
horse) caballo padre o semental // vt
(fig): **~ded with** sembrado de.
student ['stju:dənt] n estudiante m/f // a
estudiantil.
studio ['stju:dɪəu] n estudio; (sculptor's)
taller m.
studious ['stju:dɪəs] a aplicado; (studied)
calculado; **~ly** ad (carefully) con esmero.
study ['stʌdɪ] n (gen) estudio // vt estudiar;
(examine) examinar, escudriñar // vi
estudiar.
stuff [stʌf] n materia; (cloth) tela;
(substance) material m, sustancia // vt
llenar; (CULIN) rellenar; (animals) disecar;
~ing n relleno; **~y** a (room) mal
ventilado; (person) de miras estrechas.
stumble ['stʌmbl] vi tropezar, dar un
traspié; **to ~ across** (fig) tropezar con;
stumbling block n tropiezo, obstáculo.
stump [stʌmp] n (of tree) tocón m; (of
limb) muñón m // vt: **to be ~ed** quedar
perplejo.
stun [stʌn] vt dejar sin sentido.
stung [stʌŋ] pt, pp of **sting**.
stunk [stʌŋk] pp of **stink**.
stunning ['stʌnɪŋ] a (fig) pasmoso.
stunt [stʌnt] n proeza excepcional; (AVIAT)
vuelo acrobático; (publicity ~) truco
publicitario; **~ed** a enano, achaparrado;
~ man n doble m.
stupefy ['stju:pɪfaɪ] vt dejar estupefacto.
stupendous [stju:'pendəs] a estupendo,
asombroso.
stupid ['stju:pɪd] a estúpido, tonto; **~ity**
[-'pɪdɪtɪ] n estupidez f; **~ly** ad
estúpidamente.
stupor ['stju:pə*] n estupor m.
sturdy ['stɜ:dɪ] a robusto, fuerte.
stutter ['stʌtə*] n tartamudeo // vi
tartamudear.
sty [staɪ] n (for pigs) pocilga.
stye [staɪ] n (MED) orzuelo.
style [staɪl] n estilo; **stylish** a elegante, a
la moda.
stylus ['staɪləs] n (of record player) aguja.

suave [swɑːv] a cortés, fino.
sub... [sʌb] pref sub...; **~conscious** a
subconsciente // n subconsciente m;
~divide vt subdividir; **~division** n
subdivisión f.
subdue [səb'dju:] vt sojuzgar; (passions)
dominar; **~d** a (light) tenue; (person)
sumiso, manso.
subject ['sʌbdʒɪkt] n súbdito; (SCOL) tema
m, materia // vt [səb'dʒekt]: **to ~ sb to**
sth someter a uno a algo; **to be ~ to**
(law) estar sujeto a; **~ion** [-'dʒekʃən] n
sometimiento, sujeción f; **~ive** a
subjetivo; **~ matter** n materia; (content)
contenido.
subjugate ['sʌbdʒugeɪt] vt subyugar.
sublet [sʌb'let] vt subarrendar.
sublime [sə'blaɪm] a sublime.
submachine gun ['sʌbmə'ʃi:n-] n
metralleta.
submarine [sʌbmə'ri:n] n submarino.
submerge [səb'mɜ:dʒ] vt sumergir; (flood)
inundar // vi sumergirse.
submission [səb'mɪʃən] n sumisión f;
submissive [-'mɪsɪv] a sumiso.
submit [səb'mɪt] vt someter // vi
someterse.
subnormal [sʌb'nɔ:məl] a anormal;
(backward) retrasado.
subordinate [sə'bɔ:dɪnət] a, n
subordinado.
subpoena [səb'pi:nə] (LAW) n comparendo,
citación f // vt mandar comparecer.
subscribe [səb'skraɪb] vi suscribir; **to ~
to** (opinion, fund) suscribir, aprobar;
(newspaper) suscribirse a; **subscriber** n
(to periodical, telephone) abonado/a.
subscription [səb'skrɪpʃən] n abono,
suscripción f.
subsequent ['sʌbsɪkwənt] a subsiguiente,
posterior; **~ly** ad después, más tarde.
subside [səb'saɪd] vi hundirse; (flood)
bajar; (wind) amainar; **subsidence**
[-'saɪdns] n hundimiento; (in road) socavón
m.
subsidiary [səb'sɪdɪərɪ] n sucursal f, filial
f.
subsidize ['sʌbsɪdaɪz] vt subvencionar;
subsidy [-dɪ] n subvención f.
subsistence [səb'sɪstəns] n subsistencia;
(allowance) dietas fpl.
substance ['sʌbstəns] n sustancia; (fig)
esencia.
substandard [sʌb'stændəd] a inferior.
substantial [səb'stænʃl] a sustancial,
sustancioso; (fig) importante; **~ly** ad sus-
tancialmente.
substantiate [səb'stænʃɪeɪt] vt
comprobar.
substitute ['sʌbstɪtju:t] n (person)
suplente m/f; (thing) sustituto // vt: **to ~
A for B** sustituir B por A, reemplazar A
por B; **substitution** [-'tju:ʃən] n sustitución
f, reemplazo.
subterfuge ['sʌbtəfju:dʒ] n subterfugio.
subterranean [sʌbtə'reɪnɪən] a
subterráneo.

subtitle ['sʌbtaɪtl] n subtítulo.
subtle ['sʌtl] a sutil; ~ty n sutileza.
subtract [səb'trækt] vt sustraer, restar; ~ion [-'trækʃən] n sustracción f, resta.
suburb ['sʌbəːb] n arrabal m, suburbio; ~an [sə'bəːbən] a suburbano; (train etc) de cercanías.
subversive [səb'vəːsɪv] a subversivo.
subway ['sʌbweɪ] n (Brit) paso subterráneo o inferior; (US) metro.
succeed [sək'siːd] vi (person) tener éxito; (plan) salir bien // vt suceder a; to ~ in doing lograr hacer; ~ing a (following) sucesivo, seguido.
success [sək'sɛs] n éxito; (gain) triunfo; ~ful a (venture) de éxito; to be ~ful (in doing) lograr (hacer); ~fully ad con éxito.
succession [sək'sɛʃən] n (series) sucesión f, serie f; (descendants) descendencia.
successive [-'sɛsɪv] a sucesivo, consecutivo; **successor** [-'sɛsə*] n sucesor/a m/f.
succinct [sək'sɪŋkt] a sucinto.
succulent ['sʌkjulənt] a suculento.
succumb [sə'kʌm] vi sucumbir.
such [sʌtʃ] a, det tal, semejante; (of that kind): ~ a book un libro parecido; ~ books tales libros; (so much): ~ courage tanto valor; ~ a long trip un viaje tan largo; ~ a lot of tanto; ~ as (like) tal como; a noise ~ as to un ruido tal que; as ~ ad como tal // pron los/las que; ~-and- det tal o cual; until ~ time as hasta que.
suck [sʌk] vt chupar; (bottle) sorber; (breast) mamar; ~er n (BOT) serpollo; (ZOOL) ventosa; (col) bobo, primo.
suckle ['sʌkl] vt amamantar.
suction ['sʌkʃən] n succión f.
sudden ['sʌdn] a (rapid) repentino, súbito; (unexpected) imprevisto; all of a ~, ~ly ad de repente; (unexpectedly) inesperadamente.
suds [sʌdz] npl jabonaduras fpl.
sue [suː] vt demandar.
suede [sweɪd] n ante m.
suet ['suɪt] n sebo.
suffer ['sʌfə*] vt sufrir, padecer; (bear) aguantar; (allow) permitir, tolerar // vi sufrir, padecer; ~er n víctima m/f; (MED) enfermo; ~ing n sufrimiento, padecimiento; (pain) dolor m.
suffice [sə'faɪs] vi bastar, ser suficiente.
sufficient [sə'fɪʃənt] a suficiente, bastante.
suffix ['sʌfɪks] n sufijo.
suffocate ['sʌfəkeɪt] vi ahogarse, asfixiarse; **suffocation** [-'keɪʃən] n sofocación f, asfixia.
suffrage ['sʌfrɪdʒ] n sufragio; (vote) derecho de votar.
sugar ['ʃugə*] n azúcar m // vt echar azúcar a; ~ beet n remolacha; ~ cane n caña de azúcar; ~y a azucarado.
suggest [sə'dʒɛst] vt sugerir; (advise) aconsejar; ~ion [-'dʒɛstʃən] n sugerencia;

(hypnotic) sugestión f; ~ive a sugestivo; (pej) indecente.
suicidal [suɪ'saɪdl] a suicida; **suicide** ['suɪsaɪd] n suicidio; (person) suicida m/f.
suit [suːt] n (man's) traje m; (woman's) conjunto; (LAW) litigio, pleito; (CARDS) palo // vt (gen) convenir; (clothes) sentar a, ir bien a; (adapt): to ~ sth to adaptar o ajustar algo a; ~able a conveniente; (apt) indicado; ~ably ad convenientemente, en forma debida.
suitcase ['suːtkeɪs] n maleta.
suite [swiːt] n (of rooms) grupo de habitaciones; (MUS) suite f; (furniture): bedroom/dining room ~ (juego de) dormitorio/comedor m.
suitor ['suːtə*] n pretendiente m.
sulk [sʌlk] vi tener mohíno; ~y a con mohíno.
sullen ['sʌlən] a hosco, malhumorado.
sulphur, sulfur (US) ['sʌlfə*] n azufre m.
sultan ['sʌltən] n sultán m.
sultana [sʌl'tɑːnə] n (fruit) pasa de Esmirna.
sultry ['sʌltrɪ] a (weather) bochornoso; (seductive) seductor(a).
sum [sʌm] n (gen) suma; (total) total m; to ~ up vt recapitular // vi hacer un resumen.
summarize ['sʌməraɪz] vt resumir.
summary ['sʌmərɪ] n resumen m // a (justice) sumario.
summer ['sʌmə*] n verano // a de verano; ~house n (in garden) cenador m, glorieta; ~time n (season) verano; ~ time n (by clock) hora de verano.
summit ['sʌmɪt] n cima, cumbre f; ~ (conference) n conferencia cumbre.
summon ['sʌmən] vt (person) llamar; (meeting) convocar; (LAW) citar; to ~ up vt cobrar; ~s n llamamiento, llamada // vt citar, emplazar.
sump [sʌmp] n (AUT) cárter m.
sumptuous ['sʌmptjuəs] a suntuoso.
sun [sʌn] n sol m; ~bathe vi tomar el sol; ~burn n (painful) quemadura; (tan) bronceado; ~burnt a (tanned) bronceado; (painfully) quemado por el sol.
Sunday ['sʌndɪ] n domingo.
sundial ['sʌndaɪəl] n reloj m de sol.
sundry ['sʌndrɪ] a varios, diversos; all and ~ todos y cada uno; **sundries** npl géneros mpl diversos.
sunflower ['sʌnflauə*] n girasol m.
sung [sʌŋ] pp of sing.
sunglasses ['sʌnglɑːsɪz] npl gafas fpl de sol.
sunk [sʌŋk] pp of sink.
sun: ~light n luz f del sol; ~lit a iluminado por el sol; ~ny a soleado; (day) de sol; (fig) alegre; ~rise n salida del sol; ~set n puesta del sol; ~shade n (over table) sombrilla; ~shine n sol m; ~spot n mancha solar; ~stroke n insolación f; ~tan n bronceado; ~tan oil n bronceador m, crema bronceadora.
super ['suːpə*] a (col) bárbaro.

superannuation [su:pərænju'eɪʃən] *n* jubilación *f*.

superb [su:'pɔːb] *a* magnífico, espléndido.

supercilious [su:pə'sɪlɪəs] *a* (*disdainful*) desdeñoso; (*haughty*) altanero.

superficial [su:pə'fɪʃəl] *a* superficial.

superfluous [su'pɔːfluəs] *a* superfluo, de sobra.

superhuman [su:pə'hjuːmən] *a* sobrehumano.

superimpose ['su:pərɪm'pəuz] *vt* sobreponer.

superintendent [su:pərɪn'tɛndənt] *n* superintendente *m/f*; (*POLICE*) subjefe *m*.

superior [su'pɪərɪə²] *a* superior; (*smug*) desdeñoso // *n* superior *m*; ~**ity** [-'ɒrɪtɪ] *n* superioridad *f*; desdén *m*.

superlative [su'pɔːlətɪv] *a*, *n* superlativo.

superman ['su:pəmæn] *n* superhombre *m*.

supermarket ['su:pəmɑːkɪt] *n* supermercado.

supernatural [su:pə'nætʃərəl] *a* sobrenatural.

superpower ['su:pəpauə²] *n* (*POL*) superpotencia.

supersede [su:pə'siːd] *vt* suplantar.

supersonic ['su:pə'sɒnɪk] *a* supersónico.

superstition [su:pə'stɪʃən] *n* superstición *f*; **superstitious** [-ʃəs] *a* supersticioso.

supertanker ['su:pətæŋkə²] *n* superpetrolero.

supervise ['su:pəvaɪz] *vt* supervisar; **supervision** [-'vɪʒən] *n* supervisión *f*; **supervisor** *n* supervisor/a *m/f*.

supper ['sʌpə²] *n* cena; **to have** ~ cenar.

supple ['sʌpl] *a* flexible.

supplement ['sʌplɪmənt] *n* suplemento // *vt* [sʌplɪ'mɛnt] suplir; ~**ary** [-'mɛntərɪ] *a* suplementario.

supplier [sə'plaɪə²] *n* suministrador/a *m/f*; (*COMM*) distribuidor/a *m/f*.

supply [sə'plaɪ] *vt* (*provide*) suministrar, facilitar; (*equip*): **to** ~ (**with**) abastecer (de) // *n* suministro, provisión *f*; (*supplying*) abastecimiento // *a* (*teacher etc*) suplente; **supplies** *npl* (*food*) víveres *npl*; (*MIL*) pertrechos *mpl*; ~ **and demand** la oferta y la demanda.

support [sə'pɔːt] *n* (*moral, financial etc*) apoyo; (*TECH*) soporte *m* // *vt* apoyar; (*financially*) mantener; (*uphold*) sostener; ~**er** *n* (*POL etc*) partidario; (*SPORT*) aficionado.

suppose [sə'pəuz] *vt, vi* (*gen*) suponer; (*imagine*) imaginarse; **to be** ~**d to do sth** deber hacer algo; ~**dly** [sə'pəuzɪdlɪ] *ad* que se supone, según cabe suponer; **supposing** *conj* en caso de que; **supposition** [sʌpə'zɪʃən] *n* suposición *f*.

suppository [sə'pɒzɪtərɪ] *n* supositorio.

suppress [sə'prɛs] *vt* suprimir; (*yawn*) ahogar; ~**ion** [sə'prɛʃən] *n* represión *f*.

supremacy [su'prɛməsɪ] *n* supremacía; **supreme** [-'priːm] *a* supremo.

surcharge ['sɜːtʃɑːdʒ] *n* sobrecarga; (*extra tax*) recargo.

sure [ʃuə²] *a* (*gen*) seguro; (*definite, convinced*) cierto; (*aim*) certero; ~**I** (*of course*) ¡claro!, ¡por supuesto!; ~-**footed** *a* de pie firme; ~**ly** *ad* (*certainly*) seguramente.

surety ['ʃuərətɪ] *n* garantía, fianza; (*person*) fiador/a *m/f*.

surf [sɜːf] *n* olas *fpl*.

surface ['sɜːfɪs] *n* superficie *f* // *vt* (*road*) revestir // *vi* salir a la superficie.

surfboard ['sɜːfbɔːd] *n* plancha (de surfing), acuaplano.

surfeit ['sɜːfɪt] *n*: **a** ~ **of** exceso de.

surfing ['sɜːfɪŋ] *n* surfing *m*.

surge [sɜːdʒ] *n* oleada, oleaje *m* // *vi* avanzar a tropel.

surgeon ['sɜːdʒən] *n* cirujano; **dental** ~ odontólogo.

surgery ['sɜːdʒərɪ] *n* cirugía; (*room*) consultorio; **to undergo** ~ operarse; ~ **hours** *npl* horas *fpl* de consulta.

surgical ['sɜːdʒɪkl] *a* quirúrgico; ~ **spirit** *n* alcohol *m*.

surly ['sɜːlɪ] *a* hosco, malhumorado.

surmount [sɜː'maunt] *vt* superar, sobreponerse a.

surname ['sɜːneɪm] *n* apellido.

surpass [sɜː'pɑːs] *vt* superar, exceder.

surplus ['sɜːpləs] *n* (*gen*) excedente *m*; (*COMM*) superávit *m* // *a* excedente, sobrante.

surprise [sə'praɪz] *n* (*gen*) sorpresa; (*astonishment*) asombro // *vt* sorprender; asombrar; **surprising** *a* sorprendente; asombroso.

surrealist [sə'rɪəlɪst] *a* surrealista.

surrender [sə'rɛndə²] *n* rendición *f*, entrega // *vi* rendirse, entregarse.

surreptitious [sʌrəp'tɪʃəs] *a* subrepticio.

surround [sə'raund] *vt* rodar, circundar; (*MIL etc*) cercar; ~**ing** *a* circundante; ~**ings** *npl* alrededores *mpl*, cercanías *fpl*.

surveillance [sɜː'veɪləns] *n* vigilancia.

survey ['sɜːveɪ] *n* inspección *f*, examen *m*; (*inquiry*) encuesta // *vt* [sɜː'veɪ] (*gen*) examinar, inspeccionar; (*look at*) mirar, contemplar; (*make inquiries about*) hacer una encuesta sobre; ~**or** *n* agrimensor *m*.

survival [sə'vaɪvl] *n* supervivencia; **survive** *vi* sobrevivir; (*custom etc*) perdurar // *vt* sobrevivir a; **survivor** *n* superviviente *m/f*.

susceptible [sə'sɛptəbl] *a*: ~ (**to**) susceptible *o* sensible (a).

suspect ['sʌspɛkt] *a*, *n* sospechoso // *vt* [səs'pɛkt] sospechar.

suspend [səs'pɛnd] *vt* suspender; ~**er belt** *n* portaligas *m inv*; ~**ers** *npl* ligas *fpl*; (*US*) tirantes *mpl*.

suspense [səs'pɛns] *n* incertidumbre *f*, duda; (*in film etc*) suspense *m*.

suspension [səs'pɛnʃən] *n* (*gen*, *AUT*) suspensión *f*; (*of driving licence*) privación *f*; ~ **bridge** *n* puente *m* colgante.

suspicion [səs'pɪʃən] *n* (*gen*) sospecha; (*distrust*) recelo; (*trace*) traza; **suspicious**

[-ʃəs] a (suspecting) receloso; (causing ~) sospechoso.

sustain [səs'teɪn] vt sostener, apoyar; (suffer) sufrir, padecer; **~ed** a (effort) sostenido.

sustenance ['sʌstɪnəns] n sustento.

swab [swɔb] n (MED) algodón m, torunda.

swagger ['swægə°] vi pavonearse.

swallow ['swɔləu] n (bird) golondrina; (of food etc) trago // vt tragar; **to ~ up** vt (savings etc) consumir.

swam [swæm] pt of **swim.**

swamp [swɔmp] n pantano, ciénaga // vt abrumar, agobiar; **~y** a pantanoso.

swan [swɔn] n cisne m.

swap [swɔp] n canje m, intercambio // vt: **to ~ (for)** canjear (por).

swarm [swɔːm] n (of bees) enjambre m; (gen) multitud f // vi hormiguear, pulular.

swarthy ['swɔːðɪ] a moreno.

swastika ['swɔstɪkə] n suástica, cruz f gamada.

swat [swɔt] vt aplastar.

sway [sweɪ] vi mecerse, balancearse // vt (influence) mover, influir en.

swear [sweə°], pt **swore**, pp **sworn** vi jurar; **to ~ to sth** declarar algo bajo juramento; **~word** n taco, palabrota.

sweat [swɛt] n sudor m // vi sudar.

sweater ['swɛtə°] n suéter m.

sweaty ['swɛtɪ] a sudoroso.

swede [swiːd] n nabo.

Swede [swiːd] n sueco/a; **Sweden** n Suecia; **Swedish** a, n (LING) sueco.

sweep [swiːp] n (act) barredura; (of arm) golpe m; (range) extensión f, alcance m; (also: **chimney ~**) deshollinador m // (vb: pt, pp **swept**) vt barrer; (mines) rastrear // vi barrer; **to ~ away** vt barrer; (rub out) borrar; **to ~ past** vi pasar rápidamente; (brush by) rozar; **to ~ up** vi recoger la basura; **~ing** a (gesture) dramático; (generalized) generalizado.

sweet [swiːt] n (candy) dulce m, caramelo; (pudding) postre m // a dulce; (sugary) azucarado; (fresh) fresco, nuevo; (fig) dulce, amable; **~corn** n maíz m; **~en** vt endulzar; (add sugar to) poner azúcar a; **~heart** n novio/a; (in speech) amor; **~ly** ad dulcemente; (gently) suavemente; **~ness** n (gen) dulzura; (amount of sugar) lo dulce, lo azucarado; **~ pea** n guisante m de olor.

swell [swɛl] n (of sea) marejada, oleaje m // a (col: excellent) estupendo, excelente // (vb: pt **swelled**, pp **swollen** or **swelled**) vt hinchar, inflar // vi hincharse, inflarse; **~ing** n (MED) hinchazón m.

sweltering ['swɛltərɪŋ] a sofocante, de mucho calor.

swept [swɛpt] pt, pp of **sweep.**

swerve [swəːv] vi desviarse bruscamente.

swift [swɪft] n (bird) vencejo // a rápido, veloz; **~ness** n rapidez f, velocidad f.

swig [swɪg] n (col: drink) trago.

swill [swɪl] n bazofia // vt (also: ~ out, ~

down) lavar, limpiar con agua.

swim [swɪm] n: **to go for a ~** ir a nadar // (vb: pt **swam**, pp **swum**) vi nadar; (head, room) dar vueltas // vt pasar a nado; **~mer** n nadador/a m/f; **~ming** n natación f; **~ming baths** npl piscina sg; **~ming cap** n gorro de baño; **~ming costume** n bañador m, traje m de baño; **~ming pool** n piscina; **~suit** n bañador m, traje m de baño.

swindle ['swɪndl] n estafa // vt estafar; **swindler** n estafador/a m/f.

swine [swaɪn] n, pl inv cerdos mpl, puercos mpl, (col!) canalla sg.

swing [swɪŋ] n (in playground) columpio; (movement) balanceo, vaivén m; (change of direction) viraje m; (rhythm) ritmo // (vb: pt, pp **swung**) vt balancear; (on a ~) columpiar; (also: ~ **round**) voltear bruscamente // vi balancearse, columpiarse; (also: ~ **round**) volver bruscamente; **to be in full ~** estar en plena marcha; **~ bridge** n puente m giratorio; **~ door** n puerta giratoria.

swipe [swaɪp] n golpe m fuerte // vt (hit) golpear fuerte; (col: steal) guindar.

swirl [swəːl] vi arremolinarse.

Swiss [swɪs] a, n, pl inv suizo/a.

switch [swɪtʃ] n (for light, radio etc) interruptor m; (change) cambio; (of hair) trenza postiza // vt (change) cambiar de; **to ~ off** vt apagar; (engine) parar; **to ~ on** vt encender, prender; (engine, machine) arrancar; **~board** n (TEL) central f de teléfonos.

Switzerland ['swɪtsələnd] n Suiza.

swivel ['swɪvl] vi (also: ~ **round**) girar.

swollen ['swəulən] pp of **swell.**

swoon [swuːn] vi desmayarse, desvanecerse.

swoop [swuːp] n (by police etc) redada // vi (also: ~ **down**) calarse, precipitarse.

swop [swɔp] = **swap.**

sword [sɔːd] n espada; **~fish** n pez m espada.

swore [swɔː°] pt of **swear.**

sworn [swɔːn] pp of **swear.**

swot [swɔt] vt, vi empollar.

swum [swʌm] pp of **swim.**

swung [swʌŋ] pt, pp of **swing.**

sycamore ['sɪkəmɔː°] n sicomoro.

syllable ['sɪləbl] n sílaba.

syllabus ['sɪləbəs] n programa m de estudios.

symbol ['sɪmbl] n símbolo; **~ic(al)** [-'bɔlɪk(l)] a simbólico; **~ism** n simbolismo; **~ize** vt simbolizar.

symmetrical [sɪ'mɛtrɪkl] a simétrico; **symmetry** ['sɪmɪtrɪ] n simetría.

sympathetic [sɪmpə'θɛtɪk] a compasivo; (pleasant) simpático; **~ally** ad con compasión.

sympathize ['sɪmpəθaɪz] vi: **to ~ with sb** compadecerse de uno; **sympathizer** n (POL) simpatizante m/f.

sympathy ['sɪmpəθɪ] n (pity) compasión f; (liking) simpatía; **with our deepest ~**

nuestro más sentido pésame; ~ **strike** *n* huelga por solidaridad.

symphony ['sımfənı] *n* sinfonía; ~ **orchestra** *n* orquesta sinfónica.

symposium [sım'pəuzıəm] *n* simposio.

symptom ['sımptəm] *n* síntoma *m*, indicio; ~**atic** [-'mætık] *a* sintomático.

synagogue ['sınəgɔg] *n* sinagoga.

synchronize ['sıŋkrənaız] *vt* sincronizar // *vi*: to ~ **with** sincronizarse con.

syndicate ['sındıkıt] *n* (*gen*) sindicato; (*of newspapers*) cadena.

syndrome ['sındrəum] *n* síndrome *m*.

synonym ['sınənım] *n* sinónimo; ~**ous** [sı'nɔnıməs] *a*: ~**ous (with)** sinónimo (con).

synopsis [sı'nɔpsıs], *pl* **-ses** [-siːz] *n* sinopsis *f inv*.

syntax ['sıntæks] *n* sintáxis *f*.

synthesis ['sınθəsıs], *pl* **-ses** [-siːz] *n* síntesis *f inv*.

synthetic [sın'θetık] *a* sintético.

syphilis ['sıfılıs] *n* sífilis *f*.

syphon ['saıfən] = **siphon**.

Syria ['sırıə] *n* Siria; ~ *n a*, *n* sirio/a.

syringe [sı'rındʒ] *n* jeringa.

syrup ['sırəp] *n* jarabe *m*, almíbar *m*.

system ['sıstəm] *n* (*gen*) sistema; (*method*) método; (ANAT) organismo; ~**atic** [-'mætık] *a* sistemático; metódico; ~**s analyst** *n* analista *m/f* de sistemas.

T

ta [tɑː] *excl* (*Brit: col*) gracias.

tab [tæb] *n* (*gen*) lengüeta; (*label*) etiqueta; to keep ~**s on** (*fig*) vigilar.

tabby ['tæbı] *n* (*also*: ~ **cat**) gato atigrado.

table ['teıbl] *n* mesa; (*of statistics etc*) cuadro, tabla // *vt* (*motion etc*) presentar; to lay *or* set the ~ poner la mesa; ~**cloth** *n* mantel *m*; ~ **d'hôte** [tɑːbl'dəut] *n* menú *m*; ~**mat** *n* mantel *m* individual; ~**spoon** *n* cuchara grande; (*also*: ~**spoonful**: *as measurement*) cucharada.

tablet ['tæblıt] *n* (MED) tableta, pastilla; (*for writing*) bloc *m*; (*of stone*) lápida.

table: ~ **tennis** *n* ping-pong *m*, tenis *m* de mesa; ~ **wine** *n* vino de mesa.

taboo [tə'buː] *n* tabú *m* // *a* tabú.

tacit ['tæsıt] *a* tácito.

taciturn ['tæsıtəːn] *a* taciturno.

tack [tæk] *n* (*nail*) tachuela, chincheta; (*stitch*) hilván *m*; (NAUT) bordada // *vt* (*nail*) clavar con chinchetas; (*stitch*) hilvanar // *vi* virar.

tackle ['tækl] *n* (*gear*) equipo; (*also*: **fishing** ~) aparejo; (*for lifting*) polea; (RUGBY) atajo // *vt* (*difficulty*) enfrentar; (*grapple with*) agarrar; (RUGBY) atajar.

tacky ['tækı] *a* pegajoso.

tact [tækt] *n* tacto, discreción *f*; ~**ful** *a* discreto, diplomático; ~**fully** *ad* discretamente.

tactical ['tæktıkl] *a* táctico; **tactics** [-tıks] *n*, *npl* táctica *sg*.

tactless ['tæktlıs] *a* indiscreto, falto de tacto; ~**ly** *ad* indiscretamente.

tadpole ['tædpəul] *n* renacuajo.

tag [tæg] *n* (*label*) etiqueta; (*loose end*) cabo; to ~ **along with sb** acompañar a uno.

tail [teıl] *n* (*gen*) cola; (ZOOL) rabo; (*of shirt, coat*) faldón *m* // *vt* (*follow*) seguir los talones a; to ~ **away**, ~ **off** *vi* (*in size, quality etc*) ir disminuyendo; ~ **coat** *n* frac *m*; ~ **end** *n* cola, parte *f* final; ~**gate** *n* puerta trasera.

tailor ['teılə*] *n* sastre *m*; ~**ing** *n* (*cut*) corte *m*; (*craft*) sastrería; ~**-made** *a* hecho a la medida; (*fig*) especial.

tailwind ['teılwınd] *n* viento de cola.

tainted ['teıntıd] *a* (*food*) pasado; (*water, air*) contaminado; (*fig*) manchado.

take [teık], *pt* **took**, *pp* **taken** *vt* (*gen*) tomar; (*grab*) coger; (*gain: prize*) ganar; (*require: effort, courage*) exigir, hacer falta; (*tolerate*) aguantar; (*hold: passengers etc*) tener cabida para; (*accompany, bring, carry*) llevar; (*exam*) presentarse a; to ~ **sth from** (*drawer etc*) sacar algo de; (*person*) coger algo a; **I ~ it that...** supongo que...; to ~ **after** *vt fus* parecerse a; to ~ **apart** *vt* desmontar; to ~ **away** *vt* (*remove*) quitar; (*carry off*) llevar; to ~ **back** *vt* (*return*) devolver; (*one's words*) retractar; to ~ **down** *vt* (*building*) demoler; (*letter etc*) poner por escrito; to ~ **in** *vt* (*deceive*) engañar; (*understand*) entender; (*include*) abarcar; (*lodger*) acoger, recibir; to ~ **off** *vi* (AVIAT) despegar // *vt* (*remove*) quitar; (*imitate*) imitar; to ~ **on** *vt* (*work*) emprender; (*employee*) contratar; (*opponent*) desafiar; to ~ **out** *vt* sacar; (*remove*) quitar; to ~ **over** *vt* (*business*) tomar posesión de // *vi*: to ~ **over from sb** relevar a uno; to ~ **to** *vt fus* (*person*) coger simpatía a; (*activity*) aficionarse a; to ~ **up** *vt* (*a dress*) acortar; (*occupy: time, space*) ocupar; (*engage in: hobby etc*) dedicarse a; ~**away** *a* (*food*) para llevar; ~**-home pay** *n* salario neto; ~**off** *n* (AVIAT) despegue *m*; ~**over** *n* (COMM) absorción *f*; ~**over bid** *n* oferta de compra.

takings ['teıkıŋz] *npl* (COMM) ingresos *mpl*.

talc [tælk] *n* (*also*: ~**um powder**) talco.

tale [teıl] *n* (*story*) cuento; (*account*) relación *f*; to tell ~**s** (*fig: lie*) chismear.

talent ['tælnt] *n* talento; ~**ed** *a* talentoso, de talento.

talk [tɔːk] *n* (*gen*) charla; (*gossip*) habladurías *fpl*, chismes *mpl*; (*conversation*) conversación *f* // *vi* (*speak*) hablar; (*chatter*) charlar; to ~ **about** hablar de; to ~ **sb into doing sth** convencer a uno de que debe hacer algo; to ~ **sb out of doing sth** disuadir a uno de algo; to ~ **shop** hablar de asuntos profesionales; **to ~ over** *vt* hablar de; **~ative** a hablador(a).

tall [tɔːl] *a* (*gen*) alto; (*tree*) grande; **to be 6 feet ~** medir 6 pies, tener 6 pies de alto; **~boy** *n* cómoda alta; **~ness** *n* altura; **~ story** *n* historia inverosímil.

tally ['tælɪ] *n* cuenta // *vi*: **to ~ (with)** corresponder (con).

talon ['tælən] *n* garra.

tambourine [tæmbəˈriːn] *n* pandereta.

tame [teɪm] *a* (*mild*) manso; (*tamed*) domesticado; (*fig*: *story, style*) soso.

tamper ['tæmpə°] *vi*: **to ~ with** entrometerse en.

tampon ['tæmpɒn] *n* tampón *m*.

tan [tæn] *n* (*also*: **sun~**) bronceado // *vt* broncear // *vi* ponerse moreno // *a* (*colour*) marrón.

tandem ['tændəm] *n* tándem *m*.

tang [tæŋ] *n* sabor *m* fuerte.

tangerine [tændʒəˈriːn] *n* mandarina.

tangible ['tændʒəbl] *a* tangible.

tangle ['tæŋgl] *n* enredo; **to get in(to) a ~** enredarse.

tango ['tæŋgəu] *n* tango.

tank [tæŋk] *n* (*water ~*) depósito. tanque *m*; (*for fish*) acuario; (*MIL*) tanque *m*.

tanker ['tæŋkə°] *n* (*ship*) petrolero; (*truck*) camión *m* cisterna *o* tanque.

tanned [tænd] *a* (*skin*) moreno, bronceado.

tantalizing ['tæntəlaɪzɪŋ] *a* tentador(a).

tantamount ['tæntəmaunt] *a*: **~ to** equivalente a.

tantrum ['tæntrəm] *n* rabieta.

tap [tæp] *n* (*on sink etc*) grifo; (*gentle blow*) golpecito; (*gas ~*) llave *f* // *vt* dar golpecitos; (*resources*) utilizar, explotar; **~-dancing** *n* zapateado.

tape [teɪp] *n* cinta; (*also*: **magnetic ~**) cinta magnética; (*sticky ~*) cinta adhesiva // *vt* (*record*) grabar (en cinta); **~ measure** *n* cinta métrica, metro.

taper ['teɪpə°] *n* cirio // *vi* afilarse.

tape recorder ['teɪprɪkɔːdə°] *n* grabadora.

tapered ['teɪpəd], **tapering** ['teɪpərɪŋ] *a* afilado.

tapestry ['tæpɪstrɪ] *n* (*object*) tapiz *m*; (*art*) tapicería.

tapioca [tæpɪˈəukə] *n* tapioca.

tar [tɑː] *n* alquitrán *m*, brea.

tarantula [təˈræntjulə] *n* tarántula.

target ['tɑːgɪt] *n* (*gen*) blanco; **~ practice** tiro al blanco.

tariff ['tærɪf] *n* tarifa.

tarmac ['tɑːmæk] *n* (*on road*) alquitranado; (*AVIAT*) pista de aterrizaje.

tarnish ['tɑːnɪʃ] *vt* quitar el brillo a.

tarpaulin [tɑːˈpɔːlɪn] *n* alquitranado.

tarragon ['tærəgɒn] *n* estragón *m*.

tart [tɑːt] *n* (*CULIN*) tarta; (*col*: *pej*: *woman*) fulana // *a* (*flavour*) agrio, ácido.

tartan ['tɑːtn] *n* tartán *m*, escocés *m* // *a* de tartán.

tartar ['tɑːtə°] *n* (*on teeth*) sarro; **~(e) sauce** *n* salsa tártara.

task [tɑːsk] *n* tarea; **to take to ~** reprender; **~ force** *n* (*MIL, POLICE*) destacamento especial.

tassel ['tæsl] *n* borla.

taste [teɪst] *n* sabor *m*, gusto; (*also*: **after~**) dejo; (*sip*) sorbo; (*fig*: *glimpse, idea*) muestra, idea // *vt* probar // *vi*: **to ~ of** *or* **like** (*fish etc*) saber a; **you can ~ the garlic (in it)** se nota el sabor a ajo; **can I have a ~ of this wine?** ¿puedo probar el vino?; **to have a ~ for sth** ser aficionado a algo; **in good/bad ~** de buen/mal gusto; **~ful** *a* de buen gusto; **~fully** *ad* con buen gusto; **~less** *a* (*food*) insípido; (*remark*) de mal gusto; **tasty** *a* sabroso, rico.

tattered ['tætəd] *a see* **tatters**.

tatters ['tætəz] *npl*: **in ~** (*also*: **tattered**) hecho jirones.

tattoo [təˈtuː] *n* tatuaje *m*; (*spectacle*) espectáculo militar // *vt* tatuar.

tatty ['tætɪ] *a* (*col*) raído.

taught [tɔːt] *pt, pp of* **teach.**

taunt [tɔːnt] *n* burla // *vt* burlarse de.

Taurus ['tɔːrəs] *n* Tauro.

taut [tɔːt] *a* tirante, tenso.

tawdry ['tɔːdrɪ] *a* cursi, de mal gusto.

tawny ['tɔːnɪ] *a* leonado.

tax [tæks] *n* impuesto // *vt* gravar (con un impuesto); (*fig*: *test*) abrumar; (: *patience*) agotar; **direct ~** contribución directa; **~ation** [-'seɪʃən] *n* impuestos *mpl*; **~ collector** *n* recaudador/a *m/f*; **~-free** *a* libre de impuestos.

taxi ['tæksɪ] *n* taxi *m* // *vi* (*AVIAT*) rodar de suelo.

taxidermist ['tæksɪdəːmɪst] *n* taxidermista *m/f*.

taxi: ~ driver *n* taxista *m/f*; **~ rank, ~ stand** *n* parada de taxis.

tax: ~ payer *n* contribuyente *m/f*; **~ return** *n* declaración *f* de ingresos.

TB *abbr of* **tuberculosis.**

tea [tiː] *n* té *m*; (*snack*) merienda; **high ~** merienda-cena; **~ bag** *n* bolsa de té; **~ break** *n* descanso para el té; **~cake** *n* bollo.

teach [tiːtʃ], *pt, pp* **taught** *vt*: **to ~ sb sth, ~ sth to sb** enseñar algo a uno // *vi* enseñar; (*be a teacher*) ser profesor/a; **~er** *n* (*in secondary school*) profesor/a *m/f*; (*in primary school*) maestro/a; **~ing** *n* enseñanza.

tea: ~ cosy *n* cubretetera; **~cup** *n* taza para té.

teak [tiːk] *n* (*madera de*) teca.

tea leaves *npl* hojas *fpl* de té.

team [tiːm] *n* equipo; (*of animals*) pareja; **~ work** *n* trabajo de equipo.

teapot ['tiːpɒt] *n* tetera.

tear [tɛə°] *n* rasgón *m*, desgarrón *m* // *n* [tɪə°] lágrima // (*vb*: *pt* **tore**, *pp* **torn**) *vt* romper, rasgar // *vi* rasgarse; **in ~s** llorando; **to burst into ~s** deshacerse en lágrimas; **to ~ along** *vi* (*rush*) precipitarse; **~ful** *a* lloroso; **~ gas** *n* gas *m* lacrimógeno.

tearoom ['ti:ru:m] *n* salón *m* de té, cafetería.

tease [ti:z] *n* bromista *m/f* // *vt* bromear, tomar el pelo a.

tea: ~ **set** *n* juego de té; ~**spoon** *n* cucharilla; (*also*: ~**spoonful**: *as measurement*) cucharadita.

teat [ti:t] *n* (*of bottle*) tetina.

tea: ~**time** *n* hora del té; ~ **towel** *n* trapo de cocina.

technical ['teknɪkl] *a* técnico; ~**ity** [-'kælɪtɪ] *n* detalle *m* técnico; ~**ly** *ad* técnicamente.

technician [tek'nɪʃn] *n* técnico.

technique [tek'ni:k] *n* técnica.

technological [teknə'lɔdʒɪkl] *a* tecnológico; **technology** [-'nɔlədʒɪ] *n* tecnología.

teddy (bear) ['tedɪ] *n* osito de felpa.

tedious ['ti:dɪəs] *a* pesado, aburrido.

tee [ti:] *n* (GOLF) tee *m*.

teem [ti:m] *vi* abundar, pulular; **to ~ with** rebosar de; **it is ~ing (with rain)** llueve a mares.

teenage ['ti:neɪdʒ] *a* (*fashions etc*) de o para los jóvenes; **teenager** *n* joven *m/f* (de 13 a 19 años).

teens [ti:nz] *npl*: **to be in one's ~** ser un adolescente, no haber cumplido los 20.

tee-shirt ['ti:ʃə:t] *n* = **T-shirt**.

teeter ['ti:tə*] *vi* balancearse.

teeth [ti:θ] *pl* of **tooth**.

teethe [ti:ð] *vi* echar los dientes.

teething ['ti:ðɪŋ]: ~ **ring** *n* mordedor *m*; ~ **troubles** *npl* (*fig*) dificultades *fpl* iniciales.

teetotal ['ti:'təutl] *a* (*person*) abstemio.

telecommunications ['telɪkəmju:nɪ-'keɪʃənz] *n* telecomunicaciones *fpl*.

telegram ['telɪgræm] *n* telegrama *m*.

telegraph ['telɪgra:f] *n* telégrafo; ~**ic** [-'græfɪk] *a* telegráfico; ~ **pole** *n* poste *m* de telégrafos.

telepathic [telɪ'pæθɪk] *a* telepático; **telepathy** [tə'lepəθɪ] *n* telepatía.

telephone ['telɪfəun] *n* teléfono // *vt* (*person*) llamar por teléfono; (*message*) telefonear; ~ **booth**, ~ **box** *n* cabina telefónica; ~ **call** *n* llamada (telefónica); ~ **directory** *n* guía (telefónica); ~ **exchange** *n* central *f* telefónica; ~ **number** *n* número de teléfono; **telephonist** [tə'lefənɪst] *n* telefonista *m/f*.

telephoto ['telɪ'fəutəu] *a*: ~ **lens** teleobjetivo.

teleprinter ['telɪprɪntə*] *n* teletipo.

telescope ['telɪskəup] *n* telescopio; **telescopic** [-'skɔpɪk] *a* telescópico.

televise ['telɪvaɪz] *vt* televisar.

television ['telɪvɪʒən] *n* televisión *f*; ~ **set** *n* televisor *m*.

telex ['teleks] *n* telex *m*.

tell [tel], *pt*, *pp* **told** *vt* decir; (*relate*: *story*) contar; (*distinguish*): **to ~ sth from** distinguir algo de // *vi* (*have effect*) tener efecto; **to ~ sb to do sth** mandar a uno que haga algo; **to ~ sb off** reñir *o* regañar a uno; ~**er** *n* (*in bank*) cajero; ~**ing** *a* (*remark*, *detail*) revelador(a); ~**tale** *a* (*sign*) indicador(a).

telly ['telɪ] *n* (*col*) *abbr of* **television**.

temerity [tə'merɪtɪ] *n* temeridad *f*.

temper ['tempə*] *n* (*nature*) carácter *m*; (*mood*) humor *m*; (*bad* ~) genio, mal genio; (*fit of anger*) cólera; (*of child*) rabieta // *vt* (*moderate*) moderar; **to be in a ~** estar de mal humor; **to lose one's ~** perder la paciencia.

temperament ['tempərəmənt] *n* (*nature*) temperamento; ~**al** [-'mentl] *a* temperamental.

temperance ['tempərns] *n* moderación *f*; (*in drinking*) sobriedad *f*.

temperate ['tempərət] *a* moderado; (*climate*) templado.

temperature ['temprətʃə*] *n* temperatura; **to have** *or* **run a ~** tener fiebre.

tempered ['tempəd] *a* (*steel*) templado.

tempest ['tempɪst] *n* tempestad *f*.

temple ['templ] *n* (*building*) templo; (ANAT) sien *f*.

tempo ['tempəu], *pl* ~**s** *or* **tempi** [-pi:] *n* tempo; (*fig*: *of life etc*) ritmo.

temporal ['tempərl] *a* temporal.

temporarily ['tempərərɪlɪ] *ad* temporalmente.

temporary ['tempərərɪ] *a* provisional, temporal; (*passing*) transitorio; (*worker*) temporero.

tempt [tempt] *vt* tentar; **to ~ sb into doing sth** tentar *o* inducir a uno a hacer algo; ~**ation** [-'teɪʃən] *n* tentación *f*; ~**ing** *a* tentador(a).

ten [ten] *num* diez.

tenable ['tenəbl] *a* sostenible.

tenacious [tə'neɪʃəs] *a* tenaz; **tenacity** [-'næsɪtɪ] *n* tenacidad *f*.

tenancy ['tenənsɪ] *n* alquiler *m*; (*of house*) inquilinato; **tenant** *n* (*rent-payer*) inquilino; (*occupant*) habitante *m/f*.

tend [tend] *vt* cuidar // *vi*: **to ~ to do sth** tener tendencia a hacer algo.

tendency ['tendənsɪ] *n* tendencia.

tender ['tendə*] *a* tierno, blando; (*delicate*) delicado; (*sore*) sensible, dolorido; (*affectionate*) †ierno, cariñoso // *n* (COMM: *offer*) oferta; (*money*): **legal** ~ moneda de curso legal // *vt* ofrecer; ~**ize** *vt* (CULIN) ablandar; ~**ness** *n* ternura; (*of meat*) blandura.

tendon ['tendən] *n* tendón *m*.

tenement ['tenəmənt] *n* casa de pisos.

tennis ['tenɪs] *n* tenis *m*; ~ **ball** *n* pelota de tenis; ~ **court** *n* pista de tenis; ~ **racket** *n* raqueta de tenis.

tenor ['tenə*] *n* (MUS) tenor *m*.

tenpin bowling ['tenpɪn-] *n* los bolos *mpl*.

tense [tens] *a* tenso; (*stretched*) tirante; (*stiff*) rígido, tieso // *n* (LING) tiempo; ~**ness** *n* tensión *f*.

tension ['tenʃən] *n* tensión *f*.

tent [tɛnt] *n* tienda (de campaña).
tentacle ['tɛntəkl] *n* tentáculo.
tentative ['tɛntətɪv] *a* experimental; (*conclusion*) provisional.
tenterhooks ['tɛntəhuks] *npl*: **on ~** sobre ascuas.
tenth [tɛnθ] *a* décimo.
tent: ~ peg *n* clavija, estaquilla; **~ pole** *n* mástil *m*.
tenuous ['tɛnjuəs] *a* tenue.
tenure ['tɛnjuə°] *n* posesión *f*, tenencia.
tepid ['tɛpɪd] *a* tibio.
term [tɜːm] *n* (*limit*) límite *m*; (*COMM*) plazo; (*word*) término; (*period*) período; (*SCOL*) trimestre *m* // *vt* llamar; **~s** *npl* (*conditions*) condiciones *fpl*; (*COMM*) precio, tarifa; **in the short/long ~** a corto/largo plazo; **to be on good ~s with sb** llevarse bien con uno; **to come to ~s with** (*person*) llegar a un acuerdo con; (*problem*) adaptarse a.
terminal ['tɜːmɪnl] *a* terminal; (*disease*) mortal // *n* (*ELEC*) borne *m*; (*also*: **air ~**) terminal *f*; (*also*: **coach ~**) estación *f* terminal.
terminate ['tɜːmɪneɪt] *vt* terminar // *vi*: **to ~ in** acabar por; **termination** [-'neɪʃən] *n* terminación *f*; (*of contract*) conclusión *f*.
terminology [tɜːmɪ'nɔlədʒɪ] *n* terminología.
terminus ['tɜːmɪnəs], *pl* **-mini** [-mɪnaɪ] *n* término, estación *f* terminal.
termite ['tɜːmaɪt] *n* termita.
terrace ['tɛrəs] *n* terraza; (*row of houses*) hilera de casas adosadas; **the ~s** (*SPORT*) gradas *fpl*; **~d** (*garden*) escalonado; (*house*) adosado.
terrain [tɛ'reɪn] *n* terreno.
terrible ['tɛrɪbl] *a* terrible, horrible; (*fam*) malísimo; **terribly** *ad* terriblemente; (*very badly*) malísimamente.
terrier ['tɛrɪə°] *n* terrier *m*.
terrific [tə'rɪfɪk] *a* fantástico, fenomenal; (*wonderful*) maravilloso.
terrify ['tɛrɪfaɪ] *vt* aterrorizar.
territorial [tɛrɪ'tɔːrɪəl] *a* territorial.
territory ['tɛrɪtərɪ] *n* territorio.
terror ['tɛrə°] *n* terror *m*; **~ism** *n* terrorismo; **~ist** *n* terrorista *m/f*; **~ize** *vt* aterrorizar.
terse [tɜːs] *a* (*style*) conciso, (*reply*) brusco.
test [tɛst] *n* (*trial, check*) prueba, ensayo; (: *of goods in factory*) control *m*; (*of courage etc, CHEM*) prueba; (*MED*) examen *m*; (*exam*) examen *m*, test *m*; (*also*: **driving ~**) examen *m* de conducir // *vt* probar, poner a prueba.
testament ['tɛstəmənt] *n* testamento; **the Old/New T~** el Antiguo/Nuevo Testamento.
testicle ['tɛstɪkl] *n* testículo.
testify ['tɛstɪfaɪ] *vi* (*LAW*) prestar declaración; **to ~ to sth** atestiguar algo.
testimonial [tɛstɪ'məunɪəl] *n* (*reference*) recomendación *f*; (*gift*) obsequio.
testimony ['tɛstɪmənɪ] *n* (*LAW*) testimonio, declaración *f*.
test: ~ match *n* (*CRICKET, RUGBY*) partido internacional; **~ pilot** *n* piloto de pruebas; **~ tube** *n* probeta.
testy ['tɛstɪ] *a* irritable.
tetanus ['tɛtənəs] *n* tétano.
tether ['tɛðə°] *vt* atar (con una cuerda) // *n*: **at the end of one's ~** a punto de perder la paciencia.
text [tɛkst] *n* texto; **~book** *n* libro de texto.
textiles ['tɛkstaɪlz] *npl* textiles *mpl*, tejidos *mpl*.
texture ['tɛkstʃə°] *n* textura.
Thai [taɪ] *a, n* tailandés/esa *m/f*; **~land** *n* Tailandia.
Thames [tɛmz] *n*: **the ~** el (río) Támesis.
than [ðæn, ðən] *conj* que; (*with numerals*): **more ~ 10/once** más de 10/una vez; **I have more/less ~ you** tengo más/menos que tú.
thank [θæŋk] *vt* dar las gracias a, agradecer; **~ you (very much)** muchas gracias; **~s** *npl* gracias *fpl*; **~s to** *prep* gracias a; **~ful (for)** agradecido por; **~less** *a* ingrato; **Thanksgiving (Day)** *n* día *m* de acción de gracias.
that [ðæt, ðət] *conj* que // *det* ese/esa; (*more remote*) aquel/ aquella // *pron* ése/ésa; aquél/ aquélla; (*neuter*) eso; aquello; (*relative: subject*) que; (: *object*) que, el cual/la cual *etc*; (*with time*) **on the day ~ he came** el día que vino // *ad*: **~ high** tan alto, así de alto; **it's about ~ high** es más o menos así de alto; **~ one** ése/ésa; aquél/aquélla; **what's ~?** ¿qué es eso?; **who's ~?** ¿quién es?; **is ~ you?** ¿eres tú?; (*formal*) ¿es Usted?; **~'s what he said** eso es lo que dijo; **all ~** todo eso; **I can't work ~ much** no puedo trabajar tanto.
thatched [θætʃt] *a* (*roof*) de paja; **~ cottage** casita con tejado de paja.
thaw [θɔː] *n* deshielo // *vi* (*ice*) derretirse; (*food*) descongelarse // *vt* (*food*) descongelar.
the [ðiː, ðə] *def art* el/la; (*pl*) los/las; (*neuter*) lo; **~ sooner ~ better** cuanto antes mejor.
theatre, theater (*US*) ['θɪətə°] *n* teatro; **~-goer** *n* aficionado al teatro.
theatrical [θɪ'ætrɪkl] *a* teatral.
theft [θɛft] *n* robo.
their [ðɛə°] *a* su; **~s** *pron* (el) suyo/(la) suya *etc*; **a friend of ~s** un amigo suyo.
them [ðɛm, ðəm] *pron* (*direct*) los/las; (*indirect*) les; (*stressed, after prep*) ellos/ellas; **I see ~** los veo; **give ~ the book** dales el libro.
theme [θiːm] *n* tema *m*; **~ song** tema (musical).
themselves [ðəm'sɛlvz] *pl pron* (*subject*) ellos mismos/ellas mismas; (*complement*) se; (*after prep*) sí (mismos/as).
then [ðɛn] *ad* (*at that time*) entonces; (*next*) pues; (*later*) luego, después; (*and also*)

además // *conj* (*therefore*) en ese caso, entonces // *a*: the ~ **president** el entonces presidente; from ~ **on** desde entonces.

theological [θɪə'lɔdʒɪkl] *a* teológico; **theology** [θɪ'ɔlədʒɪ] *n* teología.

theorem ['θɪərəm] *n* teorema *m*.

theoretical [θɪə'rɛtɪkl] *a* teórico; **theorize** ['θɪəraɪz] *vi* elaborar una teoría; **theory** ['θɪərɪ] *n* teoría.

therapeutic(al) [θɛrə'pju:tɪk(l)] *a* terapéutico.

therapist ['θɛrəpɪst] *n* terapeuta *m/f*; **therapy** *n* terapia.

there [ðɛəʳ] *ad* allí, allá, ahí; ~, ~! ¡cálmate!; it's ~ está ahí; ~ **is**, ~ **are** hay; ~ **he is** ahí está; on/in ~ allí encima/dentro; ~abouts *ad* por ahí; ~after *ad* después; ~fore *ad* por lo tanto; ~'s = ~ **is**; ~ **has**.

thermal ['θə:ml] *a* termal.

thermometer [θə'mɔmɪtəʳ] *n* termómetro.

Thermos ['θə:mɔs] *n* termo.

thermostat ['θə:məustæt] *n* termostato.

thesaurus [θɪ'sɔ:rəs] *n* tesoro.

these [ði:z] *pl det* estos/as // *pl pron* éstos/as.

thesis ['θi:sɪs], *pl* **-ses** [-si:z] *n* tesis *f*.

they [ðeɪ] *pl pron* ellos/ellas; (*stressed*) ellos ~mismos/ellas (mismas); ~ **say that...** (*it is said that*) se dice que...; ~'d = they had; they would; ~'ll = they shall, they will; ~'re = they are; ~'ve = they have.

thick [θɪk] *a* espeso; (*fat*) grueso; (*dense*) denso, espeso; (*stupid*) torpe // *n*: **in the** ~ **of the battle** en plena batalla; **it's 20 cm** ~ tiene 20 cm de espesor; ~**en** *vi* espesarse // *vt* (*sauce etc*) espesar; ~**ness** *n* espesor *m*, grueso; ~**set** *a* rechoncho; ~**skinned** *a* (*fig*) insensible.

thief [θi:f], *pl* **thieves** [θi:vz] *n* ladrón/ona *m/f*.

thieving ['θi:vɪŋ] *n* robo.

thigh [θaɪ] *n* muslo.

thimble ['θɪmbl] *n* dedal *m*.

thin [θɪn] *a* (*gen*) delgado; (*watery*) aguado; (*light*) tenue; (*hair, crowd*) escaso; (*fog*) poco denso // *vt*: **to** ~ (**down**) (*sauce, paint*) diluir.

thing [θɪŋ] *n* (*gen*) cosa; (*object*) objeto, artículo; (*matter*) asunto; (*mania*) manía; ~**s** *npl* (*belongings*) efectos *mpl* (personales); **the best** ~ **would be to...** lo mejor sería...; **how are** ~**s?** ¿qué tal?

think [θɪŋk], *pt, pp* **thought** *vi* pensar // *vt* pensar, creer; (*imagine*) imaginar; **what did you** ~ **of them?** ¿qué te parecieron?; **to** ~ **about sth/sb** pensar en algo/alguien; **I'll** ~ **about it** lo pensaré; **to** ~ **of doing sth** pensar en hacer algo; **I** ~ **so/not** creo que sí/no; **to** ~ **well of sb** tener buen concepto de alguien; **to** ~ **over** *vt* reflexionar sobre, meditar; **to** ~ **up** *vt* imaginar; ~**ing** *a* pensante.

thinly ['θɪnlɪ] *ad* (*cut*) en lonchas finas; (*spread*) con una capa fina.

thinness ['θɪnnɪs] *n* delgadez *f*.

third [θə:d] *a* tercer(a) // *n* tercero; (*fraction*) tercio; (*scol: degree*) de tercera clase; ~**ly** *ad* en tercer lugar; ~ **party insurance** *n* seguro contra terceras personas; ~~**rate** *a* (de calidad) mediocre; **the T**~ **World** *n* el Tercer Mundo.

thirst [θə:st] *n* sed *f*; ~**y** *a* (*person*) sediento; **to be** ~**y** tener sed.

thirteen ['θə:'ti:n] *num* trece.

thirty ['θə:tɪ] *num* treinta.

this [ðɪs] *det* este/esta // *pron* éste/ésta; (*neuter*) esto; ~ **is what he said** esto es lo que dijo; ~ **high** así de alto.

thistle ['θɪsl] *n* cardo.

thong [θɔŋ] *n* correa.

thorn [θɔ:n] *a* espina; ~**y** *a* espinoso.

thorough ['θʌrə] *a* (*search*) minucioso; (*knowledge, research*) profundo; ~**bred** *a* (*horse*) de pura sangre; ~**fare** *n* calle *f*; '**no** ~**fare**' "prohibido el paso"; ~**ly** *ad* minuciosamente; profundamente, a fondo.

those [ðəuz] *pl pron* esos/esas; (*more remote*) aquellos/as // *pl det* ésos/ésas; aquéllos/as.

though [ðəu] *conj* aunque // *ad* sin embargo.

thought [θə:t] *pt, pp of* **think** // *n* pensamiento; (*opinion*) opinión *f*; (*intention*) intención *f*; ~**ful** *a* considerado; ~**less** *a* desconsiderado.

thousand ['θauzənd] *num* mil; **two** ~ dos mil; ~**s of** miles de; ~**th** *a* milésimo.

thrash [θræʃ] *vt* apalear; (*defeat*) derrotar; **to** ~ **about** *vi* revolcarse; **to** ~ **out** *vt* discutir largamente.

thread [θrɛd] *n* hilo; (*of screw*) rosca // *vt* (*needle*) enhebrar; ~**bare** *a* raído.

threat [θrɛt] *n* amenaza; ~**en** *vi* amenazar // *vt*: **to** ~**en sb with sth/to do** amenazar a uno con algo/ con hacer.

three [θri:] *num* tres; ~~**dimensional** *a* tridimensional; ~**fold** *ad*: **to increase** ~**fold** triplicar; ~~**piece suit** *n* traje *m* de tres piezas; ~~**piece suite** *n* tresillo; ~~**ply** *a* (*wool*) triple; ~~**wheeler** *n* (*car*) coche *m* de tres ruedas.

thresh [θrɛʃ] *vt* (*AGR*) trillar.

threshold ['θrɛʃhəuld] *n* umbral *m*.

threw [θru:] *pt of* **throw**.

thrift [θrɪft] *n* economía; ~**y** *a* económico.

thrill [θrɪl] *n* (*excitement*) emoción *f*; (*shudder*) estremecimiento // *vt* emocionar; estremecer; **to be** ~**ed** (*with gift etc*) estar encantado; ~**er** *n* película/novela de suspense.

thrive [θraɪv], *pt* **thrived** *or* **throve** [θrəuv], *pp* **thrived** *or* **thriven** ['θrɪvn] *vi* (*grow*) crecer; (*do well*) prosperar; **thriving** *a* próspero.

throat [θrəut] *n* garganta; **to have a sore** ~ tener dolor de garganta.

throb [θrɔb] *n* (*of heart*) latido; (*of engine*)

vibración f // vi latir; vibrar; (pain) dar punzadas.

throes [θrəuz] npl: **in the ~ of** en medio de.

thrombosis [θrɔm'bəusɪs] n trombosis f.

throne [θrəun] n trono.

throttle ['θrɔtl] n (AUT) acelerador m // vt ahogar.

through [θruː] prep por, a través de; (time) durante; (by means of) por medio de, mediante; (owing to) gracias a // a (ticket, train) directo // ad completamente, de parte a parte; **to put sb ~ to sb** (TEL) poner a alguien (en comunicación) con alguien; **to be ~** (TEL) tener comunicación; (have finished) haber terminado; **"no ~ way"** "calle sin salida"; **~out** prep (place) por todas partes de, por todo; (time) durante todo, en todo // ad por o en todas partes.

throw [θrəu] n tirada, tiro; (SPORT) lanzamiento // vt, pt **threw**, pp **thrown** tirar, echar; (SPORT) lanzar; (rider) derribar; (fig) desconcertar; **to ~ a party** dar una fiesta; **to ~ away** vt tirar; **to ~ off** vt deshacerse de; **to ~ out** vt tirar; **to ~ up** vi vomitar; **~away** a para tirar, desechable; **~-in** (SPORT) saque m.

thru [θruː] (US) = **through.**

thrush [θrʌʃ] n zorzal m, tordo.

thrust [θrʌst] n (TECH) empuje m // vt, pt, pp **thrust** empujar; (push in) introducir.

thud [θʌd] n golpe m sordo.

thug [θʌg] n (criminal) criminal m/f; (pej) bruto.

thumb [θʌm] n (ANAT) pulgar m, dedo gordo (col) // vt (book) hojear; **to ~ a lift** hacer dedo o autostop; **~tack** n (US) chinche m.

thump [θʌmp] n golpe m; (sound) porrazo // vt, vi golpear.

thunder [θʌndə*] n (gen) trueno; (sudden noise) tronido; (of applause etc) estruendo // vi tronar; (train etc): **to ~ past** pasar como un trueno; **~bolt** n rayo; **~clap** n trueno; **~storm** n tormenta; **~struck** a pasmado; **~y** a tormentoso.

Thursday ['θəːzdɪ] n jueves m.

thus [ðʌs] ad así, de este modo.

thwart [θwɔːt] vt frustrar.

thyme [taɪm] n tomillo.

thyroid ['θaɪrɔɪd] n tiroides m.

tiara [tɪ'ɑːrə] n tiara, diadema.

tic [tɪk] n tic m.

tick [tɪk] n (sound: of clock) tictac m; (mark) palomita; (ZOOL) garrapata; (col): **in a ~** en un instante // vi hacer tictac // vt marcar; **to ~ off** vt marcar; (person) poner como un trapo.

ticket ['tɪkɪt] n billete m, tíquet m; (for cinema) entrada; (in shop: on goods) etiqueta; (for library) tarjeta; **~ collector** n revisor m; **~ office** n taquilla.

tickle ['tɪkl] n cosquillas fpl // vt hacer cosquillas a; **ticklish** a que tiene cosquillas.

tidal ['taɪdl] a de marea; **~ wave** n maremoto.

tiddlywinks ['tɪdlɪwɪŋks] n juego de la pulga.

tide [taɪd] n marea; (fig: of events) curso, marcha.

tidiness ['taɪdɪnɪs] n (good order) buen orden m; (neatness) limpieza, aseo.

tidy ['taɪdɪ] a (room) ordenado; (dress, work) limpio; (person) (bien) arreglado // vt (also: **~ up**) poner en orden.

tie [taɪ] n (string etc) atadura; (also: **neck~**) corbata; (fig: link) vínculo, lazo; (SPORT: draw) empate m // vt (gen) atar // vi (SPORT) empatar; **to ~ in a bow** hacer un lazo; **to ~ a knot in sth** hacer un nudo a algo; **to ~ down** vt atar; (fig): **to ~ sb down to** obligar a uno a; **to ~ up** vt (parcel) envolver; (dog) atar; (boat) amarrar; (arrangements) concluir, despachar; **to be ~d up** (busy) estar ocupado.

tier [tɪə*] n grada; (of cake) piso.

tiger ['taɪgə*] n tigre m/f.

tight [taɪt] a (rope) tirante; (money) escaso; (clothes) ajustado; (budget, programme) apretado; (col: drunk) borracho // ad (squeeze) muy fuerte; (shut) herméticamente; **~s** npl pantimedias fpl; (for gym) malla sg; **~en** vt (rope) estirar; (screw) apretar // vi apretarse, estirarse; **~-fisted** a tacaño; **~ly** ad (grasp) muy fuerte; **~-rope** n cuerda floja.

tile [taɪl] n (on roof) teja; (on floor) baldosa; (on wall) azulejo, baldosín m; **~d** a embaldosado.

till [tɪl] n caja (registradora) // vt (land) cultivar // prep, conj = **until.**

tiller ['tɪlə*] n (NAUT) caña del timón.

tilt [tɪlt] vt inclinar // vi inclinarse.

timber [tɪmbə*] n (material) madera; (trees) árboles mpl.

time [taɪm] n tiempo; (epoch: often pl) época; (by clock) hora; (moment) momento; (occasion) vez f; (MUS) compás m // vt (gen) calcular o medir el tiempo de; (race) cronometrar; (remark etc) elegir el momento para; **a long ~** mucho tiempo; **for the ~ being** de momento, por ahora; **from ~ to ~** de vez en cuando; **in ~** (soon enough) a tiempo; (after some time) con el tiempo; (MUS) al compás; **in a week's ~** dentro de una semana; **on ~** a la hora; **5 ~s 5** 5 por 5; **what ~ is it?** ¿qué hora es?; **to have a good ~** pasarlo bien, divertirse; **~ bomb** n bomba de efecto retardado; **~keeper** n (SPORT) cronómetro; **~less** a eterno; **~ limit** n (gen) limitación f de tiempo; (COMM) plazo; **~ly** a oportuno; **~ off** n tiempo libre; **timer** n (in kitchen) reloj m programador; **~ switch** n interruptor m; **~table** n horario; **~ zone** n huso horario.

timid ['tɪmɪd] a tímido.

timing ['taɪmɪŋ] n (SPORT) cronometraje

_m_; (_gen_) elección _f_ del momento; **the ~ of his resignation** el momento que eligió para dimitir.

timpani ['tɪmpənɪ] _npl_ tímpanos _mpl_.

tin [tɪn] _n_ estaño; (_also:_ ~ **plate**) hojalata; (_can_) lata; ~ **foil** _n_ papel _m_ de estaño.

tinge [tɪndʒ] _n_ matiz _m_ // _vt_: ~**d with** teñido de.

tingle ['tɪŋgl] _n_ picotazo // _vi_ sentir picazón.

tinker ['tɪŋkə°] _n_ calderero; (_gipsy_) gitano; **to ~ with** _vt_ manosear.

tinkle ['tɪŋkl] _vi_ tintinear // _n_ (_col_): **to give sb a ~** dar un telefonazo a alguien.

tinned [tɪnd] _a_ (_food_) en lata, en conserva.

tin opener ['tɪnəupnə°] _n_ abrelatas _m inv_.

tinsel ['tɪnsl] _n_ oropel _m_.

tint [tɪnt] _n_ matiz _m_; (_for hair_) tinte _m_.

tiny ['taɪnɪ] _a_ minúsculo, pequeñito.

tip [tɪp] _n_ (_end_) punta; (_gratuity_) propina; (_for rubbish_) basurero; (_advice_) aviso // _vt_ (_waiter_) dar una propina a; (_tilt_) inclinar; (_overturn: also:_ ~ **over**) dar la vuelta a, volcar; (_empty: also:_ ~ **out**) vaciar, echar; ~**-off** _n_ (_hint_) aviso, advertencia; ~**ped** _a_ (_cigarette_) con filtro.

tipsy ['tɪpsɪ] _a_ algo borracho, mareado.

tiptoe ['tɪptəu] _n_: **on ~** de puntillas.

tiptop ['tɪp'tɔp] _a_: **in ~ condition** en perfectas condiciones.

tire ['taɪə°] _n_ (_US_) = **tyre** // _vt_ cansar // _vi_ (_gen_) cansarse; (_become bored_) aburrirse; ~**d** _a_ cansado; **to be ~d of sth** estar cansado _o_ harto de algo; **tiredness** _n_ cansancio; ~**less** _a_ incansable; ~**some** _a_ aburrido; **tiring** _a_ cansado.

tissue ['tɪʃuː] _n_ tejido; (_paper handkerchief_) pañuelo de papel, kleenex _m_; ~ **paper** _n_ papel _m_ de seda.

tit [tɪt] _n_ (_bird_) herrerillo común; **to give ~ for tat** dar ojo por ojo.

titbit ['tɪtbɪt] _n_ (_food_) golosina; (_news_) suceso.

titillate ['tɪtɪleɪt] _vt_ estimular, excitar.

titivate ['tɪtɪveɪt] _vt_ emperejilar.

title ['taɪtl] _n_ título; ~ **deed** _n_ (_LAW_) título de propiedad; ~ **role** _n_ papel _m_ principal.

titter ['tɪtə°] _vi_ reírse entre dientes.

titular ['tɪtjulə°] _a_ (_in name only_) nominal.

to [tuː, tə] _prep_ a; (_towards_) hacia; (_of time_) a, hasta; (_of_) de; **give it ~ me** dámelo; **the key ~ the front door** la llave de la puerta; **the main thing is ~...** lo importante es...; **to go ~ France/school** ir a Francia/al colegio; **a quarter ~ 5** las 5 menos cuarto; **pull/push the door ~** tirar/empujar la puerta; **to go ~ and fro** ir y venir.

toad [təud] _n_ sapo; ~**stool** _n_ hongo venenoso.

toast [təust] _n_ (_CULIN. also:_ **piece of ~**) tostada; (_drink, speech_) brindis _m_ // _vt_ (_CULIN_) tostar; (_drink to_) brindar; ~**er** _n_ tostador _m_.

tobacco [tə'bækəu] _n_ tabaco; ~**nist** _n_ estanquero; ~**nist's (shop)** _n_ estanco.

toboggan [tə'bɔgən] _n_ tobogán _m_.

today [tə'deɪ] _ad_, _n_ (_also fig_) hoy _m_.

toddler ['tɔdlə°] _n_ niño que empieza a andar.

toddy ['tɔdɪ] _n_ ponche _m_.

toe [təu] _n_ dedo (del pie); (_of shoe_) punta; **to ~ the line** (_fig_) obedecer, conformarse; ~**nail** _n_ uña del pie.

toffee ['tɔfɪ] _n_ caramelo; ~ **apple** _n_ pirulí _m_.

toga ['təugə] _n_ toga.

together [tə'gɛðə°] _ad_ juntos; (_at same time_) al mismo tiempo, a la vez; ~ **with** _prep_ junto con; ~**ness** _n_ compañerismo.

toil [tɔɪl] _n_ trabajo duro, labor _f_ // _vi_ esforzarse.

toilet ['tɔɪlət] _n_ (_lavatory_) servicios _mpl_, wáter _m_ // _cpd_ (_bag, soap etc_) de aseo; ~ **bowl** _n_ palangana; ~ **paper** _n_ papel _m_ higiénico; ~**ries** _npl_ artículos _mpl_ de aseo; (_make-up etc_) artículos _mpl_ de tocador; ~ **roll** _n_ rollo de papel higiénico; ~ **water** _n_ agua de tocador.

token ['təukən] _n_ (_sign_) señal _f_, muestra; (_souvenir_) recuerdo; (_voucher_) cupón _m_; **book/record ~** vale _m_ para comprar libros/discos.

told [təuld] _pt_, _pp of_ **tell**.

tolerable ['tɔlərəbl] _a_ (_bearable_) soportable; (_fairly good_) pasable.

tolerance ['tɔlərns] _n_ (_also:_ TECH) tolerancia; **tolerant** _a_: **tolerant of** tolerante con.

tolerate ['tɔləreɪt] _vt_ tolerar; **toleration** [-'reɪʃən] _n_ tolerancia.

toll [təul] _n_ (_of casualties_) número de víctimas; (_tax, charge_) peaje _m_ // _vi_ (_bell_) doblar; ~ **bridge** _n_ puente _m_ de peaje.

tomato [tə'mɑːtəu] _pl_ ~**es** _n_ tomate _m_.

tomb [tuːm] _n_ tumba.

tombola [tɔm'bəulə] _n_ tómbola.

tomboy ['tɔmbɔɪ] _n_ marimacho.

tombstone ['tuːmstəun] _n_ lápida.

tomcat ['tɔmkæt] _n_ gato.

tomorrow [tə'mɔrəu] _ad_, _n_ (_also fig_) mañana; **the day after ~** pasado mañana; ~ **morning** mañana por la mañana.

ton [tʌn] _n_ tonelada; ~**s of** (_col_) montones _mpl_ de.

tone [təun] _n_ tono // _vi_ armonizar; **to ~ down** _vt_ (_colour, criticism_) suavizar; (_sound_) bajar; (_MUS_) entonar; **to ~ up** _vt_ (_muscles_) tonificar; ~**-deaf** _a_ que no tiene oído.

tongs [tɔŋz] _npl_ (_for coal_) tenazas _fpl_; (_for hair_) tenacillas _fpl_.

tongue [tʌŋ] _n_ lengua; ~ **in cheek** _ad_ irónicamente; ~**-tied** _a_ (_fig_) mudo; ~**-twister** _n_ trabalenguas _m inv_.

tonic ['tɔnɪk] _n_ (_MED_) tónico; (_MUS_) tónica; (_also:_ ~ **water**) (agua) tónica.

tonight [tə'naɪt] _ad_, _n_ esta noche.

tonnage ['tʌnɪdʒ] _n_ (_NAUT_) tonelaje _m_.

tonsil ['tɔnsl] _n_ amígdala, anginas _fpl_ (_col_); ~**litis** [-'laɪtɪs] _n_ amigdalitis _f_, (inflamación _f_ de las) anginas.

too [tu:] ad (*excessively*) demasiado; (*very*) muy; (*also*) también; ~ **much** ad demasiado; ~ **many** det demasiados/as.

took [tuk] pt of **take**.

tool [tu:l] n herramienta; ~ **box** n caja de herramientas.

toot [tu:t] n (*of horn*) bocinazo; (*of whistle*) silbido // vi (*with car-horn*) tocar la bocina.

tooth [tu:θ], pl **teeth** n (ANAT, TECH) diente m; (*molar*) muela; ~**ache** n dolor m de muelas; ~**brush** n cepillo de dientes; ~**paste** n pasta de dientes; ~**pick** n palillo.

top [tɔp] n (*of mountain*) cumbre f, cima; (*of head*) coronilla; (*of ladder*) lo alto; (*of cupboard, table*) superficie f; (*lid: of box, jar*) tapa, tapadera; (: *of bottle*) tapón m; (*of list etc*) cabeza; (*toy*) peonza // a más alto; (*in rank*) principal, primero; (*best*) mejor // vt (*exceed*) exceder; (*be first in*) ir a la cabeza de; **on** ~ **of** sobre, encima de; **from** ~ **to toe** de pies a cabeza; **to** ~ **up** vt llenar; ~**coat** n sobretodo; ~ **hat** n sombrero de copa; ~-**heavy** a (*object*) desequilibrado.

topic ['tɔpɪk] n tema m, tópico; ~**al** a actual.

top: ~**less** a (*bather etc*) con el pecho al descubierto, topless; ~-**level** a (*talks*) al más alto nivel; ~**most** a más alto.

topple ['tɔpl] vt volcar, derribar // vi caerse.

topsy-turvy ['tɔpsɪ'tə:vɪ] a, ad patas arriba.

torch [tɔ:tʃ] n antorcha; (*electric*) linterna.

tore [tɔ:*] pt of **tear**.

torment ['tɔ:mɛnt] n tormento // vt [tɔ:'mɛnt] atormentar; (*fig: annoy*) fastidiar.

torn [tɔ:n] pp of **tear**.

tornado [tɔ:'neɪdəu], pl ~**es** n tornado.

torpedo [tɔ:'pi:dəu], pl ~**es** n torpedo.

torrent ['tɔrnt] n torrente m; ~**ial** [-'rɛnʃl] a torrencial.

torso ['tɔ:səu] n torso.

tortoise ['tɔ:təs] n tortuga; ~**shell** ['tɔ:təʃɛl] a de carey.

tortuous ['tɔ:tjuəs] a tortuoso.

torture ['tɔ:tʃə*] n tortura // vt torturar; (*fig*) atormentar.

Tory ['tɔ:rɪ] a, n conservador/a m/f.

toss [tɔs] vt tirar, echar; (*head*) sacudir (la cabeza); **to** ~ **a coin** echar a cara o cruz; **to** ~ **up for sth** jugar a cara o cruz algo; **to** ~ **and turn in bed** dar vueltas en la cama.

tot [tɔt] n (*drink*) copita; (*child*) nene/a m/f.

total ['təutl] a total, entero // n total m, suma // vt (*add up*) sumar; (*amount to*) ascender a.

totalitarian [təutælɪ'tɛərɪən] a totalitario.

totem pole ['təutəm-] n poste m totémico.

totter ['tɔtə*] vi tambalearse.

touch [tʌtʃ] n (*gen*) tacto; (*contact*) contacto; (*FOOTBALL*) fuera de juego // vt (*gen*) tocar; (*emotionally*) conmover; **a** ~ **of** (*fig*) una pizca o un poquito de; **to get**

in ~ **with sb** ponerse en contacto con uno; **to lose** ~ (*friends*) perder contacto; **to** ~ **on** vt fus (*topic*) aludir (brevemente) a; **to** ~ **up** vt (*paint*) retocar; ~-**and-go** a arriesgado; ~**down** n aterrizaje m; (*on sea*) amerizaje m; ~**ed** a conmovido; (*col*) chiflado; ~**ing** a conmovedor(a); ~**line** n (SPORT) línea de banda; ~**y** a (*person*) susceptible.

tough [tʌf] a (*gen*) duro; (*difficult*) difícil; (*resistant*) resistente; (*person*) fuerte; (: *pej*) bruto // n (*gangster etc*) gorila m; ~**en** vt endurecer; ~**ness** n dureza; dificultad f; resistencia; fuerza.

toupee ['tu:peɪ] n peluca.

tour ['tuə*] n viaje m, vuelta; (*also:* **package** ~) viaje m organizado; (*of town, museum*) visita // vi viajar por; ~**ing** n viajes mpl turísticos, turismo.

tourism ['tuərɪzm] n turismo.

tourist ['tuərɪst] n turista m/f // cpd turístico; ~ **office** n oficina de turismo.

tournament ['tuənəmənt] n torneo.

tousled ['tauzld] a (*hair*) despeinado.

tout [taut] vi: **to** ~ **for** solicitar clientes para // n: ~ **ticket** ~ revendedor/a m/f.

tow [təu] vt remolcar; **'on** ~' (AUT) "a remolque".

toward(s) [tə'wɔ:d(z)] prep hacia; (*of attitude*) respecto a, con; (*of purpose*) para.

towel ['tauəl] n toalla; ~**ling** n (*fabric*) felpa; ~ **rail** n toallero.

tower ['tauə*] n torre f; ~ **block** n rascacielos m inv; ~**ing** a muy alto, imponente.

town [taun] n ciudad f; **to go to** ~ ir a la ciudad; (*fig*) hacer con entusiasmo; ~ **clerk** n secretario del Ayuntamiento; ~ **council** n consejo municipal; ~ **hall** n ayuntamiento; ~ **planning** n urbanismo.

towrope ['təurəup] n cable m de remolque.

toxic ['tɔksɪk] a tóxico.

toy [tɔɪ] n juguete m; **to** ~ **with** vt fus jugar con; (*idea*) acariciar; ~**shop** n juguetería.

trace [treɪs] n rastro // vt (*draw*) trazar, delinear; (*follow*) seguir la pista de; (*locate*) encontrar.

track [træk] n (*mark*) huella, pista; (*path: gen*) camino, senda; (: *of bullet etc*) trayectoria; (: *of suspect, animal*) pista, rastro; (RAIL) vía; (*on tape, SPORT*) pista // vt seguir la pista de; **to keep** ~ **of** mantenerse al tanto de, seguir; **to** ~ **down** vt (*prey*) averiguar el paradero de; (*sth lost*) buscar y encontrar; ~ **suit** n chandal m.

tract [trækt] n (GEO) región f; (*pamphlet*) folleto.

tractor ['træktə*] n tractor m.

trade [treɪd] n comercio, negocio; (*skill, job*) oficio, empleo // vi negociar, comerciar; **to** ~ **in** vt (*old car etc*) ofrecer como parte del pago; ~-**in price** n valor m de un objeto usado que se descuenta del precio de otro nuevo; ~**mark** n marca de fábrica; ~ **name** n marca registrada;

trader n comerciante m/f; **tradesman** n (shopkeeper) tendero; ~ **union** n sindicato; ~ **unionism** n sindicalismo; **trading** n comercio; **trading estate** n zona comercial.

tradition [trəˈdɪʃən] n tradición f; ~**al** a tradicional.

traffic [ˈtræfɪk] n (gen, AUT) tráfico, circulación f; (air ~ etc) tránsito // vi: to ~ in (pej: liquor, drugs) traficar en; ~ **circle** n (US) cruce m giratorio; ~ **jam** n embotellamiento; ~ **lights** npl semáforo sg; ~ **warden** n guardia m/f de tráfico.

tragedy [ˈtrædʒədɪ] n tragedia.

tragic [ˈtrædʒɪk] a trágico.

trail [treɪl] n (tracks) rastro, pista; (path) camino, sendero; (wake) estela // vt (drag) arrastrar; (follow) seguir la pista de; (follow closely) vigilar // vi arrastrarse; to ~ **behind** vi quedar a la zaga; ~**er** n (AUT) remolque m; (US) caravana; (CINEMA) trailer m, avance m.

train [treɪn] n tren m; (of dress) cola; (series) serie f; (followers) séquito // vt (educate) formar; (teach skills to) adiestrar; (sportsman) entrenar; (dog) amaestrar; (point: gun etc): to ~ **on** apuntar a // vi (SPORT) entrenarse; (be educated) recibir una formación; ~**ed** a (worker) cualificado, adiestrado; (teacher) diplomado; (animal) amaestrado; ~**ee** [treɪˈniː] n persona que está aprendiendo; (in trade) aprendiz/a m/f; ~**er** n (SPORT) entrenador/a m/f; (of animals) domador/a m/f; ~**ing** n formación f; adiestramiento, entrenamiento; in ~**ing** (SPORT) en forma; ~**ing college** n (for teachers) escuela normal; (gen) colegio de formación profesional.

traipse [treɪps] vi andar con desgana.

trait [treɪt] n rasgo.

traitor [ˈtreɪtə*] n traidor/a m/f.

tram [træm] n (also: ~**car**) tranvía m.

tramp [træmp] n (person) vagabundo // vi andar con pasos pesados.

trample [ˈtræmpl] vt: to ~ (**underfoot**) pisotear.

trampoline [ˈtræmpəliːn] n trampolín n.

trance [trɑːns] n trance m; (MED) catalepsia.

tranquil [ˈtræŋkwɪl] a tranquilo; ~**lity** n tranquilidad f; ~**lizer** n (MED) tranquilizante m.

transact [trænˈzækt] vt (business) tramitar; ~**ion** [-ˈzækʃən] n transacción f, negocio.

transatlantic [ˈtrænzətˈlæntɪk] a transatlántico.

transcend [trænˈsɛnd] vt trascender.

transcript [ˈtrænskrɪpt] n copia; ~**ion** [-ˈskrɪpʃən] n transcripción f.

transept [ˈtrænsɛpt] n crucero.

transfer [ˈtrænsfə*] n (gen) transferencia; (SPORT) traspaso; (picture, design) calcomanía // vt [trænsˈfə*] trasladar, pasar; to ~ **the charges** (TEL) llamar a cobro revertido; ~**able** [-ˈfɜːrəbl] a trans-

ferible; 'not ~**able**' "intransferible".

transform [trænsˈfɔːm] vt transformar; ~**ation** [-ˈmeɪʃən] n transformación f; ~**er** n (ELEC) transformador m.

transfusion [trænsˈfjuːʒən] n transfusión f.

transient [ˈtrænzɪənt] a transitorio.

transistor [trænˈzɪstə*] n (ELEC) transistor m; ~ **radio** n radio f a transistores.

transit [ˈtrænzɪt] n: **in** ~ de tránsito, de paso.

transition [trænˈzɪʃən] n transición f; ~**al** a transitorio.

transitive [ˈtrænzɪtɪv] a (LING) transitivo.

transitory [ˈtrænzɪtərɪ] a transitorio.

translate [trænzˈleɪt] vt traducir; **translation** [-ˈleɪʃən] n traducción f; **translator** n traductor/a m/f.

transmission [trænzˈmɪʃən] n transmisión f.

transmit [trænzˈmɪt] vt transmitir; ~**ter** n transmisor m; (station) emisora.

transparency [trænsˈpɛərnsɪ] n (PHOT) diapositiva.

transparent [trænsˈpærnt] a transparente.

transplant [trænsˈplɑːnt] vt transplantar // n [ˈtrænsplɑːnt] (MED) transplante m.

transport [ˈtrænspɔːt] n (gen) transporte m; (also: **road/rail** ~) transportes mpl // vt [-ˈpɔːt] transportar; (carry) acarrear; ~**ation** [-ˈteɪʃən] n transporte m; ~ **café** n cafetería de carretera.

transverse [ˈtrænzvɔːs] a transversal.

transvestite [trænzˈvɛstaɪt] n travesti m/f.

trap [træp] n (snare, trick) trampa; (carriage) cabriolé m // vt coger en una trampa; (immobilize) bloquear; (jam) atascar; ~ **door** n escotilla.

trapeze [trəˈpiːz] n trapecio.

trappings [ˈtræpɪŋz] npl adornos mpl.

trash [træʃ] n (pej: goods) pacotilla; (: nonsense) basura; ~ **can** n (US) cubo de la basura.

trauma [ˈtrɔːmə] n trauma m; ~**tic** [-ˈmætɪk] a traumático.

travel [ˈtrævl] n viaje m // vi viajar // vt (distance) recorrer; ~ **agency** n agencia de viajes; ~**ler**, ~**er** (US) n viajero/a; ~**ler's cheque** n cheque m de viajero; ~**ling**, ~**ing** (US) n los viajes mpl, el viajar; ~ **sickness** n mareo.

traverse [ˈtrævəs] vt atravesar, cruzar.

travesty [ˈtrævəstɪ] n parodia.

trawler [ˈtrɔːlə*] n barco rastreador o de rastra.

tray [treɪ] n (for carrying) bandeja; (on desk) cajón m.

treacherous [ˈtrɛtʃərəs] a traidor(a); **treachery** n traición f.

treacle [ˈtriːkl] n melaza.

tread [trɛd] n (step) paso, pisada; (sound) ruido de pasos; (of tyre) banda de rodadura // vi, pt **trod**, pp **trodden** pisar; to ~ **on** vt fus pisar sobre.

treason [ˈtriːzn] n traición f.

treasure ['trɛʒə°] n tesoro // vt (value) apreciar, valorar; ~ **hunt** n caza del tesoro.

treasurer ['trɛʒərə°] n tesorero.

treasury ['trɛʒərɪ] n: **the T~** (POL) el Ministerio de Hacienda.

treat [tri:t] n (present) regalo; (pleasure) placer m // vt tratar; **to ~ sb to sth** invitar a uno a algo.

treatise ['tri:tɪz] n tratado.

treatment ['tri:tmənt] n tratamiento.

treaty ['tri:tɪ] n tratado.

treble ['trɛbl] a triple // n (MUS) triple m // vt triplicar // vi triplicarse.

tree [tri:] n árbol m; ~ **trunk** n tronco de árbol.

trek [trɛk] n (long journey) viaje m largo y peligroso; (tiring walk) caminata; (as holiday) excursión f.

trellis ['trɛlɪs] n enrejado.

tremble ['trɛmbl] vi temblar; **trembling** n temblor m // a tembloroso.

tremendous [trɪ'mɛndəs] a tremendo; (enormous) enorme; (excellent) estupendo.

tremor ['trɛmə°] n temblor m; (also: **earth ~**) temblor m de tierra.

trench [trɛntʃ] n trinchera.

trend [trɛnd] n (tendency) tendencia; (of events) curso; (fashion) moda; ~ **y a** (idea) según las tendencias actuales; (clothes) a la última moda.

trepidation [trɛpɪ'deɪʃən] n agitación f; (fear) ansia.

trespass ['trɛspəs] vi: **to ~ on** entrar sin permiso en; **"no ~ ing"** "prohibido el paso".

tress [trɛs] n trenza.

trestle ['trɛsl] n caballete m; ~ **table** n mesa de caballete.

trial ['traɪəl] n (LAW) juicio, proceso; (test: of machine etc) prueba; (hardship) desgracia; **by ~ and error** por tanteo.

triangle ['traɪæŋgl] n (MATH, MUS) triángulo; **triangular** [-'æŋgjulə°] a triangular.

tribal ['traɪbəl] a tribal.

tribe [traɪb] n tribu f; **tribesman** n miembro de una tribu.

tribulation [trɪbju'leɪʃən] n tribulación f, sufrimiento.

tribunal [traɪ'bju:nl] n tribunal m.

tributary ['trɪbjutərɪ] n (river) afluente m.

tribute ['trɪbju:t] n homenaje m; (payment) tributo; **to pay ~ to** rendir homenaje a.

trice [traɪs] n: **in a ~** en un santiamén.

trick [trɪk] n trampa; (deceit) truco; (joke) broma; (CARDS) baza // vt engañar; **to play a ~ on sb** gastar una broma a uno; ~ **ery** n astucia.

trickle ['trɪkl] n (of water etc) hililo // vi gotear.

tricky ['trɪkɪ] a difícil, delicado.

tricycle ['traɪsɪkl] n triciclo.

trifle ['traɪfl] n bagatela; (CULIN) dulce m de bizcocho, fruta y natillas // ad: **a ~ long** un poquito largo; **trifling** a insignificante.

trigger ['trɪgə°] n (of gun) gatillo; **to ~ off** vt desencadenar.

trigonometry [trɪgə'nɔmətrɪ] n trigonometría.

trill [trɪl] n (of bird) trino.

trim [trɪm] a (elegant) aseado; (house, garden) en buen estado; (figure) con buen tipo // n (haircut etc) recorte m; (on car) tapicería // vt arreglar; (cut) recortar; (decorate) adornar; (NAUT: a sail) orientar; ~ **mings** npl decoraciones fpl; (cuttings) recortes mpl.

Trinity ['trɪnɪtɪ] n: **the ~** la Trinidad.

trinket ['trɪŋkɪt] n chuchería; (piece of jewellery) baratija.

trio ['tri:əu] n trío.

trip [trɪp] n viaje m; (excursion) excursión f; (stumble) traspié m // vi (also: ~ **up**) tropezar; (go lightly) andar a paso ligero // vt poner la zancadilla a.

tripe [traɪp] n (CULIN) callos mpl; (pej: rubbish) bobadas fpl.

triple ['trɪpl] a triple.

triplets ['trɪplɪts] npl trillizos/as m/fpl.

triplicate ['trɪplɪkət] n: **in ~** por triplicado.

tripod ['traɪpɔd] n trípode m.

trite [traɪt] a gastado, trillado.

triumph ['traɪʌmf] n triunfo // vi: **to ~ (over)** vencer; ~ **ant** [-'ʌmfənt] a triunfante.

trivia ['trɪvɪə] npl trivialidades fpl.

trivial ['trɪvɪəl] a insignificante; (commonplace) trivial; ~ **ity** [-'ælɪtɪ] n trivialidad f.

trod [trɔd], **trodden** ['trɔdn] pt, pp of **tread.**

trolley ['trɔlɪ] n carrito; ~ **bus** n trolebús m.

trombone [trɔm'bəun] n trombón m.

troop [tru:p] n grupo, banda; ~ **s** npl (MIL) tropas fpl; **to ~ in/out** vi entrar/salir en grupo; ~ **er** n (MIL) soldado de caballería.

trophy ['trəufɪ] n trofeo.

tropic ['trɔpɪk] n trópico; ~ **al a** tropical.

trot [trɔt] n trote m // vi trotar; **on the ~** (fig: col) de corrido.

trouble ['trʌbl] n problema m, dificultad f; (worry) preocupación f; (bother, effort) molestia, esfuerzo; (unrest) inquietud f; (MED): **stomach ~** problemas mpl gástricos // vt molestar; (worry) preocupar, inquietar // vi: **to ~ to do sth** molestarse en hacer algo; ~ **s** npl (POL etc) conflictos mpl; **to be in ~** estar en un apuro; **to go to the ~ of doing sth** tomarse la molestia de hacer algo; **what's the ~?** ¿qué pasa?; ~ **d a** (person) preocupado; (epoch, life) agitado; ~ **maker** n elemento perturbador; (child) niño alborotado; ~ **shooter** n (in conflict) conciliador m; ~ **some** a molesto, inoportuno.

trough [trɔf] n (also: **drinking ~**)

abrevadero; (*also:* **feeding** ~) comedero; (*channel*) canal *m*.

troupe [tru:p] *n* grupo.

trousers ['trauzəz] *npl* pantalones *mpl*.

trousseau ['tru:səu], *pl* ~**x** *or* ~**s** [-z] *n* ajuar *m*.

trout [traut] *n*, *pl inv* trucha.

trowel ['trauəl] *n* paleta.

truant ['truənt] *n*: **to play** ~ hacer novillos.

truce [tru:s] *n* tregua.

truck [trʌk] *n* camión *m*; (*RAIL*) vagón *m*; ~ **driver** *n* camionero; ~ **farm** *n* (*US*) huerto de hortalizas.

truculent ['trʌkjulənt] *a* agresivo.

trudge [trʌdʒ] *vi* andar con dificultad *o* pesadamente.

true [tru:] *a* verdadero; (*accurate*) exacto; (*genuine*) auténtico; (*faithful*) fiel.

truffle ['trʌfl] *n* trufa.

truly ['tru:lɪ] *ad* auténticamente; (*truthfully*) verdaderamente; (*faithfully*) fielmente; **yours** ~ (*in letter*) (le saluda) atentamente.

trump [trʌmp] *n* triunfo; ~**ed-up** *a* inventado.

trumpet ['trʌmpɪt] *n* trompeta.

truncheon ['trʌntʃən] *n* porra.

trundle ['trʌndl] *vt, vi*: **to** ~ **along** rodar haciendo ruido.

trunk [trʌŋk] *n* (*of tree, person*) tronco; (*of elephant*) trompa; (*case*) baúl *m*; ~**s** *npl* (*also:* **swimming** ~**s**) bañador *m*; ~ **call** *n* (*TEL*) llamada interurbana.

truss [trʌs] *n* (*MED*) braguero; **to** ~ (**up**) *vt* atar.

trust [trʌst] *n* confianza; (*COMM*) trust *m*, cartel *m*; (*obligation*) responsabilidad *f*; (*LAW*) fideicomiso // *vt* (*rely on*) tener confianza en; (*entrust*): **to** ~ **sth to sb** confiar algo a uno; ~**ed** *a* de confianza; ~**ee** [trʌsˈtiː] *n* (*LAW*) depositario, fideicomisario; (*of school etc*) administrador/a *m/f*; ~**ful**, ~**ing** *a* confiado; ~**worthy** *a* digno de confianza; ~**y** *a* fiel.

truth [tru:θ], *pl* ~**s** [tru:ðz] *n* verdad *f*; ~**ful** *a* (*person*) que dice la verdad; ~**fully** *ad* sinceramente; ~**fulness** *n* veracidad *f*.

try [traɪ] *n* tentativa, intento; (*RUGBY*) ensayo // *vt* (*LAW*) juzgar, procesar; (*test: sth new*) probar, someter a prueba; (*attempt*) intentar; (*strain*) hacer sufrir // *vi* probar; **to** ~ **to do sth** intentar hacer algo; **to** ~ **on** *vt* (*clothes*) probarse; **to** ~ **out** *vt* probar, poner a prueba; ~**ing** *a* penoso, cansado.

tsar [zɑːˈ] *n* zar *m*.

T-shirt ['tiːʃəːt] *n* camiseta.

tub [tʌb] *n* cubo; (*bath*) tina, bañera.

tuba ['tjuːbə] *n* tuba.

tubby ['tʌbɪ] *a* regordete.

tube [tjuːb] *n* tubo; (*underground*) metro; (*for tyre*) cámara de aire; ~**less** *a* sin cámara.

tuberculosis [tjubəːkjuˈləusɪs] *n* tuberculosis *f*.

tube station *n* estación *f* de metro.

tubing ['tjuːbɪŋ] *n* tubería; **a piece of** ~ un trozo de tubo.

tubular ['tjuːbjuləˈ] *a* tubular; (*furniture*) de tubo.

TUC *n abbr of* **Trades Union Congress.**

tuck [tʌk] *n* (*SEWING*) pliegue *m* // *vt* (*put*) poner; **to** ~ **away** *vt* esconder; **to** ~ **in** *vt* meter; (*child*) arropar // *vi* (*eat*) comer con mucho apetito; **to** ~ **up** *vt* (*child*) arropar; ~ **shop** *n* tienda de golosinas.

Tuesday ['tjuːzdɪ] *n* martes *m*.

tuft [tʌft] *n* mechón *m*; (*of grass etc*) manojo.

tug [tʌg] *n* (*ship*) remolcador *m* // *vt* remolcar; ~**-of-war** *n* lucha de la cuerda.

tuition [tjuːˈɪʃən] *n* enseñanza; (*private* ~) clases *fpl* particulares.

tulip ['tjuːlɪp] *n* tulipán *m*.

tumble ['tʌmbl] *n* (*fall*) caída // *vi* caerse, tropezar // *vt* tirar; ~**down** *a* destartalado; ~ **dryer** *n* secador *m* de ropa automático.

tumbler ['tʌmbləˈ] *n* vaso.

tummy ['tʌmɪ] *n* (*col: belly*) barriga; (: *stomach*) vientre *m*.

tumour ['tjuːməˈ] *n* tumor *m*.

tumult ['tjuːmʌlt] *n* tumulto; ~**uous** [-ˈmʌltjuəs] *a* tumultuoso.

tuna ['tjuːnə] *n*, *pl inv* (*also:* ~ **fish**) atún *m*.

tune [tjuːn] *n* (*melody*) melodía // *vt* (*MUS*) afinar; (*RADIO, TV, AUT*) sintonizar; **to be in/out of** ~ (*instrument*) estar afinado/desafinado; (*singer*) cantar bien/ mal; **to be in/out of** ~ **with** (*fig*) armonizar/desentonar con; **to** ~ **up** *vi* (*musician*) afinar (su instrumento); ~**ful** *a* melodioso; **tuner** *n* (*radio set*) sintonizador *m*; **piano tuner** afinador *m* de pianos.

tunic ['tjuːnɪk] *n* túnica.

tuning ['tjuːnɪŋ] *n* sintonización *f*; (*MUS*) afinación *f*; ~ **fork** *n* diapasón *m*.

Tunisia [tjuːˈnɪzɪə] *n* Tunez *m*.

tunnel ['tʌnl] *n* túnel *m*; (*in mine*) galería // *vi* construir un túnel/una galería.

tunny ['tʌnɪ] *n* atún *m*.

turban ['təːbən] *n* turbante *m*.

turbine ['təːbaɪn] *n* turbina.

turbulence ['təːbjuləns] *n* (*AVIAT*) turbulencia; **turbulent** *a* turbulento.

tureen [təˈriːn] *n* sopera.

turf [təːf] *n* turba; (*clod*) césped *m* // *vt* poner césped; **to** ~ **out** *vt* (*col*) echar a la calle.

turgid ['təːdʒɪd] *a* (*speech*) pesado.

Turk [təːk] *n* turco/a.

turkey ['təːkɪ] *n* pavo.

Turkey ['təːkɪ] *n* Turquía; **Turkish** *a*, *n* turco; **Turkish bath** *n* baño turco.

turmoil ['təːmɔɪl] *n* desorden *m*, alboroto.

turn [təːn] *n* turno; (*in road*) curva; (*tendency: of mind, events*) disposición *f*, propensión f; (THEATRE) número; (MED) desmayo // vt girar, volver; (collar, steak) dar la vuelta a; (change): to ~ sth into convertir algo en // vi volver; (person: look back) volverse; (reverse direction) dar la vuelta; (milk) cortarse; (change) cambiar; (become) convertirse en; a good ~ un favor; it gave me quite a ~ me dio un susto (bastante grande); 'no left ~' (AUT) 'prohibido girar a la izquierda'; it's your ~ te toca a ti; in ~ por turnos; to take ~s turnarse; to ~ about vi dar una vuelta completa; to ~ away vi volver la cabeza; to ~ back vi volverse atrás; to ~ down vt (refuse) rechazar; (reduce) bajar; (fold) doblar (hacia abajo); to ~ in vi (col: go to bed) acostarse // vt (fold) doblar hacia dentro; to ~ off vi (from road) desviarse // vt (light, radio etc) apagar; (engine) parar; to ~ on vt (light, radio etc) encender; (engine) poner en marcha; to ~ out vt (light, gas) apagar // vi: to ~ out to be... resultar ser...; to ~ up vi (person) llegar, presentarse; (lost object) aparecer // vt (gen) subir; ~ing n (in road) vuelta; ~ing point n (fig) momento decisivo.

turnip ['tɔ:nɪp] n nabo.

turnout ['tɔ:naut] n asistencia, número de asistentes.

turnover ['tɔ:nəuvə°] n (COMM: amount of money) cifra de negocios; (: of goods) movimiento.

turnpike ['tɔ:npaɪk] n (US) autopista de peaje.

turnstile ['tɔ:nstaɪl] n torniquete m.

turntable ['tɔ:nteɪbl] n (on record player) plato.

turn-up ['tɔ:nʌp] n (on trousers) vuelta.

turpentine ['tɔ:pəntaɪn] n (also: turps) trementina.

turquoise ['tɔ:kwɔɪz] n (stone) turquesa // a color turquesa.

turret ['tʌrɪt] n torrecilla.

turtle ['tɔ:tl] n tortuga marina.

tusk [tʌsk] n colmillo.

tussle ['tʌsl] n (fight) lucha; (scuffle) pelea.

tutor ['tju:tə°] n (gen) profesor/a m/f; ~ial [-'tɔ:rɪəl] n (SCOL) seminario.

T.V. [ti:'vi:] n abbr of **television.**

twaddle ['twɔdl] n tonterías fpl, bobadas fpl.

twang [twæŋ] n (of instrument) punteado; (of voice) timbre m nasal // vi vibrar // vt (guitar) puntear.

tweed [twi:d] n tweed m.

tweezers ['twi:zəz] npl pinzas fpl de depilar.

twelfth [twelfθ] a duodécimo; T~ Night n Día de Reyes.

twelve [twelv] num doce.

twentieth ['twentɪθ] a vigésimo.

twenty ['twentɪ] num veinte.

twerp [twə:p] n (col) imbécil m/f.

twice [twaɪs] ad dos veces; ~ as much dos veces más.

twig [twɪg] n ramita // vi (col) caer en la cuenta.

twilight ['twaɪlaɪt] n crepúsculo, ocaso.

twin [twɪn] a, n gemelo/a // vt tener como gemelo.

twine [twaɪn] n bramante m // vi (plant) enroscarse.

twinge [twɪndʒ] n (of pain) punzada; (of conscience) remordimiento.

twinkle ['twɪŋkl] n centelleo // vi centellear; (eyes) parpadear.

twirl [twə:l] n giro // vt dar vueltas a // vi girar rápidamente.

twist [twɪst] n (action) torsión f; (in road, coil) vuelta; (in wire, flex) enroscadura; (in story) cambio imprevisto // vt torcer, retorcer; (weave) entrelazar; (roll around) enrollar; (fig) deformar // vi serpentear.

twit [twɪt] n (col) tonto.

twitch [twɪtʃ] n sacudida; (nervous) tic m nervioso // vi moverse nerviosamente.

two [tu:] num dos; to put ~ and ~ together (fig) atar cabos; ~-door a (AUT) de dos puertas; ~-faced a (pej: person) falso; ~fold ad: to increase ~fold duplicar; ~-piece (suit) n traje m de dos piezas; ~-piece (swimsuit) n dos piezas m inv, bikini m; ~-seater n (plane) avión m biplaza; (car) coche m de dos plazas; ~some n (people) pareja; ~-way a: ~-way traffic circulación f en ambas direcciones.

tycoon [taɪ'ku:n] n: (business) ~ magnate m.

type [taɪp] n (category) tipo, género; (model) modelo; (TYP) tipo, letra // vt (letter etc) escribir a máquina; ~-cast a (actor) encasillado; ~script n texto mecanografiado; ~writer n máquina de escribir; ~written a mecanografiado.

typhoid ['taɪfɔɪd] n tifoidea.

typhoon [taɪ'fu:n] n tifón m.

typhus ['taɪfəs] n tifus m.

typical ['tɪpɪkl] a típico; **typify** [-faɪ] vt ser típico de.

typing ['taɪpɪŋ] n mecanografía; **typist** n mecanógrafa.

tyranny ['tɪrənɪ] n tiranía.

tyrant ['taɪərnt] n tirano/a.

tyre, tire (US) ['taɪə°] n neumático, llanta.

tzar [zɑ:°] n = tsar.

U

U-bend ['ju:'bend] n (in pipe) recodo.

ubiquitous [ju:'bɪkwɪtəs] a ubicuo, omnipresente.

udder ['ʌdə°] n ubre f.

UFO ['ju:fəu] n abbr of **unidentified flying object** O.V.N.I. m (objeto volante no identificado).

ugliness ['ʌglɪnɪs] n fealdad f; **ugly** a feo; (dangerous) peligroso.

U.K. n abbr of **United Kingdom.**

ulcer ['ʌlsə°] n úlcera.

Ulster ['ʌlstəˢ] n Úlster m, Irlanda del Norte.

ulterior [ʌl'tɪərɪəˢ] a ulterior; ~ **motive** motivo oculto.

ultimate ['ʌltɪmət] a último, final; (authority) supremo; ~**ly** ad (in the end) por último, al final; (fundamentally) en el fondo.

ultimatum [ʌltɪ'meɪtəm] n ultimátum m.

ultraviolet ['ʌltrə'vaɪəlɪt] a ultravioleta.

umbilical cord [ʌmbɪ'laɪkl-] n cordón m umbilical.

umbrella [ʌm'brɛlə] n paraguas m inv.

umpire ['ʌmpaɪəˢ] n árbitro // vt arbitrar.

umpteen [ʌmp'tiːn] a tantísimos; **for the** ~**th time** por enésima vez.

UN, UNO abbr of **United Nations (Organization)**.

unable [ʌn'eɪbl] a: to be ~ to do sth ser incapaz o no poder hacer algo.

unabridged [ʌnə'brɪdʒd] a íntegro.

unaccompanied [ʌnə'kʌmpənɪd] a no acompañado.

unaccountably [ʌnə'kauntəblɪ] ad inexplicablemente.

unaccustomed [ʌnə'kʌstəmd] a: to be ~ to no tener costumbre de.

unaided [ʌn'eɪdɪd] a sin ayuda, por sí solo.

unanimous [juː'nænɪməs] a unánime; ~**ly** ad unánimemente.

unarmed [ʌn'ɑːmd] a (without a weapon) desarmado; (defenceless) inerme.

unassuming [ʌnə'sjuːmɪŋ] a modesto, sin pretensiones.

unattached [ʌnə'tætʃt] a (person) libre; (part etc) suelto, separable.

unattended [ʌnə'tɛndɪd] a (car, luggage) sin vigilancia.

unattractive [ʌnə'træktɪv] a poco atractivo.

unauthorized [ʌn'ɔːθəraɪzd] a des- autorizado.

unavoidable [ʌnə'vɔɪdəbl] a inevitable.

unaware [ʌnə'wɛəˢ] a: to be ~ of ignorar, no darse cuenta de; ~**s** ad de improviso.

unbalanced [ʌn'bælənst] a desequili- brado; (mentally) trastornado.

unbearable [ʌn'bɛərəbl] a insoportable.

unbeatable [ʌn'biːtəbl] a (team) imbatible; (price) inmejorable.

unbeaten [ʌn'biːtn] a imbatido.

unbeknown(st) [ʌnbɪ'nəun(st)] ad: ~ to me sin saberlo yo.

unbelievable [ʌnbɪ'liːvəbl] a increíble.

unbend [ʌn'bɛnd] (irg: like bend) vi suavizarse // vt (wire) enderezar.

unblock [ʌn'blɔk] vt (pipe) desatascar.

unborn [ʌn'bɔːn] a sin nacer.

unbounded [ʌn'baundɪd] a ilimitado, sin límite.

unbreakable [ʌn'breɪkəbl] a irrompible.

unbridled [ʌn'braɪdld] a (fig) desenfrenado.

unbroken [ʌn'brəukən] a (seal) intacto;

(series) continuo; (record) imbatido; (spirit) indómito.

unburden [ʌn'bɜːdn] vr: to ~ o.s. desahogarse.

unbutton [ʌn'bʌtn] vt desabrochar.

uncalled-for [ʌn'kɔːldfɔːˢ] a gratuito, inmerecido.

uncanny [ʌn'kænɪ] a extraño, extraordinario.

unceasing [ʌn'siːsɪŋ] a incesante.

uncertain [ʌn'sɜːtn] a incierto; (character) indeciso; ~**ty** n incertidumbre f.

unchanged [ʌn'tʃeɪndʒd] a sin cambiar o alterar.

uncharitable [ʌn'tʃærɪtəbl] a poco caritativo.

uncharted [ʌn'tʃɑːtɪd] a inexplorado.

unchecked [ʌn'tʃɛkt] a desenfrenado.

uncivil [ʌn'sɪvɪl] a grosero.

uncle ['ʌŋkl] n tío.

uncomfortable [ʌn'kʌmfətəbl] a incómodo; (uneasy) molesto.

uncommon [ʌn'kɔmən] a poco común, raro.

unconcerned [ʌnkən'sɜːnd] a indiferente, despreocupado.

unconditional [ʌnkən'dɪʃənl] a incondicional.

unconscious [ʌn'kɔnʃəs] a sin sentido; (unaware) inconsciente // n: the ~ el inconsciente; ~**ly** ad inconscientemente.

uncontrollable [ʌnkən'trəuləbl] a (temper) ingobernable; (laughter) incontenible.

uncouth [ʌn'kuːθ] a grosero, inculto.

uncover [ʌn'kʌvəˢ] vt (gen) descubrir; (take lid off) destapar.

undecided [ʌndɪ'saɪdɪd] a (character) indeciso; (question) no resuelto, pendiente.

undeniable [ʌndɪ'naɪəbl] a innegable.

under ['ʌndəˢ] prep debajo de; (less than) menos de; (according to) según, de acuerdo con // ad debajo, abajo; ~ **there** allí abajo; ~ **repair** en reparación.

under... [ʌndəˢ] pref sub; ~**age** a menor de edad; ~**carriage** n tren m de aterrizaje; ~**clothes** npl ropa sg interior; ~**coat** n (paint) primera mano; ~**cover** a clandestino; ~**current** n corriente f submarina; (fig) tendencia oculta; ~**cut** vt irg rebajar los precios para competir con; ~**developed** a subdesarrollado; ~**dog** n desvalido; ~**done** a (CULIN) poco hecho; ~**estimate** vt subestimar; ~**exposed** a (PHOT) subexpuesto; ~**fed** a subalimentado; ~**foot** ad bajo los pies; ~**go** vt irg sufrir; (treatment) recibir; ~**graduate** n estudiante m/f; ~**ground** n (railway) metro; (POL) movimiento clandestino // a subterráneo; ~**growth** n maleza; ~**hand(ed)** a (fig) turbio; ~**lie** vt irg estar debajo de; (fig) ser la razón fundamental de; ~**line** vt subrayar; ~**ling** ['ʌndəlɪŋ] n (pej) subalterno; ~**mine** vt socavar, minar; ~**neath** [ʌndə'niːθ] ad debajo // prep debajo de, bajo; ~**paid** a mal pagado; ~**pants** npl

(Brit) calzoncillos *mpl*; ~**pass** *n* paso subterráneo; ~**price** *vt* vender demasiado barato; ~**privileged** *a* desamparado; ~**rate** *vt* menospreciar, subestimar; ~**side** *n* parte *f* inferior, revés *m*; ~**skirt** *n* enaguas *fpl*.

understand [ʌndə'stænd] *(irg: like* **stand***)* *vt, vi* entender, comprender; *(assume)* sobreentender; ~**able** *a* comprensible; ~**ing** *a* comprensivo // *n* comprensión *f*, entendimiento; *(agreement)* acuerdo.

understatement [ʌndə'steitmənt] *n* descripción *f* insuficiente; *(quality)* modestia (excesiva).

understood [ʌndə'stud] *pt, pp of* **understand** // *a* entendido; *(implied)* sobreentendido.

understudy ['ʌndəstʌdi] *n* suplente *m/f*.

undertake [ʌndə'teik] *(irg: like* **take***)* *vt* acometer; **to** ~ **to do sth** comprometerse a hacer algo.

undertaker ['ʌndəteikə°] *n* director *m* de pompas fúnebres, sepulturero.

undertaking [ʌndə'teikiŋ] *n* empresa; *(promise)* promesa.

underwater [ʌndə'wɔːtə°] *ad* bajo el agua // *a* submarino.

underwear ['ʌndəwɛə°] *n* ropa interior.

underweight [ʌndə'weit] *a* de peso insuficiente; *(person)* demasiado delgado.

underworld ['ʌndəwɔːld] *n* *(of crime)* hampa, inframundo.

underwriter ['ʌndəraitə°] *n* *(INSURANCE)* (re)asegurador/a *m/f*.

undesirable [ʌndi'zaiərəbl] *a* indeseable.

undies ['ʌndiz] *npl* *(col)* paños *mpl* menores.

undignified [ʌn'dignifaid] *a* indecoroso.

undisputed [ʌn'spjuːtid] *a* incontestable.

undo [ʌn'duː] *(irg: like* **do***)* *vt* deshacer; ~**ing** *n* ruina, perdición *f*.

undoubted [ʌn'dautid] *a* indudable; ~**ly** *ad* indudablemente, sin duda.

undress [ʌn'dres] *vi* desnudarse.

undue [ʌn'djuː] *a* indebido, excesivo.

undulating ['ʌndjuleitiŋ] *a* ondulante.

unduly [ʌn'djuːli] *ad* excesivamente, demasiado.

unearth [ʌn'ɔːθ] *vt* desenterrar.

unearthly [ʌn'ɔːθli] *a* *(hour)* inverosímil.

uneasy [ʌn'iːzi] *a* intranquilo; *(worried)* preocupado.

uneconomic(al) ['ʌniːkə'nɔmik(l)] *a* antieconómico.

uneducated [ʌn'edjukeitid] *a* sin educación, inculto.

unemployed [ʌnim'plɔid] *a* parado, sin trabajo // *n*: **the** ~ los parados sin trabajo; **unemployment** [-'plɔimənt] *n* paro, desempleo.

unending [ʌn'endiŋ] *a* interminable.

unenthusiastic [ʌninθuːzi'æstik] *a* poco entusiasta.

unerring [ʌn'ɔːriŋ] *a* infalible.

uneven [ʌn'iːvn] *a* desigual; *(road etc)* quebrado, accidentado.

unexpected [ʌnik'spektid] *a* inesperado.

unfair [ʌn'feə°] *a*: ~ **(to)** injusto (con); ~**ly** *ad* injustamente.

unfaithful [ʌn'feiθful] *a* infiel.

unfamiliar [ʌnfə'miliə°] *a* nuevo, desconocido.

unfashionable [ʌn'fæʃnəbl] *a* pasado *o* fuera de moda.

unfasten [ʌn'fɑːsn] *vt* desatar.

unfavourable, unfavorable *(US)* [ʌn'feivərəbl] *a* desfavorable.

unfeeling [ʌn'fiːliŋ] *a* insensible.

unfinished [ʌn'finiʃt] *a* incompleto, sin terminar.

unfit [ʌn'fit] *a* con mala salud, enfermo; *(incompetent)* incompetente, incapaz; ~ **for work** no apto para trabajar.

unflagging [ʌn'flæɡiŋ] *a* incansable.

unfold [ʌn'fəuld] *vt* desdoblar; *(fig)* revelar // *vi* abrirse; revelarse.

unforeseen ['ʌnfɔː'siːn] *a* imprevisto.

unforgettable [ʌnfə'ɡetəbl] *a* inolvidable.

unforgivable [ʌnfə'ɡivəbl] *a* imperdonable.

unfortunate [ʌn'fɔːtʃnət] *a* desgraciado; *(event, remark)* inoportuno; ~**ly** *ad* desgraciadamente.

unfounded [ʌn'faundid] *a* infundado.

unfriendly [ʌn'frendli] *a* antipático.

unfurnished [ʌn'fɜːniʃt] *a* desamueblado.

ungainly [ʌn'ɡeinli] *a* desgarbado.

unhappiness [ʌn'hæpinis] *n* tristeza; **unhappy** *a* *(sad)* triste; *(unfortunate)* desgraciado; *(childhood)* infeliz; **unhappy with** *(arrangements etc)* poco contento con, descontento de.

unharmed [ʌn'hɑːmd] *a* ileso; *(col)* sano y salvo.

unhealthy [ʌn'helθi] *a* *(gen)* malsano; *(person)* enfermizo, con poca salud.

unheard-of [ʌn'hɔːdɔv] *a* inaudito, sin precedente.

unhook [ʌn'huk] *vt* desenganchar; *(from wall)* descolgar; *(dress)* desabrochar.

unhurt [ʌn'hɔːt] *a* ileso.

unidentified [ʌnai'dentifaid] *a* no identificado.

uniform ['juːnifɔːm] *n* uniforme *m* // *a* uniforme; ~**ity** [-'fɔːmiti] *n* uniformidad *f*.

unify ['juːnifai] *vt* unificar, unir.

unilateral [juːni'lætərəl] *a* unilateral.

unintentional [ʌnin'tenʃənəl] *a* involuntario.

union ['juːnjən] *n* unión *f*; *(also: trade* ~) sindicato // *a* sindical; **U~ Jack** *n* bandera del Reino Unido.

unique [juː'niːk] *a* único.

unison ['juːnisn] *n*: **in** ~ en armonía.

unit ['juːnit] *n* unidad *f*; *(team, squad)* grupo; **kitchen** ~ mueble *m* de cocina.

unite [juː'nait] *vt* unir // *vi* unirse; ~**d** *a* unido; **U~d Kingdom (U.K.)** *n* Reino Unido; **U~d Nations (Organization) (UN, UNO)** *n* (Las) Naciones Unidas *fpl* (O.N.U.); **U~d States (of America)**

(US, USA) n (Los) Estados Unidos mpl (EE.UU.).

unity ['ju:nɪtɪ] n unidad f.

universal [ju:nɪ'vɜ:sl] a universal.

universe ['ju:nɪvɜ:s] n universo.

university [ju:nɪ'vɜ:sɪtɪ] n universidad f.

unjust [ʌn'dʒʌst] a injusto.

unkempt [ʌn'kɛmpt] a descuidado; (hair) despeinado.

unkind [ʌn'kaɪnd] a poco amable; (comment etc) cruel.

unknown [ʌn'nəʊn] a desconocido.

unladen [ʌn'leɪdn] a (ship, weight) vacío.

unleash [ʌn'li:ʃ] vt soltar; (fig) desencadenar.

unless [ʌn'lɛs] conj a menos que, a no ser que; ~ he comes a menos que venga; ~ otherwise stated salvo indicación contraria.

unlike [ʌn'laɪk] a distinto // prep a diferencia de.

unlikely [ʌn'laɪklɪ] a improbable.

unlimited [ʌn'lɪmɪtɪd] a ilimitado.

unload [ʌn'ləʊd] vt descargar.

unlock [ʌn'lɔk] vt abrir (con llave).

unlucky [ʌn'lʌkɪ] a desgraciado; (object, number) que da mala suerte; **to be ~** tener mala suerte.

unmarried [ʌn'mærɪd] a soltero.

unmask [ʌn'mɑ:sk] vt desenmascarar.

unmistakable [ʌnmɪs'teɪkəbl] a inconfundible.

unmitigated [ʌn'mɪtɪgeɪtɪd] a no mitigado, absoluto.

unnatural [ʌn'nætʃrəl] a (gen) antinatural; (manner) afectado; (habit) perverso.

unnecessary [ʌn'nɛsəsərɪ] a innecesario, inútil.

unnoticed [ʌn'nəʊtɪst] a: **to go ~** pasar desapercibido.

unobtainable [ʌnəb'teɪnəbl] a inconseguible.

unoccupied [ʌn'ɔkjupaɪd] a (seat etc) libre.

unofficial [ʌnə'fɪʃl] a no oficial; (strike) espontáneo, sin la aprobación de la central.

unorthodox [ʌn'ɔːθədɔks] a poco ortodoxo.

unpack [ʌn'pæk] vi deshacer las maletas.

unpalatable [ʌn'pælətəbl] a (truth) desagradable.

unparalleled [ʌn'pærəlɛld] a (unequalled) sin par; (unique) sin precedentes.

unpleasant [ʌn'plɛznt] a (disagreeable) desagradable; (person, manner) antipático.

unplug [ʌn'plʌg] vt desenchufar, desconectar.

unpopular [ʌn'pɔpjʊlə*] a poco popular.

unprecedented [ʌn'prɛsɪdəntɪd] a sin precedentes.

unpredictable [ʌnprɪ'dɪktəbl] a imprevisible.

unproductive [ʌnprə'dʌktɪv] a improductivo.

unqualified [ʌn'kwɔlɪfaɪd] a (teacher) sin

título, no cualificado; (success) total, incondicional.

unravel [ʌn'rævl] vt desenmarañar.

unreal [ʌn'rɪəl] a irreal.

unrealistic [ʌnrɪə'lɪstɪk] a poco realista.

unreasonable [ʌn'ri:znəbl] a poco razonable; (demand) excesivo.

unrelated [ʌnrɪ'leɪtɪd] a sin relación; (family) sin parentesco.

unrelenting [ʌnrɪ'lɛntɪŋ] a implacable.

unreliable [ʌnrɪ'laɪəbl] a (person) informal; (machine) de poca confianza.

unrelieved [ʌnrɪ'li:vd] a (monotony) monótono.

unrepeatable [ʌnrɪ'pi:təbl] a (offer) irrepetible.

unrepresentative [ʌnrɛprɪ'zɛntətɪv] a poco representativo o característico.

unrest [ʌn'rɛst] n inquietud f, malestar m; (POL) disturbios mpl.

unroll [ʌn'rəʊl] vt desenrollar.

unruly [ʌn'ru:lɪ] a indisciplinado.

unsafe [ʌn'seɪf] a (journey) peligroso; (car etc) inseguro.

unsaid [ʌn'sɛd] a: **to leave sth ~** dejar algo sin decir.

unsatisfactory ['ʌnsætɪs'fæktərɪ] a insatisfactorio.

unsavoury, unsavory (US) [ʌn'seɪvərɪ] a (fig) repugnante.

unscathed [ʌn'skeɪðd] a ileso.

unscrew [ʌn'skru:] vt destornillar.

unscrupulous [ʌn'skru:pjʊləs] a sin escrúpulos.

unsettled [ʌn'sɛtld] a inquieto, inestable; (weather) variable.

unshaven [ʌn'ʃeɪvn] a sin afeitar.

unsightly [ʌn'saɪtlɪ] a feo.

unskilled [ʌn'skɪld] a: **~ worker** obrero no cualificado.

unspeakable [ʌn'spi:kəbl] a indecible; (bad) horrible.

unsteady [ʌn'stɛdɪ] a inestable.

unstuck [ʌn'stʌk] a: **to come ~** despegarse; (fig) fracasar.

unsuccessful [ʌnsək'sɛsfʊl] a (attempt) infructuoso; (writer, proposal) sin éxito; **to be ~** (in attempting sth) no tener éxito, fracasar; **~ly** ad en vano, sin éxito.

unsuitable [ʌn'su:təbl] a inconveniente, inapropiado.

unsure [ʌn'ʃʊə*] a inseguro, poco seguro.

unsuspecting [ʌnsə'spɛktɪŋ] a confiado.

unswerving [ʌn'swɜ:vɪŋ] a inquebrantable.

untangle [ʌn'tæŋgl] vt desenredar.

untapped [ʌn'tæpt] a (resources) sin explotar.

unthinkable [ʌn'θɪŋkəbl] a inconcebible, impensable.

untidy [ʌn'taɪdɪ] a (room) desordenado, en desorden; (appearance) descuidado.

untie [ʌn'taɪ] vt desatar.

until [ən'tɪl] prep hasta // conj hasta que; **~ he comes** hasta que venga; **~ then** hasta entonces.

untimely [ʌn'taɪmlɪ] a inoportuno; (death) prematuro.

untold [ʌn'təʊld] a (story) inédito; (suffering) indecible; (wealth) incalculable.

untoward [ʌntə'wɔːd] a desfavorable.

unused [ʌn'juːzd] a sin usar, nuevo.

unusual [ʌn'juːʒʊəl] a insólito, poco común.

unveil [ʌn'veɪl] vt (statue) descubrir.

unwavering [ʌn'weɪvərɪŋ] a inquebrantable.

unwelcome [ʌn'wɛlkəm] a (at a bad time) inoportuno; (unpleasant) desagradable.

unwell [ʌn'wɛl] a: to feel ~ estar indispuesto; to be ~ estar enfermo.

unwieldy [ʌn'wiːldɪ] a difícil de manejar.

unwilling [ʌn'wɪlɪŋ] a: to be ~ to do sth estar poco dispuesto a hacer algo; ~ly ad de mala gana.

unwind [ʌn'waɪnd] (irg: like **wind**) vt desenvolver // vi (relax) relajarse.

unwitting [ʌn'wɪtɪŋ] a inconsciente.

unworthy [ʌn'wɜːðɪ] a indigno.

unwrap [ʌn'ræp] vt desenvolver.

up [ʌp] prep: to go/be ~ sth subir/estar encima de algo // ad hacia arriba, arriba; ~ there allí arriba; ~ above encima, allí arriba; to be ~ (out of bed) estar levantado; it is ~ to you Ud. decide/tú decides; what is he ~ to? ¿qué es lo que quiere?, ¿qué está tramando?; he is not ~ to it no es capaz de hacerlo; ~-and-coming a prometedor(a); ~s and downs npl (fig) altibajos mpl.

upbringing ['ʌpbrɪŋɪŋ] n educación f.

update [ʌp'deɪt] vt poner al día, modernizar; (contract etc) actualizar.

upgrade [ʌp'greɪd] vt ascender; (job) revalorizar.

upheaval [ʌp'hiːvl] n trastorno, conmoción f.

uphill [ʌp'hɪl] a cuesta arriba; (fig: task) penoso, difícil // ad: to go ~ ir cuesta arriba.

uphold [ʌp'həʊld] (irg: like **hold**) vt sostener.

upholstery [ʌp'həʊlstərɪ] n tapicería.

upkeep ['ʌpkiːp] n mantenimiento.

upon [ə'pɒn] prep sobre.

upper ['ʌpə*] a superior, de arriba // n (of shoe) pala; ~-**class** a de clase alta; ~**most** a el más alto; what was ~**most** in my mind lo que más me preocupaba más.

upright ['ʌpraɪt] a vertical; (fig) honrado.

uprising ['ʌpraɪzɪŋ] n sublevación f.

uproar ['ʌprɔː*] n tumulto, escándalo.

uproot [ʌp'ruːt] vt desarraigar.

upset ['ʌpsɛt] n (to plan etc) revés m, contratiempo; (MED) trastorno // vt [ʌp-'sɛt] (irg: like **set**) (glass etc) volcar; (spill) derramar; (plan) alterar; (person) molestar, perturbar // a [ʌp'sɛt] preocupado, perturbado; (stomach) trastornado.

upshot ['ʌpʃɒt] n resultado.

upside-down ['ʌpsaɪddaʊn] ad al revés.

upstairs [ʌp'stɛəz] ad arriba // a (room) de arriba // n el piso superior.

upstart ['ʌpstɑːt] n advenedizo.

upstream [ʌp'striːm] ad río arriba.

uptake ['ʌpteɪk] n: he is quick/slow on the ~ es muy listo/ algo torpe.

up-to-date ['ʌptə'deɪt] a moderno, actual.

upturn ['ʌptɜːn] n (in luck) mejora.

upward ['ʌpwəd] a ascendente; ~(s) ad hacia arriba.

uranium [juə'reɪnɪəm] n uranio.

urban ['ɜːbən] a urbano.

urbane [ɜː'beɪn] a cortés.

urchin ['ɜːtʃɪn] n pilluelo, golfillo.

urge [ɜːdʒ] n (force) impulso; (desire) deseo // vt: to ~ sb to do sth incitar a uno a hacer algo.

urgency ['ɜːdʒənsɪ] n urgencia; (of tone) insistencia; **urgent** a urgente.

urinal ['juərɪnl] n urinario.

urinate ['juərɪneɪt] vi orinar; **urine** n orina, orines mpl.

urn [ɜːn] n urna; (also: tea ~) tetera.

us [ʌs] pron nos; (after prep) nosotros/as.

US, USA n abbr of **United States (of America).**

usage ['juːzɪdʒ] n uso, costumbre f.

use [juːs] n uso, empleo; (usefulness) utilidad f // vt [juːz] usar, emplear; she ~d to do it (ella) solía hacerlo; in ~ en uso; out of ~ anticuado, que ya no se usa; to be of ~ servir; it's no ~ (pointless) es inútil; (not useful) no sirve; to be ~d to estar acostumbrado a; to ~ up vt agotar, consumir; ~d a (car) usado; ~ful a útil; to be ~ful servir; ~less a inútil; **user** n usuario/a.

usher ['ʌʃə*] n ujier m, portero; ~**ette** [-'rɛt] n (in cinema) acomodadora.

USSR n: the ~ la U.R.S.S.

usual ['juːʒʊəl] a normal, corriente; ~ly ad normalmente.

usurp [juː'zɜːp] vt usurpar.

utensil [juː'tɛnsl] n utensilio; **kitchen** ~s batería sg de cocina.

uterus ['juːtərəs] n útero.

utilitarian [juːtɪlɪ'tɛərɪən] a utilitario.

utility [juː'tɪlɪtɪ] n utilidad f; ~ **room** n trascocina.

utilize ['juːtɪlaɪz] vt utilizar.

utmost ['ʌtməʊst] a mayor // n: to do one's ~ hacer todo lo posible.

utter ['ʌtə*] a total, completo // vt pronunciar, proferir; ~**ance** n palabras fpl, declaración f; ~ly ad completamente, totalmente.

U-turn ['juː'tɜːn] n viraje m en U.

V

v. abbr of **verse; versus; volt; vide** véase.

vacancy ['veɪkənsɪ] n (job) vacante f; (room) cuarto libro; **vacant** a desocupado, libre; (expression) distraído; **vacate**

[vəˈkeɪt] vt (house) desocupar; (job) salir de; (throne) renunciar a.
vacation [vəˈkeɪʃən] n vacaciones fpl.
vaccinate [ˈvæksɪneɪt] vt vacunar; **vaccination** [-ˈneɪʃən] n vacunación f.
vaccine [ˈvæksi:n] n vacuna.
vacuum [ˈvækjum] n vacío; ~ **cleaner** n aspiradora; ~ **flask** n termo.
vagabond [ˈvægəbɒnd] n vagabundo.
vagina [vəˈdʒaɪnə] n vagina.
vagrant [ˈveɪgrnt] n vagabundo.
vague [veɪg] a vago; (blurred: memory) borroso; (uncertain) incierto, impreciso; (person) distraído; ~ly ad vagamente.
vain [veɪn] a (conceited) vanidoso; (useless) vano, inútil; **in** ~ en vano.
vale [veɪl] n valle m.
valentine [ˈvæləntaɪn] n: **V~'s Day** Día m de los Enamorados.
valid [ˈvælɪd] a válido; (ticket) valedero; (law) vigente; ~**ity** [-ˈlɪdɪtɪ] n validez f; vigencia.
valley [ˈvælɪ] n valle m.
valour, valor (US) [ˈvælə*] n valor m, valentía.
valuable [ˈvæljuəbl] a (jewel) de valor; (time) valioso; ~**s** npl objetos mpl de valor.
valuation [væljuˈeɪʃən] n tasación f, valuación f.
value [ˈvælju:] n valor m; (importance) importancia // vt (fix price of) tasar, valorar; (esteem) apreciar; (cherish) tener en mucho; ~ **added tax (VAT)** n tasa al valor añadido o agregado; ~**d** (appreciated) apreciado.
valve [vælv] n (gen) válvula; (MED) valva.
vampire [ˈvæmpaɪə*] n vampiro/vampiresa.
van [væn] n (AUT) furgoneta; (RAIL) furgón m (de equipajes).
vandal [ˈvændl] n vándalo; ~**ism** n vandalismo; ~**ize** vt dañar, destruir.
vanilla [vəˈnɪlə] n vainilla.
vanish [ˈvænɪʃ] vi desvanecerse, esfumarse.
vanity [ˈvænɪtɪ] n vanidad f; ~ **case** n neceser m.
vantage point [ˈvɑːntɪdʒ-] n posición f ventajosa.
vapour, vapor (US) [ˈveɪpə*] n vapor m; (steam) vaho.
variable [ˈvɛərɪəbl] a variable.
variance [ˈvɛərɪəns] n: **to be at** ~ (with) desentonar (con), estar en desacuerdo (con).
variation [vɛərɪˈeɪʃən] n variedad f; (in opinion) variación f.
varicose [ˈværɪkəus] a: ~ **veins** varices fpl.
varied [ˈvɛərɪd] a variado.
variety [vəˈraɪətɪ] n variedad f, diversidad f; (quantity) surtido; ~ **show** n variedades fpl.
various [ˈvɛərɪəs] a varios(as), diversos(as).

varnish [ˈvɑːnɪʃ] n (gen) barniz m; (nail ~) esmalte m // vt (gen) barnizar; (nails) pintar (con esmalte).
vary [ˈvɛərɪ] vt variar; (change) cambiar // vi variar; (disagree) discrepar; (deviate) desviarse; ~**ing** a diversos(as).
vase [vɑːz] n florero.
vaseline [ˈvæsɪli:n] n vaselina.
vast [vɑːst] a enorme; (success) abrumador(a); ~**ness** n inmensidad f.
vat [væt] n tina, tinaja.
VAT [væt] n abbr of **Value Added Tax.**
Vatican [ˈvætɪkən] n: **the** ~ el Vaticano.
vault [vɔːlt] n (of roof) bóveda; (tomb) tumba; (in bank) sótano // vt (also: ~ over) saltar (por encima de).
veal [vi:l] n ternera.
veer [vɪə*] vi virar.
vegetable [ˈvɛdʒtəbl] n (BOT) vegetal m; (edible plant) legumbre f, hortaliza; ~**s** npl (cooked) verduras fpl // a vegetal; ~ **garden** n huerto.
vegetarian [vɛdʒɪˈtɛərɪən] a, n vegetariano/a.
vegetate [ˈvɛdʒɪteɪt] vi vegetar.
vegetation [vɛdʒɪˈteɪʃən] n vegetación f.
vehement [ˈviːmənt] a vehemente; (impassioned) apasionado.
vehicle [ˈviːɪkl] n vehículo.
veil [veɪl] n velo // vt velar.
vein [veɪn] n vena; (of ore etc) veta.
velocity [vɪˈlɒsɪtɪ] n velocidad f.
velvet [ˈvɛlvɪt] n terciopelo // a aterciopelado.
vendetta [vɛnˈdɛtə] n vendetta.
vending machine [ˈvɛndɪŋ-] n distribuidor m automático.
vendor [ˈvɛndə*] n vendedor/a m/f.
veneer [vəˈnɪə*] n chapa, enchapado; (fig) barniz m, apariencia.
venereal [vɪˈnɪərɪəl] a: ~ **disease (VD)** enfermedad f venérea.
Venetian blind [vɪˈniːʃən-] n persiana.
Venezuela [vɛnɛˈzweɪlə] n Venezuela; ~**n** a, n venezolano/a.
vengeance [ˈvɛndʒəns] n venganza; **with a** ~ (fig) con creces.
venison [ˈvɛnɪsn] n carne f de venado.
venom [ˈvɛnəm] n veneno; ~**ous** a venenoso.
vent [vɛnt] n (opening) abertura; (air-hole) respiradero; (in wall) rejilla (de ventilación) // vt (fig: feelings) desahogar.
ventilate [ˈvɛntɪleɪt] vt ventilar; **ventilation** [-ˈleɪʃən] n ventilación f; **ventilator** n ventilador m.
ventriloquist [vɛnˈtrɪləkwɪst] n ventrílocuo.
venture [ˈvɛntʃə*] n empresa // vt aventurar; (opinion) ofrecer // vi arriesgarse, lanzarse.
venue [ˈvɛnjuː] n lugar m; (meeting place) lugar m de reunión.
veranda(h) [vəˈrændə] n terraza; (with glass) galería.
verb [vɜːb] n verbo; ~**al** a verbal.

verbatim [vɑː'beɪtɪm] a, ad palabra por palabra.

verbose [vɔː'bəus] a prolijo.

verdict ['vɜːdɪkt] n veredicto, fallo; (fig) opinión f, juicio.

verge [vɜːdʒ] n borde m, margen m; **to be on the ~ of doing sth** estar a punto de hacer algo; **to ~ on** vt fus rayar en.

verify ['vɛrɪfaɪ] vt comprobar, verificar.

vermin ['vɜːmɪn] npl (animals) bichos mpl; (insects, fig) sabandijas fpl.

vermouth ['vɜːməθ] n vermut m.

vernacular ['və'nækjulə*] n vernáculo.

versatile ['vɜːsətaɪl] a (person) de talentos variados; (machine, tool etc) que tiene muchos usos; (mind) ágil, flexible.

verse [vɜːs] n versos mpl, poesía; (stanza) estrofa; (in bible) versículo.

versed [vɜːst] a: (well-)~ in versado en, conocedor de.

version ['vɜːʃən] n versión f.

versus ['vɜːsəs] prep contra.

vertebra ['vɜːtɪbrə], pl ~e [-briː] n vértebra; **vertebrate** [-brɪt] n vertebrado.

vertical ['vɜːtɪkl] a vertical.

vertigo ['vɜːtɪgəu] n vértigo.

very ['vɛrɪ] ad muy // a: **the ~ book which** el mismo libro que; **the ~ last** el último (de todos); **at the ~ least** al menos; **~ much** muchísimo.

vespers ['vɛspəz] npl vísperas fpl.

vessel ['vɛsl] n (ANAT, NAUT) vaso; (container) vasija.

vest [vɛst] n camiseta; (US: waistcoat) chaleco; **~ed interests** npl (COMM) intereses mpl creados.

vestibule ['vɛstɪbjuːl] n vestíbulo.

vestige ['vɛstɪdʒ] n vestigio, rastro.

vestry ['vɛstrɪ] n sacristía.

vet [vɛt] n abbr of veterinary surgeon // vt repasar, revisar.

veteran ['vɛtərn] n veterano; **~ car** n coche m antiguo.

veterinary ['vɛtrɪnərɪ] a veterinario; **~ surgeon** n veterinario.

veto ['viːtəu] pl ~es n veto // vt vetar, vedar.

vex [vɛks] vt (irritate) fastidiar; (make impatient) impacientar; **~ed** a (question) batallón(ona), controvertido.

via ['vaɪə] prep por, por vía de.

viable ['vaɪəbl] a viable.

viaduct ['vaɪədʌkt] n viaducto.

vibrate [vaɪ'breɪt] vi vibrar; **vibration** [-'breɪʃən] n vibración f.

vicar ['vɪkə*] n párroco; **~age** n parroquia.

vice [vaɪs] n (evil) vicio; (TECH) torno de banco.

vice- [vaɪs] pref vice; **~chairman** n vicepresidente m.

vice versa ['vaɪsɪ'vɜːsə] ad viceversa.

vicinity [vɪ'sɪnɪtɪ] n (area) vecindad f; (nearness) proximidad f.

vicious ['vɪʃəs] a (violent) violento; (depraved) depravado; (cruel) cruel;

(bitter) rencoroso; **~ness** n violencia; depravación f; crueldad f; rencor m.

victim ['vɪktɪm] n víctima m/f; **~ization** [-'zeɪʃən] n (gen) persecución f; (in strike) represalias fpl; **~ize** vt (strikers etc) tomar represalias contra.

victor ['vɪktə*] n vencedor/a m/f.

Victorian [vɪk'tɔːrɪən] a victoriano.

victorious [vɪk'tɔːrɪəs] a vencedor(a).

victory ['vɪktərɪ] n victoria.

video ['vɪdɪəu] cpd video; **~(-tape) recorder** n video-grabadora.

vie [vaɪ] vi: **to ~ with** competir con.

Vienna [vɪ'ɛnə] n Viena.

view [vjuː] n vista, perspectiva; (landscape) paisaje m; (opinion) opinión f, criterio // vt (look at) mirar; (examine) examinar; **on ~** (in museum etc) expuesto; **in full ~ (of)** en plena vista (de); **in ~ of the fact that** en vista del hecho de que; **~er** n (small projector) visionadora; (TV) televidente m/f; **~finder** n visor m de imagen; **~point** n punto de vista.

vigil ['vɪdʒɪl] n vigilia; **to keep ~** velar; **~ance** n vigilancia; **~ant** a vigilante.

vigorous ['vɪgərəs] a enérgico, vigoroso; **vigour, vigor** (US) n energía, vigor m.

vile [vaɪl] a (action) vil, infame; (smell) asqueroso.

vilify ['vɪlɪfaɪ] vt vilipendiar.

villa ['vɪlə] n (country house) casa de campo; (suburban house) chalet m.

village ['vɪlɪdʒ] n aldea; **villager** n aldeano/a.

villain ['vɪlən] n (scoundrel) malvado; (criminal) maleante m/f.

vindicate ['vɪndɪkeɪt] vt vindicar, justificar.

vindictive [vɪn'dɪktɪv] a vengativo.

vine [vaɪn] n vid f.

vinegar ['vɪnɪgə*] n vinagre m.

vineyard ['vɪnjɑːd] n viña, viñedo.

vintage ['vɪntɪdʒ] n (year) vendimia, cosecha; **~ wine** n vino añejo.

vinyl ['vaɪnl] n vinilo.

violate ['vaɪəleɪt] vt violar; **violation** [-'leɪʃən] n violación f.

violence ['vaɪələns] n violencia; **violent** a (gen) violento; (intense) intenso.

violet ['vaɪələt] a violado, violeta // n (plant) violeta.

violin [vaɪə'lɪn] n violín m; **~ist** n violinista m/f.

VIP n abbr of very important person.

viper ['vaɪpə*] n víbora.

virgin ['vɜːdʒɪn] n virgen m/f // a virgen; **the Blessed V~** la Santísima Virgen; **~ity** [-'dʒɪnɪtɪ] n virginidad f.

Virgo ['vɜːgəu] n Virgo.

virile ['vɪraɪl] a viril; **virility** [vɪ'rɪlɪtɪ] n virilidad f; (fig) machismo.

virtually ['vɜːtjuəlɪ] ad (almost) virtualmente.

virtue ['vɜːtjuː] n virtud f; **by ~ of** en virtud de.

virtuoso [vɜːtju'əuzəu] n virtuoso.

virtuous ['vɜːtjuəs] a virtuoso.

virulent ['vɪrulənt] a virulento.

virus ['vaɪərəs] n virus m.

visa ['viːzə] n visado, visa (AM).

vis-à-vis [viːzə'viː] prep respecto de.

visibility [vɪzɪ'bɪlɪtɪ] n visibilidad f.

visible ['vɪzəbl] a visible; **visibly** ad visiblemente.

vision ['vɪʒən] n (sight) vista; (foresight, in dream) visión f; ~**ary** n visionario.

visit ['vɪzɪt] n visita // vt (person) visitar, hacer una visita a; (place) ir a, (ir a) conocer; ~ **or in** (gen) visitante m/f; (to one's house) visita; (tourist) turista m/f; (tripper) excursionista m/f; ~**ors' book** n libro de visitas.

visor ['vaɪzə*] n visera.

vista ['vɪstə] n vista, panorama.

visual ['vɪzjuəl] a visual; ~**ize** vt imaginarse; (foresee) prever.

vital ['vaɪtl] a (essential) esencial, imprescindible; (important) de suma importancia; (crucial) crítico; (person) enérgico, vivo; (of life) vital; ~**ity** [-'tælɪtɪ] n energía, vitalidad f; ~**ly** ad: ~**ly important** de primera importancia.

vitamin ['vɪtəmɪn] n vitamina.

vivacious [vɪ'veɪʃəs] a vivaz, alegre.

vivid ['vɪvɪd] a (account) gráfico; (light) intenso; (imagination) vivo.

vivisection [vɪvɪ'sɛkʃən] n vivisección f.

V-neck ['viːnɛk] n cuello de pico.

vocabulary [vəu'kæbjulərɪ] n vocabulario.

vocal ['vəukl] a (noisy) ruidoso; ~ **chords** npl cuerdas fpl vocales; ~**ist** n cantante m/f.

vocation [vəu'keɪʃən] n vocación f; ~**al** a vocacional.

vociferous [və'sɪfərəs] a vocinglero.

vodka ['vɔdkə] n vodka.

vogue [vəug] n boga, moda.

voice [vɔɪs] n voz f // vt (opinion) expresar.

void [vɔɪd] n vacío; (hole) hueco // a (gen) vacío; (vacant) vacante; (null) nulo, inválido.

volatile ['vɔlətaɪl] a volátil.

volcanic [vɔl'kænɪk] a volcánico; **volcano** [-'keɪnəu], pl ~**es** n volcán m.

volley ['vɔlɪ] n (of gunfire) descarga; (of stones etc) lluvia; (TENNIS etc) voleo; ~**ball** n balonvolea, vol(e)ibol m (AM).

volt [vəult] n voltio; ~**age** n voltaje m.

voluble ['vɔljubl] a locuaz, hablador(a).

volume ['vɔljuːm] n (gen) volumen m; (book) tomo.

voluntarily ['vɔləntrɪlɪ] ad libremente, de su propia voluntad.

voluntary ['vɔləntərɪ] a voluntario, espontáneo; (unpaid) (a título) gratuito.

volunteer [vɔlən'tɪə*] n voluntario // vi ofrecerse de (voluntario).

voluptuous [və'lʌptjuəs] a voluptuoso.

vomit ['vɔmɪt] n vómito // vt, vi vomitar.

vote [vəut] n voto; (votes cast) votación f; (right to ~) derecho de votar; (franchise) sufragio // vt (chairman) elegir // vi votar, ir a votar; **voter** n votante m/f; **voting** n votación f.

vouch [vautʃ]: **to ~ for** vt garantizar, responder de.

voucher ['vautʃə*] n (for meal, petrol) vale m.

vow [vau] n voto // vi hacer voto.

vowel ['vauəl] n vocal f.

voyage ['vɔɪdʒ] n (journey) viaje m; (crossing) travesía.

vulgar ['vʌlgə*] a (rude) ordinario, grosero; (in bad taste) de mal gusto; ~**ity** [-'gærɪtɪ] n grosería; mal gusto.

vulnerable ['vʌlnərəbl] a vulnerable.

vulture ['vʌltʃə*] n buitre m.

W

wad [wɔd] n (of cotton wool, paper) bolita; (of banknotes etc) fajo.

waddle ['wɔdl] vi anadear.

wade [weɪd] vi: **to ~ through** caminar por el agua; (fig: a book) leer con dificultad.

wafer ['weɪfə*] n (biscuit) galleta, barquillo; (REL) oblea.

waffle ['wɔfl] n (CULIN) buñuelo, panqueque m // vi meter paja.

waft [wɔft] vt hacer flotar // vi flotar.

wag [wæg] vt menear, agitar // vi moverse, menearse.

wage [weɪdʒ] n (also: ~**s**) sueldo, salario // vt: **to ~ war** hacer la guerra; ~ **claim** n demanda de aumento de sueldo; ~ **earner** n asalariado/a; ~ **freeze** n congelación f de salarios.

wager ['weɪdʒə*] n apuesta // vt apostar.

waggle ['wægl] vt menear, mover.

wag(g)on ['wægən] n (horse-drawn) carro; (truck) camión m; (RAIL) vagón m.

wail [weɪl] n gemido // vi gemir.

waist [weɪst] n cintura, talle m; ~**coat** n chaleco; ~**line** n talle m.

wait [weɪt] n espera; (interval) pausa // vi esperar; **to lie in ~ for** acechar a; **I can't ~ to** (fig) estoy deseando; **to ~ for** esperar (a); **to ~ on** vt fus servir a; '**no ~ing**' (AUT) 'prohibido aparcar'; ~**er** n camarero; ~**ing list** n lista de espera; ~**ing room** n sala de espera; ~**ress** n camarera.

waive [weɪv] vt renunciar a.

wake [weɪk], pt **woke** or **waked**, pp **woken** or **waked** vt (also: ~ **up**) despertar // vi (also: ~ **up**) despertarse // n (for dead person) vela, velatorio; (NAUT) estela; **waken** vt, vi = **wake**.

Wales [weɪlz] n País m de Gales.

walk [wɔːk] n paseo; (hike) excursión f a pie, caminata; (gait) paso, andar m; (in park etc) paseo, alameda // vi andar; (for pleasure, exercise) pasearse // vt (distance) recorrer a pie, andar; (dog) sacar de paseo, pasear; **10 minutes'** ~ **from here** desde aquí hay 10 minutos a pie; **people from all** ~**s of life** gente de todas las esferas; ~**er** n (person) paseante *m/f*, caminante *m/f*; ~**ie-talkie** ['wɔːkɪ'tɔːkɪ] *n* walkie-talkie *m*, transmisor-receptor *m* (portátil); ~**ing** *n* el andar; ~**ing shoes** *npl* zapatos *mpl* para andar; ~**ing stick** *n* bastón *m*; ~**out** *n* (*of workers*) huelga sorpresa; ~**over** *n* (*col*) triunfo fácil; ~**way** *n* paseo.

wall [wɔːl] *n* pared *f*; (*exterior*) muro; (*city* ~ *etc*) muralla; ~**ed** *a* (*city*) amurallado; (*garden*) con tapia.

wallet ['wɔlɪt] *n* cartera.

wallflower ['wɔːlflauə*] *n* alhelí *m*; **to be a** ~ (*fig*) comer pavo.

wallop ['wɔləp] *vt* (*col*) zurrar.

wallow ['wɔləu] *vi* revolcarse.

wallpaper ['wɔːlpeɪpə*] *n* papel *m* pintado.

walnut ['wɔːlnʌt] *n* nuez *f*; (*tree*) nogal *m*.

walrus ['wɔːlrəs], *pl* ~ *or* ~**es** *n* morsa.

waltz [wɔːlts] *n* vals *m* // *vi* bailar el vals.

wand [wɔnd] *n* (*also:* **magic** ~) varita (mágica).

wander ['wɔndə*] *vi* (*person*) vagar, deambular; (*thoughts*) divagar; (*get lost*) extraviarse // *vt* recorrer, vagar por; ~**er** *n* vagabundo; ~**ing** *a* errante; (*thoughts*) distraído.

wane [weɪn] *vi* menguar.

wangle ['wæŋgl] *vt* (*col*): **to** ~ **sth** agenciarse algo.

want [wɔnt] *vt* (*wish for*) querer, desear; (*demand*) exigir; (*need*) necesitar; (*lack*) carecer de // *n*: **for** ~ **of** por falta de; ~**s** *npl* (*needs*) necesidades *fpl*; **to** ~ **to do** querer hacer; **to** ~ **sb to do sth** querer que uno haga algo; ~**ing** *a* falto, deficiente; **to be found** ~**ing** no estar a la altura de las circunstancias.

wanton ['wɔntn] *a* (*playful*) juguetón(ona); (*licentious*) lascivo.

war [wɔː*] *n* guerra; **to make** ~ hacer la guerra.

ward [wɔːd] *n* (*in hospital*) sala; (*POL*) distrito electoral; (*LAW: child*) pupilo; **to** ~ **off** *vt* desviar, parar; (*attack*) rechazar.

warden ['wɔːdn] *n* (*of institution*) director *m*; (*of park, game reserve*) guardián *m*; (*also:* **traffic** ~) guardia *m/f*.

warder ['wɔːdə*] *n* guardián *m*, carcelero.

wardrobe ['wɔːdrəub] *n* (*cupboard*) armario; (*clothes*) guardarropa.

warehouse ['weəhaus] *n* almacén *m*, depósito.

wares [weəz] *npl* mercancías *fpl*.

war: ~**fare** *n* guerra; ~**head** *n* cabeza armada.

warily ['weərɪlɪ] *ad* con cautela, cautelosamente.

warlike ['wɔːlaɪk] *a* guerrero.

warm [wɔːm] *a* caliente; (*thanks*) efusivo; (*clothes etc*) cálido; (*welcome, day*) caluroso; **it's** ~ hace calor; **I'm** ~ tengo calor; **to** ~ **up** *vi* (*person, room*) calentarse; (*athlete*) hacer ejercicios de calentamiento; (*discussion*) acalorarse // *vt* calentar; ~**-hearted** *a* afectuoso; ~**ly** *ad* afectuosamente; ~**th** *n* calor *m*.

warn [wɔːn] *vt* avisar, prevenir; ~**ing** *n* aviso, advertencia; ~**ing light** *n* luz *f* de advertencia.

warp [wɔːp] *vi* disformarse.

warrant ['wɔrnt] *n* (*guarantee*) garantía; (*LAW*) mandato judicial.

warranty ['wɔrəntɪ] *n* garantía.

warren ['wɔrən] *n* (*of rabbits*) madriguera; (*house*) conejera.

warrior ['wɔrɪə*] *n* guerrero.

warship ['wɔːʃɪp] *n* buque *m* o barco de guerra.

wart [wɔːt] *n* verruga.

wartime ['wɔːtaɪm] *n*: **in** ~ en tiempos de guerra, en la guerra.

wary ['weərɪ] *a* cauteloso, cauto.

was [wɔz] *pt of* **be**.

wash [wɔʃ] *vt* lavar // *vi* lavarse // *n* (*clothes etc*) lavado; (*bath*) baño; (*of ship*) estela; **to have a** ~ lavarse; **to** ~ **away** *vt* (*stain*) quitar lavando; (*subj: river etc*) llevarse; (*fig*) regar; **to** ~ **off** *vt* quitar lavando; **to** ~ **up** *vi* fregar los platos; ~**able** *a* lavable; ~**basin** *n* lavabo; ~**er** *n* (*TECH*) arandela; ~**ing** *n* (*dirty*) ropa sucia; (*clean*) colada; ~**ing machine** *n* lavadora; ~**ing powder** *n* jabón *m* en polvo; ~**ing-up** *n* fregado, platos *mpl* (para fregar); ~**out** *n* (*col*) fracaso; ~**room** *n* servicios *mpl*.

wasn't ['wɔznt] = **was not**.

wasp [wɔsp] *n* avispa.

wastage ['weɪstɪdʒ] *n* desgaste *m*; (*loss*) pérdida; **natural** ~ desgaste natural.

waste [weɪst] *n* derroche *m*, despilfarro; (*wastage*) desgaste *m*; (*of time*) pérdida; (*food*) sobras *fpl*; (*rubbish*) basura, desperdicios *mpl* // *a* (*material*) de desecho; (*left over*) sobrante; (*land*) baldío // *vt* (*squander*) malgastar, derrochar; (*time*) perder; (*opportunity*) desperdiciar; (*use up*) consumir; **to** ~ **away** *vi* consumirse; ~**bin** *n* cubo de la basura; ~**disposal unit** *n* triturador *m* de basura; ~**ful** *a* derrochador(a); (*process*) antieconómico; ~ **ground** *n* terreno baldío; ~**paper basket** *n* papelera; ~ **pipe** *n* tubo de desagüe.

watch [wɔtʃ] *n* reloj *m*; (*act of watching*) vigilia; (*vigilance*) vigilancia; (*guard: MIL*) centinela *m*; (*NAUT: spell of duty*) guardia // *vt* (*look at*) mirar, observar; (: *match, programme*) ver; (*spy on, guard*) vigilar; (*be careful of*) cuidarse de, tener cuidado de // *vi* ver, mirar; (*keep guard*) montar guardia; **to** ~ **out** *vi* cuidarse, tener cuidado; ~**dog** *n* perro guardián; ~**ful** *a* vigilante, observador(a); ~**maker** *n* relojero; ~**man** *n* guardián *m*; (*also:* **night** ~**man**) sereno, (*in factory*) vigilante *m* nocturno; ~**strap** *n* pulsera (de reloj); ~**word** *n* lema *m*.

water ['wɔːtə*] *n* agua // *vt* (*plant*) regar; **to** ~ **down** *vt* (*milk*) aguar; ~**closet** *n* wáter *m*; ~**colour** *n* acuarela; ~**cress** *n* berro; ~**fall** *n* cascada, salto de agua; ~**hole** *n* charco; ~**ing can** *n* regadera; ~

level n nivel m del agua; ~ **lily** n nenúfar m; ~ **line** n (NAUT) línea de flotación; ~**logged** a empapado; ~ **main** n cañería del agua; ~**mark** n (on paper) filigrana; ~**melon** n sandía; ~ **polo** n polo acuático; ~**proof** a impermeable; ~**shed** n (GEO) cuenca; (fig) momento crítico; ~**skiing** n esquí m acuático; ~ **tank** n depósito de agua; ~**tight** a hermético; ~**works** npl central f depuradora; ~**y** a (colour) desvaído; (coffee) aguado; (eyes) lloroso.

watt [wɔt] n vatio.

wave [weiv] n ola; (of hand) ademán m, señal f; (RADIO) onda; (in hair) ondulación f; (fig) oleada // vi agitar la mano; (flag) ondear // vi (handkerchief) agitar; (weapon) blandir; (hair) ondular; ~**length** n longitud f de onda.

waver ['weivə°] vi oscilar; (person) vacilar.

wavy ['weivi] a ondulado.

wax [wæks] n cera // vt encerar // vi (moon) crecer; ~**works** npl museo sg de cera.

way [wei] n (gen) camino; (distance) trayecto, recorrido; (direction) dirección f, sentido; (manner) modo, manera; (habit) costumbre f; (condition) estado; **which** ~? ¿en qué dirección?; to be on one's ~ estar en camino; to be in the ~ bloquear el camino; to go out of one's ~ to do sth desvivirse por hacer algo; to lose one's ~ extraviarse; in a ~ en cierto modo o sentido; by the ~ a propósito; '~ out' 'salida'; the ~ back el camino de vuelta; 'give ~' (AUT) 'ceda el paso'.

waylay [wei'lei] (irg: like lay) vt acechar.

wayward ['weiwəd] a (wilful) voluntarioso; (capricious) caprichoso; (naughty) travieso.

W.C. ['dʌblju'si:] n wáter m.

we [wi:] pl pron nosotros/as.

weak [wi:k] a (gen) débil, flojo; (tea) claro; ~**en** vi debilitarse; (give way) ceder // vt debilitar; (lessen) disminuir; ~**ling** n persona débil o delicada; ~**ness** n debilidad f; (fault) punto débil.

wealth [welθ] n (money, resources) riqueza; (of details) abundancia; ~**y** a rico.

wean [wi:n] vt destetar.

weapon ['wepən] n arma.

wear [wɛə°] n (use) uso; (deterioration through use) desgaste m; (clothing): **sports/baby**~ ropa de deportes/para niños // (vb: pt **wore**, pp **worn**) vt (clothes) llevar; (shoes) calzar; (put on) ponerse; (damage: through use) gastar, usar // vi (last) durar; (rub through etc) desgastarse; ~ **and tear** n desgaste m; to ~ **away** vt gastar // vi desgastarse; to ~ **down** vt (strength) agotar; to ~ **off** vi (pain etc) pasar, desaparecer; to ~ **out** vt desgastar; (person, strength) agotar.

weariness ['wiərinis] n cansancio; (boredom) aburrimiento, hastío.

weary ['wiəri] a (tired) cansado; (dispirited) abatido // vt cansar // vi: to ~ of cansarse de, aburrirse de.

weasel ['wi:zl] n (ZOOL) comadreja.

weather ['wɛðə°] n tiempo // vt (storm, crisis) hacer frente a; ~**beaten** a curtido; ~ **cock** n veleta; ~ **forecast** n boletín m meteorológico; ~ **vane** n = ~ **cock.**

weave [wi:v] pt **wove**, pp **woven** vt (cloth) tejer; (fig) entretejer; **weaver** n tejedor/a m/f; **weaving** n tejeduría.

web [web] n (of spider) telaraña; (on foot) membrana; (network) red f; ~**bed** a (foot) palmeado; ~**bing** n (on chair) cinchas fpl.

wed [wed], pt, pp **wedded** vt casar // vi casarse // n: **the newly**-~**s** los recién casados.

we'd [wi:d] = we had; we would.

wedded ['wedid] pt, pp of wed.

wedding ['wedin] n boda, casamiento; **silver/golden** ~ bodas fpl de plata/de oro; ~ **day** n día m de la boda; ~ **dress** n traje m de novia; ~ **present** n regalo de boda; ~ **ring** n anillo de boda.

wedge [wedʒ] n (of wood etc) cuña; (of cake) porción f // vt acuñar; (pack tightly) apretar.

wedlock ['wedlɔk] n matrimonio.

Wednesday ['wednzdi] n miércoles m.

wee [wi:] a (Scottish) pequeñito.

weed [wi:d] n mala hierba, maleza // vt escardar, desherbar; ~**killer** n herbicida m.

week [wi:k] n semana; ~**day** n día m laborable; ~**end** n fin m de semana; ~**ly** ad semanalmente, cada semana // a semanal // n semanario.

weep [wi:p] pt, pp **wept** vi, vt llorar; ~**ing willow** n sauce m llorón.

weigh [wei] vt, vi pesar; to ~ **down** vt sobrecargar; (fig: with worry) agobiar; to ~ **up** vt pesar; ~**bridge** n báscula-puente f.

weight [weit] n peso; (on scale) pesa; to **lose/put on** ~ adelgazarse/engordarse; ~**lessness** n ingravidez f; ~ **lifter** n levantador m de pesos; ~**y** a pesado.

weir [wiə°] n presa.

weird [wiəd] a raro, extraño.

welcome ['welkəm] a bienvenido // n bienvenida // vt dar la bienvenida a; (be glad of) alegrarse de; **welcoming** a acogedor(a); (speech) de bienvenida.

weld [weld] n soldadura // vt soldar; ~**er** n (person) soldador m; ~**ing** n soldadura.

welfare ['welfɛə°] n bienestar m; (social aid) asistencia social; ~ **state** n estado de bienestar.

well [wel] n fuente f, pozo // ad bien // a: to be ~ estar bien (de salud) // excl ¡vaya!, ¡bueno!; as ~ también; as ~ as igual que; ~ **done!** ¡bien hecho!; **get** ~ **soon!** ¡que te mejores pronto!; to do ~ ir o salir bien; to ~ **up** vi brotar.

we'll [wi:l] = we will, we shall.

well: ~-behaved a bien educado, formal; ~-being n bienestar m; ~-built a (person) fornido; ~-deserved a merecido; ~-developed a bien desarrollado; ~-dressed a bien vestido; ~-heeled a (col: wealthy) rico; ~-informed a enterado.

wellingtons ['wclɪŋtənz] n (also: wellington boots) botas fpl de goma.

well: ~-known a (person) conocido; ~-mannered a educado; ~-meaning a bienintencionado; ~-off a pudiente, con dinero; ~-read a culto; ~-to-do a acomodado; ~-wisher n admirador/a m/f, amigo.

Welsh [wclʃ] a galés(esa) // n (LING) galés m; ~ man/woman n galés/esa m/f.

went [wcnt] pt of go.

wept [wcpt] pt, pp of weep.

were [wəː°] pt of be.

we're [wɪəᵃ] = we are.

weren't [wəːnt] = were not.

west [wcst] n oeste m // a occidental, del oeste // ad hacia el o al oeste; the W~ n el Oeste, el Occidente; the W~ Country n el suroeste de Inglaterra; ~erly a (situation) oeste; (wind) del oeste; ~ern a occidental // n (CINEMA) película del oeste; W~ Germany n Alemania Occidental; W~ Indies npl Antillas fpl; ~ward(s) ad hacia el oeste.

wet [wct] a (damp) húmedo; (~ through) mojado; (rainy) lluvioso; to get ~ mojarse; '~ paint' 'recién pintado'; to be a ~ blanket (fig) ser un/una aguafiestas; ~ness n humedad f; ~ suit n traje m de buzo.

we've [wi:v] = we have.

whack [wæk] vt dar un buen golpe a; ~ed a (col: tired) reventado.

whale [weɪl] n (ZOOL) ballena.

wharf [wɔːf] pl wharves [wɔːvz] n muelle m.

what [wɔt] excl ¡qué!, ¡cómo! // det que // pron (interrogative) ¿qué?, ¿cómo?; (relative, indirect: object) lo que; (: subject) el/la que; ~ are you doing? ¿qué haces?; I saw ~ you did he visto lo que hiciste; ~ a mess! ¡qué lío!; ~ is it called? ¿cómo se llama?; ~ about me? ¿y yo?; ~ever det: ~ever book you choose cualquier libro que elijas // pron: do ~ever is necessary haga lo que sea necesario; no reason ~ever or ~soever ninguna razón sea la que sea; nothing ~ever nada en absoluto.

wheat [wi:t] n trigo.

wheel [wi:l] n rueda; (AUT: also: steering ~) volante m; (NAUT) timón m // vt (pram etc) empujar // vi (also: ~ round) dar la vuelta, girar; ~barrow n carretilla; ~chair n silla de ruedas; ~house n timonera.

wheeze [wi:z] n respiración f ruidosa // vi resollar.

when [wcn] ad cuándo // conj cuando; (whereas) mientras; on the day ~ I met him el día que le conocí; ~ever conj cuando, todas las veces que; (every time that) siempre que.

where [wcəᵃ] ad dónde // conj donde; this is ~ aquí es donde; ~abouts ad ¿dónde? // n: nobody knows his ~abouts nadie conoce su paradero; ~as conj visto que, mientras; wherever [-'cvᵃ°] ad dondequiera que; (interrogative) ¿dónde?; ~withal n recursos mpl.

whet [wct] vt estimular.

whether ['wcðᵃ°] conj si; I don't know ~ to accept or not no sé si aceptar o no; ~ you go or not vayas o no vayas.

which [wɪtʃ] det (interrogative) ¿qué?, ¿cuál?; ~ one of you? ¿cuál de vosotros?; ~ picture do you want? ¿qué cuadro quieres? // pron (interrogative) ¿cuál?; (relative: subject) que, lo que; (: object) el que etc, el cual etc, lo cual; I don't mind ~ no me importa cuál; the apple ~ is on the table la manzana que está sobre la mesa; the chair on ~ you are sitting la silla sobre la que estás sentado; he said he knew, ~ is true el dijo que sabía, lo cual es cierto; in ~ case en cuyo caso; ~ever det: take ~ever book you prefer coja el libro que prefiera; ~ever book you take cualquier libro que coja.

whiff [wɪf] n bocanada.

while [waɪl] n rato, momento // conj durante; (as long as) mientras; (although) aunque; for a ~ durante algún tiempo.

whim [wɪm] n capricho.

whimper ['wɪmpᵃ°] n (weeping) lloriqueo; (moan) quejido // vi lloriquear; quejarse.

whimsical ['wɪmzɪkl] a (person) caprichoso; (look) extraño.

whine [waɪn] n (of pain) gemido; (of engine) zumbido // vi gemir; zumbar.

whip [wɪp] n látigo; (for riding) fusta; (Brit: POL) oficial disciplinario del partido // vt azotar; (snatch) arrebatar; ~ped cream n crema batida; ~-round n colecta.

whirl [wɔːl] n remolino // vt hacer girar, dar vueltas a // vi girar, dar vueltas; (leaves, water etc) arremolinarse; ~pool n remolino; ~wind n torbellino.

whirr [wɔːᵃ] vi rechinar, zumbar.

whisk [wɪsk] n (CULIN) batidor m // vt batir; to ~ sth away from sb arrebatarle algo a uno; to ~ sb away or off llevar rápidamente a uno.

whisker ['wɪskᵃ°] n: ~s (of animal) bigotes mpl; (of man) patillas fpl.

whisk(e)y ['wɪskɪ] n whisky m.

whisper ['wɪspᵃ°] n cuchicheo; (rumour) rumor m; (fig) susurro, murmullo // vi cuchichear, hablar bajo; (fig) susurrar.

whist [wɪst] n whist m.

whistle ['wɪsl] n (sound) silbido; (object) silbato // vi silbar.

white [waɪt] a blanco; (pale) pálido // n blanco; (of egg) clara; ~-collar worker n oficinista m/f; ~ elephant n (fig) maula; ~ lie n mentira piadosa; ~ness n blancura; ~ **paper** n (POL) libro rojo; ~**wash** n (paint) jalbegue m, cal f // vt enjalbegar; (fig) encubrir.

whiting ['waɪtɪŋ] n, pl inv (fish) pescadilla.

Whitsun ['wɪtsn] n pentecostés m.

whittle ['wɪtl] vt: to ~ **away**, ~ **down** reducir poco a poco.

whizz [wɪz] vi: to ~ **past** or **by** pasar a toda velocidad; ~ **kid** n (col) prodigio, portento.

who [hu:] pron (relative) que, el que etc, quien; (interrogative) ¿quién?; (pl) ¿quiénes?; ~**ever** pron: ~**ever finds it** cualquiera o quienquiera que lo encuentre; **ask** ~**ever you like** pregunta a quien quieras; ~**ever he marries** no importa con quién se case.

whole [həul] a (complete) todo, entero; (not broken) intacto // n (total) total m; (sum) conjunto; **the** ~ **of the town** toda la ciudad, la ciudad entera; **on the** ~, **as a** ~ en general; ~**hearted** a sincero, cordial; ~**sale** n venta al por mayor // a al por mayor; (destruction) sistemático; ~**saler** n mayorista m/f; ~**some** a sano; **wholly** ad totalmente, enteramente.

whom [hu:m] pron que, a quien; (interrogative) ¿a quién?

whooping cough ['hu:pɪŋkɔf] n tos f ferina.

whopper ['wɔpə*] n cosa muy grande; (lie) bola; **whopping** a (col: big) enorme.

whore [hɔ:*] n (col: pej) puta.

whose [hu:z] det: ~ **book is this?** ¿de quién es este libro?; **the man** ~ **son you rescued** el hombre cuyo hijo salvaste; **the girl** ~ **sister you were speaking** to la chica con cuya hermana estabas hablando // pron: ~ **is this?** ¿de quién es esto?; **I know** ~ **it is** yo sé de quien es.

why [waɪ] ad por qué; (interrogative) ¿por qué?, ¿para qué? // excl ¡toma!, ¡cómo!; **tell me** ~ dime por qué, dime la razón; ~**ever** ad por qué.

wick [wɪk] n mecha.

wicked ['wɪkɪd] a malvado, cruel.

wicker ['wɪkə*] n (also: ~**work**) artículos mpl de mimbre.

wicket ['wɪkɪt] n (CRICKET) palos mpl.

wide [waɪd] a ancho; (region, knowledge) vasto, grande; (choice) grande // ad: to **open** ~ abrir de par en par; **to shoot** ~ errar el tiro; ~**awake** a bien despierto; (fig) despabilado; ~**ly** ad (different) muy; **it is** ~**ly believed that...** hay una convicción general de que...; **widen** vt ensanchar; ~**ness** n anchura; ~ **open** a abierto de par en par; ~**spread** a (belief etc) extendido, general.

widow ['wɪdəu] n viuda; ~**ed** a viudo; ~**er** n viudo.

width [wɪdθ] n anchura; (of cloth) ancho.

wield [wi:ld] vt (sword) manejar; (power) ejercer.

wife [waɪf], pl **wives** [waɪvz] n mujer f, esposa.

wig [wɪg] n peluca.

wiggle ['wɪgl] vt menear (rápidamente) // vi menearse.

wild [waɪld] a (animal) salvaje; (plant) silvestre; (rough) furioso, violento; (idea) disparatado, descabellado; (person) loco; ~**s** npl regiones fpl salvajes, tierras fpl vírgenes; ~**erness** ['wɪldənɪs] n desierto; ~**life** n fauna; ~**ly** ad (roughly) violentamente; (foolishly) locamente; (rashly) descabelladamente.

wilful ['wɪlful] a (person) voluntarioso; (action) deliberado; (obstinate) testarudo; (child) travieso.

will [wɪl] auxiliary vb: **he** ~ **come** vendrá // vt, pt, pp **willed**: **to** ~ **sb to do sth** desear que alguien haga algo; **he** ~**ed himself to go on** con gran fuerza de voluntad, continuó // n voluntad f; (testament) testamento; ~**ing** a (with goodwill) de buena voluntad; (submissive) complaciente; ~**ingly** ad con mucho gusto; ~**ingness** n buena voluntad.

willow ['wɪləu] n sauce m.

will power n fuerza de voluntad.

wilt [wɪlt] vi marchitarse.

wily ['waɪlɪ] a astuto.

win [wɪn] n (in sports etc) victoria, triunfo // (vb: pt, pp **won**); (obtain) conseguir, lograr // vi ganar, tener éxito; **to** ~ **over**, ~ **round** vt atraerse.

wince [wɪns] vi estremecerse.

winch [wɪntʃ] n torno.

wind [wɪnd] n viento; (breath) aliento // (vb: [waɪnd], pt, pp **wound**) vt enrollar; (wrap) envolver; (clock, toy) dar cuerda a // vi (road, river) serpentear // vt [waɪnd] (take breath away from) dejar sin aliento a; **to** ~ **up** vt (clock) dar cuerda a; (debate) concluir, terminar; ~**break** n abrigada; ~**fall** n golpe m de suerte; ~**ing** a (road) tortuoso; ~ **instrument** n (MUS) instrumento de viento; ~**mill** n molino de viento.

window ['wɪndəu] n ventana; (in car, train) ventanilla; (in shop etc) escaparate m; ~ **box** n jardinera (de ventana); ~ **cleaner** n (person) limpiacristales m inv; ~ **ledge** n alféizar m; ~ **pane** n cristal m; ~**sill** n alféizar m.

windpipe ['wɪndpaɪp] n tráquea.

windscreen ['wɪndskri:n], **windshield** ['wɪndʃi:ld] (US) n parabrisas m inv; ~ **washer** n lavaparabrisas m inv; ~ **wiper** n limpiaparabrisas m inv.

windswept ['wɪndswept] a azotado por el viento.

windy ['wɪndɪ] a de mucho viento; **it's** ~ hace viento.

wine [waɪn] n vino; ~ **cellar** n bodega; ~ **glass** n copa (para vino); ~ **list** n lista de vinos; ~ **merchant** n vinatero; ~ **tasting** n degustación f de vinos.

wing [wɪŋ] n (gen) ala; (AUT) aleta, guardabarros m inv; ~**s** npl (THEATRE) bastidores mpl; ~**er** n (SPORT) extremo.

wink [wɪŋk] n guiño, pestañeo // vi guiñar,

pestañear; (*light etc*) parpadear.

winner ['wɪnə*] *n* ganador/a *m/f.*

winning ['wɪnɪŋ] *a* (*team*) ganador(a); (*goal*) decisivo; ~s *npl* ganancias *fpl*; ~ **post** *n* meta.

winter ['wɪntə*] *n* invierno // *vi* invernar; ~ **sports** *npl* deportes *mpl* de invierno.

wintry ['wɪntrɪ] *a* invernal.

wipe [waɪp] *n:* **to give sth a** ~ pasar un trapo sobre algo // *vt* limpiar; **to** ~ **off** *vt* limpiar con un trapo; **to** ~ **out** *vt* (*debt*) liquidar; (*memory*) borrar; (*destroy*) destruir.

wire ['waɪə*] *n* alambre *m*; (*ELEC*) cable *m* (*eléctrico*); (*TEL*) telegrama *m* // *vt* (*house*) instalar el alambrado de; (*also:* ~ **up**) conectar // *vi* poner un telegrama.

wireless ['waɪəlɪs] *n* radio *f.*

wiring ['waɪərɪŋ] *n* instalación *f* eléctrica, alambrado.

wiry ['waɪərɪ] *a* nervioso, nervudo.

wisdom ['wɪzdəm] *n* sabiduría, saber *m*; (*good sense*) cordura; (*care*) prudencia; ~ **tooth** *n* muela del juicio.

wise [waɪz] *a* sabio; (*sensible*) cuerdo; (*careful*) prudente.

...wise [waɪz] *suff:* **time**~ en cuanto a *o* respecto al tiempo.

wisecrack ['waɪzkræk] *n* broma.

wish [wɪʃ] *n* (*desire*) deseo // *vt* desear; (*want*) querer; **best** ~**es** (*on birthday etc*) felicidades *fpl*; **with best** ~**es** (*in letter*) saludos *mpl*, recuerdos *mpl*; **to** ~ **sb goodbye** despedirse de uno; **he** ~**ed me well** me deseó mucha suerte; **to** ~ **to do/sb to do sth** querer hacer/que alguien haga algo; **to** ~ **for** desear; **it's** ~**ful thinking** es un espejismo.

wisp [wɪsp] *n* mechón *m*; (*of smoke*) voluta.

wistful ['wɪstful] *a* pensativo.

wit [wɪt] *n* (*wittiness*) ingenio, gracia; (*intelligence*) entendimiento; (*person*) chistoso/a.

witch [wɪtʃ] *n* bruja; ~**craft** *n* brujería.

with [wɪð, wɪθ] *prep* con; **red** ~ **anger** rojo de cólera; **the man** ~ **the grey hat** el hombre del sombrero gris; **to be** ~ **it** (*fig*) estar al tanto *o* a la moda; **I am** ~ **you** (*I understand*) te entiendo.

withdraw [wɪθ'drɔː] (*irg: like draw*) *vt* retirar, sacar // *vi* retirarse; (*go back on promise*) retractarse; **to** ~ **money (from the bank)** retirar fondos (del banco); ~**al** *n* retirada; ~**n** *a* (*person*) reservado, introvertido.

wither ['wɪðə*] *vi* marchitarse; ~**ed** *a* marchito.

withhold [wɪθ'həuld] (*irg: like hold*) *vt* (*money*) retener; (*decision*) aplazar; (*permission*) negar; (*information*) ocultar.

within [wɪð'ɪn] *prep* dentro de // *ad* dentro; ~ **reach** al alcance de la mano; ~ **sight of** a la vista de; ~ **the week** antes de acabar la semana.

without [wɪð'aut] *prep* sin.

withstand [wɪθ'stænd] (*irg: like stand*) *vt* resistir a.

witness ['wɪtnɪs] *n* (*person*) testigo; (*evidence*) testimonio // *vt* (*event*) presenciar; (*document*) atestiguar la veracidad de; ~ **box**, ~ **stand** (*US*) *n* tribuna de los testigos.

witticism ['wɪtɪsɪzm] *n* dicho ingenioso.

witty ['wɪtɪ] *a* ingenioso, salado.

wives [waɪvz] *pl of* **wife.**

wizard ['wɪzəd] *n* hechicero.

wk *abbr of* **week.**

wobble ['wɔbl] *vi* tambalearse; (*chair*) ser poco firme.

woe [wəu] *n* desgracia.

woke [wəuk], **woken** ['wəukən] *pt, pp of* **wake.**

wolf [wulf], *pl* **wolves** [wulvz] *n* lobo.

woman ['wumən], *pl* **women** *n* mujer *f*; ~**ly** a femenino.

womb [wuːm] *n* (*ANAT*) matriz *f*, útero.

women ['wɪmɪn] *pl of* **woman.**

won [wʌn] *pt, pp of* **win.**

wonder ['wʌndə*] *n* maravilla, prodigio; (*feeling*) asombro // *vi:* **to** ~ **whether** preguntarse si; **to** ~ **at** asombrarse de; **to** ~ **about** pensar sobre *o* en; **it's no** ~ **that** no es de extrañarse que; ~**ful** *a* maravilloso; ~**fully** *ad* maravillosamente, estupendamente.

won't [wəunt] = **will not.**

woo [wuː] *vt* (*woman*) cortejar.

wood [wud] *n* (*timber*) madera; (*forest*) bosque *m*; ~ **carving** *n* escultura de madera; ~**ed** *a* arbolado; ~**en** *a* de madera; (*fig*) inexpresivo; ~**pecker** *n* pájaro carpintero; ~**wind** *n* (*MUS*) instrumentos *mpl* de viento de madera; ~**work** *n* carpintería; ~**worm** *n* carcoma.

wool [wul] *n* lana; **to pull the** ~ **over sb's eyes** (*fig*) dar a uno gato por liebre; ~**len**, ~**en** (*US*) *a* de lana; ~**lens** *npl* géneros *mpl* de lana; ~**ly**, ~**y** (*US*) *a* lanudo, de lana; (*fig: ideas*) confuso.

word [wɜːd] *n* palabra; (*news*) noticia; (*message*) aviso // *vt* redactar; **in other** ~**s** en otras palabras; **to break/keep one's** ~ faltar a la palabra/cumplir la promesa; ~**ing** *n* redacción *f.*

wore [wɔː*] *pt of* **wear.**

work [wɜːk] *n* (*gen*) trabajo; (*job*) empleo, trabajo; (*ART, LITERATURE*) obra // *vi* trabajar; (*mechanism*) funcionar, marchar; (*medicine*) ser eficaz, surtir efecto // *vt* (*clay, wood etc*) tallar; (*mine etc*) explotar; (*machine*) manejar, hacer funcionar; (*cause*) producir; **to be out of** ~ estar parado, no tener trabajo; ~**s** *n* (*factory*) fábrica // *npl* (*of clock, machine*) mecanismo *sg*; **to** ~ **loose** *vi* (*part*) desprenderse; (*knot*) aflojarse; **to** ~ **on** *vt fus* trabajar en, dedicarse a; (*principle*) basarse en; **to** ~ **out** *vi* (*plans etc*) salir bien, funcionar // *vt* (*problem*) resolver; (*plan*) elaborar; **does it** ~ **out?** ¿da resultado?; **it** ~**s out at £100** suma 100 libras; **to get** ~**ed up** exaltarse; ~**able** *a* (*solution*) práctico, factible; ~**er** *n* trabajador/a, obrero; ~**ing class** *n* clase f obrera; ~**ing-class** a de clase obrera; **in** ~**ing order** en funcionamiento; ~**man** n obrero; ~**manship** n (art) hechura, arte m; (skill) habilidad f, trabajo; ~**shop** n taller m; ~**-to-rule** n huelga de celo.

world [wɔːld] n mundo // cpd (champion) del mundo; (power, war) mundial; **to think the** ~ **of sb** (fig) tener un concepto muy alto de uno; ~**ly** a mundano; ~**-wide** a mundial, universal.

worm [wɜːm] n gusano; (earth~) lombriz f.

worn [wɔːn] pp of **wear** // a usado; ~**-out** a (object) gastado; (person) rendido, agotado.

worried ['wʌrɪd] a preocupado.

worry ['wʌrɪ] n preocupación f // vt preocupar, inquietar // vi preocuparse; ~**ing** a inquietante.

worse [wɜːs] a, ad peor, inferior // n el peor, lo peor; **a change for the** ~ un empeoramiento; **worsen** vt, vi empeorar; ~ **off** a (fig): **you'll be** ~ **off this way** de esta forma estarás peor que nunca.

worship ['wɜːʃɪp] n culto; (act) adoración f // vt adorar; **Your W**~ (to mayor) señor alcalde; (to judge) señor juez; ~**per** n devoto/a.

worst [wɜːst] a (el/la) peor // ad peor // n lo peor; **at** ~ en lo peor de los casos.

worth [wɜːθ] n valor m // a: **to be** ~ valer; **it's** ~ **it** vale o merece la pena; ~**less** a sin valor; (useless) inútil; ~**while** a (activity) que merece la pena; (cause) loable.

worthy ['wɜːðɪ] a (person) respetable; (motive) honesto; ~ **of** digno de.

would [wud] auxiliary vb: **she** ~ **come** ella vendría; **he** ~ **have come** él hubiera venido; ~ **you like a biscuit?** ¿quieres una galleta?; **he** ~ **go on Mondays** solía ir los lunes; ~**-be** a (pej) presunto, aspirante.

wound [waund] pt, pp of **wind** // n [wuːnd] herida // vt [wuːnd] herir.

wove [wəuv], **woven** ['wəuvən] pt, pp of **weave**.

wrangle ['ræŋgl] n riña // vi reñir.

wrap [ræp] n (stole) chal m; (cape) capa // vt (also: ~ **up**) envolver; ~**per** n (of book) cubierta, tapa; ~**ping paper** n papel m de envolver.

wrath [rɔθ] n cólera.

wreath [riːθ], pl ~**s** [riːðz] n (funeral ~) corona; (of flowers) guirnalda.

wreathe [riːð] vt ceñir.

wreck [rɛk] n naufragio; (ship) restos mpl del barco; (pej: person) ruina // vt destruir, hundir; (fig) arruinar; ~**age** n restos mpl; (of building) escombros mpl.

wren [rɛn] n (ZOOL) reyezuelo.

wrench [rɛntʃ] n (TECH) llave f inglesa; (tug) tirón m // vt arrancar; **to** ~ **sth from sb** arrebatar algo violentamente a uno.

wrestle ['rɛsl] vi: **to** ~ (with sb) luchar (con o contra uno); **wrestler** n luchador m

(de lucha libre); **wrestling** n lucha libre; **wrestling match** n partido de lucha libre.

wretched ['rɛtʃɪd] a miserable.

wriggle ['rɪgl] n (gen) culebreo // vi (gen) serpentear.

wring [rɪŋ], pt, pp **wrung** vt torcer, retorcer; (wet clothes) escurrir; (fig): **to** ~ **sth out of sb** sacar algo por la fuerza a uno.

wrinkle ['rɪŋkl] n arruga // vt arrugar // vi arrugarse.

wrist [rɪst] n muñeca; ~ **watch** n reloj m de pulsera.

writ [rɪt] n mandato judicial; **to issue a** ~ **against sb** demandar a uno (en juicio).

write [raɪt], pt **wrote**, pp **written** vt, vi escribir; **to** ~ **down** vt escribir; (note) apuntar; **to** ~ **off** vt (debt) borrar (como incobrable); (depreciate) depreciar; **to** ~ **out** vt escribir; **to** ~ **up** vt redactar; ~**-off** n pérdida total; **the car is a** ~**-off** el coche es pura chatarra; **writer** n escritor/a m/f.

writhe [raɪð] vi retorcerse.

writing ['raɪtɪŋ] n escritura; (hand-~) letra; (of author) obra; **in** ~ por escrito; ~ **paper** n papel m de escribir.

written ['rɪtn] pp of **write**.

wrong [rɔŋ] a (bad) malo; (unfair) injusto; (incorrect) equivocado, incorrecto; (not suitable) inoportuno, inconveniente // ad mal; equivocadamente // n mal m; (injustice) injusticia // vt ser injusto con; (hurt) agraviar; **you are** ~ **to do it** estás equivocado en hacerlo, cometes un error al hacerlo; **you are** ~ **about that, you've got it** ~ en eso, estás equivocado; **to be in the** ~ no tener razón, tener la culpa; **what's** ~? ¿qué pasa?; **to go** ~ (person) equivocarse; (plan) salir mal; (machine) tener una avería; ~**ful** a injusto; ~**ly** ad injustamente.

wrote [rəut] pt of **write**.

wrought [rɔːt] a: ~ **iron** hierro forjado.

wrung [rʌŋ] pt, pp of **wring**.

wry [raɪ] a irónico.

wt. abbr of **weight**.

X

Xmas ['ɛksməs] n abbr of **Christmas**.

X-ray [ɛks'reɪ] n radiografía; ~**s** npl rayos mpl X // vt hacer una radiografía a.

xylophone ['zaɪləfəun] n xilófono.

Y

yacht [jɔt] n yate m; ~**ing** n (sport) balandrismo; **yachtsman** n balandrista m.

Yank [jæŋk] n (pej) yanqui m/f.

yap [jæp] vi (dog) aullar.

yard [jɑːd] n patio; (measure) yarda; ~**stick** n (fig) criterio, norma.

yarn [jɑːn] n hilo; (tale) cuento, historia.

yawn [jɔːn] n bostezo // vi bostezar.

yd. *abbr of* **yard(s).**

year [jɪə*] *n* año; **to be 8 ~s old** tener 8 años; **~ly** *a* anual // *ad* anualmente, cada año.

yearn [jə:n] *vi*: **to ~ for sth** añorar *o* suspirar por algo; **~ing** *n* ansia, añoranza.

yeast [ji:st] *n* levadura.

yell [jɛl] *n* grito, alarido // *vi* gritar.

yellow ['jɛləu] *a*, *n* amarillo.

yelp [jɛlp] *n* aullido // *vi* aullar.

yeoman ['jəumən] *n*: **Y~ of the Guard** alabardero de la Casa Real.

yes [jɛs] *ad*, *n* sí m.

yesterday ['jɛstədɪ] *ad*, *n* ayer m.

yet [jɛt] *ad* todavía // *conj* sin embargo, a pesar de todo; **it is not finished ~** todavía no está acabado; **the best ~** el mejor hasta ahora; **as ~** hasta ahora, todavía.

yew [ju:] *n* tejo.

Yiddish ['jɪdɪʃ] *n* judío.

yield [ji:ld] *n* producción *f*; (AGR) cosecha; (COMM) rendimiento // *vt* (gen) producir; (profit) rendir // *vi* rendirse, ceder.

yoga ['jəugə] *n* yoga.

yog(h)ourt, yog(h)urt ['jəugət] *n* yogur m.

yoke [jəuk] *n* (of oxen) yunta; (on shoulders) balancín m; (fig) yugo // *vt* acoplar.

yolk [jəuk] *n* yema (de huevo).

yonder ['jɔndə*] *ad* allá (a lo lejos).

you [ju:] *pron* tú; (pl) vosotros; (polite form) usted; (: pl) ustedes; (complement) te; (: pl) os; (after prep) tí; (: pl) vosotros; (: formal) le/la; (: pl) les; (after prep) usted; (: pl) ustedes; (one): **~ never know** uno nunca sabe; (impersonal): **~ can't do that** eso no se hace.

you'd [ju:d] = **you had; you would.**

you'll [ju:l] = **you will, you shall.**

young [jʌŋ] *a* joven // *npl* (of animal) la cría *sg*; (people): **the ~** los jóvenes, la juventud *sg*; **~er** *a* (brother etc) menor; **~ish** *a* bastante joven; **~ster** *n* joven *n*/*f*.

your [jɔ:*] *a* tu; (pl) vuestro; (formal) su.

you're [juə*] = **you are.**

yours [jɔ:z] *pron* tuyo; (: pl) vuestro; (formal) suyo; **is it ~?** ¿es tuyo etc?; **~ sincerely** *or* **faithfully** le saluda atentamente.

yourself [jɔ:'sɛlf] *pron* (reflexive) tú mismo; (complement) te; (after prep) tí (mismo); (formal) usted mismo; (: complement) se; (: after prep) sí (mismo); **yourselves** *pl pron* vosotros mismos; (after prep) vosotros (mismos); (formal) ustedes (mismos); (: complement) se; (: after prep) sí mismos.

youth [ju:θ] *n* juventud *f*; (young man: pl ~s [ju:ðz]) joven m; **~ful** *a* juvenil; **~ hostel** *n* albergue m de juventud.

you've [ju:v] = **you have.**

Yugoslav ['ju:gəu'slɑ:v] *a*, *n* yugoeslavo/a; **~ia** *n* Yugoeslavia.

Yuletide ['ju:ltaɪd] *n* Navidad *f*.

Z

zany ['zeɪnɪ] *a* tonto.

zeal [zi:l] *n* celo, entusiasmo; **~ous** ['zɛləs] *a* celoso, entusiasta.

zebra ['zi:brə] *n* cebra; **~ crossing** *n* paso de peatones.

zenith ['zɛnɪθ] *n* cénit m.

zero ['zɪərəu] *n* cero.

zest [zɛst] *n* ánimo, vivacidad *f*.

zigzag ['zɪgzæg] *n* zigzag m // *vi* zigzaguear.

zinc [zɪŋk] *n* cinc m, zinc m.

Zionism ['zaɪənɪzm] *n* sionismo; **Zionist** *n* sionista *m*/*f*.

zip [zɪp] *n* (also: **~ fastener, ~per**) cremallera // *vt* (also: **~ up**) cerrar la cremallera de.

zodiac ['zəudɪæk] *n* zodiaco.

zombie ['zɔmbɪ] *n* (fig): **like a ~** como un sonámbulo.

zone [zəun] *n* zona.

zoo [zu:] *n* (jardín m) zoológico.

zoological [zuə'lɔdʒɪkl] *a* zoológico.

zoologist [zu'ɔlədʒɪst] *n* zoólogo.

zoology [zu:'ɔlədʒɪ] *n* zoología.

zoom [zu:m] *vi*: **to ~ past** pasar zumbando; **~ lens** *n* zoom m.

SPANISH VERB TABLES

1 Gerund. *2* Imperative. *3* Present. *4* Preterite. *5* Future. *6* Present subjunctive.
7 Imperfect subjunctive. *8* Past participle. *9* Imperfect.
Etc indicates that the irregular root is used for all persons of the tense, e.g. **oír**: *6*
oiga, oigas, oigamos, oigáis, oigan.

acertar *2* acierta *3* acierto, aciertas, acierta, acierta, acierten *6* acierte, aciertes, acierte, acierten

acordar *2* acuerda *3* acuerdo, acuerdas, acuerda, acuerdan *6* acuerde, acuerdes, acuerde, acuerden

advertir *1* advirtiendo *2* advierte *3* advierto, adviertes, advierte, advierten *4* advirtió, advirtieron *6* advierta, adviertas, advierta, advirtamos, advirtáis, adviertan *7* advirtiera *etc*

agradecer *3* agradezco *6* agradezca *etc*

aparecer *3* aparezco *6* aparezca *etc*

aprobar *2* aprueba *3* apruebo, apruebas, aprueba, aprueban *6* apruebe, apruebes, apruebe, aprueben

atravesar *2* atraviesa *3* atravieso, atraviesas, atraviesa, atraviesan *6* atraviese, atravieses, atraviese, atraviesen

caber *3* quepo *4* cupe, cupiste, cupo, cupimos, cupisteis, cupieron *5* cabré *etc* *6* quepa *etc* *7* cupiera *etc*

caer *1* cayendo *3* caigo *4* cayó, cayeron *6* caiga *etc* *7* cayera *etc*

calentar *2* calienta *3* caliento, calientas, calienta, calientan *6* caliente, calientes, caliente, calienten

cerrar *2* cierra *3* cierro, cierras, cierra, cierran *6* cierre, cierres, cierre, cierren

COMER *1* comiendo *2* come, comed *3* como, comes, come, comemos, coméis, comen *4* comí, comiste, comió, comimos, comisteis, comieron *5* comeré, comerás, comerá, comeremos, comeréis, comerán *6* coma, comas, coma, comamos, comáis, coman *7* comiera, comieras, comiera, comiéramos, comierais, comieran *8* comido *9* comía, comías, comía, comíamos comíais, comían

conocer *3* conozco *6* conozca *etc*

contar *2* cuenta *3* cuento, cuentas, cuenta, cuentan *6* cuente, cuentes, cuente, cuenten

costar *2* cuesta *3* cuesto, cuestas, cuesta, cuestan *6* cueste, cuestes, cueste, cuesten

dar *3* doy *4* di, diste, dio, dimos, disteis, dieron *7* diera *etc*

decir *2* di *3* digo *4* dije, dijiste, dijo, dijimos, dijisteis, dijeron *5* diré *etc* *6* diga *etc* *7* dijera *etc* *8* dicho

despertar *2* despierta *3* despierto, despiertas, despierta, despiertan *6* despierte, despiertes, despierte, despierten

divertir *1* divirtiendo *2* divierte *3* divierto, diviertes, divierte, divierten *4* divirtió, divirtieron *6* divierta, diviertas, divierta, divirtamos, divirtáis, diviertan *7* divirtiera *etc*

dormir *1* durmiendo *2* duerme *3* duermo, duermes, duerme, duermen *4* durmió, durmieron *6* duerma, duermas, duerma, durmamos, durmáis, duerman *7* durmiera *etc*

empezar *2* empieza *3* empiezo, empiezas, empieza, empiezan *4* empecé *6* empiece, empieces, empiece, empecemos, empecéis, empiecen

entender *2* entiende *3* entiendo, entiendes, entiende, entienden *6* entienda, entiendas, entienda, entiendan

ESTAR *2* está *3* estoy, estás, está, están *4* estuve, estuviste, estuvo, estuvimos, estuvisteis, estuvieron *6* esté, estés, esté, estén *7* estuviera *etc*

HABER *3* he, has, ha, hemos, han *4* hube, hubiste, hubo, hubimos, hubisteis, hubieron *5* habré *etc 6* haya *etc 7* hubiera *etc*

HABLAR *1* hablando *2* habla, hablad *3* hablo, hablas, habla, hablamos, habláis, hablan *4* hablé hablaste, habló, hablamos, hablasteis, hablaron *5* hablaré, hablarás, hablará, hablaremos, hablaréis, hablarán *6* hable, hables, hable, hablemos, habléis, hablen *7* hablara, hablaras, hablara, habláramos, hablarais, hablaran *8* hablado *9* hablaba, hablabas, hablaba, hablábamos, hablabais, hablaban

hacer *2* haz *3* hago *4* hice, hiciste, hizo, hicimos, hicisteis, hicieron *5* haré *etc 6* haga *etc 7* hiciera *etc 8* hecho

instruir *1* instruyendo *2* instruye *3* instruyo, instruyes, instruye, instruyen *4* instruyó, instruyeron *6* instruya *etc 7* instruyera *etc*

ir *1* yendo *2* ve *3* voy, vas, va, vamos, vais, van *4* fui, fuiste, fue, fuimos, fuisteis, fueron *6* vaya, vayas, vaya, vayamos, vayáis, vayan *7* fuera *etc 9* iba, ibas, iba, íbamos, ibais, iban

jugar *2* juega *3* juego, juegas, juega, juegan *4* jugué *6* juegue *etc*

leer *1* leyendo *4* leyó, leyeron *7* leyera *etc*

morir *1* muriendo *2* muere *3* muero, mueres, muere, mueren *4* murió, murieron *6* muera, mueras, muera, muramos, muráis, mueran *7* muriera *etc 8* muerto

mostrar *2* muestra *3* muestro, muestras, muestra, muestran *6* muestre, muestres, muestre, muestren

mover *2* mueve *3* muevo, mueves, mueve, mueven *6* mueva, muevas, mueva, muevan

negar *2* niega *3* niego, niegas, niega, niegan *4* negué *6* niegue, niegues, niegue, neguemos, neguéis, nieguen

ofrecer *3* ofrezco *6* ofrezca *etc*

oír *1* oyendo *2* oye *3* oigo, oyes, oye, oyen *4* oyó, oyeron *6* oiga *etc 7* oyera *etc*

oler *2* huele *3* huelo, hueles, huele,

huelen *6* huela, huelas, huela, huelan

parecer *3* parezco *6* parezca *etc*

pedir *1* pidiendo *2* pide *3* pido, pides, pide, piden *4* pidió, pidieron *6* pida *etc 7* pidiera *etc*

pensar *2* piensa *3* pienso, piensas, piensa, piensan *6* piense, pienses, piense, piensen

perder *2* pierde *3* pierdo, pierdes, pierde, pierden *6* pierda, pierdas, pierda, pierdan

poder *1* pudiendo *2* puede *3* puedo, puedes, puede, pueden *4* pude, pudiste, pudo, pudimos, pudisteis, pudieron *5* podré *etc 6* pueda, puedas, pueda, puedan *7* pudiera *etc*

poner *2* pon *3* pongo *4* puse, pusiste, puso, pusimos, pusisteis, pusieron *5* pondré *etc 6* ponga *etc 7* pusiera *etc 8* puesto

preferir *1* prefiriendo *2* prefiere *3* prefiero, prefieres, prefiere, prefieren *4* prefirió, prefirieron *6* prefiera, prefieras, prefiera, prefiramos, prefiráis, prefieran *7* prefiriera *etc*

querer *2* quiere *3* quiero, quieres, quiere, quieren *4* quise, quisiste, quiso, quisimos, quisisteis, quisieron *5* querré *etc 6* quiera, quieras, quiera, quieran *7* quisiera *etc*

reír *2* ríe *3* río, ríes, ríe, ríen *4* rio, rieron *6* ría, rías, ría, riamos, riáis, rían *7* riera *etc*

repetir *1* repitiendo *2* repite *3* repito, repites, repite, repiten *4* repitió, repitieron *6* repita *etc 7* repitiera *etc*

rogar *2* ruega *3* ruego, ruegas, ruega, ruegan *4* rogué *6* ruegue, ruegues, ruegue, roguemos, roguéis, rueguen

saber *3* sé *4* supe, supiste, supo, supimos, supisteis, supieron *5* sabré *etc 6* sepa *etc 7* supiera *etc*

salir *2* sal *3* salgo *5* saldré *etc 6* salga *etc*

seguir *1* siguiendo *2* sigue *3* sigo, sigues, sigue, siguen *4* siguió, siguieron *6* siga *etc 7* siguiera *etc*

sentar *2* sienta *3* siento, sientas,

sienta, sientan 6 siente, sientes, siente, sienten

sentir 1 sintiendo 2 siente 3 siento, sientes, siente, sienten 4 sintió, sintieron 6 sienta, sientas, sienta, sintamos, sintáis, sientan 7 sintiera etc

SER 2 sé 3 soy, eres, es, somos, sois, son 4 fui, fuiste, fue, fuimos, fuisteis, fueron 6 sea etc 7 fuera etc 9 era, eras, era, éramos, erais, eran

servir 1 sirviendo 2 sirve 3 sirvo, sirves, sirve, sirven 4 sirvió, sirvieron 6 sirva etc 7 sirviera etc

soñar 3 sueña 3 sueño, sueñas, sueña, sueñan 6 sueñe, sueñes, sueñe, sueñen

tener 2 ten 3 tengo, tienes, tiene, tienen 4 tuve, tuviste, tuvo, tuvimos, tuvisteis, tuvieron 5 tendré etc 6 tenga etc 7 tuviera etc

traer 1 trayendo 3 traigo 4 traje, trajiste, trajo, trajimos, trajisteis, trajeron 6 traiga etc 7 trajera etc

valer 2 val 3 valgo 5 valdré etc 6 valga etc

venir 2 ven 3 vengo, vienes, viene, vienen 4 vine, viniste, vino, vinimos, vinisteis, vinieron 5 vendré etc 6 venga etc 7 viniera etc

ver 3 veo 6 vea etc 8 visto 9 veía etc

vestir 1 vistiendo 2 viste 3 visto, vistes, viste, visten 4 vistió, vistieron 6 vista etc 7 vistiera etc

VIVIR 1 viviendo 2 vive, vivid 3 vivo, vives, vive, vivimos, vivís, viven 4 viví, viviste, vivió, vivimos, vivisteis, vivieron 5 viviré, vivirás, vivirá, viviremos, viviréis, vivirán 6 viva, vivas, viva, vivamos, viváis, vivan 7 viviera, vivieras, viviera, viviéramos, vivierais, vivieran 8 vivido 9 vivía, vivías, vivía, vivíamos, vivíais, vivían

volver 2 vuelve 3 vuelvo, vuelves, vuelve, vuelven 6 vuelva, vuelvas, vuela, vuelvan 8 vuelto.

VERBOS IRREGULARES EN INGLÉS

present	pt	pp	present	pt	pp
arise	arose	arisen	eat	ate	eaten
awake	awoke	awaked	fall	fell	fallen
be (am, is, are; being)	was, were	been	feed	fed	fed
			feel	felt	felt
			fight	fought	fought
bear	bore	born(e)	find	found	found
beat	beat	beaten	flee	fled	fled
become	became	become	fling	flung	flung
befall	befell	befallen	fly	flew	flown
begin	began	begun	forbid	forbade	forbidden
behold	beheld	beheld	forecast	forecast	forecast
bend	bent	bent	forget	forgot	forgotten
beset	beset	beset	forgive	forgave	forgiven
bet	bet, betted	bet, betted	forsake	forsook	forsaken
			freeze	froze	frozen
bid	bid	bid	get	got	got, (US) gotten
bind	bound	bound			
bite	bit	bitten	give	gave	given
bleed	bled	bled	go (goes)	went	gone
blow	blew	blown			
break	broke	broken	grind	ground	ground
breed	bred	bred	grow	grew	grown
bring	brought	brought	hang	hung, hanged	hung, hanged
build	built	built			
burn	burnt, burned	burnt, burned	have	had	had
			hear	heard	heard
burst	burst	burst	hide	hid	hidden
buy	bought	bought	hit	hit	hit
can	could	(been able)	hold	held	held
cast	cast	cast	hurt	hurt	hurt
catch	caught	caught	keep	kept	kept
choose	chose	chosen	kneel	knelt, kneeled	knelt, kneeled
cling	clung	clung			
come	came	come	know	knew	known
cost	cost	cost	lay	laid	laid
creep	crept	crept	lead	led	led
cut	cut	cut	lean	leant, leaned	leant, leaned
deal	dealt	dealt			
dig	dug	dug	leap	leapt, leaped	leapt, leaped
do (3rd person; he/she/it/does)	did	done			
			learn	learnt, learned	learnt, learned
			leave	left	left
draw	drew	drawn	lend	lent	lent
dream	dreamed, dreamt	dreamed, dreamt	let	let	let
			lie (lying)	lay	lain
drink	drank	drunk			
drive	drove	driven	light	lit, lighted	lit, lighted
dwell	dwelt	dwelt			

403

present	pt	pp	present	pt	pp
lose	lost	lost	speed	sped,	sped,
make	made	made		speeded	speeded
may	might	—	spell	spelt,	spelt,
mean	meant	meant		spelled	spelled
meet	met	met	spend	spent	spent
mistake	mistook	mistaken	spill	spilt,	spilt,
mow	mowed	mown,		spilled	spilled
		mowed	spin	spun	spun
must	(had to)	(had to)	spit	spat	spat
pay	paid	paid	split	split	split
put	put	put	spoil	spoiled,	spoiled,
quit	quit,	quit,		spoilt	spoilt
	quitted	quitted	spread	spread	spread
read	read	read	spring	sprang	sprung
rend	rent	rent	stand	stood	stood
rid	rid	rid	steal	stole	stolen
ride	rode	ridden	stick	stuck	stuck
ring	rang	rung	sting	stung	stung
rise	rose	risen	stink	stank	stunk
run	ran	run	stride	strode	strode
saw	sawed	sawn	strike	struck	struck,
say	said	said			stricken
see	saw	seen	strive	strove	striven
seek	sought	sought	swear	swore	sworn
sell	sold	sold	sweep	swept	swept
send	sent	sent	swell	swelled	swollen,
set	set	set			swelled
shake	shook	shaken	swim	swam	swum
shall	should	—	swing	swung	swung
shear	sheared	shorn,	take	took	taken
		sheared	teach	taught	taught
shed	shed	shed			
shine	shone	shone	tear	tore	torn
shoot	shot	shot	tell	told	told
show	showed	shown	think	thought	thought
shrink	shrank	shrunk	throw	threw	thrown
shut	shut	shut	thrust	thrust	thrust
sing	sang	sung	tread	trod	trodden
sink	sank	sunk	wake	woke,	woken,
sit	sat	sat		waked	waked
slay	slew	slain	wear	wore	worn
sleep	slept	slept	weave	wove,	woven,
slide	slid	slid		weaved	weaved
sling	slung	slung	wed	wedded,	wedded,
slit	slit	slit		wed	wed
smell	smelt,	smelt,	weep	wept	wept
	smelled	smelled	win	won	won
sow	sowed	sown,	wind	wound	wound
		sowed	wring	wrung	wrung
speak	spoke	spoken	write	wrote	written

NOTES TO THE USER OF THIS DICTIONARY

I. Using the dictionary

In using this book, you will either want to check the meaning of a Spanish word you don't know, or find the Spanish for an English word. These two operations are quite different, and so are the problems you may face when using one side of the dictionary or the other. In order to help you, we have tried to explain below the main features of this book.

The 'wordlist' is the alphabetical list of all the items in large bold type, i.e. all the 'headwords'. Each 'entry', or article, is introduced by a headword, and may contain additional 'references' in smaller bold type, such as phrases, derivatives, and compound words. Section 1. below deals with the way references are listed.

The typography distinguishes between three broad categories of text within the dictionary. All items in bold type, large or small, are 'source language' references, for which an equivalent in the other language is provided. All items in standard type are translations. Items in italics are information about the words being translated, i.e. either labels, or 'signposts' pinpointing the appropriate translation, or explanations.

1. *Where to look for a word*

1.1 Derivatives

In order to save space, a number of derivatives have been listed within entries, provided this does not break alphabetical order. Thus, **laborar**, **laborioso**, and **laborista** are listed under the entry for **labor**, and **caller** and **calling** under **call**. You must remember this when looking for a word you don't find listed as a headword. These derivatives are always listed last within an entry (see also I.2 on entry layout).

1.2 Homographs

Homographs are words which are spelt in exactly the same way, like **pago** (payment) and **pago** (district), or **hacha** (axe) and **hacha** (torch). As a rule, in order to save space, such words have been treated under one headword only. In the very few cases where this was not possible, the presence of a feminine form helps distinguish between two consecutive homograph entries (e.g. **rapaz** and **rapaz, -a**).

1.3 Phrases

Because of the constraints of space, there can be only a limited number of idiomatic phrases in a pocket dictionary like this one. Particular emphasis is given to verbal phrases like **sacar a luz, dar a luz, dar una vuelta, dar vueltas, estar de vuelta**, etc, and also to basic constructions (see the entries for **apply, agree, ponerse, deber, dar**). Verbal phrases with the ten or so basic verbs (ser, estar, poner etc.) are listed under the noun. Other phrases and idioms are listed under the first key word, for instance de **antemano** under **antemano, no obstante** under **obstante**.

1.4 Abbreviations and proper names

For easier reference, abbreviations, acronyms and proper names have been listed alphabetically in the wordlist, as opposed to being relegated to the appendices. **M.O.T.** is used in every way like **certificate** or **permit, OVNI** like **objeto**, and these words are treated like other nouns.

1.5 Compounds

Housewife, smoke screen, caja fuerte and lámpara de pie are all compounds. One-word compounds like 'housewife' are not a problem when consulting the dictionary, since they can appear only in one place and in strict alphabetical order. When it comes to other compounds, however – hyphenated compounds and compounds made up of separate words – each language presents its own peculiar problems.

1.5.1 Spanish compounds

There are many compounds made up of two or more 'words'. When checking a Spanish compound, you might not be aware that you are dealing with a compound and not a string of autonomous words, and there may inevitably be some toing and froing between entries.

As spelling is regular in Spanish, we have listed Spanish compounds under the first word, and grouped them alphabetically within that entry. For instance, **cama de matrimonio** is within the entry for **cama** and comes before the headword **camada**. **Tos ferina** comes before the headword **tosco**, in the entry for **tos**. Remember that the meaning of a phrase or of a compound can be quite different from that of its elements taken separately, so be prepared to check through an entry thoroughly before giving up.

1.5.2 English compounds

Here there is a problem of where to find a compound because of less predictable spelling than is the case with Spanish: is it **airgun, air-gun** or **air gun**? This is why we choose to list them according to strict alphabetical order. Thus **coal field** and **coalman** are separated by **coalition.** The entries between **tax** and **technical** will provide a good illustration of the system of listing. It has drawbacks, for instance in that **tax-free** and **tax-payer** are separated by **taxi, taxidermist** and three 'taxi' compounds. However, in a short dictionary used by beginners, it has the merit of simplicity and consistency.

1.5.3 English 'phrasal verbs'

'Phrasal verbs' are verbs like **go off, blow up, cut down** etc. Here you have the advantage of knowing that these words belong together, whereas it will take the foreign user some time before he can identify these verbs immediately. They have been listed under the entry for the basic verb (e.g. **go, blow, cut**), grouped alphabetically before any other derivative or compound – for instance, **pull up** comes before **pulley.** (See also **to back out, to look up** (a word), **to look out.**)

1.6 Irregular forms

When looking up a Spanish word, you may not immediately find the form you are looking for, although the word in question has been duly entered in the dictionary. This is possibly because you are looking up an irregular noun or verb form, and these are not always given as entries in their own right.

We have assumed that you know basic Spanish grammar. Thus you will be expected to know that 'cantan' is a form of the verb **cantar,** 'luces' the plural of **luz** and so on. However, in order to help you, we have included the main irregular forms as entries in their own right, with a cross-reference to the basic form. Thus, if you come across the word 'fui' and attempt to look up a verb 'fuir', you won't find it, but what you will find between **fuga** and **fulano,** is the entry **fui** *vb ver* **ser, ir.** Similarly **hizo, hecho** etc.

With past participles, it sometimes happens that in addition to the purely verbal form there is an adjectival or noun use, for instance **herido** or **bendito.** These usages are translated as autonomous words, but they are also cross-referred to the verb whenever appropriate (see for instance entries for **abierto** or **muerto**).

2. Entry layout

All entries, however long or complex, are arranged systematically. But it may be a little difficult at first to find one's way through an entry like Spanish **parte**, or English **back, round** or **run** because homographs are grouped under the same entry (see 1.2) and the text is run on without any breakdown into paragraphs, in order to save space. Ease of reference comes with practice, but the guidelines below will make it easier for you.

2.1 'Signposting'

If you look up a Spanish word and find a string of quite different English translations, you are unlikely to have much trouble finding out which is the relevant one for the context, because you know what the English words mean, and the context will almost automatically rule out unsuitable translations. It is quite a different matter when you want to find the Spanish for, say, **lock**, in the context 'we got to the lock around lunchtime', and are faced with an entry that reads 'lock: cerradura; esclusa; mechón *m*.' You can of course go to the other side and check what each translation means. But this is time-consuming, and it doesn't always work. This is why we have provided the user with signposts which pinpoint the relevant translation. For instance with **lock**, the entry reads: ... (*of door, box*) cerradura; (*of canal*) esclusa; (*of hair*) mechón *m* ... For the context suggested above, it is now clear that 'esclusa' is the right word.

2.2 Grammatical categories and meaning categories

Complex entries are first broken down into grammatical categories, e.g.: **lock** *m* // *vt* // *vi*. Be prepared to go through entries like **run** or **back** carefully, and you will find how useful all these 'signposts' are. Each grammatical category is then split where appropriate into the various meanings, e.g.:

> **lock** *n* (*of door, box*) cerradura; (*of canal*) esclusa; (*of hair*) mechón *m* // *vt* (*with key*) cerrar con llave; (*immobilize*) inmovilizar // *vi* (*door etc*) cerrarse con llave; (*wheels*) bloquearse, trabarse.

3. Using the translations

3.1 Gender

Feminine endings for Spanish adjectives ending in -o have not been given on the English-Spanish side, but endings for other adjectives are shown: 'charming *a* encantador(a)'; 'Danish *a* danés(esa)'; 'German *a* alemán(ana)'. This may appear to duplicate information given in the Spanish-English side of the dictionary, but we feel it is a useful reminder where and when it matters. The feminine form is also given for words like **teacher, researcher** etc.

3.2 Plurals

Information on the formation of plurals in Spanish, including the plural of compounds is given in section II. Most plural forms in Spanish are regular and are not shown, but where a problem could arise, the plural is shown beside the headword on the Spanish side, e.g. **carácter,** *pl* **caracteres.** We have shown when the translation of a word used in the singular is plural; see for instance **hair, jealousy, offal.**

3.3 Verb forms

Irregular Spanish verbs appearing as translations have not been marked as such, and the user should refer to the Spanish verb tables when in doubt (pp. 400–402).

3.4 Colloquial language

You should as a rule proceed with great caution when handling foreign language which has a degree of informality. When an English word or phrase has been labelled (*col*), i.e. colloquial, you must assume that the translation belongs to a similar level of informality. If the translation is followed by (!) you should use it with extreme care, or better still avoid it unless you are with close friends!

3.5 'Grammatical words'

It is exceedingly difficult to give adequate treatment for words like **for, away, whose, which, out, off** etc. in a short dictionary such as this one. We have tried to go some way towards providing as much relevant information as possible about the most frequent uses of these words. However, for further information use a good monolingual dictionary of Spanish, and a good modern Spanish grammar.

3.6 'Approximate' translations and cultural equivalents

It is not always possible to give a genuine translation, when for instance an English word denotes a thing or institution which either doesn't exist in Spain, or is quite different. Therefore, only an approximate equivalent can be given, or else an explanation. See for instance **whip, shadow cabinet**, and on the Spanish-English side **gazpacho, doña.**

3.7 Alternative translations

As a rule, translations separated by commas can be regarded as broadly interchangeable for the meaning indicated. Translations separated by a semi-colon are not interchangeable and when in doubt you should consult either a larger bilingual dictionary such as the Collins Spanish Dictionary, or a good monolingual Spanish dictionary. You will find however that there are very few cases of translations separated by a semi-colon without an intervening 'signpost'.

II. Notes on Spanish grammar

Although a relatively easy language to learn, Spanish may seem very different from English when you first meet it in school or hear a Spanish speaker talk. Certainly the order of words and the way a Spaniard says certain things will be strange (in fact a general feeling might be that everything is the wrong way round), but if you were to compare it to languages like Arabic, Swahili or Chinese, you would soon recognize that the basic structure and pattern of Spanish is quite close to English.

We have tried here to show some of these differences, especially with the beginner and the dictionary user in mind, without dwelling on subtleties or the aspects of Spanish which are broadly similar to English. Among the greatest obstacles for the beginner are gender, verb forms and tenses, the position of adjectives, the uses of prepositions and of course, in a few cases, the sounds of Spanish (although once you have mastered each sound it is arguably one of the easiest languages to speak and understand). There are of course many more differences, some of which take us into the realm of style etc., but this is beyond the scope of this introduction.

1. *Nouns and 'satellite' words (i.e. articles, adjectives etc.)*

1.1   Gender

Note the basic difference: 'the table and the knife', but '*la* mes*a* y *el* cuchill*o*'. Gender can usually be determined by the ending of the word: 'mesa' ends in *a* and is feminine; 'cuchillo' ends in *o* and is masculine. Certain endings are always one gender, e.g. -ción is always feminine and -tor masculine. Otherwise you just have to learn the genders in each case. What *is* important, however, is that you get the article right and also the agreement of adjectives and past participles: '*un* hombre alt*o* con *la* nariz torcid*a*'. See also 1.4 (possessive adjectives).

1.2   Articles: 'el, la, lo; un; del' etc.

Apart from the problem of gender, there is the question of whether the article is used or not, and Spanish does not always follow the English pattern. For instance, you say 'I like wine', but the Spanish say 'me gusta el vino'. Conversely, 'my father is a mechanic', but 'mi padre es mecánico'.

1.2.1   'el, la, lo; los, las'

(a)   In almost all cases where 'the' is not used in English, the article must be used in Spanish. For instance:

apples are good for you   las manzanas son buenas para la salud
salmon is expensive   el salmón es caro

patience is a virtue   la paciencia es una virtud
I don't like fighting   no me gustan las peleas

N.B.   With names of countries, Spanish is gradually losing the habit of using the article, but you may still find a few cases where it persists:

e.g.   el Canadá, el Japón, la China.

(b)   Use of 'el/la' with parts of the body

Where the possessive is used in English, 'el/la' tends to be used in Spanish (often in conjunction with a pronoun):

I've twisted my ankle   me he torcido el tobillo
Put up your hand   levante la mano
My nose is bleeding   me está sangrando la nariz

(c)   'a + el; de + el'

Remember the contracted forms (shown in the dictionary under a and de):
voy al cine; vengo del huerto

(d)   'lo'

Spanish also has a neuter gender: 'lo' is often used with an adjective to express general or abstract ideas, e.g. 'eso es lo bueno' (that's the good thing about it)

1.2.2 'un, una, uno; unos, unas'

(a) In structures like 'my father is a postman' (i.e. expressing occupation, nationality or rank), Spanish does not use the indefinite article:

my brother is a mechanic   mi hermano es mecánico
he's a Frenchman   es francés

(b) After negatives, the article 'un/una' is not used with unspecified nouns:

I don't have a car   no tengo coche
she went out without saying a word   ella salió sin decir palabra

(c) The form 'uno' is used either to express the number 'one' when a masculine noun is understood, or to express the neuter idea of 'one' (i.e. we, people)

how many cats have you? One   ¿cuántos gatos tiene? Uno
(whereas: he has only one cat   tiene sólo un gato)

when one thinks about it   cuando uno lo piensa

(d) 'unos/unas'

Remember to use the plural of the article, even though there may be no article in English:

friends from Madrid have arrived   unos amigos de Madrid han llegado

1.2.3 'some/any'

Unless 'some/any' expresses something specific, it is normally not translated in Spanish, especially after a negative:

me quedan unas pesetas   I have some pesetas left

BUT: ¿quiere usted patatas?   do you want *some/any* potatoes?
quiero pan   I want *some* bread
no tengo cigarillos   I haven't *any* cigarettes

1.3 Adjectives

Apart from the question of gender, the main difficulty is the position of adjectives. As a general rule, they follow the noun (las leyes físicas, una comida sabrosísima, unos guantes rojos). Some adjectives or types of adjectives will *always* go after the noun, especially if their meaning can only be literal (una casa desmoronada, las leyes físicas, un vestido rojo). Others can also go before the noun in a figurative sense or for stylistic effect (una sabrosísima comida).

Adjectives, however, which 'limit' rather than 'describe' (mucho, poco, demasiado, tanto, primero, último) always come in front of the noun.

Finally, many common adjectives like 'bueno, malo; grande, pequeño; viejo, joven; nuevo, antiguo; pobre, rico' and others like 'mismo, cierto' will be found before or after, but with different meanings: before the meaning is usually figurative, after it is literal (the dictionary makes these differences clear).

1.3.1
Remember that certain adjectives have a shortened masculine form before nouns: bueno, BUT: un buen hombre

1.4 Possessives:

1.4.1 *'su/sus'*

Since this form can be ambiguous (his, hers, its; yours, theirs), Spanish often substitutes 'el ... de él, de ella; de usted, de ellos':

e.g. their father   su padre: el padre de ellos

1.4.2 *'el mío/la mía; los míos/las mías'* etc.

The possessive pronouns vary according to the gender of the noun they qualify as well as the number:

¿de quién es este coche?   es mío   whose is this car?   it's mine.
aquí están las entradas; las tuyas costaron más   here are the tickets; yours cost more

1.5 Demonstratives: *'este, ese, aquel; esta, esa, aquella; esto'* etc.

1.5.1

Demonstrative adjectives agree in gender and number with the noun they qualify. Spanish also has a neuter form for the pronouns 'this' and 'that'.

¿qué es eso? what's that? ¿qué es esto? what's this?

The main problem, however, is choosing between the three forms of demonstrative: the 'este' forms are straightforward and mean 'this'; the 'ese' forms mean 'that' in the sense of 'that nearby or near you'; the 'aquel' forms mean 'that yonder':

este libro   this book
¿qué es eso que tienes en la mano?   what is that you have (*there*) in your hand?
¿cómo se llaman aquellas montañas?   what are those mountains called (*yonder*)?

1.6   Comparative and superlative: '*más … que*' etc.

1.6.1

Generally you use 'más' + *adjective* or *adverb* to form the comparative; the superlative is slightly more complicated because you use the definite article with the 'más' and the article must agree in gender and number with the adjective. The superlative adverb is formed with 'lo' + 'más' + *adverb*.

más bonito/más frecuentemente   prettier/more frequently
esa casa es la *más* bonita   that is the prettiest *house*
lo *más* frecuentemente   the *most* frequent*ly*

2.   Verbs

This is one of the main areas of difficulty for English-speaking learners. There are four major problems. First, the variety of endings (hablo, hablamos etc.) and the number of irregular or 'semi-irregular' forms. Second, the difference in the formation of negative or interrogative phrases (no equivalent of 'do', 'did' etc., as in 'I didn't go; did you?'). Third, the difference in the use of tenses (e.g. two past tenses, imperfect and preterite). Fourth, the use of two verbs meaning 'to be' (ser, estar).

2.1   Verb forms

The verb tables on pp. 424 and 425 will give you the patterns for the main verb groups; irregular verb forms are shown on page 400. There is no substitute for practice on this, but try not to look upon these forms as a vast array of separate items to be learnt: there are two basic combining patterns, one relating to the person doing the action ('*I* speak vs *you* speak: habl*o*/habl*as*) and one relating to the tense (I *speak*/I *spoke*:

hablo/hablé). The present, perfect, imperfect, future and conditional will cater for most of your needs at first.

2.2 Negatives and questions

Although the simple negative 'no' is the same as English, most other negative words also need a 'no' in front when they follow the verb, but their meaning is not a 'double' negative:

no lo sé   I do *not* know
nunca lo sé   I *never* know
BUT: no lo sabía nunca   I *never* knew
ALSO: no lo sabe nunca nadie   *nobody ever* knows

The way Spanish forms questions is really a matter of the tone of voice in which the sentence is said and presents no real problem because we often use the same tone in English. When Spanish questions are written therefore, they need a special question mark at the beginning to warn you that it is a question:

es loco   he is mad
¿es loco?   is he mad?

2.3 Tenses

2.3.1

The Spanish equivalent to our continuous '-ing' form is just the same but you must remember to use the 'estar' verb 'to be' and not 'ser':

estoy ley*endo*   I am read*ing*
estaré ley*endo*   I shall be read*ing*

2.3.2

The perfect tense in English (I have done it) corresponds fairly closely to the Spanish (lo he hecho); but what seems to be a preterite in English (I did it) can in certain circumstances be translated by any of the three past tenses in Spanish (lo hice, lo he hecho, lo hacía). Basically it is a question of 'when' and 'how often'.

2.3.2.1 The imperfect

The 'imperfect' describes an action done repeatedly in the past or which went on for some time (often being a replacement for the continuous tense), e.g. lo *hacían* means 'they *used to* do it' or 'they *were doing it*', which is what the English preterite implies in a sentence such as 'they *did* it *all the time*'.

2.3.2.2. The perfect

The perfect in Spanish describes an action which has been carried out recently, usually that day. Because it expresses recent time, it can therefore translate English 'preterites': such as 'they *did* it this morning' lo *han hecho* esta mañana.

2.3.2.3 The preterite

The preterite denotes completed actions in the more distant past and is more a tense of written Spanish, e.g. 'he *did* it yesterday/the day before lo *hizo* ayer/el día anterior.

2.3.3

Don't be surprised to see Spanish use a present tense instead of the future in phrases like 'I *shall go* tomorrow': me *voy* mañana.

2.3.4 The subjunctive: 'quiero que lo haga' *vs* 'sé que lo hace' etc.

Good command of both the present and imperfect subjunctive is necessary in order to speak good Spanish, but you can probably cover a lot of situations with just the present. Even without the subjunctive you would probably be understood, except that is with verbs like 'decir' where misunderstandings might arise, e.g. dígale que **venga** means 'tell him *to come*', but dígale que **viene** means 'tell him he *is coming*'.

It is not possible to give you all the rules governing the use of the subjunctive but here are a few basic ideas explaining its use:

(a) The subjunctive is used to express a command when the polite form 'usted' is implied:
hágalo usted   you do it
lea esto   read this

(b) The subjunctive is used in subordinate clauses when doubt, hypothesis and denial are expressed (i.e. it is not a fact):

dudo que lo tenga   I doubt if he has it
no creo que lo tenga   I don't believe he has it

(c) The best guide perhaps is to see whether the subjects of the clauses
change: if they do, then there will probably be a subjunctive.

I want *him* to do it   quiero que lo **haga** él
it is good for *him* to do it   es bueno que él lo **haga**

(d) It is also used for actions which are not yet facts.
until he comes   hasta que *venga*.

2.4   Spanish has two verbs 'to be': ser, estar.

2.4.1   *ser*

Ser means 'to exist' but it also covers the meanings of 'to be' which
express qualities or permanent states: 'es bueno'   he is good (always);
'es profesor'   he is a teacher. It is also used to form the passive tense:
'fui herido'   I was wounded.

2.4.2   *estar*

Estar means 'to be situated' or 'to be in a state of ...': ' ¿dónde está el
banco?'   where is the bank (situated)?; 'estaba herido'   I was (in a)
wounded (state); 'está sentado'   he is (in a) sitting down (state); 'está
bueno'   he is well.

3. *Prepositions*

Most prepositions present no problems. The main confusion will be
about when to use 'por' and when to use 'para' when translating English
'for'. Essentially, 'por' expresses *cause* or *reason* and 'para' expresses
purpose:

lo hizo *por* mí   he did it *for* me (because of me, for my sake)
¿*para* qué lo quieres?   what do you want it *for*?

'por' also expresses exchange: ¿cuánto me da *por* esto?   how much
will you give me *for* this?

3.1   Don't forget that many verbs in English are followed by
prepositions but they are usually contained in the Spanish verb: to go
up   'subir'; to sit *down*   'sentarse' etc.

4. *Adverbs*

Adverbs can be formed from most adjectives by taking the feminine form and adding '-mente': quick-ly rápida-mente; easi-ly fácil-mente. Spanish often uses idiomatic constructions, such as 'por lo general' (generally).

5. *Pronouns*: yo, te, le, sí etc.

5.1 Subject pronouns are not normally used in Spanish except for emphasis since the verb form tells you who is doing the action: hablo *I* speak; *él* lo tiene, *yo* no *he* has it, not *me*.

5.2 Pronoun table

	SUBJECT	REFLEX.	INDIRECT OBJECT	OBJECT	PREPOSITIONAL
I	yo	me	me	me	para mí/conmigo
you	tu	te	te	te	para ti/contigo
he	él	se	le (se)	le, lo	para él
she	ella	se	le (se)	le, la	para ella
it	(ello)	se		lo, la	para (ello)
you	usted	se	le (se)	le	para usted
we	nosotros/as	nos	nos	nos	para nosotros/as
you	vosotros/as	os	os	os	para vosotros/as
they	ellos	se	les (se)	les, los	para ellos
they	ellas	se	les (se)	les, las	para ellas

III. Spanish verb conjugations

1. The table of irregular verbs on p. 400 is self-explanatory. Unless stated otherwise, if one form only is given it is the first person singular; if two forms are given, they are the third person singular and plural; if four forms are shown, they are the first, second and third person singular plus the third person plural. Any forms not shown are regular and can be found by consulting the model verb tables below: table A for an infinitive ending in '-ar' and table B for infinitives ending in '-er' or '-ir'.

2. Do not forget to use the appropriate pronoun with reflexive verbs: *me* lavo, *te* lavaste, *se* había cortado.

3. 'Semi-irregular' verbs.
   Some verbs appear to be irregular but they are in fact predictable with reference to the following guidelines:

   3.1   Because a 'c' or a 'g' in Spanish is pronounced differently depending on the vowel which follows, these letters will change in certain cases in order to maintain the original root sound:
   Roots ending in 'c': sac-ar, saqu-é; venc-er, venz-o; zurc-ir, zurz-o
   Roots ending in 'g': pag-ar, pagu-é; proteg-er, protej-o; fing-ir, finj-o
   Roots ending in 'qu' and 'gu': delinquir, delinc-o; averiguar, averigüé; distinguir, distingo
   Roots ending in 'z': cazar, cacé

   3.2   A root ending in 'i' or 'u' has to be strengthened by an accent when it takes the stress:
   'i' – confiar: confío, confías, confía, confiamos, confiáis, confían
   'u' – situar: sitúo, sitúas, sitúa, situamos, situáis, sitúan
   (N.B. there are exceptions, e.g. cambiar: cambio, cambias, cambia, etc.)

3.3.1 When a root ends in 'ñ', 'll' and 'ch' it will 'absorb' any unstressed 'i' which follows: thus 'gruñ + iendo' becomes 'gruñendo', 'gruñ + ió' 'gruñó'.

3.3.2 The opposite happens when the root is a vowel itself: when an unstressed 'i' follows, it is strengthened into a 'y', e.g. 'o + iendo' becomes 'oyendo', 'argui + iendo' 'arguyendo'.

3.4 Spanish also has what are called 'root-changing' verbs, where the vowel within the root becomes a diphthong when stressed: e > ie; o > ue. The common verbs like 'acertar' and 'acordar' are already in the verb tables, but be prepared for other verbs to follow this model, e.g. fregar friego; doler duele.

4. The 'compound tenses' are formed as follows:

Indicative:

(a) 'perfect': *present* of 'haber' + *past participle* (he hablado/comido)

(b) 'pluperfect': *imperfect* of 'haber' + *past participle* (había hablado/comido)

(c) 'future perfect': *future* of 'haber' + *past participle* (habré hablado/comido)

(d) 'conditional perfect': *conditional* of 'haber' + *past participle* (habría hablado/comido)

Subjunctive:

(a) 'perfect': *present subjunctive* of 'haber' + *past participle* (haya hablado/comido)

(b) 'pluperfect': *imperfect subjunctive* of 'haber' + *past participle* (hubiera/hubiese hablado)

5. The passive is formed by using the verb 'ser' + *past participle*. The past participle agrees in number and gender with the subject: la televisión *fue* inventada en el año... television was invented in... (Note that Spanish often avoids the passive by using a reflexive construction: la televisión *se inventó* en el año...)

6. Irregular past participles not appearing in the verb tables are formed as follows:
abrir *abierto*; cubrir *cubierto*; escribir *escrito*; imprimir *impreso*; freír *frito*; romper *roto*.

7. Imperative forms:
The familiar imperative forms are found in the verb tables (tú, vosotros). The formal imperative (usted, ustedes) adopts the form of the subjunctive: hable (usted); hablen (ustedes).

A. A regular '-ar' verb: 'hablar'

PRESENT: Indicative		Subjunctive	
	o		e
	as		es
habl	a	habl	e
	amos		emos
	áis		éis
	an		en

IMPERFECT: Indicative		Subjunctive	
	aba		ara/ase
	abas		aras/ases
habl	aba	habl	ara/ase
	ábamos		áramos/ásemos
	ábais		arais/aseis
	aban		aran/asen

PRETERITE	
	é
	aste
habl	ó
	amos
	asteis
	aron

FUTURE		CONDITIONAL	
	é		ía
	ás		ías
hablar	á	hablar	ía
	emos		íamos
	éis		íais
	án		ían

IMPERATIVE: habla, hablad

PAST PARTICIPLE: hablado

GERUND: hablando

B. Regular '-er' and '-ir' verbs: 'comer' and 'partir'

PRESENT: Indicative		Subjunctive	
com/part	o es e emos/imos éis/ís en	com/part	a as a amos áis an

IMPERFECT: Indicative		Subjunctive	
com/part	ía ías ía íamos íais ían	com/part	iera/iese ieras/ieses iera/iese iéramos/iésemos ierais/ieseis ieran/iesen

PRETERITE	
com/part	í iste ió imos isteis ieron

FUTURE		CONDITIONAL	
comer/partir	é ás á emos éis án	comer/partir	ía ías ía íamos íais ían

IMPERATIVE: come/parte, comed/partid

PAST PARTICIPLE: comido/partido

GERUND: comiendo/partiendo

IV. The sounds of Spanish

Learning to pronounce Spanish well is, as with all foreign languages, largely a matter of adopting different 'speech habits' from those used in speaking English.

A 'foreign accent' results from using the sounds of one's own language to approximate the sounds of the foreign language. This is particularly tempting when the same letter or letters represent similar sounds in each language. For instance the letter 'i' is used in both Spanish and English, but to represent slightly different sounds in each, and many Spanish speakers are unable to pronounce it in the English manner. It is possible that many do not even realise that the English speaker uses a different sound from the Spanish – hence the typical Spanish pronunciation of 'it is' which to the English speaker sounds as if it were written 'eet eess'.

These are the main ways in which Spanish 'speech habits' differ from the English:

1. *Activity of the lips, tongue etc.*

When you first hear (or even just see) a Spaniard talking, your immediate impression will probably be one of great activity and speed. However the truth is that he/she is not necessarily talking any quicker, but merely using all the 'instruments' of speech (lips, tongue, cheeks, jaw, throat, etc.) to their fullest extent.

English-speakers, on the other hand, tend to be 'lazy' in the use of these instruments – lip position, especially, is fairly unimportant and as a result vowel sounds tend to merge together, whereas in Spanish the activity of the lips etc. means that every vowel sound is clearly distinct from every other.

2. *Fewer diphthongs*

A diphthong is a glide between two vowel sounds in the same syllable. In English there are few 'pure' vowel sounds and a great many diphthongs instead. Although speakers of English may think they produce one vowel sound in the word 'day', in fact they use a diphthong, which in this instance is a glide between the vowels [e] and [ɪ] : [deɪ]. In Spanish the tension maintained in the lips, tongue and the mouth in general prevents diphthongs occurring, as the vowel sound is kept constant throughout. Hence the Spanish word corresponding to the above example, 'de', is pronounced with no final [ɪ] sound, but is phonetically represented thus: [de]. Spanish does have diphthongs, of course, but they are always a combination of two 'pure' vowel sounds.

3. *Consonants*

Consonants in Spanish are always given their full value (except in regional dialects). In English, consonants are often pronounced with a degree of laxness that can result in their becoming 'muted' but not entirely silent. In a relaxed pronunciation of a word such as 'hat', the 't' is often scarcely heard, or may even be replaced by a 'glottal stop' (a sort of 'stutter' in the throat, as in Cockney: bottle = bo'le). Hence a Spaniard sounds unmistakeably foreign to an English speaker if he 'over'-pronounces the 't' and 'l' in 'bottle' as if it were Spanish.

4. *Stress*

In English, each word has its own particular stress pattern – for instance, the two different stress patterns for the word 'escort' produces two different words, one a noun and one a verb (*an escort bureau*; *may I escort you*). This does not happen in Spanish because each word can only be stressed in one way, the rules for which are as follows:

(a) When a word ends in a *vowel* or in 'n' or 's', the *next to last* syllable is stressed: pat*a*ta, pat*a*tas, com*e*dia, c*o*me, c*o*men.

(b) When a word ends in a consonant *other* than 'n' or 's', the stress falls on the last syllable: par*e*d, habl*a*r, aud*a*z.

(c) Whenever these rules (a,b) are not applied, then an acute accent appears over the stressed vowel: hablar*á*, comi*ó*, geograf*í*a.

(d) Normally the same syllable is stressed in the plural as in the singular, so that accents may appear or disappear accordingly: c*a*rmen, c*á*rmenes; ingl*é*s, ingleses. There are two exceptions to this rule: car*á*cter, caract*e*res; r*é*gimen, reg*í*menes.

Pronunciation of the sounds of Spanish

I. Vowel

symbol	as in	hints on pronunciation
[a]	amo	not as long as 'a' in English far
[æ]	amante	in a closed syllable (ending in a consonant) the 'a' is short, as in English 'bat'
[e]	celo	like 'e' in the 'they' (or even 'a' in 'pay') but without the 'y' sound
[ɛ]	gente	in a closed syllable the 'e' is short, as in English 'pet'
[i]	mina	as in English 'mean', 'machine', but without slight 'y' sound
[o]	loco	as in English 'local', but without slight 'w' sound
[ɔ]	control	in a closed syllable the 'o' is short as in English 'cot'
[u]	mula	as in English 'rule', 'rue', but without slight 'w' sound. It is silent after 'q' and in the groups 'gue', 'gui' unless marked with a diaeresis (argüir, averigüe).

II. Diphthongs

[ai]	baile, caray	like the 'i' in English 'ride'
[au]	fraude	like the 'ou' in English 'shout'
[eɪ]	peine, rey	like the 'ey' in English 'grey'
[eu]	deuda	like 'ay' as in 'bay' plus 'oo' as in 'too', in rapid succession
[oɪ]	oigo, hoy	like the 'oy' in English 'toy'

III. Semiconsonants

[j]	bien, yugo	both 'i' and 'y' can stand for the sound 'y' in English 'yacht'
[w]	agua, fuera	the Spanish 'u' can also convey the 'w' sound of English

IV. Consonants

[b]	voy, enviar, bola	'b' and 'v' are pronounced the same in Spanish. Here at the beginning of a phrase, or after 'm' or 'n', they are pronounced like English 'b' in 'boy', 'ember'
[ß]	hubo, de veras	in any other position they are pronounced like an English 'v' but with *both lips* and not lip and teeth together
[k]	coco, calculo	'c' before 'a', 'o' or 'u' is pronounced as in English 'cat'
[θ]	cero, cinco	before 'e' or 'i' it is pronounced like 'th' in English 'think'
[d]	doy, balde	at the beginning of a phrase, or after 'l' or 'n', 'd' is pronounced as in English
[ð]	modo, Madri(d)	in any other position it is pronounced something like the 'th' in English 'the'; at the end of words it almost disappears
[g]	gano, pongo	'g' before 'a', 'o' or 'u' is pronounced as in English 'gap' if at the beginning of a phrase or after 'n'
[ɤ]	haga	'g' before 'a', 'o', 'u' but in median position and not after 'n' is pronounced more softly
[x]	giro, gente	before 'e' or 'i' it is pronounced as the Spanish 'j' below
[x]	joven	'j' (and 'ge', 'gi') is similar to the 'ch' sound of Scottish 'loch' or Welsh 'bach'

[ʎ]	ca*ll*e, *ll*uvia	'll' is like the 'lli' in English 'mi*lli*on', but is being pronounced more and more like 'y' in '*ye*t'
[n]–[m]	e*n*viar	when followed by a 'v', an 'n' changes to 'm'
[ñ]	ca*ñ*a	something like the 'ni' in English 'o*ni*on
[k]	*qu*ien, *qu*ince	'q' is always followed by a silent 'u' and pronounced as 'k' in English '*k*ing'
[rr]	*r*ápido, co*rr*e	('r' is *always* pronounced in Spanish, unlike the often silent 'r' in English 'dance*r*'); after 'l', 'n' or 's', at the beginning of a phrase or when the 'r' is doubled, it is trilled something like a Scottish or Welsh 'r'
[s]	pa*s*a, ca*s*tillo	's' is usually pronounced as in English 'pa*ss*'
[z]	mi*s*mo, de*s*de	before 'b', 'd', 'g', 'l', 'm' or 'n' it sounds like the 's' in English 'ro*s*e'
[ks]	pró*x*imo	as in English 'pro*x*y'
[gs]	e*x*amen	like the 'gs' in 'pi*gs*kin
[s]	se*x*ta	before a consonant (and even in the other cases above) the 'x' is more and more being pronounced as an English 's' as in 'pest'
[i]	*y*	by itself the 'y' is pronounced as the Spanish 'i'
[θ]	*z*ona, lu*z*	like the 'th' in English '*th*ink' (but in many regions it will be pronounced as an 's')

Note that the 'h' is always silent in Spanish: 'haya' ['aja], 'ahora' [a'ɔra]

From Spelling to Sounds

1. Spanish is an *almost* 'phonetic' language, by which we mean that every vowel and consonant has a fixed sound value. As you will have seen from the previous list, this value changes for only a few letters, and even

431

then in only one alternative position: pongo; cacé etc. Some letters also duplicate the same sound (i/y; b/v) or are not even pronounced (h).

If you look at the language in this manner, you will soon appreciate how simple it is to pronounce. There are only two important factors, therefore, which hinder this: first, the temptation (as with any foreign language) to see the language as if it were written in English, e.g. Spanish 'lee' [lee] might be seen as English 'lee' [liː]; and secondly, the related problem of knowing when two or more vowels *do* form a diphthong or are pronounced separately.

1.2.1   The solution to the first is always to look upon Spanish vowels as clearly distinct, individual sounds which are *always* pronounced.

1.2.2   The second is solved according to the following rules:

(a)   to start with, vowels are either *weak* or *strong*: 'i' and 'u' are weak, whereas 'a', 'e' and 'o' are strong.
(b)   a *weak* and *strong* combination forms a diphthong in which the stress falls on the *strong* vowel: baile, vuestro, sierra, peine, pausa.
(c)   a *weak* and *weak* combination forms a diphthong and the stress falls on the *second* vowel: fui, ruido, viuda.
(d)   a *strong* and *strong* combination remains as two separate vowels, and stress follows the normal rules (4a,b): ca-er; cre-er; cre-e; ca-os.
(e)   any word which is to be pronounced otherwise will carry an accent on the stressed vowel: caído, río, creí, baúl.

2. The letters of the Spanish alphabet

When a Spaniard wishes to spell out a word he pronounces the letters like this:

a [a]	b [be]	c [θe]	ch [tʃe]	d [de]	e [e]
f [efe]	g [xe]	h [atʃe]	i [i]	j [xota]	k [ka]
l [ele]	ll [eʎe]	m [eme]	n [ene]	o [o]	p [pe]
q [ku]	r [ere]	rr [erre]	s [ese]	t [te]	u [u]
v [uße]	x [ekis]	y [iɣrjeɣa]	z [θeta]		

The letters are feminine and you therefore talk of 'una a' or 'la a'. 'Miguel se escribe con una *m* mayúscula'.

3. It is virtually impossible for a Spaniard to pronounce an 's' at the beginning of a word without an 'e' in front: this explains why English loan-words which are established in the language already are spelled with an 'e' (*e*snob), or why you will hear new additions *pronounced* with an 'e' though not written with one (slip = 'eslip').

V. The time

what is the time ?   ¿qué hora es?

it's...   es... (*midnight, noon, 1 o'clock*), son... (*other times*)

00.00	*es* medianoche; *son* las doce (de la noche)
01.00	*es* la una (de la noche)
01.10	la una y diez
01.15	la una y cuarto
	la una y quince
01.30	la una y media
01.45	*son* las dos menos quarto
01.50	las dos menos diez
	la una cincuenta
02.00	*son* las dos
12.00	mediodía
	las doce (de la tarde)
13.00	la una
	las trece (horas)
18.00	las seis
	las dieciocho
22.30	las diez y media
	las veintidós horas y media

at what time ?   ¿a qué hora?

at one   a la una

at 2.15   a las dos y cuarto

just after 3.00   a las tres y pico

about 4.30   hacia las cuatro y media

from 6.00 to 8.00   de seis a ocho

it's nearly 9.00   son casi las nueve

at 4.00 sharp   a las cuatro en punto

Dates and numbers

1. The date

what is the date today? ¿qué día es hoy?

the first of May   el primero de mayo

the 2nd of March   el dos de marzo (*cardinals are used from 2nd to 31st*)

today is the 14th   hoy es catorce; estamos a catorce

on the 10th of June   el diez de junio

on Tuesday   el martes

on Tuesdays   los martes

from the 1st to the 3rd desde el día uno hasta el día tres

Letter headings: dates on Spanish letters are usually written thus:

22nd October, 1949   22 de octubre de 1949

Years: **1981**   mil novecientos ochenta y uno
       2000 B.C.   2000 a. de J.C. (= antes de Jesucristo)
       70 A.D.   70 d. de J.C. (= después de Jesucristo)
       in the 12th century   en el siglo doce
       in the 1940s   durante los años cuarenta

2. Notes on numbers

Cardinals

(a) 'uno' (+ 'veintiuno' etc.) agrees in gender (but not number) with its noun: treinta y un*a* person*a*s; the masculine form is shortened to 'un' unless it stands alone: veinti*un* caballos, veinti*uno*

(b) 'cien' is the commonest form; 'ciento' is mainly used for the compound numbers (except when it multiplies: 'cien mil')

(c) large numbers are divided by a full stop in Spanish:
3.461.203 = English 3,461,203

Ordinals

(a) they are adjectives and therefore agree in number and gender.

(b) 'primero' and 'tercero' lose the final 'o' in front of masculine nouns: 'el primer año', 'en tercer lugar'.

(c) they are not commonly used above 21, except for 100th and 1,000th.

(d) in the case of centuries and titles, the ordinals are only used up to 9th, and from then on the cardinals are used: 'en el siglo *quinto*' BUT 'en el siglo *diecinueve*'; 'Alfonso *primero*' BUT 'Alfonso *doce*'.

(e) the ordinals are also used for fractions:
a third   un tercio
a quarter of a kilo   un cuarto de kilo

(f) Spanish abbreviations for 1st, 2nd, 3rd etc. depend on gender and are written thus:
1st $1°$ (masculine), $1ª$ (feminine)
4th $4°$, $4ª$ etc.

Decimals
Where English uses a point, Spanish uses a comma:

101.7   101,7 (ciento uno coma siete)
0.031   0,031 (cero coma cero tres uno)

Calculations
4 + 7 = 11   cuatro *más* siete *son* once
12 − 3 = 9   doce *menos* tres *resta* nueve
3 × 7 = 21   tres *por* siete *son* veintiuno
16 ÷ 4 = 4   dieciséis *dividido por* cuatro *es* cuatro

Telephone numbers
Spaniards normally read telephone numbers by dividing them into two-figure numbers:

019567   01-95-67 (cero uno, noventa y cinco, sesenta y siete)

Numbers

1	uno(un, una)*	1st	primero(primer, primera)*
2	dos	2nd	segundo(a)
3	tres	3rd	tercero(tercer, tercera)*
4	cuatro	4th	cuarto(a)
5	cinco	5th	quinto(a)
6	seis	6th	sexto(a)
7	siete	7th	séptimo(a)
8	ocho	8th	octavo(a)
9	nueve	9th	noveno(a); nono(a)
10	diez	10th	décimo(a)
11	once	11th	undécimo(a)
12	doce	12th	duodécimo(a)
13	trece	13th	decimotercero(a)***
14	catorce	14th	decimocuarto(a)
15	quince	15th	decimoquinto(a)
16	dieciséis	16th	decimosexto(a)
17	diecisiete	17th	decimoséptimo(a)
18	dieciocho	18th	decimoctavo(a)
19	diecinueve	19th	decimonono(a)
20	veinte	20th	vigésimo(a)
21	veintiuno(-ún, -una)*	21st	vigésimo primero(a)**
22	veintidós	22nd	vigésimo segundo(a)
30	treinta	30th	trigésimo(a)
31	treinta y uno(un, una)*	31st	trigésimo primero(a)**
32	treinta y dos	32nd	trigésimo segundo(a)
40	cuarenta	40th	cuadragésimo(a)
50	cincuenta	50th	quincuagésimo(a)
60	sesenta	60th	sexagésimo(a)
70	setenta	70th	septuagésimo(a)
80	ochenta	80th	octogésimo(a)
90	noventa	90th	nonogésimo(a)
100	cien(ciento)*	100th	centésimo(a)
101	ciento uno(un, una)*		
102	ciento dos	5 1/2	cinco y medio
156	ciento cincuenta y seis	0.31	cero coma tres uno (0,31)
200	doscientos(as)	10%	diez por ciento
500	quinientos(as)		
1,000	mil	1000th	milésimo(a)
1,003	mil tres		
2,000	dos mil	2^2	dos al cuadrado
1,000,000	un millón	2^4	dos a la cuarta potencia

*, **, ***: *see notes on pages 434, 435*